CW01020320

Lee Mckelvey
Martin Crozier

Cambridge International
AS & A Level

Further Mathematics

Coursebook

CAMBRIDGE
UNIVERSITY PRESS

CAMBRIDGE
UNIVERSITY PRESS

University Printing House, Cambridge CB2 8BS, United Kingdom

One Liberty Plaza, 20th Floor, New York, NY 10006, USA

477 Williamstown Road, Port Melbourne, VIC 3207, Australia

314–321, 3rd Floor, Plot 3, Splendor Forum, Jasola District Centre, New Delhi – 110025, India

79 Anson Road, #06-04/06, Singapore 079906

Cambridge University Press is part of the University of Cambridge.

It furthers the University's mission by disseminating knowledge in the pursuit of education, learning and research at the highest international levels of excellence.

www.cambridge.org
Information on this title: www.cambridge.org/9781108403375

First published 2018

20 19 18 17 16 15 14 13 12 11 10 9 8 7 6 5 4 3

Printed in the United Kingdom by Latimer Trend

A catalogue record for this publication is available from the British Library

ISBN 978-1-108-40337-5 Paperback

Contents

Further Probability & Statistics

Introduction

Cambridge International AS & A Level Further Mathematics is a very rigorous and rewarding course that builds on the A Level Mathematics course. The Further Mathematics course is designed for students who wish to understand mathematics at a much higher level, and who have already successfully completed the A Level Mathematics course. With careful planning, Further Mathematics can be studied alongside A Level Mathematics.

The course is divided into three major areas: Pure Mathematics, Probability & Statistics and Mechanics. There are 13 Pure Mathematics topics, 5 Probability & Statistics topics and 6 Mechanics topics, which make up the four examination papers that are available to students. Due to the flexible nature of the modules, students can take either AS Further Mathematics or A Level Further Mathematics. The 24 topics build on knowledge already acquired in the A Level Mathematics course.

This coursebook has been written to reflect the rigour and flexibility of the Further Mathematics course. The authors have almost 30 years of Further Mathematics teaching experience between them, and have used their experience to create a comprehensive and supportive companion to the course. While the majority of the examples are within the scope of the course, there are opportunities for discussion and examples that will stretch the curious mind.

The book is designed not only to instruct students in what is required, but also to help them develop their own understanding of important concepts. Frequent worked examples guide students through the steps in a solution. Numerous practice questions and past paper questions provide opportunities for students to apply their learning. In addition, there are cross-topic review exercises and practice exam-style papers for students to consolidate what they have covered during the course. The questions have been written to provide a rich and diverse approach to solving problems with the intention of enhancing deep learning. Every care has been taken to ensure that the English used in this book is accessible to students with English as an additional language. This is supported by a glossary of the key terms that are essential to the course.

The authors wish you the very best as you embark on this course.

Lee Mckelvey
Martin Crozier

Past exam paper questions throughout are reproduced by permission of Cambridge Assessment International Education. Cambridge Assessment International Education bears no responsibility for the example answers to questions taken from its past question papers that are contained in this publication.

The questions, example answers, marks awarded and/or comments that appear in this book were written by the author(s). In an examination, the method in which marks would be awarded to answers similar to these may be different.

How to use this book

Throughout this book you will notice particular features that are designed to help your learning. This section provides a brief overview of these features.

In this chapter you will learn how to:

- recall and use the relations between the roots and coefficients of polynomial equations
- use a substitution to obtain an equation whose roots are related in a simple way to those of the original equation.

Learning objectives indicate the important concepts within each chapter and help you to navigate through the coursebook.

KEY POINT 1.2

$$(\Sigma\alpha)^2 = (\alpha + \beta + \gamma)^2 = \alpha^2 + \beta^2 + \gamma^2 + 2\alpha\beta + 2\alpha\gamma + 2\beta\gamma$$

Key point boxes contain a summary of the most important methods, facts and formulae.

In this section we will be looking at **cubic equations**.

Key terms are important terms in the topic that you are learning. They are highlighted in orange bold. The **glossary** contains clear definitions of these key terms.

EXPLORE 14.1

Consider a solid uniform hemisphere, having centre O and radius r, with a smaller hemisphere, also with centre O but with radius x, removed from it. In groups, investigate what happens to the centre of mass of the remaining body as $x \to r$.

Explore boxes contain enrichment activities for extension work. These activities promote group-work and peer-to-peer discussion, and are intended to deepen your understanding of a concept.

PREREQUISITE KNOWLEDGE

Where it comes from	What you should be able to do	Check your skills
AS & A Level Mathematics Pure Mathematics 1	Work with parametric curves.	1 a Given that $x = 2\cos\theta$ and $y = \sin 2\theta$, find $y = f(x)$. b If $x = t + \frac{1}{t}$ and $y = t - \frac{1}{t}$, find an equation relating x and y.
AS & A Level Mathematics Pure Mathematics 1	Recall how to integrate.	2 Evaluate the following. a $\int_{x=0}^{x=\frac{\pi}{4}} \cos^2 x \, dx$ b $\int_{x=1}^{x=2} e^{2x} \, dx$

Prerequisite knowledge exercises identify prior learning that you need to have covered before starting the chapter. Try the questions to identify any areas that you need to review before continuing with the chapter.

WORKED EXAMPLE 13.6

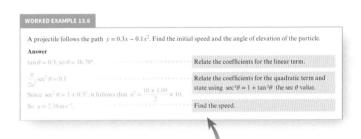

A projectile follows the path $y = 0.3x - 0.1x^2$. Find the initial speed and the angle of elevation of the particle.

Answer

$\tan\theta = 0.3$, so $\theta = 16.70°$. — Relate the coefficients for the linear term.

$\frac{g}{2u^2}\sec^2\theta = 0.1$ — Relate the coefficients for the quadratic term and state using $\sec^2\theta = 1 + \tan^2\theta$ the $\sec\theta$ value.

Since $\sec^2\theta = 1 + 0.3^2$, it follows that $u^2 = \frac{10 \times 1.09}{2} \times 10$.

So $u = 7.38\,\text{m s}^{-1}$. — Find the speed.

Worked examples provide step-by-step approaches to answering questions. The left side shows a worked solution, while the right side contains a commentary explaining each step in the working.

TIP

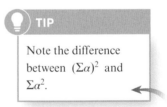

Note the difference between $(\Sigma\alpha)^2$ and $\Sigma\alpha^2$.

Tip boxes contain helpful guidance about calculating or checking your answers.

DID YOU KNOW?

Galileo rolled inked bronze balls down an inclined plane to determine where a projectile would land. This experiment allowed Galileo to determine that the path of the projectiles was very close to being parabolic.

Did you know? boxes contain interesting facts showing how Mathematics relates to the wider world.

Checklist of learning and understanding

Standard summations:

- $\sum_{r=1}^{n} r = \frac{1}{2}n(n+1)$
- $\sum_{r=1}^{n} r^2 = \frac{1}{6}n(n+1)(2n+1)$

At the end of each chapter there is a **Checklist of learning and understanding**. The checklist contains a summary of the concepts that were covered in the chapter. You can use this to quickly check that you have covered the main topics.

END-OF-CHAPTER REVIEW EXERCISE 4

1 Given that $\mathbf{A} = \begin{pmatrix} 6 & 5 \\ 2 & 3 \end{pmatrix}$ and $\mathbf{B} = \begin{pmatrix} -1 & 2 \\ 1 & -4 \end{pmatrix}$:

a find $\mathbf{C}$ such that $\mathbf{BC} = \mathbf{A} + \mathbf{A}^2$

b determine $\mathbf{D}$, where $\mathbf{ADB} = \mathbf{I}$.

The **End-of-chapter review** contains exam-style questions covering all topics in the chapter. You can use this to check your understanding of the topics you have covered.

Cross-topic review exercises appear after several chapters, and cover topics from across the preceding chapters.

CROSS-TOPIC REVIEW EXERCISE 1

1 Prove by mathematical induction that $\sum_{r=1}^{n}(r^2 - r) = \frac{1}{3}n(n^2 - 1)$.

Hence, determine an expression for $\sum_{r=n+1}^{2n}(r^2 - r)$.

REWIND

Recall from Chapter 15 that, for particles travelling in horizontal circles, the tension component is directed towards the centre.

FAST FORWARD

You will meet these formulae again in Chapter 7, when you will prove them in a more rigorous way.

Rewind and **Fast forward** boxes direct you to related learning. **Rewind** boxes refer to earlier learning, in case you need to revise a topic. **Fast forward** boxes refer to topics that you will cover at a later stage, in case you would like to extend your study.

E

Extension material goes beyond the syllabus. It is highlighted by a red line to the left of the text.

Throughout each chapter there are multiple exercises containing practice questions. The questions are coded:

PS These questions focus on problem-solving.

P These questions focus on proofs.

M These questions focus on modelling.

You should not use a calculator for these questions.

You can use a calculator for these questions.

These questions are taken from past examination papers.

Acknowledgements

The authors and publishers acknowledge the following sources of copyright material and are grateful for the permissions granted. While every effort has been made, it has not always been possible to identify the sources of all the material used, or to trace all copyright holders. If any omissions are brought to our notice, we will be happy to include the appropriate acknowledgements on reprinting.

Past exam paper questions throughout are reproduced by permission of Cambridge Assessment International Education.

Cambridge Assessment International Education bears no responsibility for the example answers to questions taken from its past question papers that are contained in this publication.

Thanks to the following for permission to reproduce the images:

Cover image darios44/Getty Images

Inside (*in order of appearance*) S. Lowry/Univ Ulster/Getty Images, John Crouch/Getty Images, franckreporter/Getty Images, Ann Monn/Getty Images, Ian Hobson/Getty Images, Paul Bradbury/Getty Images, Derek Bacon/Getty Images, Mitchell Funk/Getty Images, Martin Barraud/Getty Images, Aidan Richards/EyeEm/Getty Images, Frederic Cirou/Getty Images, Jay's photo/Getty Images, t_kimura/Getty Images, Tawan Prakaisakul/EyeEm/Getty Images, Ken Reid/Getty Images, MirageC/Getty Images, tobishinobi/Getty Images, Michelle Pedone/Getty Images, Matt Nolan/EyeEm/Getty Images, Andy Crawford/Getty Images, joe daniel price/Getty Images, Frank Krahmer/Getty Images, Derrick Argent Photography/Getty Images, John Thurm/EyeEm/Getty Images, Richard Kail/Getty Images

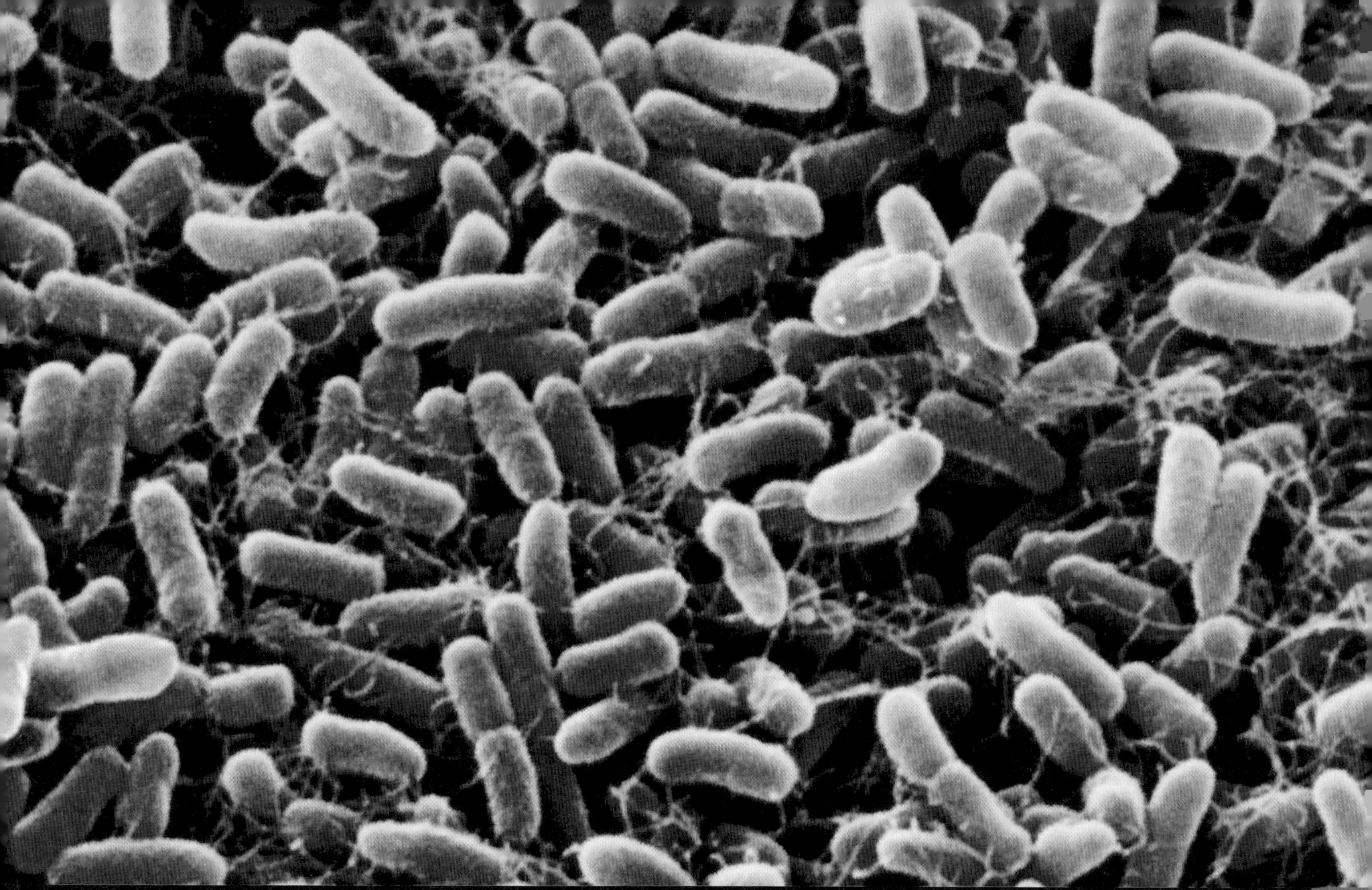

Chapter 1
Roots of polynomial equations

In this chapter you will learn how to:

- recall and use the relations between the roots and coefficients of polynomial equations
- use a substitution to obtain an equation whose roots are related in a simple way to those of the original equation.

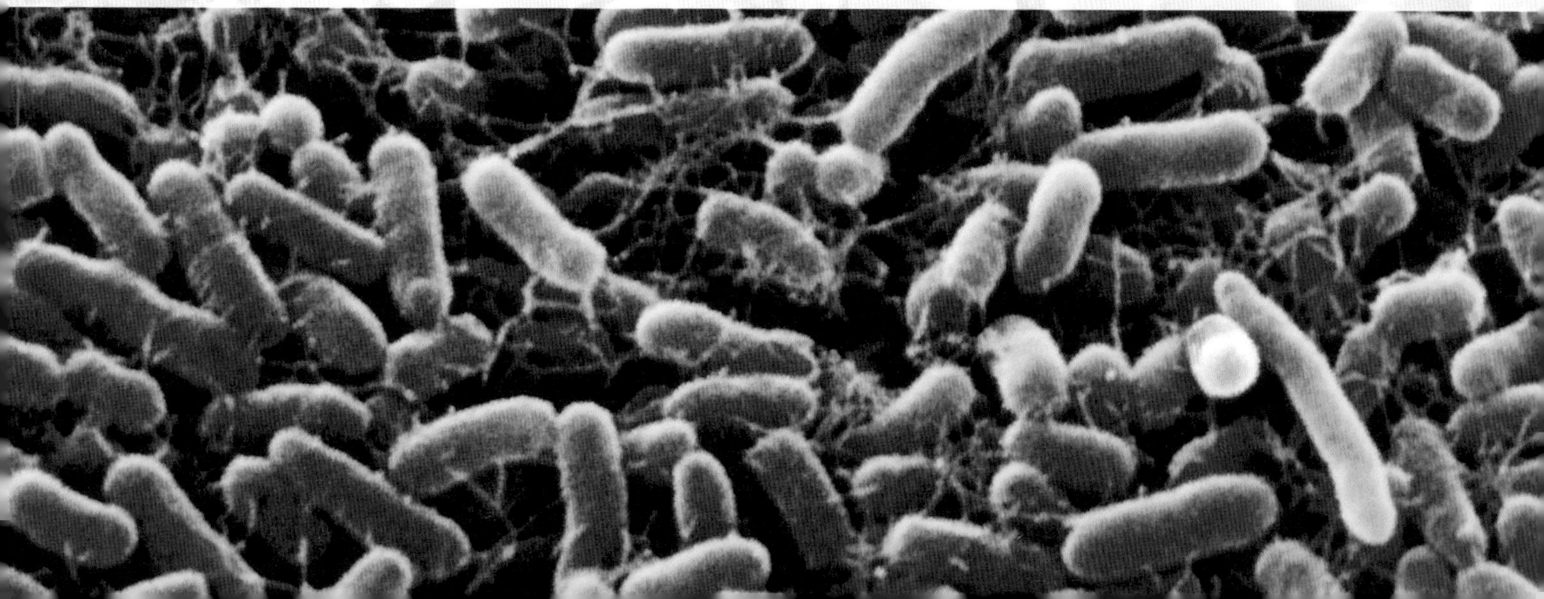

PREREQUISITE KNOWLEDGE

Where it comes from	What you should be able to do	Check your skills
AS & A Level Mathematics Pure Mathematics 1, Chapter 2	Use simple substitutions to make another variable the subject.	**1** Rewrite the following equations in terms of the new variable. **a** $x^2 - 3x + 5 = 0$, $y = x - 2$ **b** $x^3 + 2x^2 - 4 = 0$, $y = \frac{2}{x}$ **c** $x^3 - 3x + 7 = 0$, $y = \frac{1}{x+1}$
AS & A Level Mathematics Probability & Statistics 1, Chapter 2	Work with basic sigma notation, such as Σx and Σx^2.	**2** Evaluate the following. **a** $\sum_{r=1}^{10} r$ **b** $\sum_{r=1}^{10} 3$ **c** $\sum_{r=1}^{10} (r+2)$
AS & A Level Mathematics Pure Mathematics 1, Chapter 6	Work with basic recurrence relations.	**3** Write the first six terms for the following relations. **a** $u_{n+1} = 3u_n + 2$, $u_1 = 1$ **b** $u_{n+2} = 2u_{n+1} - u_n + 5$, $u_1 = 1$, $u_2 = 1$

What are polynomials?

Polynomials are algebraic expressions made up of one or more variables and a sum of terms involving non-negative integer powers of variables. For example, $2x^2 - 3xy + 5x$ is a polynomial, but neither $3x^{\frac{1}{2}}$ nor $\frac{5}{y}$ are polynomials. Engineers use polynomials to ensure that a new building can withstand the force of an earthquake. Medical researchers use them to model the behaviour of bacterial colonies.

We already know how to divide a polynomial by a linear term and identify the quotient and any remainder. We have worked with simpler polynomials when completing the square of a quadratic or finding the **discriminant**. Now we will extend this knowledge to work with higher powers. We will also use algebraic manipulation to understand the conditions for complex solutions and to combine polynomials with summation notation and recurrence relations.

In this chapter, we will look at ways to find characteristics of polynomials, finding the sum and product of roots as well as other properties linked to their roots.

1.1 Quadratics

To begin with, let us look back at the **quadratic** equation $ax^2 + bx + c = 0$. If we write this in the form $x^2 + \frac{b}{a}x + \frac{c}{a} = 0$, then we can compare it to the form $(x - \alpha)(x - \beta) = 0$. This shows that the sum of the **roots** is $\alpha + \beta = -\frac{b}{a}$, and the product of the roots is $\alpha\beta = \frac{c}{a}$, as shown in Key point 1.1. Hence, we can say that $x^2 - (\alpha + \beta)x + \alpha\beta = 0$.

KEY POINT 1.1

If we write a quadratic equation in the form $x^2 + \frac{b}{a}x + \frac{c}{a} = 0$, the sum of the roots is $\alpha + \beta = -\frac{b}{a}$.

The product of the roots of the quadratic equation is $\alpha\beta = \frac{c}{a}$.

WORKED EXAMPLE 1.1

The quadratic equation $x^2 - 2px + p = 0$ is such that one root is three times the value of the other root. Find p.

Answer

$\alpha + 3\alpha = 2p$ — Using $\alpha + \beta = -\frac{b}{a}$.

$p = 2\alpha$

$\alpha \times 3\alpha = p$ — Using $\alpha\beta = \frac{c}{a}$.

$p = 3\alpha^2$

$\frac{p}{3} = \left(\frac{p}{2}\right)^2$ — Equate the two results.

$4p - 3p^2 = 0$ — Cross multiply.

$p = \frac{4}{3}$ — Factorise and omit the case when $p = 0$.

Using $\alpha + \beta = -\frac{b}{a}$ and $\alpha\beta = \frac{c}{a}$, we can begin to define many other results, but first we must introduce some new notation. The sum of the roots can be written as $\Sigma\alpha = \alpha + \beta$ and the product can be written as $\Sigma\alpha\beta = \alpha\beta$.

Let us consider how to determine the value of $\alpha^2 + \beta^2$. The natural first step is to expand $(\alpha + \beta)^2 = \alpha^2 + \beta^2 + 2\alpha\beta$. Hence, we can say that $\alpha^2 + \beta^2 = (\Sigma\alpha)^2 - 2\Sigma\alpha\beta$. We denote $\alpha^2 + \beta^2$ as $\Sigma\alpha^2$.

TIP

Note the difference between $(\Sigma\alpha)^2$ and $\Sigma\alpha^2$.

Next, look at $(\alpha - \beta)^2$. Again, expanding the brackets is a good start. So $(\alpha - \beta)^2 = \alpha^2 + \beta^2 - 2\alpha\beta$. Hence, we can see that $(\alpha - \beta)^2 = \Sigma\alpha^2 - 2\Sigma\alpha\beta$.

We can write $\frac{1}{\alpha} + \frac{1}{\beta}$ as $\Sigma\frac{1}{\alpha}$. How do we find the sum of $\frac{1}{\alpha} + \frac{1}{\beta}$? First, combine the two fractions to get $\frac{\alpha + \beta}{\alpha\beta}$. We can see that this is $\frac{\Sigma\alpha}{\Sigma\alpha\beta}$. Similarly, we can write $\frac{1}{\alpha^2} + \frac{1}{\beta^2}$ as $\Sigma\frac{1}{\alpha^2}$ and we can show $\frac{1}{\alpha^2} + \frac{1}{\beta^2} = \frac{\Sigma\alpha^2}{(\Sigma\alpha\beta)^2}$.

WORKED EXAMPLE 1.2

Find $\alpha^3 + \beta^3$ in summation notation.

Answer

$(\alpha + \beta)^3 = \alpha^3 + 3\alpha^2\beta + 3\alpha\beta^2 + \beta^3$ — Use the binomial expansion for $(x + y)^n$.

$\alpha^3 + \beta^3 = (\alpha + \beta)^3 - 3\alpha\beta(\alpha + \beta)$ — Rearrange and factorise.

$\Sigma\alpha^3 = (\Sigma\alpha)^3 - 3\Sigma\alpha\beta\Sigma\alpha$ — Sum for each possible root.

Alternatively, use $-3\Sigma\alpha^2\beta$ in place of $-3\Sigma\alpha\beta\Sigma\alpha$. However, it is not as easy to calculate with this form.

Some of the results found can be written in alternative forms, using a recurrence relation such as $S_n = \alpha^n + \beta^n$. If we consider the quadratic equation $x^2 + 5x + 7 = 0$, we can see that $\alpha + \beta = -5$. This result can also be viewed as $S_1 = \alpha + \beta = -5$. To determine the value of $\alpha^2 + \beta^2$, we can approach this from another angle.

Given that α and β are roots of the original equation, we can state that $\alpha^2 + 5\alpha + 7 = 0$ and $\beta^2 + 5\beta + 7 = 0$. Adding these together gives the result $(\alpha^2 + \beta^2) + 5(\alpha + \beta) + 14 = 0$ or $S_2 + 5S_1 + 14 = 0$. Now we can work out the value of S_2 or $\alpha^2 + \beta^2$. From $S_2 + 5S_1 + 14 = 0$ and $S_1 = -5$ we have $S_2 = \alpha^2 + \beta^2 = 11$. Note this could also have been found from $\alpha^2 + \beta^2 = (\Sigma\alpha)^2 - 2\Sigma\alpha\beta = (-5)^2 - 2(7) = 11$.

WORKED EXAMPLE 1.3

Given that $2x^2 + 3x - 2 = 0$ has roots α, β, find the values of $\alpha^2 + \beta^2$ and $\alpha^3 + \beta^3$.

Answer

$2\alpha^2 + 3\alpha - 2 = 0$

$2\beta^2 + 3\beta - 2 = 0$

$\Rightarrow 2S_2 + 3S_1 - 4 = 0$ — Add the two equations to get the recurrence form.

$S_1 = -\frac{3}{2}$ — State $S_1 = -\frac{b}{a}$ from the original quadratic equation.

$S_2 = \alpha^2 + \beta^2 = \frac{17}{4}$ — Substitute the S_1 value into the equation.

$2x^2 + 3x - 2 = 0$

$\Rightarrow 2x^3 + 3x^2 - 2x = 0$ — Multiply by x.

$\Rightarrow 2S_3 + 3S_2 - 2S_1 = 0$ — Add $2\alpha^3 + 3\alpha^2 - 2\alpha = 0$ and $2\beta^3 + 3\beta^2 - 2\beta = 0$.

$S_3 = \alpha^3 + \beta^3 = -\frac{63}{8}$ — Use the values of S_1 and S_2.

EXERCISE 1A

1 Each of the following quadratic equations has roots α, β. Find the values of $\alpha+\beta$ and $\alpha\beta$.

a $x^2+5x+9=0$ b $x^2-4x+8=0$ c $2x^2+3x-7=0$

2 Given that $3x^2+4x+12=0$ has roots α, β, find:

a $\alpha+\beta$ and $\alpha\beta$ b $\alpha^2+\beta^2$

3 $x^2-(2+p)x+(7+p)=0$ has roots that differ by 1. Find the value of p given that $p>0$.

PS 4 If $a+b=-3$ and $a^2+b^2=7$, find the value of ab and, hence, write down a quadratic equation with roots a and b.

P 5 If $x^2+bx+c=0$ has roots α and β, prove that:

a if $\alpha=3\beta$, then $b^2=\frac{16}{3}c$

b if $\alpha=\beta-2$, then $b^2=4(c+1)$.

PS 6 You are given the quadratic equation $px^2+qx-16=0$, which has roots α and β. Given also that $\alpha+\beta=-\frac{1}{2}$ and $\alpha\beta=-8$, find the values of p and q.

7 The quadratic equation $x^2+2x-6=0$ has roots α and β. Find the values of $(\alpha-\beta)^2$ and $\frac{1}{\alpha^2}+\frac{1}{\beta^2}$.

PS 8 A quadratic equation has roots α and β. Given that $\frac{1}{\alpha}+\frac{1}{\beta}=\frac{1}{2}$ and $\alpha^2+\beta^2=12$, find two possible quadratic equations that satisfy these values.

9 The quadratic equation $3x^2+2x-4=0$ has roots α and β. Find the values of S_1, S_2 and S_{-1}.

PS 10 You are given the quadratic equation $4x^2-x+6=0$ which has roots α and β.

a Find $\alpha^2+\beta^2$.

b Without solving the quadratic equation, state what your value for part **a** tells you about the roots.

1.2 Cubics

In this section we will be looking at **cubic equations**. We will use the same concepts as in Section 1.1, but this time the roots will be α, β and γ.

Beginning with $ax^3+bx^2+cx+d=0$, the first step is to divide by the constant a to get $x^3+\frac{b}{a}x^2+\frac{c}{a}x+\frac{d}{a}=0$.

Next, relate this to $(x-\alpha)(x-\beta)(x-\gamma)=0$ to establish the relation:

$$x^3-(\alpha+\beta+\gamma)x^2+(\alpha\beta+\alpha\gamma+\beta\gamma)x-\alpha\beta\gamma=0$$

Then $\alpha+\beta+\gamma=-\frac{b}{a}$, which is known as $\Sigma\alpha$ or S_1.

Other results are $\alpha\beta+\alpha\gamma+\beta\gamma=\frac{c}{a}$, written as $\Sigma\alpha\beta$, and $\alpha\beta\gamma=-\frac{d}{a}$, written as $\Sigma\alpha\beta\gamma$.

Recall from quadratics that $\Sigma\alpha^2=(\Sigma\alpha)^2-2\Sigma\alpha\beta$. This is the same result for a cubic equation, where the term $(\Sigma\alpha)^2=(\alpha+\beta+\gamma)^2=\alpha^2+\beta^2+\gamma^2+2\alpha\beta+2\alpha\gamma+2\beta\gamma$, as shown in Key point 1.2.

> **TIP**
>
> Following on from the idea you saw in Worked example 1.3, if we consider the notation $S_n=\alpha^n+\beta^n+\gamma^n$ and then use it to represent our roots, just as with quadratic equations, we can use S_2 to represent $\alpha^2+\beta^2+\gamma^2$ and so on.

KEY POINT 1.2

$$(\Sigma\alpha)^2 = (\alpha + \beta + \gamma)^2 = \alpha^2 + \beta^2 + \gamma^2 + 2\alpha\beta + 2\alpha\gamma + 2\beta\gamma$$

WORKED EXAMPLE 1.4

Find the summation form for the results $\frac{1}{\alpha} + \frac{1}{\beta} + \frac{1}{\gamma}$ and $\frac{1}{\alpha^2} + \frac{1}{\beta^2} + \frac{1}{\gamma^2}$.

Answer

$\frac{1}{\alpha} + \frac{1}{\beta} + \frac{1}{\gamma} = \frac{\alpha\beta + \alpha\gamma + \beta\gamma}{\alpha\beta\gamma}$ — Combine the fractions.

$\Rightarrow \Sigma\frac{1}{\alpha} = \frac{\Sigma\alpha\beta}{\Sigma\alpha\beta\gamma}$ — State the result.

$\frac{1}{\alpha^2} + \frac{1}{\beta^2} + \frac{1}{\gamma^2} = \frac{\alpha^2\beta^2 + \alpha^2\gamma^2 + \beta^2\gamma^2}{\alpha^2\beta^2\gamma^2}$ — Combine the fractions, as before.

$\Sigma\frac{1}{\alpha^2} = \frac{\Sigma(\alpha\beta)^2}{(\Sigma\alpha\beta\gamma)^2}$ — State the result.

All of the results derived for quadratic equations can also be written for cubics, but the algebra is more complicated. Try to convince yourself that for a cubic it is true that $\Sigma\alpha^3 = (\Sigma\alpha)^3 - 3\Sigma\alpha\beta\Sigma\alpha + 3\Sigma\alpha\beta\gamma$.

WORKED EXAMPLE 1.5

Given that $x^3 + 2x^2 + 5 = 0$, find, using summation form, the values of S_1, S_2, S_3 and S_{-1}.

Answer

$S_1 = -2$ — Recall this is $-\frac{b}{a} = -\frac{2}{1}$.

$S_2 = (\Sigma\alpha)^2 - 2\Sigma\alpha\beta$

$\Rightarrow S_2 = (-2)^2 - 2 \times 0 = 4$ — Recall the value of $\Sigma\alpha\beta$ is given by $\frac{c}{a} = \frac{0}{1}$ as the linear term coefficient is 0.

$S_3 = (\Sigma\alpha)^3 - 3\Sigma\alpha\beta\Sigma\alpha + 3\Sigma\alpha\beta\gamma$ — The last term is $3\alpha\beta\gamma$.

$S_3 = (-2)^3 - 3 \times (0) \times (-2) + 3 \times (-5)$ — Substitute the values into the equation.

$S_3 = -23$

$S_{-1} = \frac{0}{-5} = 0$ — Recall that this result is equivalent to $\frac{c}{-d}$, which is obtained by taking the negative of the coefficient of the linear term and dividing by the constant term.

Worked example 1.5 uses the summation form, but there is a more efficient way of finding S_3 and higher powers.

In Worked example 1.6 we will use the recurrence form to evaluate results such as S_3 and S_4.

Consider the equation $x^3 + 3x^2 + 6 = 0$. Since α, β, γ all satisfy our cubics, we can see that $\alpha^3 + 3\alpha^2 + 6 = 0, \beta^3 + 3\beta^2 + 6 = 0$ and $\gamma^3 + 3\gamma^2 + 6 = 0$.

Adding the three equations gives $\alpha^3 + \beta^3 + \gamma^3 + 3(\alpha^2 + \beta^2 + \gamma^2) + 18 = 0$ or $S_3 + 3S_2 + 18 = 0$.

WORKED EXAMPLE 1.6

For the cubic equation $3x^3 + 2x^2 - 4x + 1 = 0$, find the value of S_3.

Answer

$S_1 = -\frac{2}{3}$	From $-\frac{b}{a}$.
$S_2 = \left(-\frac{2}{3}\right)^2 - 2 \times \left(-\frac{4}{3}\right) = \frac{28}{9}$	Using $S_2 = (\Sigma\alpha)^2 - 2\Sigma\alpha\beta$.
$3S_3 + 2S_2 - 4S_1 + 3 = 0$	We know that $3\alpha^3 + 2\alpha^2 - 4\alpha + 1 = 0$ and similar equations can be made for β and γ. We add the three equations.
$S_3 = -\frac{107}{27}$	Substitute for the final result.

We have already seen how to manipulate a polynomial to get a higher power result, such as obtaining S_3 from a quadratic equation. Imagine we want to obtain a value such as S_{-2} from a cubic equation, using only recurrence methods.

The first step would be to multiply our cubic by x^{-2} to give $ax + b + \frac{c}{x} + \frac{d}{x^2} = 0$. The recurrence formula would then be $aS_1 + 3b + cS_{-1} + dS_{-2} = 0$. Note the constant term, b, is multiplied by 3. Now we need to find only S_1 and S_{-1}, and from the original equation this is straightforward.

WORKED EXAMPLE 1.7

For the cubic equation $x^3 - 3x^2 + 4 = 0$, find the value of S_{-3}.

Answer

$S_{-1} = \frac{0}{-4} = 0$	Recall that $S_{-1} = \frac{\Sigma\alpha\beta}{\Sigma\alpha\beta\gamma}$.
$x^3 - 3x^2 + 4 = 0$ $\Rightarrow 1 - \frac{3}{x} + \frac{4}{x^3} = 0$	Divide by x^3.
$3 - 3S_{-1} + 4S_{-3} = 0$	Remember that the 1 is counted three times when adding the three equations for α, β and γ.
$S_{-3} = -\frac{3}{4}$	Substitute values into the equation.

We can generalise from Worked example 1.7. For a general cubic of the form $ax^3 + bx^2 + cx + d = 0$, if we multiply by x^n then our recurrence formula is $aS_{n+3} + bS_{n+2} + cS_{n+1} + dS_n = 0$. Note that only constant terms get counted multiple times.

EXERCISE 1B

1 Each of the following cubic equations has roots α, β, γ. Find, for each case, $\alpha + \beta + \gamma$ and $\alpha\beta\gamma$.

a $x^3 + 3x^2 - 5 = 0$ b $2x^3 + 5x^2 - 6 = 0$ c $x^3 + 7x - 9 = 0$

2 Given that $x^3 - 3x^2 + 12 = 0$ has roots α, β, γ, find the following values:

a $\alpha + \beta + \gamma$ and $\alpha\beta + \alpha\gamma + \beta\gamma$ b $\alpha^2 + \beta^2 + \gamma^2$

3 The roots of each of the following cubic equations are α, β, γ. In each case, find the values of S_2 and S_{-1}.

a $x^3 - 2x^2 + 5 = 0$ b $3x^3 + 4x - 1 = 0$ c $x^3 + 3x^2 + 5x - 7 = 0$

4 The cubic equation $x^3 - x + 7 = 0$ has roots α, β, γ. Find the values of $\Sigma\alpha$ and $\Sigma\alpha^2$.

M 5 Given that $2x^3 + 5x^2 + 1 = 0$ has roots α, β, γ, and that $S_n = \alpha^n + \beta^n + \gamma^n$, find the values of S_2 and S_3.

M PS 6 The cubic equation $x^3 + ax^2 + bx + a = 0$ has roots α, β, γ, and the constants a, b are real and positive.

a Find, in terms of a and b, the values of $\Sigma\alpha$ and $\Sigma\frac{1}{\alpha}$.

b Given that $\Sigma\alpha = \Sigma\frac{1}{\alpha}$, does this cubic equation have complex roots? Give a reason for your answer.

M PS 7 The cubic equation $x^3 - x + 3 = 0$ has roots α, β, γ.

a Using the relation $S_n = \alpha^n + \beta^n + \gamma^n$, or otherwise, find the value of S_4.

b By considering S_1 and S_4, determine the value of $\alpha^3(\beta + \gamma) + \beta^3(\alpha + \gamma) + \gamma^3(\alpha + \beta)$.

P 8 A cubic polynomial is given as $2x^3 - x^2 + x - 5 = 0$, having roots α, β, γ.

a Show that $2S_{n+3} - S_{n+2} + S_{n+1} - 5S_n = 0$.

b Find the value of S_{-2}.

M 9 The cubic equation $px^3 + qx^2 + r = 0$ has roots α, β, γ. Find, in terms of p, q, r:

a S_1 b S_2 c S_3

10 The equation $x^3 + px^2 + qx + r = 0$ is such that $S_1 = 0$, $S_2 = -2$ and $S_{-1} = \frac{1}{5}$.

Find the values of the constants p, q, r.

1.3 Quartics

Now that we are working with **quartics**, it is best to use the recurrence formula whenever we can. This is especially true for the sum of the cubes $(\alpha^3 + \beta^3 + \gamma^3 + \delta^3)$. If we want to determine the sum of the cubes of a general quartic, the best way is to first note down S_1, then determine S_2 and S_{-1}. After this, we can use the form $aS_4 + bS_3 + cS_2 + dS_1 + 4e = 0$, then divide by x to obtain S_3. This process allows us to work out other values, especially those beyond the highest power.

As we have seen with previous polynomials, there are standard results that are defined by observation from previous cases, but the algebra for some results is too complicated to be discussed here.

So, with our roots $\alpha, \beta, \gamma, \delta$, we have $\Sigma\alpha = -\frac{b}{a}$, $\Sigma\alpha\beta = \frac{c}{a}$, $\Sigma\alpha\beta\gamma = -\frac{d}{a}$ and $\Sigma\alpha\beta\gamma\delta = \frac{e}{a}$.

We also have $S_2 = (\Sigma\alpha)^2 - 2\Sigma\alpha\beta$ and $S_{-1} = \frac{\Sigma\alpha\beta\gamma}{\Sigma\alpha\beta\gamma\delta}$ and so on.

Algebraically it is much more sensible to use $S_n = \alpha^n + \beta^n + \gamma^n + \delta^n$.

When converting a polynomial to a recurrence formula, the constant is always multiplied by n from the original equation. As an example, $x^4 - 3x^3 - 5 = 0$ would give $S_4 - 3S_3 - 20 = 0$.

WORKED EXAMPLE 1.8

A quartic polynomial is given as $x^4 + 3x^2 - x + 5 = 0$ and has roots $\alpha, \beta, \gamma, \delta$. Find the values of S_2 and S_4.

Answer

$S_1 = 0$	Simply state the negative of the coefficient of x^3, as the coefficient of x^4 is 1.
$S_2 = 0^2 - 2 \times 3 = -6$	Use $S_2 = (\Sigma\alpha)^2 - 2\Sigma\alpha\beta$.
$S_4 + 3S_2 - S_1 + 20 = 0$	Use $S_n = \alpha^n + \beta^n + \gamma^n + \delta^n$.
$S_4 = -2$	Final answer.

TIP

Remember that for any polynomial, $\Sigma\frac{1}{\alpha}$ is always obtained using the negative of the coefficient of the linear term over the constant term.

WORKED EXAMPLE 1.9

For the quartic $x^4 - x^3 + 2x^2 - 2x - 5 = 0$, state the values of S_1 and S_{-1}, and determine the value of S_2. State whether or not there are any complex solutions.

Answer

$S_1 = 1$	$-1 \times (-1)$
$S_{-1} = \frac{-(-2)}{-5} = -\frac{2}{5}$	Use $S_{-1} = \frac{\Sigma\alpha\beta\gamma}{\Sigma\alpha\beta\gamma\delta}$.
$S_2 = (1)^2 - 2 \times 2 = -3$	Use $S_2 = (\Sigma\alpha)^2 - 2\Sigma\alpha\beta$.

$S_2 < 0$ so there are complex solutions.

TIP

Don't try to use an algebraic approach for quartics, especially for S_3 and higher. Use the recurrence method.

KEY POINT 1.3

For quartics, use $S_n = \alpha^n + \beta^n + \gamma^n + \delta^n$ as a recurrence model to determine results.

EXERCISE 1C

1 For each of the following quartic equations, find the values of $\Sigma\alpha$ and $\Sigma\alpha\beta$.

a $x^4 - 2x^3 + 5x^2 + 7 = 0$ b $2x^4 + 5x^3 - 3x + 4 = 0$ c $3x^4 - 2x^2 + 9x - 11 = 0$

2 The quartic equation $5x^4 - 3x^3 + x - 13 = 0$ has roots $\alpha, \beta, \gamma, \delta$. Find:

a $\Sigma\alpha$ and $\Sigma\alpha^2$

b $\Sigma\frac{1}{\alpha}$

3 A quartic equation is given as $x^4 + x + 2 = 0$. It has roots $\alpha, \beta, \gamma, \delta$. State the values of S_1 and S_{-1}, and find the value of S_2.

PS 4 The quartic equation $2x^4 + x^3 - x + 7 = 0$ has roots $\alpha, \beta, \gamma, \delta$. Given that $S_3 = \frac{11}{8}$, and using S_n, find the value of S_4.

5 You are given that $x^4 - x^3 + x + 2 = 0$, where the roots are $\alpha, \beta, \gamma, \delta$. Find the values of $\Sigma\alpha$, $\Sigma\alpha^2$ and $\Sigma\frac{1}{\alpha}$. Hence, determine the value of $\Sigma\alpha^3$.

PS 6 The quartic polynomial $x^4 + ax^2 + bx + 1 = 0$ has roots $\alpha, \beta, \gamma, \delta$. Given that $S_2 = S_{-1}$, find S_3 in terms of a.

PS 7 The polynomial $3x^4 + 2x^3 + 7x^2 + 4 = 0$ has roots $\alpha, \beta, \gamma, \delta$, where $S_n = \alpha^n + \beta^n + \gamma^n + \delta^n$.

a Find the values of S_1 and S_2.

b Find the values of S_3 and S_4.

c Are there any complex roots? Give a reason for your answer.

PS 8 For the polynomial $x^4 + ax^3 + bx^2 + c = 0$, with roots α, β, γ and δ, it is given that $\alpha + \beta + \gamma + \delta = 2$, $\alpha\beta\gamma\delta = 1$ and $\alpha^2 + \beta^2 + \gamma^2 + \delta^2 = 0$. Find the values of the coefficients a, b and c.

P 9 The roots of the quartic $x^4 - 2x^3 + x^2 - 4 = 0$ are $\alpha, \beta, \gamma, \delta$. Show that $S_4 = 9S_3$.

1.4 Substitutions

Imagine that we are given the quadratic equation $x^2 + 3x + 5 = 0$ with roots α, β and we are asked to find a quadratic that has roots $2\alpha, 2\beta$. There are two approaches that we can take.

First, consider the quadratic $(y - 2\alpha)(y - 2\beta) = 0$, then $y^2 - (2\alpha + 2\beta)y + 4\alpha\beta = 0$. If we compare this with the original, which is $\alpha + \beta = -3, \alpha\beta = 5$, then $y^2 + 6y + 20 = 0$ is the new quadratic. This method requires us to know some results, or at least spend time working them out.

A second method is to start with $y = 2x$, since each root of y is twice that of x. Then, substituting $x = \frac{y}{2}$ into the original gives $\left(\frac{y}{2}\right)^2 + 3\left(\frac{y}{2}\right) + 5 = 0$. Alternatively, multiplying by 4, $y^2 + 6y + 20 = 0$. This second approach does not need the values of roots. It just needs the relationship between the roots of each polynomial.

TIP

You learned in AS & A Level Mathematics Pure Mathematics 1 Coursebook how to find inverse functions by interchanging x and y. The same process is helpful here.

WORKED EXAMPLE 1.10

Given that $x^2 - 2x + 12 = 0$ has roots α, β, find the quadratic equation with roots $\frac{\alpha}{3}, \frac{\beta}{3}$.

Answer

$y = \frac{x}{3} \Rightarrow x = 3y$ — Rearrange to make x the subject.

$(3y)^2 - 2(3y) + 12 = 0$ — Substitute for x.

$3y^2 - 2y + 4 = 0$ — Multiply out terms and simplify.

More complicated substitutions include reciprocal functions. For example, consider the cubic function $x^3 + x^2 - 7 = 0$ with roots α, β, γ. If we are asked to find a cubic function with roots $\frac{1}{\alpha}, \frac{1}{\beta}, \frac{1}{\gamma}$, we would begin with $y = \frac{1}{x} \Rightarrow x = \frac{1}{y}$. Then $\left(\frac{1}{y}\right)^3 + \left(\frac{1}{y}\right)^2 - 7 = 0$, which simplifies to the cubic $7y^3 - y - 1 = 0$.

WORKED EXAMPLE 1.11

Given that $x^3 + x^2 - 5 = 0$ has roots α, β, γ, find the cubic equation with roots $\frac{1}{\alpha - 2}, \frac{1}{\beta - 2}, \frac{1}{\gamma - 2}$.

Answer

$y = \frac{1}{x - 2} \Rightarrow xy - 2y = 1$

$x = \frac{1 + 2y}{y}$ — Rearrange to make x the subject.

$\left(\frac{1 + 2y}{y}\right)^3 + \left(\frac{1 + 2y}{y}\right)^2 - 5 = 0$ — Substitute for x.

$\frac{1 + 6y + 12y^2 + 8y^3}{y^3} + \frac{1 + 4y + 4y^2}{y^2} - 5 = 0$ — Expand brackets.

$7y^3 + 16y^2 + 7y + 1 = 0$ — Multiply by y^3 and simplify.

EXPLORE 1.1

The polynomial $x^3 + x - 3 = 0$ has roots α, β, γ. If $\frac{a\alpha + 1}{\alpha - b}, \frac{a\beta + 1}{\beta - b}, \frac{a\gamma + 1}{\gamma - b}$ are the roots of another cubic, what are the conditions on a and b to ensure that these cubics are the same?

Powers of roots require a different method. For example, if we have the cubic equation $2x^3 + 7x^2 - 1 = 0$ with roots α, β, γ and we want to determine the cubic with roots $\alpha^2, \beta^2, \gamma^2$, there are two ways of approaching this.

First, we could state that $y = x^2$ and so $x = \sqrt{y}$. Substituting gives $2y^{\frac{3}{2}} + 7y - 1 = 0$. Next, write as $7y - 1 = -2y^{\frac{3}{2}}$ and square both sides, giving $49y^2 - 14y + 1 = 4y^3$. So $4y^3 - 49y^2 + 14y - 1 = 0$ is the cubic that we are looking for.

In the second approach we first rearrange the cubic to $2x^3 = 1 - 7x^2$. Doing this allows us to square both sides and get even powers of x for every term, so $4x^6 = 1 - 14x^2 + 49x^4$. Substituting in $x^2 = y$ gives the same cubic as before.

In the first approach we substitute $y = x^2$ before rearranging the equation. In the second approach we do the steps in the reverse order. For both approaches we need to make sure the powers of x are appropriate.

WORKED EXAMPLE 1.12

The polynomial $x^4 + x^3 - x + 12 = 0$ has roots $\alpha, \beta, \gamma, \delta$. Find the polynomial with roots $\alpha^2, \beta^2, \gamma^2, \delta^2$.

Answer

$y = x^2$	State the substitution.
$x^4 + 12 = x - x^3$	Rearrange so that both sides when squared give even terms.
$x^8 + 24x^4 + 144 = x^2 - 2x^4 + x^6$	Square both sides.
$x^8 - x^6 + 26x^4 - x^2 + 144 = 0$	Simplify.
$y^4 - y^3 + 26y^2 - y + 144 = 0$	Use $x^2 = y$.

These substitution methods are useful when dealing with problems such as finding the value of S_6 or even S_8.

Consider the quartic $x^4 + x^3 - 5 = 0$. For this polynomial, we would like to determine the value of S_4. The process for finding $S_4 = \alpha^4 + \beta^4 + \gamma^4 + \delta^4$ can be time consuming. Now, consider that there is another quartic such that $y = x^2$. If this quartic exists, then for y we would have $S_n = \alpha^{2n} + \beta^{2n} + \gamma^{2n} + \delta^{2n}$. Since we have doubled the power for each root, once we have determined the quartic for y we only need to find S_2, which is straightforward.

Rewrite the original quartic as $x^4 - 5 = -x^3$, then square both sides to get $x^8 - 10x^4 + 25 = x^6$. Next, replace x^2 with y so that $y^4 - y^3 - 10y^2 + 25 = 0$. Finally, for the new quartic, $S_1 = 1$ and $S_2 = 1^2 - 2 \times (-10) = 21$. Hence, for the original quartic, $S_4 = 21$.

This is an effective method and can save lots of time, particularly for much higher values of n.

TIP

Ensure both sides of the rearranged polynomial will give appropriate powers when the squaring or cubing operation has taken place. For example, $x^3 - 5x + 7 = 0$ with $y = x^2$ would be written as $x^3 - 5x = -7$ to ensure that, when squared, both sides produce only even powers.

If the same equation is used with $y = x^3$, then rearrange to $x^3 + 7 = 5x$ so that, when it is cubed, the powers of x are multiples of 3 on both sides.

WORKED EXAMPLE 1.13

The cubic polynomial $x^3 + 5x^2 + 1 = 0$ has roots α, β, γ. Using the substitution $y = x^3$, or otherwise, find the value of S_6.

Answer

$x^3 + 5x^2 + 1 = 0$	(1)	Label the original equation.
$x^3 + 1 = -5x^2$		Since we are using x^3, ensure all terms are arranged so when both sides are cubed, they produce powers that are multiples of 3.
$x^9 + 3x^6 + 3x^3 + 1 = -125x^6$		Cube both sides.
$\Rightarrow x^9 + 128x^6 + 3x^3 + 1 = 0$		Simplify.
$\Rightarrow y^3 + 128y^2 + 3y + 1 = 0$	(2)	Use $x^3 = y$, label the new equation.

$S_1 = -128$	Determine S_1.
$S_2 = (-128)^2 - 2 \times 3 = 16378$ for (2)	Substitute for S_2.
Hence, for (1), $S_6 = 16378$	State S_6.

DID YOU KNOW?

The term 'polynomials' was not used until the 17th century. Before the 15th century, equations were represented by words, not symbols. A famous Chinese algebraic problem was written: 'Three bundles of good crop, two bundles of mediocre crop, and one bundle of bad crop are sold for 29 dou.' In modern times we would phrase this as $3a + 2b + c = 29$.

EXERCISE 1D

M 1 The quadratic equation $x^2 + 5x + 3 = 0$ has roots α, β. Find the quadratic equation with roots 3α, 3β.

M 2 The quadratic equation $2x^2 - 4x + 7 = 0$ has roots α, β.

a Find the quadratic equation with roots α^2, β^2.

b Find the quadratic equation with roots $2\alpha - 3$, $2\beta - 3$.

M 3 Given that $3x^2 - 2x + 9 = 0$ has roots α, β, find the quadratic equation with roots $\frac{\alpha + 1}{\alpha}$, $\frac{\beta + 1}{\beta}$.

M 4 The quadratic equation $x^2 - 4x + 9 = 0$ has roots α, β. Find the quadratic that has roots $\frac{1}{\alpha}, \frac{1}{\beta}$.

PS 5 Given that $2x^3 - 5x + 1 = 0$ has roots α, β, γ, find the cubic equation with roots $\alpha^2, \beta^2, \gamma^2$. Hence, find the value of S_4.

P PS 6 The cubic equation $x^3 + 3x^2 - 1 = 0$ has roots α, β, γ. Show that the cubic equation with roots $\frac{\alpha + 2}{\alpha}, \frac{\beta + 2}{\beta}, \frac{\gamma + 2}{\gamma}$ is $y^3 - 3y^2 - 9y + 3 = 0$. Hence, determine the values of:

a $\frac{(\alpha + 2)(\beta + 2)(\gamma + 2)}{\alpha\beta\gamma}$

b $\frac{\alpha}{\alpha + 2} + \frac{\beta}{\beta + 2} + \frac{\gamma}{\gamma + 2}$

P PS 7 A quartic equation, $2x^4 - x^3 - 6 = 0$, has roots $\alpha, \beta, \gamma, \delta$. Show that the quartic equation with roots $\alpha^3, \beta^3, \gamma^3, \delta^3$ is $8y^4 - y^3 - 18y^2 - 108y - 216 = 0$. Hence, find the values of S_6 and S_{-3}.

PS 8 The cubic equation $x^3 - x + 4 = 0$ has roots α, β, γ. Find the cubic equation that has roots $\alpha^2, \beta^2, \gamma^2$. Hence, or otherwise, determine the values of S_6, S_8 and S_{10}.

WORKED PAST PAPER QUESTION

The equation $x^3 + x - 1 = 0$ has roots α, β, γ.

Show that the equation with roots $\alpha^3, \beta^3, \gamma^3$ is $y^3 - 3y^2 + 4y - 1 = 0$.

Hence, find the value of $\alpha^6 + \beta^6 + \gamma^6$.

Cambridge International AS & A Level Further Mathematics 9231 Paper 1 Q5 June 2008

Answer

Start with $x^3 - 1 = -x$.

Then rewrite this as $(x^3 - 1)^3 = -x^3$. This gives $x^9 - 3x^6 + 4x^3 - 1 = 0$.

Let $y = x^3$ to give $y^3 - 3y^2 + 4y - 1 = 0$.

Note that $S_n = \alpha^n + \beta^n + \gamma^n$.

S_6 for the original equation is S_2 for the new equation, so $S_2 = 3^2 - 2 \times 4 = 1$.

Hence, $\alpha^6 + \beta^6 + \gamma^6 = 1$.

Checklist of learning and understanding

For quadratic equations ($ax^2 + bx + c = 0$):

- $\Sigma\alpha = \alpha + \beta = -\frac{b}{a}$
- $\Sigma\alpha\beta = \alpha\beta = \frac{c}{a}$
- $S_n = \alpha^n + \beta^n$

For cubic equations ($ax^3 + bx^2 + cx + d = 0$):

- $\Sigma\alpha = \alpha + \beta + \gamma = -\frac{b}{a}$
- $\Sigma\alpha\beta = \alpha\beta + \alpha\gamma + \beta\gamma = \frac{c}{a}$
- $\Sigma\alpha\beta\gamma = \alpha\beta\gamma = -\frac{d}{a}$
- $S_n = \alpha^n + \beta^n + \gamma^n$

For quartic equations ($ax^4 + bx^3 + cx^2 + dx + e = 0$):

- $\Sigma\alpha = \alpha + \beta + \gamma + \delta = -\frac{b}{a}$
- $\Sigma\alpha\beta = \alpha\beta + \alpha\gamma + \alpha\delta + \beta\gamma + \beta\delta + \gamma\delta = \frac{c}{a}$
- $\Sigma\alpha\beta\gamma = \alpha\beta\gamma + \alpha\beta\delta + \alpha\gamma\delta + \beta\gamma\delta = -\frac{d}{a}$
- $\Sigma\alpha\beta\gamma\delta = \alpha\beta\gamma\delta = \frac{e}{a}$
- $S_n = \alpha^n + \beta^n + \gamma^n + \delta^n$

For recurrence notation:

- $\Sigma\alpha$ is also known as S_1.
- $\Sigma\alpha^2 = (\Sigma\alpha)^2 - 2\Sigma\alpha\beta$ is also known as S_2.
- $\Sigma\frac{1}{\alpha}$ is known as S_{-1}. It is always equal to the negative of the coefficient of the linear term divided by the coefficient of the constant term.

END-OF-CHAPTER REVIEW EXERCISE 1

1 The roots of the equation $x^3 + 4x - 1 = 0$ are α, β and γ. Use the substitution $y = \frac{1}{1+x}$ to show that the equation $6y^3 - 7y^2 + 3y - 1 = 0$ has roots $\frac{1}{\alpha+1}, \frac{1}{\beta+1}$ and $\frac{1}{\gamma+1}$.

For the cases $n = 1$ and $n = 2$, find the value of $\frac{1}{(\alpha+1)^n} + \frac{1}{(\beta+1)^n} + \frac{1}{(\gamma+1)^n}$.

Deduce the value of $\frac{1}{(\alpha+1)^3} + \frac{1}{(\beta+1)^3} + \frac{1}{(\gamma+1)^3}$.

Hence show that $\frac{(\beta+1)(\gamma+1)}{(\alpha+1)^2} + \frac{(\gamma+1)(\alpha+1)}{(\beta+1)^2} + \frac{(\alpha+1)(\beta+1)}{(\gamma+1)^2} = \frac{73}{36}$.

Cambridge International AS & A Level Further Mathematics 9231 Paper 1 Q7 November 2010

2 The roots of the quartic equation $x^4 + 4x^3 + 2x^2 - 4x + 1 = 0$ are α, β, γ and δ.

Find the values of

i $\alpha + \beta + \gamma + \delta$,

ii $\alpha^2 + \beta^2 + \gamma^2 + \delta^2$,

iii $\frac{1}{\alpha} + \frac{1}{\beta} + \frac{1}{\gamma} + \frac{1}{\delta}$,

iv $\frac{\alpha}{\beta\gamma\delta} + \frac{\beta}{\alpha\gamma\delta} + \frac{\gamma}{\alpha\beta\delta} + \frac{\delta}{\alpha\beta\gamma}$.

Using the substitution $y = x + 1$, find a quartic equation in y. Solve this quartic equation and hence find the roots of the equation $x^4 + 4x^3 + 2x^2 - 4x + 1 = 0$.

Cambridge International AS & A Level Further Mathematics 9231 Paper 11 Q11 November 2014

3 The cubic equation $x^3 - x^2 - 3x - 10 = 0$ has roots α, β, γ.

i Let $u = -\alpha + \beta + \gamma$. Show that $u + 2\alpha = 1$, and hence find a cubic equation having roots $-\alpha + \beta + \gamma, \alpha - \beta + \gamma, \alpha + \beta - \gamma$.

ii State the value of $\alpha\beta\gamma$ and hence find a cubic equation having roots $\frac{1}{\beta\gamma}, \frac{1}{\gamma\alpha}, \frac{1}{\alpha\beta}$.

Cambridge International AS & A Level Further Mathematics 9231 Paper 13 Q8 June 2012

Chapter 2
Rational functions

In this chapter you will learn how to:

- sketch graphs of simple rational functions, including the determination of oblique asymptotes, in cases where the degree of the numerator and the denominator are, at most, 2
- understand and use relationships between the graphs of $y = \mathrm{f}(x)$, $y^2 = \mathrm{f}(x)$, $y = \dfrac{1}{\mathrm{f}(x)}$, $y = |\mathrm{f}(x)|$ and $y = \mathrm{f}(|x|)$.

PREREQUISITE KNOWLEDGE

Where it comes from	What you should be able to do	Check your skills
AS & A Level Mathematics Pure Mathematics 2 & 3, Chapter 7	Split functions into partial fractions.	1 Split the following into partial fractions. a $\frac{x^2+1}{x-3}$ b $\frac{1}{(x-1)(x-2)}$ c $\frac{x^2}{x^2-1}$
AS & A Level Mathematics Pure Mathematics 1, Chapter 5	Know about asymptotes and how to determine horizontal and linear cases.	2 Write down the asymptotes for: a $y=\frac{1}{x-1}$ b $y=\frac{2x-3}{x+1}$ c $y=\frac{1}{x^2-4}$
AS & A Level Mathematics Pure Mathematics 1, Chapter 5 Pure Mathematics 2 & 3, Chapter 1	Work with the modulus function in the forms $y=\lvert f(x)\rvert$ and $y=f(\lvert x\rvert)$.	3 Make sketches of the functions: a $y=\lvert\sin x\rvert$ b $y=\sin\lvert x\rvert$ c $y=\left\lvert\frac{1}{x}\right\rvert$

What are rational functions?

A **rational function** is any function that can be defined as an algebraic fraction with polynomials as numerator and **denominator**. Rational functions are used to predict outcomes, from international trade balances in Economics to the amount of anaesthetic a patient will need for surgery.

You are already familiar with plotting graphs as functions and identifying simple **asymptotes**. You should already have the algebraic skills to use partial fractions to rearrange and simplify functions.

In this chapter, you will sketch several different types of function, including $y = f(x)$, $y^2 = f(x)$, $y = \frac{1}{f(x)}$, $y = |f(x)|$ and $y = f(|x|)$. You will also work with asymptotes (horizontal, vertical and oblique); identify symmetries of curves and similarities between curves; and determine ranges, turning points and x-intercepts and y-intercepts.

2.1 Vertical asymptotes

An asymptote is generally a line that a curve approaches but does not touch.

KEY POINT 2.1

An asymptote is generally a line that a curve approaches but does not touch. We can say the curve converges to an asymptote.

Consider the graph of the function $y = \frac{1}{x}$ (see the diagram). We can see that this curve tends towards both the coordinate axes. This is because there are two asymptotes: their equations are $x = 0$ and $y = 0$. These asymptotes are straight lines and come from the condition that $x \neq 0$ and $y \neq 0$.

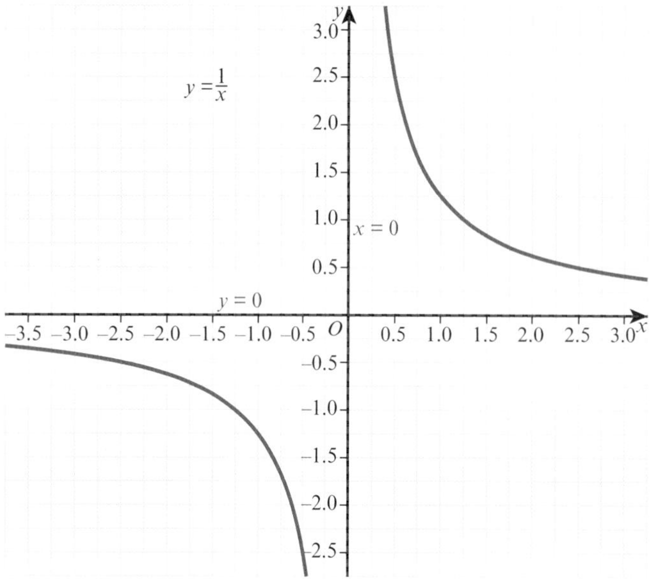

If we then consider the graph of the function $y = \frac{1}{x-1}$ (as seen in the following diagram), it is clear that $x \neq 1$ and $y \neq 0$, and these give us two asymptotes: $x = 1$ and $y = 0$. If we have any doubts about the shape of the curve, we can test either side of the line $x = 1$, where the curve has a **discontinuity**. So when $x = 1.0001$, the value of y is large and positive, and when $x = 0.9999$, the value of y is large and negative, as shown. Lastly, this curve has one **intersection** point with the coordinate axes, when $x = 0, y = -1$.

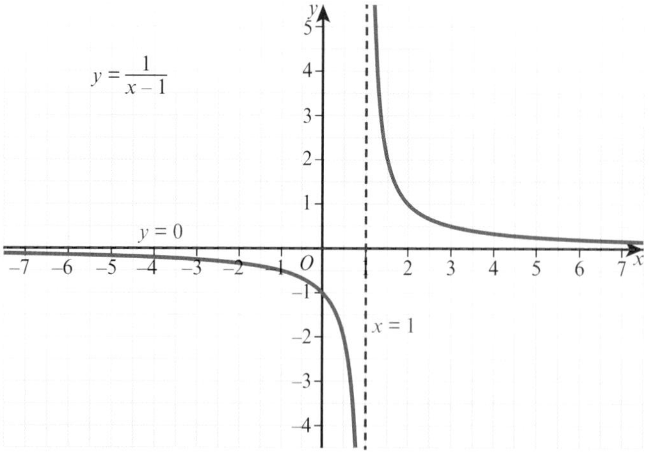

Extending this idea even further to the function $y = \frac{x+1}{x-1}$ (see the following diagram), we need to simplify the fraction before we can find the asymptotes. First, note that this function has a vertical asymptote at $x = 1$, since the denominator is zero. Also note that the numerator is larger than the denominator.

A **top-heavy** or improper fraction is a fraction where the degree of the polynomial in the numerator is greater than or equal to the degree of the denominator. Examples are $\frac{x}{x+3}, \frac{x^2}{x-5}$ and $\frac{2x^2}{x^2+7}$.

For improper fractions, the horizontal asymptote can be found in two ways. We can consider $|x| \to \infty$, when the curve $y = \frac{x+1}{x-1}$ is close to $y \approx \frac{x}{x}$ and so $y = 1$ is the asymptote. Alternatively, we can split the function into smaller parts. Since the numerator of the fraction is larger than the denominator, we can assume that $\frac{x+1}{x-1} = A + \frac{B}{x-1}$. Hence, $x + 1 = A(x - 1) + B$. We can solve this to get $A = 1, B = 2$. The equation can then be written as $y = 1 + \frac{2}{x-1}$. As $|x| \to \infty$ we can see that $\frac{2}{x-1} \to 0$, so y approaches 1. Lastly, we consider specific values to work out the shape of the curve. When $x = 0, y = -1$ and when $y = 0, x = -1$. Now we can sketch the curve.

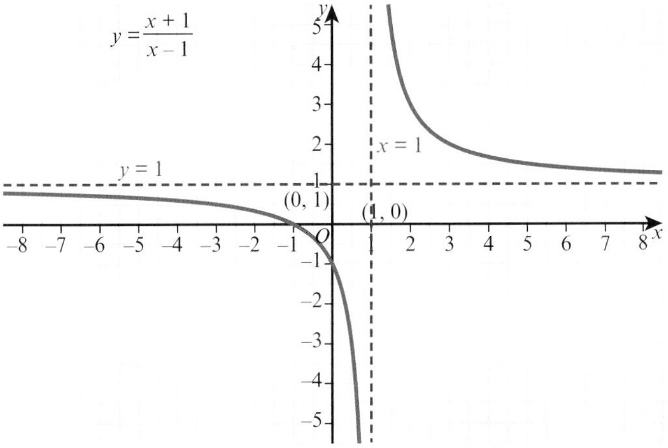

WORKED EXAMPLE 2.1

Sketch the curve $y = \frac{x+3}{x+2}$, showing all points of intersection with the coordinate axes. State the equations of the asymptotes.

Answer

When $x = 0, y = \frac{3}{2}$, when $y = 0, x = -3$	Determine the points of intersection.
$x = -2$	State the vertical asymptote.
$\lvert x\rvert \to \infty \Rightarrow y \approx 1$ so $y = 1$	Determine the horizontal asymptote. Note that partial fractions are not needed for the simpler cases.
$x = -2.0001, y < 0$ $x = -1.9999, y > 0$	Check the value of y on either side of the vertical asymptote.

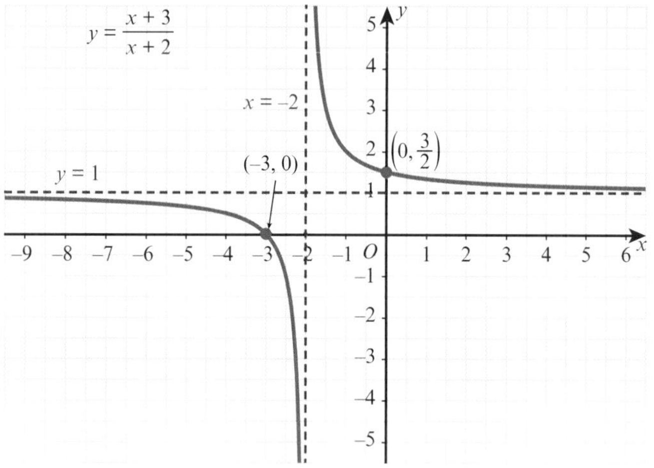

Sketch the curve, labelling all the important features. Include asymptotes, turning points and any intersections with the axes.

The examples we have looked at so far all have a linear denominator. In the next example, the denominator is a quadratic.

Consider the function $y = \frac{1}{(x-1)(x-2)}$ (shown in the following diagram). The first point to note is that we now have two vertical asymptotes: $x = 1$ and $x = 2$. Determine the horizontal asymptote next. If $|x| \to \infty$, then $y = 0$ is clearly our horizontal asymptote.

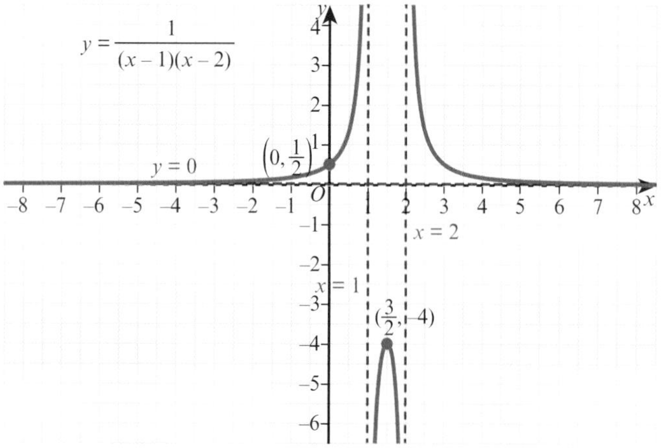

For this curve, $y \neq 0$ and when $x = 0, y = \frac{1}{2}$. You will notice in the diagram that there is at least one **turning point**. To determine the turning points we can use one of two methods.

We could just differentiate to get $\frac{dy}{dx} = \frac{3-2x}{(x^2-3x+2)^2}$. When $\frac{dy}{dx} = 0, x = \frac{3}{2}$. This value also happens to be the midpoint between 1 and 2.

The other method is to start with $y = \frac{1}{x^2-3x+2}$, then rearrange the equation to give $yx^2 - 3yx + (2y-1) = 0$. We can consider this as a quadratic equation in x and use the discriminant $b^2 - 4ac$. Use the condition that the discriminant is < 0 to set up an inequality in y. In this way, we can find which y values are invalid for the function. $b^2 - 4ac = 9y^2 - 4y(2y-1) < 0$ so $y(y+4) < 0$ and therefore $-4 < y < 0$.

Remember that these are the values of y that we *cannot* have. With the asymptote condition included, the range of values for y is $y > 0$ and $y \leqslant -4$. We can also see that the turning point occurs when $y = -4$.

TIP

Note that this second method is *only* applicable when the function does not have a full range of values. Some functions can exist for all $y \in \mathbb{R}$.

KEY POINT 2.2

For any curve of the form $y = \dfrac{ax^2 + bx + c}{dx^2 + ex + f}$, it is possible to multiply through by the denominator, then rearrange to get $(dy - ay)x^2 + (ey - by)x + (fy - cy) = 0$. Then, for this quadratic equation in x, using the discriminant $b^2 - 4ac < 0$ will tell you what values of y your curve cannot have.

WORKED EXAMPLE 2.2

The curve $y = \dfrac{x}{(x+1)(x-3)}$ is denoted as C. Determine the points of intersection with the coordinate axes, find all asymptotes and determine any turning points. Hence, sketch C.

Answer

$x = -1, x = 3$ — State the two vertical asymptotes.

$|x| \to \infty, y \to 0 \Rightarrow y = 0$ — Determine the horizontal asymptote.

$x = 0, y = 0$ — Find the only intersection point with the axes.

$\dfrac{dy}{dx} = \dfrac{1(x^2 - 2x - 3) - x(2x - 2)}{(x^2 - 2x - 3)^2}$ — Differentiate the function.

$\dfrac{dy}{dx} = \dfrac{-x^2 - 3}{(x^2 - 2x - 3)^2} \Rightarrow \dfrac{dy}{dx} \neq 0$ — Simplify and determine that there are no turning points.

$x = -1.0001, y < 0$ and $x = -0.9999, y > 0$
$x = 2.9999, y < 0$ and $x = 3.0001, y > 0$ — Test the behaviour of C either side of the discontinuities.

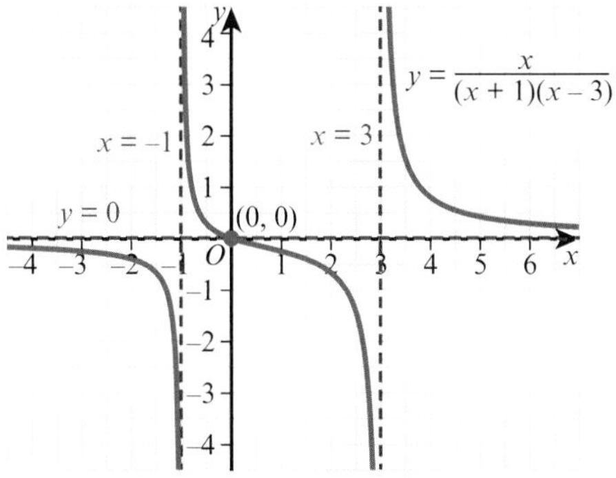

Sketch the curve. Note that, in this example, the curve actually cuts the horizontal asymptote at the point (0, 0).

EXPLORE 2.1

Consider the two curves $y = \dfrac{a}{(bx + c)(dx + e)}$ and $y = \dfrac{ax + b}{(cx + d)(ex + f)}$, where a, b, c, d, e, f are constants.

Discuss in groups what features these two curves have. Do their asymptotes differ? Do they have the same number of turning points?

So far, we have seen improper fractions where the numerator and denominator are linear functions. Now we will consider a function in which both the numerator and denominator are quadratics.

One major difference is that $y = \dfrac{ax^2 + bx + c}{x^2 + d}$ will have a horizontal asymptote at $y = a$.

Depending on the numerator, there will be 0, 1 or 2 turning points.

WORKED EXAMPLE 2.3

Sketch the curve $y = \dfrac{(x-1)(x-2)}{(2x-1)(x+1)}$, showing all points of intersection and asymptotes and determine the number of turning points.

Answer

$x = -1, x = \dfrac{1}{2}$ — State the vertical asymptotes.

$|x| \to \infty, y = \dfrac{1}{2}$ — Evaluate the horizontal asymptote.

$y = 0 \Rightarrow x = 1, x = 2$
$x = 0 \Rightarrow y = -2$ — Obtain the points of intersection.

$\dfrac{dy}{dx} = \dfrac{7x^2 - 10x + 1}{(2x^2 + x - 1)^2}$ — Differentiate and simplify.

$7x^2 - 10x + 1 = 0$ — Set $\dfrac{dy}{dx} = 0$.

$b^2 - 4ac = 72$ — The discriminant is greater than 0 so there are two solutions. Hence, there are two turning points. In fact, the stationary points are $\left(\dfrac{5 - 3\sqrt{2}}{7}, -1 - \dfrac{2\sqrt{2}}{3}\right)$ and $\left(\dfrac{5 + 3\sqrt{2}}{7}, -1 + \dfrac{2\sqrt{2}}{3}\right)$.

$x = -1.0001, y > 0$ and $x = -0.9999, y < 0$
$x = 0.4999, y < 0$ and $x = 0.50001, y > 0$ — Test values either side of each vertical asymptote.

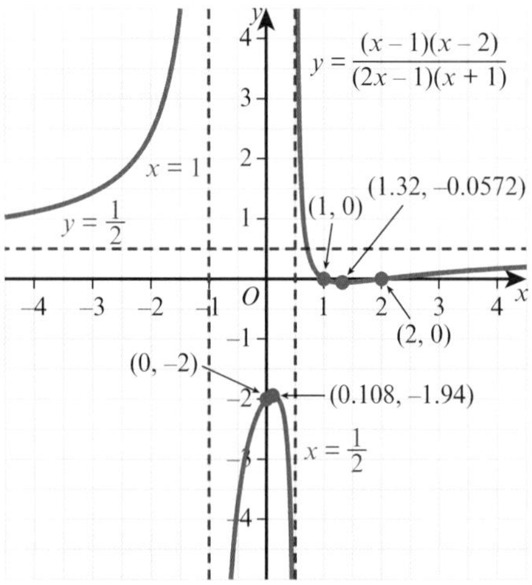

Notice that the curve has one turning point between $x = 1$ and $x = 2$. Recall that at both these values $y = 0$.

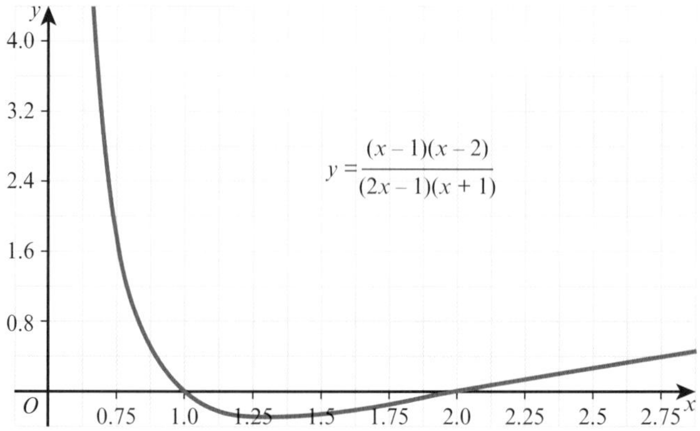

When dealing with this type of function, differentiation can be rather time consuming, but there are ways of making it more efficient. For example, if we look back at Worked example 2.3 and split the function into partial fractions, we have $y = \frac{1}{2} + \frac{1}{2(2x-1)} - \frac{2}{x+1}$.

Differentiate this to give $\frac{dy}{dx} = -\frac{1}{(2x-1)^2} + \frac{2}{(x+1)^2}$. Solving this leads to the same quadratic as before but in fewer steps.

WORKED EXAMPLE 2.4

A curve, C, is given as $y = \frac{(x-1)(x+3)}{(x-2)(x+1)}$. Find all asymptotes and points of intersection and hence sketch the curve.

You are encouraged to consider turning points.

Answer

$x = -1, x = 2$ — State the vertical asymptotes and determine the horizontal asymptote.

$|x| \to \infty,\ y = \frac{x^2+2x-3}{x^2-x-2} \Rightarrow y = 1$

When $x = 0, y = \frac{3}{2}$ — Determine the points of intersection.

When $y = 0, x = -3$ and $x = 1$

$x = -1.0001, y < 0$ and $x = -0.9999, y > 0$ — Describe the behaviour around each asymptote.

$x = 1.9999, y < 0$ and $x = 2.0001, y > 0$

$\frac{dy}{dx} = \frac{-3x^2+2x-7}{(x^2-x-2)^2} = 0$ — Differentiate and set $\frac{dy}{dx} = 0$.

$(2)^2 - 4(-3)(-7) = -80$ — Consider the numerator. A discriminant of less than 0 means there are no turning points.

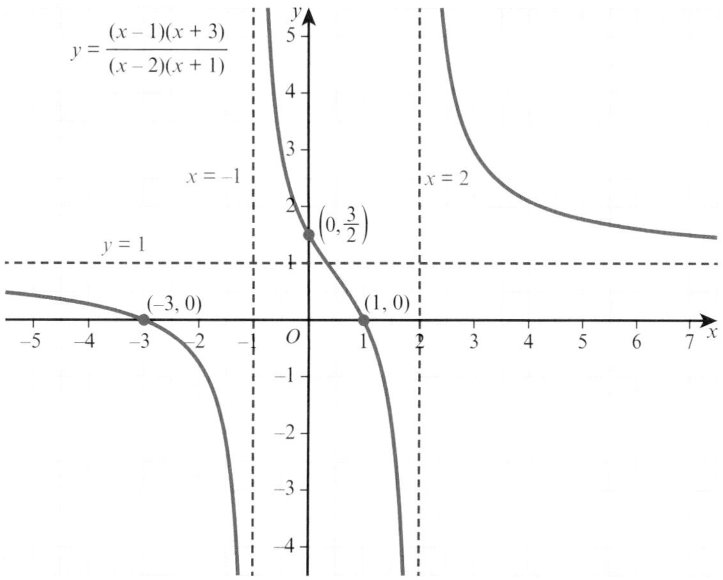

EXERCISE 2A

1 For each of the following, determine the equations of the asymptotes of the curves.

a $y = \dfrac{2x + 3}{x^2 + 3x + 2}$ b $y = \dfrac{4x + 3}{x - 2}$ c $y = \dfrac{x^2 - 2x - 3}{x^2 - 2x - 8}$

2 Write $y = \dfrac{2x^2}{x^2 - 5x - 6}$ in partial fractions. Hence, state the equations of the asymptotes.

PS 3 Determine the number of turning points for each of the following curves.

a $y = \dfrac{x}{(x + 1)(x - 3)}$ b $y = \dfrac{x^2 + 2x}{x^2 + x + 4}$

4 The curve, C, is given as $y = \dfrac{2x + 4}{x - 1}$. Find the equations of the asymptotes for C.

5 Sketch the curve $y = \dfrac{3x - 1}{x + 2}$, showing all points of intersection with the coordinate axes.

6 A curve is given as $y = \dfrac{x - 1}{x - 2}$.

a Write this in the form $y = A + \dfrac{B}{x - 2}$.

b State the equations of the asymptotes.

c Sketch the curve, showing points of intersection with the coordinate axes.

PS 7 A curve has equation $y = \dfrac{3 - x}{x^2 - 1}$.

a Write down the equations of the asymptotes.

b Find the x-coordinates of any stationary points.

c Sketch the curve.

P 8 The curve, C, is written as $y = \dfrac{2x}{(x - 1)(x + 3)}$.

a Show that C has no turning points.

b Sketch the curve C. Show on your sketch all the points of intersection with the coordinate axes.

PS 9 The curve $y = \dfrac{x^2 - 5}{(x - 1)(x + 3)}$ has two vertical asymptotes and one horizontal asymptote.

a Find the equations of these asymptotes.

b Determine the number of turning points.

c Sketch the curve.

2.2 Oblique asymptotes

In this section we will work with curves where the numerator is a quadratic and the denominator is linear. This produces an asymptote called an **oblique** asymptote, which is neither horizontal nor vertical. The curve will have one vertical asymptote that is easy to identify. To find the oblique asymptote, we need to write the equation of the curve in partial fraction form first.

If we consider the curve $y = \frac{x^2}{x+1}$, the denominator indicates that the vertical asymptote is $x = -1$. To find the oblique asymptote, we must first consider $\frac{x^2}{x+1} = Ax + B + \frac{C}{x+1}$, hence $x^2 = (Ax + B)(x + 1) + C$.

With $x = -1$ and $x = 0$ we get $C = 1, B = -1$ and it follows that $A = 1$.

This gives $y = x - 1 + \frac{1}{x+1}$ and the oblique asymptote is $y = x - 1$.

For any curve of the form $y = \frac{ax^2 + bx + c}{dx + e}$, split the function into the form $y = Ax + B + \frac{C}{dx + e}$. The vertical asymptote is $x = -\frac{e}{d}$ and the oblique asymptote is $y = Ax + B$, where $A = \frac{a}{d}$.

KEY POINT 2.3

For any curve of the form $y = \frac{ax^2 + bx + c}{dx + e}$ the vertical asymptote is $x = -\frac{e}{d}$ and the oblique asymptote is $y = Ax + B$, where $A = \frac{a}{d}$.

WORKED EXAMPLE 2.5

The curve, C, is defined as $y = \frac{x^2 + 1}{x - 2}$. Write down the vertical asymptote, and determine the equation of the oblique asymptote.

Answer

$x = 2$	Identify the vertical asymptote.
$\frac{x^2 + 1}{x - 2} = Ax + B + \frac{C}{x - 2}$	Write the function in partial fraction form.
$A = 1$	State the value of A.
$x^2 + 1 = (x + B)(x - 2) + C$	Simplify to find the coefficients.
$x = 2 \Rightarrow C = 5$ and $x = 0 \Rightarrow B = 2$	Determine the coefficients.
$y = x + 2$	State the oblique asymptote.

Once we can find oblique asymptotes, we will be able to sketch the curve. As before, we can check x-values either side of the vertical asymptote. We can also test if a curve is above or below the oblique asymptote.

Look again at the function from Worked example 2.5. We are going to determine how the curve relates to the oblique asymptote. For $x = 100$, we can see that the y-value is 102.05, which is just above the asymptote where $y = 102$. For $x = -100$, the y-value is -98.05, which is just below the asymptote where $y = -98$.

WORKED EXAMPLE 2.6

Sketch the curve $y = \frac{x^2 - 1}{2x - 3}$, stating the equations of the asymptotes and coordinates of the points of intersection.

Answer

$x = \frac{3}{2}$ — State the vertical asymptote.

$\frac{x^2 - 1}{2x - 3} = \frac{1}{2}x + B + \frac{C}{2x - 3}$ — State the value of A.

$x^2 - 1 = \left(\frac{1}{2}x + B\right)(2x - 3) + C$ — Rearrange to find the coefficients.

Using $x = \frac{3}{2}$, $C = \frac{5}{4}$ and using $x = 0$, $B = \frac{3}{4}$ — Find B and C.

$y = \frac{1}{2}x + \frac{3}{4}$ — State the oblique asymptote.

$x = 0 \Rightarrow y = \frac{1}{3}$ and $y = 0 \Rightarrow x = -1, x = 1$ — Find the points of intersection.

$x = 1.4999, y < 0$ and $x = 1.5001, y > 0$ — Examine the behaviour close to the asymptotes.

$x = 100, y_c = 50.76, y_a = 50.75$
$x = -100, y_c = -49.26, y_a = -49.25$ — Here y_a is the asymptote value, and y_c is the curve value.

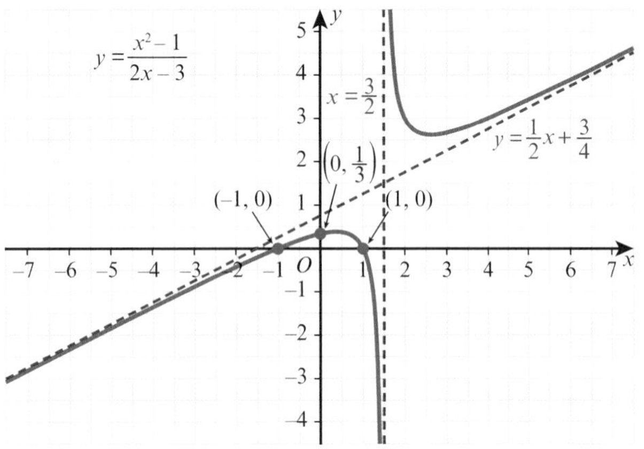

For large positive values of x the curve is above the oblique asymptote. For large negative values of x the curve is below the oblique asymptote.

EXPLORE 2.2

For a curve of type $y = \frac{ax^2 + bx + c}{dx + e}$, investigate what happens when you differentiate the equation of the curve. How many different curves can be sketched for this type of equation?

This type of curve always has two branches, which are separated by the asymptotes and lie in two of the four regions created.

Consider the curve $y = \frac{x^2 - 4}{x - 1}$. We will sketch this curve using differentiation. Start by stating the vertical asymptote $x = 1$. Next, rewrite the function as $\frac{x^2 - 4}{x - 1} = x + B + \frac{C}{x - 1}$, noticing that $A = 1$. Then, as $x^2 - 4 = (x + B)(x - 1) + C$, using $x = 1$ and $x = 0$ gives $C = -3$ and $B = 1$. So $y = x + 1 - \frac{3}{x - 1}$. Differentiating gives $\frac{dy}{dx} = 1 + \frac{3}{(x - 1)^2}$.

Setting $\frac{dy}{dx} = 0$ and rearranging this as $(x - 1)^2 = -3$, it is clear that there are no turning points. The oblique asymptote is $y = x + 1$. Therefore, the curve must appear as shown in the diagram. The points of intersection $(-2, 0)$, $(2, 0)$, $(0, 4)$ reinforce this.

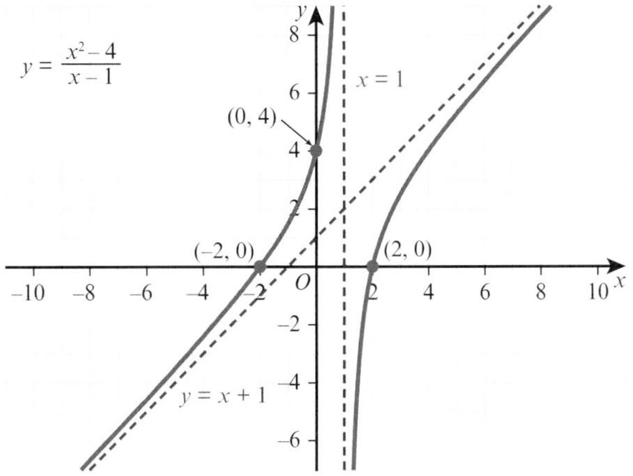

WORKED EXAMPLE 2.7

A curve has equation $y = \frac{x^2 - 9}{1 - x}$. Find the equations of the asymptotes and the coordinates of any points of intersection. Hence sketch the curve.

Answer

$x = 1$	State the vertical asymptote.
$A = -1$	State the value of A for the partial fraction form.
$\frac{x^2 - 9}{1 - x} = -x + B + \frac{C}{1 - x}$ $x = 1 \Rightarrow C = -8$ and $x = 0 \Rightarrow B = -1$	Find the coefficients.
$y = -x - 1$	State the oblique asymptote.
$x = 0 \Rightarrow y = -9$ and $y = 0 \Rightarrow x = -3, x = 3$	Determine the coordinates of the points of intersection.
$\frac{dy}{dx} = -1 - \frac{8}{(1 - x)^2} \Rightarrow \frac{dy}{dx} \neq 0$	Show that no turning points exist.

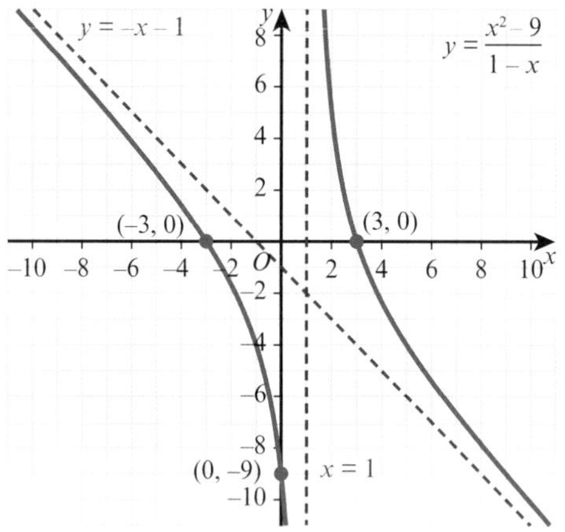

Sketch the curve.

EXERCISE 2B

1 For each curve given, find the equations of the asymptotes.

a $y = \dfrac{3x^2 + x + 3}{x + 1}$ b $y = \dfrac{x^2 + 3x - 31}{x - 4}$

2 Find the number of turning points for each of the following curves.

a $y = \dfrac{x^2 - 5}{x + 3}$ b $y = \dfrac{x^2 + 5x - 4}{2x - 1}$

PS 3 A curve is given as $y = \dfrac{6x^2 + x - 6}{2x - 1}$. Write the curve in the form $y = Ax + B + \dfrac{C}{2x - 1}$ and state the equations of the asymptotes.

4 The curve, C, is denoted as $y = \dfrac{x^2 + 3}{x - 2}$. Find the equations of the asymptotes and, hence, sketch C.

PS 5 The equation of a curve is given as $y = \dfrac{x^2 + \lambda x}{x + 1}$, where λ is a constant.

a Given that one of the asymptotes is $y = x + 2$, find the value of λ.

b State the other asymptote and sketch the curve.

PS P 6 A curve is given as $y = \dfrac{x^2 - 2x + 1}{x - 4}$.

a Find the equations of the asymptotes.

b Show that one of the turning points is (1, 0) and determine the other turning point.

c Sketch the curve.

PS 7 The curve, C, is given as $y = \dfrac{x^2 + ax + b}{2x - 1}$. Given that one of the asymptotes is $y = \frac{1}{2}x + \frac{5}{4}$ and that one of the points of intersection is (0, 4):

a find the values of a and b

b determine the number of turning points

c sketch C.

P 8 An equation is given as $y = \frac{x^2 - x + 1}{3 - x}$.

a Show that the curve can be written in the form $y = \alpha x + \beta + \frac{\gamma}{3 - x}$, stating the values of α, β and γ.

b Show that there are two turning points.

c Sketch the curve.

2.3 Inequalities

Consider the curve $y = \frac{2x^2}{2x + 3}$, and how we could find x for $\frac{2x^2}{2x + 3} < 2$.

Rearrange this to get $x^2 - 2x - 3 < 0$ and then solve, which gives $-1 < x < 3$.

To confirm that this is true we sketch the curve, as shown here.

We must be very careful to choose intervals that correctly satisfy the inequality. Sketching the curve is a very reliable method. We can see from the sketch that, when $y < 2$, there is a second interval to consider: $x < -\frac{3}{2}$.

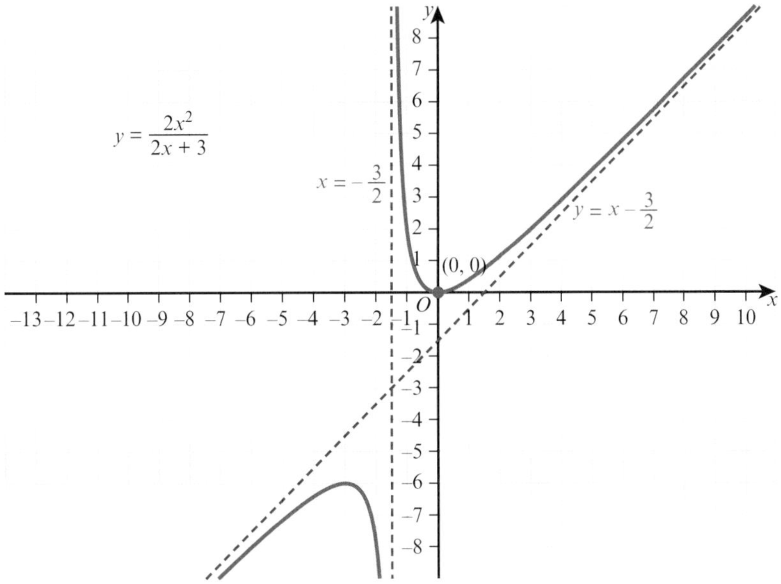

Using the curve $y = \frac{x^2 + 4x - 9}{3x - 1}$, we can see from the following diagram that, for $y > 0$, there are two distinct intervals to consider.

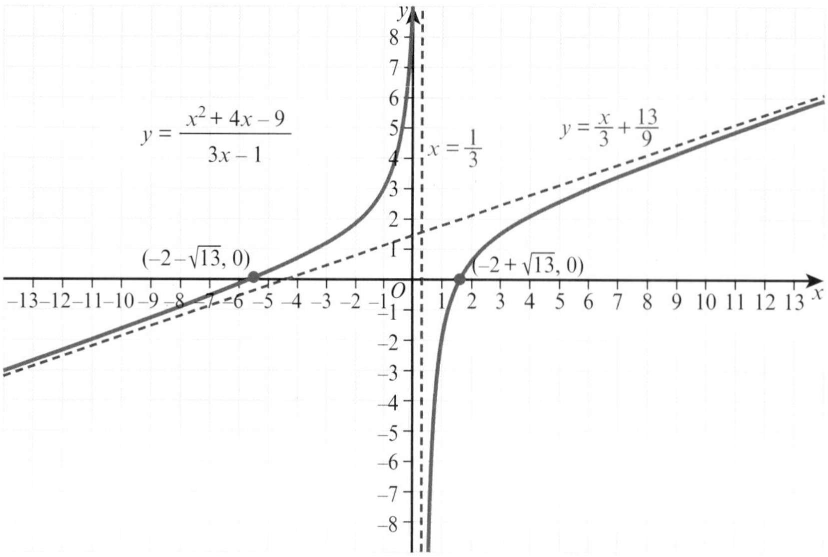

So $-2-\sqrt{13} < x < \frac{1}{3}$ and $x > -2+\sqrt{13}$ are the two intervals required.

WORKED EXAMPLE 2.8

For the equation $y = \frac{x+4}{(2x+3)(x+1)}$, determine the values of x for which $y > 1$.

Answer

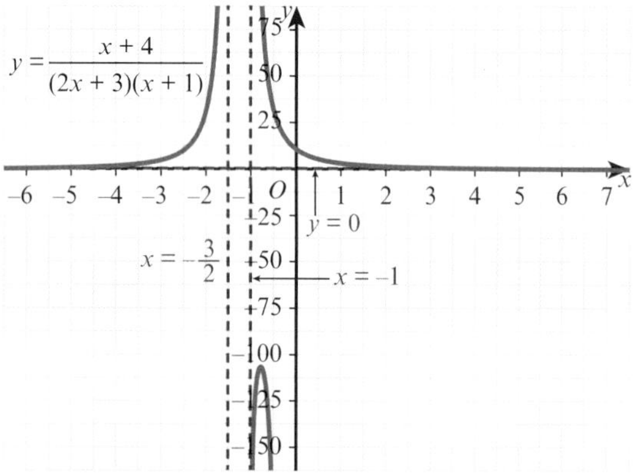

First sketch the curve.

$x = -\frac{3}{2}$, $x = -1$ and $y = 0$ — Identify the asymptotes.

Let $\frac{x+4}{(2x+3)(x+1)} = 1 \Rightarrow 2x^2 + 4x - 1 = 0$ — Set up an equation to find the critical values.

$x = -1 \pm \frac{1}{2}\sqrt{6}$ — Solve the equation.

$-1 - \frac{1}{2}\sqrt{6} < x < -\frac{3}{2}$, $-1 < x < -1 + \frac{1}{2}\sqrt{6}$ — Based on the sketch, determine which intervals are required.

TIP

Always remember to sketch the curve to ensure you don't miss any vital information. Most curves will have an interval that includes an asymptote. The asymptote will cut the interval into smaller regions.

As well as determining intervals above or below $y = k$, we can also consider the range of the functions themselves. For example, if we want to determine the range of the curve $y = \frac{x^2 + 2x - 1}{2x - 1}$, there are two approaches we can take.

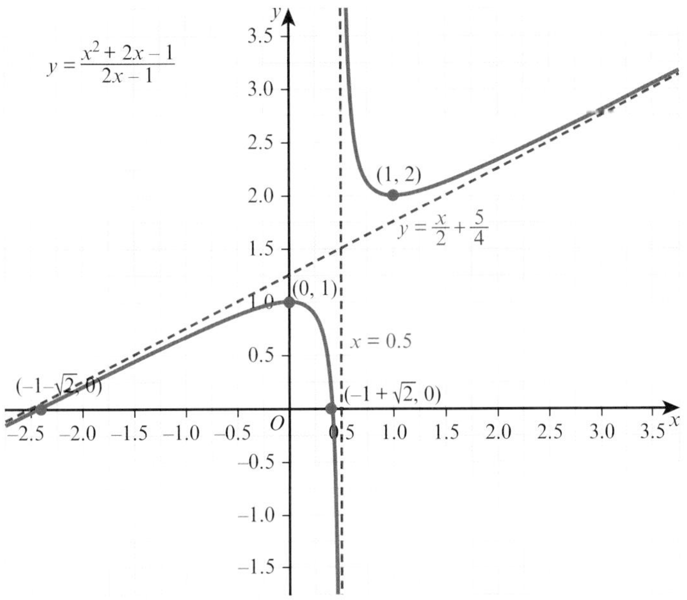

For the first method, we write the function in a simpler form and differentiate. So $y = \frac{1}{2}x + \frac{5}{4} + \frac{1}{4(2x - 1)}$, which gives $\frac{dy}{dx} = \frac{1}{2} - \frac{1}{2(2x - 1)^2}$. If this is equal to zero then $x = 0, x = 1$. From these values we find that $y = 1, y = 2$.

Using the shape of the curve from the sketch, we can see that the range of the curve is $y \leqslant 1$ or $y \geqslant 2$.

Note that we do not need the sketch to determine the range. Remember that curves of the type $y = \frac{ax^2 + bx + c}{dx + e}$ have either 0 or 2 turning points. If they have 2 turning points, the y value for the minimum for the top branch is always greater than the y value for the maximum for the bottom branch. Both branches must converge to the oblique asymptote. This means the minimum must always have a greater y value than the maximum.

The second method is one that we have met previously. Start with $y = \frac{x^2 + 2x - 1}{2x - 1}$, then cross multiply and simplify to get $x^2 + (2 - 2y)x + (y - 1) = 0$. Use the condition that the discriminant is < 0 to set up an inequality in y and solve it. This will give us the values of y that do not exist for our curve.

$4(1 - y)^2 - 4(y - 1) < 0$ leads to $y^2 - 3y + 2 < 0$, so the result is $1 < y < 2$. Hence, the values we can have are $y \leqslant 1$ or $y \geqslant 2$, just as before.

WORKED EXAMPLE 2.9

Determine the range of the curve $y = \dfrac{x^2 - 5}{3x + 4}$.

Answer

Method 1:

$3yx + 4y = x^2 - 5$ — Cross multiply.

$x^2 - 3yx - (4y + 5) = 0$ — Create a quadratic equation in x.

$(-3y)^2 + 4(4y + 5) < 0$ — Use $b^2 - 4ac < 0$.

$9\left(y + \dfrac{8}{9}\right)^2 + \dfrac{116}{9} < 0$ — Complete the square or use the quadratic formula to conclude there are no solutions we can't have. Hence, $y \in \mathbb{R}$.

Method 2:

$\dfrac{x^2 - 5}{3x + 4} = \dfrac{x}{3} - \dfrac{4}{9} - \dfrac{29}{9(3x + 4)}$ — Change into partial fractions.

$\dfrac{dy}{dx} = \dfrac{1}{3} + \dfrac{29}{3(3x + 4)^2}$ — Differentiate.

$\dfrac{dy}{dx} \neq 0$ — Conclude that the gradient is always positive. This leads to the same conclusion.

The next type of curve we will look at is different. Consider the curve $y = \dfrac{1}{x^2 + 3x + 6}$. $x^2 + 3x + 6 = 0$ clearly has no solutions, which implies that this curve can have no vertical asymptotes. More importantly, it also tells us that the curve must have a finite range. We should also note that as $|x|$ becomes large, y tends to 0, so there is a horizontal asymptote at $y = 0$.

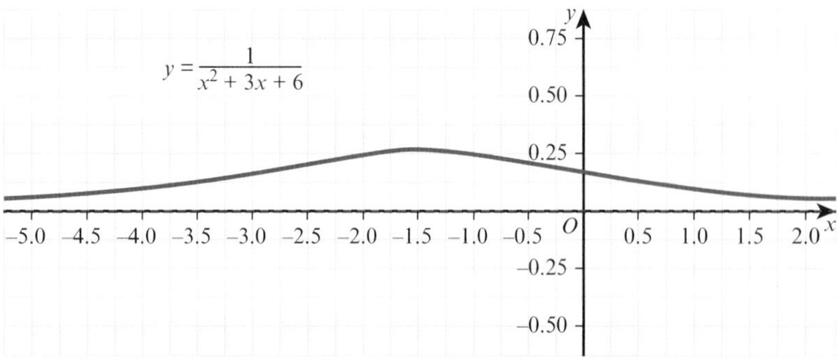

Writing the equation as $yx^2 + 3yx + (6y - 1) = 0$ and then using $b^2 - 4ac < 0$ gives the quadratic inequality $-15y^2 + 4y < 0$. This leads to $y < 0$ or $y > \dfrac{4}{15}$, and these are the values we cannot have. And so our range is $0 < y \leqslant \dfrac{4}{15}$.

Using differentiation, we could determine the coordinates of the maximum point, and hence the range.

WORKED EXAMPLE 2.10

The curve, C, is given as $y = \frac{x^2 - x - 2}{x^2 - x + 5}$. State any asymptotes, find the range of y and hence sketch the curve showing points of intersection.

Answer

$x^2 - x + 5 \neq 0$	There are no vertical asymptotes.
$y = \frac{x^2 - x - 2}{x^2 - x + 5} \Rightarrow y = 1$	This is the horizontal asymptote. As $\lvert x \rvert$ gets large, y tends to 1.
$yx^2 - yx + 5y = x^2 - x - 2$	Cross multiply.
$(y - 1)x^2 + (1 - y)x + (5y + 2) = 0$	Create a quadratic equation in x.
$19y^2 - 10y - 9 > 0$	Use $b^2 - 4ac < 0$.
$y > 1, y < -\frac{9}{19}$	State the y values that cannot be obtained.
$-\frac{9}{19} \leqslant y < 1$	State the correct range.
$x = 0 \Rightarrow y = -\frac{2}{5}$ and $y = 0 \Rightarrow x = -1, x = 2$	Find the points of intersection.
	Sketch the curve.

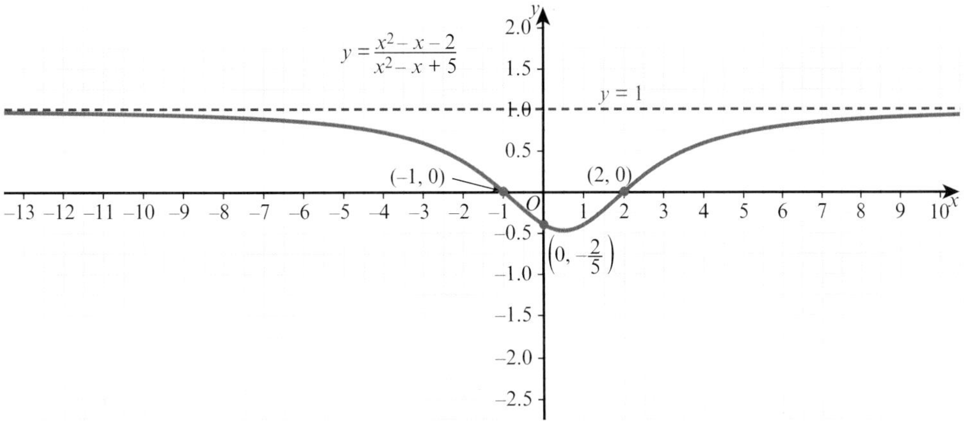

TIP

If the numerator = 0 has no solutions, the curve never meets the x-axis.

If the denominator = 0 has no solutions, then there are no vertical asymptotes.

EXERCISE 2C

PS **1** For the curve $y = \frac{2x - 3}{x + 2}$, determine the values of x such that $y > 3$.

PS **2** For the curve $y = \frac{x^2}{x + 3}$, find the range of values that y can have.

PS 3 Given that $y = \dfrac{x^2 - 2x - 4}{3x - 2}$, show that the range of the curve is $y \in R$.

PS 4 For the curve $y = \dfrac{x - 2}{x + 1}$, determine the values of x that satisfy $y < 5$.

PS 5 The curve, C, is given as $y = \dfrac{x^2 + x - 3}{x - 3}$.

a Find the range of values of y that the curve cannot have.

b Determine the exact coordinates of the turning points.

P PS 6 The curve $y = \dfrac{3x - 2 - 4x^2}{x - 2 - 3x^2}$ has a horizontal asymptote at $y = k$.

a State the value of k.

b Show that there are no vertical asymptotes.

c Determine the range for y.

P PS 7 The equation of a curve is $y = \dfrac{x}{x^2 + x - 2}$.

a Write down the equations of the asymptotes.

b Show that $y \in \mathbb{R}$.

c Determine the values of x that satisfy $y > 1$.

PS 8 The curve, C, is given as $y = \dfrac{1 - 3x}{x^2 + 3x - 10}$. Determine the values of x that satisfy $y < 2$.

2.4 Relationships between curves

From a known curve, we can determine the shapes of other related curves. For example, if we know the curve $f(x) = x^2 - 3x + 2$, then we can use this curve to determine the curve $\dfrac{1}{f(x)}$.

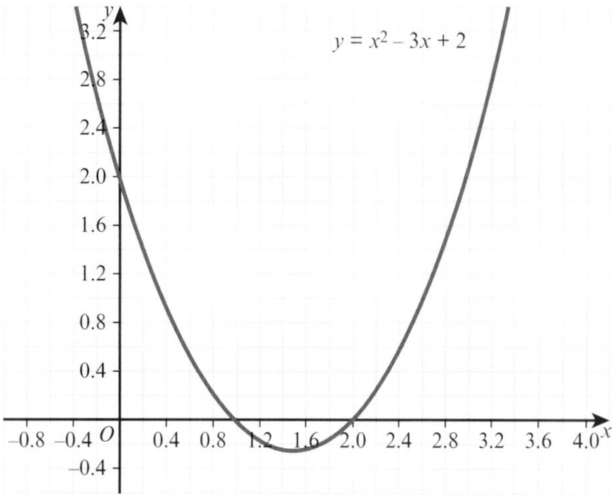

First, consider where the curve crosses the x-axis. These are the locations of the asymptotes. So when $x = 1, x = 2$ the curve will be infinite and discontinuities will exist at these points.

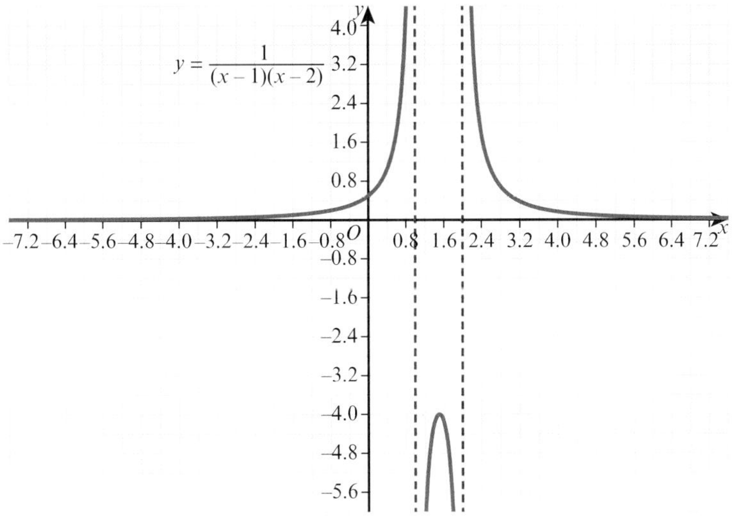

You first saw this curve in Section 2.1. We can see that, as $|x|$ tends to infinity, the original curve tends to infinity, and this new function tends to zero. The original curve crosses the y-axis at $y = 2$, and so our new curve crosses the y-axis at $y = \frac{1}{2}$. If there are solutions to the equation for $f(x) = 0$ for the original curve then we have asymptotes for the new curve. Consider, instead, the curve $y = x^2 + x + 2$. For $y = 0$ there are no solutions and, hence, $y = \frac{1}{x^2 + x + 2}$ has no discontinuities. The curve has a finite range.

You should now be familiar with both types of asymptotic curve as you have seen examples earlier in this book.

WORKED EXAMPLE 2.11

Given the curves $f(x) = x^2 + x - 2$ and $g(x) = x^2 + 2x + 7$, sketch $\frac{1}{f(x)}$ and $\frac{1}{g(x)}$.

Answer

$f(x) = (x + 2)(x - 1)$ — Factorise the function.

Hence, discontinuities at $x = -2, x = 1$. — Determine the vertical asymptotes for $\frac{1}{f(x)}$.

Horizontal asymptote at $y = 0$. — State the horizontal asymptote for $\frac{1}{f(x)}$.

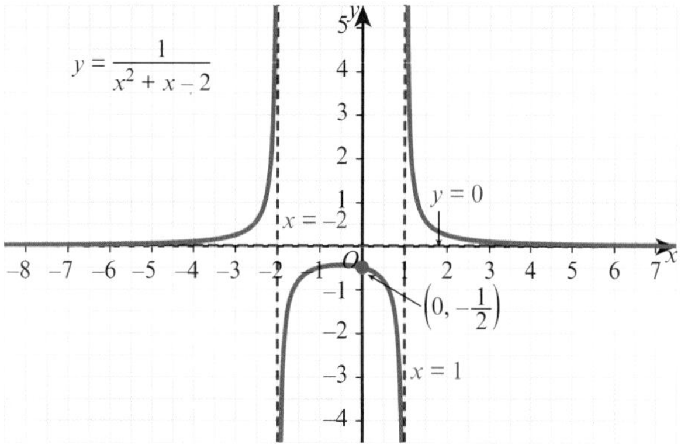

Sketch the curve.

Point of intersection at $\left(0, -\frac{1}{2}\right)$.

$x^2 + 2x + 7 = 0$ has no real solutions, therefore there are no vertical asymptotes for our graph.

Solve $yx^2 + 2yx + 7y - 1 = 0$.

Then $-24y^2 + 4y = 0$ yields $y = 0$ and $y = \frac{1}{6}$.

Use $b^2 - 4ac = 0$.

Hence, the range of the function is $0 < y < \frac{1}{6}$.

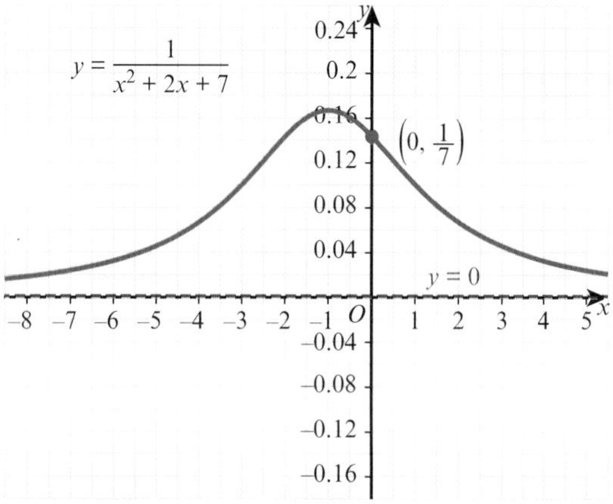

Point of intersection at $\left(0, \frac{1}{7}\right)$.

Horizontal asymptote at $y = 0$.

From a known curve, it is also possible to determine the graphs of the forms $y = |\,f(x)|$ and $y = f|x|$. We will look at the form $y = |\,f(x)|$ first.

Consider the curve $y = \frac{1}{x^2 - 1}$. This curve has two positive branches $(y > 0)$ and one negative branch $(y < 0)$.

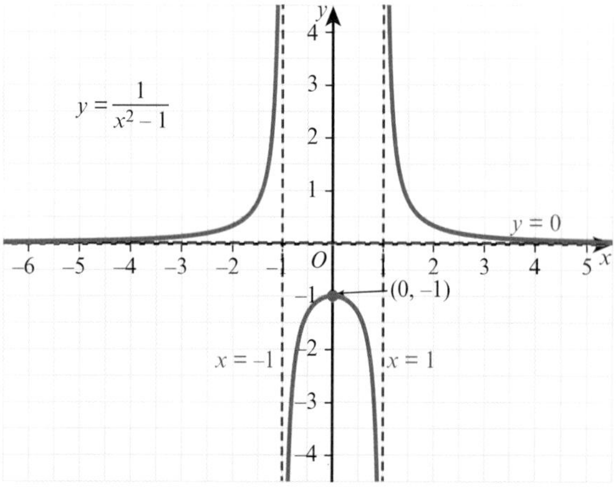

If we then consider the curve $y = \left|\frac{1}{x^2 - 1}\right|$, we need to make the negative y-values positive.

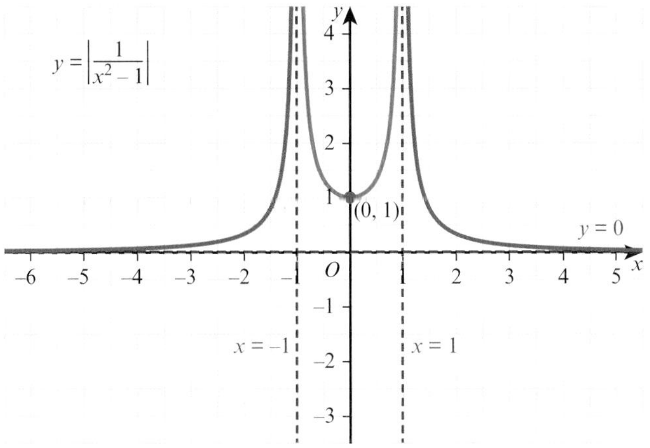

Notice that the green part of the curve has been reflected in the x-axis. This is true for all curves of the form $y = |f(x)|$.

Now we will look at curves in the form $y = f|x|$.

Consider the curve $y = \frac{x^2 + 4}{x - 1}$, shown below. We can see that there are two distinct branches.

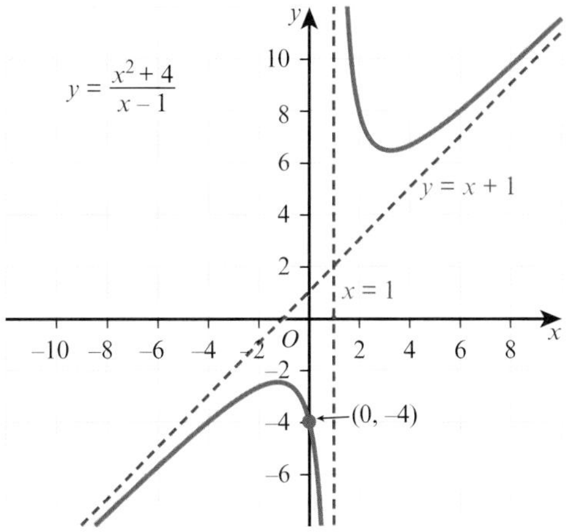

Consider the function $y = \frac{|x|^2 + 4}{|x| - 1}$. We can first note that $|x|^2 = x^2$. Next, we can see that $x = \pm a$ will have the same y-values so we can sketch the curve. This is shown in the following diagram.

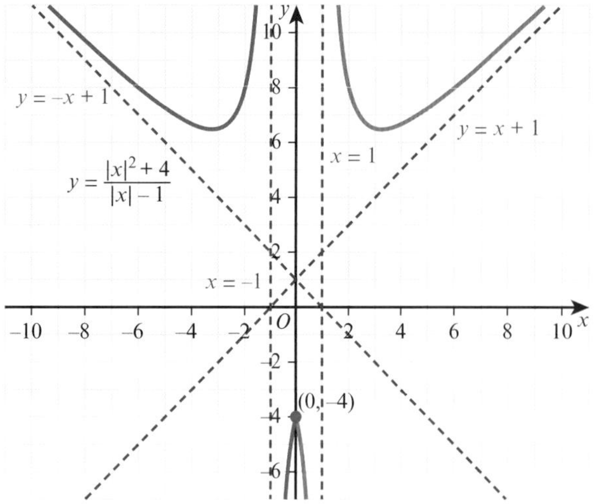

Notice that the curve is symmetrical about the y-axis. All parts of the curve that exist for $x > 0$ have been reflected to the other side of the y-axis. There are now four asymptotes, since the asymptotes are also reflected in the y-axis.

All curves that are of the form $y = f|x|$ consist of the original curve for $x \geqslant 0$. This region is reflected in the y-axis to form the other half of the curve.

WORKED EXAMPLE 2.12

Given that $f(x) = \frac{x^2}{x - 3}$, sketch the curves $y = |f(x)|$ and $y = f(|x|)$.

Answer

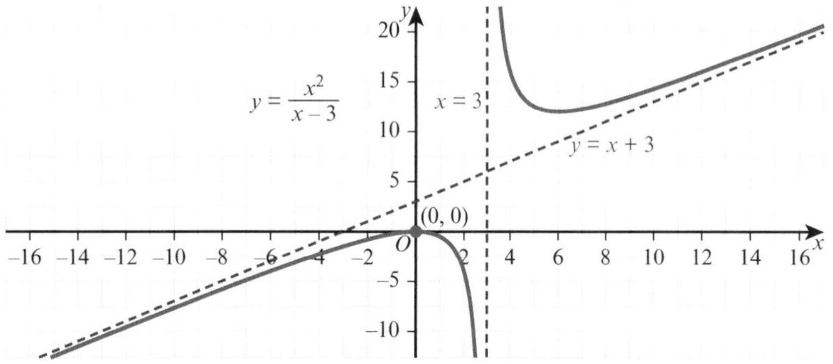

Sketch the original curve.

Note that the asymptotes are $x = 3$ and $y = x + 3$.

One branch should be below the x-axis.

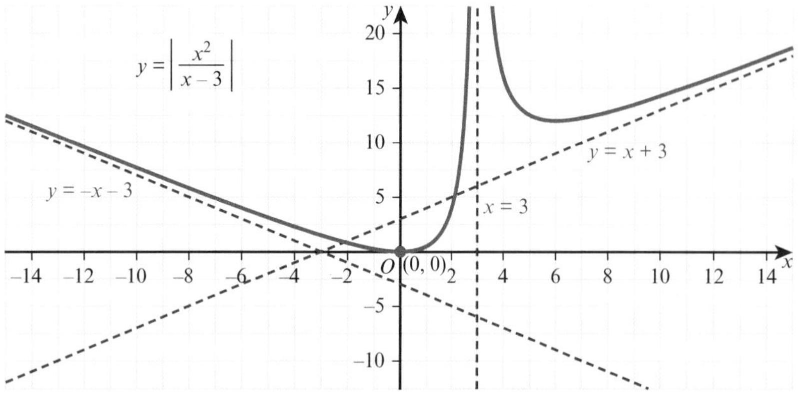

Ensure that the negative branch has now been reflected in the x-axis.

Note that there is now another asymptote that governs the curve: $y = -x - 3$.

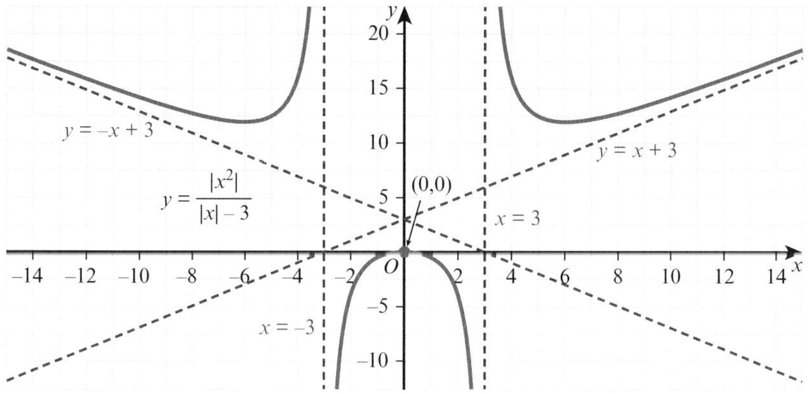

For the last sketch, note that the parts of the curve in the positive x region are reflected in the y-axis to form the other side of the curve.

Now there are four asymptotes. As well as the original ones, we have $x = -3$ and $y = -x - 3$.

Finally, we shall look at graphs of the form $y^2 = f(x)$. Consider the curve $y^2 = x$. This is parabolic in shape. To sketch this type of graph, we use a systematic approach.

First, ensure that $f(x) \geqslant 0$ and then sketch both $y = \sqrt{x}$ and $y = -\sqrt{x}$. Note that the domain for this function is $x \geqslant 0$.

When sketching this curve, notice that it is symmetrical about the x-axis. This is the case with all functions of the form $y^2 = f(x)$.

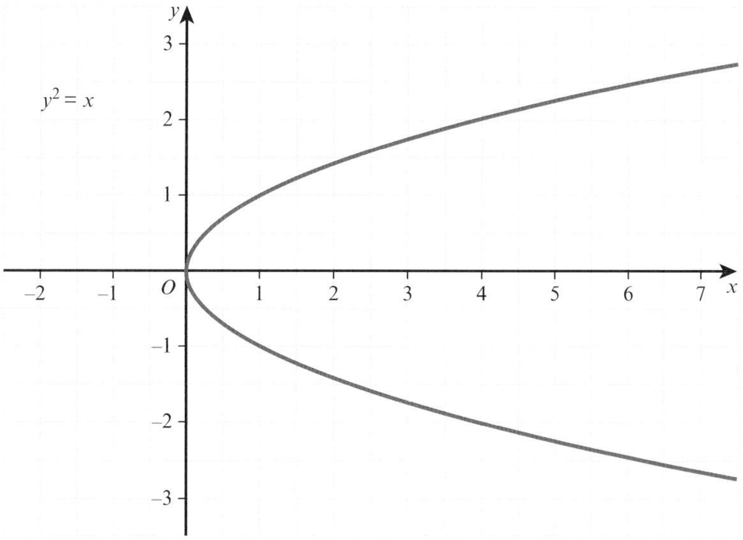

Next consider the curve $y^2 = 2x + 3$. The right-hand side is $\geqslant 0$ provided that $x \geqslant -\frac{3}{2}$.

We just need to sketch $y = \sqrt{2x + 3}$ and reflect this curve in the x-axis.

In this example, we should also notice that when $x = -\frac{3}{2}$, $y = 0$ and $y^2 = 0$, and when $x = -1, y = \pm 1$.

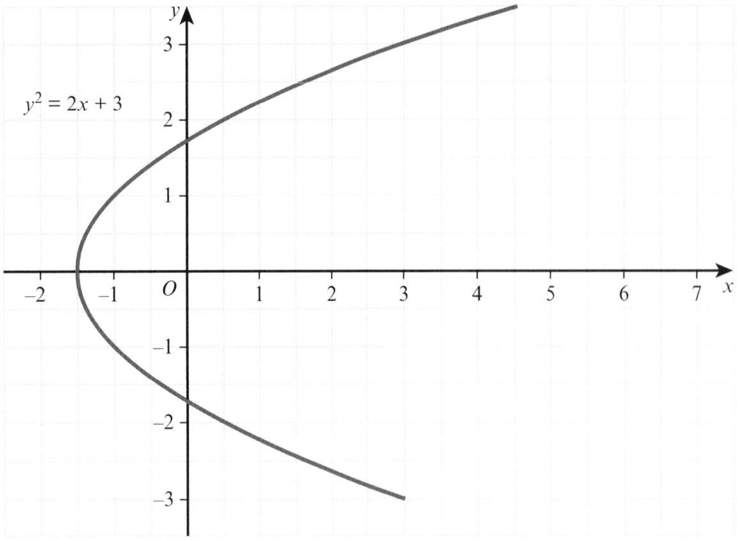

WORKED EXAMPLE 2.13

By considering $y = \sqrt{5 - 4x}$, sketch the curve $y^2 = 5 - 4x$, stating any points of intersection with the coordinate axes.

Answer

For $y^2 \geqslant 0$ we need $x \leqslant \frac{5}{4}$. — State the domain of the function.

when $x = 0, y = \pm\sqrt{5}$ and when $y = 0, x = \frac{5}{4}$ — Determine the points of intersection.

Sketch $y = \sqrt{5 - 4x}$ and then reflect the curve in the x-axis.

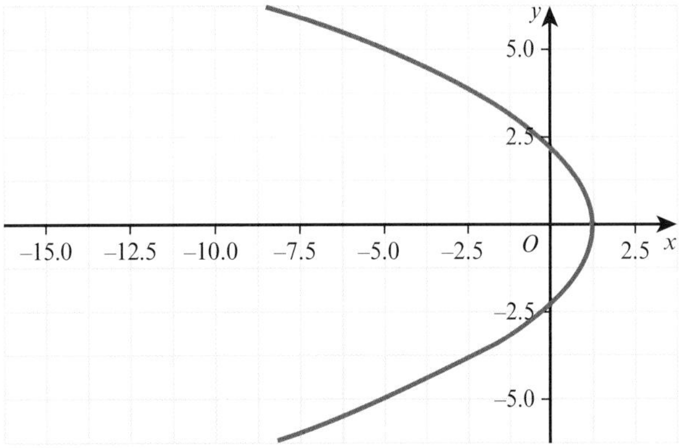

DID YOU KNOW?

The term *asymptote* was introduced by Apollonius of Perga more than 2200 years ago, when he was working on conic sections. The term asymptote is derived from the Greek word *asumptōtos*, which means 'not falling together'.

WORKED PAST PAPER QUESTION

The curve C has equation

$$y = \frac{x^2}{x + \lambda},$$

where λ is a non-zero constant. Obtain the equation of each of the asymptotes of C.

In separate diagrams, sketch C for the cases $\lambda > 0$ and $\lambda < 0$. In both cases the coordinates of the turning points must be included.

Cambridge International AS & A Level Further Mathematics 9231 Paper 1 Q10 June 2009

Answer

Let $\frac{x^2}{x+\lambda} = Ax + B + \frac{C}{x+\lambda}$, where $A = 1$.

So $x^2 = x(x+\lambda) + B(x+\lambda) + C$.

$x = -\lambda$ leads to $C = \lambda^2$, and $x = 0$ leads to $B = -\lambda$.

So $y = x - \lambda + \frac{\lambda^2}{x+\lambda}$ and the asymptotes are $y = x - \lambda$ and $x = -\lambda$.

$\frac{dy}{dx} = 1 - \frac{\lambda^2}{(x+\lambda)^2}$, and if $\frac{dy}{dx} = 0$ then $1 = \frac{\lambda^2}{(x+\lambda)^2}$. Simplifying this gives $x^2 + 2\lambda x = 0$.

Hence, there are always two turning points, located at $x = 0, y = 0$ and $x = -2\lambda, y = -4\lambda$.

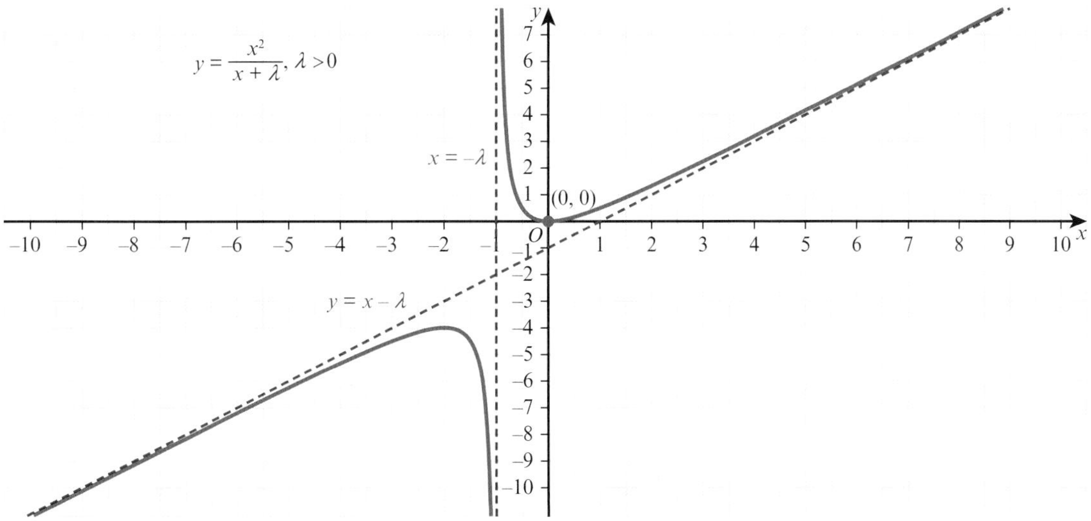

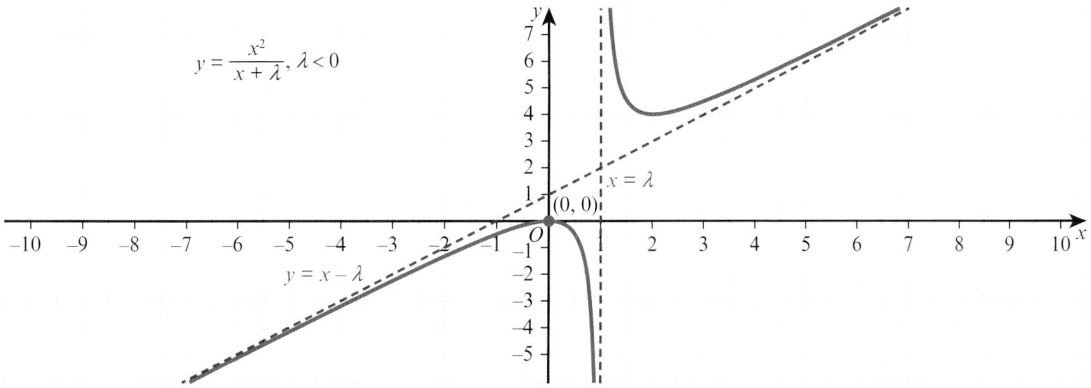

EXERCISE 2D

Do not use a calculator in this exercise.

1 Determine the number of solutions for each of the following equations.

a $\frac{|x|^2 - 2|x| - 3}{|x| - 2} = 0$ b $\frac{|x|^2 - 3|x| + 2}{|x| - 1} = 0$

2 Find the number of vertical asymptotes for the following curves.

a $y = \frac{1}{x^2 - 5x - 6}$ b $y = \frac{1}{x^2 + 2x + 3}$

3 Determine the equations of the asymptotes of the curve in the following cases.

a $y = \frac{1}{x^2 - 4}$ b $y = \frac{1}{x^2 + 2x + 5}$

PS 4 Given that $f(x) = x^2 - x - 6$, sketch the curve $y = \frac{1}{f(x)}$, showing all the asymptotes and points of intersection.

5 Sketch the curve $y^2 = 7 - 3x$, showing any points of intersection with the coordinate axes.

6 Given that $f(x) = \frac{x}{x^2 - x - 2}$, sketch the following curves. Show any asymptotes in each case.

a $y = |f(x)|$ b $y = f(|x|)$

P PS 7 You are given that $f(x) = \frac{x^2 + 2x - 5}{x + 3}$.

a Show that $f(x)$ has no turning points.

b Show also that the asymptotes are $y = x - 1$ and $x = -3$.

c Sketch the curve $|f(x)|$, showing all the asymptotes and points of intersection.

Checklist of learning and understanding

Graph types:

- For the form $y=\dfrac{ax+b}{cx+d}$ the horizontal asymptote is $y=\dfrac{a}{c}$ and the vertical asymptote is $x=-\dfrac{d}{c}$.
- The points of intersection are $\left(0,\dfrac{b}{d}\right)$ and $\left(-\dfrac{b}{a},0\right)$.
- For the form $y=\dfrac{ax+b}{(cx+d)(ex+f)}$ the horizontal asymptote is $y=0$ and the vertical asymptotes are $x=-\dfrac{d}{c}$ and $x=-\dfrac{f}{e}$.
- The points of intersection are $\left(0,\dfrac{b}{df}\right)$ and $\left(-\dfrac{b}{a},0\right)$.
- For the form $y=\dfrac{(ax+b)(cx+d)}{(ex+f)(gx+h)}$ the horizontal asymptote is $y=\dfrac{ac}{eg}$ and the vertical asymptotes are $x=-\dfrac{f}{e}$ and $x=-\dfrac{h}{g}$.
- The points of intersection are $\left(0,\dfrac{bd}{fh}\right)$, $\left(-\dfrac{b}{a},0\right)$ and $\left(-\dfrac{d}{c},0\right)$.
- For the form $y=\dfrac{(ax+b)(cx+d)}{ex^2+fx+g}$, where ex^2+fx+g gives no real solutions, the horizontal asymptote is $y=\dfrac{ac}{e}$.
- The points of intersection are $\left(0,\dfrac{bd}{g}\right)$, $\left(-\dfrac{b}{a},0\right)$ and $\left(-\dfrac{d}{c},0\right)$.
- For the form $y=\dfrac{(ax+b)(cx+d)}{ex+f}$, the vertical asymptote is $x=-\dfrac{f}{e}$ and the oblique asymptote, determined by using partial fractions, is $y=\dfrac{ac}{e}x+B$, where B is to be determined.
- The points of intersection are $\left(0,\dfrac{bd}{f}\right)$, $\left(-\dfrac{b}{a},0\right)$ and $\left(-\dfrac{d}{c},0\right)$.

For special curve types:

- For $y=\dfrac{1}{\text{f}(x)}$, consider all points where $\text{f}(x)=0$, $\text{f}(x)=\infty$ and also $\text{f}(0)=k$. All of these values can be used to construct the new graph.
- For $y=|\text{f}(x)|$, consider the original curve $y=\text{f}(x)$ and then reflect all negative parts $(y<0)$ in the x-axis.
- For $y=\text{f}(|x|)$, consider the original curve for $x\geqslant 0$, draw this section and then reflect this in the y-axis for the complete curve.
- For $y^2=\text{f}(x)$, consider the domain such that $\text{f}(x)\geqslant 0$, sketch $\sqrt{\text{f}(x)}$ and then reflect this part of the curve in the x-axis.
- In all of these cases, make sure you consider the effect on the asymptotes.

END-OF-CHAPTER REVIEW EXERCISE 2

1 A curve is given as $f(x) = \dfrac{x^2 - x - 5}{x - 3}$.

Find the equations of the asymptotes of the curve.

Sketch the curve.

Hence, or otherwise, sketch the curve $\dfrac{1}{f(x)}$. State the equations of the vertical asymptotes.

2 The curve C has equation $y = \dfrac{2x^2 + 5x - 1}{x + 2}$.

Find the equations of the asymptotes of C.

Show that $\dfrac{dy}{dx} > 2$ at all points on C.

Sketch C.

Cambridge International AS & A Level Further Mathematics 9231 Paper 13 Q7 November 2013

3 The curve C has equation $y = \dfrac{2x^2 - 3x - 2}{x^2 - 2x + 1}$. State the equations of the asymptotes of C.

Show that $y \leqslant \dfrac{25}{12}$ at all points of C.

Find the coordinates of any stationary points of C.

Sketch C, stating the coordinates of any intersections of C with the coordinate axes and the asymptotes.

Cambridge International AS & A Level Further Mathematics 9231 Paper 11 Q10 June 2013

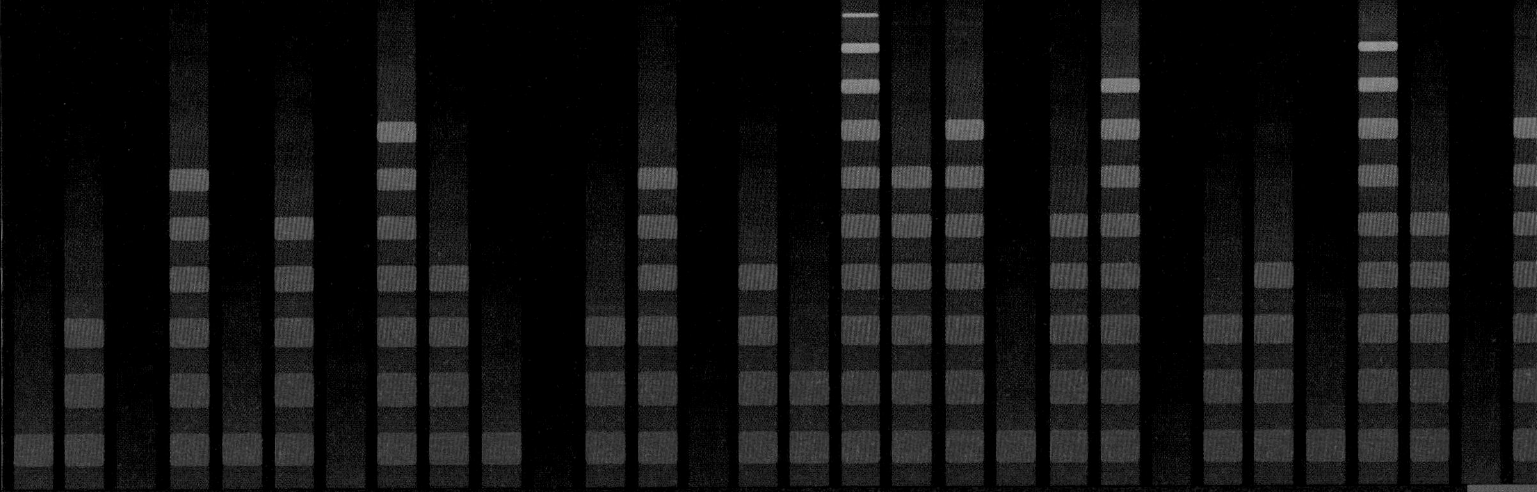

Chapter 3
Summation of series

In this chapter you will learn how to:

- use the standard results for Σr, Σr^2 and Σr^3 to find related sums
- use the method of differences to obtain the sum of a finite series
- recognise, by direct consideration of a sum to n terms, when a series is convergent, and find the sum to infinity in such cases.

PREREQUISITE KNOWLEDGE

Where it comes from	What you should be able to do	Check your skills
AS & A Level Mathematics Pure Mathematics 2 & 3, Chapter 7	Work with basic partial fractions, particularly those with a higher power in the denominator than in the numerator.	**1** Split the following into partial fractions. **a** $\frac{1}{(x+1)(x-1)}$ **b** $\frac{2}{x^2 - 3x + 2}$
AS & A Level Mathematics Pure Mathematics 1, Chapter 6	Have a basic understanding of arithmetic sequences, as well as an appreciation for convergent series.	**2** Evaluate: $S_\infty - S_{10}$, where $S_n = \frac{2(1 - 0.5^n)}{0.5}$

What is the summation of series?

A **series** is the sum of terms in a mathematical **sequence**. Historically, mathematicians needed to use infinite series to approximate values such as π, and to develop polynomials to approximate other functions. Today, we can use series to work out the value of financial investments or to help musicians mix recorded tracks to achieve the sound they want.

You are already familiar with arithmetic and geometric series and how to sum them to a given term or to infinity in the case of geometric series. This chapter will build on some of these concepts and extend them, incorporating **convergent** series and squares and cubes of numbers. You will also work with partial fractions to recognise and simplify number patterns.

3.1 The summation formulae Σr, Σr^2, Σr^3

KEY POINT 3.1

The expression for the sum of a series consisting of a constant k, added together n times, is written as $\sum_{r=1}^{n} k$ and its value is kn.

In your AS & A Level work you will have seen a variety of sequences. We know that the sum of an **arithmetic sequence** is $S_n = \frac{n}{2}[2a + (n-1)d]$. For the case when $a = 1, d = 1$ then $S_n = \frac{n}{2}[2 + (n-1)]$. This result is written as $S_n = \frac{n(n+1)}{2}$. It is known as the sum of the first n natural numbers as it represents $1 + 2 + 3 + 4 + \ldots + n$.

In summation notation, this is written as $\sum_{r=1}^{n} r = \frac{n(n+1)}{2}$. Another way to derive this is to consider the expression $(r+1)^2 = r^2 + 2r + 1$, then write down the expression as r goes from 1 to n.

$r = 1 \Rightarrow 2^2 = 1^2 + 2 \times 1 + 1$

$r = 2 \Rightarrow 3^2 = 2^2 + 2 \times 2 + 1$

$r = 3 \Rightarrow 4^2 = 3^2 + 2 \times 3 + 1$

$\vdots \quad \vdots$

$r = n \Rightarrow (n + 1)^2 = n^2 + 2 \times n + 1$

Consider the right-hand side of the equations, summed from top to bottom. Write it in summation form. This gives the expression $\sum_{r=1}^{n} r^2 + 2\sum_{r=1}^{n} r + n$.

Next, add 1 to both sides to get $1^2 + 2^2 + 3^2 + \cdots + n^2 + (n + 1)^2 = \sum_{r=1}^{n} r^2 + 2\sum_{r=1}^{n} r + n + 1$.

The left- and right-hand sides both include $\sum_{r=1}^{n} r^2$. Cancelling this term leaves

$(n + 1)^2 = 2 \times \sum_{r=1}^{n} r + n + 1$. This simplifies to $\sum_{r=1}^{n} r = \frac{n(n + 1)}{2}$.

WORKED EXAMPLE 3.1

Find $\sum_{r=1}^{n}(4r + 1)$. Hence determine the value of $\sum_{17}^{48}(4r + 1)$.

Answer

$\sum_{1}^{n}(4r + 1) = 4\sum_{1}^{n} r + \sum_{1}^{n} 1$ — Split the sum into smaller parts.

$= 4 \times \frac{n(n + 1)}{2} + n$ — Use the sum of natural numbers.

$= 2n^2 + 3n$ — Combine terms.

$\therefore \sum_{17}^{48}(4r + 1) = (2 \times 48^2 + 3 \times 48) - (2 \times 16^2 + 3 \times 16)$ — Write out as the difference of two separate sums, one with limits of 1 and 16, the other with limits of 1 and 48.

$= 4192$ — Determine the final answer.

We can use $\sum r$ instead of $\sum_{r=1}^{n} r$ provided we remember the correct limits.

Since the sum has a variable upper limit, we can write anything we want as this limit. For example, we might want to determine the value of $\sum_{r=1}^{2n} r$, which would be $\frac{(2n)(2n + 1)}{2} = 2n^2 + n$.

This result can be used to deduce the result of $\sum_{n+1}^{2n} r$. Carefully consider what the limits mean: this is the sum of the first $2n$ terms minus the sum of the first n terms.

So $2n^2 + n - \frac{n(n+1)}{2} = \frac{3}{2}n^2 + \frac{1}{2}n$.

WORKED EXAMPLE 3.2

Find an expression for $1 + 3 + 5 + 7 + \cdots$, for the first n terms, using two different approaches.

Answer

Method 1:

$$1 + 3 + 5 + 7 + \cdots = \sum_{r=1}^{n}(2r-1)$$ Write the sum of n odd terms.

$$= 2\sum_{r=1}^{n} r - n$$ Use the standard result.

$$= n(n+1) - n$$ Simplify.

$$\Rightarrow 1 + 3 + 5 + 7 + \cdots = n^2$$

Method 2:

$$1 + 3 + 5 + 7 + \cdots = \sum_{r=1}^{2n} r - \sum_{r=1}^{n}(2r)$$ Write a sum of $2n$ terms and subtract all even terms, leaving n terms.

$$= \frac{1}{2}(2n)(2n+1) - 2 \times \frac{1}{2}n(n+1)$$ The second sum is twice the sum of the first n natural numbers.

$$= n^2$$ This gives the same result.

The next case to look at is the sum of $1^2 + 2^2 + 3^2 + 4^2 + \cdots$. We will use the same method as shown previously.

Start with the expression $(r+1)^3 = r^3 + 3r^2 + 3r + 1$, then write this for $r = 1$ to n.

$$r = 1 \Rightarrow 2^3 = 1^3 + 3 \times 1^2 + 3 \times 1 + 1$$

$$r = 2 \Rightarrow 3^3 = 2^3 + 3 \times 2^2 + 3 \times 2 + 1$$

$$r = 3 \Rightarrow 4^3 = 3^3 + 3 \times 3^2 + 3 \times 3 + 1$$

$$\vdots \quad \vdots$$

$$r = n \Rightarrow (n+1)^3 = n^3 + 3 \times n^2 + 3 \times n + 1$$

Sum the right side to get $\sum_{r=1}^{n} r^3 + 3\sum_{r=1}^{n} r^2 + 3\sum_{r=1}^{n} r + n$. Then add 1 to both sides to get $1^3 + 2^3 + 3^3 + \cdots + (n+1)^3 = \sum_{r=1}^{n} r^3 + 3\sum_{r=1}^{n} r^2 + 3\sum_{r=1}^{n} r + n + 1$. After cancelling like terms, this reduces to $n^3 + 3n^2 + 3n + 1 = 3\sum_{r=1}^{n} r^2 + 3\sum_{r=1}^{n} r + n + 1$.

Since $\sum_{r=1}^{n} r = \frac{n(n+1)}{2}$, we have

$$3\sum_{r=1}^{n} r^2 = n^3 + 3n^2 + 3n + 1 - 3\frac{n(n+1)}{2} - n - 1$$

$$3\sum_{r=1}^{n} r^2 = n(n+1)(n+2) - 3\frac{n(n+1)}{2}$$

$$3\sum_{r=1}^{n} r^2 = n(n+1)\left(n+\frac{1}{2}\right)$$

$$3\sum_{r=1}^{n} r^2 = \frac{n}{2}(n+1)(2n+1)$$

and it follows that $\sum_{r=1}^{n} r^2 = \frac{1}{6}n(n+1)(2n+1)$.

This is the sum of the squares of the first n natural numbers.

WORKED EXAMPLE 3.3

Find an expression in terms of n for $\sum_{r=1}^{n}(3r^2 - 4r + 2)$.

Answer

$\sum_{r=1}^{n}(3r^2 - 4r + 2) = 3\sum_{r=1}^{n} r^2 - 4\sum_{r=1}^{n} r + \sum_{r=1}^{n} 2$ Split into individual sums.

$= 3 \times \frac{1}{6}n(n+1)(2n+1) - 4 \times \frac{1}{2}n(n+1) + 2n$ Use the result for each sum.

$= \frac{n}{2}(2n^2 + 3n + 1) - 2n^2 - 2n + 2n$

$= n^3 + \frac{3}{2}n^2 + \frac{1}{2}n - 2n^2$

$= n^3 - \frac{1}{2}n^2 + \frac{1}{2}n$ Simplify.

Using an approach similar to the one in Worked example 3.2, we are going to find an expression for $1^2 + 4^2 + 7^2 + \cdots$, for the first n terms.

There are, again, two ways to achieve this. First, write $\sum_{r=1}^{n}(3r-2)^2$ and then expand it to get $9\sum_{r=1}^{n} r^2 - 12\sum_{r=1}^{n} r + \sum_{r=1}^{n} 4$.

This gives $9 \times \frac{1}{6}n(n+1)(2n+1) - 12 \times \frac{1}{2}n(n+1) + 4n$

$= \frac{3n}{2}(2n^2 + 3n + 1) - 6n^2 - 6n + 4n$

$= 3n^3 + \frac{9}{2}n^2 + \frac{3}{2}n - 6n^2 - 2n$ which simplifies to $\frac{1}{2}n(6n^2 - 3n - 1)$.

The alternative method is to assume we have $3n$ terms and write the expression as

$1^2 + 4^2 + 7^2 + \cdots = \sum_{r=1}^{3n} r^2 - \sum_{r=1}^{n}(3r-1)^2 - \sum_{r=1}^{n}(3r)^2$. The second sum removes $2^2, 5^2, 8^2, \ldots$ from the total and the third sum removes $3^2, 6^2, 9^2, \ldots$.

Working through the algebra will lead to the same result as before. The first method is simpler, but there are cases when an alternative approach is needed.

DID YOU KNOW?

Carl Friedrich Gauss added $1 + 2 + 3 + \cdots + 100$ in a matter of seconds. He did this by considering the pairs $(1 + 100) + (2 + 99) + \cdots + (50 + 51) = 5050$.

This became formally known as $\sum_{r=1}^{n} r = \frac{n(n+1)}{2}$.

EXPLORE 3.1

Working in groups, try to work out the sum of $1^2 - 2^2 + 3^2 - 4^2 + \cdots$.

Can you write this as one summation, or do you need a series of summations?

We will now consider the sum of the cubes of natural numbers. This is the sum $1^3 + 2^3 + 3^3 + \cdots$.

As with the previous two examples, start with $(r+1)^4 = r^4 + 4r^3 + 6r^2 + 4r + 1$, then list the terms as before, from $r = 1$ to $r = n$.

$r = 1 \Rightarrow 2^4 = 1^4 + 4 \times 1^3 + 6 \times 1^2 + 4 \times 1 + 1$

$r = 2 \Rightarrow 3^4 = 2^4 + 4 \times 2^3 + 6 \times 2^2 + 4 \times 2 + 1$

$r = 3 \Rightarrow 4^4 = 3^4 + 4 \times 3^3 + 6 \times 3^2 + 4 \times 3 + 1$

$\vdots \quad \vdots$

$r = n \Rightarrow (n+1)^4 = n^4 + 4 \times n^3 + 6 \times n^2 + 4 \times n + 1$

Following the same procedure as in Worked examples 3.2 and 3.3, we find $\sum_{r=1}^{n} r^3 = \frac{1}{4}n^2(n+1)^2$.

This is the sum of the cubes of the first n natural numbers.

WORKED EXAMPLE 3.4

Find an expression in terms of n for $\sum_{r=1}^{n} r^2(r-1)$.

Answer

$\sum_{r=1}^{n} r^2(r-1) = \sum_{r=1}^{n} r^3 - \sum_{r=1}^{n} r^2$ — Write as two separate sums.

$= \frac{1}{4}n^2(n+1)^2 - \frac{1}{6}n(n+1)(2n+1)$ — Replace with the appropriate formulae.

$= n(n+1)\left(\frac{n^2}{4} + \frac{n}{4} - \frac{n}{3} - \frac{1}{6}\right)$ — Note we do not need to expand all the brackets to simplify.

$= \frac{1}{12}n(n+1)(3n^2 - n - 2)$

$= \frac{1}{12}n(n+1)(n-1)(3n+2)$ — Simplify.

E **EXPLORE 3.2**

As a class, or in groups, can you derive an expression for $\sum_{r=1}^{n} r^4$? This is beyond the syllabus but will reinforce your understanding of summations.

FAST FORWARD

You will meet these formulae again in Chapter 7, when you will prove them in a more rigorous way.

EXERCISE 3A

P 1 Show that $\sum_{r=1}^{n}(3r-5)=\frac{n}{2}(3n-7)$.

P 2 Prove that $\sum_{r=1}^{n}2r(r-3)=\frac{2}{3}n(n+1)(n-4)$.

PS 3 Determine the value of $1-2+3-4+\ \dots + (2n-1)-(2n)$.

P 4 Without using a calculator, show that $\sum_{r=1}^{n}(r+2)(r+3)=\frac{n(n^2-19)}{3}$.

PS 5 Without using a calculator, find a simplified expression for
$1^2+2^2-3^2+4^2+5^2-6^2+\cdots+(3n-2)^2+(3n-1)^2-(3n)^2$.

PS 6 Find, in terms of n, an expression for $\sum_{r=n+1}^{2n} r(r+1)$.

M 7 Find the sum of the terms $1^2+2^2+3^2+5^2+6^2+7^2+\cdots+97^2+98^2+99^2$.

P PS 8 Show that $\sum_{r=1}^{n}(2r+1)(3r+2)=\frac{n(4n^2+13n+13)}{2}$. Hence, find the result of $\sum_{r=11}^{25}(2r+1)(3r+2)$.

M PS 9 Find the sum of the cubes of the first 100 even terms.

3.2 Converging series

For the series in this section, we will reach a finite sum as the number of terms tends to infinity. This will be achieved by setting up the series in an appropriate form to help us spot a recognisable pattern.

Consider the summation $\sum_{r=1}^{n}\frac{1}{r(r+1)}$. How could we represent this in terms of n?

If we write down a few terms, $\frac{1}{2}+\frac{1}{6}+\frac{1}{12}+\frac{1}{20}+\cdots$, it appears that there is no recognisable pattern.

So, go back to the original form of the summation, and this time split the fraction into partial fractions.

Now we have $\frac{1}{r(r+1)}=\frac{A}{r}+\frac{B}{r+1}$, which gives $1=A(r+1)+Br$. From $r=-1$, $B=-1$ and from $r=0$, $A=1$.

We are now working with $\sum_{r=1}^{n}\left(\frac{1}{r}-\frac{1}{r+1}\right)$. Write down a few terms, from the start and the end of the series,

$$\sum_{r=1}^{n}\left(\frac{1}{r}-\frac{1}{r+1}\right)=\left(\frac{1}{1}-\frac{1}{2}\right)+\left(\frac{1}{2}-\frac{1}{3}\right)+\left(\frac{1}{3}-\frac{1}{4}\right)+\cdots+\left(\frac{1}{n-1}-\frac{1}{n}\right)+\left(\frac{1}{n}-\frac{1}{n+1}\right)$$

Lots of the terms cancel, and we are left with $\sum_{r=1}^{n}\left(\frac{1}{r}-\frac{1}{r+1}\right)=1-\frac{1}{n+1}$.

The cancelling of terms in this way to simplify the summation is known as the method of differences.

TIP

It is always a good idea to write down some terms. To determine which terms cancel you need to see some of the pattern. Ensure you write down terms at the start and at the end of the series.

WORKED EXAMPLE 3.5

Find, in terms of n, the sum of $\sum_{r=1}^{n}\frac{1}{(r+1)(r+2)}$.

Answer

$$\frac{1}{(r+1)(r+2)}=\frac{A}{r+1}+\frac{B}{r+2}$$ Split into partial fractions.

$$1=A(r+2)+B(r+1)$$ Find the coefficients.

using $r=-1$, $A=1$ and using $r=-2$, $B=-1$

$$\sum_{r=1}^{n}\left(\frac{1}{r+1}-\frac{1}{r+2}\right)=\left(\frac{1}{2}-\frac{1}{3}\right)+\left(\frac{1}{3}-\frac{1}{4}\right)+\left(\frac{1}{4}-\frac{1}{5}\right)+\ldots+\left(\frac{1}{n}-\frac{1}{n+1}\right)+\left(\frac{1}{n+1}-\frac{1}{n+2}\right)$$ Write down enough terms to see the cancellations.

$$=\left(\frac{1}{2}-\frac{1}{3}\right)+\left(\frac{1}{3}-\frac{1}{4}\right)+\left(\frac{1}{4}-\frac{1}{5}\right)+\ldots+\left(\frac{1}{n}-\frac{1}{n+1}\right)+\left(\frac{1}{n+1}-\frac{1}{n+2}\right)$$

$$\therefore\sum_{r=1}^{n}\frac{1}{(r+1)(r+2)}=\frac{1}{2}-\frac{1}{n+2}$$ Cancel terms to get the final answer.

For the two previous examples, the difference between the factors of the denominator was 1 in both cases. Recall we had $r(r+1)$ and then $(r+1)(r+2)$.

If we now consider the summation $\sum_{r=1}^{n}\frac{1}{r(r+2)}$, the procedure will be the same as before.

Split it into partial fractions first to give $\frac{1}{2}\sum_{r=1}^{n}\left(\frac{1}{r}-\frac{1}{r+2}\right)$, then write down some terms, initially ignoring the $\frac{1}{2}$ in front of the summation:

$$\left(\frac{1}{1}-\frac{1}{3}\right)+\left(\frac{1}{2}-\frac{1}{4}\right)+\left(\frac{1}{3}-\frac{1}{5}\right)+\left(\frac{1}{4}-\frac{1}{6}\right)+\cdots+\left(\frac{1}{n-2}-\frac{1}{n}\right)+\left(\frac{1}{n-1}-\frac{1}{n+1}\right)+\left(\frac{1}{n}-\frac{1}{n+2}\right)$$

Cancel like terms to get $1 + \frac{1}{2} - \frac{1}{n+1} - \frac{1}{n+2}$. If we then multiply by the $\frac{1}{2}$ we ignored previously, the summation can be written as $\sum_{r=1}^{n} \frac{1}{r(r+2)} = \frac{3}{4} - \frac{1}{2(n+1)} - \frac{1}{2(n+2)}$.

In this example, notice that two terms from the start and finish are included in the final answer. Previously it was only one term from each end.

EXPLORE 3.3

Consider the summation $\sum_{r=1}^{n} \frac{1}{(ar+b)(ar+c)}$. In groups, investigate the effect of changing these values. For example, what happens when $a = 2$?

WORKED EXAMPLE 3.6

For the summation $\sum_{r=2}^{n} \frac{1}{(r-1)(r+1)}$, find an expression in terms of n.

Answer

$\frac{1}{(r-1)(r+1)} = \frac{A}{r-1} + \frac{B}{r+1}$ Split into partial fractions.

$1 = A(r+1) + B(r-1)$

$A = \frac{1}{2}, B = -\frac{1}{2}$ Determine the coefficients.

$$\sum_{r=2}^{n} \frac{1}{(r-1)(r+1)} = \left(\frac{1}{1} - \frac{1}{3}\right) + \left(\frac{1}{2} - \frac{1}{4}\right) + \left(\frac{1}{3} - \frac{1}{5}\right) + \cdots + \left(\frac{1}{n-3} - \frac{1}{n-1}\right) + \left(\frac{1}{n-2} - \frac{1}{n}\right) + \left(\frac{1}{n-1} - \frac{1}{n+1}\right)$$

Initially ignore the $\frac{1}{2}$ in front of every term, and note that this sum starts at $r = 2$.

$= 1 + \frac{1}{2} - \frac{1}{n} - \frac{1}{n+1}$ Cancel terms.

$\sum_{r=2}^{n} \frac{1}{(r-1)(r+1)} = \frac{3}{4} - \frac{1}{2n} - \frac{1}{2(n+1)}$ Simplify and remember the factor of $\frac{1}{2}$ we previously ignored.

Finally, let us consider these summations as the upper limit tends to infinity. Since the powers of r are always dominant in the denominator, these summations will always tend to a limit.

TIP

Pay close attention to the limit of your sum. This may not be 1.

Look back at the example of $\sum_{r=1}^{n} \frac{1}{r(r+1)} = 1 - \frac{1}{n+1}$. As $n \to \infty$ this will tend to 1.

WORKED EXAMPLE 3.7

Given that $S_n = \sum_{r=2}^{n} \frac{5}{r(r-1)}$, find the sum of the terms as $n \to \infty$.

Answer

$\frac{5}{r(r-1)} = \frac{A}{r} + \frac{B}{r-1}$ — Split into partial fractions.

$5 = A(r-1) + Br$

$A = -5, B = 5$ — Determine the coefficients.

$\left(\frac{1}{1} - \frac{1}{2}\right) + \left(\frac{1}{2} - \frac{1}{3}\right) + \cdots + \left(\frac{1}{n-2} - \frac{1}{n-1}\right) + \left(\frac{1}{n-1} - \frac{1}{n}\right)$ — Initially ignoring the 5 in front of every term, write down enough terms to spot a pattern.

$\therefore S_n = \sum_{r=2}^{n} \frac{5}{r(r-1)} = 5 - \frac{5}{n}$ — State S_n, remembering to include the 5 we previously ignored.

$n \to \infty, S_n \to 5$ — Write down the limit.

EXERCISE 3B

PS **1** Find, in terms of n, an expression for $\sum_{r=2}^{n} \frac{3}{(r-1)r}$.

P **2** Show that $\sum_{r=1}^{n} \frac{1}{(r+4)(r+5)}$ can be written as $\frac{n}{5n+25}$.

PS **3** Determine the value of $\sum_{r=1}^{\infty} \frac{1}{(2r+3)(2r+5)}$.

PS **4** Without using a calculator, find, in terms of n, an expression for $\sum_{r=1}^{n} \frac{1}{(r+3)(r+4)}$.

P **5** Without using a calculator, given that $S_n = \sum_{r=0}^{n} \frac{1}{(2r+1)(2r+3)}$, show that $S_n = \frac{n+1}{2n+3}$.

P PS **6** Without using a calculator, show that $\sum_{r=3}^{n} \frac{1}{r(r-2)} = \frac{3}{4} - \frac{1}{2n-2} - \frac{1}{2n}$. Hence, determine, in terms of n, the result of $\sum_{r=n+1}^{2n} \frac{1}{r(r-2)}$.

PS 7 Without using a calculator, determine the value of $\sum_{r=2}^{\infty} \frac{4}{r^2 - 1}$.

PS 8 Let $S_n = \sum_{r=4}^{n} \frac{1}{r^2 - 5r + 6}$.

a Find, in terms of n, an expression for S_n.

b Given that $S = \lim_{n \to \infty} S_n$, write down the value of S.

c Find the range of values of n such that $S - S_n < 0.001$.

WORKED PAST PAPER QUESTION

Verify that, for all positive values of n,

$$\frac{1}{(n+2)(2n+3)} - \frac{1}{(n+3)(2n+5)} = \frac{4n+9}{(n+2)(n+3)(2n+3)(2n+5)}.$$

For the series $\sum_{n=1}^{N} \frac{4n+9}{(n+2)(n+3)(2n+3)(2n+5)}$, find

i the sum to N terms,

ii the sum to infinity.

Cambridge International AS & A Level Further Mathematics 9231 Paper 1 Q2 June 2009

Answer

$$\frac{1}{(n+2)(2n+3)} - \frac{1}{(n+3)(2n+5)} = \frac{2n^2 + 11n + 15 - (2n^2 + 7n + 6)}{(n+2)(n+3)(2n+3)(2n+5)}$$

$$= \frac{4n+9}{(n+2)(n+3)(2n+3)(2n+5)}$$

i $$\sum_{n=1}^{N} \frac{4n+9}{(n+2)(n+3)(2n+3)(2n+5)} = \frac{1}{3 \times 5} - \frac{1}{4 \times 7} + \frac{1}{4 \times 7} - \frac{1}{5 \times 9} + \cdots + \frac{1}{(N+2)(2N+3)} - \frac{1}{(N+3)(2N+5)}$$

$$= \frac{1}{15} - \frac{1}{(N+3)(2N+5)}$$

ii As $N \to \infty$, sum becomes $\frac{1}{15}$.

Checklist of learning and understanding

Standard summations:

- $\sum_{r=1}^{n} r = \frac{1}{2}n(n+1)$
- $\sum_{r=1}^{n} r^2 = \frac{1}{6}n(n+1)(2n+1)$
- $\sum_{r=1}^{n} r^3 = \frac{1}{4}n^2(n+1)^2$
- When we consider summations such as $\sum_{r=n+b}^{2n} \mathrm{f}(r)$, it is often best to first determine $\sum_{r=1}^{n} \mathrm{f}(r)$, then replace n with $2n$ to determine $\sum_{r=1}^{2n} \mathrm{f}(r)$. Finally, write $\sum_{r=n+b}^{2n} \mathrm{f}(r) = \sum_{r=1}^{2n} \mathrm{f}(r) - \sum_{r=1}^{n+b-1} \mathrm{f}(r)$.
- When we use the method of differences, first split $\sum_{r=1}^{n} \frac{a}{(r+b)(r+c)}$ into partial fractions such as $\sum_{r=1}^{n} \left(\frac{A}{r+b} + \frac{B}{r+c}\right)$. Next, list as many terms as needed to effectively cancel terms and get a reduced form.
- For convergence, first get the summation in the form $\sum_{r=a}^{n} \mathrm{f}(n) = b + \frac{c}{dn+e} + \cdots$. Allowing $n \to \infty$ will lead to the result of b.

END-OF-CHAPTER REVIEW EXERCISE 3

Do not use a calculator in this exercise.

1 Find the sum of the first n terms of the series $\frac{1}{1\times 3}+\frac{1}{2\times 4}+\frac{1}{3\times 5}+\cdots$ and deduce the sum to infinity.

Cambridge International AS & A Level Further Mathematics 9231 Paper 13 Q1 June 2012

2 Find $2^2+4^2+\cdots+(2n)^2$.

Hence find $1^2-2^2+3^2-4^2+\cdots-(2n)^2$, simplifying your answer.

Cambridge International AS & A Level Further Mathematics 9231 Paper 13 Q1 June 2011

3 Use the method of differences to show that $\sum_{r=1}^{N}\frac{1}{(2r+1)(2r+3)}=\frac{1}{6}-\frac{1}{2(2N+3)}$.

Deduce that $\sum_{r=N+1}^{2N}\frac{1}{(2r+1)(2r+3)}<\frac{1}{8N}$.

Cambridge International AS & A Level Further Mathematics 9231 Paper 11 Q5 June 2013

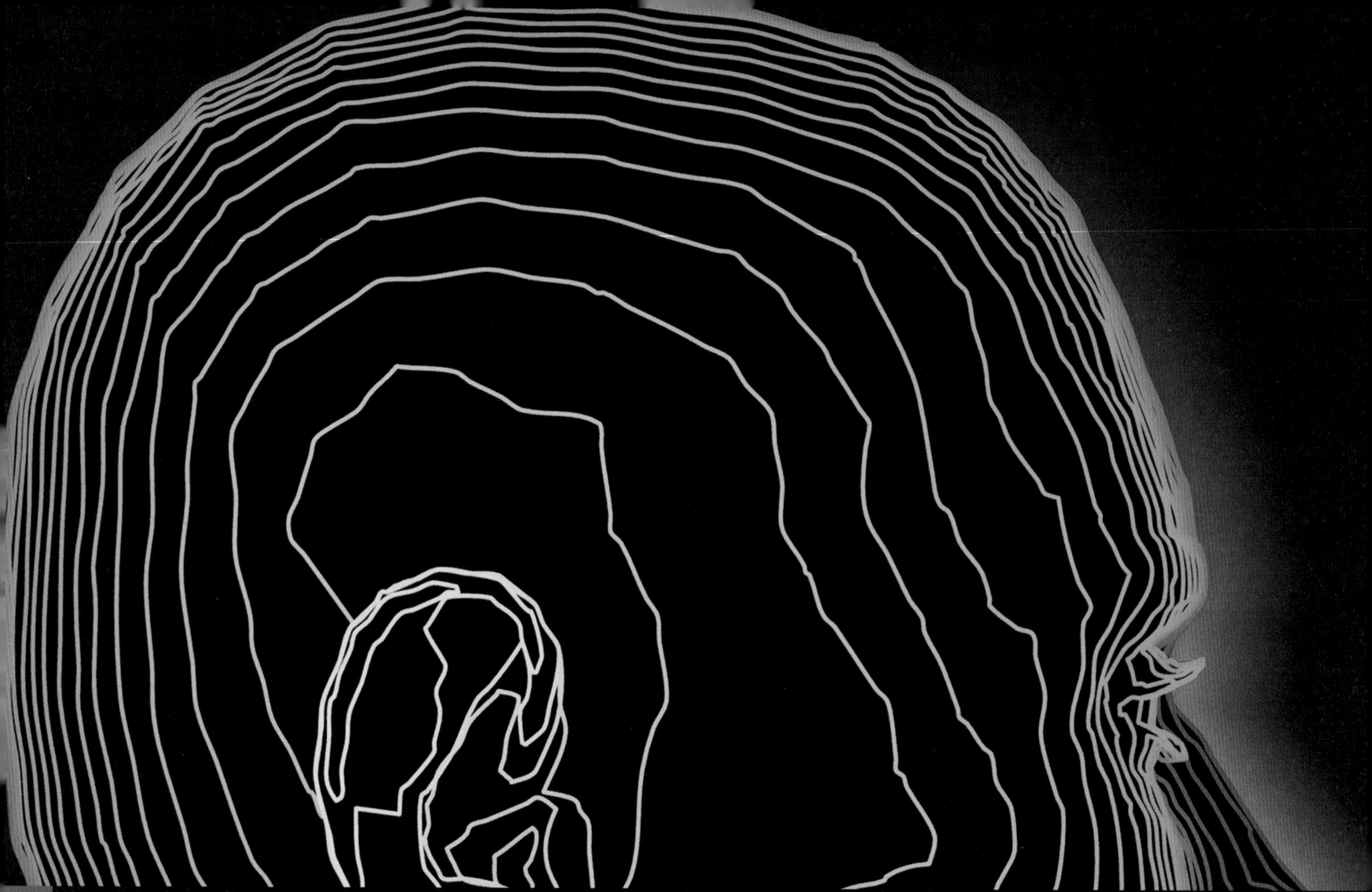

Chapter 4
Matrices 1

In this chapter you will learn how to:

- carry out matrix operations such as addition, subtraction and multiplication
- recognise the terms zero matrix, identity matrix, singular and non-singular
- evaluate determinants, find inverse matrices and know to use identities such as $(\mathbf{AB})^{-1} = \mathbf{B}^{-1}\mathbf{A}^{-1}$
- apply geometric transformations, such as rotations and enlargements, as well as being aware of the relation between scale factor and determinants.

PREREQUISITE KNOWLEDGE

Where it comes from	What you should be able to do	Check your skills
AS & A Level Mathematics Pure Mathematics 2 & 3, Chapter 9	Find the scalar product of 2- and 3-dimensional vectors.	1 Find the scalar product of the following. a $(2\mathbf{i}+\mathbf{j})\cdot(3\mathbf{i}-4\mathbf{j})$ b $(-\mathbf{i}+4\mathbf{j}+5\mathbf{k})\cdot(-6\mathbf{j}+2\mathbf{k})$

What are matrices?

Matrices (singular, **matrix**) are rectangular arrays of numbers, variables or expressions arranged in rows and columns. They are widely used in computing processes, for instance reflection and refraction in computer graphics or computer modelling of probabilities for weather forecasting.

Matrices can be used to represent information such as the coordinates of an object in 3-dimensional space. You might have a basic understanding of how matrices work from your IGCSE® course.

In this chapter we will focus on matrix operations, inverse matrices, special types of matrices and matrix transformations.

4.1 Matrix operations

The size of a matrix is defined by its **rows**, m, and **columns**, n. We refer to matrices by their **order** or size, $m \times n$.

For a general matrix of order $m \times n$ we have $\begin{pmatrix} a_{11} & a_{12} & a_{13} & \cdots \\ a_{21} & a_{22} & a_{23} & \cdots \\ a_{31} & a_{32} & a_{33} & \cdots \\ \vdots & \vdots & \vdots & \ddots \end{pmatrix}$.

Each a_{mn} inside represents an **element** of the matrix.

For example, the column vector $\begin{pmatrix} 2 \\ 5 \\ 6 \end{pmatrix}$ is a 3×1 matrix and $\begin{pmatrix} 2 & 4 & -1 \\ 3 & 0 & 1 \end{pmatrix}$ is a 2×3 matrix. The size of a matrix is important when considering addition, subtraction and multiplication.

A matrix that has the same number of rows and columns is called a square matrix.

Addition and subtraction of matrices

For matrices $\mathbf{A} = \begin{pmatrix} 3 & 2 \\ 4 & 6 \end{pmatrix}$ and $\mathbf{B} = \begin{pmatrix} 5 & -4 \\ 1 & 3 \end{pmatrix}$, adding gives $\mathbf{A} + \mathbf{B} = \begin{pmatrix} 8 & -2 \\ 5 & 9 \end{pmatrix}$ and subtracting gives $\mathbf{A} - \mathbf{B} = \begin{pmatrix} -2 & 6 \\ 3 & 3 \end{pmatrix}$.

We cannot add matrices $\mathbf{C} = \begin{pmatrix} 1 & 0 & 3 \\ 5 & -4 & 6 \end{pmatrix}$ and $\mathbf{D} = \begin{pmatrix} 1 & 2 \\ 3 & 1 \end{pmatrix}$ together because there are elements in the first matrix that have no corresponding elements to add to in the second matrix. Matrices can be added (or subtracted) only when the number of columns and rows is the same in both matrices.

To add two matrices, each element of the first matrix is added to the corresponding element of the second matrix. Subtraction uses the same method, but elements are subtracted. To add or subtract two general 2×2 matrices together, we use the formula shown in Key point 4.1.

KEY POINT 4.1

To add or subtract two general 2×2 matrices together, use:

$$\begin{pmatrix} a & b \\ c & d \end{pmatrix} \pm \begin{pmatrix} e & f \\ g & h \end{pmatrix} = \begin{pmatrix} a \pm e & b \pm f \\ c \pm g & d \pm h \end{pmatrix}$$

Matrices may be added or subtracted only when they have the same order. The result will be a matrix of the same order.

Multiplication of matrices

To multiply a matrix by a scalar, multiply each element of the matrix by the scalar.

For example, if $\mathbf{A} = \begin{pmatrix} a & b \\ c & d \end{pmatrix}$, then $k\mathbf{A} = k\begin{pmatrix} a & b \\ c & d \end{pmatrix}$, which is $\begin{pmatrix} ka & kb \\ kc & kd \end{pmatrix}$.

Consider two matrices $\mathbf{A} = \begin{pmatrix} a & b \\ c & d \end{pmatrix}$ and $\mathbf{B} = \begin{pmatrix} e & f \\ g & h \end{pmatrix}$. The product of these matrices is given as $\mathbf{AB} = \begin{pmatrix} ae + bg & af + bh \\ ce + dg & cf + dh \end{pmatrix}$.

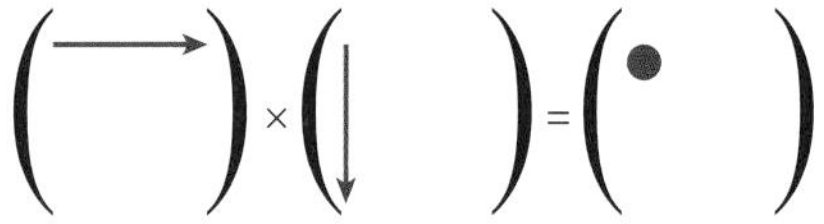

The elements of the first row of the first matrix are multiplied by the elements of the first column of the second matrix. For each row × column, sum the products. This produces new element a_{11} for the solution matrix.

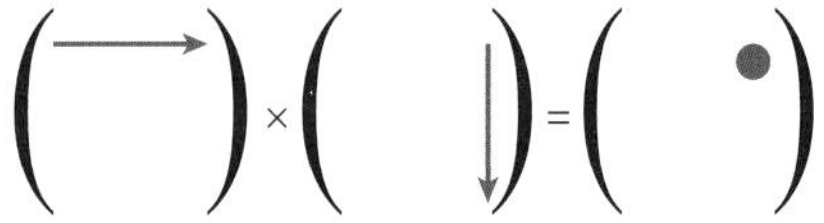

Multiplying the first row of the first matrix and the second column of the second matrix produces the element a_{12} and so on.

So if $\mathbf{E} = \begin{pmatrix} 1 & 2 \\ 3 & 4 \end{pmatrix}$ and $\mathbf{F} = \begin{pmatrix} 5 & 6 \\ 7 & 8 \end{pmatrix}$, then $\mathbf{EF} = \begin{pmatrix} 1 \times 5 + 2 \times 7 & 1 \times 6 + 2 \times 8 \\ 3 \times 5 + 4 \times 7 & 3 \times 6 + 4 \times 8 \end{pmatrix} = \begin{pmatrix} 19 & 22 \\ 43 & 50 \end{pmatrix}$.

To multiply matrices, the number of columns in the first matrix must be the same as the number of rows in the second matrix.

It is important to understand the process of matrix multiplication before we move on to any more examples.

WORKED EXAMPLE 4.1

Given that $\mathbf{A} = \begin{pmatrix} 4 & 3 \\ 2 & 1 \end{pmatrix}$ and $\mathbf{B} = \begin{pmatrix} 8 & 7 \\ 6 & 5 \end{pmatrix}$, determine the solution matrix for:

a $\mathbf{A} + 3\mathbf{B}$ b $\mathbf{B} - 4\mathbf{A}$ c $\mathbf{A}^2$ d $\mathbf{AB}$ e $\mathbf{BA}$

Answer

a $\mathbf{A} + 3\mathbf{B} = \begin{pmatrix} 4 & 3 \\ 2 & 1 \end{pmatrix} + 3\begin{pmatrix} 8 & 7 \\ 6 & 5 \end{pmatrix}$

Multiply the matrix by the scalar first, then add the two matrices.

$= \begin{pmatrix} 4 & 3 \\ 2 & 1 \end{pmatrix} + \begin{pmatrix} 24 & 21 \\ 18 & 15 \end{pmatrix}$

$= \begin{pmatrix} 28 & 24 \\ 20 & 16 \end{pmatrix}$

b $\mathbf{B} - 4\mathbf{A} = \begin{pmatrix} 8 & 7 \\ 6 & 5 \end{pmatrix} - 4\begin{pmatrix} 4 & 3 \\ 2 & 1 \end{pmatrix}$

Multiply the matrix by the scalar first, then subtract.

$= \begin{pmatrix} -8 & -5 \\ -2 & 1 \end{pmatrix}$

c $\mathbf{A}^2 = \begin{pmatrix} 4 & 3 \\ 2 & 1 \end{pmatrix}\begin{pmatrix} 4 & 3 \\ 2 & 1 \end{pmatrix}$

The square of a matrix is the result of multiplying the matrix by itself.

$= \begin{pmatrix} 22 & 15 \\ 10 & 7 \end{pmatrix}$

d $\mathbf{AB} = \begin{pmatrix} 4 & 3 \\ 2 & 1 \end{pmatrix}\begin{pmatrix} 8 & 7 \\ 6 & 5 \end{pmatrix}$

$= \begin{pmatrix} 50 & 43 \\ 22 & 19 \end{pmatrix}$

e $\mathbf{BA} = \begin{pmatrix} 8 & 7 \\ 6 & 5 \end{pmatrix}\begin{pmatrix} 4 & 3 \\ 2 & 1 \end{pmatrix}$

In general, $\mathbf{AB} \neq \mathbf{BA}$. The order in which matrices are multiplied is very important.

$= \begin{pmatrix} 46 & 31 \\ 34 & 23 \end{pmatrix}$

In general, matrix multiplication is non-commutative, as shown in Key point 4.2.

KEY POINT 4.2

For two matrices **A** and **B**, $\mathbf{AB} \neq \mathbf{BA}$.

To multiply 3×3 matrices, we use the same method as before. However, there will be more elements in each calculation.

In general, $\begin{pmatrix} a & b & c \\ * & * & * \\ * & * & * \end{pmatrix} \times \begin{pmatrix} d & * & * \\ e & * & * \\ f & * & * \end{pmatrix} = \begin{pmatrix} ad + be + cf & * & * \\ * & * & * \\ * & * & * \end{pmatrix}$.

For example, if $\mathbf{A} = \begin{pmatrix} 1 & 2 & 5 \\ 0 & -2 & 3 \\ 2 & 0 & 4 \end{pmatrix}$ and $\mathbf{B} = \begin{pmatrix} 3 & 4 & -1 \\ 5 & 2 & 1 \\ -2 & 1 & 4 \end{pmatrix}$, then

$$\mathbf{AB} = \begin{pmatrix} 1 & 2 & 5 \\ 0 & -2 & 3 \\ 2 & 0 & 4 \end{pmatrix}\begin{pmatrix} 3 & 4 & -1 \\ 5 & 2 & 1 \\ -2 & 1 & 4 \end{pmatrix} = \begin{pmatrix} 3 & 13 & 21 \\ -16 & -1 & 10 \\ -2 & 12 & 14 \end{pmatrix}.$$

Note that **BA** gives $\begin{pmatrix} 3 & 4 & -1 \\ 5 & 2 & 1 \\ -2 & 1 & 4 \end{pmatrix}\begin{pmatrix} 1 & 2 & 5 \\ 0 & -2 & 3 \\ 2 & 0 & 4 \end{pmatrix} = \begin{pmatrix} 1 & -2 & 23 \\ 7 & 6 & 35 \\ 6 & -6 & 9 \end{pmatrix}$. So $\mathbf{AB} \neq \mathbf{BA}$.

WORKED EXAMPLE 4.2

Given that $\mathbf{A} = \begin{pmatrix} 0 & 3 & -2 \\ 1 & 1 & 1 \\ -5 & 1 & 0 \end{pmatrix}$, $\mathbf{B} = \begin{pmatrix} 4 & 8 & 3 \\ 6 & 2 & 1 \\ 3 & 2 & 5 \end{pmatrix}$ and $\mathbf{C} = \begin{pmatrix} -1 & 0 & 2 \\ 2 & -1 & -1 \\ 1 & -1 & 3 \end{pmatrix}$, find the values of **AB**, **CA** and **BC**.

Answer

$$\mathbf{AB} = \begin{pmatrix} 0 & 3 & -2 \\ 1 & 1 & 1 \\ -5 & 1 & 0 \end{pmatrix}\begin{pmatrix} 4 & 8 & 3 \\ 6 & 2 & 1 \\ 3 & 2 & 5 \end{pmatrix} = \begin{pmatrix} 12 & 2 & -7 \\ 13 & 12 & 9 \\ -14 & -38 & -14 \end{pmatrix}$$

Remember to multiply elements in rows by elements in columns.

$$\mathbf{CA} = \begin{pmatrix} -1 & 0 & 2 \\ 2 & -1 & -1 \\ 1 & -1 & 3 \end{pmatrix}\begin{pmatrix} 0 & 3 & -2 \\ 1 & 1 & 1 \\ -5 & 1 & 0 \end{pmatrix} = \begin{pmatrix} -10 & -1 & 2 \\ 4 & 4 & -5 \\ -16 & 5 & -3 \end{pmatrix}$$

Where the row and column intersect, this shows which element is being calculated.

$$\mathbf{BC} = \begin{pmatrix} 4 & 8 & 3 \\ 6 & 2 & 1 \\ 3 & 2 & 5 \end{pmatrix}\begin{pmatrix} -1 & 0 & 2 \\ 2 & -1 & -1 \\ 1 & -1 & 3 \end{pmatrix} = \begin{pmatrix} 15 & -11 & 9 \\ -1 & -3 & 13 \\ 6 & -7 & 19 \end{pmatrix}$$

Multiply the matrices in the correct order.

EXPLORE 4.1

Investigate the multiplication of non-square matrices.

How is the size of the resulting matrix related to the matrices being multiplied together?

We have stated previously that, in general, $\mathbf{AB} \neq \mathbf{BA}$. There are a few exceptions to this rule.

Any matrix in which all the elements are zero is known as the **zero matrix**. This matrix can be any size and is represented by $0_{mn} = \begin{pmatrix} 0 & 0 & 0 & \cdots \\ 0 & 0 & 0 & \cdots \\ 0 & 0 & 0 & \cdots \\ \vdots & \vdots & \vdots & \ddots \end{pmatrix}$.

If $\mathbf{A} = \begin{pmatrix} a & b \\ c & d \end{pmatrix}$ and $\mathbf{B} = \begin{pmatrix} 0 & 0 \\ 0 & 0 \end{pmatrix}$, then we can see that $\mathbf{AB} = \begin{pmatrix} 0 & 0 \\ 0 & 0 \end{pmatrix}$ and $\mathbf{BA} = \begin{pmatrix} 0 & 0 \\ 0 & 0 \end{pmatrix}$. So $\mathbf{AB} = \mathbf{BA}$ when one of the matrices is a zero matrix.

Now consider the matrix $\mathbf{A} = \begin{pmatrix} 2 & 5 \\ 1 & 2 \end{pmatrix}$, and let $\mathbf{B} = \mathbf{A}^2 = \begin{pmatrix} 9 & 20 \\ 4 & 9 \end{pmatrix}$.

Then $\mathbf{AB} = \mathbf{AA}^2 = \begin{pmatrix} 2 & 5 \\ 1 & 2 \end{pmatrix}\begin{pmatrix} 9 & 20 \\ 4 & 9 \end{pmatrix} = \begin{pmatrix} 38 & 85 \\ 17 & 38 \end{pmatrix}$,

and $\mathbf{BA} = \mathbf{A}^2\mathbf{A} = \begin{pmatrix} 9 & 20 \\ 4 & 9 \end{pmatrix}\begin{pmatrix} 2 & 5 \\ 1 & 2 \end{pmatrix} = \begin{pmatrix} 38 & 85 \\ 17 & 38 \end{pmatrix}$.

It can then be shown that $\mathbf{AA}^3 = \mathbf{A}^3\mathbf{A} = \mathbf{A}^4$ and, in general, $\mathbf{A}^m\mathbf{A}^n = \mathbf{A}^n\mathbf{A}^m = \mathbf{A}^{m+n}$, as shown in Key point 4.3. This result shows that matrix multiplication does not depend on order when the matrices are both powers of the same base matrix, in this case A.

KEY POINT 4.3

$\mathbf{A}^m\mathbf{A}^n = \mathbf{A}^n\mathbf{A}^m = \mathbf{A}^{m+n}$

There is another special matrix to look at. Consider matrix $\mathbf{A} = \begin{pmatrix} a & b \\ c & d \end{pmatrix}$ and multiply it by $\begin{pmatrix} 1 & 0 \\ 0 & 1 \end{pmatrix}$

$$\begin{pmatrix} a & b \\ c & d \end{pmatrix}\begin{pmatrix} 1 & 0 \\ 0 & 1 \end{pmatrix} = \begin{pmatrix} a & b \\ c & d \end{pmatrix} \text{ and } \begin{pmatrix} 1 & 0 \\ 0 & 1 \end{pmatrix}\begin{pmatrix} a & b \\ c & d \end{pmatrix} = \begin{pmatrix} a & b \\ c & d \end{pmatrix}.$$

The matrix $\begin{pmatrix} 1 & 0 \\ 0 & 1 \end{pmatrix}$ is known as the identity matrix. We denote this matrix as **I**.

The identity matrix is a square matrix of the form $\mathbf{I} = \begin{pmatrix} 1 & 0 & 0 & \dots & 0 \\ 0 & 1 & 0 & \dots & 0 \\ 0 & 0 & 1 & \dots & 0 \\ \vdots & \vdots & \vdots & \ddots & \vdots \\ 0 & 0 & 0 & \dots & 1 \end{pmatrix}$.

This matrix behaves in a special way. When any matrix is multiplied by **I** it is unchanged. It is just like multiplying any number by 1.

In general, we can say that $\mathbf{AI} = \mathbf{IA} = \mathbf{A}$, provided that the matrix multiplication is allowed.

WORKED EXAMPLE 4.3

Given matrix $\mathbf{A} = \begin{pmatrix} -2 & 5 \\ 1 & -3 \end{pmatrix}$ and matrix $\mathbf{B} = \begin{pmatrix} a & b \\ c & d \end{pmatrix}$, prove that if $\mathbf{AB} = \mathbf{A}$ then the matrix **B** must be of the form $\begin{pmatrix} 1 & 0 \\ 0 & 1 \end{pmatrix}$.

Answer

$\begin{pmatrix} -2 & 5 \\ 1 & -3 \end{pmatrix} \times \begin{pmatrix} a & b \\ c & d \end{pmatrix}$ — Multiply the matrices together.

$-2a + 5c = -2$ (1) — Obtain four simultaneous equations.

$-2b + 5d = 5$ (2)

$a - 3c = 1$ (3)

$b - 3d = -3$ (4)

(1) + 2(3) gives $c = 0$, hence $a = 1$. — Solve the equations to find the elements.

(2) + 2(4) gives $d = 1$, hence $b = 0$.

Hence, $\mathbf{B} = \begin{pmatrix} 1 & 0 \\ 0 & 1 \end{pmatrix}$. — Confirm this is the correct matrix.

Let us look at the order of matrix multiplication in slightly more detail. Consider the three matrices $\mathbf{A} = \begin{pmatrix} 3 & 0 & 0 \\ 1 & 2 & 6 \\ 6 & 4 & -1 \end{pmatrix}$, $\mathbf{B} = \begin{pmatrix} 4 & 9 & 12 \\ -1 & -1 & 1 \\ 3 & 1 & 4 \end{pmatrix}$ and $\mathbf{C} = \begin{pmatrix} 2 & 5 & 0 \\ 8 & 1 & 7 \\ 0 & 4 & 0 \end{pmatrix}$. If we want to determine the result **ABC**, we can do this in two ways.

First, find $\mathbf{AB} = \begin{pmatrix} 12 & 27 & 36 \\ 20 & 13 & 38 \\ 17 & 49 & 72 \end{pmatrix}$ and then $(\mathbf{AB})\mathbf{C} = \begin{pmatrix} 240 & 231 & 189 \\ 144 & 265 & 91 \\ 426 & 422 & 343 \end{pmatrix}$.

Alternatively, calculate $\mathbf{BC} = \begin{pmatrix} 80 & 77 & 63 \\ -10 & -2 & -7 \\ 14 & 32 & 7 \end{pmatrix}$, and then $\mathbf{A}(\mathbf{BC}) = \begin{pmatrix} 240 & 231 & 189 \\ 144 & 265 & 91 \\ 426 & 422 & 343 \end{pmatrix}$.

So, in general, $(\mathbf{AB})\mathbf{CD} = \mathbf{A}(\mathbf{BC})\mathbf{D} = \mathbf{AB}(\mathbf{CD}) = (\mathbf{AB})(\mathbf{CD})$. We get the same result when we multiply matrices in different ways, provided the matrices stay in the same sequences, in this case **ABCD**.

EXERCISE 4A

1 Verify that $\mathbf{AB} \neq \mathbf{BA}$, where $\mathbf{A} = \begin{pmatrix} 2 & 7 \\ -9 & 4 \end{pmatrix}$ and $\mathbf{B} = \begin{pmatrix} 3 & -5 \\ 4 & 12 \end{pmatrix}$.

2 Given that $\mathbf{A} = \begin{pmatrix} 6 & 7 \\ 1 & 2 \end{pmatrix}$ and $\mathbf{B} = \begin{pmatrix} 2 & 0 \\ 1 & -4 \end{pmatrix}$, evaluate the following:

a $\mathbf{A}^2 + 2\mathbf{AB}$ b $\mathbf{B}^2\mathbf{A}$ c $\mathbf{A}^3 - \mathbf{BA}$

3 Given that $\mathbf{A} = \begin{pmatrix} 2 & -5 & 1 \\ 6 & 1 & 0 \\ 3 & 0 & -2 \end{pmatrix}$ and $\mathbf{B} = \begin{pmatrix} 1 & -2 & 1 \\ 0 & 4 & 2 \\ 0 & 0 & 2 \end{pmatrix}$, find:

a $\mathbf{AB}^2$ b $\mathbf{A}^2 - \mathbf{AB}$

4 State which of the following pairs of matrices can be multiplied together, and if they can, determine the result.

a $\begin{pmatrix} 2 & 3 \\ 1 & 5 \end{pmatrix} \times \begin{pmatrix} 0 \\ 4 \end{pmatrix}$ b $\begin{pmatrix} 5 \\ 6 \end{pmatrix} \times \begin{pmatrix} 7 & 8 \\ 10 & -2 \end{pmatrix}$

c $(5 \ \ 2 \ \ 1) \times \begin{pmatrix} 2 & 6 \\ 4 & 0 \\ 3 & 8 \end{pmatrix}$ d $\begin{pmatrix} 2 & 7 & 5 & -1 \\ 4 & -4 & 0 & 3 \end{pmatrix} \times \begin{pmatrix} 12 & 3 \\ 2 & 5 \end{pmatrix}$

5 Given that $\mathbf{A} = \begin{pmatrix} 1 & 2 & -5 \\ 0 & 9 & 3 \\ -1 & -5 & 10 \end{pmatrix}$ and $\mathbf{B} = \begin{pmatrix} 3 & 1 & -2 \\ 0 & 0 & 4 \\ 5 & -3 & -6 \end{pmatrix}$, calculate the matrices:

a $2\mathbf{A} + 5\mathbf{B}$ b $\mathbf{AB}^2$ c $\mathbf{BA}^2$ d $2\mathbf{A} + 3\mathbf{A}^2$

P 6 If $\mathbf{A} = \begin{pmatrix} 1 & -1 \\ 0 & 1 \end{pmatrix}$, show that $\mathbf{A}^n = \begin{pmatrix} 1 & -n \\ 0 & 1 \end{pmatrix}$.

7 You are given the matrices $\mathbf{A} = \begin{pmatrix} 2 & 1 & 3 \\ 4 & 6 & 0 \\ 0 & -1 & 0 \end{pmatrix}$, $\mathbf{B} = \begin{pmatrix} 0 & -3 & 0 \\ 1 & 0 & -1 \\ 3 & 0 & 1 \end{pmatrix}$ and $\mathbf{C} = \begin{pmatrix} 5 & 9 & -3 \\ -2 & 1 & 7 \\ 1 & 8 & 4 \end{pmatrix}$. Evaluate **BICIA**, where **I** is the identity matrix.

PS 8 The matrix $\mathbf{A}$ is given as $\mathbf{A} = \begin{pmatrix} 2 & 0 & 0 \\ -1 & 0 & -1 \\ 1 & 0 & 1 \end{pmatrix}$.

a Find $\mathbf{A}^2$ and $\mathbf{A}^3$.

b Determine $\mathbf{A}^n$. (You do not need to prove your result.)

4.2 The inverse matrix

In Section 4.1 we looked at how to add, subtract and multiply matrices. We did not look at division because matrices *cannot* be divided.

Consider the matrix equation $\mathbf{AB} = \mathbf{I}$, in which $\mathbf{A} = \begin{pmatrix} 2 & 5 \\ 2 & 1 \end{pmatrix}$. To determine the matrix $\mathbf{B}$, we consider what is known as an **augmented matrix**.

An augmented matrix is created by combining the columns of two matrices. We use an augmented matrix so that we can observe the row operations acting on both the original matrix and the identity matrix.

Row operations are used to change the elements of matrices. There are three types of row operation:

- row switching, where $r_i \leftrightarrow r_j$
- row multiplication, where $r_i \rightarrow kr_i$
- row addition, where $r_i \rightarrow r_i + kr_j$

We will use a combination of addition and multiplication.

In this example, we shall use the matrix $\begin{pmatrix} 2 & 5 & \vdots & 1 & 0 \\ 2 & 1 & \vdots & 0 & 1 \end{pmatrix}$. On the left side of the dotted lines we have the elements of $\mathbf{A}$; on the right side we have the elements of the identity matrix.

By changing the left side to the identity matrix, the right side will become the **inverse matrix** of $\mathbf{A}$, or $\mathbf{A}^{-1}$.

Use row operations on the augmented matrix, to change the elements of matrix $\mathbf{A}$ into the identity matrix.

Our first operation is $r_2 \rightarrow r_2 - r_1$, which changes the matrix to $\begin{pmatrix} 2 & 5 & \vdots & 1 & 0 \\ 0 & -4 & \vdots & -1 & 1 \end{pmatrix}$.

Then $r_1 \rightarrow 4r_1 + 5r_2$ gives $\begin{pmatrix} 8 & 0 & \vdots & -1 & 5 \\ 0 & -4 & \vdots & -1 & 1 \end{pmatrix}$. Next, use $r_1 \rightarrow \frac{1}{8}r_1$ and $r_2 \rightarrow -\frac{1}{4}r_2$ to get

$$\begin{pmatrix} 1 & 0 & \vdots & -\frac{1}{8} & \frac{5}{8} \\ 0 & 1 & \vdots & \frac{1}{4} & -\frac{1}{4} \end{pmatrix}.$$

Hence, $\mathbf{A}^{-1} = \begin{pmatrix} -\frac{1}{8} & \frac{5}{8} \\ \frac{1}{4} & -\frac{1}{4} \end{pmatrix}$, or we can write $\mathbf{A}^{-1} = -\frac{1}{8}\begin{pmatrix} 1 & -5 \\ -2 & 2 \end{pmatrix}$.

In general, for a 2×2 square matrix $\mathbf{A} = \begin{pmatrix} a & b \\ c & d \end{pmatrix}$, the inverse is given by

$\mathbf{A}^{-1} = \frac{1}{ad - bc}\begin{pmatrix} d & -b \\ -c & a \end{pmatrix}$, as shown in Key point 4.4. The determinant, $ad - bc = \det(\mathbf{A})$, helps to determine whether or not an inverse matrix exists.

FAST FORWARD

This will be explained in more detail in Section 4.3.

The inverse matrix now behaves just like a reciprocal in the sense that $\mathbf{A}^{-1}\mathbf{A} = \mathbf{I}$ and $\mathbf{A}\mathbf{A}^{-1} = \mathbf{I}$. This is similar to $5 \times \frac{1}{5} = 1$. This is a useful alternative to division in matrix algebra since matrices cannot be divided.

Let us go back to our original question where $\mathbf{AB} = \mathbf{I}$. Multiply both sides by the inverse matrix $\mathbf{A}^{-1}$ to give $\mathbf{A}^{-1}\mathbf{AB} = \mathbf{A}^{-1}\mathbf{I}$. Since $\mathbf{A}^{-1}\mathbf{A} = \mathbf{I}$ and $\mathbf{A}^{-1}\mathbf{I} = \mathbf{A}^{-1}$, then $\mathbf{B} = \mathbf{A}^{-1}$.

WORKED EXAMPLE 4.4

Find the matrices **B** and **C**, where $\mathbf{AB} = \mathbf{I}$ and $\mathbf{BC} = \mathbf{A}$, and $\mathbf{A} = \begin{pmatrix} 1 & 3 \\ 2 & 7 \end{pmatrix}$.

Answer

$\mathbf{A}^{-1}\mathbf{AB} = \mathbf{A}^{-1}\mathbf{I}$ — Multiply by the inverse of **A**.

$\mathbf{B} = \mathbf{A}^{-1} = \frac{1}{1}\begin{pmatrix} 7 & -3 \\ -2 & 1 \end{pmatrix} = \begin{pmatrix} 7 & -3 \\ -2 & 1 \end{pmatrix}$ — Determine the result which is **B**.

Hence, $\mathbf{B} = \begin{pmatrix} 7 & -3 \\ -2 & 1 \end{pmatrix}$.

$\mathbf{BC} = \mathbf{A} \Rightarrow \mathbf{B}^{-1}\mathbf{BC} = \mathbf{B}^{-1}\mathbf{A} \Rightarrow \mathbf{C} = \mathbf{B}^{-1}\mathbf{A}$ — Use matrix algebra to show the result for **C**.

$\mathbf{B}^{-1} = \frac{1}{1}\begin{pmatrix} 1 & 3 \\ 2 & 7 \end{pmatrix} = \mathbf{A}$ — Find the value of the inverse of **B**.

$\therefore \mathbf{C} = \mathbf{B}^{-1}\mathbf{A} = \mathbf{A}^2 = \begin{pmatrix} 1 & 3 \\ 2 & 7 \end{pmatrix}\begin{pmatrix} 1 & 3 \\ 2 & 7 \end{pmatrix}$ — Determine that **C** is the matrix $\mathbf{A}^2$.

Hence, $\mathbf{C} = \begin{pmatrix} 7 & 24 \\ 16 & 55 \end{pmatrix}$. — Find the final result for **C**.

KEY POINT 4.4

The inverse of any 2×2 matrix $\mathbf{A} = \begin{pmatrix} a & b \\ c & d \end{pmatrix}$ is given as $\mathbf{A}^{-1} = \frac{1}{ad - bc}\begin{pmatrix} d & -b \\ -c & a \end{pmatrix}$.

Let us try to determine the inverse for a 3×3 matrix, too.

Starting with the matrix $\mathbf{A} = \begin{pmatrix} 1 & 2 & 1 \\ 0 & -1 & 2 \\ 2 & 3 & 1 \end{pmatrix}$, we then use $\left(\begin{array}{ccc:ccc} 1 & 2 & 1 & 1 & 0 & 0 \\ 0 & -1 & 2 & 0 & 1 & 0 \\ 2 & 3 & 1 & 0 & 0 & 1 \end{array}\right)$ as our augmented matrix. Again, our purpose will be to convert the left side of the dotted line so that it becomes the identity matrix and the right side will become the inverse.

Again, we will be using row operations to reduce elements to 0.

Start with the row operation $r_3 \to r_3 - 2r_1$ to get $\left(\begin{array}{ccc:ccc} 1 & 2 & 1 & 1 & 0 & 0 \\ 0 & -1 & 2 & 0 & 1 & 0 \\ 0 & -1 & -1 & -2 & 0 & 1 \end{array}\right)$.

Then apply $r_3 \to r_3 - r_2$ to get $\begin{pmatrix} 1 & 2 & 1 & \vdots & 1 & 0 & 0 \\ 0 & -1 & 2 & \vdots & 0 & 1 & 0 \\ 0 & 0 & -3 & \vdots & -2 & -1 & 1 \end{pmatrix}$.

Notice that there is now a lower triangle of zeros. This is known as row echelon form.

Then apply $r_1 \to r_1 + 2r_2$ to give the matrix $\begin{pmatrix} 1 & 0 & 5 & \vdots & 1 & 2 & 0 \\ 0 & -1 & 2 & \vdots & 0 & 1 & 0 \\ 0 & 0 & -3 & \vdots & -2 & -1 & 1 \end{pmatrix}$.

Follow this with $r_1 \to 3r_1 + 5r_3$ and $r_2 \to 3r_2 + 2r_3$ to get $\begin{pmatrix} 3 & 0 & 0 & \vdots & -7 & 1 & 5 \\ 0 & -3 & 0 & \vdots & -4 & 1 & 2 \\ 0 & 0 & -3 & \vdots & -2 & -1 & 1 \end{pmatrix}$.

Lastly, apply $r_1 \to \frac{1}{3}r_1$, $r_2 \to -\frac{1}{3}r_2$ and $r_3 \to -\frac{1}{3}r_3$ to get the augmented matrix

$$\begin{pmatrix} 1 & 0 & 0 & \vdots & -\frac{7}{3} & \frac{1}{3} & \frac{5}{3} \\ 0 & 1 & 0 & \vdots & \frac{4}{3} & -\frac{1}{3} & -\frac{2}{3} \\ 0 & 0 & 1 & \vdots & \frac{2}{3} & \frac{1}{3} & -\frac{1}{3} \end{pmatrix}.$$

The right-hand side is the inverse matrix, $\mathbf{A}^{-1} = \begin{pmatrix} -\frac{7}{3} & \frac{1}{3} & \frac{5}{3} \\ \frac{4}{3} & -\frac{1}{3} & -\frac{2}{3} \\ \frac{2}{3} & \frac{1}{3} & -\frac{1}{3} \end{pmatrix}$.

We can also write this as $\mathbf{A}^{-1} = \frac{1}{3}\begin{pmatrix} -7 & 1 & 5 \\ 4 & -1 & -2 \\ 2 & 1 & -1 \end{pmatrix}$. It is generally better to take out the fraction as this makes calculations simpler.

The left side is now in **reduced row echelon form** with ones in the leading diagonal and zeros everywhere else.

WORKED EXAMPLE 4.5

Find the inverse matrix for $\mathbf{B} = \begin{pmatrix} 4 & 1 & -1 \\ 2 & 0 & 1 \\ 3 & -2 & 4 \end{pmatrix}$.

Answer

Using the six operations below:

$r_3 \to 4r_3 - 3r_1$
$r_2 \to 2r_2 - r_1$
$r_3 \to r_3 - 11r_2$
$r_1 \to 14r_1 - r_3$
$r_2 \to 14r_2 + 3r_3$
$r_1 \to r_1 + r_2$

Apply operations to rows to create lower and upper triangles of 0s on the left side of the matrix.

leads to: $\begin{pmatrix} 56 & 0 & 0 & \vdots & 16 & -16 & 8 \\ 0 & -14 & 0 & \vdots & 10 & -38 & 12 \\ 0 & 0 & -14 & \vdots & 8 & -22 & 4 \end{pmatrix}$

This should not take more than six operations for a 3×3 matrix.

Then: $\begin{pmatrix} 1 & 0 & 0 & : & \frac{2}{7} & -\frac{2}{7} & \frac{1}{7} \\ 0 & 1 & 0 & : & -\frac{5}{7} & \frac{19}{7} & -\frac{6}{7} \\ 0 & 0 & 1 & : & -\frac{4}{7} & \frac{11}{7} & -\frac{2}{7} \end{pmatrix}$

Once in this form, turn the elements on the left into 1s by dividing by 56 , −14 and −14 respectively for each row.

The left side is now in reduced row echelon form, the identity matrix. This then gives the inverse matrix on the right side.

So $\mathbf{B}^{-1} = \frac{1}{7}\begin{pmatrix} 2 & -2 & 1 \\ -5 & 19 & -6 \\ -4 & 11 & -2 \end{pmatrix}$.

Factor out the $\frac{1}{7}$ and write the elements as integers.

TIP

Remember that there are six elements in a 3×3 matrix that must be converted to 0 to determine the inverse. This means that, at most, we will need to perform six row operations.

Consider the matrix $\mathbf{C} = \begin{pmatrix} 2 & 1 & 4 \\ 5 & 4 & 7 \\ 9 & 6 & 15 \end{pmatrix}$. By performing the operations $r_2 \to 2r_2 - 5r_1$ and $r_3 \to 2r_3 - 9r_1$ the matrix becomes $\begin{pmatrix} 2 & 1 & 4 \\ 0 & 3 & -6 \\ 0 & 3 & -6 \end{pmatrix}$. It is not possible to turn this matrix into the identity matrix. Any $n \times n$ matrix with a repeated row cannot have an inverse, since one row combined with another will always create a row of zeros. This means that the matrix **C** has no inverse. Any matrix with no inverse is known as a **singular matrix**. Conversely, any matrix that does have an inverse is known as a **non-singular matrix**.

WORKED EXAMPLE 4.6

Determine which of the following matrices are singular.

a $\mathbf{A} = \begin{pmatrix} 1 & 2 & -4 \\ 6 & 1 & 2 \\ 2 & 37 & -86 \end{pmatrix}$ **b** $\mathbf{B} = \begin{pmatrix} 1 & 2 & 3 \\ 4 & 1 & 2 \\ 0 & 6 & 3 \end{pmatrix}$ **c** $\mathbf{C} = \begin{pmatrix} 1 & 4 & 7 \\ 2 & 5 & 8 \\ 3 & 6 & 9 \end{pmatrix}$

Answer

a $r_2 \to r_2 - 6r_1$ and $r_3 \to r_3 - 2r_1$ lead to $\begin{pmatrix} 1 & 2 & -4 \\ 0 & -11 & 26 \\ 0 & 33 & -78 \end{pmatrix}$.

Perform row operations until you can see if rows 2 and 3 are related or not.

Then $r_3 \to -\frac{1}{3}r_3$ to give $\begin{pmatrix} 1 & 2 & -4 \\ 0 & -11 & 26 \\ 0 & -11 & 26 \end{pmatrix}$.

The repeated row shows us that there is no inverse.

This means **A** is singular.

b $r_2 \to r_2 - 4r_1$ and $r_3 \to 7r_3 + 6r_2$ lead to $\begin{pmatrix} 1 & 2 & 3 \\ 0 & -7 & -10 \\ 0 & 0 & -39 \end{pmatrix}$

and so this matrix is non-singular.

So **B** is invertible.

If a matrix can be written in the form $\begin{pmatrix} a & b & c \\ 0 & d & e \\ 0 & 0 & f \end{pmatrix}$ then it must be invertible, provided all values present are non-zero.

c $r_2 \to r_2 - 2r_1$ and $r_3 \to r_3 - 3r_1$ lead to $\begin{pmatrix} 1 & 4 & 7 \\ 0 & -3 & -6 \\ 0 & -6 & -12 \end{pmatrix}$.

When the first element is 1, row operations are more straightforward.

Then $r_3 \to \frac{1}{2}r_3$ to give $\begin{pmatrix} 1 & 4 & 7 \\ 0 & -3 & -6 \\ 0 & -3 & -6 \end{pmatrix}$.

So **C** is also singular.

EXPLORE 4.2

What would happen if you performed column operations instead of row operations? Would the same results be observed? Can column operations work on augmented matrices?

Consider the matrices $\mathbf{A} = \begin{pmatrix} 1 & 2 \\ 3 & 4 \end{pmatrix}$ and $\mathbf{B} = \begin{pmatrix} 5 & 6 \\ 7 & 8 \end{pmatrix}$.

We first determine the inverses to be $\mathbf{A}^{-1} = -\frac{1}{2}\begin{pmatrix} 4 & -2 \\ -3 & 1 \end{pmatrix}$ and $\mathbf{B}^{-1} = -\frac{1}{2}\begin{pmatrix} 8 & -6 \\ -7 & 5 \end{pmatrix}$.

If we consider the matrix **AB** which is $\begin{pmatrix} 19 & 22 \\ 43 & 50 \end{pmatrix}$, then its inverse is

$(\mathbf{AB})^{-1} = \frac{1}{4}\begin{pmatrix} 50 & -22 \\ -43 & 19 \end{pmatrix}$.

By considering $\mathbf{B}^{-1}\mathbf{A}^{-1} = -\frac{1}{2} \times -\frac{1}{2}\begin{pmatrix} 8 & -6 \\ -7 & 5 \end{pmatrix}\begin{pmatrix} 4 & -2 \\ -3 & 1 \end{pmatrix}$, we get $\frac{1}{4}\begin{pmatrix} 50 & -22 \\ -43 & 19 \end{pmatrix}$.

In general, $(\mathbf{AB})^{-1} = \mathbf{B}^{-1}\mathbf{A}^{-1}$.

The order in which the matrices occur in the calculation is important. Note that $(\mathbf{AB})^{-1} \neq \mathbf{A}^{-1}\mathbf{B}^{-1}$.

EXPLORE 4.3

With the matrices $\mathbf{A} = \begin{pmatrix} 2 & 1 \\ 0 & 3 \end{pmatrix}$, $\mathbf{B} = \begin{pmatrix} 4 & -2 \\ 1 & 3 \end{pmatrix}$ and $\mathbf{C} = \begin{pmatrix} 0 & -1 \\ 5 & 2 \end{pmatrix}$, investigate the relationship between the matrices $\mathbf{A}^{-1}$, $\mathbf{B}^{-1}$ and $\mathbf{C}^{-1}$, and the matrices $(\mathbf{CAB})^{-1}$ and $(\mathbf{BAC})^{-1}$.

The same principles apply to any $n \times n$ matrix. So, given $\mathbf{A} = \begin{pmatrix} 1 & 2 & 0 \\ 0 & 2 & 1 \\ 3 & 0 & 2 \end{pmatrix}$ and $\mathbf{B} = \begin{pmatrix} 1 & -1 & 2 \\ 0 & 0 & 3 \\ 1 & 4 & 2 \end{pmatrix}$, we can determine the result of $(\mathbf{AB})^{-1}$ as $\mathbf{B}^{-1}\mathbf{A}^{-1}$. However, to save time, it is best to find **AB** first as we only need to find one inverse.

In this example, $\mathbf{A}^{-1} = \frac{1}{10}\begin{pmatrix} 4 & -4 & 2 \\ 3 & 2 & -1 \\ -6 & 6 & 2 \end{pmatrix}$, $\mathbf{B}^{-1} = \frac{1}{15}\begin{pmatrix} 12 & -10 & 3 \\ -3 & 0 & 3 \\ 0 & 5 & 0 \end{pmatrix}$ and the product, $\mathbf{B}^{-1}\mathbf{A}^{-1}$, works out to be $\frac{1}{150}\begin{pmatrix} 0 & -50 & 40 \\ -30 & 30 & 0 \\ 15 & 10 & -5 \end{pmatrix}$.

Working out **AB** gives the result $\begin{pmatrix} 1 & -1 & 8 \\ 1 & 4 & 8 \\ 5 & 5 & 10 \end{pmatrix}$.

Following the method shown earlier, with six row operations we will arrive at

$$(\mathbf{AB})^{-1} = \frac{1}{150}\begin{pmatrix} 0 & -50 & 40 \\ -30 & 30 & 0 \\ 15 & 10 & -5 \end{pmatrix}.$$

The advantage of using **AB** followed by $(\mathbf{AB})^{-1}$ is that this requires, at most, only six row operations to find the inverse matrix. The alternative method can take up to 12 row operations to complete.

WORKED EXAMPLE 4.7

Given that $\mathbf{A} = \begin{pmatrix} 1 & 0 & 1 \\ 0 & 1 & 1 \\ 1 & 1 & 0 \end{pmatrix}$ and $\mathbf{B} = \begin{pmatrix} -1 & 1 & 0 \\ 1 & 0 & 1 \\ 0 & 0 & -1 \end{pmatrix}$, determine the result of **C**, where $\mathbf{ABC} = \mathbf{I}$.

Answer

$\mathbf{A}^{-1}\mathbf{ABC} = \mathbf{A}^{-1}\mathbf{I} \Rightarrow \mathbf{BC} = \mathbf{A}^{-1}$ — Use matrix algebra to determine the matrix **C**.

$\mathbf{B}^{-1}\mathbf{BC} = \mathbf{B}^{-1}\mathbf{A}^{-1} \Rightarrow \mathbf{C} = \mathbf{B}^{-1}\mathbf{A}^{-1}$ — Use the result $(\mathbf{AB})^{-1} = \mathbf{B}^{-1}\mathbf{A}^{-1}$.

Hence, $\mathbf{C} = (\mathbf{AB})^{-1}$.

$\mathbf{AB} = \begin{pmatrix} 1 & 0 & 1 \\ 0 & 1 & 1 \\ 1 & 1 & 0 \end{pmatrix}\begin{pmatrix} -1 & 1 & 0 \\ 1 & 0 & 1 \\ 0 & 0 & -1 \end{pmatrix}$ — Determine the matrix **AB**.

$= \begin{pmatrix} -1 & 1 & -1 \\ 1 & 0 & 0 \\ 0 & 1 & 1 \end{pmatrix}$

Using the following row operations: — Apply the following row operations to turn the left side of the augmented matrix into reduced row echelon form.

$r_2 \to r_2 + r_1$
$r_3 \to r_3 - r_2$
$r_1 \to r_1 - r_2$
$r_2 \to 2r_2 + r_3$

gives $\left(\begin{array}{ccc|ccc} -1 & 0 & 0 & 0 & -1 & 0 \\ 0 & 2 & 0 & 1 & 1 & 1 \\ 0 & 0 & 2 & -1 & -1 & 1 \end{array}\right)$. — Factor out values to change the left side into **I**.

Hence, $(\mathbf{AB})^{-1} = \frac{1}{2}\begin{pmatrix} 0 & 2 & 0 \\ 1 & 1 & 1 \\ -1 & -1 & 1 \end{pmatrix}$. — State the result.

Finally, consider the matrix $\mathbf{A} = \begin{pmatrix} 0 & 0 & 1 \\ 1 & 2 & 0 \\ 1 & 3 & 1 \end{pmatrix}$. If we were to find the inverse of this matrix, we may notice that the top row should really be at the bottom. This can be fixed by switching the rows.

So, first, let our augmented matrix be $\left(\begin{array}{ccc|ccc} 0 & 0 & 1 & 1 & 0 & 0 \\ 1 & 2 & 0 & 0 & 1 & 0 \\ 1 & 3 & 1 & 0 & 0 & 1 \end{array}\right)$.

Apply the following row operations, $r_1 \leftrightarrow r_3$, $r_2 \to r_2 - r_1$, $r_1 \to r_1 + 3r_2 + 2r_3$ and $r_2 \to r_2 + r_3$ to get the augmented matrix $\left(\begin{array}{ccc|ccc} 1 & 0 & 0 & 2 & 3 & -2 \\ 0 & -1 & 0 & 1 & 1 & -1 \\ 0 & 0 & 1 & 1 & 0 & 0 \end{array}\right)$.

Then $\mathbf{A}^{-1} = \begin{pmatrix} 2 & 3 & -2 \\ -1 & -1 & 1 \\ 1 & 0 & 0 \end{pmatrix}$.

Notice that switching the two rows saved two row operations since the bottom row needs to be in 0 0 1 form anyway. In this example, we were also a little adventurous. The row operation $r_1 \to r_1 + 3r_2 + 2r_3$ saved a little time, too. Since the numbers in the example were very simple, the row operations were more straightforward.

EXERCISE 4B

PS 1 Given that $\mathbf{A} = \begin{pmatrix} 3 & 1 \\ 0 & 5 \end{pmatrix}$ and $\mathbf{B} = \begin{pmatrix} 2 & 1 \\ 3 & 1 \end{pmatrix}$, find **C** such that $\mathbf{ACB} = \mathbf{I}$.

PS 2 a Determine the value of k such that $\mathbf{A} = \begin{pmatrix} 2 & 3 \\ 5 & k \end{pmatrix}$ has no inverse.

b Given that $k = 8$, determine **B** where $\mathbf{BA}^2 = \mathbf{I}$.

3 Find the inverse of the matrix $\mathbf{A} = \begin{pmatrix} 1 & 3 & -2 \\ 0 & 4 & 1 \\ 1 & 1 & 2 \end{pmatrix}$.

4 Find the inverse matrix of the following matrices.

a $\begin{pmatrix} 1 & 7 \\ -2 & -5 \end{pmatrix}$

b $\begin{pmatrix} 3 & 2 \\ -8 & 12 \end{pmatrix}$

c $\begin{pmatrix} 4 & 5 \\ 3 & -4 \end{pmatrix}$

d $\begin{pmatrix} 0 & 3 \\ 8 & 11 \end{pmatrix}$

P PS 5 Given that $\mathbf{A} = \begin{pmatrix} 1 & 2 \\ 3 & 4 \end{pmatrix}$, find the matrix $\mathbf{A}^2$ and, hence, show that $\mathbf{A}(\mathbf{A} - 5\mathbf{I}) = 2\mathbf{I}$, where **I** is the identity matrix. From this equation show that the inverse matrix $\mathbf{A}^{-1} = -\frac{1}{2}\begin{pmatrix} 4 & -2 \\ -3 & 1 \end{pmatrix}$.

6 Determine if the following matrices are singular or non-singular.

a $\begin{pmatrix} 1 & 2 & 3 \\ 2 & 8 & 7 \\ 1 & 10 & 11 \end{pmatrix}$

b $\begin{pmatrix} 1 & 2 & 1 \\ -1 & -2 & 0 \\ 3 & 6 & 6 \end{pmatrix}$

PS 7 You are given the matrix $\mathbf{A} = \begin{pmatrix} 1 & 0 & 2 \\ 2 & 1 & 1 \\ 0 & 1 & 1 \end{pmatrix}$.

a Find $\mathbf{A}^2$ and $\mathbf{A}^3$.

b Find the value of k such that $\mathbf{A}^3 - k\mathbf{A}^2 + 2\mathbf{A} - 4\mathbf{I} = 0$.

c Hence, determine $\mathbf{A}^{-1}$.

PS 8 Given that $\mathbf{A} = \begin{pmatrix} 1 & 0 & 2 \\ 0 & 2 & 1 \\ -1 & -1 & 0 \end{pmatrix}$ and that $\mathbf{B} = \begin{pmatrix} 0 & 1 & 0 \\ -1 & 0 & 2 \\ 2 & 0 & 0 \end{pmatrix}$, determine **C**, where $\mathbf{ACB} = \mathbf{I}$.

PS 9 If $\mathbf{A} = \begin{pmatrix} 1 & 1 & 2 & 1 \\ 2 & 3 & 6 & 8 \\ 1 & 2 & 6 & 10 \\ 3 & 3 & 8 & 7 \end{pmatrix}$, find **B** such that $\mathbf{AB} = \mathbf{I}$.

4.3 Determinants

In Section 4.2 we looked at the inverse of a matrix. This was briefly linked to the **determinant** of the matrix.

Consider the matrix $\mathbf{A} = \begin{pmatrix} 1 & 2 \\ 3 & 6 \end{pmatrix}$.

If we attempt the row operation $r_2 \to r_2 - 3r_1$ this gives the result $\begin{pmatrix} 1 & 2 \\ 0 & 0 \end{pmatrix}$. Now we will try to find its inverse. Using $\mathbf{A} = \begin{pmatrix} a & b \\ c & d \end{pmatrix}$ we know that $\mathbf{A}^{-1} = \frac{1}{ad - bc}\begin{pmatrix} d & -b \\ -c & a \end{pmatrix}$, then $\mathbf{A}^{-1} = \frac{1}{1 \times 6 - 2 \times 3}\begin{pmatrix} 6 & -2 \\ -3 & 1 \end{pmatrix}$, or $\mathbf{A}^{-1} = \frac{1}{0}\begin{pmatrix} 6 & -2 \\ -3 & 1 \end{pmatrix}$.

We can see that the determinant, $\det(\mathbf{A}) = 0$ and the matrix $\mathbf{A}$ has no inverse.

Now, using $r_2 \to r_2 - 3r_1$ with the matrix $\mathbf{B} = \begin{pmatrix} 2 & -5 \\ 6 & 7 \end{pmatrix}$, we have $\begin{pmatrix} 2 & -5 \\ 0 & 22 \end{pmatrix}$, which looks as if it should lead to an inverse matrix. To confirm, we look at $\det(\mathbf{B}) = 2 \times 7 - (-5 \times 6) = 44$. This is, of course, non-zero, which confirms that $\mathbf{B}^{-1}$ exists.

So for any 2×2 matrix of the form $\begin{pmatrix} a & b \\ ka & kb \end{pmatrix}$, where a, b are both non-zero, the determinant will always be $kab - kab = 0$. This can also be confirmed with a row operation that leads to $\begin{pmatrix} a & b \\ 0 & 0 \end{pmatrix}$.

Any matrix that is not of the form $\begin{pmatrix} a & b \\ ka & kb \end{pmatrix}$, where a, b are both non-zero, will have a determinant that is non-zero and it will also have an inverse matrix.

Another way of writing the determinant is $\begin{vmatrix} a & b \\ c & d \end{vmatrix} = ad - bc$, as shown in Key point 4.5.

KEY POINT 4.5

If $\mathbf{A} = \begin{pmatrix} a & b \\ c & d \end{pmatrix}$, $\det(\mathbf{A}) = \begin{vmatrix} a & b \\ c & d \end{vmatrix} = ad - bc$.

We have not yet looked at the determinant for a 3×3 matrix, so consider the matrix $\mathbf{A} = \begin{pmatrix} 1 & 6 & 3 \\ 1 & 4 & 8 \\ 5 & 20 & 4 \end{pmatrix}$. The determinant is $\begin{vmatrix} 1 & 6 & 3 \\ 1 & 4 & 8 \\ 5 & 20 & 4 \end{vmatrix}$ and this can be solved by multiplying each top element by a corresponding 2×2 determinant. The overall determinant is made of three smaller determinants called minors such that $\det(\mathbf{A}) = 1\begin{vmatrix} 4 & 8 \\ 20 & 4 \end{vmatrix} - 6\begin{vmatrix} 1 & 8 \\ 5 & 4 \end{vmatrix} + 3\begin{vmatrix} 1 & 4 \\ 5 & 20 \end{vmatrix}$, which works out to be 72. Here, the scalar multiples are the elements in the top row of matrix $\mathbf{A}$.

The reason that there is a -6 is that, for a 3×3 determinant, the signs are $\begin{vmatrix} + & - & + \\ - & + & - \\ + & - & + \end{vmatrix}$

These signs when multiplied by their minors are called cofactors, and they are determined by considering $(-1)^{m+n}$ for each element.

For the matrix $\mathbf{B} = \begin{pmatrix} 1 & 2 & -1 \\ 2 & 1 & 4 \\ 3 & -2 & 2 \end{pmatrix}$ the determinant is $\det(\mathbf{B}) = \begin{vmatrix} 1 & 4 \\ -2 & 2 \end{vmatrix} - 2\begin{vmatrix} 2 & 4 \\ 3 & 2 \end{vmatrix} - \begin{vmatrix} 2 & 1 \\ 3 & -2 \end{vmatrix}$.

This works out to be 33.

WORKED EXAMPLE 4.8

Find the determinants of the following matrices.

a $\begin{pmatrix} 1 & 1 & 0 \\ 2 & 1 & 0 \\ 3 & 1 & 2 \end{pmatrix}$ b $\begin{pmatrix} 2 & 4 & 5 \\ 0 & 1 & 2 \\ 1 & -1 & 3 \end{pmatrix}$ c $\begin{pmatrix} 1 & 2 & 3 \\ 0 & 2 & 4 \\ 0 & 0 & -1 \end{pmatrix}$

Answer

a $\begin{vmatrix} 1 & 1 & 0 \\ 2 & 1 & 0 \\ 3 & 1 & 2 \end{vmatrix} = \begin{vmatrix} 1 & 0 \\ 1 & 2 \end{vmatrix} - \begin{vmatrix} 2 & 0 \\ 3 & 2 \end{vmatrix} = -2$

Don't forget the negative sign for the second minor-determinant.

b $\begin{vmatrix} 2 & 4 & 5 \\ 0 & 1 & 2 \\ 1 & -1 & 3 \end{vmatrix} = 2\begin{vmatrix} 1 & 2 \\ -1 & 3 \end{vmatrix} - 4\begin{vmatrix} 0 & 2 \\ 1 & 3 \end{vmatrix} + 5\begin{vmatrix} 0 & 1 \\ 1 & -1 \end{vmatrix} = 13$

Remember that each minor-determinant is $ad - bc$.

c $\begin{vmatrix} 1 & 2 & 3 \\ 0 & 2 & 4 \\ 0 & 0 & -1 \end{vmatrix} = \begin{vmatrix} 2 & 4 \\ 0 & -1 \end{vmatrix} - 2\begin{vmatrix} 0 & 4 \\ 0 & -1 \end{vmatrix} + 3\begin{vmatrix} 0 & 2 \\ 0 & 0 \end{vmatrix} = -2$

In this case, two of the minor-determinants are zero so only one of them contributes to the answer.

Consider the matrix $\begin{pmatrix} 1 & 1 & 0 \\ 1 & 3 & 1 \\ 2 & 1 & 4 \end{pmatrix}$. Its determinant is $\begin{vmatrix} 3 & 1 \\ 1 & 4 \end{vmatrix} - \begin{vmatrix} 1 & 1 \\ 2 & 4 \end{vmatrix} = 9$.

If we then use the operation $r_2 \rightarrow r_2 - r_1$ we get $\begin{pmatrix} 1 & 1 & 0 \\ 0 & 2 & 1 \\ 2 & 1 & 4 \end{pmatrix}$. The determinant works out to be $\begin{vmatrix} 2 & 1 \\ 1 & 4 \end{vmatrix} - \begin{vmatrix} 0 & 1 \\ 2 & 4 \end{vmatrix} = 9$. So this row operation has no effect on the determinant.

Next, if we use $r_3 \rightarrow r_3 - 2r_1$ to get $\begin{pmatrix} 1 & 1 & 0 \\ 0 & 2 & 1 \\ 0 & -1 & 4 \end{pmatrix}$, then $\begin{vmatrix} 2 & 1 \\ -1 & 4 \end{vmatrix} - \begin{vmatrix} 0 & 1 \\ 0 & 4 \end{vmatrix} = 9$, so still no change.

Next, use $r_3 \rightarrow 2r_3 + r_2$ to get $\begin{pmatrix} 1 & 1 & 0 \\ 0 & 2 & 1 \\ 0 & 0 & 9 \end{pmatrix}$, then $\begin{vmatrix} 2 & 1 \\ 0 & 9 \end{vmatrix} - \begin{vmatrix} 0 & 1 \\ 0 & 9 \end{vmatrix} = 18$, or 9×2.

So this last operation doubles the value of the determinant.

One last operation, using $r_1 \rightarrow 3r_1 + r_2$ gives us $\begin{pmatrix} 3 & 5 & 1 \\ 0 & 2 & 1 \\ 0 & 0 & 9 \end{pmatrix}$. The determinant of this matrix is $3\begin{vmatrix} 2 & 1 \\ 0 & 9 \end{vmatrix} - 5\begin{vmatrix} 0 & 1 \\ 0 & 9 \end{vmatrix} + \begin{vmatrix} 0 & 2 \\ 0 & 0 \end{vmatrix} = 54$, or 18×3, or even $9 \times 2 \times 3$.

So it appears that any row operation that multiplies the row being changed by a factor k scales the value of the determinant by this same factor k.

Take, for example, $\begin{pmatrix} a & b \\ c & d \end{pmatrix}$ whose determinant is $ad - bc$, and apply the row operation $r_2 \to r_2 - kr_1$. This gives us $\begin{pmatrix} a & b \\ c - ka & d - kb \end{pmatrix}$, for which the determinant is $ad - kab - bc + kab = ad - bc$, so there is no change in the determinant.

But if we apply $r_2 \to kr_2 - r_1$, then our matrix is $\begin{pmatrix} a & b \\ kc - a & kd - b \end{pmatrix}$. The determinant works out to be $akd - ab - bkc + ab = k(ad - bc)$, which is k times bigger than before.

EXPLORE 4.4

Investigate the effect on the value of the determinant of switching two rows in a matrix.

How can we make this useful? Consider the matrix $\begin{pmatrix} 2 & 3 & 1 \\ 0 & 3 & 5 \\ 0 & 0 & -4 \end{pmatrix}$. Its determinant is the product of the elements in the leading diagonal, which is $2 \times 3 \times (-4) = -24$.

So if a matrix can be reduced to row echelon form, then the calculation of a determinant is straightforward.

Take the matrix $\mathbf{B} = \begin{pmatrix} 4 & 1 & -1 \\ 2 & 4 & 0 \\ 1 & -1 & 5 \end{pmatrix}$. Using the row operations $r_3 \to 4r_3 - r_1$ and $r_2 \to 2r_2 - r_1$ gives us $\begin{pmatrix} 4 & 1 & -1 \\ 0 & 7 & 1 \\ 0 & -5 & 21 \end{pmatrix}$, then $r_3 \to 7r_3 + 5r_2$ leads to $\begin{pmatrix} 4 & 1 & -1 \\ 0 & 7 & 1 \\ 0 & 0 & 152 \end{pmatrix}$.

The determinant of this new matrix is $4 \times 7 \times 152 = 4256$, but our row operations have row multiples of 4, 2 and 7, so the actual size of $\det(\mathbf{B}) = \frac{4256}{4 \times 2 \times 7} = 76$.

Checking: $\begin{vmatrix} 4 & 1 & -1 \\ 2 & 4 & 0 \\ 1 & -1 & 5 \end{vmatrix} = 4\begin{vmatrix} 4 & 0 \\ -1 & 5 \end{vmatrix} - \begin{vmatrix} 2 & 0 \\ 1 & 5 \end{vmatrix} - \begin{vmatrix} 2 & 4 \\ 1 & -1 \end{vmatrix} = 80 - 10 + 6 = 76$

WORKED EXAMPLE 4.9

Find, using row operations, the size of the determinants of the following matrices.

a $\begin{pmatrix} 2 & 0 & 5 \\ 1 & -1 & 4 \\ 3 & 1 & 2 \end{pmatrix}$ **b** $\begin{pmatrix} 3 & -1 & -3 \\ 0 & 4 & 1 \\ 1 & -1 & 2 \end{pmatrix}$

Answer

a Operations $r_3 \to 2r_3 - 3r_1$, $r_2 \to 2r_2 - r_1$ and $r_3 \to r_3 + r_2$ reduce the matrix to $\begin{pmatrix} 2 & 0 & 5 \\ 0 & -2 & 3 \\ 0 & 0 & -8 \end{pmatrix}$.

So the determinant is $\frac{2 \times (-2) \times (-8)}{2 \times 2} = 8$.

The values from $2r_3$ and $2r_2$ make the determinant 4 times bigger. We need to scale this down by a factor of 2×2 to find the value of the determinant. (The third operation does not affect the size.)

b Operations $r_3 \to 3r_3 - r_1$ and $r_3 \to 2r_3 + r_2$ reduce the matrix to $\begin{pmatrix} 3 & -1 & -3 \\ 0 & 4 & 1 \\ 0 & 0 & 19 \end{pmatrix}$.

The two values $3r_3$ and $2r_3$ increase the determinant size by 3 and 2, respectively. Therefore, we need to scale this down by a factor of 3×2 to find the value of the original determinant.

So the determinant is $\frac{3 \times 4 \times 19}{3 \times 2} = 38$.

Given two matrices $\mathbf{A} = \begin{pmatrix} 2 & 5 \\ 1 & 8 \end{pmatrix}$ and $\mathbf{B} = \begin{pmatrix} 3 & 4 \\ -1 & 6 \end{pmatrix}$, we can find their determinants to be $\det(\mathbf{A}) = 11$ and $\det(\mathbf{B}) = 22$. If we then consider $\mathbf{AB} = \begin{pmatrix} 1 & 38 \\ -5 & 52 \end{pmatrix}$, its determinant works out to be $52 + 190 = 242$. Now 242 also happens to be 11×22.

$\mathbf{BA} = \begin{pmatrix} 10 & 47 \\ 4 & 43 \end{pmatrix}$ and its determinant is also 242.

Using another example with $\mathbf{A} = \begin{pmatrix} 1 & 2 & 1 \\ 0 & 1 & 3 \\ 1 & -1 & 0 \end{pmatrix}$ and $\mathbf{B} = \begin{pmatrix} 2 & 1 & 0 \\ 1 & -1 & 1 \\ 3 & 0 & 2 \end{pmatrix}$, working out their determinants, we get $\det(\mathbf{A}) = 8$ and $\det(\mathbf{B}) = -3$.

Then $\mathbf{AB} = \begin{pmatrix} 1 & 2 & 1 \\ 0 & 1 & 3 \\ 1 & -1 & 0 \end{pmatrix}\begin{pmatrix} 2 & 1 & 0 \\ 1 & -1 & 1 \\ 3 & 0 & 2 \end{pmatrix} = \begin{pmatrix} 7 & -1 & 4 \\ 10 & -1 & 7 \\ 1 & 2 & -1 \end{pmatrix}$, and its determinant works out to be

$7\begin{vmatrix} -1 & 7 \\ 2 & -1 \end{vmatrix} + \begin{vmatrix} 10 & 7 \\ 1 & -1 \end{vmatrix} + 4\begin{vmatrix} 10 & -1 \\ 1 & 2 \end{vmatrix} = -91 - 17 + 84 = -24$.

Also, $\mathbf{BA} = \begin{pmatrix} 2 & 1 & 0 \\ 1 & -1 & 1 \\ 3 & 0 & 2 \end{pmatrix}\begin{pmatrix} 1 & 2 & 1 \\ 0 & 1 & 3 \\ 1 & -1 & 0 \end{pmatrix} = \begin{pmatrix} 2 & 5 & 5 \\ 2 & 0 & -2 \\ 5 & 4 & 3 \end{pmatrix}$, and its determinant is also -24.

So, for determinants of size $n \times n$, $\det(\mathbf{AB}) = \det(\mathbf{BA}) = \det(\mathbf{A})\det(\mathbf{B})$.

EXPLORE 4.5

Discuss in groups, with the aid of your teacher, the process for finding the determinant of the matrix $\mathbf{A} = \begin{pmatrix} 1 & 2 & -1 & 4 \\ 2 & 3 & 0 & 1 \\ 5 & -1 & 1 & 1 \\ 0 & 2 & 1 & 3 \end{pmatrix}$. Does the row reduction method speed up the process now?

EXERCISE 4C

1 Given that $\mathbf{A} = \begin{pmatrix} 3 & 4 \\ 1 & 5 \end{pmatrix}$ and $\mathbf{B} = \begin{pmatrix} -1 & 2 \\ 6 & -3 \end{pmatrix}$, confirm that $\det(\mathbf{AB}) = \det(\mathbf{A}) \times \det(\mathbf{B})$ and $\det(\mathbf{BA}) = \det(\mathbf{A}) \times \det(\mathbf{B})$.

PS 2 The matrix **A** is such that $\mathbf{A} = \begin{pmatrix} x & 4 \\ 1 & x-3 \end{pmatrix}$. Find the values of x such that **A** is singular.

PS P 3 Show that $\mathbf{B} = \begin{pmatrix} x & -2 \\ 5 & x+1 \end{pmatrix}$ can always be inverted for all values of x.

4 State which of the following matrices are invertible.

a $\begin{pmatrix} 5 & 8 \\ 4 & 2 \end{pmatrix}$ **b** $\begin{pmatrix} 3 & 7 \\ -6 & -14 \end{pmatrix}$ **c** $\begin{pmatrix} 1 & 4 \\ -1 & 0 \end{pmatrix}$

5 Find the determinant of each of the following matrices.

a $\begin{pmatrix} 3 & 3 & 5 \\ 3 & 1 & 4 \\ 3 & -5 & 3 \end{pmatrix}$ **b** $\begin{pmatrix} 1 & 2 & 7 \\ -3 & 0 & -13 \\ 4 & 11 & 32 \end{pmatrix}$ **c** $\begin{pmatrix} 1 & 8 & 6 \\ 0 & -8 & 4 \\ 0 & 0 & 12 \end{pmatrix}$

P **6** You are given the matrix $\mathbf{A} = \begin{pmatrix} a & d & g \\ b & e & h \\ c & f & i \end{pmatrix}$.

Show that the row operation $r_1 \rightarrow cr_1 - ar_3$ changes the determinant by a factor of c.

PS **7** Given that $\begin{vmatrix} a & a & 2a \\ 3a & -a & 0 \\ 4a & 2a & a \end{vmatrix} = 2$, find the value of the constant a.

8 Given that $\mathbf{A} = \begin{pmatrix} 1 & 2 & 3 \\ 0 & 1 & 4 \\ 1 & 2 & 0 \end{pmatrix}$ and $\mathbf{B} = \begin{pmatrix} 1 & 5 & 2 \\ 2 & 3 & 0 \\ 1 & -1 & 0 \end{pmatrix}$, find the determinant of the matrix $\mathbf{AB}$.

4.4 Matrix transformations

Matrices can be used to represent certain transformations. For example, if we consider the rectangle $A(1, 1)$, $B(1, 3)$, $C(5, 3)$ and $D(5, 1)$, we can put these coordinates into a matrix to get $\begin{pmatrix} 1 & 1 & 5 & 5 \\ 1 & 3 & 3 & 1 \end{pmatrix}$. This is formed by considering each vertex of the rectangle as a position vector.

If we multiply this matrix by a 2×2 matrix to produce a transformation, we need to multiply in the correct order. For example $\begin{pmatrix} 1 & 0 \\ 0 & 1 \end{pmatrix}\begin{pmatrix} 1 & 1 & 5 & 5 \\ 1 & 3 & 3 & 1 \end{pmatrix} = \begin{pmatrix} 1 & 1 & 5 & 5 \\ 1 & 3 & 3 & 1 \end{pmatrix}$. There is no change when multiplying by the identity matrix.

Consider the transformation $\begin{pmatrix} 1 & 0 \\ 0 & 2 \end{pmatrix}\begin{pmatrix} 1 & 1 & 5 & 5 \\ 1 & 3 & 3 & 1 \end{pmatrix}$. Multiplying these matrices gives $\begin{pmatrix} 1 & 1 & 5 & 5 \\ 2 & 6 & 6 & 2 \end{pmatrix}$. Each y value has now doubled. This **stretches** the shape based on the distance of each vertex from the x-axis. The original shape is in red and the transformed image is in blue.

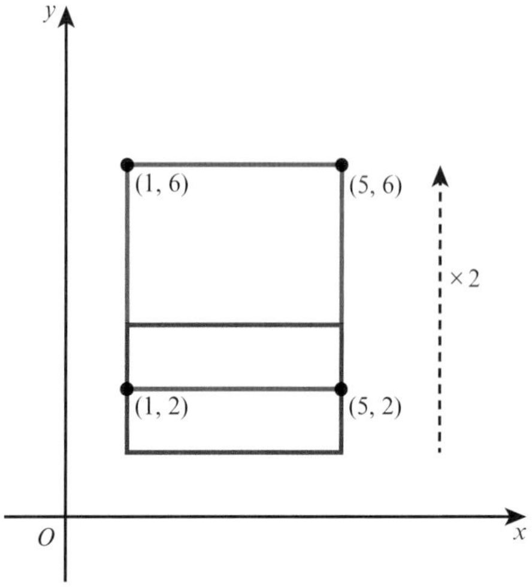

Next, consider the rectangle with vertices (1, 1), (1, 3), (4, 3) and (4, 1).

As a matrix this can be written as $\begin{pmatrix} 1 & 1 & 4 & 4 \\ 1 & 3 & 3 & 1 \end{pmatrix}$.

If we multiply it by the matrix $\begin{pmatrix} 2 & 0 \\ 0 & 1 \end{pmatrix}$, we get $\begin{pmatrix} 2 & 2 & 8 & 8 \\ 1 & 3 & 3 & 1 \end{pmatrix}$ and each x value has doubled.

This is a stretch of scale factor 2 in the x-direction: the distance relative to the y-axis has been doubled.

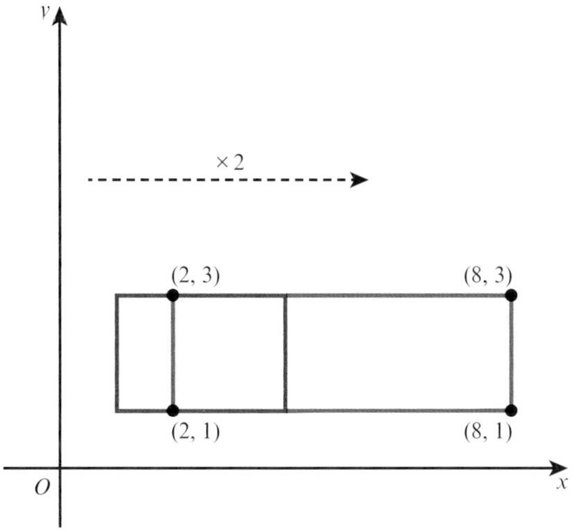

Combining the previous two examples, we can see that the matrix $\begin{pmatrix} 2 & 0 \\ 0 & 2 \end{pmatrix}$ has the effect of an **enlargement** of scale factor 2. Here we can see the matrix $\begin{pmatrix} 2 & 0 \\ 0 & 2 \end{pmatrix}$ applied to $\begin{pmatrix} 1 & 1 & 4 & 4 \\ 1 & 3 & 3 & 1 \end{pmatrix}$ to produce the matrix $\begin{pmatrix} 2 & 2 & 8 & 8 \\ 2 & 6 & 6 & 2 \end{pmatrix}$. This time the enlargement is measured from the origin, so we can say the origin is the centre of the enlargement.

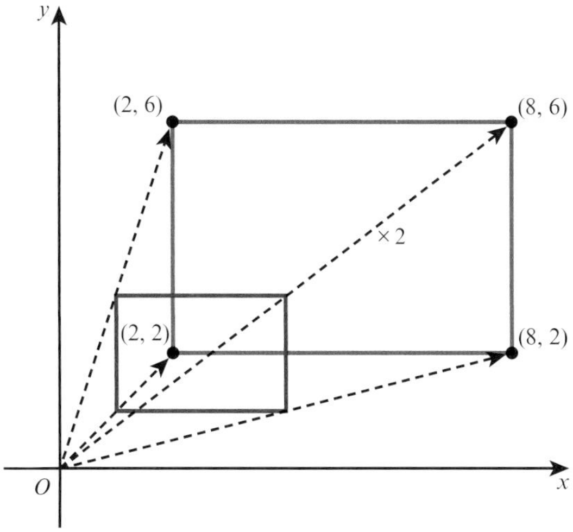

In each of these three examples we can see an **invariant** line or point. In the first example, any point on the line $y = 0$ will not change its y value. It is, therefore, invariant.

In the second example, any point on the line $x = 0$ will not change its x value. It is also, therefore, invariant. In the third example, both $x = 0$ and $y = 0$ are invariant lines. The point where they meet, in this case the origin, is known as an invariant point. The matrices for stretches are shown in Key point 4.6.

KEY POINT 4.6

For a stretch in the x-direction of scale factor k, the matrix is represented by $\begin{pmatrix} k & 0 \\ 0 & 1 \end{pmatrix}$.

For a stretch in the y-direction of scale factor k, the matrix is represented by $\begin{pmatrix} 1 & 0 \\ 0 & k \end{pmatrix}$.

For an enlargement relative to the point (0, 0) of scale factor k, the matrix is represented by $\begin{pmatrix} k & 0 \\ 0 & k \end{pmatrix}$.

Any point that is unchanged by a transformation is known as an invariant point. If that point is not the origin, then it must lie on an invariant line.

The origin is always invariant for matrix transformations.

Now consider the matrix $\begin{pmatrix} 2 & 2 & 8 & 8 \\ 2 & 6 & 6 & 2 \end{pmatrix}$ and apply the transformation $\begin{pmatrix} \frac{1}{2} & 0 \\ 0 & \frac{1}{2} \end{pmatrix}$ to it. The result is $\begin{pmatrix} 1 & 1 & 4 & 4 \\ 1 & 3 & 3 & 1 \end{pmatrix}$. We have a scale factor again, but this time it is a reducing factor. What is more interesting is if $\mathbf{A} = \begin{pmatrix} 2 & 0 \\ 0 & 2 \end{pmatrix}$, then $\mathbf{A}^{-1} = \frac{1}{4}\begin{pmatrix} 2 & 0 \\ 0 & 2 \end{pmatrix} = \begin{pmatrix} \frac{1}{2} & 0 \\ 0 & \frac{1}{2} \end{pmatrix}$. Applying an inverse matrix will revert any transformation to its original state since $\mathbf{A}^{-1}\mathbf{A} = \mathbf{I}$.

In all of the previous cases the area of the shape is increased by a factor that is equal to the size of the determinant that is transforming the shape. Take, for example, the matrix $\mathbf{A} = \begin{pmatrix} 3 & 0 \\ 0 & 2 \end{pmatrix}$. This stretches by factors 3 and 2, so the area of the new shape is six times as large since $|\det(\mathbf{A})| = 6$.

EXPLORE 4.6

Apply the matrix $\begin{pmatrix} 4 & 3 \\ 1 & 1 \end{pmatrix}$ to the triangle represented by the points (1, 1), (4, 1) and (4, 5).

What do you notice about the area of the image of the triangle?

How does this relate to the determinant of the matrix being applied?

As well as stretching and enlarging, we can also consider rotations and reflections as transformations.

Consider the triangle represented by the points $(1, 1), (1, 4), (4, 1)$. As always, we write these coordinates in matrix form $\begin{pmatrix} 1 & 1 & 4 \\ 1 & 4 & 1 \end{pmatrix}$.

If we apply the transformation matrix $\begin{pmatrix} -1 & 0 \\ 0 & 1 \end{pmatrix}$ to our triangle, we get $\begin{pmatrix} -1 & 0 \\ 0 & 1 \end{pmatrix}\begin{pmatrix} 1 & 1 & 4 \\ 1 & 4 & 1 \end{pmatrix} = \begin{pmatrix} -1 & -1 & -4 \\ 1 & 4 & 1 \end{pmatrix}$. The effect of this is a **reflection** in the y-axis; that is, the effect of this matrix is to change the sign of each x value but not to change the y values.

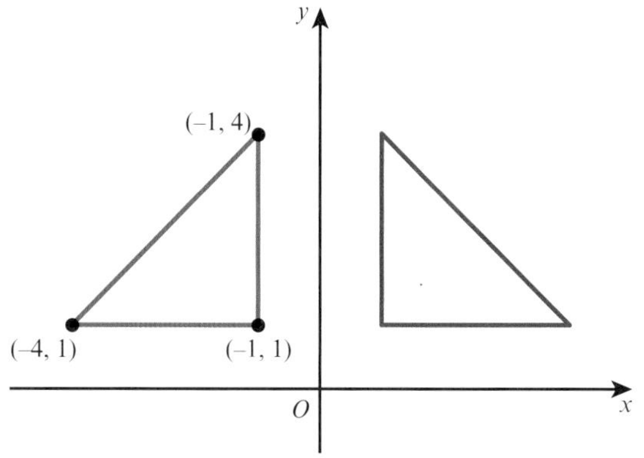

If we apply the matrix $\begin{pmatrix} 1 & 0 \\ 0 & -1 \end{pmatrix}$, this gives $\begin{pmatrix} 1 & 1 & 4 \\ -1 & -4 & -1 \end{pmatrix}$ which represents a reflection in the x-axis.

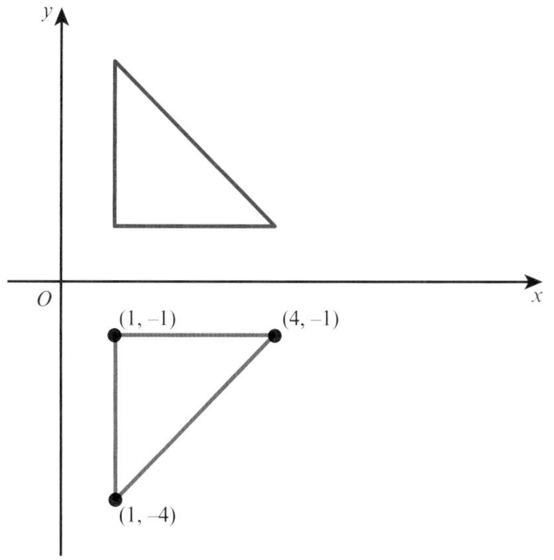

So these two matrices are responsible for reflections in axes.

Let T_1 be the transformation $\begin{pmatrix} -1 & 0 \\ 0 & 1 \end{pmatrix}$ and let T_2 be the transformation $\begin{pmatrix} 1 & 0 \\ 0 & -1 \end{pmatrix}$.

When we apply both of these transformations, in either order, to the triangle $\begin{pmatrix} 1 & 1 & 4 \\ 1 & 4 & 1 \end{pmatrix}$, then the result is $\begin{pmatrix} 1 & 0 \\ 0 & -1 \end{pmatrix}\begin{pmatrix} -1 & 0 \\ 0 & 1 \end{pmatrix}\begin{pmatrix} 1 & 1 & 4 \\ 1 & 4 & 1 \end{pmatrix} = \begin{pmatrix} -1 & -1 & -4 \\ -1 & -4 & -1 \end{pmatrix}$.

This effect is a **rotation** about the origin by 180°.

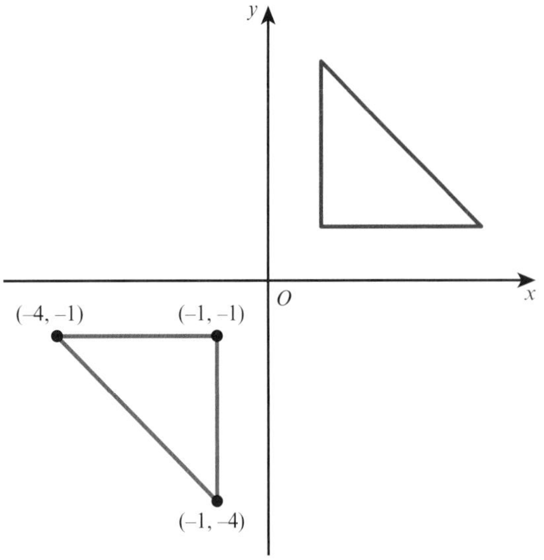

If we multiply the matrices represented by T_1 and T_2, in either order, we get the matrix $\begin{pmatrix} -1 & 0 \\ 0 & -1 \end{pmatrix}$. This rotation of 180° can be considered to be clockwise or anticlockwise. This example leads nicely to a generalised matrix that produces a rotation.

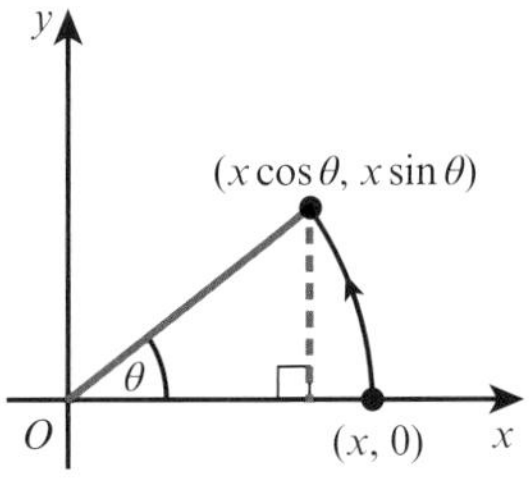

Consider the point $(x, 0)$ lying on the x-axis. Then apply the matrix $\begin{pmatrix} a & b \\ c & d \end{pmatrix}$ so that $\begin{pmatrix} a & b \\ c & d \end{pmatrix}\begin{pmatrix} x \\ 0 \end{pmatrix} = \begin{pmatrix} x\cos\theta \\ x\sin\theta \end{pmatrix}$, where θ represents an anticlockwise rotation about the origin; hence, $a = \cos\theta$ and $c = \sin\theta$. Next, consider the fact that the magnitude of this position vector does not change, so we know that the determinant must be 1. Then we have another equation $ad - bc = 1$, or $d\cos\theta - b\sin\theta = 1$.

Making use of $\cos^2\theta + \sin^2\theta = 1$ we can find solutions to the equation: $b = -\sin\theta$ and $d = \cos\theta$. The matrix for any anticlockwise rotation about the origin is $\begin{pmatrix} \cos\theta & -\sin\theta \\ \sin\theta & \cos\theta \end{pmatrix}$.

So for a 90° rotation anticlockwise about the origin, the corresponding matrix is $\begin{pmatrix} 0 & -1 \\ 1 & 0 \end{pmatrix}$,

and the matrix $\begin{pmatrix} -\frac{\sqrt{2}}{2} & \frac{\sqrt{2}}{2} \\ -\frac{\sqrt{2}}{2} & -\frac{\sqrt{2}}{2} \end{pmatrix}$ would result in a rotation of 135° clockwise about the origin.

WORKED EXAMPLE 4.10

Describe the effect of the following matrices on the triangle given by (1, 1), (3, 1) and (1, 3). Illustrate your findings.

a $\begin{pmatrix} -2 & 0 \\ 0 & 1 \end{pmatrix}$ **b** $\begin{pmatrix} 1 & 0 \\ 0 & -2 \end{pmatrix}$ **c** $\begin{pmatrix} -2 & 0 \\ 0 & -2 \end{pmatrix}$

Answer

a

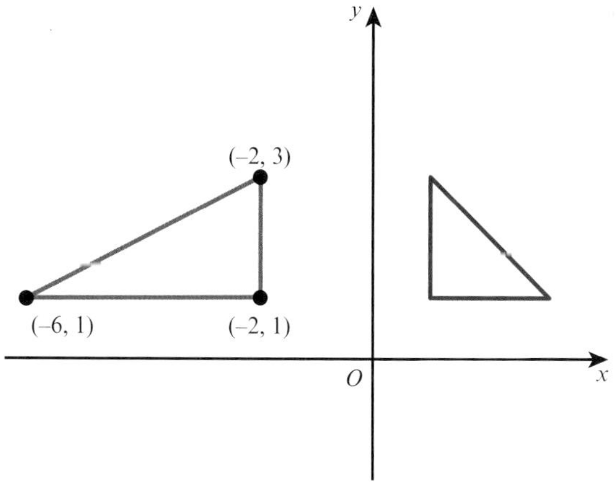

Shape is reflected in the y-axis.

Shape is stretched by a scale factor of 2 in the x-direction.

Area is doubled since the magnitude of the determinant is 2.

Stretch is related to the distance between the y-axis and each point.

b

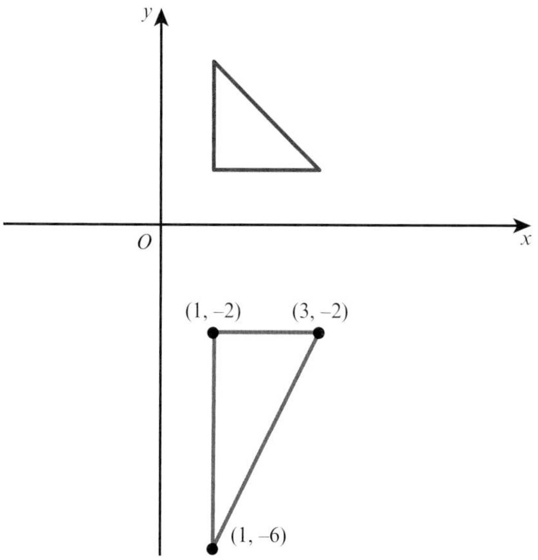

Shape is reflected in the x-axis.

Shape is stretched by a scale factor of 2 in the y-direction.

Area is doubled since the magnitude of the determinant is 2.

Stretch is related to distance between the x-axis and each point.

c

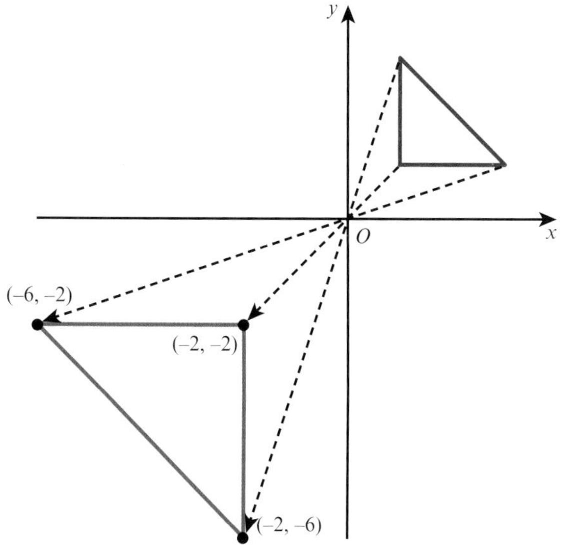

Shape is rotated 180° clockwise or anticlockwise about the origin.

Shape is enlarged relative to the origin by a scale factor of 2.

For 2×2 matrices there is one more important transformation, which is known as **shearing**. Consider the matrix $\begin{pmatrix} 1 & 1 \\ 0 & 1 \end{pmatrix}$. If we apply it to the rectangle $(1, 1), (3, 1), (3, 5), (1, 5)$, then each point is translated parallel to the x-axis since the new x-coordinates are based on $x + y$. This effect is called a shear. The distance through which points are displaced depends on their distance from the line $x = 0$.

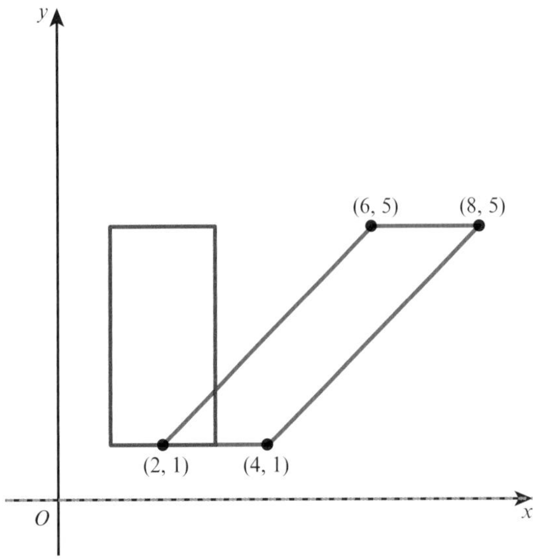

A shape being sheared in the x-direction.

Consider the rectangle $(1, 0), (3, 0), (3, 4), (1, 4)$. If we apply the same matrix to these points, we get a different shear. This time only the top points move since the two bottom vertices lie on an invariant line, $y = 0$.

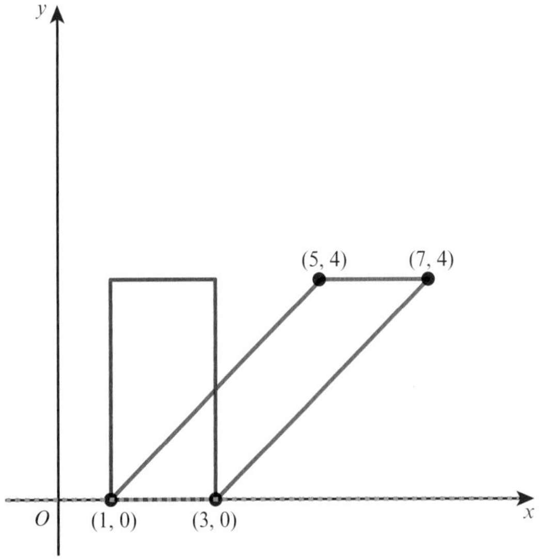

Another shear in the x-direction where the bottom vertices lie on the invariant line.

As we can see in this diagram, the top points have a y value that is unchanged by the shearing factor. So a matrix of the form $\begin{pmatrix} 1 & k \\ 0 & 1 \end{pmatrix}$ will produce a shear in the x-direction, and the distance each point is moved is equal to ky_0, where y_0 is the original y value.

A matrix of the form $\begin{pmatrix} 1 & 0 \\ 2 & 1 \end{pmatrix}$ should give a shearing effect in the y-direction instead. Apply this matrix to the rectangle with vertices $(0, 0)$, $(0, 3)$, $(2, 3)$ and $(2, 0)$.

This gives $\begin{pmatrix} 1 & 0 \\ 2 & 1 \end{pmatrix}\begin{pmatrix} 0 & 0 & 2 & 2 \\ 0 & 3 & 3 & 0 \end{pmatrix} = \begin{pmatrix} 0 & 0 & 2 & 2 \\ 0 & 3 & 7 & 4 \end{pmatrix}$.

We can see that the line $x = 0$ is invariant and any point on this line does not change.

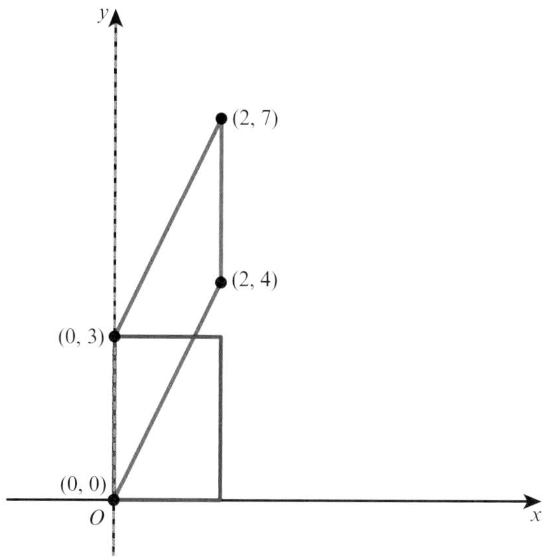

So any matrix of the form $\begin{pmatrix} 1 & 0 \\ k & 1 \end{pmatrix}$ will produce a shear in the y-direction.

EXPLORE 4.7

Apply the matrix $\begin{pmatrix} 1 & k \\ 0 & 1 \end{pmatrix}$ to sets of points and investigate with different values of k. What happens in the cases where $0 < k < 1$ or $k < 0$?

Some shears are not obvious to spot. For example, if we take the matrix $\begin{pmatrix} 4 & 3 \\ -3 & -2 \end{pmatrix}$ and apply it to the point $(1, 1)$ we get the image $\begin{pmatrix} 7 \\ -5 \end{pmatrix}$. It is not obvious that there is a shear or what the invariant line could be. Instead, consider the square $(0, 0)$, $(1, 1)$, $(2, 0)$, $(1, -1)$. Apply our matrix to these points to get $(0, 0)$, $(7, -5)$, $(8, -6)$, $(1, -1)$.

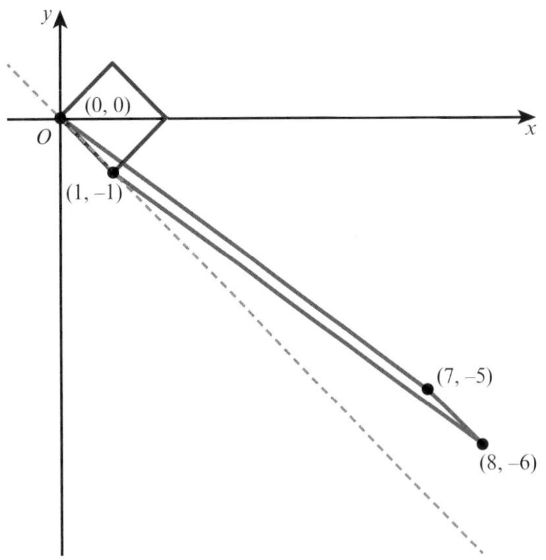

We can see from the diagram that there is an invariant line and it appears to be $y = -x$. But how can we be sure? First, since (0, 0) will always be unchanged by any matrix, we can say that all invariant lines must pass through the origin. Second, if points on the invariant line are unchanged, we can say that $\begin{pmatrix} 4 & 3 \\ -3 & -2 \end{pmatrix}\begin{pmatrix} x \\ y \end{pmatrix} = \begin{pmatrix} x \\ y \end{pmatrix}$. Multiplying out gives $4x + 3y = x$, $-3x - 2y = y$. Both equations simplify to $y = -x$, which confirms the equation of the line.

Consider the matrix $\begin{pmatrix} 1 & -2 \\ -2 & 1 \end{pmatrix}$. If we try the same method as before, then $\begin{pmatrix} 1 & -2 \\ -2 & 1 \end{pmatrix}\begin{pmatrix} x \\ y \end{pmatrix} = \begin{pmatrix} x \\ y \end{pmatrix}$ leads to $x - 2y = x$, $-2x + y = y$. This simplifies to $x = 0, y = 0$, which tells us that there is an invariant point. To find the invariant lines we must adopt a different approach.

Consider $\begin{pmatrix} 1 & -2 \\ -2 & 1 \end{pmatrix}\begin{pmatrix} t \\ mt \end{pmatrix} = \begin{pmatrix} T \\ mT \end{pmatrix}$. This is the same as before, where the line is of the form $y = mx$.

The two equations are $t - 2mt = T$ and $-2t + mt = mT$. Divide the first of these equations by the second to get $\frac{1 - 2m}{-2 + m} = \frac{1}{m}$. Solve this equation to give $m^2 = 1$, or $m = \pm 1$. Remember the invariant line is of the form $y = mx$. This means there are two invariant lines, $y = \pm x$. They meet at the origin, which is always an invariant point.

Let us use $\begin{pmatrix} 4 & 3 \\ -3 & -2 \end{pmatrix}\begin{pmatrix} t \\ mt \end{pmatrix} = \begin{pmatrix} T \\ mT \end{pmatrix}$ as another example. This gives equations $4t + 3mt = T$ and $-3t - 2mt = mT$. Dividing gives $\frac{4 + 3m}{-3 - 2m} = \frac{1}{m}$, then solving gives $(m + 1)^2 = 0$. The only solution is $m = -1$, so the line is $y = -x$.

WORKED EXAMPLE 4.11

Find any invariant lines for the following matrices.

a $\begin{pmatrix} -3 & 2 \\ -8 & 5 \end{pmatrix}$

b $\begin{pmatrix} 4 & -2 \\ -1 & 4 \end{pmatrix}$

Answer

a Start with $\begin{pmatrix} -3 & 2 \\ -8 & 5 \end{pmatrix}\begin{pmatrix} t \\ mt \end{pmatrix} = \begin{pmatrix} T \\ mT \end{pmatrix}$. — State the correct form.

Then $-3t + 2mt = T$ and $-8t + 5mt = mT$. — Obtain two equations.

Dividing gives $\frac{-3 + 2m}{-8 + 5m} = \frac{1}{m}$, then $2m^2 - 3m = 5m - 8$. — Divide, then multiply through.

So $2m^2 - 8m + 8 = 0$, hence $(m - 2)^2 = 0$. — Solve the quadratic.

$\therefore m = 2$, hence $y = 2x$. — State the correct form.

b Start with $\begin{pmatrix} 4 & -2 \\ -1 & 4 \end{pmatrix}\begin{pmatrix} t \\ mt \end{pmatrix} = \begin{pmatrix} T \\ mT \end{pmatrix}$.

Then $4t - 2mt = T$ and $-t + 4mt = mT$. — Obtain two equations.

Dividing gives $\frac{4 - 2m}{-1 + 4m} = \frac{1}{m}$, then $4m - 2m^2 = -1 + 4m$. — Obtain a quadratic.

So $2m^2 = 1$, hence $m = \pm\frac{\sqrt{2}}{2}$.

So $y = \pm\frac{\sqrt{2}}{2}x$. — Solve to give two values for y.

E For 3-dimensional space, we will focus on enlargement, rotation and reflection.

Consider the matrix $\begin{pmatrix} 2 & 0 & 0 \\ 0 & 1 & 0 \\ 0 & 0 & 1 \end{pmatrix}$. This matrix will multiply all the x values by 2, and therefore represents a stretch by a scale factor of 2 in the x-direction.

Similarly, $\begin{pmatrix} 1 & 0 & 0 \\ 0 & 3 & 0 \\ 0 & 0 & 1 \end{pmatrix}$ and $\begin{pmatrix} 1 & 0 & 0 \\ 0 & 1 & 0 \\ 0 & 0 & 4 \end{pmatrix}$ represent stretches in the y-direction by a scale factor of 3 and in the z-direction, respectively, by a scale factor of 4.

Hence, the matrix $\begin{pmatrix} k & 0 & 0 \\ 0 & k & 0 \\ 0 & 0 & k \end{pmatrix}$ represents an enlargement of scale factor k with the origin as the centre of enlargement.

For rotations, let us consider the matrix we saw previously: $\begin{pmatrix} \cos\theta & -\sin\theta \\ \sin\theta & \cos\theta \end{pmatrix}$. This is an anticlockwise rotation of angle θ about the origin. Consider the case where we wish to rotate a shape about the x-axis. The diagram is drawn so that this axis comes out of the page. Hence, the shape rotates on the page.

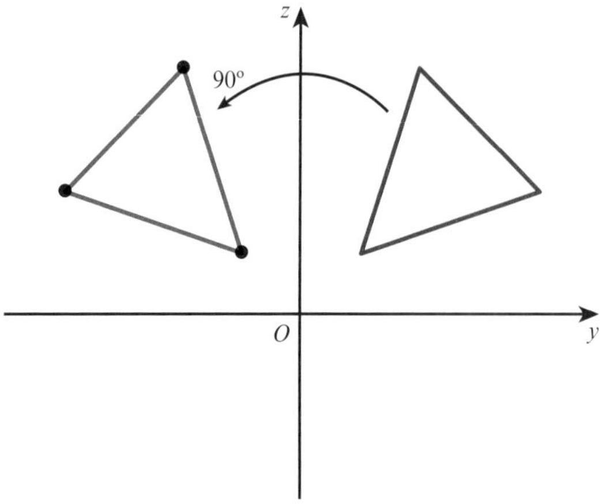

So the triangle represented by $\begin{pmatrix} x & x & x \\ 1 & 4 & 2 \\ 1 & 2 & 4 \end{pmatrix}$ is to be rotated to form the image $\begin{pmatrix} x & x & x \\ -1 & -2 & -4 \\ 1 & 4 & 2 \end{pmatrix}$. The x values do not change. We simply represent them by x. This means our matrix must be of the form $\begin{pmatrix} 1 & 0 & 0 \\ 0 & . & . \\ 0 & . & . \end{pmatrix}$. The first column must contain zeros to avoid any elements for y and z being added to the value of x.

To ensure that only y and z are rotated, we therefore use the matrix $\begin{pmatrix} 1 & 0 & 0 \\ 0 & \cos\theta & -\sin\theta \\ 0 & \sin\theta & \cos\theta \end{pmatrix}$ for anticlockwise rotations about the x-axis.

Similarly, anticlockwise rotations about the y- and z-axes require matrices $\begin{pmatrix} \cos\theta & 0 & \sin\theta \\ 0 & 1 & 0 \\ -\sin\theta & 0 & \cos\theta \end{pmatrix}$ and $\begin{pmatrix} \cos\theta & -\sin\theta & 0 \\ \sin\theta & \cos\theta & 0 \\ 0 & 0 & 1 \end{pmatrix}$, respectively.

WORKED EXAMPLE 4.12

Rotate the following matrices about the axis and by the angle given.

a $\begin{pmatrix} 1 & 0 & 2 \\ -1 & 1 & 3 \\ 4 & 1 & 1 \end{pmatrix}$, rotated about the z-axis by 45° anticlockwise

b $\begin{pmatrix} 0 & 0 & 2 \\ 1 & 1 & -2 \\ -1 & 0 & 0 \end{pmatrix}$, rotated about the x-axis by 90° clockwise

Answer

a Rotation matrix is $\begin{pmatrix} \cos 45° & -\sin 45° & 0 \\ \sin 45° & \cos 45° & 0 \\ 0 & 0 & 1 \end{pmatrix}$

Write down the rotation matrix with the correct angle.

Multiplying, $\begin{pmatrix} \frac{\sqrt{2}}{2} & -\frac{\sqrt{2}}{2} & 0 \\ \frac{\sqrt{2}}{2} & \frac{\sqrt{2}}{2} & 0 \\ 0 & 0 & 1 \end{pmatrix} \times \begin{pmatrix} 1 & 0 & 2 \\ -1 & 1 & 3 \\ 4 & 1 & 1 \end{pmatrix}$

Determine the elements of the rotation matrix.

gives the result $\begin{pmatrix} \sqrt{2} & -\frac{\sqrt{2}}{2} & -\frac{\sqrt{2}}{2} \\ 0 & \frac{\sqrt{2}}{2} & \frac{5\sqrt{2}}{2} \\ 4 & 1 & 1 \end{pmatrix}$. — Determine the result.

b Rotation matrix is $\begin{pmatrix} 1 & 0 & 0 \\ 0 & \cos(-90°) & -\sin(-90°) \\ 0 & \sin(-90°) & \cos(-90°) \end{pmatrix}$. — Write down the rotation matrix, noting that the angle is negative this time. Alternatively we could use an angle of 270° anticlockwise.

Multiplying, $\begin{pmatrix} 1 & 0 & 0 \\ 0 & 0 & 1 \\ 0 & -1 & 0 \end{pmatrix}\begin{pmatrix} 0 & 0 & 2 \\ 1 & 1 & -2 \\ -1 & 0 & 0 \end{pmatrix}$ — Recall that the elements in the first row should be unchanged.

gives the result $\begin{pmatrix} 0 & 0 & 2 \\ -1 & 0 & 0 \\ -1 & -1 & 2 \end{pmatrix}$. — Determine the result.

For reflections in 3-dimensional space we will consider reflections in planes, rather than lines.

So, for example, the matrix $\begin{pmatrix} 1 & 0 & 0 \\ 0 & 1 & 0 \\ 0 & 0 & -1 \end{pmatrix}$ would make all z values change sign. This is a reflection in the x–y plane.

Similarly, the matrices $\begin{pmatrix} -1 & 0 & 0 \\ 0 & 1 & 0 \\ 0 & 0 & 1 \end{pmatrix}$ and $\begin{pmatrix} 1 & 0 & 0 \\ 0 & -1 & 0 \\ 0 & 0 & 1 \end{pmatrix}$ are reflections in the y–z plane and x–z plane respectively.

EXPLORE 4.8

What matrices can produce reflections in the planes $x - y = 0$, $x - z = 0$ and $y - z = 0$?

Can you think of any other reflections in planes?

WORKED EXAMPLE 4.13

Find a matrix that produces a reflection in the plane $x + y = 0$.

Answer

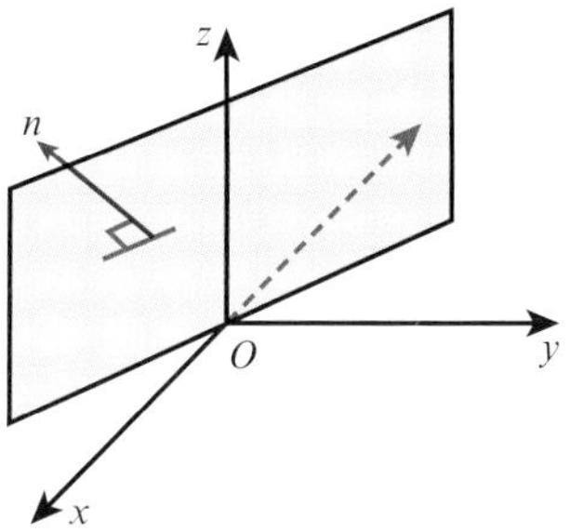

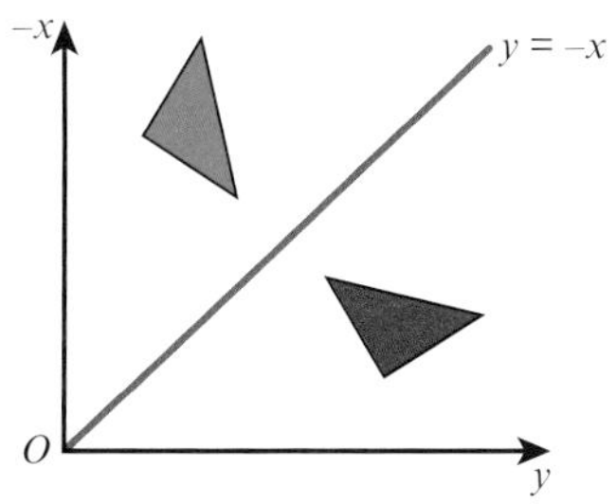

The plane has normal $\begin{pmatrix} 1 \\ 1 \\ 0 \end{pmatrix}$ or $\begin{pmatrix} -1 \\ -1 \\ 0 \end{pmatrix}$, so the plane can be visualised.

Looking down the z-axis shows the line $y = -x$.

z value unchanged, hence bottom row is 0 0 1. — Note that the z value will be unchanged by the reflection.

$-x$ and y switch places.

Hence, $\begin{pmatrix} 0 & -1 & 0 \\ -1 & 0 & 0 \\ 0 & 0 & 1 \end{pmatrix}$. — Determine the matrix.

EXERCISE 4D

1 Find the matrix represented by each of the following transformations.

a A reflection in the x-axis followed by an enlargement of scale factor 2 centered at the origin.

b A rotation of 90° anticlockwise about the origin followed by a reflection in the line $y = x$.

c An enlargement of scale factor 3 centered at the origin, followed by a reflection in the line $y = -x$.

P PS 2 a You are given the matrix $\mathbf{A} = \begin{pmatrix} 1 & 2 \\ 4 & -1 \end{pmatrix}$. Show that $\mathbf{A}\begin{pmatrix} 1 \\ -2 \end{pmatrix} = k\begin{pmatrix} 1 \\ -2 \end{pmatrix}$ and state the value of k.

b Given also that $\mathbf{A}\begin{pmatrix} b \\ 2 \end{pmatrix} = m\begin{pmatrix} 2 \\ 2 \end{pmatrix}$, find the values of b and m.

PS 3 The following transformations are given.

T_1 is a rotation of 90° clockwise about the origin.

T_2 is a reflection in the line $y = -x$.

T_3 is an enlargement of factor 2 centered at the origin.

Given that $\mathbf{A} = \begin{pmatrix} 1 & 5 \\ 6 & -3 \end{pmatrix}$, find the image of $\mathbf{A}$ using transformations T_2 followed by T_3 followed by T_1.

4 For the matrix $\begin{pmatrix} 1 & 5 & 6 \\ 2 & 2 & 4 \end{pmatrix}$, determine the transformation matrix that produces the following image.

a $\begin{pmatrix} 2 & 2 & 4 \\ 1 & 5 & 6 \end{pmatrix}$

b $\begin{pmatrix} -1 & -5 & -6 \\ 4 & 4 & 8 \end{pmatrix}$

c $\begin{pmatrix} -6 & -6 & -12 \\ 2 & 10 & 12 \end{pmatrix}$

5 Determine the area of the image produced in each case.

a triangle $A(1, 3)$, $B(1, 7)$, $C(4, 3)$ transformed by $\begin{pmatrix} 2 & 0 \\ 0 & 2 \end{pmatrix}$

b square $A(1, 1)$, $B(7, 2)$, $C(6, 8)$, $D(0, 7)$ transformed by $\begin{pmatrix} 4 & 1 \\ 5 & 2 \end{pmatrix}$

c trapezium represented by $\begin{pmatrix} 2 & 2 & 4 & 8 \\ 1 & 5 & 5 & 1 \end{pmatrix}$ transformed by $\begin{pmatrix} 1 & 4 \\ 3 & 9 \end{pmatrix}$

6 Find the invariant lines for each of the following shearing matrices.

a $\begin{pmatrix} 1 & 4 \\ 3 & 1 \end{pmatrix}$

b $\begin{pmatrix} 4 & -1 \\ 2 & 1 \end{pmatrix}$

c $\begin{pmatrix} 6 & 5 \\ 2 & 3 \end{pmatrix}$

M 7 Find the single matrix that is a combination of 90° anticlockwise rotation about the origin, followed by an enlargement of factor 2 with centre of enlargement origin, followed by a reflection in the y-axis.

Show this effect on the triangle with vertices $(1, 1), (4, 2), (3, 4)$.

E M 8 Determine the single matrix required for each of the following transformation combinations.

a Rotation about the z-axis by 90° clockwise, followed by a stretch of factor 2 in the x-direction, followed by a reflection in the x–z plane.

b Reflection in the plane $x - y = 0$, followed by an enlargement of factor $\frac{1}{2}$ with centre of enlargement origin, followed by a rotation of 45° anticlockwise about the y-axis.

WORKED EXAM-STYLE QUESTION

a Given that $\mathbf{T} = \begin{pmatrix} 2 & 3 \\ 1 & 2 \end{pmatrix}$, find the two invariant lines under the transformation represented by this matrix and show that the angle between them is $\frac{\pi}{3}$.

b The triangle ABC has vertices $A(1, 1)$, $B(5, 1)$, $C(4, 3)$. Determine the image when this triangle is transformed by $\mathbf{T}$.

c Determine the inverse of the matrix $\mathbf{T}$ and state the difference in area between the original triangle and the image created.

Answer

a Start with $\begin{pmatrix} 2 & 3 \\ 1 & 2 \end{pmatrix}\begin{pmatrix} t \\ mt \end{pmatrix} = \begin{pmatrix} T \\ mT \end{pmatrix}$, giving equations $2t + 3mt = T$ and $t + 2mt = mT$.

Divide the first equation by the second equation to get $\frac{2 + 3m}{1 + 2m} = \frac{1}{m}$, then solving gives $2m + 3m^2 = 1 + 2m$ or $3m^2 = 1$.

So $m = \pm\frac{1}{\sqrt{3}}$ and so the invariant lines are $y = -\frac{1}{\sqrt{3}}x$ and $y = \frac{1}{\sqrt{3}}x$.

Since $m = \tan\theta$, the angle between the invariant lines is $2 \times \tan^{-1}\frac{1}{\sqrt{3}} = \frac{\pi}{3}$.

b For the transformation, $\begin{pmatrix} 2 & 3 \\ 1 & 2 \end{pmatrix}\begin{pmatrix} 1 & 5 & 4 \\ 1 & 1 & 3 \end{pmatrix} = \begin{pmatrix} 5 & 13 & 17 \\ 3 & 7 & 10 \end{pmatrix}$. The image of ABC has vertices at $(5, 3)$, $(13, 7)$ and $(17, 10)$.

c The inverse matrix of $\mathbf{T}$ is $\mathbf{T}^{-1} = \frac{1}{4-3}\begin{pmatrix} 2 & -3 \\ -1 & 2 \end{pmatrix}$. Since the determinant of $\mathbf{T}$ is 1 there is no difference in the area of the triangles.

Checklist of learning and understanding

Standard operations:

- $\begin{pmatrix} a & b \\ c & d \end{pmatrix} \pm \begin{pmatrix} e & f \\ g & h \end{pmatrix} = \begin{pmatrix} a \pm e & b \pm f \\ c \pm g & d \pm h \end{pmatrix}$
- $\begin{pmatrix} a & b \\ c & d \end{pmatrix}\begin{pmatrix} e & f \\ g & h \end{pmatrix} = \begin{pmatrix} ae + bg & af + bh \\ ce + dg & cf + dh \end{pmatrix}$
- In general, $\mathbf{AB} \neq \mathbf{BA}$.
- For square matrices $\mathbf{A} \times \mathbf{A} \times \mathbf{A} \times \ldots \times \mathbf{A} = \mathbf{A}^n$.
- The identity matrix is a square matrix of the form $\mathbf{I} = \begin{pmatrix} 1 & 0 & 0 & \ldots & 0 \\ 0 & 1 & 0 & \ldots & 0 \\ 0 & 0 & 1 & \ldots & 0 \\ \vdots & \vdots & \vdots & \ddots & \vdots \\ 0 & 0 & 0 & \ldots & 1 \end{pmatrix}$, and it has the property such that $\mathbf{A} \times \mathbf{A}^{-1} = \mathbf{I}$ or $\mathbf{A}^{-1} \times \mathbf{A} = \mathbf{I}$.

Inverse matrices:

- For 2×2 matrices if $\mathbf{A} = \begin{pmatrix} a & b \\ c & d \end{pmatrix}$ then $\mathbf{A}^{-1} = \frac{1}{ad - bc}\begin{pmatrix} d & -b \\ -c & a \end{pmatrix}$.
- For $n \times n$ matrices we can use row operations on an augmented matrix of the form $\left(\begin{array}{ccc|ccc} a & b & c & 1 & 0 & 0 \\ d & e & f & 0 & 1 & 0 \\ g & h & i & 0 & 0 & 1 \end{array}\right)$.
- For any two square matrices $\mathbf{A}$ and $\mathbf{B}$, $(\mathbf{AB})^{-1} = \mathbf{B}^{-1}\mathbf{A}^{-1}$.
- A matrix without an inverse is known as singular.
- A matrix with an inverse is non-singular.

Determinants:

- The determinant of a 3×3 matrix $\mathbf{A} = \begin{pmatrix} a & b & c \\ d & e & f \\ g & h & i \end{pmatrix}$ is calculated as $\det(A) = a\begin{vmatrix} e & f \\ h & i \end{vmatrix} - b\begin{vmatrix} d & f \\ g & i \end{vmatrix} + c\begin{vmatrix} d & e \\ g & h \end{vmatrix}$.
- When the determinant of a matrix is 0, the matrix will be singular.
- The value of the determinant changes by factor k when row operations of the form $r_i \to kr_i + mr_j$ are used.
- The value of the determinant is also the factor increase of the area, or volume, when the matrix is used as a transformation.
- For two matrices $\mathbf{A}$ and $\mathbf{B}$, $\det(\mathbf{AB}) = \det(\mathbf{BA}) = \det(\mathbf{A}) \times \det(\mathbf{B})$.

Transformations:

- The following transformations are for 2×2 matrices.

Transformation	Matrix
Stretch by a scale factor of factor k in the x-direction	$\begin{pmatrix} k & 0 \\ 0 & 1 \end{pmatrix}$
Stretch by a scale factor of factor k in the y-direction	$\begin{pmatrix} 1 & 0 \\ 0 & k \end{pmatrix}$
Enlargement with centre of enlargement the origin by a scale factor of factor k	$\begin{pmatrix} k & 0 \\ 0 & k \end{pmatrix}$
Reflection in the x-axis	$\begin{pmatrix} 1 & 0 \\ 0 & -1 \end{pmatrix}$
Reflection in the y-axis	$\begin{pmatrix} -1 & 0 \\ 0 & 1 \end{pmatrix}$
Reflection in the line $y = x$	$\begin{pmatrix} 0 & 1 \\ 1 & 0 \end{pmatrix}$
Rotation about the origin by θ in the anticlockwise direction	$\begin{pmatrix} \cos\theta & -\sin\theta \\ \sin\theta & \cos\theta \end{pmatrix}$

E

- The following transformations are for 3×3 matrices.

Transformation	Matrix
Rotation about the x-axis by angle θ in the anticlockwise direction	$\begin{pmatrix} 1 & 0 & 0 \\ 0 & \cos\theta & -\sin\theta \\ 0 & \sin\theta & \cos\theta \end{pmatrix}$
Rotation about the y-axis by angle θ in the anticlockwise direction	$\begin{pmatrix} \cos\theta & 0 & \sin\theta \\ 0 & 1 & 0 \\ -\sin\theta & 0 & \cos\theta \end{pmatrix}$
Rotation about the z-axis by angle θ in the anticlockwise direction	$\begin{pmatrix} \cos\theta & -\sin\theta & 0 \\ \sin\theta & \cos\theta & 0 \\ 0 & 0 & 1 \end{pmatrix}$
Enlargement with centre of enlargement the origin by a scale factor of factor k	$\begin{pmatrix} k & 0 & 0 \\ 0 & k & 0 \\ 0 & 0 & k \end{pmatrix}$

Invariant lines:

- For 2-dimensional cases, use $\begin{pmatrix} a & b \\ c & d \end{pmatrix}\begin{pmatrix} t \\ mt \end{pmatrix} = \begin{pmatrix} T \\ mT \end{pmatrix}$ to determine two equations of the form $at + bmt = T, ct + dmt = mT$. Divide to get $\frac{a + bm}{c + dm} = \frac{1}{m}$, then solve for value(s) of m to find the invariant line(s) of the transformation in the form $y = mx$.

END-OF-CHAPTER REVIEW EXERCISE 4

1 Given that $\mathbf{A} = \begin{pmatrix} 6 & 5 \\ 2 & 3 \end{pmatrix}$ and $\mathbf{B} = \begin{pmatrix} -1 & 2 \\ 1 & -4 \end{pmatrix}$:

a find $\mathbf{C}$ such that $\mathbf{BC} = \mathbf{A} + \mathbf{A}^2$

b determine $\mathbf{D}$, where $\mathbf{ADB} = \mathbf{I}$.

2 You are given the matrix $\mathbf{A} = \begin{pmatrix} 1 & 2 & a \\ 0 & 2 & a-3 \\ 1 & 0 & a+4 \end{pmatrix}$.

a If the matrix is singular, find the value of the constant a.

b If $a = 4$, find $\mathbf{A}^{-1}$.

3 The matrix $\mathbf{A}$ is given as $\mathbf{A} = \begin{pmatrix} 3 & 4 \\ 2 & 5 \end{pmatrix}$.

a Find the invariant lines for this matrix.

b The matrix $\mathbf{A}$ is applied to the vertices of the triangle PQR, and the resulting image has vertices at the points $(11, 12)$, $(19, 15)$ and $(40, 43)$. Find the coordinates of the vertices of the original triangle.

Chapter 5
Polar coordinates

In this chapter, you will learn how to:

- understand the relations between Cartesian and polar coordinates, and convert equations of curves from Cartesian to polar and vice versa
- sketch simple polar curves, for $0 \leqslant \theta \leqslant 2\pi$ or $-\pi < \theta \leqslant \pi$ or a subset of either of these intervals
- recall the formula $\frac{1}{2}\int r^2 \, \mathrm{d}\theta$ for the area of a sector, and use this formula in simple cases.

PREREQUISITE KNOWLEDGE

Where it comes from	What you should be able to do	Check your skills
AS & A Level Mathematics Pure Mathematics 2 & 3, Chapter 4	Work with parametric curves.	**1 a** Given that $x = 2\cos\theta$ and $y = \sin 2\theta$, find $y = f(x)$. **b** If $x = t + \frac{1}{t}$ and $y = t - \frac{1}{t}$, find an equation relating x and y.
AS & A Level Mathematics Pure Mathematics 2 & 3, Chapters 5 & 8	Recall how to integrate.	**2** Evaluate the following. **a** $\int_{x=0}^{x=\frac{\pi}{4}} \cos^2 x \, dx$ **b** $\int_{x=1}^{x=2} e^{2x} \, dx$

What are polar coordinates?

In AS & A Level Mathematics you met Cartesian equations and parametric equations. Now you will learn about another type of 2-dimensional coordinate system, **polar coordinates**. In this system, a point on a plane is identified by an angle and a distance rather than two linear dimensions. Polar curves are described by the distance from the origin, r, and the angle formed with the positive x-axis, θ.

Polar coordinates are used for applications involving circular geometry or radial movement, where rectangular (Cartesian) coordinates would be awkward to use. Engineers use polar coordinates in the design and manufacture of gears. Polar coordinates also help scientists to understand electric and magnetic fields.

Polar curves can be used to create some beautiful graphs, including **cardioids** and rose petals.

5.1 The polar system

Rather than using Cartesian coordinates (x, y) to describe the position of a point we use polar coordinates (r, θ). We define an origin O called the pole, and a line in a fixed direction, conventionally the x-axis, called the initial line.

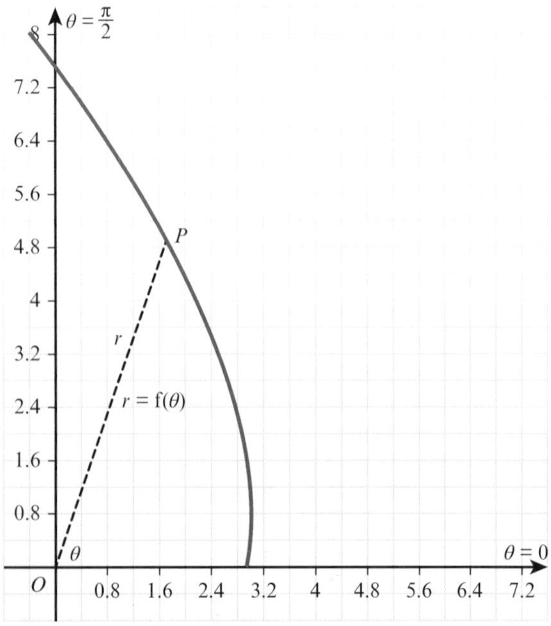

The point, P, shown on the graph has polar coordinates (r, θ). r is defined as the distance of P from the pole. The angle OP makes with the initial line is θ. Note that if θ is measured anticlockwise from the initial line the convention is for θ to be positive. If θ is measured clockwise from the initial line the convention is for θ to be negative.

The initial line, which is the x-axis when using Cartesian coordinates, is where $\theta = 0$. The y-axis for Cartesian coordinates is where $\theta = \frac{\pi}{2}$ for polar coodinates. Instead of writing functions in the form $y = f(x)$, we work with functions in the form $r = f(\theta)$.

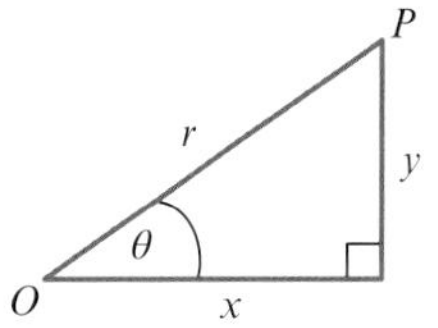

Using this right-angled triangle, and some trigonometry, we can deduce that $x = r\cos\theta$ and $y = r\sin\theta$. We can combine these using the identity (or use Pythagoras on the right-angled triangle) to deduce $x^2 + y^2 = r^2$. These equations are useful when converting between polar and Cartesian coordinates. Note that this equation does not imply that the graph is a circle. It merely describes a geometrical relationship between the x and y values at every point on the curve.

The correct way to write this is $x = \mathrm{f}(\theta)\cos\theta$, $y = \mathrm{f}(\theta)\sin\theta$. Remember that $r = \mathrm{f}(\theta)$. This is shown in Key point 5.1.

We would only have a circle in the case where $\mathrm{f}(\theta)$ is a constant.

KEY POINT 5.1

For all polar curves $x = r\cos\theta$, $y = r\sin\theta$ and $x^2 + y^2 = r^2 \Rightarrow r \geqslant 0$. The function is given in the form $r = \mathrm{f}(\theta)$.

Changing from polar to Cartesian form is quite straightforward.

For example, if $r = 2$ then using $x^2 + y^2 = r^2$ we get $x^2 + y^2 = 4$. This is a circle with radius 2 and centre $(0, 0)$.

Consider a different example: start with $y = r\sin\theta$ and multiply both sides by r.

Using $r^2 = x^2 + y^2$ and $y = r\sin\theta$ we get $x^2 + y^2 = y$, or $x^2 + y^2 - y = 0$.

By completing the square on the y terms we find $x^2 + \left(y - \frac{1}{2}\right)^2 = \frac{1}{4}$.

This is also a circle, centre $\left(0, \frac{1}{2}\right)$ and radius $\frac{1}{2}$. We will look at this curve again in Worked example 5.4.

WORKED EXAMPLE 5.1

Convert the following polar curves into Cartesian form.

a $r = \sec\theta$ **b** $r^2\cos 2\theta = 4$

Answer

a $r = \dfrac{1}{\cos\theta}$ Change $\sec\theta$ to $\dfrac{1}{\cos\theta}$.

$r\cos\theta = 1$ Multiply across.

$x = 1$ Change $r\cos\theta$ to x.

b $r^2(\cos^2\theta - \sin^2\theta) = 4$ Use the double angle formula.

$x^2 - y^2 = 4$ Use $x = r\cos\theta$, $y = r\sin\theta$.

Changing from Cartesian to polar form is also relatively straightforward.

For example, if $y = 1$ then $r\sin\theta = 1$, the polar curve is $r = \dfrac{1}{\sin\theta}$ or $r = \operatorname{cosec}\theta$

WORKED EXAMPLE 5.2

Find the polar form for the following equations.

a $y^4 = x^2 + y^2$ **b** $x^2 = \dfrac{y^4}{1 - y^2}$

Answer

a

$r^4\sin^4\theta = r^2$ — Use $y = r\sin\theta$ for the left side, and $x^2 + y^2 = r^2$ for the right side.

$r^2(r^2\sin^4\theta) = r^2$

$r^2(r^2\sin^4\theta - 1) = 0$ — $r = 0$ is not our curve, so divide by r^2 (or factorise out).

$r^2\sin^4\theta = 1$

$r^2 = \dfrac{1}{\sin^4\theta} = \operatorname{cosec}^4\theta$ — Find the equation of the curve.

b

$r^2\cos^2\theta = \dfrac{r^4\sin^4\theta}{1 - r^2\sin^2\theta}$ — Use $x = r\cos\theta$ for the left side and $y = r\sin\theta$ for the right side.

$r^2\cos^2\theta - r^4\sin^2\theta\cos^2\theta = r^4\sin^4\theta$

$r^2\cos^2\theta - r^4\sin^2\theta(1 - \sin^2\theta) = r^4\sin^4\theta$ — Use $\cos^2\theta = 1 - \sin^2\theta$ to simplify the expression.

$r^2\cos^2\theta - r^4\sin^2\theta = 0$

$r^2(\cos^2\theta - r^2\sin^2\theta) = 0$ — Factorise out the r^2 term.

$\cos^2\theta = r^2\sin^2\theta$

$r^2 = \dfrac{\cos^2\theta}{\sin^2\theta}$

$r^2 = \cot^2\theta$ — State the equation of the curve.

Now we shall look at sketching polar curves. The simplest type is the curve $r = a$ which is a circle. The distance of each point from the origin is a.

If we look at the curve $r = \theta$, this is slightly different. As θ changes, the distance also changes so the curve formed is a spiral.

Note that the curve tends to the initial line as $\theta \to 0$.

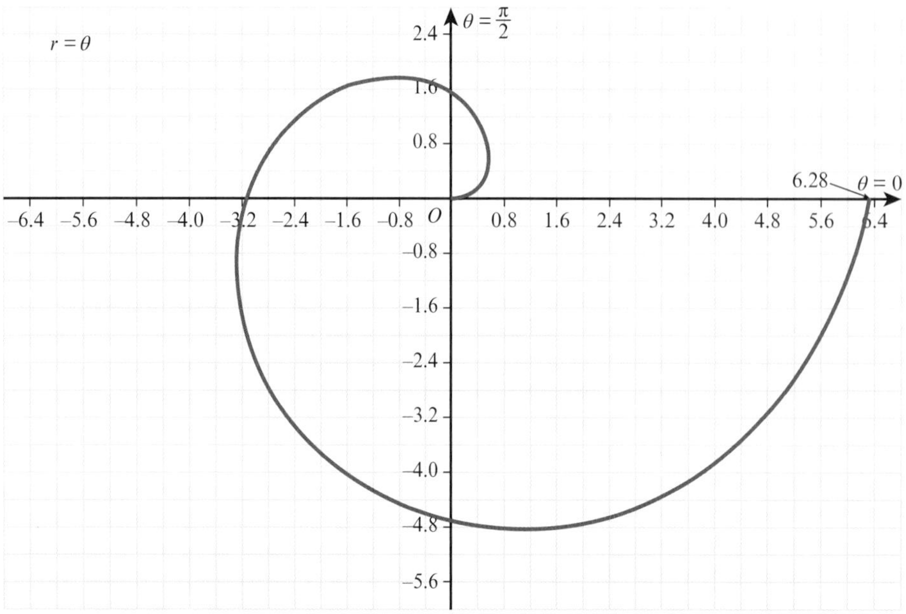

θ	$\frac{\pi}{2}$	π	$\frac{3\pi}{2}$	2π
r	1.57	3.14	4.71	6.28

One very useful tool when sketching polar curves is a table of values for (r, θ). From the table we can see that the sketch matches the values.

WORKED EXAMPLE 5.3

Sketch the curve $r\theta = 1$, for $0 < \theta \leqslant 2\pi$, noting any special features of the curve.

Answer

$r = \frac{1}{\theta}$ — Rearrange.

θ	$\frac{\pi}{2}$	π	$\frac{3\pi}{2}$	2π
r	0.637	0.318	0.212	0.159

Use specific values to form the general shape of the curve.

$\theta \neq 0$, therefore consider $\theta \to 0$. — Note the issue as $\theta \to 0$.

For small angles $\sin\theta \approx \theta$ so $r \approx \frac{1}{\sin\theta}$.

Therefore, $r\sin\theta \approx 1 \Rightarrow y \approx 1$. — Use small angles such that $\sin\delta\theta \approx \delta\theta$.

Hence, there is an asymptote at $y = 1$. — Determine the equation of the asymptote as θ tends to 0.

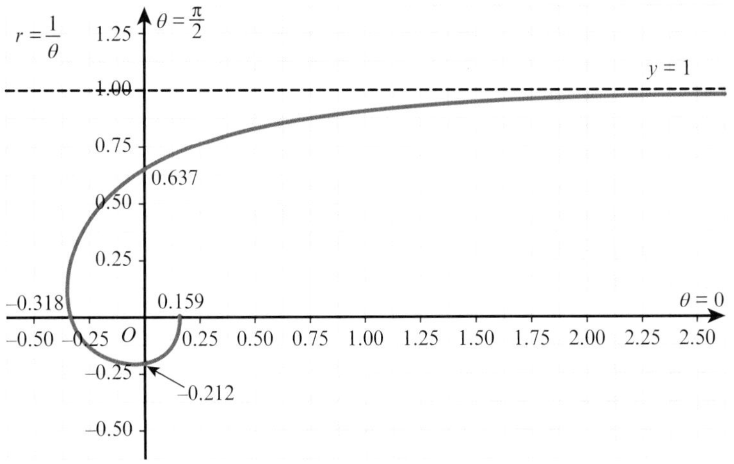

Ensure points of intersection are noted and labelled.

Since polar curves are defined with $r \geqslant 0$, we need to consider some restrictions for certain curves.

For example, if we attempted to sketch $r = \ln\theta$, the domain for θ would have to exclude $\theta < 1$. For the domain $1 \leqslant \theta \leqslant 2\pi$ we would have another spiral curve. The red dashed line represents the section of the curve that we can't sketch. The solid blue line is for $\theta > 1$.

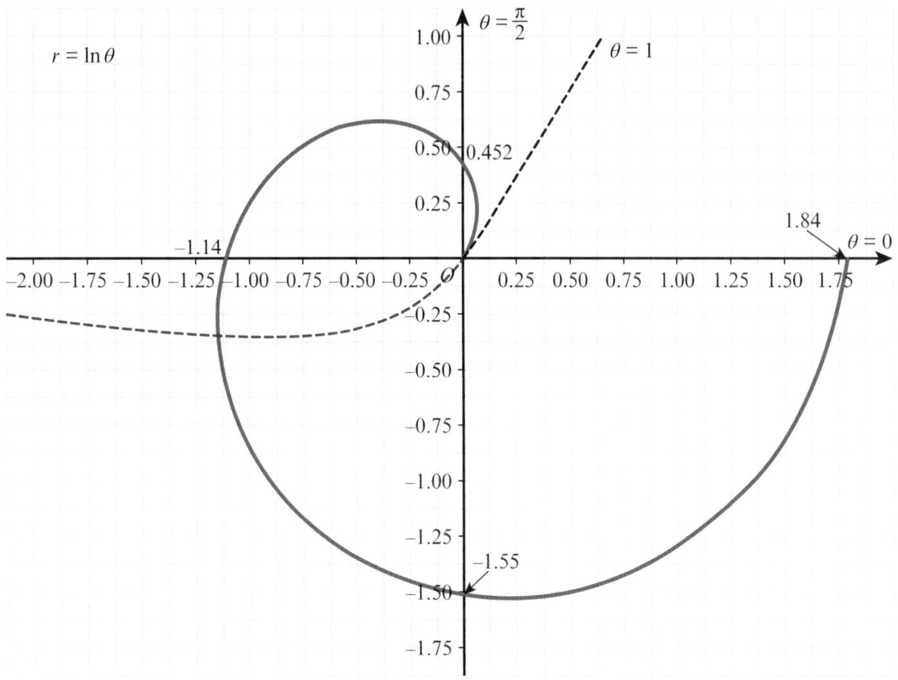

Consider the curve $r = \cos\theta$. This curve can be completed over an interval of π. But if we try to use $0 \leqslant \theta \leqslant \pi$, this will produce negative values for r for the interval $\left[\frac{\pi}{2}, \pi\right]$. You can see this in the following diagram.

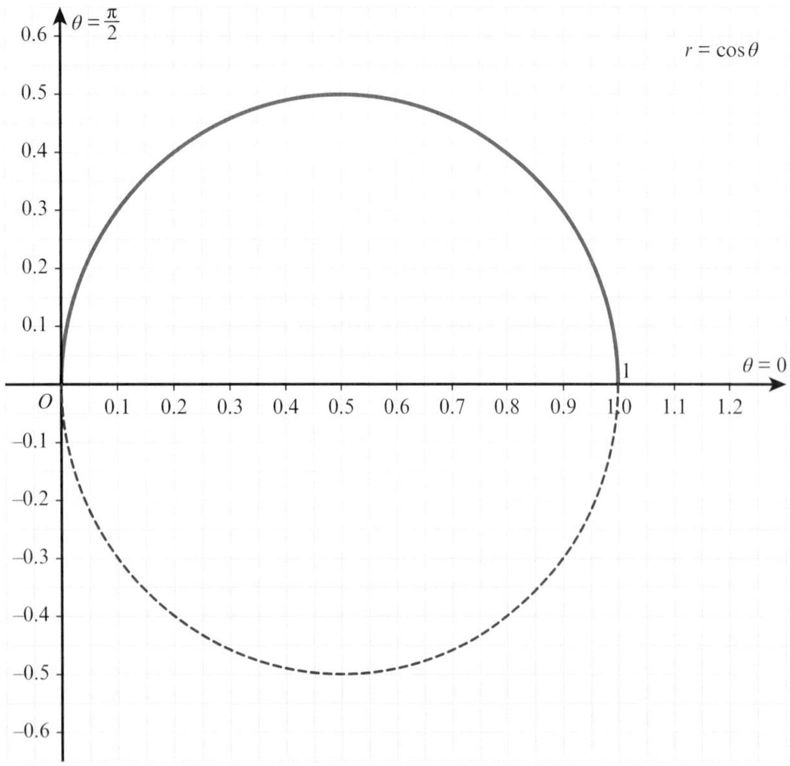

So in order to sketch $r = \cos\theta$ correctly, we must use the interval $\left[-\frac{\pi}{2}, \frac{\pi}{2}\right]$ since this interval is non-negative for $\cos\theta$. If you are not convinced that this is a circle, start with $r = \cos\theta$ and then multiply both sides by r to get $r^2 = r\cos\theta$, or $x^2 + y^2 = x$.

This simplifies to $\left(x - \frac{1}{2}\right)^2 + y^2 = \frac{1}{4}$. This is a circle with centre $\left(\frac{1}{2}, 0\right)$ and radius $\frac{1}{2}$.

WORKED EXAMPLE 5.4

Sketch the curve $r = \sin\theta$ using a table of values. State the domain for θ that ensures $r \geqslant 0$.

Answer

θ	0	$\frac{\pi}{6}$	$\frac{\pi}{4}$	$\frac{\pi}{3}$	$\frac{\pi}{2}$	$\frac{2\pi}{3}$	$\frac{3\pi}{4}$	$\frac{5\pi}{6}$	π
r	0	0.5	0.707	0.866	1	0.866	0.707	0.5	0

Work out the key values.

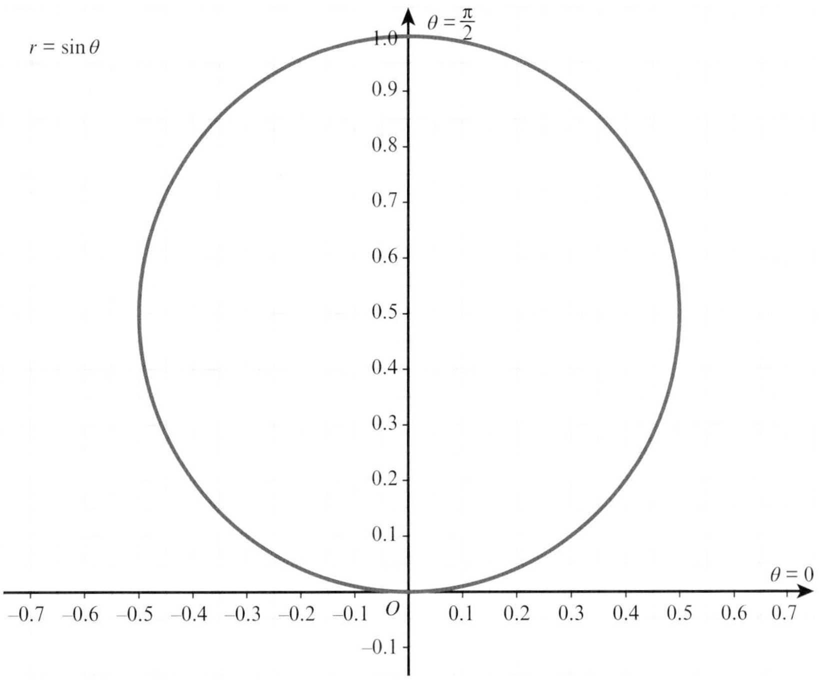

Recognise that this is a closed loop, since it starts and finishes at 0.

Valid for $0 \leqslant \theta \leqslant \pi$.

State the correct domain to avoid negative r values.

Earlier we converted $r = \sin\theta$ into $x^2 + \left(y - \frac{1}{2}\right)^2 = \frac{1}{4}$, reinforcing the fact that this is a circle. One very convincing additional fact is that the two curves $r = \cos\theta$ and $r = \sin\theta$ are $\frac{\pi}{2}$ radians apart.

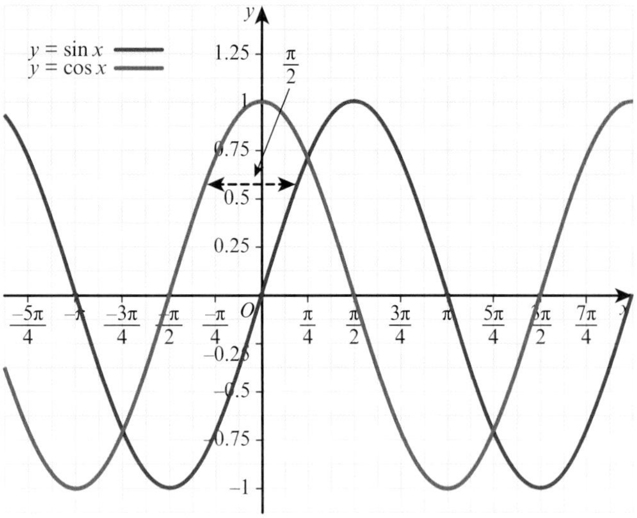

In Cartesian form, this is a translation but in polar form it is a rotation. We can see from the previous graphs that rotating $r = \cos\theta$ by $\frac{\pi}{2}$ anticlockwise about the pole gives the curve $r = \sin\theta$.

Let us now consider the curve $r = 1 + \cos\theta$. At first this looks like it could be a larger circle, perhaps a circle of radius 1.

To be sure, it is best to construct a table of values, as shown.

θ	0	$\frac{\pi}{4}$	$\frac{\pi}{2}$	$\frac{3\pi}{4}$	π	$\frac{5\pi}{4}$	$\frac{3\pi}{2}$	$\frac{7\pi}{4}$
r	2	1.71	1	0.293	0	0.293	1	1.71

From this table, it is possible to construct the curve, noting that there are no negative values of r. The smallest value r can take is 0, and at this point a **cusp** is created. This curve is known as a cardioid, or heart-shaped curve.

> **TIP**
>
> A cusp is a point where two branches of a curve meet, such that the two tangents of the curve are equal.

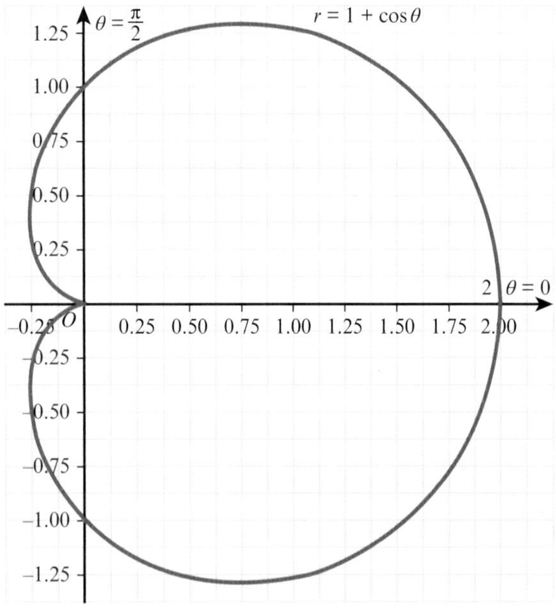

Notice that this curve, just like the function $y = \cos x$, has a line of symmetry at $\theta = 0$. This is generally the case with polar curves that contain factors of $\cos\theta$.

The curve $r = 1 + \sin\theta$ is the same shape as the curve $r = 1 + \cos\theta$. However, it is symmetrical about the line $\theta = \frac{\pi}{2}$ in the same way as the curve $y = \sin x$ is. If the angle is 2θ rather than θ then the relationship between the sin and cos curves still holds, but now the angle between them is $2\theta = \frac{\pi}{2}$, or rather $\theta = \frac{\pi}{4}$.

We can see in the following diagram the relationship between the curves $r = \cos 2\theta$ and $r = \sin 2\theta$. Note that there are no negative regions.

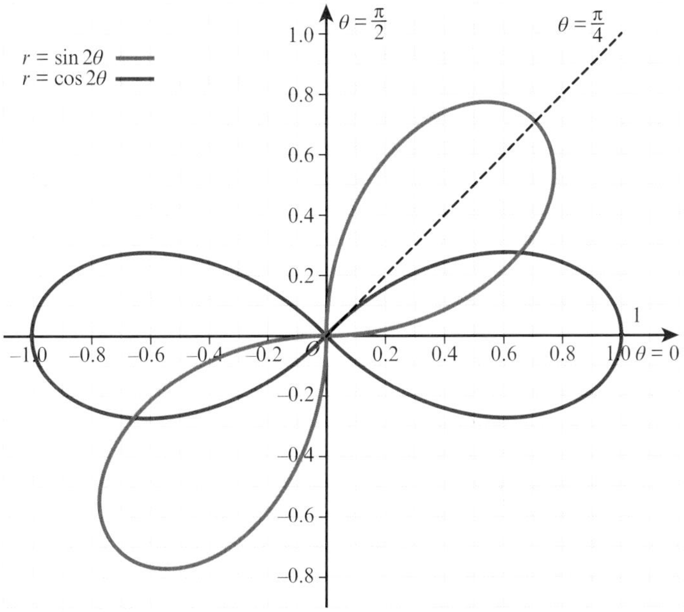

WORKED EXAMPLE 5.5

Sketch the curve $r = \sin 3\theta$ using a table of values. State the domains for θ where $r \geqslant 0$.

Answer

θ	0	$\frac{\pi}{6}$	$\frac{\pi}{4}$	$\frac{\pi}{3}$	$\frac{2\pi}{3}$	$\frac{3\pi}{4}$	$\frac{5\pi}{6}$	π	$\frac{4\pi}{3}$
r	0	1	0.707	0	0	0.707	1	0	0

Work out the key values.

θ	$\frac{3\pi}{2}$	$\frac{5\pi}{3}$
r	1	0

Determine where $r = 0$ to find the values that are allowed.

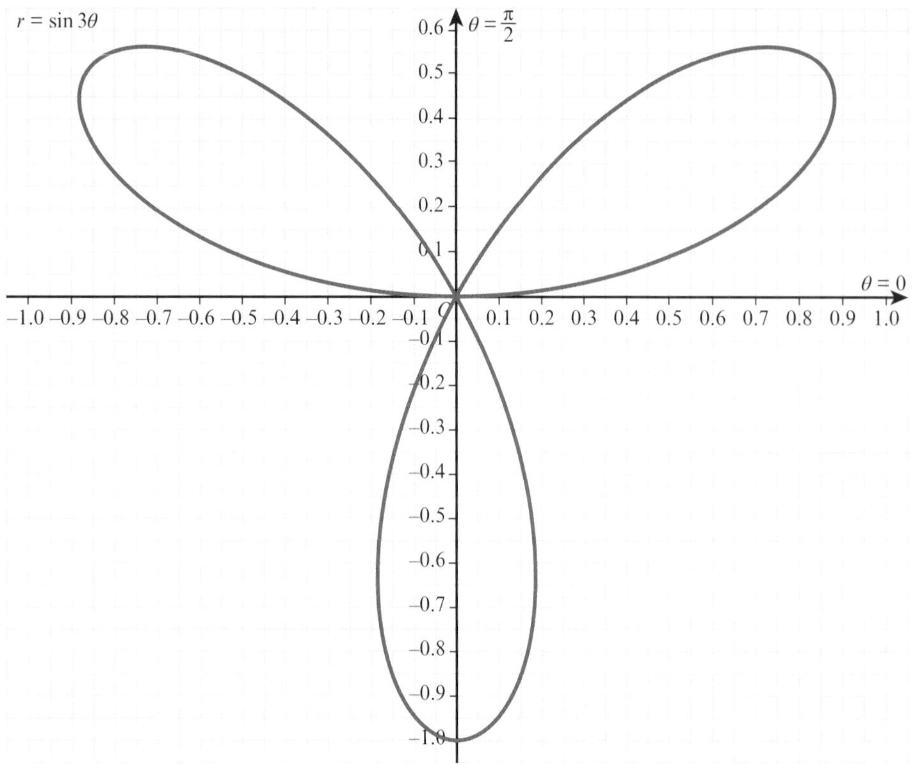

The curve has three petals, or leaves.

Note that the domains we can use are $\left[0, \frac{\pi}{3}\right], \left[\frac{2\pi}{3}, \pi\right], \left[\frac{4\pi}{3}, \frac{5\pi}{3}\right]$.

EXPLORE 5.1

Investigate curves of the form $r = \cos k\theta$ and $r = \sin k\theta$ for odd and even values of k.

You must consider the points of intersection of polar curves with the initial line and show them on your graph. The initial line will not always be when $\theta = 0$, as you have seen with both $r = \frac{1}{\theta}$ and $r = \ln\theta$.

If your function does not permit the use of $\theta = 0$ then use the value $\theta = 2\pi$, provided that your domain allows this value.

EXERCISE 5A

Do not use a calculator in this exercise.

1 Find the Cartesian form for the polar equation $r = \sin\theta$.

2 Find the coordinates of all the points where the curve $r = \cos\theta + 2$ meets the coordinates axes.

3 A curve, C, has polar equation $r = 2 - \sin\theta$, for $0 \leqslant \theta \leqslant 2\pi$. Sketch C.

PS 4 A Cartesian equation is given as $x^3 - y + y^2x = 0$. Find the polar equivalent.

5 Sketch the curve $r = 1 - 2\sin\theta$ for the interval $[0, 2\pi]$. Sketch also the inner loop and state its domain.

6 Sketch the curve $r = \sec^2\theta$ for the interval $0 \leqslant \theta \leqslant 2\pi$.

P 7 A polar curve is given as $r = \cos 2\theta$. Show that the Cartesian form is $(x^2 + y^2)^{\frac{3}{2}} = x^2 - y^2$.

8 Sketch the curve $r = \cos^2\theta$, for $-\frac{\pi}{2} \leqslant \theta \leqslant \frac{\pi}{2}$.

9 Sketch the curve $r = \sec\left(\theta - \frac{\pi}{4}\right)$, showing the coordinates of all points of intersection with the coordinate axes.

10 The curve, C, is defined as $r = \cos 3\theta$, for $0 \leqslant \theta \leqslant 2\pi$. Sketch C.

11 Sketch the curve in question **4**.

5.2 Applications of polar coordinates

When polar curves intersect, we find these points of intersection in the same way as for Cartesian equations. Consider, for example, the two curves $r = \cos\theta$ and $r = \cos 2\theta$.

When these two curves meet, $\cos 2\theta = \cos\theta$, or $2\cos^2\theta - 1 = \cos\theta$. Hence, $(2\cos\theta + 1)(\cos\theta - 1) = 0$. We can see in the following diagram that the only point of intersection is when $\theta = 0$. So our point is $(1, 0)$.

Note that these are polar coordinates and not (x, y) coordinates. Although $\cos\frac{\pi}{2} = 0$ for the circle $r = \cos\theta$, the value $\theta = \frac{\pi}{2}$ is not defined on $r = \cos 2\theta$.

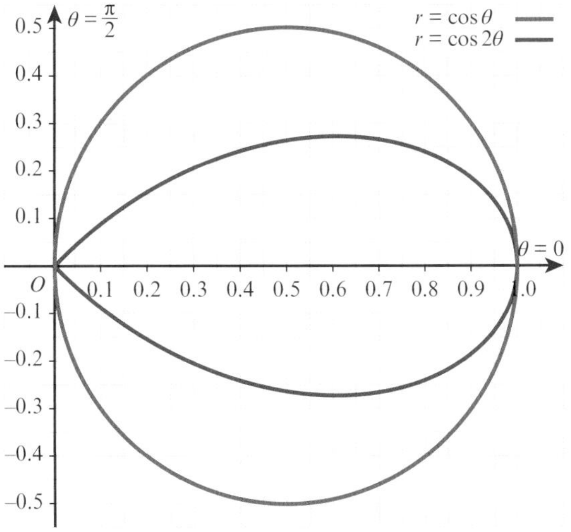

It is advisable to sketch the curves you are given so that you can be clear how the two curves interact in polar coordinates. This is stated in Key point 5.2.

KEY POINT 5.2

Always sketch the curves you are given, to make it clear how the two curves interact in polar coordinates.

WORKED EXAMPLE 5.6

Determine the points of intersection of the curves $r = \tan\theta$ and $r = \sin 2\theta$.

Answer

$\tan\theta = \sin 2\theta$ — Form an equation.

$\frac{\sin\theta}{\cos\theta} = 2\sin\theta\cos\theta$ — Use trigonometric identities.

$\sin\theta(1 - 2\cos^2\theta) = 0$

$\theta = 0, \frac{\pi}{4}, \frac{3\pi}{4}, \pi, \frac{5\pi}{4}, \frac{7\pi}{4}$ — Do not divide by $\sin\theta$ or you will lose solutions.

Hence, $(0, 0), (0, \pi), \left(1, \frac{\pi}{4}\right), \left(1, \frac{5\pi}{4}\right)$. — Write down all the possible values in polar coordinates, checking where r is non-negative.

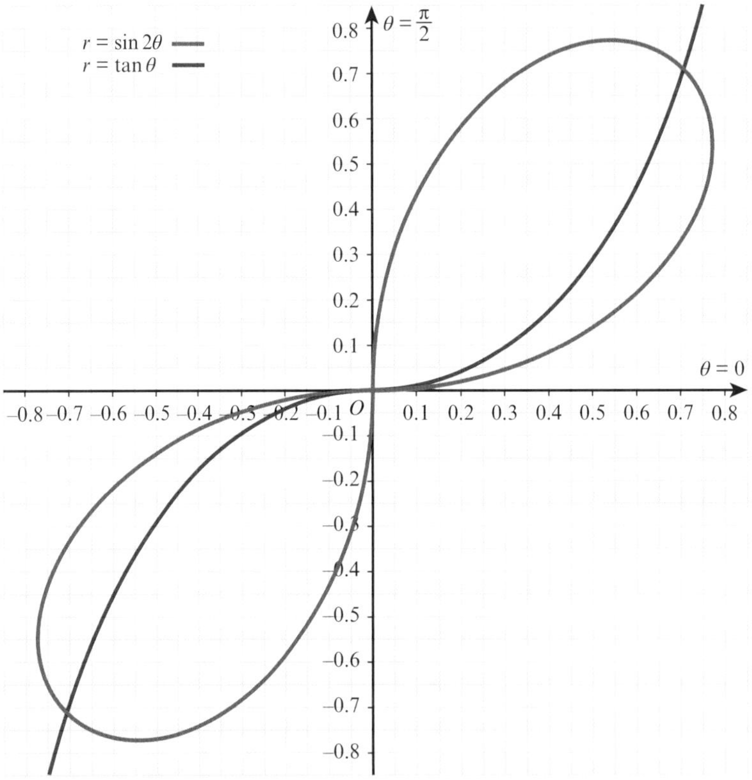

Next we will consider the area contained inside a polar curve. The concept is very similar to the area under the curve for Cartesian equations.

We have two points, $P(r, \theta)$ and $Q(r + \delta r, \theta + \delta\theta)$, on a polar curve, such that the area OPQ is δA.

Then as $\delta\theta \to 0$ we can say that $\delta r \to 0$. So we will assume that the area OPQ is a sector with area $\frac{1}{2}r^2\,\delta\theta$. Once we have set a limit, we can use $d\theta$ instead of $\delta\theta$.

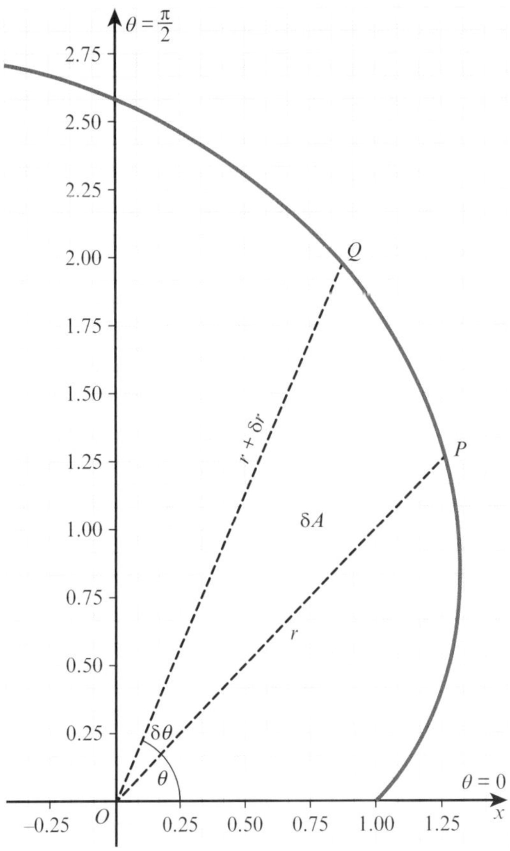

Adding these small areas over an interval $\alpha \leqslant \theta \leqslant \beta$, we can write $A = \frac{1}{2}\int_{\alpha}^{\beta} r^2\,d\theta$.

This is the area inside a polar curve over the specified interval.

For example, let us look at the area inside the polar curve $r = 1 + \cos\theta$ over $0 \leqslant \theta \leqslant \pi$.

Start with $A = \frac{1}{2}\int_0^{\pi} r^2\,d\theta$, which leads to $A = \frac{1}{2}\int_0^{\pi}(1+\cos\theta)^2\,d\theta$.

Expanding leads to $\frac{1}{2}\int_0^{\pi}(1 + 2\cos\theta + \cos^2\theta)\,d\theta$ and simplifying leads to $A = \frac{1}{2}\int_0^{\pi}\left(\frac{3}{2} + 2\cos\theta + \frac{1}{2}\cos 2\theta\right)d\theta$. (Note the use of $\cos^2\theta = \frac{1}{2} + \frac{1}{2}\cos 2\theta$.)

So $A = \left[\frac{3\theta}{4} + \sin\theta + \frac{1}{8}\sin 2\theta\right]_0^{\pi}$, which is $\frac{3\pi}{4}$.

WORKED EXAMPLE 5.7

Find the area enclosed by the curve $r = \cos 2\theta$ over the interval $[0, 2\pi]$.

Answer

$A = \frac{1}{2}\int_0^{2\pi}\cos^2 2\theta\,d\theta$ — Start with the full interval.

$= \frac{1}{4}\int_0^{2\pi}(1 + \cos 4\theta)\,d\theta$

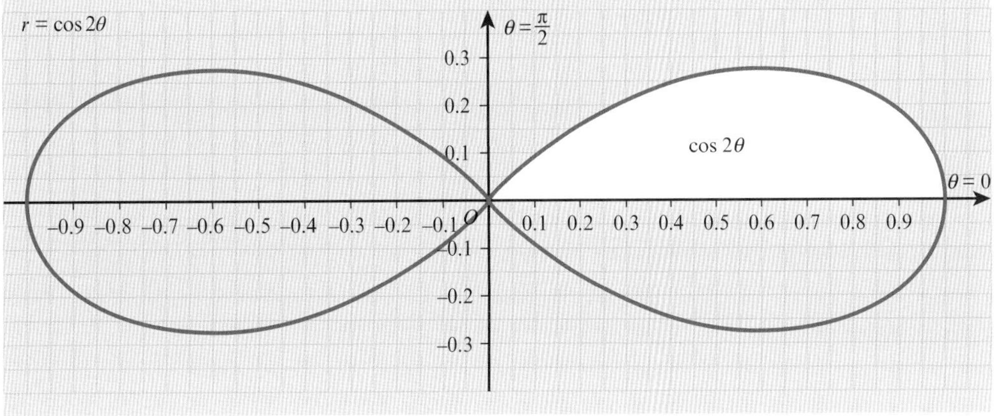

$= 4 \times \frac{1}{4}\int_0^{\frac{\pi}{4}} (1 + \cos 4\theta)\,d\theta$ — Recognise the symmetry in the curve.

$= \left[\theta + \frac{1}{4}\sin 4\theta\right]_0^{\frac{\pi}{4}}$ — Use reduced limits.

$\therefore A = \frac{\pi}{4}$ — Evaluate the total area.

If we evaluate $\frac{1}{4}\left[\theta + \frac{1}{4}\sin 4\theta\right]_0^{2\pi}$ we get $\frac{\pi}{2}$, which is twice as large as the true answer. This is because the area of the curve for the regions with $r < 0$ has also been included.

DID YOU KNOW?

Polar curves have been known for about 2200 years, although they have not been used formally as a coordinate system for all this time. Archimedes described his Archimedean spiral as a function whose radius depends on the angle. However, it was not until the 17th century that mathematicians such as Cavalieri, Pascal, Newton and Bernoulli started to write functions in polar form and use them to determine results such as the area inside an Archimedean spiral.

TIP

Always use the symmetry of curves to help you work out the area of a polar curve.

Finding the area between polar curves is similar to finding the area between Cartesian curves.

Consider two curves, r_1 and r_2, as shown in the diagram.

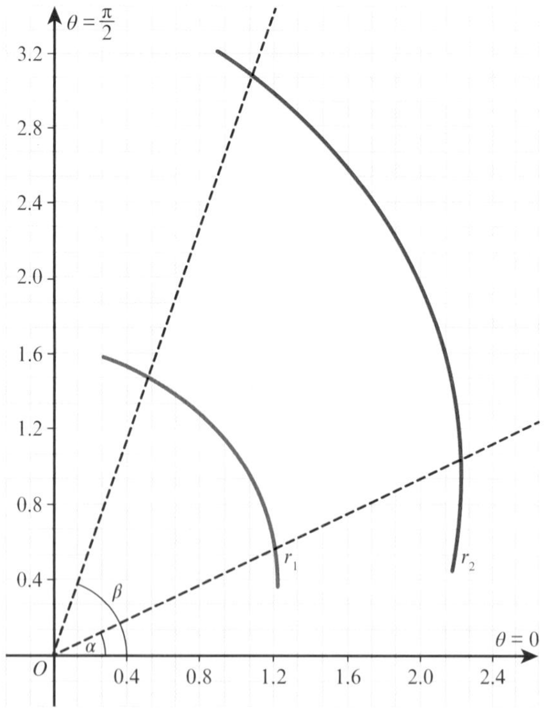

The area between them can be found using $A = \frac{1}{2}\int_\alpha^\beta (r_2^2 - r_1^2)\,d\theta$.

(Note that this is *not* the same as $A = \frac{1}{2}\int_\alpha^\beta (r_2 - r_1)^2\,d\theta$: that is a very different integral.)

For example, consider the two curves $r = \sin\theta$ and $r = 2\sin\theta$ over the interval $\frac{\pi}{6} \leqslant \theta \leqslant \frac{\pi}{2}$. Note that $2\sin\theta$ is the bigger curve, so square and subtract the functions.

Integrate $\frac{1}{2}\int_{\frac{\pi}{6}}^{\frac{\pi}{2}} (4\sin^2\theta - \sin^2\theta)\,d\theta$, which simplifies to $3 \times \frac{1}{2} \times \frac{1}{2}\int_{\frac{\pi}{6}}^{\frac{\pi}{2}} (1 - \cos 2\theta)\,d\theta$.

This integrates to give $\frac{3}{4}\left[\theta - \frac{1}{2}\sin 2\theta\right]_{\frac{\pi}{2}}^{\frac{\pi}{6}}$. So $A = \frac{\pi}{4} + \frac{3\sqrt{3}}{16}$.

WORKED EXAMPLE 5.8

Find the area contained between the curves $r=\theta$ and $r=e^{\theta}$ and the lines $\theta=1, \theta=1.2$.

Answer

$A=\frac{1}{2}\int_{1}^{1.2}(e^{2\theta}-\theta^2)\,d\theta$ — Write the integral. Note that the exponential has a larger area.

$=\frac{1}{2}\left[\frac{1}{2}e^{2\theta}-\frac{1}{3}\theta^3\right]_1^{1.2}$ — Integrate and determine the area.

$=0.787$

If we want to find the area between $r=\cos\theta$ and $r=\sin\theta$, we can see that the curves meet twice. However, these two points are Cartesian points of intersection. The only true point of intersection in polar coordinates is $\left(\frac{\sqrt{2}}{2},\frac{\pi}{4}\right)$. As the two curves have different θ values when $r=0$, we must take care when integrating.

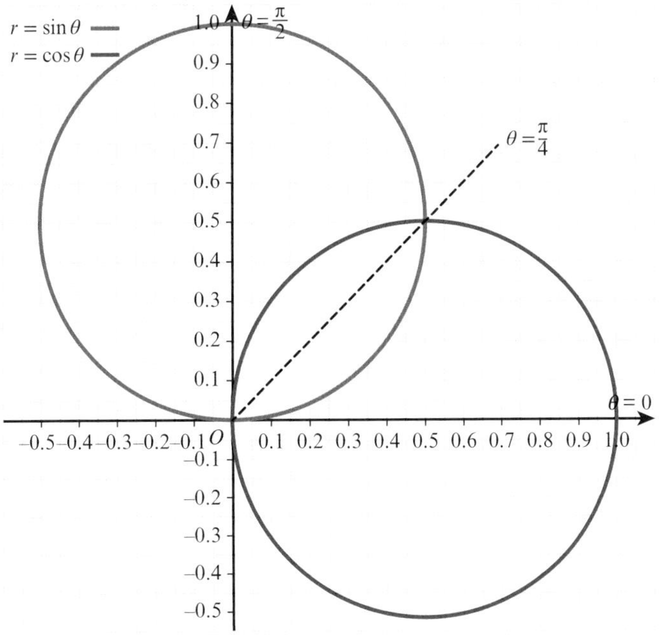

To find the area between them we must consider the limits of both each curves separately.

So $A=\frac{1}{2}\int_0^{\frac{\pi}{4}}\sin^2\theta\,d\theta+\frac{1}{2}\int_{\frac{\pi}{4}}^{\frac{\pi}{2}}\cos^2\theta\,d\theta$. We cannot combine these two integrals because the limits are different. Use the double angle formula for $\cos 2\theta$, to give

$A=\frac{1}{4}\int_0^{\frac{\pi}{4}}(1-\cos 2\theta)\,d\theta+\frac{1}{4}\int_{\frac{\pi}{4}}^{\frac{\pi}{2}}(1+\cos 2\theta)\,d\theta$.

Integrate to give $A=\frac{1}{4}\left[\theta-\frac{1}{2}\sin 2\theta\right]_0^{\frac{\pi}{4}}+\frac{1}{4}\left[\theta+\frac{1}{2}\sin 2\theta\right]_{\frac{\pi}{4}}^{\frac{\pi}{2}}$. Evaluate this to give $A=\frac{\pi}{8}-\frac{1}{4}$.

Because of the geometry of the two curves, we can obtain the same area by considering $2\times\frac{1}{2}\int_0^{\frac{\pi}{4}}\sin^2\theta\,d\theta$.

TIP

Pay close attention to the limits of both the curves in your integral. If they differ, you cannot combine the integrals and must keep them separate. Also pay special attention to the polar points of intersection. The Cartesian points of intersection may not be actual points of intersection.

WORKED EXAMPLE 5.9

Find the area enclosed between the curves $r = \sin\theta$ and $r = 1 - \sin\theta$.

Answer

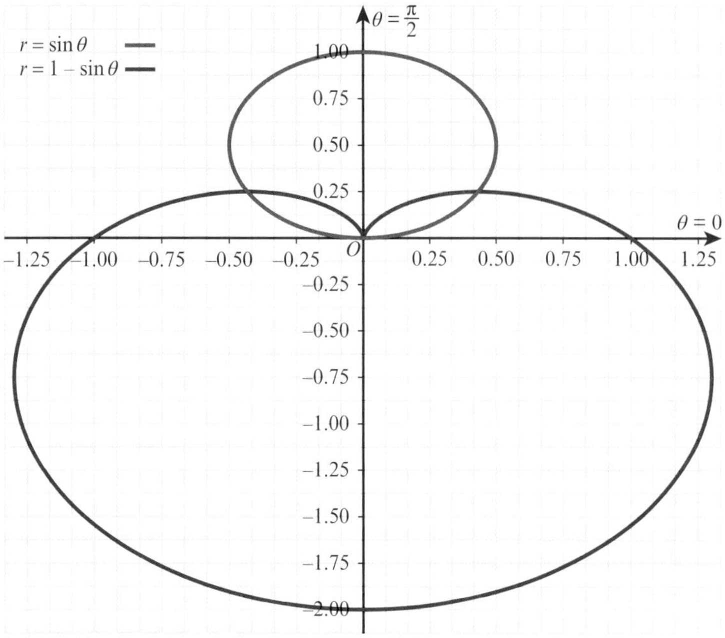

Make a sketch of the curves to identify the enclosed area.

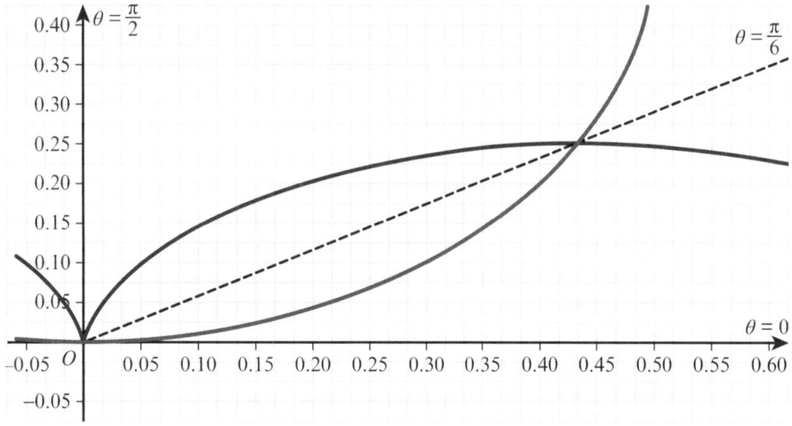

Recognise that the two areas on each side of the line $\theta = \frac{\pi}{2}$ are equal, so you only need to consider one of them.

$$A = 2 \times \frac{1}{2}\left(\int_0^{\frac{\pi}{6}} \sin^2\theta \, d\theta + \int_{\frac{\pi}{6}}^{\frac{\pi}{2}} (1 - \sin\theta)^2 \, d\theta\right)$$

Use different limits for each part of the area.

$$= \frac{1}{2}\int_0^{\frac{\pi}{6}} (1 - \cos 2\theta) \, d\theta + \int_{\frac{\pi}{6}}^{\frac{\pi}{2}} \left(\frac{3}{2} - 2\sin\theta - \frac{1}{2}\cos 2\theta\right) d\theta$$

Use the double angle formula for $\cos 2\theta$ twice.

$$= \left[\frac{\theta}{2} - \frac{1}{4}\sin 2\theta\right]_0^{\frac{\pi}{6}} + \left[\frac{3\theta}{2} + 2\cos\theta - \frac{1}{4}\sin 2\theta\right]_{\frac{\pi}{6}}^{\frac{\pi}{2}}$$

Integrate the parts separately.

$$\therefore A = \frac{7\pi}{12} - \sqrt{3}$$

Evaluate the area.

Polar curves that are looped usually contain $\sin(f(\theta))$ or $\cos(f(\theta))$. Looped regions have a maximum distance from the origin. To find this maximum distance we can look very carefully at the curve: at the point P the curve is at its greatest distance, but on either side of this point the curve gets closer to the origin.

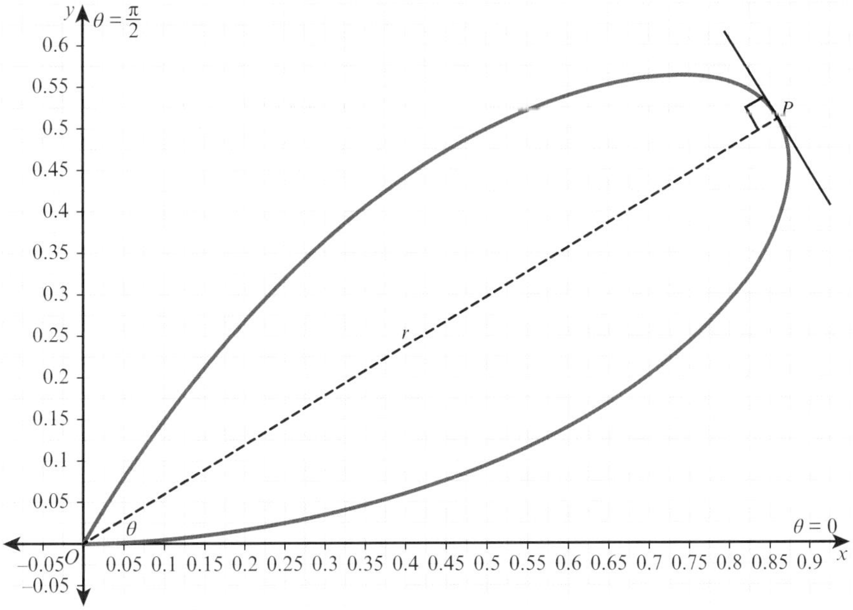

So it must be true that $\frac{dr}{d\theta} = 0$ at P. That is, r is greatest at this point. Also at this point the line OP is perpendicular to the tangent to the curve.

Consider the curve $r = e^{\theta}\sin\theta$, which is a closed loop over the interval $[0, \pi]$.

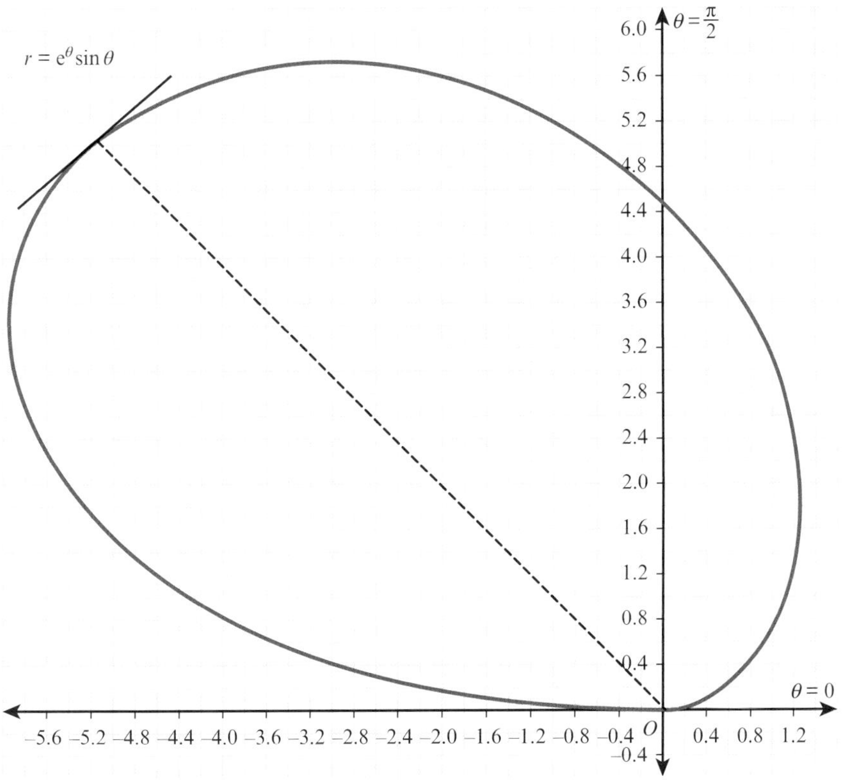

To find the maximum value for r we find $\frac{dr}{d\theta}$, which is $e^{\theta}\sin\theta + e^{\theta}\cos\theta$.

Then $e^{\theta}\sin\theta + e^{\theta}\cos\theta = 0$. So $e^{\theta}(\sin\theta + \cos\theta) = 0$. Since $e^{\theta} \neq 0$, we know $\sin\theta = -\cos\theta$.

This means $\tan\theta = -1$, and $\theta = \frac{3\pi}{4}$.

Hence, $r_{max} = e^{\frac{3\pi}{4}}\sin\frac{3\pi}{4}$, or $\frac{\sqrt{2}e^{\frac{3\pi}{4}}}{2} \approx 7.46$.

Note that not all curves will give a useful result for $\frac{dr}{d\theta}$. The curve $r = \theta$ has $\frac{dr}{d\theta} = 1$, which implies the distance of the curve from the origin is always increasing.

WORKED EXAMPLE 5.10

Determine the maximum distance of the curve $r = \theta e^{-\theta}$ from the origin.

Answer

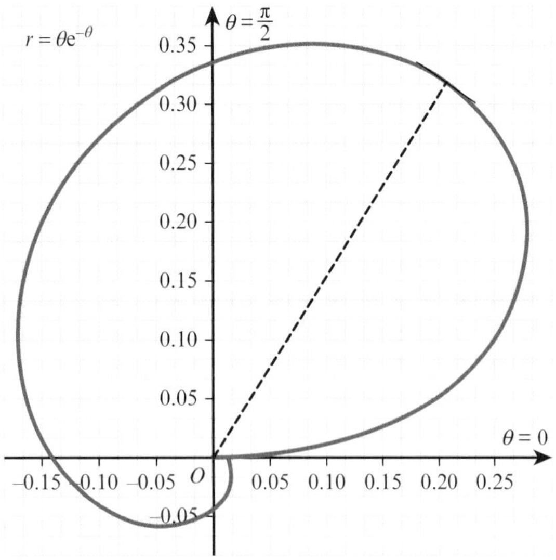

Sketch the curve first to see the approximate location of the maximum value.
(A sketch is not always necessary.)
Note: This curve is not looped but does have a maximum distance.

$\frac{dr}{d\theta} = e^{-\theta} - \theta e^{-\theta}$ — Differentiate the function.

$e^{-\theta}(1 - \theta) = 0 \Rightarrow \theta = 1$ — Set equal to zero, noting that $e^{-\theta} \neq 0$.

$r_{max} = e^{-1} = \frac{1}{e} \approx 0.368$ — Determine the maximum distance.

Since these curves also lie in the Cartesian plane, we can consider the maximum and minimum values of x and y. To do this, we must go back to the original parametric equations for polar curves.

Recall from Section 5.1 that $x = f(\theta)\cos\theta$ and $y = f(\theta)\sin\theta$. To determine maxima and minima we simply need to find $\frac{dx}{d\theta}$ or $\frac{dy}{d\theta}$.

Let us look at a curve that we have seen before: $r = 1 + \cos\theta$. We want to determine the maximum value for y.

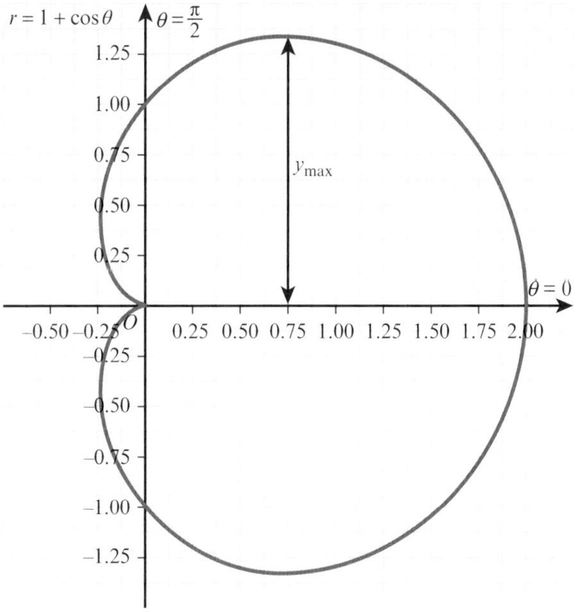

So if $y = (1 + \cos\theta)\sin\theta$, then $\dfrac{dy}{d\theta} = \cos\theta - \sin^2\theta + \cos^2\theta = \cos\theta - 1 + \cos^2\theta + \cos^2\theta$ $= 2\cos^2\theta + \cos\theta - 1$. This simplifies to $(2\cos\theta - 1)(\cos\theta + 1) = 0$.

From the derivative, it seems that $\theta = \dfrac{\pi}{3}, \pi, \dfrac{5\pi}{3}$. So for the maximum y value we use $\theta = \dfrac{\pi}{3}$.

So $y_{max} = \left(1 + \dfrac{1}{2}\right)\dfrac{\sqrt{3}}{2} = \dfrac{3\sqrt{3}}{4}$.

Note that using $\theta = \dfrac{5\pi}{3}$ gives $y_{min} = -\dfrac{3\sqrt{3}}{4}$. Using $\theta = \pi$ we get $y = 0$, since at $\theta = \pi$ we are at the cusp of the curve.

WORKED EXAMPLE 5.11

Find the minimum y value for $r = 1 + \sin\theta$.

Answer

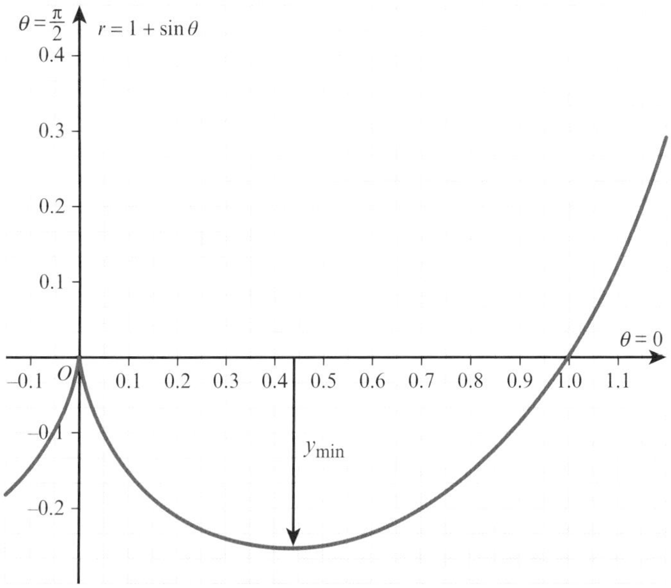

Sketch the graph first.
Note: This graph is a zoomed in portion of the curve showing the minimum y value.

$y = (1 + \sin\theta)\sin\theta$ — Write y in a simplified form.

$= \sin\theta + \sin^2\theta$

$\frac{dy}{d\theta} = \cos\theta + 2\sin\theta\cos\theta$ — Differentiate and put equal to 0.

$\Rightarrow \cos\theta(1 + 2\sin\theta) = 0$

$\theta = \frac{\pi}{2}, \frac{7\pi}{6}, \frac{3\pi}{2}, \frac{11\pi}{6}$ — Identify all possible values.

$\theta = \frac{11\pi}{6} \Rightarrow y = \left(1 - \frac{1}{2}\right) \times \left(-\frac{1}{2}\right) = -\frac{1}{4}$ — Determine the correct value for minimum y.

Finally, consider the curve $r = \sin 2\theta$ for which we want to maximise x.

Starting with $x = \sin 2\theta\cos\theta$, this gives $\frac{dx}{d\theta} = 2\cos 2\theta\cos\theta - \sin 2\theta\sin\theta$.

Using double angle formulae will lead to $\frac{dx}{d\theta} = 6\cos^3\theta - 4\cos\theta$. Then factorise to get $2\cos\theta(3\cos^2\theta - 2) = 0$.

If $\cos\theta = 0$ then $\theta = \frac{\pi}{2}, \frac{3\pi}{2}$, and we do not want these values. But if $\cos^2\theta = \frac{2}{3}$, we can see from the diagram that $\cos\theta = \sqrt{\frac{2}{3}}$ is the value we need.

If $\cos\theta = \sqrt{\frac{2}{3}}$, then $\sin\theta = \frac{1}{\sqrt{3}}$. Hence, $x_{max} = 2 \times \frac{1}{\sqrt{3}} \times \left(\sqrt{\frac{2}{3}}\right)^2 = \frac{4\sqrt{3}}{9}$.

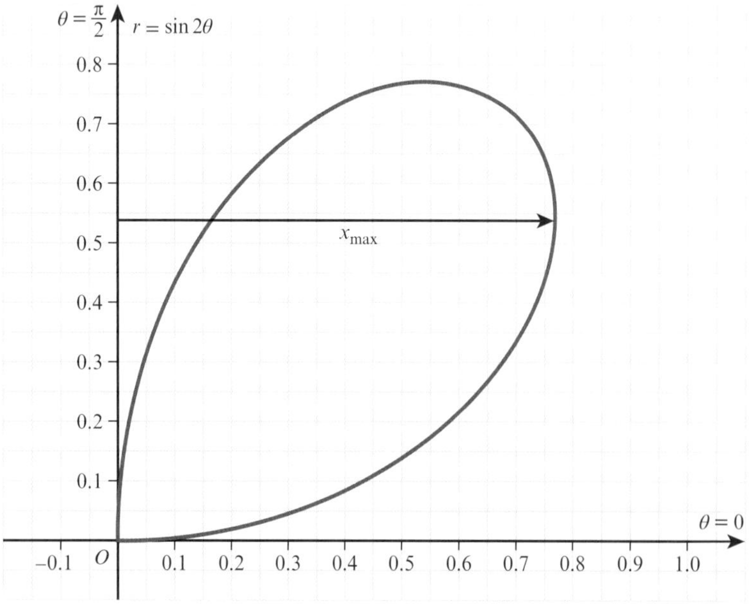

TIP

Even a basic sketch of a curve can be very helpful when you are attempting to work out maximum and minimum values.

EXERCISE 5B

M 1 Find the area contained in the curve $r = \theta$ between $\theta = \frac{\pi}{4}$ and $\theta = \frac{\pi}{2}$.

PS 2 Find the maximum distance of the curve $r = \cos\theta - \sin\theta$ from the origin, and the coordinates at which this happens.

P PS 3 Given that $r = 1 + \cos\theta$, show that the maximum value of y is $\frac{3\sqrt{3}}{4}$.

M 4 Without using a calculator, find the area bounded by the curve $r = e^{\theta}$ and the lines $\theta = 1$ and $\theta = 2$.

M 5 The curve $r = \sqrt{(\ln\theta)}$ is defined for $\frac{\pi}{2} \leqslant \theta \leqslant \pi$. Find the area bounded by the curve over this interval, giving your answer correct to 3 significant figures.

PS 6 Find the maximum distance of the curve $r = e^{\theta}\cos\left(\theta - \frac{\pi}{6}\right)$ from the origin for the interval $0 \leqslant \theta \leqslant \frac{\pi}{2}$.

PS 7 The diagram shows the curves $r = 1 + \cos\theta$ and $r = 1 + \sin\theta$. Without using a calculator, find the area of the shaded region, giving your answer in an exact form.

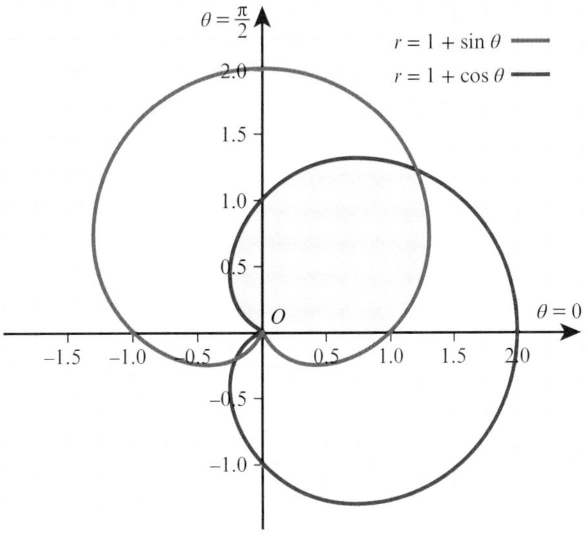

P PS 8 A polar curve is given as $r = \cos 2\theta + \cos\theta$.

a Show that $x = \cos\theta + \cos^2\theta - 2\cos^3\theta$.

b Differentiate the result in part **a** and show that for stationary points $\sin\theta(6\cos^2\theta + \cos\theta - 1) = 0$.

c Deduce the minimum value of x.

PS 9 Without using a calculator, find the area enclosed by the curve $r = \theta e^{\theta}$ and the lines $\theta = 1$ and $\theta = 2$.

WORKED PAST PAPER QUESTION

Draw a sketch of the curve C whose polar equation is $r = \theta$, for $0 \leqslant \theta \leqslant \frac{1}{2}\pi$.

On the same diagram draw the line $\theta = \alpha$, where $0 < \alpha < \frac{1}{2}\pi$.

The region bounded by C and the line $\theta = \frac{1}{2}\pi$ is denoted by R. Find the exact value of α for which the line $\theta = \alpha$ divides R into two regions of equal area.

Cambridge International AS & A Level Further Mathematics 9231 Paper 1 Q5 June 2009

Answer

Sketch of $r = \theta$ and $\theta = \alpha$.

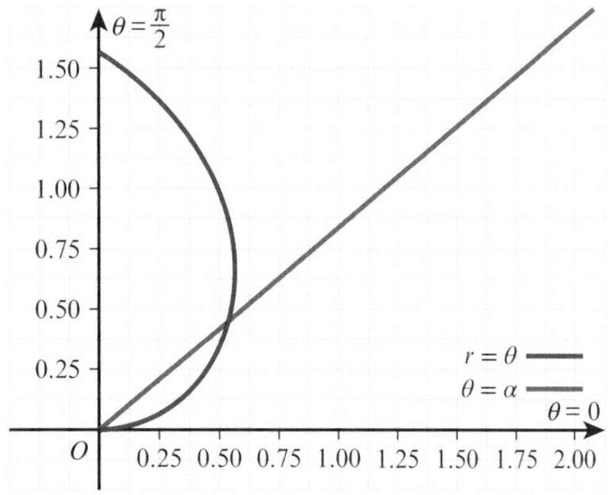

Start with $\displaystyle\int_0^{\alpha} \frac{1}{2}\theta^2 \, d\theta = \int_{\alpha}^{\frac{\pi}{2}} \frac{1}{2}\theta^2 \, d\theta$

Then $\left[\frac{1}{6}\theta^3\right]_0^{\alpha} = \left[\frac{1}{6}\theta^3\right]_{\alpha}^{\frac{\pi}{2}}$

So $\frac{1}{6}\alpha^3 = \frac{1}{6} \times \frac{\pi^3}{8} - \frac{1}{6}\alpha^3$

Therefore, $2\alpha^3 = \frac{\pi^3}{8} \Rightarrow \alpha = \frac{\pi}{2^{\frac{4}{3}}}$

Checklist of learning and understanding

Notation:

- Written as $r = f(\theta)$, where r represents the distance from the origin and θ is the angle measured from the initial line in an anticlockwise direction.
- All polar curves are such that $x = r\cos\theta$, $y = r\sin\theta$ and $x^2 + y^2 = r^2$.
- Parametric polar form is $x = f(\theta)\cos\theta$ and $y = f(\theta)\sin\theta$.

Curve sketching:

- Use a small table to work out the key values of r and θ to get a general idea of the shape.
- Determine, if any, the values of θ when $r = 0$.
- Make full use of curve symmetry and lines of symmetry; for example, cosine-based curves have symmetry about the line $\theta = 0$.

Example curves:

- Spirals

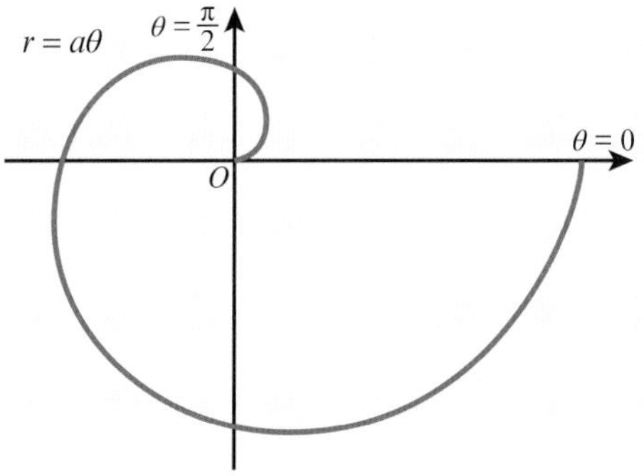

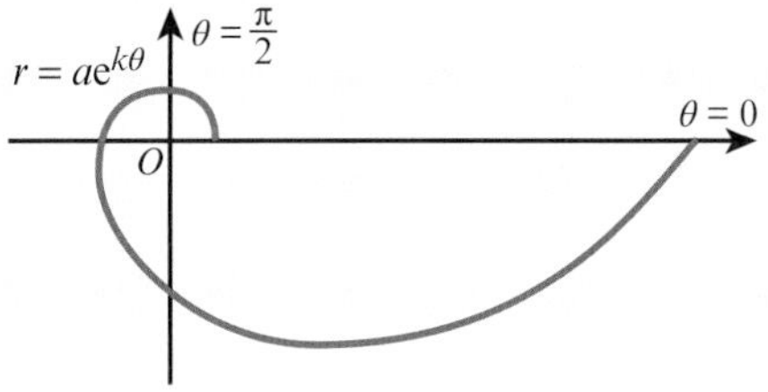

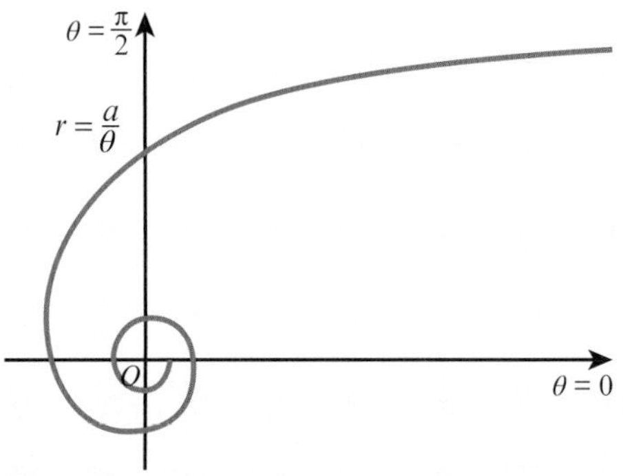

- Cardioids $(r = a + b\cos\theta)$

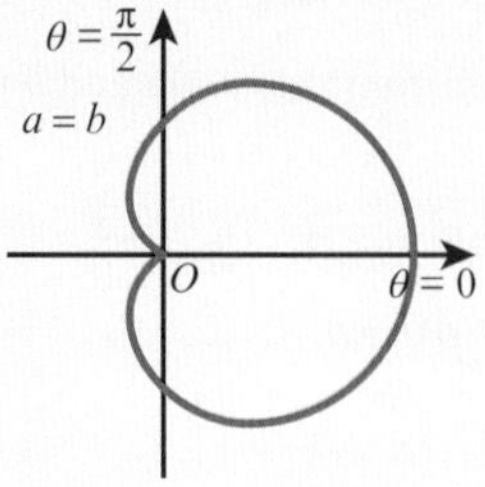

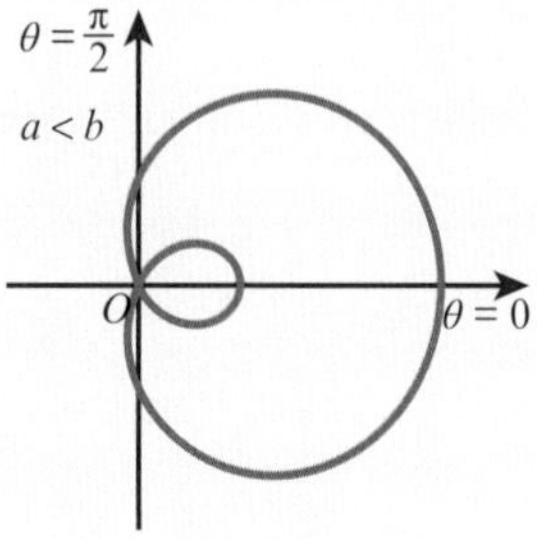

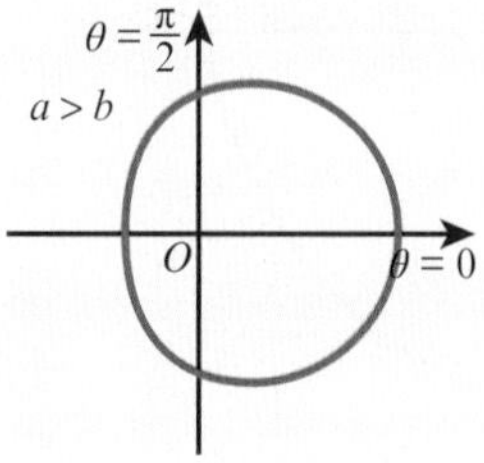

Area of a polar curve:

- The formula for area is $A = \frac{1}{2}\int_{\alpha}^{\beta} r^2\,\mathrm{d}\theta$.
- For the area between two curves, use $A = \frac{1}{2}\int_{\alpha}^{\beta}\left(r_2^2 - r_1^2\right)\mathrm{d}\theta$.
- If the limits for two curves differ, their integrals cannot be combined.

Maxima/minima:

- For the greatest distance from the origin use $\frac{\mathrm{d}r}{\mathrm{d}\theta}$.
- For the maximum or minimum distance from the line $\theta = 0$ use $\frac{\mathrm{d}y}{\mathrm{d}\theta}$.
- For the maximum or minimum distance from the line $\theta = \frac{\pi}{2}$ use $\frac{\mathrm{d}x}{\mathrm{d}\theta}$.

END-OF-CHAPTER REVIEW EXERCISE 5

1 The curve C has polar equation $r = a(1 - e^{-\theta})$, where a is a positive constant and $0 \leqslant \theta < 2\pi$.

i Draw a sketch of C.

ii Show that the area of the region bounded by C and the lines $\theta = \ln 2$ and $\theta = \ln 4$ is $\frac{1}{2}a^2\left(\ln 2 - \frac{13}{32}\right)$.

Cambridge International AS & A Level Further Mathematics 9231 Paper 11 Q2 June 2010

2 The curve C has polar equation $r = 3 + 2\cos\theta$, for $-\pi < \theta \leqslant \pi$. The straight line l has polar equation $r\cos\theta = 2$.

Sketch both C and l on a single diagram.

Find the polar coordinates of the points of intersection of C and l.

The region R is enclosed by C and l, and contains the pole. Find the area of R.

Cambridge International AS & A Level Further Mathematics 9231 Paper 11 Q10 November 2011

3 The curve C has polar equation $r = 2\sin\theta(1 - \cos\theta)$, for $0 \leqslant \theta \leqslant \pi$.

Find $\frac{dr}{d\theta}$ and hence find the polar coordinates of the point of C that is furthest from the pole.

Sketch C.

Find the exact area of the sector from $\theta = 0$ to $\theta = \frac{1}{4}\pi$.

Cambridge International AS & A Level Further Mathematics 9231 Paper 13 Q10 November 2013

Chapter 6
Vectors

In this chapter you will learn how to:

- use the equation of a plane in any form
- use the vector product to determine a common perpendicular, as well as understanding its applications
- use the equations of lines and planes together with scalar and vector products to solve problems concerning distances, angles and intersections.

PREREQUISITE KNOWLEDGE

Where it comes from	What you should be able to do	Check your skills
AS & A Level Mathematics Pure Mathematics 2 & 3, Chapter 9	Find the vector equation of a line.	1 Use the points given to determine the vector equation of the line passing through them. a $A(2, 3, 1)$, $B(4, 5, -3)$ b $A(3, 0, 1)$, $B(5, 6, 2)$
AS & A Level Mathematics Pure Mathematics 2 & 3, Chapter 9	Apply the scalar product to help to determine the angle between two vectors.	2 Find the angle between the following pairs of vectors. a $\mathbf{u} = \mathbf{i} + 3\mathbf{j} + \mathbf{k}$, $\mathbf{v} = -\mathbf{j} + 3\mathbf{k}$ b $\mathbf{u} = 2\mathbf{i} + 5\mathbf{j} - \mathbf{k}$, $\mathbf{v} = 4\mathbf{i} - 2\mathbf{j} + 4\mathbf{k}$

Why do we need vectors?

Vectors describe anything that has both magnitude and direction. You may not realise it but we use vectors when we consider how to kick a football into a goal, and how to create high-resolution, believable graphics in a computer game.

You have already learned about vectors in AS & A Level Mathematics Pure Mathematics 3, including work on vector equations of lines and the scalar product. This chapter extends these ideas to planes, links planes to systems of linear equations and matrices, and introduces the vector product and some of its applications.

KEY POINT 6.1

The **scalar product** is $\mathbf{a}\cdot\mathbf{b} = |\mathbf{a}||\mathbf{b}|\cos\theta$, where θ is the angle between the directions of vectors **a** and **b**.

6.1 The vector product rule

You have already met the scalar product (as shown in Key point 6.1) in the AS & A Level Mathematics course. Now we will examine the relationship between two non-parallel vectors and a common perpendicular. This rule is known as the **cross product** or **vector product**.

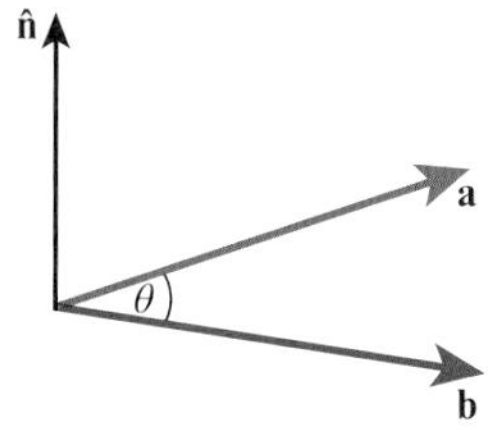

This is written as $\mathbf{a} \times \mathbf{b} = |\mathbf{a}||\mathbf{b}|\sin\theta\,\hat{\mathbf{n}}$, where $\hat{\mathbf{n}}$ is a **unit vector** that is a **common perpendicular** to **a** and **b**. We will concentrate on the left-hand side first.

If two vectors, $\mathbf{a} = a_1\mathbf{i} + a_2\mathbf{j} + a_3\mathbf{k}$ and $\mathbf{b} = b_1\mathbf{i} + b_2\mathbf{j} + b_3\mathbf{k}$, both have a common perpendicular $x\mathbf{i} + y\mathbf{j} + z\mathbf{k}$, we can use the scalar product twice to produce $a_1x + a_2y + a_3z = 0$ and $b_1x + b_2y + b_3z = 0$. Solving these (you do not need to solve these) gives $x = a_2b_3 - a_3b_2$, $y = a_3b_1 - a_1b_3$, $z = a_1b_2 - a_2b_1$.

So our common perpendicular is $\begin{pmatrix} a_2b_3 - a_3b_2 \\ a_3b_1 - a_1b_3 \\ a_1b_2 - a_2b_1 \end{pmatrix}$.

Another way of getting the same result is to consider the **vector determinant** $\begin{vmatrix} \mathbf{i} & \mathbf{j} & \mathbf{k} \\ a_1 & a_2 & a_3 \\ b_1 & b_2 & b_3 \end{vmatrix}$, then write this as $\begin{vmatrix} a_2 & a_3 \\ b_2 & b_3 \end{vmatrix}\mathbf{i} - \begin{vmatrix} a_1 & a_3 \\ b_1 & b_3 \end{vmatrix}\mathbf{j} + \begin{vmatrix} a_1 & a_2 \\ b_1 & b_2 \end{vmatrix}\mathbf{k}$. Simplifying each minor determinant will lead to the same result as before.

We have seen this method in Chapter 4. We will use the determinant method throughout this text.

Consider the two vectors $3\mathbf{i} - \mathbf{j} + 5\mathbf{k}$ and $2\mathbf{i} + 7\mathbf{j} - \mathbf{k}$. Denote a normal vector as $\mathbf{n}$, so

$$\mathbf{n} = \begin{vmatrix} \mathbf{i} & \mathbf{j} & \mathbf{k} \\ 3 & -1 & 5 \\ 2 & 7 & -1 \end{vmatrix} = (1-35)\mathbf{i} - (-3-10)\mathbf{j} + (21-(-2))\mathbf{k} = -34\mathbf{i} + 13\mathbf{j} + 23\mathbf{k}.$$

So $\mathbf{n} = -34\mathbf{i} + 13\mathbf{j} + 23\mathbf{k}$ is a vector perpendicular to both of the given vectors.

REWIND

We saw in Chapter 4 that for the 3×3 matrix $\begin{pmatrix} a & b & c \\ d & e & f \\ g & h & i \end{pmatrix}$, the determinant is given by $a\begin{vmatrix} e & f \\ h & i \end{vmatrix} - b\begin{vmatrix} d & f \\ g & i \end{vmatrix} + c\begin{vmatrix} d & e \\ g & h \end{vmatrix}$.

WORKED EXAMPLE 6.1

In each case, find a vector perpendicular to each pair of vectors given.

a $-4\mathbf{i} + 2\mathbf{j} + \mathbf{k}$ and $3\mathbf{i} - 7\mathbf{k}$
b $-2\mathbf{i} + 12\mathbf{j} - 9\mathbf{k}$ and $4\mathbf{j} + 5\mathbf{k}$
c $\mathbf{i} + \mathbf{j} + 2\mathbf{k}$ and $2\mathbf{i} + 7\mathbf{j} - 6\mathbf{k}$

Answer

a $\mathbf{n} = \begin{vmatrix} \mathbf{i} & \mathbf{j} & \mathbf{k} \\ -4 & 2 & 1 \\ 3 & 0 & -7 \end{vmatrix} = (-14-0)\mathbf{i} - (28-3)\mathbf{j} + (0-6)\mathbf{k}$ — Find the cross product of the vectors.

$= -14\mathbf{i} - 25\mathbf{j} - 6\mathbf{k}$ or $\mathbf{n} = 14\mathbf{i} + 25\mathbf{j} + 6\mathbf{k}$ — Take out the factor -1.

Note that a multiple of the normal vector found is still normal to the given vectors.

b $\mathbf{n} = \begin{vmatrix} \mathbf{i} & \mathbf{j} & \mathbf{k} \\ -2 & 12 & -9 \\ 0 & 4 & 5 \end{vmatrix} = (60-(-36))\mathbf{i} - (-10-0)\mathbf{j} + (-8-0)\mathbf{k}$ — Find the cross product of the vectors.

$= 96\mathbf{i} + 10\mathbf{j} - 8\mathbf{k}$ or $\mathbf{n} = 48\mathbf{i} + 5\mathbf{j} - 4\mathbf{k}$ — Take out the factor 2.

c $\mathbf{n} = \begin{vmatrix} \mathbf{i} & \mathbf{j} & \mathbf{k} \\ 1 & 1 & 2 \\ 2 & 7 & -6 \end{vmatrix} = (-6-14)\mathbf{i} - (-6-4)\mathbf{j} + (7-2)\mathbf{k}$ — Find the cross product of the vectors.

$= -20\mathbf{i} + 10\mathbf{j} + 5\mathbf{k}$ or $\mathbf{n} = -4\mathbf{i} + 2\mathbf{j} + \mathbf{k}$ — Take out the factor 5.

Recall the vector product $\mathbf{a} \times \mathbf{b} = |\mathbf{a}||\mathbf{b}|\sin\theta\,\hat{\mathbf{n}}$. Next, let us focus on the right side of the equation for the vector product, $|\mathbf{a}||\mathbf{b}|\sin\theta\,\hat{\mathbf{n}}$.

Work out the magnitude of this. As the unit vector is magnitude 1, this expression reduces to the area of a parallelogram as shown in the diagram. This means that the area of a parallelogram can also be written as $|\mathbf{a} \times \mathbf{b}|$.

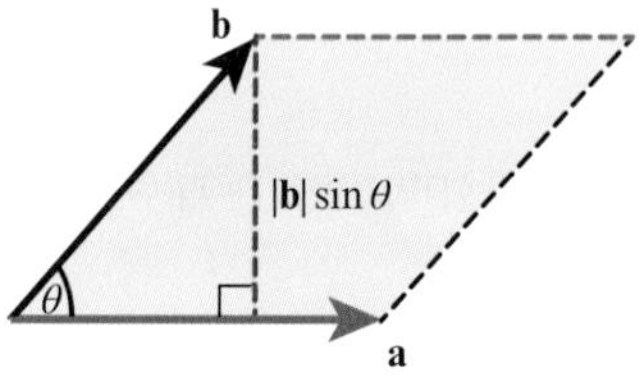

So the magnitude of the vector normal to both **a** and **b** is actually the area of a parallelogram.

Look at the magnitude of the right side of the vector product again and halve this result. This gives $\frac{1}{2}|\mathbf{a}||\mathbf{b}|\sin\theta$ which is the area of a triangle. It implies that the area of a triangle can be written as $\frac{1}{2}|\mathbf{a}\times\mathbf{b}|$.

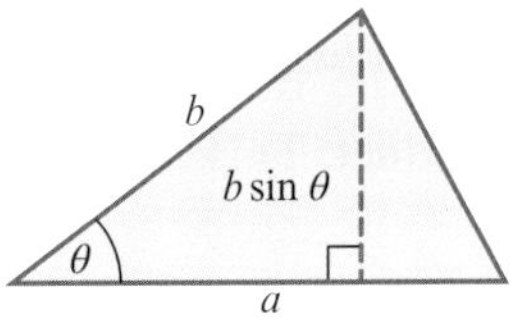

Consider the three points $O(0, 0, 0)$, $A(-2, 3, 6)$ and $B(2, 2, 1)$. We will find the area of the triangle OAB, using both the vector product and scalar product methods. Here the vectors are $\overrightarrow{OA} = -2\mathbf{i} + 3\mathbf{j} + 6\mathbf{k}$ and $\overrightarrow{OB} = 2\mathbf{i} + 2\mathbf{j} + \mathbf{k}$.

Vector (cross) product:

Let $\mathbf{n} = \begin{vmatrix} \mathbf{i} & \mathbf{j} & \mathbf{k} \\ -2 & 3 & 6 \\ 2 & 2 & 1 \end{vmatrix} = -9\mathbf{i} + 14\mathbf{j} - 10\mathbf{k}$, so $|\mathbf{n}| = |\mathbf{a}\times\mathbf{b}| = \sqrt{9^2 + 14^2 + 10^2} = \sqrt{377}$.

Hence, the area is $\frac{1}{2}|\mathbf{a}\times\mathbf{b}| = \frac{1}{2}\sqrt{377}$.

Scalar (dot) product:

$|\overrightarrow{OA}| = \sqrt{2^2 + 3^2 + 6^2} = 7$ and $|\overrightarrow{OB}| = \sqrt{2^2 + 2^2 + 1^2} = 3$.

$$\cos\theta = \frac{\overrightarrow{OA}\cdot\overrightarrow{OB}}{|\overrightarrow{OA}||\overrightarrow{OB}|} = \frac{-4+6+6}{21} = \frac{8}{21}, \text{ so } \sin\theta = \sqrt{\left(1 - \frac{64}{441}\right)} = \frac{\sqrt{377}}{21}.$$

So the area of the triangle is $\frac{1}{2}|\mathbf{a}||\mathbf{b}|\sin\theta = \frac{1}{2}\times 7\times 3\times\frac{\sqrt{377}}{21} = \frac{1}{2}\sqrt{377}$.

We can see that the area is the same in both cases. The vector product method is more convenient as we do not need to find the angle to determine the area of the triangle.

WORKED EXAMPLE 6.2

Find the area of the triangle ABC, given that the vertices are $A(4, 1, -2)$, $B(5, 5, 6)$ and $C(0, 3, 7)$.

Answer

$\overrightarrow{AB} = \mathbf{i} + 4\mathbf{j} + 8\mathbf{k}$
$\overrightarrow{BC} = -5\mathbf{i} - 2\mathbf{j} + \mathbf{k}$ — Find any two sides in vector form.

$\begin{vmatrix} \mathbf{i} & \mathbf{j} & \mathbf{k} \\ 1 & 4 & 8 \\ -5 & -2 & 1 \end{vmatrix} = 20\mathbf{i} - 41\mathbf{j} + 18\mathbf{k}$ — Find the cross product of the two vectors to get a common perpendicular.

$|20\mathbf{i} - 41\mathbf{j} + 18\mathbf{k}| = \sqrt{20^2 + 41^2 + 18^2}$
$= \sqrt{2405}$ — Find the magnitude of the common perpendicular. This is $|\mathbf{a}\times\mathbf{b}|$.

$\therefore$ Area $= \frac{1}{2}\sqrt{2405}$ — Divide by 2 to get the area.

E An extension of this is the calculation of the volume of a tetrahedron. The volume of any tetrahedron is given as $\frac{1}{3}\times$ base area $\times$ perpendicular height. From the diagram, we can say this is $\frac{1}{3}\times\frac{1}{2}|\mathbf{a}\times\mathbf{b}|\times h$.

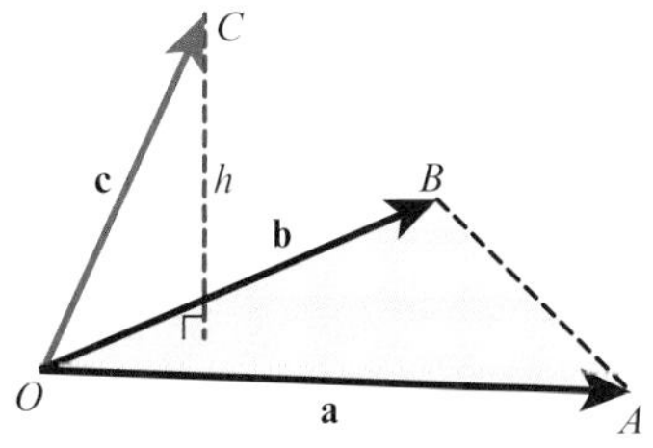

Now the height, h, is the projection of $\mathbf{c}$ in the direction of $\mathbf{n}$, where $\mathbf{n} = \mathbf{a}\times\mathbf{b}$.

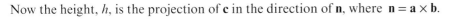

The volume can be written as $\frac{1}{6}|(\mathbf{a} \times \mathbf{b})\cdot\mathbf{c}|$. The part $(\mathbf{a} \times \mathbf{b})\cdot\mathbf{c}$ is known as the scalar triple product. This is not part of the syllabus, but is interesting to know.

For example, consider the three points $A(2, -1, 1)$, $B(-3, 2, 2)$ and $C(4, 2, -7)$, all relative to an origin at $O(0, 0, 0)$.

So $\overrightarrow{OA} = 2\mathbf{i} - \mathbf{j} + \mathbf{k}$, $\overrightarrow{OB} = -3\mathbf{i} + 2\mathbf{j} + 2\mathbf{k}$ and $\overrightarrow{OC} = 4\mathbf{i} + 2\mathbf{j} - 7\mathbf{k}$. Then find the vector product of any two of these, such as $\overrightarrow{OA} \times \overrightarrow{OB} = \begin{vmatrix} \mathbf{i} & \mathbf{j} & \mathbf{k} \\ 2 & -1 & 1 \\ -3 & 2 & 2 \end{vmatrix} = -4\mathbf{i} - 7\mathbf{j} + \mathbf{k}$. Then $(\overrightarrow{OA} \times \overrightarrow{OB})\cdot\overrightarrow{OC} = -16 - 14 - 7 = -37$.

The last step to find $\frac{1}{6}|(\mathbf{a} \times \mathbf{b})\cdot\mathbf{c}|$ is to take the positive value of -37 and divide by 6 to get $\frac{37}{6}$.

WORKED EXAMPLE 6.3

Find the volume of the tetrahedron $OABC$, where $\overrightarrow{OA} = \mathbf{i} + 2\mathbf{j} + 2\mathbf{k}$, $\overrightarrow{OB} = 3\mathbf{i} - 4\mathbf{j} + \mathbf{k}$ and $\overrightarrow{OC} = 6\mathbf{i} - 2\mathbf{j} - \mathbf{k}$.

Answer

$\overrightarrow{OA} \times \overrightarrow{OB} = \begin{vmatrix} \mathbf{i} & \mathbf{j} & \mathbf{k} \\ 1 & 2 & 2 \\ 3 & -4 & 1 \end{vmatrix} = 10\mathbf{i} + 5\mathbf{j} - 10\mathbf{k}$ — Find the cross product of any two directions to get a normal.

$(\overrightarrow{OA} \times \overrightarrow{OB})\cdot\overrightarrow{OC} = 60 - 10 + 10 = 60$ — Dot this normal with the other vector.

$\therefore V = \frac{1}{6} \times 60 = 10$ — Take the magnitude and divide by 6.

EXPLORE 6.1

Using the four points $A(0, 5, 2)$, $B(3, -3, 1)$, $C(2, 7, -1)$, $D(3, 0, -2)$ and working in groups, confirm that no matter what vectors are used, you will always get the same volume for the tetrahedron $ABCD$.

EXERCISE 6A

1 In each case, find the value of p such that the vectors given are perpendicular.

a $p\mathbf{i} + 2\mathbf{j} + 3\mathbf{k}$ and $4\mathbf{i} + \mathbf{j} + 2\mathbf{k}$

b $3\mathbf{i} + 5\mathbf{j} + 2\mathbf{k}$ and $\mathbf{i} + p\mathbf{j} - 4\mathbf{k}$

PS 2 The cross product of $\mathbf{i} + \alpha\mathbf{j} + \mathbf{k}$ and $3\mathbf{i} + 4\mathbf{k}$ is $8\mathbf{i} - \mathbf{j} - 6\mathbf{k}$. What is the value of α?

PS 3 Given that the cross product of $2\mathbf{i} + \alpha\mathbf{j} - \mathbf{k}$ and $\beta\mathbf{i} + 4\mathbf{j} + 2\mathbf{k}$ is $10\mathbf{i} - 5\mathbf{j} + 5\mathbf{k}$, find the values of α and β.

4 Find the common perpendicular to the two vectors given in each case.

a $\mathbf{a} = 5\mathbf{i} - 8\mathbf{j} + 2\mathbf{k}$, $\mathbf{b} = 3\mathbf{i} - 4\mathbf{j} - \mathbf{k}$

b $\mathbf{a} = 2\mathbf{i} - 10\mathbf{j} + 3\mathbf{k}$, $\mathbf{b} = 5\mathbf{i} - 7\mathbf{j} + 4\mathbf{k}$

c $\mathbf{a} = 12\mathbf{j} + 7\mathbf{k}$, $\mathbf{b} = -6\mathbf{i} + \mathbf{j} + 9\mathbf{k}$

d $\mathbf{a} = 2\mathbf{i} + 17\mathbf{j}$, $\mathbf{b} = 4\mathbf{i} + 8\mathbf{j} - 13\mathbf{k}$

5 Find the area of the triangle in each of the following cases.

a Triangle OAB with $A(6, -7, 21)$ and $B(3, 2, -5)$.

b Triangle ABC with $A(0, 0, 2)$, $B(-4, 9, 3)$ and $C(2, 0, 7)$.

c Triangle ABQ with $A(5, 1, 2)$, $B(6, -9, 0)$ and $\overrightarrow{OB} = 3\overrightarrow{OQ}$.

d Triangle BPQ with $A(1, 3, 4)$, $B(3, 7, 8)$, $C(7, 0, 16)$, $\overrightarrow{AP} = \frac{1}{2}\overrightarrow{AB}$ and $3\overrightarrow{PC} = 5\overrightarrow{PQ}$.

PS 6 Two points are given as $A(2, 1, 3)$ and $B(5, k, 7)$. Given that the triangle OAB has area $\frac{\sqrt{3}}{2}$, determine the possible values of k.

E 7 In each of the following cases, determine the volume of the tetrahedron.

a Tetrahedron $OABC$ with $A(-2, 4, 1)$, $B(8, 1, 0)$ and $C(5, 6, -7)$.

b Tetrahedron $ABCD$ with $A(1, 1, -1)$, $B(0, 4, 0)$, $C(0, 6, 7)$ and $D(3, -7, 7)$.

c Tetrahedron $ABCP$ with $A(2, 5, 0)$, $B(3, -1, 4)$, $C(0, 6, 7)$ and $\overrightarrow{OP} = 3\overrightarrow{OA}$.

PS 8 The tetrahedron $A(2, 5, m)$, $B(1, 7, 2)$, $C(1, 8, 3)$ and $D(9, 8, -1)$ has volume 2. Determine the value of m.

6.2 Vector equation of a line

You have met the vector equation of a line in the AS & A Level Mathematics course. This section will build on what you have learned and extend these ideas.

The **vector equation of a line** is $\mathbf{r} = \mathbf{a} + \mathbf{b}t$, where $\mathbf{a}$ is a **position vector** that goes from the origin to the line, and $\mathbf{b}$ is the direction vector of the line. t is a variable scalar, and different values of t can be used to find different points that are on the line.

Consider two points P and Q with coordinates $P(1, 2, 4)$ and $Q(2, -1, 3)$. The direction $\mathbf{b} = \overrightarrow{PQ}$ is $\mathbf{i} - 3\mathbf{j} - \mathbf{k}$. Then, using either point for the vector $\mathbf{a}$, $\mathbf{r} = \mathbf{i} + 2\mathbf{j} + 4\mathbf{k} + (\mathbf{i} - 3\mathbf{j} - \mathbf{k})t$. This represents the vector equation of a line which passes through P and Q. Making $t = 0$ in this equation gives the position vector of point P and making $t = 1$ gives the position vector of Q.

WORKED EXAMPLE 6.4

Find the vector equation of the line in each case.

a $A(2, 3, 5)$, $B(1, 1, 2)$. The line through A and B.
b $A(-1, 4, 1)$, $B(0, 2, -3)$, $C(1, 1, 5)$. The line through C parallel to the line through A and B.

Answer

a $\overrightarrow{AB} = -\mathbf{i} - 2\mathbf{j} - 3\mathbf{k}$ — Find the vector between the two points.

$\mathbf{r} = 2\mathbf{i} + 3\mathbf{j} + 5\mathbf{k} + (-\mathbf{i} - 2\mathbf{j} - 3\mathbf{k})t$ — State the equation of the line.

b $\overrightarrow{AB} = \mathbf{i} - 2\mathbf{j} - 4\mathbf{k}$ — Find the direction vector $\overrightarrow{AB}$.

$\mathbf{r} = \mathbf{i} + \mathbf{j} + 5\mathbf{k} + (\mathbf{i} - 2\mathbf{j} - 4\mathbf{k})t$ — State the equation of the line. We use the position vector of C and the direction vector $\overrightarrow{AB}$ since the line is parallel to the line through A and B.

One application that you may have met before is the shortest distance between a point and a line. The diagram shows a line with direction vector **b** where the distance from P to the line is to be minimised.

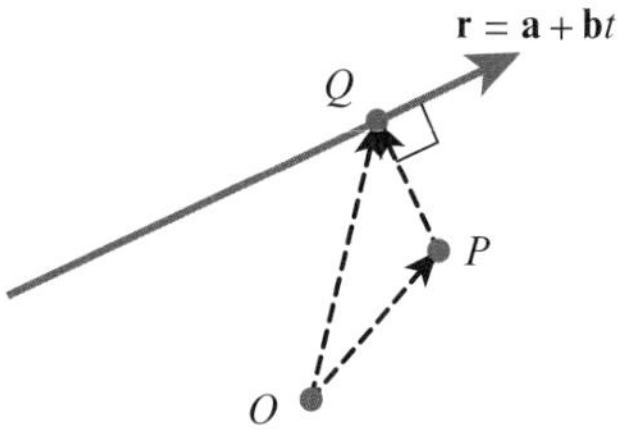

Note that, for some point Q, the vector $\overrightarrow{PQ}$ is perpendicular to **b**, or $\overrightarrow{PQ}\cdot\mathbf{b} = 0$. Since Q is on the line, it follows that $\overrightarrow{OQ} = \mathbf{r}$. If we know $\overrightarrow{OQ}$ in terms of t and we know $\overrightarrow{OP}$ in terms of t, we can find $\overrightarrow{PQ}$ which is $\overrightarrow{OQ} - \overrightarrow{OP}$.

Using $\overrightarrow{PQ}\cdot\mathbf{b} = 0$, we can determine the t value for Q and the vector $\overrightarrow{PQ}$. We can now find $|\overrightarrow{PQ}|$ which is the shortest distance from P to the line.

For example, consider a line with equation $\mathbf{r} = \mathbf{i} + \mathbf{j} + 5\mathbf{k} + (2\mathbf{i} - 2\mathbf{j} + \mathbf{k})t$ and let the point be $P(1, 1, 2)$. To find the shortest distance from P to the line, first state that $\overrightarrow{OP} = \mathbf{i} + \mathbf{j} + 2\mathbf{k}$ and $\overrightarrow{OQ} = (1 + 2t)\mathbf{i} + (1 - 2t)\mathbf{j} + (5 + t)\mathbf{k}$.

Then $\overrightarrow{PQ} = 2t\mathbf{i} - 2t\mathbf{j} + (3 + t)\mathbf{k}$.

We use the component form of $\overrightarrow{PQ}\cdot\mathbf{b} = 0$ to get $4t + 4t + 3 + t = 0 \Rightarrow t = -\frac{1}{3}$. Hence, $\overrightarrow{PQ} = -\frac{2}{3}\mathbf{i} + \frac{2}{3}\mathbf{j} + \frac{8}{3}\mathbf{k}$.

Therefore, the shortest distance from P to the line is $\sqrt{\frac{4}{9} + \frac{4}{9} + \frac{64}{9}} = 2\sqrt{2}$.

WORKED EXAMPLE 6.5

Find the shortest distance between the point $P(2, 1, 4)$ and the line $\mathbf{r} = 4\mathbf{i} + 4\mathbf{j} + 5\mathbf{k} + (\mathbf{i} + \mathbf{j} + \mathbf{k})t$.

Answer

$\overrightarrow{OP} = 2\mathbf{i} + \mathbf{j} + 4\mathbf{k}$ — State position of point.

$\overrightarrow{OQ} = (4 + t)\mathbf{i} + (4 + t)\mathbf{j} + (5 + t)\mathbf{k}$ — State a general point on the line.

$\Rightarrow \overrightarrow{PQ} = (2 + t)\mathbf{i} + (3 + t)\mathbf{j} + (1 + t)\mathbf{k}$ — Determine the vector $\overrightarrow{PQ}$ in terms of t.

Let line direction be $\mathbf{b} = \mathbf{i} + \mathbf{j} + \mathbf{k}$ — Dot vectors and determine the value of t.

$\overrightarrow{PQ}.\mathbf{b} = 0 \Rightarrow 6 + 3t = 0$

$\therefore t = -2$

$\therefore \overrightarrow{PQ} = \mathbf{j} - \mathbf{k}$ — Find $\overrightarrow{PQ}$ and hence the shortest distance.

$\Rightarrow |\overrightarrow{PQ}| = \sqrt{2}$

TIP

Make a sketch of this type of problem. Draw any vector through a point P, then construct a vector triangle from an origin.

An alternative method to the one shown in Worked example 6.5 is to make use of the vector product. If we first consider the vector $\overrightarrow{AP}$, then the shortest distance from P to the line is $|\overrightarrow{AP}|\sin\theta$. Next, multiply by the magnitude of the unit vector $|\mathbf{u}|$. This does not change the distance.

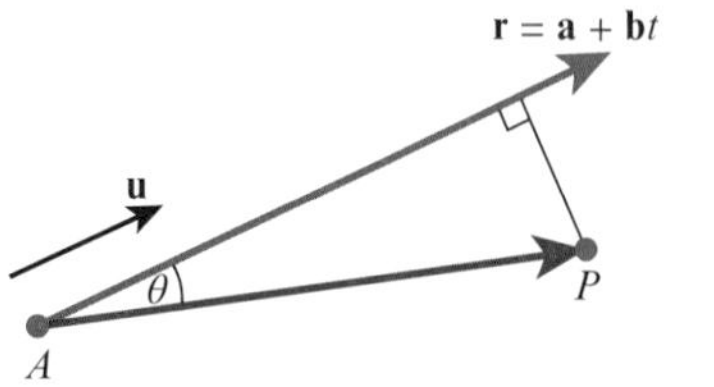

Now the distance is $|\overrightarrow{AP}||\mathbf{u}|\sin\theta$ or $|\overrightarrow{AP} \times \mathbf{u}|$, using the vector product. So, in this example, the unit vector is $\mathbf{u} = \frac{1}{\sqrt{3}}(\mathbf{i} + \mathbf{j} + \mathbf{k})$. The magnitude of $\mathbf{i} + \mathbf{j} + \mathbf{k}$ is $\sqrt{1^2 + 1^2 + 1^2} = \sqrt{3}$. Given $A(4, 4, 5)$ and $P(2, 1, 4)$, $\overrightarrow{AP} = -2\mathbf{i} - 3\mathbf{j} - \mathbf{k}$.

Then $\overrightarrow{AP} \times \mathbf{u} = \frac{1}{\sqrt{3}}\begin{vmatrix} \mathbf{i} & \mathbf{j} & \mathbf{k} \\ -2 & -3 & -1 \\ 1 & 1 & 1 \end{vmatrix} = \frac{1}{\sqrt{3}}(-2\mathbf{i} + \mathbf{j} + \mathbf{k})$. Hence, $|\overrightarrow{AP} \times \mathbf{u}| = \frac{1}{\sqrt{3}} \times \sqrt{6} = \sqrt{2}$.

This is the same result but takes much less work. Remember that the vector **u** is the unit vector of the line's direction **b**.

WORKED EXAMPLE 6.6

Find the shortest distance between the point $P(3, 2, -1)$ and the line $\mathbf{r} = 3\mathbf{j} - 4\mathbf{k} + (-\mathbf{i} + 2\mathbf{j} - \mathbf{k})t$.

Answer

$A(0, 3, -4) \Rightarrow \overrightarrow{AP} = 3\mathbf{i} - \mathbf{j} + 3\mathbf{k}$ — State the vector $\overrightarrow{AP}$.

$\mathbf{b} = -\mathbf{i} + 2\mathbf{j} - \mathbf{k} \Rightarrow \mathbf{u} = \frac{1}{\sqrt{6}}(-\mathbf{i} + 2\mathbf{j} - \mathbf{k})$ — Determine the unit vector in the direction **b**.

$\therefore \overrightarrow{AP} \times \mathbf{u} = \frac{1}{\sqrt{6}}\begin{vmatrix} \mathbf{i} & \mathbf{j} & \mathbf{k} \\ 3 & -1 & 3 \\ -1 & 2 & -1 \end{vmatrix} = \frac{1}{\sqrt{6}}(-5\mathbf{i} + 5\mathbf{k})$ — Find the cross product of the two vectors.

Hence $|\overrightarrow{AP} \times \mathbf{u}| = \frac{1}{\sqrt{6}} \times \sqrt{(-5)^2 + 5^2} = \frac{1}{\sqrt{6}} \times \sqrt{50}$

$= \frac{1}{\sqrt{6}} \times 5\sqrt{2} = \frac{5\sqrt{3}}{3}$ — Find the shortest distance.

This leads us to another useful result. Finding the shortest distance between two straight lines uses a similar approach.

Imagine two lines, $\mathbf{r}_1 = \mathbf{a}_1 + \mathbf{b}_1 t$ and $\mathbf{r}_2 = \mathbf{a}_2 + \mathbf{b}_2 t$, passing through points P and Q, respectively. These lines are also such that $\mathbf{a}_1 = \overrightarrow{OS}$ and $\mathbf{a}_2 = \overrightarrow{OT}$, and the direction $\overrightarrow{PQ}$ is parallel to $\mathbf{b}_1 \times \mathbf{b}_2$. We are looking for the distance $|\overrightarrow{PQ}|$. This is equal to $|\overrightarrow{ST}|\cos\theta$.

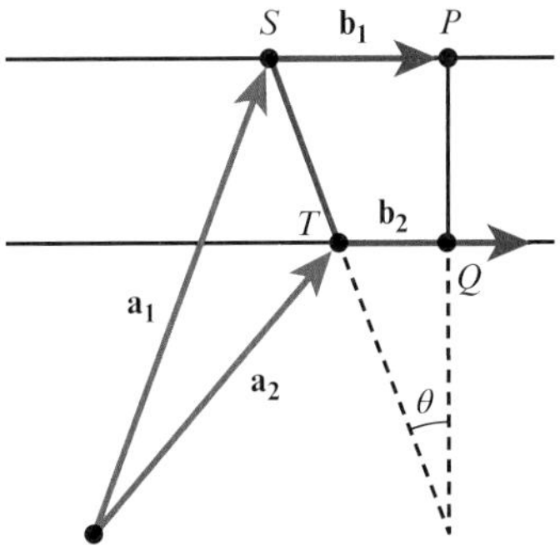

Remember that $|\overrightarrow{ST}|$ must be greater than $|\overrightarrow{PQ}|$ since $|\overrightarrow{PQ}|$ is the shortest distance between the two lines.

So if the distance is $|\overrightarrow{ST}|\cos\theta$, note that $\cos\theta = \frac{\overrightarrow{ST}\cdot\overrightarrow{PQ}}{|\overrightarrow{ST}||\overrightarrow{PQ}|} = \frac{\overrightarrow{ST}\cdot(\mathbf{b}_1 \times \mathbf{b}_2)}{|\overrightarrow{ST}|\cdot|\mathbf{b}_1 \times \mathbf{b}_2|}$.

Substituting this new form for $\cos\theta$ and noting that $\overrightarrow{ST} = \mathbf{a}_2 - \mathbf{a}_1$, the distance is $\left|\frac{(\mathbf{a}_2 - \mathbf{a}_1)\cdot(\mathbf{b}_1 \times \mathbf{b}_2)}{|\mathbf{b}_1 \times \mathbf{b}_2|}\right|$.

The outer modulus signs are used to ensure that the distance is positive.

For example, let $\mathbf{r}_1 = 2\mathbf{i} + \mathbf{j} + \mathbf{k} + (\mathbf{i} + 2\mathbf{j} + 3\mathbf{k})s$ and $\mathbf{r}_2 = 3\mathbf{i} + 4\mathbf{k} + (-2\mathbf{i} - \mathbf{j} + 5\mathbf{k})t$. We will find the shortest distance between them. For the distance, we have $|\overrightarrow{PQ}| = \left|\frac{(\mathbf{a}_2 - \mathbf{a}_1)\cdot(\mathbf{b}_1 \times \mathbf{b}_2)}{|\mathbf{b}_1 \times \mathbf{b}_2|}\right|$.

Calculate each part in turn. First, $\mathbf{a}_2 - \mathbf{a}_1 = \mathbf{i} - \mathbf{j} + 3\mathbf{k}$.

Then $\mathbf{b}_1 \times \mathbf{b}_2 = \begin{vmatrix} \mathbf{i} & \mathbf{j} & \mathbf{k} \\ 1 & 2 & 3 \\ -2 & -1 & 5 \end{vmatrix} = 13\mathbf{i} - 11\mathbf{j} + 3\mathbf{k}$, and $|\mathbf{b}_1 \times \mathbf{b}_2| = \sqrt{299}$.

Hence, $|\overrightarrow{PQ}| = \left|\dfrac{(\mathbf{i} - \mathbf{j} + 3\mathbf{k})\cdot(13\mathbf{i} - 11\mathbf{j} + 3\mathbf{k})}{\sqrt{299}}\right| = \dfrac{33\sqrt{299}}{299}$.

WORKED EXAMPLE 6.7

Find the shortest distance between the lines $\mathbf{r}_1 = 2\mathbf{i} + 3\mathbf{k} + (-\mathbf{i} - \mathbf{j} + \mathbf{k})s$ and $\mathbf{r}_2 = \mathbf{i} - \mathbf{j} + 2\mathbf{k} + 2\mathbf{k}t$.

Answer

$\mathbf{a}_2 - \mathbf{a}_1 = -\mathbf{i} - \mathbf{j} - \mathbf{k}$ — Find the vector $\overrightarrow{ST}$.

$\mathbf{b}_1 \times \mathbf{b}_2 = \begin{vmatrix} \mathbf{i} & \mathbf{j} & \mathbf{k} \\ -1 & -1 & 1 \\ 0 & 0 & 2 \end{vmatrix} = -2\mathbf{i} + 2\mathbf{j}$ — Find the cross product of the directions of the two lines.

$\Rightarrow |\mathbf{b}_1 \times \mathbf{b}_2| = 2\sqrt{2}$ — Find the modulus of the normal vector.

$(-\mathbf{i} - \mathbf{j} - \mathbf{k})\cdot(-2\mathbf{i} + 2\mathbf{j}) = 0$ — Determine the value of $(\mathbf{a}_2 - \mathbf{a}_1)\cdot(\mathbf{b}_1 \times \mathbf{b}_2)$.

$\therefore |\overrightarrow{PQ}| = 0$ — State the distance between the two lines.

You may need to find the position vectors of the points P and Q rather than the distance between them.

Consider the two lines $\mathbf{r}_1 = \mathbf{i} + \mathbf{j} + 2\mathbf{k} + (\mathbf{i} - \mathbf{j} + \mathbf{k})s$ and $\mathbf{r}_2 = 2\mathbf{i} + \mathbf{k} + (\mathbf{i} + \mathbf{j} - \mathbf{k})t$. Let P be on $\mathbf{r}_1$ such that $\overrightarrow{OP} = (1 + s)\mathbf{i} + (1 - s)\mathbf{j} + (2 + s)\mathbf{k}$, and let Q be on $\mathbf{r}_2$ such that $\overrightarrow{OQ} = (2 + t)\mathbf{i} + t\mathbf{j} + (1 - t)\mathbf{k}$. Then $\overrightarrow{PQ} = (1 - s + t)\mathbf{i} + (-1 + s + t)\mathbf{j} - (1 + s + t)\mathbf{k}$. This direction is perpendicular to both direction vectors so $\overrightarrow{PQ}\cdot(\mathbf{i} - \mathbf{j} + \mathbf{k}) = 0$ and $\overrightarrow{PQ}\cdot(\mathbf{i} + \mathbf{j} - \mathbf{k}) = 0$.

From these two scalar products we have $3s + t = 1$ and $s + 3t = -1$. Solving the equations gives $s = \frac{1}{2}$, $t = -\frac{1}{2}$. Hence, $\overrightarrow{OP} = \frac{3}{2}\mathbf{i} + \frac{1}{2}\mathbf{j} + \frac{5}{2}\mathbf{k}$, $\overrightarrow{OQ} = \frac{3}{2}\mathbf{i} - \frac{1}{2}\mathbf{j} + \frac{3}{2}\mathbf{k}$.

WORKED EXAMPLE 6.8

The points P and Q lie on the lines $\mathbf{r}_1 = 2\mathbf{i} + 3\mathbf{j} + (-\mathbf{i} + 2\mathbf{j} + \mathbf{k})s$ and $\mathbf{r}_2 = 3\mathbf{i} + \mathbf{j} + (-\mathbf{i} + \mathbf{j})t$, respectively, such that $\overrightarrow{PQ}$ is perpendicular to both lines. Find the coordinates of P and Q, and find the distance between them.

Answer

$\overrightarrow{OP} = (2 - s)\mathbf{i} + (3 + 2s)\mathbf{j} + s\mathbf{k}$
$\overrightarrow{OQ} = (3 - t)\mathbf{i} + (1 + t)\mathbf{j}$ — State the position vectors of P and Q.

$\therefore \overrightarrow{PQ} = (1 + s - t)\mathbf{i} + (-2 - 2s + t)\mathbf{j} - s\mathbf{k}$ — Form the perpendicular vector $\overrightarrow{PQ}$.

$\overrightarrow{PQ}\cdot(-\mathbf{i} + 2\mathbf{j} + \mathbf{k}) = 0$, $\overrightarrow{PQ}\cdot(-\mathbf{i} + \mathbf{j}) = 0$
$-1 - s + t - 4 - 4s + 2t - s = 0$ and
$-1 - s + t - 2 - 2s + t = 0$ — Find the scalar product of $\overrightarrow{PQ}$ with the two direction vectors.

$\Rightarrow -6s + 3t = 5,\ -3s + 2t = 3$ — Form equations in s and t.

$\therefore s = -\frac{1}{3},\ t = 1.$ — Solve the equations to find s and t.

$\Rightarrow P\left(\frac{7}{3}, \frac{7}{3}, -\frac{1}{3}\right), Q(2,2,0)$ — Find the coordinates of P and Q, and hence the distance between them.

$$\therefore |\overrightarrow{PQ}| = \sqrt{\left(2-\frac{7}{3}\right)^2 + \left(2-\frac{7}{3}\right)^2 + \left(0-\frac{-1}{3}\right)^2}$$

$$= \sqrt{\left(-\frac{1}{3}\right)^2 + \left(-\frac{1}{3}\right)^2 + \left(\frac{1}{3}\right)^2} = \frac{\sqrt{3}}{3}$$

EXERCISE 6B

1 For each case, find the vector equation of the line through the points given. Give your answer in the form $\mathbf{r} = \mathbf{a} + \mathbf{b}t$.

a (2, 3, 5) and (−7, 1, 6)

b (4, 1, 1) and (−5, 6, 1)

c (0, 2, 4) and (1, 1, −1)

2 Determine the equation of the line that passes through (1, 7, −2) and is perpendicular to both $2\mathbf{i} - 3\mathbf{j} + 5\mathbf{k}$ and $4\mathbf{i} - \mathbf{j} + 2\mathbf{k}$.

3 Determine the equation of the line that passes through (3, −5, 1) and is perpendicular to both $-\mathbf{i} + 2\mathbf{j} - 4\mathbf{k}$ and $3\mathbf{i} + 2\mathbf{j}$.

M 4 Three points are given as $A(2, 2, 1)$, $B(1, 0, 4)$ and $C(2, -3, 1)$. Find the shortest distance between the point C and the line through A and B. Give your answer in the form $\frac{a\sqrt{b}}{c}$.

PS 5 The points P and Q are on the lines $\mathbf{r} = \mathbf{k} + (2\mathbf{i} + 3\mathbf{j} + \mathbf{k})s$ and $\mathbf{r} = \mathbf{i} + \mathbf{j} + 4\mathbf{k} + 4\mathbf{j}t$, respectively. Given that $\overrightarrow{PQ}$ is perpendicular to both lines, find the position vectors $\overrightarrow{OP}$ and $\overrightarrow{OQ}$.

P PS 6 The lines $\mathbf{r} = \mathbf{i} - 2\mathbf{j} + 3\mathbf{k} + (4\mathbf{i} - \mathbf{j})s$ and $\mathbf{r} = 3\mathbf{i} - 5\mathbf{k} + (\mathbf{i} + 4\mathbf{j} + 3\mathbf{k})t$ are skew.

a Show that the lines do not intersect.

b Find the angle between the lines.

c Find the shortest distance between the lines.

P 7 The lines L_1 $\mathbf{r} = \mathbf{i} - \mathbf{k} + (\mathbf{i} - \mathbf{j} - 2\mathbf{k})t$ and L_2 $\mathbf{r} = 2\mathbf{i} + \mathbf{j} + (3\mathbf{i} + \cos\theta\mathbf{j} + \mathbf{k})s$, where $0 \leqslant \theta < 2\pi$, are skew.

a Show that these lines do not intersect regardless of the value of θ.

b Determine the shortest distance between them.

PS 8 In both of the following cases, determine the value(s) of the unknown constants for which the two lines intersect.

a $\mathbf{r} = a\mathbf{i} + 4\mathbf{j} + 2\mathbf{k} + (\mathbf{i} - \mathbf{j} - 3\mathbf{k})s$ and $\mathbf{r} = 4\mathbf{i} + 3\mathbf{j} - \mathbf{k} + (2\mathbf{i} + 2\mathbf{j} - \mathbf{k})t$

b $\mathbf{r} = 2\mathbf{j} + 5\mathbf{k} + (\mathbf{i} + 2\mathbf{j} + b\mathbf{k})s$ and $\mathbf{r} = 3\mathbf{i} - 2\mathbf{j} + 4\mathbf{k} + (\mathbf{i} + \mathbf{j})t$

6.3 Planes

In Mathematics, a plane is an infinite two-dimensional surface. It can be represented in different ways, but one property about planes is very important. Inside a plane it is clear that there are many direction vectors, but for each individual plane there is one direction that is important, the direction normal to the plane.

Suppose the normal to a plane is given as $\mathbf{n} = a\mathbf{i} + b\mathbf{j} + c\mathbf{k}$ and we know one point $A(p, q, r)$ in the plane. Using a general point $R(x, y, z)$ in the plane we can generate a vector $\overrightarrow{AR}$ in the plane, so it is perpendicular to the normal.

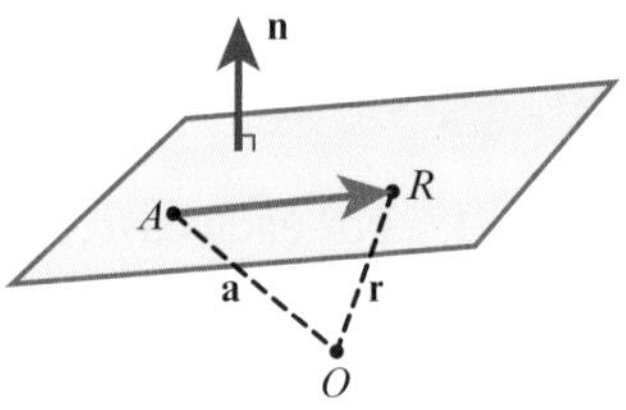

With $\overrightarrow{AR} = \mathbf{r} - \mathbf{a}$ it is clear that $\overrightarrow{AR}\cdot\mathbf{n} = 0$. Then $(\mathbf{r} - \mathbf{a})\cdot\mathbf{n} = 0$, which leads to the **scalar equation of a plane**, $\mathbf{r}\cdot\mathbf{n} = \mathbf{a}\cdot\mathbf{n}$.

Using the scalar product leads to $ax + by + cz = d$, the Cartesian equation of a plane.

For example, if we consider a plane with $\mathbf{n} = \mathbf{i} - 3\mathbf{j} + \mathbf{k}$, and we know the point $(3, -5, 4)$ is in the plane, then $(\mathbf{i} - 3\mathbf{j} + \mathbf{k})\cdot(3\mathbf{i} - 5\mathbf{j} + 4\mathbf{k}) = 22$ such that $\mathbf{r}\cdot(\mathbf{i} - 3\mathbf{j} + \mathbf{k}) = 22$ is the scalar form and $x - 3y + z = 22$ is the Cartesian form.

The last form is the **vector equation of a plane**. Consider, relative to an origin, a position vector **a** of a point in a plane. Then consider two non-parallel vectors **b** and **c** in the plane with appropriate scalars s and t. Any point in the plane can then be defined by $\mathbf{r} = \mathbf{a} + \mathbf{b}s + \mathbf{c}t$.

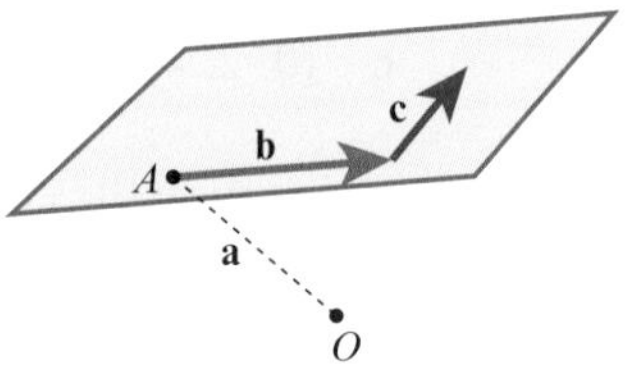

This is an extension of the idea of the vector equation of a line. We can define a point on a line in vector form using a point on the line plus the direction of the line (its direction vector). Similarly, we can define a plane in vector form using a point in the plane plus two direction vectors in the plane.

Finding the vector product of the two direction vectors produces a common perpendicular, a vector that is normal to the plane. From this we can find the Cartesian equation of the plane, $ax + by + cz = d$.

For example, suppose we want to find the equation of the plane passing through the points $A(2, 1, 2)$, $B(3, 0, -1)$ and $C(4, 5, 1)$. We can write $\overrightarrow{AB} = \mathbf{i} - \mathbf{j} - 3\mathbf{k}$ and $\overrightarrow{AC} = 2\mathbf{i} + 4\mathbf{j} - \mathbf{k}$, so the vector equation of the plane is $\mathbf{r} = 2\mathbf{i} + \mathbf{j} + 2\mathbf{k} + (\mathbf{i} - \mathbf{j} - 3\mathbf{k})s + (2\mathbf{i} + 4\mathbf{j} - \mathbf{k})t$.

To determine the other two forms of the equation, we need to find the normal,

$\mathbf{n} = \begin{vmatrix} \mathbf{i} & \mathbf{j} & \mathbf{k} \\ 1 & -1 & -3 \\ 2 & 4 & -1 \end{vmatrix}$. Using the cross product gives $\mathbf{n} = 13\mathbf{i} - 5\mathbf{j} + 6\mathbf{k}$. Next

$\mathbf{a}\cdot\mathbf{n} = (2 \times 13) + (1 \times (-5)) + (2 \times 6) = 33$, and so $\mathbf{r}\cdot(13\mathbf{i} - 5\mathbf{j} + 6\mathbf{k}) = 33$ is the scalar form. The equivalent Cartesian form is $13x - 5y + 6z = 33$.

DID YOU KNOW?

Vectors came about from the work on the geometric representation of complex numbers in the first two decades of the 19th century. Mathematicians such as Caspar Wessel, Jean Robert Argand and Carl Friedrich Gauss were major contributors.

Isaac Newton worked with quantities such as force and velocity, which are vector quantities, much earlier. However, Newton never mentioned the concept of a vector.

WORKED EXAMPLE 6.9

Given that the plane Π contains the points $A(2, -5, 1)$, $B(0, 3, 2)$ and $C(-4, 1, 1)$, find the equation of the plane in both vector and Cartesian form.

Answer

$\overrightarrow{BA} = 2\mathbf{i} - 8\mathbf{j} - \mathbf{k}$ — Find two directions in the plane that are non-parallel.

$\overrightarrow{CA} = 6\mathbf{i} - 6\mathbf{j}$

$\therefore \mathbf{r} = 3\mathbf{j} + 2\mathbf{k} + (2\mathbf{i} - 8\mathbf{j} - \mathbf{k})s + (6\mathbf{i} - 6\mathbf{j})t$ — Write down the vector equation of the plane.

So $\mathbf{n} = \begin{vmatrix} \mathbf{i} & \mathbf{j} & \mathbf{k} \\ 2 & -8 & -1 \\ 6 & -6 & 0 \end{vmatrix} = -6\mathbf{i} - 6\mathbf{j} + 36\mathbf{k}$ or dividing by -6 we get $\mathbf{i} + \mathbf{j} - 6\mathbf{k}$. — Find the cross product of the directions to get the normal direction.

$\mathbf{r}\cdot\mathbf{n} = \mathbf{a}\cdot\mathbf{n}$, where $\mathbf{a}\cdot\mathbf{n} = (2 \times 1) + ((-5) \times 1) + (1 \times (-6)) = -9$. — Use the scalar product to find the scalar form. Finally, determine the Cartesian form.

This leads to $x + y - 6z = -9$.

Two planes in space can interact in one of two ways: either they meet or they don't meet. When two planes meet there is a **line of intersection** rather than a point.

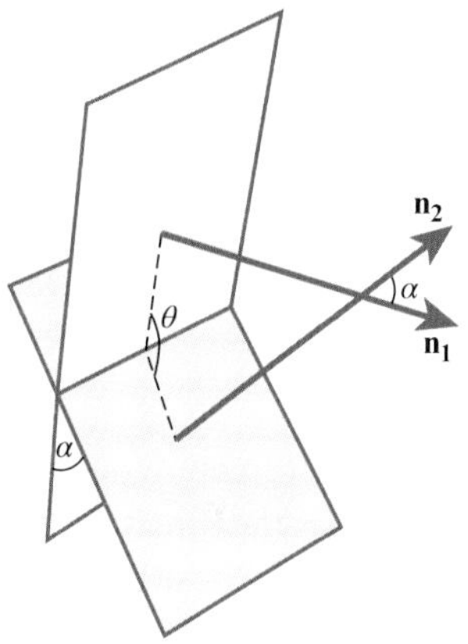

Clearly, when two planes meet there will be an angle between them. In fact, there are two angles, as you can see in the diagram on the right.

Using the scalar product, $\cos\theta = \dfrac{\mathbf{n}_1\cdot\mathbf{n}_2}{|\mathbf{n}_1||\mathbf{n}_2|}$. This angle θ is also one of the angles between the planes. If each normal is at right angles to the plane, we have $\theta + \alpha = 180°$, which means that, for example, we either find the acute angle straight away or use $\theta = 180° - \alpha$.

Another way of viewing this is shown in the following diagram. A kite is formed between the normals and the planes to show the link between the angles. A question will usually ask for the acute angle or the obtuse angle, rather than asking simply for 'the angle'.

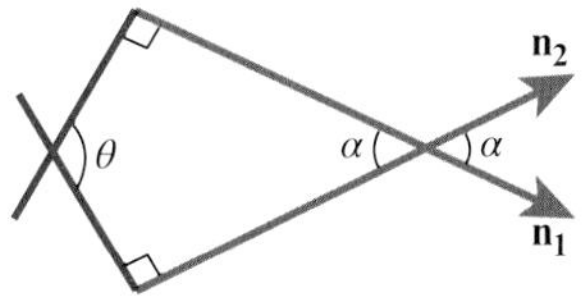

For example, consider the two planes $x - y + 3z = 4$ and $2x + y - 5z = 12$. We are going to find the acute angle between them.

Start with $\cos\alpha = \dfrac{(\mathbf{i} - \mathbf{j} + 3\mathbf{k})\cdot(2\mathbf{i} + \mathbf{j} - 5\mathbf{k})}{\sqrt{11}\sqrt{30}}$. Then using the scalar product gives $\cos\alpha = \dfrac{-14}{\sqrt{11}\sqrt{30}}$, which leads to $\alpha = 140.4°$. This is not the acute angle, so $\theta = 180° - 140.4° = 39.6°$.

Note that if $\mathbf{n}_1\cdot\mathbf{n}_2 > 0$ then α is acute. If $\mathbf{n}_1\cdot\mathbf{n}_2 < 0$ then α is obtuse. If $\mathbf{n}_1\cdot\mathbf{n}_2 = 0$ then the normals are at right angles. This implies the planes are also at right angles.

WORKED EXAMPLE 6.10

Four points are given as $A(2, 3, 1)$, $B(-4, -2, 5)$, $C(3, 3, 2)$ and $D(0, 0, 4)$. Find the acute angle between the planes ABC and ACD.

Answer

$\overrightarrow{AB} = -6\mathbf{i} - 5\mathbf{j} + 4\mathbf{k}$ — Find the three directions related to the two planes.

$\overrightarrow{AC} = \mathbf{i} + \mathbf{k}$

$\overrightarrow{AD} = -2\mathbf{i} - 3\mathbf{j} + 3\mathbf{k}$

$\mathbf{n}_1 = \begin{vmatrix} \mathbf{i} & \mathbf{j} & \mathbf{k} \\ -6 & -5 & 4 \\ 1 & 0 & 1 \end{vmatrix} = -5\mathbf{i} + 10\mathbf{j} + 5\mathbf{k}$ — Find $\mathbf{n}_1 = \overrightarrow{AB} \times \overrightarrow{AC}$.

$\mathbf{n}_2 = \begin{vmatrix} \mathbf{i} & \mathbf{j} & \mathbf{k} \\ 1 & 0 & 1 \\ -2 & -3 & 3 \end{vmatrix} = 3\mathbf{i} - 5\mathbf{j} - 3\mathbf{k}$ — Find $\mathbf{n}_2 = \overrightarrow{AC} \times \overrightarrow{AD}$.

$\cos\alpha = \dfrac{(-5\mathbf{i} + 10\mathbf{j} + 5\mathbf{k})\cdot(3\mathbf{i} - 5\mathbf{j} - 3\mathbf{k})}{\sqrt{150}\sqrt{43}}$ — Use the scalar product.

$\cos\alpha = -\dfrac{80}{\sqrt{150}\sqrt{43}} \Rightarrow \alpha = 174.95°$ — Find the obtuse angle.

$\therefore \theta = 5.05°$ — State the acute angle.

When two planes intersect, their line of intersection is a line that is parallel to both of the planes. This means that the line of intersection is also perpendicular to both of the normals.

Since the direction of the line is perpendicular to both normals, then $\mathbf{b} = \mathbf{n}_1 \times \mathbf{n}_2$, where $\mathbf{b}$ is the direction vector of the line. To find the vector equation of the line, we still need the position vector of a point on the line.

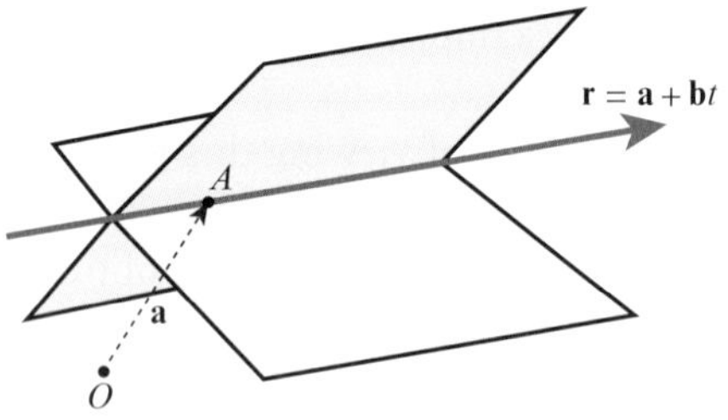

So, using the example $3x + y - z = 2$ and $x - y + 5z = 2$, we know the two normals are $\mathbf{n}_1 = 3\mathbf{i} + \mathbf{j} - \mathbf{k}$ and $\mathbf{n}_2 = \mathbf{i} - \mathbf{j} + 5\mathbf{k}$. From these, the direction vector of the line is $\mathbf{b} = \begin{vmatrix} \mathbf{i} & \mathbf{j} & \mathbf{k} \\ 3 & 1 & -1 \\ 1 & -1 & 5 \end{vmatrix} = 4\mathbf{i} - 16\mathbf{j} - 4\mathbf{k}$.

For the position vector $\mathbf{a}$ there are two methods that we can use.

First, take $3x + y - z = 2$ and $x - y + 5z = 2$ and let $z = 0$. This gives $3x + y = 2$ and $x - y = 2$. Solving these gives $x = 1$ and $y = -1$. Hence, the position vector of a point on the line of intersection is $\mathbf{i} - \mathbf{j}$, so the line of intersection is given as $\mathbf{r} = \mathbf{i} - \mathbf{j} + (\mathbf{i} - 4\mathbf{j} - \mathbf{k})t$. Note we have divided $\mathbf{b}$ by 4 to get the direction vector of the line of intersection in a simpler form.

The reason for choosing, for example $z = 0$, is that it simplifies the algebra and it makes us aware of the fact that somewhere on the line there must be a point where z actually is 0. This is, of course, assuming that neither plane is parallel to the xy-plane.

WORKED EXAMPLE 6.11

Find the vector equation of the line of intersection of the planes $x + 3y - z = 1$ and $2x + 4y + z = 6$.

Answer

$$\mathbf{b} = \begin{vmatrix} \mathbf{i} & \mathbf{j} & \mathbf{k} \\ 1 & 3 & -1 \\ 2 & 4 & 1 \end{vmatrix} = 7\mathbf{i} - 3\mathbf{j} - 2\mathbf{k}$$

Find the direction of the line by finding the cross product of the normals.

Let $x = 0 \Rightarrow 3y - z = 1, 4y + z = 6$
So $x = 0, y = 1, z = 2.$

Let $x = 0$ to determine the values of y and z of a point on the line of intersection.

$\therefore \mathbf{r} = \mathbf{j} + 2\mathbf{k} + (7\mathbf{i} - 3\mathbf{j} - 2\mathbf{k})t$

Write down the vector equation of the line of intersection.

For the second method, start by adding the equations of the two planes $3x + y - z = 2$ and $x - y + 5z = 2$ together to eliminate one variable. This gives $4x + 4z = 4$, and so $x = 1 - z$. Substituting this into the equation for the second plane gives $1 - z - y + 5z = 2$ or $y = -1 + 4z$. Next, let $z = t$ such that $x = 1 - t$ and $y = -1 + 4t$ so we have $\begin{pmatrix} x \\ y \\ z \end{pmatrix} = \begin{pmatrix} 1 \\ -1 \\ 0 \end{pmatrix} + \begin{pmatrix} -1 \\ 4 \\ 1 \end{pmatrix} t$, which is now the equation of the line of intersection of the two planes.

Note that $\begin{pmatrix} -1 \\ 4 \\ 1 \end{pmatrix} = -\begin{pmatrix} 1 \\ -4 \\ -1 \end{pmatrix}$, so this is parallel to the same direction vector as before.

This method allows us to create a free variable, in this case z, which can be changed to any value and hence behaves as a parameter.

WORKED EXAMPLE 6.12

By setting y as a free variable, determine the equation of the line of intersection of the planes $3x - y + 2z = 3$ and $x + 3y - z = 6$.

Answer

$$3x - y + 2z = 3$$
$$2x + 6y - 2z = 12$$

Hence, $5x + 5y = 15 \Rightarrow x + y = 3$

Add the first equation to twice the second equation to eliminate z.

So $x = 3 - y$

Determine x in terms of y.

Hence, $3 - y + 3y - z = 6 \Rightarrow z = -3 + 2y$

Find z in terms of y by substituting $3 - y$ into the equation of the second plane.

Let $y = t$.

So $\begin{pmatrix} x \\ y \\ z \end{pmatrix} = \begin{pmatrix} 3 \\ 0 \\ -3 \end{pmatrix} + \begin{pmatrix} -1 \\ 1 \\ 2 \end{pmatrix} t.$

Write x and z in terms of t to form the equation of the line.

As well as planes intersecting planes, we can also have lines intersecting planes. Lines are either parallel to planes or they will intersect them.

To determine where a line and a plane meet, write the equation of the line in parametric form first. Substitute this into the plane's equation to determine the value of t. This will allow you to find the point, if it exists, where the line and plane meet.

For example, let the plane P be $3x + 4y - 5z = 22$ and the line be $\mathbf{r} = 2\mathbf{i} + \mathbf{j} + 4\mathbf{k} + (-\mathbf{i} + \mathbf{j} - 3\mathbf{k})t$. Write the equation of the line in parametric form $(2 - t)\mathbf{i} + (1 + t)\mathbf{j} + (4 - 3t)\mathbf{k}$. Substitute this into the equation of the plane to give $3(2 - t) + 4(1 + t) - 5(4 - 3t) = 22$, or $6 - 3t + 4 + 4t - 20 + 15t = 22$. Solving for t gives $t = 2$.

If we substitute this value for t into the equation of the line, it tells us where the line and the plane meet. In this case, that point is $\mathbf{r} = 3\mathbf{j} - 2\mathbf{k}$ when given as a position vector.

If a line and a plane are parallel, there are two more cases to consider. Either the line really is parallel to the plane and never meets the plane, or the line is wholly contained in the plane.

First consider the plane $3x + y + 2z = 6$ and the line $\mathbf{r} = \mathbf{i} - \mathbf{j} + 2\mathbf{k} + (4\mathbf{i} - 2\mathbf{j} - 5\mathbf{k})t$. If we find the scalar product of the direction of the normal and the direction vector of the line we get $(3 \times 4) + (1 \times (-2)) + (2 \times (-5)) = 12 - 2 - 10$. The result is 0, meaning the line and the normal to the plane are perpendicular. This confirms that the line is either in the plane or parallel to the plane.

If we substitute the parametric form of the equation of the line into the equation of the plane, this gives $3(1 + 4t) - 1 - 2t + 2(2 - 5t) = 6$. Simplifying to $3 + 12t - 1 - 2t + 4 - 10t = 6$ then solving gives us $6 = 6$. What does this solution mean? It tells us that the line meets the plane for all values of t or, simply put, the line lies in the plane.

Suppose we want to find the relationship between the line $\mathbf{r} = 2\mathbf{i} + \mathbf{j} + 3\mathbf{k} + (4\mathbf{i} - 2\mathbf{j} - 5\mathbf{k})t$ and the plane. Substituting the parametric form of the equation of the line into the equation of the plane we get $3(2 + 4t) + 1 - 2t + 2(3 - 5t) = 6$. This simplifies to $6 + 12t + 1 - 2t + 6 - 10t = 6$, and we get the result $13 = 6$. This is not possible, it suggests that the line is parallel to the plane but never meets the plane.

WORKED EXAMPLE 6.13

Show that the line $\mathbf{r} = \mathbf{i} - \mathbf{j} + 8\mathbf{k} + (2\mathbf{i} - \mathbf{k})t$ lies in the plane $x + 5y + 2z = 12$.

Answer

Method 1:

$$\begin{pmatrix} x \\ y \\ z \end{pmatrix} = \begin{pmatrix} 1 + 2t \\ -1 \\ 8 - t \end{pmatrix}$$

Write the parametric form of the equation of the line.

$$\therefore (1 + 2t) + 5(-1) + 2(8 - t) = 12$$
$$\Rightarrow 12 = 12$$

Substitute the parametric form into the equation of the plane. Therefore, all t values work.

Method 2:

$t = 0$: $\mathbf{r} = \mathbf{i} - \mathbf{j} + 8\mathbf{k}$. Substituting this into the plane's equation gives $1 - 5 + 16 = 12$

$t = 1$: $\mathbf{r} = 3\mathbf{i} - \mathbf{j} + 7\mathbf{k}$. Substituting this into the plane's equation gives $3 - 5 + 14 = 12$

Choose any two values of t to find two points on the line, then show both points on the line lie in the plane also.

Hence, in both cases, the line lies wholly in the plane.

If a plane and a line meet only once, there must be an angle between the line and the plane. This angle can be determined from the scalar product of the normal of the plane and the direction vector of the line.

Using $\cos\alpha = \frac{\mathbf{b}\cdot\mathbf{n}}{|\mathbf{b}||\mathbf{n}|}$ will give α and then using either $\theta = 90° - \alpha$ or $\theta = \alpha - 90°$ will give the desired angle. Note that if $\mathbf{b}\cdot\mathbf{n} > 0$ then α will be acute, and if $\mathbf{b}\cdot\mathbf{n} < 0$ then α is obtuse.

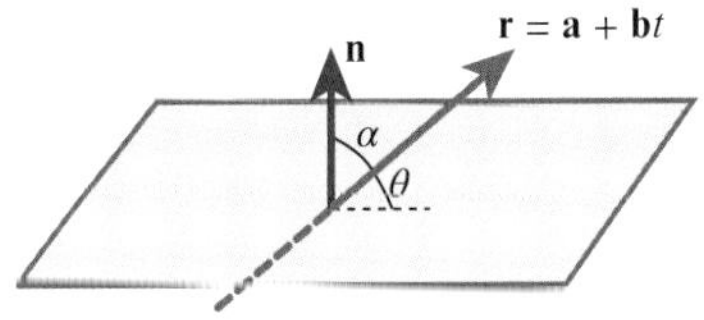

Of course, when $\mathbf{b}\cdot\mathbf{n} = 0$ the line is perpendicular to the normal, or parallel to the plane.

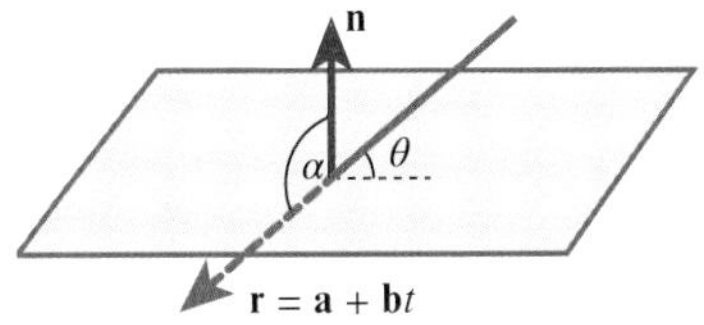

For example, consider the line $\mathbf{r} = \mathbf{i} + 4\mathbf{j} - 3\mathbf{k} + (\mathbf{i} + 2\mathbf{j} - 6\mathbf{k})t$ and the plane $x + 2y + z = 5$.

First, use $\cos\alpha = \frac{\mathbf{b}\cdot\mathbf{n}}{|\mathbf{b}||\mathbf{n}|}$ to get $\cos\alpha = \frac{(\mathbf{i} + 2\mathbf{j} - 6\mathbf{k})\cdot(\mathbf{i} + 2\mathbf{j} + \mathbf{k})}{\sqrt{41}\sqrt{6}}$, which simplifies to $\cos\alpha = \frac{-1}{\sqrt{41}\sqrt{6}}$. So $\alpha = 93.66°$, which implies that the angle between the line and the plane is $3.66°$ (3 sf).

WORKED EXAMPLE 6.14

Find the angle between the line $\mathbf{r} = 8\mathbf{i} - 3\mathbf{j} + \mathbf{k} + (2\mathbf{i} + 2\mathbf{j} - \mathbf{k})t$ and the plane $3x - y = 2$.

Answer

$\cos\alpha = \frac{(2\mathbf{i} + 2\mathbf{j} - \mathbf{k})\cdot(3\mathbf{i} - \mathbf{j})}{\sqrt{9}\sqrt{10}}$	Find the scalar product of the line's direction vector and the normal to the plane. Divide by the moduli.
$\therefore \cos\alpha = \frac{4}{3\sqrt{10}} \Rightarrow \alpha = 65.06°$	Substitute into the scalar product rule.
Hence, $\theta = 24.9°$.	Use $90° - \alpha$ to get the desired angle.

We will now look at two ways of finding the shortest distance between a point and a plane. The first method is very similar to the one we used to find when lines are parallel to planes. First, form a new line that is parallel to the normal of the plane, passing through the point P. Then write the equation of the line in parametric form and find where the line meets the plane. This gives us a position vector of the point, labelled R. We can now determine the distance PR.

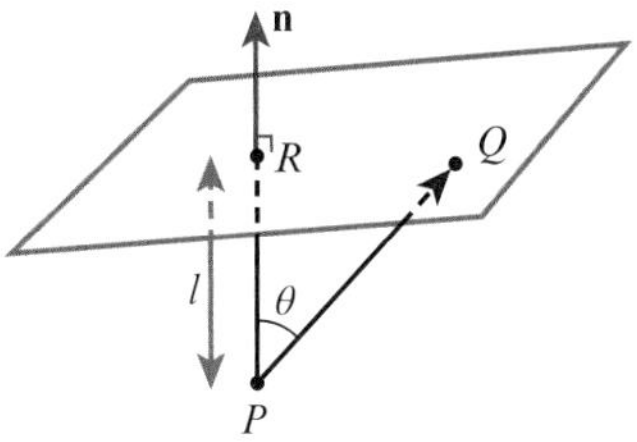

For example, consider the plane $2x - 3y + 6z = -14$ and the point $P(4, -5, 2)$. To find the distance between them, we first create the line $\mathbf{r} = 4\mathbf{i} - 5\mathbf{j} + 2\mathbf{k} + (2\mathbf{i} - 3\mathbf{j} + 6\mathbf{k})t$.

Now let the line intersect our plane, giving $2(4 + 2t) - 3(-5 - 3t) + 6(2 + 6t) = -14$, giving $8 + 4t + 15 + 9t + 12 + 36t = -14$, which leads to $t = -1$. Therefore, the point where the line meets the plane is $R(2, -2, -4)$.

There are two ways to determine the distance PR. We can find $\overrightarrow{PR} = (2 - 4)\mathbf{i} + ((-2) - (-5))\mathbf{j} + (-4 - 2)\mathbf{k} = -2\mathbf{i} + 3\mathbf{j} - 6\mathbf{k}$ and show the distance is 7. Alternatively, we can see that the distance is actually $|-1 \times \mathbf{n}|$ as $\overrightarrow{PR} = -\mathbf{n}$ in this particular case and $t = -1$. Since $|\mathbf{n}| = \sqrt{4 + 9 + 36} = 7$ we get the same result.

WORKED EXAMPLE 6.15

Find the shortest distance between the point (1, 2, 3) and the plane $4x + y - z = 12$.

Answer

Let $\mathbf{r} = \mathbf{i} + 2\mathbf{j} + 3\mathbf{k} + (4\mathbf{i} + \mathbf{j} - \mathbf{k})t$ — State the equation of the line through the point in the direction of the normal.

$\therefore 4(1 + 4t) + (2 + t) - (3 - t) = 12$
$4 + 16t + 2 + t - 3 + t = 12$
$\Rightarrow t = \frac{1}{2}$ — Substitute the parametric form of the equation of the line into the equation of the plane to get the value of t.

$|4\mathbf{i} + \mathbf{j} - \mathbf{k}| = \sqrt{18}$ — Find the magnitude of the normal.

Hence, the shortest distance of the point from the plane is $\frac{1}{2} \times \sqrt{18} = \frac{3\sqrt{2}}{2}$. — Multiply the magnitude of the normal by $\frac{1}{2}$ as in this case $t = \frac{1}{2}$.

The second way to determine the shortest distance between a point and a plane is using the scalar product. In the previous diagram, the distance $|\overrightarrow{PQ}|\cos\theta$ represents the shortest distance.

From the scalar product, $\cos\theta = \frac{\overrightarrow{PQ}\cdot\mathbf{n}}{|\overrightarrow{PQ}||\mathbf{n}|}$. Substituting this into the previous result gives the distance as $\left|\frac{\overrightarrow{PQ}\cdot\mathbf{n}}{|\mathbf{n}|}\right|$. Notice that there are modulus signs on the outside since $\overrightarrow{PQ}\cdot\mathbf{n}$ can be positive or negative.

For example, consider the point $P(2, 0, 4)$ and the plane $-x + 4y + 5z = 2$.
To determine the point Q we just need to find any point in the plane, such as $(-2, 0, 0)$.
This gives $\overrightarrow{PQ} = -4\mathbf{i} - 4\mathbf{k}$.

Then the distance is $\left|\frac{(-4\mathbf{i} - 4\mathbf{k})\cdot(-\mathbf{i} + 4\mathbf{j} + 5\mathbf{k})}{|-\mathbf{i} + 4\mathbf{j} + 5\mathbf{k}|}\right|$, which is $\left|\frac{-16}{\sqrt{42}}\right|$, or $\frac{8\sqrt{42}}{21}$.

Choosing a different point for Q, such as $\left(0, \frac{1}{2}, 0\right)$, we find $\overrightarrow{PQ} = -2\mathbf{i} + \frac{1}{2}\mathbf{j} - 4\mathbf{k}$. Therefore, the distance is $\left|\frac{\left(-2\mathbf{i} + \frac{1}{2}\mathbf{j} - 4\mathbf{k}\right)\cdot(-\mathbf{i} + 4\mathbf{j} + 5\mathbf{k})}{|-\mathbf{i} + 4\mathbf{j} + 5\mathbf{k}|}\right|$, which is also $\left|\frac{-16}{\sqrt{42}}\right|$, as before. In fact any point in the plane will work.

WORKED EXAMPLE 6.16

Find the shortest distance between the point $P(4, 1, -5)$ and the plane $2x + 7y - 6z = 14$.

Answer

Let Q be (7, 0, 0). — Choose any point in the plane.

$\therefore \overrightarrow{PQ} = 3\mathbf{i} - \mathbf{j} + 5\mathbf{k}$ — Form $\overrightarrow{PQ}$.

$\mathbf{n} = 2\mathbf{i} + 7\mathbf{j} - 6\mathbf{k}$	State the normal of the plane.
Distance $= \left\| \dfrac{(3\mathbf{i} - \mathbf{j} + 5\mathbf{k})\cdot(2\mathbf{i} + 7\mathbf{j} - 6\mathbf{k})}{\sqrt{89}} \right\|$	Substitute into the distance formula.
Hence, distance $= \dfrac{31\sqrt{89}}{89}$.	Determine the distance.

EXERCISE 6C

1 Find the equation of the plane passing through the points given in each case.

a $A(2, 4, 1)$, $B(3, 0, -1)$, $C(8, 1, 1)$

b $A(3, -2, 3)$, $B(1, -8, 9)$, $C(1, 0, 2)$

c $A(1, -3, 0)$, $B(5, 2, -4)$, $C(3, -2, 6)$

2 Find the equation of the plane that contains the line $\mathbf{r} = 2\mathbf{i} - \mathbf{j} + 3\mathbf{k} + (-\mathbf{i} + 4\mathbf{j} - 5\mathbf{k})t$ and the point $(2, 6, 3)$.

3 Find the equation of the plane that is perpendicular to the planes $2x - 4y + z = 10$ and $x - 4z = 2$ and that contains the point $(2, 3, 1)$.

4 Find, in Cartesian form, the equation of the plane containing the points $A(1, -1, 1)$, $B(0, 0, 5)$ and $C(2, 3, 7)$.

5 Find the shortest distance between the point $(5, 2, 6)$ and the plane that passes through the point $(2, -3, 2)$ and is perpendicular to the direction $\mathbf{i} + \mathbf{j}$.

6 Find the acute angle between the planes Π_1: $2x - y + 4z = 13$ and Π_2: $3y - 2z = 4$.

PS 7 The plane P is given as $x + 2y - 5z = 7$ and the line l as $\mathbf{r} = -3\mathbf{i} + 4\mathbf{j} + 6\mathbf{k} + (11\mathbf{i} + \mathbf{j} + 8\mathbf{k})t$.

a Find the angle between the line and the plane.

b Find the equation of the plane that contains the line l and is perpendicular to the plane P.

PS 8 Find the line of intersection of the planes Π_1: $3x - y + z = 4$ and Π_2: $5x + y - 3z = 6$. Hence, find the equation of the plane that contains this line of intersection and is perpendicular to Π_1.

PS 9 Find the distance of the point (p, q, r) from the plane $ax + by + cz = d$, giving your answer in a simplified form.

PS 10 Four points are given as $A(-1, -2, 3)$, $B(0, 0, 9)$, $C(-2, 4, -1)$ and $D(2, 7, 1)$. Find the shortest distance between the plane through ABD and the point C, giving your answer to 3 significant figures.

WORKED PAST PAPER QUESTION

The plane Π_1 has equation $\mathbf{r} = \mathbf{i} + 2\mathbf{j} + \mathbf{k} + \theta(2\mathbf{j} - \mathbf{k}) + \phi(3\mathbf{i} + 2\mathbf{j} - 2\mathbf{k})$.

Find a vector normal to Π_1 and hence show that the equation of Π_1 can be written as $2x + 3y + 6z = 14$.

The line l has equation $\mathbf{r} = 3\mathbf{i} + 8\mathbf{j} + 2\mathbf{k} + t(4\mathbf{i} + 6\mathbf{j} + 5\mathbf{k})$.

The point on l where $t = \lambda$ is denoted by P. Find the set of values of λ for which the perpendicular distance of P from Π_1 is not greater than 4.

The plane Π_2 contains l and the point with position vector $\mathbf{i} + 2\mathbf{j} + \mathbf{k}$. Find the acute angle between Π_1 and Π_2.

Cambridge International AS & A Level Further Mathematics 9231 Paper 1 Q11 November 2008

Answer

Finding the cross product of the direction vectors in the plane gives $\begin{vmatrix} \mathbf{i} & \mathbf{j} & \mathbf{k} \\ 0 & 2 & -1 \\ 3 & 2 & -2 \end{vmatrix} = -2\mathbf{i} - 3\mathbf{j} - 6\mathbf{k}$, the normal vector.

Use $\mathbf{r}\cdot\mathbf{n} = \mathbf{a}\cdot\mathbf{n}$ to find $\mathbf{a}\cdot\mathbf{n} = (1 \times 2) + (2 \times 3) + (1 \times 6) = 14$ so Π_1: $2x + 3y + 6z = 14$, hence $\mathbf{n} = 2\mathbf{i} + 3\mathbf{j} + 6\mathbf{k}$.
Be sure to show all working since the answer is given in the question.

Let $\overrightarrow{OP} = (3 + 4\lambda)\mathbf{i} + (8 + 6\lambda)\mathbf{j} + (2 + 5\lambda)\mathbf{k}$ and $\overrightarrow{OQ} = 7\mathbf{i}$, where Q is a point on the plane.

Then $\overrightarrow{PQ} = (7 - 3 - 4\lambda)\mathbf{i} + (-8 - 6\lambda)\mathbf{j} + (-2 - 5\lambda)\mathbf{k}$.

$\overrightarrow{PQ}\cdot\mathbf{n} = 8 - 8\lambda - 24 - 18\lambda - 12 - 30\lambda = -28 - 56\lambda$ and $|\mathbf{n}| = \sqrt{2^2 + 3^2 + 6^2} = \sqrt{49} = 7$.

So $\left|\dfrac{-28 - 56\lambda}{7}\right| \leqslant 4$, so $-28 \leqslant 28 + 56\lambda \leqslant 28$, or $-56 \leqslant 56\lambda \leqslant 0$, which gives $-1 \leqslant \lambda \leqslant 0$.

To find the acute angle between the planes, first find vector equations of two lines parallel to the second plane so you can find a normal to this plane. $(3\mathbf{i} + 8\mathbf{j} + 2\mathbf{k}) - (\mathbf{i} + 2\mathbf{j} + \mathbf{k}) = 2\mathbf{i} + 6\mathbf{j} + \mathbf{k}$,

then $\begin{vmatrix} \mathbf{i} & \mathbf{j} & \mathbf{k} \\ 4 & 6 & 5 \\ 2 & 6 & 1 \end{vmatrix} = -24\mathbf{i} + 6\mathbf{j} + 12\mathbf{k}$, which is $\mathbf{n}_2$.

Then use the scalar product to find the angle between the planes, $\cos\alpha = \dfrac{\mathbf{n}_1\cdot\mathbf{n}_2}{|\mathbf{n}_1||\mathbf{n}_2|}$, so

$$\cos\alpha = \frac{(2\mathbf{i} + 3\mathbf{j} + 6\mathbf{k})\cdot(-24\mathbf{i} + 6\mathbf{j} + 12\mathbf{k})}{\sqrt{49}\sqrt{756}} = \frac{42}{7\sqrt{756}} = \frac{42}{42\sqrt{21}} = \frac{1}{\sqrt{21}}.$$

Hence, $\alpha = 77.4°$.

Checklist of learning and understanding

The vector product:

- The vector product is $|\mathbf{a} \times \mathbf{b}| = |\mathbf{a}||\mathbf{b}|\hat{\mathbf{n}} \sin \theta$.
- The result $\mathbf{a} \times \mathbf{b}$ produces a vector perpendicular to the plane that is parallel to both **a** and **b**.
- The area of the triangle OAB is given as $\frac{1}{2}|\mathbf{a} \times \mathbf{b}|$.
- E The volume of a tetrahedron is given as $\frac{1}{6}|(\mathbf{a} \times \mathbf{b})\cdot\mathbf{c}|$.

Vector equation of a line:

- The vector equation of a line is $\mathbf{r} = \mathbf{a} + \mathbf{b}t$, where **a** is a position vector of a point on the line and **b** is the direction vector of the line.
- The shortest distance between a point and a line is derived from $\overrightarrow{PQ}\cdot\mathbf{b} = 0$, where P is the point and Q is a point on the line.
- The shortest distance between the skew lines $\mathbf{r}_1 = \mathbf{a}_1 + \mathbf{b}_1 s$ and $\mathbf{r}_2 = \mathbf{a}_2 + \mathbf{b}_2 t$ is given by the formula $\left|\frac{(\mathbf{a}_2 - \mathbf{a}_1)\cdot(\mathbf{b}_1 \times \mathbf{b}_2)}{|\mathbf{b}_1 \times \mathbf{b}_2|}\right|$.

Planes:

- The scalar equation of a plane is $\mathbf{r}\cdot\mathbf{n} = \mathbf{a}\cdot\mathbf{n}$.
- The Cartesian equation of a plane is $ax + by + cz = d$.
- The vector equation of a plane is $\mathbf{r} = \mathbf{a} + \mathbf{b}s + \mathbf{c}t$.
- For the angle between the planes $\mathbf{r}\cdot\mathbf{n}_1 = d_1$ and $\mathbf{r}\cdot\mathbf{n}_2 = d_2$, use $\cos\alpha = \frac{\mathbf{n}_1\cdot\mathbf{n}_2}{|\mathbf{n}_1||\mathbf{n}_2|}$. The two possible angles are α and $180° - \alpha$.
- For the line of intersection of two planes, set one variable as a free variable (e.g. z) and then obtain a set of equations such as:

  $x = a + bt$
  $y = c + dt$
  $z = e + ft$

  The equation of the line of intersection is then $\mathbf{r} = a\mathbf{i} + c\mathbf{j} + e\mathbf{k} + (b\mathbf{i} + d\mathbf{j} + f\mathbf{k})t$.
- For a line meeting a plane, substitute the parametric form of the equation of the line into the equation of the plane to determine the position vector of their point of intersection.
- For the angle θ between the line $\mathbf{r} = \mathbf{a} + \mathbf{b}t$ and the plane with normal **n**, use $\cos\alpha = \frac{\mathbf{n}\cdot\mathbf{b}}{|\mathbf{n}||\mathbf{b}|}$.
- Depending on the size of α, use either $\theta = 90° - \alpha$ or $\theta = \alpha - 90°$.
- For the shortest distance between the point P and the plane $\mathbf{r}\cdot\mathbf{n} = d$ use $\left|\frac{\overrightarrow{PQ}\cdot\mathbf{n}}{|\mathbf{n}|}\right|$, where Q can be any point in the plane.

END-OF-CHAPTER REVIEW EXERCISE 6

1 The lines l_1 and l_2 have equations $\mathbf{r} = 8\mathbf{i} + 2\mathbf{j} + 3\mathbf{k} + \lambda(\mathbf{i} - 2\mathbf{j})$ and $\mathbf{r} = 5\mathbf{i} + 3\mathbf{j} - 14\mathbf{k} + \mu(2\mathbf{j} - 3\mathbf{k})$ respectively. The point P on l_1 and the point Q on l_2 are such that PQ is perpendicular to both l_1 and l_2. Find the position vector of the point P and the position vector of the point Q.

The points with position vectors $8\mathbf{i} + 2\mathbf{j} + 3\mathbf{k}$ and $5\mathbf{i} + 3\mathbf{j} - 14\mathbf{k}$ are denoted by A and B respectively.

Find

i $\overrightarrow{AP} \times \overrightarrow{AQ}$ and hence the area of the triangle APQ,

ii the volume of the tetrahedron $APQB$. (You are given that the volume of a tetrahedron is $\frac{1}{3} \times$ area of base $\times$ perpendicular height.)

Cambridge International AS & A Level Further Mathematics 9231 Paper 11 Q11 June 2015

2 Find a Cartesian equation of the plane Π_1 passing through the points with coordinates $(2, -1, 3)$, $(4, 2, -5)$ and $(-1, 3, -2)$.

The plane Π_2 has Cartesian equation $3x - y + 2z = 5$. Find the acute angle between Π_1 and Π_2.

Find a vector equation of the line of intersection of the planes Π_1 and Π_2.

Cambridge International AS & A Level Further Mathematics 9231 Paper 11 Q8 June 2016

3 The points A, B, C have position vectors $4\mathbf{i} + 5\mathbf{j} + 6\mathbf{k}$, $5\mathbf{i} + 7\mathbf{j} + 8\mathbf{k}$, $2\mathbf{i} + 6\mathbf{j} + 4\mathbf{k}$, respectively, relative to the origin O. Find a Cartesian equation of the plane ABC.

The point D has position vector $6\mathbf{i} + 3\mathbf{j} + 6\mathbf{k}$. Find the coordinates of E, the point of intersection of the line OD with the plane ABC.

Find the acute angle between the line ED and the plane ABC.

Cambridge International AS & A Level Further Mathematics 9231 Paper 13 Q8 November 2013

Chapter 7
Proof by induction

In this chapter you will learn how to:

- use the method of mathematical induction to establish a given result
- recognise situations where conjecture based on a limited trial followed by inductive proof is a useful strategy, and carry this out in simple cases.

PREREQUISITE KNOWLEDGE

Where it comes from	What you should be able to do	Check your skills
AS & A Level Mathematics Pure Mathematics 2 & 3, Chapter 5	Differentiate functions such as polynomials, exponentials and trigonometric functions, to 2nd derivative form.	1 Find the derivative stated for each function. a $y = xe^x$, $\frac{d^4y}{dx^4}$ b $y = \sin^2 2x$, $\frac{d^6y}{dx^6}$
Probability & Statistics 1, Chapter 2 Pure Mathematics 1, Chapter 6	Work with recurrence relations and general series summation formulae.	2 Simplify $\sum_{r=1}^{n}(2r+3)+2n+5$.
Chapter 4	Multiply matrices together.	3 Given that $\mathbf{A} = \begin{pmatrix} 1 & 2 \\ -1 & 4 \end{pmatrix}$ and $\mathbf{B} = \begin{pmatrix} -3 & 0 \\ 2 & 5 \end{pmatrix}$, evaluate: a $\mathbf{AB}$ b $\mathbf{A}^3$

What is proof?

If we consider the sequence $1, 2, 4, 8, 16, \ldots$ we can see that the terms increase by a factor of 2. It also appears that every term in this sequence will continue to be of the form 2^n for $n \geqslant 0$. Let us look at a way of proving that this is always true.

We can define the sequence by $u_{n+1} = 2u_n$, where $u_0 = 1$. We can also see that $u_n = 2^n$ for $n \geqslant 0$. But for true mathematical proof, we need to be certain that a relationship is true (or false) for all values being considered, without exception.

In this chapter, we will look at one kind of mathematical proof, proof by **induction**. We will learn how to set up a mathematical inductive process, using the first term and a general term given. We need to form a convincing argument to prove a statement is true for all values in the interval.

7.1 The inductive process

The condition for proof by induction is shown in Key point 7.1.

KEY POINT 7.1

If a statement is defined for $u_n \geqslant a$, then your proof must reflect this exact interval in the final conclusion.

Using the example mentioned in the introduction, we shall prove by mathematical induction that $u_n = 2^n$ for $n \geqslant 0$ (recall $u_{n+1} = 2u_n$).

Start with the case $n = 0$: $u_0 = 2^0 = 1$. Since we know this is the first term in the sequence, we can say that the $n = 0$ case is true. (Later we will denote this P_0.)

A general way to say the next part is:

Let P_k be the statement that, for some integer k, $u_k = 2^k$.

This is what we are trying to prove, so we make the assumption that it is true. We should be very clear with this statement.

Next, place this assumed result into our recurrence relation, so $u_{k+1} = 2 \times u_k = 2 \times 2^k = 2^{k+1}$. Hence, we have shown that $P_k \Rightarrow P_{k+1}$. That is to say, a general term implies the next term must also be true.

To complete the inductive process, we must now conclude what we have found.

Hence, by mathematical induction, since P_0 is true and $P_k \Rightarrow P_{k+1}$, P_n is true for all $n \geqslant 0$.

WORKED EXAMPLE 7.1

Prove, by mathematical induction, that $\sum_{r=1}^{n} r = \frac{1}{2}n(n+1)$.

Answer

Let P_k be the statement that, for some value $n = k$:

$$\sum_{r=1}^{k} r = \frac{1}{2}k(k+1)$$

Write your opening inductive statement.

For P_1, $n = 1$: So $\sum_{r=1}^{1} r = \frac{1}{2} \times 1 \times 2 = 1$, and the sum of only the first term is 1.
Hence, P_1 is true.

Show the first case works, that is the left side and the right side of the equation are equal when $n = 1$.

Next, consider $\sum_{r=1}^{k+1} r = \frac{1}{2}k(k+1) + k + 1$

Set up the $k + 1$ case.

$$= \frac{1}{2}k^2 + \frac{3}{2}k + 1$$

$$= \frac{1}{2}(k^2 + 3k + 2)$$

$$= \frac{1}{2}(k+1)(k+2)$$

$$= \frac{1}{2}(k+1)((k+1)+1)$$

This is in the same form as the original statement for P_k, with k replaced by $k + 1$.

Hence, $P_k \Rightarrow P_{k+1}$.

Show it leads to what you would expect to be true.

Hence, since P_1 is true and $P_k \Rightarrow P_{k+1}$, by mathematical induction, P_n is true for all $n \geqslant 1$.

Conclude the inductive process.

Your task is to set up the process to verify the validity of the statement. Remember to note that each statement is actually true.

As well as the standard summation formulae, we can also use this method for any summation.

For example, let us assume we are asked to prove by induction that

$$\sum_{r=1}^{n} r(r+1) = \frac{1}{3}n(n+1)(n+2).$$

We make our statement for P_k, which is $\sum_{r=1}^{k} r(r+1) = \frac{1}{3}k(k+1)(k+2)$.

Start with $n = 1$ to get the usual initial case:

left side is $1(2) = 2$ and right side is $\frac{1}{3} \times 1 \times 2 \times 3 = 2$

Hence P_1 is true.

Then add the next term to the sum. This means adding $r(r + 1)$ with $r = k + 1$ to the sum, that is adding $(k + 1)(k + 2)$. The right side is $\frac{1}{3}k(k + 1)(k + 2) + (k + 1)(k + 2) = (k + 1)(k + 2)\left(\frac{k}{3} + 1\right)$.

This simplifies to $\frac{1}{3}(k + 1)(k + 2)(k + 3)$, which is the sum shown with k replaced by $k + 1$. This shows that $P_k \Rightarrow P_{k+1}$.

Finally, conclude and ensure that we mention the valid values for n. Hence, since P_1 is true and $P_k \Rightarrow P_{k+1}$, by mathematical induction, P_n is true for all $n \geqslant 1$.

WORKED EXAMPLE 7.2

Use mathematical induction to prove $\sum_{r=1}^{n} (r^2 - r) = \frac{n(n^2 - 1)}{3}$ for all $n \geqslant 1$.

Answer

Let P_k be the statement that, for some $n = k$:

$$\sum_{r=1}^{k} (r^2 - r) = \frac{k(k^2 - 1)}{3}$$

Write your opening inductive statement.

P_1: When $n = 1$, $\sum_{r=1}^{1} (r^2 - r) = 0$ and $\frac{1(1 - 1)}{3} = 0$.

Therefore, P_1 is true.

Show that the first case works.

Next consider $\frac{k(k^2 - 1)}{3} + (k + 1)^2 - (k + 1)$

Set up the $k + 1$ case.

$$= \frac{(k + 1)}{3}[k(k - 1) + 3(k + 1) - 3]$$
$$= \frac{(k + 1)}{3}[k^2 + 2k + 3 - 3]$$

Be aware we are aiming to reach the right side of the P_k statement with k replaced by $k + 1$. It is best to keep factors where possible.

$= \frac{1}{3}(k + 1)[(k + 1)^2 - 1]$, and so $P_k \Rightarrow P_{k+1}$.

Show it leads to what you would expect to be true.

Hence, since P_1 is true and $P_k \Rightarrow P_{k+1}$, by mathematical induction, P_n is true for all $n \geqslant 1$.

Conclude the inductive process.

As well as working with summation of series, we also need to be able to work with derivatives of functions.

Starting with a very simple example, we are going to prove by mathematical induction that if $y = e^{2x}$, then $\frac{d^n y}{dx^n} = 2^n e^{2x}$.

Let P_k be the statement that, for some value $n = k$, $\frac{d^k y}{dx^k} = 2^k e^{2x}$.

To confirm the initial case, we need to differentiate at least once, so $n = 1$.

Thus, $\frac{dy}{dx} = 2e^{2x}$, confirming from the result $\frac{d^1y}{dx^1} = 2^1 \times e^{2x}$. So P_1 is true.

Next $\frac{d}{dx}(2^k e^{2x}) = 2^k \times 2 \times e^{2x} = 2^{k+1} e^{2x}$. This is convincing enough to say it is the $(k + 1)$th derivative. Therefore, $P_k \Rightarrow P_{k+1}$.

Hence, since P_1 is true and $P_k \Rightarrow P_{k+1}$, by mathematical induction, P_n is true for all $n \geqslant 1$.

Suppose, however, the function is $y = \sin 3x$ and we are asked to prove that $\frac{d^{2n}y}{dx^{2n}} = (-1)^n 3^{2n} \sin 3x$. It is important to consider the number of times we need to differentiate. When determining the base case, we need to differentiate twice, but this counts as $n = 1$.

Also, when considering the kth case, we must differentiate this twice to obtain first $\frac{d^{2k+1}y}{dx^{2k+1}}$, then $\frac{d^{2k+2}y}{dx^{2k+2}}$, which can also be written as $\frac{d^{2(k+1)}y}{dx^{2(k+1)}}$. This will generally occur when we are dealing with a $\sin f(x)$ or $\cos f(x)$ form.

WORKED EXAMPLE 7.3

Prove by mathematical induction that the $2n$th derivative of $y = \cos(1 - 2x)$ is $\frac{d^{2n}y}{dx^{2n}} = (-1)^n 2^{2n} \cos(1 - 2x)$.

Answer

Let P_k be the statement that, for some value $n = k$:

$$\frac{d^{2k}y}{dx^{2k}} = (-1)^k 2^{2k} \cos(1 - 2x)$$

Write your opening inductive statement.

$$\frac{dy}{dx} = 2\sin(1 - 2x), \quad \frac{d^2y}{dx^2} = -4\cos(1 - 2x)$$

Differentiate twice for the $n = 1$ case.

So for $n = 1$:

$$\frac{d^2y}{dx^2} = (-1)^1 \times 2^2 \cos(1 - 2x) = -4\cos(1 - 2x)$$

This shows that P_1 is true.

$$\frac{d}{dx}((-1)^k 2^{2k} \cos(1 - 2x)) = (-1)^k(-1)2 \times 2^{2k} \sin(1 - 2x)$$

$$\frac{d}{dx}((-1)^{k+1} 2^{2k+1} \sin(1 - 2x)) = (-1)^{k+1}(-1)2 \times 2^{2k+1} \cos(1 - 2x)$$

Differentiate the kth case twice to obtain the $(k + 1)$th case.

$$= (-1)^{k+1} 2^{2(k+1)} \cos(1 - 2x)$$

Note this is the P_k statement with k replaced by $k + 1$.

Therefore, $P_k \Rightarrow P_{k+1}$.

Note the inductive step.

Hence, since P_1 is true and $P_k \Rightarrow P_{k+1}$, by mathematical induction, P_n is true for all $n \geqslant 1$.

Finish the inductive proof.

Next, let us consider recurrence relations. As an example, we will first look at $u_{n+1} = \frac{4u_n + 3}{u_n + 2}$, where $u_1 = 1$. Our task is to show that $u_n < 3$; that is, all terms are smaller than 3.

We state our P_k, which is $u_k < 3$, and is what we are trying to show.

For the case when $n = 1$ we know $u_1 = 1$ so it is definitely less than 3, as it is stated as 1.

Next take $u_{k+1} = \frac{4u_k + 3}{u_k + 2}$ and subtract 3 from both sides to get $u_{k+1} - 3 = \frac{4u_k + 3}{u_k + 2} - 3 = \frac{4u_k + 3 - 3(u_k + 2)}{u_k + 2} = \frac{u_k - 3}{u_k + 2}$. It is easier to show this is greater or less than 0 rather than greater than or less than some value a.

After simplifying we get $u_{k+1} - 3 = 1 - \frac{5}{u_k + 2}$. If $u_k < 3$ then $\frac{5}{u_k + 2} > 1$ so $1 - \frac{5}{u_k + 2} < 0$.

This implies that $u_{k+1} - 3 < 0$ and $u_{k+1} < 3$. Thus, $P_k \Rightarrow P_{k+1}$. Hence, since P_1 is true and $P_k \Rightarrow P_{k+1}$, by mathematical induction P_n is true for all $n \geqslant 1$.

TIP

You don't always need to subtract from both sides, but it does make the process more straightforward.

WORKED EXAMPLE 7.4

Prove by mathematical induction the two following problems.

a If $u_{n+1} = \frac{5u_n - 2}{u_n + 2}$, where $u_1 = 5$. Show that $u_n > 2$ for all $n \geqslant 1$.

b If $u_{n+1} = 3u_n + 2$, where $u_1 = 1$. Show that $u_n = 2 \times 3^{n-1} - 1$ for all $n \geqslant 1$.

Answer

a Let P_k be the statement that, for some value $n = k$, $u_k > 2$. — Subtract 2 from both sides.

$u_1 = 5 > 2$. Hence, P_1 is true. — Show $n = 1$ case is true.

Then $u_{k+1} - 2 = \frac{5u_k - 2}{u_k + 2} - 2$

$= \frac{5u_k - 2 - 2(u_k + 2)}{u_k + 2}$ — Simplify the algebra.

$= \frac{3u_k - 6}{u_k + 2}$

$= 3 - \frac{12}{u_k + 2}$

So if $u_k > 2$, $\frac{12}{u_k + 2} < 3$, then $3 - \frac{12}{u_k + 2} > 0$. — Simplify and show right side is positive.

Hence $u_{k+1} - 2 > 0$.

Therefore $P_k \Rightarrow P_{k+1}$.

So by mathematical induction, P_n is true for all $n \geqslant 1$. — Conclude mathematical induction.

b Let P_k be the statement that, for some value $n = k$, $u_k = 2 \times 3^{k-1}$. — Make general statement.

$u_1 = 2 \times 3^0 - 1 = 1$ so P_1 is true. — Show $n = 1$ is true.

Then $u_{k+1} = 3(2 \times 3^{k-1} - 1) + 2$

$= 2 \times 3^k - 3 + 2$ — Show by substituting that P_k leads to P_{k+1}.

$\therefore u_{k+1} = 2 \times 3^k - 1$

Therefore $P_k \Rightarrow P_{k+1}$.

So by mathematical induction, P_n is true for all $n \geqslant 1$. — Complete the inductive process.

Finally, let us look at matrices. Consider the matrix $\mathbf{A} = \begin{pmatrix} 1 & 0 \\ 1 & 1 \end{pmatrix}$. It is given that $\mathbf{A}^n = \begin{pmatrix} 1 & 0 \\ n & 1 \end{pmatrix}$.

Let P_k be the statement that, for some value $n = k$, $\mathbf{A}^k = \begin{pmatrix} 1 & 0 \\ k & 1 \end{pmatrix}$.

To show this result is true we must show the first case is true. This is achieved by considering $\mathbf{A}^1 = \begin{pmatrix} 1 & 0 \\ 1 & 1 \end{pmatrix}$, which is true. Hence P_1 is true.

Then consider $\mathbf{A}^k\mathbf{A}$, which is $\begin{pmatrix} 1 & 0 \\ k & 1 \end{pmatrix}\begin{pmatrix} 1 & 0 \\ 1 & 1 \end{pmatrix} = \begin{pmatrix} 1 & 0 \\ k+1 & 1 \end{pmatrix}$. So it is true that $P_k \Rightarrow P_{k+1}$.

Since P_1 is true and $P_k \Rightarrow P_{k+1}$, by mathematical induction, P_n is true for all $n \geqslant 1$.

WORKED EXAMPLE 7.5

The matrix $\mathbf{B} = \begin{pmatrix} 2 & 1 \\ 0 & 1 \end{pmatrix}$ is to be raised to the power n to give $\mathbf{B}^n = \begin{pmatrix} 2^n & 2^n - 1 \\ 0 & 1 \end{pmatrix}$. Prove this is true by mathematical induction.

Answer

Let P_k be the statement that, for some value $n = k$:

$\mathbf{B}^k = \begin{pmatrix} 2^k & 2^k - 1 \\ 0 & 1 \end{pmatrix}$

State P_k.

For P_1: When $n = 1$, $\mathbf{B}^1 = \begin{pmatrix} 2^1 & 2^1 - 1 \\ 0 & 1 \end{pmatrix} = \begin{pmatrix} 2 & 1 \\ 0 & 1 \end{pmatrix} = \mathbf{B}$.

Show the first case is true.

Hence, true for the case when $n = 1$.

$\mathbf{B}^k\mathbf{B} = \begin{pmatrix} 2^k & 2^k - 1 \\ 0 & 1 \end{pmatrix}\begin{pmatrix} 2 & 1 \\ 0 & 1 \end{pmatrix}$.

Show that P_k leads to P_{k+1}.

This is $\begin{pmatrix} 2 \times 2^k & 2^k + 2^k - 1 \\ 0 & 1 \end{pmatrix} = \begin{pmatrix} 2^{k+1} & 2^{k+1} - 1 \\ 0 & 1 \end{pmatrix} = \mathbf{B}^{k+1}$.

Therefore, $P_k \Rightarrow P_{k+1}$.

So since P_1 is true and $P_k \Rightarrow P_{k+1}$, by mathematical induction, P_n is true for all $n \geqslant 1$.

Finish inductive proof.

EXPLORE 7.1

If a matrix is given as $\mathbf{C} = \begin{pmatrix} \frac{1}{2} & 1 \\ 0 & 1 \end{pmatrix}$, work in groups to determine $\mathbf{C}^n$ and find out what happens as $n \to \infty$.

EXERCISE 7A

Do not use a calculator in this exercise.

P 1 Prove, by mathematical induction, that $\sum_{r=1}^{n} r(r+3) = \frac{1}{3}n(n+1)(n+5)$ for all $n \geqslant 1$.

P 2 Prove, by mathematical induction, that the sum of the first n terms of an arithmetic sequence is $\frac{n}{2}[2a + (n - 1)d]$, where a is the first term and d is the common difference.

P 3 Given that $u_{n+1} = 2u_n + 1$ and that $u_1 = 1$, show, by mathematical induction, that $u_n = 2^n - 1$ for all $n \geqslant 1$.

P 4 Use mathematical induction to prove that $\sum_{r=1}^{n} r(r^2 - 1) = \frac{1}{4}n(n + 1)(n - 1)(n + 2)$.

P 5 A function is given as $y = \cos 2x + 2\sin 2x$.

a Find the second derivative.

b Using mathematical induction, show that $\frac{\mathrm{d}^{2n}y}{\mathrm{d}x^{2n}} = (-1)^n 2^{2n}[\cos 2x + 2\sin 2x]$ for values $n \geqslant 1$.

6 The recurrence relation $u_{n+1} = 2u_n - 2$ has first term $u_1 = 10$.

a Find the values of u_2, u_3 and u_4.

b Prove by mathematical induction that $u_n = 4 \times 2^n + 2$.

P 7 Prove, by mathematical induction, that $u_n > \frac{1}{2}$ is true for the relation $u_{n+1} = \frac{u_n^2 + 1}{u_n + 2}$ where $u_1 = 1$.

P 8 Using mathematical induction, prove that $\sum_{r=1}^{n} (3r^2 + r) = n(n + 1)^2$.

P PS 9 A matrix is given as $\mathbf{A} = \begin{pmatrix} \frac{1}{3} & 0 \\ -1 & 1 \end{pmatrix}$.

a Determine the values of $\mathbf{A}^2$, $\mathbf{A}^3$ and $\mathbf{A}^4$.

b Prove, by mathematical induction, that $\mathbf{A}^n = \begin{pmatrix} \frac{1}{3^n} & 0 \\ \frac{3}{2}\left(\frac{1}{3^n} - 1\right) & 1 \end{pmatrix}$.

c State $\mathbf{A}^n$ when $n \to \infty$.

7.2 Proof by induction for divisibility

Consider the function $f(n) = 2^{2n+2} + 5$ for $n \geqslant 0$. We are given that each term is divisible by 3.

We check a few terms. For example, $f(0) = 9$, $f(1) = 21$ and $f(2) = 69$ so it seems as though they are all divisible by 3.

How can this be proved by mathematical induction?

Let P_k be the statement that, for some value $n = k$, $f(k) = 2^{2k+2} + 5$ is divisible by 3.

The first case, $n = 0$, is certainly true so we can say that P_0 is true. All the previous examples had a way of getting to the next term, by adding, multiplying, differentiating and so on.

For this function we are going to write down the case for $n = k + 1$. This is $f(k + 1) = 2^{2(k+1)+2} + 5$. Then consider $f(k + 1) - f(k) = 2^{2k+4} - 2^{2k+2}$. Now, before we progress, recall that our statement was to assume that $f(k)$ is divisible by 3. If this is true, then by writing $f(k + 1) = 2^{2k+4} - 2^{2k+2} + f(k)$ we just need to show that $2^{2k+4} - 2^{2k+2}$ is divisible by 3.

$2^{2k+4} - 2^{2k+2} = 2^4 \times 2^{2k} - 2^2 \times 2^{2k} = 16 \times 2^{2k} - 4 \times 2^{2k} = 12 \times 2^{2k}$ or $3 \times 4 \times 2^{2k}$. This is divisible by 3.

So if $2^{2k+4} - 2^{2k+2}$ and $f(k)$ are both divisible by 3, then $f(k+1)$ must be divisible by 3.

Therefore, $P_k \Rightarrow P_{k+1}$, and since P_0 is true and $P_k \Rightarrow P_{k+1}$, by mathematical induction P_n is true for all $n \geqslant 0$.

This process is summarised in Key point 7.2.

KEY POINT 7.2

If $f(a)$ is assumed to be divisible by b, and k is divisible by b, then $f(a+1) - f(a) = k$ implies that $f(a+1)$ must also be divisible by b.

WORKED EXAMPLE 7.6

A function is defined as $f(n) = 3^{n+2} + 5$. Using mathematical induction, prove that $3^{n+2} + 5$ is always divisible by 2 for $n \geqslant 0$.

Answer

Let P_k be the statement that, for some value $n = k$, $3^{k+2} + 5$ is divisible by 2. — State P_k.

For P_0: when $n = 0$, $f(0) = 14$. So P_0 is true. — Show base case is true.

Then $f(k+1) = 3^{k+1+2} + 5 = 3 \times 3^{k+2} + 5$. — Write down the difference.

So $f(k+1) - f(k) = 3 \times 3^{k+2} + 5 - 3^{k+2} - 5$

We assumed $f(k)$ was divisible by 2, so we can then say that — State initial assumption..

$f(k+1) = 2 \times 3^{k+2} + f(k)$, which is clearly divisible by 2. — Show $f(k+1)$ must be divisible by 2.

Therefore $P_k \Rightarrow P_{k+1}$. — Inductive step.

Hence, for all $n \geqslant 0$, by mathematical induction P_n is always true. — Final conclusion.

This approach also works with polynomials, for example, showing that $f(n) = n^2 + (n+2)^2$ is divisible by 2.

We may have identified that this will be an even number, but we are going to prove it using mathematical induction.

Let P_k be the statement that, for some value $n = k$, $f(k) = k^2 + (k+2)^2$ is divisible by 2.

We see that $f(0) = 0^2 + 2^2 = 4$, so $f(0)$ is divisible by 2. We can say that P_0 is true.

Then $f(k+1) = (k+1)^2 + (k+1+2)^2 = (k+1)^2 + (k+3)^2$.

$$\begin{aligned}\text{Next, } f(k+1) - f(k) &= (k+1)^2 + (k+3)^2 - k^2 - (k+2)^2 \\ &= k^2 + 2k + 1 + k^2 + 6k + 9 - k^2 - k^2 - 4k - 4 \\ &= 2k^2 + 8k + 10 - (2k^2 + 4k + 4) \\ &= 4k + 6 = 2(2k+3)\end{aligned}$$

which is divisible by 2 and so it follows that $P_k \Rightarrow P_{k+1}$.

We can now conclude our argument. Since P_0 is true and $P_k \Rightarrow P_{k+1}$, by mathematical induction P_n is true for all $n \geqslant 0$.

WORKED EXAMPLE 7.7

A function is given as $f(n) = (n+2)^3 + (2n+1)^3$. Prove by induction that $f(n)$ is divisible by 3 for all values $n \geqslant 0$.

Answer

Let P_k be the statement that, for some value $n = k$, $(k+2)^3 + (2k+1)^3$ is divisible by 3. — State P_k.

For P_0: Let $n = 0 \Rightarrow f(0) = (0+2)^3 + (0+1)^3 = 9 = 3 \times 3$ which is divisible by 3 so f(0) is divisible by 3. So P_0 is true. — Show the first value works.

$f(k+1) = (k+3)^3 + (2k+3)^3$, then using — Find the difference between successive values.

$$f(k+1) - f(k) = (k+3)^3 + (2k+3)^3 - (k+2)^3 - (2k+1)^3$$
$$= k^3 + 9k^2 + 27k + 27 + 8k^3 + 36k^2 + 54k + 27 - k^3 - 6k^2 - 12k - 8 - 8k^3 - 12k^2 - 6k - 1$$

which gives $27k^2 + 63k + 45$.

Hence, $f(k+1) = 3(9k^2 + 21k + 15) + f(k)$ which is divisible by 3 as $3(9k^2 + 21k + 15)$ has a factor of 3. We have stated earlier that $f(k)$ is divisible by 3, and therefore $P_k \Rightarrow P_{k+1}$. — Show the inductive step.

Thus, since P_0 is true and $P_k \Rightarrow P_{k+1}$, P_n is true by mathematical induction for all $n \geqslant 0$. — State the conclusion.

EXERCISE 7B

Do not use a calculator in this exercise.

P 1 Prove, by mathematical induction, that $n^3 + 2n$ is divisible by 3 for all $n \geqslant 1$.

P 2 Prove, by mathematical induction, that $8^n - 3^n$ is divisible by 5 for all $n \geqslant 1$.

P 3 Prove, by mathematical induction, that $3^{2n} - 1$ is divisible by 8 for all $n \geqslant 1$.

P 4 Prove, by mathematical induction, that $3^{(3n+2)} + 4$ is divisible by 13 for $n \geqslant 0$.

P 5 A function is given as $f(n) = (2n+1)^3 + (3n-2)^2 + n + 3$. Using mathematical induction, prove that $f(n)$ is always even for $n \geqslant 0$.

P 6 Using mathematical induction, prove that $8^n - 1$ is always divisible by 7.

P 7 Prove, by mathematical induction, that $n^3 - n$ is divisible by 6 for $n \geqslant 2$.

P 8 A function is given as $f(n) = 3^{4n+3} + 7^{2n+1} + 6$. Show by using proof by induction that $f(n)$ is always divisible by 8 for $n \geqslant 0$.

WORKED PAST PAPER QUESTION

Prove by induction that $\sum_{r=1}^{n}(3r^5 + r^3) = \frac{1}{2}n^3(n+1)^3$ for all $n \geqslant 1$.

Cambridge International AS & A Level Further Mathematics 9231 Paper 1 Q7 (first part) June 2008

Answer

Let P_k be the statement that, for some value $n = k$, $\sum_{r=1}^{k}(3r^5 + r^3) = \frac{1}{2}k^3(k+1)^3$.

For $n = 1$: P_1 is $\sum_{r=1}^{1}(3r^5 + r^3) = (3 \times 1 + 1) = 4$, and also $\frac{1}{2} \times 1 \times (1+1)^3 = 4$.

Therefore, P_1 is true.

Then $\sum_{r=1}^{k+1}(3r^5 + r^3) = \frac{1}{2}k^3(k+1)^3 + 3(k+1)^5 + (k+1)^3$,

which is $(k+1)^3\left[\frac{1}{2}k^3 + 3(k+1)^2 + 1\right] = \frac{1}{2}(k+1)^3[k^3 + 6k^2 + 12k + 8] = \frac{1}{2}(k+1)^3(k+2)^3$

$= \frac{1}{2}(k+1)^3(k+1+1)^3$

Therefore $P_k \Rightarrow P_{k+1}$.

Hence, since P_1 is true and $P_k \Rightarrow P_{k+1}$, P_n is true by mathematical induction for all values $n \geqslant 1$.

DID YOU KNOW?

As far back as 370 BCE, ancient mathematicians such as Plato were using inductive proof in an implicit way. Even Euclid used a form of induction when proving the number of primes is infinite.

The first mathematician to explicitly state the inductive procedure in the correct manner was Blaise Pascal in 1665.

Checklist of learning and understanding

Setting up the proof:

- Let P_k be the statement that, for some value k, your expression is true.
- Start with the smallest possible value for n and show the statement is true for P_0, or P_1, or whichever P_n has been found to be true.
- Show this statement leads to the next value $k+1$. See the separate sections below for the method.
- Complete the proof with a conclusion that mentions your P_n is true for all values as stated in the question. The statement should be similar to 'Since P_0 is true and $P_k \Rightarrow P_{k+1}$, by mathematical induction P_n is true for all $n \geqslant 0$.'

Summations:

- If $\sum_{r=1}^{n} \mathrm{f}(r) = \mathrm{g}(n)$ is given, assume $\sum_{r=1}^{k} \mathrm{f}(r) = \mathrm{g}(k)$ is true for P_k and add $\mathrm{f}(k+1)$ to $\mathrm{g}(k)$ to show that $P_k \Rightarrow P_{k+1}$.

Derivatives:

- If $y = \mathrm{f}(x)$, $\frac{\mathrm{d}^n y}{\mathrm{d}x^n} = \mathrm{f}^{(n)}(x)$ is given, assume $\frac{\mathrm{d}^k y}{\mathrm{d}x^k} = \mathrm{f}^{(k)}(x)$ is true for P_k. Differentiate $\frac{\mathrm{d}^k y}{\mathrm{d}x^k} = \mathrm{f}^{(k)}(x)$ as many times as required to show $P_k \Rightarrow P_{k+1}$.

Recurrence relations:

- If $u_{n+1} = \mathrm{f}(u_n)$ and $u_n = \mathrm{g}(n)$ are given, assume $u_k = \mathrm{g}(k)$ is true for P_k and put this into $\mathrm{f}(u_k)$ to obtain u_{k+1}. This leads to the inductive step where $P_k \Rightarrow P_{k+1}$.

Matrices:

- If $\mathbf{A}^n$ and $\mathbf{A}$ are given, assume $\mathbf{A}^k$ is true for P_k and determine $\mathbf{A}^k\mathbf{A}$ to show $P_k \Rightarrow P_{k+1}$.

Divisibility:

- If $\mathrm{f}(n)$ is given as being divisible by b, assume $\mathrm{f}(k)$ is divisible by b for P_k and show that $\mathrm{f}(k+1) - \mathrm{f}(k) = ab$, which leads to $P_k \Rightarrow P_{k+1}$.

END-OF-CHAPTER REVIEW EXERCISE 7

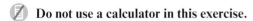

Do not use a calculator in this exercise.

1 Prove by mathematical induction that, for all non-negative integers n, $11^{2n} + 25^n + 22$ is divisible by 24.

Cambridge International AS & A Level Further Mathematics 9231 Paper 11 Q3 June 2014

2 It is given that $u_r = r \times r!$ for $r = 1, 2, 3, \ldots$. Let $S_n = u_1 + u_2 + u_3 + \cdots + u_n$. Write down the values of $2! - S_1$, $3! - S_2$, $4! - S_3$, $5! - S_4$.

Conjecture a formula for S_n.

Prove, by mathematical induction, a formula for S_n, for all positive integers n.

Cambridge International AS & A Level Further Mathematics 9231 Paper 11 Q3 November 2014

3 The sequence $a_1, a_2, a_3, \ldots$ is such that $a_1 > 5$ and $a_{n+1} = \frac{4a_n}{5} + \frac{5}{a_n}$ for every positive integer n.

Prove by mathematical induction that $a_n > 5$ for every positive integer n.

Prove also that $a_n > a_{n+1}$ for every positive integer n.

Cambridge International AS & A Level Further Mathematics 9231 Paper 11 Q3 June 2015

CROSS-TOPIC REVIEW EXERCISE 1

1 Prove by mathematical induction that $\sum_{r=1}^{n}(r^2 - r) = \frac{1}{3}n(n^2 - 1)$.

Hence, determine an expression for $\sum_{r=n+1}^{2n}(r^2 - r)$.

2 The cubic equation $x^3 - 5x^2 + 1 = 0$ has roots α, β, γ.

a Find the values of S_1 and S_3.

Another cubic equation has roots $\alpha^2, \beta^2, \gamma^2$.

b Find the cubic equation with these roots.

c Hence, or otherwise, determine the result of S_6.

3 The curve C is given as $y = \dfrac{2+x}{x^2+5x+4}$.

a Write down the asymptotes of C.

b Find $\dfrac{dy}{dx}$.

c Determine the number of turning points.

d Sketch the curve C, showing all asymptotes, and stating intercepts with the coordinate axes.

4 Three planes are given as:

Π_1: $x - 2y + 3z = 5$, Π_2: $-x + 4y + z = -5$ and Π_3: $2x - 2y + 9z = 9$.

By writing these three equations in the form $\mathbf{A}x = b$, state the matrix $\mathbf{A}$ and perform row operations on your augmented matrix until it is in row echelon form.

5 The polar curve C is given as $r = 2\sin 2\theta$, for $0 \leqslant \theta \leqslant \frac{\pi}{2}$.

a Sketch the curve C.

b Find the greatest distance of the curve from the y-axis.

c Evaluate the area inside the polar curve C, for the interval $0 \leqslant \theta \leqslant \frac{\pi}{2}$.

6 Four points $A(2, 3, 1)$, $B(0, 4, -3)$, $C(2, 2, 0)$ and $D(-1, 0, 1)$ are given.

The line l_1 passes through A and B, and the line l_2 passes through C and D.

a Find the angle between the lines l_1 and l_2.

b Find the shortest distance between the lines l_1 and l_2.

7 Prove by mathematical induction that, for all values $n \geqslant 1$, $7^n + 2^{3n} - 1$ is divisible by 7.

8 The equation $x^3 - 4x + 2 = 0$ has roots α, β, γ.

a Find the value of $\dfrac{1}{\alpha^2} + \dfrac{1}{\beta^2} + \dfrac{1}{\gamma^2}$.

b Show that the matrix $\begin{pmatrix} 1 & \alpha & 1 \\ 2\gamma & 0 & \beta \\ \gamma & 0 & 3\beta \end{pmatrix}$ is non-singular.

9 Express $u_n = \frac{1}{4n^2 - 1}$ in partial fractions, and hence find $\sum_{n=1}^{n} u_n$ in terms of n.

Deduce that the infinite series $u_1 + u_2 + u_3 + \ldots$ is convergent and state the sum to infinity.

Cambridge International AS & A Level Mathematics 9231 Paper 1 Q1 June 2006

10 The curve C has equation $y = \frac{5(x-1)(x+2)}{(x-2)(x+3)}$.

i Express y in the form $P + \frac{Q}{x-2} + \frac{R}{x+3}$.

ii Show that $\frac{dy}{dx} = 0$ for exactly one value of x and find the corresponding value of y.

iii Write down the equations of all the asymptotes of C.

iv Find the set of values of k for which the line $y = k$ does not intersect C.

Cambridge International AS & A Level Further Mathematics 9231 Paper 1 Q11a November 2003

11 Given that the matrix $\mathbf{A} = \begin{pmatrix} 2 & 2 & 4 \\ 2 & 2 & 2 \\ 2 & 3 & 2 \end{pmatrix}$ is non-singular, find the matrix $\mathbf{B}$ such that $\mathbf{BA}^2 = \mathbf{I}$.

12 Given that $u_{n+1} = \frac{4u_n + 7}{u_n + 2}$ has first term $u_1 = 3$, prove, by mathematical induction, that $u_n < 4$ for all $n \geqslant 1$.

Chapter 8
Continuous random variables

In this chapter you will learn how to:

- use a probability density function that may be defined as a piecewise function
- use the general result $E(g(X)) = \int f(x)\, g(x)\, dx$, where $f(x)$ is the probability density function of the continuous random variable X, and $g(X)$ is a function of X
- understand and use the relationship between the probability density function (PDF) and the cumulative distribution function (CDF), and use either to evaluate probabilities or percentiles
- use cumulative distribution functions of related variables in simple cases.

PREREQUISITE KNOWLEDGE

<table>
<tr><th>Where it comes from</th><th>What you should be able to do</th><th>Check your skills</th></tr>
<tr><td>AS & A Level Mathematics Probability & Statistics 1, Chapter 4</td><td>Calculate E(X) and Var(X).</td><td>1 <table><tr><td>x</td><td>1</td><td>2</td><td>3</td><td>4</td></tr><tr><td>P($X = x$)</td><td>0.2</td><td>0.4</td><td>0.3</td><td>0.1</td></tr></table>Find E(X) and Var(X).</td></tr>
<tr><td>AS & A Level Mathematics Pure Mathematics 1, Chapter 9</td><td>Integrate and evaluate simple functions in a given interval.</td><td>2 Evaluate $\int_3^5 x^2 \, dx$.</td></tr>
</table>

What are continuous random variables?

A continuous random variable is a random variable that can take all values in an interval. It can be used to model quantities we measure, such as time or length.

A random variable could be a set of possible values from a random experiment. If the data can take any value within a given range then we say it is a continuous random variable. Suppose we measure the times people spend waiting for a bus at a bus stop. We know that a bus arrives every 13 minutes, but we do not know when the last bus arrived. Here, the waiting time is continuous and so we can model this situation with a continuous random variable. We can calculate mean waiting times, for example, the probability we will need to wait more than eight minutes.

In this chapter we shall study continuous random variables as well as their expectation and variance.

We shall use the **probability density function** (PDF) and **cumulative distribution function** (CDF) to calculate percentiles and probabilities. There are similarities with the work you did on discrete random variables and the normal distribution in AS & A Level Mathematics Probability & Statistics 1, Chapter 4 and Chapter 8. This work will help you to understand how the normal distribution is created.

We shall link related variables to find the PDF and CDF of functions of a variable.

8.1 The probability density function

A probability density function describes the probability of a continuous random variable in a similar way that a probability distribution table describes the probability of a discrete random variable.

The probability that a continuous random variable is equal to a particular value is always zero. This means we cannot use a table to describe the probability, so we use a function instead.

We need to know the conditions for a function on a given interval to represent a probability density function. Probability cannot be negative, and so a probability density function can *never* be negative, as shown in Key point 8.1.

KEY POINT 8.1

The function that defines the probability density function is always positive.

Condition 1: For $f(x)$ to represent a probability density function, $f(x) \geqslant 0$ for all values of x.

As the random variable is continuous, instead of adding values to evaluate probabilities over an interval, we must integrate the probability density function. Remember that integration can be used to evaluate the area bounded by a curve and the x-axis between particular limits. The area between the function and the x-axis defines the probability over an interval. The total area between the function and the x-axis must equal 1, as it represents the total probability of the probability density function, as shown in Key point 8.2.

KEY POINT 8.2

The area under the probability density function must equal 1.

This statement is equivalent to saying that the sum of all probabilities must equal 1.

Condition 2: For $f(x)$ to represent a probability density function, $\int f(x)\,dx = 1$ for all values of x.

Conditions 1 and 2 must both be true for $f(x)$ to represent a probability density function.

Consider the following grouped continuous data.

	Frequency	Relative frequency	Relative frequency density
$0 \leqslant x < 10$	40	$0.2\dot{6}$	$0.02\dot{6}$
$10 \leqslant x < 15$	30	0.2	0.04
$15 \leqslant x < 20$	20	$0.1\dot{3}$	$0.02\dot{6}$
$20 \leqslant x < 30$	10	$0.0\dot{6}$	$0.00\dot{6}$
$30 \leqslant x < 40$	20	$0.2\dot{6}$	$0.02\dot{6}$
$40 \leqslant x \leqslant 50$	30	0.2	0.02

If we were to draw a histogram of the continuous random variable, allowing the frequency to equal the area, we would have a histogram whose total area equals the frequency. If, instead, we considered the relative frequencies, then the area of the histogram would be 1. We know that relative frequency can represent probabilities.

The data are displayed in a histogram with a total area of 1.

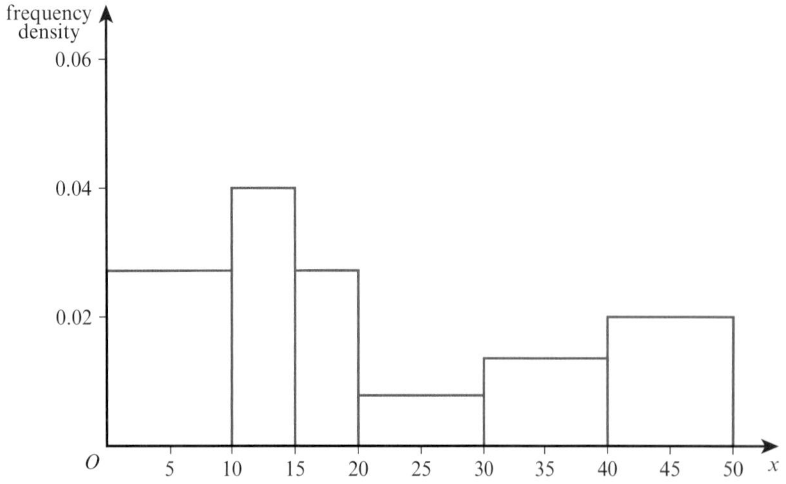

In fact, this continuous data can be modelled using the following curve.

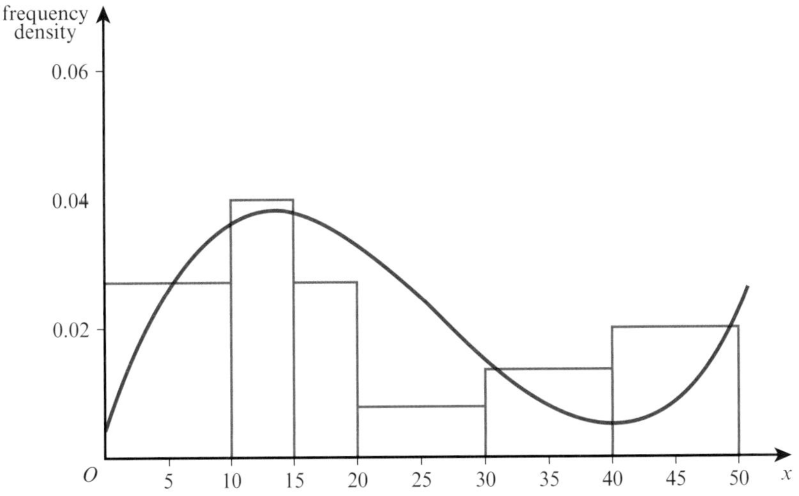

The area under this curve is also equal to 1.

WORKED EXAMPLE 8.1

Find the value of k for which $f(x) = kx^2$ could represent a probability density function over the interval $1 \leqslant x \leqslant 3$.

Answer

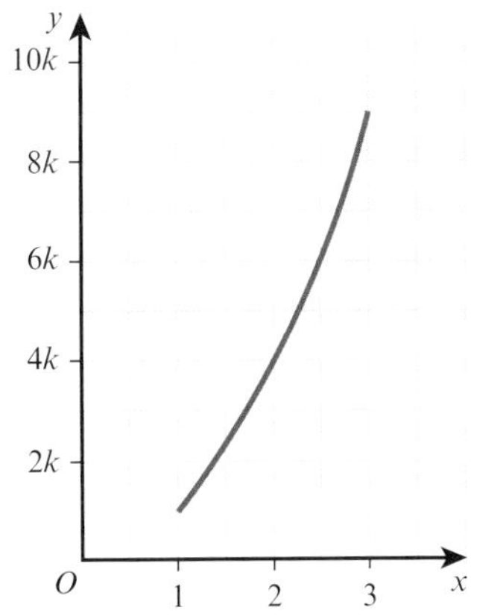

Check that the function is not negative. It is helpful to draw a sketch.

Alternatively, you may be required to show that a function is *always* positive for an interval.

$$\int_1^3 kx^2\,dx = 1$$

Evaluate the integral with limits of 3 and 1, and equate to 1.

$$\left[\frac{kx^3}{3}\right]_1^3 = 1$$

Substitute in the limits.

$$k\left(\frac{3^3}{3} - \frac{1^3}{3}\right) = 1$$

Take out the common factor k.

$$\frac{26k}{3} = 1$$

Therefore, $k = \frac{3}{26}$.

Rearrange.

To find the probability between two values of the continuous random variable, integrate the PDF, $f(x)$, between those values, as shown in Key point 8.3. Note that, as $P(X = a) = 0$, $P(X < a)$ and $P(X \leqslant a)$ have the same value.

KEY POINT 8.3

The probability between two values of the continuous random variable is:

$$P(a < X < b) = \int_a^b f(x)\,dx = F(b) - F(a)$$

DID YOU KNOW?

In calculus, if we differentiate $f(x)$, we label it $f'(x)$ and call it the **derivative**.

If we integrate $f(x)$, we get $F(x)$ and call it the **primitive**.

We will learn more about this later but, in simple terms, when we integrate a probability density function $f(x)$ we find the cumulative distribution function $F(x)$. We can use cumulative distribution functions to calculate percentiles of distributions and probabilities. For example, $P(a \leqslant X \leqslant b) = F(b) - F(a)$.

When dealing with the normal distribution, we use $\Phi(z)$ to represent the cumulative distribution function. Φ is upper case phi in Greek. Its Latin equivalent is F. The probabilities are calculated in the same way from tables:

$$P(a \leqslant X \leqslant b) = \Phi(b) - \Phi(a)$$

REWIND

This is why, when dealing with discrete random variables in AS & A Level Probability & Statistics 1, Chapter 6, we used the following to represent the cumulative probability.

$F(x_0) = P(X \leqslant x_0)$

It is important to define fully the probability density function for all values of x. We must state for which values the PDF is valid, and for which values it is 0.

Consider the probability density function from Worked example 8.1: $f(x) = \frac{3x^2}{26}$ for $1 \leqslant x \leqslant 3$.

We should define this function for all values of x, so we write it as:

$$f(x) = \begin{cases} \frac{3x^2}{26} & 1 \leqslant x \leqslant 3 \\ 0 & \text{otherwise} \end{cases}$$

Now the function is defined for all values of x.

This notation can be used when dealing with probability density functions that are **piecewise functions**, as shown in Key point 8.4.

KEY POINT 8.4

Sometimes, probability density functions are represented by a combination of different functions, each corresponding to a part of the domain. Such probability density functions are called piecewise functions.

WORKED EXAMPLE 8.2

Consider the continuous random variable X, which has probability density function:

$$f(x) = \begin{cases} k(x+1) & 1 \leqslant x < 4 \\ k & 4 \leqslant x \leqslant 8 \\ 0 & \text{otherwise} \end{cases}$$

a Find the value of k.

b Calculate $P(2 \leqslant X < 6)$.

Answer

a

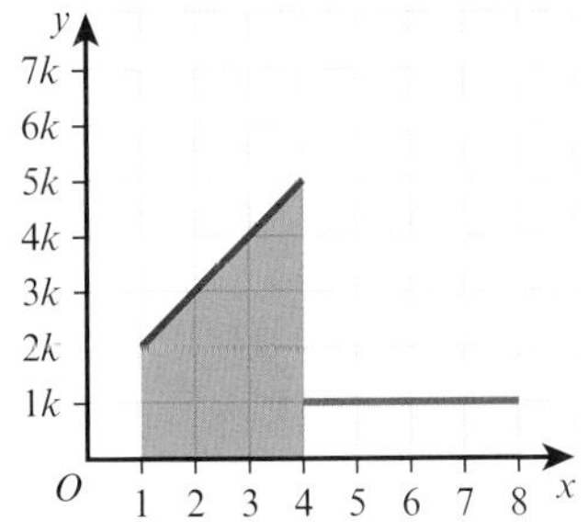

The function does *not* need to be piecewise continuous.

$$\int_1^4 k(x+1)\,dx + \int_4^8 k\,dx = 1$$

The total area must be 1.

$$k\left[\frac{x^2}{2}+x\right]_1^4 + k[x]_4^8 = 1$$

Take out k as a common factor to make the integration and algebra easier. Integrate and solve for k.

$$k\left(12-\frac{3}{2}\right)+k(8-4)=1$$

$$\frac{29k}{2}=1$$

$$k=\frac{2}{29}$$

b

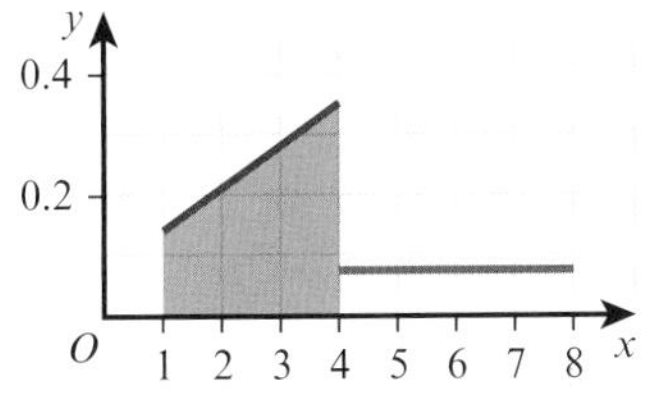

Ensure that the probabilities correspond to the domains of the PDF.

It is easy to make a numerical mistake, so show *all* of your working.

$$P(2 \leqslant X < 6) = P(2 \leqslant X < 4) + P(4 \leqslant X < 6)$$

$$\int_2^4 \frac{2}{29}(x+1)\,dx + \int_4^6 \frac{2}{29}\,dx$$

$$= \frac{2}{29}\left(\left[\frac{x^2}{2}+x\right]_2^4 + [x]_4^6\right)$$

$$= \frac{2}{29}((12-4)+(6-4))$$

$$P(2 \leqslant X < 6) = \frac{20}{29}$$

Alternatively:

Work out the area of the trapezium and the rectangle instead of using integration.

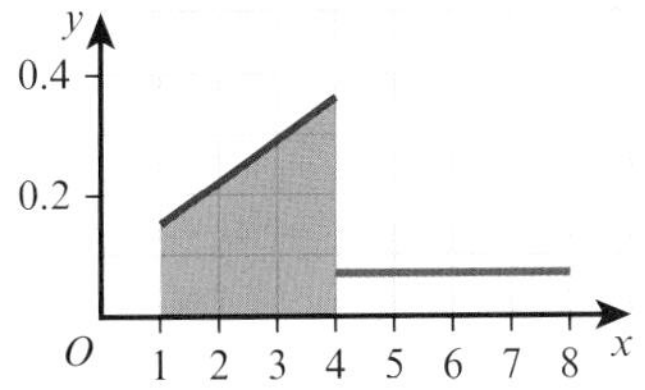

$$P(2 \leqslant X < 6) = P(2 \leqslant X < 4) + P(4 \leqslant X < 6)$$

For the trapezium: Find the area of the trapezium.

$f(2) = \frac{6}{29}$, $f(4) = \frac{10}{29}$

$$P(2 \leqslant X < 4) = \frac{2\left(\frac{6}{29} + \frac{10}{29}\right)}{2} = \frac{16}{29}$$

For the rectangle: Find the area of the rectangle, and add this to the area of the trapezium.

$$P(4 \leqslant X < 6) = 2 \times \frac{2}{29} = \frac{4}{29}$$

Total area $= \frac{16}{29} + \frac{4}{29} = \frac{20}{29}$ as before.

EXERCISE 8A

1 For each of the following, state whether or not it is a valid probability density function, giving a reason.

a $f(x) = \begin{cases} \frac{1}{10}(x+3) & 1 \leqslant x \leqslant 3 \\ 0 & \text{otherwise} \end{cases}$

b $f(x) = \begin{cases} -3x^2 + \frac{9}{2}x & 0 \leqslant x \leqslant 2 \\ 0 & \text{otherwise} \end{cases}$

c $f(x) = \begin{cases} x & 0 \leqslant x < 1 \\ 2 - x & 1 \leqslant x \leqslant 2 \\ 0 & \text{otherwise} \end{cases}$

d $f(x) = \begin{cases} x^2 & -1 \leqslant x \leqslant 2 \\ 0 & \text{otherwise} \end{cases}$

2 Sketch the following probability density functions.

a $f(x) = \begin{cases} \frac{1}{12}(x^2+3) & -1 \leqslant x \leqslant 2 \\ 0 & \text{otherwise} \end{cases}$

b $f(x) = \begin{cases} \frac{x}{4} & 0 \leqslant x < 2 \\ \frac{1}{2} & 2 \leqslant x \leqslant 3 \\ 0 & \text{otherwise} \end{cases}$

c $f(x) = \begin{cases} \frac{1}{20} & 0 \leqslant x < 5 \\ \frac{1}{96}(x-5) & 5 \leqslant x \leqslant 17 \\ 0 & \text{otherwise} \end{cases}$

3 Find the value of k for which $f(x) = \begin{cases} kx(3-x) & 0 \leqslant x \leqslant 3 \\ 0 & \text{otherwise} \end{cases}$ represents a probability density function.

4 Find the exact value of k for which $f(x) = \begin{cases} ke^{2(x-5)} & 3 \leqslant x \leqslant 4 \\ 0 & \text{otherwise} \end{cases}$ represents a probability density function.

5 For the given probability density function $f(x) = \begin{cases} k(x+1) & 5 \leqslant x \leqslant 9 \\ 0 & \text{otherwise} \end{cases}$, find:

a the value of k

b $P(X = 7)$

c $P(X < 8)$

d $P(X > 6)$

6 For the given probability density function $f(x) = \begin{cases} k(x^2 - 2x + 3) & 1 \leqslant x \leqslant 4 \\ 0 & \text{otherwise} \end{cases}$, find:

a the value of k

b $P(X < 2)$

c $P(1.5 \leqslant X < 3.5)$

7 Find the value of k for which $f(x) = \begin{cases} kx & 0 \leqslant x < 6 \\ \frac{k}{2}(9 - x) & 6 \leqslant x < 9 \\ 0 & \text{otherwise} \end{cases}$ represents a probability density function.

8 Find the value of k for which $f(x) = \begin{cases} \frac{k}{2}(x+1) & -1 \leqslant x < 3 \\ 2k & 3 \leqslant x < 4 \\ -\frac{2k}{3}(x+7) & 4 \leqslant x \leqslant 7 \\ 0 & \text{otherwise} \end{cases}$ represents a probability density function.

9 For the given probability density function $f(x) = \begin{cases} 4k & 5 \leqslant x < 7 \\ k(11 - x) & 7 \leqslant x < 11 \\ 0 & \text{otherwise} \end{cases}$, find:

a the value of k

b $P(X < 6)$

c $P(X > 8)$

d $P(6 < X \leqslant 10)$

10 For the given probability density function $f(x) = \begin{cases} k(6x - x^2) & 0 \leqslant x < 3 \\ 9k(5 - x) & 3 \leqslant x \leqslant 5 \\ 0 & \text{otherwise} \end{cases}$, find:

a the value of k

b $P(X < 3)$

c $P(X < 4.5)$

8.2 The cumulative distribution function

In this section, we shall see how to find a cumulative distribution function (CDF) from a probability density function (PDF), and vice versa.

We know from Section 8.1 that the area between the graph of a probability density function and the x-axis represents the probability. This area is found by integrating the PDF between suitable limits. If we integrate the PDF between the smallest value in the domain and use a variable as the upper limit, it will create a function that we can use to find the cumulative probability. We will not need to integrate the PDF every time. This is called the cumulative distribution function. We must define this for all values of x, as shown in Key point 8.5.

KEY POINT 8.5

Let the continuous random variable X have a probability density function $f(x)$. Then the cumulative distribution function is defined as:

$$F(x) = P(X \leqslant x) = \int_{-\infty}^{x} f(t)\,dt$$

Note that in Key point 8.5, since the limit is the variable x, we should not use x as the variable in the PDF. We simply choose a different letter here, known as a dummy variable.

Alternatively, instead of using limits, we could perform an indefinite integration. Then we would use the fact that the cumulative value at the right-hand end of the domain is 1 to find the constant of integration.

In Worked example 8.3, the probability density function consists of a single function. The first method shows the use of limits. The second method shows how we can use indefinite integration.

WORKED EXAMPLE 8.3

The continuous random variable X has probability density function $f(x) = \begin{cases} \frac{1}{12}x & 1 \leqslant x \leqslant 5 \\ 0 & \text{otherwise} \end{cases}$.

Find the cumulative distribution function.

Answer

Method 1: Using the limits

$F(x) = \int_1^x \frac{1}{12}t\,dt$ — Set up the integral. The lower limit is now 1. This is the smallest value in the domain.

$F(x) = \left[\frac{t^2}{24}\right]_1^x$ — Use t within the integral since x is within the limit.

$F(x) = \frac{x^2 - 1}{24}$ — Integrate and substitute in the limits.

It is worth checking that $F(5) = 1$ and $F(1) = 0$.

Method 2: Using indefinite integration

$F(x) = \int \frac{x}{12}\,dx$ — Since we are not using limits here, we can still use x as our variable.

$F(x) = \frac{x^2}{24} + c$

Using $F(1) = 0$ — We can use either $F(1) = 0$ or $F(5) = 1$ to find c: $F(1) = 0$ since *no* probabilities have yet been added; $F(5) = 1$ since *all* probabilities have been added.

$0 = \frac{1^2}{24} + c$

$c = -\frac{1}{24}$

$F(x) = \frac{x^2}{24} - \frac{1}{24}$

$$F(x) = \begin{cases} 0 & x < 1 \\ \frac{x^2 - 1}{24} & 1 \leqslant x \leqslant 5 \\ 1 & x > 5 \end{cases}$$

For both methods, define the cumulative distribution fully.

In Worked example 8.3, the probability density function has only one function. If the probability density function is a piecewise function, we need to find the cumulative distribution function for *each* piece of the function. We need to ensure that the cumulative probability from previous parts of the function is added. Worked example 8.4 shows two parts to the piecewise function.

Notice that in Worked example 8.4, the probability density function is not continuous. However, the cumulative distribution function *must* be continuous.

WORKED EXAMPLE 8.4

The continuous random variable X has probability density function $f(x) = \begin{cases} \frac{2}{29}(x+1) & 1 \leqslant x < 4 \\ \frac{2}{29} & 4 \leqslant x \leqslant 8 \\ 0 & \text{otherwise.} \end{cases}$

a Find the cumulative distribution function.

b Find $P(2 < X < 5)$.

c Find the value of a for which $P(X > a) = 0.1$.

Answer

a **Method 1**

Take each function in turn. A sketch graph is useful.

If $1 \leqslant x < 4$:

$$F(x) = \int_1^x \frac{2}{29}(t+1)\,dt$$

Find the cumulative distribution function for the first function.

$$= \left[\frac{2}{29}\left(\frac{t^2}{2} + t\right)\right]_1^x$$

$$= \frac{2}{29}\left(\frac{x^2}{2} + x\right) - \frac{2}{29}\left(\frac{1}{2} + 1\right)$$

$$F(x) = \frac{x^2}{29} + \frac{2x}{29} - \frac{3}{29}$$

And when $x = 4$, $F(4) = \frac{21}{29}$.

If $4 \leqslant x \leqslant 8$:

$$F(x) = F(4) + \int_4^x \frac{2}{29}\,dt$$

Since the cumulative distribution is continuous, the second domain starts at 4.

$$= \frac{21}{29} + \left[\frac{2t}{29}\right]_4^x$$

$$= \frac{21}{29} + \left(\frac{2x}{29} - \frac{8}{29}\right)$$

$$= \frac{13}{29} + \frac{2x}{29}$$

Check that $F(8) = 1$.

Method 2

If $1 \leqslant x < 4$:

Treat each part separately.

$$F(x) = \int \frac{2}{29}(x+1)\,dx$$

$$= \frac{x^2}{29} + \frac{2x}{29} + c$$

Since $F(1) = 0$:

$$0 = \frac{1}{29} + \frac{2}{29} + c$$

Use the condition $F(1) = 0$.

Leading to $c = -\frac{3}{29}$.

Therefore, for this domain:

$$F(x) = \frac{x^2}{29} + \frac{2x}{29} - \frac{3}{29}$$

If $4 \leqslant x \leqslant 8$: $F(x) = \int \frac{2}{29}\,dx$

$$= \frac{2}{29}x + k$$

Here there is no need to add F(4) since it becomes absorbed into the constant of integration.

Since $F(8) = 1$:

There are two values we can use to calculate k. $F(4) = \frac{21}{29}$ and $F(8) = 1$. It is best to use $F(8) = 1$, since we may have calculated $F(4)$ incorrectly.

$$1 = \frac{16}{29} + k$$

So, $k = \frac{13}{29}$

And therefore for $4 \leqslant x < 8$:

$$F(x) = \frac{2x}{29} + \frac{13}{29}$$

$$F(x) = \begin{cases} 0 & x < 1 \\ \dfrac{x^2}{29} + \dfrac{2x}{29} - \dfrac{3}{29} & 1 \leqslant x < 4 \\ \dfrac{2x}{29} + \dfrac{13}{29} & 4 \leqslant x \leqslant 8 \\ 1 & x > 8 \end{cases}$$

Define F(x).

These can be factorised.

b Find $P(2 < X < 5)$.

Make sure that you use the correct part of F(x) when evaluating the probability.

$$P(2 < X < 5) = P(X < 5) - P(X < 2)$$

$$= F(5) - F(2)$$

$$= \frac{2 \times 5 + 13}{29} - \frac{2^2 + 2 \times 2 - 3}{29}$$

$$= \frac{23}{29} - \frac{5}{29}$$

$$P(2 < X < 5) = \frac{18}{29}$$

c Find the value of a for which $P(X > a) = 0.1$.

Consider carefully in which domain the value of a will lie.

$F(a) = 0.9$

But since $F(4) = \dfrac{21}{29}$ and $F(8) = 1$ then

$F(4) < F(a) < F(8)$.

This implies $4 < a < 8$:

Check that your answer is in the correct domain.

$$F(a) = \frac{(2a + 13)}{29} = 0.9$$

$$a = 6.55$$

Percentiles

A **percentile** is a value that has a cumulative probability equal to a given probability.

For example, the 90th percentile, α, of a continuous random variable, X, is such that $P(X \leqslant \alpha) = 0.9$. Part **c** of Worked example 8.4 demonstrates how we find percentiles using the cumulative distribution function. a is the value below which 90% of the area lies. It is known as the 90th percentile. We need to be able to find a percentile, or show it correct to a given accuracy.

More generally, the nth percentile, α, of a continuous random variable, X, is $P(X \leqslant \alpha) = \dfrac{n}{100}$, as shown in Key point 8.6.

KEY POINT 8.6

The nth percentile, α, of a continuous random variable, X, is $P(X \leqslant \alpha) = \frac{n}{100}$.

For the cumulative distribution function, $F(\alpha) = \frac{n}{100}$, as shown in Key point 8.7.

KEY POINT 8.7

For the cumulative distribution function, $F(\alpha) = \frac{n}{100}$ where α is the nth percentile.

The important percentiles are shown in Key point 8.8.

KEY POINT 8.8

The median	$F(m) = 0.5$
The lower quartile	$F(q_1) = 0.25$
The upper quartile	$F(q_3) = 0.75$

WORKED EXAMPLE 8.5

Let X be a random variable with cumulative distribution function $F(x) = \begin{cases} 0 & x < 0 \\ \frac{e^x - 1}{e^3 - 1} & 0 \leqslant x \leqslant 3 \\ 1 & x > 3. \end{cases}$

a Calculate the median.

b Calculate the lower and upper quartiles.

c Calculate the 40th percentile.

Answer

a $F(m) = \frac{e^m - 1}{e^3 - 1} = \frac{1}{2}$ — Set the cumulative distribution function equal to $\frac{1}{2}$.

$e^m = \frac{e^3 - 1}{2} + 1$ — Rearrange and solve.

$m = \ln\left(\frac{e^3 - 1}{2} + 1\right)$

$m = 2.355$

b $F(q_1) = \frac{e^{q_1} - 1}{e^3 - 1} = \frac{1}{4}$ — Set the cumulative distribution function equal to $\frac{1}{4}$.

$e^{q_1} = \frac{e^3 - 1}{4} + 1$ — Rearrange and solve.

$q_1 = \ln\left(\frac{e^3 - 1}{4} + 1\right)$

$q_1 = 1.753$

$F(q_3) = \frac{e^{q_3} - 1}{e^3 - 1} = \frac{3}{4}$ Set the cumulative distribution function equal to $\frac{3}{4}$.

$e^{q_3} = \frac{3(e^3 - 1)}{4} + 1$ Rearrange and solve.

$q_3 = \ln\left(\frac{3(e^3 - 1)}{4} + 1\right)$

$q_3 = 2.729$

c $F(\alpha) = \frac{e^\alpha - 1}{e^3 - 1} = 0.4$ Set the cumulative distribution function equal to 0.4.

$e^\alpha = 0.4(e^3 - 1) + 1$ Rearrange and solve.

$\alpha = \ln[0.4(e^3 - 1) + 1]$

$\alpha = 2.156$

In Worked example 8.5, we were given the cumulative distribution function to start with. Sometimes we may need to find the CDF before calculating the median. Also, we may need to use some numerical methods to show that the value of a median, or in fact any percentile, is correct to a given level of accuracy.

WORKED EXAMPLE 8.6

Let X be a continuous random variable with probability density function $f(x) = \begin{cases} \frac{3}{10}\left(x^2 + \frac{1}{3}\right) & 0 \leqslant x \leqslant 2 \\ 0 & \text{otherwise.} \end{cases}$

Show that the median is 1.52, correct to 3 significant figures.

Answer

There are two methods we can use to solve this. First, we can find $F(x)$ and equate it to 0.5. Second, we could build this value into the limits for integration.

Method 1: Evaluating the integral directly

$F(m) = P(X \leqslant m) = \int_0^m \frac{3}{10}\left(t^2 + \frac{1}{3}\right) dt = 0.5$

$\frac{3}{10}\left[\frac{t^3}{3} + \frac{t}{3}\right]_0^m = 0.5$

$\frac{1}{10}(m^3 + m) = 0.5$

This leads to:

$g(m) = m^3 + m - 5 = 0$

This is a cubic that does not factorise.

You should not use a calculator to solve this as the question asks you to show that the median is 1.52 correct to 3 significant figures.

Since $m = 1.52$ (3 significant figures)

$m \in (1.515, 1.525)$.

$g(1.515) = 1.515^3 + 1.515 - 5 = -0.0077\ldots$.negative

$g(1.525) = 1.525^3 + 1.525 - 5 = 0.0715\ldots$.positive

This is covered in AS & A Level Pure Mathematics 3, Chapter 6.

Since $g(m)$ is continuous and there is a change in sign, m must be within the interval.

So $m = 1.52$ (3 significant figures).

Method 2

The advantage of finding the cumulative distribution function $F(x)$ rather than the probability directly is that it is possible to use this for other percentiles as well.

$$F(x) = \int_0^x \frac{3}{10}\left(t^2 + \frac{1}{3}\right) dt$$

$$F(x) = \begin{cases} 0 & x < 0 \\ \frac{1}{10}(x^3 + x) & 0 \leqslant x \leqslant 2 \\ 1 & x > 2 \end{cases}$$

If $1.515 \leqslant m < 1.525$,

then $F(1.515) \leqslant 0.5 < F(1.525)$ and vice versa.

The principle here is the same. Instead of looking for a change in sign, we look for the values being either side of 0.5.

$F(1.515) = \frac{1}{10}(1.515^3 + 1.515) = 0.499\ldots < 0.5$

The $F(x)$ values are either side of 0.5.

$F(1.525) = \frac{1}{10}(1.525^3 + 1.525) = 0.507\ldots > 0.5$

Therefore $m = 1.52$ (3 significant figures).

Method 2 of Worked example 8.6 can be used to show any percentile to a given level of accuracy. We may not always be able to calculate the exact value.

We can find a cumulative distribution function from a probability density function by integrating. We may also need to find the PDF from a given CDF. This helps us calculate the mean or variance for a continuous random variable, as we cannot find this directly from the cumulative distribution function. We differentiate $F(x)$ to find $f(x)$, since differentiation is the inverse operation to integration. This is shown in Key point 8.9.

KEY POINT 8.9

Let the continuous random variable X have a cumulative distribution function $F(x)$. The probability density function is defined as:

$$f(x) = \frac{dF(x)}{dx}$$

If the function is piecewise, then, as in Worked example 8.7, make sure that all parts are differentiated.

WORKED EXAMPLE 8.7

A continuous random variable, X, has cumulative distribution function $F(x) = \begin{cases} 0 & x < 0 \\ \frac{x^2}{108} & 0 \leqslant x < 6 \\ \frac{1}{54}\left(9x - \frac{x^2}{4} - 27\right) & 6 \leqslant x \leqslant 18 \\ 1 & \text{otherwise.} \end{cases}$

Find $f(x)$, the probability density function.

Answer

If $0 \leqslant x < 6$:

$\frac{dF(x)}{dx} = \frac{x}{54}$

Differentiate $F(x)$ to find $f(x)$.

If $6 < x \leqslant 18$:

$\frac{dF(x)}{dx} = \frac{1}{54}\left(9 - \frac{x}{2}\right)$

$f(x) = \begin{cases} \frac{x}{54} & 0 \leqslant x < 6 \\ \frac{1}{54}\left(9 - \frac{x}{2}\right) & 6 \leqslant x \leqslant 18 \\ 0 & \text{otherwise} \end{cases}$

In the regions $x < 0$ and $x > 18$ we differentiate to 0. This is reflected in the 'otherwise' comment.

We can use the probability density function to find the mode of a function, as shown in Key point 8.10.

KEY POINT 8.10

The mode is the highest point on a probability density function and so is either a stationary point or at the end points of the domain.

Given f(x) defined as > 0 for $a \leqslant x \leqslant b$, then the mode is at $\frac{d}{dx}f(x) = 0\left[\frac{d^2}{dx^2}f(x) < 0\right]$ or a or b.

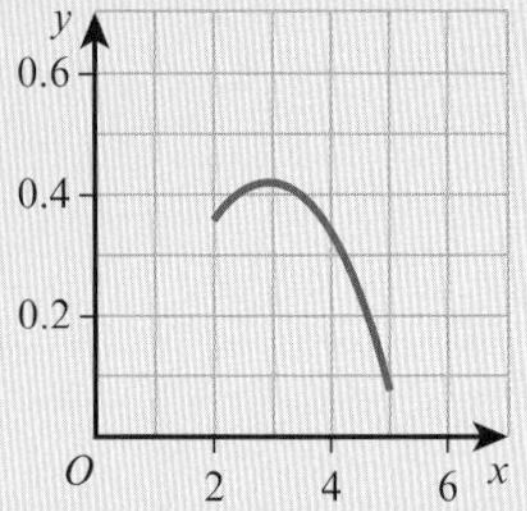

Here the mode is at the stationary point and is found at $\frac{df(x)}{dx} = 0$.

It is also a maximum $\left[\frac{d^2f(x)}{dx^2} < 0\right]$.

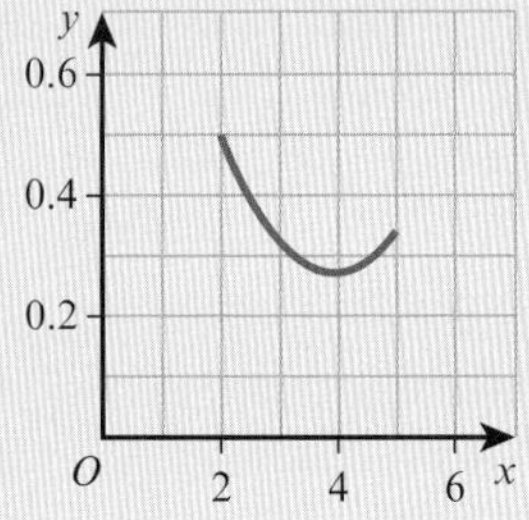

Here, we have a stationary point, but it is a minimum. We can see that the maximum value is at the start of the function.

The mode is a useful measure of central tendency, particularly if the data are highly skewed. We can also use the mode to discuss whether a dataset is positively or negatively skewed.

WORKED EXAMPLE 8.8

For each of the following probability density functions, find the mode.

a $f(x) = \begin{cases} \frac{1}{72}(8x - x^2) & 0 \leqslant x \leqslant 6 \\ 0 & \text{otherwise} \end{cases}$

b $f(x) = \begin{cases} \frac{1}{60}(2x + 3) & 2 \leqslant x \leqslant 7 \\ 0 & \text{otherwise} \end{cases}$

c $f(x) = \begin{cases} \frac{1}{48}(x^2 - 10x + 29) & 1 \leqslant x \leqslant 7 \\ 0 & \text{otherwise} \end{cases}$

Answer

a $f(x) = \begin{cases} \frac{1}{72}(8x - x^2) & 0 \leqslant x \leqslant 6 \\ 0 & \text{otherwise} \end{cases}$ We know that the stationary point is a maximum.

Stationary point:

$\frac{d}{dx}(f(x)) = \frac{1}{72}(8 - 2x) = 0$

Maximum where $x = 4$: We need to work out the values of potential maxima.

$f(0) = 0$

$f(4) = \frac{2}{9}$

$f(6) = \frac{1}{6}$

The mode is therefore when $x = 4$. Choose the greatest value.

b $f(x) = \begin{cases} \frac{1}{60}(2x + 3) & 2 \leqslant x \leqslant 7 \\ 0 & \text{otherwise} \end{cases}$ Since the function is linear, it has no stationary points.

$f(2) = \frac{7}{60}$

$f(7) = \frac{17}{60}$

The mode is therefore when $x = 7$. Choose the greater value.

Alternatively, since the function is linear and always increasing, we can deduce the maximum value will be at $x = 7$.

c $f(x) = \begin{cases} \frac{1}{48}(x^2 - 10x + 29) & 1 \leqslant x \leqslant 7 \\ 0 & \text{otherwise} \end{cases}$ Find the stationary point.

Stationary point:

$\frac{d}{dx}(f(x)) = \frac{1}{48}(2x - 10) = 0$

Maximum where $x = 5$: Work out the values of potential maxima.

$f(1) = \frac{5}{12}$

$f(5) = \frac{1}{12}$

$f(7) = \frac{1}{6}$

The mode is therefore when $x = 1$. Choose the greatest value.

If the functions are more complicated, use a graph to help you, as shown in Worked example 8.9.

WORKED EXAMPLE 8.9

Given $f(x) = \begin{cases} \frac{1}{128}x & 0 \leqslant x < 8 \\ \frac{5}{24} - \frac{x}{96} & 8 \leqslant x \leqslant 20 \\ 0 & \text{otherwise} \end{cases}$, find the mode.

Answer

Mode = 8 It is easy to see where the mode is from the graph.

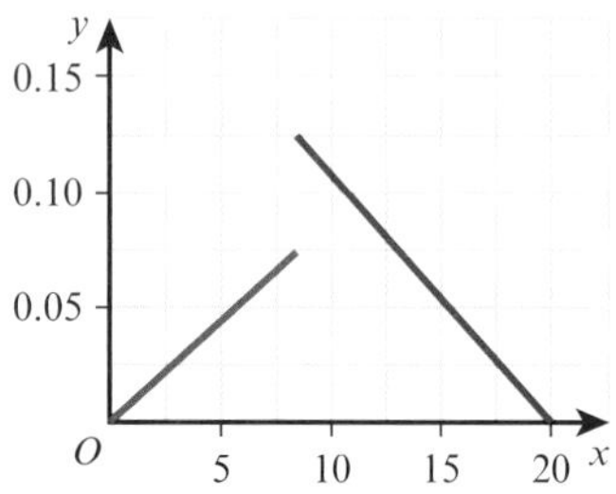

EXERCISE 8B

1 Find F(x), the cumulative distribution function for:

$$f(x) = \begin{cases} \frac{2}{95}(5 - 3x) & -4 \leqslant x \leqslant 1 \\ 0 & \text{otherwise} \end{cases}$$

2 Find F(x), the cumulative distribution function for:

$$f(x) = \begin{cases} \frac{1}{9}(x^2 - 8x + 18) & 2 \leqslant x \leqslant 5 \\ 0 & \text{otherwise} \end{cases}$$

3 Find F(x), the cumulative distribution function for:

$$f(x) = \begin{cases} \frac{1}{16} & 3 \leqslant x < 7 \\ \frac{1}{8} & 7 \leqslant x \leqslant 13 \\ 0 & \text{otherwise} \end{cases}$$

4 Find F(x), the cumulative distribution function for:

$$f(x) = \begin{cases} \frac{4}{27}(x - 1) & 1 \leqslant x < 4 \\ \frac{4}{27}(11 - 2x) & 4 \leqslant x \leqslant \frac{11}{2} \\ 0 & \text{otherwise} \end{cases}$$

5 Find F(x), the cumulative distribution function for:

$$f(x) = \begin{cases} \frac{1}{24} & 0 \leqslant x < 5 \\ \frac{1}{24}(x-4) & 5 \leqslant x < 7 \\ \frac{1}{8} & 7 \leqslant x < 12 \\ 0 & \text{otherwise} \end{cases}$$

6 For the given probability density function: $f(x) = \begin{cases} \frac{1}{28}(12-x) & 3 \leqslant x \leqslant 7 \\ 0 & \text{otherwise} \end{cases}$

a find F(x)

b calculate F(5)

c find P($4 \leqslant x < 6$)

d find m such that F(m) = 0.5. Give your answer to 2 decimal places.

7 For the given probability density function: $f(x) = \begin{cases} \frac{3}{100}(x-2)(8-x) & 2 \leqslant x \leqslant 7 \\ 0 & \text{otherwise} \end{cases}$

a find F(x), writing your answer in the form $\frac{-a}{100}(x-b)(x-c)^2$, where a, b, c are positive integers

b find P($X \leqslant 4$)

c find P($X > 5$).

8 For the given probability density function: $f(x) = \begin{cases} \frac{1}{90}(13-x) & 4 \leqslant x < 7 \\ \frac{1}{270}(x+11) & 7 \leqslant x \leqslant 16 \\ 0 & \text{otherwise} \end{cases}$

a find F(x)

b find P($X \leqslant 6$)

c find P($X \leqslant 11$)

d find a such that P($X \geqslant a$) = 0.75

e find m such that F(m) = 0.5, giving your answer to 3 significant figures.

9 For the given probability density function: $f(x) = \begin{cases} \frac{1}{99}(x^2 - 18x + 83) & 6 \leqslant x \leqslant 15 \\ 0 & \text{otherwise} \end{cases}$

a find F(x)

b find P($X > 8$)

c show that the upper quartile is 14.3, to 1 decimal place.

PS 10 For the given probability density function: $f(x) = \begin{cases} \frac{12}{335}(x^3 + 4x^2 + 1) & -4 \leqslant x \leqslant 1 \\ 0 & \text{otherwise} \end{cases}$

a find the mode

b show that the 40th percentile is −2.56, correct to 2 decimal places.

8.3 Calculating E(g(X)) for a continuous random variable

REWIND

In AS & A Level Mathematics Probability & Statistics 2, Chapter 2, we found both $E(aX + b)$ and $Var(aX + b)$ for discrete random variables. Also, in Chapter 4, we found $E(X)$ and $Var(X)$ for continuous random variables.

For discrete random variables we could simply recalculate the expectation and variance by redefining the variable, for example:

x	1	2	3
$P(X = x)$	$\frac{1}{3}$	$\frac{1}{6}$	$\frac{1}{2}$

When $Y = 3X + 7$, we can write the probability distribution of Y as:

y	10	13	16
$P(Y = y)$	$\frac{1}{3}$	$\frac{1}{6}$	$\frac{1}{2}$

We can calculate $E(3X + 7)$ and $Var(3X + 7)$ from this table.

For continuous random variables we cannot use this method. We need to be able to find $E(g(X))$ and $Var(g(X))$ from their probability density function, as shown in Key point 8.11.

TIP

$\forall x$ means 'for all x'. This notation allows us to find the area when there are many domains for the continuous random variable.

KEY POINT 8.11

Let X be a continuous random variable with probability density function $f(x)$. Then:

$$E(X) = \int_{\forall x} x f(x)\,dx \text{ and } E(g(X)) = \int_{\forall x} g(x) f(x)\,dx$$

There are similar integrals in AS & A Level Mathematics Probability & Statistics 2.

You may have used these to calculate $E(X^2)$ to find $Var(X)$: $E(X^2) = \int_{\forall x} x^2 f(x)\,dx$ and $Var(X) = E(X^2) - [E(X)]^2$.

WORKED EXAMPLE 8.10

A continuous random variable, X, has probability density function $f(x) = \begin{cases} \frac{1}{5}\left(\frac{6x}{5} + \frac{1}{2}\right) & 0 \leqslant x \leqslant 2.5 \\ 0 & \text{otherwise.} \end{cases}$

a Find $E(X)$.

b Find $E(X(X + 1))$.

Answer

a $E(X) = \int_{\forall x} x f(x)\,dx$ — From the definition.

$$E(X) = \int_0^{2.5} x \times \frac{1}{5}\left(\frac{6x}{5} + \frac{1}{2}\right) dx$$

$$= \frac{1}{5}\int_0^{2.5} \frac{6x^2}{5} + \frac{x}{2} dx$$ Multiply and simplify.

$$= \frac{1}{5}\left[\frac{2x^3}{5} + \frac{x^2}{4}\right]_0^{2.5}$$

$$= \frac{1}{5}\left(\left(\frac{2(2.5)^3}{5} + \frac{2.5^2}{4}\right) - 0\right)$$ Substitute in limits.

$$= 1.5625$$ Always check to see if the answer makes sense. It must be between 0 and 2.5.

b $E(g(X)) = \int_{\forall x} g(x) f(x) dx$ From the definition.

$$E(X(X+1)) = \int_0^{2.5} x(x+1) \times \frac{1}{5}\left(\frac{6x}{5} + \frac{1}{2}\right) dx$$

$$= \frac{1}{5}\int_0^{2.5} \frac{6x^3}{5} + \frac{17x^2}{10} + \frac{x}{2} dx$$ Multiply out and collect like terms.

$$= \frac{1}{5}\left[\frac{3x^4}{10} + \frac{17x^3}{30} + \frac{x^2}{4}\right]_0^{2.5}$$

$$= \frac{1}{5}\left(\left(\frac{3(2.5)^4}{10} + \frac{17(2.5)^3}{30} + \frac{2.5^2}{4}\right) - 0\right)$$ Substitute in limits.

$$E(X(X+1)) = 4.427083\ldots$$

$$= 4.43 \text{ (to 3 significant figures)}$$ Evaluate.

WORKED EXAMPLE 8.11

A continuous random variable, X, has probability density function $f(x) = \begin{cases} \frac{x}{12} & 0 \leqslant x < 3 \\ \frac{1}{8} & 3 \leqslant x < 8 \\ 0 & \text{otherwise} \end{cases}$.

Find $E\left(\frac{1}{X}\right)$.

Answer

$E(g(X)) = \int_{\forall x} g(x) f(x) dx$ From the definition.

$$\mathrm{E}\left(\frac{1}{X}\right) = \int_0^3 \frac{1}{x}\left(\frac{x}{12}\right)\mathrm{d}x + \int_3^8 \frac{1}{x}\left(\frac{1}{8}\right)\mathrm{d}x$$

Since there are two domains, integrate over all values of x. Split the integral into sections to do this using the given domains.

$$= \int_0^3 \frac{1}{12}\,\mathrm{d}x + \int_3^8 \frac{1}{8x}\,\mathrm{d}x$$

$$= \left[\frac{x}{12}\right]_0^3 + \left[\frac{1}{8}\ln x\right]_3^8$$

Integrate.

$$= \left(\frac{1}{4} - 0\right) + \left(\frac{1}{8}\ln 8 - \frac{1}{8}\ln 3\right)$$

Evaluate.

$$= \frac{1}{8}\left(2 + \ln\left(\frac{8}{3}\right)\right)$$

Simplify.

$$= 0.372\,603\,6\ldots$$

Make sure you read the question carefully. You may be required to leave your answer in exact form.

$$= 0.373 \text{ (to 3 significant figures)}$$

DID YOU KNOW?

Another name for $\mathrm{E}(X)$ is the first moment of the distribution of X and, using this, we can find a measure of centrality. It links to finding a centre of mass, using moments, in Mechanics.

$\mathrm{E}(X^2)$ is called the second moment and links to measures of dispersion.

$\mathrm{E}(X^n)$ is called the nth moment of the distribution of X. When $n = 3$, we can calculate some measures of skewness and, when $n = 4$, we are able to analyse kurtosis, a measure of how 'flat' a distribution is.

EXERCISE 8C

1 $\mathrm{f}(x) = \begin{cases} \dfrac{x}{200} & 0 \leqslant x \leqslant 20 \\ 0 & \text{otherwise.} \end{cases}$

a Find $\mathrm{E}(X)$. b Find $\mathrm{E}(X^2)$. c Find $\mathrm{Var}(X)$.

2 The continuous random variable X has probability density function given by $\mathrm{f}(x) = \begin{cases} \dfrac{2}{21}(7 - x) & 2 \leqslant x \leqslant 5 \\ 0 & \text{otherwise.} \end{cases}$

a Find $\mathrm{E}(X)$. b Find $\mathrm{E}(X^2)$. c Find $\mathrm{Var}(X)$.

3 The continuous random variable X has probability density function given by $\mathrm{f}(x) = \begin{cases} \dfrac{1}{5} & 5 \leqslant x < 8 \\ \dfrac{1}{15} & 8 \leqslant x \leqslant 14 \\ 0 & \text{otherwise.} \end{cases}$

a Find $\mathrm{E}(X)$. b Find $\mathrm{E}(X^2)$. c Find $\mathrm{Var}(X)$. d Find $\mathrm{SD}(X)$.

4 The continuous random variable X has probability density function given by $f(x) = \begin{cases} \frac{3}{20} & 1 \leqslant x \leqslant 6 \\ \frac{1}{200}(16 - x) & 6 < x \leqslant 16 \\ 0 & \text{otherwise.} \end{cases}$

a Find $E(X)$.
b Find $E(X^2)$.
c Find $\text{Var}(X)$.

5 The continuous random variable X has probability density function given by $f(x) = \begin{cases} \frac{5}{64}\left(3 + \frac{1}{x^2}\right) & 1 \leqslant x \leqslant 5 \\ 0 & \text{otherwise.} \end{cases}$

Find $E(X)$, giving your answer in the form $a(b + \ln c)$.

PS 6 The continuous random variable X has probability density function given by $f(x) = \begin{cases} \frac{1}{56}(23 - x) & 7 \leqslant x \leqslant 11 \\ 0 & \text{otherwise.} \end{cases}$

Find $E(X(X - 1))$.

7 The continuous random variable X has probability density function given by $f(x) = \begin{cases} 1 - \frac{x}{4} & 1 \leqslant x \leqslant 3 \\ 0 & \text{otherwise.} \end{cases}$

Find the exact value of $E(e^X)$.

8 The continuous random variable X has probability density function given by

$$f(x) = \begin{cases} -\frac{3}{16}(x^2 - 10x + 22) & 4 \leqslant x \leqslant 6 \\ 0 & \text{otherwise.} \end{cases}$$

Find $E\left(\frac{1}{X^2}\right)$. Give your answer in the form $a \ln b + c$.

9 The continuous random variable X has probability density function given by $f(x) = \begin{cases} \frac{4}{15} & 0 \leqslant x \leqslant 3 \\ \frac{1}{10} & 3 < x \leqslant 5 \\ 0 & \text{otherwise.} \end{cases}$

Find $E((X - 2)^2)$.

10 The continuous random variable X has probability density function given by $f(x) = \begin{cases} \frac{1}{8}(5 - x) & 1 \leqslant x < 3 \\ \frac{1}{32}(x - 3) & 3 \leqslant x \leqslant 7 \\ 0 & \text{otherwise.} \end{cases}$

Find $E\left(\frac{1}{X}\right)$.

PS 11 For the given cumulative distribution function: $F(x) = \begin{cases} 0 & x < 1 \\ \frac{1}{36}(x^3 + 5x - 6) & 1 \leqslant x \leqslant 3 \\ 1 & x > 3 \end{cases}$

a show that the median is 2.32, correct to 3 significant figures
b find the mode
c find $E(X)$
d use your answers to parts **a**, **b** and **c** to comment on the skewness of the distribution.

8.4 Finding the probability density function and cumulative distribution function of $Y = g(X)$

In Section 8.3 we saw how to find E(Y), where $Y = g(X)$. We now need to calculate the probability density function and the cumulative distribution function for the continuous random variable $Y = g(X)$. This will allow us to calculate percentiles and probabilities for these functions. With a discrete random variable, we can simply recalculate the probability distribution and cumulative distribution. We will work with a discrete random variable with the following probability distribution. This will help us to develop some ideas that we can use later with continuous random variables.

x	1	2	3
$P(X = x)$	$\frac{1}{2}$	$\frac{1}{8}$	$\frac{3}{8}$

And cumulative distribution:

x	1	2	3
$F(x)$	$\frac{1}{2}$	$\frac{5}{8}$	1

Consider $Y = X^2$. The probability distribution is:

y	1	4	9
$P(Y = y)$	$\frac{1}{2}$	$\frac{1}{8}$	$\frac{3}{8}$

Or, equivalently, using X:

x	1	2	3
$P(X = \sqrt{y})$	$\frac{1}{2}$	$\frac{1}{8}$	$\frac{3}{8}$

And cumulative distribution G(y):

y	1	4	9
$G(y)$ $P(Y \leqslant y)$	$\frac{1}{2}$	$\frac{5}{8}$	1

Or, equivalently, using X:

x	1	2	3
$F(\sqrt{y})$ $P(X \leqslant \sqrt{y})$	$\frac{1}{2}$	$\frac{5}{8}$	1

If $Y = h(X)$, then $G(y) = P(X \leqslant h^{-1}(y))$.

Consider $Y = -X$. The probability distribution is:

y	-3	-2	-1
$P(Y = y)$	$\frac{3}{8}$	$\frac{1}{8}$	$\frac{1}{2}$

And cumulative distribution $G(y)$:

y	-3	-2	-1
$G(y) = P(Y \leqslant y)$	$\frac{3}{8}$	$\frac{1}{2}$	1

Or equivalently, using X:

x	1	2	3
$F(-y)$ $P(X \geqslant y) = 1 - P(X \leqslant -y)$	$\frac{1}{2}$	$\frac{5}{8}$	1

Here, we can see that if $Y = h(X)$, then $G(y) = 1 - P(X \leqslant h^{-1}(y))$.

Consider $Y = \frac{1}{X}$. The probability distribution is:

y	$\frac{1}{3}$	$\frac{1}{2}$	1
$P(Y = y)$	$\frac{3}{8}$	$\frac{1}{8}$	$\frac{1}{2}$

And cumulative distribution $G(y)$:

y	$\frac{1}{3}$	$\frac{1}{2}$	1
$G(y) = P(Y \leqslant y)$	$\frac{3}{8}$	$\frac{1}{2}$	1

Or, equivalently, using X:

x	1	2	3
$F\left(\frac{1}{y}\right)$ $P\left(X \geqslant \frac{1}{y}\right) = 1 - P\left(X \leqslant \frac{1}{y}\right)$	$\frac{1}{2}$	$\frac{5}{8}$	1

Here, we can see also that if $Y = h(X)$, then $G(y) = 1 - P(X \leqslant h^{-1}(y))$ for a discrete random variable.

For continuous variables we cannot do this. Instead, we use a similar idea with the cumulative distribution function of $Y = g(X)$, as shown in Key point 8.12.

KEY POINT 8.12

For a continuous random variable, X, with cumulative distribution function $F(x)$ and a function $Y = h(X)$, we find the cumulative distribution function $G(y)$ by:

$$G(y) = P(Y \leqslant y) = \begin{cases} P(X \leqslant h^{-1}(y)) = F(h^{-1}(y)) \\ \text{or} \\ P(X \geqslant h^{-1}(y)) = 1 - F(h^{-1}(y)) \end{cases}$$

WORKED EXAMPLE 8.12

Consider the continuous random variable X with cumulative distribution function $F(x) = \begin{cases} 0 & x < 0 \\ \dfrac{x^2}{16} & 0 \leqslant x \leqslant 4 \\ 1 & x > 4. \end{cases}$

Find the cumulative distribution function of $Y = X^2$.

Answer

$$F(x) = \begin{cases} 0 & x < 0 \\ \dfrac{x^2}{16} & 0 \leqslant x \leqslant 4 \\ 1 & x > 4 \end{cases}$$

$Y = X^2$

Note that as X increases, so does Y.

This becomes important later.

Consider $G(y) = P(Y \leqslant y)$, which is also $P(X \leqslant \sqrt{y}) = F(\sqrt{y})$

Apply this now to the CDF.

$$F(\sqrt{y}) = \begin{cases} 0 & \sqrt{y} < 0 \\ \dfrac{(\sqrt{y})^2}{16} & 0 \leqslant \sqrt{y} \leqslant 4 \\ 1 & \sqrt{y} > 4 \end{cases}$$

This is the same as $F(x)$ with the function applied.

$$G(y) = \begin{cases} 0 & y < 0 \\ \dfrac{y}{16} & 0 \leqslant y \leqslant 16 \\ 1 & y > 16 \end{cases}$$

Write in terms of y.

This is the full description of the cumulative distribution function for X^2.

In Worked example 8.12 we saw how to find the CDF of a function of X from the CDF of the continuous random variable X.

What if we start with the probability density function of X and need to find the PDF of $Y = g(X)$?

We cannot do this directly, but there is a way, using the material covered so far:

$f(x)$ the PDF of $X \rightarrow F(x)$ the CDF of $X \rightarrow G(y)$ the CDF of $Y \rightarrow g(y)$ the PDF of Y

WORKED EXAMPLE 8.13

A continuous random variable, X, has probability density function $f(x) = \begin{cases} \dfrac{8}{3x^3} & 1 \leqslant x \leqslant 2 \\ 0 & \text{otherwise} \end{cases}$. Find the probability density function of $Y = \dfrac{X^2}{4}$.

Answer

Find $F(x)$ first: — Always calculate the cumulative distribution function first.

$$F(x) = \int_1^x \frac{8}{3t^3}\,dt$$

$$= \left[-\frac{4}{3t^2}\right]_1^x$$

$$= -\frac{4}{3x^2} - \left(-\frac{4}{3}\right)$$

$$= \frac{4}{3}\left(1 - \frac{1}{x^2}\right)$$

Therefore, $F(x) = \begin{cases} 0 & x < 1 \\ \frac{4}{3}\left(1 - \frac{1}{x^2}\right) & 1 \leqslant x \leqslant 2 \\ 1 & x > 2 \end{cases}$

Now consider the function $Y = \frac{X^2}{4}$. — Make X the subject.

$X = 2\sqrt{Y}$

$G(y) = P(Y \leqslant y) = P(X \leqslant 2\sqrt{y})$ — Apply this to the cumulative function.

$G(y) = F(2\sqrt{y})$

$$F(2\sqrt{y}) = \frac{4}{3}\left(1 - \frac{1}{(2\sqrt{y})^2}\right)$$

$$G(y) = \frac{4}{3} - \frac{1}{3y}$$

The domain of $F(x)$ is $1 \leqslant x \leqslant 2$. — Now consider the domain.

And of $F(2\sqrt{y})$: $1 \leqslant 2\sqrt{y} \leqslant 2$ — Apply the function, rearranging to make y the subject.

$1 \leqslant 4y \leqslant 4$

$\frac{1}{4} \leqslant y \leqslant 1$

Therefore, $G(y) = \begin{cases} 0 & y < \frac{1}{4} \\ \frac{4}{3} - \frac{1}{3y} & \frac{1}{4} \leqslant y \leqslant 1 \\ 1 & y > 1 \end{cases}$

It is useful to check:

$$G\left(\frac{1}{4}\right) = \frac{4}{3} - \frac{1}{3\left(\frac{1}{4}\right)} = 0$$

$$G(1) = \frac{4}{3} - \frac{1}{3(1)} = 1$$

$g(y) = \frac{dG(y)}{dy}$ — Differentiate.

$g(y) = \frac{1}{3y^2}$

And $g(y) = \begin{cases} \frac{1}{3y^2} & \frac{1}{4} \leqslant y \leqslant 1 \\ 0 & \text{otherwise} \end{cases}$ — As required. Remember to define fully the probability density function.

When we deal with reciprocal or negative functions, we need to be very careful about how we define the cumulative distribution function. For example, as in Worked example 8.14, if the function is $Y = \frac{1}{X}$, ensure that you define the correct domain.

WORKED EXAMPLE 8.14

Let the continuous random variable X have probability density function

$$f(x) = \begin{cases} \frac{8}{3x^3} & 1 \leqslant x \leqslant 2 \\ 0 & \text{otherwise.} \end{cases}$$

Find the probability density function of $Y = \frac{1}{X}$.

Answer

$F(x) = \int \frac{8}{3x^3}\,dx$ — Find F(x).

$= -\frac{4}{3x^2} + c$ — Find the constant of integration instead of using limits.

$-\frac{4}{3(2)^2} + c = 1$ — Use F(2) = 1.

Therefore, $c = \frac{4}{3}$.

And $F(x) = \frac{4}{3}\left(1 - \frac{1}{x^2}\right)$.

Now consider the function $Y = \frac{1}{X}$. — Since we are taking the reciprocal, change the inequality. Think about why the inequality switches over in this example.

$G(y) = P(Y \leqslant y) = P\left(X \geqslant \frac{1}{y}\right) = 1 - P\left(X \leqslant \frac{1}{y}\right)$

$G(y) = 1 - F\left(\frac{1}{y}\right)$

$= 1 - \frac{4}{3}(1 - y^2)$

$= \frac{1}{3}(4y^2 - 1)$

The domain for F(x) is $1 \leqslant x \leqslant 2$.

$1 \leqslant \frac{1}{y} \leqslant 2$

The domain for G(y) is therefore $\frac{1}{2} \leqslant y \leqslant 1$.

The same care is required for the domain.

Check the domain for the reciprocal function.

Therefore, $G(y) = \begin{cases} 0 & y < \frac{1}{2} \\ \frac{1}{3}(4y^2 - 1) & \frac{1}{2} \leqslant y \leqslant 1 \\ 1 & y > 1 \end{cases}$

Check:

$G\left(\frac{1}{2}\right) = \frac{1}{3}\left(4\left(\frac{1}{2}\right)^2 - 1\right) = 0$

$G(1) = \frac{1}{3}(4(1)^2 - 1) = 1$

$g(y) = \frac{dG(y)}{dy}$

$g(y) = \frac{8y}{3}$

Differentiate to find g(y).

$g(y) = \begin{cases} \frac{8y}{3} & \frac{1}{2} \leqslant y \leqslant 1 \\ 0 & \text{otherwise} \end{cases}$

Define fully g(y).

TIP

Always take your time when finding the CDF of a function of X, and notice when you need to change the inequality.

EXERCISE 8D

1 $F(x) = \begin{cases} 0 & x < 0 \\ \frac{x^2}{400} & 0 \leqslant x \leqslant 20 \\ 1 & x > 20 \end{cases}$. Find the cumulative distribution function of $A = X^2$.

2 $F(x) = \begin{cases} 0 & x < 0 \\ \frac{1}{10}(x^3 + x) & 0 \leqslant x \leqslant 2 \\ 1 & x > 2 \end{cases}$. Find the cumulative distribution function of $A = X^3$.

3 $F(x) = \begin{cases} 0 & x < -4 \\ \frac{1}{95}(-3x^2 + 10x + 88) & -4 \leqslant x \leqslant 1 \\ 1 & \text{otherwise} \end{cases}$. Find the cumulative distribution function $A = 3X - 22$.

4 The continuous random variable X has cumulative distribution function given by

$F(x) = \begin{cases} 0 & x < 1 \\ \frac{1}{3}(x^2 - 1) & 1 \leqslant x \leqslant 2 \\ 1 & x > 2 \end{cases}$. Find the cumulative distribution function of:

a $A = X^2$

b $B = \sqrt{X}$

5 The continuous random variable X has cumulative distribution function given by

$$F(x) = \begin{cases} 0 & x < 0 \\ \frac{1}{300}(x^2 + 20x) & 0 \leqslant x \leqslant 10 \\ 1 & x > 10 \end{cases}$$

Find the cumulative distribution function of $Y = 100X^2$.

6 The continuous random variable X has probability density function given by $f(x) = \begin{cases} \frac{1}{8}(4 - x) & 0 \leqslant x \leqslant 4 \\ 0 & \text{otherwise.} \end{cases}$

a Find $F(x)$.

b Find the cumulative distribution function of $Y = 3X - 2$.

c Find the probability density function of Y.

7 The continuous random variable X has probability density function given by $f(x) = \begin{cases} \frac{2}{x^2} & 1 \leqslant x \leqslant 2 \\ 0 & \text{otherwise.} \end{cases}$

a Find $F(x)$.

b Find the cumulative distribution of $Y = \frac{X^2}{4}$.

c Find the probability density function of Y.

8 The continuous random variable X has cumulative distribution function given by

$$F(x) = \begin{cases} 0 & x < 1 \\ -\frac{25}{24}\left(\frac{1}{x^2} - 1\right) & 1 \leqslant x \leqslant 5 \\ 1 & \text{otherwise.} \end{cases}$$

a Find the cumulative distribution function of $Y = \frac{1}{X}$.

b Find the probability density function of Y.

9 The continuous random variable X has probability density function given by $f(x) = \begin{cases} \frac{2}{25}(5 - x) & 0 \leqslant x \leqslant 5 \\ 0 & \text{otherwise.} \end{cases}$

a Find $F(x)$.

b Find the cumulative distribution of $Y = 5 - 2X$.

c Find $P(Y < 2)$.

d Find $P(-2 < Y < 2)$.

e Find the probability density function of Y.

M 10 A circular ink blot has radius r, described by the probability distribution $\mathrm{f}(r) = \begin{cases} \frac{2}{25}(6-r) & 1 \leqslant r \leqslant 6 \\ 0 & \text{otherwise.} \end{cases}$

a Find $\mathrm{F}(r)$, the cumulative density function.

b Find $\mathrm{G}(A)$, the cumulative distribution function for the area of the ink blot.

c Find the probability density function for the area of the ink blot.

WORKED PAST PAPER QUESTION

The continuous random variable X has probability density function f given by

$$\mathrm{f}(x) = \begin{cases} \frac{1}{6}x & 2 \leqslant x \leqslant 4 \\ 0 & \text{otherwise} \end{cases}$$

i Find the cumulative distribution function of X.

The continuous random variable Y is defined by $Y = X^3$. Find

ii the probability density function of Y

iii the value of k for which $\mathrm{P}(Y \geqslant k) = \frac{7}{12}$

Cambridge International AS & A Level Further Mathematics 9231 Paper 21 Q7 November 2016

Answer

i $\mathrm{f}(x) = \begin{cases} \frac{1}{6}x & 2 \leqslant x \leqslant 4 \\ 0 & \text{otherwise} \end{cases}$

For $2 \leqslant x \leqslant 4$: — Integrate to find $\mathrm{F}(x)$.

$\mathrm{F}(x) = \int_2^x \frac{1}{6}t \, \mathrm{d}t = \left[\frac{t^2}{12}\right]_2^x$ — Use a dummy variable.

$= \frac{x^2}{12} - \frac{2^2}{12}$ — Evaluate.

$\mathrm{F}(x) = \frac{x^2}{12} - \frac{1}{3}$

$\mathrm{F}(x) = \begin{cases} 0 & x < 2 \\ \frac{x^2}{12} - \frac{1}{3} & 2 \leqslant x \leqslant 4 \\ 1 & x > 4 \end{cases}$ — Define fully.

ii $G(y) = P(Y < y) = P(X^3 < y)$ State G(y) in terms of X.

$$= P\left(X < y^{\frac{1}{3}}\right) = F\left(y^{\frac{1}{3}}\right)$$

$$G(y) = \frac{y^{\frac{2}{3}}}{12} - \frac{1}{3}$$ Define G(y).

$$g(y) = \frac{1}{18}y^{-\frac{1}{3}}$$ Differentiate to get g(y).

$$2 \leqslant y^{\frac{1}{3}} \leqslant 4$$

$$8 \leqslant y \leqslant 64$$

$$g(y) = \begin{cases} \frac{1}{18}y^{-\frac{1}{3}} & 8 \leqslant y \leqslant 64 \\ 0 & \text{otherwise} \end{cases}$$ Define g(y) fully.

iii $P(Y \geqslant k) = 1 - P(Y \leqslant k)$ Consider the cumulative probability.

$$= 1 - G(k)$$

$$1 - \frac{k^{\frac{2}{3}}}{12} + \frac{1}{3} = \frac{7}{12}$$

$$\frac{16}{12} - \frac{k^{\frac{2}{3}}}{12} = \frac{7}{12}$$

$$k^{\frac{2}{3}} = 9$$

$$k = 9^{\frac{3}{2}}$$ Solve for k.

$$k = 27$$

Checklist of learning and understanding

Probability density functions:

- For f(x) to represent a probability density function, $f(x) \geqslant 0$ for all values of x.
- $\int_{\forall x} f(x)\,dx = 1$

Cumulative distribution functions:

- $F(x) = \int_{-\infty}^{x} f(t)\,dt$
- $\frac{dF(x)}{dx} = f(x)$

Expectation of functions of X:

- $E[g(X)] = \int_{\forall x} g(x)f(x)\,dx$

Finding the cumulative distribution function of a function of X:

- $G(y) = P(Y \leqslant y) = \begin{cases} P(X \leqslant h^{-1}(y)) = F(h^{-1}(y)) \\ \text{or} \\ P(X \geqslant h^{-1}(y)) = 1 - F(h^{-1}(y)) \end{cases}$

END-OF-CHAPTER REVIEW EXERCISE 8

1 The time, T seconds, between successive cars passing a particular checkpoint on a wide road has probability density function f given by $f(t) = \begin{cases} \frac{1}{100}e^{-0.01t} & t \geqslant 0 \\ 0 & \text{otherwise.} \end{cases}$

i State the expected value of T.

ii Find the median value of T.

iii Sally wishes to cross the road at this checkpoint and she needs 20 seconds to complete the crossing. She decides to start out immediately after a car passes. Find the probability that she will complete the crossing before the next car passes.

Cambridge International AS & A Level Further Mathematics 9231 Paper 21 Q7 November 2014

2 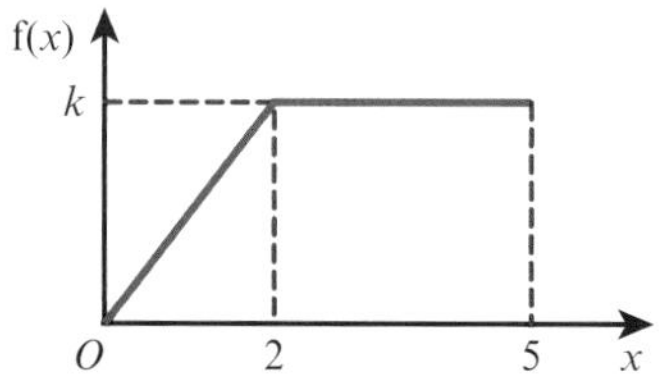

The continuous random variable X takes values in the interval $0 \leqslant x \leqslant 5$ only. For $0 \leqslant x \leqslant 5$ the graph of its probability density function f consists of two straight line segments, as shown in the diagram.

a Find k and show that f is given by $f(x) = \begin{cases} \frac{1}{8}x & 0 \leqslant x \leqslant 2 \\ \frac{1}{4} & 2 \leqslant x \leqslant 5 \\ 0 & \text{otherwise.} \end{cases}$

b The random variable Y is given by $Y = X^2$.

i Find the probability density function of Y.

ii Show that $E(Y) = 10.25$.

iii Show that the median of Y is the square of the median of X.

Cambridge International AS & A Level Further Mathematics 9231 Paper 23 Q11 November 2012

3 The lifetime, in years, of an electrical component is the random variable T, with probability density function f given by

$$f(t) = \begin{cases} Ae^{-\lambda t} & t \geqslant 0, \\ 0 & \text{otherwise,} \end{cases}$$

where A and λ are positive constants.

i Show that $A = \lambda$.

It is known that out of 100 randomly chosen components, 16 failed within the first year.

ii Find an estimate for the value of λ, and hence find an estimate for the median value of T.

Cambridge International AS & A Level Further Mathematics 9231 Paper 22 Q8 November 2013

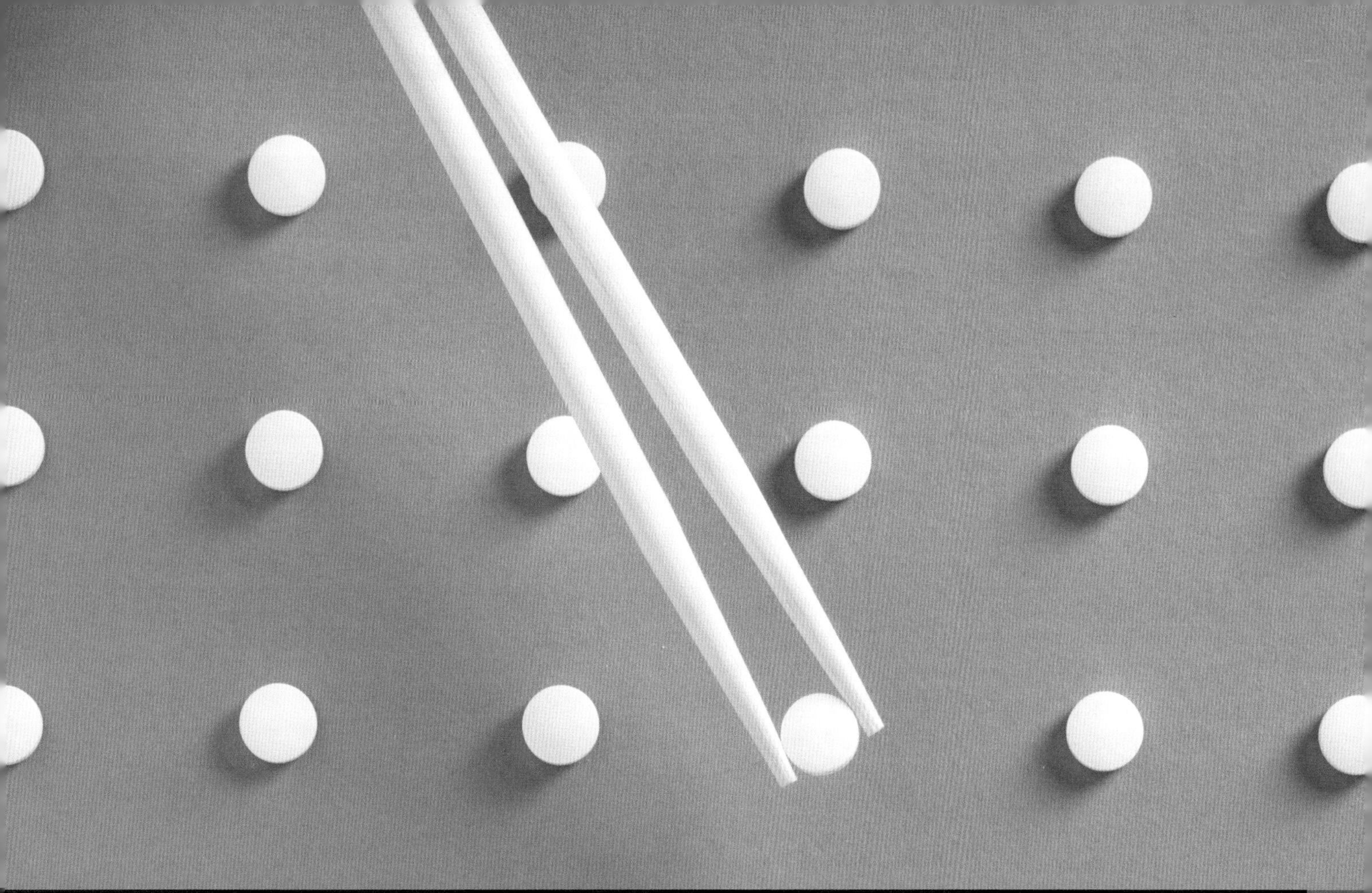

Chapter 9
Inferential statistics

In this chapter you will learn how to:

- formulate and carry out a hypothesis test concerning the mean for a small sample, using the *t*-test
- calculate a pooled estimate of a population variance from two samples
- formulate and carry out a hypothesis test concerning the difference in means, using:
  - a two-sample *t*-test
  - a paired sample *t*-test
  - a test using the normal distribution
- determine a confidence interval for a population mean based on a small sample, using the *t*-distribution
- determine a confidence interval for the difference in population means.

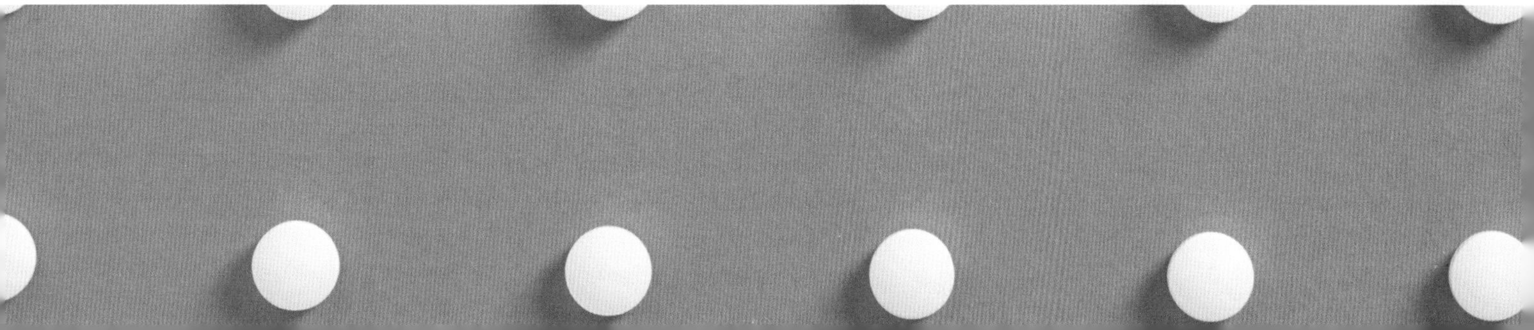

PREREQUISITE KNOWLEDGE

Where it comes from	What you should be able to do	Check your skills
AS & A Level Mathematics Probability & Statistics 1, Chapter 8 AS & A Level Mathematics Probability & Statistics 2, Chapter 3	Standardise and find critical values from a cumulative normal distribution table.	**1** Let $X \sim N(24, 2^2)$. Find $P(X \leqslant 26.34)$.
AS & A Level Mathematics Probability & Statistics 2, Chapter 6	Find an unbiased estimator of the variance.	**2** Given that $\sum x = 126$, $\sum x^2 = 514$ and $n = 37$, find the unbiased estimator of the variance.

Hypothesis testing and making inferences

This chapter builds on work covered in AS & A Level Mathematics Probability & Statistics 2, to develop techniques based on the mean of a distribution. We shall consider situations that have small samples or populations for which the variance is unknown. We shall then carry out hypothesis tests concerning the mean. Being able to test the mean is very important in industry and medicine, for example, to test if the amount of effective drug in a headache tablet is correct. If not enough of the active drug is present, the medicine may not have the desired effect. We can also use this type of test to see whether the machine that is making the tablets is putting enough of the effective drug into the tablets.

9.1 *t*-distribution

When we collect a sample from a normal distribution to carry out a hypothesis test concerning the mean, we need to make some assumptions in order to use the normal distribution. We assume that the population variance is known, or that the sample size is sufficiently large that we can use s^2, the unbiased estimator of the variance, instead of the population variance, σ^2.

If the sample size is small, and we do not know what the variance is, then it is no longer appropriate to use the unbiased estimator. The t-distribution was developed so that the unbiased estimator could be used. It is a better model in this situation.

The diagram shows that the t-distribution is different from the normal distribution because the density in the tails is greater than the density in the tails of the standard normal distribution. This means that the t-distribution has greater probability in the tails and less probability in the centre compared to the standard normal distribution. The t-distribution is a family of distributions with $(n - 1)$ **degrees of freedom**. The number of degrees of freedom refers to the number of independent observations in a set of data. The number of degrees of freedom of the t-distribution relate to the sample size, n, and as the sample size increases, the t-distribution looks more like the normal distribution.

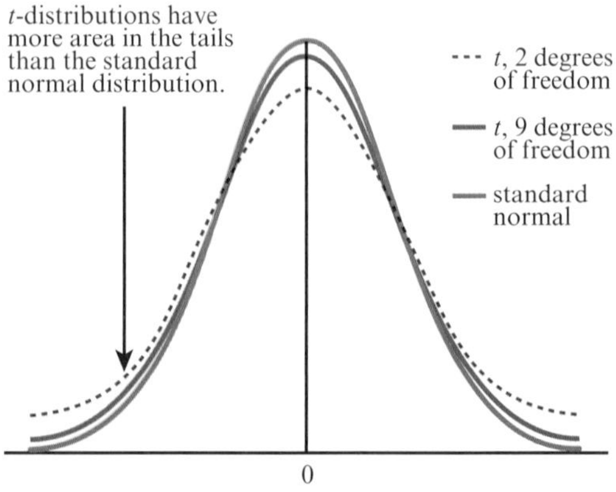

Hence, the distribution of the t statistic from samples of size 8 would be described by a t-distribution having $8 - 1$ or 7 degrees of freedom. Similarly, a t-distribution having 15 degrees of freedom would be used with a sample of size 16. As the degrees of freedom tend to infinity, the distribution becomes more like the normal distribution.

KEY POINT 9.1

Given n data points, the unbiased estimator of the variance, s^2, is calculated using:

$$s^2 = \frac{1}{n-1}\sum(x-\bar{x})^2$$

or

$$s^2 = \frac{1}{n-1}\left(\sum x^2 - \frac{\left(\sum x\right)^2}{n}\right) = \frac{1}{n-1}\left(\sum x^2 - n\bar{x}^2\right)$$

This can be written as $s^2 = \frac{S_{xx}}{n-1}$.

TIP

The unbiased estimator of the variance is also sometimes written as $\hat{\sigma}^2$. Generally, if θ is a parameter, then $\hat{\theta}$ is an estimator. In this book, we will use s^2.

Key point 9.1 gives a convenient way of calculating the unbiased estimator of the variance, s^2.

WORKED EXAMPLE 9.1

The wingspans of six Monarch butterflies are measured (in cm) and recorded as:

8.8, 9.6, 9.2, 9.1, 9.9, 8.7

Calculate the unbiased estimator for the variance of these data.

Answer

Method 1

$\sum x = 55.3$

First calculate the estimator of the mean, $\bar{x}$, using $\bar{x} = \frac{\Sigma x}{n}$.

$\bar{x} = \frac{55.3}{6} = 9.2166\ldots$

$x - \bar{x}$	$(x - \bar{x})^2$
−0.41667	0.173611
0.383333	0.146944
−0.01667	0.000278
−0.11667	0.013611
0.683333	0.466944
−0.51667	0.266944

Use the most accurate values when working to avoid rounding errors.

$\sum(x-\bar{x})^2 = 1.068333$

So $s^2 = \frac{1.068333}{6-1} = 0.214$ (to 3 significant figures)

Use $s^2 = \frac{1}{n-1}\sum(x-\bar{x})^2$

Method 2: Using summative data

This method helps with analysis of variance (ANOVA) which is studied at degree level.

$\sum x = 55.3$

$\sum x^2 = 510.75$

$$S_{xx} = \sum x^2 - \frac{(\Sigma x)^2}{n}$$
$$= 510.75 - \frac{55.3^2}{6}$$
$$= 1.068333$$

So $s^2 = \frac{1.068333}{6-1} = 0.214$ (to 3 significant figures)

We now have the tools to perform a hypothesis test concerning the population mean. This is where a small sample is taken from an underlying normal distribution with unknown variance. In other words, we assume the population is normally distributed.

There are several important steps when performing a hypothesis test for significance. First, we define the null hypothesis H_0. When dealing with a parametric test, H_0 is the assumed value of the parameter. It is this assumption that we are testing. Then we propose an alternative hypothesis H_1. There could be many different versions of this but, for the purposes of this course, it depends on whether we are looking at a one-tailed or a two-tailed test. Consequently, we refer only to H_0 and state whether we reject or do not reject it. Does rejecting H_0 mean that H_1 is accepted?

For an underlying normal distribution with unknown variance, a small sample of size n is taken. To carry out a hypothesis test on the mean, the t-distribution with $(n - 1)$ degrees of freedom is used to find the critical value. In fact, $\overline{X} \sim t_{n-1}$. We state the null and alternative hypotheses as shown in Key point 9.2.

KEY POINT 9.2

For an underlying population that is normally distributed, with unknown variance, the null and alternative hypotheses will be:

H_0: $\mu = k$, where k is the assumed value of the mean that we are testing

H_1: $\begin{cases} \mu < k \\ \mu > k \\ \mu \neq k \end{cases}$ depending on whether we are performing a one-tailed or two-tailed test

The test statistic $= \frac{\overline{x} - \mu}{s/\sqrt{n}}$, where $\overline{x}$ is the sample mean and $s = \sqrt{\frac{S_{xx}}{n-1}}$ is the unbiased estimator of the standard deviation.

The critical value for a significance level $100(1 - \alpha)\%$ is:

One-tailed	$t_{\alpha, n-1}$
Two-tailed	$t_{\frac{\alpha}{2}, n-1}$

WORKED EXAMPLE 9.2

Monarch butterflies are bred at a butterfly farm. Monarch butterflies should grow to have a mean wingspan of 9.4 cm. The breeders are concerned that their butterflies are not growing as well as they could be, so a sample of six Monarch butterflies is taken and their wingspans measured (in cm). These are recorded as: 8.8, 9.6, 9.2, 9.1, 9.9, 8.7. Assuming that the wingspans are normally distributed and using a 10% significance level, investigate whether the wingspans of the butterflies are less than 9.4 cm.

Answer

Important facts:

- assume underlying normal distribution
- variance is unknown
- sample size is small.

This suggests that we need a t-test.

We are testing whether the population mean is **below** 9.4.
This is a one-tailed test.
The significance level is 10%.

Make sure that you state whether you have a one- or two-tailed test.

H_0: $\mu = 9.4$, H_1: $\mu < 9.4$
Test statistics:

$\bar{x} = 9.22$ (3 significant figures) as found in Worked example 9.1

Define the null and alternative hypotheses. We must use parameters in the hypothesis test. This is the assumed value for μ when calculating the test statistic.

$s = 0.462$ (3 significant figures) as found in Worked example 9.1

Note $s^2 = 0.214$ was found earlier, so $s = 0.462$

$$\text{Test statistic} = \frac{\bar{x} - \mu}{s/\sqrt{n}} = \frac{9.22 - 9.4}{0.462/\sqrt{6}} = -0.9715$$

Use $\frac{\bar{x} - \mu}{s/\sqrt{n}}$ and make the critical value positive or negative accordingly.

The critical value for this test is $t_{0.9,\,5} = -1.476$.

p	0.75	0.90	0.95
$\nu = 1$	1.000	3.078	6.314
2	0.816	1.886	2.920
3	0.765	1.638	2.353
4	0.741	1.533	2.132
5	0.727	1.476	2.015
6	0.718	1.440	1.943
7	0.711	1.415	1.895
8	0.706	1.397	1.860

We look at the t-distribution table. Since the test is one-tailed, at the 10% significance level we need the 90th percentile with 5 degrees of freedom.

Our test statistic is negative, so we need to consider the negative value for t too.

Now we need to decide whether to reject H_0 or not.

Since $-0.9715 > -1.476$ this means the test statistic is not in the critical region, so we do not reject H_0.

Consider H_0, the assumption we made. Note we do not state we accept H_1 but instead state we do not reject H_0.

There is insufficient evidence to suggest that the mean wingspan of the Monarch butterflies is less than 9.4 cm.

Write a conclusion in context.

Worked example 9.3 demonstrates a two-tailed test.

WORKED EXAMPLE 9.3

A random sample of 12 workers from a mobile phone assembly line is selected from a large number of workers. A manager asks each of these workers to assemble a phone at their normal working speed. The times taken, in minutes, to complete these tasks are recorded below.

43.2, 41.6, 49.3, 48.2, 44.2, 40.6, 39.7, 43.4, 44.9, 45.1, 46.2, 43.2

Assuming that this sample comes from an underlying normal population, investigate the claim that the population mean is 45 minutes. Use a 5% significance level.

Answer

Important facts:

- underlying normal distribution assumed
- variance is unknown
- sample size is small.

This suggests that we need a t-test.

Test whether the population mean is different from 45.

This is a two-tailed test.

The significance level is 5%.

Decide whether this is a one- or two-tailed test.

H_0: $\mu = 45$

H_1: $\mu \neq 45$

Define the null and alternative hypotheses. Use parameters in the hypothesis test. This is the assumed value for μ when calculating the test statistic.

Test statistic:

$\Sigma x = 529.6$

$\Sigma x^2 = 23\,462.88$

$$S_{xx} = \Sigma x^2 - \frac{(\Sigma x)^2}{n}$$

$$S_{xx} = 23462.88 - \frac{529.6^2}{12} = 89.8666...$$

$$s = \sqrt{\frac{89.8666...}{11}} = 2.858\,268...$$

Use $s^2 = \frac{S_{xx}}{n-1}$, where $S_{xx} = \Sigma x^2 - \frac{(\Sigma x)^2}{n}$.

$$\bar{x} = \frac{\Sigma x}{n} = \frac{529.6}{12} = 44.133...$$

$s = 2.86$ (to 3 significant figures)

$\bar{x} = 44.1$ (to 3 significant figures)

$$\text{Test statistic} = \frac{\bar{x} - \mu}{s/\sqrt{n}} = \frac{44.1 - 45}{2.86/\sqrt{12}} = -1.05$$

Always use $\frac{\bar{x} - \mu}{s/\sqrt{n}}$ and make the critical value positive or negative accordingly.

The critical value for this test is $t_{0.975,\,11} = -2.201$.

p	0.75	0.90	0.95	0.975
$\nu = 1$	1.000	3.078	6.314	12.71
2	0.186	1.886	2.920	4.303
3	0.765	1.638	2.353	3.182
4	0.741	1.533	2.132	2.776
5	0.727	1.476	2.015	2.571
6	0.718	1.440	1.943	2.447
7	0.711	1.415	1.895	2.365
8	0.706	1.397	1.860	2.306
9	0.703	1.383	1.833	2.262
10	0.700	1.372	1.812	2.228
11	0.697	1.363	1.796	2.201
12	0.695	1.356	1.782	2.179

Since this is a two-tailed test at the 5% significance level, look at the 97.5th percentile with 11 degrees of freedom, in the t-distribution table.

See if the test statistic is in the critical region. In this case, this will be when the test statistic is less than the critical value, if negative, or greater than the critical value, if positive. Since the test statistic is negative, we will need to compare it with the negative critical value.

Since $-1.05 > -2.201$, the test statistic is not in the critical region and hence we do not reject H_0.

It is best to refer to H_0.

There is insufficient evidence to claim that the population mean is not 45 minutes.

We should always write full conclusions in context. Note we should not state there is sufficient evidence the population mean is 45 minutes, but instead state there is insufficient evidence the population mean is not 45 minutes.

It is very important to know which test to perform when testing the mean. In AS & A Level Mathematics Probability & Statistics 2, Chapter 5, you carried out a hypothesis test concerning the mean. In that case, the underlying distribution was known to be normal, or the sample size was large enough to use the central limit theorem. You were also given the population variance. In this chapter, you have carried out hypothesis tests for small samples or where the population variance was unknown. It is very important that you choose the most appropriate test to carry out.

The flowchart shown in Key point 9.3 can help you to decide which is the most appropriate test to use.

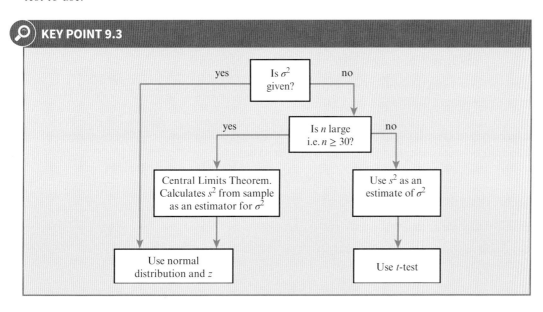

KEY POINT 9.3

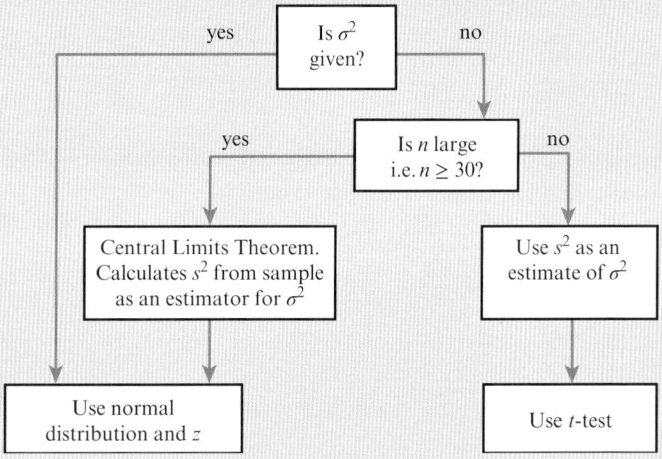

FAST FORWARD

If the underlying distribution is not normal, and the sample size is small, we can use non-parametric tests, as shown in Chapter 11.

EXERCISE 9A

1 For the given data, find unbiased estimates for the mean and variance.

a 12, 16, 17, 19, 13, 14, 11, 16, 19, 21, 14, 15

b 143, 154, 156, 145, 144, 132, 135, 148, 171, 124

2 In each case, state the magnitude of the test statistic for the given value of n and stated significance level.

a $n = 11$, one-tailed 5%

b $n = 21$, one-tailed 2.5%

c $n = 15$, two-tailed 5%

d $n = 25$, two-tailed 1%

e $n = 8$, one-tailed 10%

f $n = 18$, two-tailed 10%

3 State the null and alternative hypotheses for the following tests.

a The population mean differs from 41.

b The population mean is greater than 7.3.

c The population mean has decreased from 54.2.

d The population mean has not changed from 6.5.

4 For the given test statistic, sample sizes and significance levels, state whether you would reject or not reject the null hypothesis.

a Test statistic = 1.96, $n = 10$, 5% one-tailed

b Test statistic = −2.764, $n = 8$, 1% one-tailed

c Test statistic = 1.451, $n = 15$, 10% two-tailed

d Test statistic = −2.341, $n = 11$, 5% two-tailed

5 In a given week, 12 babies are born in hospital. Assume that this sample came from an underlying normal population. The length of each baby is routinely measured and is listed below (in cm):

$$49, 50, 45, 51, 47, 49, 48, 54, 53, 55, 45, 50$$

a Find unbiased estimators for the mean and variance.

The average length of babies is thought to be 50.5 cm. There is a concern that this is an overestimate.

b Test this claim at the 5% significance level based on this sample.

6 A drugs manufacturer claims that the amount of paracetamol in tablets is 60 mg. A sample of ten tablets is taken and the amount of paracetamol in each is recorded:

$$59.1, 59.7, 61.0, 59.1, 60.6, 68.9, 60.2, 58.6, 58.7, 58.9$$

Assuming that this sample came from an underlying normal population, test the claim at the 5% significance level that the amount of paracetamol is different from 60 mg.

7 The weight, X g, of a large bag of crisps is said to be normally distributed with a mean of 175 g. A sample of eight bags is opened and the contents weighed. The results are listed below.

$$173.2, 171.5, 176.3, 175.1, 174.7, 174.2, 176, 174.5$$

A consumer group believes that the bags are underfilled.

a Test this claim at the 5% significance level.

b Suggest why only a small sample of packets was tested.

8 At a petrol station, the manager thinks that one of the pumps is not working properly and is giving out more petrol than it should. She decides to test this claim by filling up ten buckets with 5 litres, according to the pump. The results, in cm^3, are given below (1 litre $= 1000\ cm^3$).

It is assumed that the amounts given are from a normal distribution.

5001, 5002, 5009, 4996, 4997, 5001, 5003, 5006, 5013, 5013

Using this sample, test at the 5% significance level whether or not the petrol pump is giving out too much petrol.

9.2 Hypothesis tests concerning the difference in means

We may test whether two populations have equal population means. In Section 9.1 we learned that the type of test we need to perform depends on a number of factors. These factors include: whether or not we know the population variances; whether the underlying distribution is normal, or the means approximate to a normal distribution by the application of the central limit theorem; and the size of the sample.

To start with, we will assume three things:

- the underlying distributions are normal
- the populations are independent
- the population variance of the two populations is the same (but may be unknown).

> **TIP**
>
> The second assumption can be tested using an F-test, but this is beyond the scope of this course.

From AS & A Level Mathematics Probability & Statistics 2, Chapter 4:

If $X \sim \text{N}(\mu, \sigma^2)$, then $\bar{X} \sim \text{N}\left(\mu, \dfrac{\sigma^2}{n}\right)$.

If $X \sim \text{N}(\mu_x, \sigma_x^2)$ is independent of $Y \sim \text{N}(\mu_y, \sigma_y^2)$, then $X - Y \sim \text{N}(\mu_x - \mu_y, \sigma_x^2 + \sigma_y^2)$ and

$\bar{X} - \bar{Y} \sim \text{N}\left(\mu_x - \mu_y, \dfrac{\sigma_x^2}{n_x} + \dfrac{\sigma_y^2}{n_y}\right)$.

We standardise to find a z-value, as shown in Key point 9.4. This acts as the test statistic for the difference in means.

KEY POINT 9.4

z-value is given by $Z = \dfrac{(\bar{X} - \bar{Y}) - (\mu_x - \mu_y)}{\sqrt{\dfrac{\sigma_x^2}{n_x} + \dfrac{\sigma_y^2}{n_y}}} \sim \text{N}(0, 1)$.

WORKED EXAMPLE 9.4

A group of 50 children and 70 adults participate in a maths activity. The mean time taken for the children to complete the activity is 45.3 seconds, with a standard deviation of 3.2 seconds. For the adults, the mean time is 46.1 seconds with a standard deviation of 2.8 seconds. Assuming the completion times are normally distributed with equal variances, test at the 5% significance level whether or not the children are faster at completing the activity.

Answer

First consider the conditions and assumptions:

- n is large for both populations
- both have an underlying mean
- the variances are equal but unknown.

Estimate σ^2 with s_x^2 and s_y^2.

Let $C \sim N(45.3, 3.2^2)$ represent the population of children.

Let $A \sim N(46.1, 2.8^2)$ represent the population of adults.

If the children are faster than the adults, then $\mu_A > \mu_C$.

Rewrite this as $\mu_A - \mu_C > 0$.

$H_0: \mu_A - \mu_C = 0$
$H_1: \mu_A - \mu_C > 0$

You could have this the other way round, but a positive value for H_1 will reduce errors in interpretation.

$$\text{Test statistic} = \frac{(\bar{A} - \bar{C}) - (\mu_A - \mu_C)}{\sqrt{\frac{s_A^2}{n_A} + \frac{s_C^2}{n_C}}}$$

Estimate σ^2 with s_x^2 and s_y^2 under the assumption of $H_0: \mu_A - \mu_C = 0$.

$$= \frac{(46.1 - 45.3) - 0}{\sqrt{\frac{2.8^2}{70} + \frac{3.2^2}{50}}} = 1.4213\ldots$$

This is a one-tailed test at the 5% significance level so the critical value is 1.96.
Since $1.4213 < 1.96$, the test statistic is not in the critical region and we should not reject H_0.

Always discuss H_0, the assumption you made.

There is insufficient evidence to suggest that the children perform the maths activity faster than the adults.

Always write full contextualised conclusions.

FAST FORWARD

In Worked example 9.4, we are given data that is normally distributed. We are given large samples and can therefore use s^2 in place of σ^2. In other situations we must use different techniques, as shown in Section 9.3.

Sometimes we need to carry out two-sample tests, such as comparing the mean of two distributions of unknown but equal variances. If the sample sizes are too small to allow us to use s_x^2 and s_y^2 as estimators, we need to pool these variances (combine them).

Consider two samples of size n_x and n_y. From underlying normal distributions the pooled estimate of the population variance is:

$$s_p^2 = \frac{\sum(x - \bar{x})^2 + \sum(y - \bar{y})^2}{n_x + n_y - 2}$$

However, if you are given the unbiased estimators of the variance for each sample,

$$s_x^2 = \frac{\sum(x - \bar{x})^2}{n_x - 1} \text{ and } s_y^2 = \frac{\sum(y - \bar{y})^2}{n_y - 1},$$

then $\sum(x - \bar{x})^2 + \sum(y - \bar{y})^2 = (n_x - 1)s_x^2 + (n_y - 1)s_y^2$.

Then the pooled estimate of the population variance, as shown in Key point 9.5, is $s_p^2 = \dfrac{(n_x - 1)s_x^2 + (n_y - 1)s_y^2}{n_x + n_y - 2}$.

But how small should n be? Generally, we would need $n < 15$.

KEY POINT 9.5

For two samples of size n_x and n_y the pooled estimate of the population variance is:

$$s_p^2 = \frac{\sum (x - \bar{x})^2 + \sum (y - \bar{y})^2}{n_x + n_y - 2}$$

If you know the unbiased estimators of the variance for each sample, $s_x^2 = \dfrac{\sum (x - \bar{x})^2}{n_x - 1}$ and $s_y^2 = \dfrac{\sum (y - \bar{y})^2}{n_y - 1}$, then $\sum (x - \bar{x})^2 + \sum (y - \bar{y})^2 = (n_x - 1)s_x^2 + (n_y - 1)s_y^2$.

So the pooled estimate of the population variance is $s_p^2 = \dfrac{(n_x - 1)s_x^2 + (n_y - 1)s_y^2}{n_x + n_y - 2}$.

Let's consider how Key point 9.5 affects the test statistic:

$$\frac{(\bar{X} - \bar{Y}) - (\mu_x - \mu_y)}{\sqrt{\dfrac{\sigma_x^2}{n_x} + \dfrac{\sigma_y^2}{n_y}}}$$

If we make the assumption that the variances are equal and that the pooled estimator can be used, $\sigma_x^2 = \sigma^2{}_y = s_p^2$, we have:

$$\frac{\sigma_x^2}{n_x} + \frac{\sigma_y^2}{n_y} = s_p^2\left(\frac{1}{n_x} + \frac{1}{n_y}\right)$$

Since n is small, we know that this will be modelled as a t-distribution, as shown in Key point 9.6.

KEY POINT 9.6

t-distribution:

$$T = \frac{(\bar{X} - \bar{Y}) - (\mu_x - \mu_y)}{\sqrt{s_p^2\left(\dfrac{1}{n_x} + \dfrac{1}{n_y}\right)}} \sim t_{n_x + n_y - 2}$$

WORKED EXAMPLE 9.5

A shopkeeper believes that playing music in his shop encourages customers to spend more money. To test this belief, he records how much money is collected for a ten-day period while music is playing and then for an eight-day period without music. The sales, in thousands of dollars, are summarised as follows.

With music	$\sum x = 960.1$	$\sum x^2 = 92\,274.44$
Without music	$\sum y = 748.2$	$\sum y^2 = 70\,041.16$

Assuming these data are randomly sampled from normal distributions with the same variance, test the shopkeeper's claim, using a 5% significance level.

Answer

First consider the assumptions and conditions:

- n is small for both populations
- both have an underlying mean
- the variances are equal but unknown.

Since n is small and the variances are unknown, we must use a t-test and hence the pooled estimator.

Let X represent the sales with music and Y represent the sales without music.

Define the variables to be used.

If the sales with music are greater than without, then $\mu_x > \mu_y$.

Rewrite this as $\mu_x - \mu_y > 0$.

H_0: $\mu_x - \mu_y = 0$

H_1: $\mu_x - \mu_y > 0$

The test statistic is:

$$\frac{(\overline{X} - \overline{Y}) - (\mu_x - \mu_y)}{\sqrt{s_p^2\left(\frac{1}{n_x} + \frac{1}{n_y}\right)}}$$

If the sample variances are given, then $s_p^2 = \frac{(n_x - 1)s_x^2 + (n_y - 1)s_y^2}{n_x + n_y - 2}$ is used.

$$S_{xx} = \Sigma x^2 - \frac{(\Sigma x)^2}{n_x} = 92\,274.44 - \frac{960.1^2}{10} = 95.239$$

$$S_{yy} = \Sigma y^2 - \frac{(\Sigma y)^2}{n_y} = 70\,041.16 - \frac{748.2^2}{8} = 65.755$$

$$s_p^2 = \frac{S_{xx} + S_{yy}}{n_x + n_y - 2} = \frac{95.239 + 65.755}{10 + 8 - 2} = 10.062125$$

Calculate s_p^2.

We can use the form:

$$s_p^2 = \frac{S_{xx} + S_{yy}}{n_x + n_y - 2}$$

$$\overline{x} = \frac{\Sigma x}{n_x} = \frac{960.1}{10} = 96.01$$

$$\overline{y} = \frac{\Sigma y}{n_y} = \frac{748.2}{8} = 93.525$$

Calculate $\overline{x}$ and $\overline{y}$.

Test statistic:

$$\frac{(96.01 - 93.525) - 0}{\sqrt{10.062125\left(\frac{1}{10} + \frac{1}{8}\right)}} = 1.65154$$

The critical value is $t_{0.95,\,16} = 1.746$.

We have $10 + 8 - 2 = 16$ degrees of freedom here.

p	0.75	0.90	0.95
10	0.700	1.372	1.812
11	0.697	1.363	1.796
12	0.695	1.356	1.782
13	0.694	1.350	1.771
14	0.692	1.345	1.761
15	0.691	1.341	1.753
16	0.690	1.337	1.746
17	0.689	1.333	1.740

Since $1.65154 < 1.746$, the test statistic is not in the critical region so we do not reject H_0.

Always refer to H_0, the assumption you made.

There is insufficient evidence to suggest that playing music increases the sales in the shop.

Write a full contextualised conclusion.

EXERCISE 9B

1 Given the sample variance and sample size of each set of data, find the pooled estimate of variance.

a $s_x^2 = 13.2 \quad n_x = 15$

$s_y^2 = 11.9 \quad n_y = 13$

b $s_x^2 = 161.2 \quad n_x = 21$

$s_y^2 = 158.7 \quad n_y = 24$

c $s_x^2 = 32.1 \quad n_x = 60$

$s_y^2 = 48.6 \quad n_y = 40$

2 For the following pairs of data sets, find an estimate for the pooled variance.

a

X	27	19	15	19	21
	18	17	16	20	28

Y	32	31	27	26
	29	30	28	14

b

X	23	25	26	19	22	21
	28	25	26	19	23	

Y	14	19	21	20	17
	16	18	15	21	

3 For each question, state the magnitude of the test statistic for the given values of n_x and n_y and stated significance level.

a $n_x = 8, n_y = 6$, one-tailed 5%

b $n_x = 14, n_y = 10$, one-tailed 2.5%

c $n_x = 8, n_y = 7$, two-tailed 5%

d $n_x = 20, n_y = 12$, two-tailed 1%

e $n_x = 11, n_y = 14$, one-tailed 10%

f $n_x = 17, n_y = 12$, two-tailed 10%

4 For each of the following, state the null and alternate hypotheses.

a The difference in population means is not 0.

b The population mean for X is greater than the population mean for Y.

c The population mean for X is five units greater than the population mean for Y.

d The difference in the population means is not six units.

M 5 Two examiners are marking an examination paper, and it is believed that examiner A is more strict than examiner B. The results from several papers are added together for each examiner, and presented in the following table.

	Sample size	Sum of marks
Examiner A	16	689
Examiner B	12	636

Test the claim at the 5% significance level, assuming that the marks are normally distributed with a standard deviation of 15.

M 6 Takahē birds are native to New Zealand and are very rare. The male birds and female birds look very similar. The only way of differentiating males from females is to measure their weights. It is known that the female bird is slightly smaller than the male, and so weighing them could be a way of identifying the gender of an adult Takahē bird.

The weights of ten male and eight female Takahē birds are measured, and the summative statistics are presented in the following table.

	Sample size	Sum	Sum of squares
Male	10	28.1	79.4
Female	8	21.5	58.3

a Find s_p^2, the pooled estimator of the population variance.

b Test, at the 5% significance level, whether male Takahē birds are heavier than female Takahē birds assuming the weights are normally distributed.

M 7 A company that makes computers must transport them from its warehouse to the delivery centre, with one lorry delivery per day. In three weeks' time, the usual route will have roadworks stopping the traffic for six weeks. The local council says that the alternative route will add not more than ten minutes to the route. The manager of the company does not think that this is true and so, for the next 14 days, he asks eight of the company's lorry drivers to travel the new route, and six to travel the old route.

Old	34	45	36	47	42	43		
New	47	51	47	50	53	51	50	45

a Find s_p^2, the pooled estimate of the population variance.

b Test, at the 5% significance level, whether the manager is justified in his complaint assuming the times are normally distributed.

M 8 Samples are taken from two different types of honey and the viscosity (i.e. how 'runny' the honey is) is measured.

Honey	Mean	Standard deviation	Sample size
A	114.44	0.62	4
B	114.93	0.94	6

Assuming normal distributions, test at the 5% significance level whether there is a difference in the viscosity of the two types of honey.

9.3 Paired t-tests

In Section 9.2, we looked at whether or not two samples with the same variances have the same mean. We looked at the difference in means, sometimes referred to as an 'unpaired test', since there is no mechanism to 'pair' the data values.

If we need to measure the effect of a variable on a set of data, then we measure twice: before the change in variable, and after. This repeated measures design allows us to pair the points in the two datasets. In this situation, a paired t-test would be the most appropriate test to perform. Instead of measuring the difference in the means, we measure the mean of the differences, as shown in Key point 9.7.

TIP

In Social Sciences, the unpaired test is also known as an independent samples design.

KEY POINT 9.7

For a paired t-test, with n pairs of data, and H_0: $\mu_d = k$ (typically $\mu_d = 0$)

the test statistic $= \dfrac{\bar{d} - k}{\dfrac{s_d}{\sqrt{n}}}$

where $d_i = x_i - y_i$, and $\bar{d}$ and s_d are the sample mean and standard deviation of $D \sim \mathrm{N}\left(\mu_d, \dfrac{s_d^2}{n}\right)$.

We test using a t-distribution with $(n - 1)$ degrees of freedom.

The only assumption for this test is that the difference is approximately normally distributed. As a consequence, if your dataset has outliers, this test is not appropriate. Worked example 9.6 works through a paired t-test.

WORKED EXAMPLE 9.6

A diagnostic test is taken by ten students before a revision session, and then again after completing the revision session. Their scores are presented in the following table.

Student	A	B	C	D	E	F	G	H	I	J
Before	45	54	49	51	53	64	71	55	78	43
After	49	56	56	54	61	70	72	60	82	51

Using a paired t-test, and assuming the differences in scores are normally distributed, test at the 5% significance level whether the revision was effective.

Answer

	Before	After	Difference
A	45	49	4
B	54	56	2
C	49	56	7
D	51	54	3
E	53	61	8
F	64	70	6
G	71	72	1
H	55	60	5
I	78	82	4
J	43	51	8

First, calculate all of the differences so we can calculate s_d and $\bar{d}$.

$\Sigma d = 48$

$\Sigma d^2 = 284$

$\bar{d} = \frac{\Sigma d}{n} = \frac{48}{10} = 4.8$

$S_{dd} = \Sigma d^2 - \frac{(\Sigma d)^2}{n}$

Find the summative values.

$S_{dd} = 284 - \frac{48^2}{10} = 53.6$

$s_d^2 = \frac{S_{dd}}{n-1} = \frac{53.6}{9} = 5.96$ (to 3 significant figures)

$\bar{d} = 4.8$

Now find the unbiased estimates.

$s_d^2 = 5.96$ (to 3 significant figures)

Carrying out the test, let $\bar{D} \approx \mathrm{N}\left(\mu_d, \frac{s_d^2}{n}\right)$.

We can now perform our hypothesis test. We require an approximately normal distribution.

H_0: $\mu_d = 0$

H_1: $\mu_d > 0$

If the revision has been effective, then we would anticipate the difference to increase, and so the test is one-tailed test.

Test statistic $= \frac{\bar{d}}{\frac{s_d}{\sqrt{n}}} = \frac{4.8}{\sqrt{\frac{5.96}{10}}} = 6.22$

The critical value is $t_{0.95,\,9} = 1.833$.

The critical value at the 5% significance level must be found.

Since the test statistic is greater than the critical value, the test statistic is in the critical region. So we reject H_0 as there is sufficient evidence to suggest that the difference in scores has increased and so the revision has been effective.

A well-formed conclusion is required. We reject the null hypothesis and state there is sufficient evidence to suggest the revision has been effective.

In Worked example 9.6 we are measuring whether there is a difference in the mean. Worked example 9.7 considers whether the difference in the mean is greater than, or less than, a certain value.

WORKED EXAMPLE 9.7

This uses the same scenario as in Worked example 9.6.

Student	A	B	C	D	E	F	G	H	I	J
Before	45	54	49	51	53	64	71	55	78	43
After	49	56	56	54	61	70	72	60	82	51

Using a paired t-test, and assuming the differences in scores are normally distributed, test at the 5% significance level whether students have increased their scores by four marks or more.

Answer

$\overline{d} = 4.8$
$s_d^2 = 5.96$ (to 3 significant figures)

Use the same estimators as before.

Let $\overline{D} \approx \mathrm{N}\left(\mu_d, \frac{s_d^2}{n}\right)$.

H_0: $\mu_d = 4$

H_1: $\mu_d > 4$

Test statistic $= \dfrac{\overline{d} - 4}{\frac{s_d}{\sqrt{n}}} = \dfrac{0.8}{\sqrt{\frac{5.96}{10}}} = 1.04$

Carry out the test.

The critical value is $t_{0.95,9} = 1.833$.

We need the critical value at the 5% significance level.

Since the test statistic is less than the critical value, the test statistic is not in the critical region. We do not reject H_0. There is insufficient evidence to suggest that the difference in scores has increased by four or more.

A well-formed conclusion is required.

EXERCISE 9C

1 For each of the following pairs of data, find the sample mean of the difference, $\overline{d}$, and the unbiased estimator of the variance of the distance, s_d^2.

a

X	124	139	128	119	119	112	113	128	113
Y	127	117	121	126	119	125	118	118	127

b

X	34.3	30.8	32.8	27.5	26.3	27.8	35.1	31.1
Y	27.3	28.5	30.5	29	28	33	31.6	28

X	28.5	31.5	30.7	29.5
Y	32.8	28.1	30.9	30

c

X	75	84	80	66	78	97	68	86
Y	81	81	86	90	87	76	88	89

X	86	73	97	70	72
Y	84	92	85	90	91

2 For the given null hypotheses, find the test statistic of the following summative data.

a H_0: $\mu_d = 0$
$\mu_d = 0.344$, $s_d^2 = 121$, $n = 11$

b H_0: $\mu_d = 0$
$\mu_d = -0.688$, $s_d^2 = 11.62$, $n = 10$

c H_0: $\mu_d = -5$
$\mu_d = -5.82$, $s_d^2 = 182.3$, $n = 12$

3 For the data in question **2a–c**, state the magnitude of critical value, given the following alternate hypothesis and significance level.

a $H_1: \mu_d \neq 0$, significance level 5%

b $H_1: \mu_d > 0$, significance level 5%

c $H_1: \mu_d < -5$, significance level 2.5%

M 4 A biologist investigates the effect of a new food on Takahē male birds. Eight birds are weighed (in kg). They are then fed the new food for 14 days and weighed again.

Let us assume that the weight gains are normally distributed.

Initial weight (kg)	2.67	2.93	3.12	3.21	2.64	2.73	2.86	2.91
Weight after 14 days (kg)	2.71	3.01	3.19	3.24	2.6	2.78	2.84	2.97

Test, at the 2.5% significance level, to investigate whether there has been a significant increase in the weight of the Takahē male birds.

M 5 A diet programme aims at trying to help people lose at least 2 kg in weight within five weeks of starting the programme. A sample of eight participants are asked to volunteer to take part in the experiment and their weight at the beginning of the programme and after five weeks is measured and recorded. The following estimators were calculated: $\bar{d} = 2.225$; $s_d^2 = 0.931589$. Test, at the 5% significance level, the claim that participants will lose at least 2 kg of weight within the first five weeks of the programme, assuming the weight losses are normally distributed.

M 6 Police trainees are given a test to assess how good their memory is. After seeing ten car plates for 15 seconds each, they must write down as many as they can remember. The trainees then attend a memory improvement course. After this week-long course, they are retested. The results of the tests for eight police trainees are presented in the following table.

Number correct before course	6	5	6	5	7	5	4	6
Number correct after course	6	8	6	7	9	8	9	6

Test, at the 5% significance level, whether the course has made a difference to the trainees' scores, assuming the differences in scores are normally distributed.

M 7 A company sends its employees to a psychologist to try to improve their sales productivity. The following table shows the sales figures, in thousands of dollars, of six employees before and after seeing the psychologist.

	A	B	C	D	E	F
Before	10	8	15	38	60	90
After	14	9	16	42	80	83

Test, at the 5% significance level, whether the visits to the psychologist have improved sales productivity, assuming the increases in sales are normally distributed.

9.4 Confidence intervals for the mean of a small sample

Confidence intervals are another useful tool in statistical inference.

In a hypothesis test, we are interested in finding the critical region for the test. A confidence interval can be thought of as the **acceptance region** instead.

Confidence intervals are commonly misinterpreted so it is important to know the following concepts:

- A confidence interval is created from a sample taken.
- If another sample is taken, then a different confidence interval will be found.
- The population mean, although unknown, is fixed and so we assess whether the confidence interval contains the population mean.

If $\bar{x}$ is the mean of a random sample of size n from a normal distribution with population mean μ, and unbiased estimator of the variance s^2, a $100(\alpha - 1)\%$ confidence interval for μ is as shown in Key point 9.8.

KEY POINT 9.8

A $100(\alpha - 1)\%$ confidence interval for μ is given by:

$$\bar{x} \pm t_{\frac{\alpha}{2}, n-1}\frac{s}{\sqrt{n}}$$

Consider that $\bar{X} \sim N(\mu, \sigma^2)$ and that $\bar{x}$, the sample mean and s^2 the unbiased estimator of the variance are calculated with a small sample size.

Let us consider performing a hypothesis test at the 90% significance level. The critical values for this test would be $\pm t_{0.95, n-1}$.

We could now unstandardise the critical values to calculate the limits for μ which would lead us to not reject the null hypothesis.

$$\pm t_{0.95, n-1} = \frac{\bar{x} - \mu}{\frac{s}{\sqrt{n}}}$$

$$\pm t_{0.95, n-1}\frac{s}{\sqrt{n}} = \bar{x} - \mu$$

$$\mu = \bar{x} \pm t_{0.95, n-1}\frac{s}{\sqrt{n}}$$

And so

$$\bar{x} - t_{0.95, n-1}\frac{s}{\sqrt{n}} \leqslant \mu \leqslant \bar{x} + t_{0.95, n-1}\frac{s}{\sqrt{n}}$$

is the acceptance region for this hypothesis test. We can also call this the 90% confidence interval for μ.

It is written as:

$$\left(\bar{x} - t_{0.95, n-1}\frac{s}{\sqrt{n}}, \bar{x} + t_{0.95, n-1}\frac{s}{\sqrt{n}}\right)$$

More generally,

Let us consider performing a hypothesis test at the $100(\alpha - 1)\%$ significance level. The critical values for this test would be $\pm t_{\frac{\alpha}{2}, n-1}$.

We could now unstandardise the critical values to calculate the limits for μ which would lead us to not reject the null hypothesis.

$$\pm t_{\frac{\alpha}{2}, n-1} = \frac{\overline{x} - \mu}{\frac{s}{\sqrt{n}}}$$

$$\pm t_{\frac{\alpha}{2}, n-1}\frac{s}{\sqrt{n}} = \overline{x} - \mu$$

$$\mu = \overline{x} \pm t_{\frac{\alpha}{2}, n-1}\frac{s}{\sqrt{n}}$$

And so

$$\overline{x} - t_{\frac{\alpha}{2}, n-1}\frac{s}{\sqrt{n}} \leqslant \mu \leqslant \overline{x} + t_{\frac{\alpha}{2}, n-1}\frac{s}{\sqrt{n}}$$

is the acceptance region for this hypothesis test. We can also call this the $100(\alpha - 1)\%$ confidence interval for μ.

It is written as:

$$\left(\overline{x} - t_{\frac{\alpha}{2}, n-1}\frac{s}{\sqrt{n}}, \overline{x} + t_{\frac{\alpha}{2}, n-1}\frac{s}{\sqrt{n}}\right)$$

WORKED EXAMPLE 9.8

A random sample of people queueing for a train ticket are asked how long they have been waiting in the queue before buying their ticket. Their replies, in minutes, are 12, 17, 21, 9, 14, 19.

a Assuming a normal distribution, calculate a 90% confidence interval for the mean stated waiting time.
b Comment on the train company's claim that the mean waiting time is ten minutes.

Answer

a Since we have a small sample, and the population variance is unknown, we must consider a t-distribution.

$\Sigma x = 92$
$\Sigma x^2 = 1512$

Calculate the unbiased estimators of the mean and variance.

$$\overline{x} = \frac{\Sigma x}{n} = \frac{92}{6} = 15.333$$

$$S_{xx} = \Sigma x^2 - \frac{(\Sigma x)^2}{n} = 1512 - \frac{92^2}{6} = 101.333\ldots$$

$$s^2 = \frac{S_{xx}}{n - 1} = \frac{101.33\ldots}{5} = 20.267$$

We are creating a 90% confidence interval, so:

$100(\alpha - 1)\% = 90\%$

Therefore, $\frac{\alpha}{2} = 0.95$

The confidence interval required is:

$\bar{x} \pm t_{0.95,\,5}\frac{s_x}{\sqrt{n}}$ — The interval can be stated each time – it does not need to be derived.

From tables, $t_{0.95,\,5} = 2.015$. — Use the correct p-value when reading from the t-tables.

And so the confidence interval is:

$15.33 \pm 2.015\frac{\sqrt{20.267}}{\sqrt{6}}$

And the 90% confidence interval is (11.627, 19.033). — Write the confidence interval like this.

b The confidence interval (CI) does not contain the claimed value of ten minutes. In fact, the confidence interval is wholly above the claimed value.

This means that the train company is underestimating the waiting time in the queue.

EXERCISE 9D

1 For the following confidence intervals, find the value from the t-distribution that must be used.

a 90% confidence interval, $n = 6$

b 90% confidence interval, $n = 8$

c 95% confidence interval, $n = 12$

d 80% confidence interval, $n = 7$

2 For the given sample sizes and values of s_x^2, find the value of the standard error $\left(\frac{s}{\sqrt{n}}\right)$.

a $n = 8 \quad s_x^2 = 9$

b $n = 6 \quad s_x^2 = 12$

c $n = 9 \quad s_x^2 = 22$

d $n = 5 \quad s_x^2 = 4.2$

3 Given that the data comes from an underlying normal distribution, and that $\bar{x} = 13.2$, $s_x^2 = 18$, find the confidence interval for the sample size stated.

a 90% confidence interval, $n = 8$

b 90% confidence interval, $n = 6$

c 90% confidence interval, $n = 9$

d 95% confidence interval, $n = 7$

e 99% confidence interval, $n = 9$

f 80% confidence interval, $n = 10$

4 For the following dataset, find a 95% confidence interval.

12, 15, 16, 18, 17, 15

Write each end of the interval to 2 decimal places.

M 5 A car rental company claims that, on average, its class C-type car will use 7.1 litres of fuel per 100 km when travelling at 60 km/h. Seven class C cars are tested on a test track and their fuel use over 100 km is measured.

Fuel usage	7.236	7.113	7.098	7.198	7.143	7.151	7.132

a Assuming a normal distribution, find a 95% confidence interval for the mean amount of fuel used.

b Comment on the claim by the car rental company that its class C cars use 7.1 litres of fuel per 100 km.

M 6 While on holiday, Yushan likes to stay in youth hostels. The company that owns the hostels claims that the average price of a night's stay is \$43. Yushan spends one night each in six different hostels. The prices that she pays are:

\$46, \$46, \$48, \$42, \$40, \$38

Calculate a 90% confidence interval for these data, assuming a normal distribution for the prices paid.

7 The contents of jars of beans may be assumed to be normally distributed. The contents, in grams, of a random sample of nine jars are as follows.

$$460, 449, 458, 455, 461, 456, 459, 457, 453$$

a Calculate a 95% confidence interval for these data.

b The jar has 'Contains 454 g' written on the label. Comment on this claim based on your calculated confidence interval.

8 The waiting time for a particular train that runs daily is measured over 36 days. The average waiting time is found to be 37.2 minutes, with a standard deviation of 3.2 minutes. Find a 99% confidence interval for the waiting times for the train, assuming the waiting times are normally distributed.

9.5 Confidence intervals for the difference in means

In Section 9.2, we considered setting up a hypothesis test for the difference in means with the following assumptions:

- the underlying distributions are normal
- the populations are independent
- the population variance of the two populations is the same (but may be unknown)
- n is large.

For this, we modelled the difference on the means as a normal distribution as:

$$\overline{X} - \overline{Y} \sim \mathrm{N}\left(\mu_x - \mu_y, \frac{\sigma_x^2}{n_x} + \frac{\sigma_y^2}{n_y}\right)$$

Upon standardising, this creates a z-value of:

$$z = \frac{(\overline{X} - \overline{Y}) - (\mu_x - \mu_y)}{\sqrt{\frac{\sigma_x^2}{n_x} + \frac{\sigma_y^2}{n_y}}} \sim \mathrm{N}(0, 1)$$

The confidence interval can be derived from this test statistic. Consider using the value of z for a known percentage value. In Section 9.4, we used the t-statistic, but this time we will use the z-statistic. Depending on the assumptions and types of distribution, it is possible to create confidence intervals for many mean calculations. For example, an estimated confidence interval for the mean of a Poisson distribution can be calculated by approximating it to a normal distribution. Let $\overline{x}$ be the mean of a random sample of size

n_x from a normal distribution with population mean μ_x and unbiased estimator of the variance s_x^2, and let $\overline{y}$ be the mean of a random sample of size n_y from a normal distribution with population mean μ_y and unbiased estimator of the variance s_y^2, with the conditions:

- X and Y are independent populations
- the population variance of the two populations is the same (but may be unknown)
- n is large.

Then a $100(\alpha - 1)\%$ confidence interval for the difference in means can be calculated as shown in Key point 9.9.

KEY POINT 9.9

A $100(\alpha - 1)\%$ confidence interval for the difference in means is:

$$\overline{x} - \overline{y} \pm z_{\frac{\alpha}{2}} \sqrt{\frac{s_x^2}{n_x} + \frac{s_y^2}{n_y}}$$

We also need to consider small samples, for which $n < 30$. Here, we pool the variances to get the best estimate, and then model the difference as a t-distribution.

When we pool the variances like this, the hypothesis yields the following test statistic where s_p^2 is the pooled estimate of the population variance.

$$t_{\frac{\alpha}{2}, n_x+n_y-2} = \frac{(X - Y) - (\mu_x - \mu_y)}{\sqrt{s_p^2\left(\frac{1}{n_x} + \frac{1}{n_y}\right)}}$$

A $100(\alpha - 1)\%$ confidence interval for the difference in means for small samples can be calculated as shown in Key point 9.10.

KEY POINT 9.10

The $100(\alpha - 1)\%$ confidence interval for the difference in means for small samples is:

$$(\overline{x} - \overline{y}) \pm t_{\frac{\alpha}{2}, n_x+n_y-2} \times s_p \sqrt{\frac{1}{n_x} + \frac{1}{n_y}}$$

where $s_p^2 = \dfrac{\sum (x - \overline{x})^2 + \sum (y - \overline{y})^2}{n_x + n_y - 2}$.

We can calculate s_p^2 using $\dfrac{(n_x - 1)s_x^2 + (n_y - 1)s_y^2}{n_x + n_y - 2}$ if we know the unbiased estimators s_x^2 and s_y^2.

It is very important to use the correct test based on the sample size.

WORKED EXAMPLE 9.9

A group of 60 men and 70 women participate in a maths activity. The mean time taken for the men to complete the activity is 45.3 seconds, with a standard deviation of 3.2 seconds. For the women, the mean time is 46.1 seconds with a standard deviation of 2.8 seconds. Assuming the completion times are normally distributed with equal variances, find a 90% confidence interval for the difference in the means.

Answer

$\bar{x} - \bar{y} \pm z_{\frac{\alpha}{2}}\sqrt{\frac{s_x^2}{n_x} + \frac{s_y^2}{n_y}}$ — Since n_x and n_y are large in this case, we can use a normal distribution.

Let X represent the completion times for women and Y the completion times for men.

$\bar{x} = 46.1,\ s_x = 2.8,\ n_x = 70$

$\bar{y} = 45.3,\ s_y = 3.2,\ n_y = 60$

$46.1 - 45.3 \pm 1.6449\sqrt{\frac{2.8^2}{70} + \frac{3.2^2}{60}}$ — Since we are looking for a 90% confidence interval, we consider $z_{0.95} = 1.6449$.

$= 0.8 \pm 0.874\,534\ldots$

$(-0.0745, 1.6745)$

Given one confidence interval, it is possible to calculate a different confidence interval for the same sample.

WORKED EXAMPLE 9.10

Given that a 90% confidence interval is $(-0.0745, 1.6745)$, calculate a 99% confidence interval.

Answer

We currently know the following. — From the tables: $z_{0.95} = 1.6449$.

$\bar{x} - 1.6449 \times \frac{s}{\sqrt{n}} = -0.0745$

and $\bar{x} + 1.6449 \times \frac{s}{\sqrt{n}} = 1.6745$

$2\bar{x} = 1.6$

$\bar{x} = 0.8$ — Solve simultaneously for $\bar{x}$ and $\frac{s}{\sqrt{n}}$.

$\frac{3.2898s}{\sqrt{n}} = 1.749$

Therefore:

$\frac{2.576s}{\sqrt{n}} = 1.749 \times \frac{2.576}{3.2898} = 1.370$ — For a 99% CI, we consider $z_{0.995} = 2.576$.

And the 99% confidence interval becomes:

$(0.8 - 1.370, 0.8 + 1.370)$

$(-0.570, 2.170)$

In Worked example 9.11, we shall find the pooled estimate of the population variance and construct the confidence interval, as shown in Key point 9.11.

KEY POINT 9.11

A $100(\alpha - 1)\%$ confidence interval for the difference in means is:

$$(\bar{x} - \bar{y}) \pm t_{\frac{\alpha}{2}, n_x + n_y - 2} \times s_p \sqrt{\frac{1}{n_x} + \frac{1}{n_y}}$$

WORKED EXAMPLE 9.11

A shopkeeper believes that playing music in his shop encourages customers to spend more money in his shop. To test this, he records how much money was collected for a ten-day period while music was playing and then an eight-day period when it wasn't. The sales, in thousands of dollars, are summarised as follows.

With music	$\sum x = 960.1$	$\sum x^2 = 92\,274.44$
Without music	$\sum y = 748.2$	$\sum y^2 = 70\,041.16$

Assuming these data are randomly sampled from normal distributions with the same variance, find the 90% confidence interval for the difference in means.

Answer

$\bar{x} = 96.01$

$\bar{y} = 93.525$

$s_p^2 = 10.062125$

We saw this in Worked example 9.5, and so we can state the statistics calculated.

The confidence interval can be calculated by:

$$(\bar{x} - \bar{y}) \pm t_{\frac{\alpha}{2}, n_x + n_y - 2} \times s_p \sqrt{\frac{1}{n_x} + \frac{1}{n_y}}$$

$$= (96.01 - 93.525) \pm 1.746 \times \sqrt{10.062125}\sqrt{\frac{1}{10} + \frac{1}{8}}$$

We are using $t_{0.95, 16} = 1.746$.

$$= 2.485 \pm 1.746 \times 1.5047$$

So the 90% confidence interval is:

$(-0.142, 5.112)$

WORKED EXAMPLE 9.12

A chemist has developed a fuel additive and claims that it reduces the fuel consumption of cars. Eight randomly selected cars were each filled with 20 litres of fuel and driven around a race circuit. Each car was tested twice, once with the additive and once without it. The distances in miles that each car travelled before running out of fuel are given in the table below.

Car	1	2	3	4	5	6	7	8
Distance without additive	163	172	195	170	183	185	161	176
Distance with additive	168	185	187	172	180	189	172	175

Assuming a normal distribution, find a 90% confidence interval for the difference in the distances travelled.

Answer

Since this is a matched pairs design, we are repeating the experiment on each car then we consider the difference between each pair of data points.

With additive	Without additive	Difference
168	163	5
185	172	13
187	195	−8
172	170	2
180	183	−3
189	185	4
172	161	11
175	176	−1

First, find the differences.

$\sum d = 23, \sum d^2 = 409$

Calculate $\bar{d}$ and s_d^2.

$\bar{d} = \frac{23}{8} = 2.875$

$S_{dd} = 409 - \frac{23^2}{8} = \frac{2743}{8} = 342.875$

$s_d = \sqrt{\frac{342.875}{7}} = 6.999$

We use: $s_d^2 = \frac{S_{dd}}{7}$

$\bar{d} \pm t_{0.95,7} \times \frac{s_d}{\sqrt{8}}$

Calculate the confidence interval.

$2.875 \pm 1.895 \times \frac{6.999}{\sqrt{8}}$

$t_{0.95,7} = 1.895$ from tables.

$2.875 - 4.68855 = -1.814$

$2.875 + 4.68855 = 7.564$

$(-1.814, 7.564)$

EXERCISE 9E

1 For the following confidence intervals, find the value that must be used from the z-distribution.

a 90% confidence interval, $n_x = 40, n_y = 60$

b 95% confidence interval, $n_x = 30, n_y = 40$

c 99% confidence interval, $n_x = 40, n_y = 35$

d 80% confidence interval, $n_x = 80, n_y = 100$

2 For the following confidence intervals, find the value that must be used from the t-distribution.

a 90% confidence interval, $n_x = 8, n_y = 6$

b 95% confidence interval, $n_x = 14, n_y = 9$

c 99% confidence interval, $n_x = 15, n_y = 15$

d 80% confidence interval, $n_x = 8, n_y = 12$

3 By first calculating either $\sqrt{\frac{s_x^2}{n_x}+\frac{s_y^2}{n_y}}$ or $s_p\sqrt{\frac{1}{n_x}+\frac{1}{n_y}}$, as appropriate, find the stated confidence interval for $\mu_x - \mu_y$. You may assume that the data has come from an underlying normal distribution.

a

$s_x^2 = 13.2$	$n_x = 40$	$\bar{x} = 8.31$
$s_y^2 = 14.6$	$n_y = 50$	$\bar{y} = 7.92$

90% confidence interval

b

$s_x^2 = 11.356$	$n_x = 12$	$\bar{x} = 36.08$
$s_y^2 = 11.643$	$n_y = 8$	$\bar{y} = 36.75$

90% confidence interval

c

$s_x^2 = 433.9$	$n_x = 8$	$\bar{x} = 127.25$
$s_y^2 = 292.9$	$n_y = 7$	$\bar{y} = 124.42$

95% confidence interval

4 A 95% confidence interval using z values is (9.642, 14.558).

a Calculate a 90% confidence interval.

b Calculate a 99% confidence interval.

M 5 Two newly discovered trees, X and Y, are thought to belong to the same species. Leaf measurements are made on each tree and the estimators tabulated.

Tree	Number of leaves sampled	Mean length (cm)	Variance (cm^2)
X	10	14.3	0.50
Y	12	15.1	1.52

a Calculate a pooled estimate for the population variance.

b Find the 90% confidence interval for the difference in the means of the leaf lengths.

M 6 A psychologist wishes to investigate the effect of sleep deprivation on reaction times. Eight students volunteer to take a test, which measures their reaction time, and then re-take the test after being awake for 36 hours. Their reaction times, in milliseconds, are recorded.

	A	B	C	D	E	F	G	H
Before	19.3	11.1	10.3	12.4	13.6	13.2	14.6	15.2
After	20.5	13.5	14.2	12.9	15.3	15.2	16.2	15.9

a Calculate the 99% confidence interval for the difference in reaction times.

b Interpret your confidence interval regarding the effect of sleep deprivation on reaction times.

M 7 In a large school, a sample of 50 boys and 60 girls complete a 100 m race. The estimators of the data are given.

	Sample size	Mean time taken (s)	Variance (s^2)
Boys	50	13.7	2.56
Girls	60	14.9	3.43

Find the 95% confidence interval for the difference in times between the boys and girls to complete the 100 m race.

M 8 An economist believes that a typical basket of weekly food, bought by a family of four, costs more in Eastville than in Weston. Seven stores are randomly selected in each of these two towns and the cost of the basket recorded (in \$).

Eastville	13.21	13.97	13.76	13.11	13.25	13.98	13.03
Weston	12.93	13.13	12.98	13.01	12.99	13.21	13.01

Calculate the 95% confidence interval for the difference in means, assuming the costs are normally distributed.

WORKED PAST PAPER QUESTION

A company decides that its employees should follow an exercise programme for 30 minutes each day, with the aim that they lose weight and increase productivity. The weights, in kg, of a random sample of 8 employees at the start of the programme and after following the programme for 6 weeks are shown in the table.

Employee	A	B	C	D	E	F	G	H
Weight before (kg)	98.6	87.3	90.4	85.2	100.5	92.4	89.9	91.3
Weight after (kg)	93.5	85.2	88.2	84.6	95.4	89.3	86.0	87.6

a Assuming that loss in weight is normally distributed, find a 95% confidence interval for the mean loss in weight of the company's employees.

b Test at the 5% significance level whether, after the exercise programme, there is a reduction of more than 2.5 kg in the population mean weight.

Cambridge International AS & A Level Further Mathematics 9231 Paper 23 Q8 June 2011

Answer

a

Difference	5.1	2.1	2.2	0.6	5.1	3.1	3.9	3.7

First, calculate the differences in weight.

$\sum d = 25.8,\ \sum d^2 = 100.14$

$\bar{d} = \frac{25.8}{8} = 3.225$

$s_d^2 = \frac{1}{8-1}\left(100.14 - \frac{25.8^2}{8}\right) = 1.555^2$

95% confidence interval

$\bar{d} \pm t_{0.975,7} \times \frac{s}{\sqrt{n}}$

$= 3.225 \pm 2.365 \times \frac{1.555}{\sqrt{8}}$

Use the unbiased estimators.

$[1.92, 4.53]$

Since the sample size is small, we must consider the t-distribution.

b $H_0: \mu_b - \mu_a = 2.5$, $H_1: \mu_b - \mu_a > 2.5$

State the hypotheses. When setting the parameters, label them sensibly, for example, μ_b for before and μ_a for after.

$\bar{d} = 3.225$

$s_d^2 = 1.555^2$

Calculate $\bar{d}$ and s_d^2.

$t = \frac{\bar{d} - (\mu_b - \mu_a)}{\frac{s}{\sqrt{n}}} = \frac{3.225 - 2.5}{\frac{1.555}{\sqrt{8}}} = 1.32$ Calculate the test statistic.

$t_{0.95,7} = 1.89$ We are assuming an underlying normal distribution. We have a small sample size with unknown variance. We need to use the t-distribution for our critical value.

Since $1.32 < 1.89$, we do not reject H_0. There is insufficient evidence that the difference in the means is greater than 2.5.

Checklist of learning and understanding

Hypothesis test for the mean, with a small sample:

- The test statistic is $\frac{\bar{X} - \mu}{\frac{\sigma}{\sqrt{n}}} \sim t_{n-1}$.
- s can be used in place of σ when the population variance is unknown.

Pooled estimate of a population variance from two samples:

- The pooled estimate of the population variance, s_p^2 can be found from $s_p^2 = \frac{\sum(x - \bar{x})^2 + \sum(y - \bar{y})^2}{n_x + n_y - 2}$.

Difference in means: two-sample *t*-test:

- Assume:
  - underlying distributions are normal
  - populations are independent
  - population variance of the two populations is the same (but may be unknown).
- The test statistic is $T = \frac{(\bar{X} - \bar{Y}) - (\mu_x - \mu_y)}{\sqrt{s_p^2\left(\frac{1}{n_x} + \frac{1}{n_y}\right)}} \sim t_{n_x + n_y - 2}$.

Difference in means: paired sample *t*-test:

- Assume:
  - differences are normally distributed
  - population variance of the two populations is the same (but may be unknown)
  - data are matched pairs (repeated measures design).
- The test statistic is $\frac{\bar{d} - k}{\frac{s_d}{\sqrt{n}}}$.

Difference in means: normal distribution:

- Assume:
  - underlying distributions are normal
  - large sample sizes
  - populations are independent
  - population variance of the two populations is the same (but may be unknown).

- The test statistic is $Z = \dfrac{(\overline{X} - \overline{Y}) - (\mu_x - \mu_y)}{\sqrt{\dfrac{\sigma_x^2}{n_x} + \dfrac{\sigma_y^2}{n_y}}} \sim \text{N}(0, 1)$.

Confidence interval for a mean from a small sample:

- If $\overline{x}$ is the mean of a random sample of size n from a normal distribution with population mean μ, a $100(\alpha - 1)\%$ confidence interval for μ is given by $\overline{x} \pm t_{\frac{\alpha}{2}, n-1}\dfrac{s}{\sqrt{n}}$.

Confidence interval for the difference in population means:

- A $100\,(\alpha - 1)\%$ confidence interval for the difference in means for small samples is given as:

$$(\overline{x} - \overline{y}) \pm t_{\frac{\alpha}{2}, n_x + n_y - 2} \times s_p\sqrt{\frac{1}{n_x} + \frac{1}{n_y}}$$

- A $100(\alpha - 1)\%$ confidence interval for the difference in means (for large n) is given as:

$$(\overline{x} - \overline{y}) \pm z_{\frac{\alpha}{2}}\sqrt{\frac{s_x^2}{n_x} + \frac{s_y^2}{n_y}}$$

- A $100(\alpha - 1)\%$ confidence interval for the difference in means for matched pairs is given as:

$$\overline{d} \pm t_{\left(\frac{\alpha}{2}, n-1\right)} \times \frac{s_d}{\sqrt{n}}$$

END-OF-CHAPTER REVIEW EXERCISE 9

1 a A gardener P claims that a new type of fruit tree produces a higher annual mass of fruit than the type that he has previously grown. The old type of tree produced 5.2 kg of fruit per tree, on average. A random sample of 10 trees of the new type is chosen. The masses, x kg, of fruit produced are summarised as follows.

$$\sum x = 61.0$$

$$\sum x^2 - 384.0$$

Test, at the 5% significance level, whether gardener P's claim is justified, assuming a normal distribution.

b Another gardener Q has his own type of fruit tree. The masses, y kg, of fruit produced by a random sample of 10 trees grown by gardener Q are summarised as follows.

$$\sum y = 70.0$$

$$\sum y^2 = 500.6$$

Test, at the 5% significance level, whether the mean mass of fruit produced by gardener Q's trees is greater than the mean mass of fruit produced by gardener P's trees. You may assume that both distributions are normal and you should state any additional assumption.

Cambridge International AS & A Level Further Mathematics 9231 Paper 21 Q9 June 2013

2 A random sample of 10 observations of a normally distributed random variable X gave the following summarised data, where $\bar{x}$ denotes the sample mean.

$$\sum x = 70.4, \sum (x - \bar{x})^2 = 8.48$$

Test, at the 10% significance level, whether the population mean of X is less than 7.5.

Cambridge International AS & A Level Further Mathematics 9231 Paper 22 Q7 November 2013

3 A random sample of 50 observations of a random variable X and a random sample of 60 observations of a random variable Y are taken. The results for the sample means, $\bar{x}$ and $\bar{y}$, and the unbiased estimates for the population variances, s_x^2 and s_y^2, respectively, are as follows.

$$\bar{x} = 25.4 \quad \bar{y} = 23.6 \quad s_x^2 = 23.2 \quad s_y^2 = 27.8$$

A test at the α% significance level, of the null hypothesis that the population means of X and Y are equal, against the alternative hypothesis that they are not equal, is carried out. Given that the null hypothesis is not rejected, find the set of possible values of α.

Cambridge International AS & A Level Further Mathematics 9231 Paper 21 Q6 November 2014

Chapter 10
Chi-squared tests

In this chapter you will learn how to:

- fit a theoretical distribution, as prescribed by a given hypothesis, to given data
- use a χ^2-test, with the appropriate number of degrees of freedom, to carry out the corresponding goodness of fit analysis
- use a χ^2-test, with the appropriate number of degrees of freedom, for independence in a contingency table.

PREREQUISITE KNOWLEDGE

Where it comes from	What you should be able to do	Check your skills
AS & A Level Mathematics Probability & Statistics 1, Chapters 6 & 7 AS & A Level Mathematics Probability & Statistics 2, Chapter 2	Calculate probabilities from discrete random variables such as binomial, Poisson and geometric.	**1** Let $X \sim \text{Bin}(10, 0.2)$. Find $P(X \leqslant 3)$. **2** Let $Y \sim \text{Po}(2.2)$. Find $P(Y > 3)$. **3** Let $G \sim \text{Geo}(0.3)$. Find $P(G \leqslant 4)$.
AS & A Level Mathematics Probability & Statistics 2, Chapter 5	Calculate probabilities from the normal distribution.	**4** Let $X \sim N(42, 6)$. Find $P(X \geqslant 40.2)$.
Chapter 8	Calculate probabilities from any continuous random variable.	**5** Let X represent a continuous random variable with a probability density function f given by: $f(x) = \begin{cases} \frac{3}{80}(x^2 + 3) & -2 \leqslant x \leqslant 3 \\ 0 & \text{otherwise} \end{cases}$ Find $P(-1 \leqslant X < 2)$.

Testing statistical models

In this chapter, we shall test whether the data provided fit a particular distribution. Sometimes the parameters will be given, but sometimes they will not.

We shall also test how closely categorical data are associated. For example, we could test if there is an association between hair colour and eye colour, or between colour blindness and gender.

These statistical tests are vital in social sciences: Psychology and Sociology, in particular. Most of the data collected in these subjects are categorical. This allows researchers to analyse any associations between these types of data.

10.1 Forming hypotheses

We shall test how well the observed data from an experiment fits the expected values from a distribution. For example, consider rolling a die. We may wish to test if the values on the die have an equal chance of being selected, that is the die is not biased. This means that we are looking to see if the data fit a **discrete uniform distribution**. A discrete uniform distribution occurs when each outcome is equally likely so it has the same probability.

To perform a hypothesis test, we need to define a null hypothesis as in Chapter 9.

For the die, we could set up these hypotheses:

H_0: There is no difference between the observed data and the expected values.

H_1: There is a difference between the observed data and the expected values.

This is vague, but it shows the fundamental premise behind the test. We need to ensure that our hypotheses are related to the situation we are testing, as shown in Key point 10.1.

We could have written these hypotheses:

H_0: A discrete uniform distribution is a good-fit model.

H_1: A discrete uniform distribution is not a good-fit model.

It is very important that the hypotheses are well written and that our conclusions refer to the initial problem.

KEY POINT 10.1

When defining your null and alternative hypotheses, make sure you refer to the distribution that you are using to model your observed data.

In your conclusion, make sure you address the initial problem. You will see this in the examples regarding rolling die.

Let us continue with the idea of rolling a die. In an experiment, we roll a die 180 times and collect the following data.

Number, n	1	2	3	4	5	6
Observed frequency	29	31	34	39	23	24

We will use N to denote $\sum O_i$, the sum of the observed frequencies.

To test whether the die is biased or not, we need to consider how well this data set fits a discrete uniform distribution.

The discrete uniform distribution will have the following probability distribution.

$$P(X = x) = \begin{cases} \frac{1}{6} & x = 1, 2, 3, 4, 5, 6 \\ 0 & \text{otherwise} \end{cases}$$

The expected frequencies from this distribution (and, in fact, any discrete distribution we choose to use) can be calculated using the formula $N \times P(X = x)$.

Number, n	1	2	3	4	5	6
Expected frequency	30	30	30	30	30	30

The last cell is coloured red for a reason. Since we know the total is 180, and we know the sum of the other expected values is 150, the last value is predetermined. It is not calculated from the probability distribution. This seems trivial at the moment, but will become very important when calculating the test statistic and modelling its distribution.

The first five expected values (these can be *any* five) are free, independent variables. The final expected value is predetermined and is not independent of the others. It is calculated from the others rather than from the probability distribution.

This is called a **constraint** and reduces the **free variables** in the system by one. We call these degrees of freedom.

We will need to refine how we find degrees of freedom, but we can make use of the formula shown in Key point 10.2.

KEY POINT 10.2

For a goodness-of-fit test, the number of degrees of freedom, ν (the Greek letter nu), in the system is found using:

ν = number of expected values − 1 − number of parameters estimated

In the case of rolling a die, we have six expected values. We subtract 1 because of the constraint on the system and we have no parameters to estimate. (This will be developed further through the following examples.)

Let's look back at our die:

Number, n	1	2	3	4	5	6
Observed frequency	29	31	34	39	23	24
Expected frequency	30	30	30	30	30	30

We need to calculate a test statistic to be able to carry out the test.

We want to calculate the *difference* relative to the expected value (E_i) and the corresponding observed value (O_i). We want this test statistic to be equal to 0 if the observed and expected frequencies are the same.

The construction is very similar to finding the sample variance.

We first calculate $\frac{(O_i - E_i)^2}{E_i}$ for each pair of values and then we add these up:

$$X^2 = \sum \left(\frac{(O_i - E_i)^2}{E_i} \right)$$

This is the test statistic that we will use.

Which distribution can we use to model the test statistic? If we meet the following necessary conditions then $X^2 \sim \chi^2(\nu)$, where ν is the number of degrees of freedom required:

- each O_i represents a frequency
- all E_i are greater than five
- the classes all form a sample space; that is, each observation taken fits uniquely into a single category.

This is shown in Key point 10.3. Note that χ^2 is a **chi-squared** (from the Greek letter chi; pronounced 'kye-squared') statistic.

KEY POINT 10.3

Given the condition that all $E_i \geqslant 5$, then $\sum \left(\frac{(O_i - E_i)^2}{E_i} \right) \sim \chi^2(\nu)$ is a good approximation.

DID YOU KNOW?

The $\chi^2(\nu)$ distribution is the sum of ν independent values from squared standardised normal distributions:

$$\chi^2(\nu) = \sum_{1}^{\nu} Z_i^2, \text{ where } Z_i \sim N(0, 1^2)$$

In the case of the die discussed previously, we have five independent variables (the final E was a constraint on the system), and so we can model the X^2 statistic, the sum of the squared normal distributions, as $Z_1^2 + Z_2^2 + Z_3^2 + Z_4^2 + Z_5^2 = \chi^2(5)$.

The condition that $E_i \geqslant 5$ is linked to the similar condition that the frequency of the bars of a histogram must also by greater than five. It is useful to research this yourself. It has something to do with the effect of outlying data on the test statistic. As the sample size grows, this condition can be relaxed as the approximations to the squared normal distributions improve. However, in this course we must use the condition that each $E_i \geqslant 5$.

WORKED EXAMPLE 10.1

Let us return to the experiment with the die.

An experiment is carried out to test whether a die is biased or not. A die is rolled 180 times and the following observations are tabulated.

Number, n	1	2	3	4	5	6
Observed frequency	29	31	34	39	23	24

Test, at the 5% significance level, whether the die is biased.

Answer

If the die is biased, then we cannot fit the data to a discrete uniform distribution. If the die is unbiased, then a discrete uniform distribution would be a good fit.

Define the hypotheses.

H_0: A discrete uniform distribution is a good fit.
H_1: A discrete uniform distribution is not a good fit.

The assumed probability distribution is:

Expected frequencies are calculated using $N \times P(X = x)$.

$$P(X = x) = \begin{cases} \frac{1}{6} & x = 1, 2, 3, 4, 5, 6 \\ 0 & \text{otherwise} \end{cases}$$

So we can calculate the expected frequencies and, hence, the value of each $\frac{(O_i - E_i)^2}{E_i}$.

Number	Observed	Expected	$\frac{(O_i - E_i)^2}{E_i}$
1	29	30	0.0333
2	31	30	0.0333
3	34	30	0.5333
4	39	30	2.7
5	23	30	1.6333
6	24	30	1.2

$$\chi^2 = \sum\left(\frac{(O_i - E_i)^2}{E_i}\right) = 6.1333$$

$\nu = 6 - 1 - 0$
$\nu = 5$

Calculate the degrees of freedom. Since we have not estimated any parameters, we have five degrees of freedom.

The critical value will be:

Find the critical value from the χ^2-distribution table.

Even though the hypothesis is two-tailed, we consider only the upper tail for goodness of fit since we are measuring how much the test statistic *exceeds* a specific value.

p	0.95
$\nu = 1$	3.841
2	5.991
3	7.815
4	9.488
5	11.07
6	12.59

$\chi_5^2(0.95) = 11.07$

Since $6.1333 < 11.07$, there is insufficient evidence to reject H_0.

Always refer to H_0.

There is insufficient evidence to state that a discrete uniform distribution is not a good fit.

Refer back to the question when writing the conclusion.

There is insufficient evidence to suggest that the die is biased.

TIP

There is another way of calculating this test statistic.

$$\Sigma\left(\frac{(O_i - E_i)^2}{E_i}\right)$$

$$= \Sigma\left(\frac{O_i^2 - 2O_iE_i + E_i^2}{E_i}\right)$$ Multiply out.

$$= \Sigma\left(\frac{O_i^2}{E_i}\right) - 2\Sigma(O_i) + \Sigma(E_i)$$ Simplify.

$$= \Sigma\left(\frac{O_i^2}{E_i}\right) - 2N + N$$ Now we have established that $\Sigma O_i = N$.

$$\chi^2 = \Sigma\left(\frac{O_i^2}{E_i}\right) - N$$ And, in fact, $\Sigma E_i = N$.

This is a convenient form to use, but some information that may be useful for further analysis may be lost. We will mention this when we consider contingency tables in Section 10.4.

EXERCISE 10A

1 Find the values of:

a $\chi_8^2(0.9)$ b $\chi_{11}^2(0.95)$ c $\chi_4^2(0.99)$ d $\chi_{21}^2(0.995)$

2 For the following distributions and sample sizes, write the table of expected values.

a $P(X = x) = \begin{cases} \frac{x^2}{30} & x = 1, 2, 3, 4 \\ 0 & \text{otherwise} \end{cases}$

$n = 150$

b Data values a, b, c, d are in the ratio 4:4:2:2; $n = 240$

c $P(X = x) = \begin{cases} \frac{1}{7} & x = 2, 3, 4, 5, 6, 7, 8 \\ 0 & \text{otherwise} \end{cases}$

$n = 280$

3 For the following sets of observed (O) and expected (E) data, calculate the value of χ^2, the test statistic.

a

O	32	59	12	14	41	32
E	40	50	20	15	40	25

b

O	8	23	39	42	42	41	36	22	11
E	11	24	35	40	45	40	35	24	11

c

O	35	61	70	55	39
E	30	60	90	50	30

4 The following dataset shows values for what is thought to have come from the probability distribution.

$$P(X = x) = \begin{cases} \frac{5 - x}{10} & x = 1, 2, 3, 4 \\ 0 & \text{otherwise} \end{cases}$$

n	1	2	3	4
Observed frequency	35	29	12	4

A test at the 5% significance level will be carried out.

a Find the expected values.

b State the hypotheses.

c Find the value of the test statistic.

d State the degrees of freedom.

e Write down the critical value.

f Conclude the hypothesis test.

M 5 The population of a country is known to have blood groups O, A, B and AB in the ratio 5:3:2:1. 220 people are randomly selected from the population of a neighbouring country. Their blood group is assessed and the results tabulated.

Blood type	O	A	B	AB
Frequency	87	73	49	11

Test at the 5% significance level whether or not the neighbouring country's population has the same proportions of blood groups.

M 6 A company is preparing invoices to send to their customers. Before they are sent, they are checked and the daily number of mistakes found over a two-week period are recorded.

	Week 1					Week 2				
	M	Tu	W	Th	F	M	Tu	W	Th	F
Errors	29	17	13	15	22	26	16	25	18	19

Test, at the 5% level of significance, whether a uniform distribution is a good-fit model.

10.2 Goodness of fit for discrete distributions

Testing a binomial distribution as a model

We can now apply these general principles to known parametric distributions. With the binomial distribution, we may be asked to see whether the dataset fits a binomial distribution with a given probability of success (p), or we may be asked whether it fits a binomial distribution without the parameter stated. In this case, we would need to estimate the parameter. This will affect the degrees of freedom, as stated in the formula:

ν = number of expected values − 1 − number of estimated parameters

The parameter is p. This can be estimated by knowing that $E(X) = np$. So the estimate of p is:

$$\hat{p} = \frac{\bar{x}}{n}, \text{ where } \bar{x} = \frac{\Sigma r_i \times O_i}{N}, \text{ where } r_i = 0, 1, 2..., n, \text{ the mean from the observed dataset.}$$

TIP

Be careful not to confuse n (the number of trials in the binomial distribution) with N (the number of times the experiment is repeated).

TIP

All values should be written to 3 decimal places. However, more accurate values should be used in calculations.

WORKED EXAMPLE 10.2

The data in the table are thought to be binomially distributed.

x	0	1	2	3	4	5	6	7
Frequency	10	34	63	48	29	10	4	2

Test, at the 5% significance level, the claim that the data are binomially distributed.

Answer

$$\bar{x} = \frac{\Sigma(r_i \times O_i)}{N} = \frac{508}{200} = 2.54$$

Since we are not given a parameter, we must estimate this first.

Therefore, $\hat{p} = \frac{2.54}{7} = 0.363$ (3 significant figures)

H_0: A binomial distribution is a good fit.
H_1: A binomial distribution is not a good fit.

Define the hypotheses. Notice there is no reference to the value of the population proportion, as this is unknown.

We calculate the expected values by $200 \times {}^nC_r(0.363)^r(0.637)^{n-r}$.

Expected values are calculated using $E_i = N \times P(X = r)$ and we have $X \sim \text{Bin}(7, 0.363)$.

x	Observed	Expected
0	10	8.525
1	34	33.985
2	63	58.064
3	48	55.113
4	29	31.387
5	10	10.725
6	4	2.036
7	2	0.166

x	Observed	Expected	$\frac{(O_i - E_i)^2}{E_i}$
0	10	8.525	0.255
1	34	33.985	0.000
2	63	58.064	0.420
3	48	55.113	0.918
4	29	31.387	0.182
5–7	16	12.927	0.731

As some $E_i < 5$ we need to combine the cells for when $x = 5, 6$ and 7.

After combining we have six expected values.

$$\chi^2 = \sum\left(\frac{(O_i - E_i)^2}{E_i}\right) = 2.506$$

$\nu = 6 - 1 - 1 = 4$

Consider the number of degrees of freedom: we need the extra −1 because we are now required to estimate a parameter.

The critical value is $\chi_4^2(0.95) = 9.488$. Since $2.506 < 9.488$, there is insufficient evidence to reject H_0. There is insufficient evidence to state that a binomial distribution is not a good fit.

Note, throughout the question, no reference has been made to the population proportion. This is because it is unknown.

Testing a Poisson distribution as a model

With the Poisson distribution, we need to see whether the dataset fits a Poisson distribution with a given rate (the parameter here is λ). Alternatively, we may need to estimate the parameter.

The parameter is λ. This can be estimated using:

$$\hat{\lambda} = \frac{\Sigma r_i \times O_i}{N}$$

WORKED EXAMPLE 10.3

The data in the table are thought to be modelled as a Poisson distribution with a mean of 2.5.

Number, n	0	1	2	3	4	5	6	7–
Frequency	8	34	42	28	26	5	5	2

Test the claim, at the 5% level of significance, that the data can be modelled as a Poisson distribution with mean 2.5.

Answer

In this case, the parameter is given and so it does not need to be estimated.

H_0: The Poisson (2.5) model is a good fit.

H_1: The Poisson (2.5) model is not a good fit.

Define the hypotheses.

Here we can refer to the population parameter in the hypotheses, as it is a known value.

We calculate the expected values here by:

$150 \times e^{-2.5} \times \dfrac{2.5^r}{r!}$

For the Poisson distribution, $P(X = r) = \dfrac{e^{-\lambda}\lambda^r}{r!}$.

The final E value is calculated as 150 – (sum of the others).

x	Observed	Expected
0	8	12.313
1	34	30.782
2	42	38.477
3	28	32.064
4	26	20.040
5	5	10.020
6	5	4.175
7–	2	2.129

x	Observed	Expected	$\dfrac{(O_i - E_i)^2}{E_i}$
0	8	12.313	1.511
1	34	30.782	0.336
2	42	38.477	0.323
3	28	32.064	0.515
4	26	20.040	1.772
5	5	10.020	2.515
6–	7	6.304	0.077

Since $E < 5$ for some values, we need to combine the final two categories.

$\chi^2 = \sum \left(\dfrac{(O_i - E_i)^2}{E_i} \right) = 7.049$

Calculate the test statistic.

$\nu = 7 - 1 = 6$

We now consider the degrees of freedom.

No parameters were estimated.

The critical value is $\chi_6^2(0.95) = 12.59$.

Since $7.049 < 12.59$, there is insufficient evidence to reject H_0.

There is insufficient evidence to state that a Poisson (2.5) model is not a good fit.

EXERCISE 10B

1 It is believed that some data, $N = 80$, can be modelled by $X \sim \text{Bin}(6, 0.3)$. The table of expected values is:

x_i	0	1	2	3	46
E_i	9.412	24.202	r	s	5.638

a Find r.

b Find s.

Write your answers to 3 decimal places.

2 It is believed that some data, $N = 100$, can be modelled by $X \sim \text{Po}(2.9)$. The table of expected values is:

x_i	0	1	2	3	4	5	6–
E_i	5.502	15.957	r	22.367	s	9.405	7.417

a Find r.

b Find s.

Write your answers to 3 decimal places.

3 It is believed that the following observed data follow a binomial distribution.

x_i	0	1	2	3	4	5	6	7
O_i	3	10	15	16	9	3	2	2

Let $\hat{p}$ be the unbiased estimator for the proportion, p.

a Show that $\hat{p} = 0.393$ to 3 significant figures.

b Using the value found in **a**, find the values of r and s in the following table of expected data.

x_i	0–1	2	3	4	5–7
E_i	10.078	r	17.304	s	5.378

c Explain why it was necessary to combine some of the columns together.

4 For the data below, calculate the test statistic and state how many degrees of freedom are required, assuming no parameters need to be estimated.

O	20	31	15	12	10	2
E	24	35	14	7	6	4

For each following question, clearly state:

- your hypotheses
- the value of your test statistic
- the degrees of freedom required
- the critical value
- your conclusion.

M 5 150 students take a multiple-choice test consisting of six questions. The numbers of correct answers are tabulated.

x	0	1	2	3	4	5	6
Observed	2	10	30	36	44	22	6

Test, at the 5% significance level, whether a binomial distribution is a good model for the data.

M 6 The number of accidents on a road per day is recorded for 80 days, giving the following results.

No. accidents	0	1	2	3	4	5
Frequency	13	21	23	11	7	5

It is thought that the dataset models a Poisson distribution with a rate of 2.5 accidents per day. Test this claim at the 5% significance level.

M 7 The owner of a small ski hostel records the demand for rooms during high season.

Rooms required	0	1	2	3	4
No. nights	13	27	41	13	6

a Show that the mean demand for rooms per night is 1.72.

A test is to be carried out at the 1% significance level to show that a Poisson distribution is a good model. The expected values are:

Rooms required	0	1	2	3	4
Expected values	17.91	p	26.49	q	9.62

b Find the value of p, and hence q.

c Carry out the hypothesis test.

10.3 Goodness of fit for continuous distributions

Testing a normal distribution as a model

With the normal distribution, as with all continuous distributions, we need to note carefully how the data are grouped so that we calculate the expected values correctly. Worked examples 10.4 and 10.5 highlight this point. We also need to be aware that two parameters may now need to be estimated: μ and σ^2.

If required, μ can be estimated by $\bar{x}$, and σ^2 can be estimated by s^2. This will affect the number of degrees of freedom, as shown in Key point 10.4.

KEY POINT 10.4

When fitting a normal distribution, the number of degrees of freedom are:

$\nu = n - 1$ if no parameters are estimated

$\nu = n - 1 - 1$ if one parameter is estimated

$\nu = n - 1 - 2$ if two parameters are estimated.

WORKED EXAMPLE 10.4

During observations on the weights of 150 newborn babies, the following data are observed and recorded to 1 decimal place.

Weight (kg)	2.0–2.4	2.5–2.9	3.0–3.4	3.5–3.9	4.0–4.4	4.5–4.9
Frequency	8	14	54	43	22	9

It is believed that the data follow a normal distribution, with variance 0.4. Test this belief at the 10% significance level.

Answer

Here, we are given the population variance, but we need to estimate the mean. We also need to set out the data in a way that will enable us to calculate the expected values.

To estimate the mean, use the midpoints of the groups in the usual calculation.

$\sum fx = 522$

$n = 150$

$\hat{\mu} = \frac{522}{150} = 3.48$

H_0: A normal distribution with variance 0.4 is a good fit.
H_1: A normal distribution with variance 0.4 is not a good fit.

Define the hypotheses.

a	b	Probability of interval	Observed value	Expected value	$\frac{(O_i - E_i^2)}{E_i}$
	2.45	0.0517	8	7.755	0.008
2.45	2.95	0.1493	14	22.397	3.148
2.95	3.45	0.2801	54	42.010	3.422
3.45	3.95	0.2902	43	43.532	0.007
3.95	4.45	0.1661	22	24.922	0.343
4.45		0.0626	9	9.383	0.016

Show the information correctly so you can calculate the expected values. It is very important that the expected values add up correctly to the total of observed data. For this to happen, we must consider the entire probability distribution and ensure that the probabilities add up to 1.

We must use the probability at the lower tail and the upper tail to include all values. This means that the lower group should be $X < 2.45$ rather than $1.95 \leqslant X < 2.45$. Similarly, for the upper tail, we should consider $X \geqslant 4.45$ rather than $4.45 \leqslant X < 4.95$.

Standardise $X \sim N(3.48, 0.4)$ to calculate the probabilities.

For example: $P(X < 2.45)$

$$= P\left(Z < \frac{2.45 - 3.48}{\sqrt{0.4}}\right) = 0.0517$$

$$\chi^2 = \sum\left(\frac{(O_i - E_i)^2}{E_i}\right) = 6.942$$

$\nu = 6 - 1 - 1 = 4$

We have estimated one parameter, $\hat{\mu} = 3.48$, and so we have $\nu = n - 1 - 1$ degrees of freedom.

The critical value is $\chi_4^2(0.9) = 7.779$.

Find the critical value.

Since $6.942 < 7.779$, there is insufficient evidence to reject H_0. There is insufficient evidence to state that a normal distribution with variance 0.4 is not a good model.

Worked example 10.5 introduces a continuous uniform distribution and fits it to the data. The grouped data are described in a different way. It is very important that you are aware of how the data are presented, as this can affect the accuracy of the estimators required.

A continuous uniform distribution is sometimes referred to as a *rectangular* distribution due to the shape of its probability density function. The distribution over an interval has the same probability density for all values.

Let $X \sim U[a, b]$.

Then $f(x) = \begin{cases} \frac{1}{b-a} & a \leqslant x \leqslant b \\ 0 & \text{otherwise.} \end{cases}$

For example, consider $X \sim U[2, 8]$:

$f(x) = \begin{cases} \frac{1}{6} & 2 \leqslant x \leqslant 8 \\ 0 & \text{otherwise} \end{cases}$

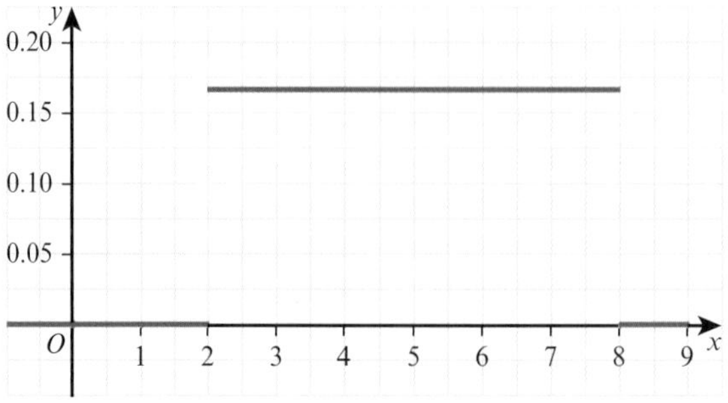

WORKED EXAMPLE 10.5

The waiting times for a bus are observed over 120 days and the results are noted.

Time, t (min)	0–	10–	20–	30–	40–	50–60
Frequency	14	25	27	25	15	14

The departure time of the previous bus is unknown in each case. It is believed that the waiting times are uniformly distributed over one hour. Test this claim at the 10% level of significance.

Answer

We are modelling this as a uniform distribution on the interval [0, 60] and so we can define our hypotheses on this basis.

Define the hypotheses.

H_0: $U[0, 60]$ is a good model.

H_1: $U[0, 60]$ is not a good model.

t (min)	Observed	Expected	$\frac{(O_i - E_i^2)}{E_i}$
$0 \leqslant t < 10$	14	20	1.8
$10 \leqslant t < 20$	25	20	1.25
$20 \leqslant t < 30$	27	20	2.45
$30 \leqslant t < 40$	25	20	1.25
$40 \leqslant t < 50$	15	20	1.25
$50 \leqslant t < 60$	14	20	1.8

The probability function for $U[a, b]$ is

$$P(X = x) = \begin{cases} \frac{1}{b-a} & a \leqslant x \leqslant b \\ 0 & \text{otherwise.} \end{cases}$$

$$\chi^2 = \sum\left(\frac{(O_i - E_i)^2}{E_i}\right) = 9.8$$

$\nu = 6 - 1 = 5$

Calculate the number of degrees of freedom.

$\chi_5^2(0.9) = 9.236$

Find the critical value.

Since $9.8 > 9.236$, there is sufficient evidence to reject H_0.

There is sufficient evidence to suggest that $U[0, 60]$ does not fit the data.

EXERCISE 10C

1 For each of the following distributions, write the table of expected values.

a $P(X = x) = \begin{cases} \frac{1}{5} & 2 \leqslant x \leqslant 7 \\ 0 & \text{otherwise} \end{cases}$

x	O_i
$2 \leqslant x < 3$	18
$3 \leqslant x < 4$	10
$4 \leqslant x < 4.5$	10
$4.5 \leqslant x < 5$	11
$5 \leqslant x \leqslant 7$	31

b $P(X = x) = \begin{cases} \frac{2}{9} & 6.5 \leqslant x \leqslant 11 \\ 0 & \text{otherwise} \end{cases}$

x	O_i
$6.5 \leqslant x < 7.5$	20
$7.5 \leqslant x < 8$	8
$8 \leqslant x < 8.5$	11
$8.5 \leqslant x < 9$	6
$9 \leqslant x < 10$	21
$10 \leqslant x < 11$	15

c $P(X = x) = \begin{cases} \frac{x^2 - 1}{228} & 3 \leqslant x \leqslant 9 \\ 0 & \text{otherwise} \end{cases}$

x	O_i
$3 \leqslant x < 6$	127
$6 \leqslant x < 7$	86
$7 \leqslant x < 8$	119
$8 \leqslant x < 8.5$	79
$8.5 \leqslant x \leqslant 9$	89

2 For each distribution in question **1a–c**, calculate the value of the test statistic, χ^2.

a

x	O_i
$2 \leqslant x < 3$	18
$3 \leqslant x < 4$	10
$4 \leqslant x < 4.5$	10
$4.5 \leqslant x < 5$	11
$5 \leqslant x \leqslant 7$	31

b

x	O_i
$6.5 \leqslant x < 7.5$	20
$7.5 \leqslant x < 8$	8
$8 \leqslant x < 8.5$	11
$8.5 \leqslant x < 9$	6
$9 \leqslant x < 10$	21
$10 \leqslant x < 11$	15

c

x	O_i
$3 \leqslant x < 6$	127
$6 \leqslant x < 7$	86
$7 \leqslant x < 8$	119
$8 \leqslant x < 8.5$	79
$8.5 \leqslant x \leqslant 9$	89

3 For each of the following sets of information, find:

i the number of degrees of freedom

ii the critical value.

a Number of E_i cells after combining = 9. The data are believed to fit a normal distribution with mean 6. Test at 5% significance.

b Number of E_i cells after combining = 7. The data are believed to fit a normal distribution.

Test at 10% significance.

c Number of E_i cells after combining = 11. The data are believed to fit a normal distribution with mean 6 and variance 4.

Test at 2.5% significance.

d Number of E_i cells after combining = 15. The data are believed to fit a normal distribution with variance 5.

Test at 5% significance.

4 Let $X \sim N(35, 4^2)$. Find:

a $P(X < 30.5)$ b $P(30.5 \leqslant X < 40.5)$ c $P(40.5 \leqslant X < 46.5)$ d $P(X \geqslant 46.5)$

For each following question, clearly state:

- your hypotheses
- the value of the test statistic
- the number of degrees of freedom required
- the critical value
- your conclusion.

M 5 A machine is designed to cut metal into strips of length 25 m, to the nearest metre. The lengths of 100 cut pieces are grouped and recorded.

Length cut (m)	Frequency
$24.5 \leqslant l < 24.75$	21
$24.75 \leqslant l < 25$	29
$25 \leqslant l < 25.25$	27
$25.25 \leqslant l < 25.5$	23

It is believed that the machine is equally likely to cut the metal to any length between 24.5 and 25.5 m. Test this claim at the 5% level of significance.

M 6 A company makes climbing rope, which is cut to lengths of 50 m with a standard deviation of 1.5 m. A sample of 150 pieces of rope is measured and the results are recorded.

Length (m)	Frequency
$l < 48$	0
$48 \leqslant l < 49$	2
$49 \leqslant l < 50$	22
$50 \leqslant l < 51$	30
$51 \leqslant l < 52$	33
$52 \leqslant l < 53$	30
$53 \leqslant l < 54$	25
$54 \leqslant l < 55$	8

Test, at the 5% significance level, whether the lengths of pieces of rope can be modelled as a normal distribution according to the parameters suggested.

M 7 At the end of a statistics course, 110 students sit an examination. The marks are grouped into classes, as shown in the following table.

Marks (X)	Number of students
0–29	22
30–34	8
35–39	8
40–49	16
50–59	20
60–69	16
70–90	20

$\sum x = 5305$, $\sum x^2 = 392\,247.5$

It is believed that the mean for the population is 47.5.

a Show that the unbiased estimator for the standard deviation of these data is 35.38.

b Test, at the 0.5% significance level, whether the data fit a normal distribution with mean 47.5.

8 It is believed that the following data fit the model $f(x) = \begin{cases} \frac{1}{40}e^{-\left(\frac{x}{4}\right)} & 0 < x \\ 0 & \text{otherwise.} \end{cases}$

x	0–	20–	40–	60–	90–	120–
Frequency	40	20	15	14	8	3

Test this claim at the 5% significance level.

EXPLORE 10.1

Sometimes, statistics can be manipulated to ensure that the outcome of a test supports a person's claim.

Consider a tree nursery. It has recently reduced its spending on the amount and quality of the fertiliser used to help the trees to grow. The expected heights of the trees after six months should be:

Height (cm)	0–10	11–20	21–30	31–40	41–50	51–60	61–70	71–80	81–90
Expected frequencies	2	2	5	4	9	11	2	3	2

The nursery manager has been told that the fertiliser is not good enough and the trees are not growing as they should be. For non-scientific reasons, the nursery manager wishes to show that this is not true. He carries out a 2.5% significance level χ^2-test to show that the observed data and expected data have the same distribution. The observed heights of the trees after six months were:

Height (cm)	0–10	11–20	21–30	31–40	41–50	51–60	61–70	71–80	81–90
Observed frequencies	4	4	5	11	6	4	3	2	1

How can the nursery manager perform a χ^2-test to show that the observed and expected data come from the same distribution and, hence, the trees are growing as they should? Think about how to group categories.

10.4 Testing association through contingency tables

Another application of the χ^2-distribution is to look for an association between two criteria. We describe this as testing whether two criteria are *independent*. This is a particularly powerful test as it allows us to deal with data in categories, such as the association between eye colour and hair colour. Again, we need to be very specific and careful with the language that we use. As long as the two criteria we want to test can be split into distinct categories, we can create a **contingency table** and then use χ^2 to test for an association between the criteria.

It is important to include row totals, column totals and the grand total when using contingency tables.

The total of each row is called R_i.

The total of each column is called C_j.

		Hair colour			Row totals
		Brown	Blonde	Red	
Eye colour	Brown	63	31	6	$100 = R_1$
	Blue	26	20	14	$60 = R_2$
	Green	11	19	10	$40 = R_3$
Column totals		$100 = C_1$	$70 = C_2$	$30 = C_3$	$200 = T$

This is a contingency table. Notice that each data point will be placed uniquely into one of the nine categories, thus satisfying one of the conditions for using a χ^2-distribution.

This contingency table shows the *observed* data.

We can see that the eye colours are in the ratio 5 : 3 : 2 and the hair colours are in the ratio 10 : 7 : 3. However, no individual row or column matches these ratios.

If there is no association between the criteria, the ratios between the totals should also be reflected in each row and in each column. We use the ratios to find each expected value, as shown in Key point 10.5.

KEY POINT 10.5

To calculate each expected value in a contingency table:

$$E_{ij} = \frac{R_i \times C_j}{T}$$

This will guarantee that the ratios between the totals are reflected in each row and each column, and will give us a table that assumes there is no association between eye colour and hair colour. We can now set up our hypotheses.

WORKED EXAMPLE 10.6

Consider the previous contingency table. Find the expected values.

Answer

		Hair colour			Row totals
		Brown	Blonde	Red	
Eye colour	Brown	$\frac{100 \times 100}{200}$	$\frac{100 \times 70}{200}$	$\frac{100 \times 30}{200}$	100
	Blue	$\frac{60 \times 100}{200}$	$\frac{60 \times 70}{200}$	$\frac{60 \times 30}{200}$	60
	Green	$\frac{40 \times 100}{200}$	$\frac{40 \times 70}{200}$	$\frac{40 \times 30}{200}$	40
Column totals		100	70	30	200

We use the formula $E_{ij} = \frac{R_i \times C_j}{T}$ for each cell.

		Hair colour			Row totals
		Brown	Blonde	Red	
Eye colour	Brown	50	35	15	100
	Blue	30	21	9	60
	Green	20	14	6	40
Column totals		100	70	30	200

Notice that in the table of expected values, each row is now in the ratio 10 : 7 : 3 and each column is in the ratio 5 : 3 : 2, as required.

To perform a χ^2-**test**, we also need to consider how many degrees of freedom there are in the system.

Consider the previous table (expected values):

		Hair colour			Row totals
		Brown	Blonde	Red	
Eye colour	Brown	50			100
	Blue			9	60
	Green	20	14		40
Column totals		100	70	30	200

Since we are given the totals, we have sufficient information (and the necessary information) to be able to generate the whole table. The four data values shown in red are the only free independent variables that exist. We can calculate the remaining five values from these four. Note that these are not the only four values that could be used. Some combinations of four values will not work as they will not allow us to calculate the rest of the values. The minimum number of expected values that must be calculated independently is four in this case. We can calculate the number of degrees of freedom as (number of rows – 1)(number of columns – 1) = (3 – 1)(3 – 1) = 4 as shown in Key point 10.6.

KEY POINT 10.6

The number of degrees of freedom of an $r \times c$ contingency table is:

$$\nu = (r - 1)(c - 1)$$

It is now possible to perform a hypothesis test to see whether there is an association between two criteria (provided the criteria are independent).

WORKED EXAMPLE 10.7

Given the data below, conduct a hypothesis test, at the 5% significance level, to see whether there is an association between eye colour and hair colour.

Observed values		Hair colour			Row totals
		Brown	Blonde	Red	
Eye colour	Brown	63	31	6	100
	Blue	26	20	14	60
	Green	11	19	10	40
Column totals		100	70	30	200

Answer

H_0: There is no association between eye colour and hair colour.

H_1: There is an association between eye colour and hair colour.

First define the hypotheses.

We could have stated the hypotheses as:

H_0: Eye colour and hair colour are independent.

H_1: Eye colour and hair colour are not independent.

Expected values		Hair colour			Row totals
		Brown	Blonde	Red	
Eye colour	Brown	50	35	15	100
	Blue	30	21	9	60
	Green	20	14	6	40
Column totals		100	70	30	200

We can now calculate the expected values.

Observed	Expected	$\frac{(O_{ij}-E_{ij})^2}{E_{ij}}$
63	50	3.38
26	30	0.533
11	20	4.05
31	35	0.457
20	21	0.048
19	14	1.786
6	15	5.4
14	9	2.778
10	6	2.667

We calculate $\frac{(O_{ij}-E_{ij})^2}{E_{ij}}$ for each pair. In this case, this is called the contribution.

$$\chi^2 = \sum\left(\frac{(O_{ij}-E_{ij})^2}{E_{ij}}\right) = 21.098$$

Calculate the test statistic.

Degrees of freedom:
$\nu = (r-1)(c-1) = 4$

Calculate the number of degrees of freedom.

$\chi_4^2(0.95) = 9.488$

Find the critical value.

Since $21.098 > 9.488$, there is sufficient evidence to reject H_0.
There is sufficient evidence to suggest an association between eye colour and hair colour.

Write your conclusion to the hypothesis test.

A different way of saying this would be:
There is sufficient evidence to suggest that eye colour and hair colour are not independent.

In Worked example 10.7, each individual $\frac{(O_{ij} - E_{ij})^2}{E_{ij}}$ was referred to as a *contribution.* This is an appropriate name since each value contributes to the test statistic. In fact, the relative size of this can give us more information when we reject the null hypothesis. It shows the major contributing factor that causes us to reject the null hypothesis.

We could use the form $\sum\left(\frac{O_{ij}^2}{E_{ij}}\right) - N$, but then we would not be able to deduce this information.

WORKED EXAMPLE 10.8

A research student collects information regarding the age of adults and the amount of debt that they have accumulated. The information collected is presented in the following table.

		Amount of debt	
		$\leqslant$ \$7500	> \$7500
Age (years)	$\leqslant$ 35	45	68
	> 35	15	32

Test, at the 5% level of significance, to decide whether there is an association between age and amount of debt.

Answer

H_0: There is no association between age and amount of debt.

H_1: There is an association between age and amount of debt.

Define the hypotheses.

Observed		Amount of debt		
		$\leqslant$ \$7500	> \$7500	
Age (years)	$\leqslant$ 35	45	68	113
	> 35	15	32	47
		60	100	160

Calculate the totals for each row and column.

Expected		Amount of debt	
		$\leqslant$ \$7500	> \$7500
Age (years)	$\leqslant$ 35	42.375	70.625
	> 35	17.625	29.375

Calculate the expected values using $E_{ij} = \frac{R_i \times C_j}{T}$.

There is no $E_{ij} < 5$, so we do not need to consider combining categories.

Observed	Expected	$\frac{(O_{ij} - E_{ij})^2}{E_{ij}}$
45	42.375	0.163
15	17.625	0.391
68	70.625	0.098
32	29.375	0.235

$$\chi^2 = \sum\left(\frac{(O_{ij} - E_{ij})^2}{E_{ij}}\right) = 0.886$$

Calculate the test statistic.

Degrees of freedom: — Calculate the number of degrees of freedom.

$\nu = (r-1)(c-1)$
$\nu = (2-1)(2-1)$

$\chi_1^2(0.95) = 3.841$ — Find the critical value.

Since $0.886 < 3.841$, there is insufficient evidence to reject H_0. There is insufficient evidence to state there is an association between age and amount of debt.

E In Worked example 10.8, the number of categories is very small and so does not yield good results. Using a 2 × 2 contingency table in this case means that the χ^2-distribution does not approximate the test statistic particularly well. In this case it would have been better to use Yates' correction, where each contribution is calculated as $\frac{(|O_{ij} - E_{ij}| - 0.5)^2}{E_{ij}}$.

For AS & A Level Further Mathematics, we are not required to use this, but it is important for further study.

WORKED EXAMPLE 10.9

In a school, the IGCSE results of 380 students are compared to see if there is an association between the grade gained in Mathematics and the grade gained in English. The results are shown in the table.

		Mathematics grade				
		A	B	C	D	E
English grade	A	33	23	9	4	1
	B	23	44	24	8	1
	C	14	30	28	11	2
	D	7	17	25	17	4
	E	1	6	19	22	7

a Calculate a table of expected values.

b Which columns would you combine and why?

c Which rows might you consider combining? State the advantages and disadvantages of combining these rows.

d Combining both rows and columns as suggested, perform a test, at the 1% significance level, to see whether there is an association between grades achieved in English and in Maths.

Answer

a

Observed values		Mathematics grade					
		A	B	C	D	E	
English grade	A	33	23	9	4	1	70
	B	23	44	24	8	1	100
	C	14	30	28	11	2	85
	D	7	17	25	17	4	70
	E	1	6	19	22	7	55
		78	120	105	62	15	380

Calculate the totals for each row and column.

Expected values		Mathematics grade				
		A	B	C	D	E
English grade	A	14.368	22.105	19.342	11.421	2.763
	B	20.526	31.579	27.632	16.316	3.947
	C	17.447	26.842	23.487	13.868	3.355
	D	14.368	22.105	19.342	11.421	2.763
	E	11.289	17.368	15.197	8.974	2.171

Calculate each expected value using $E_{ij} = \dfrac{R_i \times C_j}{T}$.

b Combining the last two columns will ensure that all $E_{ij} \geqslant 5$.

We need to combine columns if any $E_{ij} < 5$.

c We could also combine the D and E rows. An advantage of this is that we are able to compare grade groupings in the same way: A, B, C, D/E is the same for each subject. The disadvantage of this is that we have lost information and also the critical value is reduced.

d H_0: There is no association between grades achieved in Maths and in English.

Define the hypotheses.

H_1: There is an association between grades achieved in Maths and in English.

Observed data table with totals for each row and column:

Combine the necessary columns/rows.

		Mathematics grade				
		A	B	C	D/E	
English grade	A	33	23	9	5	70
	B	23	44	24	9	100
	C	14	30	28	13	85
	D/E	8	23	44	50	125
		78	120	105	77	380

Expected value table:

		Mathematics grade			
		A	B	C	D/E
English grade	A	14.37	22.11	19.34	14.18
	B	20.53	31.58	27.63	20.26
	C	17.45	26.84	23.49	17.22
	D/E	25.66	39.47	34.54	25.33

O_{ij}	E_{ij}	$\frac{(O_{ij}-E_{ij})^2}{E_{ij}}$
33	14.37	24.16
23	20.53	0.30
14	17.45	0.68
8	25.66	12.15
23	22.11	0.04
44	31.58	4.89
30	26.84	0.37
23	39.47	6.88
9	19.34	5.53
24	27.63	0.48
28	23.49	0.87
44	34.54	2.59
5	14.18	5.95
9	20.26	6.26
13	17.22	1.04
50	25.33	24.03
	Sum	96.20

Calculate the test statistic.

$\chi^2 = 96.20$

$\nu = (4-1)(4-1) = 9$

$\chi_9^2(0.99) = 21.67$

Calculate the number of degrees of freedom, using $\nu = (r-1)(c-1)$.

Since $96.20 > 21.67$ there is sufficient evidence to reject H_0.

There is an association between the grades achieved in Maths and in English.

Always add a conclusion, referring to the question.

EXERCISE 10D

1 a For the following table of observed data, calculate the expected values E_{11}, E_{31} and E_{33}.

20	30	10
30	50	20
10	20	10

b For the following table of observed data, calculate the expected values E_{12}, E_{24} and E_{13}.

14	20	24	22
8	8	13	11

Write your expected values to 2 decimal places where required.

c For the following table of observed data, calculate the table of expected data

8	12	7
12	11	8
16	23	9
18	12	4

Write your values to 2 decimal places, where required.

2 For the following observed data, write the table of expected data and calculate the test statistic.

a

10	30
20	40

b

36	30
58	76

c

36	30
24	30
58	76

d

16	4	10
14	4	20
18	5	23

3 For each given table of expected data, state how many degrees of freedom would be required.

a

13.44	14.84	13.72
16.64	18.37	16.99
17.92	19.79	18.29

b

10	20	30
21.67	43.33	65
28.33	56.67	85
40	80	120

c

10.52	21.03	31.55	1.90
21.68	43.37	65.05	3.90
28.48	56.96	85.44	5.12
39.32	78.64	117.96	7.08

4 Two categories X and Y are thought to be associated. The table of observed data is:

	Y_1	Y_2
X_1	23	36
X_2	42	136

a Give the table of expected values, to 2 decimal places.

b Calculate the test statistic.

c Test, at the 5% significance level, whether there is an association between category X and category Y. Clearly state your hypotheses.

For each following question, clearly state:

- your hypotheses
- the value of the test statistic
- the degrees of freedom required
- the critical value
- your conclusion.

M 5 A bank manager obtains information on 150 randomly selected loans made by the bank in the previous year. The loans are classified as either good or toxic. The manager also looks at the age groups of the people provided with the loan.

		Age group (years)			Total
		18–25	Over 25–35	Over 35	
Loan type	Good	41	32	27	100
	Toxic	23	17	10	50
	Total	64	49	37	150

Carry out a test, at the 10% significance level, to see if the loan type is independent of age group.

M 6 Last year, 500 students in England entered a poetry competition. Eighty of the entries were published in a book. Each student was required to state which region of England they lived in: north, south, east or west. 140 students indicated they were from the north, 120 from the south and 90 from the east. 15% of students from the north had their poems published, 10% from the south were published and 20% from the east were published.

a Complete the following contingency table.

	N	S	E	W	Total
Selected	21				
Rejected					
Total	140				500

b Test, at the 5% significance level, whether there is an association between being published and the region in which the students lived.

M 7 Residents of three towns, A, B and C, are surveyed on how good their mobile phone reception is while at home, choosing from good, satisfactory or poor. A random sample of responses are gathered from each town and tabulated.

	Good	Satisfactory	Poor
A	32	42	16
B	27	24	24
C	16	9	10

Test, at the 5% significance level, whether there is an association between the town and the quality of mobile phone reception.

WORKED PAST PAPER QUESTION

Random samples of employees are taken from two companies, A and B. Each employee is asked which of three types of coffee (cappuccino, latte, and ground) they prefer. The results are shown in the following table.

	Cappuccino	Latte	Ground
Company A	60	52	32
Company B	35	40	31

a Test, at the 5% significance level, whether coffee preferences of employees are independent of their company.

Larger random samples, consisting of N times as many employees from each company, are taken. In each company, the proportions of employees preferring the three types of coffee remain unchanged.

b Find the least possible value of N that would lead to the conclusion, at the 1% significance level, that coffee preferences of employees are not independent of their company.

Cambridge International AS & A Level Further Mathematics 9231 Paper 21 Q10 June 2012

Answer

a Calculate the totals for each row and column.

First we need to find the expected values. Remember:

$$E_{ij} = \frac{R_i \times C_j}{T}$$

	Cappuccino	Latte	Ground
Company A	$\frac{144 \times 95}{250}$	$\frac{144 \times 92}{250}$	$\frac{144 \times 63}{250}$
Company B	$\frac{106 \times 95}{250}$	$\frac{106 \times 92}{250}$	$\frac{106 \times 63}{250}$

	Cappuccino	Latte	Ground
Company A	54.72	52.992	36.288
Company B	40.28	39.008	26.712

H_0: There is no association between the company and coffee preference
H_1: There is an association between the company and coffee preference

Define the hypotheses.

O	E	$\frac{(O_{ij} - E_{ij})^2}{E_{ij}}$
60	54.72	0.509474
52	52.992	0.01857
32	36.288	0.506695
35	40.28	0.692115
40	39.008	0.025227
31	26.712	0.68834

Calculate the test statistic.

$\chi^2 = 2.44$

Because of rounding, 2.45 is also acceptable here.

$\nu = (2 - 1)(3 - 1) = 2$

Calculate number of the degrees of freedom.

$\chi_2^2(0.95) = 5.991$

Compare the critical value with the test statistic.

Since $2.44 < 5.991$, we do not reject H_0. There is insufficient evidence to suggest there is an association between the company and the coffee type.

b Since the proportions of data are the same, just N times bigger, the test statistic $X^2 = N \times 2.44$.

At the 1% significance level, with two degrees of freedom, the critical value is $\chi_2^2(0.99)$.

$\chi_2^2(0.99) = 9.21$

To reject the test, we require $N \times 2.44 > 9.21$.

$N > 3.77$

Hence, $N_{\text{min}} = 4$.

Checklist of learning and understanding

Goodness of fit:

- When fitting data to a distribution, we combine cells to ensure that $E_i \geqslant 5$.

  Then the test statistic is calculated by $\chi^2 = \sum \left(\frac{(O_i - E_i)^2}{E_i} \right) \sim \chi^2(\nu)$ and will have

  ν = number of expected values − 1 − number of estimated parameters.

Known distributions:

Distribution	Degrees of freedom
Binomial	$\nu = n - 1$ if p not estimated $\nu = n - 2$ if p estimated
Poisson	$\nu = n - 1$ if λ not estimated $\nu = n - 2$ if λ estimated
Normal	$\nu = n - 1$ if μ and σ^2 not estimated $\nu = n - 2$ if μ or σ^2 estimated $\nu = n - 3$ if μ and σ^2 estimated

Contingency tables:

- These are used to look for an association between two criteria or independence.
- Each expected value can be found from $E_{ij} = \frac{R_i \times C_j}{T}$, where R_i is the ith row total and C_j is the jth column total.
- Rows or columns can be combined to ensure that each $E_{ij} \geqslant 5$.
- The test statistic is then calculated by $\chi^2 = \sum \left(\frac{(O_{ij} - E_{ij})^2}{E_{ij}} \right)$.
- The number of degrees of freedom is $\nu = (r - 1)(c - 1)$ where r is the number of rows and c is the number of columns in the table.

END-OF-CHAPTER REVIEW EXERCISE 10

1 A family was asked to record the number of letters delivered to their house on each of 200 randomly chosen weekdays. The results are summarised below:

Number of letters	0	1	2	3	4	5	$\geqslant 6$
Number of days	57	60	53	25	4	1	0

a It is suggested that the number of letters delivered each weekday has a Poisson distribution. By finding the mean and variance for this sample, comment on the appropriateness of this suggestion.

The following table includes some of the expected values, correct to 3 decimal places, using a Poisson distribution with mean equal to the sample mean for the above data.

Number of letters	0	1	2	3	4	5	$\geqslant 6$
Expected number of days	53.964	70.693	p	q	6.622	1.735	0.463

b i Show that $p = 46.304$, correct to 3 decimal places, and find q.

ii Carry out a goodness of fit test at the 10% significance level.

Cambridge International AS & A Level Further Mathematics 9231 Paper 23 Q10 June 2011

2 A random sample of 200 is taken from the adult population of a town and classified by age group and preferred type of car. The results are given in the following table.

	Hatchback	Estate	Convertible
Under 25 years	32	11	17
Between 25 and 50 years	45	24	6
Over 50 years	31	16	18

Test, at the 5% significance level, whether preferred type of car is independent of age group.

Cambridge International AS & A Level Further Mathematics 9231 Paper 23 Q8 June 2014

3 A random sample of 80 observations of the continuous random variable X was taken and the values are summarised in the following table.

Interval	$2 \leqslant x < 3$	$3 \leqslant x < 4$	$4 \leqslant x < 5$	$5 \leqslant x < 6$
Observed frequency	36	29	9	6

It is required to test the goodness of fit of the distribution having probability density function f given by

$$f(x) = \begin{cases} \dfrac{3}{x^2} & 2 \leqslant x < 6, \\ 0 & \text{otherwise.} \end{cases}$$

a Show that the expected frequency for the interval $2 \leqslant x < 3$ is 40 and calculate the remaining expected frequencies.

b Carry out a goodness of fit test, at the 10% significance level.

Cambridge International AS & A Level Further Mathematics 9231 Paper 22 Q7 June 2013

Chapter 11
Non-parametric tests

In this chapter you will learn how to:

- understand the idea of a non-parametric test and when it might be useful
- understand the basis of the sign test, the Wilcoxon signed-rank test and the Wilcoxon rank-sum test
- use a single-sample sign test and a single-sample Wilcoxon signed-rank test to test a hypothesis concerning a population median
- use a paired-sample sign test, a Wilcoxon matched-pairs signed-rank test and a Wilcoxon rank-sum test, as appropriate, to test for identity of populations.

PREREQUISITE KNOWLEDGE

Where it comes from	What you should be able to do	Check your skills
AS & A Level Mathematics Probability & Statistics 1, Chapter 7	Find probabilities from the binomial distribution.	**1** Given $X \sim \text{Bin}(10, 0.5)$, find $\text{P}(X \leqslant 2 \cup X \geqslant 9)$.

Hypothesis testing with few distributional assumptions

In Chapter 9 we carried out hypothesis tests for the mean. We specified a number of conditions such as large/small sample size and known/unknown variance and we assumed that there was a underlying normal distribution. We carried out a test using the normal distribution or a t-test.

All of these tests are called parametric tests because we know the underlying distribution. There is a population mean which is a parameter we can test.

If we do not know the underlying distribution then we carry out a **non-parametric test**. If the sample size is small, we must develop new tests to be able to gather information regarding the data. The measure of centrality in these cases is usually the median.

11.1 Non-parametric tests

Sometimes when we wish to perform a hypothesis test, we are not able to assume the type of distribution from which the sample data came. In fact, it may not have a distribution. This causes some problems as we cannot assume a population parameter, for example, the mean or variance. In this case, we say that the data is non-parametric. A variety of non-parametric tests have been developed to cater for this. Each test is based on certain assumptions so, depending what we can assume, we can choose the correct test.

This chapter is split into two main parts, but the ideas are interlinked. In the first part we focus on single-sample statistics. In the second part we focus on two-sample statistics. Most of the ideas in the second part will be introduced in the first part. The assumptions for each test are listed in the following table.

Type of test	Test	Assumptions
Single sample	Sign test	• The underlying data are continuous • The data are independent
	Wilcoxon signed-rank test	• The underlying data are symmetric • The underlying data are continuous • The data are independent
Two sample	Paired sign test	• The data are in matched pairs • The differences between matched pairs are continuous • The data are independent
	Wilcoxon matched-pairs signed-rank test	• The data are in matched pairs • The differences between matched pairs are symmetric • The differences between matched pairs are continuous • The data are independent
	Wilcoxon rank-sum test	• The two samples are independent • The underlying data are symmetric • The underlying data are continuous

11.2 Single-sample sign test

We can use the single-sample sign test when we wish to see whether data differ from a stated value for the median. It is important to understand that the median is *not* a parameter, as we do not know the underlying distribution. This test is based on the assumptions listed in the previous table.

To perform the single-sample sign test, mark the values that are greater than the stated median with a + sign, and mark those that are less than the stated median with a – sign. If the data are well distributed about the median, we would expect an equal number of + and – signs. So there should be a probability of 0.5 that any data point is above the median and a probability of 0.5 that it is below the median.

Some people think that the single-sample sign test is quite a crude method, but it does give some useful information. The single-sample sign test is a special case of the binomial test, when n is the number of data points and the probability of 'success' is 0.5, as shown in Key point 11.1.

KEY POINT 11.1

Given n data points, a single-sample sign test is created using $X \sim \text{Bin}(n, 0.5)$. The test statistic can be the number of + signs, that is the number of data points greater than the median. We can calculate the probability that X is above this test statistic, below this test statistic, or either in the case of a two-tailed test.

This can be expressed as $P(X \leqslant ts \mid X \sim \text{Bin}(n, 0.5))$ or $P(X \geqslant ts \mid X \sim \text{Bin}(n, 0.5))$ where ts stands for test statistic.

WORKED EXAMPLE 11.1

It is believed that the following dataset comes from a population with median 135.

150	130	125	140	170
140	190	180	175	165
160	130	140	140	145

Perform a single-sample sign test, at the 5% significance level, to test this claim.

Answer

H_0: The population median is 135. — First, state the hypotheses.

H_1: The population median is not 135. — Notice that this is a two-tailed test.

Value	Sign	Value	Sign
150	+	140	+
140	+	140	+
160	+	175	+
130	–	140	+
190	+	170	+
130	–	165	+
125	–	145	+
180	+		

Consider which values are above or below the stated median.

Here, the test statistic is 12, as there are 12 values above the stated median.

Consider $X \sim \text{Bin}(15, 0.5)$:

Since 12 is greater than $\frac{n}{2}$, which is 7.5, we need consider only the top tail.

$$P(X \geqslant 12) = {}^{15}C_{12}(0.5)^{15} + {}^{15}C_{13}(0.5)^{15} + {}^{15}C_{14}(0.5)^{15} + {}^{15}C_{15}(0.5)^{15}$$

$P(X \geqslant 12) = 0.017\,578$

Since $0.017\,578 < 0.025$, the test statistic of 12 is in the critical region and, therefore, we reject H_0.

Since we are looking at a two-tailed test, we consider 2.5% as our critical value.

There is sufficient evidence to suggest the population median is not 135.

E In a situation where we have zero instead of + or –, the data point is discounted. This is not required in this course.

It is possible to approximate the sign test to a normal distribution for large n ($n > 10$ is considered large here), as shown in Key point 11.2.

KEY POINT 11.2

Let $S = min$(number of + signs, number of – signs) then $E(S) = \frac{n}{2}$, $\text{Var}(S) = \frac{n}{4}$.

For large n (> 10), $T \sim N\left(\frac{n}{2}, \frac{n}{4}\right)$, we can use the normal approximation of the binomial with $p = 0.5$. We must also make sure that we use a continuity correction. As we are approximating a discrete distribution with a continuous distribution, our z-value is:

$$z = \frac{S^+ - \mu + 0.5}{\sigma}$$

For example, if the test statistic is $S^+ = 5$, and we have approximated to $T \sim N(15, 7.5)$, we calculate the z-value as $z = \frac{5.5 - 15}{\sqrt{7.5}}$ since any value from 5 up to 5.5 rounds down to 5, and we are looking in this case at $P(X < 15)$.

EXERCISE 11A

1 For the following dataset, calculate S^+ based on each of the stated null hypotheses.

133	132	155	145	157
140	152	167	148	158
163	126	179	126	149
182	138	172	178	166

a H_0: population median is 150.

b H_0: population median is 141.

c H_0: population median is 156.

d H_0: population median is 165.

2 For each of the following, find $P(X \leqslant S^+ | X \sim \text{Bin}(n, 0.5))$.

a $S^+ = 3, n = 12$ b $S^+ = 2, n = 9$ c $S^+ = 4, n = 15$ d $S^+ = 5, n = 20$

3 For each of the following, find $P(X \geqslant S^+ | X \sim \text{Bin}(n, 0.5))$.

a $S^+ = 11, n = 14$ b $S^+ = 10, n = 12$ c $S^+ = 13, n = 15$ d $S^+ = 17, n = 25$

4 For the given hypotheses, sample size and value of S^+, state whether the null hypothesis should be rejected or not rejected at the 5% significance level. Do not use a normal approximation.

a H_0: the population median is 38.
H_1: the population median is less than 38.
$S^+ = 4, n = 15$

b H_0: the population median is 16.2.
H_1: the population median is not 16.2.
$S^+ = 5, n = 20$

c H_0: the population median is 154.
H_1: the population median is greater than 154.
$S^+ = 11, n = 15$

5 For each of the tests in question **4a–c**, state $E(S)$ and $\text{Var}(S)$ and hence the value of the test statistic, when approximating to the normal distribution.

M 6 Acid rain is a problem for many areas. Rain is described as being acidic if its pH level is below 5.2. In a city, a biologist takes 12 water samples and measures the pH.

4.73	5.06	4.87	4.88
5.04	5.16	5.07	5.09
5.11	5.24	5.25	5.25

Test, at the 5% significance level, whether the rain in this city is acidic.

M 7 During 2017, the weekly amount of pocket money given to a random sample of 15-year-old children living in Chicago is:

\$9.50, \$10.50, \$12.50, \$7.50, \$20.00, \$13.00, \$14.00, \$16.00, \$17.50, \$10.00

During 2016, the median amount of pocket money given to 15-year-olds in Chicago was \$11.00. Carry out a sign test to investigate the claim that the median weekly amount of pocket money given to 15-year-old children in Chicago has increased since 2016. Test this claim at the 10% level of significance.

M 8 A website advertises used cars for sale. During September 2018, 12 cars of similar age and of the same model are for sale. The asking prices for the cars ($AUS) are:

5999, 8900, 7000, 6499, 7500, 7999, 8450, 6500, 7250, 8150, 4999, 5600

a Investigate, at the 10% significance level, whether the median asking price for such cars is $7675.

b Still using the 10% level of significance, above what value would the median need to be to make the test significant?

M 9 The tax office claims that it takes 60 minutes to fill out their tax form. A researcher believes that it takes longer than this. A random sample of 20 people are selected, and the recorded times taken to complete the form are listed below.

55	62	63	68	70
71	58	62	64	69
69	72	59	62	66
68	69	72	69	63

Use a suitable approximation to test the claim, at the 5% significance level, that the time taken to complete the form is more than 60 minutes.

11.3 Single-sample Wilcoxon signed-rank test

If we know that our underlying data are symmetric, we can refine the sign test by performing a Wilcoxon signed-rank test. This test factors in the magnitude of the rank, as well as whether it is above or below the median. Another condition placed on the use of this test is that the underlying data are continuous.

To perform the single-sample Wilcoxon signed-rank test, we rank the differences in the data points from the stated population median. The test statistic is the smaller value of the sums of the negative ranks and the sums of the positive ranks.

As shown in Key point 11.3, a Wilcoxon signed-rank test can be performed under the conditions that:

- the underlying data are symmetric
- the underlying data are continuous
- the data are independent.

KEY POINT 11.3

Where P is the sum of the ranks corresponding to the positive differences from the stated median and N is the sum of ranks corresponding to the negative differences from the stated median:

$$T = \min(P, N)$$

T is the test statistic for the Wilcoxon signed-rank test. Critical values can be found in the statistical tables. If the test statistic is below the critical value, we reject H_0.

Even though the data are continuous, we are measuring the sums of ranks, and so the distribution of T is *discrete*. Also, it is worth noting that P can fall between the values 0 and $\frac{n(n+1)}{2}$. As all of the data points lie about the stated population median, their ranks will be between 1 and n, and the sum of these integers is $\frac{n(n+1)}{2}$.

The closer our test statistic is to 0, the more extreme the data; that is, the more likely data are to be above or below the stated population median. This is why we need our test statistic to be below the critical value from the tables.

WORKED EXAMPLE 11.2

The weights (in kg) of ten randomly selected Spanish mackerel are recorded:

1.6, 1.1, 2.1, 2.4, 2.2, 2.9, 2.6, 2.3, 2.7, 1.9

Test, at the 5% significance level, whether the median weight is greater than 1.8 kg.

Answer

H_0: The population median weight of Spanish mackerel is 1.8 kg.

H_1: The population median weight of Spanish mackerel is greater than 1.8 kg.

Define the hypotheses.

Weight, W_i	W_i – Median	P	N
1.6	−0.2		2
1.1	−0.7		7
2.1	0.3	3	
2.4	0.6	6	
2.2	0.4	4	
2.9	1.1	10	
2.6	0.8	8	
2.3	0.5	5	
2.7	0.9	9	
1.9	0.1	1	
	Sums:	46	9

To perform this test, we first need to rank the magnitude of differences of each data point from the stated population median. Ignoring signs, start with the smallest difference and give this rank 1, the next smallest difference is given rank 2 and so on.

We can check P and N here using the fact that:

$$P + N = \frac{n(n+1)}{2}$$

So the test statistic here is $T = \min(P, N) = 9$.

We look up the critical value in the statistical tables:

	Level of significance			
One-tailed	0.05	0.025	0.01	0.005
Two-tailed	0.1	0.05	0.02	0.01
$n = 6$	2	0		
7	3	2	0	
8	5	3	1	0
9	8	5	3	1
10	(10)	8	5	3
11	13	10	7	5

We are conducting a one-tailed test here at the 5% significance level.

The critical value here is 10.

Since $9 < 10$, (test statistic < critical value), there is sufficient evidence to reject H_0.

Be careful, as we require test statistic < critical value to reject H_0 here. This is different from the other tests performed in Chapter 9. We are testing whether the test statistic is significantly smaller than would happen by chance.

There is sufficient evidence to suggest that the population median is not 1.8 kg.

Write a conclusion in context.

E If the ranks are tied, for example, two values both have rank 3, they occupy the 3rd and 4th placings and so we allocate them a tied rank of 3.5. However, this is beyond the scope of this course.

It is possible to approximate the Wilcoxon signed-rank test to a normal distribution for large n, as shown in Key point 11.4.

KEY POINT 11.4

Given the statistic $T = \min(P, N)$, then:

$$E(T) = \frac{n(n+1)}{4}$$

$$\text{Var}(T) = \frac{n(n+1)(2n+1)}{24}$$

And for large n:

$$T \sim N\left(\frac{n(n+1)}{4}, \frac{n(n+1)(2n+1)}{24}\right)$$

We use a continuity correction since we are approximating a discrete distribution with a continuous distribution. Our z-value is:

$$z = \frac{T - \mu + 0.5}{\sigma}$$

WORKED EXAMPLE 11.3

In a clinical trial, the survival times, in weeks, for 19 patients with non-Hodgkin's lymphoma are recorded.

37	54	73	89	94	110	112	123	129	132
148	151	173	189	201	204	213	276	281	

Test, at the 5% significance level, whether the median differs from 150.

Answer

H_0: The population median is 150.

H_1: The population median is different from 150.

State the hypotheses.

W_i	W_i – Med	$\|W_i$ – Med$\|$	P	N
37	−113	113		17
54	−96	96		16
73	−77	77		15
89	−61	61		13
94	−56	56		12
110	−40	40		9
112	−38	38		7
123	−27	27		6
129	−21	21		4
132	−18	18		3
148	−2	2		2
151	1	1	1	
173	23	23	5	
189	39	39	8	
201	51	51	10	
204	54	54	11	
213	63	63	14	
276	126	126	18	
281	131	131	19	
		Sum	86	104

Set up the table of ranks for the data.

Ignoring signs, start with the smallest difference and give this rank 1, the next smallest difference is given rank 2 and so on.

We can check

$$P + N = 86 + 104 = 190 = \frac{19(19+1)}{2} = \frac{n(n+1)}{2}$$

$T = \min(P, N) = 86$

$$E(T) = \frac{n(n+1)}{4} = \frac{19 \times 20}{4} = 95$$

$$\text{Var}(T) = \frac{n(n+1)(2n+1)}{24} = \frac{19 \times 20 \times 39}{24} = 617.5$$

Calculate E(T) and Var(T) so we can approximate to the normal.

$z = \frac{86.5 - 95}{\sqrt{617.5}}$

$= -0.342$

Use this statistic from $T \sim N(95, 617.5)$ and standardise it using $z = \frac{T - \mu + 0.5}{\sigma}$.

$P(Z \leqslant -0.342) = 0.3662$

Since this is negative, but two-tailed, we consider only the bottom tail.

Since $0.3662 > 0.025$, we do not reject H_0.

Since this is greater than 2.5%, it is not in the critical region.

We could instead have compared -0.342 with the critical value for the two-tailed test, -1.96.

Since $-0.342 > -1.96$, we do not reject H_0.

There is insufficient evidence to suggest that the population median differs from 150.

E When using tied ranks (which is beyond this course) the calculation for the variance overestimates the variance. To compensate, we count the number of ranks that are tied, t, and reduce the variance by $\frac{t^3 - t}{48}$. So:

$$\text{Var}(T) = \frac{n(n+1)(2n+1)}{24} - \frac{t^3 - t}{48}$$

EXERCISE 11B

1 Assuming that a Wilcoxon signed-rank test is appropriate for the data, calculate T (the test statistic) based on the null hypotheses stated.

67	81	94
71	88	97
72	90	102
75	91	104
77	92	105

a H_0: population median is 85.

b H_0: population median is 100.

c H_0: population median is 70.

2 For each sample size and significance level given, state the critical value for a Wilcoxon signed-rank test.

a $n = 8$, 5% significance, one-tailed

b $n = 15$, 1% significance, one-tailed

c $n = 18$, 2% significance, two-tailed

d $n = 9$, 10% significance, two-tailed

3 State the assumptions required for the use of the Wilcoxon signed-rank test.

4 For each of the following tests, find:

- $E(T)$ and $Var(T)$
- the test statistic when approximating to the normal distribution.

Also state whether you would reject or not reject the null hypothesis.

a H_0: the population median is 142.1.
H_1: the population median is less than 142.1.
5% significance level
$T = 175$, $n = 30$

b H_0: the population median is 40.6.
H_1: the population median is not 40.6.
10% significance level
$T = 59$, $n = 20$

c H_0: the population median is 16.3.
H_1: the population median is greater than 16.3.
2.5% significance level
$T = 260$, $n = 40$

M 5 A psychology student carries out a test on short-term memory. She shows 20 commonly used words to ten 18-year-old males. As soon as the 20 words have been shown, the psychologist asks the participants to write down as many words as they can remember in five minutes. The sample of 18-year-old males can be seen as representative of the population of 18-year-old males.

The number of words correctly remembered by the participants are:

15, 7, 12, 14, 11, 10, 4, 13, 9, 2

The median number of words remembered by 65-year-old males in this test is four. Carry out a Wilcoxon signed-rank test, at the 5% level of significance, to investigate whether the median number of words remembered by the 18-year-old males is greater than that for the 65-year-old males.

M 6 Trials are carried out on a new tablet to help ease joint pain for people with chronic arthritis. A randomly selected sample of eight patients who have been suffering from arthritis are given the new tablets. Each participant measures the time it takes for the pain to stop after taking a new tablet as soon as they wake in the morning. The times, in minutes, are:

34, 44, 25, 30, 8, 27, 41, 31

The average waiting time for the old type of tablet is 43 minutes after awakening.

a Carry out a Wilcoxon signed-rank test, at the 5% significance level, to investigate whether the new tablets offer faster pain relief.

b Give a reason why the Wilcoxon signed-rank test might be preferred to a sign test.

M 7 The student council of a large school believes that the average time that the A Level students spend on individual study has increased because students are more aware of the need to achieve high grades. In 2018, the average time per week of the school term that students spent on individual study was 11.2 hours.

A random sample of ten students are asked to record the amount of time on individual study for three weeks during October 2016. The average times, in hours, per week are then calculated:

12, 13.2, 14.1, 10.8, 9.6, 11.3, 17.6, 14.3, 12.1, 19.2

Test, at the 5% level of significance, whether the average amount of time spent on individual study has increased from 2015.

M 8 Managers at a busy international airport are studying the times taken by arriving passengers to pass immigration, collect their luggage, then pass through customs. It is known that in the past this was 50 minutes. Some changes have been made to the queuing system in the hope of reducing this time. A random sample of 45 arriving passengers is taken and the rank sums calculated as $P = 55$, $N = 410$. Using a suitable approximation, test, with a 1% significance level, whether the median waiting time has reduced.

11.4 Paired-sample sign test

We can extend the idea of the sign test to work with paired-sample data by looking for a positive or negative difference. Nevertheless, the principles behind the sign test remain the same.

WORKED EXAMPLE 11.4

Data are collected on the time, in seconds, it takes nine children to tie up their left shoelace and their right shoelace.

Child	Left (s)	Right (s)
A	42	45
B	38	36
C	51	52
D	42	39
E	31	35
F	48	49
G	61	62
H	38	39
I	44	45

Test, at the 10% level of significance, whether there is a difference in the time it takes for the children to tie each shoelace.

Answer

H_0: There is no difference in the time taken to tie their left and right shoelaces.

Define the hypotheses.

H_1: There is a difference in the time taken to tie their left and right shoelaces.

Child	Left (s)	Right (s)	
A	42	45	−
B	38	36	+
C	51	52	−
D	42	39	+
E	31	35	−
F	48	49	−
G	61	62	−
H	38	39	−
I	44	45	−

Set $L_i - R_i$ as the difference.

The test statistic is 2.

Let the number of + signs be the test statistic.

$P(X \leqslant 2) = {}^9C_0(0.5)^9 + {}^9C_1(0.5)^9 + {}^9C_2(0.5)^9$

$P(X \leqslant 2) = 0.089\,844$

Use: $X \sim \text{Bin}(9, 0.5)$

The test is two-tailed, but we need to consider only the lower tail.

Since $0.089\,844 > 0.05$, the test statistic of 2 is not in the critical region. Therefore, there is insufficient evidence to reject H_0. There is insufficient evidence to say there is a difference in the times taken for children to tie their left and right shoelaces.

The probability will be 5%, as the test is two-tailed.

EXERCISE 11C

1 For the following paired datasets, a paired sign test will be performed. Calculate S^+.

a

11	7	10	7	13	6	6	9	11
12	13	7	8	8	5	6	8	12

b

16	22	12	23	19	15
17	22	14	22	18	17

c

163	162	166	157	158	153
160	162	163	158	167	156

2 a For the following dataset, state the value of n to be used in the paired sign test. Give a reason for your answer.

A	160	158
B	159	159
C	167	158
D	166	163
E	162	163
F	163	166
G	166	165
H	159	164
I	166	166
J	166	164
K	161	161
L	159	162
M	158	157
N	161	166

b Find the value of S^+ for the dataset in part **a**.

3 In each case, state whether you would reject or not reject H_0 at the stated significance level.

H_0: the population medians are equal.

H_1: the population medians are not equal.

a $n = 9$, $S^+ = 3$, 10% significance level

b $n = 6$, $S^+ = 1$, 5% significance level

c $n = 8$, $S^+ = 1$, 10% significance level

4 For the dataset in question **2a**:

a state whether a normal approximation would be appropriate, giving a reason for your answer

b find $E(S^+)$ and $Var(S^+)$

c by assuming that a normal approximation would be appropriate, find the test statistic that would be used in performing a hypothesis test.

M 5 A new drug to help ease bronchitis, a lung infection, is developed and needs to be inhaled using an aerosol. Two types of aerosol (X and Y) have been developed and the company wishes to test whether there is a difference in the average effectiveness of the aerosols. Ten patients participate in the trial, in which the patient breathes in before using the aerosol and afterwards. The percentage increase in air intake is measured and recorded.

	A	B	C	D	E	F	G	H	I	J
X	27	22	11	41	19	57	48	41	35	37
Y	23	18	7	18	24	63	31	23	21	28

Test, at the 5% significance level, whether or not there is any difference in the average effectiveness of the aerosols.

M 6 An eye hospital treats a large number of patients who have one eye normal, and the other eye suffers from a thinning of the cornea. Seven such patients are randomly selected and the thickness of their cornea on their good eye and poor eye is measured, in micrometres.

	A	B	C	D	E	F	G
Good eye	512	502	516	484	476	390	498
Poor eye	503	505	493	480	477	355	491

Using a sign test, at the 10% significance level, investigate whether there is any difference in the thickness of the cornea between the two eyes.

M 7 At a research centre, a trial is conducted to see if a new fertiliser gives a better yield of potatoes than the usual fertiliser. Ten plots of land are available for the trial. Each plot is spilt into two equal halves: one half is treated with the new fertiliser, the other half with the usual fertiliser. The following table gives the yield, in kg, per half plot.

	Plot									
	1	2	3	4	5	6	7	8	9	10
Usual	20.2	22.0	17.8	20.6	26.8	20.9	21.2	16.5	20.8	12.9
New	20.8	24.3	17.0	21.2	27.7	19.4	22.6	17.3	20.9	13.1

Using a sign test, at the 5% significance level, investigate whether the new fertiliser produces an increased average yield.

11.5 Wilcoxon matched-pairs signed-rank test

The Wilcoxon matched-pairs signed-rank test is used when we have matched pairs of data, as for the sign test, but when we can assume that the differences in the pairs of the data are symmetric, as shown in Key point 11.5. The process is the same as for the single-sample Wilcoxon signed-rank test. Worked example 11.5 demonstrates how to use the Wilcoxon matched-pairs signed-rank test.

KEY POINT 11.5

When we have matched pairs of data of unknown distributions, but the differences between them are thought to be symmetric, it is appropriate to use a Wilcoxon matched-pairs signed-rank test. We test to see whether the paired-difference median is 0.

WORKED EXAMPLE 11.5

An investigation is carried out into the effectiveness of two types of post-operative pain relief drug: Drug 1 and Drug 2. Seven adults agree to take Drug 1 on one day, and Drug 2 on the second. The time, in hours, of pain relief is recorded.

	Drug 1	Drug 2
A	4.1	3.9
B	3.2	3.3
C	5.3	5.0
D	5.1	4.6
E	4.2	4.6
F	3.8	3.2
G	3.6	4.3

Test, using the matched-pairs Wilcoxon signed-rank test, at the 5% significance level, whether Drug 2 gives longer pain relief than Drug 1.

Answer

H_0: The times are the same before and after.

H_1: The times afterwards have increased.

Define the hypotheses.

This is a one-tailed test.

Before	After	Difference	P	N
4.1	3.9	0.2	2	
3.2	3.3	−0.1		1
5.3	5	0.3	3	
5.1	4.6	0.5	5	
4.2	4.6	−0.4		4
3.8	3.2	0.6	6	
3.6	4.3	−0.7		7
		Sum	16	12

First calculate the test statistic.

Calculate differences and rank them, keeping track of positive and negative differences.

$T = \min(P, N) = 12$

And so the test statistic = 12.

Find the critical value in the statistical tables:

We are carrying out a 5% one-tailed test.

	Level of significance			
One-tailed	0.05	0.025	0.01	0.005
Two-tailed	0.1	0.05	0.02	0.01
$n = 6$	2	0		
7	(3)	2	0	
8	5	3	1	0
9	8	5	3	1
10	10	8	5	3
11	13	10	7	5

Since $12 > 3$ (test statistic > critical value), there is insufficient evidence to reject H_0.

There is insufficient evidence to suggest that Drug 2 gives longer pain relief.

EXERCISE 11D

1 For the following pairs of data, calculate the value of $T = \min(P, N)$.

a

A	B
6.2	6.7
7.6	7.3
5.7	5.3
6.2	6
8.4	7.8
7.2	7.3

b

A	B
15.4	13.8
13.1	13.4
14	14.1
13.8	14.1
15.4	15
14	14.7
15.2	15
15.4	14.4
15.1	13.6

c

A	B
12.1	13
13.6	13
14.2	13.5
15.3	14.5
14.7	14.5
14.9	13

2 For the hypotheses, sample size and test statistic given, state whether you would reject or not reject the null hypothesis.

a H_0: the population medians are equal.
H_1: the population medians are not equal.
$n = 8$, $T = 4$, significance level 5%

b H_0: the scores are the same.
H_1: the scores have decreased.
$n = 14$, $T = 20$, significance level 5%

c H_0: the weights are the same.
H_1: the weights have increased.
$n = 9$, $T = 6$, significance level 2%

3 For a sample size of $n = 18$, a Wilcoxon signed-rank test is to be carried out. Where $T = \min(P, N)$:

a Find $E(T)$.

b Find $Var(T)$.

c Given that the value of T is 59 and that a normal approximation is appropriate, calculate the test statistic to be used.

d For the given hypotheses, state whether at 5% you would reject or not reject the null hypothesis.

H_0: the population medians are equal.

H_1: the population medians are not equal.

M 4 Percentage marks are obtained for a random sample of eight A Level students for their AS & A Level examinations in Statistics and in Mechanics. The following table shows their results.

	Statistics	Mechanics
A	53	57
B	64	62
C	72	79
D	61	58
E	72	67

	Statistics	Mechanics
F	58	52
G	59	60
H	71	79

a Test, at the 10% significance level, whether there is a difference in the students' scores in Mechanics and Statistics.

b State any assumptions you have made.

M 5 The manufacturer of a brand of smartphone wishes to know what its customers think about the performance of the phone before and after introducing a new processor. The manufacturer selects, at random, ten customers. Each customer is given a phone without the new processor and a phone with the new processor. Each customer is then asked to rate 'on a scale of 1–20' the performance of each smartphone (20 being the best).

	A	B	C	D	E	F	G	H	I	J
Original processor	15	17	13	17	14	12	13	7	7	10
New processor	12	15	18	18	10	19	19	15	17	19

Test, at the 5% significance level, whether customers think that the phone with the new processor is better.

M 6 A particular type of tree can develop a virus that creates black spots on the leaves. The more spots, the more the virus has infected the tree. Two different virus treatments have been developed: treatment X and treatment Y. A sample of eight leaves is chosen. Each leaf is divided into two equal sections without removing it from the tree. On one half, treatment X is used and on the other, treatment Y. The number of black spots on each half is given in the table.

	A	B	C	D	E	F	G	H
X	41	37	34	12	7	19	23	16
Y	24	21	30	11	5	14	20	9

Test, at the 5% significance level, whether there is a difference between the two treatments.

M 7 It is believed that identical twins have similar IQ levels. Thirty pairs of identical twins participate in an IQ test and their results are recorded. There are no tied or zero ranks. The sum of positive ranks is 272, and the sum of negative ranks is 193.

a Find $E(T)$.

b Find $Var(T)$.

c Using a suitable approximation, test, at the 5% significance level, whether there is a difference between the IQ scores of a set of identical twins.

11.6 Wilcoxon rank-sum test

The Wilcoxon matched-pairs signed-rank test requires data to be paired, and groups of data must be of equal size. What if we have two independent groups of different sizes and we want to test for a difference in their medians? To do this, we perform the Wilcoxon rank-sum test to see whether the data are from the same distribution. This test is very similar in design to the independent t-test.

To perform the Wilcoxon rank-sum test, we rank the data first, as if it were from one population. We then sum the ranks for each group separately. These sums are the test statistics.

The calculation of the Wilcoxon rank-sum test statistic is quite tricky. We have two samples, one of size m and the other of size n, and we let $m \leqslant n$. Let R_m be the sum of the ranks from the group of size m. We have not defined which way we should rank the data.

Let R_m be the ranking given, then $m(n + m + 1) - R_m$ will create the rank sum of the smaller sample when ranked the opposite way round, explained as follows.

There are $n + m$ data points in total. If a data point is the ath value when ranked one way and the bth value when ranked the other, then the sum of these two ranks will be $n + m + 1$.

We have m data points in the smaller sample, so the sum of all of these sums of ranks is $m(n + m + 1)$. To find the rank sum when they are ranked the other way round, we use $m(n + m + 1) - R_m$.

To avoid having to think too carefully about the ranking order, we define the test statistic as $W = \min(R_m, m(n + m + 1) - R_m)$, as shown in Key point 11.6.

We can find the critical values from the data tables given.

KEY POINT 11.6

If two samples have sizes m and n, where $m \leqslant n$, R_m is the sum of the ranks of the items in the sample of size m, the test statistic is:

$$W = \min(R_m, m(n + m + 1) - R_m)$$

WORKED EXAMPLE 11.6

Researchers are investigating the effect of vitamin B12 on the size of the brain. A sample of males aged between 25 and 40 years is selected. Nine of them are known to have low B12 levels and seven are known to have high B12 levels. After a brain scan, the ratio of brain volume to skull capacity is recorded.

Low B12 levels	0.795	0.798	0.802	0.805	0.806	0.807	0.808	0.81	0.812
High B12 levels	0.786	0.789	0.792	0.796	0.799	0.8	0.803		

Carry out a Wilcoxon rank-sum test, at the 5% significance level, to see whether the level of vitamin B12 affects the size of the brain.

Answer

H_0: level of B12 has no effect on brain size.

We can also state H_0 as the samples are from the same population.

H_1: level of B12 has an effect on brain size.

		Low B12	High B12
0.812	1	1	
0.810	2	2	
0.808	3	3	
0.807	4	4	
0.806	5	5	
0.805	6	6	
0.803	7		7
0.802	8	8	
0.800	9		9
0.799	10		10
0.798	11	11	
0.796	12		12
0.795	13	13	
0.792	14		14
0.789	15		15
0.786	16		16
	Sum	53	83

First, rank the whole dataset. Note which group each value comes from. Then add up the ranks for each category.

Use the value of sums of the group with the smaller sample size.

The following table shows what we would get if we ranked them the other way round.

		Low B12	High B12
0.812	16	16	
0.810	15	15	
0.808	14	14	
0.807	13	13	
0.806	12	12	
0.805	11	11	
0.803	10		10
0.802	9	9	
0.800	8		8
0.799	7		7
0.798	6	6	
0.796	5		5
0.795	4	4	
0.792	3		3
0.789	2		2
0.786	1		1
	Sum	100	36

$R_m = 83$ since this is the rank sum from the smaller-sized sample.

$m(n + m + 1) - R_m = 7(9 + 7 + 1) - 83 = 36$

The test statistic is the minimum of 83 and 36, which is $W = 36$.

Calculate the test statistic.

	Level of significance		
One-tailed	0.05	0.025	0.01
Two-tailed	0.1	0.05	0.02
n	$m = 7$		
7	39	36	34
8	41	38	35
9	43	(40)	37
10	45	42	39

Find the critical value.

Since $36 < 40$, there is sufficient evidence to reject H_0.

There is evidence to suggest that level of vitamin B12 affects brain size.

For large n and m ($n \geqslant 10$, $m \geqslant 10$) it is possible to approximate W as a normal distribution, $W = \min(R_m, m(n+m+1) - R_m)$ as shown in Key point 11.7.

KEY POINT 11.7

For large n and m ($n \geqslant 10, m \geqslant 10$) it is possible to approximate W as a normal distribution:

$$E(W) = \frac{m(n+m+1)}{2}$$

$$Var(W) = \frac{mn(n+m+1)}{12}$$

We must also make sure that we use a continuity correction. Since we are approximating a discrete distribution with a continuous distribution, our z-value is $z = \frac{W - \mu + 0.5}{\sigma}$.

DID YOU KNOW?

There is another test that is statistically equivalent to the Wilcoxon rank-sum test. This is the Mann–Whitney U-test. The only difference is the measure of the test statistic, and hence the table of critical values, but it is equivalent. You may come across Mann–Whitney U-test in the Social Sciences.

WORKED EXAMPLE 11.7

A company is investigating a new production technique to improve the quality of camera lenses for a phone. Samples of the lenses are given to a camera expert who is asked to rank the lenses, with rank 1 being the highest quality. The expert does not know which production technique has been used.

Lens	*A*	*B*	*C*	*D*	*E*	*F*	*G*	*H*	*I*	*J*	*K*	*L*
Method	old	new	new	old	old	new	old	new	old	old	old	new
Rank	12	1	2	9	10	5	21	6	20	22	23	17

Lens	*M*	*N*	*O*	*P*	*Q*	*R*	*S*	*T*	*U*	*V*	*W*	*X*
Method	new	new	old	old	old	new	old	new	old	new	new	old
Rank	14	13	3	4	19	11	24	16	18	8	7	15

Using a suitable approximation as shown in Key point 11.7, test, at the 5% significance level, whether there is a difference in the quality of production techniques.

Answer

H_0: There is no difference in the quality of the two samples.

H_1: There is a difference in the quality of the two samples.

Define the hypotheses.

$m = 11$ (new)

$n = 13$ (old)

Since we are approximating, we need to know only the sizes of the two samples and the rank sum.

$$E(R_m) = \frac{m(n+m+1)}{2} = \frac{11(25)}{2} = 137.5$$

Find E(X) and Var(X).

$$Var(R_m) = \frac{mn(n+m+1)}{12} = \frac{11 \times 13(25)}{12} = 297\frac{11}{12}$$

$R_m = 1 + 2 + 5 + 6 + 17 + 14 + 13 + 11 + 16 + 8 + 7$

The test statistic is the minimum of R_m and $m(n + m + 1) - R_m$.

$R_m = 100$

$m(n + m + 1) - R_m = 175$

And so $W = \min(R_m, m(n + m + 1) - R_m) = 100$.

$$z = \frac{100.5 - 137.5}{\sqrt{\left(297\frac{11}{12}\right)}} = -2.144$$

Find the z-test statistic, remembering to make the continuity correction.

$P(Z \leqslant -2.144) = 1 - 0.984 = 0.0160$

Since we have a two-tailed test, compare the probability with the critical value for 2.5%.

Since $0.0160 < 0.025$, the test statistic is in the critical region and so we have sufficient evidence to reject H_0.

We could have compared -2.144 with the critical value for the two-tailed test, -1.96.

Since $-2.144 < -1.96$, the test statistic is in the critical region and so we have sufficient evidence to reject H_0.

There is a difference in quality between samples of camera lenses made by different production techniques.

EXPLORE 11.1

We are given a table of critical values for all of the tests that we carry out. Sometimes it is not clear where these values come from. In this activity, we shall find some of the critical values of the Wilcoxon rank-sum test.

Let us consider the situation where we have sample sizes $m = 4$ and $n = 6$. Here we have ten ranks, four of which must be assigned to the sample of size four.

The first case is the rankings $\{1, 2, 3, 4\}$, with the rank sum of 10.

The second case is a rank sum of 11, created with the rankings $\{1, 2, 3, 5\}$.

1 Find the sets of ranks that give a rank sum of:

   a 12   **b** 13 [three sets]

   c 14 [five sets]   **d** 15 [six sets]

2 How many possible sets of four ranks are there from ten?

3 Copy and complete the following table.

P(rank sum = 10)	$\frac{1}{210}$	0.004762
P(rank sum $\leqslant$ 11)	$\frac{1+1}{210}$	0.009524
P(rank sum $\leqslant$ 12)		
P(rank sum $\leqslant$ 13)		
P(rank sum $\leqslant$ 14)		
P(rank sum $\leqslant$ 15)		

The critical value, c, of a 5% one-tailed test is the greatest value of c that satisfies $P(X \leqslant c) \leqslant 0.05$.

From the work shown, we can see that this is $c = 13$.

And so we conclude that for $m = 4, n = 6$ the critical value for a one-tailed test at the 5% significance level is 13.

This is reflected in the critical value table.

	Level of significance					
One-tailed	0.05	0.025	0.01	0.05	0.025	0.01
Two-tailed	0.1	0.05	0.02	0.1	0.05	0.02
n	$m = 3$			$m = 4$		
3	6	–	–			
4	6	–	–	11	10	–
5	7	6	–	12	11	10
6	8	7	–	13	12	11

We can now also confirm that the critical values for tests at the 2.5% and 1% significance levels are correct.

EXPLORE 11.2

Use the internet to research the Kruskal–Wallis test for non-parametric data. We can use the Kruskal–Wallis test to compare three or more samples.

EXERCISE 11E

1 For each of the following datasets, calculate the values of:

i R_m

ii $m(n + m + 1) - R_m$

iii W

a

X	Y
5.7	4.8
4.4	3.9
4.9	4.1
4.6	4.2
5.2	4.7
4.5	4.3
	5.3

b

X	Y
17.3	19.8
19.7	18.1
19.4	19.2
18.3	18.6
18.7	18.4
18.9	18.0
19.1	18.5
	17.6
	17.8
	17.7

c

X	Y
21.5	22.0
21.6	22.9
21.8	22.6
22.4	22.5
23.0	22.8
	22.1
	23.1
	22.7

d

X	Y
114.2	115.8
116.1	115.1
115.4	116.0
116.8	117.1
116.2	117.2

2 For the corresponding dataset in question **1a–d**, state the critical value for the following significance levels.

a Significance level 5% one-tailed

b Significance level 10% two-tailed

c Significance level 5% two-tailed

d Significance level 1% one-tailed

3 For the following dataset sizes, find $E(R_m)$ and $Var(R_m)$.

a $n = 12, m = 9$

b $n = 13, m = 12$

c $n = 9, m = 8$

d $n = 15, m = 13$

4 a For the following dataset sizes and W values, find the test statistic if a normal approximation is used.
$n = 18, m = 12; W = 146$

b These hypotheses are given:
H_0: Population medians are equal.
H_1: Population medians are not equal.
Testing at 10%, state whether you would reject or not reject the null hypothesis.

M 5 It is believed that the calorie content of a chicken sausage is different to that of a vegetarian sausage. The calorie contents of eight vegetarian sausages and seven chicken sausages are measured and tabulated.

Vegetarian	186	181	176	135	184	190	111	132
Chicken	129	137	102	106	94	142	149	

Using a Wilcoxon rank-sum test, investigate this claim with a 5% significance level.

M 6 Plants of the same species grow on opposite sides of a river. It is thought that plants on the north side grow taller than those on the south side. Eight randomly selected plants are chosen from each side of the river, removed and their lengths measured to the nearest cm. By using a Wilcoxon rank-sum test, investigate this claim with a 5% significance level.

North side	23	21	20	28	27	19	24	25
South side	18	15	22	14	16	22	17	26

M 7 A supermarket manager wishes to investigate the quality of plums. Plums can be delivered from source to the supermarket either chilled (below 5 °C) or at a constant temperature of 12 °C. The amount of time (in days) it takes for the plums to become soft and therefore overripe is measured and ranked. The highest rank is the quickest to become overripe.

Stored at 12 °C	3	8	9	4	11	10
Chilled	2	7	1	5	6	

Carry out an appropriate non-parametric test, at the 5% level of significance, to investigate whether the chilled plums take longer to become overripe.

M 8 Mr Sum wishes to investigate whether a student's test score depends on whether the test is taken in the morning or in the afternoon. He selects a random sample of 35 students of similar ability, and randomly assigns some of them to take the test in the morning and the rest to take the test in the afternoon. The students taking the test in the morning are kept away from the students taking the test in the afternoon. The ordered scores are given in the following table (M for morning sitting, A for afternoon sitting).

M	31		M	64
M	32		A	65
M	38		A	66
M	39		M	67
A	41		A	68
A	43		A	69
M	44		M	70
A	47		A	72
M	48		A	73
A	49		A	75
M	51		A	76
A	56		A	78
M	57		M	81
A	58		A	82
M	59		A	85
M	60		A	86
M	62		A	88
A	63			

Using a suitable approximation, test, at a 2% level of significance, whether exam performance is affected by the session in which a student takes the examination.

WORKED EXAM-STYLE QUESTION

The following table shows the systolic blood pressure (mm Hg) of a random sample of eight students before and after a six-week training period.

Student	1	2	3	4	5	6	7	8
Before training	130	170	125	170	130	130	145	160
After training	120	163	120	135	143	136	144	120

a Stating clearly your hypotheses, test, using the Wilcoxon signed-rank test, whether or not there is evidence that the training has reduced blood pressure. Use a 5% level of significance.

At a later date a random sample of 30 students undertake a six-week training period. Analysis of their results using the Wilcoxon signed-rank test gives $T = 132$.

b Stating clearly your hypotheses and using a 5% level of significance, test whether or not there is evidence that the training has reduced blood pressure.

Answer

a H_0: Population median blood pressure is unchanged.

Define the hypotheses.

H_1: Population median blood pressure has decreased.

	1	2	3	4	5	6	7	8
Before–after	10	7	5	35	−13	−6	1	40
Rank	5	4	2	7	6	3	1	8
Signed rank	5	4	2	7	−6	−3	1	8

Calculate the sums of positive ranks, P, the sums of negative ranks, N, and the test statistic, T.

$P = 27$, $N = 9$

$T = \min(P, N) = 9$

Critical value is 5.

The test is one-tailed.

Since $9 > 5$, do not reject H_0.

Compare the test statistic with the critical value.

There is no evidence to suggest that the median blood pressure has decreased.

Conclude in context.

b H_0: Population median blood pressure is unchanged.

Define the hypotheses.

H_1: Population median blood pressure has decreased.

$$E(T) = \frac{n(n+1)}{4} = 232.5$$

Calculate $E(T)$ and $Var(T)$. We can approximate to the normal distribution as n is large.

$$Var(X) = \frac{n(n+1)(2n+1)}{24} = 2363.75$$

$$\text{Test statistic} = z = \frac{T - \mu + 0.5}{\sigma}$$

Calculate the test statistic, remembering continuity corrections.

$$= \frac{132 - 232.5 + 0.5}{\sqrt{2363.75}}$$

$$= -2.06$$

Critical value $= -1.645$

Find the critical value.

Since $-2.06 < -1.645$, reject H_0.

Compare the test statistic with the critical value.

The population median blood pressure has decreased.

Conclude in context.

Checklist of learning and understanding

Single-sample sign test:

- Given n data points, a sign test is created using $X \sim \text{Bin}(n, 0.5)$. The test statistic can be the number of + signs, that is the number of data points greater than the median. We can calculate the probability that X is above this test statistic, below this test statistic, or either in the case of a two-tailed test.

Wilcoxon signed-rank test:

- A Wilcoxon signed-rank test can be performed when:
  - the underlying data are symmetric
  - the underlying data are continuous.
- Where:
  - P is the sum of the ranks corresponding to the positive differences from the stated median
  - N is the sum of the ranks corresponding to the negative differences from the stated median
  - $T = \min(P, N)$ is the test statistic.
- Given the statistic $T = \min(P, N)$, then $\text{E}(T) = \frac{n(n+1)}{4}$, $\text{Var}(T) = \frac{n(n+1)(2n+1)}{24}$.

  For large n: $T \sim \text{N}\left(\frac{n(n+1)}{4}, \frac{n(n+1)(2n+1)}{24}\right)$ allowing for an approximate z-test to be done using $z = \frac{T - \mu + 0.5}{\sigma}$.

Wilcoxon matched-pairs signed-rank test:

- A Wilcoxon matched-pairs signed-rank test can be performed when:
  - the difference between matched-pairs is symmetric
  - the difference between matched-pairs is continuous.
- Where:
  - P is the sum of the ranks corresponding to the positive differences between the matched pairs
  - N is the sum of ranks corresponding to the negative differences between the matched pairs
  - $T = \min(P, N)$ is the test statistic.
- Given the statistic $T = \min(P, N)$, then $\text{E}(T) = \frac{n(n+1)}{4}$ and $\text{Var}(T) = \frac{n(n+1)(2n+1)}{24}$.

  For large n, $T \sim \text{N}\left(\frac{n(n+1)}{4}, \frac{n(n+1)(2n+1)}{24}\right)$, allowing for an approximate z-test with $z = \frac{T - \mu + 0.5}{\sigma}$.

Wilcoxon rank-sum test:

- A Wilcoxon rank-sum test can be performed when the two samples are independent, where:
  - the two samples have sizes m and n, where $m \leqslant n$
  - R_m is the sum of the ranks of the items in the sample of size m
  - the test statistic is $W = \min(R_m, m(n+m+1) - R_m)$.
- Given the test statistic W, then $\mathrm{E}(W) = \dfrac{m(n+m+1)}{2}$ and $\mathrm{Var}(W) = \dfrac{mn(n+m+1)}{12}$.

  For large n and m $(n \geqslant 10, m \geqslant 10)$ it is possible to approximate W as a normal distribution:
  - $W \sim \mathrm{N}\left(\dfrac{m(n+m+1)}{2}, \dfrac{mn(n+m+1)}{12}\right)$, allowing for an approximate z-test with

    $z = \dfrac{W - \mu + 0.5}{\sigma}$.

END-OF-CHAPTER REVIEW EXERCISE 11

M 1 The dining room in a school is some distance away from the building that has all of the classrooms in it. The school believes that students take longer walking back from the dining room after lunch than they do walking there. The school records the time taken (in seconds) by ten randomly chosen students to walk to the dining room and ten students to walk back to the main school. The recorded times are presented in the following tables.

To the dining hall	62	58	69	84	45
	96	116	89	51	75

From the dining hall	67	85	68	100	49
	121	139	87	54	88

a i Using these data, state which non-parametric test would be most appropriate. Give a reason for your choice and any assumptions you need to make.

ii Carry out a test of the school's belief at the 5% significance level.

b Later on, the school discovers that the person who collected the data has used the same ten students and has recorded them in the same order.

i Which test is now most appropriate to use? Give a reason for your answer.

ii Using this new information, carry out a test of the school's belief at the 5% significance level.

M 2 The blood cholesterol levels of 30 males and 20 females are measured. These data are shown in the following table.

Males	621	550	104	303	384
	1080	1061	771	206	1203
	810	259	610	770	382
	829	385	479	1301	551
	92	723	105	478	417
	1081	383	205	207	258
Females	208	482	94	194	370
	973	683	72	50	162
	149	215	304	127	233
	189	529	191	974	710

Using a suitable approximation, test, at the 5% significance level, whether the blood cholesterol levels of females and males differ. Is the assumption that the dataset is symmetric justified?

M 3 An investigation is conducted into the pollution levels in a major city. The number of 2.5 mm particles can be measured using the Air Quality Index (AQI). The World Health Organization recommends that an AQI of 50 or below will not have a significant effect on health. The AQI is measured for 14 consecutive days. The data are shown in the following table.

45	132	87	103	67	46	90
78	54	79	81	44	65	82

a Explain why the following tests cannot be carried out:

i a t-test

ii a single-sample Wilcoxon signed-rank test.

b Carry out an appropriate test, at the 5% significance level, to establish whether there is evidence that the AQI is above 50 in the city.

Chapter 12
Probability generating functions

In this chapter you will learn how to:

- understand the concept of a probability generating function (PGF)
- construct and use the PGF for given distributions, including:
  - discrete uniform distribution
  - binomial distribution
  - geometric distribution
  - Poisson distribution
- use formulae for the mean $(\mathrm{E}(X))$ and variance $(\mathrm{Var}(X))$ of a discrete random variable in terms of its PGF, and use these formulae to calculate the mean and variance of a given probability distribution
- use the result that the PGF of the sum of independent random variables is the product of the PGFs of those random variables (the convolution theorem)
- find the probability generating function of a linear transformation of random variables
- generalise to three or more random variables.

PREREQUISITE KNOWLEDGE

Where it comes from	What you should be able to do	Check your skills
AS & A Level Mathematics Probability & Statistics 1, Chapters 7 & 8 AS & A Level Mathematics Probability & Statistics 2, Chapters 2 & 4	You should be familiar with the binomial distribution, the Poisson distribution, and the geometric distribution.	**1** Find $\mathrm{E}(X)$ and $\mathrm{Var}(X)$ of $X \sim \mathrm{Bin}(8, 0.4)$. **2** Find $\mathrm{E}(X)$ and $\mathrm{Var}(X)$ of $X \sim \mathrm{Po}(2)$. **3** Find $\mathrm{E}(X)$ and $\mathrm{Var}(X)$ of $X \sim \mathrm{Geo}(0.3)$.
AS & A Level Mathematics Pure Mathematics 1, Chapters 6 & 21	Find the sum of a geometric series. Use some aspects of Maclaurin expansions.	**4** Find the sum to the nth term of $\frac{1}{3} + \left(\frac{1}{3}\right)^2 + \left(\frac{1}{3}\right)^3 + \ldots$ **5** Find the Maclaurin expansion of $\frac{5}{(3-2t)^2}$ up to and including the t^3 term.

Redefining probability distributions

The discrete uniform distribution is a distribution where each discrete value has the same probability of occurring. For instance, when rolling a fair die, the probability of each outcome is $\frac{1}{6}$.

x	1	2	3	4	5	6
$\mathrm{P}(X = x)$	$\frac{1}{6}$	$\frac{1}{6}$	$\frac{1}{6}$	$\frac{1}{6}$	$\frac{1}{6}$	$\frac{1}{6}$

Generally:

$$\mathrm{P}(X = x) = \begin{cases} \frac{1}{n} & x = x_1, x_2, \ldots, x_n \\ 0 & \text{otherwise} \end{cases}$$

In this chapter, we shall study a different way of describing a probability distribution. We focus on finding the probability generating functions (PGFs) of discrete probability distributions. This gives an elegant and efficient way of finding expected values and variances. A PGF gives a concise form for a probability distribution and allows much greater analysis. By recognising the expansions of functions, PGFs enable us to describe the structure of infinite discrete distributions, such as the Poisson distribution and geometric distribution. We can therefore use PGFs to find the probabilities when the value of the discrete random variable is very large indeed.

12.1 The probability generating function

Let X represent a discrete random variable, with values x_i:

x	x_1	x_2	x_3	...	x_n
$\mathrm{P}(X = x)$	$\mathrm{P}(X = x_1)$	$\mathrm{P}(X = x_2)$	$\mathrm{P}(X = x_3)$	...	$\mathrm{P}(X = x_n)$

We can create a function $G_X(t)$ using this table:

$$G_X(t) = P(X = x_1)t^{x_1} + P(X = x_2)t^{x_2} + P(X = x_3)t^{x_3} + \ldots + P(X = x_n)t^{x_n}$$

This function is called the **probability generating function** (PGF). It can be written as a single summation:

$$G_X(t) = \sum_x t^{x_i} P(X = x_i)$$

This is called the closed form of the probability generating function. Notice that the expression for $G_X(t)$ is the same as that for the expectation function, $E(t^X)$, and so $G_X(t) = \sum_x t^{x_i} P(X = x_i) = E(t^X)$, as shown in Key point 12.1.

KEY POINT 12.1

$$G_X(t) = \sum_x t^{x_i} P(X = x_i) = E(t^X)$$

The variable t is called a dummy variable in this case, and has no significance itself, but t does have an important role in finding the expectation of X and higher moments of expectation.

WORKED EXAMPLE 12.1

Consider the following probability distribution.

x	0	1	2	3	4	5	6
$P(X = x)$	0.1	0.2	0.3	0.15	0.1	0.1	0.05

Write down the PGF for the random variable X.

Answer

Apply the general form for the PGF.

$G_X(t) = \sum_x t^{x_i} P(X = x_i)$

$G_X(t) = 0.1t^0 + 0.2t^1 + 0.3t^2 + 0.15t^3 + 0.1t^4 + 0.1t^5 + 0.05t^6$

Sometimes it is useful to do this in table form first.

In Worked example 12.1, the values of the random variable occur in a sequence. This does not have to be the case, as Worked example 12.2 shows.

WORKED EXAMPLE 12.2

Consider the following probability distribution.

x	2	4	5	10
$P(X = x)$	0.1	0.2	0.3	0.4

Write down the PGF for the random variable X.

Answer

Apply the general form for the PGF.

$G_X(t) = \sum_x t^{x_i} P(X = x_i)$

$G_X(t) = 0.1t^2 + 0.2t^4 + 0.3t^5 + 0.4t^{10}$

Notice that there does not need to be any specific pattern in the values that the random variable can take.

At a trivial level, you can think of a PGF as a different way of presenting the information given by a probability distribution table. As you will discover throughout this chapter, PGFs allow us to calculate much more.

You may have noticed in Worked examples 12.1 and 12.2 that the probabilities are just the coefficients of each of the terms in t. The sum of these probabilities is 1.

We can see this by evaluating the probability generating function when $t = 1$:

$$G_X(1) = \sum_x 1^{x_i} P(X = x_i) = \sum_x P(X = x_i) = 1$$
$$G_X(1) = 1$$

Something that is a little harder to spot is that if we differentiate the probability generating function with respect to t, we will multiply each term by the value x_i:

$$G'_X(1) = \sum_x x_i(1)^{x_i - 1} P(X = x_i)$$

And then evaluating at $t = 1$ gives:

$$G'_X(1) = \sum_x x_i(1)^{x_i - 1} P(X = x_i) = E(X)$$

So $G'_X(1) = E(X)$, as shown in Key point 12.2.

KEY POINT 12.2

$$G'_X(1) = E(X)$$

You may notice that if all of the values of x are non-negative integer values, then $G_X(t)$ forms a polynomial in t. This may be finite or infinite, depending on the context.

REWIND

From your work on series in AS & A Level Pure Mathematics 1 Chapter 6, you may have observed that if there is a pattern in the PGF, it may be possible to express it as a function rather than a summation. This can lead to an efficient way of finding $E(X)$.

WORKED EXAMPLE 12.3

Let X be a discrete random variable, as shown in the probability distribution given by:

x	1	2	3	4	5
$P(X = x)$	0.2	0.2	0.2	0.2	0.2

Find the probability generating function for X.

Answer

The PGF is: — Use the definition of $G_X(t)$.

$$G_X(t) = \sum_x t^{x_i} P(X = x_i)$$

$$G_X(t) = 0.2t^1 + 0.2t^2 + 0.2t^3 + 0.2t^4 + 0.2t^5$$
$$= 0.2t(1 + t + t^2 + t^3 + t^4)$$ — Factorise.

FAST FORWARD

In the work on Maclaurin expansions in Chapter 21 Section 21.4, you should see that if there is a pattern in the PGF, it may be possible to express it as a function rather than a summation. This is an efficient way of finding $E(X)$ and higher moments of expectation.

$(1 + t + t^2 + t^3 + t^4) = S_5 = \frac{1 - t^5}{1 - t}$

Notice that this expression is the sum of the first five terms of a geometric series with first term 1 and common ratio t.

So we can use the formula $S_n = \frac{a(1 - r^n)}{1 - r}$ from AS & A Level Pure Mathematics 1.

$G_X(t) = \frac{0.2t(1 - t^5)}{1 - t}$

Notice that the distribution from the table is a uniform distribution.

Discrete uniform distribution

Let X be a discrete random variable with $P(X = x_i) = \begin{cases} \frac{1}{n} & i = 1, \ldots n \\ 0 & \text{otherwise.} \end{cases}$

Then $G_X(t) = \frac{t(1 - t^n)}{n(1 - t)}$, as shown in Key point 12.3.

KEY POINT 12.3

For a uniform distribution:

$$G_X(t) = \frac{t(1 - t^n)}{n(1 - t)}$$

WORKED EXAMPLE 12.4

Let $X \sim \text{Bin}(5, 0.2)$. Find the probability generating function for X.

Answer

As a reminder, the probability distribution would be:

Use the binomial formula from AS & A Level Probability & Statistics 1: $P(X = x) = \binom{n}{x} p^x q^{n-x}$

x	$P(X = x)$
0	0.8^5
1	$5 \times 0.8^4 \times 0.2$
2	$10 \times 0.8^3 \times 0.2^2$
3	$10 \times 0.8^2 \times 0.2^3$
4	$5 \times 0.8^1 \times 0.2^4$
5	0.2^5

The PGF is:

$G_X(t) = \sum_x t^x P(X = x)$

$G_X(t) = 0.8^5 + 5 \times 0.8^4 \times 0.2t + 10 \times 0.8^3 \times 0.2^2 t^2$
$\quad + 10 \times 0.8^2 \times 0.2^3 t^3 + 5 \times 0.8^1 \times 0.2^4 t^4 + 0.2^5 t^5$
$\quad = (0.8 + 0.2t)^5$

This is a binomial expansion and can be factorised.

Binomial distribution

Let $X \sim \text{Bin}(n, p)$. Then $G_X(t) = (q + pt)^n$, as shown in Key point 12.4.

KEY POINT 12.4

For the binomial distribution:

$$G_X(t) = (q + pt)^n$$

WORKED EXAMPLE 12.5

Let $X \sim \text{Geo}\left(\frac{1}{5}\right)$. Find the probability generating function for X.

Answer

As a reminder, the probability distribution would be:

Using the geometric formula from AS & A Level Probability & Statistics 1:

$\text{P}(X = x) = \left(\frac{4}{5}\right)^{x-1}\left(\frac{1}{5}\right)$

x	$P(X = x)$
1	$\frac{1}{5}$
2	$\left(\frac{4}{5}\right)\left(\frac{1}{5}\right)$
3	$\left(\frac{4}{5}\right)^2\left(\frac{1}{5}\right)$
...	...

The PGF is:

$$G_X(t) = \sum_x t^{x_i}\text{P}(X = x_i)$$

$$G_X(t) = \frac{1}{5}t + \left(\frac{4}{5}\right)\left(\frac{1}{5}\right)t^2 + \left(\frac{4}{5}\right)^2\left(\frac{1}{5}\right)t^3 + \ldots$$

$$= \frac{t}{5}\left(1 + \left(\frac{4t}{5}\right) + \left(\frac{4t}{5}\right)^2 + \ldots\right)$$

This is the sum of a geometric series to infinity. So we can use the formula $S_\infty = \frac{a}{1 - r}$ from AS & A Level Pure Mathematics 1.

$$= \frac{\frac{t}{5}}{\left(1 - \frac{4t}{5}\right)}$$

This gives us a generalised form, but we need to simplify it.

$$= \frac{t}{5 - 4t}$$

Geometric distribution

Let $X \sim \text{Geo}(p)$. Then $\text{G}_X(t) = \dfrac{pt}{1-qt}$, as shown in Key point 12.5.

KEY POINT 12.5

For a geometric distribution:

$$\text{G}_X(t) = \frac{pt}{1-qt}$$

Poisson distribution

Let $X \sim \text{Po}(\lambda)$. Then $\text{G}_X(t) = \text{e}^{\lambda(t-1)}$, as shown in Key point 12.6.

KEY POINT 12.6

For a Poisson distribution:

$$\text{G}_X(t) = \text{e}^{\lambda(t-1)}$$

PROOF 12.1

The following table shows the probability distribution table for $X \sim \text{Po}(\lambda)$, using $\text{P}(X = x) = \dfrac{\text{e}^{-\lambda}\lambda^x}{x!}$.

x	$\text{P}(X = x)$
0	$\text{e}^{-\lambda}$
1	$\dfrac{\lambda\text{e}^{-\lambda}}{1!}$
2	$\dfrac{\lambda^2\text{e}^{-\lambda}}{2!}$
3	$\dfrac{\lambda^3\text{e}^{-\lambda}}{3!}$
...	...

And so the PGF is:

$$\begin{aligned}\text{G}_X(t) &= \text{e}^{-\lambda} + \frac{\lambda\text{e}^{-\lambda}}{1!}t + \frac{\lambda^2\text{e}^{-\lambda}}{2!}t^2 + \frac{\lambda^3\text{e}^{-\lambda}}{3!}t^3 + \ldots \\ &= \text{e}^{-\lambda}\left(1 + \lambda t + \frac{(\lambda t)^2}{2!} + \frac{(\lambda t)^3}{3!} + \ldots\right)\end{aligned}$$

From Chapter 21, we have the following Maclaurin expansion.

$$\text{e}^x \approx 1 + x + \frac{x^2}{2!} + \frac{x^3}{3!} + \ldots$$

Therefore, the PGF becomes:

$$\begin{aligned}\text{G}_X(t) &= \text{e}^{-\lambda}(\text{e}^{\lambda t}) \\ &= \text{e}^{\lambda(t-1)}\end{aligned}$$

as required.

EXERCISE 12A

1 For each of the following distributions, write down the probability generating function, $G_X(t)$.

a $X \sim \text{Bin}(20, 0.3)$ b $X \sim \text{Bin}(10, 0.25)$ c $X \sim \text{Bin}(50, 0.04)$

2 For each of the following distributions, write down the probability generating function, $G_X(t)$.

a $X \sim \text{Po}(4)$ b $X \sim \text{Po}(2.3)$ c $X \sim \text{Po}(12)$

3 For each of the following distributions, write down the probability generating function, $G_X(t)$.

a $X \sim \text{Geo}(0.1)$ b $X \sim \text{Geo}(0.7)$ c $X \sim \text{Geo}(0.4)$

4 Find the probability generating function for:

x	1	2	3	4	5	6	7
$P(X = x)$	$\frac{1}{4}$	$\frac{1}{8}$	$\frac{1}{4}$	$\frac{1}{16}$	$\frac{1}{16}$	$\frac{1}{8}$	$\frac{1}{8}$

5 Find the probability generating function for:

x	2	4	6	8	10
$P(X = x)$	$\frac{1}{16}$	$\frac{1}{4}$	$\frac{3}{8}$	$\frac{1}{4}$	$\frac{1}{16}$

Write your answer in the form $at^b(1 + t^2)^c$.

6 Find the probability distribution for the following probability generating function.

$$G_X(t) = \frac{t^3}{6}(2 + t^4 + 2t^8)$$

7 Find the probability distribution for the following probability generating function.

$$G_X(t) = \left(\frac{4}{5} + \frac{t}{5}\right)^7$$

8 A distribution has a probability generating function of:

$$G_X(t) = \frac{1}{3}\left(\frac{2 + t}{2 - t}\right)$$

a Find the probabilities for when $x = 0, 1, 2, 3$.

b Find a general formula for $P(X = k), k \geqslant 1$.

P 9 Independent trials, each with the probability of 'success' p, are carried out. The random variable X counts the number of trials up to and including that on which the first success is obtained. Write down an expression for $P(X = x)$ for $x = 1, 2, \ldots$. Show that the probability generating function of X is $G_X(t) = pt(1 - qt)^{-1}$.

10 Consider the probability generating function $G_X(t) = \dfrac{k}{(5 - 2t)^2}$. Find the value of k.

12.2 Mean (E(X)) and variance (Var(X)) using the probability generating function

In this section, we shall find the mean and variance using the PGF of a discrete random variable. We shall discover why expressing the probabilities in a functional way using a polynomial is a very powerful tool.

Here are a few important results that we shall use:

$$\mathrm{E}(X) = \sum_{\forall x} x\mathrm{P}(X = x)$$

$$\mathrm{E}(X^2) = \sum_{\forall x} x^2\mathrm{P}(X = x)$$

$$\mathrm{Var}(X) = \mathrm{E}(X^2) - [\mathrm{E}(X)]^2$$

These lead to the following results. First, as shown in Section 12.1, Key point 12.2:

$$\mathrm{E}(X) = \mathrm{G}'_X(1)$$

Differentiating $\mathrm{G}_X(t)$ twice:

$$\mathrm{G}_X(t) = \sum_x t^x\mathrm{P}(X = x)$$

$$\mathrm{G}'_X(t) = \sum_x xt^{x-1}\mathrm{P}(X = x)$$

$$\mathrm{G}''_X(t) = \sum_x x(x-1)t^{x-2}\mathrm{P}(X = x)$$

Evaluating at $t = 1$:

$$\mathrm{G}''_X(1) = \sum_x x(x-1)\mathrm{P}(X = x)$$

$$\mathrm{G}''_X(1) = \sum_x (x^2 - x)\mathrm{P}(X = x)$$

$$\mathrm{G}''_X(1) = \sum_x x^2\mathrm{P}(X = x) - \sum_x x\mathrm{P}(X = x)$$

$$\mathrm{G}''_X(1) = \mathrm{E}(X^2) - \mathrm{E}(X)$$

$$\mathrm{E}(X^2) = \mathrm{G}''_X(1) + \mathrm{G}'_X(1)$$

Therefore:

$$\mathrm{Var}(X) = \mathrm{E}(X^2) - [\mathrm{E}(X)]^2$$

$$\mathrm{Var}(X) = \mathrm{G}''_X(1) + \mathrm{G}'_X(1) - [\mathrm{G}'_X(1)]^2$$

as shown in Key point 12.7.

KEY POINT 12.7

$$\mathrm{Var}(X) = \mathrm{G}''_X(1) + \mathrm{G}'_X(1) - [\mathrm{G}'_X(1)]^2$$

WORKED EXAMPLE 12.6

A bag contains five red balls and three green balls. The balls are taken out one at a time, the colour is noted, and then it is replaced. Let X be the number of times a ball is removed until a green ball is chosen.

a State the PGF of X.

b Calculate the mean and variance of X.

Answer

a In this question, we can see that the outcomes follow a geometric distribution:

$$X \sim \text{Geo}\left(\frac{3}{8}\right)$$

Always define a random variable before using it. Here, $p = \frac{3}{8}$ and $q = \frac{5}{8}$.

Its PGF is:

$$G_X(t) = \frac{pt}{1 - qt}$$

$$= \frac{\left(\frac{3}{8}\right)t}{1 - \left(\frac{5}{8}\right)t}$$

$$= \frac{3t}{8 - 5t}$$

Simplify.

We will need to differentiate this twice in part **b**.

b $$G'_X(t) = \frac{3(8 - 5t) - 3t(-5)}{(8 - 5t)^2}$$

The quotient rule is needed here.

$$= \frac{24}{(8 - 5t)^2}$$

$$= 24(8 - 5t)^{-2}$$

$$G''_X(t) = 24 \times -5 \times -2(8 - 5t)^{-3}$$

Find the second derivative.

Use the chain rule.

$$= \frac{240}{(8 - 5t)^3}$$

$$G'_X(1) = \frac{24}{9} = 2\frac{2}{3}$$

Evaluate at $t = 1$.

$$G''_X(1) = \frac{240}{27} = 8\frac{8}{9}$$

$$E(X) = G'_X(1) = 2\frac{2}{3}$$

Use the standard results.

$$\text{Var}(X) = G''_X(1) + G'_X(1) - [G'_X(1)]^2$$

$$= \frac{80}{9} + \frac{8}{3} - \frac{64}{9}$$

$$= \frac{40}{9} = 4\frac{4}{9}$$

Generally, the previous results offer only a different way of calculating the mean and variance. Worked examples 12.7 and 12.8 demonstrate some properties of distributions using the probability generating functions.

WORKED EXAMPLE 12.7

Prove that for $X \sim \text{Po}(\lambda)$:

a $\text{E}(X) = \lambda$

b $\text{Var}(X) = \lambda$

Answer

a $G_X(t) = e^{\lambda(t-1)}$	Consider the PGF of the Poisson distribution.
$G'_X(t) = \lambda e^{\lambda(t-1)}$	Differentiate.
$G'_X(1) = \lambda e^{\lambda(1-1)}$	Let $t = 1$.
$G'_X(1) = \lambda$	
$\text{E}(X) = \lambda$	As required.
b $G'_X(t) = \lambda e^{\lambda(t-1)}$	Consider $G'_X(t)$.
$G''_X(t) = \lambda^2 e^{\lambda(t-1)}$	Differentiate again.
$G''_X(1) = \lambda^2$	Let $t = 1$.
$\text{Var}(X) = G''_X(1) + G'_X(1) - [G'_X(1)]^2$	Use the given identity.
$\text{Var}(X) = \lambda^2 + \lambda - \lambda^2$	
$\text{Var}(X) = \lambda$	As required.

We shall use the properties of the mean and variance to calculate unknown probabilities using the PGF, as in Worked example 12.8.

WORKED EXAMPLE 12.8

A discrete random variable has the following probability distribution.

x	0	1	2
$\text{P}(X = x)$	a	b	c

The mean is $\frac{2}{3}$ and the variance is $\frac{5}{9}$. Find a, b and c.

Answer

First, express this using the PGF:	$G_X(t) = \sum_x t^{x_i} \text{P}(X = x_i)$
$G_X(t) = a + bt + ct^2$ $G'_X(t) = b + 2ct$ $G''_X(t) = 2c$	Differentiate twice to find the expectation and variance.
$G_X(1) = a + b + c$ $G'_X(1) = b + 2c$ $G''_X(1) = 2c$	Evaluate at $t = 1$.

$1 = a + b + c \quad (1)$ .... $G_X(1) = 1$

$\frac{2}{3} = b + 2c \quad (2)$ .... $E(X) = G'_X(1)$

$\frac{5}{9} = 2c + \frac{2}{3} - \frac{4}{9}$ .... $Var(X) = G''_X(1) + G'_X(1) - [G'_X(1)]^2$

$\frac{1}{3} = 2c \quad (3)$

From (3): $c = \frac{1}{6}$

From (2): $b = \frac{1}{3}$

From (1): $a = \frac{1}{2}$

We can use the derivatives of $G_X(t)$ to help us find $P(X = r)$ of probability generating functions. We use the idea that the expansion of a function of this type coincides with its Maclaurin expansion.

Consider $G_X(t) = \frac{t}{2-t}$.

This can be expanded binomially to give $\frac{t}{2} + \frac{t^2}{4} + \frac{t^3}{8} + \frac{t^4}{16} + \ldots$.

The probabilities for each r can be seen here clearly, but what if the expansion is not a known one?

We can consider the Maclaurin expansion of any function as:

$$G_X(t) = G_X(0) + G'_X(0)t + \frac{G''_X(0)t^2}{2!} + \frac{G'''_X(0)t^3}{3!} + \ldots$$

And so the probabilities could also be calculated using:

$$P(X = r) = \frac{G_X^{(r)}(0)}{r!}$$

where $G_X^{(r)}(t)$ is the rth derivative of $G_X(t)$.

EXERCISE 12B

1 For the following probability generating function:

$$G_X(t) = \frac{t^2}{10}(1 + 2t + 3t^2 + 2t^4 + t^5)$$

a Find $G'_X(1)$. b Find $G''_X(1)$. c Find $E(X)$. d Find $Var(X)$.

2 For the following probability generating function:

$$G_X(t) = \frac{t}{16}(1 + 4t + 6t^2 + 4t^3 + t^4)$$

a Find $G'_X(1)$. b Find $G''_X(1)$. c Find $E(X)$. d Find $Var(X)$.

3 Find $E(X)$ and $Var(X)$ of the following probability generating function.

$$G_X(t) = \frac{t^4}{10}(3 + 5t + t^3 + t^5)$$

4 Find E(X) and Var(X) of the following probability generating function.

$$G_X(t) = \frac{9}{(5 - 2t)^2}$$

5 In a game, the probability that player A wins on her rth go can be described as a discrete random variable X, with probability function $P(X = r) = \frac{1}{2^r}$, for $r = 1, 2, 3, \ldots$.

a Find the probability generating function.

b Find E(X) and Var(X).

6 Find E(X) and Var(X) of the following probability generating function,

$$G_X(t) = \frac{p}{1 - qt}$$

where $q = 1 - p$.

7 Find E(X) and Var(X) of the following probability generating function.

$$G_X(t) = \frac{t + 2}{(2 - t^2)(4 - t)}$$

M 8 A regular octagonal spinner is made up of eight isosceles triangles. Two of the triangles have a score of 2, three triangles have a score of 'a' and three triangles have a score of 'b', where $a < b$. The expectation and variance of the spinner are given by:

$$E(X) = 4.25$$

$$Var(X) = \frac{75}{16}$$

a Find an expression for $G_X(t)$, $G'_X(t)$ and $G''_X(t)$.

b Hence, find the values of a and b.

E All the examples covered so far have involved discrete random variables where each value of the random variable has a probability associated with it. This means we can set up the probability generating function easily and calculate the mean and variance from this.

This is not possible to do if the random variable is continuous. To calculate the mean and variance for a continuous random variable we use the **moment generating function**. This technique also works for a discrete random variable.

$M_X(\theta) = \sum_x e^{\theta x} P(X = x)$	For a discrete random variable, X.
$M_X(\theta) = \int e^{\theta x} f(x)\,dx$	For a continuous random variable, X, with a probability density function $f(x)$.

The following results come from the moment generating function.

$$E(X) = M'(0)$$
$$E(X^r) = M^r(0)$$
$$Var(X) = M''(0) - [M'(0)]^2$$

This is beyond the Further Mathematics course.

12.3 The sum of independent random variables

In AS & A Level Probability & Statistics 2, Chapter 3, you learned that, if there are two independent variables of the same distribution (for example the normal), $X \sim N(\mu_1, \sigma_1^2)$ and $Y \sim N(\mu_2, \sigma_2^2)$, we can create the distribution of $X + Y$. This will be $X + Y \sim N(\mu_1 + \mu_2, \sigma_1^2 + \sigma_2^2)$. The same is true for the Poisson distribution. We need to have some method for finding the PGF of $X + Y$ for any pairing of independent random variables X and Y. We will consider discrete random variables in this case.

Consider the following two distributions as an example. In Section 12.4, we will extend this idea to three or more random variables.

Let X have the following probability distribution.

x	0	1	2
$P(X = x)$	p_0	p_1	p_2

Let Y have the following probability distribution.

y	0	1	2
$P(Y = y)$	q_0	q_1	q_2

Then the distribution of $X + Y$ is:

$x + y$	$P(X + Y = x + y)$
0	$P(X = 0 \cap Y = 0)$
1	$P(X = 0 \cap Y = 1) + P(X = 1 \cap Y = 0)$
2	$P(X = 0 \cap Y = 2) + P(X = 1 \cap Y = 1) + P(X = 2 \cap Y = 0)$
3	$P(X = 1 \cap Y = 2) + P(X = 2 \cap Y = 1)$
4	$P(X = 2 \cap Y = 2)$

If X and Y are independent, then $P(X = x_i \cap Y = y_j) = P(X = x_i) \times P(Y = y_j) = p_i q_j$.

The previous table now becomes:

$x + y$	$P(X + Y = x + y)$
0	$p_0 q_0$
1	$p_1 q_0 + p_0 q_1$
2	$p_2 q_0 + p_1 q_1 + p_0 q_2$
3	$p_2 q_1 + p_1 q_2$
4	$p_2 q_2$

Now consider the PGF of $X + Y$:

$$G_{X+Y}(t) = p_0 q_0 + (p_1 q_0 + p_0 q_1)t + (p_2 q_0 + p_1 q_1 + p_0 q_2)t^2 + (p_2 q_1 + p_1 q_2)t^3 + p_2 q_2 t^4$$

This can be rewritten as:

$$G_{X+Y}(t) = (p_0 + p_1 t + p_2 t^2)(q_0 + q_1 t + q_2 t^2)$$

And we notice that these are the PGFs of X and of Y:

$$G_{X+Y}(t) = G_X(t) \times G_Y(t)$$

This is called the **convolution theorem**.

The convolution theorem

Let X and Y be two independent discrete random variables with PGFs $G_X(t)$ and $G_Y(t)$. The probability generating function of $X + Y$ is given as $G_{X+Y}(t) = G_X(t) \times G_Y(t)$, as shown in Key point 12.8.

KEY POINT 12.8

$$G_{X+Y}(t) = G_X(t) \times G_Y(t)$$

We will use this result directly to find the probability generating function of the sum of two independent random variables.

WORKED EXAMPLE 12.9

The discrete random variables X and Y have the following probability distributions.

x	1	2	3
$P(X = x)$	$\frac{1}{4}$	$\frac{1}{4}$	$\frac{1}{2}$

y	2	4	6
$P(Y = y)$	$\frac{1}{3}$	$\frac{1}{3}$	$\frac{1}{3}$

Assuming that X and Y are independent:

a find the PGF of $X + Y$

b write down the probability distribution of $X + Y$

c show that $E(X + Y) = E(X) + E(Y)$ and $Var(X + Y) = Var(X) + Var(Y)$.

Answer

a $G_X(t) = \frac{1}{4}t + \frac{1}{4}t^2 + \frac{1}{2}t^3$ — First, consider the PGFs of X and Y.

and $G_Y(t) = \frac{1}{3}t^2 + \frac{1}{3}t^4 + \frac{1}{3}t^6$

$G_{X+Y}(t) = G_X(t) \times G_Y(t)$ — Since X and Y are assumed to be independent, we can use the convolution theorem.

$$G_{X+Y}(t) = \left(\frac{1}{4}t + \frac{1}{4}t^2 + \frac{1}{2}t^3\right) \times \left(\frac{1}{3}t^2 + \frac{1}{3}t^4 + \frac{1}{3}t^6\right)$$

$$= \frac{t^3}{12}(1 + t + 2t^2) \times (1 + t^2 + t^4)$$

Take out $\frac{1}{4}t \times \frac{1}{3}t^2$ as a common factor.

$$= \frac{t^3}{12}(1 + t^2 + t^4 + t + t^3 + t^5 + 2t^2 + 2t^4 + 2t^6)$$

Multiply.

$$= \frac{t^3}{12}(1 + t + 3t^2 + t^3 + 3t^4 + t^5 + 2t^6)$$

Simplify.

b

$x+y$	$P(X+Y=x+y)$
3	$\frac{1}{12}$
4	$\frac{1}{12}$
5	$\frac{1}{4}$
6	$\frac{1}{12}$
7	$\frac{1}{4}$
8	$\frac{1}{12}$
9	$\frac{1}{6}$

c $G_{X+Y}(t)=\frac{1}{12}(t^3+t^4+3t^5+t^6+3t^7+t^8+2t^9)$

Remember the powers of t relate to the values of the distribution, and the coefficients relate to their respective probabilities.

$G'_{X+Y}(t)=\frac{1}{12}(3t^2+4t^3+15t^4+6t^5+21t^6+8t^7+18t^8)$

Find both derivatives first.

$G''_{X+Y}(t)=\frac{1}{12}(6t+12t^2+60t^3+30t^4+126t^5+56t^6+144t^7)$

$G'_{X+Y}(1)=\frac{1}{12}(3+4+15+6+21+8+18)$

Evaluate the derivatives at $t=1$.

$=\frac{75}{12}=6\frac{1}{4}$

$G''_{X+Y}(1)=\frac{1}{12}(6+12+60+30+126+56+144)$

$=\frac{434}{12}=36\frac{1}{6}$

$E(X+Y)=G'_{X+Y}(1)=6\frac{1}{4}$

$E(X+Y)=G'_X(1)$

$\text{Var}(X+Y)=\frac{434}{12}+\frac{75}{12}-\left[\frac{75}{12}\right]^2=\frac{161}{48}=3\frac{17}{48}$

$\text{Var}(X)=G''_X(1)+G'_X(1)-[G'_X(1)]^2$

Similarly:

$G_X(t)=\frac{1}{4}t+\frac{1}{4}t^2+\frac{1}{2}t^3$

$G'_X(t)=\frac{1}{4}+\frac{2}{4}t+\frac{3}{2}t^2$ $\qquad G'_X(1)=\frac{9}{4}$

$G''_X(t)=\frac{1}{2}+3t$ $\qquad G''_X(1)=\frac{7}{2}$

$E(X)=\frac{9}{4}$

$\text{Var}(X)=\frac{7}{2}+\frac{9}{4}-\left(\frac{9}{4}\right)^2=\frac{11}{16}$

And:

Consider $E(Y)$ and $Var(Y)$ in the same way as for $E(X)$ and $Var(X)$.

$G_Y(t) = \frac{1}{3}t^2 + \frac{1}{3}t^4 + \frac{1}{3}t^6$

$G'_Y(t) = \frac{2}{3}t + \frac{4}{3}t^3 + 2t^5$ $\quad G'_Y(1) = 4$

$G''_Y(t) = \frac{2}{3} + 4t^2 + 10t^4$ $\quad G''_Y(1) = \frac{44}{3}$

$E(Y) = 4$

$Var(Y) = \frac{44}{3} + 4 - 4^2 = \frac{8}{3}$

$E(X) + E(Y) = \frac{9}{4} + 4 = 6\frac{1}{4} = E(X + Y)$

$Var(X) + Var(Y) = \frac{11}{16} + \frac{8}{3} = \frac{161}{48} = 3\frac{17}{48} = Var(X + Y)$

Therefore, $E(X + Y) = E(X) + E(Y)$ and $Var(X + Y) = Var(X) + Var(Y)$.

Compare the two sets of results.

The PGF of a function of a random variable

Consider a discrete random variable that is a function of another variable, as seen in Chapter 8.

$Y = aX + b$, where X has PGF $G_X(t)$.

We can find the PGF of Y by considering the alternative definition of the PGF:

$$G_X(t) = E(t^X)$$

Consider $Y = aX + b$, then:

$$\begin{aligned} G_Y(t) &= E(t^Y) = E(t^{aX+b}) \\ &= E(t^{aX}t^b) = t^bE(t^{aX}) \\ &= t^bE[(t^a)^X] \\ &= t^bG_X(t^a) \end{aligned}$$

Therefore, $G_{aX+b}(t) = t^bG_X(t^a)$, as shown in Key point 12.9.

KEY POINT 12.9

$$G_{aX+b}(t) = t^bG_X(t^a)$$

From this definition, we can now formally reproduce some of the results shown in Chapter 11.

Let us find the expectation and variance of $Y = aX + b$ using the PGF of X.

$G_{aX+b}(t) = t^b G_X(t^a)$	
$G'_{aX+b}(t) = bt^{b-1}G_X(t^a) + at^{a-1}t^bG'_X(t^a)$	Differentiate using the product rule and the chain rule.
$G'_{aX+b}(1) = b1^{b-1}G_X(1^a) + a1^{a-1}1^bG'_X(1^a)$ $G'_{aX+b}(1) = b \times 1 + aG'_X(1)$ $E(aX + b) = aE(X) + b$	 $G_X(1) = 1$ $G'_X(1) = E(X)$
$G''_{aX+b}(t) = b(b-1)t^{b-2}G_X(t^a) + abt^{a-1}t^{b-1}G'_X(t^a)$ $+ a(a+b-1)t^{a+b-2}G'_X(t^a)$ $+ a^2t^{a-1}t^{a-1}t^bG''_X(t^a)$ $G''_{aX+b}(1) = b(b-1) + abG'_X(1) + a(a+b-1)G'_X(1) + a^2G''_X(1)$	Differentiate again. Let $t = 1$.
$\text{Var}(aX + b) = G''_{aX+b}(1) + G'_{aX+b}(1) - [G'_{aX+b}(1)]^2$ $\text{Var}(aX + b) = b(b-1) + abE(X) + a(a+b-1)E(X)$ $+ a^2G''_X(1) + [aE(X) + b] - [aE(X) + b]^2$ $= b^2 - b + abE(X) + a^2E(X) + abE(X) - aE(X) + a^2G''_X(1)$ $+ aE(X) + b - a^2[E(X)]^2 - 2abE(X) - b^2$ $= a^2[E(X) + G''_X(1) - [E(X)]^2]$ $\text{Var}(aX + b) = a^2\text{Var}(X)$	$\text{Var}(X) = G''_X(1) + E(X) - [E(X)]^2$

WORKED EXAMPLE 12.10

A discrete random variable, X, has the probability distribution:

x	1	2	3	4	5
$P(X = x)$	$\frac{1}{9}$	$\frac{2}{9}$	$\frac{3}{9}$	$\frac{2}{9}$	$\frac{1}{9}$

a Find $G_X(t)$, the PGF of X.

b Given that $Y = 4 - 7X$, find $G_Y(t)$, the PGF of Y.

Answer

a $G_X(t) = \frac{1}{9}t + \frac{2}{9}t^2 + \frac{3}{9}t^3 + \frac{2}{9}t^4 + \frac{1}{9}t^5$ — Use the definition for $G_X(t)$.

$= \frac{t}{9}(1 + 2t + 3t^2 + 2t^3 + t^4)$ — Factorise.

b $G_Y(t) = G_{-7X+4}(t)$ — Use the definition $G_{aX+b}(t) = t^bG_X(t^a)$.

$G_{-7X+4}(t) = t^4G_X(t^{-7})$

$G_{-7X+4}(t) = t^4 \times \frac{t^{-7}}{9}(1 + 2(t^{-7}) + 3(t^{-7})^2 + 2(t^{-7})^3 + (t^{-7})^4)$

$G_Y(t) = \frac{1}{9t^3}\left(1 + \frac{2}{t^7} + \frac{3}{t^{14}} + \frac{2}{t^{21}} + \frac{1}{t^{28}}\right)$

EXERCISE 12C

1 A discrete random variable X has probability distribution:

x	1	2
$P(X = x)$	0.4	0.6

A discrete random variable Y has probability distribution:

y	0	1	3	5
$P(Y = y)$	0.25	0.25	0.25	0.25

Given that X and Y are independent, find:

a $G_X(t)$ b $G_Y(t)$ c $G_{X+Y}(t)$

2 A discrete random variable X has probability distribution:

x	−2	−1	0	1	2
$P(X = x)$	0.1	0.2	0.4	0.2	0.1

A discrete random variable Y has probability distribution:

y	2	3	4	5	6
$P(Y = y)$	0.2	0.2	0.2	0.2	0.2

Given that X and Y are independent, find:

a $G_X(t)$ b $G_Y(t)$ c $G_{X+Y}(t)$

3 A discrete random variable, X, has the probability distribution:

x	1	3	5
$P(X = x)$	0.2	0.5	0.3

A discrete random variable, Y, has the probability distribution:

y	0	2	4
$P(Y = y)$	0.3	0.4	0.3

a Find $G_X(t)$. b Find $G_Y(t)$.

Hence, given that X and Y are independent:

c find $G_{X+Y}(t)$ d write down the probability distribution of $X + Y$.

4 Let $X \sim \text{Geo}(0.4)$ and $Y \sim \text{Geo}(0.6)$, where X and Y are independent.

a Write down an expression for $G_{X+Y}(t)$. b Express $\frac{5}{(5-2t)(5-3t)}$ in partial fractions.

c Hence, find $P(X + Y = k)$ for $k = 2, 3, 4$.

5 Let $X \sim \text{Bin}(3, 0.2)$ and $Y \sim \text{Po}(2)$, where X and Y are independent.

a Find the probability generating function for $X + Y$.

b Find the value of $E(X + Y)$.

c Find the value of $G''_{X+Y}(t)$. Write your answer in the form:

$$\frac{2e^{2t}}{125e^2}(t+4)(at^2 + bt + c)$$

d Find the value of $\text{Var}(X + Y)$.

P 6 Let $X \sim \text{Po}(a)$ and $Y \sim \text{Po}(b)$. Prove that if X and Y are independent:

a $\text{E}(X+Y) = a+b$

b $\text{Var}(X+Y) = a+b$

7 Let $\text{G}_X(t) = \dfrac{3t}{5-2t}$.

a For $Y = 5X$, find $\text{G}_Y(t)$.

b For $Y = X+7$, find $\text{G}_Y(t)$.

8 Let $\text{G}_X(t) = \text{e}^{4(t-1)}$.

a For $Y = X - 1$, find $\text{G}_Y(t)$.

b For $Y = 3 - 2X$, find $\text{G}_Y(t)$.

P 9 A discrete random variable, X, has the probability generating function:

$$\text{G}_X(t) = \frac{3}{10-7t}$$

a Find the probability generating function for $Y = 3X + 4$.

b Show that $\text{E}(Y) = 11$.

c Find $\text{P}(Y = k)$ for $k = 4, 7, 10$.

12.4 Three or more random variables

In the previous sections, we considered only two random variables and only a linear combination of one random variable. If the variables are independent, we can generalise this to deal with more than two random variables, and also linear combinations of these variables, as shown in Key points 12.10 and 12.11.

KEY POINT 12.10

For independent random variables, X_i, with corresponding PGF $\text{G}_{X_i}(t)$, then:

$$\text{G}_{X_1+\ldots+X_n}(t) = \text{G}_{X_1}(t) \times \ldots \times \text{G}_{X_n}(t)$$

If n independent discrete random variables all have the same PGF, then this formula reduces to:

$$\text{G}_{X_1+\ldots+X_n}(t) = [\text{G}_X(t)]^n$$

This is different from:

$$\text{G}_{nX}(t) = \text{G}_X(t^n)$$

KEY POINT 12.11

For independent random variables, X_i, with corresponding PGF $\text{G}_{X_i}(t)$, then:

$$\text{G}_{aX_1+bX_2} = \text{G}_{X_1}(t^a) \times \text{G}_{X_2}(t^b)$$

WORKED EXAMPLE 12.11

Find the probability generating function for the total number of 8s when a fair eight-sided die is rolled six times.

Answer

When one die is rolled, X has the following probability distribution, where X = number of 8s:

Find the PGF.

X	0	1
$P(X = x)$	$\frac{7}{8}$	$\frac{1}{8}$

And so its PGF is $G_X(t) = \frac{7}{8} + \frac{1}{8}t$.

This is called a Bernoulli distribution.

Since we are rolling the die six times, we define $Y = X_1 + X_2 + \ldots + X_6$.

And so the PGF of Y is $G_Y(t) = [G_X(t)]^6$.

These are all independent, so we can use the property $G_{aX_1 + bX_2} = G_{X_1}(t^a) \times G_{X_2}(t^b)$.

$G_Y(t) = \left(\frac{7}{8} + \frac{1}{8}t\right)^6$

Notice that this is the same as the PGF of $Y \sim \text{Bin}\left(6, \frac{1}{8}\right)$.

EXERCISE 12D

1 Consider the discrete random variable X, with probability generating function:

$$G_X(t) = \frac{t^2}{5}(4 + t)$$

X_1 and X_2 are two independent observations. Given that $Y = X_1 + X_2$, find:

a $G_Y(t)$

b the probability distribution of Y.

2 Consider the discrete random variable X, with probability distribution:

x	-1	0	1
$P(X = x)$	$\frac{1}{4}$	$\frac{1}{2}$	$\frac{1}{4}$

Three independent observations of X are taken and the values are added to form Y. Three independent observations of X are taken and the values of each X_i added to form Y where $Y = X_1 + X_2 + X_3$.

a Find $G_X(t)$.

b Find $G_y(t)$.

c Find $P(Y = 1)$.

3 Two independent random variables X and Y have corresponding probability generating functions:

$$G_X(t) = e^{3(t-1)}$$

and

$$G_Y(t) = e^{5(t-1)}$$

It is given that $A = Y - X$.

a A student made the following attempt to find $G_A(t)$:

Step 1: $G_{X+Y}(t) = G_X(t) \times G_Y(t)$

Step 2: Therefore $G_{Y-X}(t) = G_Y(t) \div G_X(t)$

Step 3: $G_{Y-X}(t) = e^{5(t-1)} \div e^{3(t-1)}$

Step 4: $G_{Y-X}(t) = e^{2(t-1)}$

Which step contains the error in the student's working?

b Find the correct probability generating function of A, $G_A(t)$.

4 Consider the discrete random variable X, with probability distribution:

X	1	2	3
$P(X = x)$	$\frac{1}{3}$	$\frac{1}{3}$	$\frac{1}{3}$

and Y, with probability distribution:

y	4	5	6
$P(Y = y)$	$\frac{1}{2}$	$\frac{1}{4}$	$\frac{1}{4}$

It is given that $A = 2Y - 3X$.

a Find $G_X(t)$. b Find $G_Y(t)$. c Find $G_A(t)$.

5 Consider the independent discrete random variables X, Y and Z, where:

$G_X(t) = (0.7 + 0.3t)^3$

$G_Y(t) = (0.3 + 0.7t)^4$

$G_Z(t) = \dfrac{3t}{10 - 7t}$

Find the probability generating function for the following.

a $A = 2X + Y + 1$ b $B = X - Y - 3Z + 4$ c $C = 3X + 2Y + Z - 1$

6 An observation from $X \sim \text{Geo}(0.3)$ is taken five times: $X_1, \ldots X_5$.

a Find the probability generating function of $Y = (X_1 + \ldots + X_5)$.

b Find $P(Y \leqslant 8)$ to 4 significant figures.

7 Let X be a discrete random variable with probability distribution:

x	1	2	3
$P(X = x)$	0.2	0.3	0.5

Four independent observations are made. Y is the sum of these observations.

a Find the probability density function of Y.

b Find $E(Y)$. c Find $\text{Var}(Y)$.

8 Let $X_1 \sim \text{Geo}(0.1)$, $X_2 \sim \text{Geo}(0.2)$ and $X_3 \sim \text{Geo}(0.3)$.

Let $Y = 3X_1 + 2X_2 + X_3$.

a Find $G_Y(t)$. b Find $P(Y = 7)$.

EXPLORE 12.1

Consider two die, A and B. Each face on each die has an equal probability of occurring.

Die A has faces 1, 3, 4, 5, 6, 8.

Die B has faces 1, 2, 2, 3, 3, 4.

1 Find the probability generating function of each die and, hence, the probability generating function for Z, the sum of the scores on both die.

2 What do you notice about the probability distribution for the sum of scores?

WORKED EXAM-STYLE QUESTION

Jamil and Yao are revising for a Maths exam by randomly selecting questions from a large question bank. They play a game by taking it in turns to answer questions. The first person to get a question right wins the game. Jamil answers a question correctly $\frac{1}{4}$ of the time. Yao answers a question correctly $\frac{1}{5}$ of the time. Assume that all question attempts are independent. Let X be the total number of questions attempted. Jamil will start the game.

a Find the probability generating function for X.

b Find $\mathrm{E}(X)$.

c Find $\mathrm{Var}(X)$.

Answer

a $X = 1$ (Jamil starts the game and wins)

$\mathrm{P}(X=1)=\frac{1}{4}$

It is worth finding a few probabilities to spot any patterns in them. There may be a standard PGF that we can apply.

$X = 2$ (Jamil is incorrect, then Yao is correct).

$\mathrm{P}(X=2)=\frac{3}{4}\times\frac{1}{5}=\frac{3}{20}$

$X = 3$ (Jamil incorrect, Yao incorrect, Jamil correct).

$\mathrm{P}(X=3)=\left(\frac{3}{4}\times\frac{4}{5}\right)\times\frac{1}{4}=\left(\frac{3}{5}\right)\times\frac{1}{4}$

$\mathrm{P}(X=4)=\frac{3}{4}\times\frac{4}{5}\times\frac{3}{4}\times\frac{1}{5}=\left(\frac{3}{5}\right)\times\frac{3}{20}$

$\mathrm{P}(X=5)=\frac{3}{4}\times\frac{4}{5}\times\frac{3}{4}\times\frac{4}{5}\times\frac{1}{4}=\left(\frac{3}{5}\right)^2\times\frac{1}{4}$

$\mathrm{P}(X=6)=\frac{3}{4}\times\frac{4}{5}\times\frac{3}{4}\times\frac{4}{5}\times\frac{3}{4}\times\frac{1}{5}=\left(\frac{3}{5}\right)^2\times\frac{3}{20}$

And so on.

$$G_X(t) = \frac{1}{4}t + \left(\frac{3}{5}\right)\left(\frac{1}{4}\right)t^3 + \left(\frac{3}{5}\right)^2\left(\frac{1}{4}\right)t^5 + \ldots$$
$$+ \left(\frac{3}{20}\right)t^2 + \left(\frac{3}{5}\right)\left(\frac{3}{20}\right)t^4 + \left(\frac{3}{5}\right)^2\left(\frac{3}{20}\right)t^6 + \ldots$$

We can look for a pattern in the odd and even values for X. When X is odd, Jamil wins. When X is even, Yao wins.

$$= \left(\frac{t}{4}\right)\left(\frac{1}{1-\frac{3}{5}t^2}\right) + \left(\frac{3t^2}{20}\right)\left(\frac{1}{1-\frac{3}{5}t^2}\right)$$

Each of these patterns is a sum to infinity of geometric series, so we can use the formula $S_\infty = \frac{a}{1-r}$ from AS & A Level Pure Mathematics 1.

$$= \frac{5t + 3t^2}{4(5 - 3t^2)}$$

Write in closed form and simplify.

b $$G_X(t) = \frac{5t + 3t^2}{4(5 - 3t^2)}$$

$$G'_X(t) = \frac{4(5 - 3t^2)(5 + 6t) - (5t + 3t^2)(4)(-6t)}{4^2(5 - 3t^2)^2}$$

Differentiate.

$$= \frac{100 + 120t - 60t^2 - 72t^3 + 120t^2 + 72t^3}{4^2(5 - 3t^2)^2}$$

$$= \frac{5(3t^2 + 6t + 5)}{4(5 - 3t^2)^2}$$

$$G'_X(1) = \frac{35}{8}$$

Set $t = 1$ to find $E(X)$.

$$E(X) = \frac{35}{8}$$

c $$G''_X(t) = \frac{4(5 - 3t^2)^2(5)(6t + 6) - 5(3t^2 + 6t + 5)(4)(2)(-6t)(5 - 3t^2)}{4^2(5 - 3t^2)^4}$$

$$= \frac{(5 - 3t^2)(5)(3t + 3) - 5(3t^2 + 6t + 5)(-6t)}{2(5 - 3t^2)^3}$$

$$= \frac{75t + 75 - 45t^3 - 45t^2 + 90t^3 + 180t^2 + 150t}{2(5 - 3t^2)^3}$$

$$= \frac{15(3t^3 + 9t^2 + 15t + 5)}{2(5 - 3t^2)^3}$$

We need $G''_X(1)$ to find $\text{Var}(X)$: $\text{Var}(X) = G''_X(1) + G'_X(1) - [G'_X(1)]^2$

$$G''_X(1) = 30$$

$$\text{Var}(X) = G''_X(1) + G'_X(1) - [G'_X(1)]^2$$

$$\text{Var}(X) = 30 + \frac{35}{8} - \left(\frac{35}{8}\right)^2$$

$$= \frac{975}{64}$$

Checklist of learning and understanding

For a discrete probability distribution:

- The probability generating function is $G_X(t) = E(t^X) = \sum_x t^x P(X = x)$.

Standard probability generating functions:

Probability distribution	$P(X = r)$	$G_X(t)$
$Bin(n, p)$	${}^nC_r q^{n-r} p^r$	$(q + pt)^n$
$Po(\lambda)$	$\frac{e^{-\lambda}\lambda^r}{r!}$	$e^{\lambda(t-1)}$
$Geo(p)$	$q^{r-1}p$	$\frac{pt}{1 - qt}$

E(X) and Var(X):

- $G_X(1) = 1$
- $E(X) = G'_X(1)$
- $Var(X) = G''_X(1) + G'_X(1) - [G'_X(1)]^2$
- $Var(X) = G''_X(1) + E(X) - [E(X)^2]$

For two independent random variables:

- $G_{X+Y}(t) = G_X(t) \times G_Y(t)$

To generalise to three or more random variables:

- $G_{X_1+\ldots+X_n}(t) = G_{X_1}(t) \times \ldots \times G_{X_n}(t)$

The probability generating function of a linear transformation:

- $G_{aX+b}(t) = t^b G_X(t^a)$

END-OF-CHAPTER REVIEW EXERCISE 12

1 The discrete random variable X is the number of times we throw a pair of fair die to get a sum of eight. Find the probability generating function, as well as the expected number of throws and the variance of X.

2 A discrete random variable, X, has the probability distribution function:

$$P(X = x) = \frac{k}{e^x} \quad x = 0, 1, 2, 3, \ldots$$

a Find the value of k and the probability generating function.

b Find $E(X)$.

c Find $Var(X)$.

P 3 A game consists of rolling two die, one die with six sides, the other die with eight sides, and adding the scores together. Both die are fair, with the first numbered 1 to 6 and the second numbered 1 to 8. Show that the probability generating function of Z, where Z is the sum of the scores on the two die, is:

$$\frac{t^2}{48} \times \frac{(1 - t^6)(1 - t^8)}{1 - t^2}$$

P 4 The variable Y can take only the values $1, 2, 3, \ldots$ and is such that $P(Y = r) = kP(X = r)$, where $X \sim Po(\lambda)$. Show that the probability generating function of Y is given by:

$$G_Y(t) = \frac{e^{\lambda t} - 1}{e^{\lambda} - 1}$$

CROSS-TOPIC REVIEW EXERCISE 2

1 A random sample of 40 observations of a random variable X, and a random sample of 25 observations of a random variable Y, are taken. The sample means and unbiased estimates are:

$\bar{x} = 13.6$ $\bar{y} = 11.2$ $s_x = 6.3$ $s_y = 7.1$

A test is performed at a significance level of $\alpha\%$ using the following hypotheses:

$$H_0: \mu_x - \mu_y = 0$$
$$H_1: \mu_x - \mu_y > 0$$

Given that H_0 is not rejected, find the possible values of α.

2 A school is considering buying a large number of safety devices to install in the classrooms. The devices are designed to activate sprinklers if the temperature in the room exceeds 65 °C. A sample of the devices are tested by slowly increasing the temperature and noting the temperatures, in °C, at which the sprinklers are activated. The results are as follows.

57.8 62.9 63.7 71.2 60.6 69.5 64.7 65.7

Use a t-test and the 10% significance level to examine whether the mean temperature at which the sprinklers are activated is 65 °C. Assume that the sample is random and mean temperatures are normally distributed.

3 A random variable X has a probability distribution, $f(x)$, given by:

$$f(x) = \begin{cases} ke^{-3x} & 0 \leqslant x \leqslant 1 \\ 0 & \text{otherwise} \end{cases}$$

a Show that $k = \dfrac{3e^3}{e^3 - 1}$.

b Find the median value of X.

4 A random sample of five metal rods produced by a machine is taken. Each rod is tested for hardness. The results, in suitable units, are as follows.

524 526 520 523 530

i Assuming a normal distribution, calculate a 95% confidence interval for the population mean.

Some adjustments are made to the machine. Assume that a normal distribution is still appropriate and that the population variance remains unchanged. A second random sample, this time of ten metal rods, is now taken. The results for hardness are as follows.

525 520 522 524 518 520 519 525 527 516

ii Stating suitable hypotheses, test at the 10% significance level whether there is any difference between the population means before and after the adjustments.

Cambridge International AS & A Level Further Mathematics 9231 Paper 22 Q9 November 2011

5 A biased die has probability p of showing a 6. The random variable X counts the number of trials up to and including the trial in which the first 6 is obtained. The random variable Y counts the number of trials up to and including the trial in which the nth 6 is obtained.

a Write down an expression for $P(X = x)$ for $X = 1, 2, \ldots$. Show that the probability generating function of X is:

$$G_X(t) = pt(1 - qt)^{-1}$$

where $q = 1 - p$. Hence show that the mean and variance of X are, respectively:

$$E(X) = \frac{1}{p}$$

$$\text{Var}(X) = \frac{q}{p^2}$$

b Given that the trials for X are independent and that $Y = X_1 + X_2 + \cdots + X_n$, find:

i the probability generating function for Y

ii $E(Y)$ and $Var(Y)$.

6 The owner of three driving schools, A, B and C, wished to assess whether there was an association between passing the driving test and the school attended. He selected a random sample of learner drivers from each of his schools and recorded the numbers of passes and failures at each school. The results that he obtained are shown in the table below.

	Driving school attended		
	A	B	C
Passes	23	15	17
Failures	27	25	43

Using a χ^2-test and a 5% level of significance, test whether there is an association between passing or failing the driving test and the driving school attended.

Cambridge International AS & A Level Further Mathematics 9231 Paper 2 Q8 November 2010

7 Trees of the same species grow on opposite sides of a river valley. The heights of eight randomly selected trees from each side of the river valley are measured and the results, in metres, are given in the table.

East side (m)	13.6	20.1	7.8	18.2	8.5	7.7	16.0	13.4
West side (m)	5.9	7.5	9.6	11.0	4.1	7.1	10.1	12.2

Carry out a Wilcoxon rank-sum test, at the 5% level of significance, to investigate whether there is any difference in the average heights of the trees from the two sides of the river valley.

Interpret your conclusion in context.

8 The continuous random variable X has probability density function, f, given by:

$$f(x) = \begin{cases} \frac{1}{15}((x-3)^2 + 2) & 0 \leqslant x \leqslant 3 \\ 0 & \text{otherwise} \end{cases}$$

The random variable Y is defined by $Y = X^2$.

a Show that the cumulative distribution function $G(y)$ is given by:

$$G(y) = \begin{cases} 0 & y < 0 \\ \frac{1}{45}\left(y^{\frac{3}{2}} - 9y + 33y^{\frac{1}{2}}\right) & 0 \leqslant y \leqslant 9 \\ 1 & y > 9 \end{cases}$$

b Show that the median is 0.75, correct to 2 decimal places.

c Find $E(Y)$.

9 A charity launched a campaign to raise awareness of low pay amongst full-time workers in company canteens. The charity now believes the median weekly wage in this job sector has increased.

After the campaign, a random sample of ten canteen workers was asked how much they earned in the previous week. The results, in NZ$, were as follows.

156.45 145.50 151.30 150.70 156.10 151.15 144.40 146.60 163.75 157.60

Before the campaign the median weekly wage for full-time workers in the company canteens was NZ$ 147.50.

Carry out a Wilcoxon signed-rank test to determine whether there has been an increase in the median wage after the campaign. Use the 5% level of significance.

10 It has been found that 60% of the computer chips produced in a factory are faulty. As part of quality control, 100 samples of 4 chips are selected at random, and each chip is tested. The number of faulty chips in each sample is recorded, with the results given in the following table.

Number of faulty chips	0	1	2	3	4
Number of samples	2	12	27	49	10

The expected values for a binomial distribution with parameters $n = 4$ and $p = 0.6$ are given in the following table.

Number of faulty chips	0	1	2	3	4
Number of samples	2.56	15.36	34.56	34.56	12.96

i Show how the expected value 34.56 corresponding to 2 faulty chips is obtained.

ii Carry out a goodness of fit test at the 5% significance level, and state what can be deduced from the outcome of the test.

Cambridge International AS & A Level Further Mathematics 9231 Paper 2 Q9 November 2009

11 The Tax Bureau claims that people typically take 140 minutes to fill in a tax form. A researcher believes that this claim is incorrect and that, generally, it takes people longer to complete the form. She recorded the time (in minutes) it took ten people to complete the form. The results are given below.

151 138 132 149 145 152 141 148 162 146

Carry out a sign test, at the 5% significance level, to investigate whether the average time to complete the form is greater than 140 minutes.

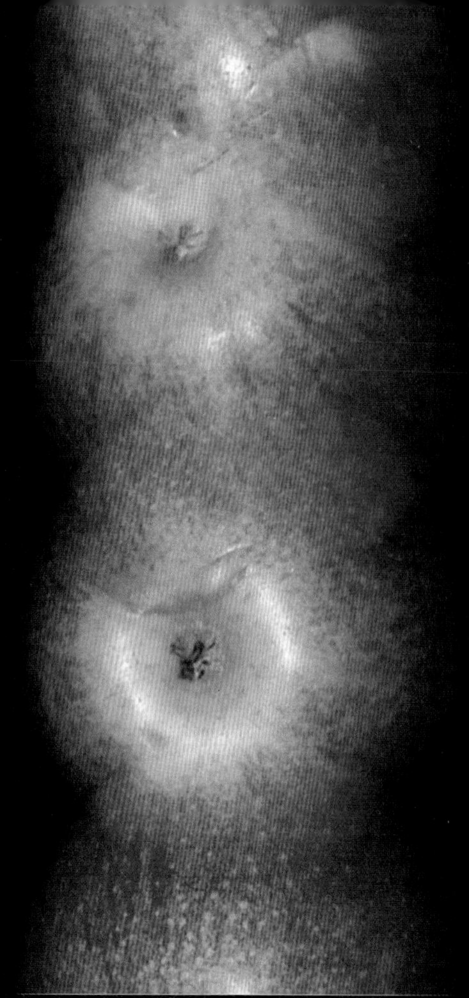

Chapter 13
Projectiles

In this chapter, you will learn how to:

- use Newton's equations of motion to determine results related to projectile motion
- use these results to solve problems involving projectiles from both ground level and raised platforms
- make use of the components of the motion to understand and solve more complicated problems.

PREREQUISITE KNOWLEDGE

Where it comes from	What you should be able to do	Check your skills
AS & A Level Mathematics Mechanics, Chapter 1	Remember and use Newton's equations of motion.	**1** A cyclist is travelling along a straight horizontal road at $6\,m\,s^{-1}$ when he sees a red traffic light 50 m ahead. He stops pedalling and applies his brakes to decelerate uniformly until he stops. Find the magnitude of his deceleration.
AS & A Level Mathematics Mechanics, Chapters 1 & 3 Pure Mathematics 2 & 3, Chapter 9	Work with basic vectors, such as the components in both horizontal and vertical directions.	**2** A particle is projected from the top of a cliff with initial speed $20\,m\,s^{-1}$ vertically upwards. The particle lands at the bottom of the cliff, 50 m below the point from which it was projected. Find the time taken for the particle to reach the bottom of the cliff and the velocity of the particle at that time.

What are projectiles?

A **projectile** is any object that, once it has been thrown, propelled or dropped, continues to move under its own **inertia** and the force of gravity. We are most likely to encounter projectiles when we play sports, when we drop things, or when we observe objects after a collision. The apple that (allegedly) fell on Isaac Newton's head was a projectile.

In this chapter, you will look at the motion of **particles** that are projected at an oblique angle to the horizontal and/or vertical directions. The paths of these particles will be analysed as horizontal and vertical components. Each direction can be dealt with separately or together.

13.1 Motion in the vertical plane

In this chapter, we use the symbols a for acceleration, u for initial velocity, v for final velocity, t for time, and x for displacement. Unless stated otherwise, $g = 10\,m\,s^{-2}$.

You will have met **Newton's equations of motion** in your earlier study of Mechanics. These equations are valid only if the acceleration of the object is constant, usually due to the mass of the object.

We use the same equations to derive some standard results for the motion of a projectile.

These equations are:

- $s = ut + \frac{1}{2}at^2$
- $v = u + at$
- $v^2 = u^2 + 2as$
- $s = \frac{(u + v)t}{2}$
- $s = vt - \frac{1}{2}at^2$

For projectile questions, we use a simplified **model** of reality. This means we usually assume there are no resisting forces such as air resistance. We model the projectile as a particle so we can assume there are no rotational forces (spin). We also assume that the force due to gravity is constant. The path travelled by the projectile is known as a **parabolic trajectory**.

The **displacement** of the particle at any time is given by $s = ut + \frac{1}{2}at^2$, a quadratic function whose graph is a parabola.

Let us use Newton's equations for a projectile. Consider a particle thrown with initial velocity u at an angle θ above the horizontal direction, as shown in the diagram. The initial velocity of the particle can be described in terms of two components: $u\cos\theta$ in the horizontal direction, and $u\sin\theta$ in the vertical direction. These directions are normally referred to in Cartesian form as x- and y-directions.

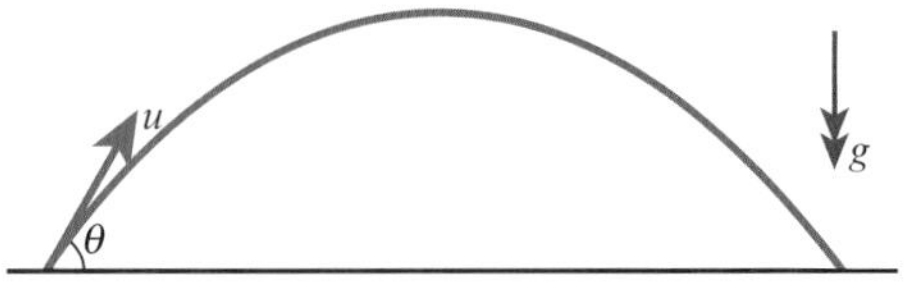

Using $v = u + at$ in the y-direction gives $v_y = u\sin\theta - gt$, and in the x-direction we can see that $v_x = u\cos\theta$. Remember that the acceleration due to gravity acts vertically downwards. Taking upwards as positive, in the vertical direction, $a = -g$ and in the horizontal direction, $a = 0$.

When the particle reaches its highest point $v_y = 0$, then $u\sin\theta = gt$, or $t = \frac{u\sin\theta}{g}$. Since we can ignore air resistance, the time it takes the particle to travel from the ground to the top of its path must be the same as the time it takes to return to the ground. This means that the total flight time is $t = \frac{2u\sin\theta}{g}$.

We will focus on the distance travelled horizontally and vertically. Let x represent the horizontal displacement travelled, and y represent the vertical displacement travelled.

Then, using $s = ut + \frac{1}{2}at^2$:

$$x = u\cos\theta t$$

$$y = u\sin\theta t - \frac{1}{2}gt^2$$

Now use the value we found earlier for total flight time, to give:

$$x = u\cos\theta \times \frac{2u\sin\theta}{g} = \frac{2u^2\sin\theta\cos\theta}{g}$$ and here we can use $2\sin\theta\cos\theta \equiv 2\sin 2\theta$

Hence, $x = \frac{u^2\sin 2\theta}{g}$.

This result is known as the range, and it represents the horizontal distance covered. This value is a maximum when $\theta = 45°$ and $\sin 2\theta = 1$. The angle at which the object is projected is known as the **angle of elevation**, and is measured upwards from the horizontal. Please note that the above results for the range and total flight time have been derived from the displacement and velocity components of a projectile, which are not in the formula booklet. It is therefore suggested that you know how to quickly derive these results when needed.

> **TIP**
>
> Differentiating these two results gives $v_x = u\cos\theta$, $v_y = u\sin\theta - gt$. These are the same values we have already established.

WORKED EXAMPLE 13.1

A particle is projected from a point on a horizontal surface with initial speed $20\,\text{m s}^{-1}$ at an angle of elevation of 25°. Find:

a the range of the particle

b the time taken to reach the highest point

c the speed of the particle when $t = 0.5$.

Answer

a Using $x = \frac{u^2\sin 2\theta}{g}$, $x = \frac{20^2\sin 50°}{10}$ — Substitute the values into the formula for the horizontal range.

Hence, $x = 30.6\,\text{m}$.

b At the highest point $v_y = 0$, so $t = \frac{u\sin\theta}{g} = \frac{20\sin 25}{10}$ — Using $v_y = u\sin\theta - gt$ leads to the time taken.

$t = 0.845\,\text{s}$

c $v_x = 20\cos 25 = 18.126$ — Determine both components of the speed at the given time.

$v_y = 20\sin 25 - 10 \times 0.5 = 3.452$ — Find the magnitude of the resultant speed.

So the speed is $\sqrt{18.126^2 + 3.452^2} = 18.5\,\text{m s}^{-1}$.

Particles that are projected from raised platforms can be viewed as following part of a parabolic path.

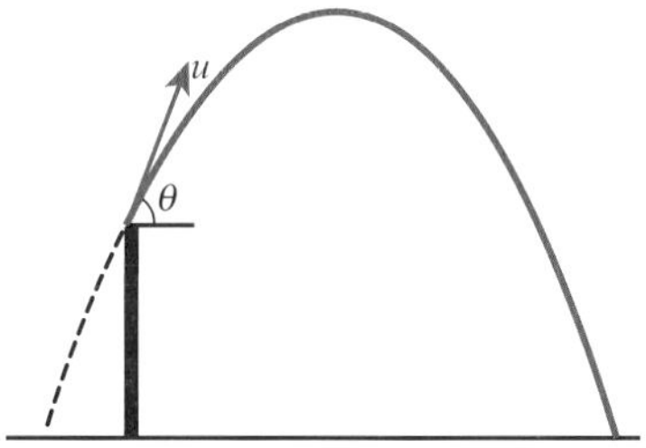

This diagram shows a particle's trajectory from a raised point. Trace the path backwards to see where it would have started if it had been launched from ground level.

Consider an example where $u = 15$, $\theta = 60°$, and the platform is 10 m above the ground. How would you go about finding the final speed of the projectile when it reaches ground level? Start with $v^2 = u^2 + 2as$ vertically, so $v_y^2 = (15\sin 60)^2 - 2 \times 10 \times (-10)$. This gives us $v_y = \frac{5\sqrt{59}}{2}$, which is the vertical component of the speed when the particle hits the ground.

Next use $v_x = 15\cos 60 = 7.5$, leading to $v = \sqrt{v_x^2 + v_y^2}$, which is equal to $5\sqrt{17}\,\text{m s}^{-1}$.

TIP

When a particle is projected upwards, any position below the starting point is a *negative* displacement. Pay close attention to negative values in your calculations.

TIP

The question usually states if the angle is above the horizontal (angle of elevation) or measured from the vertical. When the angle is 45°, this is not necessary.

WORKED EXAMPLE 13.2

A particle is projected from the top of a platform 15 m above the horizontal floor below. The angle of projection is 45° and the initial speed is $25\,\text{m s}^{-1}$. Find:

a the exact time taken to reach the horizontal floor below

b the exact speed of the particle as it hits the floor.

Answer

a $s = ut + \frac{1}{2}at^2$ — Model the vertical motion. Remember that the floor is 15 m below the starting position.

Vertically, this gives:

$-15 = 25t\sin 45 - 5t^2$.

Rearranging we get: — Calculate the two times; one is invalid as it is before the start of motion.

$5t^2 - \frac{25\sqrt{2}}{2}t - 15 = 0$ or

$t^2 - \frac{5\sqrt{2}}{2}t - 3 = 0$.

Note: The negative value for time represents the time when the particle would have started if it had been projected from ground level.

This is a quadratic equation, so using the quadratic formula we get:

$t = \frac{2.5\sqrt{2} \pm 3.5\sqrt{2}}{2}$.

So $t = 3\sqrt{2}\,\text{s}$. — This answer is given in exact form as required by the question.

b Using $v = u + at$ horizontally and vertically gives: | Find both components of the speed at the required time.

$v_x = 25\cos 45 = 12.5\sqrt{2}$

$v_y = 25\sin 45 - 10 \times 3\sqrt{2}$

$= -17.5\sqrt{2}$

Hence, $v = \sqrt{v_x^2 + v_y^2} = 5\sqrt{37}\,\text{m s}^{-1}$. | Calculate the resultant in exact form.

Projectiles can, instead, be launched at an angle below the horizontal (**angle of depression**).

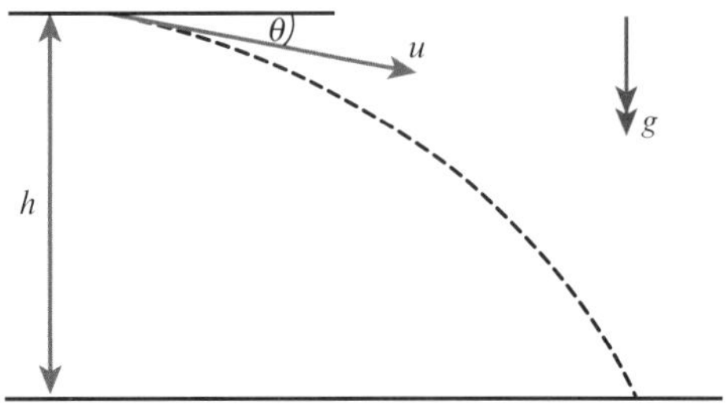

Let us consider a particle thrown with initial speed $40\,\text{m s}^{-1}$, at an angle of depression of 10°. Initially, it is at a height of 20 m above horizontal ground. To determine how far the particle travels in the horizontal direction, we must first find the time it takes to reach ground level, then apply this value of t to the horizontal displacement.

Using $s = ut + \frac{1}{2}at^2$ vertically, we have $20 = 40t\sin 10 + 5t^2$. Notice here we have taken the downwards direction as positive, so $s = 20$ and $a = 10$. This reduces the use of negatives so can make the work easier when working with an angle of depression.

This gives $5t^2 + 40t\sin 10 - 20 = 0$ so $t = \dfrac{-40\sin 10 \pm \sqrt{(-40\sin 10)^2 - 4(5)(-20)}}{2(5)}$

Solving this equation gives two values for t. The value we want is positive (the projectile starts at $t = 0$) so $t = 1.423$ s. Use $x = ut\cos\theta = 40\cos 10 \times 1.423$, which gives a distance of 56.0 m.

WORKED EXAMPLE 13.3

An aircraft is on a scientific data collection mission over an ocean. The aircraft is travelling horizontally at a speed of $50\,\text{m s}^{-1}$ when it launches a sensor at an angle of 25° below the horizontal with an initial speed of $10\,\text{m s}^{-1}$. Given that the plane is 1 km above the ocean, and assuming that the ocean surface is flat, find the speed of the sensor when it is 100 m from the surface of the ocean.

Assume that air resistance is negligible.

Answer

Using $s = ut + \frac{1}{2}at^2$ vertically and taking downwards as positive:

$900 = 10t\sin 25 + 5t^2$. | Determine the time taken to fall 900 m.

Then $t^2 + 2t\sin 25 - 180 = 0 \Rightarrow t = 13$ | Find the time taken.

So $v_y = 10\sin 25 + 10 \times 13 = 134.23$.	Calculate the vertical component of speed using $v = u + at$ vertically.
The plane is moving at the time of launch:	
So $v_x = 50 + 10\cos 25 = 59.06$.	Find the horizontal component of speed using the initial speed of the plane and $v = u + at$ horizontally.
Hence, $v = \sqrt{v_x^2 + v_y^2} = 147\,\text{m s}^{-1}$.	Find the resultant speed.

KEY POINT 13.1

When an object is projected with an angle of depression, choose downwards as the positive direction. This means your vertical displacement is positive and the value of a is also positive.

EXERCISE 13A

1 A projectile is launched from point O on horizontal ground, landing at the point A.

a $OA = 205\,\text{m}$, $\theta = 40°$. Find the speed u.

b $\theta = 30°$, $u = 32\,\text{m s}^{-1}$. Find the range OA.

c $OA = 130\,\text{m}$, $u = 40\,\text{m s}^{-1}$. Find the possible angles of projection θ.

PS 2 A projectile is launched from a point on horizontal ground with speed U. Given that the horizontal distance travelled before hitting the ground again is 140 m, and that the angle of projection is 25° above the horizontal, find U.

3 In a game a ball is kicked from the point O on horizontal ground, so that it lands on a scoring area which extends from 20 m to 25 m from O. If the angle of elevation when kicked is 35°, find the initial speed required for the ball to land in the scoring area.

M 4 A particle is projected from point A on horizontal ground with initial speed $25\,\text{m s}^{-1}$ and angle of elevation θ. Given that the range of the particle is 60 m, find the value of the angle θ.

PS 5 A football player kicks a football from a point on the ground with an angle of elevation of 15°. The ball must land on horizontal ground level between 10 m and 20 m from the player's feet. Find the possible range of values of the initial speed of the football.

PS 6 A basketball is thrown with speed $10\,\text{m s}^{-1}$ from a point 2 m above the ground, at an angle of 45° above the horizontal. Find the speed of the basketball when it is at a height of 4 m for the second time during its motion.

PS 7 A particle of mass 2 kg is fired up a smooth slope of length 4 m, with initial speed $10\,\text{m s}^{-1}$, which is inclined at 30° above the horizontal.
The bottom of the slope is at the same level as horizontal ground.

a Find the speed of the particle at the top of the slope.

b The particle now flies off the slope and travels as a projectile. Find the greatest height achieved above the ground level.

M 8 A particle is projected horizontally from a point that is 12 m above a horizontal surface, with a speed of $15\,\text{m s}^{-1}$. Find the horizontal distance travelled before the particle hits the surface below.

PS 9 A particle is projected across a horizontal area of land, with initial speed $30\,\text{m s}^{-1}$ and inclined at an angle of 40°. Find the duration of time for which the particle is at least 10 m above the ground.

PS 10 A small stone is thrown from the top of a building that is 30 m tall. The stone is given an initial speed of $5\,\text{m s}^{-1}$, and it is directed downwards with an angle of depression of 15°.

a Find the time taken for the stone to reach the ground.

b Find the speed of the stone as it hits the ground.

13.2 The Cartesian equation of the trajectory

In Section 13.1 we saw that the general motion of a projectile launched from ground level is governed by its initial speed and the angle at which it is projected.

Consider the horizontal part of the motion. We know that $x = ut\cos\theta$. This means that, at any time, the value of t is given by $t = \frac{x}{u\cos\theta}$.

Now consider the vertical part of the motion. We know that $y = ut\sin\theta - \frac{1}{2}gt^2$. Substituting the expression found for t into this result gives $y = u\sin\theta\left(\frac{x}{u\cos\theta}\right) - \frac{1}{2}g\left(\frac{x}{u\cos\theta}\right)^2$.

Simplifying this, we get $y = x\tan\theta - \frac{gx^2}{2u^2}\sec^2\theta$.

This is essentially a quadratic equation in the form of an inverted parabola. The value of θ, once chosen, is constant and so only x and y vary. The equation is known as the Cartesian equation of the trajectory of a projectile.

Consider a ball that is to be kicked over a wall. The wall is 5 m tall and is 20 m from the starting position of the ball.

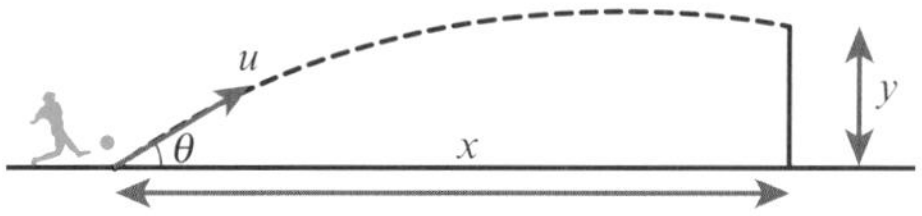

If the ball is kicked at an angle of 30° above the horizontal, how can we find the minimum speed required so that the ball just passes over the wall?

Begin with $y = x\tan\theta - \frac{gx^2}{2u^2}\sec^2\theta$. At the top of the wall, $x = 20$, $y = 5$.

So $5 = 20\tan 30 - \frac{g \times 20^2}{2u^2}\sec^2 30$. This can be written as $5 = \frac{20\sqrt{3}}{3} - \frac{8000}{3u^2}$, from which we find $u = 20.2\,\text{m s}^{-1}$.

When a particle is at ground level during its motion, $y = 0$. This means $x\tan\theta - \frac{gx^2}{2u^2}\sec^2\theta = 0$ or $x\left(\tan\theta - \frac{g}{2u^2}x\sec^2\theta\right) = 0$. This gives $x = 0$ and $x = \frac{2u^2\tan\theta}{g\sec^2\theta} = \frac{2u^2\sin\theta\cos\theta}{g} = \frac{u^2\sin 2\theta}{g}$, the start and finish points of the motion, as shown in Key point 13.2.

KEY POINT 13.2

When $y = 0$, $x\tan\theta - \dfrac{gx^2}{2u^2}\sec^2\theta = 0$ or $x\left(\tan\theta - \dfrac{g}{2u^2}x\sec^2\theta\right) = 0$.

So the start and finish points of the motion are $x = 0$ and $x = \dfrac{u^2\sin 2\theta}{g}$.

WORKED EXAMPLE 13.4

A projectile is launched from a point O, 1 m above horizontal ground level. It is given an initial speed of $20\,\text{m}\,\text{s}^{-1}$ and an angle of elevation of 25°. Find the horizontal distance from O when the particle is 2 m above the ground and descending.

Answer

Start with $y = 1$. Use $y = x\tan\theta - \dfrac{gx^2}{2u^2}\sec^2\theta$.

The projectile starts at 1 m above the ground, so $y = 1$ for the particle to be 2 m above the ground.

Then $1 = x\tan 25 - \dfrac{10x^2}{2\times 20^2}\sec^2 25$ or

Input the known values into the trajectory equation.

$\dfrac{\sec^2 25}{80}x^2 - x\tan 25 + 1 = 0$ leads to two results.

These are 2.32 and 28.3.

Obtain two results for x. One value is when the projectile is ascending and the other value is when it is descending.

Hence, $x = 28.3$ m.

Choose the larger value of x for when the projectile is descending.

Consider a particle being projected downwards instead. Remember that gravity assists when particles are descending, so it is a good idea to make the downward acceleration positive.

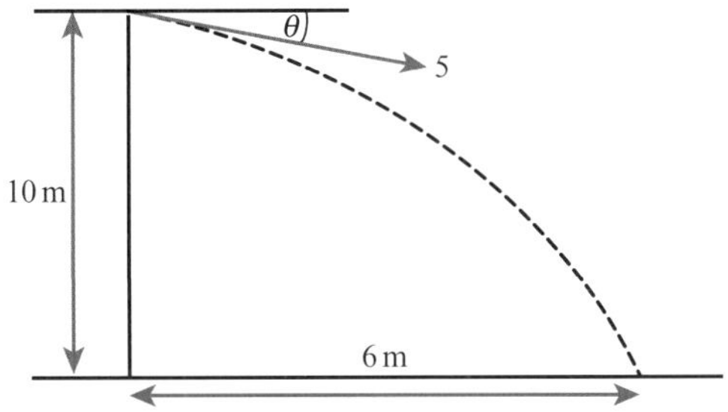

For example, consider a particle projected from a point 10 m above horizontal ground, with initial speed $5\,\text{m}\,\text{s}^{-1}$ and an angle of depression θ. Can we determine the angle if the horizontal distance travelled before hitting the ground is 6 m?

Start with the equation $y = x\tan\theta + \dfrac{gx^2}{2u^2}\sec^2\theta$, giving $10 = 6\tan\theta + \dfrac{10\times 6^2}{2\times 5^2}(1+\tan^2\theta)$,

which leads to $7.2\tan^2\theta + 6\tan\theta - 2.8 = 0$. From here, $\tan\theta = \dfrac{1}{3}$ or $\tan\theta = -\dfrac{7}{6}$. However,

$\tan\theta = -\dfrac{7}{6}$ would give a negative value for θ. The magnitude of this angle would represent the angle of elevation that would cause the particle to travel 6 m horizontally before hitting the ground. Hence we require $\tan\theta = \frac{1}{3} \Rightarrow \theta = 18.4°$.

WORKED EXAMPLE 13.5

A ball is thrown from the top of a building of height 20 m. The ball is thrown such that the initial speed is $U\,\text{m s}^{-1}$ and the angle of depression of the throw is 30°. Find:

a the horizontal distance travelled in terms of U

b the horizontal distance when $U = 5$.

Answer

a Use $y = x\tan\theta + \frac{gx^2}{2u^2}\sec^2\theta$.	Use the Cartesian equation of the trajectory.
So $20 = \frac{x\sqrt{3}}{3} + \frac{20x^2}{3U^2}$.	Substitute the values for the angle and height.
So $20x^2 + \sqrt{3}U^2x - 60U^2 = 0$.	Rearrange to get a quadratic in x.
Then $x = \frac{1}{40}\sqrt{3}(-U^2 + \sqrt{U^2(1600 + U^2)})\,\text{m}$.	Solve for x. (Ignore the negative solution.)
b When $U = 5$, $x = 7.65\,\text{m}$.	Find the solution when $U = 5$.

Consider a particle that follows a parabolic path, such as $y = 0.5x - 0.01x^2$. When we compare this equation with the trajectory, $y = x\tan\theta - \frac{gx^2}{2u^2}\sec^2\theta$, it is clear that $\tan\theta = 0.5$ and also that $\frac{10}{2u^2}\sec^2\theta = 0.01$.

To solve these we must first find $\theta = 26.57°$ then, using $\sec^2\theta = 1 + \tan^2\theta$, we obtain $\sec\theta = \frac{\sqrt{5}}{2}$ and $u = 25\,\text{m s}^{-1}$.

WORKED EXAMPLE 13.6

A projectile follows the path $y = 0.3x - 0.1x^2$. Find the initial speed and the angle of elevation of the particle.

Answer

$\tan\theta = 0.3$, so $\theta = 16.70°$.	Compare the coefficients for the linear term.
$\frac{g}{2u^2}\sec^2\theta = 0.1$ Since $\sec^2\theta = 1 + 0.3^2$, it follows that $u^2 = \frac{10 \times 1.09}{2} \times 10$.	Compare the coefficients for the quadratic term and use $\sec^2\theta = 1 + \tan^2\theta$ to find the value of $\sec\theta$.
So $u = 7.38\,\text{m s}^{-1}$.	Find the speed.

We will now look at the direction of motion of a projectile at certain points in its path.

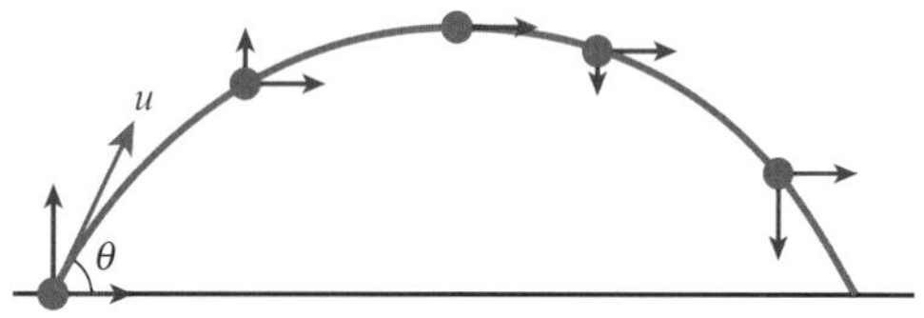

As the object follows its path the horizontal component of velocity is unchanged. However, the vertical component goes from its greatest positive value initially to zero at the highest point of the trajectory to its greatest negative value when it reaches the ground again.

This implies that the direction of motion of the particle is related to its velocity at that time. To find the direction we just need to know the components of velocity. We already know the horizontal component since it is constant throughout the motion. So we only need to find the vertical component.

Consider a particle with initial speed $20\,\text{m s}^{-1}$, projected at an angle of elevation of 50° from horizontal ground. Is it possible to find the height of the particle when it is travelling in a direction of 45° below the horizontal?

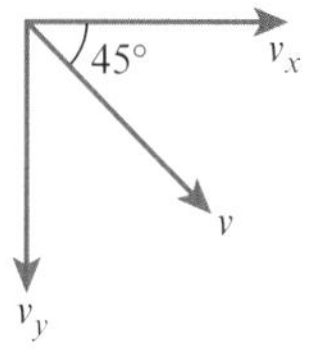

When the angle is 45° below the horizontal, from the diagram we see that $v_x = -v_y$, and so $20\cos 50 = -(20\sin 50 - gt)$. This means we can work out the time at this point and use this time to find the height. So $t = \frac{20}{g}(\cos 50 + \sin 50) = 2.818\,\text{s}$. Then, using $y = 20t\sin 50 - 5t^2$ gives a height of $3.47\,\text{m}$.

WORKED EXAMPLE 13.7

A particle is projected from the top of a tower that is 50 m tall. The initial speed is $25\,\text{m s}^{-1}$ and the angle of depression is 10°. Find the height of the particle above the ground when the downward angle of the direction of the particle is 30°.

Answer

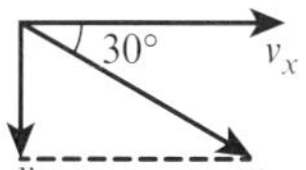

The tangent of the angle is $\frac{v_y}{v_x}$.

Note that $\tan 30 = \frac{v_y}{v_x}$. Then we have $v_y = \frac{\sqrt{3}}{3}v_x$.

Recognise the relationship between the tangent and the components.

So $25\sin 10 + gt = \frac{\sqrt{3}}{3}(25\cos 10)$.

Use this relationship with $v_y = 25\sin 10 + gt$ and $v_x = 25\cos 10$. Note that this time v_y is positive since the motion is downwards throughout.

From this $t = 0.9873\,\text{s}$.

Solve to find the time.

Then $y = 25t\sin 10 + 5t^2$ gives $y = 9.1603$.

Work out the vertical distance travelled from the point of release.

Hence, $50 - y = 40.8\,\text{m}$ above the ground.

Determine the height.

DID YOU KNOW?

Galileo rolled inked bronze balls down an inclined plane to determine where a projectile would land. This experiment allowed Galileo to determine that the path of a projectile is very close to being parabolic.

EXERCISE 13B

1 A particle is projected from horizontal ground with initial speed $15\,\text{m}\,\text{s}^{-1}$ and angle of elevation $60°$. Find the horizontal distance travelled when the particle is first at a height of 8 m above ground level.

2 A ball is thrown from a point 2 m above horizontal ground. The initial speed is $20\,\text{m}\,\text{s}^{-1}$ and the angle of elevation is $45°$. Find the horizontal distance covered when the ball is 12 m above the ground.

3 A particle is projected from ground level with initial speed $30\,\text{m}\,\text{s}^{-1}$ at an angle of elevation of $25°$. Find the horizontal distance travelled from the starting point when the height is 4 m for the first time.

PS 4 A particle is projected from a point 5 m above a horizontal plane. The angle of elevation is $10°$. Given that the particle travels 75 m before hitting the ground, find the initial speed.

PS 5 A particle is projected from a platform 4 m above horizontal ground, with an initial speed of $20\,\text{m}\,\text{s}^{-1}$ and an angle of elevation of $20°$. Find the direction of the particle as it lands on the ground.

M PS 6 A ball is kicked at a house window. The window is 4 m up a vertical wall from a horizontal floor. The ball is kicked from a position that is 12 m distance from the foot of the wall. If the ball enters the window at an angle that is $30°$ below the horizontal, find:

a the time taken to reach the window

b the initial speed of the ball.

TIP

Consider $\cos^2\theta + \sin^2\theta$.

M 7 A particle is projected from the top of an office building that is 35 m tall. The initial speed is $14\,\text{m}\,\text{s}^{-1}$ and the angle of depression is $20°$. Find the height of the particle above the ground when the downward angle of the direction of the particle is $45°$.

P 8 A particle is projected from a point on a horizontal surface with initial speed u and angle of elevation β. At any time during its motion, the particle is at the position (x, y), where x is the horizontal distance travelled and y is the vertical distance travelled.

Show that $y = x\tan\beta - \dfrac{gx^2}{2u^2}(1 + \tan^2\beta)$.

PS 9 A particle is projected from a point on a horizontal plane with speed $20\,\text{m}\,\text{s}^{-1}$ at an angle of elevation of θ. Given that the particle passes through the point $x = 20$, $y = 10$, find the possible angles of elevation.

P 10 A particle is projected from a point on horizontal ground with initial speed u and angle of elevation α. Show that $x^2 + y^2 = u^2t^2 - 10yt^2 - 25t^4$, where (x, y) is the particle's position at time t.

WORKED EXAM-STYLE QUESTION

A small stone is projected from a point O on horizontal ground, with speed $V\,\text{m s}^{-1}$ at an angle $\theta°$ above the horizontal. The horizontal and upward vertical displacements of the particle from O at time t seconds after projection are x and y respectively. The equation of the stone's trajectory is $y = 0.75x - 0.02x^2$, where x and y are in metres. Find:

a the values of θ and V
b the distance from O of the point where the stone hits the ground
c the greatest height reached by the stone.

Answer

a Comparing $y = x\tan\theta - \dfrac{gx^2}{2V^2}\sec^2\theta$ with $y = 0.75x - 0.02x^2$, it is clear that $\tan\theta = \dfrac{3}{4}$. Hence, $\theta = 36.9°$.

Then $\dfrac{g}{2V^2}\sec^2\theta = 0.02$, and since $\cos\theta = \dfrac{4}{5}$, $\sec^2\theta = \dfrac{25}{16}$. Hence, $V = \dfrac{25\sqrt{10}}{4} = 19.8\,\text{m s}^{-1}$.

b Letting $y = 0$, $0.75x - 0.02x^2 = 0$. So $x = 0$ or $0.02x = 0.75$. Hence, $x = 37.5\,\text{m}$.

c At the highest point $x = \dfrac{37.5}{2} = 18.75$, so $y = 0.75 \times 18.75 - 0.02 \times 18.75^2 = 7.03\,\text{m}$.

Checklist of learning and understanding

Governing equations:

- For displacement: $x = ut\cos\theta$ and $y = ut\sin\theta - \dfrac{1}{2}gt^2$
- For velocity: $v_x = u\cos\theta$ and $v_y = u\sin\theta - gt$
- For the range: $x_{\text{max}} = \dfrac{u^2\sin 2\theta}{g}$
- Total flight time: $t = \dfrac{2u\sin\theta}{g}$

TIP

The formulae for range and total flight time apply only to particles that start and finish their motion on the same horizontal level.

Cartesian equation of the trajectory:

- $y = x\tan\theta - \dfrac{gx^2}{2u^2}\sec^2\theta$
- If given as $y = ax - bx^2$, then $a = \tan\theta$ and $b = \dfrac{g}{2u^2}\sec^2\theta$.

Direction of motion:

- Particles projected upwards are subject to $-g$, so $y = ut\sin\theta - \dfrac{1}{2}gt^2$ and $v_y = u\sin\theta - gt$.
- Particles projected downwards have $+g$, and so $y = ut\sin\theta + \dfrac{1}{2}gt^2$ and $v_y = u\sin\theta + gt$.
- For the angle of projection use $\tan\theta = \dfrac{v_y}{v_x}$.

END-OF-CHAPTER REVIEW EXERCISE 13

1 A particle is projected from a point O on horizontal ground. The velocity of projection has magnitude $20\,\text{m}\,\text{s}^{-1}$ and direction upwards at an angle θ to the horizontal. The particle passes through the point, which is 7 m above the ground and 16 m horizontally from O, and hits the ground at the point A.

i Using the equation of the particle's trajectory and the identity $\sec^2\theta = 1 + \tan^2\theta$, show that the possible values of $\tan\theta$ are $\frac{3}{4}$ and $\frac{17}{4}$.

ii Find the distance OA for each of the two possible values of $\tan\theta$.

iii Sketch in the same diagram the two possible trajectories.

Cambridge International AS & A Level Mathematics 9709 Paper 51 Q5 June 2010

2 A particle P is projected from a point O with initial speed $10\,\text{m}\,\text{s}^{-1}$ at an angle of 45° above the horizontal. P subsequently passes through the point A, which is at an angle of elevation of 30° from O (see diagram). At time t s after projection the horizontal and vertically upward displacements of P from O are x m and y m, respectively.

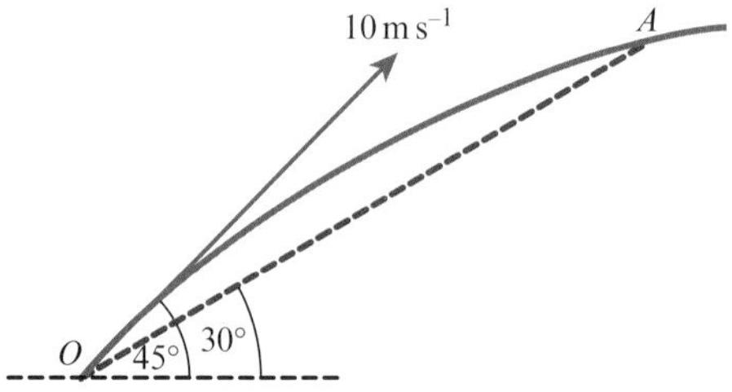

i Write down expressions for x and y in terms of t, and hence obtain the equation of the trajectory of P.

ii Calculate the value of x when P is at A.

iii Find the angle the trajectory makes with the horizontal when P is at A.

Cambridge International AS & A Level Mathematics 9709 Paper 51 Q7 November 2010

3 A particle P is projected with speed $35\,\text{m}\,\text{s}^{-1}$ from a point O on a horizontal plane. In the subsequent motion, the horizontal and vertically upwards displacements of P from O are x m and y m, respectively. The equation of the trajectory is $y = kx - \frac{(1+k^2)x^2}{245}$, where k is a constant. P passes through the points $A(14, a)$ and $B(42, 2a)$, where a is a constant.

i Calculate the two possible values of k and, hence, show that the larger of the two possible angles of projection is 63.435°, correct to 3 decimal places.

For the larger angle of projection, calculate

ii The time after projection when P passes through A,

iii The speed and direction of motion of P when it passes through B.

Cambridge International AS & A Level Mathematics 9709 Paper 51 Q7 November 2016

Chapter 14
Equilibrium of a rigid body

In this chapter you will learn how to:

- find the moment of a force and use it to determine the centre of mass of 2- and 3-dimensional shapes
- determine the centre of mass of a composite body, made up of standard shapes
- make use of the fact that the vector sum of forces is zero when objects are in equilibrium
- solve problems with coplanar forces, including objects on the point of sliding or toppling.

PREREQUISITE KNOWLEDGE

Where it comes from	What you should be able to do	Check your skills
AS & A Level Mathematics Mechanics, Chapter 2	Resolve forces in two perpendicular directions.	1 An object of mass m is sliding down a smooth slope inclined at an angle θ to the horizontal. Find the components of the weight of the object parallel and perpendicular to the slope.
AS & A Level Mathematics Mechanics, Chapter 4	Be able to determine or make use of the coefficient of friction of an object on the point of moving.	2 A particle of mass 2 kg is resting on a rough slope inclined at an angle θ to the horizontal. The maximum force that the frictional force can produce is 10 N. Find the value of θ for which the particle is on the point of slipping.

What is equilibrium?

When all forces acting on an object are balanced and the vector sum of the forces is zero, we say the object is in a state of **equilibrium**. Equilibrium is one of the most important concepts in engineering analysis. It allows you to check whether systems are stable and to calculate otherwise unknown forces.

In this chapter, we shall find the moment, or turning effect of a force, produced when we apply a force at a perpendicular distance to an object. For moments to be applied, the object must have length, so we cannot model it as a particle. Instead, we use a rigid body, a larger version of a particle. This is assumed to be inflexible so it does not bend when forces are applied.

We shall use this to find the centre of mass of standard shapes and **composite** bodies. Finally, these bodies will be placed in positions such that they are on the point of **breaking equilibrium** by sliding or toppling. To tackle the problems, we will resolve forces and take moments. The symbols we use are shown in Key point 14.1.

KEY POINT 14.1

In this chapter, you will use the symbols a for acceleration, v for velocity, and x for displacement. Unless stated otherwise, $g = 10\,\mathrm{m\,s^{-2}}$.

14.1 The moment of a force

Imagine trying to loosen a nut with a spanner (wrench). Applying the force with a short spanner would make it difficult to loosen the nut. But applying the same force with a longer spanner will result in a greater turning effect. This turning effect is known as a **moment**.

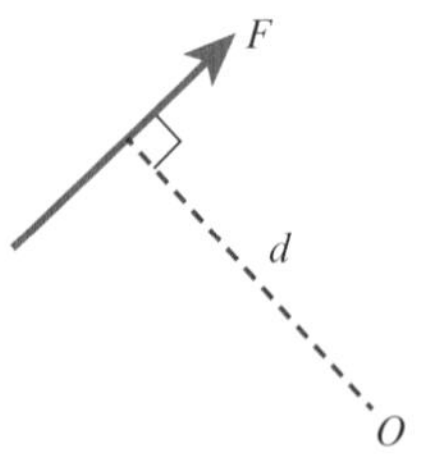

Moments are calculated by multiplying a force by a perpendicular distance, as shown in Key point 14.2. This means that moments are to be measured in newton metres (N m). When we talk about moments, we refer to the moment of that particular force.

KEY POINT 14.2

The moment of a force, F, about a point O is $F \times d$, where d is the perpendicular distance from the point O to the line of action of the force F. If the distance between the force and the point O is zero, there is no turning effect.

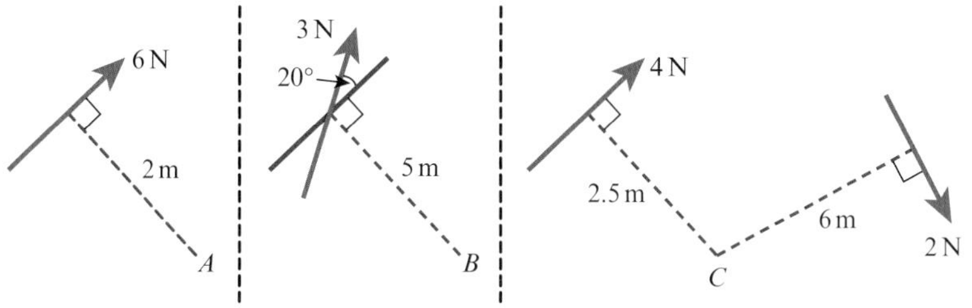

From the diagram, the moment of the 6 N force about the point A can be calculated as $6 \times 2 = 12\,\text{N m}$.

For the moment of the force about B, we first need to find the component of the force that is perpendicular to the line through B. So the moment is $3\cos 20 \times 5 = 14.1\,\text{N m}$.

The other component of the force, $3\sin 20$, passes through B, so its moment is zero.

For the moment of the forces about the point C, we add the turning effects since they both act in the same direction, which is clockwise. So the moment is $4 \times 2.5 + 2 \times 6 = 22\,\text{N m}$.

WORKED EXAMPLE 14.1

For each of the following cases, work out the moment and state whether it is a clockwise or anticlockwise turning effect.

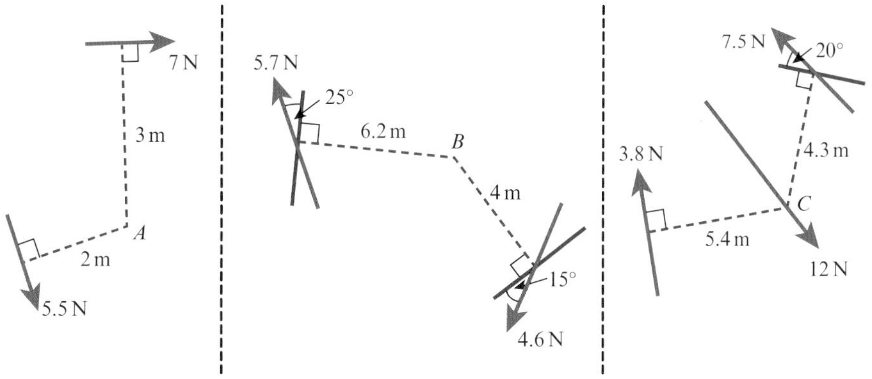

Answer

For A ↻: $7 \times 3 - 5.5 \times 2 = 10\,\text{N m}$ clockwise — Choose clockwise or anticlockwise as your positive direction.

For B ↻: $5.7\cos 25 \times 6.2 + 4.6\cos 15 \times 4 = 49.8\,\text{N m}$ clockwise — Determine the components of forces.

For C ↻: $3.8 \times 5.4 - 7.5\cos 20 \times 4.3 = -9.79$, therefore $9.79\,\text{N m}$ anticlockwise. — It is better to state a positive moment 'anticlockwise', rather than a negative moment clockwise.

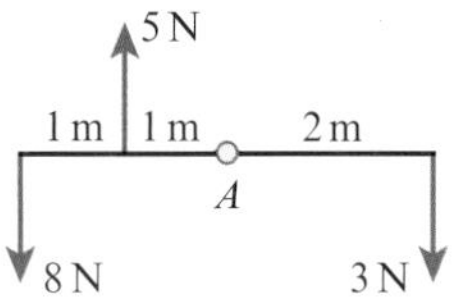

If we take a rod and apply a series of forces to it, we can observe the turning effect on the rod. We generally model it as a 'light' rod, so we can ignore the mass, and a **rigid body**, so it does not bend when forces are applied.

So taking moments about the point A, ↺: $3 \times 2 + 5 \times 1 - 8 \times 2 = 5$ N m anticlockwise. The 5 N force and the 3 N force turn the same way about the point A, whereas the 8 N is in the opposite direction. This means that the rod will turn about A as it is not in equilibrium.

WORKED EXAMPLE 14.2

In each case, a light rod is pivoted at a fixed point, A. Find the unknown values such that the rod will have a zero moment about A.

a

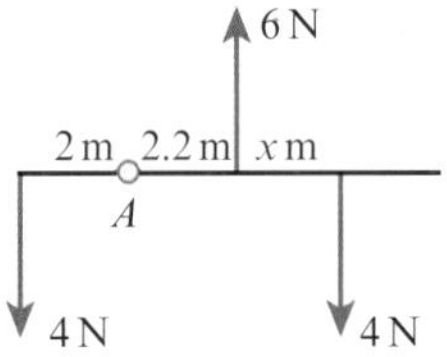

b

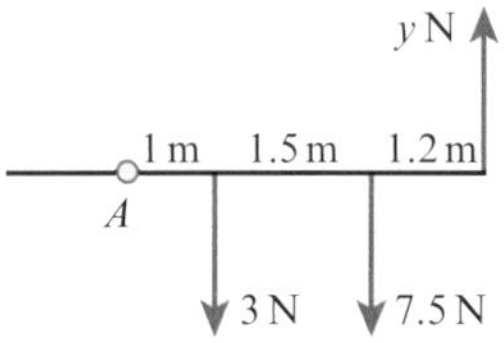

c

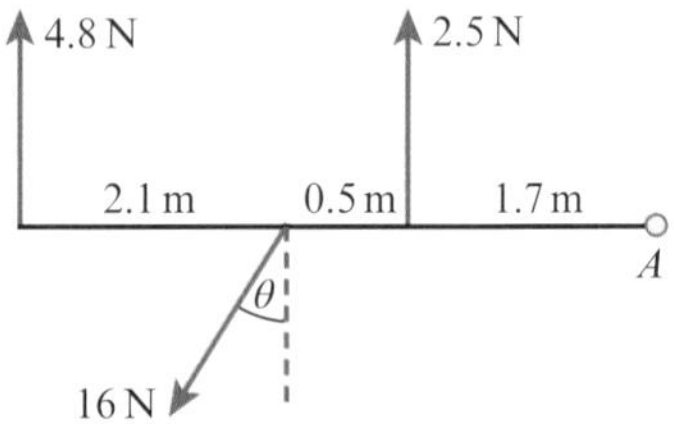

Answer

a About A ↺: $4 \times (x + 2.2) - 6 \times 2.2 - 4 \times 2 = 0$

So $4x + 8.8 = 21.2$, giving $x = 3.1$ m.

Note the distance of $x + 2.2$ between the clockwise force and A.

b About A ↺: $3 \times 1 + 7.5 \times 2.5 - y \times 3.7 = 0$

So $3.7y = 21.75$, giving $y = 5.88$ N.

Make sure the total moment is zero in order to determine y.

c About A ↺: $4.8 \times 4.3 + 2.5 \times 1.7 - 16\cos\theta \times 2.2 = 0$

So $35.2\cos\theta = 24.89$, giving $\theta = 45.0°$.

Remember to use only the component of the force perpendicular to the rod.

Consider a **uniform** rod of length 2 m and mass 2 kg resting in equilibrium over the edge of a table. The edge of the table is the point A. The mass B at the end of the rod is 3 kg.

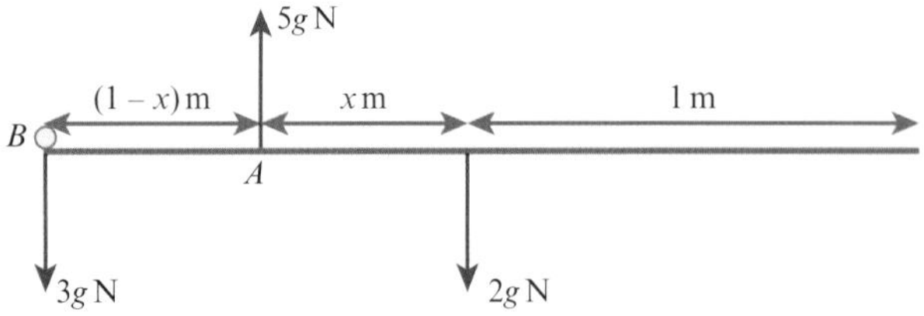

This time we consider the weight of the rod. Because the rod is modelled as uniform, its weight acts at the centre of the rod.

If we ignore the small mass at the point B, taking moments about A gives $2g \times x = 20x$ N m. This means the rod would not be in equilibrium and would turn about the point A.

So we include the mass 3 g and take moments again, now $2gx = 3g(1 - x)$, and so $x = \frac{3}{5}$ m. The reaction force has a moment of zero about the point A.

WORKED EXAMPLE 14.3

A uniform rod, AB, of length 5 m and mass 10 kg, is placed over the edge of a cliff such that B is 4 m from the edge of the cliff and hanging over the edge. A man, of mass 80 kg, stands on the cliff side of the rod, a distance of x m from the edge of the cliff.

a Find the value of x so that the rod is on the point of tipping over the cliff.

The man now stands at A and a boy of mass 35 kg walks across the rod towards B.

b Can the boy walk all the way to the end of the rod?

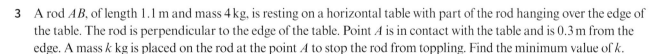

Answer

a

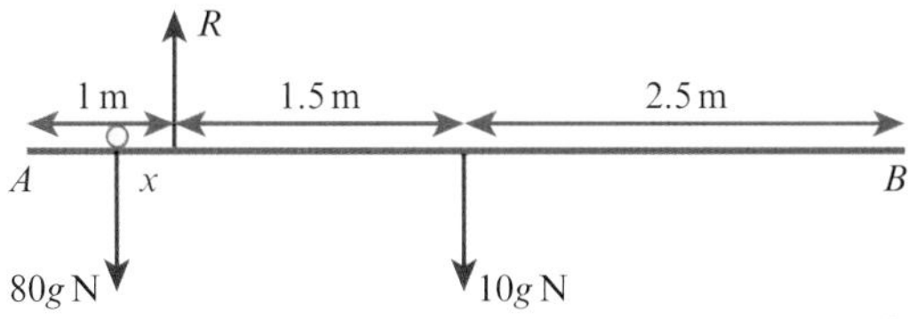

Sketch the first case, labelling your diagram fully.

About edge ↺: $10g \times 1.5 = 80g \times x$, so $x = \frac{3}{16}$ m.

Taking moments about the edge gives x.

b

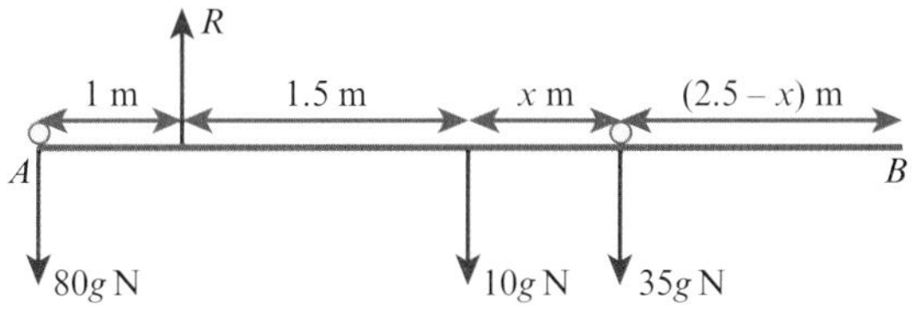

Redraw diagram with the boy included and the man now at point A.

About edge ↺: $10g \times 1.5 + 35g \times (1.5 + x) = 80g \times 1$

Then $1.5 + x = \frac{80g - 15g}{35g}$. So, at most, $x = \frac{5}{14}$ m.

So the boy cannot reach the end of the rod at B.

Taking moments about the edge shows that the distance is less than 2.5 m, so the boy can never reach B.

EXERCISE 14A

1 A rod AB of length 3.1 m and mass 8 kg is balancing on a pivot at a point C, where AC is 1.2 m. It is kept balanced by masses being placed at A and B. If the mass at A is 4 kg, determine the mass at B.

2 A rod AB of length 1.4 m and mass 6 kg is balancing on a pivot at a point C, where AC is 0.5 m. It is kept balanced by masses being placed at A and B. If the mass at A is 3 kg, determine the mass at B.

M 3 A rod AB, of length 1.1 m and mass 4 kg, is resting on a horizontal table with part of the rod hanging over the edge of the table. The rod is perpendicular to the edge of the table. Point A is in contact with the table and is 0.3 m from the edge. A mass k kg is placed on the rod at the point A to stop the rod from toppling. Find the minimum value of k.

4 Find the moment about O of the forces shown, stating if it is clockwise or anticlockwise.

a

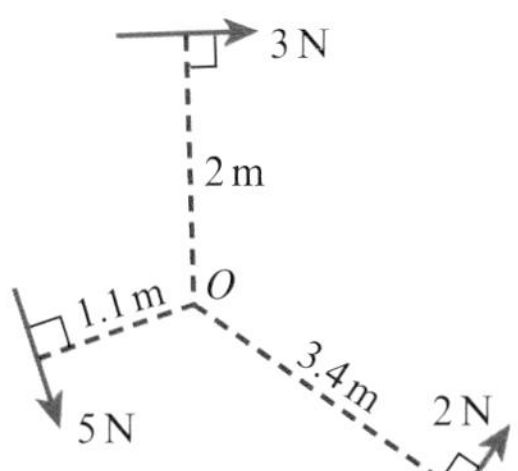

b

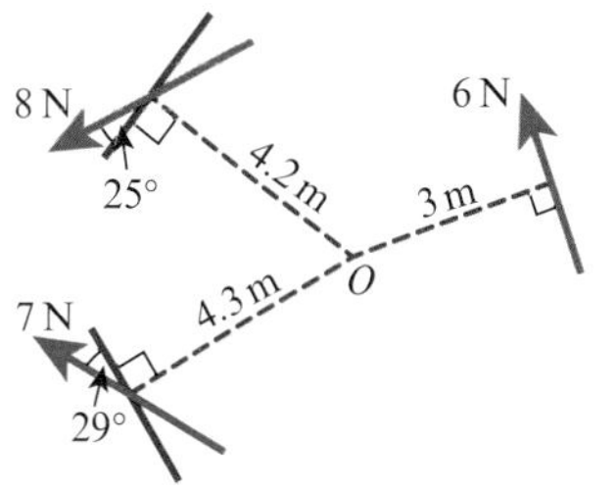

c

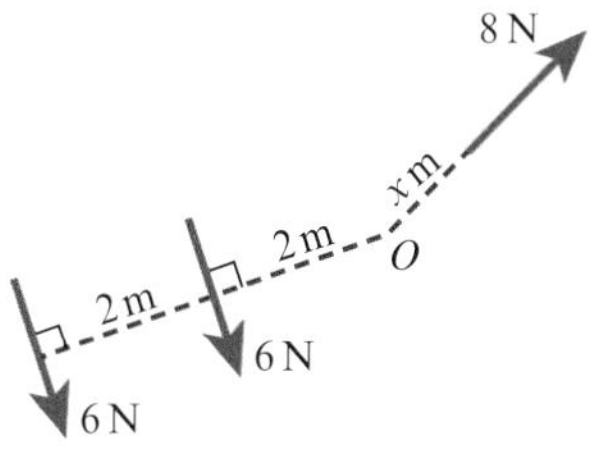

5 For each of the following rods, find the moment about the point P.

a
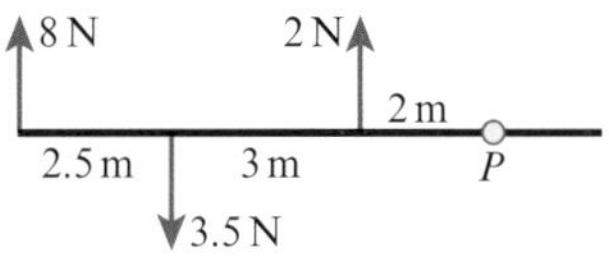

b
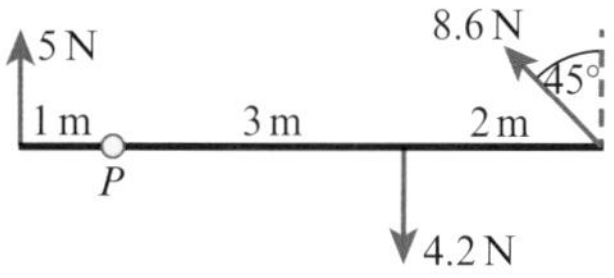

c
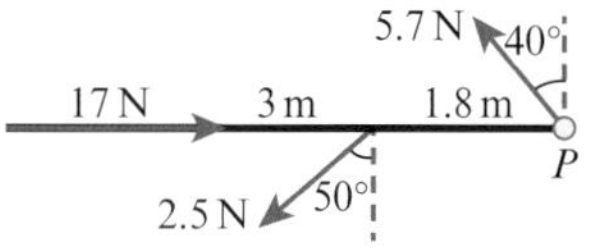

PS 6 A rod, AB, of length 0.4 m and mass 5 kg, is resting such that part of the rod is hanging over the edge of a horizontal table. The rod is positioned so that it is perpendicular to the edge of the table, and with the point A in contact with the table and 0.15 m from the edge.

a A mass of 8 kg is placed on the rod to stop the rod from falling off the table. Find its distance from the point A.

b The 8 kg mass is now placed at the point A. A second mass is added at the point B. Find the maximum mass that can be added without the rod toppling.

PS 7 A rod, AB, of length 5 m and mass 12 kg is hanging over the edge of a cliff. The end A is 1.2 m from the edge of the cliff, and the rod is assumed to be perpendicular to the cliff. A woman, of mass M, stands at the point A, and a girl, of mass m, stands at the point B. Given that the rod is on the point of tipping, find m in terms of M.

PS M 8 In each case, find the unknown such that the total moment about O is zero.

a
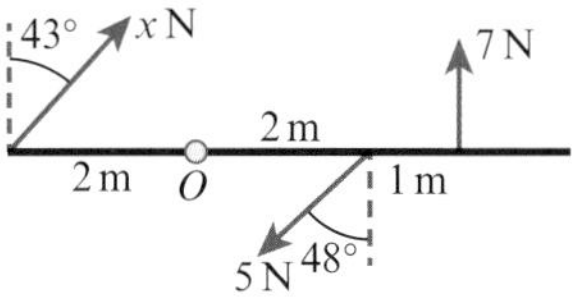

b
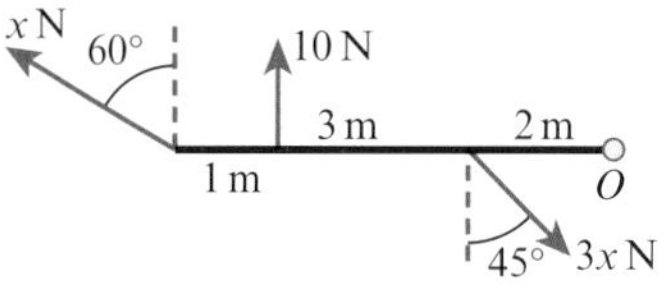

c
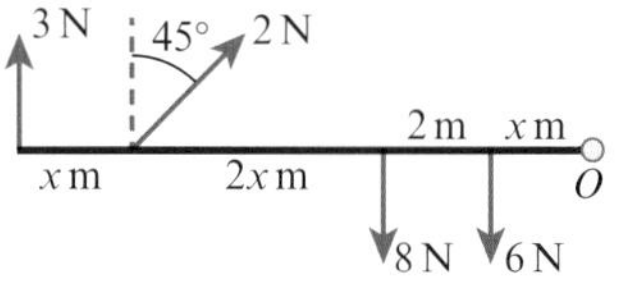

14.2 Centres of mass of rods and laminas

We can use moments in finding the **centre of mass** of an object. All the weight of an object acts through its centre of mass.

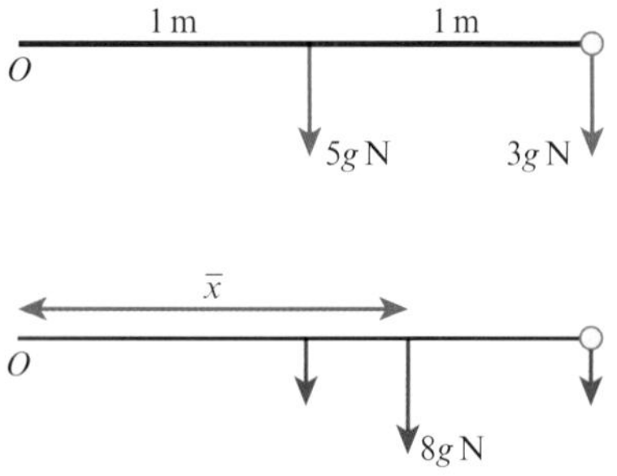

For example, consider a rod of length 2 m and mass 5 kg. We add a mass of 3 kg to one end.

If we take moments about O ↻: $5g \times 1 + 3g \times 2 = 11g$ N m.

Now consider this turning effect as coming from one force positioned where $8g \times \bar{x} = 11g$, then $\bar{x} = \frac{11}{8}$ m from the point O.

We have created a single force a distance of $\frac{11}{8}$ m from O. This force multiplied by the distance $\bar{x}$ represents the sum of all the turning effects of the system.

WORKED EXAMPLE 14.4

Find the distance, $\bar{x}$, of the single force that represents all other forces from the point O.

a
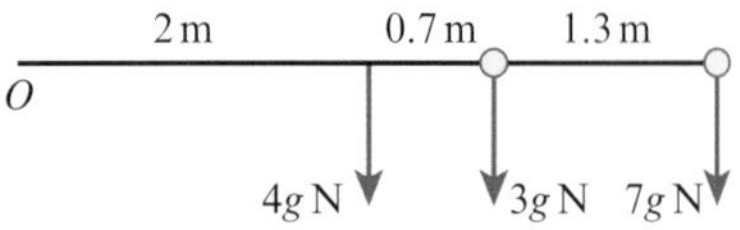

b
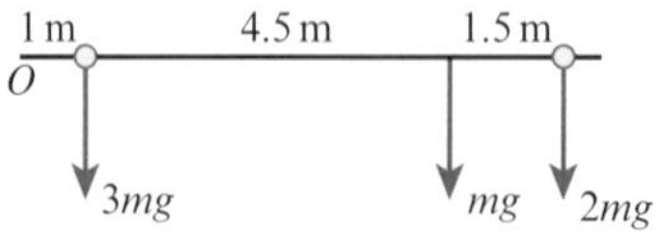

c
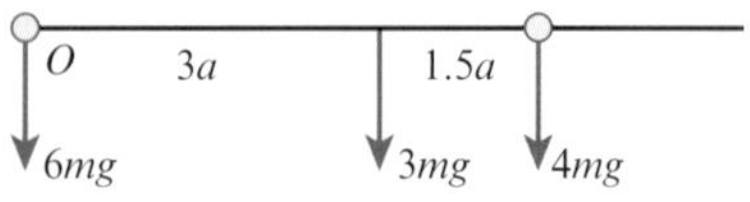

Answer

a About O ↻: $4g \times 2 + 3g \times 2.7 + 7g \times 4$
$= 44.1g = 14g \times \bar{x}$

Hence, $\bar{x} = 3.15$ m.

Take moments about O, then compare this to the sum of the forces $\times\ \bar{x}$.

b About O ↺: $3mg \times 1 + mg \times 5.5 + 2mg \times 7$

$= 22.5mg = 6mg \times \bar{x}$

Hence, $\bar{x} = 3.75$ m.

c About O ↺: $3mg \times 3a + 4mg \times 4.5a$

$= 27mga = 13mg \times \bar{x}$

Hence, $\bar{x} = \frac{27}{13}a$.

Although the moment of the $6mg$ force at O is zero, you must remember to include the weight when finding $\bar{x}$.

KEY POINT 14.3

The distance of the centre of mass $\bar{x}$ from the point of reference is equal to $\frac{m_1x_1 + m_2x_2 + m_3x_3 + \cdots}{m_1 + m_2 + m_3 + \cdots}$, where m_i is the mass of each element of the object, and x_i is the distance of each element from a point of reference about which moments are taken.

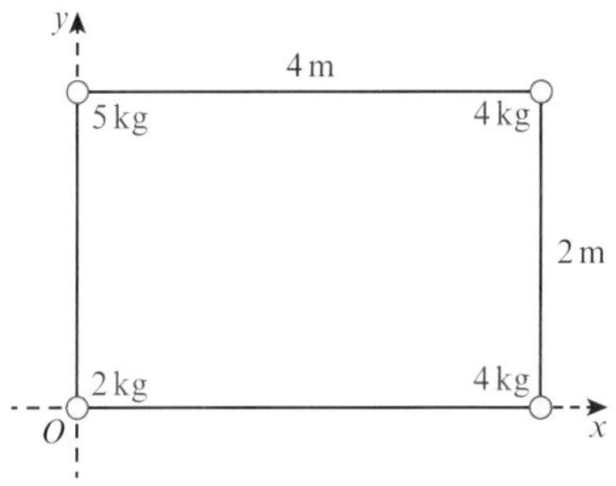

Let us look at a 2-dimensional case such as a framework with masses added.

We can now work out the centre of mass in two dimensions. This will give us coordinates relative to two perpendicular axes of reference. In this framework, we shall assume each rod is light but there are masses attached at each corner.

To take moments about a point, we assume the framework is horizontal and the weights have a turning effect on the framework.

Taking moments about Ox ↺: $5g \times 2 + 4g \times 2 = 15g \times \bar{y}$, so $\bar{y} = 1.2$ m. Remember that the masses that lie along Ox will not contribute to the turning effect.

Then moments about Oy ↺: $4g \times 4 + 4g \times 4 = 15g \times \bar{x}$, so $\bar{x} = \frac{32}{15}$ m.

So the centre of mass G has position $\left(\frac{32}{15}, 1.2\right)$ relative to the point O.

WORKED EXAMPLE 14.5

A rectangular framework, $ABCD$, is made of four light rods. There are masses on the rods at the given points.

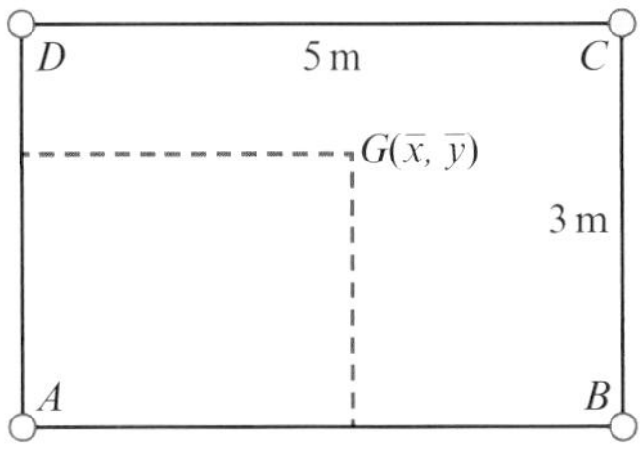

In each case, determine the coordinates of the centre of mass. Use AB and AD as your axes, with A as your origin.

a 2 kg at A, 4 kg at B, 7 kg at C, 2.5 kg at D

b 5 kg at the midpoint of AD, 6 kg at B, 4 kg at E, where $CE = \frac{1}{3}CB$

c 6 kg at A, 3 kg at the midpoint of AB, 8 kg at B, 10 kg at point F, where $DF = \frac{3}{5}DC$

Answer

a About AB ↻: $7g \times 3 + 2.5g \times 3 = 15.5 \times \bar{y}$ — Ignore the masses at A and B for this part.

So $\bar{y} = \frac{57}{31}$.

About AD ↻: $4g \times 5 + 7g \times 5 = 15.5 \times \bar{x}$ — Ignore the masses at A and D.

So $\bar{x} = \frac{110}{31}$.

Hence, centre of mass is $G\left(\frac{110}{31}, \frac{57}{31}\right)$. — State the centre of mass.

b About AB ↻: $5g \times 1.5 + 4g \times 2 = 15g \times \bar{y}$ — Note that the mass at A is zero.

So $\bar{y} = \frac{31}{30}$.

About AD ↻: $6g \times 5 + 4g \times 5 = 15g \times \bar{x}$

So $\bar{x} = \frac{10}{3}$.

Hence, centre of mass is $G\left(\frac{10}{3}, \frac{31}{30}\right)$.

c About AB ↻: $10g \times 3 = 27g \times \bar{y}$

So $\bar{y} = \frac{10}{9}$.

About AD ↻:
$3g \times 2.5 + 8g \times 5 + 10g \times 3 = 27g \times \bar{x}$ — Remember that $DF = 3\,\text{m}$.

So $\bar{x} = \frac{155}{54}$.

Hence, centre of mass is $G\left(\frac{155}{54}, \frac{10}{9}\right)$.

We shall now consider a thin, 2-dimensional shape known as a **lamina**. If a lamina is described as uniform, then we assume that its mass is spread evenly across its area.

The standard shapes you will encounter are the rectangle, circle, triangle and sector of a circle.

For a rectangle the centre of mass is in the centre, where the lines of symmetry meet.

For triangles, consider the scalene triangle ABC, with L, M, N at the midpoints of BC, AC and AB, respectively.

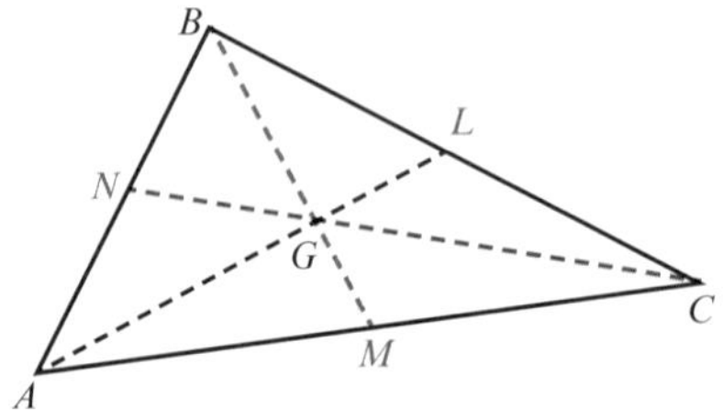

Now, relative to an origin O, we have $\overrightarrow{OA} = \mathbf{a}$, $\overrightarrow{OB} = \mathbf{b}$ and $\overrightarrow{OC} = \mathbf{c}$. We want to find $\overrightarrow{OG}$.

First, state that $\overrightarrow{OG} = \overrightarrow{OA} + \alpha\overrightarrow{AL}$, or $\overrightarrow{OG} = \overrightarrow{OB} + \beta\overrightarrow{BM}$, or $\overrightarrow{OG} = \overrightarrow{OC} + \gamma\overrightarrow{CN}$. The scalars α, β, γ are all between 0 and 1.

Next, with $\overrightarrow{AL} = (\mathbf{b} - \mathbf{a}) + \frac{1}{2}(\mathbf{c} - \mathbf{b})$, $\overrightarrow{BM} = (\mathbf{c} - \mathbf{b}) + \frac{1}{2}(\mathbf{a} - \mathbf{c})$, $\overrightarrow{CN} = (\mathbf{a} - \mathbf{c}) + \frac{1}{2}(\mathbf{b} - \mathbf{a})$, we have $\overrightarrow{OG} = (1 - \alpha)\mathbf{a} + \frac{\alpha}{2}(\mathbf{b} + \mathbf{c})$, $\overrightarrow{OG} = (1 - \beta)\mathbf{b} + \frac{\beta}{2}(\mathbf{a} + \mathbf{c})$ and $\overrightarrow{OG} = (1 - \gamma)\mathbf{c} + \frac{\gamma}{2}(\mathbf{a} + \mathbf{b})$.

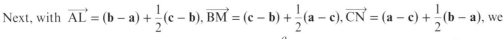

This means that each result must have the same coefficients for **a**, **b**, **c**. For example, we see that $1-\alpha=\frac{\beta}{2}=\frac{\gamma}{2}$ and $1-\beta=\frac{\alpha}{2}=\frac{\gamma}{2}$. So $1-\alpha=\frac{\alpha}{2}$, which leads to $\alpha=\beta=\gamma=\frac{2}{3}$

Hence, $\overrightarrow{OG}=\frac{1}{3}(\mathbf{a}+\mathbf{b}+\mathbf{c})$.

Next, consider the triangle ABC with $AB=6a$ and $AC=3a$. The centre of mass G can be found using A as the origin and then moving one-third of the distance along each edge to get $G(2a, a)$.

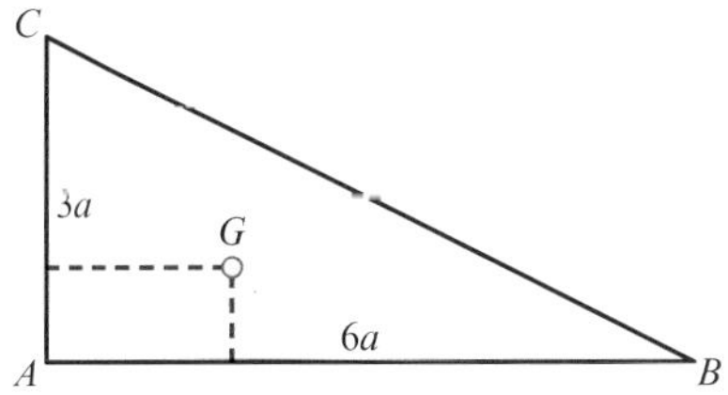

Note that this is relative to the edges AB and AC. An alternative way of doing this is to use the result $G\left(\frac{x_1+x_2+x_3}{3}, \frac{y_1+y_2+y_3}{3}\right)$, as shown in Key point 14.4, where the x_i and y_i terms are the vertices measured from an origin. In our case we used A as the origin, so $G\left(\frac{0+6a+0}{3}, \frac{0+0+3a}{3}\right)$ leads to the same result as before.

KEY POINT 14.4

The centre of mass of any triangular lamina is given by $\left(\frac{x_1+x_2+x_3}{3}, \frac{y_1+y_2+y_3}{3}\right)$, where the three vertices of the triangle are at $(x_1, y_1), (x_2, y_2), (x_3, y_3)$.

WORKED EXAMPLE 14.6

For each case, work out the centre of mass of the triangle, stating your point of reference.

1
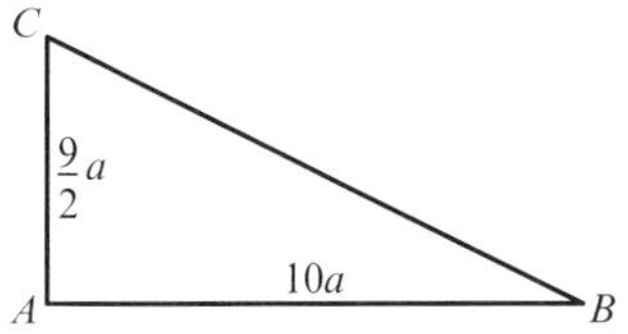

2
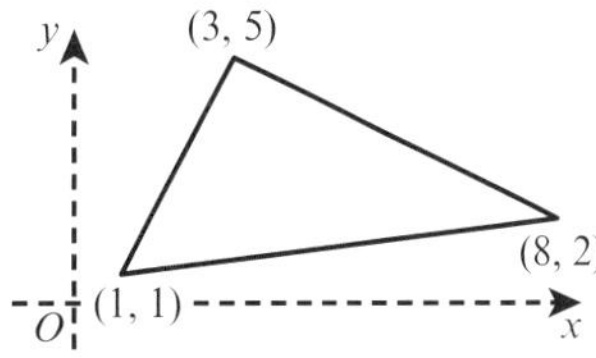

Answer

a Using AB and AC as axes, $\frac{1}{3}\times 10a$ and $\frac{1}{3}\times\frac{9}{2}a$ gives $G\left(\frac{10}{3}a, \frac{3}{2}a\right)$.
Set the axes. Then take one-third of each length from A.

b Using O as the origin, $\left(\frac{1+3+8}{3}, \frac{1+5+2}{3}\right)$ gives $G\left(4, \frac{8}{3}\right)$.
Take the mean of x and y.

Consider a lamina in the shape of a sector of a circle with an angle 2α at the centre, a radius r and a centre O. Then a smaller sector is chosen. Its angle is $\mathrm{d}\theta$, which is so small that the sector is almost a triangle, meaning we can use our results from above to find the position of the centre of mass of this small sector.

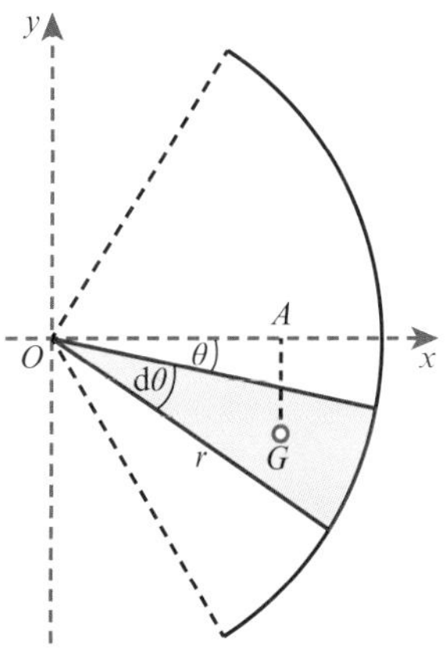

For that small sector, $OG=\frac{2}{3}r$, which means that the length $OA=\frac{2}{3}r\cos\left(\theta+\frac{1}{2}\mathrm{d}\theta\right)\approx\frac{2}{3}r\cos\theta$.

The total mass of the large sector, represented by the area of the sector × the mass per unit area, is $\frac{1}{2}r^2\times 2\alpha\times\rho=r^2\alpha\rho$, where ρ, **the Greek letter rho**, is the mass per unit area. The mass of each small sector is $\frac{1}{2}r^2\rho\,\mathrm{d}\theta$, so summing each moment contribution, $r^2\alpha\rho\bar{x}=\int_{-\alpha}^{\alpha}\frac{2}{3}r\cos\theta\times\frac{1}{2}r^2\rho\,\mathrm{d}\theta$.

So $r^2 \alpha\rho\bar{x} = \frac{1}{3}\rho r^3[\sin\theta]_{-\alpha}^{\alpha}$, leading to $\bar{x} = \frac{r(\sin\alpha - \sin(-\alpha))}{3\alpha} = \frac{2r\sin\alpha}{3\alpha}$, as shown in Key point 14.5. This result can be used for any sector, giving the distance OG, where OG bisects the angle 2α subtended at the centre of the circle. The angle must be given in radians, not degrees.

KEY POINT 14.5

The centre of mass of a sector-shaped lamina with an angle of 2α subtended at the centre is given as $\frac{2r\sin\alpha}{3\alpha}$.

WORKED EXAMPLE 14.7

Determine the centre of mass from the centre O of a sector of radius r with angle:

a $\frac{\pi}{2}$ **b** π

Answer

a

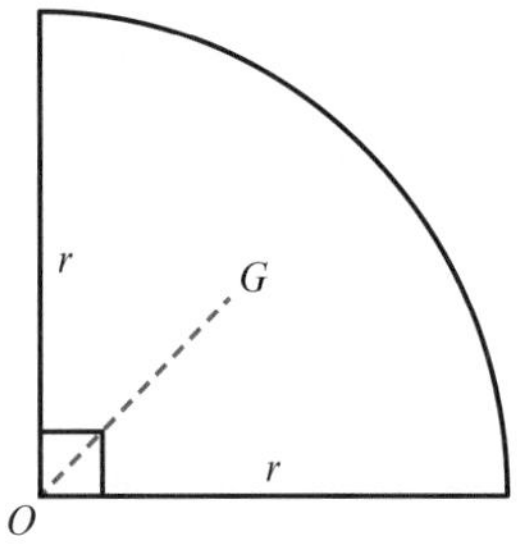

$OG = \frac{2r\sin\alpha}{3\alpha}$, — Quote the result.

here $\alpha = \frac{\pi}{4}$. — Take half the angle subtended at the centre.

Hence, $OG = \frac{2r\sin\frac{\pi}{4}}{\frac{3\pi}{4}}$ — Determine the distance OG.

which is $\frac{4r\sqrt{2}}{3\pi}$.

b

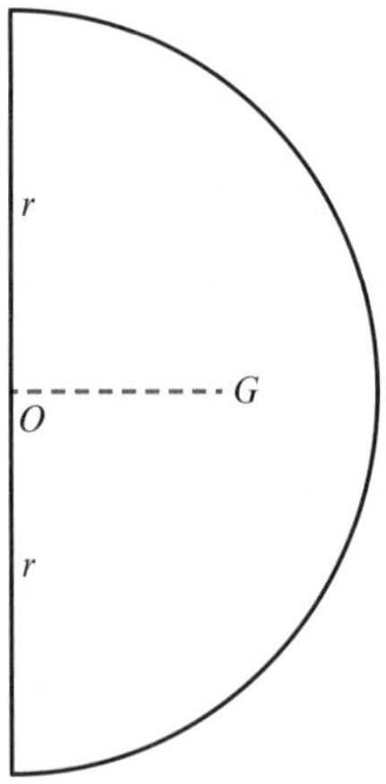

Again, using $OG = \frac{2r\sin\alpha}{3\alpha}$ with $\alpha = \frac{\pi}{2}$ gives the result — Since a semi-circle is a sector the result for the sector can be used with $\alpha = \frac{\pi}{2}$.

$OG = \frac{2r\sin\frac{\pi}{2}}{\frac{3\pi}{2}}$, — Don't forget that the angle must be in radians for this to work.

which is $\frac{4r}{3\pi}$.

Now that we have seen some standard lamina, we can look at combining these shapes to form composite bodies. In this example we have a composite lamina made of two uniform rectangular laminae. Using ρ as the mass per unit area, one rectangle has mass $3a^2\rho$ and the other has mass $2a^2\rho$, so the whole body has mass $5a^2\rho$.

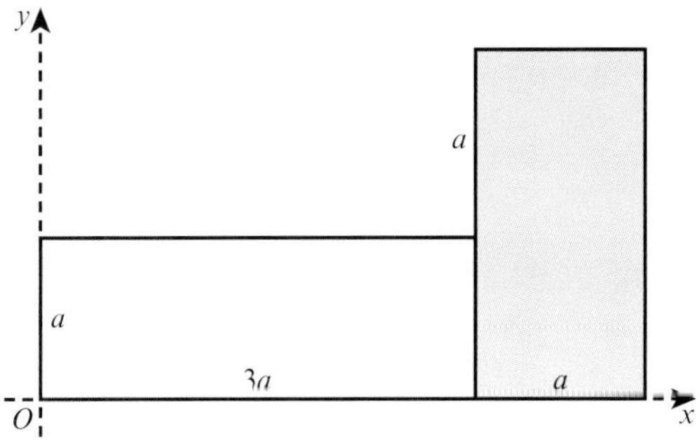

Taking moments about the y-axis ↺: $3a^2\rho \times \frac{3}{2}a + 2a^2\rho\left(3a + \frac{a}{2}\right) = 5a^2\rho\bar{x}$,
and so $\bar{x} = 2.3a$.

Then taking moments about the x-axis ↺: $3a^2\rho \times \frac{a}{2} + 2a^2\rho \times a = 5a^2\rho\bar{y}$,
and so $\bar{y} = 0.7a$.

So the centre of mass is $G(2.3a, 0.7a)$.

WORKED EXAMPLE 14.8

For each composite shape, determine the centre of mass relative to the axes shown.

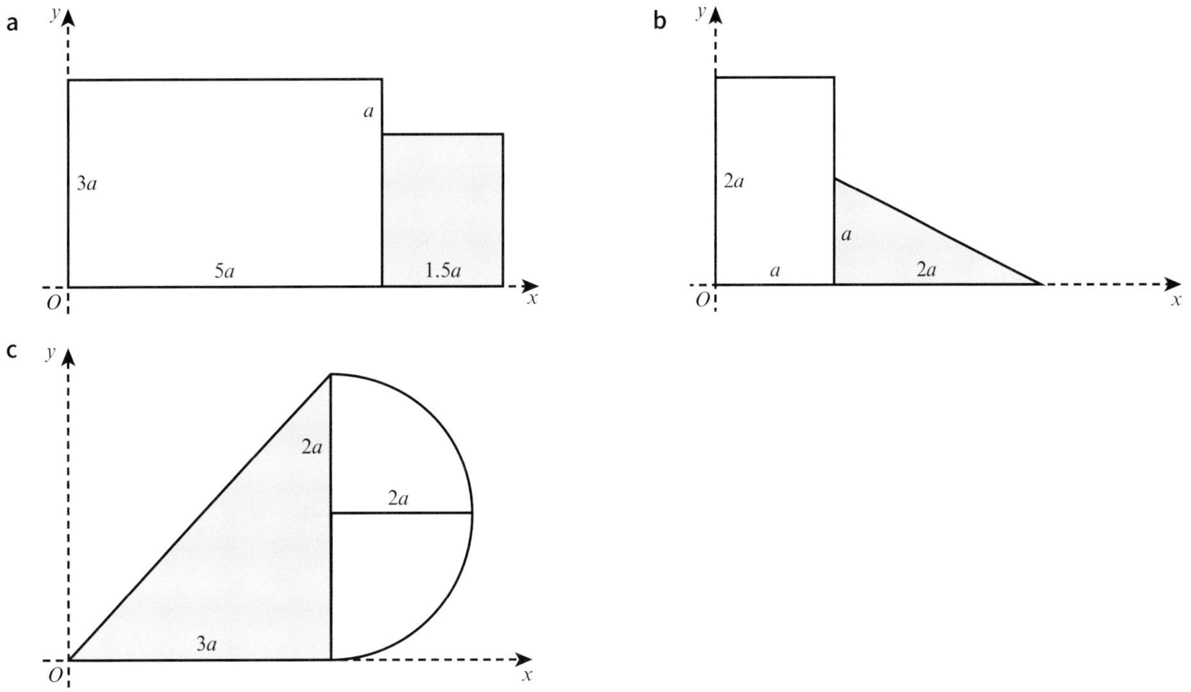

Answer

a Large rectangle has mass $15a^2\rho$, small rectangle has mass $3a^2\rho$

Work out the mass of each part first. Use ρ as the mass per unit area. You can then find the total mass.

So total mass is $18a^2\rho$.

About the y-axis ↺:

$$15a^2\rho \times \frac{5}{2}a + 3a^2\rho\left(5a + \frac{3}{4}a\right) = 18a^2\rho\bar{x}$$

Take moments about each axis to determine the coordinates of the centre of mass. The height of the smaller rectangle must be $2a$.

So $\bar{x} = \frac{73}{24}a$.

About the x-axis ↺:

$$15a^2\rho \times \frac{3}{2}a + 3a^2\rho \times a = 18a^2\rho\bar{y}$$

So $\bar{y} = \frac{17}{12}a$.

b Rectangle mass is $2a^2\rho$, triangle mass is $a^2\rho$

So total mass is $3a^2\rho$.

For the triangular lamina the centre of mass is $\frac{1}{3}$ of the distance from the bottom left corner of the triangle.

About y-axis ↺:

$$2a^2\rho \times \frac{a}{2} + a^2\rho \times \left(a + \frac{2}{3}a\right) = 3a^2\rho\bar{x}$$

This gives $\bar{x} = \frac{8}{9}a$.

About x-axis ↺: $2a^2\rho \times a + a^2\rho \times \frac{a}{3} = 3a^2\rho\bar{y}$

This gives $\bar{y} = \frac{7}{9}a$.

c Triangle mass is $6a^2\rho$, semicircle mass is $2\pi a^2\rho$

So total mass is $(6 + 2\pi)a^2\rho$.

The height of the triangle is twice the radius of the semicircle.

Centre of mass of semicircle from the vertical diameter shown is $\frac{4 \times 2a}{3\pi} = \frac{8a}{3\pi}$.

For the semicircle we know that $OG = \frac{4r}{3\pi}$. We can quote this result and use it.

About y-axis ↺:

$$6a^2\rho \times 2a + 2\pi a^2\rho \times \left(3a + \frac{8a}{3\pi}\right) = (6 + 2\pi)a^2\rho\bar{x}$$

So $\bar{x} = 2.95a$.

About x-axis ↺:

$$6a^2\rho \times \frac{4}{3}a + 2\pi a^2\rho \times 2a = (6 + 2\pi)a^2\rho\bar{y}$$

This leads to $\bar{y} = 1.67a$.

What if the lamina is a shape such as the lamina shown here? There are two ways we can deal with this.

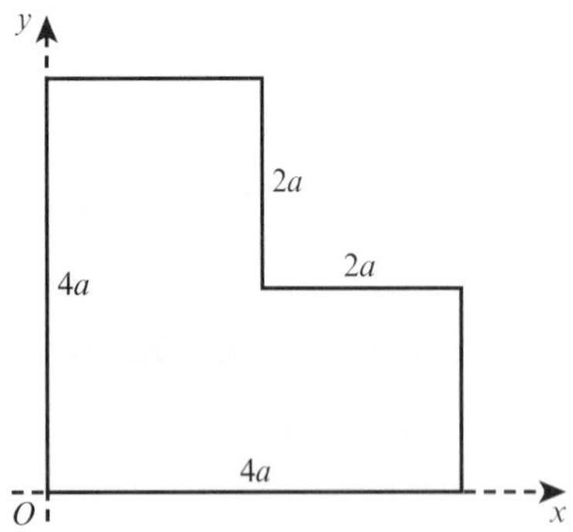

We could split the shape into a rectangle and a square, adding the moment of each shape to determine the total moment.

Alternatively, we could consider the larger square and its moment then subtract the moment of a smaller square to get the moment of the remaining shape.

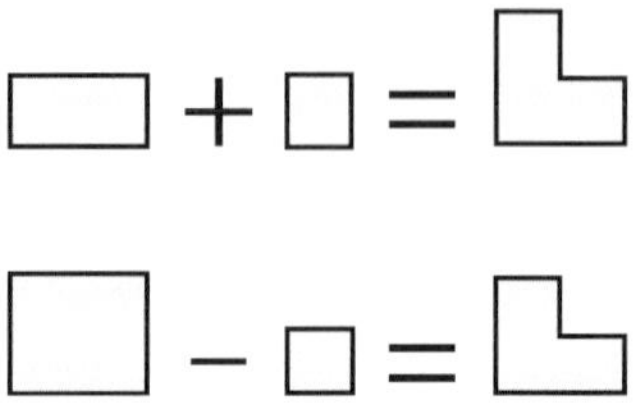

For this example, we are going to use the second method. In this example it is rather trivial, but for harder examples it is better to use this method. Note that the large square has mass $16a^2\rho$ and the small square has mass $4a^2\rho$, so our lamina has mass $12a^2\rho$.

Taking moments about Oy ↺: $16a^2\rho \times 2a - 4a^2\rho \times 3a = 12a^2\rho\bar{x}$, giving $\bar{x} = \frac{5}{3}a$.

Taking moments about Ox ↺: $16a^2\rho \times 2a - 4a^2\rho \times 3a = 12a^2\rho\bar{y}$, giving $\bar{y} = \frac{5}{3}a$.

Note that the results for $\bar{x}$ and $\bar{y}$ are the same due to symmetry.

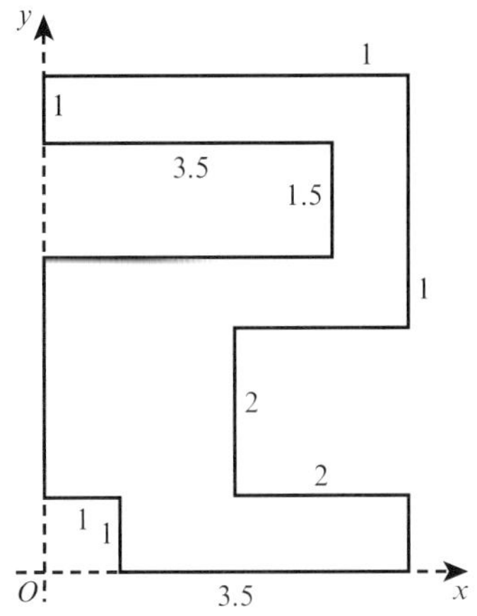

If we look at a more complicated example, such as in the diagram on the right, then we see that a large rectangle, of dimensions 4.5×6.5, has a 3.5×1.5 rectangle removed, a 2×2 square removed, and a 1×1 square removed.

The mass of the complete rectangle is 29.25ρ. The removed parts are 5.25ρ, 4ρ and ρ, respectively, so the lamina has mass 19ρ. We can now take moments about both axes to find the centre of mass.

About Oy ↺: $29.25\rho \times 2.25 - 5.25\rho \times 1.75 - 4\rho \times 3.5 - \rho \times 0.5 = 19\rho\bar{x}$, so $\bar{x} = 2.22$.

About Ox ↺: $29.25\rho \times 3.25 - \rho \times 0.5 - 4\rho \times 2 - 5.25\rho \times 4.75 = 19\rho\bar{y}$, so $\bar{y} = 3.24$.

WORKED EXAMPLE 14.9

The diagram shows a large circular-shaped lamina that is constructed by removing smaller circular areas from a circle of radius 15 cm.

The circle centred at the point $A(-6, 7)$ has radius 4 cm, the circle centred at $B(10, 3)$ has radius 2 cm, and the circle centred at $C(-3, -6)$ has radius 5 cm. Relative to the point O, find the centre of mass of the lamina. You may assume the lamina is uniform.

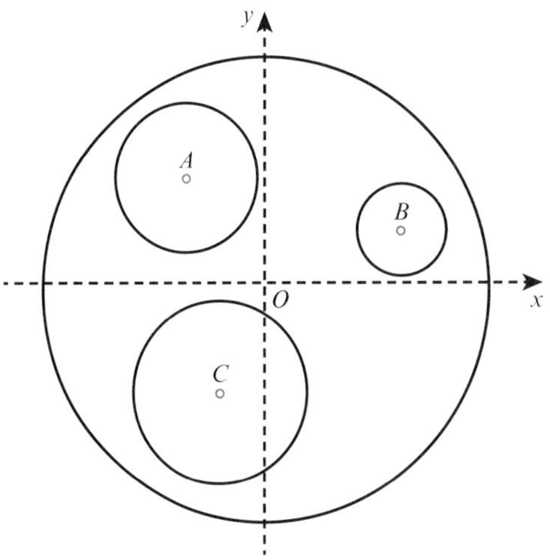

Answer

Large circle mass: $225\pi\rho$

Circle A mass: $16\pi\rho$

Circle B mass: $4\pi\rho$

Circle C mass: $25\pi\rho$

So lamina mass is $180\pi\rho$.

Determine the mass of each smaller circle to obtain the lamina's mass.

Taking moments:

About Oy ↺:

$225\pi\rho \times 0 + 25\pi\rho \times 3 + 16\pi\rho \times 6 - 4\pi\rho \times 10 = 180\pi\rho\bar{x}$

So $\bar{x} = 0.728$ cm.

Take moments; notice that some contributions are added.

This is actually $-(\text{mass} \times (-\text{length}))$, so still subtracted but with negative displacement.

About Ox ↺: Repeat for $\bar{y}$.

$225\pi\rho \times 0 + 25\pi\rho \times 6 - 16\pi\rho \times 7 - 4\pi\rho \times 3 = 180\pi\rho\bar{y}$

So $\bar{y} = 0.144$ cm.

DID YOU KNOW?

Centres of mass are very important for understanding planetary motion. The centre of mass between two objects is known as the **barycentre**. This is the point at which the two objects balance each other. For example, the barycentre between the Earth and the Moon is offset from the centre of the Earth by approximately 4700 km.

Now we will look at shapes formed from wire. For example, a piece of uniform wire could be bent into an arc of a circle with radius r, and angle 2α radians subtended at the centre.

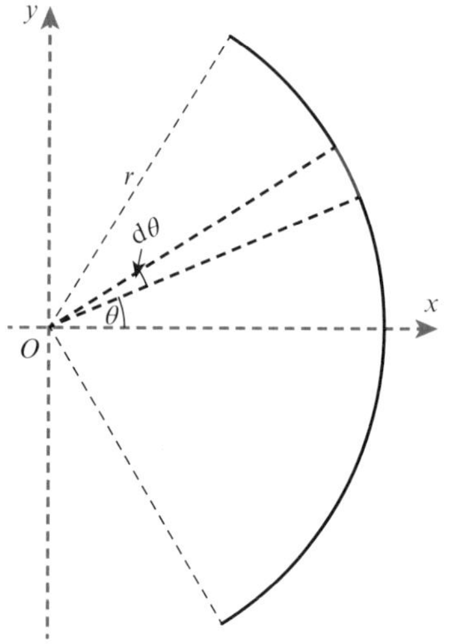

So each small arc of wire has mass $r\rho\,\mathrm{d}\theta$, and its distance from Oy is $r\cos\left(\theta + \frac{\mathrm{d}\theta}{2}\right) \approx r\cos\theta$.

The total mass of the wire is $2r\rho\alpha$, so the moment of the wire about Oy is $2r\rho\alpha\bar{x} = \int_{-\alpha}^{\alpha} r^2\rho\cos\theta\,\mathrm{d}\theta$.

So $2\alpha\bar{x} = r[\sin\theta]_{-\alpha}^{\alpha}$, which leads to $\bar{x} = \frac{r\sin\alpha}{\alpha}$.

For a semicircle, the distance of the centre of mass from O is $\frac{r\sin\frac{\pi}{2}}{\frac{\pi}{2}} = \frac{2r}{\pi}$.

For a quarter circle $\bar{x} = \frac{2\sqrt{2}r}{\pi}$.

WORKED EXAMPLE 14.10

The letter P is constructed using a uniform straight piece of wire of length $4a$ joined to another piece of uniform wire that is bent into a semicircle of radius a. Given that the semicircular piece of wire is three times as dense as the straight wire, find the position of the centre of mass $G(\bar{x}, \bar{y})$ relative to the point O.

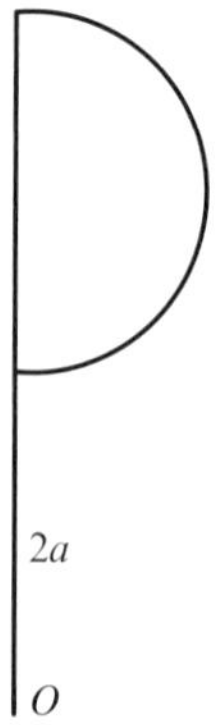

Answer

Mass of straight wire: $4a\rho$

Mass of semicircle: $\pi a \times 3\rho = 3\pi a\rho$

For $\bar{x}$ ↺: $4a\rho \times 0 + 3\pi a\rho \times \frac{2a}{\pi} = (4a\rho + 3\pi a\rho)\bar{x}$

Hence, $\bar{x} = \frac{6a}{4 + 3\pi}$.

For $\bar{y}$ ↺: $4a\rho \times 2a + 3\pi a\rho \times 3a = (4a\rho + 3\pi a\rho)\bar{y}$

Hence, $\bar{y} = \frac{(8 + 9\pi)a}{4 + 3\pi}$.

EXERCISE 14B

1 The diagram shows a lamina that is formed by removing a small rectangle from a larger rectangle. Find the distance of the centre of mass from AB and from AC.

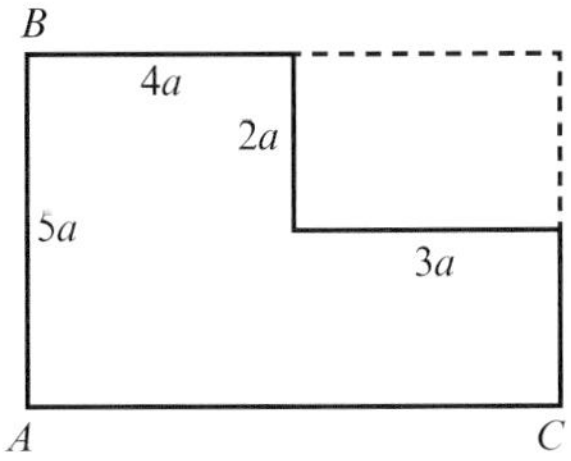

2 The diagram shows a uniform lamina in the shape of a trapezium. Find the distance of the centre of mass from edge AB and from edge AC.

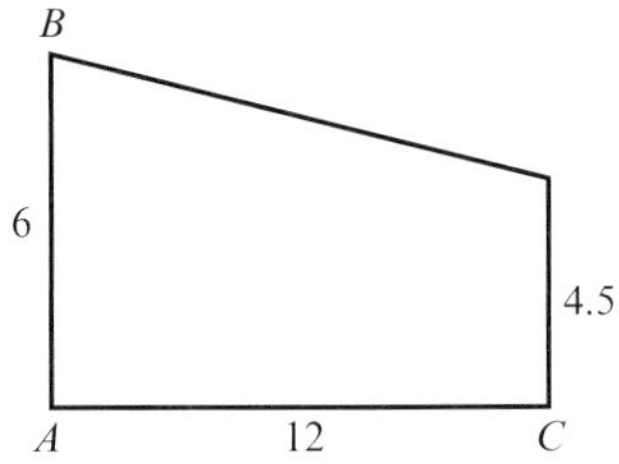

3 The diagram shows two uniform laminas, each a right-angled triangle, that are joined together at one edge, AB.

The smaller triangle is twice as dense as the larger triangle. Find the distance of the centre of mass from the edge AB.

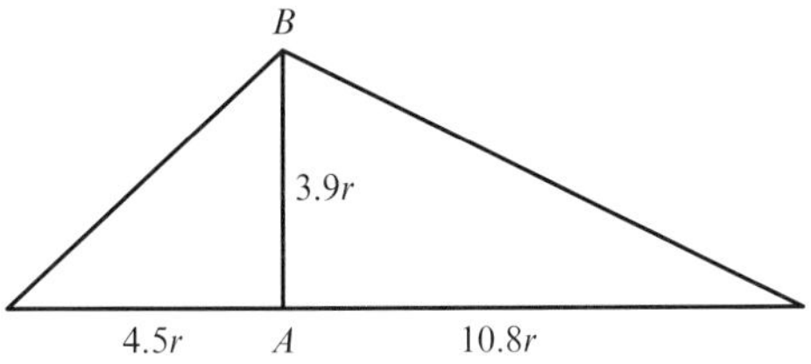

4 The image shows a uniform lamina that is formed by removing a square from a right-angled triangle. Find the coordinates of the centre of mass, as measured from the point O.

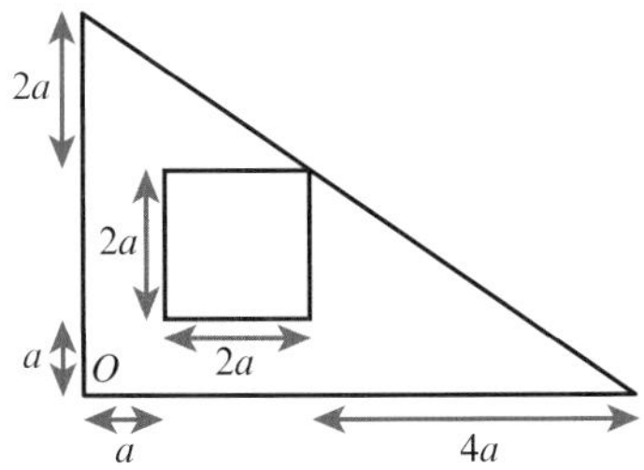

5 The diagram shows a uniform square lamina of side $4r$ and density 2ρ attached to a uniform lamina in the shape of a quarter circle of radius $4r$ and density ρ. Find the distance of the centre of mass from the edges OA and OB.

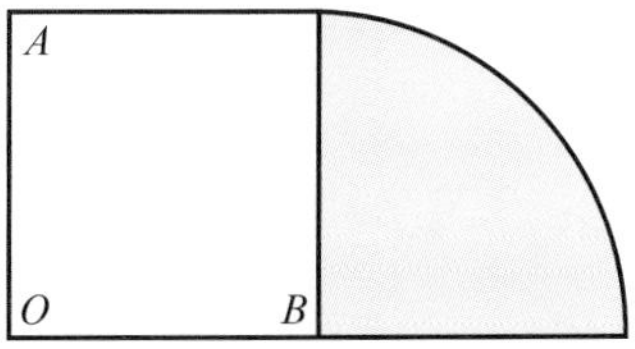

6 A piece of uniform wire is bent to form the letter D. This letter D consists of a straight edge of length 2 m, and a semicircle of radius 1 m. The letter D is held upright with the straight edge in the vertical plane. The bottom corner is denoted as O. Find the centre of mass from the corner O.

M 7 A uniform lamina is made from a square of side $2a$ joined to a semicircle of radius $2a$. This semicircle is then joined to another semicircle of radius $2a$, which is in turn joined to a smaller semicircle of radius a, as shown in the diagram. Find the centre of mass from the edges AB and AC.

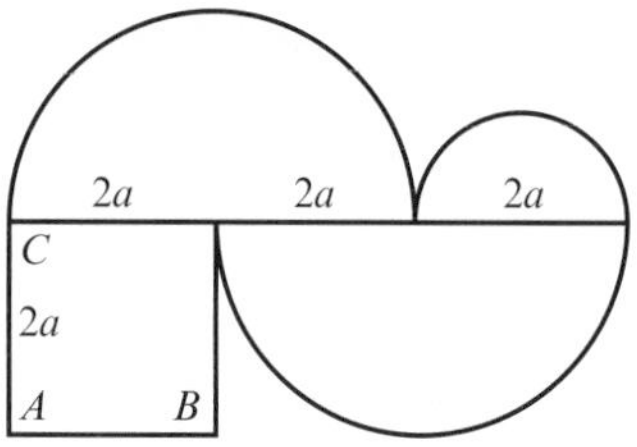

P 8 Show that the centre of mass of this uniform lamina, in the shape of a trapezium, is given by:

$$G\left(\frac{ah + 2bh}{3a + 3b}, \frac{a^2 + ab + b^2}{3a + 3b}\right)$$

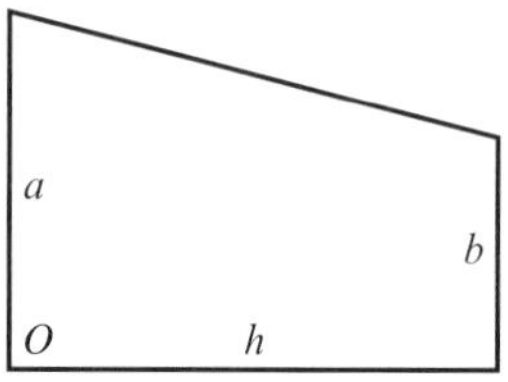

14.3 Centres of mass of solids

Moving on from 2-dimensional shapes, we shall now consider 3-dimensional solids. We shall look mainly at the cone and the hemisphere.

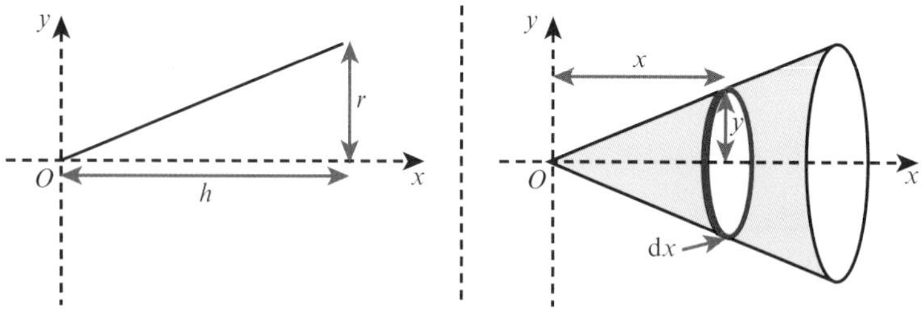

Consider rotating the line $y = \frac{r}{h}x$ about the x-axis from $x = 0$ to $x = h$, as shown in the diagram. The shape formed is a cone with height h and base radius r. It is symmetrical about the x-axis, and so $\bar{y}$ is zero.

To determine the centre of mass of the solid formed, we must consider a single 'slice' through the cone. A general slice will have radius y, thickness $\mathrm{d}x$, and its volume $\mathrm{d}V$ can be written as $\pi y^2 \mathrm{d}x$.

Each slice will have mass $\rho\pi y^2 \mathrm{d}x$ and is a distance x from the y-axis, so each slice contributes to the moment.

The mass of the cone is then $\frac{1}{3}\rho\pi r^2 h$, so $V\bar{x} = \int_0^h \pi x y^2 \mathrm{d}x$ will give us the distance of the centre of mass from (0, 0).

So, $\frac{1}{3}\rho\pi r^2 h\bar{x} = \int_0^h \rho\pi x\left(\frac{r}{h}x\right)^2 \mathrm{d}x$, which becomes $\frac{1}{3}h\bar{x} = \frac{1}{h^2}\left[\frac{1}{4}x^4\right]_0^h$. Hence, $\bar{x} = \frac{3}{4}h$.

KEY POINT 14.6

The centre of mass of a right circular cone, of height h and base radius r, is given as $G\left(\frac{3}{4}h, 0\right)$ when measured from the vertex.

WORKED EXAMPLE 14.11

A solid uniform cone of height $3a$ and base radius a has a smaller similar cone removed from it. The smaller cone has height a. The resulting shape is known as a **frustum**. Find the centre of mass of the frustum when measured from the smaller of its two plane faces.

Answer

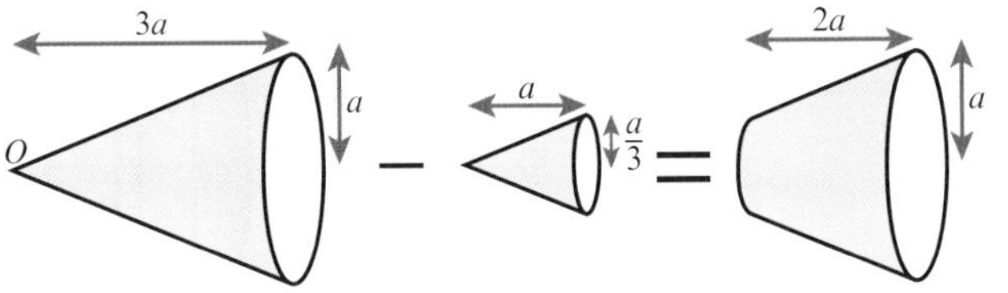

Large cone mass is $\frac{1}{3}\pi a^2\rho \times 3a = \pi a^3\rho$.

First, find the mass of the frustum from the difference in the masses of the two cones.

Small cone mass is $\frac{1}{3}\pi\left(\frac{a}{3}\right)^2\rho \times a = \frac{1}{27}\pi a^3\rho$.

So the mass of the frustum is $\frac{26}{27}\pi a^3\rho$.

From O ↻:

Use the vertex of the larger cone to take moments.

$\pi a^3\rho \times \frac{3}{4} \times 3a - \frac{1}{27}\pi a^3\rho \times \frac{3}{4} \times a = \frac{26}{27}\pi a^3\rho\bar{x}$

So $\bar{x} = \frac{30}{13}a$.

So from the smaller plane face $\frac{30}{13}a - a = \frac{17}{13}a$.

Subtract a from this result to get the distance from the smaller plane face.

WORKED EXAMPLE 14.12

A solid uniform cylinder, of radius $2a$ and length $6a$, has a cone of height $3a$ and base radius a removed from it. The cone removed has its axis of symmetry coinciding with that of the cylinder, and the plane face of the cone lies in the same plane as one end of the cylinder. Find the centre of mass of the remaining solid when measured from the opposite plane face of the cylinder.

Answer

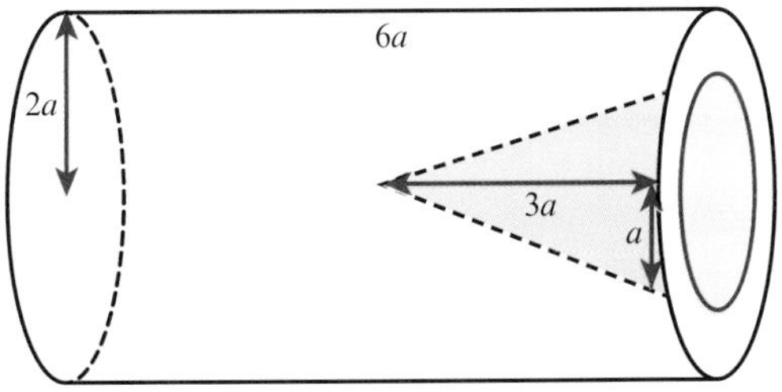

Visualising the solid makes the question much easier.

Mass of cylinder is $4\pi a^2 \times 6a\rho = 24\pi a^3\rho$.

Find the mass of each part, subtracting the mass of the cone to get the mass of the remaining solid.

Mass of cone is $\frac{1}{3}\pi a^2 \times 3a\rho = \pi a^3\rho$.

Mass of remaining solid is $23\pi a^3\rho$.

About the opposite face ↺:

Take moments about the opposite end. Remember the vertex of the cone is a distance of $3a$ from that face.

$24\pi a^3\rho \times 3a - \pi a^3\rho \times \left(3a + \frac{9}{4}a\right) = 23\pi a^3\rho\bar{x}$

So $\bar{x} = 2.90a$.

For a solid uniform hemisphere, consider a quarter circle of radius r that is rotated about the x-axis to form a solid. The hemisphere is made up of slices, and each slice has radius y and thickness $\mathrm{d}x$. As we calculated with the cone earlier, each slice has volume $\mathrm{d}V = \pi y^2\,\mathrm{d}x$.

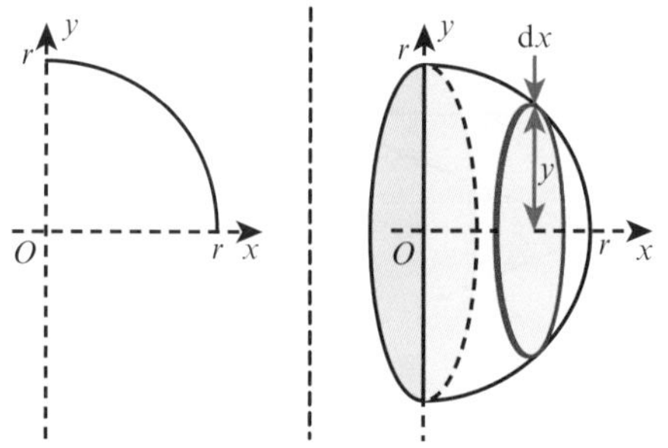

The equation of the circle is $x^2 + y^2 = r^2$.

Each slice is a distance of x from the y-axis, and so each slice is contributing to the moment of the whole hemisphere.

Let the mass of each slice be $\rho\pi y^2\mathrm{d}x$, and let the mass of the hemisphere be $\frac{2}{3}\rho\pi r^3$.

Then, taking moments about Oy for each slice, $\frac{2}{3}\rho\pi r^3\bar{x} = \int_0^r \rho\pi x(r^2 - x^2)\mathrm{d}x$, then integrating gives $\frac{2}{3}\pi r^3\bar{x} = \pi\left[\frac{1}{2}r^2x^2 - \frac{1}{4}x^4\right]_0^r$, then with the limits, $\frac{2}{3}\pi r^3\bar{x} = \pi\left(\frac{1}{4}r^4\right)$. Hence, $\bar{x} = \frac{3}{8}r$.

KEY POINT 14.7

For a solid hemisphere with radius r, the centre of mass is along the line of symmetry $\frac{3}{8}r$ from the centre of the plane face.

EXPLORE 14.1

Consider a solid uniform hemisphere, having centre O and radius r, with a smaller hemisphere, also with centre O but with radius x, removed from it. In groups, investigate what happens to the centre of mass of the remaining body as $x \to r$.

WORKED EXAMPLE 14.13

A solid uniform cylinder of radius $3r$ and length $6r$ is connected by one of its plane faces to a solid uniform hemisphere of radius $2r$. Their lines of symmetry coincide and the density of the hemisphere is twice that of the cylinder. Find the distance of the centre of mass of the solid from the plane face that is at the opposite end from where the hemisphere is connected.

Answer

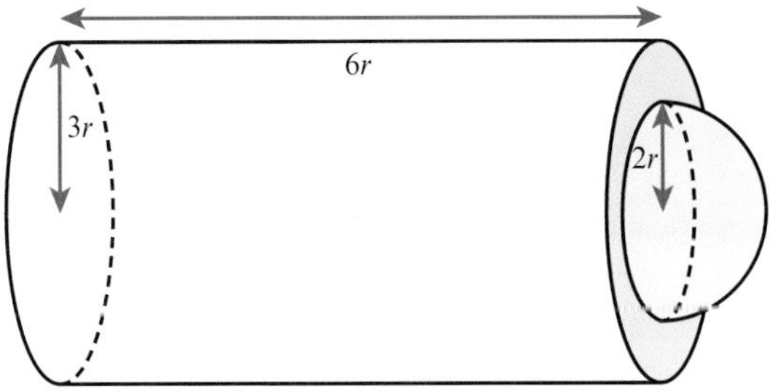

This diagram shows the situation described in the question.

You could also draw this as separate, smaller diagrams of the cylinder and the hemisphere.

Mass of cylinder: $\pi \times (3r)^2 \times 6r \times \rho = 54\pi r^3\rho$

Mass of hemisphere: $\frac{2}{3}\pi \times (2r)^3 \times 2\rho = \frac{32}{3}\pi r^3\rho$

Determine the mass of each part, remembering that the hemisphere has twice the density of the cylinder.

Mass of shape: $\frac{194}{3}\pi r^3\rho$

Add the results together.

About opposite face ↺:

Take moments about the opposite face to determine $\bar{x}$.

$$54\pi r^3\rho \times 3r + \frac{32}{3}\pi r^3\rho \times \left(6r + \frac{3}{8} \times 2r\right)$$
$$= \frac{194}{3}\pi r^3\rho\bar{x}$$

So $\bar{x} = \frac{351}{97}r$.

Consider that you are making a toy that is to be formed by attaching a hemisphere to a cone, as shown in the diagram.

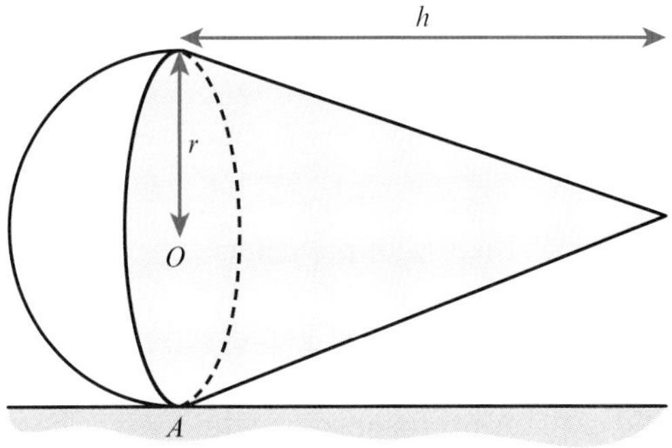

This shape will be placed with the point A on the ground, where A is a point on the rim of the hemisphere. The toy starts with OA vertical. We would like the toy to return to a stable position, that is when the apex (point) of the cone is vertically above O and OA is horizontal. We assume that the cone and the hemisphere are made from the same uniform material.

The mass of the hemisphere is $\frac{2}{3}\pi r^3\rho$ and the mass of the cone is $\frac{1}{3}\pi r^2 h\rho$.

Taking moments about OA ↺: $\frac{2}{3}\pi r^3\rho \times \frac{3}{8}r = \frac{1}{3}\pi r^2 h\rho \times \frac{1}{4}h$

Here we assume that the toy balances when OA is vertical, so we consider $h < \mathrm{f}(r)$.

Solving gives $r^2 = \frac{1}{3}h^2$, which simplifies to $h = \sqrt{3}r$. Since we want the toy to return to its upright position, this means that $h < \sqrt{3}r$.

WORKED EXAMPLE 14.14

A solid uniform hemisphere of radius $2r$ is joined to a solid uniform cone of height h and base radius r. The cone and hemisphere have their plane faces joined together. At the join, their lines of symmetry also coincide. If the cone is twice as dense as the hemisphere, find a relationship between h and r so that the shape can balance when both the plane faces are vertical.

Answer

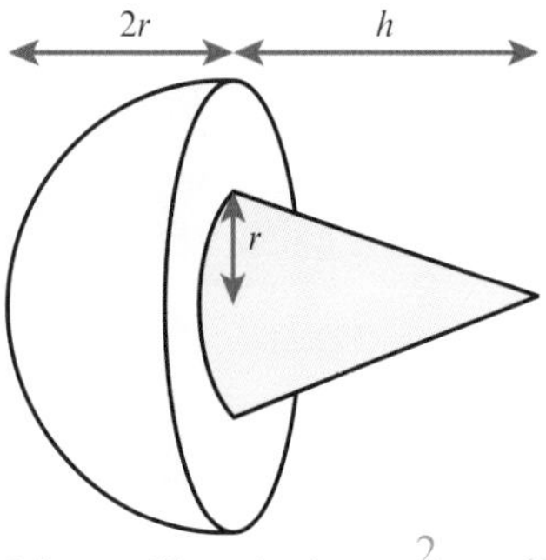

Remember that the cone is twice as dense as the hemisphere.

This object has its centre of mass at the join of the two plane faces.

Mass of hemisphere: $\frac{2}{3}\pi \times (2r)^3\rho = \frac{16}{3}\pi r^3\rho$

Mass of cone: $\frac{1}{3}\pi r^2 h \times 2\rho = \frac{2}{3}\pi r^2 h\rho$

Find the mass of each part. Notice that you do not need the total mass since the moments of the two parts must be equal for equilibrium.

Moments about the plane face:

Balance the turning effects and determine $h = \mathrm{f}(r)$.

$$\frac{16}{3}\pi r^3\rho \times \frac{3}{8} \times 2r = \frac{2}{3}\pi r^2 h\rho \times \frac{1}{4}h$$

So $4r^2 = \frac{1}{6}h^2$, which means $h = \sqrt{24}r$.

EXERCISE 14C

PS 1 A uniform solid cylinder, of radius r and length $4r$, has a uniform solid hemisphere of radius r, of the same material, attached to one of its plane faces. The plane faces of each solid coincide with each other. Find the distance of the centre of mass from the opposite plane face of the cylinder.

PS 2 Two uniform cones with base radius r are joined together by their plane faces. Their lines of symmetry are aligned. The height of one cone is $6r$ and the height of the other cone is $2r$.

Given that the smaller cone is 50% denser than the larger cone, find the distance of the centre of mass from their joint plane face.

PS 3 Find, by using integration, the centre of mass of a solid hemisphere of radius $2r$, measured from its plane face.

PS 4 A uniform solid cylinder has length $4a$ and radius $2a$ at each end. Centred on the plane faces are points A and B, respectively, such that AB is $4a$. At the plane face B, a hemisphere, of radius $2a$ and centre B, is removed from the cylinder. Find the centre of mass of the remaining solid from the point A.

PS 5 A uniform solid cone, C_1, of base radius $1.5r$ and height $4r$, is connected to another uniform solid cone, C_2, of base radius $1.5r$ and height r. Given that the cones are connected by the faces of their planes, and that C_2 is three times as dense as C_1, find the centre of mass from the vertex of C_1.

PS 6 A toy is constructed by joining a hemisphere to a cone by their plane faces. Both the hemisphere and cone have the same radius, r, and the cone has height $10r$. Given that the density of the cone is ρ, and that the density of the hemisphere is $k\rho$, find the value of k such that the toy can balance when the joint face is vertical.

PS 7 The diagram shows a cylinder with a hemisphere removed from one end, and a cone attached to the other end. Each part is solid and its mass uniformly distributed. The density of the cone is twice that of the cylinder. Find the centre of mass from the vertex of the cone.

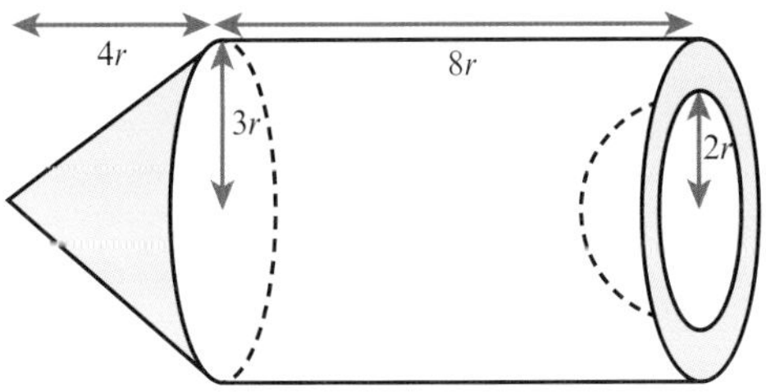

PS 8 The diagram shows two uniform solid cylinders. The larger cylinder has density ρ and the smaller cylinder has density $k\rho$. The cylinders are joined together by the faces of their planes, and their lines of symmetry coincide. Find the distance of the centre of mass from the plane face that joins the two cylinders.

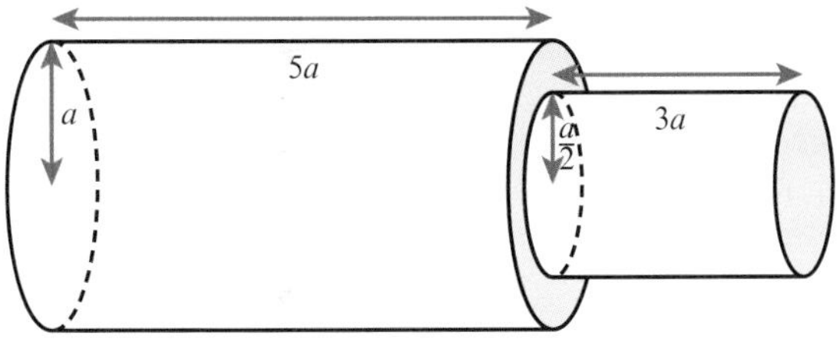

14.4 Objects in equilibrium

Consider a uniform ladder, AB, resting against a smooth vertical wall and a rough horizontal floor. The ladder has a length of $2a$ and mass m. The ladder makes an angle of θ with the wall, where $\tan\theta = \frac{3}{4}$.

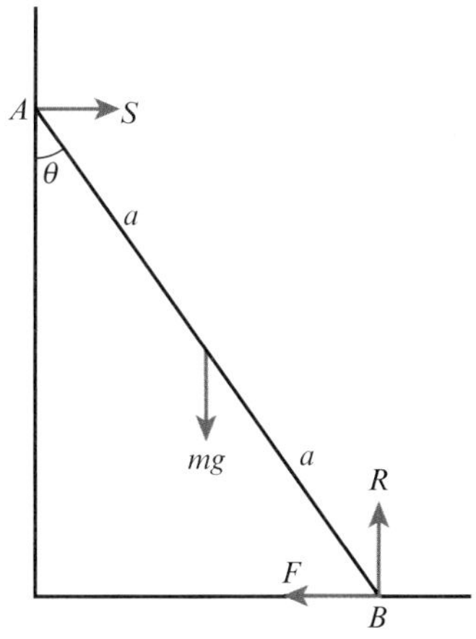

Can we find the range of values for the coefficient of friction that would keep the ladder from slipping?

First, we resolve forces horizontally to get $F = S$. Then we resolve forces vertically to get $R = mg$. If the ladder is to be prevented from slipping, then $F \leqslant \mu R$.

Next, take moments about B ↺: $S \times 2a\cos\theta = mg \times a\sin\theta$

With $\sin\theta = \frac{3}{5}$, $\cos\theta = \frac{4}{5}$, we get $S = \frac{3}{8}mg$. Since $F = S$, $F = \frac{3}{8}mg$, then $\frac{3}{8}mg \leqslant \mu mg$, which leads to $\mu \geqslant \frac{3}{8}$.

WORKED EXAMPLE 14.15

A uniform ladder is placed against a smooth vertical wall and rough horizontal floor. The ladder is of length a and mass $2m$. The ladder is placed such that the angle between the ladder and vertical wall is 30°. A painter, of mass $5m$, stands one-quarter of the way up the ladder and the ladder is on the point of slipping. Find the minimum coefficient of friction required to prevent the ladder from slipping.

Answer

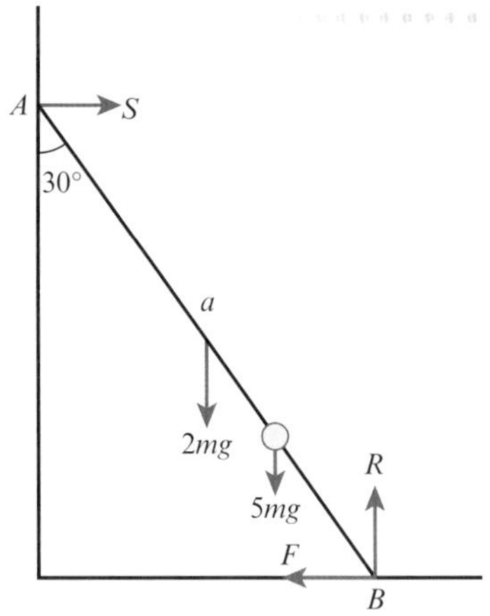

Make sure you have a fully labelled clear diagram, showing forces and angles.

$R(\rightarrow)$: $S = F$ and $R(\uparrow)$: $R = 7mg$.

Resolve forces in both directions.

About B ↻:

Take moments about a point that eliminates the most unknown forces.

$S \times a\cos 30 = 2mg \times \frac{a}{2}\sin 30 + 5mg \times \frac{a}{4}\sin 30$

Hence, $S = \frac{3\sqrt{3}}{4}mg$.

Determine S.

Then, using $F \leqslant \mu R$, $\frac{3\sqrt{3}}{4}mg \leqslant \mu \times 7mg$,

Recall that $F = S = \frac{3\sqrt{3}}{4}mg$ and use it to find μ.

so $\mu_{\text{min}} = \frac{3\sqrt{3}}{28}$.

EXPLORE 14.2

Discuss in groups the situations when μ is quite large and close to 1. Can the value of μ be greater than 1? If so, in what situations would this occur? Research online to support your discussions and findings.

WORKED EXAMPLE 14.16

A uniform rod of mass m and length $2a$ is held in equilibrium by a light, inelastic string of length $2a$, and by a frictional force due to the rod's contact with a rough vertical wall. The angle between the string and the rod is 60°, as shown in the diagram. The rod is on the point of slipping downwards.

By resolving forces, and taking moments at an appropriate point, find a range of values for μ so that the rod does slip down.

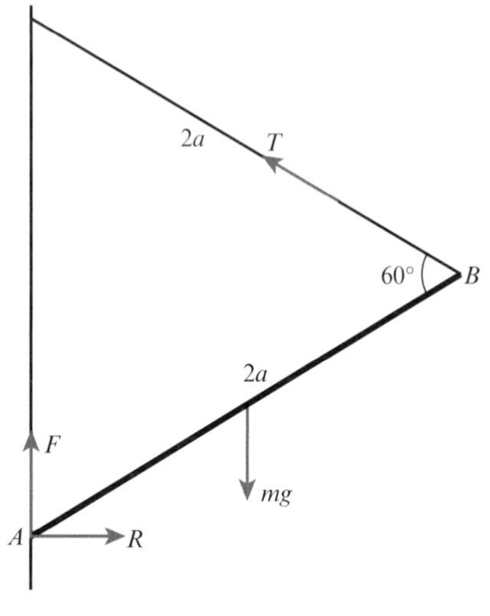

Answer

$R(\rightarrow)$: $R = T\cos 30$ — Resolve forces both horizontally and vertically.

$R(\uparrow)$: $T\cos 60 + F = mg$

About A ↺: $mg \times a\sin 60 = T\cos 30 \times 2a\cos 60 + T\sin 30 \times 2a\sin 60$ — Take moments about A.

This gives $T = \frac{1}{2}mg$. So $F = \frac{3}{4}mg$ and $R = \frac{\sqrt{3}}{4}mg$. — Evaluate T.

Then, using $F \leqslant \mu R$, $\frac{3}{4} \leqslant \frac{\mu\sqrt{3}}{4}$ or $\mu \geqslant \sqrt{3}$. — Use limiting friction to establish a range of values for μ.

Since we want the rod to slip, we need $\mu < \sqrt{3}$. — State the correct range.

Consider a rectangular block placed on a rough, sloping plane and imagine that the coefficient of friction is large enough to prevent the block from slipping. The block has dimensions $a \times 2a \times 3a$, where $3a$ is the depth of the block.

The slope is slowly raised so that the angle increases until the object topples over. We need to find the angle at which the block is about to topple.

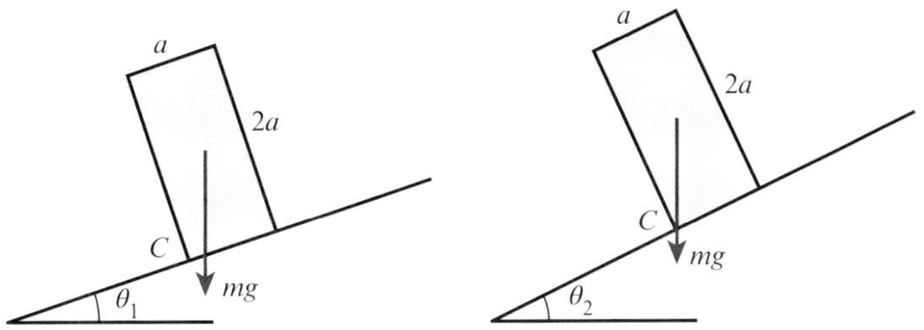

When the block is about to topple, its centre of mass will pass through the last point on the edge of the block that contacts the slope. In this case, the centre of mass is vertically above the point C.

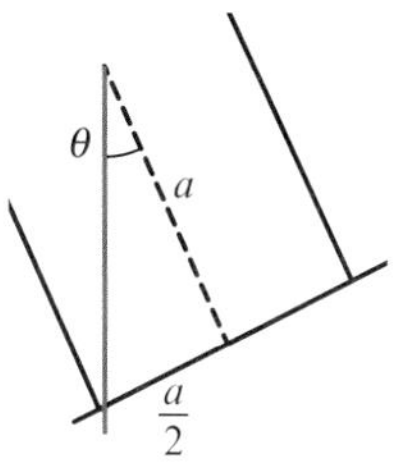

Notice that there is a small triangle that contains all the information we require. So when the block is about to topple, the angle θ can be found by considering $\tan\theta = \frac{a}{2a} = \frac{1}{2}$.

So the block topples when $\theta = 26.6°$.

WORKED EXAMPLE 14.17

A solid uniform hemisphere is placed on a rough slope, with its plane face against the slope. Assume the friction force is great enough to prevent the hemisphere from slipping.

If the slope is inclined at an angle of 65°, state whether or not the hemisphere topples. Justify your answer.

If it does not topple, what is the maximum possible angle of inclination of the slope?

Answer

Let the radius be r. — Quote the standard result for solid uniform hemispheres (see Section 14.3).

Then, using the standard formula for hemispheres, the distance from the slope to the point G is $\frac{3}{8}r$.

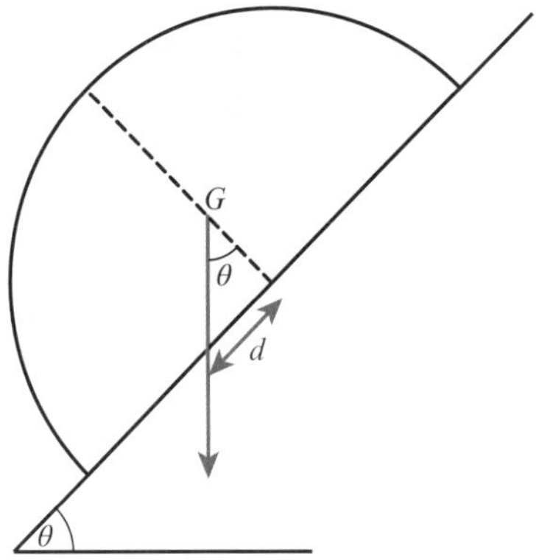

From the diagram we need the length $d = r$ for the hemisphere to topple.

Note that the weight passes through the lowest point only when $d = r$.

Clearly $\tan\theta = \frac{d}{\frac{3}{8}r}$, or $d = \frac{3}{8}r\tan\theta$.

Using $\theta = 65°$, $d = \frac{3}{8}r \times 2.145 = 0.804r$, and since this is less than r, we can conclude that the hemisphere does not topple.

Use the given angle to determine d and show it is less than r.

State that it does not topple.

The maximum angle comes from $r = \frac{3}{8}r\tan\theta$, or $\tan\theta = \frac{8}{3}$.

Find the maximum angle, derived from $d = r$.

So the maximum angle is 69.4°.

WORKED EXAMPLE 14.18

A shape is formed by joining a solid uniform cylinder to a solid uniform cone. The cylinder has radius r and height r; the cone has base radius r and height $2r$. The two solids are joined by a plane face, and the lines of symmetry of the two solids coincide. This shape is placed on a rough slope, as shown in the diagram.

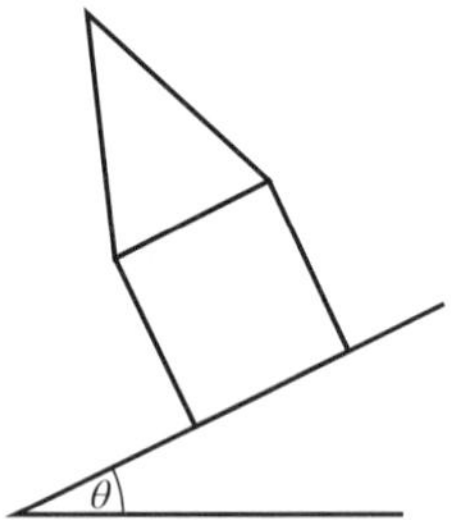

If the slope is sufficiently rough to prevent sliding, find the angle at which the shape is about to topple.

Answer

Start with the centre of mass:

Mass of cylinder is $\pi r^3\rho$.

Mass of cone is $\frac{2}{3}\pi r^3\rho$.

Find the mass of each part, then work out the total mass.

So total mass of solid is $\frac{5}{3}\pi r^3\rho$.

About base ↻: $\pi r^3\rho \times \frac{r}{2} + \frac{2}{3}\pi r^3\rho \times \left(r + \frac{r}{2}\right) = \frac{5}{3}\pi r^3\rho\bar{y}$

So $\bar{y} = \frac{9}{10}r$.

Take moments to find the position of the centre of mass above the slope.

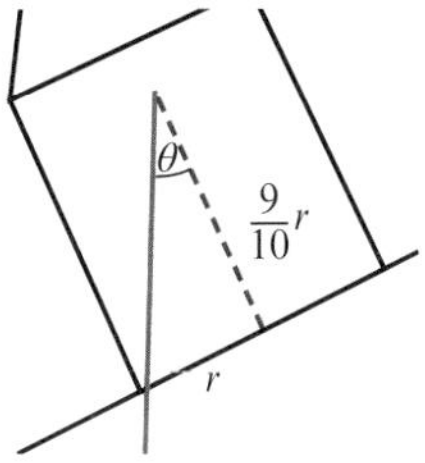

Observe from the diagram that the required angle is θ, and $\tan\theta = \frac{r}{\frac{9}{10}r}$.

Therefore, $\theta = 48.0°$.

Next, work out the angle when the shape is about to topple. Use the centre of mass along with the cylinder's radius to determine the angle required.

Until now, we have been working with objects on a surface. We shall also consider objects that are suspended by a given point.

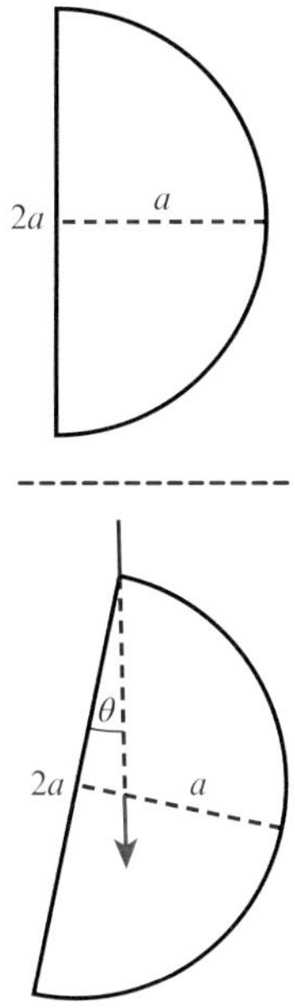

For example, consider a letter D made from uniform wire. We shall model the D as a rod of length $2a$, and a semicircle of radius a.

If we hang the letter D from one of its corners, can we find the angle between the rod and the vertical?

We must first find the centre of mass for the D (see Section 14.2). To do this we need to know the masses. The mass of the rod is $2a\rho$, the mass of the curved part is $\pi a\rho$, and the total is $(\pi + 2)a\rho$.

Take moments about the rod ↻: $2a\rho \times 0 + \pi a\rho \times \frac{2a}{\pi} = (\pi + 2)a\rho\bar{x}$, then $\bar{x} = \frac{2a}{\pi + 2}$.

From the lower part of the diagram we can see that $\tan\theta = \frac{\bar{x}}{a}$, which gives $\tan\theta = \frac{2}{\pi + 2}$.

So the angle between the rod and the vertical is $\theta = 21.3°$.

WORKED EXAMPLE 14.19

An L-shaped uniform lamina is formed by joining two rectangles together, as shown in the diagram.

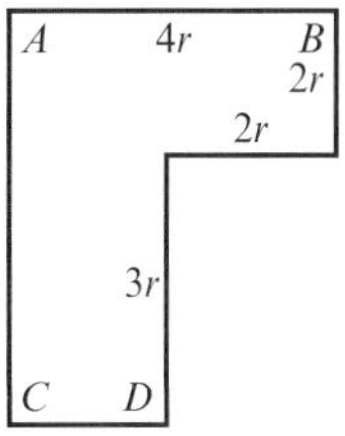

a Find the centre of mass of the lamina from the edges AB and AC.

The shape is then suspended from the point A.

b Find the angle between AB and the vertical.

Answer

a Split into $2r \times 5r$ and $2r \times 2r$. — Separate the lamina into smaller parts.

About AC ↻: — Take moments about two perpendicular edges to determine the centre of mass.

$10r^2\rho \times r + 4r^2\rho \times 3r = 14r^2\rho\bar{x}$, so $\bar{x} = \frac{11}{7}r$.

About AB ↻:

$10r^2\rho \times \frac{5}{2}r + 4r^2\rho \times r = 14r^2\rho\bar{y}$, so $\bar{y} = \frac{29}{14}r$.

b Using $\tan\theta = \frac{\bar{y}}{\bar{x}}$ leads to $\tan\theta = \frac{29}{22}$. — Write down the tangent of the angle in terms of $\bar{x}, \bar{y}$.

And so $\theta = 52.8°$.

WORKED EXAMPLE 14.20

The diagram shows a solid uniform cone joined to a solid uniform hemisphere. The cone has base radius r and height $3r$, and the hemisphere has radius r. The two shapes are joined by their plane faces, and AB is a diameter on that plane face.

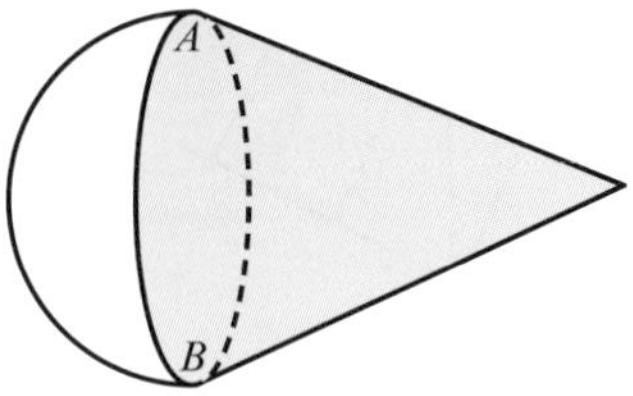

If the density of the cone is four times that of the hemisphere, find the position of the centre of mass relative to the line AB. The shape is then suspended from point A. Find the angle AB makes with the vertical.

Answer

Mass of cone is $\frac{1}{3}\pi r^2 \times 3r \times 4\rho = 4\pi r^3\rho$. — Determine the mass of each part first.

Mass of hemisphere is $\frac{2}{3}\pi r^3\rho$.

Total mass is $\frac{14}{3}\pi r^3\rho$. — Total mass for the whole solid.

About AB ↺: — Take moments about the diameter AB.

$4\pi r^3\rho \times \frac{3}{4}r - \frac{2}{3}\pi r^3\rho \times \frac{3}{8}r = \frac{14}{3}\pi r^3\rho\bar{x}$

Simplify: $\bar{x} = \frac{33}{56}r$ — Obtain $\bar{x}$.

For the angle, $\tan\theta = \frac{\frac{33}{56}r}{r}$, which gives $\theta = 30.5°$. — Use this in a triangle with adjacent side equal to the radius r.

Lastly, we shall look at objects sliding versus toppling. Consider a cuboid of dimensions $2a \times 2a \times 4a$ and mass m resting on rough, horizontal ground. We are going to apply a force X at the top edge of the cuboid. This force will either make the cuboid slide along the ground or make it topple about O.

As the force X increases, the reaction force gets closer and closer to the point O, and unless the cuboid slides it will topple over.

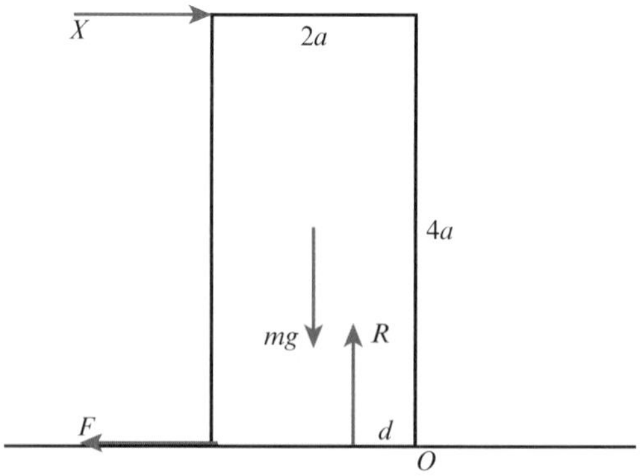

So resolving and taking moments, $R(\rightarrow)$: $X = F$, $R(\uparrow)$: $R = mg$.

Then taking moments about O ↺: $X \times 4a + R \times d = mg \times a$

So $X = \frac{mga - mgd}{4a}$.

If $X = 0$, $d = a$, so the reaction force is midway along the edge that touches the ground.

If $X = \frac{1}{4}mg$ then $mga = mga - mgd$, which gives $d = 0$. This means the cuboid is on the point of toppling. Now we consider the possibility of sliding. If $X = F = \mu R$, then if $\mu > \frac{1}{4}$, the cuboid will topple before sliding.

If $X = \frac{1}{6}mg$ and $\mu = \frac{1}{8}$, we note that $X = \frac{mga - mgd}{4a}$ gives $d = \frac{1}{3}a$, which means the shape will not topple. Then, noting that $F_{\max} = \frac{1}{8}mg$ means that $X > F$, and we can see that the cuboid slides.

WORKED EXAMPLE 14.21

A uniform right-angled triangular prism, of mass m, is resting on a rough horizontal surface, as shown in the diagram. The triangle has sides a, $2a$, $\sqrt{5}a$ and the depth of the prism is a. A force, X, is applied to the top edge, as shown.

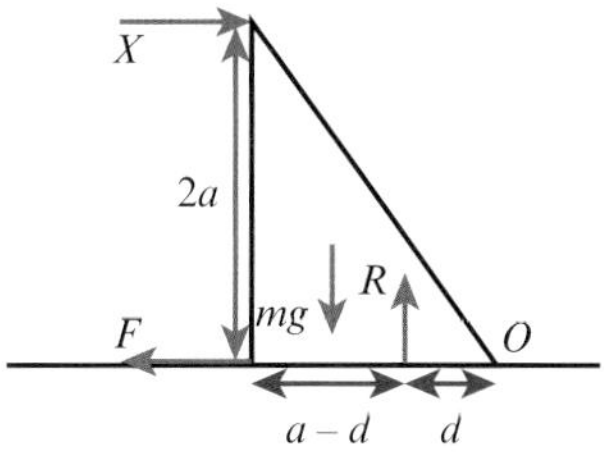

Determine in each case whether or not the prism breaks equilibrium. If it does, determine if it slides or topples.

a $X = \frac{1}{5}mg, \mu = \frac{3}{4}$ **b** $X = \frac{1}{4}mg, \mu = \frac{1}{5}$ **c** $X = \frac{1}{3}mg, \mu = \frac{1}{2}$

Answer

a Resolving $R(\rightarrow)$: $X = F$ and $R(\uparrow)$: $R = mg$.

Always resolve forces, then take moments to set up your system.

Moments about O ↺: $X \times 2a + R \times d = mg \times \frac{2}{3}a$

So $X = \dfrac{\frac{2}{3}mga - mgd}{2a}$.

So $X = \frac{1}{5}mg \Rightarrow d = \frac{4}{15}a$ so it will not topple.

$d > 0$ so it will not topple.

Using $F = \mu R$ we get $F = \frac{3}{4}mg > \frac{1}{5}mg$ so it will not slide.

$F > X$ so it will not slide.

Equilibrium is not broken.

b With $X = \frac{1}{4}mg \Rightarrow d = \frac{1}{6}a$ so it will not topple.

$d > 0$ so it will not topple.

$F = \frac{1}{5}mg < \frac{1}{4}mg$ so the prism breaks equilibrium by sliding.

$F < X$ so sliding occurs.

c With $X = \frac{1}{3}mg \Rightarrow d = 0$ so the prism is about to topple.

$d = 0$ so toppling occurs.

$F = \frac{1}{2}mg > \frac{1}{3}mg$ so the prism topples but doesn't slide.

$F > X$ so it will not slide.

WORKED EXAMPLE 14.22

A solid uniform cone, of base radius r and height $4r$, is placed on a rough plane inclined at an angle θ, as shown in the diagram.

The coefficient of friction between the cone and the plane is 0.5. The plane is hinged at the bottom, and it is slowly rotated so that θ increases. Giving a justification for your answer, determine whether or not the cone topples before it slides.

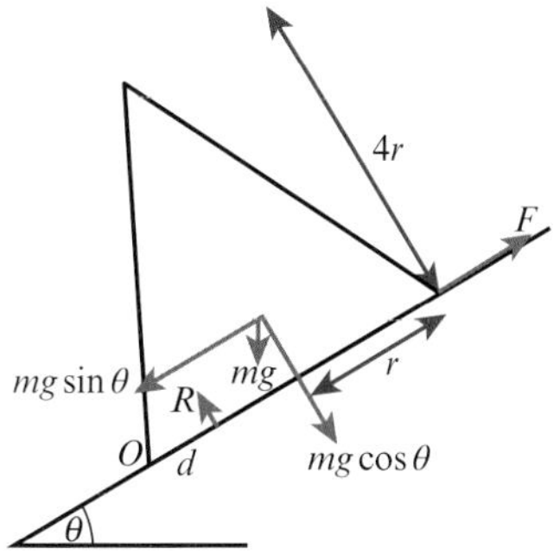

Answer

Resolving $R(\nearrow)$: $F = mg\sin\theta$ and $R(\nwarrow)$: $R = mg\cos\theta$.

Resolve forces parallel to the plane and perpendicular to the plane.

Taking moments about O ↺: $R \times d + mg\sin\theta \times \frac{1}{4} \times 4r$

$= mg\cos\theta \times r$

Split mg into components and take moments about the bottom point of contact, O.

Rearranging gives $d = \frac{mgr\cos\theta - mgr\sin\theta}{mg\cos\theta}$.

So if $d = 0$ then $\cos\theta = \sin\theta \Rightarrow \theta = 45°$. So the cone will be on the point of toppling if this angle is reached.

Determine the limit for toppling.

Assuming the cone is on the point of sliding, $mg\sin\theta = \mu mg\cos\theta$, hence $\mu = \tan\theta$.

Use the resolved results to find the sliding limit.

Since $\mu = 0.5$, $\theta = 26.6$.

So the cone will slide before it topples, when θ is 26.6°.

State how equilibrium is broken.

EXERCISE 14D

1 A uniform solid cylinder, of radius r and height $5r$, is suspended from a point on the rim of its plane face. It is allowed to rest in equilibrium. Find the angle between the plane face of the cylinder and the downwards vertical.

PS 2 A uniform solid cylinder, of radius $2r$ and height $7r$, is resting on a sufficiently rough slope. The slope is inclined at an angle α. Find the maximum value of α such that the cylinder is on the point of toppling.

PS 3 A ladder of length $4a$ is placed such that it rests against a smooth vertical wall and stands upon a rough horizontal floor. The angle between the ladder and the wall is 30°. The ladder has mass $2m$. Find the range of values of the coefficient of friction, μ, so that the ladder does not slip.

PS 4 A solid uniform cone, of base radius $2a$ and height $5a$, is suspended by a point, B, on the rim of its circular base. The centre of the circular base is denoted by C. Find the angle BC makes with the vertical.

5 The diagram shows a uniform lamina in the shape of a trapezium. The lamina is suspended from the point A. Find the angle between the vertical and the edge AB.

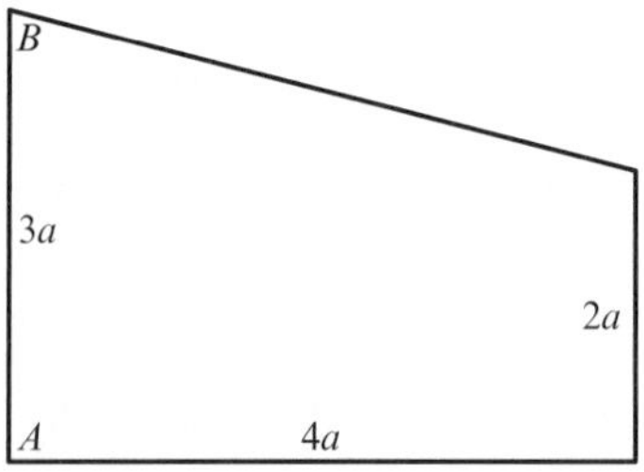

PS M 6 A uniform ladder, of length $2a$ and mass m, is resting against a smooth vertical wall and a rough horizontal floor. The ladder is making an angle of 30° with the wall, and the coefficient of friction between the ladder and the floor is $\frac{1}{2\sqrt{3}}$. An electrician, of mass $8m$, is trying to ascend the ladder. Determine how far they can walk up the ladder before it slips.

M 7 The diagram shows a uniform rod, of mass m and length $2a$, smoothly hinged to a vertical wall. A light, inelastic string connects the rod to a point on the wall above the hinge. Find the magnitude and direction of the force on the rod from the hinge.

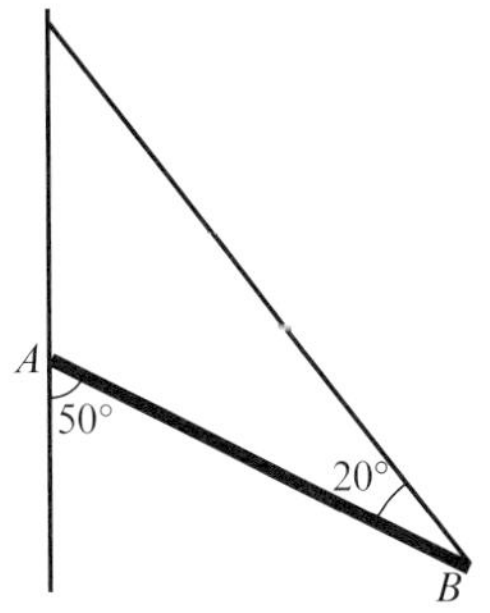

PS 8 A solid uniform cone, of base radius r and height $6r$, has a similar smaller cone of height $2r$ removed from the top to form a frustum. This frustum is placed, with its larger plane face, on a rough surface that is hinged to the floor at one edge. The surface is slowly rotated so that the incline angle increases. Given that the coefficient of friction is 0.85, find whether the frustum breaks equilibrium by toppling or sliding.

PS M 9 A solid uniform hemisphere, of radius r, is placed onto a rough plane inclined at 45° to the horizontal. A force, P, parallel to and up the plane, is applied to the hemisphere at a point that is $\frac{r}{2}$ above the surface of the plane. The highest point on the rim of the hemisphere that touches the plane is denoted by A.

a Assuming that the friction is great enough to prevent slipping, find the value of P required to make the hemisphere topple up the plane. Give your answer in terms of m and g.

b Let $\mu = \frac{3}{4}$ and let the hemisphere be on the point of slipping up the plane. Find the distance between the reaction force and the point A.

WORKED PAST PAPER QUESTION

Uniform rods AB, AC and BC have lengths 3 m, 4 m and 5 m respectively, and weights 15 N, 20 N and 25 N respectively. The rods are rigidly joined to form a right-angled triangular frame ABC. The frame is hinged at B to a fixed point and is held in equilibrium, with AC horizontal, by means of an inextensible string attached at C. The string is at right angles to BC and the tension in the string is T N (see diagram).

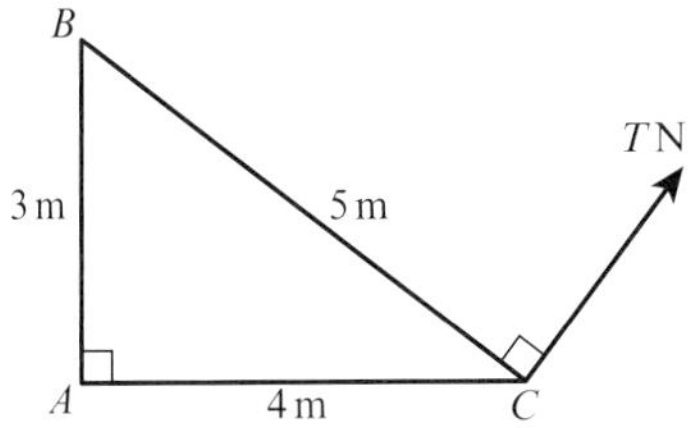

i Find the value of T.

A uniform triangular lamina PQR, of weight 60 N, has the same size and shape as the frame ABC. The lamina is now attached to the frame with P, Q and R at A, B and C respectively. The composite body is held in equilibrium with A, B and C in the same positions as before. Find

ii the new value of T.

iii the magnitude of the vertical component of the force acting on the composite body at B.

Cambridge International AS & A Level Mathematics 9709 Paper 5 Q4 June 2008

Answer

i

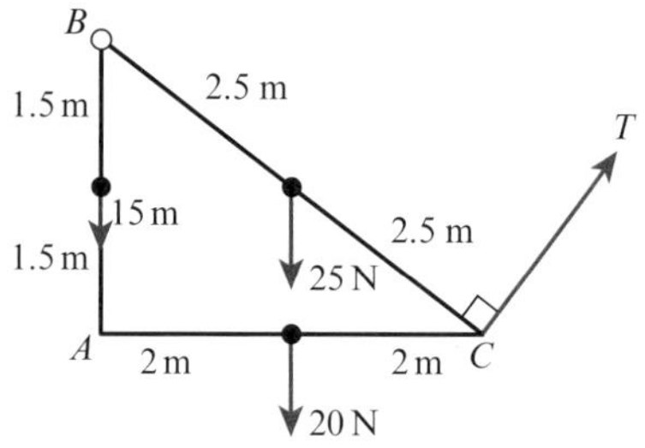

Moments about B ↻: $20 \times 2 + 25 \times 2 = 5T$. Hence, $T = 18$ N.

ii

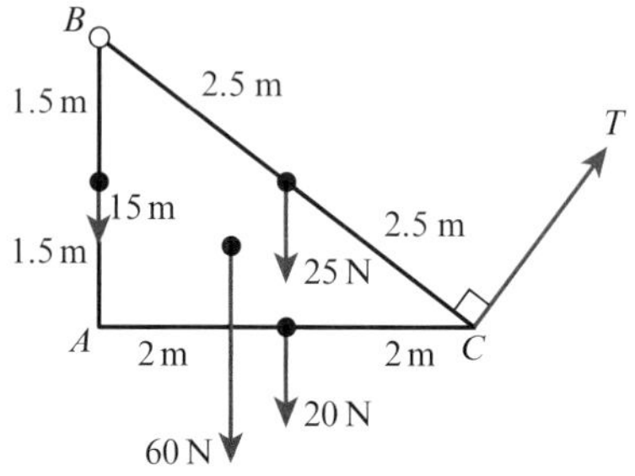

Moments about B ↻: $20 \times 2 + 25 \times 2 + 60 \times \frac{1}{3} \times 4 = 5T$. Hence, $T = 34$ N.

iii Let the force be Y, then $R(\uparrow)$: $Y + T \times \frac{4}{5} = 15 + 20 + 25 + 60$. Hence, $Y = 92.8$ N.

Checklist of learning and understanding

Moment of a force:

- A force F with perpendicular distance d from a point O has moment Fd about the point O.

Centres of mass, 2D lamina and frameworks:

- For a composite body made up of masses $m_1, m_2, \ldots$ with distances $x_1, x_2, \ldots,$ from a reference point respectively, the distance of the centre of mass from the reference point is $\bar{x} = \frac{\Sigma x_i m_i}{\Sigma m_i}$.
- For a triangular lamina the centre of mass is $\left(\frac{x_1 + x_2 + x_3}{3}, \frac{y_1 + y_2 + y_3}{3}\right)$, where (x_1, y_1), (x_2, y_2) and (x_3, x_3) are the coordinates of the vertices of the triangle.
- For a lamina of a sector of angle 2α radians from a circle centre O, with radius r, the centre of mass is $\frac{2r \sin \alpha}{3\alpha}$ from the centre of the circle.
- For an arc of a circle of angle 2α radians from a circle centre O, with radius r, the centre of mass is $\frac{r \sin \alpha}{\alpha}$ from the centre of the circle.

Centres of mass, 3D solids:

- For a right circular cone, with height h, the centre of mass is along the line of symmetry through the vertex, at a distance $\frac{3}{4}h$ from the vertex of the cone.
- For a solid hemisphere with radius r, the centre of mass is along the line of symmetry $\frac{3}{8}r$ from the centre of the plane face.

END-OF-CHAPTER REVIEW EXERCISE 14

1 A uniform beam AB has length 2 m and weight 70 N. The beam is hinged at A to a fixed point on a vertical wall, and is held in equilibrium by a light inextensible rope. One end of the rope is attached to the wall at a point 1.7 m vertically above the hinge. The other end of the rope is attached to the beam at a point 0.8 m from A. The rope is at right angles to AB. The beam carries a load of weight 220 N at B (see diagram).

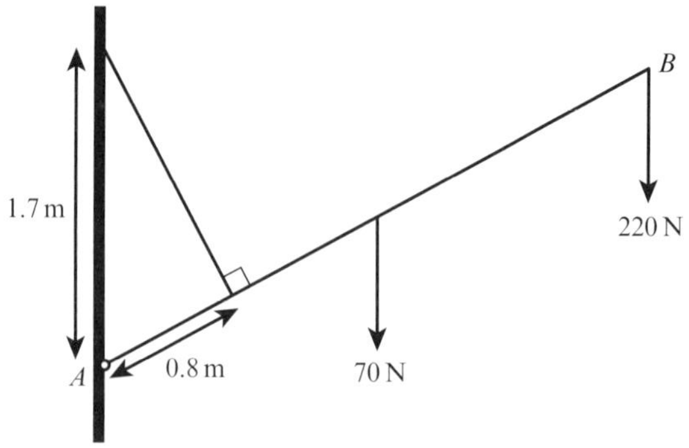

i Find the tension in the rope.

ii Find the direction of the force exerted on the beam at A.

Cambridge International AS & A Level Mathematics 9709 Paper 51 Q4 November 2010

2 A uniform rod AB has weight 6 N and length 0.8 m. The rod rests in limiting equilibrium with B in contact with a rough horizontal surface and AB inclined at 60° to the horizontal. Equilibrium is maintained by a force, in the vertical plane containing AB, acting at A at an angle of 45° to AB (see diagram). Calculate

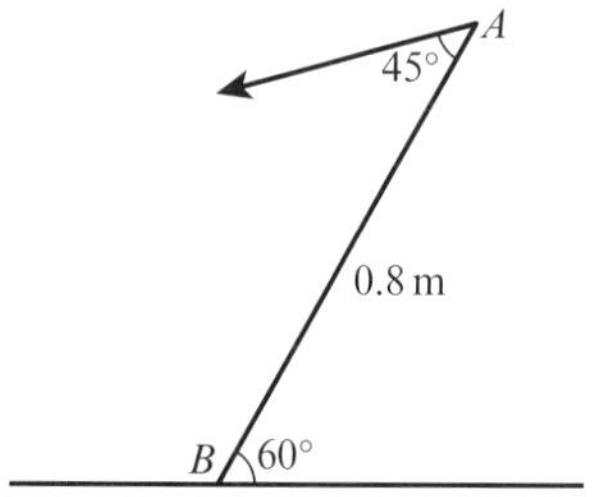

i the magnitude of the force applied at A,

ii the least possible value of the coefficient of friction at B.

Cambridge International AS & A Level Mathematics 9709 Paper 51 Q2 November 2012

3 The diagram shows the cross-section $OABCDE$ through the centre of mass of a uniform prism on a rough inclined plane. The portion $ADEO$ is a rectangle in which $AD = OE = 0.6$ m and $DE = AO = 0.8$ m; the portion BCD is an isosceles triangle in which angle BCD is a right angle, and A is the mid-point of BD. The plane is inclined at 45° to the horizontal, BC lies along a line of greatest slope of the plane and DE is horizontal.

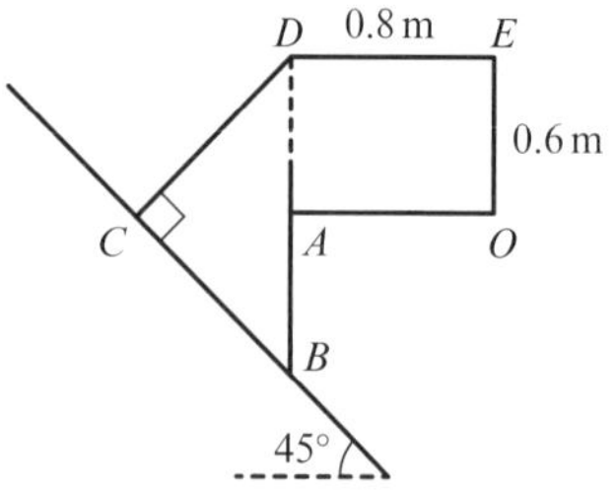

i Calculate the distance of the centre of mass of the prism from BD.

The weight of the prism is 21 N, and it is held in equilibrium by a horizontal force of magnitude P N acting along ED.

ii a Find the smallest value of P for which the prism does not topple.

b It is given that the prism is about to slip for this smallest value of P. Calculate the coefficient of friction between the prism and the plane.

The value of P is gradually increased until the prism ceases to be in equilibrium.

iii Show that the prism topples before it begins to slide, stating the value of P at which equilibrium is broken.

Cambridge International AS & A Level Mathematics 9709 Paper 51 Q7 June 2015

Chapter 15
Circular motion

In this chapter you will learn how to:

- relate angular speed (measured in rad s^{-1}) and linear speed
- apply the formula $r\omega^2$ or $\frac{v^2}{r}$ (for the acceleration towards the centre of a circle) to problems involving horizontal circles and conical pendulums with constant angular speed and to problems involving vertical circles without any loss in energy.

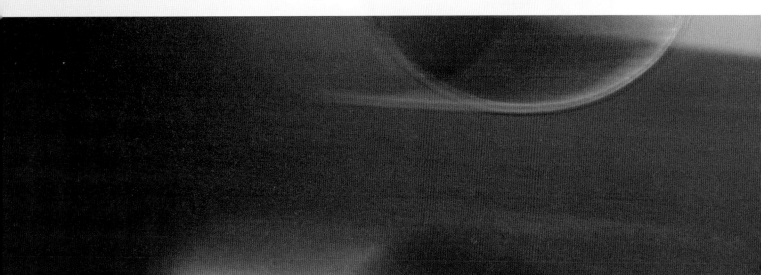

PREREQUISITE KNOWLEDGE

Where it comes from	What you should be able to do	Check your skills
AS & A Level Mathematics Mechanics, Chapter 3	Resolve forces in two perpendicular directions.	**1** Find the magnitude and direction of the resultant of the forces shown. 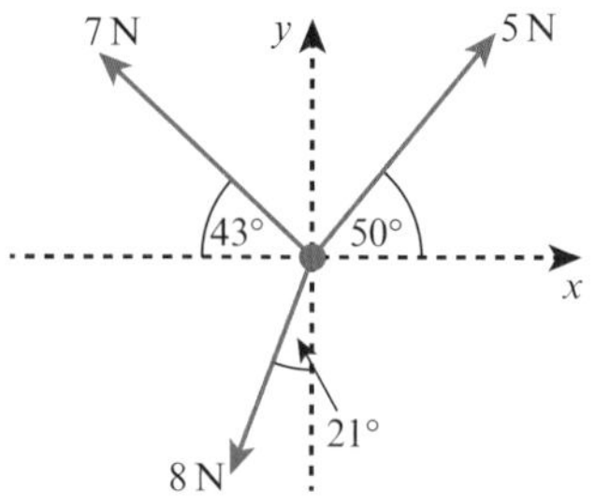
AS & A Level Mathematics Mechanics, Chapters 2 & 3	Apply Newton's second law with multiple forces.	**2** A block on rough horizontal ground is subject to three forces: a pulling force of magnitude 17.8 N acting at 20° above the horizontal; a horizontal pushing force, in the same direction as the pulling force, of magnitude 8.9 N; and a resisting force of magnitude 22.3 N. If the block has mass 4 kg, find the acceleration of the block.
AS & A Level Mathematics Mechanics, Chapters 8 & 9	Calculate the potential energy and kinetic energy of a system at any point during its motion.	**3** A particle of mass 1.5 kg is projected up a smooth slope inclined at 25°. The particle has initial speed 22 m s^{-1}. If the particle travels 5 m up the slope, what is its speed at that point?

What is circular motion?

Circular motion is the motion of a particle around part or all of a circular path. The circle may be horizontal or vertical.

Examples of **circular motion** are all around us in real life, but some are more obvious than others. The pendulum on an old clock and a conker on a string both move with circular motion, but have you ever thought of cars racing in the Indianapolis 500 in the same way? Because the track is banked, the cars are moving in the same way as a steel ball around the inside of a circular bearing.

In this chapter we shall look at two types of circular motion: horizontal and vertical. We shall discover that the acceleration of a particle moving in a circle is directed towards the centre of the circle. We shall often use **conservation of energy** and Newton's second law to solve problems of circular motion.

In this chapter we shall use the symbols v for linear speed, ω for angular speed, r for radius, and a for acceleration. We shall use the abbreviations KE for kinetic energy and PE for potential energy.

Unless stated otherwise, $g = 10\,\text{m}\,\text{s}^{-2}$.

15.1 Horizontal circles

Consider a particle moving in a horizontal circular path with constant speed.

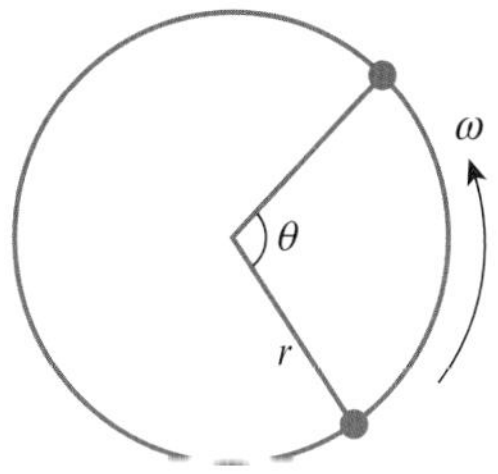

The path is an arc of a circle, measured as $r\theta$. The rate of change of this distance $\frac{d}{dt}(r\theta)$ is equal to $r\frac{d\theta}{dt}$. So we have the relation $v = r\frac{d\theta}{dt}$ or $v = r\omega$, as shown in Key point 15.1. The quantity $\omega = \frac{d\theta}{dt}$ is known as the **angular speed** and is constant.

KEY POINT 15.1

To calculate the speed of a particle moving with circular motion, use:

$$v = r\frac{d\theta}{dt} \quad \text{or} \quad v = r\omega$$

The formulae in Key point 15.1 imply that, the larger the circle, the greater the speed must be. The angular speed is the same whatever the size of the radius because it measures the angle of travel over time, as shown in Key point 15.2.

KEY POINT 15.2

The angular speed ω is measured in radians per second, denoted as rad s^{-1}. One complete cycle is 2π radians, so the frequency, the number of revolutions per second, is $\frac{2\pi}{\omega}$.

WORKED EXAMPLE 15.1

In each case, convert either angular speed to linear speed or linear speed to angular speed, or calculate both quantities, as appropriate:

a a particle travelling in a circular path of radius 5 m with angular speed $4\,\text{rad s}^{-1}$

b a particle travelling along a circular path of radius 2.5 m, with speed $4\,\text{m s}^{-1}$

c a particle travelling on a circular path with radius 2 m, where the time to cover one complete circle is 6 s

d the Earth travelling around the Sun, where the path is assumed to be circular and of radius 1.496×10^{11} m.

Answer

a Using $v = r\omega$, $v = 5 \times 4 = 20\,\text{m s}^{-1}$. — The first two examples just require you to substitute values into the formula.

b Using $v = r\omega$, $4 = 2.5\omega$. Hence, $\omega = 1.6\,\text{rad s}^{-1}$.

c Since 2π is covered in 6s, $\omega = \frac{2\pi}{6} = \frac{\pi}{3}\,\text{rad s}^{-1}$. — First determine the angular speed.

Then $v = 2 \times \frac{\pi}{3} = \frac{2\pi}{3}\,\text{m s}^{-1}$. — Then find the linear speed.

d First, consider that 365 days is 31 536 000 seconds. — Determine the number of seconds per year.

Then for a complete revolution: — Note the angular speed is very small.

$$\omega = \frac{2\pi}{31\,536\,000}$$
$$\approx 1.99 \times 10^{-7}\,\text{rad s}^{-1}$$

Use $v = r\omega$: — Calculate the linear speed.

$$v = 1.496 \times 10^{11} \times 1.992 \times 10^{-7}$$
$$= 29\,800\,\text{m s}^{-1}$$

As an object travels in a circular path, its direction of motion constantly changes.

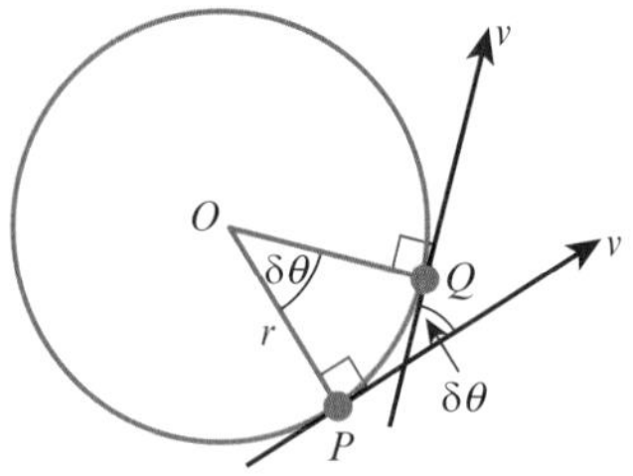

Because of this, the linear speed of the object is not actually constant. Consider two points on the path of a circle, P and Q. Let the angle POQ be very small, $\delta\theta$. At the point P we assume the speed is v. Then, since Q is very close to P, we can also assume that the speed at Q has the components $v\cos\delta\theta$ and $v\sin\delta\theta$, where these components are parallel and perpendicular to the tangent at P. Since $\sin\delta\theta \approx \delta\theta$ and $\cos\delta\theta \approx 1$, we can focus on the acceleration parallel and perpendicular to the tangent at P.

Since acceleration $= \dfrac{\text{change in speed}}{\text{change in time}}$, the parallel acceleration component is $\dfrac{v\cos\delta\theta - v}{\delta t} \approx 0$,

and the perpendicular acceleration component, acting towards the centre, is $\dfrac{v\sin\delta\theta - 0}{\delta t}$.

Hence, the acceleration acts towards the centre and is of magnitude $v\dfrac{\mathrm{d}\theta}{\mathrm{d}t}$. This is commonly written as $r\omega^2$ or $\dfrac{v^2}{r}$, as shown in Key point 15.3.

KEY POINT 15.3

The acceleration towards the centre for an object moving in circular motion is $a = \dfrac{v^2}{r}$ or $a = r\omega^2$.
The link between v and ω is $v = r\omega$.

Consider a particle travelling on a circular path of radius 1.2 m. Its speed is $3\,\text{m s}^{-1}$. If the mass of the particle is 2 kg, can we find the force towards the centre?

We begin with $F = ma = m\dfrac{v^2}{r}$.

Substituting the mass, radius and speed provided: $F = 2 \times \dfrac{3^2}{1.2}$

Hence, $F = 15\,\text{N}$.

WORKED EXAMPLE 15.2

In each case, find the force towards the centre:

a a particle of mass 1.5 kg, travelling with angular speed $4\,\text{rad s}^{-1}$, where the radius is 0.5 m

b a particle of mass 4 kg, travelling with speed $5\,\text{m s}^{-1}$, where the radius is 2.4 m

c a particle of mass 0.5 kg, travelling around a circle of radius 20 m in 12 s.

Answer

a Using $F = ma$, we have $F = mr\omega^2$.
So $F = 1.5 \times 0.5 \times 4^2$
$= 12\,\text{N}$

Note the type of speed and use the corresponding formula.

b Using $F = m\frac{v^2}{r}$, we have $4 \times \frac{5^2}{2.4}$.

So $F = \frac{125}{3}\,\text{N}$.

c First find $\omega = \frac{2\pi}{12} = \frac{\pi}{6}$.

Determine the angular speed before applying $F = ma$.

Then using $F = mr\omega^2$ gives $0.5 \times 20 \times \left(\frac{\pi}{6}\right)^2 = \frac{5\pi^2}{18} = 2.74\,\text{N}$.

Now that we understand the idea of acceleration towards the centre of the circle, let us look at an example in context. Consider a particle that is attached to one end of a light, inextensible string of length 2 m. The other end of the string is attached to a point on a smooth, horizontal table. The particle has mass 1.5 kg and it describes horizontal circles on the surface of the table with angular speed $4\,\text{rad}\,\text{s}^{-1}$. We want to find the tension in the string.

Start with $F = ma = mr\omega^2$, then $T = 1.5 \times 2 \times 4^2$, so the tension in the string is 48 N.

WORKED EXAMPLE 15.3

A particle is describing circles on a smooth, horizontal table. The particle is attached to a light, inelastic string that is attached to a point, O, where the radius of the circles is 1.2 m. Given that the tension in the string is 40 N, and that the particle can complete one circle in $\frac{5\pi}{3}$ s, find the mass of the particle.

Answer

First use $\omega = \frac{2\pi}{\frac{3\pi}{5}} = 1.2\,\text{rad}\,\text{s}^{-1}$.

Find the angular speed.

Then $F = ma$ gives $40 = m \times 1.2 \times (1.2)^2$.

Apply $F = ma$.

So $m = 23.1\,\text{kg}$.

WORKED EXAMPLE 15.4

A particle is placed on a rough horizontal disc 4 m from the centre of the disc. The particle has mass 2 kg and the coefficient of friction between the particle and the disc is 0.6. The disc begins to spin around slowly until the particle slips. Find the frictional force on the particle when the disc is spinning at $2\,\text{m}\,\text{s}^{-1}$. Find also the angular speed of the disc when the particle is on the point of slipping.

Answer

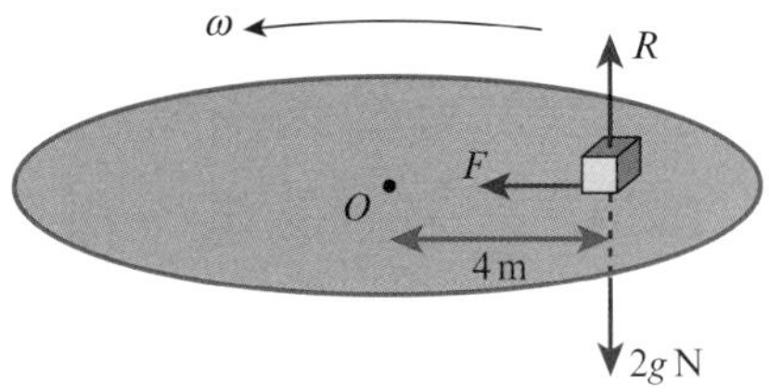

Draw a fully labelled, clear diagram.

This helps you to see what is happening.

Using $F = ma$, we have $F = 2 \times \frac{2^2}{4} = 2$ N — Use $F = m\frac{v^2}{r}$ to obtain the result.

At the slipping point, $F_{lim} = \mu R = 0.6 \times 2g = 12$ N. — State the maximum frictional force (see Rewind).

So $12 = 2 \times 4 \times \omega^2$. — Use $F = mr\omega^2$ to find the angular speed.

Hence, $\omega = \frac{\sqrt{6}}{2}$ rad s^{-1}.

REWIND

Recall from Chapter 14 that when an object is on the point of slipping on a rough surface, $F_{max} = \mu R$. We can also write F_{max} as F_{lim}, which refers to **limiting friction**.

WORKED EXAMPLE 15.5

Two particles are attached to a light, inelastic string of length $4a$. One particle, P, of mass m, is placed on a large, smooth disc. The string is then threaded through a smooth hole in the centre of the disc. At the other end of the string is the particle Q, of mass $2m$. The disc is spinning such that particle Q does not move and is $1.5a$ below the centre of the disc. Find the tension in the string, and also find the angular speed of the particle P in terms of a as it moves in circles.

Answer

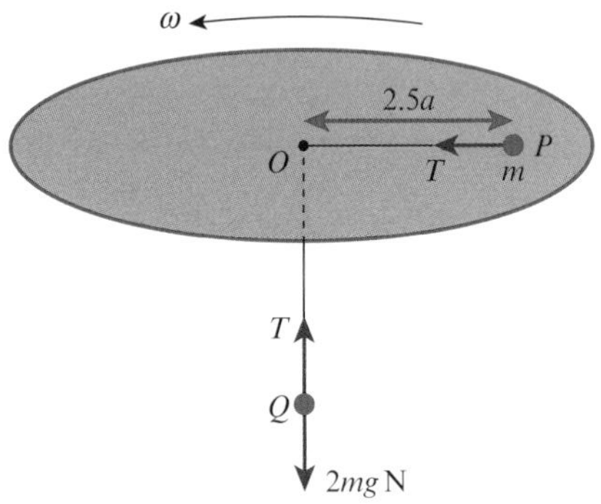

Since the string is of length $4a$ it is clear that the radius of the circle described is $2.5a$.

Q does not move, so $T = 2mg$ N — Balance forces vertically for Q.

So $T = mr\omega^2$ gives $2mg = m \times 2.5a \times \omega^2$ — Use $F = ma$ with angular speed form for particle Q.

Hence, $\omega = \sqrt{\frac{4g}{5a}}$ rad s^{-1}. — Find ω.

WORKED EXAMPLE 15.6

A particle P, is placed on a large, rough, horizontal disc. P is of mass 3 kg. P is then attached to a light, inextensible string of length 2.4 m. The string passes through a smooth hole in the centre of the disc, and at the other end is a particle, Q, of mass 6 kg. The coefficient of friction between P and the disc is 0.5. Q is hanging freely under the hole in the disc. The disc begins to spin with P at a distance of 1.6 m from the centre of the disc. If Q does not move at any point during the motion, find the range of angular speeds possible.

Answer

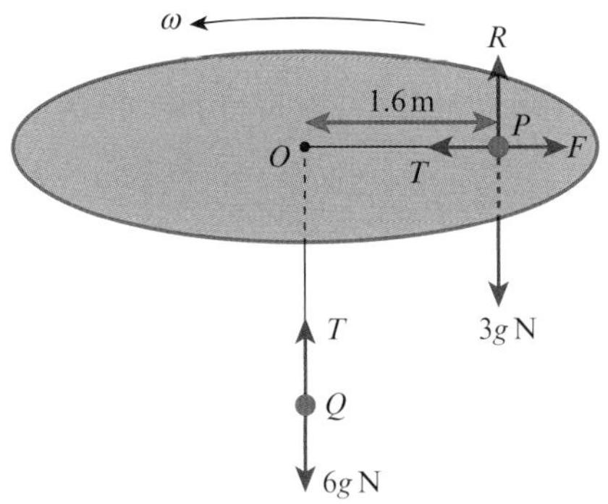

The friction force will be used in conjunction with the force towards the centre.

First, $F_{\text{lim}} = 0.5 \times 3g = 15\text{ N}$, and if Q doesn't move $T = 60\text{ N}$.

Determine the limiting friction and state the tension in the string.

Slipping inwards: $60 = F + mr\omega^2$

Then $60 = 15 + 3 \times 1.6\omega^2$

$$\omega = \frac{5\sqrt{6}}{4}\text{ rad s}^{-1}$$

For slipping inwards, ω has a *minimum* value.

Slipping outwards: $60 + F = mr\omega^2$

Then $75 = 4.8\,\omega^2$

$$\omega = \frac{5\sqrt{10}}{4}\text{ rad s}^{-1}$$

For slipping outwards, ω has a *maximum* value.

Hence, $\frac{5\sqrt{6}}{4} \leqslant \omega \leqslant \frac{5\sqrt{10}}{4}$

State the range of allowed values.

DID YOU KNOW?

Rollercoaster loops are never circular. They are actually constructed to form what is known as a clothoid loop. On a circular track, the speed would decrease as you travelled around the loop with constant acceleration and the roller coaster may not complete the loop. On a clothoid loop, the radius is smaller at the top to keep the speed high enough.

EXERCISE 15A

1 In each of the following, use the relation $v = r\omega$ to determine the unknown value.

a $v = 4, r = 6$. Find ω.

b $v = 6, \omega = 3$. Find r.

c $r = 5, \omega = 0.8$. Find v.

2 A particle of mass 0.2 kg is attached to a light inextensible string of length 1.5 m. The particle is moving in horizontal circles. Find the tension in the string if the speed of the particle is $5\,\text{m}\,\text{s}^{-1}$.

3 A particle of mass 0.8 kg is attached to a light inextensible string of length 1.2 m. The particle is moving in horizontal circles. Find the angular speed of the particle if the tension in the string is 10 N.

PS 4 A particle is describing horizontal circles on a smooth, horizontal table. The particle is fixed to its circular path by an inelastic string of length 1.5 m. Given that the tension in the string is 45 N, and that the mass of the particle is 5 kg, find the angular speed of the particle.

State also how many seconds the particle takes to describe one complete circle.

PS 5 A particle is placed on a rough horizontal disc, $2a$ from the centre of the disc. The particle is of mass $3m$.

The disc then starts to spin at an angular speed of $\sqrt{\frac{g}{4a}}$. Given that the particle is on the point of slipping, find a range of values of μ such that equilibrium is not broken.

M 6 A car is driving on a horizontal circular section of road that has radius 50 m. The car is of mass 800 kg and the coefficient of friction between the tyres and the road is 0.8. Find the maximum speed that the car can drive around the road without slipping.

PS M 7 A particle of mass 1.5 kg is resting on a smooth horizontal table. The particle is attached to a light, inextensible string of length 2.5 m. This string is passed through a smooth hole in the table. At the other end of the string is a particle of mass 4 kg. The particle on the table is set in motion and describes circles with radius 1.5 m. Find the speed of the particle on the table. Assume that the particle that is freely hanging does not move during the motion.

PS 8 A particle is describing horizontal circles of radius a; the mass of the particle is m. Given that the particle can complete one circle in τ seconds, and that the particle is held in its path by means of a light, inextensible string with tension T, find an expression for the mass m.

PS 9 A particle is placed on the inside of a rough, hollow cylinder of radius $2a$. The cylinder is placed upright and can rotate about an axis through its centre. The particle has mass m and the coefficient of friction is $\frac{3}{4}$. Given the particle does not slip as the cylinder rotates, find the speed at which the cylinder rotates.

PS M 10 A particle, P, is placed on a large, rough, horizontal disc. P is of mass 2.4 kg. The particle is then attached to a light, inextensible string of length 4 m. The string passes through a smooth hole in the centre of the disc, and at the other end is a particle, Q, of mass 3 kg. The coefficient of friction between P and the disc is 0.2. Q is hanging freely under the hole in the disc. The disc is set spinning with P at a distance of 1.2 m from the centre of the disc. If Q does not move at any point during the motion, find the range of speeds possible.

15.2 The 3-dimensional case

Consider a particle on the end of a light, inelastic string with the other end of the string attached to a fixed point O. The particle is set in motion to describe small horizontal circles. This is a **conical pendulum** model.

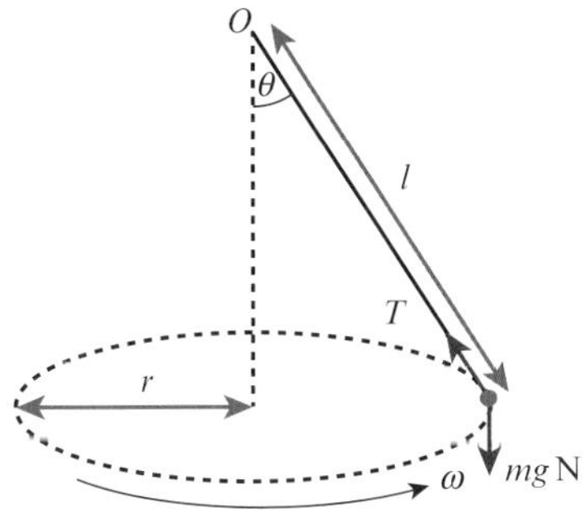

The string describes the curved surface of a cone as the particle moves in a circle below the fixed point at O. The force towards the centre is now a component of the tension in the string. The vertical component of the tension links to the weight of the particle. With this kind of problem we must resolve into horizontal and vertical components first.

$R(\uparrow)$: $T\cos\theta = mg$; hence, $T = \dfrac{mg}{\cos\theta}$.

Then $R(\leftarrow)$: $T\sin\theta = mr\omega^2$.

Since $\dfrac{r}{l} = \sin\theta$, it follows that $T\sin\theta = ml\sin\theta\,\omega^2$, or $T = ml\omega^2$.

Equating these two results gives $\omega = \sqrt{\dfrac{g}{l\cos\theta}}$.

Assigning some values, let the mass of the particle be 2 kg, the angle 30° and the string length 2.5 m.

Then the tension is $\dfrac{40\sqrt{3}}{3}$ N and the angular speed is $\sqrt{\dfrac{8\sqrt{3}}{3}}$ rad s^{-1}.

WORKED EXAMPLE 15.7

A particle of mass 1.5 kg is attached to one end of a light, inelastic string of length 1.8 m. The string is attached to a fixed point, O, at its other end. The particle is set in motion and describes horizontal circles with the string taut and at 20° to the downward vertical through the point O. Find the tension in the string and the angular speed of the particle.

Answer

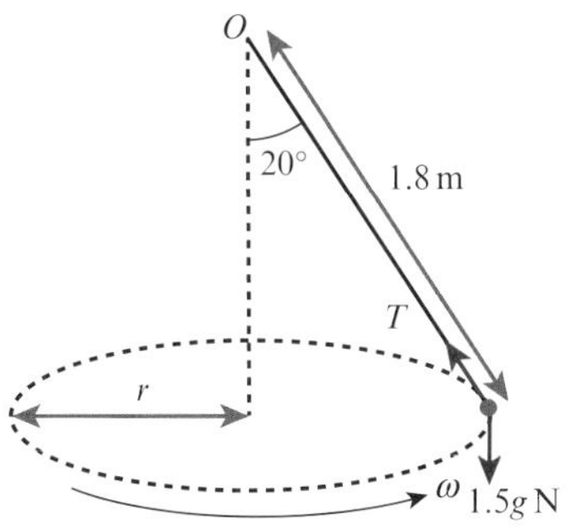

A large, well-labelled diagram is essential for mechanics problems.

Draw a diagram so you can resolve both vertically and horizontally.

$R(\uparrow)$: $T\cos 20 = 1.5g$; hence, $T = \dfrac{15}{\cos 20} = 16.0$ N.   Resolve vertically to find T.

$R(\leftarrow)$: $T\sin 20 = 1.5 \times r \times \omega^2$, where $r = 1.8\sin 20$.   Resolve horizontally using $F = ma$

$\dfrac{15}{\cos 20}\sin 20 = 1.5 \times 1.8\sin 20 \times \omega^2$ Solve to find ω.

So $\omega = 2.43$ rad s^{-1}.

If you are asked to find the speed of a particle instead of the angular speed, you need to be careful when cancelling terms.

For the general case in the diagram at the start of Section 15.2, $T = \frac{mg}{\cos\theta}$ is unchanged, but towards the centre, $T\sin\theta = m\frac{v^2}{l\sin\theta}$.

Notice that the $\sin\theta$ term does not cancel here. Keep in mind this term cancels only for angular speed.

WORKED EXAMPLE 15.8

A particle of mass $3m$ is attached to a light, inextensible string of length $5a$. The other end of the string is attached to a fixed point, O. The particle is moving in horizontal circles about a centre that is $4a$ vertically below the point O. By resolving vertically and horizontally, find the tension in the string and the speed of the particle.

Answer

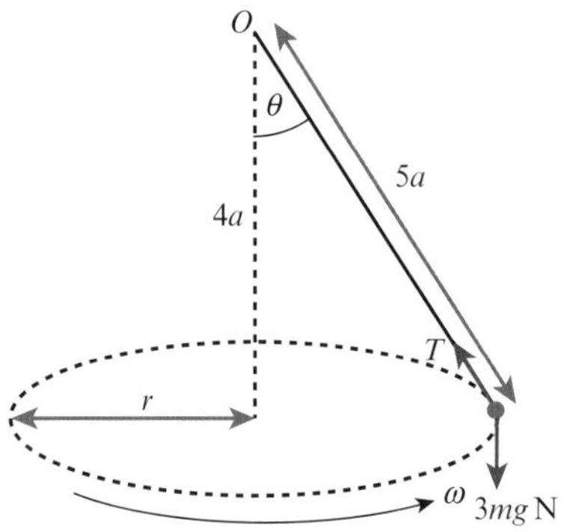

$\cos\theta = \frac{4}{5}$ and $\sin\theta = \frac{3}{5}$. — First note the sides of the triangle formed.

$R(\uparrow)$: $T\cos\theta = 3mg$, and so $T = \frac{15}{4}mg$. — Resolve vertically to find the tension.

$R(\leftarrow)$: $T\sin\theta = 3m\frac{v^2}{3a}$, then $\frac{15}{4}mg \times \frac{3}{5} = \frac{m}{a}v^2$. — Resolve horizontally with this tension to get v^2 and substitute the earlier expression found for T.

Hence, $v = \frac{3}{2}\sqrt{ga}$. — State the value of v.

Consider an object on a sloped surface, sometimes called a banked surface. Here, there is a reaction force rather than tension in a string.

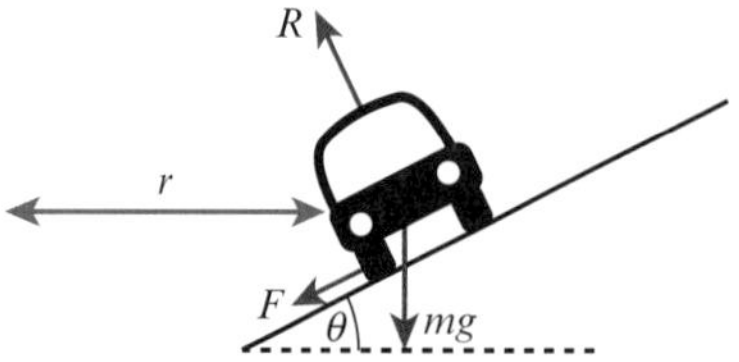

First consider the case when the surface is smooth. We shall have the same situation as that of the conical pendulum. When there is friction, it is usually considered to act down the slope. This is because the car is likely to slip up the slope due to excess speed.

Resolving vertically: $R\cos\theta = mg + F\sin\theta$

Then considering the forces towards the centre: $F\cos\theta + R\sin\theta = m\frac{v^2}{r}$

If the car is on the point of slipping, $F = \mu R$.

Resolving vertically, $R\cos\theta - \mu R\sin\theta = mg$, so $R = \dfrac{mg}{\cos\theta - \mu\sin\theta}$.

Then from the force towards the centre, $R(\mu\cos\theta + \sin\theta) = m\dfrac{v^2}{r}$, so $\dfrac{\mu\cos\theta + \sin\theta}{\cos\theta - \mu\sin\theta}mg = m\dfrac{v^2}{r}$.

If we then divide top and bottom by $\cos\theta$, this gives $\dfrac{v^2}{r} = g\dfrac{\mu + \tan\theta}{1 - \mu\tan\theta}$.

You do not have to memorise this result, but you should be able to derive it.

WORKED EXAMPLE 15.9

A car of mass 1000 kg is turning on a banked road of radius 80 m. The incline of the road is 15° and the car is travelling at 25 m s^{-1}. The car is about to slip up the road.

- **a** Resolve vertically and find an expression for the reaction force between the car and the road, in terms of the frictional force.
- **b** Resolve towards the centre of the circle.
- **c** Find the coefficient of friction between the car and the road.

Answer

a $R(\uparrow)$: $R\cos 15 = 1000g + F\sin 15$ — Resolve vertically. There are three forces.

So $R = \dfrac{10\,000 + F\sin 15}{\cos 15}$. — Determine R.

b $R\sin 15 + F\cos 15 = 1000 \times \dfrac{25^2}{80}$ — Resolve horizontally towards the centre.

c Equating: — Form an equation in terms of F only.

$(10\,000 + F\sin 15)\tan 15 + F\cos 15 = \dfrac{15\,625}{2}$

$F(\sin 15\tan 15 + \cos 15) = \dfrac{15\,625}{2} - 10\,000\tan 15$

This gives $F = 4958.105$ N, then $R = 11\,681.28$ N — Determine a numerical result for F and then for R.

Hence, $\mu = 0.424$. — Make use of $F = \mu R$.

We shall also encounter problems where there is more than one force acting towards the centre, for example, a particle with two strings attached. In Worked example 15.10, we assume that a single string with a particle attached to the centre of the string can be treated as two separate strings with different tensions.

WORKED EXAMPLE 15.10

A light, inelastic string of length $2a$ is tied to a fixed, vertical pole at two points, A and B. A is a distance a vertically above B. A particle of mass $2m$ is attached to the midpoint of the string. The particle is then set in motion to describe horizontal circles. Both parts of the string are taut at all times during the motion. Given that the speed of the particle is $\sqrt{\frac{9}{4}ga}$, find the tension in both parts of the string.

Answer

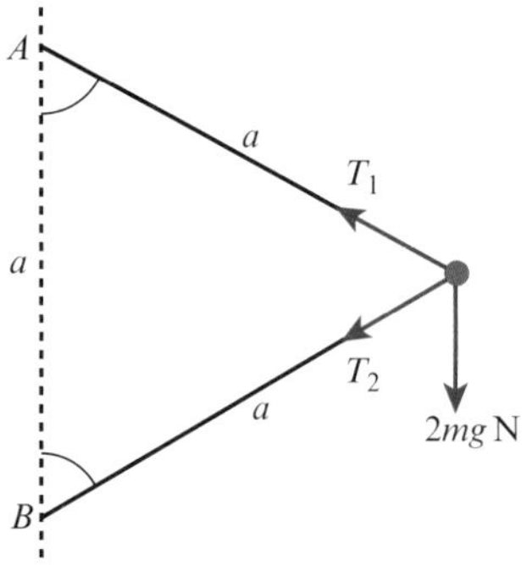

By sketching a suitable diagram, we can see that we have an equilateral triangle.

The particle at the midpoint of the string splits it into two equal parts. Note that their tensions are different.

Using a sketch shows that the upper string must have a larger tension than the lower string. This information will help you when checking for errors.

$R(\uparrow)$: $T_1 \cos 60 = T_2 \cos 60 + 2mg$

Note angles are all 60°, and resolve.

$$R(\leftarrow): T_1 \sin 60 + T_2 \sin 60 = \frac{2m \times \frac{9}{4}ga}{\frac{a\sqrt{3}}{2}}$$

Use Pythagoras or trigonometry to find the radius of the circular motion.

The force acts towards the centre.

So $(T_1 + T_2) \times \frac{\sqrt{3}}{2} = \frac{9mg}{\sqrt{3}}$, then $T_1 + T_2 = 6mg$.

Simplify the second equation.

Solving $T_1 = T_2 + 4mg$ gives $T_1 - T_2 = 4mg$.

Simplify the first equation and combine.

Gives $T_2 = mg$ and $T_1 = 5mg$.

Obtain both tensions.

EXERCISE 15B

1 A particle of mass 0.9 kg is attached to a light inextensible string of length 2.4 m. The other end of the string is attached to a fixed point on the ceiling. The particle is describing horizontal circles with the string taut and making an angle of 25° with the downward vertical. Find the speed of the particle.

2 A particle of mass 1.6 kg is attached to a light inextensible string of length 1.4 m. The other end of the string is attached to a fixed point on the ceiling. The particle is describing horizontal circles with the string taut and making an angle of 35° with the downward vertical. Find the angular speed of the particle.

3 A particle of mass 2 kg is attached to a light, inextensible string of length 3 m. The other end of the string is attached to a fixed point on the ceiling. The particle is describing horizontal circles with the string taut and making an angle of 30° with the downward vertical. Find the angular speed of the particle.

PS 4 A car is driving around a banked road inclined at 15° to the horizontal. The car has mass 1200 kg and the radius of the circular part of the road is 60 m. The coefficient of friction between the road and the tyres is 0.75, and the car is on the point of slipping up the road. Find the speed of the car.

PS 5 A particle, P, of mass 3 kg is attached to two light, inextensible strings. One string is attached at its other end to a point, A. The other string has its other end attached to a point, B. A is 4 m above B. The particle makes horizontal circles such that angle PAB is 30° and angle PBA is 60°. Given that the speed of the particle is $3.6\,\mathrm{m\,s^{-1}}$, find the tension in each string.

M 6 A hemispherical bowl of radius a is resting in a fixed position where its rim is horizontal. A small ball of mass $2m$ is moving around the inside of the bowl such that the circle described by the ball is $\frac{a}{2}$ vertically below the rim of the bowl. Find the speed of the ball.

PS 7 A light, inextensible string of length 4 m is threaded through a smooth ring at the point O. One end of the string has a particle, P, of mass 4 kg, which is 1.2 m vertically below O. Particle Q, of mass 1.6 kg, is attached to the other end of the string. Particle Q is describing horizontal circles, with the string OQ making an angle of 20° with the downward vertical.

a If particle P does not move during the motion, find the angular speed of Q.

b Find the number of complete circles described per minute.

PS 8 A car is moving on a circular section of road where the road is banked at 25° to the horizontal. The radius of this section of road is 100 m. The car has mass 1400 kg and is travelling at $30\,\mathrm{m\,s^{-1}}$. Given that the car is about to slip up the road, find the value of μ.

M 9 A toy plane of mass 0.4 kg is attached to one end of a light, inextensible string of length 6 m. The other end of the string is attached to the point O. The string is taut and makes an angle of 45° with the upward vertical. Find:

a the tension in the string

b the speed of the toy plane.

15.3 Vertical circles

The problems we have looked at so far involved motion in a horizontal circle but particles can also describe vertical circles.

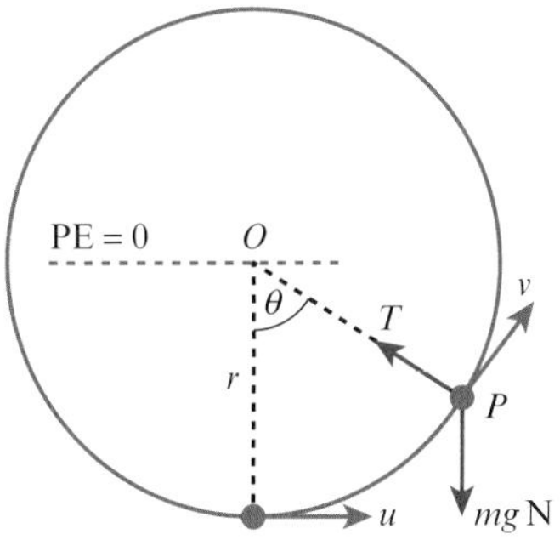

As the object moves around the circular path, it will gain potential energy due to the gain in height. This gain in potential energy comes about when the kinetic energy reduces, so in these situations the angular speed of the particle varies. This is the main reason we use the linear speed for this type of problem.

Consider a particle of mass m that is attached to a light, inelastic string of length r. The particle is at rest in equilibrium before being projected with speed u from the lowest point. Assuming there are no resisting forces, we can use the principle of conservation of energy.

Considering zero potential energy when the particle is at a height level with the centre of the circle, as seen in the diagram:

Initially, $\text{PE} = -mgr$ and $\text{KE} = \frac{1}{2}mu^2$. Generally, $\text{PE} = -mgr\cos\theta$ and $\text{KE} = \frac{1}{2}mv^2$.

For the particle to complete full circles, at the top of the circle it must have $\text{KE} > 0$. This means that the particle continues to move after reaching the top. This idea is also reinforced by the need to have tension in the string at the very top. If there was no tension in the string, then the particle would no longer be travelling along a circular path.

So considering $F = ma$ towards the centre at a general point, $T - mg\cos\theta = \frac{mv^2}{r}$.

Then from the principle of conservation of energy, $\frac{1}{2}mu^2 - mgr = \frac{1}{2}mv^2 - mgr\cos\theta$,

or $\frac{mv^2}{r} = \frac{mu^2}{r} - 2mg + 2mg\cos\theta$. Combining these two equations gives

$T - mg\cos\theta = \frac{mu^2}{r} - 2mg + 2mg\cos\theta$, and if the tension is such that $T \geqslant 0$, then

$\frac{mu^2}{r} \geqslant 2mg - 3mg\cos\theta$.

At the top point $\theta = 180°$, and so $\frac{u^2}{r} \geqslant 5g$, giving $u \geqslant \sqrt{5gr}$. This is the condition for complete vertical circles for a circle of radius r, as shown in Key point 15.4.

KEY POINT 15.4

For a particle to complete vertical circles of radius r, starting from the lowest point, the speed u must satisfy the condition $u \geqslant \sqrt{5gr}$

WORKED EXAMPLE 15.11

A particle of mass m is attached to a light, inelastic string of length $2a$. The other end of the string is attached to a fixed point, O. When the particle is resting in equilibrium below the point O, it is given a horizontal speed, u.

a Write down the minimum value of u required to complete a full circle.

b Given that $u^2 = 16ga$, find the greatest and least tension in the string.

Answer

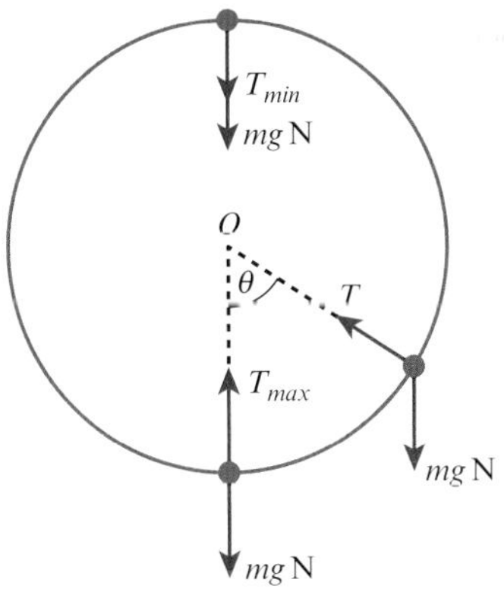

Note that the greatest tension will always be when the particle is at the bottom of the circle.

The weight component plus the tendency of the particle to 'escape' the circular path means this is where the tension is maximum.

Similarly, at the top the tension is minimum since the speed is at a minimum and both tension and weight act downwards.

a Require $u_{\min} = \sqrt{5g(2a)} = \sqrt{10ga}$.

Use $u \geqslant \sqrt{5gr}$, with new radius.

b At a general point

$T - mg\cos\theta = \dfrac{mv^2}{2a}$.

Use $F = ma$ generally.

Initially:

$\text{PE} = -2mga,\ \text{KE} = \dfrac{1}{2}mu^2$

Determine the energy of the system at the start and at a general point.

Generally: $\text{PE} = -2mga\cos\theta,\ \text{KE} = \dfrac{1}{2}mv^2$

By CoE:

$\dfrac{1}{2}mu^2 - 2mga = \dfrac{1}{2}mv^2 - 2mga\cos\theta$

Assume conservation of energy (CoE).

At the lowest point: $\theta = 0,\ u^2 = 16ga$

$\therefore T_{\max} = 9mg$ N

Find maximum tension at the lowest point.

At the highest point: $\theta = 180°$

So $\left(\dfrac{1}{2}m\right)(16ga) - 2mga = \dfrac{1}{2}mv^2 + 2mga$,

giving $v^2 = 8ga$.

Use the angle at the top to find the speed.

Then $T + mg = \dfrac{8mga}{2a}$, so $T_{\min} = 3mg$ N

Determine the minimum tension.

Consider a small ball placed on the inside of a smooth, hollow ring. We can model this in exactly the same way as the particle on a string.

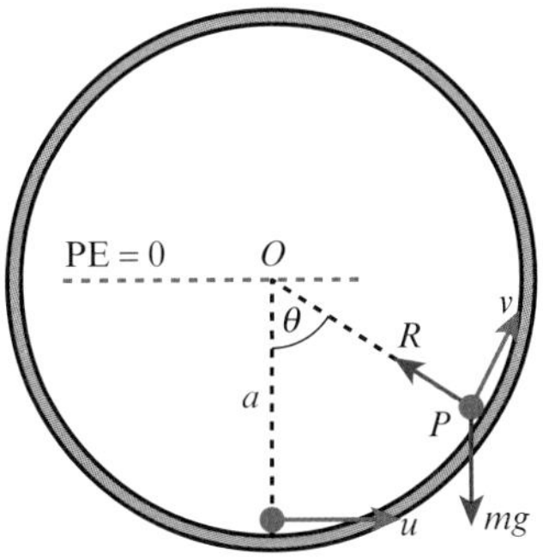

TIP

If a particle lacks the energy to complete a full circle it can behave in two ways. If the particle has enough energy to travel beyond the horizontal midline of the circle, it will leave the surface of the ring and become a projectile. If it does not have enough energy to reach the midline, it will behave like a pendulum and eventually come to rest at the lowest point of the circle.

In the absence of a string, the ball keeping contact with the inner surface of the ring produces a reaction force towards the centre of the ring. Just as with the particle on a string, if the particle does not have enough energy it will simply leave the circular path. The particle still travels, but it is no longer in contact with the inner surface of the ring.

WORKED EXAMPLE 15.12

A particle, P, of mass m is resting on the inside of a smooth, circular ring, with centre O and radius a. The particle is projected from the lowest point with a horizontal speed of $u^2 = \frac{5}{2}ga$. Find the angle between the line OP and the downward vertical at the point where the particle leaves the surface of the ring.

Answer

Initially: $\text{PE} = -mga,\ \text{KE} = \left(\frac{1}{2}m\right)\left(\frac{5}{2}ga\right) = \frac{5}{4}mga$ — Determine the energy at the start and at a general point.

Generally: $\text{PE} = -mga\cos\theta,\ \text{KE} = \frac{1}{2}mv^2$

By CoE: $\frac{1}{4}mga + mga\cos\theta = \frac{1}{2}mv^2 \quad (1)$ — Use conservation of energy.

Using $F = ma,\ R - mg\cos\theta = \frac{mv^2}{a}. \quad (2)$ — Resolve horizontally, towards the centre.

So $R - mg\cos\theta = \frac{1}{2}mg + 2mg\cos\theta.$ — Combine the equations.

Hence, $R = \frac{1}{2}mg + 3mg\cos\theta.$

When the particle leaves its circular path:

$R = 0 \Rightarrow \cos\theta = -\frac{1}{6}$ — Let the reaction be zero to find the point where the particle leaves the surface.

$\theta = 99.6°$ — Determine the angle at that point.

WORKED EXAMPLE 15.13

A particle, P, of mass m is resting on the inside of a smooth, circular ring, with centre O and radius a. The particle is projected from the lowest point with a horizontal speed of $u^2 = 3ga$. Find the greatest height above O achieved by the particle.

Answer

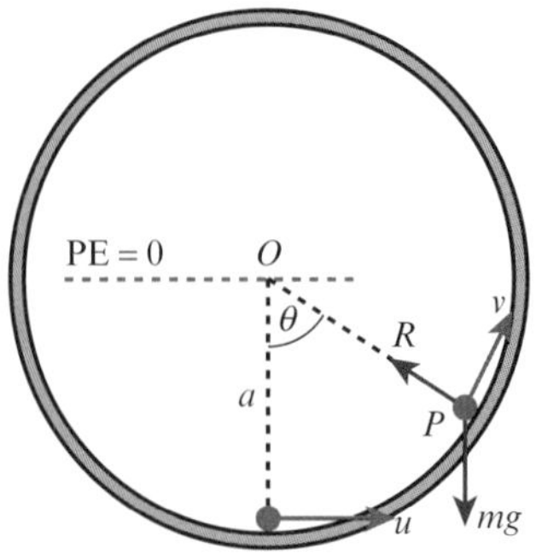

Label your diagram with the same notation and references as in the question.

Initially: KE $= \frac{3}{2}mga$, PE $= -mga$	Find the energy at the start.
Generally: KE $= \frac{1}{2}mv^2$, PE $= -mga\cos\theta$	Find the energy at a general point.
By CoE: $mg + 2mg\cos\theta = \frac{mv^2}{a}$	Use conservation of energy and multiply through by $\frac{2}{a}$.
Using $F = ma$, $R - mg\cos\theta = \frac{mv^2}{a}$.	Resolve towards the centre.
So $R - mg\cos\theta = mg + 2mg\cos\theta$.	
$R = 0$ gives $\cos\theta = -\frac{1}{3}$. With this angle $v = \sqrt{\frac{1}{3}ga}$.	Let the reaction force be zero to determine the angle and speed at the point when the particle leaves the surface of the ring.
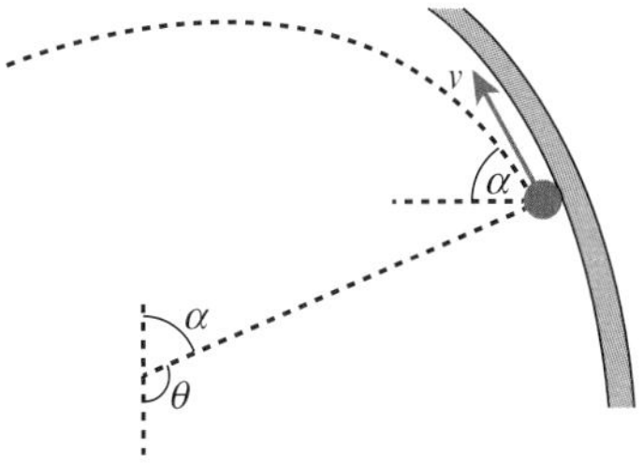	As the particle leaves the inner surface, note that the angle α is important for the height of the particle at that point, as well as the component form of the speed. Although it looks as if the particle is still moving around the circle, its path is a tangent to the circle. After this point, the particle will fall off the ring and travel as a projectile under gravity.
Since $\cos\alpha = \frac{1}{3}$, we can split the speed into components.	State $\cos\alpha$ and use it to find $\sin\alpha$.
$v_y = \sqrt{\frac{1}{3}ga}\,\sin\alpha = \frac{2\sqrt{2}}{3}\sqrt{\frac{1}{3}ga}$ (Only need ↑.)	Determine the vertical speed component.
Using $v^2 = u^2 + 2as$, so $0 = \frac{8}{27}ga - 2gs$,	Speed at the highest point is zero.
giving $s = \frac{4}{27}a$.	
So the total height above O is $a\cos\alpha + s = \frac{13}{27}a$.	State the greatest height achieved above O.

Instead of travelling on the inside or a circular surface, particles can travel on the outside. Consider a hemispherical shell resting on a horizontal surface with its plane face at the bottom. The hemisphere is smooth and has radius r. At the top of the hemisphere is a particle of mass m. The particle is given a very slight push, to produce enough speed to get the particle moving. Let us look at the situation where the particle leaves the surface of the hemisphere.

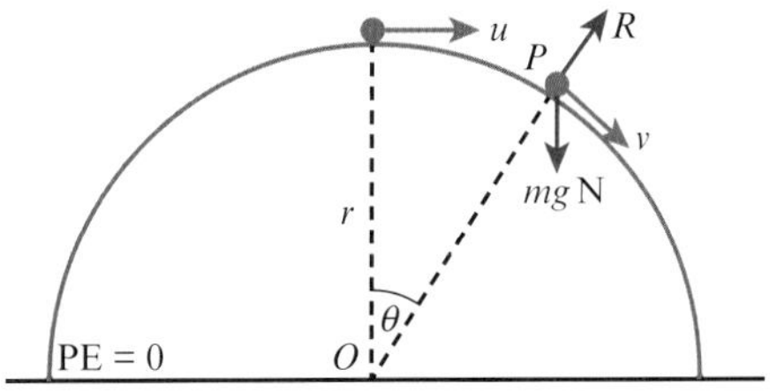

Initially, $\text{KE} = \frac{1}{2}mu^2$ and $\text{PE} = mgr$. Generally, $\text{KE} = \frac{1}{2}mv^2$ and $\text{PE} = mgr\cos\theta$.

Using conservation of energy: $\frac{1}{2}mv^2 = \frac{1}{2}mu^2 + mgr - mgr\cos\theta$

If we multiply through by $\frac{2}{r}$, we get $\frac{mv^2}{r} = \frac{mu^2}{r} + 2mg - 2mg\cos\theta$.

Next use $F = ma$ towards the centre of the hemisphere to get $mg\cos\theta - R = \frac{mv^2}{r}$

or $-R = \frac{mu^2}{r} + 2mg - 3mg\cos\theta$.

When the particle leaves the surface, $R = 0$ and so $\cos\theta = \dfrac{\frac{mu^2}{r} + 2mg}{3mg}$.

This result is quite useful. If $u \approx 0$ then $\cos\theta \approx \frac{2}{3}$, so even with the slightest push the particle will leave the surface of the hemisphere after 48.2°.

It also shows that when $u^2 = gr$, $\cos\theta = 1$, and so $\theta = 0$, implying the particle leaves the surface immediately after being given an initial speed of $\sqrt{gr}$, as shown in Key point 15.5.

KEY POINT 15.5

When a particle is projected from the top of a hemisphere, provided the initial speed is $0 < u < \sqrt{gr}$, the particle will turn through an angle θ, where $0 < \theta < \cos^{-1}\left(\frac{2}{3}\right)$.

WORKED EXAMPLE 15.14

A particle of mass m is projected from the top of a hemisphere of radius a. The hemisphere has its plane face in contact with the horizontal surface below it, and the hemisphere is to be considered smooth. If the initial speed at the top is $\sqrt{\frac{1}{4}ga}$, find the speed of the particle at the moment it loses contact with the hemisphere.

Answer

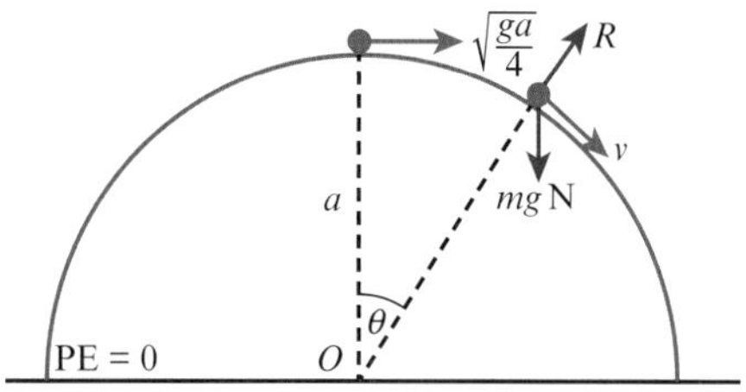

It is usually easier to consider the zero potential energy line at the centre of the 'circle'. This reduces the number of combinations of distances in your calculations.

Initially: $\text{KE} = \frac{1}{8}mga$, $\text{PE} = mga$ — Find the energy at the top.

Generally: $\text{KE} = \frac{1}{2}mv^2$, $\text{PE} = mga\cos\theta$ — Determine the energy at a general point.

CoE: $\frac{mv^2}{a} = \frac{9}{4}mg - 2mg\cos\theta$ — Use conservation of energy and combine this with the force towards the centre.

Using $F = ma$, $mg\cos\theta - R = \frac{mv^2}{a}$. Combine this with the energy result to get $mg\cos\theta - R = \frac{9}{4}mg - 2mg\cos\theta$.

Obtain a result in R and $\cos\theta$.

When $R = 0$, $\cos\theta = \frac{3}{4}$ and so $v = \sqrt{\frac{3}{4}ga}$.

Find the speed at thc point of loss of contact.

WORKED EXAMPLE 15.15

A smooth hemisphere of radius $2a$ is fixed with its plane face against a horizontal surface. The centre of the plane face is denoted as O. A particle of mass m is placed at the top of the hemisphere. The particle is then projected horizontally with speed $\sqrt{\frac{2}{3}ga}$. The particle first lands on the horizontal surface at the point B. Determine the distance OB.

Answer

The particle will lose contact with the hemisphere at some point.

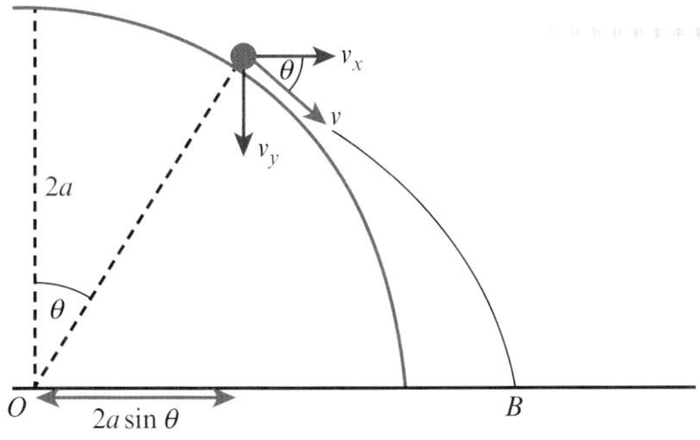

You can draw two diagrams: one for the initial calculations and one for when the particle leaves the surface.

Initially: $\text{KE} = \frac{1}{3}mga$, $\text{PE} = 2mga$

Generally: $\text{KE} = \frac{1}{2}mv^2$, $\text{PE} = 2mga\cos\theta$

Determine the energy at the two points, as for similar problems.

CoE: $\frac{mv^2}{2a} = \frac{7}{3}mg - 2mg\cos\theta$

Conservation of energy.

Using $F = ma$, $mg\cos\theta - R = \frac{mv^2}{2a}$

or $mg\cos\theta - R = \frac{7}{3}mg - 2mg\cos\theta$.

For forces towards the centre, remember that the component of the weight is greater than the reaction force.

So $R = 0 \Rightarrow \cos\theta = \frac{7}{9}$. We also have $\sin\theta = \frac{4\sqrt{2}}{9}$.

Let the reaction force be zero to find the angle at separation.

Speed at leaving point is $v = \sqrt{\frac{14}{9}ga}$.

Determine the speed at that point.

So $v_y = v\sin\theta = \frac{4\sqrt{2}}{9}\sqrt{\frac{14}{9}ga}$.

Use $s = ut + \frac{1}{2}at^2$ vertically to find the time taken to reach the ground, so $\frac{14}{9}a = \sqrt{\frac{448}{729}ga}t + \frac{1}{2}gt^2$.

Determine the time to reach the ground, where $s_y = 2a\cos\theta$.

Solving this leads to $t = 1.146\sqrt{\frac{a}{g}}$,

so $v_x = v\cos\theta = \frac{7}{9}\sqrt{\frac{14}{9}ga}$.

Use $s = ut$ to give $s = 1.146\sqrt{\frac{a}{g}}\sqrt{\frac{686}{729}ga} = 1.112a$.

Substitute into $s = ut$ for the horizontal distance covered.

So OB is $2a \times \frac{4\sqrt{2}}{9} + 1.112a = 2.37a$.

Add this distance to the initial distance covered $(2a\sin\theta)$ before losing contact.

WORKED EXAMPLE 15.16

A particle, P, of mass m, is at rest on the lowest part of a semicircular piece of metal. The semicircle has radius a and it is completely smooth. The particle is projected with a horizontal speed of $\sqrt{8ga}$.

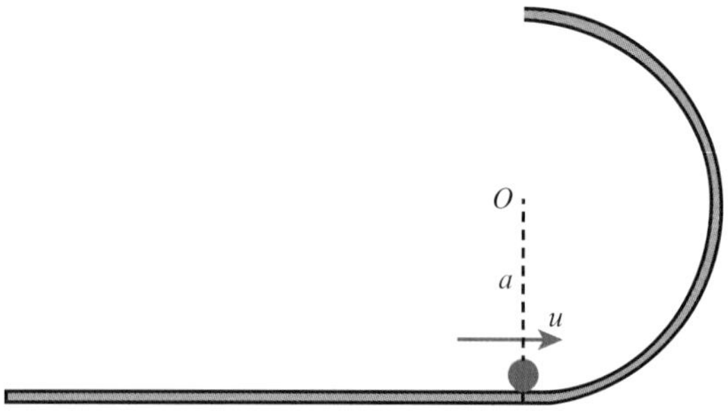

a Find the speed of the particle when it is just about to lose contact with the semicircle.

The particle then travels as a projectile until it hits the ground.

b Find the horizontal distance between O and the point where the particle hits the ground.

Answer

a Initially: PE $= -mga$, KE $= 4mga$

Generally: PE $= -mga\cos\theta$, KE $= \frac{1}{2}mv^2$

Determine the energy at the start and at a general point, using O as the level of zero potential energy.

CoE: $\frac{mv^2}{a} = 6mg + 2mg\cos\theta$

Use conservation of energy.

From here, $\theta = 180°$ leads to $v = 2\sqrt{ga}$.

Use the angle at the top to find the speed.

b Distance to the ground is $2a$, so $2a = 0 + \frac{1}{2}gt^2$. — Find the time to reach the ground below, noting that $v_y = 0$ at this point.

So $t = \sqrt{\frac{4a}{g}}$.

Then using $s = ut$, $s = 2\sqrt{ga} \times \sqrt{\frac{4a}{g}} = 4a$. — Use that value of the time to determine the horizontal distance travelled.

Hence, particle lands a horizontal distance of $4a$ from O.

We next need to look at special cases of the motion on the outer surface of an arc of a circle. Consider a track that consists of two circular arcs, as shown in the following diagram.

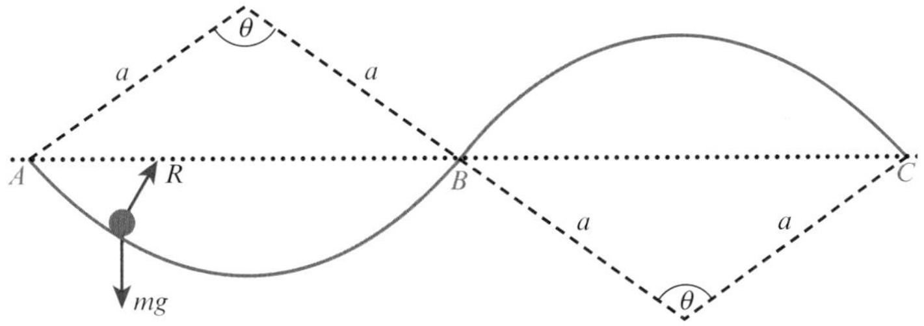

Imagine a particle starts at A and moves along the track to the point B, which is at the same horizontal level as A. The particle cannot lose contact with the track between A and B. The particle can, however, leave the track between B and C, providing it has enough energy to do so.

Let's look more closely at point B.

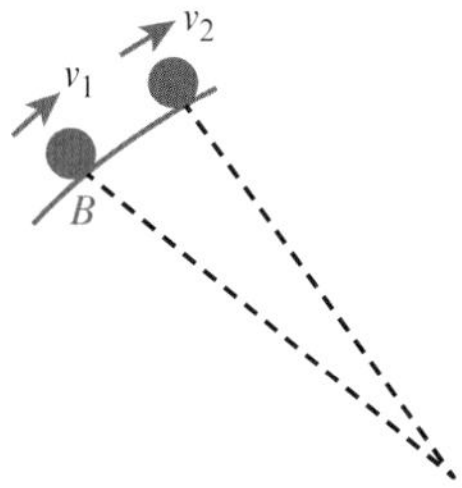

As the particle reaches B it has speed v_1, and as it climbs the arc BC the speed will reduce to v_2. This loss in kinetic energy will inhibit the particle's chance to escape from the surface. So if the particle does not escape the arc BC at the point B, it will never escape.

EXPLORE 15.1

For the previous example, discuss the different ways in which a particle could be projected from A and reach C.

WORKED EXAMPLE 15.17

A particle is projected from the point O with speed U along a track that is made up of two identical quarter circles, as shown in the diagram. Find the range of values of U such that the particle reaches B without losing contact with the track.

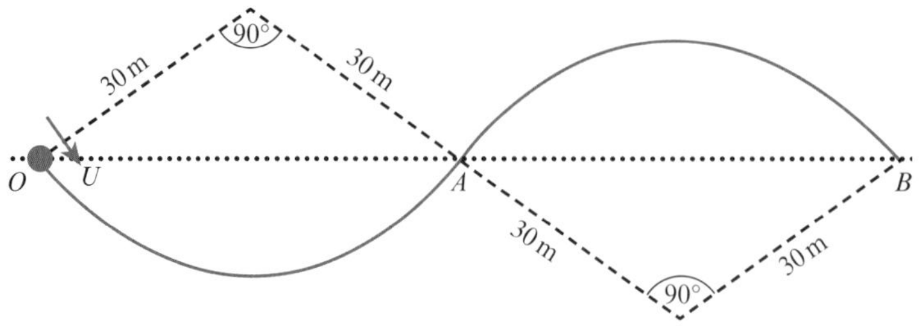

Answer

First note that $U_O = U_A$.	Since these are at the same level, the speeds are the same.
At A: KE $= \frac{1}{2}mU^2$, PE $= mg \times 30\cos 45 = 15\sqrt{2}mg$	Determine the energy at A and at the top of the arc, using the centre of the circle that forms arc AB as the level of zero potential energy.
To just reach the top of arc AB, KE $= \frac{1}{2}mv^2$, PE $= 30mg$.	If the particle just reaches the top of the arc, it can continue down to B.
CoE: $\frac{1}{2}mv^2 = \frac{1}{2}mU^2 + 15\sqrt{2}mg - 30mg$	Use conservation of energy and let the speed be positive only at the top of the arc.
Need $v > 0$, $\frac{1}{2}mU^2 > 30mg - 15\sqrt{2}mg$; hence, $U > 13.3\,\text{m s}^{-1}$.	This is the minimum speed required to reach B.
Using $F = ma$, $mg\cos\theta - R = \frac{mU^2}{30}$; let $\theta = 45°$ and assume the particle will leave the track $(R = 0)$.	Resolve towards the centre. Assume the particle leaves the track at A.
So $mg\cos 45 = \frac{mU^2}{30}$, and so $U^2 = 212.13$.	Determine the speed required to leave the track.
Therefore, $13.3\,\text{m s}^{-1} < U < 14.6\,\text{m s}^{-1}$.	State the range of values for U.

EXERCISE 15C

1 A particle of mass m is attached to the end of a light inelastic string of length $1.5a$. The other end of the string is attached to a fixed point O. When the particle is resting in equilibrium, it is given a horizontal speed of $\sqrt{ga}$. Find the angle turned through when the particle comes to instantaneous rest.

2 A particle of mass m is attached to the end of a light inelastic string of length $1.2a$. The other end of the string is attached to a fixed point O. When the particle is resting in equilibrium, it is given a horizontal speed of $\sqrt{5ga}$. Find the angle turned through when the tension in the string is zero.

PS **3** A smooth hemisphere of radius $1.6a$ is placed plane face down and fixed onto a horizontal plane. A particle of mass $2m$ is placed on the top of the hemisphere and projected with speed $\sqrt{\frac{1}{4}ga}$. As the particle travels down the curved surface of the hemisphere it turns through an angle θ, where θ is measured from the vertical through the centre of the hemisphere. Find the value of θ when the particle loses contact with the hemisphere.

PS **4** A particle of mass $2m$ is attached to the end of a light, inelastic string of length a. The other end of the string is attached to a fixed point, O. When the particle is resting in equilibrium, it is given a horizontal speed of $\sqrt{7ga}$ and consequently describes vertical circles. Find the greatest and least tension in the string.

M PS **5** A particle of mass m is attached to a light, inextensible string of length a. With the other end of the string attached to a fixed point, A, the particle rests in equilibrium. The particle is then given an initial horizontal speed u. Find the condition on u such that the particle never leaves the circular path, but never completes full circles.

M **6** A particle of mass 3 kg is resting on the inside of a smooth, circular hoop of radius 2 m. From the bottom position, the particle is projected horizontally with speed $8\,\text{m}\,\text{s}^{-1}$. Find the greatest height achieved by the particle from the point where it is projected.

PS **7** A smooth hemisphere, of radius $1.5a$, is placed plane face down and fixed onto a horizontal plane. A particle, of mass m, is placed on the top of the hemisphere and projected with speed $\sqrt{\frac{3}{4}ga}$. As the particle travels down the curved surface of the hemisphere the particle turns through an angle θ. Find the value of θ when the particle loses contact with the hemisphere.

M PS **8** A particle of mass m is resting on the inside of a smooth, circular hoop of radius $3a$. The particle is then projected from the lowest point, with horizontal speed u.

a State the minimum speed required to complete vertical circles.

b The particle is projected with speed $\sqrt{12ga}$. Find the speed when the particle has turned through 120°.

c Find also the reaction force exerted on the particle when the angle is 120°.

PS **9** A particle is held at rest on a smooth, circular track, which is an arc of radius a. The track is standing in a vertical plane, and it is fixed to a horizontal surface. The points O and A are such that OA is horizontal, as shown in the diagram. The particle is released from rest and proceeds to slide down the track.

a Find the speed of the particle at the point where it is just about to lose contact with the track.

b Find the greatest reaction force on the particle while it is in contact with the track.

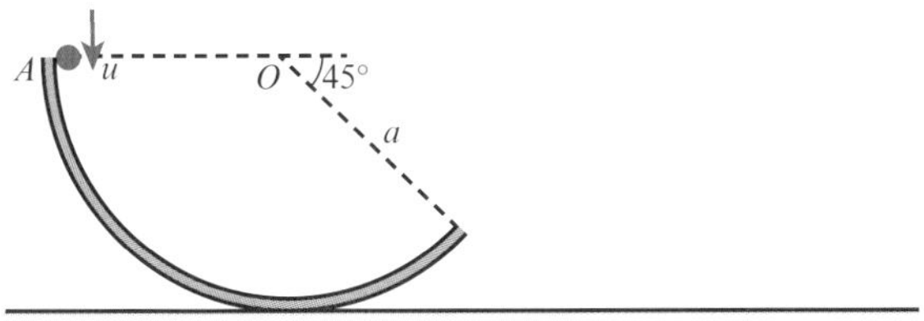

M PS **10** A string of length $2a$ is attached to a point O and has a particle of mass $3m$ attached to the other end. The particle is resting in equilibrium. The particle is then projected with horizontal speed $\sqrt{15ga}$.

a Find the speed of the particle at the highest point of its circular path.

b Find the difference between the greatest and least tension in the string.

WORKED PAST PAPER QUESTION

A small bead (B) of mass m is threaded on a smooth wire fixed in a vertical plane. The wire forms a circle of radius a and centre O. The highest point of the circle is A. The bead is slightly displaced from rest at A. When angle $AOB = \theta$, where $\theta < \cos^{-1}\left(\frac{2}{3}\right)$, the force exerted on the bead by the wire has magnitude R_1. When angle $AOB = \pi + \theta$, the force exerted on the bead by the wire has magnitude R_2. Show that $R_2 - R_1 = 4mg$.

Cambridge International AS & A Level Further Mathematics 9231 Paper 2 Q2 November 2008

Answer

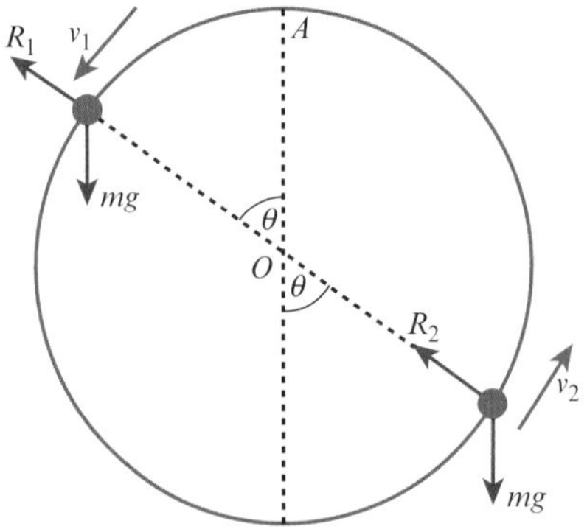

Consider the potential energy equal to zero at the level of O.

At the higher point: $mg\cos\theta - R_1 = \frac{mv_1^2}{a}$

$\text{PE} = mga\cos\theta$, $\text{KE} = \frac{1}{2}mv_1^2$

At the lower point: $R_2 - mg\cos\theta = \frac{mv_2^2}{a}$

$\text{PE} = -mga\cos\theta$, $\text{KE} = \frac{1}{2}mv_2^2$

Adding the force equations gives $R_2 - R_1 = \frac{m}{a}(v_1^2 + v_2^2)$.

Now at A: $\text{KE} = 0$, $\text{PE} = mga$, so by conservation of energy, $mga = mga\cos\theta + \frac{1}{2}mv_1^2$, leading to $v_1^2 = 2ga(1 - \cos\theta)$.

Also by conservation of energy, $mga = -mga\cos\theta + \frac{1}{2}mv_2^2$, so $v_2^2 = 2ga(1 + \cos\theta)$.

Hence, $R_2 - R_1 = \frac{m}{a}(2ga - 2ga\cos\theta + 2ga + 2ga\cos\theta)$, which leads to $R_2 - R_1 = 4mg$.

Checklist of learning and understanding

Governing equations for horizontal and vertical circles:

- For particles moving in circular paths of radius r, $v = r\omega$, where v is the linear speed and ω is the angular speed.
- For the acceleration towards the centre, $a = r\omega^2$ or $a = \frac{v^2}{r}$.
- The time for each complete circle is given by $\frac{2\pi}{\omega}$.

For vertical circles:

- Using $F = ma$ towards the centre is generally of the form $T - mg\cos\theta = \frac{mv^2}{r}$ for strings and $R - mg\cos\theta = \frac{mv^2}{r}$ for particles travelling on the inside of a circular path.
- Using $F = ma$ towards the centre for motion on a hemisphere, $mg\cos\theta - R = \frac{mv^2}{r}$.
- If the tension or reaction force is zero during motion, then the object has left the circular path and is now a projectile.
- Providing there are no resisting forces, the principle of conservation of energy states that $\frac{1}{2}mu^2 + \text{PE}_A = \frac{1}{2}mv^2 + \text{PE}_B$, where A and B are usually the starting point and a general point of the motion.

END-OF-CHAPTER REVIEW EXERCISE 15

1 One end of a light inextensible string is attached to a fixed point A and the other end of the string is attached to a particle P. The particle P moves with constant angular speed 5 rad s^{-1} in a horizontal circle which has its centre O vertically below A. The string makes an angle θ with the vertical (see diagram). The tension in the string is three times the weight of P.

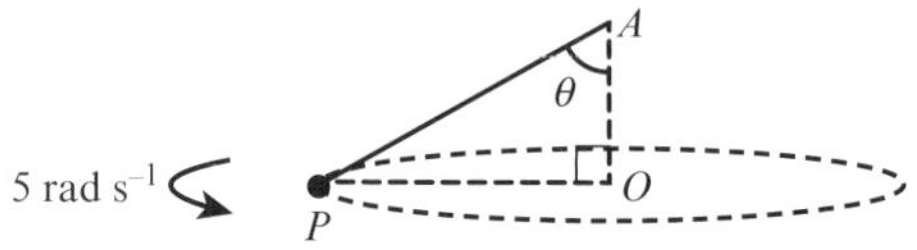

i Show that the length of the string is 1.2 m.

ii Find the speed of P.

Cambridge International AS & A Level Mathematics 9709 Paper 51 Q3 June 2015

2 A smooth bead B of mass 0.3 kg is threaded on a light inextensible string of length 0.9 m. One end of the string is attached to a fixed point A, and the other end of the string is attached to a fixed point C which is vertically below A. The tension in the string is T N, and the bead rotates with angular speed $\omega \text{ rad s}^{-1}$ in a horizontal circle about the vertical axis through A and C.

i Given that B moves in a circle with centre C and radius 0.2 m, calculate ω, and hence find the kinetic energy of B.

ii Given instead that angle $ABC = 90°$, and that AB makes an angle $\tan^{-1}\left(\frac{1}{2}\right)$ with the vertical, calculate T and ω.

Cambridge International AS & A Level Mathematics 9709 Paper 52 Q6 November 2011

3 A particle P of mass m is projected horizontally with speed $\sqrt{\frac{7}{2}ga}$ from the lowest point of the inside of a fixed hollow smooth sphere of internal radius a and centre O. The angle between OP and the downward vertical at O is denoted by θ. Show that, as long as P remains in contact with the inner surface of the sphere, the magnitude of the reaction between the sphere and the particle is $\frac{3}{2}mg(1 + 2\cos\theta)$.

Find the speed of P

i when it loses contact with the sphere,

ii when, in the subsequent motion, it passes through the horizontal plane containing O. (You may assume that this happens before P comes into contact with the sphere again.)

Cambridge International AS & A Level Mathematics 9231 Paper 21 Q3 June 2012

Chapter 16
Hooke's law

In this chapter, you will learn how to:

- use Hooke's law as a model to relate the force in an elastic string or spring with the extension or compression
- use the formula to calculate the elastic potential energy stored in a string or spring and to solve problems involving forces due to elastic strings or springs.

PREREQUISITE KNOWLEDGE

Where it comes from	What you should be able to do	Check your skills
AS & A Level Mathematics Mechanics, Chapter 2	Find the net force acting on a body.	1 Two opposing, pulling forces act on a body. Their magnitudes are 7 N and 4 N. If the mass of the body is 2.5 kg, and the body starts from rest, find the distance travelled by the body in six seconds.
AS & A Level Mathematics Mechanics, Chapters 8 & 9	Determine the kinetic energy and potential energy of a system, and be able to make use of the conservation of energy.	2 A particle slides down a smooth plane inclined at 30° to the horizontal. The initial speed of the particle is $3\,\mathrm{m\,s^{-1}}$. Find the speed of the particle after sliding for 14 m down the plane.

What is Hooke's law?

In the 17th century, physicist Robert Hooke discovered that, for part of the **deformation** of springs, the extension of the spring is directly proportional to the force used to deform it. We know this relationship as Hooke's law. It applies to the deformation of more than just springs. It can be used for a range of applications, from inflating balloons for a birthday party to calculating the amount of sway in a skyscraper in high winds.

In this chapter, we will look at questions in which strings are no longer inextensible. The force required to stretch a string or spring will relate directly to its **extension**, that is how much it lengthens. We shall also solve problems about more complicated systems, by considering the energy stored in a spring. We shall use the symbols explained in Key point 16.1.

KEY POINT 16.1

In this chapter, we shall use the symbols T for tension, x for the length of the extension, l for the natural length of a spring, and λ for the modulus of elasticity. Note that λ is measured in N.

Unless stated otherwise, $g = 10\,\mathrm{m\,s^{-2}}$.

16.1 Hooke's law

In previous work we have worked on problems involving connected particles or particles suspended by strings. The length of these strings did not change: they were considered inelastic, or **inextensible**.

For **elastic** strings, the force required to stretch the string is **directly proportional** to the length by which the string is extended. This gives us the relationship $T \propto x$, usually written as $T = kx$. The constant k varies between different materials and it also depends on the **natural length** of the string. We therefore use the form $T = \frac{\lambda x}{l}$. Here, λ is the **modulus of elasticity**, which tells us how stretchable the material is, and l is the natural length of the spring. This relationship is known as **Hooke's law**. We tend to use the constant $\frac{\lambda}{l}$, as shown in Key point 16.2.

KEY POINT 16.2

It is better to use the constant $\frac{\lambda}{l}$ than k as λ has the same value whatever the length of the string.

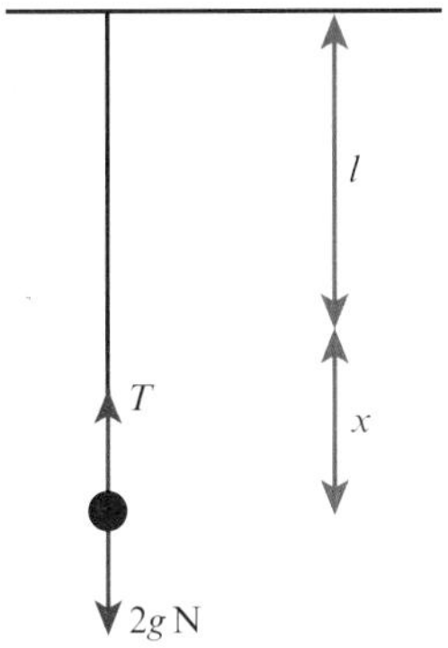

Consider a light, elastic string of length 1 m. One end of the string is attached to a ceiling, and the other end is attached to a particle of mass 2 kg. If the system is at rest in equilibrium, and the string has modulus of elasticity 50 N, find the length of the extended string.

For this example, first we resolve vertically so that $T = 2g$ N. Then using Hooke's law, $\frac{\lambda x}{l} = 2g$. Substituting the given values gives $\frac{50 \times x}{1} = 2g$; hence, $x = 0.4$ m. This means the length of the extended string is $1 + 0.4 = 1.4$ m.

In mechanics, a good diagram is the best way to start a question. You are strongly advised to try to sketch a diagram for every question you attempt.

WORKED EXAMPLE 16.1

A block of 3 kg is attached to one end of a light, elastic string of natural length 2 m. The other end of the string is attached to a ceiling, and the string and block are at rest in equilibrium. Given that the extension in the string is 0.8 m, find the value of λ.

Answer

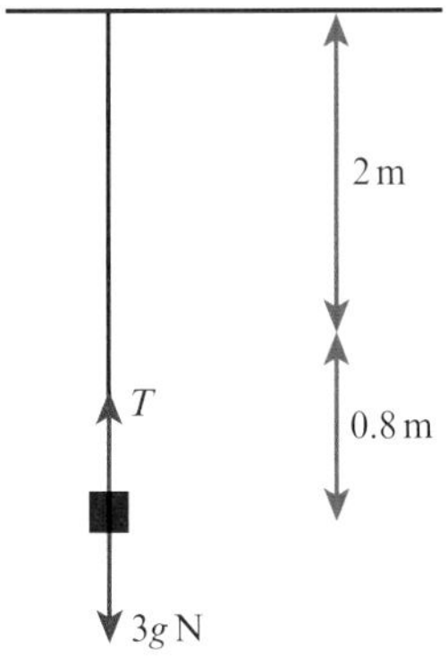

Start with a clear diagram.

Ensure all information is added.

Label distances and forces.

$$\frac{\lambda \times 0.8}{2} = 3g$$

Use Hooke's law.

$$\therefore \lambda = 7.5g = 75 \text{ N}$$

Determine λ.

We shall also encounter problems involving elastic springs.

Springs can be stretched and are modelled in exactly the same way as elastic strings but with one major difference. A spring can also be **compressed**.

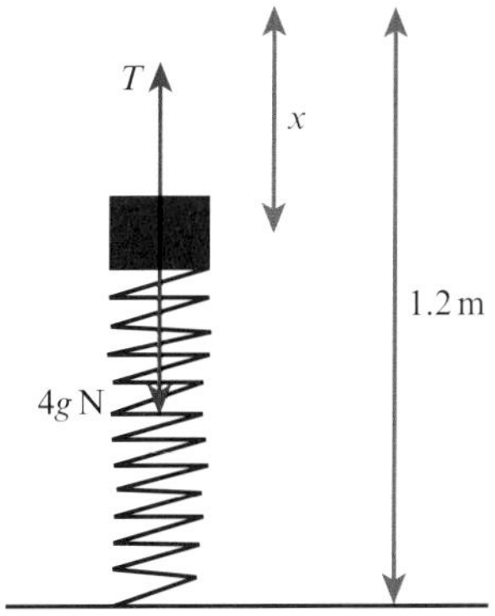

Consider a light spring of natural length 1.2 m that is fixed to a horizontal floor so that the spring stands vertically. A mass of 4 kg is placed on top of the spring so that the spring compresses by a distance x.

Given that the modulus of elasticity is 45 N, can we find the value of x?

Instead of tension, there is a force known as thrust, due to the spring resisting compression.

Using Hooke's law, $4g = \frac{45 \times x}{1.2}$. Hence, $x = 1.07$ m.

Let us consider stretching a spring. A light spring of unknown natural length is fixed to a ceiling at one end, with a mass of 0.5 kg attached to the other end. The spring is allowed to hang in equilibrium such that the length of the spring is now 12 cm.
If the modulus of elasticity is 10 N, find the natural length of the spring.

Since l and x are unknown, it is best to write first that $l + x = 0.12$. Using Hooke's law we know that $0.5g = \frac{10 \times x}{l}$, or $x = 0.5l$. Then $1.5l = 0.12$, which gives $l = 0.08$ m.

WORKED EXAMPLE 16.2

A light spring, of natural length 1.6 m and modulus of elasticity 40 N, is attached to a floor at point A. The other end of the spring is attached to a block, C, of mass 2 kg. The same block is attached to a second light spring, of natural length 1.2 m and modulus of elasticity 25 N, which is then attached to a ceiling at point B.

Both springs are vertical. A and C are vertically below B.

Given that AB is 4.5 m, find the distance AC.

Answer

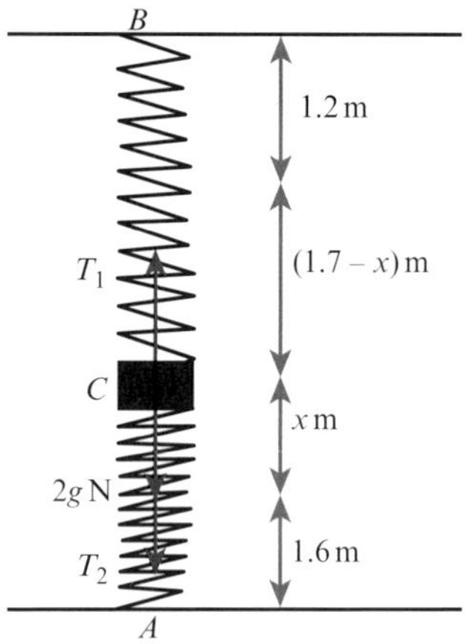

Draw a diagram.

Label all forces and lengths.

Take care that you label the extension of the top spring and the compression of the bottom spring.

$R(\uparrow)$: $T_1 = T_2 + 2g$ — Resolve the forces vertically.

$T_1 = \frac{25 \times (1.7 - x)}{1.2}$ — Determine the upper force.

$T_2 + 2g = \frac{40 \times x}{1.6} + 20$ — Determine the lower force.

So $\frac{25 \times 1.7}{1.2} - 20 = \frac{40x}{1.6} + \frac{25x}{1.2}$ — Equate the forces.

Hence, $x = 0.336$ m and AC is 1.94 m. — Determine x and, hence, AC.

WORKED EXAMPLE 16.3

A light, elastic string, of natural length $2a$, has a mass of $2m$ attached to one end. The string is in a vertical plane and the system rests in equilibrium with the aid of a horizontal force of magnitude mg.

If the string is stretched to a length of $2.5a$, find the tension in the string and the modulus of elasticity.

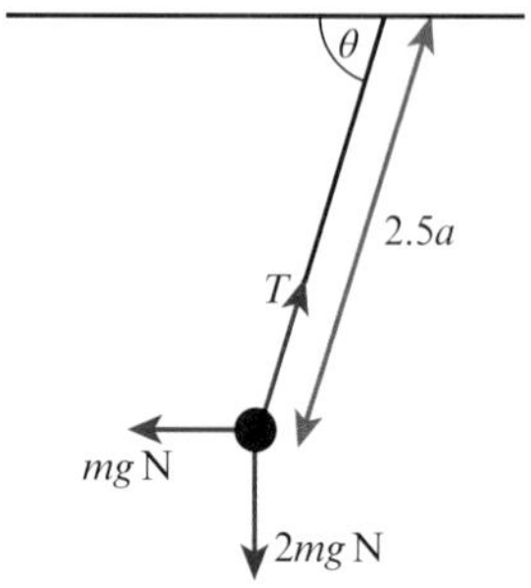

Answer

$R(\uparrow)$: $T\sin\theta = 2mg$ — Resolve forces vertically.

$R(\rightarrow)$: $T\cos\theta = mg$ — Resolve forces horizontally.

Hence, $\tan\theta = \dfrac{2mg}{mg} = 2$, therefore $\sin\theta = \dfrac{2}{\sqrt{5}}$. — Divide the equations to get $\tan\theta$. Use the triangle with sides of 1, 2, $\sqrt{5}$ to get $\sin\theta$.

Therefore, $T \times \dfrac{2}{\sqrt{5}} = 2mg \Rightarrow T = \sqrt{5}mg$ N. — Determine the tension.

$T = \dfrac{\lambda x}{l} \Rightarrow \sqrt{5}mg = \dfrac{\lambda \times 0.5a}{2a}$ — Use Hooke's law.

Therefore, $\lambda = 4\sqrt{5}mg$ N. — Substitute to get λ.

WORKED EXAMPLE 16.4

A light, elastic string of natural length 1.5 m is stretched between the points A and B. A particle, P, of mass 3 kg, is attached to the midpoint of the string. The string rests in equilibrium with the parts of the string making an angle of 40° to the horizontal, as shown in the diagram. Find the value of the modulus of elasticity.

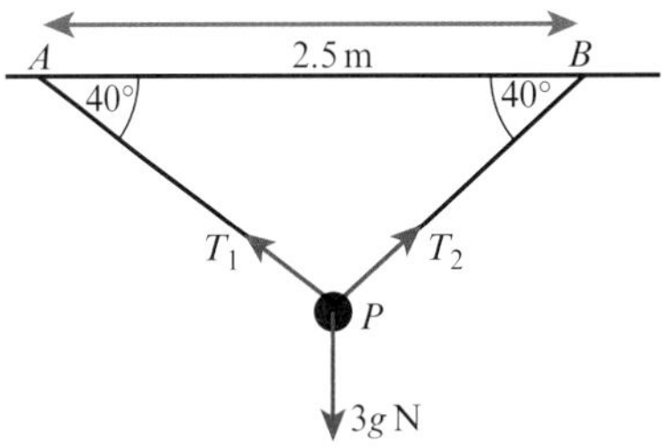

Answer

Particle at midpoint of string $\Rightarrow T_1 = T_2 = T$. — Note that the tensions are equal.

$R(\uparrow)$: $2T\sin 40 = 3g$ — Resolve forces vertically.

$T = 23.336$ N — Use the tension for one half of the string.

$23.336 = \dfrac{\lambda x}{0.75}$

Since $\cos 40 = \dfrac{1.25}{AP}$, $AP = 1.632$. — Determine the new length for one half of the string.

So $x = 1.632 - 0.75 = 0.8818$ m. — Find the extension for one half of the string.

Hence, $\lambda = \dfrac{23.336 \times 0.75}{0.8818} = 19.8$ N. — Determine the modulus of elasticity.

EXERCISE 16A

1 A light elastic string of natural length l and modulus of elasticity λ is stretched by a force T, causing the string to extend. In each of the following cases, work out the unknown value.

a $T = 15$ N, $\lambda = 40$ N, $l = 1.2$ m. Find the extension.

b $T = 25$ N, $l = 1.5$ m, $x = 0.5$ m. Find the modulus of elasticity.

c $T = (3\lambda - 11)$ N, $l = 2$ m, $x = 0.5$ m. Find the tension in the string.

TIP

It is better to use the constant $\dfrac{\lambda}{l}$ than k as λ has the same value whatever the length of the string.

2 A light string of unknown natural length is fixed to a ceiling at one end, with a mass of 0.4 kg attached to the other end. The string is allowed to hang in equilibrium such that the length of the string is now 15 cm. If the modulus of elasticity is 20 N, find the natural length of the string.

M 3 A light string is attached to a ceiling at the point A. The natural length of the string is 1.3 m and the string has a mass of $3m$ attached to the free end. The string is allowed to rest in equilibrium. Given that the string is stretched by an extra 20% in length, find the value of the modulus of elasticity.

M 4 A light, elastic string is attached to a ceiling at the point A. The natural length of the string is 1.6 m and the string has a mass of $2m$ attached to the other end. The string is allowed to rest in equilibrium. Given that the string is stretched by 40% of its length, find the value of the modulus of elasticity.

PS 5 Two points, A and B, lie 3 m apart on a smooth horizontal surface. A light, elastic string, of natural length 0.8 m and modulus of elasticity 70 N, is attached to A. Its other end is attached to a particle, P, of mass m. A second light, elastic string, of natural length 1.3 m and modulus of elasticity 50 N, is attached to the point B. Its other end is also attached to the particle P. The particle is allowed to rest in equilibrium. Find the distance BP.

PS 6 Two fixed points, A and B, are such that A is 4 m vertically above B. A light spring of natural length 1.5 m is attached to A, and at the other end it has a particle of mass 6 kg attached. A second light spring of natural length 1 m is attached to the point B. Its other end is attached to the same particle. Both springs are in the same vertical plane. Given that the modulus of elasticity of the lower spring is one-third of that of the upper spring, and that the extension of one spring is six times the compression of the other spring, find the modulus of elasticity of the lower spring.

P PS 7 A particle, P, of mass 3.5 kg is attached to one end of a light, elastic string, of natural length 1.2 m. The other end of the string is attached to a fixed point, O. The particle is allowed to rest in equilibrium with P 1.8 m below O.

a Show that the modulus of elasticity λ is $7g$ N.

b The particle is now pulled horizontally to the side by a force of magnitude X N so that the angle between the string and the downward vertical is 60°. Given that the particle is at the same vertical level as it was before, find the value of X.

M PS 8 A particle, P, of mass 4 kg is resting on a rough, horizontal table. A light, elastic string, of natural length 2 m and modulus of elasticity 50 N, is attached to P. It is then passed over a smooth pulley to a second particle, Q, of mass 3 kg. Q is hanging freely below the table and the system is on the point of slipping. Determine the coefficient of friction and find the extension of the string.

PS 9 A particle of mass 2 kg is being held in equilibrium on a smooth slope by a horizontal force, P, and a light, elastic spring. The spring has modulus of elasticity 10 N and is attached to the particle and also to the slope 1.5 m up the slope from the particle. If the slope is inclined at 25°, and the force P is of magnitude 5 N, find the two possible natural lengths of the spring.

M PS

10 A particle of mass km is placed on top of a light, vertical spring of natural length $2a$. The modulus of elasticity of the spring is $3mg$ and the spring is standing upright so that it lies in a vertical plane.

a Find the compression in the spring in terms of k and a.

b Find the value of k such that the length of the spring is halved due to the weight of the particle.

16.2 Elastic potential energy

When an elastic string or spring is stretched, or when a spring is compressed, **elastic potential energy (EPE)** is stored in the system. This is the energy stored in strings and springs as they are stretched or compressed.

For example, if an elastic string is stretched, then the work required to stretch the string is related to the force applied and the length of the extension, x.

Since work done is equal to force multiplied by distance, we can state that $W = \int_{x_1}^{x_2} F\,\mathrm{d}x$.

Here the force being applied is considered over a distance $x_2 - x_1$. If we use $\frac{\lambda x}{l}$ as the force, then the work done in stretching the string is $\int_0^x \frac{\lambda x}{l}\mathrm{d}x = \left[\frac{\lambda x^2}{2l}\right]_0^x$. So the work required, the elastic potential energy, can be written as $\text{EPE} = \frac{\lambda x^2}{2l}$. The units are joules, as shown in Key point 16.3.

KEY POINT 16.3

Work-energy principle: If a constant force acts on a body over a given distance, then the work done by the force is equal to the energy gain of the object.

For example, a light elastic string, of natural length 1.5 m and modulus of elasticity 50 N, is stretched to 1.75 m. To find the energy stored in the string use $\frac{\lambda x^2}{2l}$.

So $\text{EPE} = \frac{50 \times 0.25^2}{2 \times 1.5} = 1.04\,\text{J}$.

WORKED EXAMPLE 16.5

Find the elastic potential energy in each of the following systems.

a A light, elastic string of natural length 2 m and modulus of elasticity 100 N, is stretched by 1.2 m.

b A light, elastic spring, of natural length 1.8 m and modulus of elasticity 50 N, is compressed by one-third of its original length.

c A light spring, of natural length $3a$ and modulus of elasticity $4mg$, is stretched to $5a$.

Answer

a $\text{EPE} = \frac{100 \times 1.2^2}{2 \times 2}$ — Input all values into the formula.

$= 36\,\text{J}$ — Include the units for energy.

b $\text{EPE} = \dfrac{50 \times x^2}{2 \times 1.8}$ — Substitute in the values.

One-third of length: $x = 0.6$ — Determine the compression distance.

Therefore, $\text{EPE} = 5\,\text{J}$.

c $\text{EPE} = \dfrac{4mg \times (5a - 3a)^2}{2 \times 3a}$ — Make a note of the extension in the spring.

$= \dfrac{8}{3}mga\,\text{J}$ — State the result.

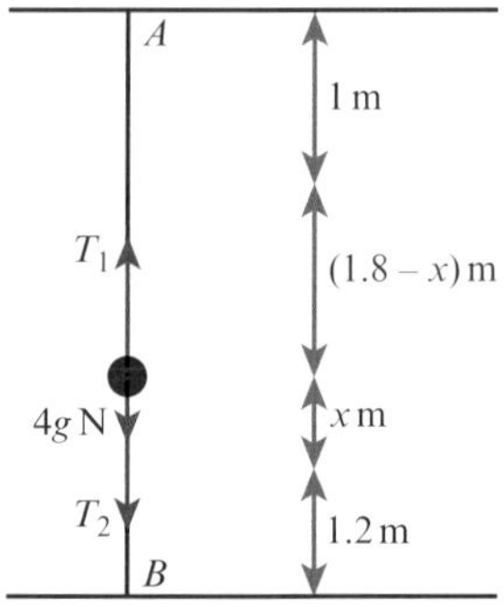

As mentioned in Section 16.1, we may encounter questions that are more complicated. Let us consider an example where a particle of mass 4 kg is tied to two light, elastic strings.

The top string has natural length 1 m and modulus of elasticity $3g$ N. The bottom string has natural length 1.2 m and modulus of elasticity $2g$ N.

To determine the elastic energy stored in the system we must find the extension of each string. Given that AB is 4 m, we can work out the middle part and then determine x.

$R(\uparrow)$: $T_1 = T_2 + 4g$, then using Hooke's law on each string and equating the forces we get

$\dfrac{3g(1.8 - x)}{1} = \dfrac{2gx}{1.2} + 4g$. This leads to $x = 0.3\,\text{m}$.

Then add the elastic potential energy stored in each string to get

$$\text{EPE} = \frac{3g \times 1.5^2}{2 \times 1} + \frac{2g \times 0.3^2}{2 \times 1.2} = 34.5\,\text{J}.$$

WORKED EXAMPLE 16.6

Two points, A and B, lie on a smooth horizontal surface a distance $5a$ apart. A light, elastic string, of natural length $2a$ and modulus of elasticity $3mg$, is attached to A and then attached to a particle, P, of mass m. A second light, elastic string, of natural length $1.5a$ and modulus of elasticity $7mg$, is attached to B and then attached to the same particle P. Determine the amount of EPE stored in the system.

Answer

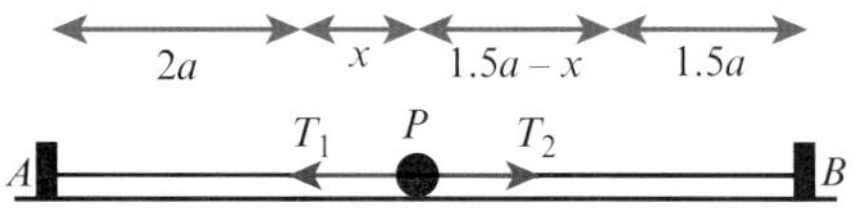

Sketch a diagram showing the forces and appropriate lengths.

$R(\rightarrow)$: $T_1 = T_2$ — Resolve horizontally.

So $\dfrac{3mg \times x}{2a} = \dfrac{7mg(1.5a - x)}{1.5a}$.

Then $4.5mgx = 21mga - 14mgx$. — Simplify the equation.

Hence, $x = \dfrac{42}{37}a \approx 1.135a$. — Determine the extension for each string.

Then $\text{EPE} = \dfrac{3mg \times (1.135a)^2}{2 \times 2a} + \dfrac{7mg \times (0.3649a)^2}{2 \times 1.5a}$ — Sum the EPE for each string.

$= 1.28mga\,\text{J}$ — Work out the result.

WORKED EXAMPLE 16.7

A light, elastic string of length 2.5 m has modulus of elasticity 65 N. Find the work done when stretching the string from 3 m to 6 m.

Answer

For 0.5 m extension: $\text{EPE} = \dfrac{65 \times 0.5^2}{2 \times 2.5} = 3.25$ — Find the smaller extension EPE.

For 3.5 m extension: $\text{EPE} = \dfrac{65 \times 3.5^2}{2 \times 2.5} = 159.25$ — Find the larger extension EPE.

Hence, work done is 156 J. — Deduce that the energy required is the difference between the two.

WORKED EXAMPLE 16.8

A light, elastic string, of natural length $2a$ and modulus of elasticity $7mg$, has one end tied to a point on a ceiling. The other end of the string is attached to a particle, P, of mass m. A second light, elastic string, of natural length $3a$ and modulus of elasticity $5mg$, is tied to P. Its other end is attached to a second particle, Q, of mass $3m$. Q is vertically below P.

With the system resting in equilibrium, both strings are taut. Find the elastic potential energy stored in the system.

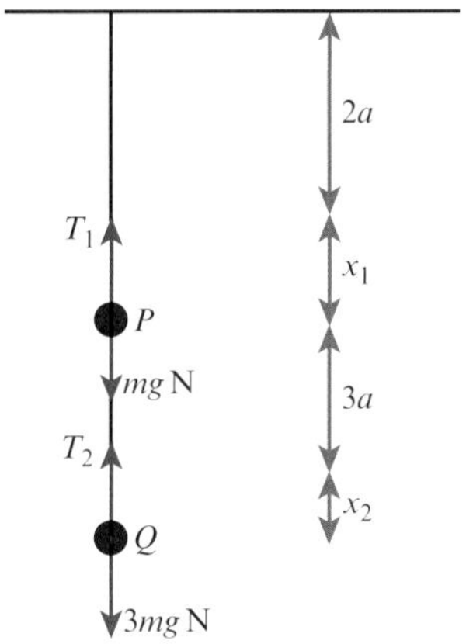

Answer

For the upper string: $4mg = \dfrac{7mg \times x_1}{2a}$, so $x_1 = \dfrac{8}{7}a$. — Upper string holds two particles.

For lower string: $3mg = \dfrac{5mg \times x_2}{3a}$, so $x_2 = \dfrac{9}{5}a$. — Lower string holds only the lower particle.

$$\text{Total EPE} = \frac{7mg \times \frac{64}{49}a^2}{2 \times 2a} + \frac{5mg \times \frac{81}{25}a^2}{2 \times 3a} = \frac{349}{70}mga \text{ J}$$ — Add the two EPEs together.

DID YOU KNOW?

Most materials, including many metals and even glass, follow Hooke's law for part of their movement in tension or compression.

Any material that, when stretched or compressed, does not return to its original form is said to be plastic.

EXERCISE 16B

1 A light elastic string of natural length l and modulus of elasticity λ is stretched by an extension x, by means of a force T, causing the string to gain elastic potential energy (EPE). Find the unknown value in each case.

a $\lambda = 50\,\text{N}$, $x = 0.5\,\text{m}$, $l = 1.5\,\text{m}$. Find the energy stored in the string.

b EPE $= 100\,\text{J}$, $\lambda = 60\,\text{N}$, $l = 1.2\,\text{m}$. Find the extension of the string.

c EPE $= 50\,\text{J}$, $x = 0.8\,\text{m}$, $l = 1.6\,\text{m}$. Find the modulus of elasticity.

P 2 Prove, using integration, that the elastic potential energy stored in a string of natural length l and modulus of elasticity λ is $\frac{\lambda x^2}{2l}$, where x is the extension of the string.

M 3 A particle of mass 5 kg is attached to one end of a light elastic string of natural length 0.8 m. The other end of the string is attached to a fixed ceiling and the particle is allowed to rest, hanging in equilibrium. If the string is stretched by an additional 80%, determine the modulus of elasticity. Hence find the elastic potential energy stored in the string.

M 4 A particle of mass 3 kg is attached to one end of a light, elastic string of natural length 1.2 m. The other end of the string is attached to a fixed ceiling and the particle is allowed to rest, hanging in equilibrium. If the string is stretched by an additional 50%, determine the modulus of elasticity and, hence, find the elastic potential energy stored in the string.

PS 5 The points A and B are 4.5 m apart, with A vertically above B. Particle P, of mass 2 kg, is connected to A and B by means of two light, elastic springs. The spring attached to point A has natural length 1 m and modulus of elasticity 50 N; the spring attached to B has natural length 1.4 m and modulus of elasticity 80 N. The system rests in equilibrium. Find the EPE stored in the system.

P PS 6 A light elastic string has one end attached to a ceiling. The other end is attached to a particle of mass $3m$. The string has natural length $2a$ and modulus of elasticity $6mg$. The particle rests in equilibrium.

a Show that the extension in the string is a.

b A smaller particle of mass km is attached to the existing particle. If the EPE increase is $\frac{8}{3}mga$ J, find the value of k.

PS 7 A light, elastic string of natural length 2.4 m is stretched between two points, A and B, on a horizontal ceiling. The distance AB is 4 m. The modulus of elasticity of the string is 60 N. A particle of mass 3.5 kg is attached to the midpoint of the string. The system rests in equilibrium, with both parts of the string making an angle of 30° with the ceiling.

a Find the extension of the string.

b Determine the amount of elastic potential energy stored in the string.

PS 8 A light, elastic string, of natural length $\frac{3}{2}a$ and modulus of elasticity $2mg$, is attached to a ceiling at the point A. The other end is attached to a particle, P, of mass $5m$. A second light, elastic string, of natural length $\frac{5}{2}a$ and modulus of elasticity $8mg$, is attached to P. The other end of this string has a particle, Q, attached to it. The system is allowed to rest in equilibrium. Given that the mass of Q is $3m$, find:

a the distance AQ

b the amount of elastic potential energy stored in the system.

16.3 The work–energy principle

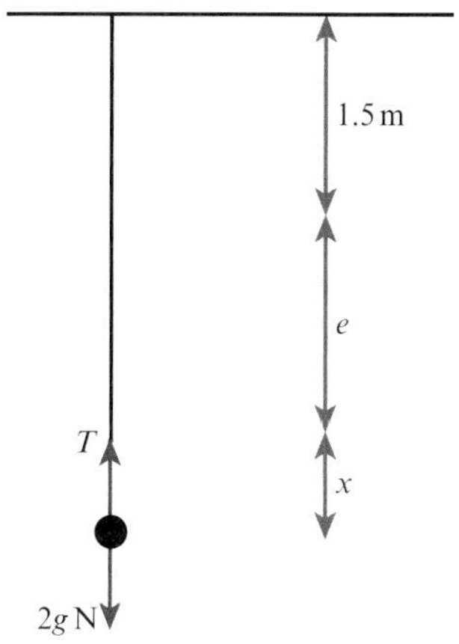

We can also model the motion of a system that is no longer in equilibrium. For example, if a particle hanging on an elastic string is pulled down further and released, what happens next? We assume motion will happen. So in this section we look at acceleration and forces at certain points in the motion. We use kinetic energy (KE), potential energy (PE), work lost due to resistance, and elastic potential energy (EPE) to analyse the motion of objects.

Consider a particle of mass 2 kg that is attached to a light, elastic string, of natural length 1.5 m and modulus of elasticity $4g$ N. The string is attached to a ceiling at its other end. The particle is allowed to rest in equilibrium before being pulled down a further 0.5 m and then released.

Suppose we want to work out the speed of the particle after it has travelled 0.4 m upwards. We need to determine PE, KE and EPE at the start and finish. To do this, we must find the initial extension e of the string. We use Hooke's law to get $2g = \frac{4g \times e}{1.5}$, and so $e = 0.75$ m.

Assign a zero potential point, then measure all potential energy relative to this point.

Initially, $\text{KE} = 0$, $\text{PE} = 0$, $\text{EPE} = \frac{4g \times (0.75 + 0.5)^2}{2 \times 1.5} = \frac{25}{12}g$ J, and then finally $\text{KE} = \frac{1}{2} \times 2v^2$, $\text{PE} = 2g \times 0.4$ and $\text{EPE} = \frac{4g \times (1.25 - 0.4)^2}{2 \times 1.5} = \frac{289}{300}g$ J. By the conservation of energy, $\frac{25}{12}g = v^2 + 0.8g + \frac{289}{300}g$, hence $v^2 = \frac{8}{25}g$, and so $v = \frac{2\sqrt{2g}}{5}$ m s^{-1}. This is about 1.79 m s^{-1}.

WORKED EXAMPLE 16.9

A light, elastic string, of natural length 2 m and modulus of elasticity 60 N, has one end attached to a point, A, on a rough horizontal surface. The other end is attached to a particle P of mass 3 kg that is on the table. The particle is pulled to the side so that the distance AP is 4 m.

a If the coefficient of friction between the table and the particle is 0.4, find the speed as the particle passes through the point A.

b Find the initial acceleration.

Answer

a

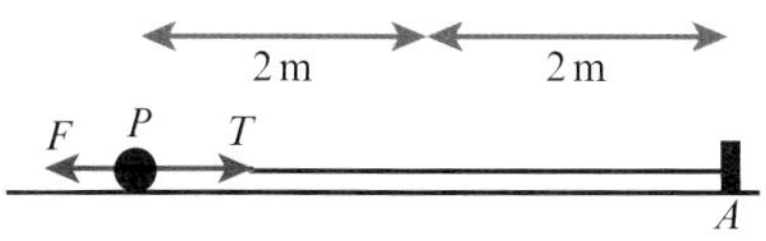

Sketch a suitable diagram.

Label the forces and add distances.

Initially: $\text{KE} = 0$, $\text{EPE} = \frac{60 \times 2^2}{2 \times 2} = 60$ — Determine the initial energy.

At A: $\text{KE} = \frac{1}{2} \times 3v^2$, $\text{EPE} = 0$ — Don't balance the energy levels yet.

$F_{max} = \frac{2}{5} \times 3g = 12$ — Determine the maximum frictional force.

Energy lost to friction: $W_F = 12 \times 4 = 48$ — Find the work done against friction.

Conservation of energy: $60 = \frac{3}{2}v^2 + 48$ — Now balance the energy.

$v = 2\sqrt{2}\,\text{m s}^{-1}$ — Determine the speed.

b $F = ma$, so $T - F = 3a$. — Use Newton's second law horizontally, followed by Hooke's law to find T.

So $\frac{60 \times 2}{2} - 12 = 3a$

$a = 16\,\text{m s}^{-2}$ — Determine the initial acceleration.

Consider a smooth, horizontal disc of radius $5a$, which has its centre at the point O. A light, elastic string, of natural length $2a$ and modulus of elasticity $3mg$, is attached to the point O. The other end of the string is attached to a particle of mass m resting on the surface of the disc. The particle remains at rest relative to the surface of the disc when the disc is rotating about the point O with angular speed ω.

REWIND

Recall from Chapter 15 that, for particles travelling in horizontal circles, the tension component is directed towards the centre.

If the particle is describing circles of radius $3a$, how can we determine the angular speed?

First, use Hooke's law, so $T = \frac{3mg \times a}{2a} = \frac{3}{2}mg$.

Next, use Newton's second law towards the centre of the circle to get $T = mr\omega^2$, and then $\frac{3}{2}mg = m \times 3a \times \omega^2$.

So $\omega = \sqrt{\frac{g}{2a}}\,\text{rad s}^{-1}$.

WORKED EXAMPLE 16.10

A smooth disc of radius 1.2 m is fixed to a horizontal plane. The centre of the disc is O. A light, elastic string, of natural length 0.8 m and modulus of elasticity 100 N, is attached to the centre O, and the other end of the string is attached to a particle of mass 0.5 kg. The particle is describing horizontal circles with constant angular speed. Given that the particle is on the point of falling off the edge of the disc, find the angular speed of the particle and the total energy in the system.

Answer

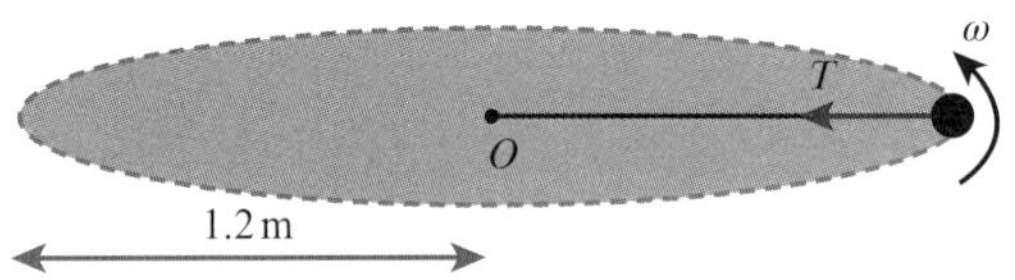

If the particle is about to fall off the edge of the disc, the radius of its circular path must be 1.2 m.

$T = \frac{\lambda x}{l}$, so $T = \frac{100 \times 0.4}{0.8} = 50$. — Use Hooke's law to find the tension.

$R(\leftarrow)$: $T = mr\omega^2$ — Resolve towards the centre. Obtain the angular speed.

Then $50 = 0.5 \times 1.2 \times \omega^2 \Rightarrow \omega = \frac{5\sqrt{30}}{3}\,\text{rad s}^{-1}$.

For the string: $\text{EPE} = \frac{100 \times 0.4^2}{2 \times 0.8} = 10$ — Find the EPE in the string.

For the particle: — Determine the linear speed of the particle.

$v = r\omega = 1.2 \times \frac{5\sqrt{30}}{3} = 2\sqrt{30}$

$KE = \frac{1}{2} \times \frac{1}{2} \times 120 = 30$ — Find the KE of the particle.

Hence, the total energy is 40 J. — Add the energies together.

WORKED EXAMPLE 16.11

A rough slope is inclined at an angle of 15° to the horizontal. A light, elastic string is attached to the top of the slope at the point A. The string has natural length 2.4 m and modulus of elasticity 150 N. A particle of mass 1 kg is attached to the other end of the string. The particle is allowed to rest in equilibrium on the slope with the string taut.

a Find the extension of the string.

b The particle is pulled down a further 0.5 m and released. Given that the coefficient of friction between the particle and slope is 0.4, find the distance of the particle from A when the particle first comes to instantaneous rest.

Answer

a

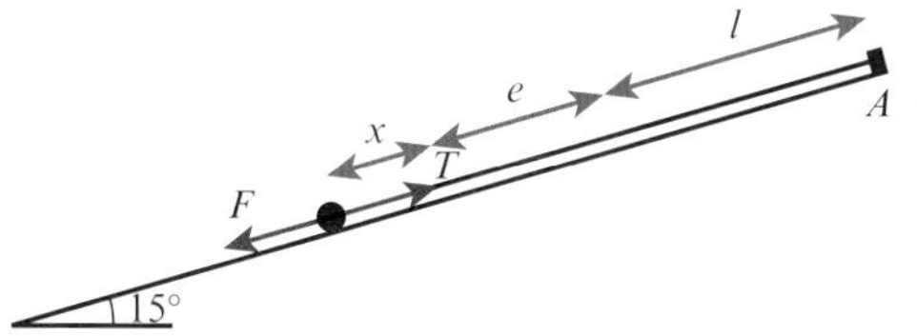

Since there are two stages for the string extension, it is best to label them e and x.

Resolving up the plane: $T = g\sin 15 = \frac{150e}{2.4}$ — Find the extension in the string.

So $e = 0.0414$ m.

b At the low point: KE = 0, PE = 0 and — Determine the energy before release.

$EPE = \frac{150 \times 0.5414^2}{2 \times 2.4}$

$= 9.16$

At the high point: KE = 0, EPE = 0 and — Find the work done against gravity.

$PE = d \times g\sin 15$

$= 2.588d$

Friction: $F = 0.4 \times g\cos 15 = 3.864$ — Determine the frictional force.

$W_F = 3.864 \times d$; hence, $9.16 = 6.452d$. — Find the work done against friction.

So $d = 1.42$.

Hence, distance $= 2.4 + 0.0414 + 0.5 - 1.42$

$= 1.52$ m from A — Total string length minus distance travelled.

> **TIP**
>
> If a particle is travelling along a rough surface, then the frictional force will be at its maximum while the motion continues.

WORKED EXAMPLE 16.12

A particle, of mass 2 kg, is attached to one end of a light, elastic string of natural length 1.5 m and modulus of elasticity $50\sqrt{3}$ N. The other end of the string is attached to a point, O, on the ceiling. The particle describes horizontal circles with the string taut and 30° to the vertical. Find the angular speed of the particle.

Answer

$R(\uparrow)$: $T\cos 30 = 2g$; hence, $T = \frac{40}{\sqrt{3}}$. — Resolve vertically to get the tension.

Using Hooke's law, $T = \frac{\lambda x}{l}$, which gives: — Use the tension to determine the extension in the string.

$$\frac{40}{\sqrt{3}} = \frac{50\sqrt{3} \times x}{1.5}$$

Hence, $x = 0.4$ m

$R(\rightarrow)$: $T\sin 30 = 2 \times 1.9 \sin 30 \times \omega^2$ — Resolve towards the centre, noting the radius of the circle is $1.9 \sin 30$.

$$\frac{40}{\sqrt{3}} = 3.8 \times \omega^2$$ — Equate results to find ω.

So $\omega = 2.47$ rad s^{-1}

WORKED EXAMPLE 16.13

A particle, P, of mass $3m$, is attached to one end of a light, elastic string of natural length $5a$ and modulus of elasticity $8mg$. The other end of the string is threaded through a small, smooth ring, S, and a second particle, Q, of mass $5m$ is attached to this end. The particle P describes horizontal circles with angular speed ω. Particle Q remains stationary at a distance of $2a$ below the ring.

Find the extension in the string and the angular speed of Q.

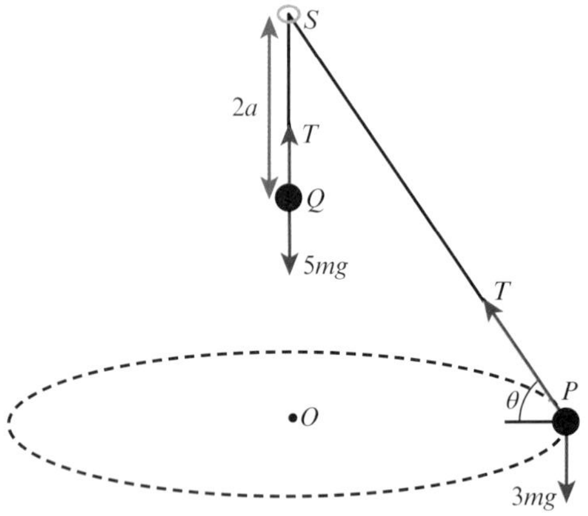

Answer

For Q: $R(\uparrow)T = 5mg$ — Particle Q is in equilibrium.

For P: $R(\uparrow)T\sin\theta = 3mg$, so $\sin\theta = \frac{3}{5}$. — The same string so the tensions are the same.

Hooke's law: $5mg = \frac{8mg \times e}{5a} \Rightarrow e = \frac{25}{8}a$ m — Use Hooke's law to find the extension.

For P: $R(\rightarrow)T\cos\theta = 3m \times \left(3a + \frac{25}{8}a\right)\cos\theta \times \omega^2$ — Resolve towards the centre noting the radius of the circular motion is $(3a + e)\cos\theta$.

$\cos\theta = \frac{4}{5}$, so this becomes $5mg \times \frac{4}{5} = 3m \times \frac{49}{8}a \times \frac{4}{5}\omega^2$ — Note that $\cos\theta$ cancels.

Hence, $\omega = \sqrt{\frac{400}{147a}}$ rad s^{-1}. — Evaluate the angular speed.

EXERCISE 16C

> **TIP**
> Always draw a fully labelled diagram. Include forces, lengths, angles and points.

1 A particle of mass 0.4 kg is hanging from a light elastic string. The string has natural length 2 m and modulus of elasticity 100 N. It is held at rest with the string extended by a total of 1.2m. If the particle is released, find the kinetic energy after it has risen by 0.6 m.

M 2 A particle of mass 2 kg is attached to one end of a light elastic string of natural length 1.5 m and modulus of elasticity 50 N. The other end of the string is attached to a fixed ceiling and the particle is allowed to rest, hanging in equilibrium. The particle is then pulled down 0.3 m and released. Find the speed of the particle after it has travelled 0.4 m upwards.

PS 3 A particle, P, of mass 3 kg is attached to one end of a light, elastic spring. The other end of the spring is attached to a ceiling at the point A. The spring has natural length 1.6 m and modulus of elasticity 45 N. The system rests in equilibrium with the spring vertical.

a Find the extension in the spring.

b The particle is pulled down a further 0.6 m and released. Find the distance of the particle below the point A when it first comes to instantaneous rest.

PS 4 A light, elastic string, of natural length 2 m and modulus of elasticity 50 N, is attached to two points, A and B, by its opposite ends. The points A and B are at the same horizontal level and they are 3.5 m apart. A particle of mass 2 kg is attached to the midpoint of the string. The particle is then projected downwards with speed u. Given that the particle comes to instantaneous rest 2 m below the level of AB, find the value of u.

M 5 One end of a light, elastic string, of natural length 1.2 m and modulus of elasticity 32 N, is attached to a fixed point, B. A particle, P, of mass 1.5 kg, is then attached to the other end of the string. The particle P is held 2 m vertically above the point B and then released.

a Find the acceleration of P when it is 1.5 m above B.

b Find the kinetic energy of P when it is at the same horizontal level as B.

c Find the distance below B when the particle first comes to instantaneous rest.

PS 6 A rough, inclined plane has a string attached to it at the point C. The string has natural length 1.4 m and modulus of elasticity 80 N. The string is then attached to a particle, P, of mass 4 kg. P is farther down the plane than C. The particle P is then pulled down the plane so that it is 4 m from C and released. Given that the coefficient of friction between the particle and the plane is 0.5, and the plane has a 30° incline, find the speed of the particle as it reaches the point C for the first time.

PS 7 A light, elastic string, of natural length 1.8 m and modulus of elasticity 45 N, is attached to a ceiling at point G. The lower end of the string is attached to a particle, P, of mass 1.8 kg. A second light, elastic string, of natural length 0.9 m and modulus of elasticity 35 N, is attached to the particle and then to the point H, where H is 4 m vertically below G. The particle rests in equilibrium with both parts of the string taut.

a Find the distance of P above H.

b P is then pulled down a further 1 m and released. Find the speed when the particle is 1.5 m above H.

PS 8 A particle, P, of mass m, is moving in a horizontal circle, having centre O, with angular speed $\sqrt{\frac{g}{4a}}$. The particle is attached to one end of a light, elastic string of natural length $3a$ and modulus of elasticity $\frac{15}{8}mg$. The other end is attached to a fixed point, C, which is vertically above O. The string makes an angle, θ, with the downward vertical, where $\tan\theta = \frac{3}{4}$. Find the elastic potential energy in the string and the kinetic energy of the particle P.

M 9 A particle, P, of mass 3 kg, rests on a rough, horizontal table, where $\mu = \frac{2}{3}$. P is attached to a light, elastic string of natural length 2 m and modulus of elasticity 49 N. The string passes over a smooth, fixed pulley at the edge of the table and is then attached to a particle, Q, of mass 1 kg. Q is held at the same level as the pulley and released. Given that P is initially 1 m from the pulley, find the speed of Q at the instant P begins to move.

WORKED PAST PAPER QUESTION

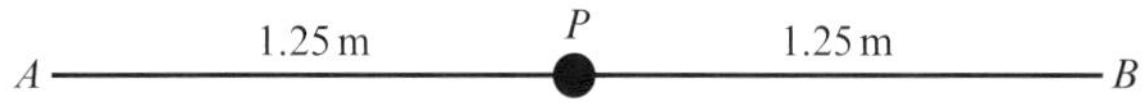

A and B are fixed points on a smooth horizontal table. The distance AB is 2.5 m. An elastic string of natural length 0.6 m and modulus of elasticity 24 N has one end attached to the table at A, and the other end attached to a particle P of mass 0.95 kg. Another elastic string of natural length 0.9 m and modulus of elasticity 18 N has one end attached to the table at B, and the other end attached to P. The particle P is held at rest at the mid-point of AB (see diagram).

i Find the tensions in the strings.

The particle is released from rest.

ii Find the acceleration of P immediately after its release.

iii P reaches its maximum speed at the point C. Find the distance AC.

Cambridge International AS & A Level Mathematics 9709 Paper 5 Q6 June 2007

Answer

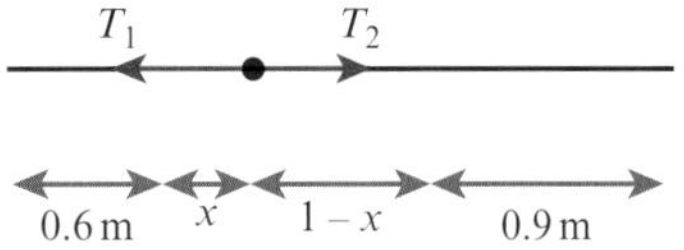

i For the string AP: $T_1 = \frac{24 \times 0.65}{0.6} = 26$ N

For the string BP: $T_2 = \frac{18 \times 0.35}{0.9} = 7$ N

ii Using $F = ma$, $26 - 7 = 0.95a$. So $a = 20\,\text{m s}^{-2}$.

iii When the maximum speed occurs, acceleration is zero, hence $T_1 = T_2$, so $\frac{24x}{0.6} = \frac{18(1-x)}{0.9}$.

Solving, $21.6x = 10.8 - 10.8x \Rightarrow x = \frac{1}{3}$; hence, $AC = 0.6 + \frac{1}{3} = \frac{14}{15}$ m.

Checklist of learning and understanding

Hooke's law:

- $T = \frac{\lambda x}{l}$, where λ is the modulus of elasticity, l is the natural length of an elastic string, and x is the extension of the string.
- Also applies to elastic springs, in which the value of x is either an extension or compression of the spring.
- When a system is resting in equilibrium, the tension is constant and proportional to the extension.

Elastic potential energy:

- Derived from the work done to extend or compress a spring or string over a certain distance.

  This work is given by $\int_0^x \frac{\lambda x}{l}\,dx$.
- Given as $\frac{\lambda x^2}{2l}$ and measured in joules.
- Used in conjunction with kinetic and potential energy (the work–energy principle).

END-OF-CHAPTER REVIEW EXERCISE 16

1 A particle P of mass 0.28 kg is attached to the mid-point of a light elastic string of natural length 4 m. The ends of the string are attached to fixed points A and B which are at the same horizontal level and 4.8 m apart. P is released from rest at the mid-point of AB. In the subsequent motion, the acceleration of P is zero when P is at a distance 0.7 m below AB.

i Show that the modulus of elasticity of the string is 20 N.

ii Calculate the maximum speed of P.

Cambridge International AS & A Level Mathematics 9709 Paper 51 Q5 November 2010

2

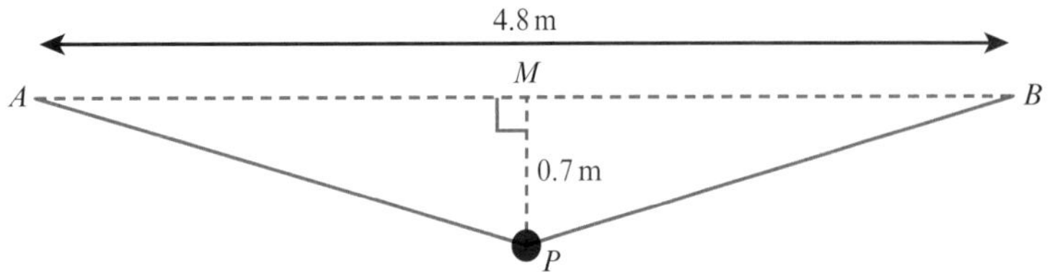

A particle P of mass 0.35 kg is attached to the mid-point of a light elastic string of natural length 4 m. The ends of the string are attached to fixed points A and B which are 4.8 m apart at the same horizontal level. P hangs in equilibrium at a point 0.7 m vertically below the mid-point M of AB (see diagram).

i Find the tension in the string and hence show that the modulus of elasticity of the string is 25 N.

P is now held at rest at a point 1.8 m vertically below M, and is then released.

ii Find the speed with which P passes through M.

Cambridge International AS & A Level Mathematics 9709 Paper 51 Q6 June 2010

3 The ends of a light elastic string of natural length 0.8 m and modulus of elasticity λ N are attached to fixed points A and B which are 1.2 m apart at the same horizontal level. A particle of mass 0.3 kg is attached to the centre of the string, and released from rest at the mid-point of AB. The particle descends 0.32 m vertically before coming to instantaneous rest.

i Calculate λ.

ii Calculate the speed of the particle when it is 0.25 m below AB.

Cambridge International AS & A Level Mathematics 9709 Paper 53 Q4 June 2011

Chapter 17
Linear motion under a variable force

In this chapter you will learn how to:

- differentiate and integrate functions in terms of the time t or the displacement x
- set up and solve separable first order differential equations, using variable forces
- determine displacement, velocity or acceleration.

PREREQUISITE KNOWLEDGE

Where it comes from	What you should be able to do	Check your skills
AS & A Level Mathematics Pure Mathematics 2 & 3, Chapters 4 & 5	Differentiate and integrate functions such as t^3, $(2t-5)^4$ and $\cos 2t$.	**1** **a** Find the derivative of $3t^4$. **b** Integrate $\sin 4t$. **c** Differentiate $e^t \cos t$.
AS & A Level Mathematics Pure Mathematics 2 & 3, Chapter 10	Separate the variables of a first order differential equation.	**2** **a** Separate and then integrate $\frac{dv}{dt} = \frac{t^2}{v}$ to find $v = f(t)$. **b** Solve $e^x \frac{dv}{dx} = -2v$ to get $v = f(x)$.

When do variable forces affect linear motion?

If an object falls through the air we like to assume that the air resistance is either negligible or constant. In fact, air resistance is a variable force that changes as the speed of an object changes. This type of variable force causes the acceleration of the object to vary, too.

Linear motion deals only with objects travelling in straight lines. When these objects experience forces that do not change, the object will either be:

- at rest or moving with a constant velocity; see Newton's first law, or
- moving with a constant acceleration, if the net force is a non-zero constant; see Newton's second law.

If the net force is non-zero, and it varies with time or distance, linear motion will be affected. This concept is the basis for motion as simple as standing up from a chair, and as complex as designing supersonic planes.

In this chapter, you will look at objects that are travelling under the influence of a variable force. This, in turn, will produce an acceleration that is variable. These systems will be:

- either set up first as **differential equations** such as $\frac{dv}{dt} = f(t)$ or $v\frac{dv}{dx} = g(x)$, before being solved with **initial conditions** or
- described in terms of displacement or velocity as functions of time.

KEY POINT 17.1

In this chapter, we shall use the symbols F for force, a for acceleration, v for velocity, x for displacement and t for time.

Unless stated otherwise, $g = 10\,\mathrm{m\,s^{-2}}$.

17.1 Acceleration with respect to time

In AS & A Level Mechanics, you saw Newton's equations of motion as well as models that involve motion with variable acceleration for basic cases.

Let us remind ourselves what we have learned previously. Acceleration is the rate of change of velocity over time. This means acceleration can be written in the form $\frac{dv}{dt}$. Another way of confirming this result is to start with displacement, differentiate once to get $\frac{dx}{dt}$, which is velocity, then differentiate again to get $\frac{d^2x}{dt^2}$. Now, since $\frac{d^2x}{dt^2} = \frac{d}{dt}\left(\frac{dx}{dt}\right)$, we can see that acceleration can also be written as $\frac{dv}{dt}$.

Consider a particle that is travelling in a straight line with variable acceleration $a = -2t\,\text{m s}^{-2}$. If the initial velocity is $4\,\text{m s}^{-1}$, can we find the velocity function in terms of time?

Start with $a = \frac{dv}{dt} = -2t$. Integrating both sides with respect to time gives $\int \frac{dv}{dt}\,dt = -2\int t\,dt$, or $\int dv = -2\int t\,dt$. Integrating, we get, $v = -t^2 + c$, and with an initial velocity of 4, this means when $v = 4$, $t = 0$ and so $c = 4$.

So, the velocity function in terms of time is, $v = 4 - t^2\,\text{m s}^{-1}$.

WORKED EXAMPLE 17.1

A particle is travelling in a straight line with $a = \sin 2t\,\text{m s}^{-2}$. It passes through the point O with speed $v = \frac{9}{2}\,\text{m s}^{-1}$ at time $t = 0\,\text{s}$. Find:

a v in terms of t

b the displacement, x, in terms of t, relative to the point O.

Answer

a Let $a = \frac{dv}{dt} = \sin 2t$, then $\int dv = \int \sin 2t\,dt$. — Write down the differential equation and separate the variables.

So $v = -\frac{1}{2}\cos 2t + c$. — Integrate both sides.

When $v = \frac{9}{2}$, $t = 0$; hence, $c = 5$. — Use the initial conditions.

Hence, $v = 5 - \frac{1}{2}\cos 2t\,\text{m s}^{-1}$.

b Let $v = \frac{dx}{dt} = 5 - \frac{1}{2}\cos 2t$. — Write down the differential equation and separate the variables.

Then $\int dx = \int \left(5 - \frac{1}{2}\cos 2t\right) dt$.

Hence, $x = 5t - \frac{1}{4}\sin 2t + k$. — Integrate both sides.

When $x = 0$, $t = 0$; hence, $k = 0$. — Use the initial conditions.

So $x = 5t - \frac{1}{4}\sin 2t\,\text{m}$.

Now we shall consider where this variable acceleration comes from. Consider a particle that has a force of $2t^2$ N acting in the direction of motion of the particle. If the particle has a mass of 2 kg, we can work out the velocity as a function of time t.

Starting with $F = ma$, we have $2t^2 = 2\frac{dv}{dt}$, then $\frac{dv}{dt} = t^2$. So $\int dv = \int t^2\,dt$, then $v = \frac{1}{3}t^3 + c$.

If we know the initial conditions, we can determine the value of the constant c.

WORKED EXAMPLE 17.2

A particle of mass 4 kg is travelling in a straight line under the influence of a single opposing force. This force has magnitude $e^{0.5t}$ N. If the particle passes through a point, O, at time $t = 0$ s with velocity $2\,\text{m}\,\text{s}^{-1}$, find expressions for both velocity and displacement in terms of t.

Answer

Use $F = ma$ to get $-e^{0.5t} = 4\frac{dv}{dt}$.	Note that the force is opposing, so it is a negative force.
Then $\frac{dv}{dt} = -\frac{1}{4}e^{0.5t}$.	Set up the differential equation.
So $\int dv = -\frac{1}{4}\int e^{0.5t}\,dt$.	
Therefore, $v = -\frac{1}{2}e^{0.5t} + c$.	Solve for v.
Using $v = 2, t = 0$ gives $c = \frac{5}{2}$.	Use the initial conditions.
Hence, $v = \frac{5}{2} - \frac{1}{2}e^{0.5t}\,\text{m}\,\text{s}^{-1}$.	Find the first expression.
Next, let $\frac{dx}{dt} = \frac{5}{2} - \frac{1}{2}e^{0.5t}$,	Set up the second equation.
then $\int dx = \frac{1}{2}\int(5 - e^{0.5t})dt$.	
So $x = \frac{5}{2}t - e^{0.5t} + k$, when measuring from O.	
When $x = 0, t = 0$:	Use the initial conditions.
And so $0 = 0 - 1 + k \Rightarrow k = 1$.	Note the constant is not always 0.
Hence, $x = \frac{5}{2}t - e^{0.5t} + 1$ m.	Find the second expression.

If you are given a velocity function such as $v = (2 - 3t)^2 - 4\,\text{m}\,\text{s}^{-1}$ and asked to find the acceleration, you can differentiate this expression using the chain rule to give $\frac{dv}{dt} = -3 \times 2 \times (2 - 3t)$. Hence, the acceleration is $a = -6(2 - 3t)\,\text{m}\,\text{s}^{-2}$.

Similarly, if you are given $x = te^t$ and you are asked for $v = f(t)$ or $a = g(t)$,

then, for this example using the product rule, $v = \frac{dx}{dt} = 1 \times e^t + t \times e^t = e^t(t + 1)$.

Then $a = \frac{d^2x}{dt^2} = \frac{dv}{dt} = 1 \times e^t + (t + 1) \times e^t = e^t(t + 2)$.

So $v = e^t(t + 1)\,\text{m}\,\text{s}^{-1}$ and $a = e^t(t + 2)\,\text{m}\,\text{s}^{-2}$.

WORKED EXAMPLE 17.3

A particle is travelling along a straight path such that its displacement at time t is given by the expression $x = 2\ln(t^2 + 1) - 2$ m. Find the time when the velocity is at a maximum.

Answer

From $x = 2\ln(t^2 + 1) - 2$, $\frac{dx}{dt} = \frac{2 \times 2t}{t^2 + 1}$. So $v = \frac{4t}{t^2 + 1}$. — Differentiate to get v.

Then using the quotient rule $\frac{dv}{dt} = \frac{(t^2 + 1) \times 4 - 4t \times 2t}{(t^2 + 1)^2}$, so $a = \frac{4(1 - t^2)}{(t^2 + 1)^2}$. — Differentiate again to get a to find when the velocity is at a maximum.

v_{max} occurs when $a = 0$, so $1 - t^2 = 0$ means $t = 1$ s. — Let $a = 0$ to find time. Notice we discard the negative value for time.

You will have learned in AS & A Level Mechanics that the area under a velocity–time graph represents the displacement. So, to determine the area we consider the integral $\int_a^b v\,dt$, where the values of a and b are times during the motion. So $x = \int_{t_1}^{t_2} v\,dt$ gives the desired result.

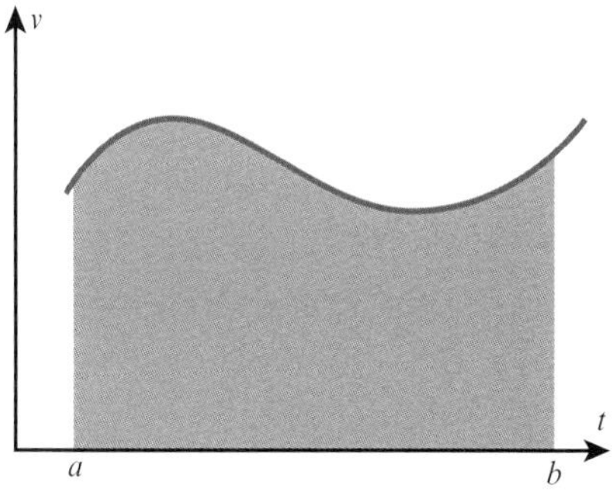

For example, if we are told that a particle is such that the velocity at time t is given as $v = t^2 + 2t$, then to find the displacement of the particle after four seconds, let $x = \int_0^4 (t^2 + 2t)\,dt$.

So $x = \left[\frac{1}{3}t^3 + t^2\right]_0^4 = \frac{112}{3}$ m.

WORKED EXAMPLE 17.4

A particle is travelling along a straight line such that $v = t^3 - t^2 + 2$ m s^{-1}. Find:

a the acceleration when $t = 2$

b the distance travelled during the third second.

Answer

a $\frac{dv}{dt} = 3t^2 - 2t$, so $a = 3t^2 - 2t$. — Differentiate to get a.

When $t = 2$: $a = 12 - 4 = 8$ m s^{-2} — Determine the value.

b For the third second, we need $t = 2$ to $t = 3$. — Note what 'third' second actually represents.

So $x = \int_2^3 (t^3 - t^2 + 2)\,dt = \left[\frac{1}{4}t^4 - \frac{1}{3}t^3 + 2t\right]_2^3$. — Integrate to get x.

This is $\left(\frac{1}{4} \times 81 - \frac{1}{3} \times 27 + 6\right) - \left(\frac{1}{4} \times 16 - \frac{1}{3} \times 8 + 4\right)$. — Substitute in limits to find the value.

So $x = \frac{143}{12}$ m.

TIP

If a particle changes its direction during its motion, then the distance travelled will not be the same as the displacement.

EXPLORE 17.1

Explore functions such as $v = t^2 - t\,\text{m}\,\text{s}^{-1}$ for $0 \leqslant t \leqslant \frac{3}{2}$, and $v = t^3 - 3t^2 + 2t\,\text{m}\,\text{s}^{-1}$ for $0 \leqslant t \leqslant 2$. How would you approach this type of problem?

EXERCISE 17A

1 In each case you are given the displacement function of a particle. Find the velocity and acceleration at the time given.

a $x = 3t^2 + 5t^3, t = 2$ b $x = e^{2t} - 5t, t = 0$ c $x = 5\ln(t + 1) + t^2, t = 3$

M 2 A force of magnitude t^2 N is applied to a particle of mass 0.3 kg, resting on a smooth horizontal surface, for two seconds. Find the speed of the particle after the two seconds.

PS 3 A particle of mass 0.5 kg is travelling on a smooth horizontal surface with a constant speed of $4\,\text{m}\,\text{s}^{-1}$. A force of magnitude kt N is applied to the particle to slow it down. Given that the particle comes to rest after three seconds, find the value of k.

PS 4 A particle is travelling with velocity function $v = \frac{1}{t^2}\,\text{m}\,\text{s}^{-1}$. Given that $x = 2$ m when $t = 1$ s, find $x = \text{f}(t)$.

What does this tell you about the displacement of the particle?

M 5 A force of magnitude $(4t + 3)$ N is applied in the direction of motion of a particle of mass 5 kg. The particle travels in a straight line. Given that the particle is already travelling at $5\,\text{m}\,\text{s}^{-1}$ when the force is initially applied, find the velocity after a further two seconds.

PS 6 An opposing force of magnitude $2t^2$ N is applied to an object of mass 2 kg. At the time when the force begins to act, the object is already travelling at $3\,\text{m}\,\text{s}^{-1}$ and is passing through the point O. Find expressions for the velocity of the object, and the displacement relative to the point O.

PS M 7 A particle is travelling in a straight line with displacement function $x = te^{-t}$ m. Determine the time when the velocity is at a maximum.

PS 8 A truck of mass 12 000 kg is driving at a constant speed of $15\,\text{m}\,\text{s}^{-1}$. The truck driver sees a red traffic light 100 m ahead and applies the brakes. This produces a braking force of magnitude $300t^2$ N. Will the truck stop before reaching the traffic lights?

M 9 A particle travels in a straight line with velocity $v = 2 + \sin t\,\text{m}\,\text{s}^{-1}$. It passes through the point O when $t = 0$ s. Find the displacement from O after four seconds.

P 10 A ball of mass m kg is dropped from a very high tower. Due to air resistance the ball is subject to an opposing force of magnitude mkv N, where k is a constant and v is the velocity of the ball. Show that $v = \frac{g}{k}(1 - e^{-kt})$ and state the terminal speed of the ball, assuming that it does not hit the ground first.

M 11 A particle passes a point, O, with speed $12\,\text{m}\,\text{s}^{-1}$, travelling in a straight line. The acceleration of the particle is $-4t\,\text{m}\,\text{s}^{-2}$. Find:

a the time taken for the particle to be at instantaneous rest

b the distance travelled during this time.

P PS 12 A toy rocket, of mass 1 kg, is modelled as a particle. It is launched from rest using its engines, which produce a force of size $(20 - t)$ N and have enough fuel for five seconds. After five seconds the rocket will be subject to one force only: its weight.

a Show that, for $0 \leqslant t \leqslant 5$, $\frac{dv}{dt} = 2(5 - t)$.

b Find the velocity when $t = 5$ s.

c Find the maximum height achieved, to the nearest metre.

17.2 Acceleration with respect to displacement

As well as measuring the motion of objects with time, we can also measure using displacement.

Consider a particle moving such that the acceleration is given as $a = -\frac{2}{x^2}$ m s^{-2}. Suppose we need to find $v = f(x)$, given that $v = 2$ m s^{-1} when $x = 1$ m. To solve this, we must set up a differential equation.

We cannot use $\frac{dv}{dt} = -\frac{2}{x^2}$ since the variables do not match. But if we use the chain rule on $\frac{dv}{dt} = \frac{dv}{dx} \times \frac{dx}{dt}$, then $v\frac{dv}{dx} = -\frac{2}{x^2}$, as shown in Key point 17.2. Separating the variables gives $\int v\, dv = -\int \frac{2}{x^2}\, dx$. Then integrating gives $\frac{1}{2}v^2 = \frac{2}{x} + c$, and using the initial conditions we find $c = 0$ and $v = \frac{2}{\sqrt{x}}$ m s^{-1}.

KEY POINT 17.2

In order to solve differential equations involving acceleration and displacement, use the acceleration form $a = v\frac{dv}{dx}$.

DID YOU KNOW?

By considering an object with initial velocity u, general velocity v and constant acceleration k, you can use $\frac{dv}{dt} = k$ and $v\frac{dv}{dx} = k$ to obtain Newton's equations of motion. These are also known as SUVAT equations since they involve the variables s, u, v, a and t.

WORKED EXAMPLE 17.5

A particle is travelling in the direction Ox away from the point O with acceleration $a = 2(x - 1)^2$ m s^{-2}. Given that the velocity is 4 m s^{-1} when $x = 1$ m, find the velocity when $x = 4$ m.

Answer

Let $v\frac{dv}{dx} = 2(x-1)^2$, then $\int v\, dv = \int 2(x-1)^2\, dx$. — Start with the differential equation and separate the variables.

So $\frac{1}{2}v^2 = \frac{2}{3}(x-1)^3 + c$. — Integrate both sides.

When $v = 4$, $x = 1 \Rightarrow c = 8$, so $\frac{1}{2}v^2 = \frac{2}{3}(x-1)^3 + 8$. — Use the initial conditions.

When $x = 4$, $\frac{1}{2}v^2 = \frac{2}{3} \times 27 + 8$, so $v = 2\sqrt{13}$ m s^{-1}. — Determine the velocity at the given point.

WORKED EXAMPLE 17.6

A particle is subject to forces that produce an acceleration of $a = -\tan x \, \text{m s}^{-2}$, where $0 \leqslant x \leqslant \frac{\pi}{3}$. The particle travels in a straight line, and when $x = 0\,\text{m}$ it passes through the point O with velocity $4\,\text{m s}^{-1}$.

a Describe what happens to the particle after passing through O.

b Find the velocity of the particle in terms of the displacement.

c Find v when $x = \frac{\pi}{3}\,\text{m}$.

Answer

a The particle slows down as the acceleration becomes more negative. — $a < 0$, so the particle must decelerate.

b $v\frac{dv}{dx} = -\tan x$, then $\int v \, dv = \int \frac{-\sin x}{\cos x} dx$. — Separate the variables and move the negative sign inside the integral.

So $\frac{1}{2}v^2 = \ln|\cos x| + c$. — Integrate both sides.

$x = 0, v = 4$, so $c = 8$. — Use the initial conditions.

Then $\frac{1}{2}v^2 = \ln|\cos x| + 8$.

Hence, $v = \sqrt{2\ln|\cos x| + 16}\,\text{m s}^{-1}$. — State the expression.

c $v = \sqrt{2\ln\left|\cos\frac{\pi}{3}\right| + 16} \approx 3.82\,\text{m s}^{-1}$. — Substitute in the values.

WORKED EXAMPLE 17.7

A particle is moving along the x-axis such that its acceleration is of magnitude $2x\,\text{m s}^{-2}$ for $0 \leqslant x \leqslant k$. The particle passes through the point O when $x = 0\,\text{m}$, and at this point $v = 12\,\text{m s}^{-1}$. Given that the acceleration is directed towards O, find:

a the velocity of the particle when $x = 4\,\text{m}$

b the value of k.

Answer

a Let $v\frac{dv}{dx} = -2x$. — State the differential equation and separate the variables.

Then $\int v \, dv = -2\int x \, dx$.

Hence, $\frac{1}{2}v^2 = -x^2 + c$.

When $x = 0, v = 12$, so $c = 72$, so $\frac{1}{2}v^2 = 72 - x^2$. — Integrate both sides and use the values to find $v = f(x)$.

Leading to $v = \sqrt{144 - 2x^2}\,\text{m s}^{-1}$. — Find the velocity at the required point.

When $x = 4$, $v = 4\sqrt{7}\,\text{m s}^{-1}$.

b Velocity function fails to work when $v^2 < 0$. — Note the condition for the function to work.

Hence, the limit of the velocity function working is when $144 = 2x^2 \Rightarrow x = \sqrt{72}$; hence, $k = \sqrt{72}$. — Determine k.

Suppose we apply a force of magnitude $\sin x$ to a particle of mass 3 kg, where x is displacement and the force is valid for $0 \leqslant x \leqslant \pi$.

If the particle passes through the point O with velocity $2\,\mathrm{m\,s^{-1}}$, and the force applied is in the direction of motion, we should be able to determine the velocity when the displacement is $\frac{\pi}{2}$ m.

We start with $F = ma$, then $\sin x = 3v\frac{\mathrm{d}v}{\mathrm{d}x}$.

So $\int 3v\,\mathrm{d}v = \int \sin x\,\mathrm{d}x$, which means $\frac{3}{2}v^2 = -\cos x + c$.

Next, with $x = 0$, $v = 2$, we get $c = 7$. Then $\frac{3}{2}v^2 = 7 - \cos x$.

When $x = \frac{\pi}{2}$ we see that $\frac{3}{2}v^2 = 7$, or $v = \sqrt{\frac{14}{3}}\,\mathrm{m\,s^{-1}}$.

WORKED EXAMPLE 17.8

A toy car, of mass 0.5 kg, is travelling in a straight line and passes through the point O with velocity $8\,\mathrm{m\,s^{-1}}$. Then an opposing force of magnitude $\frac{4}{x+1}$ N acts on the car, where x is measured from the point O. Find:

a the velocity of the particle as a function of x

b the exact distance travelled when the velocity is $6\,\mathrm{m\,s^{-1}}$.

Answer

a From $F = ma$, $-\frac{4}{x+1} = 0.5v\frac{\mathrm{d}v}{\mathrm{d}x}$. — Form the differential equation. Note the opposing force is negative.

Then $\int v\,\mathrm{d}v = -8\int \frac{1}{x+1}\,\mathrm{d}x$.

So $\frac{1}{2}v^2 = -8\ln|x+1| + c$.

When $v = 8$, $x = 0 \Rightarrow c = 32$

So $v = \sqrt{64 - 16\ln|x+1|}\,\mathrm{m\,s^{-1}}$. — Integrate both sides and use the given values to find $v = \mathrm{f}(x)$.

b Let $6 = \sqrt{64 - 16\ln|x+1|}$. — Substitute in $v = 6$ and solve for x.

Then $36 = 64 - 16\ln|x+1|$,

so $\frac{7}{4} = \ln|x+1|$.

Hence, $x = e^{\frac{7}{4}} - 1$ m.

EXERCISE 17B

1 In each of the following cases, integrate the acceleration expression using $a = v\frac{dv}{dx}$ to obtain an expression for v.

a $a = x^2 + 3$ b $a = e^{2x} - x$ c $a = 3 - \frac{1}{x^2}$

M 2 A particle of mass 2 kg is resting on a smooth horizontal surface. A force of magnitude $4x$ N is applied to the particle. Find the speed of the particle after it has travelled 6 m.

PS 3 A particle is travelling in a straight line such that its acceleration is $3x$ m s^{-2}. Find $v = f(x)$, given that when $v = 5$ ms^{-2}, $x = 0$ m.

M 4 A force of magnitude $\frac{x}{x+3}$ N is used to drive a car of mass 1200 kg. The car starts from rest. Find the velocity of the car when $x = 6$ m.

PS 5 A particle moves along the x-axis with acceleration $3e^{-2x}$ m s^{-2} directed towards the origin, O. Given that P passes through O with speed 5 m s^{-1}, find an expression for the velocity in terms of x and, hence, find the terminal speed of the particle.

M 6 A particle of mass 0.25 kg is travelling in a straight line at 6 m s^{-1} when it passes through a point, O. An opposing force of magnitude $\frac{x}{x^2+1}$ N is then applied to the particle. Find the speed of the particle when $x = 10$ m.

PS 7 A particle is travelling in a straight line with acceleration $(3 + 2x)$ m s^{-2}. As it passes through a point, O, its velocity is 2 m s^{-1}. Find v^2 in terms of x.

M 8 A particle has velocity $v = kx \sin x$ m s^{-1}, where x is the distance from the point O. The particle travels in a straight line. Given that the particle has velocity $v = 2$ m s^{-1} when $x = \frac{3\pi}{2}$ m, find the acceleration of the particle when $x = \frac{5\pi}{2}$ m.

PS 9 A particle is travelling along a straight line with acceleration $4\cos\frac{x}{4}$ m s^{-2}. As it passes through the point where $x = 0$ m its velocity is $v = 7$ m s^{-1}.

a Find an expression for the velocity in terms of the displacement x m.

b Write down the exact value of the minimum velocity of the particle.

PS 10 A particle of mass 2 kg experiences a force of magnitude $\left(3x - \frac{1}{x^2}\right)$ N being applied in the same direction as the particle's motion. When $x = 1$ m, $v = 4$ m s^{-1}. Find $v = f(x)$.

WORKED PAST PAPER QUESTION

A particle P of mass 0.5 kg moves on a horizontal surface along the straight line OA, in the direction from O to A. The coefficient of friction between P and the surface is 0.08. Air resistance of magnitude $0.2v$ N opposes the motion, where $v\,\mathrm{m\,s^{-1}}$ is the speed of P at time t s. The particle passes through O with speed $4\,\mathrm{m\,s^{-1}}$ when $t = 0$.

i Show that $2.5\frac{dv}{dt} = -(v+2)$ and hence find the value of t when $v = 0$.

ii Show that $\frac{dx}{dt} = 6e^{-0.4t} - 2$, where x m is the displacement of P from O at time t s, and hence find the distance OP when $v = 0$.

Cambridge International AS & A Level Mathematics 9709 Paper 5 Q7 June 2008

Answer

i Start with $F = ma$, then $-F_{Fr} - 0.2v = 0.5\frac{dv}{dt}$.

Since $-F_{Fr} = 0.08 \times 0.5g$, $-0.4 - 0.2v = 0.5\frac{dv}{dt}$.

Multiplying by 5 gives $2.5\frac{dv}{dt} = -(v+2)$.

Separating the variables gives $\int \frac{1}{v+2}\,dv = -\int 0.4\,dt$, which leads to $\ln(v+2) = -0.4t + c$.

When $t = 0$, $v = 4$ and so $c = \ln 6$. So $\ln(v+2) = -0.4t + \ln 6$.

When $t = 0$, $\ln 2 - \ln 6 = -0.4t$; hence, $t = \frac{5}{2}\ln 3 = 2.75$ s.

ii Starting from $\ln(v+2) - \ln 6 = -0.4t$, $\frac{v+2}{6} = e^{-0.4t}$, then $v = 6e^{-0.4t} - 2$.

Since $v = \frac{dx}{dt}$, $\frac{dx}{dt} = 6e^{-0.4t} - 2$.

Integrating, $x = \int_0^{\frac{5}{2}\ln 3} (6e^{-0.4t} - 2)\,dt$, which leads to $x = [-15e^{-0.4t} - 2t]_0^{\frac{5}{2}\ln 3}$.

So the distance is 4.51 m.

Checklist of learning and understanding

Terminology:

- Velocity is the rate of change of displacement with respect to time.
- Acceleration is the rate of change of velocity with respect to time.

Notation:

- $a = \frac{d^2x}{dt^2}$, the second derivative of displacement with respect to time.
- $a = \frac{dv}{dt}$, the derivative of velocity with respect to time.
- $a = v\frac{dv}{dx}$, derived from $\frac{dv}{dt}$, is the acceleration in terms of displacement.
- $v = \frac{dx}{dt}$, the first derivative of displacement.
- $x = \int v\,dt$
- $v = \int a\,dt$

END-OF-CHAPTER REVIEW EXERCISE 17

1 A particle P starts from rest at a point O and travels in a straight line. The acceleration of P is $(15 - 6x)\ \text{m s}^{-2}$, where x m is the displacement of P from O.

i Find the value of x for which P reaches its maximum velocity, and calculate this maximum velocity.

ii Calculate the acceleration of P when it is at instantaneous rest and $x > 0$.

Cambridge International AS & A Level Mathematics 9709 Paper 51 Q4 June 2011

2 A cyclist and his bicycle have a total mass of 81 kg. The cyclist starts from rest and rides in a straight line. The cyclist exerts a constant force of 135 N and the motion is opposed by a resistance of magnitude $9v$ N, where $v\ \text{m s}^{-1}$ is the cyclist's speed at time t s after starting.

i Show that $\frac{9}{15 - v}\frac{\mathrm{d}v}{\mathrm{d}t} = 1$.

ii Solve this differential equation to show that $v = 15\left(1 - \mathrm{e}^{-\frac{1}{9}t}\right)$.

iii Find the distance travelled by the cyclist in the first 9 s of the motion.

Cambridge International AS & A Level Mathematics 9709 Paper 51 Q6 November 2010

3 A particle P of mass 0.25 kg moves in a straight line on a smooth horizontal surface. P starts at the point O with speed $10\ \text{m s}^{-1}$ and moves towards a fixed point A on the line.

At time t s the displacement of P from O is x m and the velocity of P is $v\ \text{m s}^{-1}$. A resistive force of magnitude $(5 - x)$ N acts on P in the direction towards O.

i Form a differential equation in v and x. By solving this differential equation, show that $v = 10 - 2x$.

ii Find x in terms of t, and hence show that the particle is always less than 5 m from O.

Cambridge International AS & A Level Mathematics 9709 Paper 51 Q7 June 2010

Chapter 18
Momentum

In this chapter you will learn how to:

- recall and use the definition of the impulse of a constant force, and relate the impulse acting on a particle to the change in its momentum
- recall Newton's experimental law, also known as the law of restitution, and the definition of the coefficient of restitution
- understand and make use of the terms elastic and inelastic
- use Newton's experimental law to solve problems involving the direct and oblique impact of a smooth sphere with a smooth surface.

PREREQUISITE KNOWLEDGE

Where it comes from	What you should be able to do	Check your skills
AS & A Level Mathematics Mechanics, Chapter 3 Pure Mathematics 2 & 3, Chapter 9	Write velocity in component form.	1 A particle is moving in a straight line with velocity $12\,\text{m}\,\text{s}^{-1}$ such that the angle its path makes with the x-axis is 30° anticlockwise. Find the components of the velocity in the x and y directions.
AS & A Level Mathematics Mechanics, Chapter 8	Find the kinetic energy of an object that is in motion.	2 A particle of mass 2 kg is travelling with speed $4\,\text{m}\,\text{s}^{-1}$. Later in the motion it is travelling with speed $11\,\text{m}\,\text{s}^{-1}$. Find the change in kinetic energy.

What is momentum?

Any object that has mass and is in motion has momentum. If two objects are moving at the same velocity, the heavier object will have greater momentum.

In this chapter, we shall work with the quantities momentum and impulse, understand how the formulae are derived, and understand the units used for these quantities. We shall also look at collisions between bodies, especially elastic and inelastic collisions where momentum is always conserved, using the symbols defined in Key point 18.1.

KEY POINT 18.1

In this chapter, we shall use the symbols m for mass, u for velocity before the collision, v for velocity after the collision, P for momentum, e for coefficient of restitution, I for impulse and KE for kinetic energy. Impulse will not be examined in this course.

Newton's experimental law and the coefficient of restitution have many real-world applications. There are strict performance rules for equipment used in sports, such as golf and tennis. Manufacturers use Newton's experimental law to ensure that their sports equipment adheres to the required elastic properties and stays within the rules.

18.1 Impulse and the conservation of momentum

Consider an object of mass m, moving with velocity v. The **momentum**, P, of this object is defined as being the product of its mass and velocity. Hence, $P = mv$. This quantity is a vector: it can be either positive or negative.

For an object to change its momentum, a force must be applied. If that force is applied over time, then $\frac{\text{d}}{\text{d}t}(P) = \frac{\text{d}}{\text{d}t}(mv)$, then $\frac{\text{d}P}{\text{d}t} = m\frac{\text{d}v}{\text{d}t} + v\frac{\text{d}m}{\text{d}t}$. If you assume that the mass does not change over time, then $\frac{\text{d}P}{\text{d}t} = m\frac{\text{d}v}{\text{d}t}$.

Changing an object's momentum requires a force. We have seen how to use the equation from Newton's second law, $F = ma$.

Reversing this process by integrating should give a result that relates to momentum.

So $\int_0^t F\,dt = \int_0^t ma\,dt$. Noting that $a = \frac{dv}{dt}$, and that the velocities at the times given are u and v, $\int_0^t F\,dt = \int_0^t m\frac{dv}{dt}\,dt$ becomes $\int_0^t F\,dt = \int_u^v m\,dv$.

E

Then $Ft = mv - mu$. This is clearly a change in momentum, which we call **impulse**. Common practice is to let $I = Ft$ so that $I = m(v - u)$. The units of impulse are given in Key point 18.2.

KEY POINT 18.2

Impulse I is measured in newton seconds (N s).

WORKED EXAMPLE 18.1

A particle of mass 4 kg is travelling in a straight line on a smooth, horizontal surface. The particle is moving at a constant velocity of $3\,\text{m}\,\text{s}^{-1}$ when a force of magnitude 5 N is applied for 0.4 s. Find the impulse applied to the particle and its velocity after 0.4 s. The particle does not change direction during its motion.

Answer

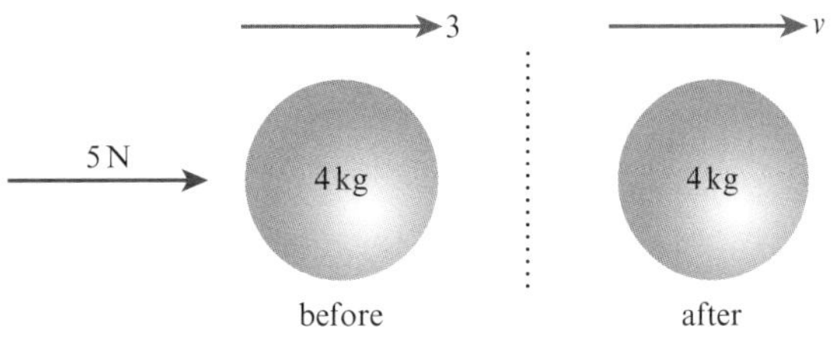

A simple clear diagram shows the before and after states of the particle.

Use $I = Ft$, $I = 5 \times 0.4 = 2\,\text{N s}$. — Use force and time to find the impulse.

Using $I = m(v - u)$, $2 = 4(v - 3)$. — Apply impulse to the right.

Hence, $v = 3.5\,\text{m}\,\text{s}^{-1}$. — Determine the final velocity.

WORKED EXAMPLE 18.2

A particle of mass 10 kg travels in a straight line. When the particle is travelling with velocity $12\,\text{m}\,\text{s}^{-1}$, a force of magnitude 18 N is applied to the particle for 12 s. Given that the particle's direction is reversed, find the velocity of the particle after 12 s.

Answer

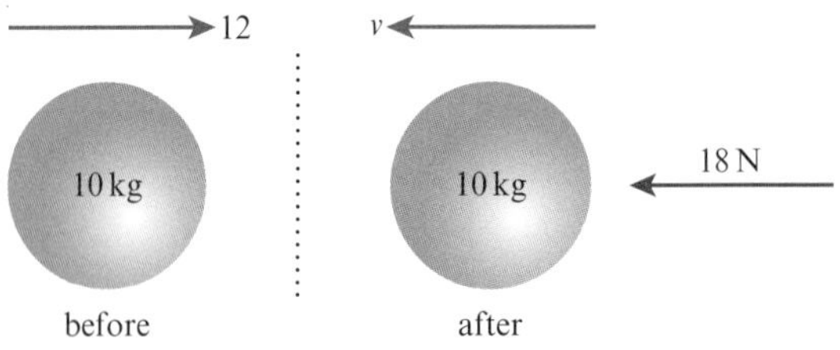

Note that the particle changes direction. This implies that the momentum of the particle before the force is applied and the momentum afterwards must be in different directions.

First take positive momentum to the left. — Choose a sensible positive direction.

Using $Ft = m(v - u)$, $18 \times 12 = 10(v - (-12))$.	Use the impulse formula.
Then $\frac{18 \times 12}{10} - 12 = v$; hence, $v = 9.6\,\mathrm{m\,s^{-1}}$.	Determine the final velocity.

WORKED EXAMPLE 18.3

A particle of mass 5 kg is travelling along a smooth, horizontal surface with velocity $15\,\mathrm{m\,s^{-1}}$. Given that the force, F, applied over 4 s reduces the velocity by $8\,\mathrm{m\,s^{-1}}$, and that the particle still travels in the same direction, find the force F.

Answer

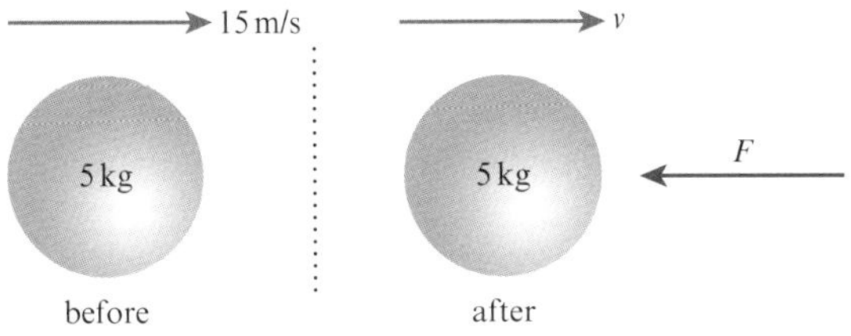

Note that the velocity is reduced, so F is in the opposite direction to v.

Use $Ft = m(v - u)$ to the right.	Take positive momentum to the right.
$-4F = 5(v - 15)$	State the value of v.
Since $v = 7$, then $4F = 40$.	
Hence, $F = 10\,\mathrm{N}$.	Determine F.

When two particles collide, whether they remain separate after impact or combine to make a single object, the law of conservation of momentum states that $m_1u_1 + m_2u_2 = m_1v_1 + m_2v_2$, as shown in Key point 18.3. m_1, m_2 are the masses of the particles; u_1, u_2 are the velocities before the collision, and v_1, v_2 are the velocities after the collision.

KEY POINT 18.3

The law of conservation of momentum:

$$m_1u_1 + m_2u_2 = m_1v_1 + m_2v_2$$

Consider a particle, P, of mass 2 kg travelling on a smooth, horizontal surface with velocity $5\,\mathrm{m\,s^{-1}}$. This particle collides with a second particle, Q, of mass 1 kg, which is at rest. The particles stick together when they collide. The particles are said to **coalesce**.

If we draw a diagram to explain what happens, then we can attempt to find the velocity of the particle afterwards.

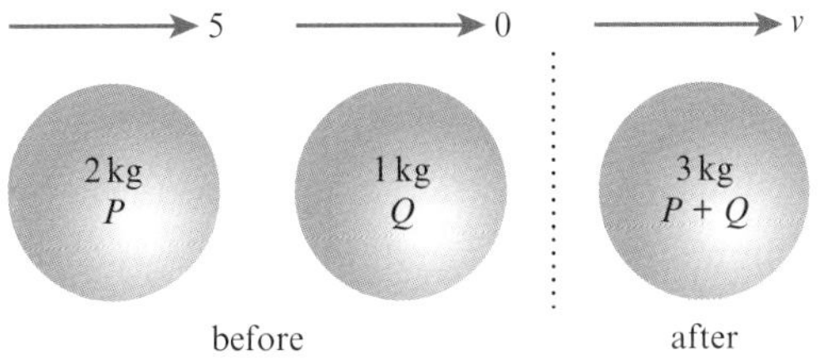

So using conservation of momentum in the direction of motion, $2 \times 5 + 0 = (2 + 1)v$.

Hence the velocity of the combined particles afterwards is $v = \frac{10}{3}\,\text{m s}^{-1}$.

This method comes from the equation $m_1u_1 + m_2u_2 = m_1v_1 + m_2v_2$, as shown in Key point 18.3. Here, each particle has its own momentum and, since momentum is conserved, both sides must balance.

In this simple case, the particles coalesce and the right side becomes:

$$m_1v + m_2v = (m_1 + m_2)v$$

KEY POINT 18.4

When two particles collide, the amount of kinetic energy (KE) lost can be found by comparing the KE before and after the collision. If the collision is perfectly elastic, we can use conservation of energy to equate KE before and after the collision.

When two particles collide and coalesce, or stick together, they are said to be inelastic. That means there is no bounce between them. If two particles collide and there is no loss in kinetic energy, the collision is said to be **perfectly elastic**. We can use conservation of energy, as shown in Key point 18.4.

Consider the example of two particles that are both of mass m. They are travelling with velocities $2u$ and u, as shown. To find a relationship for the velocities after a perfectly elastic collision, we must first find the kinetic energy before they collide.

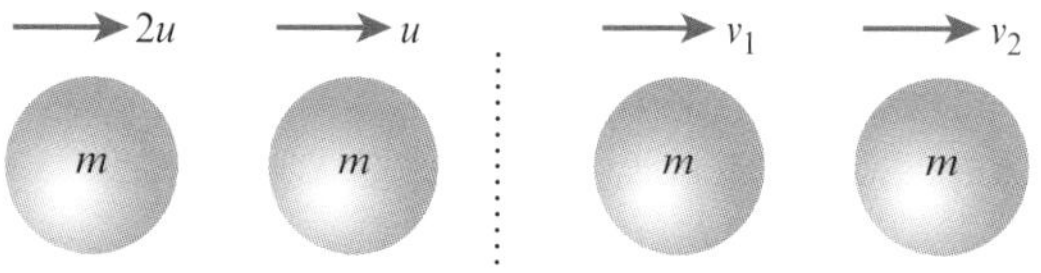

$\text{KE}_{\text{before}} = \frac{1}{2}m(2u)^2 + \frac{1}{2}mu^2 = \frac{5}{2}mu^2$, and $\text{KE}_{\text{after}} = \frac{1}{2}m(v_1^2 + v_2^2)$.

Using conservation of energy means $5u^2 = v_1^2 + v_2^2$ is the equation we need to solve. There are many solutions to this, so we shall not be able to solve this at present.

To help us deal with this, we are going to use **Newton's experimental law**, which is also known as Newton's law of restitution.

This law states that the constant $e = \frac{\text{speed of separation}}{\text{speed of approach}}$, where $0 \leqslant e \leqslant 1$. e is called the **coefficient of restitution**. When $e = 0$ the objects colliding have no elasticity. This means that they will coalesce.

When $e = 1$, the objects are said to be perfectly elastic, as in this example.

To determine v_1 and v_2, let $e = \frac{v_2 - v_1}{2u - u}$. In this expression, $v_2 - v_1$ shows how quickly the second particle escapes the first one and $2u - u$ shows how quickly the particles approach each other.

So $1 = \frac{v_2 - v_1}{u}$, which means $v_2 - v_1 = u$. Then from the law of conservation of momentum we have $2mu + mu = mv_1 + mv_2$, or $3u = v_1 + v_2$. Combining these two equations gives $v_1 = u$ and $v_2 = 2u$.

WORKED EXAMPLE 18.4

Two particles, P and Q, are travelling on a smooth, horizontal plane. P has mass 3 kg and Q has mass 1 kg. P has velocity $3u$ and Q velocity u. P then collides with Q, such that the collision is perfectly elastic. Find the velocity of each particle after the collision. Confirm that the kinetic energy is the same before and after the collision.

Answer

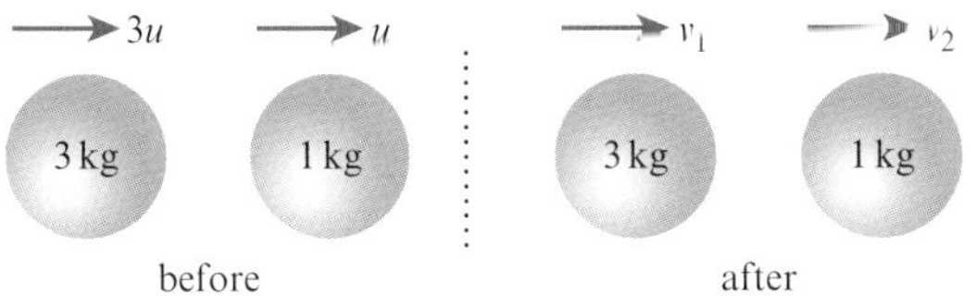

Using conservation of momentum: $9u + u = 3v_1 + v_2$ ------------(1) — Use conservation of momentum.

Using Newton's experimental law: $1 = \frac{v_2 - v_1}{3u - u}$, so $v_2 - v_1 = 2u$. (2) — Use Newton's experimental law (NEL) with $e = 1$ as we have a perfectly elastic collision.

Combining (1) and (2) gives $v_1 = 2u\,\text{m s}^{-1}$, $v_2 = 4u\,\text{m s}^{-1}$ — Solve the simultaneous equations.

Before: $\text{KE} = \frac{1}{2} \times 3 \times 9u^2 + \frac{1}{2} \times 1 \times u^2 = 14u^2\,\text{J}$ — Find the KE before the collision.

After: $\text{KE} = \frac{1}{2} \times 3 \times 4u^2 + \frac{1}{2} \times 1 \times 16u^2 = 14u^2\,\text{J}$ — Confirm that the KE after the collision is the same.

When collisions are neither inelastic nor perfectly elastic, we have a coefficient of restitution that reduces the energy of the system. In most cases $0 < e < 1$.

EXPLORE 18.1

Table tennis balls are made to have the value $e \approx 0.95$. Carry out some online research into different types of sporting equipment, such as footballs and tennis balls, and find out their coefficients of restitution.

WORKED EXAMPLE 18.5

Two smooth spheres of equal radius are resting on a smooth surface. Sphere A has mass $2m$ and sphere B has mass $3m$. The coefficient of restitution between the spheres is $\frac{2}{3}$. Sphere A is projected towards B with velocity $2u$ and sphere B is projected towards A with velocity u. Find the velocity of each sphere after the collision.

Find also the loss in kinetic energy.

Answer

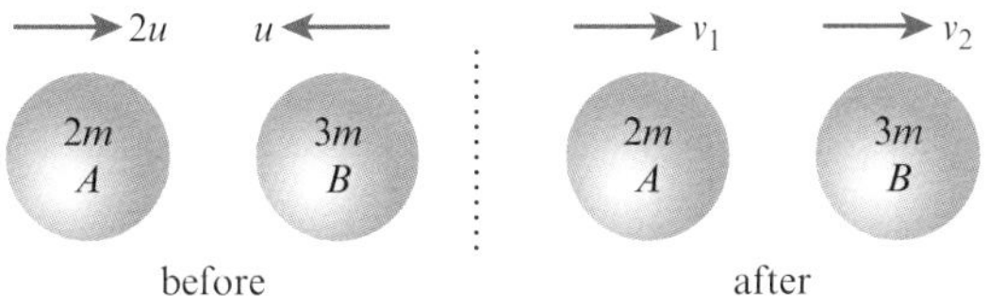

It is best to make no assumptions about the directions of particles after a collision. The solutions will tell you what is happening.

Conservation of momentum: $4mu - 3mu = 2mv_1 + 3mv_2$, so $2v_1 + 3v_2 = u$.

Use conservation of momentum and law of restitution equations.

Newton's experimental law: $\frac{2}{3} = \frac{v_2 - v_1}{2u + u}$, so $3v_2 - 3v_1 = 6u$.

Combining gives $v_1 = -u\,\text{m s}^{-1}$, $v_2 = u\,\text{m s}^{-1}$.

Since $v_1 < 0$, A changes direction. B also changes direction.

Before: $\text{KE} = \frac{1}{2} \times 2m \times 4u^2 + \frac{1}{2} \times 3m \times u^2 = \frac{11}{2}mu^2$

Find the energy before and after the collision to determine the loss in kinetic energy.

After: $\text{KE} = \frac{1}{2} \times 2m \times u^2 + \frac{1}{2} \times 3m \times u^2 = \frac{5}{2}mu^2$

Hence, the energy loss is $3mu^2$ J.

WORKED EXAMPLE 18.6

Two smooth spheres of equal radius are resting on a smooth surface. Sphere P has mass m and sphere Q has mass $2m$. The coefficient of restitution between the spheres is e. Sphere P is projected towards Q with velocity u. Find a condition on e such that P's direction is changed.

Answer

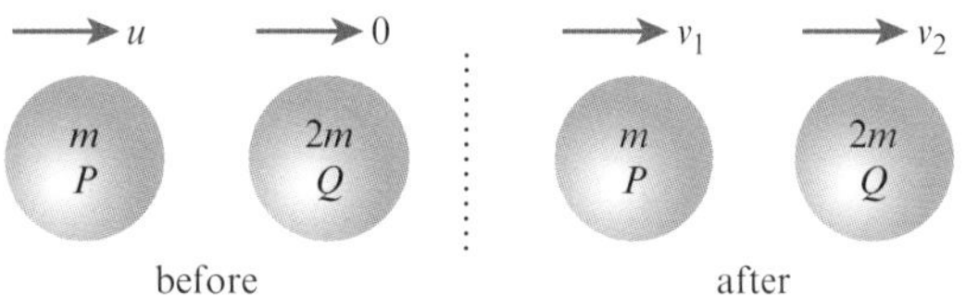

Conservation of momentum: $mu = mv_1 + 2mv_2$, so $v_1 + 2v_2 = u$.

Write down the two standard equations.

Newton's experimental law: $e = \frac{v_2 - v_1}{u}$, so $v_2 - v_1 = eu$.

Combining gives $v_2 = \frac{u}{3}(1 + e)$, and so $v_1 = \frac{u}{3}(1 - 2e)$.

Equate to get v_1 and v_2 in terms of e.

Consider $v_1 < 0$, and so $1 - 2e < 0 \Rightarrow e > \frac{1}{2}$.

Note P's change in direction.

$v_1 < 0$ leads to the result.

DID YOU KNOW?

Newton's cradle was first demonstrated by a French physicist known as Abbe Mariotte in the 17th century. An English actor saw a toy version in 1967 and gave it the name Newton's cradle.

EXERCISE 18A

PS 1 Two particles, P and Q, are resting on a smooth, horizontal surface. P is projected towards Q with velocity $2u$ and they collide directly. Given that the masses of P and Q are $2m$ and m, respectively, and that the collision is perfectly elastic, find the velocity of P and Q afterwards.

PS 2 Two particles, P and Q, are resting on a smooth surface. They are connected by a light string of length 4 m. The particles are of mass $2m$ and $3m$, respectively, and are resting 2 m apart. Q is projected directly away from P with velocity u. Given that the string is inextensible, find the velocity of the particles when the string becomes taut.

M 3 Two identical, 1 kg, smooth spheres, A and B, of equal radius, are travelling on a smooth surface. The velocity of A is $3\,\text{m s}^{-1}$ and the velocity of B is $2\,\text{m s}^{-1}$. Given that the spheres are moving in opposite directions, and that the coefficient of restitution is 0.7, find the loss in kinetic energy due to the collision.

PS 4 A particle, P, of mass $4m$, is projected with velocity $2u$ towards another particle, Q, of mass $5m$, which is at rest. Both particles are on a smooth, horizontal surface. The coefficient of restitution between the particles is e. Find the condition on e so that both particles are travelling in the same direction after the collision.

PS 5 Two particles, P and Q, are resting on a smooth, horizontal surface. Their masses are 2 kg and 3 kg, respectively. Particle P is projected towards Q with velocity $5\,\text{m s}^{-1}$. It subsequently strikes Q and Q moves off with velocity $2.5\,\text{m s}^{-1}$. Find the value of e, and also find the loss in kinetic energy due to the collision.

PS 6 Two particles, P and Q, are resting on a smooth, horizontal surface. P has mass $2m$ and Q has mass m. P is projected towards Q with velocity u and Q is projected towards P with velocity $3u$. Given that Q has velocity $\frac{5}{9}u$, and has its direction changed due to the collision, find the value of e.

P PS 7 Two smooth spheres of equal size are resting on a smooth, horizontal surface. Particle P, of mass m, is projected towards particle Q, of mass $2m$, with velocity $3u$. Particle Q is initially at rest. The coefficient of restitution between the spheres is e.

a Show that particle P has its direction changed provided $e > \frac{1}{2}$.

b Given that the kinetic energy after the collision is half the initial kinetic energy, find the value of e and state the velocity of P.

18.2 Oblique collisions and other examples

Consider a particle travelling towards a wall with velocity u at an angle of θ. If we split the velocity into component form we have u_y parallel to the wall, and u_x perpendicular to the wall.

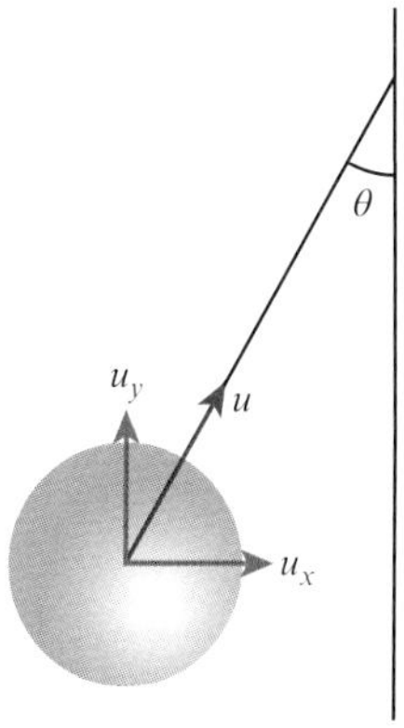

When the particle bounces off the wall, the component u_y is unaffected by the collision, but the component u_x will be subject to the conservation of momentum.

After bouncing off the wall, the component u_x will become eu_x. Note that the angles α and θ are not the same, unless $e = 1$.

When an object collides with a wall at an angle other than 90°, this is known as an **oblique collision**.

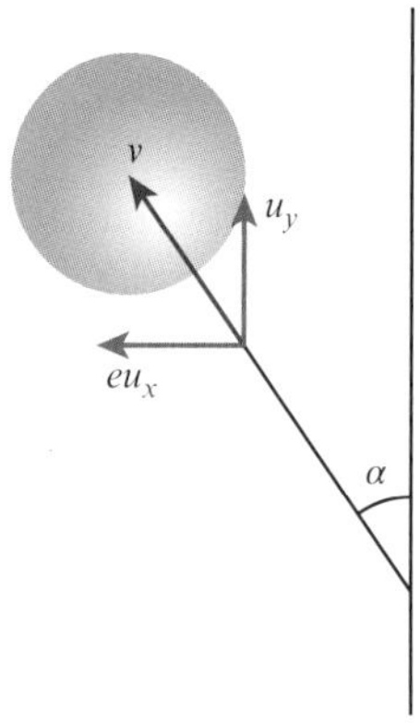

As an example, consider a particle travelling with velocity $2u$, directed at an angle of 30° to a wall, with coefficient of restitution $\frac{1}{2}$ between the particle and the wall. Find the velocity of the particle after the collision.

We have $u_y = 2u\cos 30 = u\sqrt{3}$, and $u_x = 2u\sin 30 = u$.

The particle bounces off the wall so $eu_x = \frac{u}{2}$. Then for the velocity afterwards, we have $\sqrt{(u\sqrt{3})^2 + \left(\frac{u}{2}\right)^2}$, which is $\frac{u\sqrt{13}}{2}$ m s^{-1}. We can also find the angle that the particle makes with the wall afterwards, using $\tan\alpha = \frac{eu_x}{u_y} = \frac{\frac{u}{2}}{u\sqrt{3}}$, which gives $\alpha = 16.1°$.

WORKED EXAMPLE 18.7

A particle is projected along a smooth, horizontal surface with velocity u. The particle collides with a smooth, vertical wall at an angle of 60°. Given that the coefficient of restitution between the particle and the wall is 0.3, find the angle between the wall and the path of the particle after the collision.

Answer

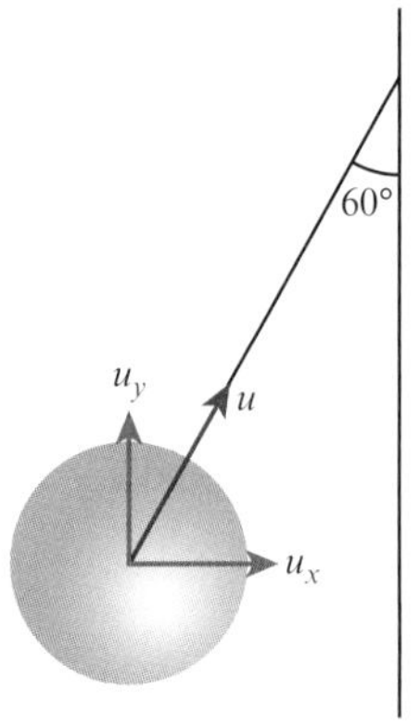

First: $u_y = u\cos 60 = \frac{u}{2}$ — Split the velocity into its components.

Then $u_x = u\sin 60 = \frac{u\sqrt{3}}{2}$.

Then after bouncing, $eu_x = \frac{3}{10} \times \frac{u\sqrt{3}}{2} = \frac{3\sqrt{3}u}{20}$. — Find the component that is perpendicular to the wall after colliding.

Then $\tan\alpha = \frac{3\sqrt{3}}{20} \times \frac{2}{1}$. — Use components to find the tangent of the angle.

So $\alpha = 27.5°$. — Determine α.

WORKED EXAMPLE 18.8

A particle of mass 3 kg is travelling on a smooth, horizontal surface with velocity $4\,\text{m s}^{-1}$. The particle collides obliquely with a smooth, vertical wall where the coefficient of restitution is $\frac{1}{3}$. Given that the angle between the path of the particle and the wall before the collision is 40°, find the loss in kinetic energy due to the collision.

Answer

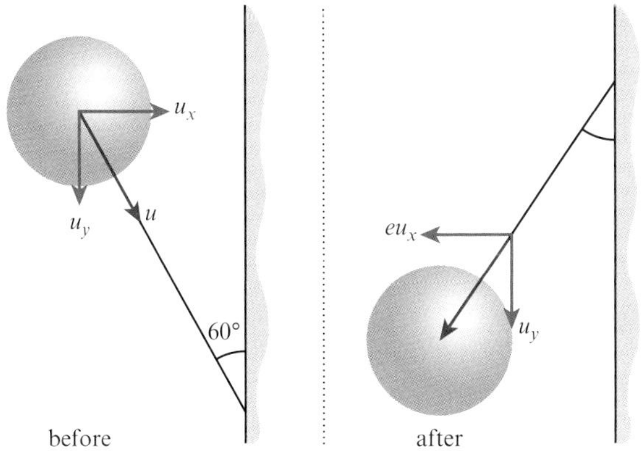

Parallel to wall: $u_y = 4\cos 40 = 3.0642$ — Find both components before the collision.

Perpendicular to wall: $u_x = 4\sin 40 = 2.5712$

After collision, $eu_x = 0.8571$. — Find the perpendicular component after the collision.

Before: $\text{KE} = \frac{1}{2} \times 3 \times 4^2 = 24$ — Determine the KE before and after the collision.

After: $\text{KE} = \frac{1}{2} \times 3 \times (3.0642^2 + 0.8571^2) = 15.186$

Hence, the energy loss is 8.81 J. — Determine the difference in kinetic energy.

WORKED EXAMPLE 18.9

When a smooth sphere travelling on smooth horizontal ground collides obliquely with a smooth vertical wall, it rebounds off the wall at right angles to its original direction. If the sphere is travelling with velocity u and its path makes an angle of 60° with the wall before the collision, find e, the coefficient of restitution.

Answer

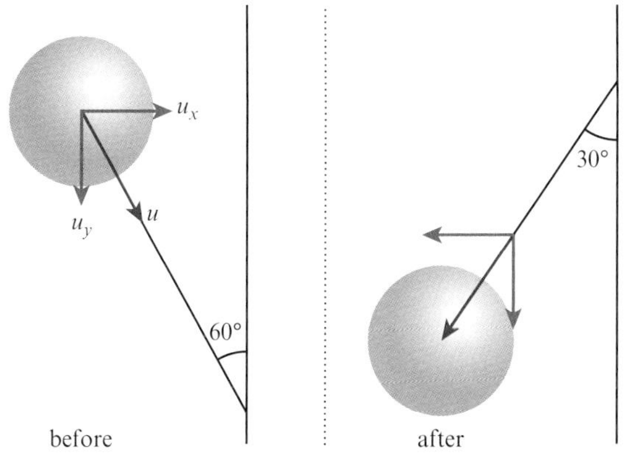

Draw a clear diagram showing the situation before and after the collision.

Parallel: $u_y = u\cos 60 = \frac{u}{2}$ — Find the velocity components before the collision.

This is unchanged after the collision.

Perpendicular: $u_x = u\sin 60 = \frac{\sqrt{3}}{2}u$ — State the perpendicular component.

After the collision, $eu_x = \frac{\sqrt{3}}{2}eu$.

Since the angle after is 30°, $\tan 30 = \frac{\sqrt{3}}{2}eu \times \frac{2}{u}$. — Use the tangent of the angle to relate the components.

So $\frac{1}{\sqrt{3}} = \sqrt{3}e \Rightarrow e = \frac{1}{3}$. — Determine e.

Particles can also rebound off walls at 90°.

Consider two particles, A and B, of masses m and $2m$. They are resting on a smooth horizontal surface. Particle A is projected towards B with velocity u. A strikes B and then B will go on to strike a smooth vertical wall, rebounding off at 90°. If the coefficient of restitution between the particles is $\frac{7}{8}$, and the coefficient of restitution between B and the wall is $\frac{1}{3}$, can we show that there are no further collisions?

To start with, we need to draw two diagrams: one for the A–B collision, and one for B and the wall.

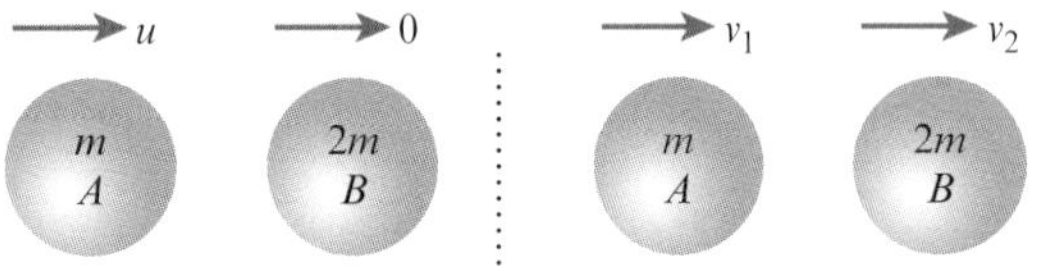

before after

First we use conservation of momentum: $mu = mv_1 + 2mv_2$ to get $u = v_1 + 2v_2$.

Then use Newton's experimental law: $\frac{7}{8} = \frac{v_2 - v_1}{u}$, or $v_2 - v_1 = \frac{7}{8}u$

Adding these two gives $v_2 = \frac{5}{8}u$ and $v_1 = -\frac{1}{4}u$. So we know that A travels in the opposite direction away from the wall.

B hits the wall and bounces off with velocity $\frac{1}{3} \times \frac{5}{8}u = \frac{5}{24}u$. It is now travelling in the same direction as A.

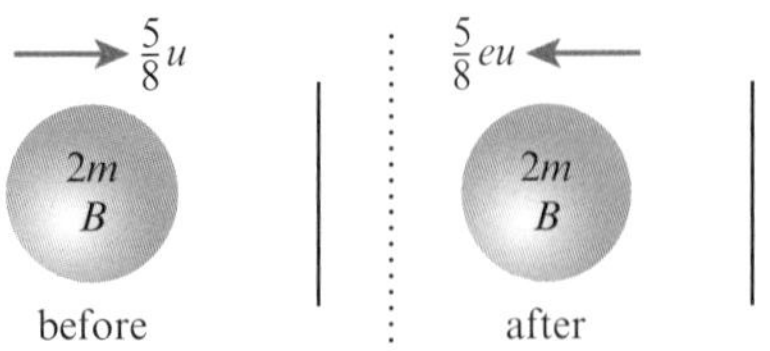

before after

Since $\frac{1}{4}u > \frac{5}{24}u$, B will never catch up with A, and so there will be no more collisions.

WORKED EXAMPLE 18.10

Two smooth spheres, P and Q, of masses $2m$ and $3m$, respectively, are resting on a smooth, horizontal surface. Sphere P is projected towards Q with velocity $2u$. P strikes Q and Q begins to travel towards a smooth, vertical wall. The coefficient of restitution between the spheres is e. Q strikes the wall at right angles and rebounds off the wall, where the coefficient of restitution between Q and the wall is $\frac{1}{8}$. Given that P's direction is reversed, and that Q strikes P again, find the range of values of e.

Answer

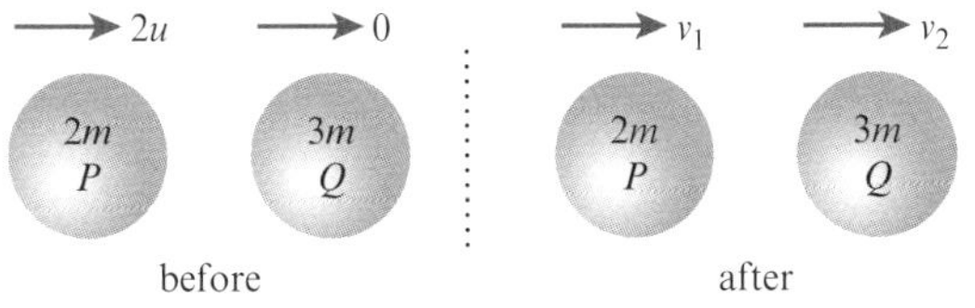

Conservation of momentum: $4mu = 2mv_1 + 3mv_2$, so $2v_1 + 3v_2 = 4u$. Newton's experimental law: $e = \frac{v_2 - v_1}{2u}$, so $2v_2 - 2v_1 = 4eu$.	Write down the two standard equations.
Adding gives $5v_2 = 4u + 4eu$, or $v_2 = \frac{4}{5}u(1 + e)$.	Equate them to find both velocities in terms of e.
Hence, $v_1 = \frac{2}{5}u(2 - 3e)$.	v_1 result to be used later.

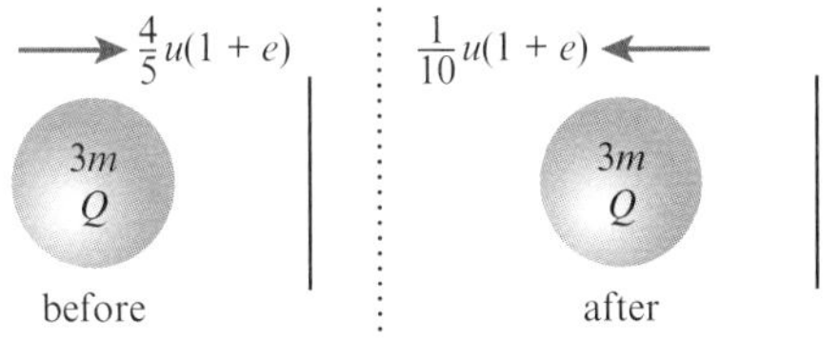

Since $e_{\text{wall}} = \frac{1}{8}$, Q bounces off with velocity $\frac{1}{10}u(1 + e)$.	Allow Q to bounce off the wall.
For P to change direction $2 - 3e < 0$, so $e > \frac{2}{3}$.	State how P changing direction affects the value of e.
For Q to strike P again, $\frac{1}{10}u(1 + e) > \frac{2}{5}u(3e - 2)$. This gives $e < \frac{9}{11}$.	Assume P is moving to the left, and allow Q to travel faster than P.
Hence, $\frac{2}{3} < e < \frac{9}{11}$.	State the final range of values.

Let us now look at multiple objects colliding. We shall consider three smooth spheres, A, B and C, all of equal size, resting on a smooth, horizontal surface.

Let A have mass m, B have mass $2m$ and C have mass m. The coefficient of restitution between A and B is $\frac{1}{3}$, and the coefficient of restitution between B and C is $\frac{2}{3}$. So, assuming A, B and C are collinear (arranged in a straight line), let us project A towards B with velocity u.

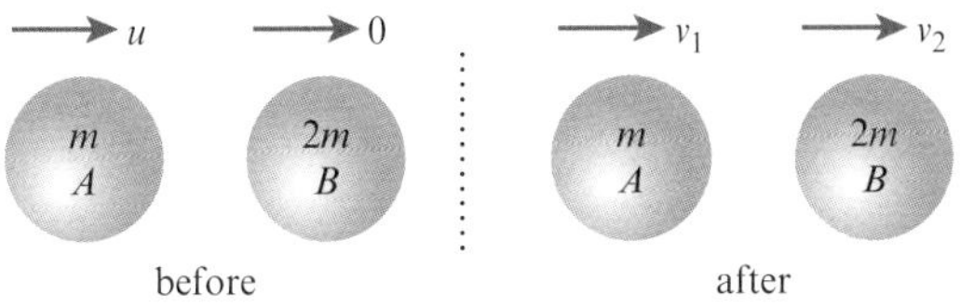

Conservation of momentum: $mu = mv_1 + 2mv_2$, so $u = v_1 + 2v_2$.

Newton's experimental law: $\frac{1}{3} = \frac{v_2 - v_1}{u}$, which leads to $v_2 - v_1 = \frac{1}{3}u$.

Equating gives $v_1 = \frac{1}{9}u$ and $v_2 = \frac{4}{9}u$.

Next, we observe B and C colliding.

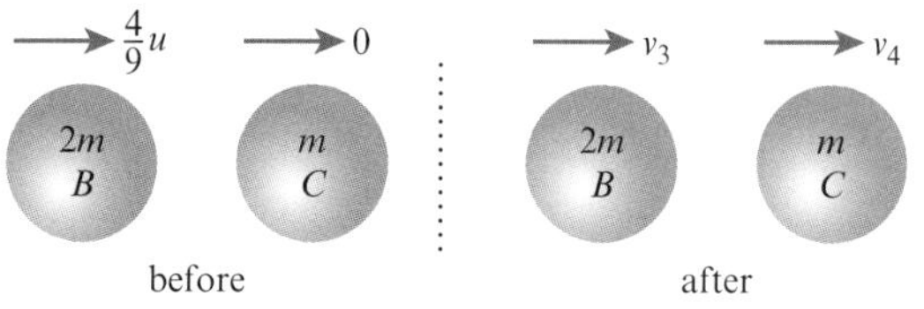

So conservation of momentum: $\frac{8}{9}mu = 2mv_3 + mv_4$, so $2v_3 + v_4 = \frac{8}{9}u$.

Using Newton's experimental law: $\frac{2}{3} = \frac{v_4 - v_3}{\frac{4}{9}u}$, leading to $v_4 - v_3 = \frac{8}{27}u$.

Equating gives $v_3 = \frac{16}{81}u$ and $v_4 = \frac{40}{81}u$.

Also, according to the velocity of B, A will not collide with B again. There are no further collisions.

We can then work out the loss in kinetic energy at this point. So, initially $\text{KE} = \frac{1}{2}mu^2$, then finally we have $\text{KE} = \frac{1}{2}m\left(\frac{1}{9}u\right)^2 + \frac{1}{2} \times 2m\left(\frac{16}{81}u\right)^2 + \frac{1}{2}m\left(\frac{40}{81}u\right)^2 = \frac{731}{4374}mu^2$. So the loss in kinetic energy is $\frac{728}{2187}mu^2$ J.

TIP

You are unlikely to encounter an example with more than three particles colliding.

WORKED EXAMPLE 18.11

Three particles, P, Q and R, are of masses 2 kg, 3 kg and 1 kg, respectively. They are all at rest on a smooth, horizontal surface. P is projected towards Q with velocity $5\,\text{m}\,\text{s}^{-1}$. At the same time, Q is projected towards P with velocity $1\,\text{m}\,\text{s}^{-1}$. Given that P, Q and R are all in the same line, and that the coefficient of restitution between all spheres is 0.6, find the speed of R after it is hit by Q.

Answer

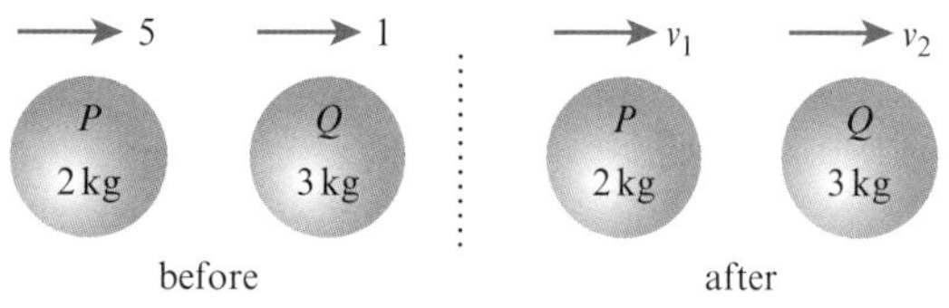

P–Q conservation of momentum: $2 \times 5 - 3 \times 1 = 2v_1 + 3v_2$, so $2v_1 + 3v_2 = 7$.

Consider the collision of P and Q first. Make sure you draw a diagram as the problems will be easier to solve.

Newton's experimental law: $\frac{3}{5} = \frac{v_2 - v_1}{6}$, and thus $v_2 - v_1 = 3.6$.

Combining these two equations gives $v_2 = 2.84$ and $v_1 = -0.76$ (to the left).

Solve to find the velocities after the first collision.

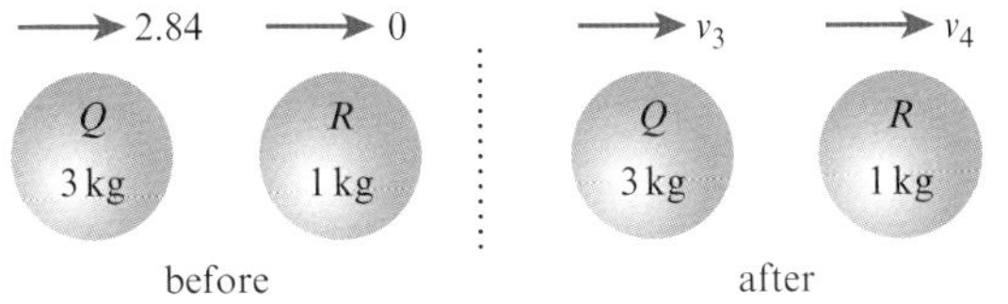

Q–R conservation of momentum: $3 \times 2.84 = 3v_3 + v_4$, so $3v_3 + v_4 = 8.52$.

Consider the Q and R collision. Create the necessary equations.

Newton's experimental law: $\frac{3}{5} = \frac{v_4 - v_3}{2.84}$ giving $v_4 - v_3 = 1.704$.

Combine to solve.

Then $v_3 = 1.704\,\mathrm{m\,s^{-1}}$ and $v_4 = 3.408\,\mathrm{m\,s^{-1}}$.

Calculate the velocity of R.

Finally, we look at oblique collisions between two spheres or particles. It is important to note the line of centres between the two objects. When the two particles meet, we consider the conservation of momentum in two directions: along the line of centres and perpendicular to the line of centres. The general case is shown in the diagram.

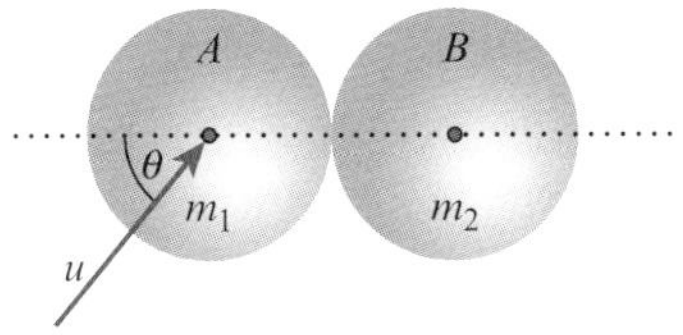

Consider two spheres, A and B, of equal radii, on a smooth horizontal surface, and with masses $2m$ and m, respectively. Initially, sphere B is at rest and sphere A is projected with speed u towards B. When the spheres collide, the direction of A is at 45° to the line through the centres of A and B. Given that the coefficient of restitution between the spheres is $\frac{1}{2}$, find the speeds of the particles after colliding.

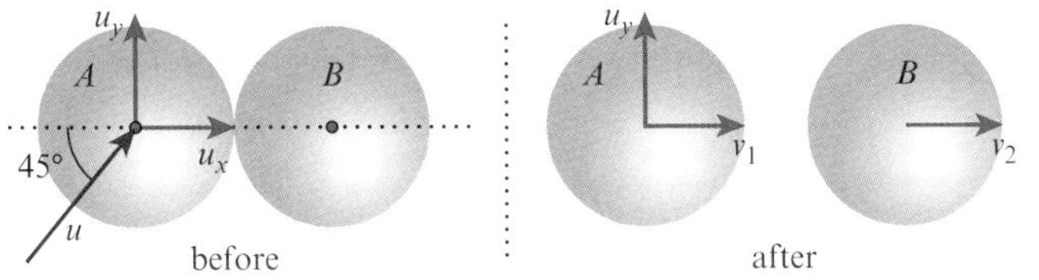

Begin by considering the components of the speed of A. We notice that the only component affecting the collision is u_x. Note that $u_x = u\cos 45$, $u_y = u\sin 45$.

Using conservation of momentum, we find the vertical components will cancel to give: $2mu\cos 45 = 2mv_1 + mv_2$, which we write as $u\sqrt{2} = 2v_1 + v_2$.

Using Newton's experimental law: $\frac{1}{2} = \frac{v_2 - v_1}{u\cos 45}$ which can be written as $\frac{u\sqrt{2}}{4} = v_2 - v_1$.

Combining these leads to $v_1 = \frac{u\sqrt{2}}{4}$ and $v_2 = \frac{u\sqrt{2}}{2}$. So the speed of sphere B after the collision is $\frac{u\sqrt{2}}{2}\,\mathrm{m\,s^{-1}}$.

For sphere A the final speed is given by $\sqrt{u_y^2 + v_1^2} = \sqrt{\left(\frac{u\sqrt{2}}{2}\right)^2 + \left(\frac{u\sqrt{2}}{4}\right)^2}$. Hence, the speed is $\frac{u\sqrt{5}}{2\sqrt{2}}\,\text{m s}^{-1}$.

We can also determine the angle of deflection caused by the collision. This is the angle that shows the change in direction travelled before and after the collision. The direction relative to the line through the centres is 45°, then after the collision the angle is $\tan^{-1}\left(\frac{u_y}{v_1}\right)$. This gives an angle of $\tan^{-1} 2 = 63.4°$. So the angle of deflection is $63.4° - 45° = 18.4°$.

WORKED EXAMPLE 18.12

Two smooth spheres of equal radii, P and Q, are at rest on a smooth horizontal surface. The coefficient of restitution between them is $\frac{1}{4}$. Sphere P has mass m and sphere Q has mass $3m$. Sphere P is given an initial speed of $4u$ and is projected in a direction such that it will collide with Q. Given that the angle between the direction of P and the line through the centres of P and Q at the point of impact is 60°, find the angle of deflection for P.

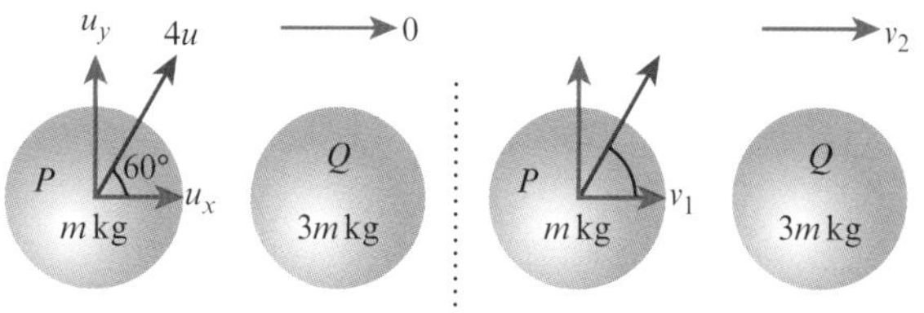

Answer

For P: $u_x = 4u\cos 60 = 2u$, $u_y = 4u\sin 60 = 2\sqrt{3}u$ — Work out the two components for P.

Then, along the line PQ:
conservation of momentum: $4u\cos 60 = mv_1 + 3mv_2$,
or $2u = v_1 + 3v_2$. — Along the line of centres we consider conservation of momentum and Newton's experimental law.

Newton's experimental law: $\frac{1}{4} = \frac{v_2 - v_1}{2u}$, or $v_2 - v_1 = \frac{u}{2}$.

Adding these two gives $\frac{5u}{2} = 4v_2$, and so $v_2 = \frac{5}{8}u$.
Hence, $v_1 = \frac{1}{8}u$. — Combine the equations to find the speeds of both spheres.

Before the collision, the angle between P's direction and the line through the centres is 60°. — Note the angle before the collision.

After, it is $\tan^{-1}\left(\frac{u_y}{v_1}\right) = \tan^{-1}(16\sqrt{3})$, which is 87.9°. — Determine the angle of P relative to the line of centres after the collision.

Hence, the angle of deflection is 27.9°. — State the angle of deflection.

EXERCISE 18B

M 1 A small smooth ball of mass m is travelling on a smooth horizontal floor with speed u. The ball then goes on to strike a fixed smooth vertical wall at an angle $\theta = 30°$ to the wall. The coefficient of restitution between the ball and the wall is 0.5. Find the speed of the ball after bouncing off the wall.

PS 2 A small smooth ball of mass $3m$ is travelling on a smooth horizontal floor with speed $2u$. The ball then goes on to strike a fixed smooth vertical wall at an angle $\theta = 60°$ to the wall. The coefficient of restitution between the ball and the wall is 0.25. Find the loss in kinetic energy due to the collision with the wall.

PS 3 Three rail carriages are on a smooth, horizontal rail track. They are equally spaced apart. The carriages are labelled A, B and C, and their masses are $2m$, $6m$ and $3m$, respectively. Carriage A is projected towards carriage B with speed u, where B is in between A and C. Given that the coefficient of restitution between each carriage is 0, find the velocity of the carriages after B collides with C.

PS 4 A particle is travelling on a smooth, horizontal surface with velocity $3u$. The particle collides with a smooth, vertical wall at an oblique angle of 30° to the wall. Find the angle between the path of the particle and the wall after the collision, given that $e = \frac{1}{8}$.

P PS 5 Two smooth, identical spheres, P and Q, are resting on a smooth, horizontal surface. The masses of the spheres are $3m$ and m, respectively. P is projected towards Q with velocity u.

a Given that the coefficient of restitution between P and Q is e, show that, no matter the value of e, P will travel in the same direction as Q after the collision.

b Given that $e = \frac{2}{5}$, find the loss in kinetic energy due to the collision.

PS 6 Three particles are lying in a straight line on a smooth, horizontal surface. The particles are labelled A, B and C, with B between A and C. The masses of the particles are 5 kg, 3 kg and 2 kg, respectively. The coefficient of restitution between A and B is $\frac{1}{2}$, and the collision between B and C is perfectly elastic. Particle C is projected towards particle B with velocity $8\,\text{m s}^{-1}$. Find the velocity of each particle after the second collision, stating whether or not there will be any further collisions.

M 7 The diagram shows a smooth sphere, travelling horizontally, that is colliding with two smooth vertical walls at a corner point. The sphere has an initial velocity u, and given that the coefficient of restitution between the sphere and wall is e, find a relationship between the initial velocity and the final velocity after two collisions.

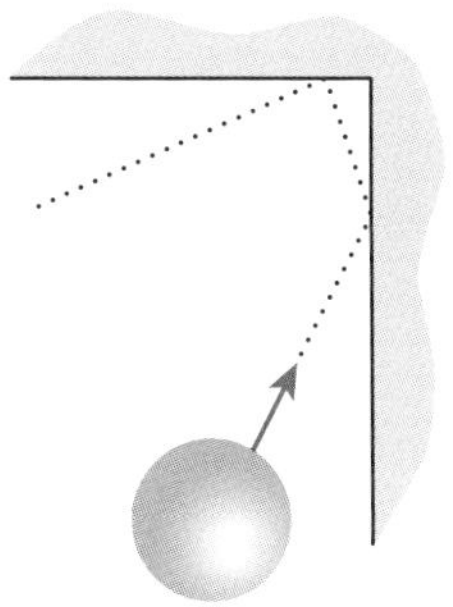

PS 8 Particles P and Q are resting on a smooth, horizontal surface. A smooth, vertical wall is at a distance $2r$ from Q, and the wall is perpendicular to the line through P and Q. The masses of P and Q are $2m$ and m, respectively. The coefficient of restitution between P and Q is $\frac{2}{3}$, and the coefficient of restitution between Q and the wall is $\frac{2}{5}$. P is projected towards Q with velocity u. Find the distance of the particles from the wall when they collide for a second time.

PS 9 Three identical smooth spheres, A, B and C, of masses $2m$, M and m, respectively, are resting on a smooth, horizontal surface. The coefficient of restitution between A and B is $\frac{4}{5}$, and the coefficient of restitution between B and C is $\frac{1}{2}$. Sphere A is projected towards B with velocity $2u$. Given that A, B and C are collinear, and that the velocity of B is zero after it collides with C, find the loss in kinetic energy after the second collision.

PS 10 Two spheres, P and Q, which are of equal radii, are placed on a smooth, horizontal surface. Their masses are m and $2m$, respectively. Initially, sphere Q is at rest and sphere P is projected with speed u towards Q. When the spheres collide, the direction of P is 30° to the line through the centres of P and Q. Given that the coefficient of restitution between the spheres is $\frac{4}{5}$, find the loss in kinetic energy due to the collision.

WORKED PAST PAPER QUESTION

Two smooth spheres A and B, of equal radii, have masses 0.1 kg and m kg respectively. They are moving towards each other in a straight line on a smooth horizontal table and collide directly. Immediately before the collision the speed of A is $5\,\text{m}\,\text{s}^{-1}$ and the speed of B is $2\,\text{m}\,\text{s}^{-1}$.

i Assume that in the collision A does not change direction. The speeds of A and B after the collision are $v_A\,\text{m}\,\text{s}^{-1}$ and $v_B\,\text{m}\,\text{s}^{-1}$ respectively. Express m in terms of v_A and v_B, and hence show that $m < 0.25$.

Cambridge International AS & A Level Further Mathematics 9231 Paper 2 Q4 November 2008

Answer

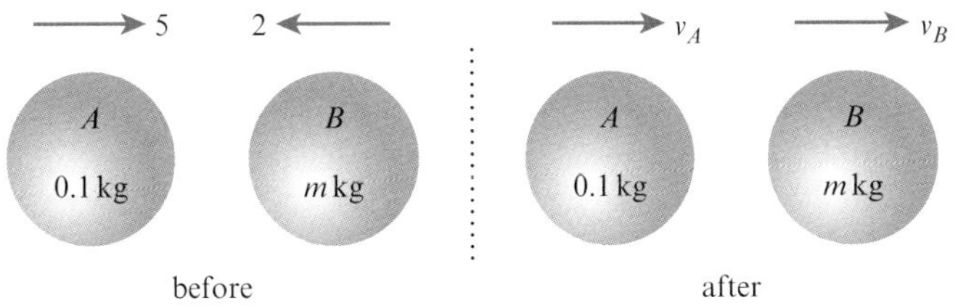

i Conservation of momentum: $0.1 \times 5 - m \times 2 = 0.1v_A + mv_B$, then $m = \dfrac{0.5 - 0.1v_A}{2 + v_B}$.

Since $v_A > 0$ and $v_B > 0$, $0.5 - 0.1v_A < 0.5$ and $2 + v_B > 2$. So $m < 0.25$.

Checklist of learning and understanding

Momentum and impulse:

- Momentum is the product of mass and velocity such that $P = mv$.
- The rate of change of momentum is a force such that $F = \frac{\mathrm{d}P}{\mathrm{d}t}$.
- Impulse is given as $I = m(v - u)$, measured in newton seconds, N s.
- Impulse is a force applied over time, so $I = Ft$, or $Ft = mv - mu$.

Collisions:

- For the conservation of momentum, $m_1u_1 + m_2u_2 = m_1v_1 + m_2v_2$.
- For particles that coalesce ($e = 0$), $m_1u_1 + m_2u_2 = (m_1 + m_2)v$.
- For perfectly elastic collisions, $e = 1$.
- Newton's experimental law states that $e = \frac{\text{speed of separation}}{\text{speed of approach}}$, where e is known as the coefficient of restitution and can take values $0 \leqslant e \leqslant 1$.
- When two objects collide directly, conservation of momentum is considered along the line through their centres.
- When an object collides obliquely with a wall, only the component of the velocity that is perpendicular to the wall is considered for conservation of momentum.

END-OF-CHAPTER REVIEW EXERCISE 18

1 Two smooth spheres A and B, of equal radius, are moving in the same direction in the same straight line on a smooth horizontal table. Sphere A has mass m and speed u and sphere B has mass αm and speed $\frac{1}{4}u$.
The spheres collide and A is brought to rest by the collision. Find the coefficient of restitution in terms of α.

Deduce that $\alpha \geqslant 2$.

Cambridge International AS & A Level Further Mathematics 9231 Paper 2 Q3 November 2010

2 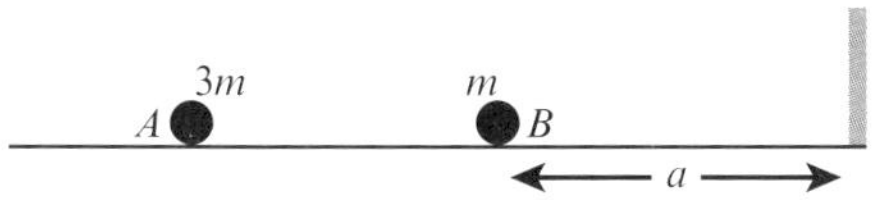

Two perfectly elastic small smooth spheres A and B have masses $3m$ and m respectively. They lie at rest on a smooth horizontal plane with B at a distance a from a smooth vertical barrier. The line of centres of the spheres is perpendicular to the barrier, and B is between A and the barrier (see diagram). Sphere A is projected towards sphere B with speed u and, after the collision between the spheres, B hits the barrier. The coefficient of restitution between B and the barrier is $\frac{1}{2}$. Find the speeds of A and B immediately after they first collide, and the distance from the barrier of the point where they collide for the second time.

Cambridge International AS & A Level Further Mathematics 9231 Paper 21 Q3 June 2010

3 Three small spheres, A, B and C, of masses m, km and $6m$ respectively, have the same radius. They are at rest on a smooth horizontal surface, in a straight line with B between A and C. The coefficient of restitution between A and B is $\frac{1}{2}$ and the coefficient of restitution between B and C is e. Sphere A is projected towards B with speed u and is brought to rest by the subsequent collision.
Show that $k = 2$.
Given that there are no further collisions after B has collided with C, show that $e \leqslant \frac{1}{3}$.

Cambridge International AS & A Level Further Mathematics 9231 Paper 23 Q1 June 2011

CROSS-TOPIC REVIEW EXERCISE 3

1 A light, elastic string, of natural length 2 m and modulus of elasticity 40 N, has one end attached to a ceiling at the point O. A particle of mass 0.5 kg is attached to the other end of the string, and the system is allowed to rest in equilibrium with the string taut.

a Find the extension in the string.

The particle is then pulled down a further 0.75 m and released.

b Find the shortest distance between the particle and O in the subsequent motion.

c Show that while the string is taut the particle performs simple harmonic motion.

2 The diagram shows a lamina that consists of a uniform semicircular plate of radius a attached to a uniform rectangular plate of dimensions a and $2a$.

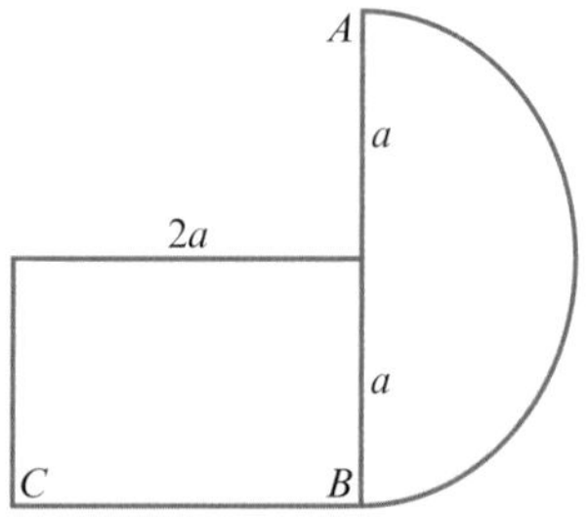

The density of the rectangular section is twice the density of the semicircular section.

a Find the centre of mass of the combined lamina from the edges AB and BC.

b The lamina is suspended from the point A and allowed to hang in equilibrium. Find the angle between AB and the vertical.

3 A particle of mass m is dropped from a great height. The air resistance on the particle is given as mkv N.

a Show that $\frac{dv}{dt} = g - kv$.

b Hence, show that $v = \frac{g}{k}(1 - e^{-kt})$.

c State the speed of the particle after a very long time.

4 A smooth hemisphere, of radius $2a$, is placed with its plane face on a horizontal surface. A particle, of mass $3m$, is placed on the highest point of the hemisphere. The particle is then projected horizontally with speed $\sqrt{\frac{1}{4}ga}$.

a Find the height of the particle above the horizontal surface when it leaves the surface of the hemisphere.

b Find the speed of the particle when it strikes the horizontal surface.

5 A particle is projected from the top of a cliff that is 25 m above the sea below. The speed of the projection is $40\,\text{m}\,\text{s}^{-1}$ and the angle of elevation is 15°. The particle travels as a projectile and lands in the sea.

a Find the horizontal distance the particle travels before landing in the sea.

b Find the duration of time for which the particle is 30 m above the sea below.

c Find the direction of the particle just before it hits the water.

6 Two particles, P and Q, of masses $2m$ and $3m$, respectively, are resting on a smooth, horizontal surface. Particle P is projected towards Q with speed u. It strikes Q directly and the coefficient of restitution between the particles is e.

a Find the velocity of P and Q after the collision, in terms of e and u.

b Find the range of values of e such that P's direction does not change due to the collision.

c Find the loss in kinetic energy due to the collision, giving your answer in terms of e, m and u.

Chapter 19
Hyperbolic functions

In this chapter you will learn how to:

- relate the hyperbolic functions to the exponential function
- sketch graphs of the hyperbolic functions
- prove and use identities involving hyperbolic functions
- use the definitions of the inverse hyperbolic functions and use the logarithmic forms.

PREREQUISITE KNOWLEDGE

Where it comes from	What you should be able to do	Check your skills
AS & A Level Mathematics Pure Mathematics 2 & 3, Chapter 3	Use the trigonometric identities.	**1** Prove: $\frac{\cos A}{\sin B} - \frac{\sin A}{\cos B} \equiv \frac{\cos(A+B)}{\sin B \cos B}$
AS & A Level Mathematics Pure Mathematics 2 & 3, Chapter 2	Manipulate equations involving the natural logarithm and exponential functions.	**2** Solve: $e^{2x} - e^{x} - 6 = 0$

What are hyperbolic functions?

In the Pure Mathematics 2 & 3 Coursebook, Chapter 4, you learned uses for trigonometric functions other than solving problems based on a triangle. In fact, trigonometric functions are also called **circular functions**, as they all have geometric meaning and derivations from the equation of the unit circle. There are similar relationships between the structure of circles, **hyperbolas**, **parabolas** and **ellipses**. These shapes are all called **conic sections**, because they are shapes produced when we slice a cone. Horizontal slices produce circles; oblique slices produce ellipses; slices parallel to the slope of the cone produce parabolas; steeper slices than this produce hyperbolas.

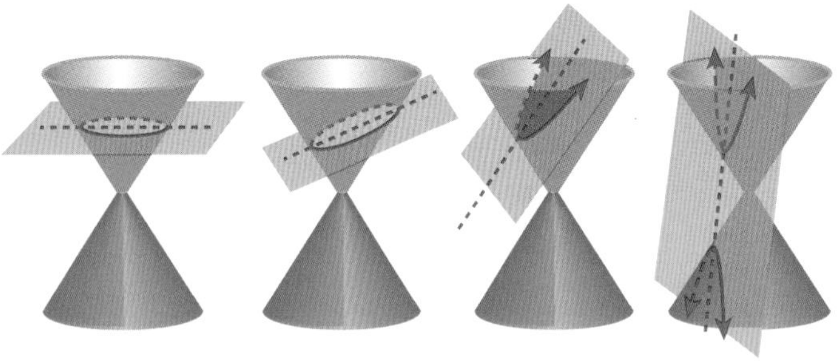

Hyperbolic functions are a class of functions that are derived from the **unit hyperbola**, $x^2 - y^2 = 1$. They are a significant tool in an engineer's toolkit. They also allow us to find highly elegant solutions to differential equations.

19.1 Exponential forms of hyperbolic functions

In the introduction, we discussed the relationships between hyperbolic functions and trigonometric functions. Hyperbolics link to apparently vastly different function types, but as you read this chapter and do subsequent work on complex numbers, you will start to see the connections.

We shall start by relating hyperbolic functions to exponentials. It is not clear from the ideas and development of hyperbolics whether the exponential definitions came first or the relationships with trigonometry came first. We shall use the exponential forms to develop the idea. Let us begin with the hyperbolic sine function:

$$y = \sinh x$$

The first challenge is the pronunciation of the hyperbolic functions. The hyperbolic sine is pronounced 'shine' and its exponential definition is:

$$\sinh x = \frac{e^x - e^{-x}}{2}$$

Based on this, we can define the domain, find the range and draw the function. It is helpful to consider this graph as the average of $y = e^x$ and $y = -e^{-x}$.

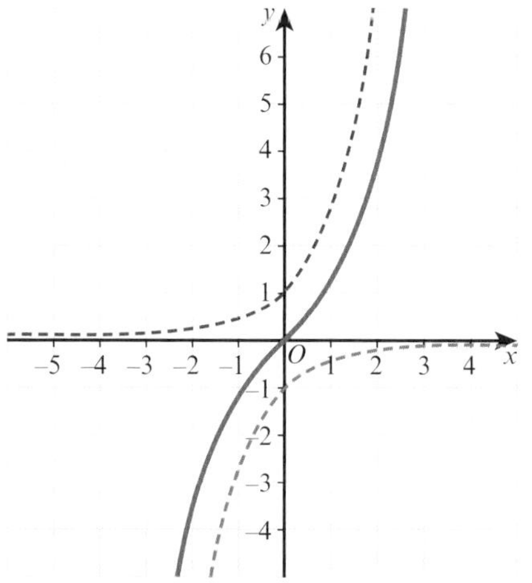

From this, we can see that the function is a one–one mapping. The domain is $x \in \mathbb{R}$. The range is $f(x) \in \mathbb{R}$. It is also an odd function.

$$y = \cosh x$$

The hyperbolic cosine is pronounced 'cosh' and its exponential definition is:

$$\cosh x = \frac{e^x + e^{-x}}{2}$$

We consider this graph as the average of $y = e^x$ and $y = e^{-x}$.

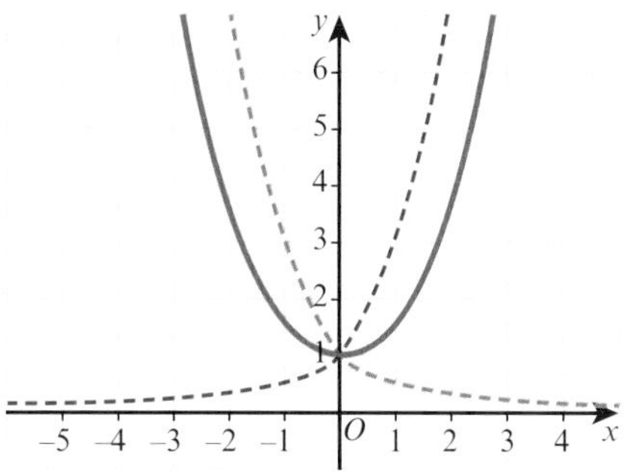

From this, we can see that the function is *not* a one–one mapping. However, it can be evaluated with both positive and negative values for x.

The domain is $x \in \mathbb{R}$. The range is $f(x) \geqslant 1$. It is an even function.

For the function to be one–one, we need to restrict the domain to $x \geqslant 0$. This will be very important later.

DID YOU KNOW?

The hyperbolic cosine is a very special curve and has many occurrences in nature. It is called a **catenary**, and is the shape of a hanging chain.

EXPLORE 19.1

Based on the exponential definitions of $\sinh x$ and $\cosh x$, find:

$$\frac{d}{dx}(\sinh x) \text{ and } \frac{d}{dx}(\cosh x)$$

The exponential forms of $\sinh x$ and $\cosh x$ are shown in Key point 19.1.

KEY POINT 19.1

The exponential forms of $\sinh x$ and $\cosh x$:

$$\sinh x = \frac{e^x - e^{-x}}{2}, \quad x \in \mathbb{R}, \ f(x) \in \mathbb{R}$$

$$\cosh x = \frac{e^x + e^{-x}}{2}, \quad x \in \mathbb{R}, \ f(x) \geqslant 1$$

From this, we can deduce that $e^x = \cosh x + \sinh x$.

We can now derive further hyperbolic functions:

Hyperbolic function	Pronunciation	Exponential form
$\tanh x$	'tanch' (preferred) 'than' (a long thhhhhh as in 'thank you') 'tank'	$\tanh x = \frac{e^x - e^{-x}}{e^x + e^{-x}}$
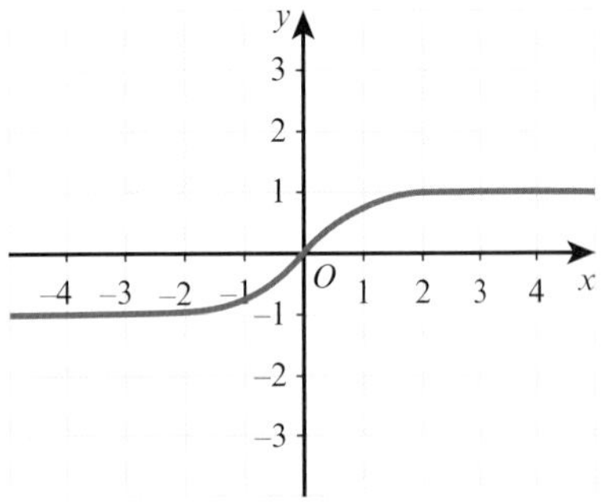		Domain: $x \in \mathbb{R}$
		Range: $-1 < f(x) < 1$
		Odd function

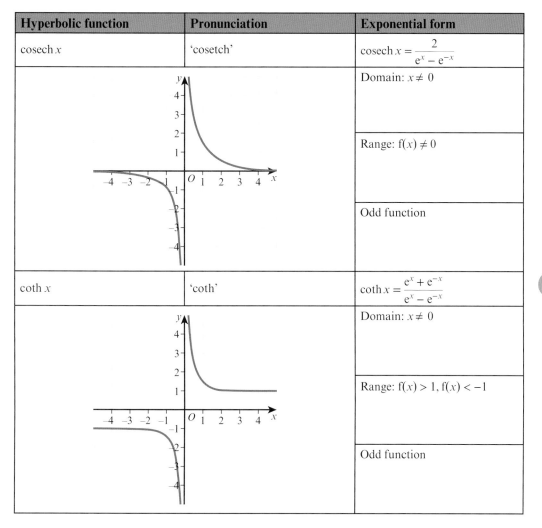

Hyperbolic function	Pronunciation	Exponential form
sech x	'setch'	$\operatorname{sech} x = \dfrac{2}{e^x + e^{-x}}$
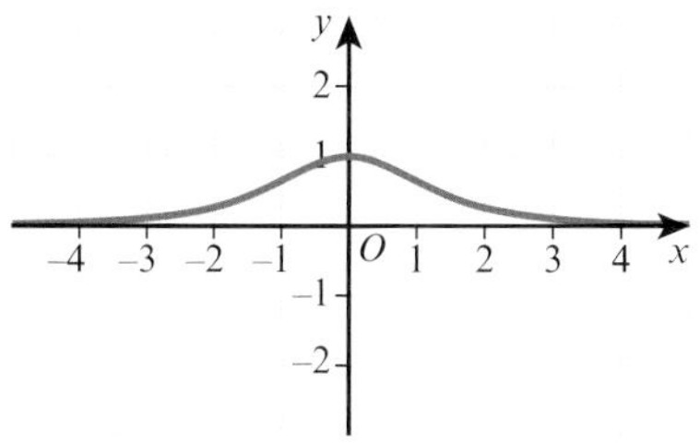		Domain: $x \in \mathbb{R}$
		Range: $0 < f(x) \leqslant 1$
		Even function

DID YOU KNOW?

The graph of $y = \operatorname{sech}^2 x$ is a very important curve. It is used to model tsunamis and to model wavelets in wave–particle duality. We call this type of wave a soliton. It is a very special type of wave that does not lose energy as it travels. Its velocity is proportional to the amplitude of the wave. This is why tsunamis have such a destructive force. You might study more about solitons at university level.

Hyperbolic function	Pronunciation	Exponential form
cosech x	'cosetch'	$\operatorname{cosech} x = \dfrac{2}{e^x - e^{-x}}$
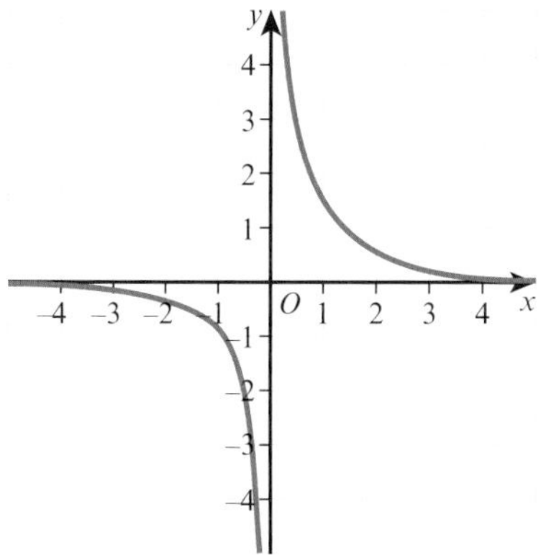		Domain: $x \neq 0$
		Range: $f(x) \neq 0$
		Odd function
coth x	'coth'	$\coth x = \dfrac{e^x + e^{-x}}{e^x - e^{-x}}$
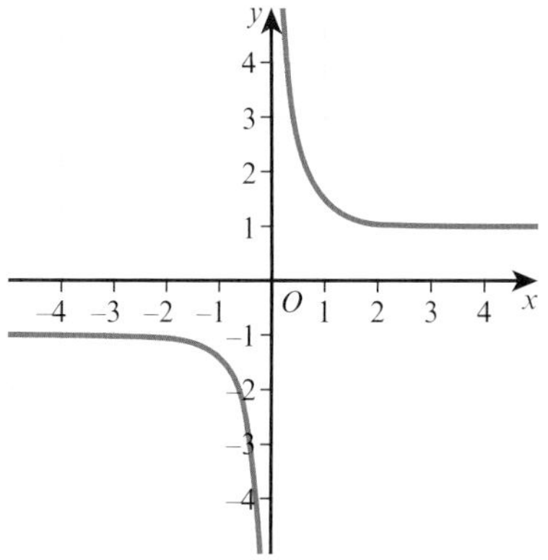		Domain: $x \neq 0$
		Range: $f(x) > 1, f(x) < -1$
		Odd function

TIP

To help us remember the reciprocal functions of sech x, cosech x and coth x, we can apply the third letter rule as with trigonometric reciprocal functions:

$\operatorname{sech} x = \dfrac{1}{\cosh x}$

$\operatorname{cosech} x = \dfrac{1}{\sinh x}$

$\coth x = \dfrac{1}{\tanh x}$

WORKED EXAMPLE 19.1

Sketch the graph of $y = |3\cosh(x + 1) - 4|$.

Answer

Given that $f(x) = \cosh x$:

Consider each transformation in turn.

$y = f(x + 1)$

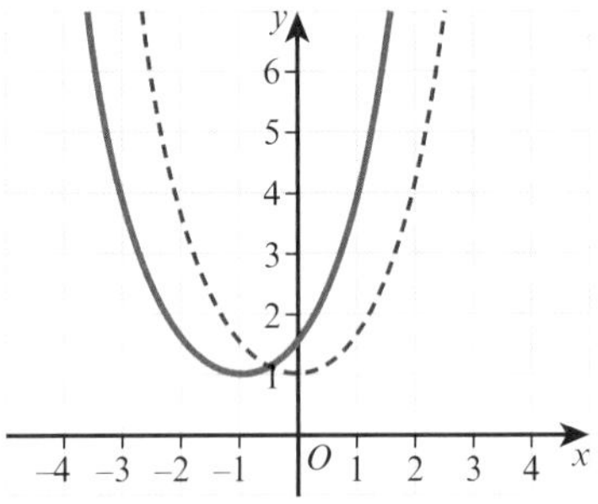

$y = 3f(x + 1)$

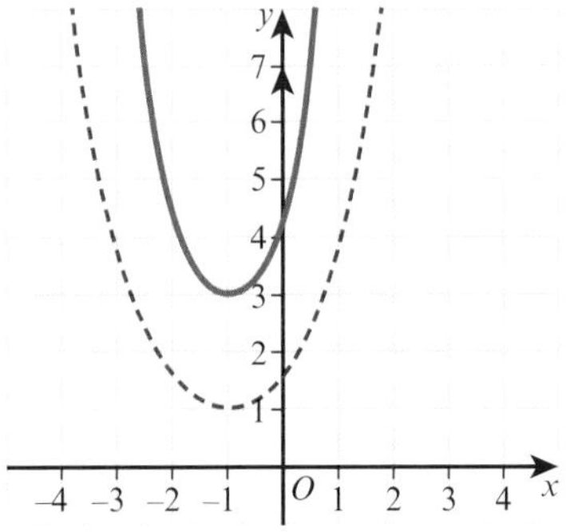

$y = 3f(x + 1) - 4$

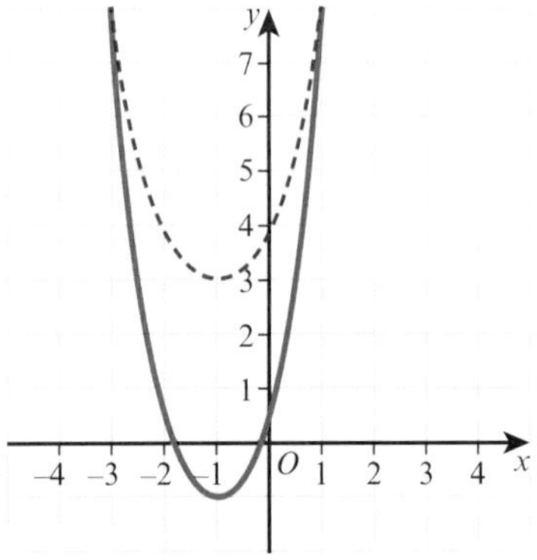

This is the graph of $|3\cosh(x + 1) - 4|$.

$y = |3f(x + 1) - 4|$

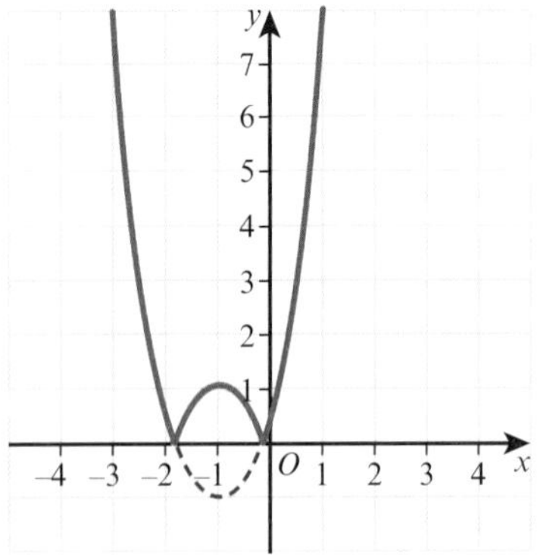

These functions can all be evaluated using a calculator, in the same way as for trigonometric functions. However, generally you will be required to write in exact form, unless told otherwise. We can use the previous definitions to solve equations involving hyperbolic forms.

WORKED EXAMPLE 19.2

Leaving your answer in exact form, solve $4\cosh x - 3\sinh x = 4$.

Answer

$$4\cosh x - 3\sinh x = 4$$

$$4\left(\frac{e^x + e^{-x}}{2}\right) - 3\left(\frac{e^x - e^{-x}}{2}\right) = 4$$

First, use the exponential definitions:

$$\sinh x = \frac{e^x - e^{-x}}{2}$$

$$\cosh x = \frac{e^x + e^{-x}}{2}$$

$$4e^{2x} + 4 - 3e^{2x} + 3 = 8e^x$$

Now multiply up by $2e^x$.

$$e^{2x} - 8e^x + 7 = 0$$

This is now a quadratic in terms of e^x and so can be solved.

$$(e^x - 7)(e^x - 1) = 0$$

Leading to two solutions: $x = \ln 7$, $x = \ln 1 = 0$

We are usually asked to give our solutions in exact form.

It is possible to approach this problem using a similar technique as that for trigonometric equations using hyperbolic forms. However, this rarely gives such elegant solutions. We need to understand both inverse hyperbolic functions and their logarithmic forms.

WORKED EXAMPLE 19.3

Solve $3\tanh^2 x - 4\tanh x = 4$.

Answer

$$3\tanh^2 x - 4\tanh x - 4 = 0$$

First, recognise that this is a quadratic equation in terms of $\tanh x$.

$$3T^2 - 4T - 4 = 0$$

To make it simpler, replace $\tanh x$ with T.

$$3T^2 - 6T + 2T - 4 = 0$$
$$3T(T-2) + 2(T-2) = 0$$
$$(T-2)(3T+2) = 0$$
$$T = 2$$
$$\text{Or } T = -\frac{2}{3}$$

Solve the equation.

We are left then to solve:

$$\tanh x = -\frac{2}{3}$$

$$x = \tanh^{-1}\left(-\frac{2}{3}\right)$$

Remember: since the range of $\tanh x$ cannot exceed 1, $T = 2$ will not lead to any solutions.

EXERCISE 19A

Write all solutions in exact form unless otherwise stated.

1 Solve $19\sinh x + 16\cosh x = 8$.

2 Solve $29\cosh x = 11\sinh x + 27$.

3 Solve $17\sinh x + 16\cosh x = 8$.

4 Solve $7 = 17\tanh x + 28\,\text{sech}\,x$.

5 Solve $\text{cosech}\,x - 2\coth x = 2$.

6 Sketch the graph of $y = |3\cosh x - 5|$.

7 Sketch the graph of $y = 4 - \text{cosech}(x - 2)$.

8 Sketch the graph of $y = \left|2 + \frac{1}{2}\coth(x + 1)\right|$.

PS 9 Solve $4\cosh x + \sinh x = 8$. Write your answers in the form $b \ln a$, where a and b are integers.

PS 10 Solve $10\cosh x + 2\sinh x = 11$, giving your answers in the form $\ln a$, where a is a rational number.

PS 11 Given that $\text{sech}^{-1} x = \ln\left(\frac{1 + \sqrt{1 - x^2}}{x}\right)$, solve $4\,\text{sech}\,x - 3\tanh^2 x = 1$.

19.2 Hyperbolic identities

If we consider that hyperbolic functions are similar to trigonometric functions, it is reasonable to consider that **hyperbolic identities** exist in the same way. We can use the exponential forms to prove that they are true.

TIP

When forming a proof, it is very important to either start at the left-hand side and show it is the same as the right-hand side, or start at the right-hand side to show it is the same as the left-hand side. Starting from both ends until you get a common expression will not make a formal proof. You can use this to help you see how to formulate your proof, but the final written answer must be in the correct order. Make sure that you state every algebraic step: tell the whole story!

WORKED EXAMPLE 19.4

Prove that $\cosh^2 x - \sinh^2 x \equiv 1$.

Answer

$\cosh^2 x - \sinh^2 x$

$\equiv \left(\frac{e^x + e^{-x}}{2}\right)^2 - \left(\frac{e^x - e^{-x}}{2}\right)^2$ First, convert to exponential form and consider the left-hand side.

$\equiv \frac{1}{4}((e^{2x} + 2 + e^{-2x}) - (e^{2x} - 2 + e^{-2x}))$ Expand and take out a factor of $\frac{1}{4}$.

$\equiv \frac{1}{4}(e^{2x} + 2 + e^{-2x} - e^{2x} + 2 - e^{-2x})$

$\equiv \frac{1}{4}(4) \equiv 1$ This is the right-hand side.

Therefore, $\cosh^2 x - \sinh^2 x \equiv 1$. Therefore, the left-hand side becomes the right-hand side.

WORKED EXAMPLE 19.5

Prove that $\sinh(A+B) \equiv \sinh A \cosh B + \sinh B \cosh A$.

Answer

$\sinh A \cosh B + \sinh B \cosh A$

$\equiv \left(\frac{e^A - e^{-A}}{2}\right)\left(\frac{e^B + e^{-B}}{2}\right) + \left(\frac{e^B - e^{-B}}{2}\right)\left(\frac{e^A + e^{-A}}{2}\right)$ — Consider the right-hand side and convert it to exponential form.

$\equiv \frac{1}{4}(e^Ae^B - e^{-A}e^B + e^Ae^{-B} - e^{-A}e^{-B} + e^Be^A - e^{-B}e^A + e^Be^{-A} - e^{-B}e^{-A})$ — Expand and take out a factor of $\frac{1}{4}$.

$\equiv \frac{1}{4}(2e^{A+B} - 2e^{-(A+B)})$ — Use $e^Ae^B = e^{A+B}$ and $e^{-A}e^{-B} = e^{-(A+B)}$.

$\equiv \frac{e^{(A+B)} - e^{-(A+B)}}{2} \equiv \sinh(A+B)$ — This proof works from right-hand side to left-hand side.

as required.

You should have noticed that these two proofs are similar to trigonometric identities. It is possible to use **Osborne's rule**, as shown in Key point 19.2, to move from a trigonometric identity to a hyperbolic identity. Nevertheless, this does not constitute a proof!

KEY POINT 19.2

Osborne's rule

To move from a trigonometric identity to a hyperbolic identity: change a cos to a cosh and change the *sign* of a product of sinhs.

We can use Osborne's rule when we are required to use a hyperbolic identity without needing its proof.

WORKED EXAMPLE 19.6

Using Osborne's rule, state the angle addition formula for $\tanh(A+B)$.

Answer

Start by considering the trigonometric identity: — We consider replacing tan with tanh.

$\tan(A+B) \equiv \frac{\tan A + \tan B}{1 - \tan A \tan B}$

$\tanh(A+B) \equiv \frac{\tanh A + \tanh B}{1 + \tanh A \tanh B}$ — sinh is the numerator of tanh. Applying Osborne's rule, we notice that $\tanh A \tanh B$ will require a sign change since it includes a product of sinhs.

as required.

EXERCISE 19B

P 1 Prove that $\cosh^2 x \equiv \dfrac{\text{cosech}^2 x + 1}{\coth^2 x - 1}$.

P 2 Prove that $\cosh 3x \equiv 4\cosh^3 x - 3\cosh x$.

P 3 Prove that $\coth 2x - \coth x \equiv \dfrac{1}{2}(\tanh x - \coth x)$.

P 4 Prove the following hyperbolic identities.

a $\cosh(A - B) \equiv \cosh A \cosh B - \sinh A \sinh B$

b $\sinh 3x \equiv 3\sinh x + 4\sinh^3 x$

c $\sinh A - \sinh B \equiv 2\cosh\left(\dfrac{A+B}{2}\right)\sinh\left(\dfrac{A-B}{2}\right)$

P 5 Given that $\tanh\left(\dfrac{x}{2}\right) = t$, prove that $\sinh x = \dfrac{2t}{1-t^2}$.

19.3 Inverse hyperbolic functions

As with trigonometric functions, the hyperbolic inverse functions must exist and be well defined. As with any function, the inverse function will be a reflection in the line $y = x$ for the one–one aspect of the function (otherwise the inverse will not be well defined).

Take care to use the correct notation.

You may have noticed by now that the notation for inverse trigonometric functions is a little ambiguous and it can be easily confused with reciprocal functions. There is another commonly used notation for them:

$$\sin^{-1} x = \arcsin x$$
$$\cos^{-1} x = \arccos x$$
$$\tan^{-1} x = \arctan x$$

DID YOU KNOW?

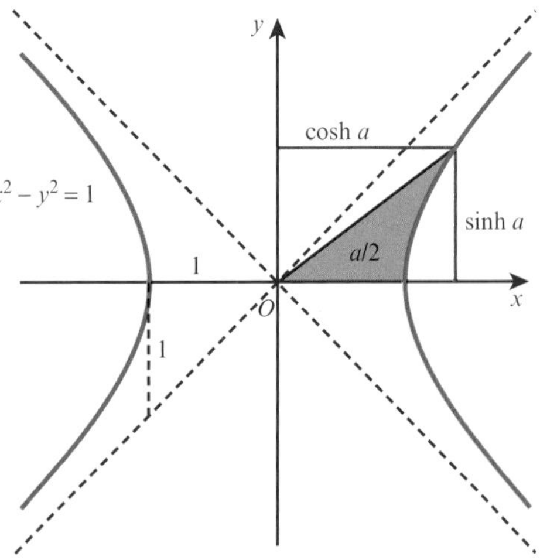

The origin of the prefix *arc*- comes from the unit circle, and the fact that the arc length is equal to the angle ($l = r\theta$, where $r = 1$). Finding the angle θ is then equivalent to finding the arc length. So finding the angle, which requires inverting the sine function, is equivalent to finding the *arcsine*.

There is a similar idea with hyperbolics, although beyond the scope of this course. Finding the hyperbolic angle is equivalent to finding twice the *area* of the hyperbolic sector of $x^2 - y^2 = 1$, the unit hyperbola.

KEY POINT 19.3

The inverse hyperbolic functions are:

Function (green)	Inverse function (red)	Graph	Domain and range of the inverse function
$\sinh x$	$\sinh^{-1} x$	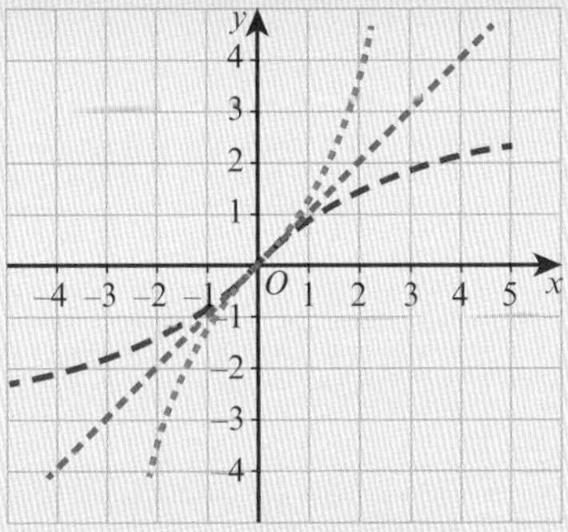	$x \in \mathbb{R}$ $f(x) \in \mathbb{R}$
$\cosh x$	$\cosh^{-1} x$	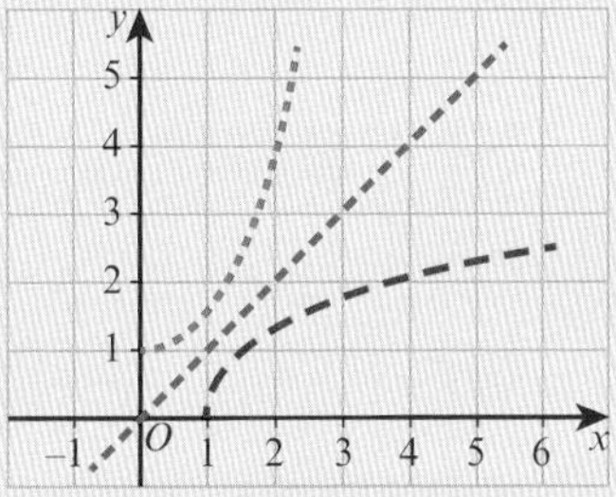	$x \geqslant 1$ $f(x) \geqslant 0$
$\tanh x$	$\tanh^{-1} x$	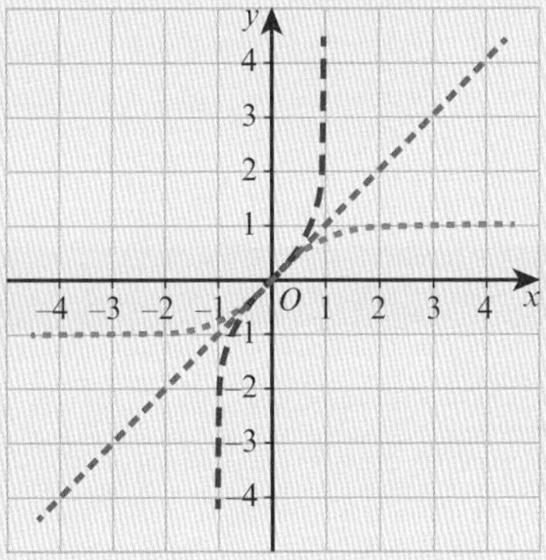	$-1 < x < 1$ $f(x) \in \mathbb{R}$

WORKED EXAMPLE 19.7

Solve the equation $\sinh^2 x - 5\sinh x + 4 = 0$. Give your answers to 3 significant figures.

Answer

$\sinh^2 x - 5\sinh x + 4 = 0$

$(\sinh x - 4)(\sinh x - 1) = 0$

First, notice that this is a quadratic equation in terms of $\sinh x$, and it will factorise.

When $\sinh x = 4$, $x = \sinh^{-1} 4$:

$x = 2.09$

When $\sinh x = 1$, $x = \sinh^{-1} 1$:

$x = 0.881$

Make sure solutions are written to the required level of accuracy.

It is possible to write the answer exactly, using natural logarithms.

19.4 Logarithmic form for inverse hyperbolic functions

If hyperbolic functions can be described in terms of exponential functions, then it is reasonable to assume that inverse hyperbolic functions can be described using the natural logarithm function. This is indeed the case and is shown in Key point 19.4.

WORKED EXAMPLE 19.8

Find the **logarithmic form** of $\sinh^{-1} x$.

Answer

$y = \sinh^{-1} x$

$\sinh y = x$ — Rewrite x in terms of $\sinh y$.

$\frac{e^y - e^{-y}}{2} = x$ — Express in exponential form.

$e^{2y} - 1 = 2e^y x$ — Rearrange to make y the subject.

$e^{2y} - 2e^y x - 1 = 0$

$(e^y - x)^2 - x^2 - 1 = 0$

$(e^y - x)^2 = x^2 + 1$ — To do that here, complete the square.

$e^y = x \pm \sqrt{x^2 + 1}$

$y = \ln(x + \sqrt{x^2 + 1})$ — Take logs to make y the subject.

Therefore, $\sinh^{-1} x = \ln(x + \sqrt{x^2 + 1})$. — Since we can only take logs of positive numbers, take only the positive root here. Consider why we do this rather than take the modulus.

KEY POINT 19.4

The logarithmic forms of the inverse hyperbolic functions are:

$\sinh^{-1} x$	$\ln(x + \sqrt{x^2 + 1})$
$\cosh^{-1} x$	$\ln(x + \sqrt{x^2 - 1})$
$\tanh^{-1} x$	$\frac{1}{2}\ln\left(\frac{1 + x}{1 - x}\right)$
$\coth^{-1} x$	$\frac{1}{2}\ln\left(\frac{x + 1}{x - 1}\right)$
$\text{sech}^{-1} x$	$\ln\left(\frac{1 + \sqrt{1 - x^2}}{x}\right)$
$\text{cosech}^{-1} x$	$\ln\left(\frac{1 + \sqrt{1 + x^2}}{x}\right)$

TIP

Why do we consider only the positive root here?

You need to be able to derive the logarithmic form for inverse hyperbolics.

You are now equipped to give your answers in exact form. In the next example, we will solve the equation we had in Worked example 19.7 but this time we will give our answers in exact form.

WORKED EXAMPLE 19.9

Solve the equation $\sinh^2 x - 5\sinh x + 4 = 0$. Give your answers in exact logarithmic form.

Answer

$\sinh^2 x - 5\sinh x + 4 = 0$
$(\sinh x - 4)(\sinh x - 1) = 0$

Notice that this is a quadratic equation in terms of $\sinh x$, and it will factorise.

When $\sinh x = 4$, $x = \sinh^{-1} 4$:

$\sinh^{-1} 4 = \ln(4 + \sqrt{4^2 + 1})$

$x = \ln(4 + \sqrt{17})$

When $\sinh x = 1$, $x = \sinh^{-1} 1$:

$\sinh^{-1} 1 = \ln(1 + \sqrt{1^2 + 1})$

$x = \ln(1 + \sqrt{2})$

Note the answer has been requested in exact logarithmic form.

WORKED EXAMPLE 19.10

Prove that $\sinh^{-1} A + \sinh^{-1} B \equiv \sinh^{-1}(A\sqrt{1 + B^2} + B\sqrt{1 + A^2})$.

Answer

$1 + (A\sqrt{1 + B^2} + B\sqrt{1 + A^2})^2$

Consider $1 + (A\sqrt{1 + B^2} + B\sqrt{1 + A^2})^2$.

$\equiv 1 + 2A^2B^2 + 2AB\sqrt{A^2 + 1}\sqrt{B^2 + 1} + A^2 + B^2$

$\equiv A^2B^2 + 2AB\sqrt{A^2 + 1}\sqrt{B^2 + 1} + (A^2 + 1)(B^2 + 1)$

$(1 + A^2)(1 + B^2) \equiv 1 + A^2 + B^2 + A^2B^2$

$\equiv (AB + \sqrt{A^2 + 1}\sqrt{B^2 + 1})^2$

Call this result (1).

$\sinh^{-1}(A\sqrt{1 + B^2} + B\sqrt{1 + A^2})$

$\equiv \ln(A\sqrt{1 + B^2} + B\sqrt{1 + A^2}$

$\quad + \sqrt{1 + (A\sqrt{1 + B^2} + B\sqrt{1 + A^2})^2})$

$\equiv \ln(A\sqrt{1 + B^2} + B\sqrt{1 + A^2} + AB + \sqrt{A^2 + 1}\sqrt{B^2 + 1})$

$\equiv \ln((A + \sqrt{1 + A^2})(B + \sqrt{1 + B^2}))$

Use result (1).

This is of the form $AC + BD + AB + CD$.

It will factorise to $(A + D)(B + C)$.

$\equiv \ln(A + \sqrt{1 + A^2}) + \ln(B + \sqrt{1 + B^2})$

Rewrite, using the laws of logarithms.

$\equiv \sinh^{-1} A + \sinh^{-1} B$

as required.

There are some very interesting relationships between the inverse hyperbolic functions. We do not need to know these but they will help with some of the hyperbolic and trigonometric integration later. For example:

$$\sinh(\cosh^{-1} x) = \sqrt{x^2 - 1}$$

$$\ln x = \tanh^{-1}\left(\frac{x^2 - 1}{x^2 + 1}\right)$$

EXERCISE 19C

1 Find the exact value of:

a $\sinh^{-1} 3$ b $\tanh^{-1} \frac{2}{3}$ c $\cosh^{-1} \frac{5}{4}$

2 Solve, giving your answers as logarithms.

a $3\cosh^2 x = -10 \sinh x$

b $\tanh^2 x + 5 \operatorname{sech} x - 5 = 0$

c $\sinh 2x = \cosh x$

P 3 Prove that $\cosh^{-1} x \equiv \ln(x + \sqrt{x^2 - 1})$.

P 4 Prove that $\tanh^{-1} x \equiv \frac{1}{2} \ln\left(\frac{1+x}{1-x}\right)$.

P 5 Prove that $\operatorname{sech}^{-1} x \equiv \ln\left(\frac{1+\sqrt{1-x^2}}{x}\right)$.

P 6 Prove that $\tanh^{-1} A + \tanh^{-1} B \equiv \tanh^{-1}\left(\frac{A+B}{1+AB}\right)$.

P 7 a Prove that $4\cosh^3 x - 3\cosh x \equiv \cosh 3x$.

b Hence, solve $\cosh 3x = 5\cosh x$.

WORKED EXAM-STYLE QUESTION

Given that $\sinh y = x$, show that:

a $y = \ln(x + \sqrt{1 + x^2})$

By differentiating this result, show that:

b $\frac{dy}{dx} = \frac{1}{\sqrt{1+x^2}}$

Answer

a $\sinh y = x$ — Use the exponential definition.

$$\frac{e^y - e^{-y}}{2} = x$$

$$e^{2y} - 1 = 2e^y x$$

$$e^{2y} - 2e^y x - 1 = 0$$

$(e^y - x)^2 - x^2 - 1 = 0$ — Complete the square.

$$(e^y - x)^2 = x^2 + 1$$

$$e^y = x \pm \sqrt{x^2 + 1}$$

$y = \ln(x + \sqrt{x^2 + 1})$ — Rearrange and take the positive root.

b Let $y = \ln u$.

Therefore, $\frac{dy}{du} = \frac{1}{u}$.

$u = x + (1 + x^2)^{\frac{1}{2}}$

Therefore, $\frac{du}{dx} = 1 + \left(\frac{1}{2}\right)2x(1 + x^2)^{-\frac{1}{2}}$. ······ Simplify.

$$= 1 + \frac{x}{\sqrt{1 + x^2}}$$

$$= \frac{\sqrt{1 + x^2} + x}{\sqrt{1 + x^2}}$$

$\frac{dy}{dx} = \frac{dy}{du} \times \frac{du}{dx}$ ······ Use the chain rule.

$\frac{dy}{dx} = \frac{1}{x + (1 + x^2)^{\frac{1}{2}}} \times \frac{\sqrt{1 + x^2} + x}{\sqrt{1 + x^2}}$ ······ Use $u = x + (1 + x^2)^{\frac{1}{2}}$.

$\frac{dy}{dx} = \frac{1}{\sqrt{1 + x^2}}$ as required.

Checklist of learning and understanding

For hyperbolic functions:

- $\sinh x = \frac{e^x - e^{-x}}{2}$
- $\cosh x = \frac{e^x + e^{-x}}{2}$
- $\tanh x = \frac{e^x - e^{-x}}{e^x + e^{-x}} = \frac{e^{2x} - 1}{e^{2x} + 1}$

For inverse functions:

- $\text{arcsinh}\, x = \sinh^{-1} x = \ln(x + \sqrt{x^2 + 1})$
- $\text{arccosh}\, x = \cosh^{-1} x = \ln(x + \sqrt{x^2 - 1})$
- $\text{arctanh}\, x = \tanh^{-1} x = \frac{1}{2}\ln\left(\frac{1 + x}{1 - x}\right)$

END-OF-CHAPTER REVIEW EXERCISE 19

P 1 Solve $5\cosh x - \cosh 2x = 3$. Leave your answer in exact logarithmic form.

P 2 Starting from the definitions of $\sinh x$ and $\cosh x$ in terms of exponentials, prove that:

a $1 + 2\sinh^2 x \equiv \cosh 2x$

b $2\cosh 2x + \sinh x \equiv 5$

P 3 a Show, by using exponential form, that the curve with equation $y = \cosh 2x + \sinh x$ has exactly one stationary point.

b Determine, in exact logarithmic form, the x-coordinate of the turning point.

Chapter 20
Matrices 2

In this chapter you will learn how to:

- formulate and solve systems of three simultaneous equations with three unknowns
- relate solutions of matrices geometrically to lines and planes
- understand the terms eigenvalue and eigenvector, and be able to find them
- diagonalise matrices and use them to find matrices of the form A^n.

PREREQUISITE KNOWLEDGE

Where it comes from	What you should be able to do	Check your skills
Chapter 4	Find determinants of matrices up to 3×3.	**1** Find the determinant of each of the following matrices: **a** $\begin{vmatrix} 2 & 3 \\ 5 & 1 \end{vmatrix}$ **b** $\begin{vmatrix} 1 & 2 & 1 \\ 3 & 2 & 0 \\ 4 & -1 & -1 \end{vmatrix}$
Chapter 4	Multiply matrices.	**2** Work out the following calculations: **a** $\begin{pmatrix} -1 & 2 \\ 3 & 6 \end{pmatrix}\begin{pmatrix} 0 & 4 \\ -2 & 1 \end{pmatrix}$ **b** $\begin{pmatrix} 1 & -2 & 3 \\ 2 & 0 & 1 \\ 4 & 3 & 3 \end{pmatrix}\begin{pmatrix} 0 & 2 & 3 \\ -1 & 2 & 1 \\ 0 & 0 & 4 \end{pmatrix}$
Chapter 6	Find the normal of a plane.	**3** Write down the normal of each of the following planes: **a** $3x + 2y - z = 5$ **b** $-2x + 5z = 6$ **c** $3y = -11$

What else can we do with matrices?

In this chapter we shall look at a special type of vector called an eigenvector.

Eigenvectors are widely used. Applications include vibration models for bridge and building design and the page-ranking algorithm that is used to prioritise the results from search engines.

We shall also develop our knowledge of matrices that we studied in Chapter 4.

20.1 Eigenvalues and eigenvectors

To begin, let us consider the matrix $\mathbf{A} = \begin{pmatrix} 1 & 2 \\ 3 & 0 \end{pmatrix}$. If we multiply this matrix by the vectors $\begin{pmatrix} 1 \\ 2 \end{pmatrix}$, $\begin{pmatrix} -3 \\ 4 \end{pmatrix}$ and $\begin{pmatrix} 1 \\ 1 \end{pmatrix}$, then the results are $\begin{pmatrix} 5 \\ 3 \end{pmatrix}$, $\begin{pmatrix} 5 \\ -9 \end{pmatrix}$ and $\begin{pmatrix} 3 \\ 3 \end{pmatrix}$. Notice that the magnitude of the third vector increased, but its direction remained the same.

So why do some vectors *not* change direction?

To answer this question, first consider the statement $\mathbf{Ax} = \lambda\mathbf{x}$. This says that a matrix $\mathbf{A}$ applied to a non-zero vector $\mathbf{x}$ results in a vector $\lambda\mathbf{x}$. Since λ is a scalar quantity, the direction of the original vector is unchanged.

Now multiply both sides of the equation by the identity matrix to get $\mathbf{IAx} = \mathbf{I}\lambda\mathbf{x}$. Then $\mathbf{Ax} = \lambda\mathbf{Ix}$, which can be written as $(\mathbf{A} - \lambda\mathbf{I})\mathbf{x} = 0$. Note that here $\lambda\mathbf{I} = \begin{pmatrix} \lambda & 0 & 0 & \dots & 0 \\ 0 & \lambda & 0 & \dots & 0 \\ 0 & 0 & \lambda & \dots & 0 \\ \vdots & \vdots & \vdots & \ddots & \vdots \\ 0 & 0 & 0 & \dots & \lambda \end{pmatrix}$.

If $(\mathbf{A} - \lambda\mathbf{I})^{-1}$ were to exist, then $\mathbf{x}$ would always be the zero vector, which is *not* the case. This means that the inverse *cannot* exist. The only way the inverse cannot exist is if $\det(\mathbf{A} - \lambda\mathbf{I}) = 0$.

We shall use this result to help determine the values of λ. This will enable us to determine the eigenvectors of a matrix.

Look again at the previous example, this time with $\mathbf{A} = \begin{pmatrix} 1 & 2 \\ 3 & 0 \end{pmatrix}$.

We first find $\det(\mathbf{A} - \lambda\mathbf{I}) = \begin{vmatrix} 1-\lambda & 2 \\ 3 & -\lambda \end{vmatrix} = 0$, and from here $-\lambda(1-\lambda) - 6 = 0$, or $\lambda^2 - \lambda - 6 = 0$. This equation is known as the **characteristic equation**, and the λ values which satisfy this equation are known as **eigenvalues**. The word *eigen* is German for 'self'.

Solving the equation gives $\lambda = -2, 3$. We can use these values in the original statement: $\mathbf{Ax} = \lambda\mathbf{x}$, or $\begin{pmatrix} 1 & 2 \\ 3 & 0 \end{pmatrix}\begin{pmatrix} x \\ y \end{pmatrix} = \lambda\begin{pmatrix} x \\ y \end{pmatrix}$, which is then written as $\begin{matrix} x + 2y = \lambda x \\ 3x = \lambda y \end{matrix}$.

For the case when $\lambda = -2$, $\begin{matrix} x + 2y = -2x \\ 3x = -2y \end{matrix}$; both equations give $y = -\frac{3}{2}x$. This result implies that any vector of the form $\begin{pmatrix} 2 \\ -3 \end{pmatrix}$ will not change direction when $\mathbf{A}$ is applied to it.

If we test this, $\begin{pmatrix} 1 & 2 \\ 3 & 0 \end{pmatrix}\begin{pmatrix} 2 \\ -3 \end{pmatrix} = \begin{pmatrix} -4 \\ 6 \end{pmatrix}$, which is parallel to the original vector.

For the case when $\lambda = 3$, $\begin{matrix} x + 2y = 3x \\ 3x = 3y \end{matrix}$ and so $y = x$. This is the vector $\begin{pmatrix} 1 \\ 1 \end{pmatrix}$, which we already know has an unchanged direction. The vectors we have just found, $\begin{pmatrix} 2 \\ -3 \end{pmatrix}$ and $\begin{pmatrix} 1 \\ 1 \end{pmatrix}$, are known as **eigenvectors**. Their directions are unchanged when the matrix $\mathbf{A}$ is applied to them.

The use of the word *eigen* is appropriate here, since the vectors map to a scalar multiple of themselves.

WORKED EXAMPLE 20.1

Find the eigenvalues and eigenvectors of the matrix $\mathbf{B} = \begin{pmatrix} -2 & 1 \\ 6 & 3 \end{pmatrix}$.

Answer

Let $\det(\mathbf{B} - \lambda\mathbf{I}) = 0$, so $\begin{vmatrix} -2-\lambda & 1 \\ 6 & 3-\lambda \end{vmatrix} = 0$. — Use the determinant to find the characteristic equation.

Hence, $-6 - \lambda + \lambda^2 - 6 = 0$, or $\lambda^2 - \lambda - 12 = 0$.

Solving: $\lambda = -3, 4$ — Solve the equation to get the eigenvalues.

From $\mathbf{Bx} = \lambda\mathbf{x}$, $\begin{pmatrix} -2 & 1 \\ 6 & 3 \end{pmatrix}\begin{pmatrix} x \\ y \end{pmatrix} = \lambda\begin{pmatrix} x \\ y \end{pmatrix}$, or $\begin{matrix} -2x + y = \lambda x \\ 6x + 3y = \lambda y \end{matrix}$.

For $\lambda = -3$: $\begin{matrix} -2x + y = -3x \\ 6x + 3y = -3y \end{matrix}$, from which $y = -x$.

So when $\lambda = -3$, an eigenvector is $\begin{pmatrix} 1 \\ -1 \end{pmatrix}$.

For $\lambda = 4$: $\begin{matrix} -2x + y = 4x \\ 6x + 3y = 4y \end{matrix}$, from which $y = 6x$

So when $\lambda = 4$, an eigenvector is $\begin{pmatrix} 1 \\ 6 \end{pmatrix}$.

Use each eigenvalue to produce a corresponding eigenvector. Remember any scalar product of an eigenvector is also an eigenvector for the matrix.

With 2×2 matrices, the eigenvectors can be determined by considering a linear function. This function is the gradient of the line passing through the origin that has been converted to a vector.

For 3×3 matrices, this is not the same. Since we cannot represent lines correctly in 3-dimensional space, we must find an alternative approach.

Consider the matrix $\mathbf{A} = \begin{pmatrix} 1 & 2 & 4 \\ 0 & 2 & 2 \\ 0 & 0 & 3 \end{pmatrix}$, which is already conveniently in row echelon form.

Then using $\det(\mathbf{A} - \lambda\mathbf{I}) = 0$ leads to $\begin{vmatrix} 1-\lambda & 2 & 4 \\ 0 & 2-\lambda & 2 \\ 0 & 0 & 3-\lambda \end{vmatrix} = 0$.

Then $(1-\lambda)\begin{vmatrix} 2-\lambda & 2 \\ 0 & 3-\lambda \end{vmatrix} - 2\begin{vmatrix} 0 & 2 \\ 0 & 3-\lambda \end{vmatrix} + 4\begin{vmatrix} 0 & 2-\lambda \\ 0 & 0 \end{vmatrix} = 0$.

Use the determinant to find the characteristic equation $(1-\lambda)(2-\lambda)(3-\lambda) = 0$.

Now, our expression $\mathbf{Ax} = \lambda\mathbf{x}$ gives us $\begin{pmatrix} 1 & 2 & 4 \\ 0 & 2 & 2 \\ 0 & 0 & 3 \end{pmatrix}\begin{pmatrix} x \\ y \\ z \end{pmatrix} = \lambda\begin{pmatrix} x \\ y \\ z \end{pmatrix}$, or $\begin{aligned} x + 2y + 4z &= \lambda x \\ 2y + 2z &= \lambda y. \\ 3z &= \lambda z \end{aligned}$

Use the characteristic equation to select values for λ.

When $\lambda = 1$: $\begin{aligned} x + 2y + 4z &= x \\ 2y + 2z &= y \\ 3z &= z \end{aligned}$, which shows $z = 0, y = 0$ and $x = x$. This means that x can be any value, so an eigenvector corresponding to $\lambda = 1$ is $\begin{pmatrix} 1 \\ 0 \\ 0 \end{pmatrix}$.

When $\lambda = 2$: $\begin{aligned} x + 2y + 4z &= 2x \\ 2y + 2z &= 2y \\ 3z &= 2z \end{aligned}$, which shows that $z = 0, y = y$ and $x = 2y$. So this time y can be any value, and x will be twice the value of y. Hence, an eigenvector corresponding to $\lambda = 2$ is $\begin{pmatrix} 2 \\ 1 \\ 0 \end{pmatrix}$.

When $\lambda = 3$: $\begin{aligned} x + 2y + 4z &= 3x \\ 2y + 2z &= 3y \\ 3z &= 3z \end{aligned}$, which shows $z = z, y = 2z$ and $x = 4z$. So x and y both depend on z. Hence, an eigenvector corresponding to $\lambda = 3$ is $\begin{pmatrix} 4 \\ 2 \\ 1 \end{pmatrix}$.

WORKED EXAMPLE 20.2

Find the eigenvalues and corresponding eigenvectors for $\mathbf{B} = \begin{pmatrix} 3 & 2 & 4 \\ 1 & 2 & 0 \\ 1 & -2 & 1 \end{pmatrix}$.

Answer

From $\det(\mathbf{B} - \lambda\mathbf{I}) = 0$, we have $\begin{vmatrix} 3-\lambda & 2 & 4 \\ 1 & 2-\lambda & 0 \\ 1 & -2 & 1-\lambda \end{vmatrix} = 0$.

Use the determinant to find the characteristic equation.

So $(3-\lambda)\begin{vmatrix} 2-\lambda & 0 \\ -2 & 1-\lambda \end{vmatrix} - 2\begin{vmatrix} 1 & 0 \\ 1 & 1-\lambda \end{vmatrix} + 4\begin{vmatrix} 1 & 2-\lambda \\ 1 & -2 \end{vmatrix} = 0$.

Then $(3-\lambda)(2-\lambda)(1-\lambda) - 2(1-\lambda) + 4(-4+\lambda) = 0$.

Fully factorise to determine the eigenvalues.

This leads to $\lambda^3 - 6\lambda^2 + 5\lambda + 12 = 0$.
One solution is $\lambda = -1$, which means $\lambda + 1$ is a factor.

The degree of the characteristic equation (polynomial) will be the same as the dimension of the square matrix.

So factorising gives $(\lambda+1)(\lambda-3)(\lambda-4) = 0$, and $\lambda = -1, 3, 4$.

Use this equation to determine each eigenvector.

$\mathbf{Bx} = \lambda\mathbf{x}$ leads to $\begin{pmatrix} 3 & 2 & 4 \\ 1 & 2 & 0 \\ 1 & -2 & 1 \end{pmatrix}\begin{pmatrix} x \\ y \\ z \end{pmatrix} = \lambda\begin{pmatrix} x \\ y \\ z \end{pmatrix}$.

From which $\begin{aligned} 3x + 2y + 4z &= \lambda x \\ x + 2y &= \lambda y. \\ x - 2y + z &= \lambda z \end{aligned}$

For $\lambda = -1$: $\begin{aligned} 3x + 2y + 4z &= -x \\ x + 2y &= -y. \\ x - 2y + z &= -z \end{aligned}$

The second equation gives $x = -3y$, which goes into the third equation to give the result for z.

From here $x = -3y$ and then $z = \frac{5}{2}y$, so they both depend on y. An eigenvector is $\begin{pmatrix} -6 \\ 2 \\ 5 \end{pmatrix}$.

Eigenvectors are normally written without fractions.

For $\lambda = 3$: $\begin{aligned} 3x + 2y + 4z &= 3x \\ x + 2y &= 3y. \text{ From here } x = y, y = -2z. \\ x - 2y + z &= 3z \end{aligned}$

The second equation gives $x = y$. Substituting this into the third equation gives $y = -2z$.

So an eigenvector is $\begin{pmatrix} -2 \\ -2 \\ 1 \end{pmatrix}$.

Can also be $\begin{pmatrix} 2 \\ 2 \\ -1 \end{pmatrix}$.

For $\lambda = 4$: $\begin{aligned} 3x + 2y + 4z &= 4x \\ x + 2y &= 4y, \\ x - 2y + z &= 4z \end{aligned}$

and so $x = 2y$, which leads to $z = 0$.

The second equation gives $x = 2y$, which goes into the third equation to show that $z = 0$.

So an eigenvector is $\begin{pmatrix} 2 \\ 1 \\ 0 \end{pmatrix}$.

WORKED EXAMPLE 20.3

Find the eigenvalues and corresponding eigenvectors of $\mathbf{C} = \begin{pmatrix} 2 & 1 & 1 \\ -1 & 1 & 2 \\ 1 & 2 & 1 \end{pmatrix}$.

Answer

Start with $\det(\mathbf{C} - \lambda\mathbf{I}) = 0$, so $\begin{vmatrix} 2-\lambda & 1 & 1 \\ -1 & 1-\lambda & 2 \\ 1 & 2 & 1-\lambda \end{vmatrix} = 0$. — Set the determinant of the matrix equal to zero.

Then $(2-\lambda)\begin{vmatrix} 1-\lambda & 2 \\ 2 & 1-\lambda \end{vmatrix} - \begin{vmatrix} -1 & 2 \\ 1 & 1-\lambda \end{vmatrix} + \begin{vmatrix} -1 & 1-\lambda \\ 1 & 2 \end{vmatrix} = 0$, — Work through the algebra to find the characteristic equation.

Then $(2-\lambda)[(1-\lambda)^2 - 4] - (\lambda - 3) - 3 + \lambda = 0$

Or $(2-\lambda)(\lambda^2 - 2\lambda - 3) = 0$ which gives the characteristic equation $(\lambda+1)(\lambda-2)(\lambda-3) = 0$.

So the eigenvalues are $\lambda = -1, 2, 3$. — State the eigenvalues.

From $\mathbf{Cx} = \lambda\mathbf{x}$ we get $\begin{matrix} 2x + y + z = \lambda x \\ -x + y + 2z = \lambda y. \\ x + 2y + z = \lambda z \end{matrix}$ — Write down the general form before substituting in the λ values.

For $\lambda = -1$: $\begin{matrix} 2x + y + z = -x \\ -x + y + 2z = -y. \\ x + 2y + z = -z \end{matrix}$ — Choose the second and third equations since they can be combined easily.

So $-x + 2y + 2z = 0$ and $x + 2y + 2z = 0$.

Adding these gives $y = -z$ and $x = 0$.

So an eigenvector is $\begin{pmatrix} 0 \\ 1 \\ -1 \end{pmatrix}$. — State an eigenvector.

For $\lambda = 2$: $\begin{matrix} 2x + y + z = 2x \\ -x + y + 2z = 2y, \\ x + 2y + z = 2z \end{matrix}$ then $y = -z$ and $x = 3z$. — Start with the first equation, then use the result in the third equation.

So a corresponding eigenvector is $\begin{pmatrix} 3 \\ -1 \\ 1 \end{pmatrix}$. — State an eigenvector.

For $\lambda = 3$: $\begin{matrix} 2x + y + z = 3x \\ -x + y + 2z = 3y. \\ x + 2y + z = 3z \end{matrix}$ — Choose the first and second equations since they can be combined easily.

So $-x + y + z = 0$ and also $-x - 2y + 2z = 0$.

Subtracting gives $z = 3y$ and $x = 4y$.

An eigenvector is therefore $\begin{pmatrix} 4 \\ 1 \\ 3 \end{pmatrix}$. — State an eigenvector.

We now know that $\mathbf{Ax} = \lambda\mathbf{x}$ for a square matrix $\mathbf{A}$, its eigenvectors $\mathbf{x}$ and corresponding eigenvalues λ. It follows that knowing an eigenvector and applying the matrix to it will give us an eigenvalue, as shown in Key point 20.1. For example, if we let $\mathbf{A} = \begin{pmatrix} 2 & 1 \\ 7 & -4 \end{pmatrix}$ and $\begin{pmatrix} 1 \\ 1 \end{pmatrix}$ is an eigenvector, then $\begin{pmatrix} 2 & 1 \\ 7 & -4 \end{pmatrix}\begin{pmatrix} 1 \\ 1 \end{pmatrix} = \begin{pmatrix} 3 \\ 3 \end{pmatrix} = 3\begin{pmatrix} 1 \\ 1 \end{pmatrix}$, which means the eigenvalue is 3.

KEY POINT 20.1

If a matrix, $\mathbf{A}$, has eigenvalue λ and corresponding eigenvector $\mathbf{e}$, then $\mathbf{Ae} = \lambda\mathbf{e}$.

Suppose $\mathbf{B} = \begin{pmatrix} 0 & -1 & 0 \\ k & -9 & -6 \\ 5 & 11 & 7 \end{pmatrix}$ has a known eigenvector $\begin{pmatrix} 1 \\ 2 \\ -3 \end{pmatrix}$. We will find the corresponding eigenvalue and the value of k.

We start with $\begin{pmatrix} 0 & -1 & 0 \\ k & -9 & -6 \\ 5 & 11 & 7 \end{pmatrix}\begin{pmatrix} 1 \\ 2 \\ -3 \end{pmatrix} = \begin{pmatrix} -2 \\ k \\ 6 \end{pmatrix}$. By comparing the third elements of the eigenvectors we can see that $\lambda = -2$, leading to $k = -4$.

EXERCISE 20A

1 In each case, state whether or not the given vectors are eigenvectors of the matrix. If they are eigenvectors, write down their corresponding eigenvalues.

a $\mathbf{A} = \begin{pmatrix} 1 & 2 \\ 4 & 3 \end{pmatrix}$, $\mathbf{e}_1 = \begin{pmatrix} 1 \\ 2 \end{pmatrix}$ and $\mathbf{e}_2 = \begin{pmatrix} 1 \\ -2 \end{pmatrix}$

b $\mathbf{B} = \begin{pmatrix} 1 & 0 \\ 6 & -5 \end{pmatrix}$, $\mathbf{e}_1 = \begin{pmatrix} 3 \\ 2 \end{pmatrix}$ and $\mathbf{e}_2 = \begin{pmatrix} 1 \\ 1 \end{pmatrix}$

c $\mathbf{C} = \begin{pmatrix} 2 & 3 \\ 7 & -2 \end{pmatrix}$, $\mathbf{e}_1 = \begin{pmatrix} 3 \\ -7 \end{pmatrix}$ and $\mathbf{e}_2 = \begin{pmatrix} 1 \\ 4 \end{pmatrix}$

2 Given that $\mathbf{A} = \begin{pmatrix} 1 & 2 & 4 \\ 0 & 1 & 0 \\ 3 & 1 & 2 \end{pmatrix}$, show that the following vectors are eigenvectors, and determine their eigenvalues:

$\mathbf{e}_1 = \begin{pmatrix} 4 \\ 0 \\ -3 \end{pmatrix}$, $\mathbf{e}_2 = \begin{pmatrix} 1 \\ 0 \\ 1 \end{pmatrix}$, $\mathbf{e}_3 = \begin{pmatrix} 1 \\ -6 \\ 3 \end{pmatrix}$

PS 3 Given that $\mathbf{M} = \begin{pmatrix} 7 & 0 \\ 4 & -1 \end{pmatrix}$ has eigenvectors $\mathbf{e}_1 = \begin{pmatrix} 0 \\ 1 \end{pmatrix}$, $\mathbf{e}_2 = \begin{pmatrix} 2 \\ 1 \end{pmatrix}$, determine the corresponding eigenvalues.

By considering $\mathbf{M}^2\mathbf{e}_1$ and $\mathbf{Me}_1$, find the eigenvalues for $\mathbf{M}^2$.

Hence determine the eigenvalues and corresponding eigenvectors of $\mathbf{M}^5$.

M 4 Find the eigenvalues and corresponding eigenvectors for the following matrices.

a $\begin{pmatrix} 3 & 4 \\ 1 & 0 \end{pmatrix}$

b $\begin{pmatrix} 1 & 3 \\ 5 & -1 \end{pmatrix}$

PS 5 The matrix $\mathbf{G} = \begin{pmatrix} -11 & 3 & -6 \\ 8 & -2 & 4 \\ r & -6 & 9 \end{pmatrix}$ has eigenvector $\begin{pmatrix} 9 \\ -8 \\ -16 \end{pmatrix}$. Find the value of r.

PS 6 Given that $\mathbf{A} = \begin{pmatrix} p & -3 & 0 \\ 1 & 2 & 1 \\ -1 & q & 4 \end{pmatrix}$ has eigenvectors $\begin{pmatrix} 1 \\ 1 \\ -1 \end{pmatrix}$, $\begin{pmatrix} 3 \\ 1 \\ -1 \end{pmatrix}$, $\begin{pmatrix} 1 \\ 0 \\ -1 \end{pmatrix}$, find the values of the corresponding eigenvalues, as well as p and q.

P 7 Show that the characteristic equation for the matrix $\begin{pmatrix} 5 & 4 & 1 \\ -6 & -2 & 3 \\ 8 & 8 & 3 \end{pmatrix}$ is $\lambda^3 - 6\lambda^2 - 9\lambda + 14 = 0$.

PS 8 Find the eigenvalues and corresponding eigenvectors for the matrix $\begin{pmatrix} -3 & a & 2 \\ -2b & 2 & b \\ 0 & 2a & 1 \end{pmatrix}$.

20.2 Matrix algebra

Consider the matrix $\mathbf{A} = \begin{pmatrix} 2 & 5 \\ 1 & 6 \end{pmatrix}$, which has eigenvalues $\lambda = 1, 7$ and corresponding eigenvectors $\begin{pmatrix} -5 \\ 1 \end{pmatrix}$ and $\begin{pmatrix} 1 \\ 1 \end{pmatrix}$. Let $\mathbf{B} = \mathbf{A} + 2\mathbf{I}$ such that $\mathbf{B} = \begin{pmatrix} 4 & 5 \\ 1 & 8 \end{pmatrix}$. **B** should have the same eigenvectors as **A**.

Let one eigenvector be $\mathbf{e}_1$. Then $\mathbf{Be}_1 = \mathbf{Ae}_1 + 2\mathbf{Ie}_1$. Since **A** and **I** do not change the direction of $\mathbf{e}_1$, then it follows that **B** does not change its direction either. Hence, **B** must have the same eigenvectors as **A**.

So $\begin{pmatrix} 4 & 5 \\ 1 & 8 \end{pmatrix}\begin{pmatrix} -5 \\ 1 \end{pmatrix} = \begin{pmatrix} -15 \\ 3 \end{pmatrix} = 3\begin{pmatrix} -5 \\ 1 \end{pmatrix}$. Notice that the eigenvalue is not the same as it was for **A**.

Then $\begin{pmatrix} 4 & 5 \\ 1 & 8 \end{pmatrix}\begin{pmatrix} 1 \\ 1 \end{pmatrix} = 9\begin{pmatrix} 1 \\ 1 \end{pmatrix}$, which also has a different eigenvalue. Notice that each eigenvalue for **B** is two more than the eigenvalue for **A**.

It appears that adding $k\mathbf{I}$ to a matrix increases the eigenvalues by k.

We will check this with another example. Let $\mathbf{C} = \begin{pmatrix} 1 & 2 & 0 \\ 0 & 5 & 3 \\ 0 & 2 & 4 \end{pmatrix}$ with eigenvalues 1, 2, 7 and corresponding eigenvectors $\begin{pmatrix} 1 \\ 0 \\ 0 \end{pmatrix}, \begin{pmatrix} 2 \\ 1 \\ -1 \end{pmatrix}, \begin{pmatrix} 1 \\ 3 \\ 2 \end{pmatrix}$.

Then let $\mathbf{D} = \mathbf{C} - 4\mathbf{I}$, so that $\mathbf{D} = \begin{pmatrix} -3 & 2 & 0 \\ 0 & 1 & 3 \\ 0 & 2 & 0 \end{pmatrix}$.

Now $\begin{pmatrix} -3 & 2 & 0 \\ 0 & 1 & 3 \\ 0 & 2 & 0 \end{pmatrix}\begin{pmatrix} 1 \\ 0 \\ 0 \end{pmatrix} = \begin{pmatrix} -3 \\ 0 \\ 0 \end{pmatrix}$ gives an eigenvalue of -3.

$\begin{pmatrix} -3 & 2 & 0 \\ 0 & 1 & 3 \\ 0 & 2 & 0 \end{pmatrix}\begin{pmatrix} 2 \\ 1 \\ -1 \end{pmatrix} = \begin{pmatrix} -4 \\ -2 \\ 2 \end{pmatrix}$ gives an eigenvalue of -2.

Lastly, $\begin{pmatrix} -3 & 2 & 0 \\ 0 & 1 & 3 \\ 0 & 2 & 0 \end{pmatrix}\begin{pmatrix} 1 \\ 3 \\ 2 \end{pmatrix} = \begin{pmatrix} 3 \\ 9 \\ 6 \end{pmatrix}$ gives an eigenvalue of 3.

So the eigenvalues of **D** are $-3, -2, 3$. These are all four less than the eigenvalues of **C**. Again, adding $k\mathbf{I}$ to the matrix has increased the eigenvalues by k, since k was negative in this example.

If matrix **A** has eigenvalue λ and corresponding eigenvector **e**, and matrix **B** has eigenvalue μ and corresponding eigenvector **e**, then $(\mathbf{A} + \mathbf{B})\mathbf{e}$ is equal to $\mathbf{Ae} + \mathbf{Be} = \lambda\mathbf{e} + \mu\mathbf{e}$.
So $(\mathbf{A} + \mathbf{B})\mathbf{e} = (\lambda + \mu)\mathbf{e}$, as shown in Key point 20.2.

KEY POINT 20.2

If matrix **A** has eigenvalue λ and corresponding eigenvector **e**, and matrix **B** has eigenvalue μ and corresponding eigenvector **e**, then $(\mathbf{A} + \mathbf{B})\mathbf{e} = (\lambda + \mu)\mathbf{e}$.

WORKED EXAMPLE 20.4

The matrix $\mathbf{A} = \begin{pmatrix} -1 & 12 & 1 \\ 1 & 3 & 3 \\ 0 & 0 & -4 \end{pmatrix}$ has eigenvalues $\lambda = -3, -4, 5$. For each of the following cases, write down the corresponding eigenvalues and write down the relationship between each matrix and **A**.

a $\mathbf{B} = \begin{pmatrix} 1 & 12 & 1 \\ 1 & 5 & 3 \\ 0 & 0 & -2 \end{pmatrix}$ b $\mathbf{C} = \begin{pmatrix} -2 & 12 & 1 \\ 1 & 2 & 3 \\ 0 & 0 & -5 \end{pmatrix}$ c $\mathbf{D} = \begin{pmatrix} 3 & 12 & 1 \\ 1 & 7 & 3 \\ 0 & 0 & 0 \end{pmatrix}$

Answer

a For **B**: $\lambda = -1, -2, 7$; relationship is $\mathbf{B} = \mathbf{A} + 2\mathbf{I}$.

b For **C**: $\lambda = -4, -5, 4$; relationship is $\mathbf{C} = \mathbf{A} - \mathbf{I}$.

c For **D**: $\lambda = 1, 0, 9$; relationship is $\mathbf{D} = \mathbf{A} + 4\mathbf{I}$.

Relate each case to the original matrix. The difference in the leading diagonal leads to the new eigenvalues.

WORKED EXAMPLE 20.5

The matrix **A** is given by $\begin{pmatrix} -6 & 2 & 3 \\ -14 & 3 & 10 \\ -4 & 2 & 1 \end{pmatrix}$. The matrix **B** is given by $\mathbf{A} + 3\mathbf{I}$.

Two eigenvalues of **A** are $\lambda = -2, 1$ and their corresponding eigenvectors are $\begin{pmatrix} 5 \\ -2 \\ 8 \end{pmatrix}, \begin{pmatrix} 1 \\ 2 \\ 1 \end{pmatrix}$.

Find the eigenvalues and corresponding eigenvectors for **B**.

Answer

With $\det(\mathbf{A} - \lambda\mathbf{I}) = 0$, $\begin{vmatrix} -6-\lambda & 2 & 3 \\ -14 & 3-\lambda & 10 \\ -4 & 2 & 1-\lambda \end{vmatrix} = 0$.

Find the characteristic equation first.

So $(-6-\lambda)\begin{vmatrix} 3-\lambda & 10 \\ 2 & 1-\lambda \end{vmatrix} - 2\begin{vmatrix} -14 & 10 \\ -4 & 1-\lambda \end{vmatrix} + 3\begin{vmatrix} -14 & 3-\lambda \\ -4 & 2 \end{vmatrix} = 0$,

which simplifies to $(-6-\lambda)(\lambda^2 - 4\lambda - 17) - 40\lambda - 100 = 0$

and then finally $\lambda^3 + 2\lambda^2 - \lambda - 2 = 0$.

Since we have been told $\lambda = -2, 1$ then $(\lambda + 2)(\lambda - 1)(\lambda + 1) = 0$.

So the last eigenvalue is -1.

Then determine the last eigenvalue.

From $\mathbf{Ax} = \lambda\mathbf{x}$, $\begin{matrix} -6x + 2y + 3z = -x \\ -14x + 3y + 10z = -y \\ -4x + 2y + z = -z \end{matrix}$, and so $x = z$ and $y = z$.

Use the value found to produce the final eigenvector.

So an eigenvector is $\begin{pmatrix} 1 \\ 1 \\ 1 \end{pmatrix}$.

Determine the last eigenvector.

For **B** the eigenvectors are clearly $\begin{pmatrix} 5 \\ -2 \\ 8 \end{pmatrix}, \begin{pmatrix} 1 \\ 2 \\ 1 \end{pmatrix}, \begin{pmatrix} 1 \\ 1 \\ 1 \end{pmatrix}$.

State that the eigenvectors are the same for **B** as for **A**.

The eigenvalues are 1, 4, 2, respectively.

Write down each eigenvalue for **B** by adding 3 to the eigenvalues for **A**.

Consider the matrix $\mathbf{A} = \begin{pmatrix} 2 & 2 \\ 5 & -1 \end{pmatrix}$, with eigenvalues $-3, 4$ and corresponding eigenvectors $\begin{pmatrix} 2 \\ -5 \end{pmatrix}$ and $\begin{pmatrix} 1 \\ 1 \end{pmatrix}$. Let $\mathbf{B} = \mathbf{A} + 2\mathbf{I}$ such that $\mathbf{B} = \begin{pmatrix} 4 & 2 \\ 5 & 1 \end{pmatrix}$, with eigenvalues $-1, 6$ and the same eigenvectors as $\mathbf{A}$.

We find $\mathbf{AB} = \begin{pmatrix} 2 & 2 \\ 5 & -1 \end{pmatrix}\begin{pmatrix} 4 & 2 \\ 5 & 1 \end{pmatrix} = \begin{pmatrix} 18 & 6 \\ 15 & 9 \end{pmatrix}$ and then multiply this matrix by the eigenvectors: $\begin{pmatrix} 18 & 6 \\ 15 & 9 \end{pmatrix}\begin{pmatrix} 2 \\ -5 \end{pmatrix} = 3\begin{pmatrix} 2 \\ -5 \end{pmatrix}$ and $\begin{pmatrix} 18 & 6 \\ 15 & 9 \end{pmatrix}\begin{pmatrix} 1 \\ 1 \end{pmatrix} = 24\begin{pmatrix} 1 \\ 1 \end{pmatrix}$.

So it looks as if the eigenvalues of **AB** are the product of the eigenvalues of **A** and **B**.

Let us try another example: $\mathbf{C} = \begin{pmatrix} 2 & 1 & 1 \\ -1 & 1 & 2 \\ 1 & 2 & 1 \end{pmatrix}$ has eigenvalues $-1, 2, 3$ and eigenvectors $\begin{pmatrix} 0 \\ 1 \\ -1 \end{pmatrix}, \begin{pmatrix} 3 \\ -1 \\ 1 \end{pmatrix}, \begin{pmatrix} 4 \\ 1 \\ 3 \end{pmatrix}$. Let $\mathbf{D} = \mathbf{C} - 4\mathbf{I}$ where $\mathbf{D} = \begin{pmatrix} -2 & 1 & 1 \\ -1 & -3 & 2 \\ 1 & 2 & -3 \end{pmatrix}$. Matrix **D** has eigenvalues $-5, -2, -1$ and the same eigenvectors as **C**.

We find **CD**: $\begin{pmatrix} -4 & 1 & 1 \\ 3 & 0 & -5 \\ -3 & -3 & 2 \end{pmatrix}$.

So $\begin{pmatrix} -4 & 1 & 1 \\ 3 & 0 & -5 \\ -3 & -3 & 2 \end{pmatrix}\begin{pmatrix} 0 \\ 1 \\ -1 \end{pmatrix} = \begin{pmatrix} 0 \\ 5 \\ -5 \end{pmatrix}$ gives an eigenvalue of 5.

$\begin{pmatrix} -4 & 1 & 1 \\ 3 & 0 & -5 \\ -3 & -3 & 2 \end{pmatrix}\begin{pmatrix} 3 \\ -1 \\ 1 \end{pmatrix} = \begin{pmatrix} -12 \\ 4 \\ -4 \end{pmatrix}$ gives an eigenvalue of -4.

$\begin{pmatrix} -4 & 1 & 1 \\ 3 & 0 & -5 \\ -3 & -3 & 2 \end{pmatrix}\begin{pmatrix} 4 \\ 1 \\ 3 \end{pmatrix} = \begin{pmatrix} -12 \\ -3 \\ -9 \end{pmatrix}$ gives an eigenvalue of -3.

Again, the eigenvalues of **CD** are the product of the eigenvalues of **C** and **D**, as shown in Key point 20.3.

KEY POINT 20.3

If matrix **A** has eigenvalue λ and corresponding eigenvector **e**, and matrix **B** has eigenvalue μ and corresponding eigenvector **e**, then $\mathbf{ABe} = \mathbf{A}(\mu\mathbf{e})$. We can write this as $\mu\mathbf{Ae} = \mu\lambda\mathbf{e}$. Hence, the matrix **AB** with eigenvector **e** has eigenvalue $\mu\lambda$.

Consider the matrix $\mathbf{A} = \begin{pmatrix} 2 & 6 \\ 5 & 3 \end{pmatrix}$ with eigenvalues $-3, 8$ and corresponding eigenvectors $\begin{pmatrix} 6 \\ -5 \end{pmatrix}$ and $\begin{pmatrix} 1 \\ 1 \end{pmatrix}$. Then $\mathbf{A}^2$ should have eigenvalues of 9 and 64. To confirm this, we find $\mathbf{A}^2 = \begin{pmatrix} 34 & 30 \\ 25 & 39 \end{pmatrix}$. Then $\begin{pmatrix} 34 & 30 \\ 25 & 39 \end{pmatrix}\begin{pmatrix} 6 \\ -5 \end{pmatrix} = \begin{pmatrix} 54 \\ -45 \end{pmatrix} = 9\begin{pmatrix} 6 \\ -5 \end{pmatrix}$, and $\begin{pmatrix} 34 & 30 \\ 25 & 39 \end{pmatrix}\begin{pmatrix} 1 \\ 1 \end{pmatrix} = \begin{pmatrix} 64 \\ 64 \end{pmatrix} = 64\begin{pmatrix} 1 \\ 1 \end{pmatrix}$.

This follows the statement in Key point 20.3. It also suggests that $\mathbf{A}^3$, which is $\mathbf{A}^2\mathbf{A}$, will have eigenvalues $-27, 512$.

Given that the matrix $\mathbf{A}$ has eigenvalue λ and corresponding eigenvector $\mathbf{e}$, the result of $\mathbf{A}^n\mathbf{e}$ is given as $\mathbf{A}^{n-1}\mathbf{Ae} = \lambda\mathbf{A}^{n-1}\mathbf{e}$. This leads to $\lambda\mathbf{A}^{n-2}\mathbf{Ae} = \lambda^2\mathbf{A}^{n-2}\mathbf{e}$ and so on.

The result is that $\mathbf{A}^n\mathbf{e}$ has eigenvalue λ^n.

WORKED EXAMPLE 20.6

The matrix $\mathbf{A}$ is given as $\begin{pmatrix} -3 & 0 \\ 5 & 2 \end{pmatrix}$. Determine the eigenvalues and corresponding eigenvectors of the matrix $\mathbf{A}^6$.

Answer

With $\det(\mathbf{A} - \lambda\mathbf{I}) = 0$, $\begin{vmatrix} -3-\lambda & 0 \\ 5 & 2-\lambda \end{vmatrix} = 0$.

Find the determinant of $\mathbf{A} - \lambda\mathbf{I}$ to get the characteristic equation.

So $(-3-\lambda)(2-\lambda) = 0$, giving $\lambda = -3, 2$.

Note we do not always need to expand the determinant fully to find the eigenvalues.

Then $\mathbf{Ax} = \lambda\mathbf{x}$ gives $\begin{matrix} -3x = \lambda x \\ 5x + 2y = \lambda y. \end{matrix}$

Determine the eigenvalues.

For $\lambda = -3$: $\begin{matrix} -3x = -3x \\ 5x + 2y = -3y \end{matrix}$, giving $x = x, y = -x$ so an eigenvector is $\begin{pmatrix} 1 \\ -1 \end{pmatrix}$.

Find each eigenvector for its respective eigenvalue.

For $\lambda = 2$: $\begin{matrix} -3x = 2x \\ 5x + 2y = 2y \end{matrix}$, giving $x = 0, y = y$ so an eigenvector is $\begin{pmatrix} 0 \\ 1 \end{pmatrix}$.

Hence for $\mathbf{A}^6$ the eigenvalues are 729, 64 with corresponding eigenvectors $\begin{pmatrix} 1 \\ -1 \end{pmatrix}$ and $\begin{pmatrix} 0 \\ 1 \end{pmatrix}$.

Use $(-3)^6$ and 2^6 to get the eigenvalues. State the eigenvectors.

An interesting property of matrices is that the sum of powers of a matrix still has the same eigenvectors. For example, let $\mathbf{B} = \begin{pmatrix} 1 & 3 \\ 7 & 5 \end{pmatrix}$, which has eigenvalues $\lambda = -2, 8$ and corresponding eigenvectors $\begin{pmatrix} 1 \\ -1 \end{pmatrix}$ and $\begin{pmatrix} 3 \\ 7 \end{pmatrix}$.

Then $\mathbf{B}^2 = \begin{pmatrix} 22 & 18 \\ 42 & 46 \end{pmatrix}$ has eigenvalues 4, 64 for the same eigenvectors. $\mathbf{B}^3 = \begin{pmatrix} 148 & 156 \\ 364 & 356 \end{pmatrix}$ has eigenvalues -8, 512 and again has the same eigenvectors.

If we let $\mathbf{C} = \mathbf{B} + \mathbf{B}^2 + \mathbf{B}^3$, we find that $\mathbf{C} = \begin{pmatrix} 171 & 177 \\ 413 & 407 \end{pmatrix}$. So $\begin{pmatrix} 171 & 177 \\ 413 & 407 \end{pmatrix}\begin{pmatrix} 1 \\ -1 \end{pmatrix} = \begin{pmatrix} -6 \\ 6 \end{pmatrix}$, which is $-6\begin{pmatrix} 1 \\ -1 \end{pmatrix}$. Also $\begin{pmatrix} 171 & 177 \\ 413 & 407 \end{pmatrix}\begin{pmatrix} 3 \\ 7 \end{pmatrix} = \begin{pmatrix} 1752 \\ 4088 \end{pmatrix} = 584\begin{pmatrix} 3 \\ 7 \end{pmatrix}$.

These eigenvalues are actually the sum of the eigenvalues of $\mathbf{B}$, $\mathbf{B}^2$, $\mathbf{B}^3$.

If we consider $\mathbf{Ce} = (\mathbf{B} + \mathbf{B}^2 + \mathbf{B}^3)\mathbf{e}$, which is $(\lambda + \lambda^2 + \lambda^3)\mathbf{e}$, we can see why the previous example works.

WORKED EXAMPLE 20.7

Given that $\mathbf{A} = \begin{pmatrix} -7 & k & -8 \\ 2 & l & m \\ 5 & 4 & 6 \end{pmatrix}$, and that two eigenvectors are $\begin{pmatrix} 0 \\ 2 \\ -1 \end{pmatrix}$, $\begin{pmatrix} 2 \\ 1 \\ -2 \end{pmatrix}$, find the values of k, l, m, the eigenvalues and the last eigenvector.

Hence, determine the eigenvalues and eigenvectors of $\mathbf{B} = \mathbf{A} + 2\mathbf{A}^3$.

Answer

Start with $\begin{pmatrix} -7 & k & -8 \\ 2 & l & m \\ 5 & 4 & 6 \end{pmatrix}\begin{pmatrix} 0 \\ 2 \\ -1 \end{pmatrix} = \begin{pmatrix} 2k+8 \\ 2l-m \\ 2 \end{pmatrix}$.

Use the known eigenvectors to determine the first eigenvalue and k.

Hence, by comparing the first elements of the eigenvectors we can find $k = -4$ and by comparing the third elements of the eigenvectors we have $\lambda_1 = -2$. We also have $2l - m = -4$ by using the eigenvalue of -2 and the second elements of the eigenvectors.

Then $\begin{pmatrix} -7 & k & -8 \\ 2 & l & m \\ 5 & 4 & 6 \end{pmatrix}\begin{pmatrix} 2 \\ 1 \\ -2 \end{pmatrix} = \begin{pmatrix} k+2 \\ 4+l-2m \\ 2 \end{pmatrix}$.

For both eigenvectors generate an equation in terms of l and m.

Hence, $\lambda_2 = -1$, and $4 + l - 2m = -1$.

Obtain the second eigenvalue.

Solving the two equations for l and m gives $l = -1, m = 2$.

Find l and m.

So $\det(\mathbf{A} - \lambda\mathbf{I}) = 0$ gives $\begin{vmatrix} -7-\lambda & -4 & -8 \\ 2 & -1-\lambda & 2 \\ 5 & 4 & 6-\lambda \end{vmatrix} = 0$.

Use the determinant to obtain the characteristic equation.

So $(-7-\lambda)\begin{vmatrix} -1-\lambda & 2 \\ 4 & 6-\lambda \end{vmatrix} + 4\begin{vmatrix} 2 & 2 \\ 5 & 6-\lambda \end{vmatrix} - 8\begin{vmatrix} 2 & -1-\lambda \\ 5 & 4 \end{vmatrix} = 0$.

Then $-(7+\lambda)(\lambda^2 - 5\lambda - 14) + 4(2 - 2\lambda) - 8(13 + 5\lambda) = 0$,

which simplifies to $\lambda^3 + 2\lambda^2 - \lambda - 2 = 0$.

Since we know two eigenvalues already, then

Since two eigenvalues are known, we can factorise easily to find the third eigenvalue.

$(\lambda + 2)(\lambda + 1)(\lambda - 1) = 0$. So $\lambda_3 = 1$.

Obtain the third eigenvalue.

Using $\mathbf{A}\mathbf{x} = \lambda\mathbf{x}$:
$$\begin{aligned} -7x - 4y - 8z &= \lambda x \\ 2x - y + 2z &= \lambda y \\ 5x + 4y + 6z &= \lambda z \end{aligned}$$

With $\lambda = 1$ we have $-8x - 4y - 8z = 0$ and $2x - 2y + 2z = 0$,

which leads to $y = 0$ and $z = -x$. So the last eigenvector is $\begin{pmatrix} 1 \\ 0 \\ -1 \end{pmatrix}$.

Determine the last eigenvector.

For $\mathbf{B}$, the eigenvalues are $-2 + 2(-8), -1 + 2(-1), 1 + 2$. which become $-18, -3, 3$.

For the eigenvalues of $\mathbf{B}$, work out $\lambda + 2\lambda^3$ for each of the original eigenvalues.

The eigenvectors are $\begin{pmatrix} 0 \\ 2 \\ -1 \end{pmatrix}, \begin{pmatrix} 2 \\ 1 \\ -2 \end{pmatrix}, \begin{pmatrix} 1 \\ 0 \\ -1 \end{pmatrix}$.

DID YOU KNOW?

The terms eigenvalue and eigenvector were referred to as 'proper' until David Hilbert from Germany used the term *eigen*, meaning 'own' or 'self'. This led to the terminology we use today.

A very quick and effective way to determine the inverse of a matrix is to make use of the **Cayley–Hamilton theorem.**

For a square matrix $\mathbf{A}$, assume that the characteristic equation is $P_A(\lambda) = \det(\mathbf{A} - \lambda\mathbf{I})$.

The Cayley–Hamilton theorem states that $P_A(\mathbf{A}) = 0$.

So for the characteristic equation $a\lambda^3 + b\lambda^2 + c\lambda + d = 0$, it is also true that $a\mathbf{A}^3 + b\mathbf{A}^2 + c\mathbf{A} + d\mathbf{I} = 0$.

Note that our equation is now a matrix equation. This requires us to change d, which is just a number, into matrix form, $d\mathbf{I}$.

To find the inverse let $a\mathbf{A}^3 + b\mathbf{A}^2 + c\mathbf{A} = -d\mathbf{I}$.

This can be factorised to be $\mathbf{A}(a\mathbf{A}^2 + b\mathbf{A} + c\mathbf{I}) = -d\mathbf{I}$.

Finally, $\dfrac{a\mathbf{A}^2 + b\mathbf{A} + c\mathbf{I}}{-d} = \mathbf{A}^{-1}\mathbf{I}$. Since $\mathbf{A}^{-1}\mathbf{I} = \mathbf{A}^{-1}$ we have $\dfrac{a\mathbf{A}^2 + b\mathbf{A} + c\mathbf{I}}{-d} = \mathbf{A}^{-1}$.

For example, the matrix $\mathbf{A} = \begin{pmatrix} -2 & -4 & 2 \\ -2 & 1 & 2 \\ 4 & 2 & 5 \end{pmatrix}$ has the characteristic equation $\lambda^3 - 4\lambda^2 - 27\lambda + 90 = 0$. By the Cayley–Hamilton theorem, $\mathbf{A}^3 - 4\mathbf{A}^2 - 27\mathbf{A} + 90\mathbf{I} = 0$. Then $\mathbf{A}(\mathbf{A}^2 - 4\mathbf{A} - 27\mathbf{I}) = -90\mathbf{I}$. Multiplying both sides by the inverse $\mathbf{A}^{-1}$ gives $\mathbf{A}^2 - 4\mathbf{A} - 27\mathbf{I} = -90\mathbf{A}^{-1}$, as shown in Key point 20.4.

Then

$$\mathbf{A}^{-1} = -\frac{1}{90}\left[\begin{pmatrix} 20 & 8 & -2 \\ 10 & 13 & 8 \\ 8 & -4 & 37 \end{pmatrix} - 4\begin{pmatrix} -2 & -4 & 2 \\ -2 & 1 & 2 \\ 4 & 2 & 5 \end{pmatrix} - \begin{pmatrix} 27 & 0 & 0 \\ 0 & 27 & 0 \\ 0 & 0 & 27 \end{pmatrix}\right] = \begin{pmatrix} -\frac{1}{90} & -\frac{4}{15} & \frac{1}{9} \\ -\frac{1}{5} & \frac{1}{5} & 0 \\ \frac{4}{45} & \frac{2}{15} & \frac{1}{9} \end{pmatrix}$$

KEY POINT 20.4

If matrix $\mathbf{A}$ has characteristic equation $P_A(\lambda)$, then the Cayley–Hamilton theorem states that $P_A(\mathbf{A}) = 0$.

The characteristic equation $\lambda^n + a_{n-1}\lambda^{n-1} + a_{n-2}\lambda^{n-2} + \cdots + a_1\lambda + a_0 = 0$ can be converted to $\mathbf{A}^n + a_{n-1}\mathbf{A}^{n-1} + a_{n-2}\mathbf{A}^{n-2} + \cdots + a_1\mathbf{A} + a_0\mathbf{I} = 0$. From this we can determine the inverse matrix.

WORKED EXAMPLE 20.8

The matrix $\mathbf{A}$ is given as $\begin{pmatrix} 1 & 2 & -1 \\ 0 & 2 & 4 \\ 0 & 0 & -3 \end{pmatrix}$. Determine the characteristic equation of $\mathbf{A}$ and use it to determine the matrix $\mathbf{A}^{-1}$.

Answer

Since the matrix is in row echelon form, the eigenvalues are $\lambda = 1, 2, -3$.

With a lower triangle of zeroes, the eigenvalues are the elements of the leading diagonal.

This is from $(\lambda - 1)(\lambda - 2)(\lambda + 3) = 0$.

The characteristic equation:

$P_A(\lambda)$ is $\lambda^3 - 7\lambda + 6 = 0$

By the Cayley–Hamilton theorem $\mathbf{A}^3 - 7\mathbf{A} + 6\mathbf{I} = 0$.

State $P_A(\mathbf{A}) = 0$.

Then $\mathbf{A}(\mathbf{A}^2 - 7\mathbf{I}) = -6\mathbf{I}$, and so $\mathbf{A}^2 - 7\mathbf{I} = -6\mathbf{A}^{-1}$.

Factorise and multiply by $\mathbf{A}^{-1}$.

So $\mathbf{A}^{-1} = -\frac{1}{6}[\mathbf{A}^2 - 7\mathbf{I}]$, where $\mathbf{A}^2 = \begin{pmatrix} 1 & 6 & 10 \\ 0 & 4 & -4 \\ 0 & 0 & 9 \end{pmatrix}$.

Find the value of $\mathbf{A}^2$.

Thus $\mathbf{A}^{-1} = -\frac{1}{6}\left[\begin{pmatrix} 1 & 6 & 10 \\ 0 & 4 & -4 \\ 0 & 0 & 9 \end{pmatrix} - \begin{pmatrix} 7 & 0 & 0 \\ 0 & 7 & 0 \\ 0 & 0 & 7 \end{pmatrix}\right]$

and $\mathbf{A}^{-1} = \begin{pmatrix} 1 & -1 & -\frac{5}{3} \\ 0 & \frac{1}{2} & \frac{2}{3} \\ 0 & 0 & -\frac{1}{3} \end{pmatrix}$.

Evaluate the inverse and simplify the result.

EXERCISE 20B

PS 1 Given that the matrix $\mathbf{A}$ has eigenvalue λ and corresponding eigenvector $\mathbf{e}$, find the eigenvalue for $\mathbf{A}^2$.

P 2 The matrix $\mathbf{A}$ has eigenvalue λ and corresponding eigenvector $\mathbf{e}$, and the matrix $\mathbf{B}$ has eigenvalue μ and corresponding eigenvector $\mathbf{e}$. Show that the matrices $\mathbf{AB}$ and $\mathbf{BA}$ have the same eigenvalues and corresponding eigenvectors.

PS 3 The matrix $\mathbf{A}$ has eigenvalue λ and corresponding eigenvector $\mathbf{e}$, and the matrix $\mathbf{B}$ has eigenvalue μ and corresponding eigenvector $\mathbf{e}$. Find the eigenvalue and corresponding eigenvector of $\mathbf{A} - 2\mathbf{B}$.

M 4 Find the eigenvalues and eigenvectors for each of the following matrices.

a $\begin{pmatrix} 4 & -2 \\ -6 & 5 \end{pmatrix}$ b $\begin{pmatrix} 3 & 8 \\ 0 & 2 \end{pmatrix}$

M 5 For each of the following matrices, find its eigenvalues and eigenvectors. Find also the eigenvalues of $\mathbf{B} = \mathbf{A}^2 - 3\mathbf{I}$.

a $\mathbf{A} = \begin{pmatrix} 2 & 1 & -2 \\ 0 & 1 & 0 \\ 1 & 2 & 5 \end{pmatrix}$ b $\mathbf{A} = \begin{pmatrix} 1 & 0 & 0 \\ 4 & 2 & 0 \\ 0 & 0 & 5 \end{pmatrix}$

PS 6 The matrix $\mathbf{A} = \begin{pmatrix} 4 & 0 & 1 \\ 0 & 5 & 0 \\ 0 & 3 & -6 \end{pmatrix}$ has eigenvectors $\begin{pmatrix} 1 \\ 0 \\ -10 \end{pmatrix}, \begin{pmatrix} 1 \\ 0 \\ 0 \end{pmatrix}, \begin{pmatrix} 3 \\ 11 \\ 3 \end{pmatrix}$.

a Find the eigenvalues of $\mathbf{A}^3$.

b The matrix $\mathbf{B} = \mathbf{A} - \mathbf{A}^2$. Find the eigenvalues and eigenvectors of $\mathbf{B}$.

PS 7 Given that $\mathbf{A} = \begin{pmatrix} 1 & 5 & 7 \\ 1 & 3 & -1 \\ a & 1 & 5 \end{pmatrix}$ has eigenvector $\begin{pmatrix} 1 \\ -1 \\ 1 \end{pmatrix}$, find the corresponding eigenvalue and the value of a.
Hence, find the remaining eigenvalues and eigenvectors.

P 8 If a matrix, $\mathbf{A}$, has eigenvalue λ and corresponding eigenvector $\mathbf{e}$, show the following.

a $\mathbf{Ae} + \mathbf{A}^2\mathbf{e} = (\lambda + \lambda^2)\mathbf{e}$

b $\mathbf{Ae} + \mathbf{A}^{-1}\mathbf{e} = \left(\lambda + \frac{1}{\lambda}\right)\mathbf{e}$

M 9 Using the Cayley–Hamilton theorem, find the inverse of the matrix $\mathbf{A} = \begin{pmatrix} 0 & -4 & -6 \\ -1 & 0 & -3 \\ 1 & 2 & 5 \end{pmatrix}$.

20.3 Diagonalisation

Consider the matrix $\mathbf{A} = \begin{pmatrix} -3 & -1 \\ 8 & 6 \end{pmatrix}$. Finding $\mathbf{A}^2$ is simple but finding $\mathbf{A}^{25}$ would take a great deal of calculation. For a 3×3 matrix it would take even longer.

Fortunately, there is a more efficient way of doing this.

For $\mathbf{A} = \begin{pmatrix} -3 & -1 \\ 8 & 6 \end{pmatrix}$ we can determine that the eigenvalues are $\lambda = -2, 5$ and the corresponding eigenvectors work out to be $\begin{pmatrix} 1 \\ -1 \end{pmatrix}, \begin{pmatrix} 1 \\ -8 \end{pmatrix}$.

Next we shall form two new matrices:

$\mathbf{P} = \begin{pmatrix} 1 & 1 \\ -1 & -8 \end{pmatrix}$ which is made up of the eigenvectors

$\mathbf{D} = \begin{pmatrix} -2 & 0 \\ 0 & 5 \end{pmatrix}$ which has a leading diagonal consisting of the eigenvalues that correspond to the eigenvectors in $\mathbf{P}$. Now, we can calculate $\mathbf{AP} = \begin{pmatrix} -3 & -1 \\ 8 & 6 \end{pmatrix}\begin{pmatrix} 1 & 1 \\ -1 & -8 \end{pmatrix} = \begin{pmatrix} -2 & 5 \\ 2 & -40 \end{pmatrix}$.

This new matrix shows the effect of each eigenvalue on its respective eigenvector.

Next we calculate $\mathbf{PD}$, to get $\begin{pmatrix} 1 & 1 \\ -1 & -8 \end{pmatrix}\begin{pmatrix} -2 & 0 \\ 0 & 5 \end{pmatrix} = \begin{pmatrix} -2 & 5 \\ 2 & -40 \end{pmatrix}$. Here each eigenvector is multiplied by its own eigenvalue. So, for this example, $\mathbf{AP} = \mathbf{PD}$.

Now consider $\mathbf{B} = \begin{pmatrix} 1 & 0 & 2 \\ 1 & 3 & 0 \\ 0 & 0 & 4 \end{pmatrix}$. This matrix has eigenvalues $\lambda = 1, 3, 4$, with corresponding eigenvectors $\begin{pmatrix} 2 \\ -1 \\ 0 \end{pmatrix}, \begin{pmatrix} 0 \\ 1 \\ 0 \end{pmatrix}, \begin{pmatrix} 2 \\ 2 \\ 3 \end{pmatrix}$.

Let $\mathbf{P} = \begin{pmatrix} 2 & 0 & 2 \\ -1 & 1 & 2 \\ 0 & 0 & 3 \end{pmatrix}$ where, again, the eigenvectors form the matrix.

Let $\mathbf{D} = \begin{pmatrix} 1 & 0 & 0 \\ 0 & 3 & 0 \\ 0 & 0 & 4 \end{pmatrix}$ where, again, the leading diagonal consists of the eigenvalues corresponding to their respective eigenvectors.

$\mathbf{BP} = \begin{pmatrix} 1 & 0 & 2 \\ 1 & 3 & 0 \\ 0 & 0 & 4 \end{pmatrix}\begin{pmatrix} 2 & 0 & 2 \\ -1 & 1 & 2 \\ 0 & 0 & 3 \end{pmatrix} = \begin{pmatrix} 2 & 0 & 8 \\ -1 & 3 & 8 \\ 0 & 0 & 12 \end{pmatrix}$ and $\mathbf{PD} = \begin{pmatrix} 2 & 0 & 2 \\ -1 & 1 & 2 \\ 0 & 0 & 3 \end{pmatrix}\begin{pmatrix} 1 & 0 & 0 \\ 0 & 3 & 0 \\ 0 & 0 & 4 \end{pmatrix} =$ $\begin{pmatrix} 2 & 0 & 8 \\ -1 & 3 & 8 \\ 0 & 0 & 12 \end{pmatrix}$. So, again, $\mathbf{BP} = \mathbf{PD}$.

EXPLORE 20.1

Let $\mathbf{A} = \begin{pmatrix} a & b \\ c & d \end{pmatrix}$, where the eigenvalues are λ_1, λ_2 and the eigenvectors are $\begin{pmatrix} x_1 \\ x_2 \end{pmatrix}$, $\begin{pmatrix} y_1 \\ y_2 \end{pmatrix}$.

Investigate, with this general case, whether or not $\mathbf{AP} = \mathbf{PD}$. This can be extended as shown in Key point 20.5.

KEY POINT 20.5

If matrix $\mathbf{A}$ has eigenvalues $\lambda_1, \lambda_2, \lambda_3, \ldots \lambda_n$ and corresponding eigenvectors $\begin{pmatrix} x_1 \\ x_2 \\ x_3 \\ \vdots \\ x_n \end{pmatrix}, \begin{pmatrix} y_1 \\ y_2 \\ y_3 \\ \vdots \\ y_n \end{pmatrix}, \begin{pmatrix} z_1 \\ z_2 \\ z_3 \\ \vdots \\ z_n \end{pmatrix}, \ldots$ then the matrix $\mathbf{D} = \begin{pmatrix} \lambda_1 & 0 & 0 & \ldots & 0 \\ 0 & \lambda_2 & 0 & \ldots & 0 \\ 0 & 0 & \lambda_3 & \ldots & 0 \\ \vdots & \vdots & \vdots & \ddots & \vdots \\ 0 & 0 & 0 & \ldots & \lambda_n \end{pmatrix}$ and matrix

$\mathbf{P} = \begin{pmatrix} x_1 & y_1 & z_1 & \ldots & \ldots \\ x_2 & y_2 & z_2 & \ldots & \ldots \\ x_3 & y_3 & z_3 & \ldots & \ldots \\ \vdots & \vdots & \vdots & \ddots & \vdots \\ x_n & y_n & z_n & \ldots & \ddots \end{pmatrix}$ are such that $\mathbf{AP} = \mathbf{PD}$. Hence, $\mathbf{A} = \mathbf{PDP}^{-1}$. Note that

$\mathbf{D}^m = \begin{pmatrix} \lambda_1 & 0 & 0 & \ldots & 0 \\ 0 & \lambda_2 & 0 & \ldots & 0 \\ 0 & 0 & \lambda_3 & \ldots & 0 \\ \vdots & \vdots & \vdots & \ddots & \vdots \\ 0 & 0 & 0 & \ldots & \lambda_n \end{pmatrix}^m = \begin{pmatrix} \lambda_1{}^m & 0 & 0 & \ldots & 0 \\ 0 & \lambda_2{}^m & 0 & \ldots & 0 \\ 0 & 0 & \lambda_3{}^m & \ldots & 0 \\ \vdots & \vdots & \vdots & \ddots & \vdots \\ 0 & 0 & 0 & \ldots & \lambda_n{}^m \end{pmatrix}$ so it is easy to find powers of $\mathbf{D}$.

Any matrix that can be written in the form $\mathbf{A} = \mathbf{PDP}^{-1}$ is said to be **diagonalisable**.

To make use of this relationship, consider the matrix $\mathbf{A} = \begin{pmatrix} 1 & -2 \\ 0 & -1 \end{pmatrix}$. Consider, for example, that we wish to determine $\mathbf{A}^{20}$. If we use the form $\mathbf{A} = \mathbf{PDP}^{-1}$ then $\mathbf{A}^{20} = (\mathbf{PDP}^{-1})^{20}$, which can be written as $\mathbf{PDP}^{-1} \times \mathbf{PDP}^{-1} \times \ldots \times \mathbf{PDP}^{-1}$. Note that all internal products of the form $\mathbf{P}^{-1}\mathbf{P}$ are equal to $\mathbf{I}$. So $\mathbf{A}^{20} = \mathbf{PDDD} \ldots \mathbf{DDP}^{-1} \Rightarrow \mathbf{A}^{20} = \mathbf{PD}^{20}\mathbf{P}^{-1}$.

REWIND

You can review basic matrix operations in Chapter 4 of this book.

The matrix $\mathbf{A}$ has eigenvalues $\lambda = -1, 1$ and corresponding eigenvectors $\begin{pmatrix} 1 \\ 1 \end{pmatrix}$, $\begin{pmatrix} 1 \\ 0 \end{pmatrix}$.

So $\mathbf{D} = \begin{pmatrix} -1 & 0 \\ 0 & 1 \end{pmatrix}$ and $\mathbf{P} = \begin{pmatrix} 1 & 1 \\ 1 & 0 \end{pmatrix}$. We also need the inverse of the matrix $\mathbf{P}$, so $\mathbf{P}^{-1} = \begin{pmatrix} 0 & 1 \\ 1 & -1 \end{pmatrix}$.

Hence, $\mathbf{A}^{20} = \begin{pmatrix} 1 & 1 \\ 1 & 0 \end{pmatrix}\begin{pmatrix} -1 & 0 \\ 0 & 1 \end{pmatrix}^{20}\begin{pmatrix} 0 & 1 \\ 1 & -1 \end{pmatrix} = \begin{pmatrix} 1 & 1 \\ 1 & 0 \end{pmatrix}\begin{pmatrix} 1 & 0 \\ 0 & 1 \end{pmatrix}\begin{pmatrix} 0 & 1 \\ 1 & -1 \end{pmatrix}$. Matrix multiplication yields $\mathbf{A}^{20} = \begin{pmatrix} 1 & 0 \\ 0 & 1 \end{pmatrix}$.

WORKED EXAMPLE 20.9

A matrix is given as $\mathbf{B} = \begin{pmatrix} 1 & 2 & 0 \\ 0 & 3 & 1 \\ 0 & 0 & 2 \end{pmatrix}$. It is known to have eigenvalues $\lambda = 1, 2, 3$ and corresponding eigenvectors $\begin{pmatrix} 1 \\ 0 \\ 0 \end{pmatrix}, \begin{pmatrix} 2 \\ 1 \\ -1 \end{pmatrix}, \begin{pmatrix} 1 \\ 1 \\ 0 \end{pmatrix}$. Find $\mathbf{B}^6$.

Answer

Let $\mathbf{D} = \begin{pmatrix} 1 & 0 & 0 \\ 0 & 2 & 0 \\ 0 & 0 & 3 \end{pmatrix}$ and $\mathbf{P} = \begin{pmatrix} 1 & 2 & 1 \\ 0 & 1 & 1 \\ 0 & -1 & 0 \end{pmatrix}$.

State matrices **D** and **P**.

Then performing the row operations $r_3 \rightarrow r_3 + r_2$, $r_1 \rightarrow r_1 - 2r_2$, $r_1 \rightarrow r_1 + r_3$, $r_2 \rightarrow r_2 - r_3$ on the augmented matrix

$$\begin{pmatrix} 1 & 2 & 1 & \vdots & 1 & 0 & 0 \\ 0 & 1 & 1 & \vdots & 0 & 1 & 0 \\ 0 & -1 & 0 & \vdots & 0 & 0 & 1 \end{pmatrix} \text{ leads to the matrix } \mathbf{P}^{-1} = \begin{pmatrix} 1 & -1 & 1 \\ 0 & 0 & -1 \\ 0 & 1 & 1 \end{pmatrix}.$$

Use row operations on an augmented matrix for **P** to change the right-hand side into the inverse of the matrix **P**.

So with $\mathbf{P}^{-1}$ and $\mathbf{D}^6 = \begin{pmatrix} 1 & 0 & 0 \\ 0 & 64 & 0 \\ 0 & 0 & 729 \end{pmatrix}$

State the matrix $\mathbf{D}^6$ using Key point 20.5.

we can now say that $\mathbf{B}^6 = \begin{pmatrix} 1 & 2 & 1 \\ 0 & 1 & 1 \\ 0 & -1 & 0 \end{pmatrix} \begin{pmatrix} 1 & 0 & 0 \\ 0 & 64 & 0 \\ 0 & 0 & 729 \end{pmatrix} \begin{pmatrix} 1 & -1 & 1 \\ 0 & 0 & -1 \\ 0 & 1 & 1 \end{pmatrix}$.

Calculate $\mathbf{B}^6$.

which works out to be $\begin{pmatrix} 1 & 728 & 602 \\ 0 & 729 & 665 \\ 0 & 0 & 64 \end{pmatrix}$.

WORKED EXAMPLE 20.10

Given that one of the eigenvectors of the matrix $\mathbf{A} = \begin{pmatrix} 2 & -5 & 0 \\ 1 & a & 3 \\ 0 & 0 & 5 \end{pmatrix}$ is $\begin{pmatrix} 5 \\ 1 \\ 0 \end{pmatrix}$, find matrices **P** and **E** such that $\mathbf{A}^5 = \mathbf{PEP}^{-1}$. (You are *not* required to find $\mathbf{P}^{-1}$.)

Answer

Start with $\begin{pmatrix} 2 & -5 & 0 \\ 1 & a & 3 \\ 0 & 0 & 5 \end{pmatrix} \begin{pmatrix} 5 \\ 1 \\ 0 \end{pmatrix} = \begin{pmatrix} 5 \\ 5+a \\ 0 \end{pmatrix}$.

Use the first eigenvector to determine the corresponding eigenvalue and the value of a.

Hence, $\lambda_1 = 1$ and $a = -4$.

Then $\begin{vmatrix} 2-\lambda & -5 & 0 \\ 1 & -4-\lambda & 3 \\ 0 & 0 & 5-\lambda \end{vmatrix} = 0$ gives the characteristic equation $(2-\lambda)(-4-\lambda)(5-\lambda) + 5(5-\lambda) = 0$.

Use $\det(\mathbf{A} - \lambda\mathbf{I}) = 0$ to determine the other eigenvalues.

Then $(5-\lambda)[(2-\lambda)(-4-\lambda) + 5] = 0$.

Simplifying gives the equation $(5-\lambda)(\lambda+3)(\lambda-1) = 0$.

Hence, $\lambda_2 = -3, \lambda_3 = 5$

$$\text{Then } \mathbf{Ax} = \lambda\mathbf{x} \Rightarrow \begin{aligned} 2x - 5y &= \lambda x \\ x - 4y + 3z &= \lambda y \\ 5z &= \lambda z \end{aligned}$$

Let $\mathbf{Ax} = \lambda\mathbf{x}$ so that the other eigenvectors can be determined.

$2x - 5y = -3x$

When $\lambda = -3$, $x - 4y + 3z = -3y$,

$5z = -3z$

Look for the one equation that explicitly determines one of your values.

giving $z = 0$, $y = x$, and so an eigenvector is $\begin{pmatrix} 1 \\ 1 \\ 0 \end{pmatrix}$.

Combine results if necessary to obtain the eigenvectors.

$2x - 5y = 5x$

When $\lambda = 5$, $x - 4y + 3z = 5y$, giving $y = -\frac{3}{5}x$ and

$5z = 5z$

$z = -\frac{32}{15}x$. Hence, an eigenvector is $\begin{pmatrix} 15 \\ -9 \\ -32 \end{pmatrix}$.

So now $\mathbf{P} = \begin{pmatrix} 1 & 5 & 15 \\ 1 & 1 & -9 \\ 0 & 0 & -32 \end{pmatrix}$ and then with $\mathbf{E} = \mathbf{D}^5$ we

State **P** formed by the three eigenvectors.

have $\mathbf{E} = \begin{pmatrix} -243 & 0 & 0 \\ 0 & 1 & 0 \\ 0 & 0 & 3125 \end{pmatrix}$.

Note that $\mathbf{A}^5$ requires $\mathbf{D}^5$, which is denoted by **E**.

It was stated earlier that a matrix written in the form $\mathbf{A} = \mathbf{PDP}^{-1}$ is diagonalisable. From this expression, the only matrix that might cause a problem is $\mathbf{P}^{-1}$. If $\mathbf{P}^{-1}$ does not exist, then our relationship does not exist: **A** can be diagonalised only if $\mathbf{P}^{-1}$ exists.

E Consider the matrix $\mathbf{A} = \begin{pmatrix} 2 & 3 & 1 \\ 0 & 2 & 4 \\ 0 & 0 & 1 \end{pmatrix}$. It has characteristic equation $(\lambda - 2)^2(\lambda - 1) = 0$.

Since there are only two eigenvalues, there are only two different independent eigenvectors. These are $\begin{pmatrix} 1 \\ 0 \\ 0 \end{pmatrix}$ and $\begin{pmatrix} 11 \\ -4 \\ 1 \end{pmatrix}$. So now $\mathbf{P} = \begin{pmatrix} 1 & 0 & 11 \\ 0 & 0 & -4 \\ 0 & 0 & 1 \end{pmatrix}$, which cannot possibly have an inverse. So the matrix **A** is *not* diagonalisable.

TIP

Any matrix that is non-square does *not* have an inverse. This implies that non-square matrices *cannot* be diagonalised.

WORKED EXAMPLE 20.11

Show that the matrix $\mathbf{A} = \begin{pmatrix} 2 & -3 \\ 3 & -4 \end{pmatrix}$ is not diagonalisable.

Answer

Using $\det(\mathbf{A} - \lambda\mathbf{I}) = 0$, $\begin{vmatrix} 2-\lambda & -3 \\ 3 & -4-\lambda \end{vmatrix} = 0$, and so the characteristic equation is $\lambda^2 + 2\lambda + 1 = 0$, or $(\lambda + 1)^2 = 0$.

Use the determinant to find the characteristic equation.

So $\lambda = -1$.

Note that only one value of λ exists.

Hence, there is only one distinct eigenvector. So **P** is not a square matrix, which means it has no inverse.

Only one eigenvector means **P** is not an $n \times n$ matrix.

Therefore, **A** is not diagonalisable.

Hence, we cannot form $\mathbf{A} = \mathbf{PDP}^{-1}$.

EXERCISE 20C

E 1 State whether or not the following matrices are diagonalisable.

a $\begin{pmatrix} 3 & -2 \\ 2 & -1 \end{pmatrix}$ b $\begin{pmatrix} 1 & 1 \\ 8 & 2 \end{pmatrix}$ c $\begin{pmatrix} -10 & -9 \\ 4 & 2 \end{pmatrix}$

E PS 2 Given that the matrix $\begin{pmatrix} -1 & k \\ 7 & 3 \end{pmatrix}$ is not diagonalisable over reals, find the values of k.

PS 3 Given that the matrix $\begin{pmatrix} -7 & -10 \\ k & 4 \end{pmatrix}$ is diagonalisable, find the smallest positive value of k, where k is an integer, that gives integer eigenvalues.

M 4 Find the values of the following matrices.

a $\begin{pmatrix} -3 & 4 \\ 0 & 2 \end{pmatrix}^6$ b $\begin{pmatrix} -5 & 7 \\ -4 & 6 \end{pmatrix}^7$

E PS 5 Find which of the following matrices are diagonalisable.

a $\begin{pmatrix} 1 & 0 & 2 \\ 0 & 3 & 2 \\ 2 & 0 & 1 \end{pmatrix}$ b $\begin{pmatrix} 1 & -1 & 0 \\ 1 & 3 & 0 \\ 0 & 0 & 2 \end{pmatrix}$ c $\begin{pmatrix} 3 & 0 & -1 \\ 0 & 1 & 0 \\ 2 & 0 & 0 \end{pmatrix}$

PS 6 The matrix $\mathbf{A} = \begin{pmatrix} 3 & 3 & 2 \\ 1 & 5 & 0 \\ 0 & 0 & 4 \end{pmatrix}$ has eigenvectors $\begin{pmatrix} 3 \\ -1 \\ 0 \end{pmatrix}, \begin{pmatrix} 1 \\ -1 \\ 2 \end{pmatrix}, \begin{pmatrix} 1 \\ 1 \\ 0 \end{pmatrix}$. Find the matrices $\mathbf{P}$ and $\mathbf{H}$ such that $\mathbf{B}^4 = \mathbf{PHP}^{-1}$, where $\mathbf{B} = \mathbf{A} - 3\mathbf{I}$.

E M 7 For the matrix $\mathbf{A} = \begin{pmatrix} k & 1 & 2 \\ 0 & 2 & 3 \\ 0 & 0 & 1 \end{pmatrix}$, find the eigenvalues and eigenvectors for the cases when $k = 0$ and $k = 2$. Explain why the matrix $\mathbf{A}$ cannot be diagonalised when $k = 2$.

PS 8 You are given the matrix $\mathbf{A} = \begin{pmatrix} 1 & 0 & 3 & 2 \\ 0 & 2 & 1 & 1 \\ 0 & 0 & -1 & 5 \\ 0 & 0 & 0 & -2 \end{pmatrix}$, where the eigenvalues are $\lambda_1, \lambda_2, \lambda_3, \lambda_4$.

a Write down the values of $\lambda_1, \lambda_2, \lambda_3, \lambda_4$.

b If $\mathbf{P}^{-1} = \frac{1}{6}\begin{pmatrix} 6 & 0 & 9 & 19 \\ 0 & 6 & 2 & 4 \\ 6 & 0 & -1 & -5 \\ 0 & 0 & 0 & 2 \end{pmatrix}$, determine the value of $\mathbf{A}^6$.

TIP

Use the leading diagonal.

20.4 Systems of equations

Consider the system of equations $\begin{aligned} 2x - y + 3z &= 4 \\ 3x + 2y + 8z &= 13 \\ 4x + 2y + 11z &= 16 \end{aligned}$. We want to find a solution for x, y, z.

First, rewrite this system as $\begin{pmatrix} 2 & -1 & 3 \\ 3 & 2 & 8 \\ 4 & 2 & 11 \end{pmatrix}\begin{pmatrix} x \\ y \\ z \end{pmatrix} = \begin{pmatrix} 4 \\ 13 \\ 16 \end{pmatrix}$.

There is a very good way of approaching this using row reduction methods.

For the augmented matrix $\begin{pmatrix} 2 & -1 & 3 & \vdots & 4 \\ 3 & 2 & 8 & \vdots & 13 \\ 4 & 2 & 11 & \vdots & 16 \end{pmatrix}$, the operations $r_3 \to r_3 - 2r_1$, $r_2 \to 2r_2 - 3r_1$ and $r_3 \to 7r_3 - 4r_2$ will give $\begin{pmatrix} 2 & -1 & 3 & \vdots & 4 \\ 0 & 7 & 7 & \vdots & 14 \\ 0 & 0 & 7 & \vdots & 0 \end{pmatrix}$. From here we have

$$\begin{aligned} 2x - y + 3z &= 4 \\ 7y + 7z &= 14 \\ 7z &= 0 \end{aligned}$$

and, hence, $z = 0, y = 2, x = 3$.

So the system has a unique solution (3, 2, 0).

WORKED EXAMPLE 20.12

Find the unique solution for the system of equations $\begin{aligned} 2x + 5z &= -3 \\ x + y + 2z &= 0. \\ x - y + 4z &= -4 \end{aligned}$

Answer

Let $\begin{pmatrix} 2 & 0 & 5 \\ 1 & 1 & 2 \\ 1 & -1 & 4 \end{pmatrix}\begin{pmatrix} x \\ y \\ z \end{pmatrix} = \begin{pmatrix} -3 \\ 0 \\ -4 \end{pmatrix}$. — Write down the matrix form.

Then for the augmented matrix $\begin{pmatrix} 2 & 0 & 5 & \vdots & -3 \\ 1 & 1 & 2 & \vdots & 0 \\ 1 & -1 & 4 & \vdots & -4 \end{pmatrix}$ — Create the augmented matrix.

apply the row operations $r_2 \to 2r_2 - r_1$, $r_3 \to 2r_3 - r_1$, $r_3 \to r_3 + r_2$ to get the matrix $\begin{pmatrix} 2 & 0 & 5 & \vdots & -3 \\ 0 & 2 & -1 & \vdots & 3 \\ 0 & 0 & 2 & \vdots & -2 \end{pmatrix}$. — Apply operations to get row echelon form.

Hence, $z = -1, y = 1, x = 1$. — Solve for a unique solution.

What happens if there is no unique solution? Consider the system $\begin{aligned} x + 2y + 3z &= 1 \\ 3x + 4y + 13z &= 5. \\ 4x + 7y + 14z &= 5 \end{aligned}$

First, write this as $\begin{pmatrix} 1 & 2 & 3 \\ 3 & 4 & 13 \\ 4 & 7 & 14 \end{pmatrix}\begin{pmatrix} x \\ y \\ z \end{pmatrix} = \begin{pmatrix} 1 \\ 5 \\ 5 \end{pmatrix}$, so the augmented matrix is $\begin{pmatrix} 1 & 2 & 3 & \vdots & 1 \\ 3 & 4 & 13 & \vdots & 5 \\ 4 & 7 & 14 & \vdots & 5 \end{pmatrix}$. Perform operations $r_2 \to r_2 - 3r_1$, $r_3 \to r_3 - 4r_1$ and $r_3 \to 2r_3 - r_2$, giving $\begin{pmatrix} 1 & 2 & 3 & \vdots & 1 \\ 0 & -2 & 4 & \vdots & 2 \\ 0 & 0 & 0 & \vdots & 0 \end{pmatrix}$.

In $\mathbf{Ax} = \mathbf{b}$ form, this is $\begin{pmatrix} 1 & 2 & 3 \\ 0 & -2 & 4 \\ 0 & 0 & 0 \end{pmatrix}\begin{pmatrix} x \\ y \\ z \end{pmatrix} = \begin{pmatrix} 1 \\ 2 \\ 0 \end{pmatrix}$, which gives $x + 2y + 3z = 1, -2y + 4z = 2$.

Simplify these equations to give $y = -1 + 2z$ and $x = 3 - 7z$.

Now let z be a free variable t. We can write the equations as $\begin{pmatrix} x \\ y \\ z \end{pmatrix} = \begin{pmatrix} 3 \\ -1 \\ 0 \end{pmatrix} + \begin{pmatrix} -7 \\ 2 \\ 1 \end{pmatrix}t$.

Note that, since both x and y depend on z, we can introduce this parameter into our system. As z is a free variable, it is free to change in value. This means that there is an infinite number of solutions.

WORKED EXAMPLE 20.13

Find a solution set for the system of equations $\begin{matrix} 2x + 3y + z = 1 \\ 4x + 10y + 5z = 3. \\ 2x + 11y + 7z = 3 \end{matrix}$

Answer

The augmented matrix is $\begin{pmatrix} 2 & 3 & 1 & : & 1 \\ 4 & 10 & 5 & : & 3 \\ 2 & 11 & 7 & : & 3 \end{pmatrix}$.

Write all the coefficients in an augmented matrix.

The row operations $r_2 \to r_2 - 2r_1$, $r_3 \to r_3 - r_1$, $r_3 \to r_3 - 2r_2$ give $\begin{pmatrix} 2 & 3 & 1 & : & 1 \\ 0 & 4 & 3 & : & 1 \\ 0 & 0 & 0 & : & 0 \end{pmatrix}$.

Apply row operations until the last row cannot be altered any further.

So $2x + 3y + z = 1$, $4y + 3z = 1$ can be simplified to $y = \frac{1}{4} - \frac{3}{4}z$ and $x = \frac{1}{8} + \frac{5}{8}z$.

Write down the equations that relate two variables against the free variable.

Then letting $\frac{z}{8} = t$ gives $\begin{pmatrix} x \\ y \\ z \end{pmatrix} = \begin{pmatrix} \frac{1}{8} \\ \frac{1}{4} \\ 0 \end{pmatrix} + \begin{pmatrix} 5 \\ -6 \\ 8 \end{pmatrix}t$.

State the solution.

If a system of equations is given as $\begin{matrix} 3x - y + 4z = 1 \\ 3x + y + 3z = 2, \\ 6x - 4y + 9z = 3 \end{matrix}$ can we determine whether or not the system actually has any solutions?

Starting with $\begin{pmatrix} 3 & -1 & 4 \\ 3 & 1 & 3 \\ 6 & -4 & 9 \end{pmatrix}\begin{pmatrix} x \\ y \\ z \end{pmatrix} = \begin{pmatrix} 1 \\ 2 \\ 3 \end{pmatrix}$ we have the augmented matrix $\begin{pmatrix} 3 & -1 & 4 & : & 1 \\ 3 & 1 & 3 & : & 2 \\ 6 & -4 & 9 & : & 3 \end{pmatrix}$.

With the row operations $r_3 \to r_3 - 2r_2$, $r_2 \to r_2 - r_1$, $r_3 \to r_3 + 3r_2$ the augmented matrix becomes $\begin{pmatrix} 3 & -1 & 4 & : & 1 \\ 0 & 2 & -1 & : & 1 \\ 0 & 0 & 0 & : & 2 \end{pmatrix}$. Notice that the last row states that $0 = 2$. Of course, this cannot be true so this system has no solutions.

WORKED EXAMPLE 20.14

Show that the system of equations $\begin{matrix} x + 4y - 2z = 1 \\ x + 5y = 2 \\ 3x + 13y - 4z = 3 \end{matrix}$ has no solutions.

Answer

Start with $\begin{pmatrix} 1 & 4 & -2 & : & 1 \\ 1 & 5 & 0 & : & 2 \\ 3 & 13 & -4 & : & 3 \end{pmatrix}$, then use the row

Use the augmented matrix with row operations to get to row echelon form.

operations $r_2 \to r_2 - r_1, r_3 \to r_3 - 3r_1, r_3 \to r_3 - r_2$ to give $\begin{pmatrix} 1 & 4 & -2 & \vdots & 1 \\ 0 & 1 & 2 & \vdots & 1 \\ 0 & 0 & 0 & \vdots & -1 \end{pmatrix}$.

The last row states that $0 = -1$, so there are no solutions.

Inconsistent values mean no solutions.

If we have the system $\begin{matrix} x + 2y - z = 1 \\ 2x + 5y + z = 9 \\ x + 3y + 3z = 10 \end{matrix}$ and we are to interpret these systems of equations, performing row operations will reduce the augmented matrix to $\begin{pmatrix} 1 & 2 & -1 & \vdots & 1 \\ 0 & 1 & 3 & \vdots & 7 \\ 0 & 0 & 1 & \vdots & 2 \end{pmatrix}$.

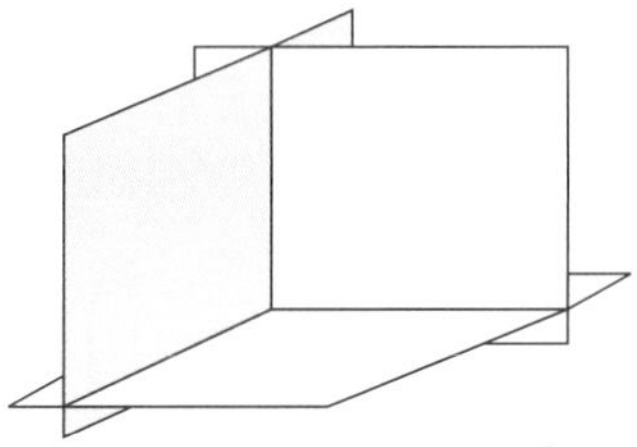

Since the bottom row has a distinct solution for z, we can see that there is just one unique answer. The three equations can be modelled as planes, and the unique solution is the one point where the planes meet.

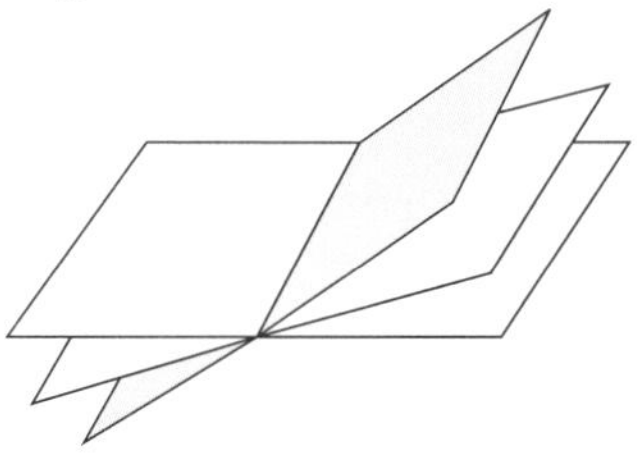

For the system $\begin{matrix} x + 3y + 2z = 1 \\ 2x + 4y + 3z = 3 \\ x + 7y + 4z = -1 \end{matrix}$ we perform row operations until our augmented matrix is of the form $\begin{pmatrix} 1 & 3 & 2 & \vdots & 1 \\ 0 & -2 & -1 & \vdots & 1 \\ 0 & 0 & 0 & \vdots & 0 \end{pmatrix}$. This system has an infinite number of solutions, so all three planes meet on a line of intersection.

Finally, consider the system $\begin{matrix} x + 4y - 3z = 1 \\ x + 3y - 2z = 2 \\ 2x + 9y - 7z = 3 \end{matrix}$. When we perform row operations on the augmented matrix we get the result $\begin{pmatrix} 1 & 4 & -3 & \vdots & 1 \\ 0 & -1 & 1 & \vdots & 1 \\ 0 & 0 & 0 & \vdots & 2 \end{pmatrix}$, which has no solutions.

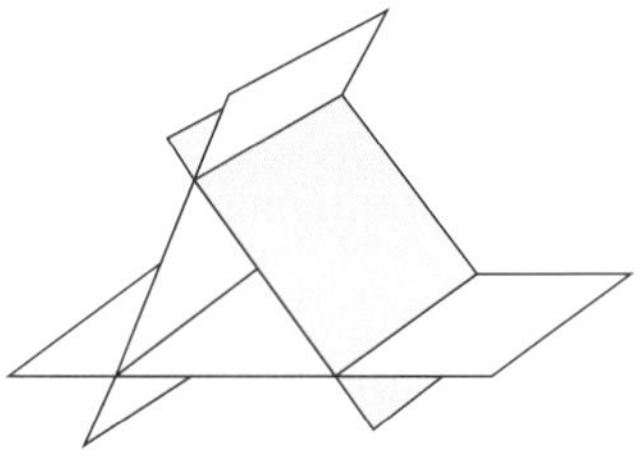

The diagram on the right shows one example of three planes without a solution.

EXERCISE 20D

M **1** Using matrix algebra, determine whether each of the following has unique solutions and, if so, state those solutions.

a $\begin{matrix} 3x - y = 6 \\ -6x + 2y = -13 \end{matrix}$ **b** $\begin{matrix} 2x + y = 4 \\ 3x - y = 7 \end{matrix}$ **c** $\begin{matrix} 5x - 4y = 2 \\ 10x - 8y = 4 \end{matrix}$

PS **2** Matrix $\mathbf{A} = \begin{pmatrix} 2 & \alpha \\ 3 & -2 \end{pmatrix}$ and matrix $\mathbf{B} = \begin{pmatrix} 3 \\ \beta \end{pmatrix}$. By considering $\mathbf{AX} = \mathbf{B}$, where $\mathbf{X} = \begin{pmatrix} x \\ y \end{pmatrix}$, find:

a α and β such that there are no solutions

b α and β such that there are an infinite number of solutions

c α and β such that there is a unique solution.

PS 3 Determine if the following systems of equations have a unique solution, an infinite number of solutions or no solution. If there is a unique solution or an infinite number of solutions, calculate the solutions.

a $\begin{aligned} x + 4y - 2z &= 2 \\ -2x - 10y - 6z &= 3 \\ 3x + 14y + 4z &= 7 \end{aligned}$ b $\begin{aligned} 2x + y + z &= 1 \\ 2x + 3y + 10z &= 3 \\ 4x - z &= 1 \end{aligned}$ c $\begin{aligned} x + 5y - z &= 1 \\ 2x + 7y - 4z &= 0 \\ 4x + 11y - 10z &= -2 \end{aligned}$

PS 4 For the system of equations $\begin{aligned} x - y &= 1 \\ 2x - y + 5z &= 4 \\ x + 2y + 15z &= k \end{aligned}$, find the value of k such that there is an infinite number of solutions.

M 5 Three planes are given:

$$\begin{aligned} x - 4y + 4z &= 3 \\ x - 7y + 11z &= 4 \\ 2x - 5y + 3z &= 5 \end{aligned}$$

Find the unique point where all planes intersect.

M 6 For the three planes $\begin{aligned} x - 6y &= 2 \\ 2x + 4y - 17z &= 4 \\ 3x + 12y - 33z &= 6 \end{aligned}$, find the point of intersection.

7 For the system of equations $\begin{aligned} x + y + 3z &= 1 \\ x - 2y + 2z &= -1 \\ 3x + 6y + az &= b \end{aligned}$, state the number of solutions when:

a $a = 5, b = 5$ b $a = 10, b = 10$ c $a = 10, b = 5$

WORKED PAST PAPER QUESTION

Show that if λ is an eigenvalue of the square matrix **A** with **e** as a corresponding eigenvector, and μ is an eigenvalue of the square matrix **B** for which **e** is also a corresponding eigenvector, then $\lambda + \mu$ is an eigenvalue of the matrix **A** + **B** with **e** as a corresponding eigenvector.

The matrix

$$\mathbf{A} = \begin{pmatrix} 3 & -1 & 0 \\ -4 & -6 & -6 \\ 5 & 11 & 10 \end{pmatrix}$$

has $\begin{pmatrix} 1 \\ -1 \\ 1 \end{pmatrix}$ as an eigenvector. Find the corresponding eigenvalue.

The other two eigenvalues of **A** are 1 and 2, with corresponding eigenvectors $\begin{pmatrix} 1 \\ 2 \\ -3 \end{pmatrix}$ and $\begin{pmatrix} 1 \\ 1 \\ -2 \end{pmatrix}$ respectively.

The matrix **B** has eigenvalues 2, 3, 1 with corresponding eigenvectors $\begin{pmatrix} 1 \\ -1 \\ 1 \end{pmatrix}$, $\begin{pmatrix} 1 \\ 2 \\ -3 \end{pmatrix}$ and $\begin{pmatrix} 1 \\ 1 \\ -2 \end{pmatrix}$ respectively.

Find a matrix **P** and a diagonal matrix **D** such that $(\mathbf{A} + \mathbf{B})^4 = \mathbf{PDP}^{-1}$.

Cambridge International AS & A Level Further Mathematics 9231 Paper 1 Q3 June 2008

Answer

Start with $(\mathbf{A} + \mathbf{B})\mathbf{e} = \mathbf{Ae} + \mathbf{Be}$, which is $\lambda\mathbf{e} + \mu\mathbf{e} = (\lambda + \mu)\mathbf{e}$.

$\mathbf{A}\begin{pmatrix} 1 \\ -1 \\ 1 \end{pmatrix} = \begin{pmatrix} 3 & -1 & 0 \\ -4 & -6 & -6 \\ 5 & 11 & 10 \end{pmatrix}\begin{pmatrix} 1 \\ -1 \\ 1 \end{pmatrix} = 4\begin{pmatrix} 1 \\ -1 \\ 1 \end{pmatrix}$ gives an eigenvalue of 4.

By adding the eigenvalues of **A** and **B**, we find the eigenvalues of $\mathbf{A}+\mathbf{B}$ are 6, 4, 3, so $\mathbf{D}=\begin{pmatrix}1296 & 0 & 0\\ 0 & 256 & 0\\ 0 & 0 & 81\end{pmatrix}$ and $\mathbf{P}=\begin{pmatrix}1 & 1 & 1\\ -1 & 2 & 1\\ 1 & -3 & -2\end{pmatrix}$. Note the columns of **D** and **P** may be swapped but the columns of eigenvectors must correspond to the columns of eigenvalues.

Checklist of learning and understanding

For eigenvalues and eigenvectors:

- To determine a characteristic equation, use $\det(\mathbf{A}-\lambda\mathbf{I})=0$.
- To find the eigenvectors, use the relation $\mathbf{Ax}=\lambda\mathbf{x}$.
- Eigenvectors do not change direction when a matrix is applied to them.

For matrix algebra: Given that $\mathbf{Ae}=\lambda\mathbf{e}$ and $\mathbf{Be}=\mu\mathbf{e}$:

- The matrix $\mathbf{A}+\mathbf{B}$ has eigenvalue $\lambda+\mu$ and corresponding eigenvector **e**.
- The matrix **AB** has eigenvalue $\lambda\mu$ and corresponding eigenvector **e**.
- The matrix $\mathbf{A}+k\mathbf{I}$ has eigenvalue $\lambda+k$ and corresponding eigenvector **e**.
- The matrix $\mathbf{A}^p+\mathbf{A}^q+\ldots$ has eigenvalue $\lambda^p+\lambda^q+\ldots$ and corresponding eigenvector **e**.

For diagonalisation:

- A matrix, **A**, that can be written in the form $\mathbf{A}=\mathbf{PDP}^{-1}$ is said to be diagonalisable.
- The diagonal matrix $\mathbf{D}=\begin{pmatrix}\lambda_1 & 0 & 0 & \ldots & 0\\ 0 & \lambda_2 & 0 & \ldots & 0\\ 0 & 0 & \lambda_3 & \ldots & 0\\ \vdots & \vdots & \vdots & \ddots & \vdots\\ 0 & 0 & 0 & \ldots & \lambda_n\end{pmatrix}$, where each eigenvalue is placed in the leading diagonal of a square matrix.
- The matrix **P** has its columns made up of eigenvectors that correspond to the eigenvalues in **D**.
- If there are fewer eigenvalues than the dimension of the matrix, then there will be insufficient distinct eigenvectors. This means that, in general, the matrix **P** cannot have an inverse, and so the matrix **A** cannot be diagonalised. There are exceptions to this but they are not covered in this course.

For systems of linear equations:

- For a system of equations, where the reduced augmented matrix is of the form $\begin{pmatrix}* & * & * & \vdots & *\\ * & * & * & \vdots & *\\ 0 & 0 & \alpha & \vdots & \beta\end{pmatrix}$, there are three cases to consider.
  - If $\alpha=0$ and $\beta=0$, then there is an infinite number of solutions.
  - If $\alpha=0$ and $\beta\neq 0$, then there are no solutions.
  - If $\alpha\neq 0$, then for all $\beta\in\mathbb{R}$ there will be a unique solution.

For inverse matrices:

- For a matrix, **A**, with characteristic equation $\mathrm{P}_A(\lambda)=a\lambda^3+b\lambda^2+c\lambda+d=0$, the equation $a\mathbf{A}^3+b\mathbf{A}^2+c\mathbf{A}+d\mathbf{I}=0$ is also true.

END-OF-CHAPTER REVIEW EXERCISE 20

1 Find the eigenvalues and corresponding eigenvectors of the matrix $\mathbf{A} = \begin{pmatrix} 3 & -1 & 0 \\ -1 & 2 & -1 \\ 0 & -1 & 3 \end{pmatrix}$.

Find a non-singular matrix $\mathbf{M}$ and a diagonal matrix $\mathbf{D}$ such that $(\mathbf{A} - 2\mathbf{I})^3 = \mathbf{MDM}^{-1}$, where $\mathbf{I}$ is the 3×3 identity matrix.

Cambridge International AS & A Level Further Mathematics 9231 Paper 1 Q9 November 2010

2 You are given the matrix $\mathbf{A} = \begin{pmatrix} 1 & 0 & 2 \\ 0 & 2 & 0 \\ 0 & 1 & -1 \end{pmatrix}$.

Find the characteristic equation of $\mathbf{A}$.

Hence, or otherwise, determine the unknown constants for $\mathbf{A}^3 + \alpha\mathbf{A}^2 + \beta\mathbf{A} + \gamma\mathbf{I} = 0$.

Hence, or otherwise, find $\mathbf{A}^{-1}$.

3 A 3×3 matrix $\mathbf{A}$ has eigenvalues $-1, 1, 2$, with corresponding eigenvectors $\begin{pmatrix} 0 \\ 1 \\ -1 \end{pmatrix}, \begin{pmatrix} -1 \\ 0 \\ 1 \end{pmatrix}, \begin{pmatrix} 1 \\ 1 \\ 0 \end{pmatrix}$, respectively.

Find

i the matrix $\mathbf{A}$,

ii $\mathbf{A}^{2n}$, where n is a positive integer.

Cambridge International AS & A Level Further Mathematics 9231 Paper 13 Q11a June 2011

Chapter 21
Differentiation

In this chapter you will learn how to:

- obtain expressions for $\dfrac{d^2y}{dx^2}$ in cases where the relation between x and y is defined both implicitly and parametrically
- differentiate hyperbolic functions, inverse hyperbolic functions and inverse trigonometric functions
- derive and use the first few terms of Maclaurin's series for a function.

PREREQUISITE KNOWLEDGE

Where it comes from	What you should be able to do	Check your skills
AS & A Level Mathematics Pure Mathematics 2 & 3, Chapter 4	Differentiate functions such as $e^{f(x)}$, $a\cos(f(x))$ and $a\ln f(x)$.	1 Differentiate the following functions. a xe^{2x} b $2\sin(x^2+1)$ c $\ln\left(\frac{x^3}{x-1}\right)$
AS & A Level Mathematics Pure Mathematics 2 & 3, Chapter 4	Differentiate functions implicitly.	2 Find $\frac{dy}{dx}$ for the expression $x^2y - y^3 = 2y + x$.
AS & A Level Mathematics Pure Mathematics 2 & 3, Chapter 4	Differentiate functions defined parametrically.	3 Find $\frac{dy}{dx}$ for the set of parametric equations $x = t^2 - t, y = t^3$.

What else can we do with differentiation?

In this chapter we shall look at the **differentiation** of some new functions, such as hyperbolic functions and inverse functions. We shall extend the **implicit** and parametric differentiation techniques you learned in your A Level Mathematics Pure Mathematics 2 & 3 course.

We shall also study Maclaurin's series for a variety of functions. This will allow us to approximate functions with a polynomial.

Differentiation is the section of calculus that looks at rates of change of variables. It is used in many different areas, such as Physics, Chemistry, Engineering, Medicine and Economics. Calculus was developed by both Isaac Newton and Gottfried Leibniz. It has become a pivotal part of modern science and engineering.

21.1 Implicit functions

You will have met implicit functions within A Level Mathematics Pure Mathematics 2 & 3, Chapter 4, where you will have found only the first derivative. In this section we shall be extending this to incorporate the second derivative.

Implicit differentiation allows us to differentiate functions that are not explicitly written as $y = f(x)$. For example, consider the function $y^2 = x$. Differentiating both sides with respect to x, we can write $2y\frac{dy}{dx} = 1$, and so $\frac{dy}{dx} = \frac{1}{2y}$.

When differentiating y, think of this as $\frac{d}{dx}(y)$, as shown in Key point 21.1. This is the same as $\frac{dy}{dx}$. If your function is, for example, $y^2x + y = \ln y$, do not start with $\frac{dy}{dx} =$. Instead, start with $\frac{d}{dx}(y^2x + y) = \frac{d}{dx}(\ln y)$ and then differentiate. This is also an application of the chain rule.

KEY POINT 21.1

To differentiate, start with $\frac{\mathrm{d}}{\mathrm{d}x}(\ldots) =$ instead of $\frac{\mathrm{d}y}{\mathrm{d}x} =$ and then differentiate.

Consider $x^3 + y^2 = 2y$. Suppose we want to find the first and second derivatives with respect to x. We write $\frac{\mathrm{d}}{\mathrm{d}x}(x^3 + y^2) = \frac{\mathrm{d}}{\mathrm{d}x}(2y)$ and so $3x^2 + 2y\frac{\mathrm{d}y}{\mathrm{d}x} = 2\frac{\mathrm{d}y}{\mathrm{d}x}$ ...(1). Rearranging gives us $\frac{\mathrm{d}y}{\mathrm{d}x} = \frac{3x^2}{2-2y}$ ...(2). To determine the second derivative, it is generally not a good idea to consider (2), since differentiating this result would mean having to deal with a quotient.

Instead, we differentiate (1), the original form of the first derivative:

$\frac{\mathrm{d}}{\mathrm{d}x}\left(3x^2 + 2y\frac{\mathrm{d}y}{\mathrm{d}x}\right) = \frac{\mathrm{d}}{\mathrm{d}x}\left(2\frac{\mathrm{d}y}{\mathrm{d}x}\right)$ and so $6x + 2\left(\frac{\mathrm{d}y}{\mathrm{d}x}\right)^2 + 2y\frac{\mathrm{d}^2y}{\mathrm{d}x^2} = 2\frac{\mathrm{d}^2y}{\mathrm{d}x^2}$, then

$$\frac{\mathrm{d}^2y}{\mathrm{d}x^2} = \frac{6x + 2\left(\frac{\mathrm{d}y}{\mathrm{d}x}\right)^2}{2-2y}.$$

Using the previous result, $\frac{\mathrm{d}^2y}{\mathrm{d}x^2} = \frac{6x + 2\left(\frac{3x^2}{2-2y}\right)^2}{2-2y}$, which simplifies to

$$\frac{\mathrm{d}^2y}{\mathrm{d}x^2} = \frac{6x(2-2y)^2 + 18x^4}{(2-2y)^3}.$$

WORKED EXAMPLE 21.1

Given that $\mathrm{e}^x + \mathrm{e}^{2y} = \ln y$, find the first and second derivatives with respect to x.

Answer

First, $\mathrm{e}^x + 2\mathrm{e}^{2y}\frac{\mathrm{d}y}{\mathrm{d}x} = \frac{1}{y}\frac{dy}{\mathrm{d}x}$. — Find the first derivative.

Then $\mathrm{e}^x + 4\mathrm{e}^{2y}\left(\frac{\mathrm{d}y}{\mathrm{d}x}\right)^2 + 2\mathrm{e}^{2y}\frac{\mathrm{d}^2y}{\mathrm{d}x^2} = -\frac{1}{y^2}\left(\frac{\mathrm{d}y}{\mathrm{d}x}\right)^2 + \frac{1}{y}\frac{\mathrm{d}^2y}{\mathrm{d}x^2}$. — Differentiate the first derivative in its current form to get the second derivative.

So $\frac{\mathrm{d}y}{\mathrm{d}x} = \frac{y\mathrm{e}^x}{1-2y\mathrm{e}^{2y}}$, and $\frac{\mathrm{d}^2y}{\mathrm{d}x^2} = \frac{y^2\mathrm{e}^x + (1+4y^2\mathrm{e}^{2y})\left(\frac{\mathrm{d}y}{\mathrm{d}x}\right)^2}{y-2y^2\mathrm{e}^{2y}}$. — Rearrange both results.

Using the result for $\frac{\mathrm{d}y}{\mathrm{d}x}$, rewrite the second derivative as — Substitute $\frac{\mathrm{d}y}{\mathrm{d}x}$ into the result for the second derivative.

$$\frac{\mathrm{d}^2y}{\mathrm{d}x^2} = \frac{y^2\mathrm{e}^x + (1+4y^2\mathrm{e}^{2y})\left(\frac{y\mathrm{e}^x}{1-2y\mathrm{e}^{2y}}\right)^2}{y(1-2y\mathrm{e}^{2y})}.$$

Then $\frac{\mathrm{d}^2y}{\mathrm{d}x^2} = \frac{y\mathrm{e}^x[(1-2y\mathrm{e}^{2y})^2 + \mathrm{e}^x(1+4y^2\mathrm{e}^{2y})]}{(1-2y\mathrm{e}^{2y})^3}$. — Simplify as required.

Obtain the result, or any equivalent form.

We shall now look at a slightly more complicated example: $x^3y^2 + y = \sin x$.

Differentiating, $3x^2y^2 + 2x^3y\frac{dy}{dx} + \frac{dy}{dx} = \cos x$. Notice that we now have a triple product, $2x^3y\frac{dy}{dx}$. In order to deal with this we need to see how to differentiate a triple product.

If $y = uvw$, where $u = f(x)$, $v = g(x)$, $w = h(x)$, then $y + \delta y = (u + \delta u)(v + \delta v)(w + \delta w)$. Multiplying out the brackets leads to:

$y + \delta y = uvw + u\delta v\delta w + v\delta u\delta w + w\delta u\delta v + uv\delta w + uw\delta v + vw\delta u + \delta u\delta v\delta w$

Notice that $y = uvw$ will now cancel. We then divide through by δx to get:

$\frac{\delta y}{\delta x} = \frac{u\delta v\delta w}{\delta x} + \frac{v\delta u\delta w}{\delta x} + \frac{w\delta u\delta v}{\delta x} + \frac{uv\delta w}{\delta x} + \frac{uw\delta v}{\delta x} + \frac{vw\delta u}{\delta x} + \frac{\delta u\delta v\delta w}{\delta x}$, and then let δx tend to 0.

This means that the terms $\frac{u\delta v\delta w}{\delta x}, \frac{v\delta u\delta w}{\delta x}, \frac{w\delta u\delta v}{\delta x}$ and $\frac{\delta u\delta v\delta w}{\delta x}$ are all small enough to be ignored.

So $\frac{dy}{dx} = uv\frac{dw}{dx} + uw\frac{dv}{dx} + vw\frac{du}{dx}$, as shown in Key point 21.2.

KEY POINT 21.2

If a function is of the form $y = uvw$, where each factor is a function of x, then the triple product differentiates to give $\frac{dy}{dx} = uv\frac{dw}{dx} + uw\frac{dv}{dx} + vw\frac{du}{dx}$.

In our example, we got to the point where $3x^2y^2 + 2x^3y\frac{dy}{dx} + \frac{dy}{dx} = \cos x$.

Differentiating again gives $6xy^2 + 6x^2y\frac{dy}{dx} + 6x^2y\frac{dy}{dx} + 2x^3\left(\frac{dy}{dx}\right)^2 + 2x^3y\frac{d^2y}{dx^2} + \frac{d^2y}{dx^2} = -\sin x$.

We could rearrange the algebra to find expressions for $\frac{dy}{dx}$ and $\frac{d^2y}{dx^2}$.

WORKED EXAMPLE 21.2

An implicit equation is given as $xe^{x+y} = (x+1)^2$. Find the first and second derivatives with respect to x.

Answer

Begin with $e^{x+y} + x\left(1 + \frac{dy}{dx}\right)e^{x+y} = 2(x+1)$.

Differentiate once.

Then $\left(1 + \frac{dy}{dx}\right)e^{x+y} + \left(1 + \frac{dy}{dx}\right)e^{x+y} + xe^{x+y}\frac{d^2y}{dx^2}$

$+ x\left(1 + \frac{dy}{dx}\right)^2 e^{x+y} = 2.$

Note the triple product when differentiating a second time.

So $\frac{dy}{dx} = \frac{2(x+1) - e^{x+y} - xe^{x+y}}{xe^{x+y}}$ is the first derivative.

State the first derivative.

And $\frac{d^2y}{dx^2} = \frac{2e^{-(x+y)}}{x} - \frac{2}{x}\left(1 + \frac{dy}{dx}\right) - \left(1 + \frac{dy}{dx}\right)^2$ is the second derivative.

The algebra has become too complicated to write the second derivative just in terms of x and y.

EXPLORE 21.1

Discuss in groups how you could attempt to differentiate the functions $y = x^x$ and $y = x^{x^x}$.

TIP

Deal with $y = x^x$ first.

Looking at Worked example 21.2, there is a good reason why we did not simplify the second derivative. If we only need to find numerical values for the first and second derivatives, we do not need to simplify the expressions.

Consider the function $x^2 + xy^2 = (y+1)^3$, where it is known that when $x = 1$, $y = -1$. To find numerical values for $\frac{dy}{dx}$ and $\frac{d^2y}{dx^2}$, we start with the first derivative.

So $2x + 2xy\frac{dy}{dx} + y^2 = 3(y+1)^2\frac{dy}{dx}$. Then with $x = 1$, $y = -1$, $2 - 2\frac{dy}{dx} + 1 = 0$, which gives us $\frac{dy}{dx} = \frac{3}{2}$. We do not need to find $\frac{dy}{dx}$ explicitly as we only need its numerical value.

Differentiating again, $2 + 4y\frac{dy}{dx} + 2x\left(\frac{dy}{dx}\right)^2 + 2xy\frac{d^2y}{dx^2} = 3\frac{d^2y}{dx^2}(y+1)^2 + 6\left(\frac{dy}{dx}\right)^2(y+1)$.

Using the values $x = 1$, $y = -1$ and $\frac{dy}{dx} = \frac{3}{2}$ we have $2 - 6 + \frac{9}{2} - 2\frac{d^2y}{dx^2} = 0$.

Hence, $\frac{d^2y}{dx^2} = \frac{1}{4}$.

WORKED EXAMPLE 21.3

Given that $y^3 + yx^2 = e^x$ passes through the point $A(0, 1)$, find the values of the first and second derivatives at the point A.

Answer

First, $3y^2\frac{dy}{dx} + x^2\frac{dy}{dx} + 2yx = e^x$. — Differentiate once.

Using $x = 0$ and $y = 1$ we get $3\frac{dy}{dx} = 1$. So $\frac{dy}{dx} = \frac{1}{3}$. — Use the given values. There is no need to rearrange to find $\frac{dy}{dx}$ explicitly.

Then $6y\left(\frac{dy}{dx}\right)^2 + 3y^2\frac{d^2y}{dx^2} + x^2\frac{d^2y}{dx^2} + 2x\frac{dy}{dx} + 2x\frac{dy}{dx} + 2y = e^x$. — Differentiate again.

Using $x = 0$, $y = 1$ and $\frac{dy}{dx} = \frac{1}{3}$ we get $\frac{2}{3} + 3\frac{d^2y}{dx^2} + 2 = 1$. — Use the given values and the result for $\frac{dy}{dx}$.

Hence, $\frac{d^2y}{dx^2} = -\frac{5}{9}$. — Determine the value of the second derivative.

EXERCISE 21A

1 For each case, find the first derivative $\frac{dy}{dx}$.

a $xy = e^x$ b $y^2x = e^y$ c $\tan(x + y) = y$

M 2 Find the value of the second derivative $\frac{d^2y}{dx^2}$ of $x^2 = ye^x + y^2$ at the point (0, 0).

M 3 Find the value of the first and second derivatives of $\ln(x + y) = 2y$ at the point (1, 0).

PS 4 Given that $xy = \sin(x + y)$, find the first and second derivatives with respect to x.

M 5 An implicit curve, C, is defined as $y^2 = \ln x + e^y - 1$. Given that C passes through the point (1, 0), find the values of $\frac{dy}{dx}$ and $\frac{d^2y}{dx^2}$ at this point.

P 6 A curve is given as $xy^\alpha = \beta$, where α, β are constants.

a Find $\frac{dy}{dx}$. b Show that $\frac{d^2y}{dx^2} = \frac{y(1+\alpha)}{\alpha^2x^2}$.

M 7 The curve C is given as $(x + y)^6 = x$. Given that the curve also passes through the point (1, 0), determine the values of $\frac{dy}{dx}$ and $\frac{d^2y}{dx^2}$ at this point.

M 8 An implicit curve is defined as $\sin 2x \cos 2y = \frac{\sqrt{3}}{4}$. It is known that the curve passes through the point $P\left(\frac{\pi}{3}, \frac{\pi}{6}\right)$. Find, at the point P:

a $\frac{dy}{dx}$ b $\frac{d^2y}{dx^2}$

DID YOU KNOW?

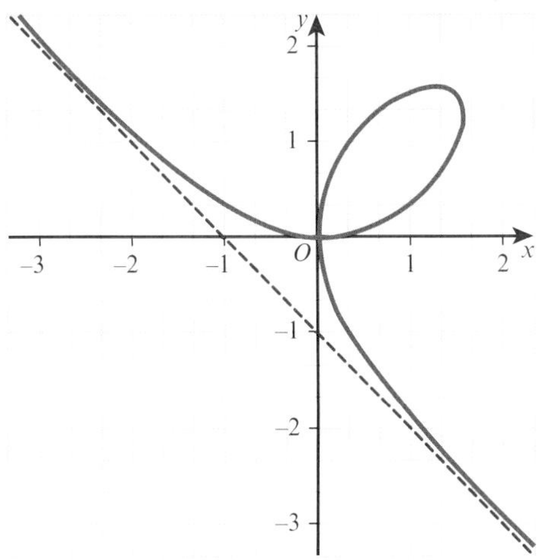

The French mathematician René Descartes worked on the now famous curve $x^3 + y^3 = 3axy$. In 1638 Descartes challenged Fermat to determine the tangent line to the curve. Fermat did this without any knowledge of calculus! Once calculus was discovered, differentiating this function was a much easier way to find the tangent.

21.2 Parametric equations

You have met parametric equations in your A Level Mathematics course: two functions are dependent on a common parameter, for example, $x = \mathrm{f}(t)$ and $y = \mathrm{g}(t)$, where t is the parameter.

To determine the gradient of a curve represented by a set of parametric equations, we must first determine $\frac{\mathrm{d}x}{\mathrm{d}t}$ and $\frac{\mathrm{d}y}{\mathrm{d}t}$. Then, using the chain rule, $\frac{\mathrm{d}y}{\mathrm{d}x} = \frac{\mathrm{d}y}{\mathrm{d}t} \times \frac{\mathrm{d}t}{\mathrm{d}x}$, or $\frac{\mathrm{d}y}{\mathrm{d}x} = \frac{\frac{\mathrm{d}y}{\mathrm{d}t}}{\frac{\mathrm{d}x}{\mathrm{d}t}}$.

Another way of writing this is $\frac{\mathrm{d}y}{\mathrm{d}x} = \frac{\mathrm{d}}{\mathrm{d}t}(y) \times \frac{\mathrm{d}t}{\mathrm{d}x}$, where y is differentiated with respect to t and then multiplied by $\frac{\mathrm{d}t}{\mathrm{d}x}$.

For example, if $x = t^2$ and $y = t + 1$, then $\frac{\mathrm{d}y}{\mathrm{d}t} = 1$ and $\frac{\mathrm{d}x}{\mathrm{d}t} = 2t$. This means $\frac{\mathrm{d}y}{\mathrm{d}x} = \frac{1}{2t}$.
Notice that the first derivative is a function of t, so to determine the second derivative we must differentiate $\frac{\mathrm{d}y}{\mathrm{d}x}$ with respect to t.

Thus $\frac{\mathrm{d}^2y}{\mathrm{d}x^2} = \frac{\mathrm{d}}{\mathrm{d}t}\left(\frac{\mathrm{d}y}{\mathrm{d}x}\right) \times \frac{\mathrm{d}t}{\mathrm{d}x}$, as shown in Key point 21.3. Notice that the first and second derivatives are obtained using a very similar approach.

KEY POINT 21.3

For the parametric equations $x = \mathrm{f}(t), y = \mathrm{g}(t)$, the first and second derivatives are given by:

$$\frac{\mathrm{d}y}{\mathrm{d}x} = \frac{\mathrm{d}}{\mathrm{d}t}(y) \times \frac{\mathrm{d}t}{\mathrm{d}x}$$

$$\frac{\mathrm{d}^2y}{\mathrm{d}x^2} = \frac{\mathrm{d}}{\mathrm{d}t}\left(\frac{\mathrm{d}y}{\mathrm{d}x}\right) \times \frac{\mathrm{d}t}{\mathrm{d}x}$$

Going back to our example with $x = t^2, y = t + 1$, we have already found that $\frac{\mathrm{d}y}{\mathrm{d}x} = \frac{1}{2t}$. For the second derivative, first find $\frac{\mathrm{d}}{\mathrm{d}t}\left(\frac{1}{2t}\right) = \frac{1}{2}\frac{\mathrm{d}}{\mathrm{d}t}\left(\frac{1}{t}\right) = -\frac{1}{2t^2}$. Then using $\frac{\mathrm{d}^2y}{\mathrm{d}x^2} = \frac{\mathrm{d}}{\mathrm{d}t}\left(\frac{\mathrm{d}y}{\mathrm{d}x}\right) \times \frac{\mathrm{d}t}{\mathrm{d}x}$ our second derivative is $\frac{\mathrm{d}^2y}{\mathrm{d}x^2} = -\frac{1}{2t^2} \times \frac{1}{2t} = -\frac{1}{4t^3}$.

WORKED EXAMPLE 21.4

Given that $x = \frac{1}{t+1}$ and $y = t^2$, find the first and second derivatives of y with respect to x.

Answer

Start with $\frac{dx}{dt} = -\frac{1}{(t+1)^2}$ and $\frac{dy}{dt} = 2t$. — Differentiate both equations.

Then $\frac{dy}{dx} = 2t \times -(t+1)^2 = -2t(1+t)^2$. — Use the chain rule to determine $\frac{dy}{dx}$.

Then $\frac{d}{dt}\left(\frac{dy}{dx}\right) = -2(1+t)^2 - 4t(1+t)$.

This simplifies to $-2(t+1)(3t+1)$. — Differentiate the first derivative with respect to t.

Then $\frac{d^2y}{dx^2} = \frac{d}{dt}\left(\frac{dy}{dx}\right) \times \frac{dt}{dx} = -2(t+1)(3t+1) \times -(t+1)^2$. — Use the form of the second derivative with your result from above.

Hence, $\frac{d^2y}{dx^2} = 2(3t+1)(t+1)^3$. — Simplify to give the final answer.

WORKED EXAMPLE 21.5

If $x = te^t$, $y = t^3 - t$ determine the functions $\frac{dy}{dx}$ and $\frac{d^2y}{dx^2}$.

Answer

First, $\frac{dy}{dt} = 3t^2 - 1$ and $\frac{dx}{dt} = e^t + te^t = e^t(1+t)$ — Differentiate x and y with respect to t.

Then $\frac{dy}{dx} = \frac{3t^2 - 1}{e^t(1+t)}$. — Divide $\frac{dy}{dt}$ by $\frac{dx}{dt}$.

Next, $\frac{d}{dt}\left(\frac{3t^2-1}{e^t(1+t)}\right) = \frac{e^t(1+t)6t - (3t^2-1)(e^t + e^t + te^t)}{e^{2t}(1+t)^2} = \frac{7t + 2 - 3t^3}{e^t(1+t)^2}$. — Differentiate $\frac{dy}{dx}$ with respect to t.

So with $\frac{d^2y}{dx^2} = \frac{d}{dt}\left(\frac{dy}{dx}\right) \times \frac{dt}{dx}$, $\frac{d^2y}{dx^2} = \frac{7t+2-3t^3}{e^{2t}(1+t)^3}$. — Multiply the result by $\frac{dt}{dx}$, or $\frac{1}{\frac{dx}{dt}}$.

Consider the curve represented by $x = \cos t$, $y = \sin 2t$ for $0 \leqslant t \leqslant \pi$. Suppose we want to find the coordinates of all the stationary points, and to determine their nature.

The first step is to obtain $\frac{dx}{dt} = -\sin t$, $\frac{dy}{dt} = 2\cos 2t$ and, hence, $\frac{dy}{dx} = -\frac{2\cos 2t}{\sin t}$.

Then for turning points we need $\frac{dy}{dx} = 0$, or for parametric-based derivatives, we just need $\frac{dy}{dt} = 0$.

So let $2\cos 2t = 0$. This leads to $t = \frac{\pi}{4}, \frac{3\pi}{4}$.

When $t = \frac{\pi}{4}$: $x = \frac{\sqrt{2}}{2}$, $y = 1$. When $t = \frac{3\pi}{4}$: $x = -\frac{\sqrt{2}}{2}$, $y = -1$.

To determine the nature of the stationary points, first find

$\frac{d}{dt}\left(\frac{dy}{dx}\right) = -\frac{\sin t(-4\sin 2t) - 2\cos 2t(\cos t)}{\sin^2 t}$, then multiplying by $-\frac{1}{\sin t}$ leads to

$\frac{d^2y}{dx^2} = -\frac{2(\cos 2t \cos t + 2\sin 2t \sin t)}{\sin^3 t}$.

When $t = \frac{\pi}{4}$: $\frac{d^2y}{dx^2} = -\frac{4\frac{\sqrt{2}}{2}}{\frac{1}{2\sqrt{2}}} = -8 < 0$. Hence, we have a maximum at $\left(\frac{\sqrt{2}}{2}, 1\right)$.

When $t = \frac{3\pi}{4}$: $\frac{d^2y}{dx^2} = -\frac{-4\frac{\sqrt{2}}{2}}{\frac{1}{2\sqrt{2}}} = 8 > 0$. Hence, we have a minimum at $\left(-\frac{\sqrt{2}}{2}, -1\right)$.

WORKED EXAMPLE 21.6

A parametric curve is represented by the pair of equations $x = t^4 + t, y = t^3 - 3t^2$. Find the coordinates of any stationary points, and determine their nature.

Answer

Begin with $\frac{dx}{dt} = 4t^3 + 1, \frac{dy}{dt} = 3t^2 - 6t$. Hence, $\frac{dy}{dx} = \frac{3t^2 - 6t}{4t^3 + 1}$.

Find the derivatives of each variable with respect to t and determine $\frac{dy}{dx}$.

For turning points we need $\frac{dy}{dt} = 0$, so $3t^2 - 6t = 0$, giving $t = 0, 2$.

For turning points let $\frac{dy}{dt} = 0$.

Determine $\frac{d}{dt}\left(\frac{dy}{dx}\right) = \frac{(4t^3 + 1)(6t - 6) - (3t^2 - 6t)(12t^2)}{(4t^3 + 1)^2} = \frac{48t^3 - 12t^4 + 6t - 6}{(4t^3 + 1)^2}$.

Differentiate $\frac{dy}{dx}$ with respect to t.

So $\frac{d^2y}{dx^2} = \frac{d}{dt}\left(\frac{dy}{dx}\right) \times \frac{dt}{dx} = \frac{48t^3 - 12t^4 + 6t - 6}{(4t^3 + 1)^3}$

When $t = 0$, $\frac{d^2y}{dx^2} = -6 < 0$. Hence we have a maximum point when $t = 0$.

Since $\frac{d^2y}{dx^2} < 0$ we have a maximum.

When $t = 2$, $\frac{d^2y}{dx^2} = \frac{2}{363} > 0$. Hence we have a minimum point when $t = 2$.

Since $\frac{d^2y}{dx^2} > 0$ we have a minimum.

Also, when $t = 0, x = 0$ and $y = 0$, and when $t = 2, x = 18, y = -4$.

Determine the coordinates of both stationary points.

So at (0, 0) we have a maximum point, and at (18, −4) we have a minimum point.

Write down the coordinates of each stationary point and state whether it is a maximum or minimum.

EXERCISE 21B

M 1 For each case, differentiate the set of parametric equations to obtain the second derivative $\frac{d^2y}{dx^2}$.

a $x = t^2, y = 3t + 1$

b $x = e^t, y = t^2$

M 2 Find the value of the second derivative $\frac{d^2y}{dx^2}$ of the parametric equations $x = t^3, y = \frac{4}{t}$, at the point where $t = 2$.

M 3 Find the values of $\frac{dy}{dx}$ and $\frac{d^2y}{dx^2}$ of the parametric equations $x = e^{3t}, y = e^t$, at the point where $t = 1$.

M 4 Given that $x = t^3, y = 3t^2$, find the value of $\frac{d^2y}{dx^2}$ when $t = 2$.

P PS 5 A parametric curve is defined as $x = \ln(t + 1)$ and $y = e^t$, where $t > 0$.

a Find $\frac{dy}{dx}$ in terms of t.

b Show that the second derivative with respect to x is always positive.

P 6 The parametric curve $x = t^2 + t, y = \ln t$ is valid for $t > 0$.

a Show that there are no turning points.

b Show that the second derivative with respect to x is $-\frac{4t + 1}{t^2(2t + 1)^3}$.

PS 7 If $x = \sin^2 t, y = \cos^3 t$ is valid for $0 \leqslant t \leqslant 2\pi$, find the second derivative with respect to x in terms of t.

PS 8 Given that $x = t^2 - \frac{1}{t}, y = t^2 + \frac{1}{t}$, find:

a the value(s) of t for any stationary point(s)

b the nature of any turning point(s).

P PS 9 The parametric curve represented by $x = e^{2t} + e^{-2t}, y = e^{2t} - e^{-2t}$ is valid for all t.

a Find $\frac{dy}{dx}$ and state the number of turning points.

b Show that the second derivative with respect to x is $-\frac{4e^{6t}}{(e^{4t} - 1)^3}$.

21.3 Hyperbolic and inverse functions

The hyperbolic functions were introduced in Chapter 19:

- $\sinh x = \frac{e^x - e^{-x}}{2}$
- $\cosh x = \frac{e^x + e^{-x}}{2}$
- $\tanh x = \frac{e^x - e^{-x}}{e^x + e^{-x}}$

Starting with $y = \sinh x = \frac{e^x - e^{-x}}{2}$, $\frac{dy}{dx} = \frac{e^x + e^{-x}}{2}$. Hence $\frac{dy}{dx} = \cosh x$.

Differentiating $y = \cosh x = \frac{e^x + e^{-x}}{2}$ gives $\frac{e^x - e^{-x}}{2}$. So $\frac{dy}{dx} = \sinh x$. These relationships are shown in Key point 21.4.

KEY POINT 21.4

If $y = \sinh x$, then $\frac{dy}{dx} = \cosh x$.

If $y = \cosh x$, then $\frac{dy}{dx} = \sinh x$.

WORKED EXAMPLE 21.7

Find the derivatives of the following functions.

a $y = \sinh 2x$　　b $y = \cosh x^2$　　c $y = \sinh^2 x$　　d $y = \cosh 3x \sinh 4x$

Answer

a Let $u = 2x$, then $y = \sinh u$. — Use a substitution to simplify the function.

So $\frac{dy}{du} = \cosh u$ and $\frac{du}{dx} = 2$.

So $\frac{dy}{dx} = \frac{dy}{du} \times \frac{du}{dx} = 2\cosh 2x$. — Use the chain rule to get $\frac{dy}{dx}$.

b Let $u = x^2$, then $y = \cosh u$. — Again, make use of a substitution.

So $\frac{dy}{du} = \sinh u$ and $\frac{du}{dx} = 2x$.

So $\frac{dy}{dx} = 2x \sinh x^2$. — From the chain rule we get the result.

c $y = (\sinh x)^2$

So $\frac{dy}{dx} = 2\sinh x \cosh x$, or $\sinh 2x$. — Treat this as $[f(x)]^n$, finishing with $\frac{dy}{dx} = nf'(x)[f(x)]^{n-1}$ and use $\sinh 2A = 2\sinh A \cosh A$.

d $\frac{dy}{dx} = 3\sinh 3x \sinh 4x + 4\cosh 3x \cosh 4x$. — Differentiate using the product rule and chain rule.

Notice that hyperbolic functions behave in a very similar way to trigonometric functions.

Let us consider the derivatives of $\tanh x$, $\text{sech}\, x$, $\text{cosech}\, x$ and $\coth x$.

If $y = \tanh x = \dfrac{\sinh x}{\cosh x}$ then, using the quotient rule, $\dfrac{dy}{dx} = \dfrac{\cosh x \cosh x - \sinh x \sinh x}{\cosh^2 x}$.

Using $\cosh^2 x - \sinh^2 x = 1$, $\dfrac{dy}{dx} = \dfrac{1}{\cosh^2 x} = \text{sech}^2 x$.

If $y = \text{sech}\, x = \dfrac{1}{\cosh x}$, $\dfrac{dy}{dx} = \dfrac{\cosh x \times 0 - 1 \times \sinh x}{\cosh^2 x} = -\text{sech}\, x \tanh x$.

If $y = \text{cosech}\, x = \dfrac{1}{\sinh x}$, $\dfrac{dy}{dx} = \dfrac{\sinh x \times 0 - 1 \times \cosh x}{\sinh^2 x} = -\text{cosech}\, x \coth x$.

If $y = \coth x = \dfrac{\cosh x}{\sinh x}$, $\dfrac{dy}{dx} = \dfrac{\sinh x \sinh x - \cosh x \cosh x}{\sinh^2 x}$. Again, using $\cosh^2 x - \sinh^2 x = 1$,

$\dfrac{dy}{dx} = -\text{cosech}^2 x$.

These results are shown in Key point 21.5.

KEY POINT 21.5

If $y = \tanh x$, then $\dfrac{dy}{dx} = \text{sech}^2 x$.

If $y = \text{sech}\, x$, then $\dfrac{dy}{dx} = -\text{sech}\, x \tanh x$.

If $y = \text{cosech}\, x$, then $\dfrac{dy}{dx} = -\text{cosech}\, x \coth x$.

If $y = \coth x$, then $\dfrac{dy}{dx} = -\text{cosech}^2 x$.

WORKED EXAMPLE 21.8

Find $\dfrac{dy}{dx}$ for each of the following functions.

a $y = 2x\,\text{sech}(3x - 1)$

b $y = \ln(\tanh x)$

c $y = x^2 e^{\coth x}$

d $\sinh(x + y) = y^2 x^3$

Answer

a $\dfrac{dy}{dx} = 2 \times \text{sech}(3x - 1) + 2x \times (-)3\,\text{sech}(3x - 1)\tanh(3x - 1)$

Differentiate and take out the common factors.

This simplifies to $2\,\text{sech}(3x - 1)[1 - 3x\tanh(3x - 1)]$.

b Using the chain rule we have

Recall the method for differentiating logarithms from your A level Mathematics course.

$\dfrac{dy}{dx} = \dfrac{\text{sech}^2 x}{\tanh x} = \dfrac{1}{\cosh x \sinh x}$, or $\dfrac{dy}{dx} = \dfrac{2}{\sinh 2x}$.

Also make use of the double angle formula for $\sinh 2A$.

c Using the chain rule: $\frac{dy}{dx} = 2x \times e^{\coth x} + x^2 \times (-\text{cosech}^2 x)e^{\coth x}$.	Using the product rule and chain rule.
This can be simplified to $xe^{\coth x}(2 - x\,\text{cosech}^2 x)$.	Take out common factors.
d $\left(1 + \frac{dy}{dx}\right)\cosh(x + y) = 2yx^3\frac{dy}{dx} + 3x^2y^2$	Differentiate implicitly.
$\frac{dy}{dx} = \frac{3x^2y^2 - \cosh(x + y)}{\cosh(x + y) - 2yx^3}$.	Rearrange and state $\frac{dy}{dx}$.

We shall move on to the inverse functions of trigonometric and hyperbolic functions.

Consider, for example, the function $y = \sin^{-1} x$. This is also known as $y = \arcsin x$. We want to be able to determine the derivative of this function, as shown in Key point 21.6. How do we begin? Since we have already met implicit differentiation, and we know how to differentiate the sine function, let us first take the sine of both sides.

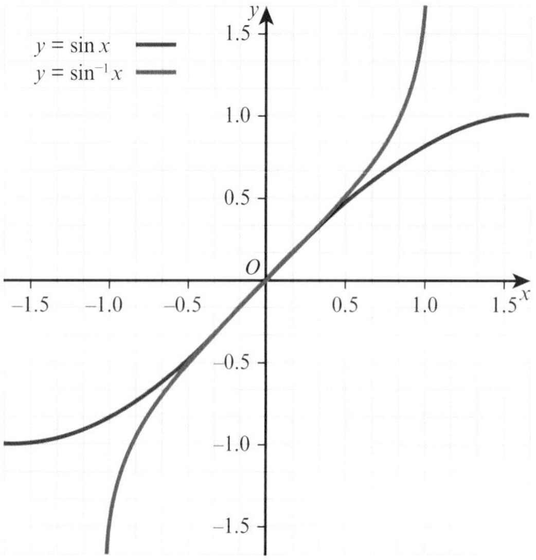

So $\sin y = x$, then $\cos y\frac{dy}{dx} = 1$, and so $\frac{dy}{dx} = \frac{1}{\cos y}$. Since $\cos y = \pm\sqrt{1 - \sin^2 y}$ we can say that $\cos y = \pm\sqrt{1 - x^2}$. Then from the diagram we see that the curve of $y = \sin^{-1} x$ is always increasing. Hence we take the positive root and $\frac{dy}{dx} = \frac{1}{\sqrt{1 - x^2}}$.

Similarly, for $y = \cos^{-1} x$, we start with $\cos y = x$, then $-\sin y \dfrac{dy}{dx} = 1$.

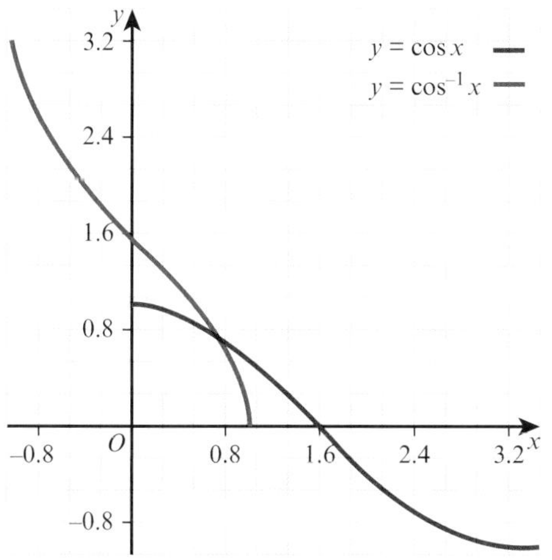

So with $\dfrac{dy}{dx} = -\dfrac{1}{\sin y}$ we look at the denominator. Since $\sin y = \pm\sqrt{1 - \cos^2 y}$ it follows that $\sin y = \pm\sqrt{1 - x^2}$. From the graph we can confirm that $\dfrac{dy}{dx} = -\dfrac{1}{\sqrt{1 - x^2}}$, as shown in Key point 21.6.

WORKED EXAMPLE 21.9

Given that $y = \tan^{-1} x$, find $\dfrac{dy}{dx}$.

Answer

From $y = \tan^{-1} x$ let $\tan y = x$. — Take tan of both sides.

Then $\sec^2 y \dfrac{dy}{dx} = 1$. — Differentiate implicitly and use trigonometric identities.

Given that $1 + \tan^2 y = \sec^2 y$:

$$\frac{dy}{dx} = \frac{1}{1 + \tan^2 y}$$

So $\dfrac{dy}{dx} = \dfrac{1}{1 + x^2}$. — State $\dfrac{dy}{dx}$.

KEY POINT 21.6

If $y = \sin^{-1} x$, then $\dfrac{dy}{dx} = \dfrac{1}{\sqrt{1 - x^2}}$.

If $y = \cos^{-1} x$, then $\dfrac{dy}{dx} = -\dfrac{1}{\sqrt{1 - x^2}}$.

If $y = \tan^{-1} x$, then $\dfrac{dy}{dx} = \dfrac{1}{1 + x^2}$.

WORKED EXAMPLE 21.10

Find the derivatives of the following functions.

a $y = x\cos^{-1} x$ b $y = \tan^{-1} 3x$ c $xy = \sin^{-1} 2x$

Answer

a $\frac{dy}{dx} = 1 \times \cos^{-1} x - x \times \frac{1}{\sqrt{1-x^2}} = \cos^{-1} x - \frac{x}{\sqrt{1-x^2}}$ — Differentiate as a product and quote the standard result for $\cos^{-1} x$.

b We have a slightly different form, so $\tan y = 3x$, and then $\sec^2 y \frac{dy}{dx} = 3.$ — Since we have $3x$ it is best to take tan of both sides.

So $\frac{dy}{dx} = \frac{3}{\sec^2 y} = \frac{3}{1+\tan^2 y} = \frac{3}{1+9x^2}.$ — State the result.

c $\sin xy = 2x$, then $\left(x\frac{dy}{dx} + y\right)\cos xy = 2.$ — After taking sin of both sides, differentiate implicitly.

Then $\frac{dy}{dx} = \frac{2 - y\cos xy}{x\cos xy}.$ — Simplify the result.

We have seen how to differentiate inverse trigonometric functions. Now we will differentiate inverse hyperbolic functions.

Starting with $y = \sinh^{-1}x$, we write $\sinh y = x$. Then $\cosh y\frac{dy}{dx} = 1$ so $\frac{dy}{dx} = \frac{1}{\cosh y}$. Using the result $\cosh^2 y - \sinh^2 y = 1$, we have $\cosh y = \pm\sqrt{1+x^2}$.

From the following graph it is clear that the gradient of $\sinh^{-1}x$ is always positive. So $\frac{dy}{dx} = \frac{1}{\sqrt{1+x^2}}$, as shown in Key point 21.7.

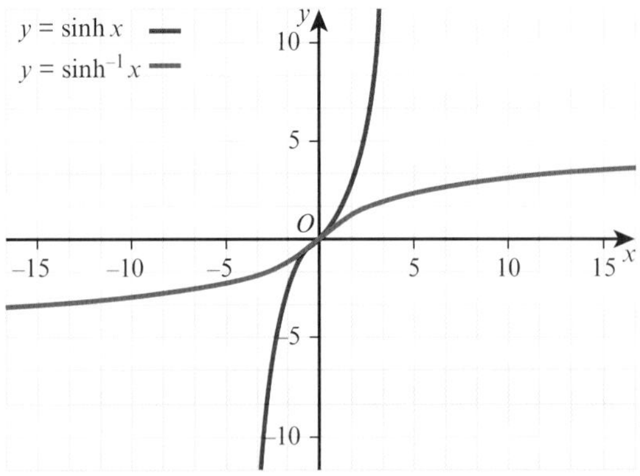

Next consider $y = \cosh^{-1}x$. Writing it as $\cosh y = x$ gives us $\sinh y\frac{dy}{dx} = 1.$

Again we use the identity $\cosh^2 y - \sinh^2 y = 1$, giving $\sinh y = \pm\sqrt{x^2-1}.$

From the graph, we see that the function $\cosh^{-1}x$ has a positive gradient for all values of x in its domain. So $\frac{dy}{dx} = \frac{1}{\sqrt{x^2-1}}$.

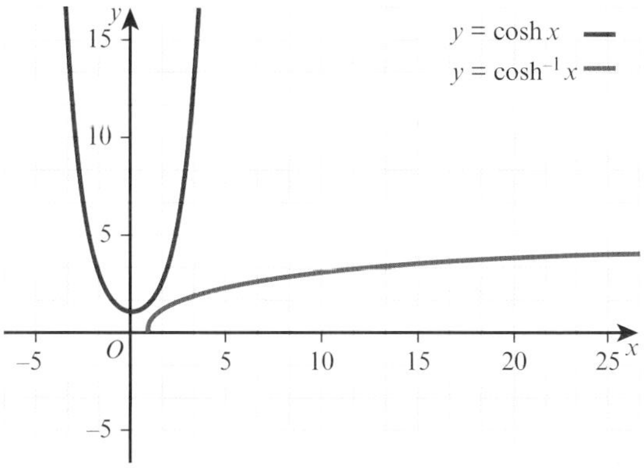

WORKED EXAMPLE 21.11

Find the gradient of the curve $y = \tanh^{-1}x$.

Answer

Start with $\tanh y = x$.

$\text{sech}^2 y \frac{dy}{dx} = 1$	Use implicit differentiation.
Then using $\text{sech}^2 y = 1 - \tanh^2 y$,	Then use the identity to rearrange the result.
we can say that $\frac{dy}{dx} = \frac{1}{1-x^2}$.	State the derivative.

KEY POINT 21.7

If $y = \sinh^{-1}x$, then $\frac{dy}{dx} = \frac{1}{\sqrt{1+x^2}}$.

If $y = \cosh^{-1}x$, then $\frac{dy}{dx} = \frac{1}{\sqrt{x^2-1}}$.

If $y = \tanh^{-1}x$, then $\frac{dy}{dx} = \frac{1}{1-x^2}$.

EXERCISE 21C

P 1 By differentiating $y = \frac{1}{2}e^{2x} + \frac{1}{2}e^{-2x}$, show that $\frac{dy}{dx} = 2\sinh 2x$.

M 2 Given that $y = \tanh^{-1}(2x+3)$, find $\frac{dy}{dx}$.

M 3 Find the first derivative of $y = \sin^{-1}(x^3)$.

M 4 Differentiate the following functions with respect to x. Simplify your answer where possible.

a $y = \ln \cosh 4x$

b $y = x^2 \sinh(2x^2 - 1)$

c $y = x \cosh^{-1} 5x$

d $y = \tan^{-1}(x + y)$

M 5 Given that $y = x \sinh^{-1} 2x$, find $\frac{d^2y}{dx^2}$.

PS 6 A curve is defined as $y = \cosh^3 x^2$.

a Find the first derivative with respect to x, stating the number of turning points.

b Find the second derivative with respect to x.

PS 7 Establish a result for the first derivative with respect to x for the following functions.

a $ay = \sin^{-1} bx$

b $ay = \tan^{-1} bx$

c $ay = \sinh^{-1} bx$

d $ay = \cosh^{-1} bx$

e $ay = \tanh^{-1} bx$

M 8 A curve, C, is defined as being $x = 3\tanh^{-1} t, y = \sin 2t$, where $-1 \leqslant t \leqslant 1$.

a Find the values of t where the gradient is zero.

b Find the second derivative with respect to x when $t = 0$.

21.4 Maclaurin series

You have already met binomial expansions in your A Level Mathematics course. The expansions that are particularly important involve approximating a function using a polynomial.

Consider, for example, the function $\frac{1}{1-x} = 1 + x + x^2 + x^3 + \ldots$. Provided $|x| < 1$ this approximation is valid. To get a better approximation we want x to be as close to zero as possible.

But what if the function we want to approximate is not of the form $(a + bx)^n$? For example, we might want to approximate $y = e^x$.

To do this we are going to use a special case of Taylor series.

The Taylor series of a function $f(x)$ is given as:

$$f(a) + f'(a)(x-a) + \frac{f''(a)(x-a)^2}{2!} + \frac{f'''(a)(x-a)^3}{3!} + \ldots$$

where $f(x)$ is differentiable an infinite number of times, and the constant a denotes the point $x = a$ at which we evaluate the function.

We shall work with a special case of Taylor series, where $a = 0$. This is known as a Maclaurin series, where $f(x) = f(0) + f'(0)x + \frac{f''(0)x^2}{2!} + \frac{f'''(0)x^3}{3!} + \ldots$

The Maclaurin series can also be represented in summation form, as $\sum_{n=0}^{\infty} \frac{f^{(n)}(0)}{n!} x^n$, as shown in Key point 21.8, where $f^{(n)}(0)$ is the nth derivative evaluated at the point $x = 0$.

KEY POINT 21.8

The Maclaurin series for an infinitely differentiable function $f(x)$ about the point $x = 0$, is given by

$$f(x) = f(0) + f'(0)x + \frac{f''(0)x^2}{2!} + \frac{f'''(0)x^3}{3!} + \dots$$

In summation form this is written as $\sum_{n=0}^{\infty} \frac{f^{(n)}(0)}{n!}x^n$.

How does this work? Consider the function $f(x) = \frac{1}{1-x}$, for which we have already found the expansion.

Then $f(x) = (1-x)^{-1}$ gives $f(0) = 1$.

$f'(x) = (-1)(-1)(1-x)^{-2} = (1-x)^{-2}$ gives $f'(0) = 1$.

$f''(x) = (-2)(-1)(1-x)^{-3} = 2(1-x)^{-3}$ gives $f''(0) = 2$.

$f'''(x) = 2(-3)(-1)(1-x)^{-4} = 6(1-x)^{-4}$ gives $f'''(0) = 6$.

$f^{(4)}(x) = 6(-4)(-1)(1-x)^{-5} = 24(1-x)^{-5}$ gives $f^{(4)}(0) = 24$.

So $f(x) \approx 1 + x + \frac{2x^2}{2!} + \frac{6x^3}{3!} + \frac{24x^4}{4!}$, which is $1 + x + x^2 + x^3 + x^4$ as before.

Note that this is the same as the binomially expanded result.

Let us find the Maclaurin series for $f(x) = e^x$ about the point $x = 0$.

$f(x) = e^x$, giving $f(0) = 1$.

$f'(x) = e^x$, giving $f'(0) = 1$.

$f''(x) = e^x$, giving $f''(0) = 1$.

$f'''(x) = e^x$, giving $f'''(0) = 1$.

$f^{(4)}(x) = e^x$, giving $f^{(4)}(0) = 1$.

$f^{(5)}(x) = e^x$, giving $f^{(5)}(0) = 1$.

So $e^x = 1 + x + \frac{x^2}{2!} + \frac{x^3}{3!} + \frac{x^4}{4!} + \frac{x^5}{5!} \dots$

The following diagrams show the Maclaurin series for e^x fitting more closely to the curve $f(x) = e^x$ as we add more terms.

In the summation form $\sum_{n=0}^{\infty} \frac{f^{(n)}(0)x^n}{n!}$, we are considering what happens as n increases.

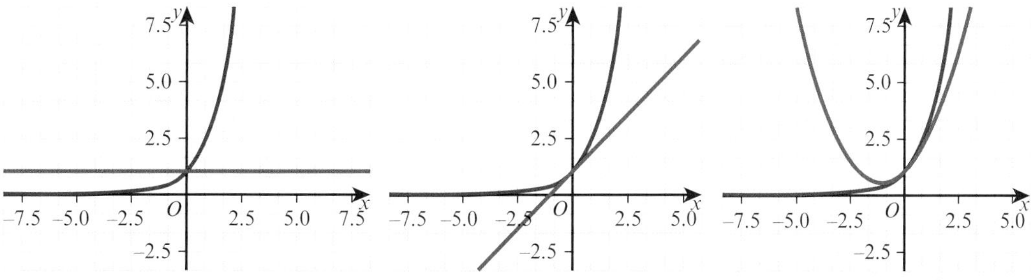

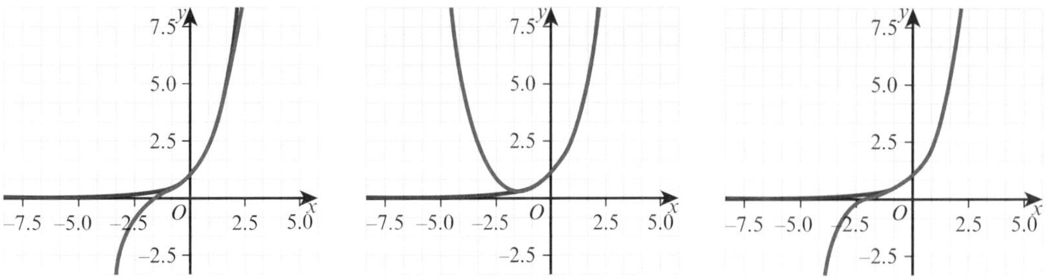

$n = 3$ $n = 4$ $n = 5$

If $x = 0$ we have $f(0) = e^0 = 1$ for the original curve, and this is also true for our Maclaurin series.

If $x = 0.01$, then $e^{0.01} = 1.010\,050\,167\,084\,168$, and from our series we have $1.010\,050\,167\,084\,17$. These are remarkably close with only six terms, but our value of x is close to zero.

If $x = 1$, then $e^1 = 2.718\,281\,828\,459\,045$, and from our series we get $2.716\,666\,666\,666\,67$, which is not as accurate as the previous approximation.

Since this series is centred on $x = 0$, the further away from zero we try to approximate, the more terms we need.

WORKED EXAMPLE 21.12

Find the Maclaurin series for $f(x) = \sin x$ about $x = 0$, giving the first four non-zero terms.

Answer

$f(0) = 0$ — Substitute zero into the function.

$f'(x) = \cos x$, giving $f'(0) = 1$. — Differentiate the function sufficient times to obtain four non-zero terms.

$f''(x) = -\sin x$, giving $f''(0) = 0$.

$f'''(x) = -\cos x$, giving $f'''(0) = -1$. — Notice that, due to the cyclic nature of sine and cosine, we get a non-zero term every other term.

$f^{(4)}(x) = \sin x$, giving $f^{(4)}(0) = 0$.

$f^{(5)}(x) = \cos x$, giving $f^{(5)}(0) = 1$. — Remember to use $\frac{f^{(n)}(0)}{n!}x^n$ for each term in the series.

$f^{(6)}(x) = -\sin x$, giving $f^{(6)}(0) = 0$.

$f^{(7)}(x) = -\cos x$, giving $f^{(7)}(0) = -1$.

Hence, $\sin x \approx x - \frac{x^3}{3!} + \frac{x^5}{5!} - \frac{x^7}{7!}$. — State the result.

Suppose we want to find the Maclaurin series for $\cos x$, there are two ways to do this. We can either differentiate the function enough times to find sufficient non-zero terms, or we can simply differentiate the Maclaurin series for $\sin x$.

So $\cos x \approx \frac{d}{dx}\left(x - \frac{x^3}{3!} + \frac{x^5}{5!} - \frac{x^7}{7!}\right) = 1 - \frac{x^2}{2!} + \frac{x^4}{4!} - \frac{x^6}{6!}$.

EXPLORE 21.2

Investigate the link between the Maclaurin series for e^x, $\sin x$ and $\cos x$.

WORKED EXAMPLE 21.13

If $f(x) = \sin^{-1} x$, find the first three non-zero terms of the Maclaurin series for this function. Find also an estimate, to 9 decimal places, for $\sin^{-1} 0.1$.

Answer

$f(0) = 0$ — Find the first term.

$f'(x) = (1 - x^2)^{-\frac{1}{2}}$, giving $f'(0) = 1$. — Differentiate using Key point 21.6.

$f''(x) = \left(-\frac{1}{2}\right)(-2x)(1 - x^2)^{-\frac{3}{2}} = x(1 - x^2)^{-\frac{3}{2}}$,

giving $f''(0) = 0$.

$f'''(x) = (1 - x^2)^{-\frac{3}{2}} + x\left(-\frac{3}{2}\right)(-2x)(1 - x^2)^{-\frac{5}{2}}$, — Use the product rule for the third derivative onwards.

which simplifies to $(1 - x^2)^{-\frac{3}{2}} + 3x^2(1 - x^2)^{-\frac{5}{2}}$. — Try to simplify expressions as much as possible; these derivatives have many terms.

So $f'''(0) = 1$.

$f^{(4)}(x) = \left(-\frac{3}{2}\right)(-2x)(1 - x^2)^{-\frac{5}{2}} + 6x(1 - x^2)^{-\frac{5}{2}} + 3x^2\left(-\frac{5}{2}\right)(-2x)(1 - x^2)^{-\frac{7}{2}}$,

which simplifies to $9x(1 - x^2)^{-\frac{5}{2}} + 15x^3(1 - x^2)^{-\frac{7}{2}}$.

This gives $f^{(4)}(0) = 0$.

$f^{(5)}(x) = 9(1 - x^2)^{-\frac{5}{2}} + 9x\left(-\frac{5}{2}\right)(-2x)(1 - x^2)^{-\frac{7}{2}} + 45x^2(1 - x^2)^{-\frac{7}{2}} + 15x^3\left(-\frac{7}{2}\right)(-2x)(1 - x^2)^{-\frac{9}{2}}$

This simplifies to $9(1 - x^2)^{-\frac{5}{2}} + 90x^2(1 - x^2)^{-\frac{7}{2}} + 105x^4(1 - x^2)^{-\frac{9}{2}}$.

Hence, $f^{(5)}(0) = 9$. — Write out each expression before simplifying to avoid errors.

So $\sin^{-1} x \approx x + \frac{x^3}{6} + \frac{3x^5}{40}$. — State the correct series.

Now, $\sin^{-1} 0.1 = 0.1 + \frac{0.001}{6} + \frac{3(0.00001)}{40} = 0.100\,167\,417$. — You have found an approximation without using the $\sin^{-1}$ button on your calculator.

Another way to determine a series for a function is to link it to a known series. Take, for example, $y = \sin 2x$. Since we know that $\sin x = x - \frac{x^3}{3!} + \frac{x^5}{5!} - \frac{x^7}{7!} + \ldots$ we have

$\sin 2x = 2x - \frac{(2x)^3}{3!} + \frac{(2x)^5}{5!} - \frac{(2x)^7}{7!} + \ldots$, which simplifies to $\sin 2x = 2x - \frac{4x^3}{3} + \frac{4x^5}{15} - \frac{8x^7}{315} + \ldots$.

WORKED EXAMPLE 21.14

Using calculus, find the Maclaurin series for $\tan x$, giving the first three non-zero terms.

Use your result to determine $\tan\left(\frac{1}{2}x\right)$ and $\ln(\sec x)$.

Answer

$f(x) = \tan x$ gives $f(0) = 0$. — State the first term.

$f'(x) = \sec^2 x$ gives $f'(0) = 1$.

$f''(x) = \frac{d}{dx}\left(\frac{1}{\cos^2 x}\right) = \frac{d}{dx}(\cos x)^{-2} = -2(\cos x)^{-3} \times -\sin x$

$= 2\sec^2 x \tan x$ gives $f''(0) = 0$. — Differentiate $\sec^2 x$ as $(\cos x)^{-2}$ or use the quotient rule to differentiate $\frac{1}{\cos^2 x}$.

$f'''(x) = 4\sec^2 x \tan^2 x + 2\sec^4 x$ gives $f'''(0) = 2$.

$f^{(4)}(x) = 8\sec^2 x \tan^3 x + 8\sec^4 x \tan x + 8\sec^4 x \tan x$,

which simplifies to $f^{(4)}(x) = 8\sec^2 x \tan^3 x + 16\sec^4 x \tan x$,

giving $f^{(4)}(0) = 0$. — Combine like terms before finding the next derivative.

$f^{(5)}(x) = 16\sec^2 x \tan^4 x + 24\sec^4 x \tan^2 x + 64\sec^4 x \tan^2 x + 16\sec^6 x$ — Look for terms that are only in the form $\sec^n x$ as these lead to the coefficients.

This simplifies to:

$16\sec^2 x \tan^4 x + 88\sec^4 x \tan^2 x + 16\sec^6 x$

which then leads to $f^{(5)}(0) = 16$.

So $\tan x \approx x + \frac{x^3}{3} + \frac{2x^5}{15}$. — State the Maclaurin series.

Hence, $\tan\left(\frac{x}{2}\right) \approx \frac{x}{2} + \frac{1}{3}\left(\frac{x}{2}\right)^3 + \frac{2}{15}\left(\frac{x}{2}\right)^5$. — Replace each x with $\frac{x}{2}$ and then simplify the terms.

This can then be simplified to give $\tan\left(\frac{x}{2}\right) \approx \frac{x}{2} + \frac{x^3}{24} + \frac{x^5}{240}$.

For $\ln(\sec x)$, differentiating gives $\frac{\sec x \tan x}{\sec x} = \tan x$. — Note that $\frac{d}{dx}(\ln(\sec x)) = \tan x$ or $\ln(\sec x) = \int \tan x \, dx$.

This means $\ln(\sec x) \approx \int\left(x + \frac{x^3}{3} + \frac{2x^5}{15}\right)dx$.

This integrates to give $\ln(\sec x) \approx \frac{x^2}{2} + \frac{x^4}{12} + \frac{x^6}{45} + c$. — Integrate and add a constant of integration.

Notice that Worked example 21.14 took a lot of work for only three non-zero terms. Let us look at an alternative approach.

Consider $y = \tan x$, then $y' = \sec^2 x$. But using $1 + \tan^2 x = \sec^2 x$ we have $y' = 1 + y^2$. We can differentiate this to get $y'' = 2yy'$, which can then be written as $y'' = 2y(1 + y^2) = 2y + 2y^3$.

Then $y''' = 2y' + 6y^2y' = 2(1 + y^2) + 6y^2(1 + y^2) = 2 + 8y^2 + 6y^4$. If we continue doing this we should notice that each derivative can be written in terms of $y = \tan x$. Since $\tan 0 = 0$, we only need to consider terms that are independent of y, and these give us the values of our coefficients.

For example, $y' = 1 + y^2$, so when $x = 0$, $\frac{dy}{dx} = 1$, and with $\frac{d^2y}{dx^2} = 2y + 2y^3$, $x = 0$ means $\frac{d^2y}{dx^2} = 0$.

Instead of $f(x), f'(x), f''(x), \ldots$ we now have $y, y', y'', \ldots$.

KEY POINT 21.9

For derivatives of a function, the shorthand notation for each successive derivative can be written as:

$$y' = \frac{dy}{dx},\ y'' = \frac{d^2y}{dx^2},\ y''' = \frac{d^3y}{dx^3},\ \ldots,\ y^{(n)} = \frac{d^ny}{dx^n}$$

Note that this is the same as the binomially expanded result.

WORKED EXAMPLE 21.15

Using shorthand notation, find the Maclaurin series for $y = \ln(1 + x)$, giving four non-zero terms. Use your result to estimate $\ln 1.1$, to 6 decimal places.

Answer

$y = \ln(1 + x)$, so $e^y = 1 + x$ and $e^{-y} = \frac{1}{1 + x}$.

Rearrange since the differentiated log function can be expressed as an exponential.

Also note that $e^{-ny} = \left(\frac{1}{1 + x}\right)^n$.

So when $x = 0$, $y = 0$.

Use this relation for each term when $x = 0$.

Then $y' = \frac{1}{1 + x} = e^{-y}$, when $x = 0$, $y' = 1$.

Next $y'' = -y'e^{-y} = -e^{-2y}$. When $x = 0$, $y'' = -1$.

Change each derivative so that it is expressed as ke^{-ny} since this is always equal to k when $x = 0$.

Then $y''' = 2y'e^{-2y} = 2e^{-3y}$ and when $x = 0$, $y''' = 2$.

Then $y^{(4)} = -6y'e^{-3y} = -6e^{-4y}$ and when $x = 0$, $y^{(4)} = -6$.

So $\ln(1 + x) \approx x - \frac{x^2}{2} + \frac{x^3}{3} - \frac{x^4}{4}$.

Use the coefficients to state the result.

When $x = 0.1$, $\ln(1.1) = 0.1 - \frac{0.01}{2} + \frac{0.001}{3} - \frac{0.0001}{4}$.

Use $x = 0.1$ to estimate the result. Note this is *not* the same as the actual value.

This is approximately 0.095 308.

EXERCISE 21D

1 Find the fourth derivative of each of the following functions.

a $y = e^{x^2}$

b $y = x\cos x$

M 2 Find the first three non-zero terms of the Maclaurin series for $f(x) = \frac{2}{(2x^2 + 1)^{\frac{3}{2}}}$.

M 3 By considering the expansion of $y = \ln(2x + 4)$, find an approximation, using five terms, to $\ln 4.02$. Give your answer to 7 decimal places.

M 4 Find the Maclaurin series for the following functions, in each case giving the first four non-zero terms.

a $f(x) = \sec x$ b $f(x) = \tan^{-1} x$ c $f(x) = \sinh x$

PS 5 You are given the function $f(x) = \cot^{-1} x$.

a Find the Maclaurin series for $f(x)$, giving the first four non-zero terms.

b Use your result from part **a** to find the series for $\frac{1}{1+x^2}$, also giving the first four non-zero terms.

M 6 Using standard results, or otherwise, find the Maclaurin series, giving the first four non-zero terms, for the following functions.

a $f(x) = \cos 3x$ b $f(x) = \frac{x^2}{1-3x}$ c $f(x) = \cosh\left(\frac{3x}{2}\right)$

PS 7 By first finding a four-term Maclaurin series for $f(x) = \sinh^{-1}x$, determine an approximation with respect to x for $\sinh^{-1} 0.2$. Give your answer to 8 decimal places.

P PS 8 Consider the function $y = \tanh x$.

a By differentiating twice, show that $y'' = -2y + 2y^3$.

b Differentiate with respect to x up to $y^{(5)}$ and use this to determine the Maclaurin series of $y = \tanh x$.

WORKED PAST PAPER QUESTION

A curve has parametric equations $x = 2\theta - \sin 2\theta$, $y = 1 - \cos 2\theta$, for $-3\pi \leqslant \theta \leqslant 3\pi$.

Show that $\frac{dy}{dx} = \cot\theta$, except for certain values of θ, which should be stated.

Find the value of $\frac{d^2y}{dx^2}$ when $\theta = \frac{1}{4}\pi$.

Cambridge International AS & A Level Further Mathematics 9231 Paper 13 Q4 November 2013

Answer

Start with $\frac{dy}{d\theta} = 2\sin 2\theta$ and $\frac{dx}{d\theta} = 2 - 2\cos 2\theta$. Then $\frac{dy}{dx} = \frac{\sin 2\theta}{1 - \cos 2\theta}$.

Using $\sin 2\theta = 2\sin\theta\cos\theta$ and $\cos 2\theta = 1 - 2\sin^2\theta$, we have $\frac{dy}{dx} = \frac{2\sin\theta\cos\theta}{2\sin^2\theta}$.

This simplifies to $\frac{dy}{dx} = \cot\theta$.

Values of θ not permitted are $-3\pi, -2\pi, -\pi, 0, \pi, 2\pi, 3\pi$.

For the second derivative: $\frac{d^2y}{dx^2} = \frac{d}{d\theta}(\cot\theta) \times \frac{d\theta}{dx}$, which is $-\operatorname{cosec}^2\theta \times \frac{1}{2(1-\cos 2\theta)}$.

When $\theta = \frac{\pi}{4}$, we have $-(\sqrt{2})^2 \times \frac{1}{2(1-0)} = -1$.

Checklist of learning and understanding

For general differentiation:

- If $y = [f(x)]^n$, then $\frac{dy}{dx} = nf'(x)[f(x)]^{n-1}$.
- If $y = \ln[f(x)]$, then $\frac{dy}{dx} = \frac{f'(x)}{f(x)}$.
- If $y = e^{f(x)}$, then $\frac{dy}{dx} = f'(x)e^{f(x)}$.
- If $y = uvw$, where u, v, w are all functions of x, then $\frac{dy}{dx} = uv\frac{dw}{dx} + uw\frac{dv}{dx} + vw\frac{du}{dx}$.

For parametric differentiation:

- If $x = f(t)$ and $y = g(t)$, then $\frac{dy}{dx} = \frac{dy}{dt} \times \frac{dt}{dx}$ and $\frac{d^2y}{dx^2} = \frac{d}{dt}\left(\frac{dy}{dx}\right) \times \frac{dt}{dx}$.

For the derivatives of standard functions:

- $y = \sinh x, \frac{dy}{dx} = \cosh x$ $y = \coth x, \frac{dy}{dx} = -\text{cosech}^2 x$
- $y = \cosh x, \frac{dy}{dx} = \sinh x$ $y = \text{sech}\, x, \frac{dy}{dx} = -\text{sech}\, x \tanh x$
- $y = \tanh x, \frac{dy}{dx} = \text{sech}^2 x$ $y = \text{cosech}\, x, \frac{dy}{dx} = -\text{cosech}\, x \coth x$
- $y = \sin^{-1} x, \frac{dy}{dx} = \frac{1}{\sqrt{1-x^2}}$ $y = \cos^{-1} x, \frac{dy}{dx} = -\frac{1}{\sqrt{1-x^2}}$
- $y = \tan^{-1} x, \frac{dy}{dx} = \frac{1}{1+x^2}$ $y = \sinh^{-1} x, \frac{dy}{dx} = \frac{1}{\sqrt{x^2+1}}$
- $y = \cosh^{-1} x, \frac{dy}{dx} = \frac{1}{\sqrt{x^2-1}}$ $y = \tanh^{-1} x, \frac{dy}{dx} = \frac{1}{1-x^2}$

For Maclaurin series:

- For an infinitely differentiable function $f(x)$ about the point $x = 0$, the Maclaurin series is given by $f(x) = f(0) + f'(0)x + \frac{f''(0)x^2}{2!} + \frac{f'''(0)x^3}{3!} + \ldots$.
- In summation form the Maclaurin series can be represented by $\sum_{n=0}^{\infty} \frac{f^{(n)}(0)}{n!}x^n$.
- $\sin x = x - \frac{x^3}{3!} + \frac{x^5}{5!} - \frac{x^7}{7!} + \ldots$
- $\cos x = 1 - \frac{x^2}{2!} + \frac{x^4}{4!} - \frac{x^6}{6!} + \ldots$
- $e^x = 1 + x + \frac{x^2}{2!} + \frac{x^3}{3!} + \ldots$
- $\ln(1 + x) = x - \frac{x^2}{2} + \frac{x^3}{3} - \frac{x^4}{4} + \ldots$
- $\sinh x = x + \frac{x^3}{3!} + \frac{x^5}{5!} + \frac{x^7}{7!} + \ldots$
- $\cosh x = 1 + \frac{x^2}{2!} + \frac{x^4}{4!} + \frac{x^6}{6!} + \ldots$

END-OF-CHAPTER REVIEW EXERCISE 21

1 The point $P(2, 1)$ lies on the curve with equation $x^3 - 2y^3 = 3xy$.

Find

i the value of $\frac{dy}{dx}$ at P,

ii the value of $\frac{d^2y}{dx^2}$ at P.

Cambridge International AS & A Level Further Mathematics 9231 Paper 11 Q5 November 2011

2 A curve has equation $x^2 - 6xy + 25y^2 = 16$. Show that $\frac{dy}{dx} = 0$ at the point $(3, 1)$.

By finding the value of $\frac{d^2y}{dx^2}$ at the point $(3, 1)$, determine the nature of this turning point.

Cambridge International AS & A Level Further Mathematics 9231 Paper 11 Q6 June 2015

3 Given that $y = \cos^{-1}\left(\frac{1}{2}x\right)$, find $\frac{dy}{dx}$ and $\frac{d^2y}{dx^2}$.

Hence, determine the Maclaurin expansion of $y = \cos^{-1}\left(\frac{1}{2}x\right)$, giving the first three non-zero terms.

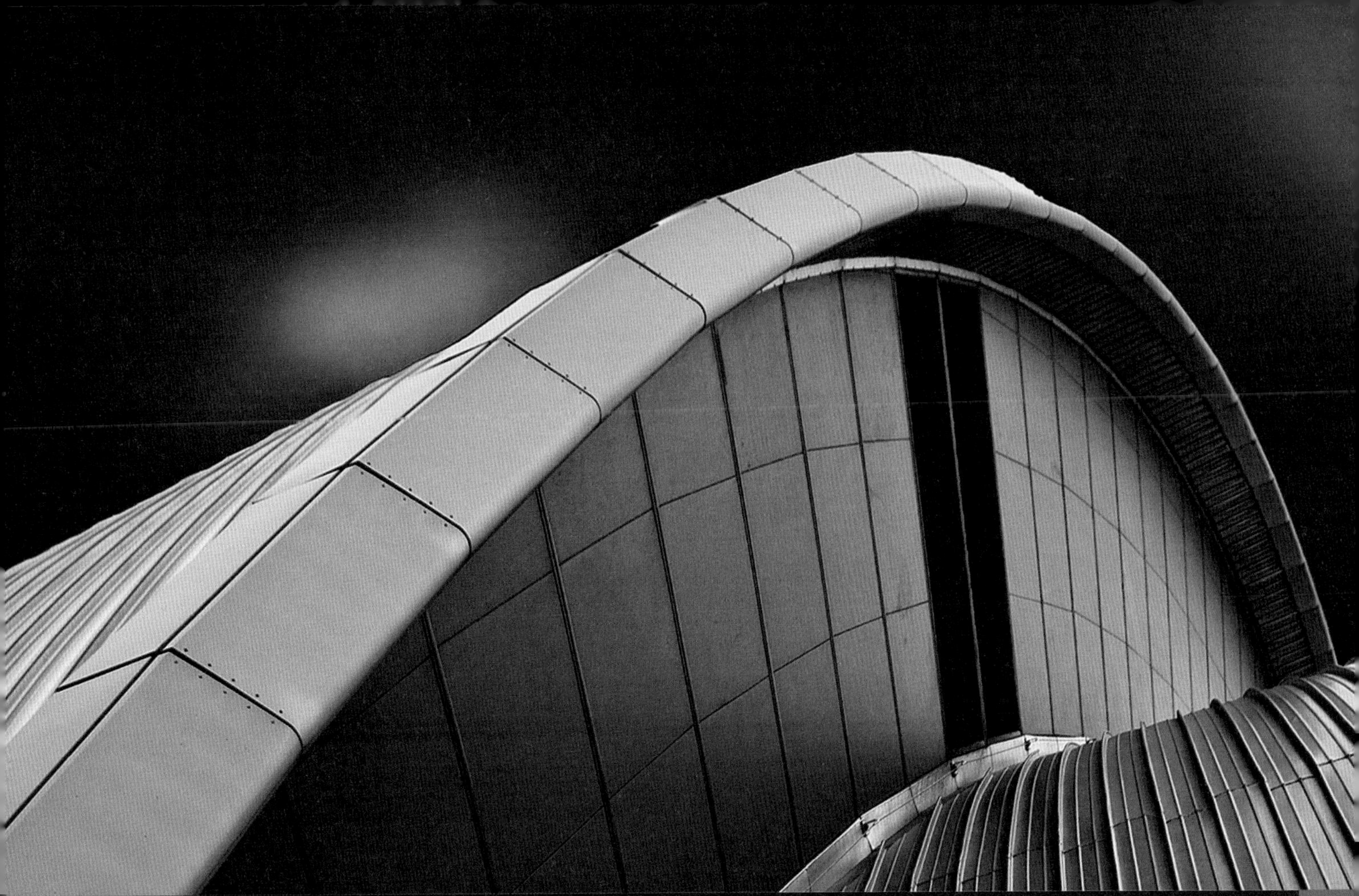

Chapter 22
Integration

In this chapter you will learn how to:

- integrate hyperbolic functions and recognise integrals of the form $\frac{1}{\sqrt{a^2 - x^2}}, \frac{1}{\sqrt{a^2 + x^2}}$
- define and use reduction formulae for evaluation of definite integrals
- use rectangles to estimate or set bounds for the area under a curve
- use integration to find arc lengths and surface areas of revolution.

PREREQUISITE KNOWLEDGE

Where it comes from	What you should be able to do	Check your skills
AS & A Level Mathematics Pure Mathematics 2 & 3, Chapter 8	Use integration by parts.	**1** Evaluate $\int_0^1 xe^{2x}\,dx$.
AS & A Level Mathematics Pure Mathematics 2 & 3, Chapter 8	Work with trigonometric identities.	**2** Using a suitable trigonometric identity, determine $\int \sqrt{1-\cos x}\,dx$.

What is integration?

We can consider integration as the reverse of differentiation. It is also the process of combining smaller parts to find the whole, for example, when finding lengths, areas and volumes.

In this chapter we shall integrate a variety of functions, including functions that lead to hyperbolic solutions. We shall learn new techniques, such as constructing **reduction** formulae, to solve more complicated integrals involving high powers. We shall use these new skills to find the length of an arc and the area of a surface of revolution. Finally, we shall set up **boundaries**, and use summation techniques to calculate the area under a curve between the boundaries.

22.1 Integration techniques

You will have met several integration techniques in your A Level Mathematics Pure Mathematics 3 course, such as integration by parts and integration by substitution.

Consider the integral $I = \int \frac{1}{\sqrt{1-x^2}}\,dx$. The denominator is the square root of two terms. If we can change this to the square root of one term, then the integration will be much easier.

Thinking about the trigonometric identity $\cos^2 u = 1 - \sin^2 u$, if we try $x = \sin u$ as a substitution, then $\frac{dx}{du} = \cos u$.

Next replace x with $\sin u$ and dx with $\frac{dx}{du}du$. We get $I = \int \frac{\cos u}{\sqrt{1-\sin^2 u}}\,du$, which is $\int 1\,du = u + c$. Then $I = u + c$, but since $u = \sin^{-1} x$ we have $I = \sin^{-1} x + c$.

WORKED EXAMPLE 22.1

Determine the indefinite integral $I = \int \frac{4}{4+x^2}\,dx$.

Answer

Let $x = 2\tan u$.

Then $\frac{dx}{du} = 2\sec^2 u$, giving $dx = 2\sec^2 u\,du$.

Choose a substitution that replaces two terms with one term, so here we can use the trigonometric identity $1 + \tan^2 u = \sec^2 u$.

So $I = 4\int \frac{8\sec^2 u}{4 + 4\tan^2 u}\,du$, which is $\int 2\,du$.	Differentiate the substitution and simplify the integral.
Integrating then gives $I = 2u + c$, or $I = 2\tan^{-1}\left(\frac{x}{2}\right) + c$.	Integrate and change back to the original variable which is x.

WORKED EXAMPLE 22.2

Find the exact value of the integral $\int_0^{1.5} \sqrt{9 - x^2}\,dx$.

Answer

Let $x = 3\sin u$, so $\frac{dx}{du} = 3\cos u$.	Choose a substitution, and differentiate it. Considering the integral, the trigonometric identity $\cos^2 u = 1 - \sin^2 u$ will again be useful.
Also when $x = 0, u = 0$ and when $x = 1.5, u = \frac{\pi}{6}$.	Using the substitution, work out the new limits, remembering to work in radians.
Let $I = \int_0^{\frac{\pi}{6}} \sqrt{9 - 9\sin^2 u} \times 3\cos u\,du$.	Substitute all values and results into the integral.
Simplify this integral to $I = 9\int_0^{\frac{\pi}{6}} \cos^2 u\,du$.	
Next use $\cos^2 u = \frac{1}{2} + \frac{1}{2}\cos 2u$.	Make use of the double angle formula.
So $I = \frac{9}{2}\int_0^{\frac{\pi}{6}} (1 + \cos 2u)du$.	
Integrating gives $I = \frac{9}{2}\left[u + \frac{1}{2}\sin 2u\right]_0^{\frac{\pi}{6}} = \frac{9\sqrt{3}}{8} + \frac{3\pi}{4}$.	Integrate and evaluate.

Consider the integral $I = \int \frac{1}{\sqrt{x^2 - 1}}\,dx$. We could substitute $x = \sec u$, since $\tan^2 u = \sec^2 u - 1$.

Then $\frac{dx}{du} = \sec u \tan u$, giving $dx = \sec u \tan u\,du$.

So $I = \int \frac{\sec u \tan u}{\sqrt{\sec^2 u - 1}}\,du$ becomes $I = \int \sec u\,du$. Multiplying top and bottom by $\sec u + \tan u$ gives $I = \int \frac{\sec^2 u + \sec u \tan u}{\sec u + \tan u}\,du$, which is now of the form $\frac{f'(x)}{f(x)}$.

Integrating gives $I = \ln|\sec u + \tan u| + c$. Since $x = \sec u$ and $\tan u = \sqrt{x^2 - 1}$, the answer is $I = \ln|x + \sqrt{x^2 - 1}| + c$.

An alternative substitution is $x = \cosh u$. Since $\cosh^2 u - \sinh^2 u = 1$, then $\frac{dx}{du} = \sinh u$.

So $I = \int \frac{\sinh u}{\sinh u}\,du = u + c$. This integration is much easier than the previous one.

Hyperbolic substitutions can make some integrals extremely simple. The last step is to write $I = \cosh^{-1} x + c$. We could write the answer in terms of logs as in the first method, using the identity for $\cosh^{-1} x$ from Chapter 19.

WORKED EXAMPLE 22.3

Using an appropriate substitution, determine the result of $\int \frac{3}{\sqrt{x^2+4}}\,\mathrm{d}x$.

Answer

Start with $x = 2\sinh u$, then $\frac{\mathrm{d}x}{\mathrm{d}u} = 2\cosh u$. — Use $x = 2\sinh u$ as the substitution.

So $I = 3\int \frac{2\cosh u}{\sqrt{4\sinh^2 u + 4}}\,\mathrm{d}u = 3u + c$. — Substitute all values and simplify the integral to just a constant.

Therefore, $I = 3\sinh^{-1}\left(\frac{x}{2}\right) + c$. — Integrate and convert u back to the original variable, x.

In Worked example 22.4 it is important to know when hyperbolic substitutions are appropriate.

WORKED EXAMPLE 22.4

Using an appropriate substitution, determine the result of $\int \frac{1}{\sqrt{9-4x^2}}\,\mathrm{d}x$. Discuss your findings.

Answer

Let $2x = 3\tanh u$, then $2\frac{\mathrm{d}x}{\mathrm{d}u} = 3\,\mathrm{sech}^2 u$. — This substitution requires much more work.

So $I = \frac{3}{2}\int \frac{\mathrm{sech}^2 u}{\sqrt{9-9\tanh^2 u}}\,\mathrm{d}u = \frac{1}{2}\int \mathrm{sech}\, u\,\mathrm{d}u$. — This is not as simple as integrating $\sec u$.

Since $\mathrm{sech}\, u = \frac{1}{\cosh u}$, then $\mathrm{sech}\, u = \frac{2}{e^u + e^{-u}}$.

So $I = \frac{1}{2}\int \frac{2e^u}{e^{2u}+1}\,\mathrm{d}u$. Let $t = e^u$ so that $\frac{\mathrm{d}t}{\mathrm{d}u} = e^u$. — A second substitution is required at this point.

Then $I = \int \frac{1}{t^2+1}\,\mathrm{d}t$, which is $\tan^{-1} t + c$. — This is a standard result.

So, working backwards, $I = \tan^{-1}(e^u) + c$ then $I = \tan^{-1}\left(e^{\tanh^{-1}\frac{2x}{3}}\right) + c$.

This result is much more complicated. — The result is not in a very suitable format.

Using $2x = 3\sin u$ instead gives $2\frac{\mathrm{d}x}{\mathrm{d}u} = 3\cos u$ and so $\frac{3}{2}\int \frac{\cos u}{\sqrt{9-9\sin^2 u}}\,\mathrm{d}u = \frac{1}{2}\int \mathrm{d}u$ which leads to $\frac{1}{2}\sin^{-1}\left(\frac{2x}{3}\right) + c$. — This substitution is more suitable, and the result is found more quickly.

Consider $I = \int \frac{1}{x^2+2x+2}\,\mathrm{d}x$. If you try a trigonometric substitution, you will have rather a complicated expression in the denominator.

Instead, we are going to complete the square: $x^2 + 2x + 2 = (x+1)^2 + 1$.

Now $I = \int \frac{1}{(x+1)^2+1}\,\mathrm{d}x$.

Let $x + 1 = \tan u$ so $\mathrm{d}x = \sec^2 u\,\mathrm{d}u$ and $I = \int \frac{1}{1+\tan^2 u}\sec^2 u\,\mathrm{d}u = \int \mathrm{d}u$.

Integrating gives us $I = u + c$, then since $u = \tan^{-1}(x+1)$ we have $I = \tan^{-1}(x+1) + c$.

WORKED EXAMPLE 22.5

Using an appropriate substitution, determine the result of $\int \frac{1}{x^2 - 4x + 7}\mathrm{d}x$.

Answer

First $x^2 - 4x + 7 = (x-2)^2 + 3$.	Complete the square.
Then $I = \int \frac{1}{(x-2)^2 + 3}\mathrm{d}x$.	Rewrite the integral.
Using $\sqrt{3}\tan u = x - 2$, we have $\mathrm{d}x = \sqrt{3}\sec^2 u\,\mathrm{d}u$.	Recognise that you have a tan substitution.
So $I = \int \frac{\sqrt{3}\sec^2 u}{3 + 3\tan^2 u}\mathrm{d}u = \int \frac{1}{\sqrt{3}}\mathrm{d}u$.	Substitute in.
Integrating gives $I = \frac{1}{\sqrt{3}}u + c$.	Integrate.
Substituting back leads to $I = \frac{1}{\sqrt{3}}\tan^{-1}\left(\frac{x-2}{\sqrt{3}}\right) + c$.	Rewrite solution in terms of the original variable.

WORKED EXAMPLE 22.6

Using a hyperbolic substitution, determine the result of $\int \frac{1}{x^2 + 4x}\mathrm{d}x$.

Answer

First $x^2 + 4x = (x+2)^2 - 4$.	Complete the square.
Then $I = \int \frac{1}{(x+2)^2 - 4}\mathrm{d}x$.	Rewrite the integral.
Let $x + 2 = 2\tanh u$, then $\mathrm{d}x = 2\operatorname{sech}^2 u\,\mathrm{d}u$.	Recognise that you have a tanh substitution.
Now $I = \int \frac{1}{4\tanh^2 u - 4}2\operatorname{sech}^2 u\,\mathrm{d}u$.	Substitute in.
Then use $\operatorname{sech}^2 u = 1 - \tanh^2 u$.	Use the identity to simplify.
So $I = -\frac{1}{2}\int \mathrm{d}u$.	Rewrite integral.
Integrating gives $I = -\frac{1}{2}u + c$.	Integrate to get a solution.
Finally $I = -\frac{1}{2}\tanh^{-1}\left(\frac{x+2}{2}\right) + c$.	Use $u = \tanh^{-1}\left(\frac{x+2}{2}\right)$.

The work we did with derivatives of hyperbolic functions will help us to integrate them.

So $\int \sinh x\,dx = \cosh x + c$ and $\int \cosh x\,dx = \sinh x + c$ are two standard results.

Integrating $\tanh x$ takes a little more thought: $\int \tanh x\,dx = \int \frac{\sinh x}{\cosh x}\,dx = \ln|\cosh x| + c$.

Similarly, we can shown that $\int \cosh x\,dx = \int \frac{\cosh x}{\sinh x}\,dx = \ln|\sinh x| + c$.

WORKED EXAMPLE 22.7

Find a solution for the following integrals.

a $\int 2\sinh 3x\,dx$ b $\int \frac{1}{\sinh x}\,dx$ c $\int_{\ln 2}^{\ln 3} 3\cosh 4x\,dx$

Answer

a From the standard result, $I = \frac{2}{3}\cosh 3x + c$. Divide by 3.

b $I = \int \frac{2}{e^x - e^{-x}}\,dx$, then $I = 2\int \frac{e^x}{e^{2x} - 1}\,dx$. Rewrite as exponentials.

Then let $u = e^x$, so $\frac{du}{dx} = e^x$ Substitute to remove the exponentials.

Our integral becomes $I = 2\int \frac{u}{u^2 - 1}\frac{1}{u}\,du = 2\int \frac{1}{u^2 - 1}\,du$.

Then let $u = \coth t$ so $\frac{du}{dt} = -\text{cosech}^2 t$ so that Substitute again with $u = \coth t$.

our integral becomes $I = 2\int \frac{-\text{cosech}^2 t}{\text{cosech}^2 t}\,dt$, which is $-2t + c$.

Then $I = -2\coth^{-1} u + c = -2\coth^{-1}(e^x) + c$. State the result in the original variable.

c $I = \int_{\ln 2}^{\ln 3} 3\cosh 4x\,dx = \frac{3}{4}[\sinh 4x]_{\ln 2}^{\ln 3}$ Integrate using the standard result.

This is then $\frac{3}{8}[e^{4x} - e^{-4x}]_{\ln 2}^{\ln 3}$, which is 24.4. Evaluate, using the exponential form for $\sinh 4x$.

We saw how to differentiate inverse hyperbolic functions in Chapter 21.

To integrate inverse hyperbolic functions, let us consider $\int \cosh^{-1} x\,dx$. To integrate this by parts, re-write this as $\cosh^{-1} x \times 1$ and let $u = \cosh^{-1} x$, so $\frac{du}{dx} = \frac{1}{\sqrt{x^2 - 1}}$, and $\frac{dv}{dx} = 1$, so $v = x$. Then $I = x\cosh^{-1} x - \int \frac{x}{\sqrt{x^2 - 1}}\,dx$ and integrating the second term leads to

$I = x\cosh^{-1} x - \sqrt{x^2 - 1} + c$.

WORKED EXAMPLE 22.8

Determine the result of the integral $\int \tanh^{-1} x \, dx$.

Answer

Let $u = \tanh^{-1} x$, so $\frac{du}{dx} = \frac{1}{1-x^2}$. — Differentiate $\tanh^{-1} x$.

Then $\frac{dv}{dx} = 1$ and $v = x$. — Include a '1' to be able to integrate by parts.

So $I = x \tanh^{-1} x - \int \frac{x}{1-x^2} dx$. — Note the second term is of the form $\int \frac{kf'(x)}{f(x)} dx$.

Integrating the second term leads to $I = x \tanh^{-1} x + \frac{1}{2} \ln|1-x^2| + c$. — Determine the final result.

EXERCISE 22A

1 Determine the integral $\int \frac{-2}{\sqrt{25-9x^2}} dx$.

2 Evaluate the integral $\int_0^{\frac{\pi}{4}} \tan^{-1} x \, dx$, giving your answer in an exact form.

M 3 Find the area under the curve $y = \sinh 2x$ from $x = \ln 3$ to $x = \ln 5$.

4 Determine the integral $\int \frac{2}{\sqrt{2+x^2}} dx$.

5 Evaluate $\int_2^3 \frac{1}{\sqrt{x^2-4}} dx$.

M PS 6 Find the volume generated when $y = \frac{6}{\sqrt{9-x^2}}$ is rotated about the x-axis from $x = 1$ to $x = 2$.

7 Evaluate $\int_{0.75}^1 \coth 2x \, dx$.

8 Determine the integral $\int \frac{6}{\sqrt{4-9x^2}} dx$.

9 Integrate $x \cosh x$.

M 10 The curve $y = \sinh x$ is rotated about the x-axis from $x = 0$ to $x = 1$. Determine the volume generated.

11 Determine $\int \sinh^{-1} x \, dx$.

22.2 Reduction formulae

Beginning with $\int \cos^2 x \, dx$, we have already seen that using the double angle formulae can make this integral straightforward. We are now going to solve this integral using integration by parts.

Start with $I = \int \cos^2 x \, dx = \int \cos x \times \cos x \, dx$. Let $u = \cos x$, $\frac{du}{dx} = -\sin x$ and $\frac{dv}{dx} = \cos x$, $v = \sin x$. So $I = \cos x \sin x + \int \sin^2 x \, dx$.

Then with $\sin^2 x = 1 - \cos^2 x$ we have $I = \cos x \sin x + \int (1 - \cos^2 x) dx$. Split the integral into $\int 1 \, dx - \int \cos^2 x \, dx$. Notice that the integral of $\cos^2 x$ is I, so $2I = \cos x \sin x + x + c$.

Hence, $I = \frac{1}{2}(\cos x \sin x + x) + c$.

WORKED EXAMPLE 22.9

Given that $I_3 = \int \cos^3 x \, dx$, find the result for I_3, using integration by parts.

Answer

Let $I_3 = \int \cos^2 x \cos x \, dx$. — Rewrite $\cos^3 x$ as $\cos^2 x \cos x$ and differentiate the higher power for integration by parts.

Then $u = \cos^2 x$, $\frac{du}{dx} = -2\cos x \sin x$, and $\frac{dv}{dx} = \cos x$, $v = \sin x$. — Integrate the single powered term.

So $I_3 = \cos^2 x \sin x + 2\int \cos x \sin^2 x \, dx$.

After replacing the $\sin^2 x$ with $1 - \cos^2 x$, the integral becomes $I_3 = \cos^2 x \sin x + 2\int \cos x \, dx - 2\int \cos^3 x \, dx$. — Use the identity $\cos^2 x + \sin^2 x = 1$ to replace the sine part.

Then we have $3I_3 = \cos^2 x \sin x + 2\sin x + c$. — Add $2I_3$ to both sides of the equation.

Hence, $I_3 = \frac{1}{3}(\cos^2 x \sin x + 2\sin x) + c$. — Divide by 3 to find I_3.

We should now be able to attempt $I_n = \int \cos^n x \, dx$. First split this function into two functions, so $I_n = \int \cos^{n-1} x \cos x \, dx$.

$u = \cos^{n-1} x$, $\frac{du}{dx} = -(n-1)\cos^{n-2} x \sin x$, and $\frac{dv}{dx} = \cos x$, $v = \sin x$.

So $I_n = \cos^{n-1} x \sin x + (n-1)\int \cos^{n-2} x \sin^2 x \, dx$. Again, using $\sin^2 x = 1 - \cos^2 x$ we have

$I_n = \cos^{n-1} x \sin x + (n-1)\int \cos^{n-2} x \, dx - (n-1)\int \cos^n x \, dx$.

Now, if $I_n = \int \cos^n x \, dx$, then using the same notation, $I_{n-2} = \int \cos^{n-2} x \, dx$, and we then have:

$$I_n = \cos^{n-1} x \sin x + (n-1)I_{n-2} - (n-1)I_n$$

Hence, $I_n = \frac{1}{n}[\cos^{n-1} x \sin x] + \frac{n-1}{n} I_{n-2}$. This is only valid for $n \geqslant 2$. This is known as a **reduction formula**. It allows us to integrate a function, and with each **iteration** the power reduces by 2. It is called a reduction formula because each time we integrate there is a loss in power.

Using this reduction formula is simple enough. Consider $\int \cos^4 x \, dx$, which we shall denote as I_4.

From our formula, $I_4 = \frac{1}{4}(\cos^3 x \sin x) + \frac{3}{4}I_2$, and $I_2 = \frac{1}{2}(\cos x \sin x) + \frac{1}{2}I_0$. The last part of our expression is $I_0 = \int 1\,\mathrm{d}x = x$, so $I_4 = \frac{1}{4}(\cos^3 x \sin x) + \frac{3}{8}(\cos x \sin x + x) + c$.

WORKED EXAMPLE 22.10

If $I_n = \int \sin^n x\,\mathrm{d}x$, show, using integration by parts, that $I_n = \frac{1}{n}[-\cos x \sin^{n-1} x] + \frac{n-1}{n}I_{n-2}$ for $n \geqslant 2$.

Answer

Let $I_n = \int \sin^{n-1} x \sin x\,\mathrm{d}x$, so $u = \sin^{n-1} x$, $\frac{\mathrm{d}v}{\mathrm{d}x} = \sin x$ such that $\frac{\mathrm{d}u}{\mathrm{d}x} = (n-1)\sin^{n-2} x \cos x$, $v = -\cos x$.

Rewrite $\sin^n x$ as $\sin^{n-1} x \sin x$ to create a single power that can be integrated.

So $I_n = [-\cos x \sin^{n-1} x] + (n-1)\int \sin^{n-2} x \cos^2 x\,\mathrm{d}x$.

Using $\cos^2 x = 1 - \sin^2 x$, we get the expression:

Make use of the identities to simplify the expression.

$I_n = [-\cos x \sin^{n-1} x] + (n-1)\int \sin^{n-2} x\,\mathrm{d}x - (n-1)\int \sin^n x\,\mathrm{d}x$

Note that $I_n = \int \sin^n x\,\mathrm{d}x$ means $I_{n-2} = \int \sin^{n-2} x\,\mathrm{d}x$.

This gives $I_n = \frac{1}{n}[-\cos x \sin^{n-1} x] + \frac{n-1}{n}I_{n-2}$.

This is valid for $n \geqslant 2$.

State the solution, and state the requirement for n.

We can also split hyperbolic functions such as $I_n = \int \cosh^n 2x\,\mathrm{d}x$ in a similar way:

$I_n = \int \cosh^{n-1} 2x \cosh 2x\,\mathrm{d}x$.

Let $u = \cosh^{n-1} 2x$, $\frac{\mathrm{d}u}{\mathrm{d}x} = 2(n-1)\cosh^{n-2} 2x \sinh 2x$ and $\frac{\mathrm{d}v}{\mathrm{d}x} = \cosh 2x$, $v = \frac{1}{2}\sinh 2x$. Then $I_n = \frac{1}{2}\sinh 2x \cosh^{n-1} 2x - (n-1)\int \cosh^{n-2} 2x \sinh^2 2x\,\mathrm{d}x$. Since $\sinh^2 2x = \cosh^2 2x - 1$, we can say that $I_n = \frac{1}{2}\sinh 2x \cosh^{n-1} 2x - (n-1)\int \cosh^n 2x\,\mathrm{d}x + (n-1)\int \cosh^{n-2} 2x\,\mathrm{d}x$.

Then $I_n = \frac{1}{2}\sinh 2x \cosh^{n-1} 2x - (n-1)I_n + (n-1)I_{n-2}$. This can be simplified to the form $I_n = \frac{1}{2n}(\sinh 2x \cosh^{n-1} 2x) + \frac{n-1}{n}I_{n-2}$ for $n \geqslant 2$.

WORKED EXAMPLE 22.11

If $I_n = \int \coth^n x\,\mathrm{d}x$, show that the reduction formula is $I_n = \frac{1}{n-1}(-\coth^{n-1} x) + I_{n-2}$ for $n \geqslant 2$.

Answer

Let $I_n = \int \coth^{n-2} x \coth^2 x\,\mathrm{d}x$. Using $\coth^2 x = 1 + \mathrm{cosech}^2 x$, we have $I_n = \int \coth^{n-2} x\,\mathrm{d}x + \int \coth^{n-2} x\,\mathrm{cosech}^2 x\,\mathrm{d}x$.

Rewrite $\coth^n x$ as $\coth^{n-2} x \coth^2 x$ and make use of the result $\coth^2 x = 1 + \mathrm{cosech}^2 x$.

Let $u = \coth^{n-2}x$, $\frac{du}{dx} = -(n-2)\coth^{n-3}x\,\text{cosech}^2 x$ and also $\frac{dv}{dx} = \text{cosech}^2 x$, $v = -\coth x$.

Use integration by parts on the second integral and note that the first integral does not need integrating, as we can write this as I_{n-2}.

Then noting that $\int \coth^{n-2}x\,dx = I_{n-2}$ we have:

$I_n = I_{n-2} + -\coth^{n-1}x - (n-2)\int \coth^{n-2}x\,\text{cosech}^2 x\,dx$

Use $\coth^2 x = 1 + \text{cosech}^2 x$ to simplify the integral term.

Use the same identity again to simplify and collect terms.

So $I_n = I_{n-2} - \coth^{n-1}x - (n-2)I_n + (n-2)I_{n-2}$.

Hence, $I_n = \frac{1}{n-1}(-\coth^{n-1}x) + I_{n-2}$.

State the result.

We can also deal with non-trigonometric functions. For example, consider $I_n = \int x^n e^x\,dx$. Using integration by parts, let $u = x^n$, $\frac{du}{dx} = nx^{n-1}$ and $\frac{dv}{dx} = e^x$, $v = e^x$.

Then $I_n = x^n e^x - n\int x^{n-1}e^x\,dx$. So with $I_{n-1} = \int x^{n-1}e^x\,dx$, $I_n = x^n e^x - nI_{n-1}$ for $n \geqslant 1$.

So if we have the integral $\int x^4 e^x\,dx$, $I_4 = x^4e^x - 4I_3$, $I_3 = x^3e^x - 3I_2$, $I_2 = x^2e^x - 2I_1$ and $I_1 = xe^x - I_0$, where $I_0 = e^x$.

Hence, $I_4 = x^4e^x - 4x^3e^x + 12x^2e^x - 24xe^x + 24e^x + c$.

Another example is $I_n = \int x^2(1+x^6)^n\,dx$. Using integration by parts, $u = (1+x^6)^n$, $\frac{du}{dx} = 6nx^5(1+x^6)^{n-1}$, $\frac{dv}{dx} = x^2$, and $v = \frac{1}{3}x^3$.

So $I_n = \frac{1}{3}x^3(1+x^6)^n - 2n\int x^8(1+x^6)^{n-1}\,dx$, but this looks as if the second part could never relate to I_n. We can do the algebra to rewrite $x^8 = x^2(1 + x^6 - 1)$. Substituting this into the expression gives $I_n = \frac{1}{3}x^3(1+x^6)^n - 2n\int x^2(1+x^6-1)(1+x^6)^{n-1}\,dx$.

$I_n = \frac{1}{3}x^3(1+x^6)^n - 2n\int x^2(1+x^6)^n\,dx + 2n\int x^2(1+x^6)^{n-1}\,dx$. As $I_n = \int x^2(1+x^6)^n\,dx$ and $I_{n-1} = \int x^2(1+x^6)^{n-1}\,dx$, the expression becomes $I_n = \frac{1}{3}x^3(1+x^6)^n - 2nI_n + 2nI_{n-1}$.

So $I_n = \frac{x^3(1+x^6)^n}{3(2n+1)} + \frac{2n}{2n+1}I_{n-1}$ for $n \geqslant 1$.

WORKED EXAMPLE 22.12

If $I_n = \int x^n(x^2 - 1)^9\,dx$, show, using integration by parts, that $I_n = \frac{x^{n-1}(x^2-1)^{10}}{n+19} + \frac{n-1}{n+19}I_{n-2}$ for $n \geqslant 2$.

Answer

Let $I_n = \int x^{n-1}x(x^2 - 1)^9\,dx$ then let $u = x^{n-1}$, $\frac{du}{dx} = (n-1)x^{n-2}$

and $\frac{dv}{dx} = x(x^2-1)^9$, $v = \frac{1}{20}(x^2-1)^{10}$.

Rewrite x^n as $x^{n-1}x$ so that we can integrate $x(x^2 - 1)^9$.

Then $I_n = \frac{x^{n-1}}{20}(x^2-1)^{10} - \frac{n-1}{20}\int x^{n-2}(x^2-1)^{10}\,dx$.

Let $(x^2-1)^{10} = (x^2-1)(x^2-1)^9$.

Rewrite $(x^2 - 1)^{10}$ as $(x^2 - 1)(x^2 - 1)^9$ so we get $(x^2 - 1)^9$ back in our expression.

Then $I_n = \frac{x^{n-1}}{20}(x^2-1)^{10} - \frac{n-1}{20}\int x^n(x^2-1)^9\,dx$
$+ \frac{n-1}{20}\int x^{n-2}(x^2-1)^9\,dx$.

Replace the integrals with their respective I_n form.

So $I_n = \frac{x^{n-1}}{20}(x^2-1)^{10} - \frac{n-1}{20}I_n + \frac{n-1}{20}I_{n-2}$.

Rearranging gives $I_n = \frac{x^{n-1}(x^2-1)^{10}}{n+19} + \frac{n-1}{n+19}I_{n-2}$.

If we have a definite integral (with limits) such as $I_4 = \int_0^{\frac{\pi}{6}} \tan^4 x\,dx$, it is best to find a reduction formula before substituting the limits.

Let $I_n = \int_0^{\frac{\pi}{6}} \tan^n x\,dx = \int_0^{\frac{\pi}{6}} \tan^2 x \tan^{n-2} x\,dx$. We choose $\tan^2 x$ because we can change this to $\sec^2 x - 1$ which we can integrate.

$$I_n = \int_0^{\frac{\pi}{6}} \sec^2 x \tan^{n-2} x\,dx - \int_0^{\frac{\pi}{6}} \tan^{n-2} x\,dx$$

The first term integrates to give $\frac{1}{n-1}\tan^{n-1} x$ so $I_n = \left[\frac{1}{n-1}\tan^{n-1} x\right]_0^{\frac{\pi}{6}} - I_{n-2}$. This is valid for $n \geqslant 2$.

Using limits in the integrated expression leads to $I_n = \frac{1}{n-1}\left(\frac{\sqrt{3}}{3}\right)^{n-1} - I_{n-2}$.

Look back at the original problem, $I_4 = \int_0^{\frac{\pi}{6}} \tan^4 x\,dx$.

$I_4 = \frac{1}{3} \times \frac{3\sqrt{3}}{27} - I_2$ and $I_2 = \frac{\sqrt{3}}{3} - I_0$ and $I_0 = \int_0^{\frac{\pi}{6}} 1\,dx = \frac{\pi}{6}$.

We find $I_2 = \frac{\sqrt{3}}{3} - \frac{\pi}{6}$. This leads to $I_4 = \frac{\pi}{6} - \frac{8\sqrt{3}}{27}$.

WORKED EXAMPLE 22.13

Show that $I_n = \int_0^{\frac{\pi}{2}} x^n \cos x \, dx$ has the reduction formula $I_n = \left(\frac{\pi}{2}\right)^n - n(n-1)I_{n-2}$ for $n \geqslant 2$. Hence, find the exact value of $\int_0^{\frac{\pi}{2}} x^3 \cos x \, dx$.

Answer

Let $u = x^n$, $\frac{dv}{dx} = \cos x$, so that $\frac{du}{dx} = nx^{n-1}$, $v = \sin x$. — State u and $\frac{dv}{dx}$ for integration by parts.

Then $I_n = [x^n \sin x]_0^{\frac{\pi}{2}} - n\int_0^{\frac{\pi}{2}} x^{n-1} \sin x \, dx$. — Notice that integration by parts will be needed twice.

Using integration by parts a second time, let $u = x^{n-1}$, $\frac{dv}{dx} = \sin x$ such that $\frac{du}{dx} = (n-1)x^{n-2}$, $v = -\cos x$. — Use integration by parts again and note that the last integral is kI_{n-2}.

Now $I_n = [x^n \sin x]_0^{\frac{\pi}{2}} - n([-x^{n-1} \cos x]_0^{\frac{\pi}{2}} + (n-1)\int_0^{\frac{\pi}{2}} x^{n-2} \cos x \, dx)$,

giving $I_n = [x^n \sin x + nx^{n-1} \cos x]_0^{\frac{\pi}{2}} - n(n-1)I_{n-2}$.

Thus $I_n = \left(\frac{\pi}{2}\right)^n - n(n-1)I_{n-2}$ for $n \geqslant 2$. — Simplify and show the result given.

So $I_3 = \left(\frac{\pi}{2}\right)^3 - 3 \times 2I_1$, and $I_1 = \int_0^{\frac{\pi}{2}} x \cos x \, dx$. — Use the reduction formula, then evaluate I_1.

Let $u = x$, $\frac{dv}{dx} = \cos x$, then $\frac{du}{dx} = 1$, $v = \sin x$.

So $I_1 = [x \sin x]_0^{\frac{\pi}{2}} - \int_0^{\frac{\pi}{2}} \sin x \, dx = [x \sin x + \cos x]_0^{\frac{\pi}{2}} = \frac{\pi}{2} - 1$. — Determine the value of I_1.

Hence, $I_3 = \frac{\pi^3}{8} - 3\pi + 6$. — Substitute I_1 into the reduction formula to find I_3.

EXERCISE 22B

PS 1 You are given that $I_5 = \int_0^{\frac{\pi}{4}} \tan^5 x \, dx$. Find, without using a reduction formula, a relationship between I_5 and I_3. [Hint: Use $\tan^2 x \equiv \sec^2 x - 1$.]

PS 2 Given that $I_6 = \int_0^1 x^6 e^x \, dx$, find a relationship between I_6 and I_4.

PS 3 Given that $I_4 = \int_0^1 x^6(1 + x^3)^4 \, dx$, find a relationship between I_4 and I_3.

PS 4 Find a reduction formula for $I_n = \int_0^{\frac{\pi}{4}} \sin^n 2x \, dx$, stating the values of n for which it is valid.

P 5 Given that $I_n = \int_0^{\frac{\pi}{4}} \sec^n x \, dx$, show that $I_n = \frac{(\sqrt{2})^{n-2}}{n-1} + \frac{n-2}{n-1}I_{n-2}$ for $n \geqslant 2$. Hence, determine the exact value of I_6.

P 6 You are given that $I_n = \int_0^1 x(1 - 2x^4)^n \, \mathrm{d}x$.

a Show that $I_n = \frac{(-1)^n}{4n + 2} + \frac{2n}{2n + 1} I_{n-1}$ for $n \geqslant 1$.

b Find the exact value of I_4.

P 7 Show that the reduction formula for $I_n = \int_0^1 x^n \mathrm{e}^{3x} \mathrm{d}x$ is $I_n = \frac{1}{3}\mathrm{e}^3 - \frac{n}{3} I_{n-1}$ for $n \geqslant 1$. Hence, find I_3, giving your answer in terms of e.

P 8 You are given that $I_n = \int_1^2 (\ln x)^n \mathrm{d}x$. Show that $I_n = 2(\ln 2)^n - nI_{n-1}$ for $n \geqslant 1$. Hence, determine the value of I_5, giving your answer correct to 4 decimal places.

M 9 Find the exact volume generated when $\sin^3 x$ is rotated about the x-axis from $x = 0$ to $x = \frac{\pi}{2}$.

22.3 Arc lengths and surface areas

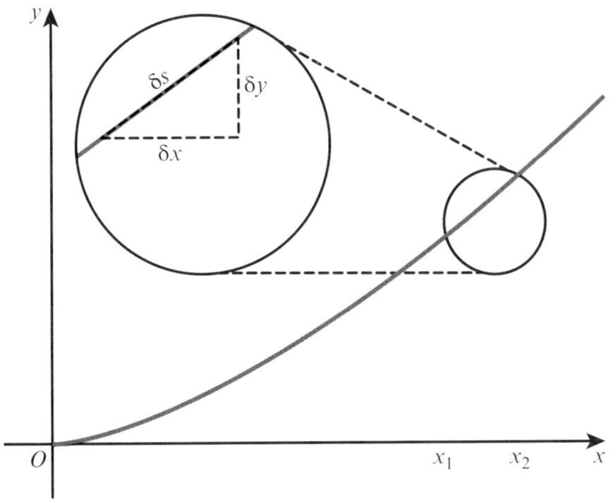

Consider the curve $y = \frac{1}{4}x^{\frac{3}{2}}$. We would like to know the length of this curve from $x = x_1$ to $x = x_2$.

To find the length, let us first call it s. So a small part of the curve is of length δs.

If we zoom in far enough, as in the diagram, that small section of curve now looks like a line segment. We can approximate its length with $(\delta s)^2 = (\delta x)^2 + (\delta y)^2$.

Next, divide all terms by $(\delta x)^2$ to get the relationship $\left(\frac{\delta s}{\delta x}\right)^2 = 1 + \left(\frac{\delta y}{\delta x}\right)^2$. Finding the square root gives $\frac{\delta s}{\delta x} = \sqrt{1 + \left(\frac{\delta y}{\delta x}\right)^2}$. Then we let $\delta x \to 0$, and integrate the expression to get $\int_{x_1}^{x_2} \frac{\mathrm{d}s}{\mathrm{d}x} \mathrm{d}x = \int_{x_1}^{x_2} \sqrt{1 + \left(\frac{\mathrm{d}y}{\mathrm{d}x}\right)^2} \mathrm{d}x$. Hence, $s = \int_{x_1}^{x_2} \sqrt{1 + \left(\frac{\mathrm{d}y}{\mathrm{d}x}\right)^2} \mathrm{d}x$. This is the Cartesian form for arc length, as shown in Key point 22.1.

Going back to the previous curve $y = \frac{1}{4}x^{\frac{3}{2}}$, to find the length of the curve from $x = 0$ to $x = 1$, we first differentiate to get $\frac{\mathrm{d}y}{\mathrm{d}x} = \frac{3}{8}x^{\frac{1}{2}}$, then $s = \int_0^1 \sqrt{1 + \frac{9}{64}x} \, \mathrm{d}x$.

Integrating gives $s = \left[\frac{128}{27}\left(1 + \frac{9}{64}x\right)^{\frac{3}{2}}\right]_0^1$. This gives $s = 1.03$.

KEY POINT 22.1

The length of an arc in Cartesian form is given by $s = \int_{x_1}^{x_2} \sqrt{1 + \left(\frac{dy}{dx}\right)^2}\, dx$.

DID YOU KNOW?

There is evidence of forms of calculus as far back as the 18th century BCE. Although this work does not have the rigour of calculus, it certainly tackled some applications of the calculus we know and use today.

WORKED EXAMPLE 22.14

Find the length of the curve $y = \cosh x$ from $x = 0$ to $x = \ln 2$.

Answer

If $y = \cosh x$, then $\frac{dy}{dx} = \sinh x$. — Differentiate y with respect to x.

So $s = \int_0^{\ln 2} \sqrt{1 + \sinh^2 x}\, dx$. — Put the result into the formula.

Use the identity $\cosh^2 x - \sinh^2 x = 1$.
$s = \int_0^{\ln 2} \sqrt{\cosh^2 x}\, dx$ — Use the identity to simplify the integral.

$s = [\sinh x]_0^{\ln 2} = \frac{3}{4}$ — Integrate and evaluate.

EXPLORE 22.1

One of the hyperbolic functions has the property that, over a finite interval, its arc length is always equal to the area under the curve. Investigate the hyperbolic functions and determine which one it is.

If a curve is given in parametric form, such as $x = t^2, y = t^3$, we need a different way of working out arc length.

It is still true that $(\delta s)^2 = (\delta x)^2 + (\delta y)^2$, but since our curve is parametric, we shall now divide by $(\delta t)^2$ instead. This gives $\left(\frac{\delta s}{\delta t}\right)^2 = \left(\frac{\delta x}{\delta t}\right)^2 + \left(\frac{\delta y}{\delta t}\right)^2$.

Taking the square root and letting $\delta t \to 0$ gives $\frac{ds}{dt} = \sqrt{\left(\frac{dx}{dt}\right)^2 + \left(\frac{dy}{dt}\right)^2}$.

Finally, integrating over the interval $t_1 \leqslant t \leqslant t_2$ gives $s = \int_{t_1}^{t_2} \sqrt{\left(\frac{dx}{dt}\right)^2 + \left(\frac{dy}{dt}\right)^2}\, dt$.

This is the parametric form for arc length, as shown in Key point 22.2.

For example, if $x = t^2, y = t^3$, we first differentiate both functions with respect to t. This gives $\frac{dx}{dt} = 2t$ and $\frac{dy}{dt} = 3t^2$. Let the limits be, for example, $t = 1$ and $t = 2$.

So $s = \int_1^2 \sqrt{4t^2 + 9t^4}\,dt$, which is $s = \int_1^2 t\sqrt{4 + 9t^2}\,dt$. This simple integral is $\left[\frac{1}{27}(4 + 9t^2)^{\frac{3}{2}}\right]_1^2$, and when it is evaluated the result is $s = 7.63$.

KEY POINT 22.2

The length of an arc in parametric form is given by $s = \int_{t_1}^{t_2} \sqrt{\left(\frac{dx}{dt}\right)^2 + \left(\frac{dy}{dt}\right)^2}\,dt$.

WORKED EXAMPLE 22.15

If $x = \cos^2 t$ and $y = \sin^2 t$, determine the length of the parametric curve from $t = 0$ to $t = \frac{\pi}{4}$.

Answer

$\frac{dx}{dt} = -2\sin t\cos t$ and $\frac{dy}{dt} = 2\sin t\cos t$. — Differentiate both parametric functions with respect to t.

Then $s = \int_0^{\frac{\pi}{4}} \sqrt{8\sin^2 t\cos^2 t}\,dt = \int_0^{\frac{\pi}{4}} \sqrt{2\sin^2 2t}\,dt$ using the double angle formula for $\sin 2t$. — Recognise that when squared the differentiated expressions are the same. Use the sine double angle formula and simplify the result.

So $s = \int_0^{\frac{\pi}{4}} \sqrt{2}\sin 2t\,dt$. Integrating gives $\left[-\frac{\sqrt{2}}{2}\cos 2t\right]_0^{\frac{\pi}{4}}$. — Integrate.

This evaluates to $\frac{\sqrt{2}}{2}$. — Evaluate to get the result.

If a curve is given in polar form, such as $r = e^\theta$, we need a different way of working out arc length.

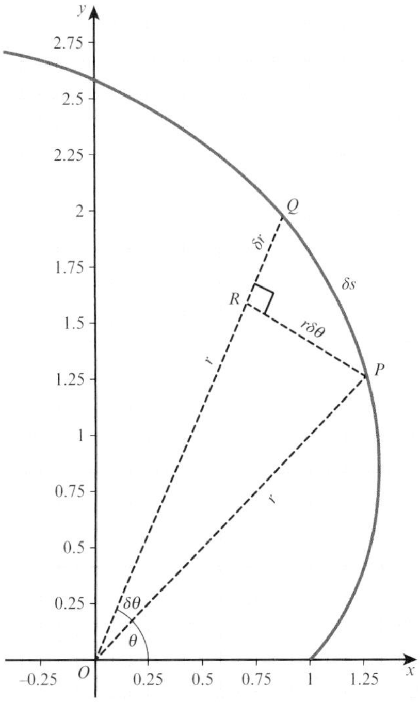

Begin with a general curve as shown. We can think of a small part of the curve PQ as our small length δs.

Then we have $RQ = \delta r$. If we consider OPR as a sector, as $\delta\theta \to 0$, $RP \approx r\delta\theta$, and also the angle at R approaches a right angle.

As this happens, we can say that $PQ^2 = (\delta r)^2 + (r\delta\theta)^2$.

Letting $PQ = \delta s$, $\left(\frac{\delta s}{\delta\theta}\right)^2 = \left(\frac{\delta r}{\delta\theta}\right)^2 + r^2$

so $\frac{\delta s}{\delta\theta} = \sqrt{r^2 + \left(\frac{\delta r}{\delta\theta}\right)^2}$. If we consider $\delta\theta \to 0$ and integrate this gives us the result $s = \int_{\theta_1}^{\theta_2} \sqrt{r^2 + \left(\frac{dr}{d\theta}\right)^2}\,d\theta$.

Returning to our example of $r = e^\theta$, let us try to find the arc length over the interval 0 to $\frac{\pi}{2}$.

$\frac{dr}{d\theta} = e^\theta$, then $s = \int_0^{\frac{\pi}{2}} \sqrt{e^{2\theta} + e^{2\theta}}\,d\theta$ which simplifies to $s = \int_0^{\frac{\pi}{2}} \sqrt{2}e^\theta\,d\theta$.

Integrating, $s = \sqrt{2}[e^\theta]_0^{\frac{\pi}{2}}$, which gives $s = \sqrt{2}(e^{\frac{\pi}{2}} - 1)$.

KEY POINT 22.3

The length of an arc in polar form is given by $s = \int_{\theta_1}^{\theta_2} \sqrt{r^2 + \left(\frac{\mathrm{d}r}{\mathrm{d}\theta}\right)^2}\,\mathrm{d}\theta$.

WORKED EXAMPLE 22.16

If $r = \sin\theta$, determine the length of the polar curve over the interval $\left[0, \frac{\pi}{4}\right]$.

Answer

Differentiating, $\frac{\mathrm{d}r}{\mathrm{d}\theta} = \cos\theta$. — Differentiate the polar function.

Then $s = \int_0^{\frac{\pi}{4}} \sqrt{\sin^2\theta + \cos^2\theta}\,\mathrm{d}\theta = \int_0^{\frac{\pi}{4}} 1\,\mathrm{d}\theta$ — Substitute into the formula and simplify.

using $\sin^2\theta + \cos^2\theta = 1$.

Integrating gives $[\theta]_0^{\frac{\pi}{4}}$ which evaluates to be $\frac{\pi}{4}$. — Integrate and substitute in limits to get the result.

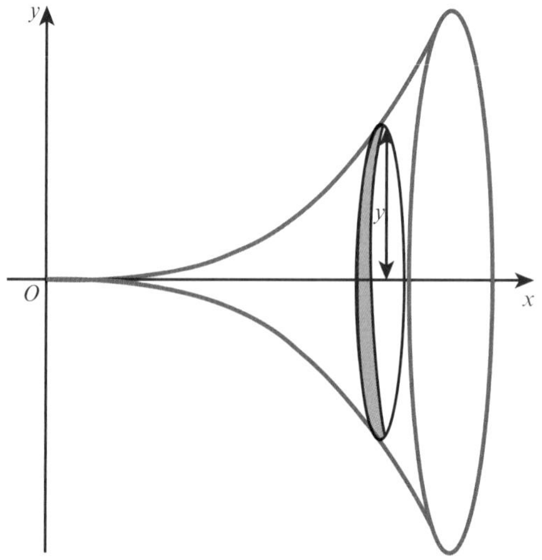

We can also determine the surface area generated when an arc of a curve is rotated about an axis, as shown in the diagram. We can imagine a strip generating a solid which approximates to a frustum. Its curved surface area is what we are trying to find.

Let S be the surface area when the curve is rotated about the x-axis. The small piece of surface area generated by a small arc δs is approximately $\delta S = 2\pi y\,\delta s$.

As $\delta\theta \to 0$, using a similar argument as for arc length, we obtain these two results:

$S = \int_{x_1}^{x_2} 2\pi y \sqrt{1 + \left(\frac{\mathrm{d}y}{\mathrm{d}x}\right)^2}\,\mathrm{d}x$ for Cartesian curves, and $S = \int_{t_1}^{t_2} 2\pi y \sqrt{\left(\frac{\mathrm{d}x}{\mathrm{d}t}\right)^2 + \left(\frac{\mathrm{d}y}{\mathrm{d}t}\right)^2}\,\mathrm{d}t$ for parametric curves. The radius, y, appears in both formulae and the expression under the square root sign in both cases is $\frac{\mathrm{d}s}{\mathrm{d}t}$.

Consider the curve $y = \frac{1}{3}x^3$. We would like to determine the surface area generated when the curve is rotated about the x-axis from $x = 0$ to $x = 1$.

Differentiate with respect to x to get $\frac{dy}{dx} = x^2$. Then

$$S = \int_0^1 2\pi \frac{1}{3}x^3\sqrt{1 + (x^2)^2}\,dx = \frac{2}{3}\pi\int_0^1 x^3\sqrt{1 + x^4}\,dx.$$

Integrating gives $S = \frac{2}{3}\pi\left[\frac{1}{6}(1 + x^4)^{\frac{3}{2}}\right]_0^1$. So the surface area generated is $S = \frac{\pi}{9}(2\sqrt{2} - 1)$.

TIP

For an integral of the form $\int\sqrt{a^2 + b^2x^2}\,dx$ it is best to use a hyperbolic substitution of the form $bx = a\sinh\theta$. This gives $\int\frac{a^2}{b}\cosh^2\theta\,d\theta$.

The alternative is to use $bx = a\tan\theta$. This transforms the integral to $\int\frac{a^2}{b}\sec^3\theta\,d\theta$ which is a little more difficult.

WORKED EXAMPLE 22.17

Given that $y = x^{\frac{1}{2}}$, determine the surface area generated when the curve is rotated about the x-axis from $x = 2$ to $x = 12$.

Answer

Since $y = x^{\frac{1}{2}}$, then $\frac{dy}{dx} = \frac{1}{2\sqrt{x}}$. — Differentiate the curve with respect to x.

So $S = \int_2^{12} 2\pi\sqrt{x}\sqrt{1 + \frac{1}{4x}}\,dx$.

$S = \int_2^{12} 2\pi\sqrt{x}\frac{\sqrt{4x + 1}}{2\sqrt{x}}\,dx$, — Take the $4x$ out of the square root.

giving $S = \int_2^{12} \pi\sqrt{4x + 1}\,dx$. — Cancel terms to simplify the integral.

Integrating, $S = \pi\left[\frac{1}{6}(4x + 1)^{\frac{3}{2}}\right]_2^{12}$. — Integrate and evaluate.

This gives the surface area $S = \frac{158}{3}\pi$.

WORKED EXAMPLE 22.18

The equation for the movement of an asteroid is given by $x = a\cos^3 t$, $y = a\sin^3 t$, where a is a constant. Determine the surface area formed when the curve is rotated about the x-axis from $t = 0$ to $t = \frac{\pi}{2}$.

Answer

$\frac{dx}{dt} = -3a\cos^2 t\sin t$, $\frac{dy}{dt} = 3a\sin^2 t\cos t$ — Differentiate both parametric functions with respect to t.

$S = 2\pi\int_0^{\frac{\pi}{2}} a\sin^3 t\sqrt{9a^2\cos^4 t\sin^2 t + 9a^2\sin^4 t\cos^2 t}\,dt$ — Substitute into the formula.

Simplify by taking out the common terms from under the square root. — Note that $9a^2$, $\cos^2 t$, $\sin^2 t$ are common terms.

This gives $S = 2\pi\int_0^{\frac{\pi}{2}} 3a^2\cos t\sin^4 t\sqrt{\cos^2 t + \sin^2 t}\,dt$.	Use $\cos^2 t + \sin^2 t = 1$.
So $S = 6\pi a^2\int_0^{\frac{\pi}{2}} \cos t\sin^4 t\,dt$	Note that $\frac{d}{dt}(\sin^5 t) = 5\cos t\sin^4 t$
Next integrate to get $S = 6\pi a^2\left[\frac{1}{5}\sin^5 t\right]_0^{\frac{\pi}{2}}$.	
This gives a result of $\frac{6\pi a^2}{5}$.	Evaluate with limits given.

Instead of rotating the curve about the x-axis, we can rotate it about the y-axis. The difference between these two rotations is that the radius x appears in our formulae rather than y.

The result for the surface area is $S = \int_{x_1}^{x_2} 2\pi x\sqrt{1 + \left(\frac{dy}{dx}\right)^2}\,dx$ in Cartesian form, and $S = \int_{t_1}^{t_2} 2\pi x\sqrt{\left(\frac{dx}{dt}\right)^2 + \left(\frac{dy}{dt}\right)^2}\,dt$ in parametric form.

Consider rotating the curve $y = x^2$ about the y-axis between $x = 1$ and $x = 2$. First find $\frac{dy}{dx} = 2x$. Next substitute into $S = \int_{x_1}^{x_2} 2\pi x\sqrt{1 + \left(\frac{dy}{dx}\right)^2}\,dx$ to get $S = \int_1^2 2\pi x\sqrt{1 + 4x^2}\,dx$.

This integrates to give $S = \left[\frac{\pi}{6}(1 + 4x^2)^{\frac{3}{2}}\right]_1^2$.

Evaluating leads to the answer $S = \frac{\pi}{6}(17\sqrt{17} - 5\sqrt{5})$.

WORKED EXAMPLE 22.19

A curve is defined parametrically as $x = \cos^2 2t$, $y = \sin^2 2t$ for $0 \leqslant t \leqslant \frac{\pi}{4}$. Determine the surface area generated when this curve is rotated about the y-axis.

Answer

$\frac{dx}{dt} = -4\sin 2t\cos 2t$ and $\frac{dy}{dt} = 4\sin 2t\cos 2t$.	Differentiate both functions with respect to t.
$\frac{ds}{dt} = \sqrt{32\cos^2 2t\sin^2 2t}$	Determine the result of $\frac{ds}{dt}$.
So $S = \int_0^{\frac{\pi}{4}} 2\pi\cos^2 2t \times 4\sqrt{2}\cos 2t\sin 2t\,dt$,	Substitute it into the formula and simplify the integral.
which simplifies to $S = 8\pi\sqrt{2}\int_0^{\frac{\pi}{4}} \cos^3 2t\sin 2t\,dt$.	Note that $\frac{d}{dt}(\cos^4 2t) = -8\sin 2t\cos^3 2t$
Integrating gives $S = 8\pi\sqrt{2}\left[-\frac{1}{8}\cos^4 2t\right]_0^{\frac{\pi}{4}}$, giving $S = \pi\sqrt{2}$.	Use the limits to get the result.

EXERCISE 22C

M 1 Find the length of the curve $y = 4x^{\frac{3}{2}}$ from $x = 1$ to $x = 2$. Give your answer to 3 decimal places.

M 2 Find the surface area of revolution formed when the curve represented by $x = \sin t, y = \cos t$, for $t = 0, t = \frac{\pi}{2}$, is rotated about the x-axis by 2π radians.

M 3 The curve C is given as $y = \frac{1}{3}(x-4)^{\frac{3}{2}}$. Find the length of the curve from $x = 4$ to $x = 9$.

M 4 Find the length of the curve $y = \frac{1}{2}e^x + \frac{1}{2}e^{-x}$ from $x = \ln 2$ to $x = \ln 3$.

M 5 Find, to 1 decimal place, the surface area of revolution formed when $y = (x-2)^3$ is rotated about the x-axis from $x = 3$ to $x = 4$.

P PS 6 Given that $x = \frac{1}{3}t^3, y = \frac{1}{2}t^2$, show that the arc length of the curve can be represented as $s = \int_{t_1}^{t_2}(t^2 + t^4)^{\frac{1}{2}}\,dt$.
Hence, determine, to 3 significant figures, the length of the curve for $1 \leqslant t \leqslant 2$.

P 7 The curve C is given as $y = \frac{1}{2}x^2$.

a Show that the surface area of revolution of the curve about the x-axis from $x = 0$ to $x = 1$ is $S = \int_0^1 \pi x^2(1 + x^2)^{\frac{1}{2}}\,dx$.

b Using the substitution $x = \tan\theta$, or otherwise, show that the surface area of revolution can then be written as $S = \pi\int_0^{\frac{\pi}{4}}(\sec^5\theta - \sec^3\theta)d\theta$.

c Hence, find the surface area of revolution.

M 8 The polar curve C is given as $r = \theta$. Find, to three decimal places, the length of the curve from $\theta = 0.1$ to $\theta = 0.3$.

22.4 Limits of areas

Imagine we wish to determine the result of an infinite summation such as $\sum_{n=1}^{\infty} f(n)$. We can consider that each unit step is a rectangle of height $f(n)$, and then draw the analogy between the sum of these areas and an integral of the form $\int_1^{\infty} f(x)\,dx$. In this way, we can determine whether the summation converges or diverges.

A very famous series is the harmonic series, given as $\sum_{n=1}^{\infty}\frac{1}{n} = 1 + \frac{1}{2} + \frac{1}{3} + \frac{1}{4} + \cdots$.

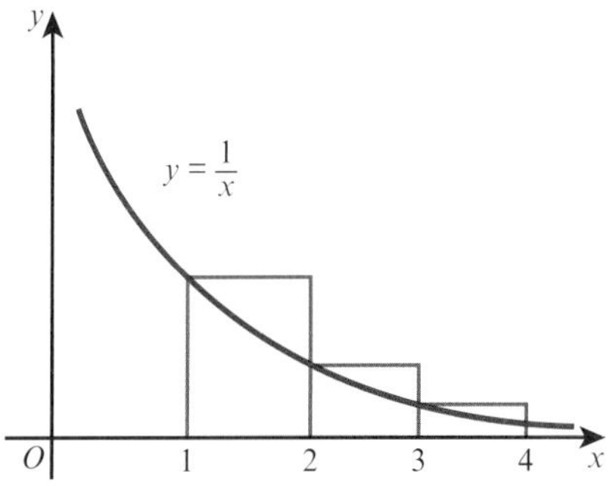

This series actually diverges, and to confirm this, we consider the result of $\int_1^n \frac{1}{x}\,dx$.

Integrating, $\int_1^n \frac{1}{x}dx = [\ln x]_1^n = \ln n$. Then as $n \to \infty$ our area is infinite. Looking at the diagram it is clear that the area between the curve and the x-axis is less than the area of the rectangles. However, we just determined that the area under the curve is infinite, which implies that the series $\sum_{n=1}^{\infty}\frac{1}{n} = 1 + \frac{1}{2} + \frac{1}{3} + \frac{1}{4} + \cdots$ must also tend to infinity. This is known as the **integral test**.

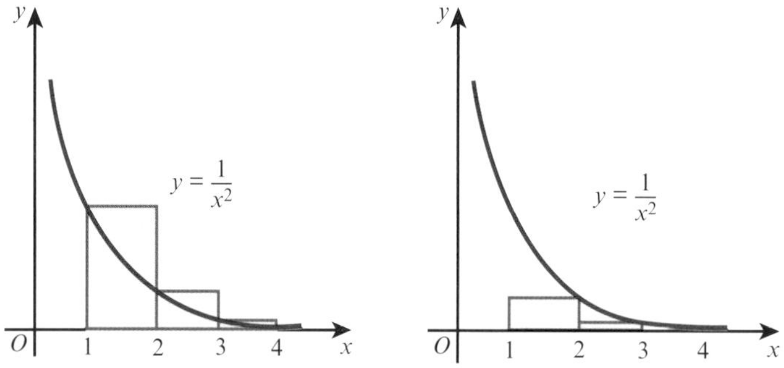

Consider this again with $\sum_{n=1}^{\infty}\frac{1}{n^2}$. We do not know whether this series converges. Let us consider calculating an upper bound using the integral. See the graph of $y = \frac{1}{x^2}$ above. The first graph shows the area between the curve and the x-axis estimated using rectangles of unit width where the top left corner of each rectangle determines each rectangle's height. With this method the curve acts as a lower bound.

If instead we use the top right corner of each rectangle to determine each rectangle's height, as in the second graph, we can see that the curve can act as an upper bound. In fact, the curve is an upper bound for $\frac{1}{2^2} + \frac{1}{3^2} + \frac{1}{4^2} + \ldots + \frac{1}{n^2} = \sum_{r=2}^{n}\frac{1}{r^2}$ so to find an upper bound for $\sum_{r=1}^{n}\frac{1}{r^2}$ we require the area under the curve plus one.

Therefore, $\sum_{r=1}^{n}\frac{1}{r^2} < 1 + \int_{1}^{n}\frac{1}{x^2}\,dx$

$$\sum_{r=1}^{n}\frac{1}{r^2} < 1 + \left[-\frac{1}{x}\right]_1^n$$

$$\sum_{r=1}^{n}\frac{1}{r^2} < 2 - \frac{1}{n}$$

As $n \to \infty$, this tends to 2. We see that $\sum_{r=1}^{n}\frac{1}{r^2}$ must also converge since the right side summation converges.

We can also calculate a lower bound for the sum by considering the first graph. Here, the curve underestimates the summation so makes a lower bound.

Note that we are finding the area of rectangles with the left-hand edge of the first rectangle at 1. The last rectangle will *end* at $n + 1$ and so we can state that:

$$\sum_{r=1}^{n}\frac{1}{r^2} > \int_{1}^{n+1}\frac{1}{x^2}\,dx$$

$$\sum_{r=1}^{n}\frac{1}{r^2} > \left[-\frac{1}{x}\right]_1^{n+1}$$

$$\sum_{r=1}^{n}\frac{1}{r^2} > 1 - \frac{1}{n+1}$$

So we can deduce the limit as $n \to \infty$ is 1.

WORKED EXAMPLE 22.20

a Find the upper and lower bounds for $\sum_{r=1}^{n} \frac{1}{r\sqrt{r}}$.

b Evaluate the infinite sum $\sum_{n=1}^{\infty} \frac{1}{n\sqrt{n}}$. If the summation converges, give an estimate for the upper bound.

Answer

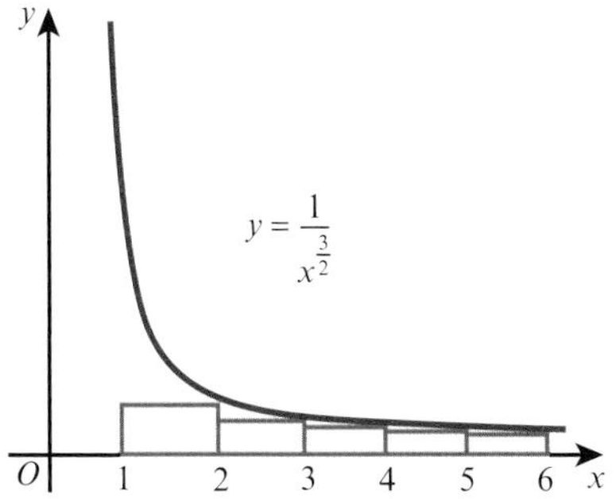

a We need to recognise that $\sum_{r=2}^{n} \frac{1}{r\sqrt{r}} < \int_1^n x^{-\frac{3}{2}} dx$.

Therefore $\sum_{r=1}^{n} \frac{1}{r\sqrt{r}} < 1 + \int_1^n x^{-\frac{3}{2}} dx$ — Relate the integral to those terms we are evaluating and adjust accordingly (by adding 1 in this case).

$\sum_{r=1}^{n} \frac{1}{r\sqrt{r}} < 1 + [-2x^{-\frac{1}{2}}]_1^n$ — Integrate.

$\sum_{r=1}^{n} \frac{1}{r\sqrt{r}} < 1 + \left(2 - \frac{2}{\sqrt{n}}\right)$

$\sum_{r=1}^{n} \frac{1}{r\sqrt{r}} < 3 - \frac{2}{\sqrt{n}}$

So the upper bound is $3 - \frac{2}{\sqrt{n}}$.

Now for the lower bound:

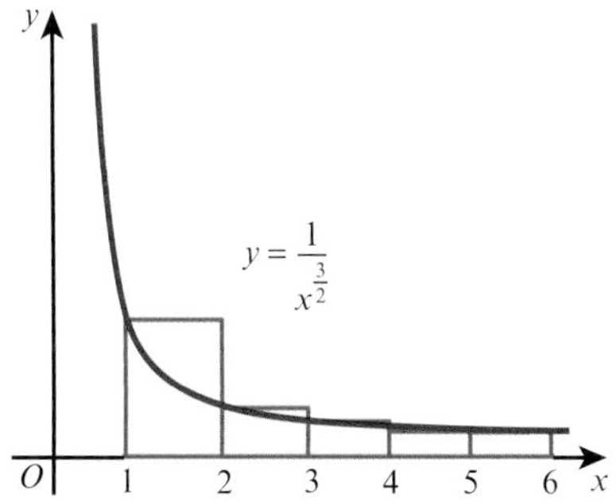

$$\sum_{r=1}^{n} \frac{1}{r\sqrt{r}} > \int_1^{n+1} x^{-\frac{3}{2}}\,dx$$

Make sure that the upper value on the integral covers all of the rectangles to be summed.

$$\sum_{r=1}^{n} \frac{1}{r\sqrt{r}} > \left[-2x^{-\frac{1}{2}}\right]_1^{n+1}$$

$$\sum_{r=1}^{n} \frac{1}{r\sqrt{r}} > 2 - \frac{2}{\sqrt{n+1}}$$

So the lower bound is $2 - \frac{2}{\sqrt{n+1}}$.

b The upper bound is $3 - \frac{2}{\sqrt{n}}$.

We consider $n \to \infty$, then $\sum_{r=1}^{\infty} \frac{1}{r\sqrt{r}} < 3$ since $\frac{1}{\sqrt{n}} \to 0$,

so the upper bound is 3.

Let the area under a curve be denoted R and the area of a summation of rectangles be denoted by S.

- If $R > S$ and R converges, then S also converges.
- If $R < S$ and R diverges, then S also diverges.
- If $R > S$ and R diverges, this does not imply anything about S.
- If $R < S$ and R converges, this does not imply anything about S.

In either of the last two cases, we need to approach the problem in a different way.

EXPLORE 22.2

Investigate the summation $\sum_{n=1}^{\infty} \frac{1}{n^p}$ with varying powers of p. When does it converge and when does it diverge? Can you devise a proof to confirm your findings?

So if we are asked to determine whether $\sum_{n=1}^{\infty} \frac{n}{n^2+1}$ converges or diverges, we first relate this to the integral $\int_1^{\infty} \frac{x}{x^2+1}\,dx$. This has a smaller area than the summation of rectangles for $\sum_{n=1}^{\infty} \frac{n}{n^2+1}$.

Integrating, we get $\left[\frac{1}{2}\ln|x^2+1|\right]_1^{\infty}$, which diverges. Hence, $\sum_{n=1}^{\infty} \frac{n}{n^2+1}$ also diverges.

WORKED EXAMPLE 22.21

Find the upper bound for $\sum_{r=2}^{n} \frac{1}{r \ln r}$. Hence, show that $\sum_{n=2}^{\infty} \frac{1}{n \ln n}$ diverges.

Answer

Consider the integral that will be the upper bound and summation it will relate to.

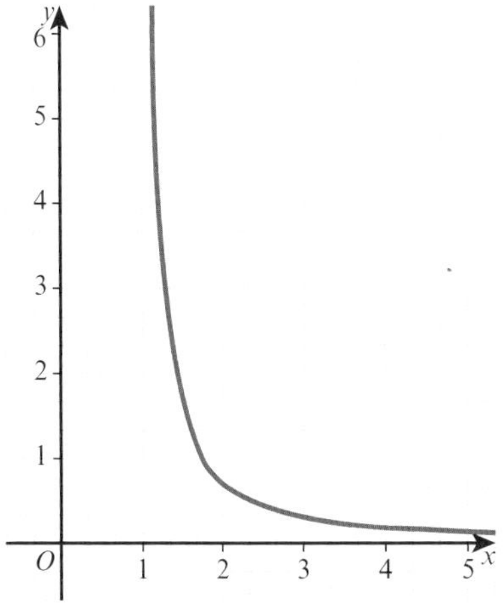

$$\sum_{r=3}^{n} \frac{1}{r \ln r} < \int_{2}^{n} \frac{1}{x \ln x} \mathrm{d}x$$

Relate the summation to an integral.

$$\sum_{r=2}^{n} \frac{1}{r \ln r} < 2 \ln 2 + \int_{2}^{n} \frac{1}{x \ln x} \mathrm{d}x$$

Recognise that the integral, when considered as $\int_{2}^{n} \frac{1/x}{\ln x}$ is of the form $\int_{2}^{\infty} \frac{\mathrm{f}'(x)}{\mathrm{f}(x)} \mathrm{d}x$.

$$\sum_{r=2}^{n} \frac{1}{r \ln r} < 2 \ln 2 + [\ln |\ln x|]_{2}^{n}$$

Integrate.

$$\sum_{r=2}^{n} \frac{1}{r \ln r} < 2 \ln 2 + \ln |\ln n| - \ln |\ln 2|$$

Evaluate.

If we consider $n \to \infty$, this upper bound diverges.

State that the summation diverges.

Another way to determine convergence or divergence is to compare summations with known integrals. For example:

$\sum_{n=2}^{\infty} \frac{1}{n^2}$ can be replaced by $\int_{2}^{\infty} \frac{1}{x^2 - 1} \mathrm{d}x$, which is larger than $\int_{2}^{\infty} \frac{1}{x^2} \mathrm{d}x$.

Integrating $\int_{2}^{\infty} \frac{1}{x^2 - 1} \mathrm{d}x$ leads to $\left[\frac{1}{2} \ln \left(\frac{x-1}{x+1}\right)\right]_{2}^{\infty}$.

$\left[\frac{1}{2} \ln \left(\frac{x-1}{x+1}\right)\right]_{2}^{\infty}$ then evaluates to be $\frac{1}{2} \ln 3$, which is finite in size.

Hence, if $\int_{2}^{\infty} \frac{1}{x^2 - 1} \mathrm{d}x$ is finite and larger than $\int_{2}^{\infty} \frac{1}{x^2} \mathrm{d}x$, this tells us that $\int_{2}^{\infty} \frac{1}{x^2} \mathrm{d}x$ must also be finite. Hence $\sum_{n=2}^{\infty} \frac{1}{n^2}$ must converge.

WORKED EXAMPLE 22.22

Show that $\sum_{n=1}^{\infty} \frac{1}{\sqrt{n}}$ diverges by using a comparison.

Answer

Since $\frac{1}{\sqrt{n}} > \frac{1}{\sqrt{n+1}}$, the integral $\int_1^{\infty} \frac{1}{\sqrt{x+1}} \mathrm{d}x$ can be used. — State a function that is known to be smaller than $\frac{1}{\sqrt{n}}$.

So $\int_1^{\infty} \frac{1}{\sqrt{x+1}} \mathrm{d}x = \int_1^{\infty} (x+1)^{-\frac{1}{2}} \mathrm{d}x$, which is $\left[2(x+1)^{\frac{1}{2}}\right]_1^{\infty}$. — Integrate.

Evaluating leads to a result which tends to infinity. — Evaluate to show that the value tends to infinity.

So if $\int_1^{\infty} \frac{1}{\sqrt{x+1}} \mathrm{d}x$ diverges, $\sum_{n=1}^{\infty} \frac{1}{\sqrt{n}}$ also diverges. — State the comparison that leads to the conclusion that the original summation diverges.

WORKED EXAMPLE 22.23

Using a similar function, show that $\sum_{n=2}^{\infty} \frac{1}{\sqrt{n^2-3}}$ diverges.

Answer

Start with $\frac{1}{\sqrt{n^2-3}} > \frac{1}{\sqrt{n^2}} = \frac{1}{n}$. — State a function that is both smaller and easier to integrate.

As we saw earlier, $\sum_{n=2}^{\infty} \frac{1}{n}$ diverges. — Recall that the harmonic series diverges.

So $\sum_{n=2}^{\infty} \frac{1}{\sqrt{n^2-3}}$ must also diverge. — State the result.

When an alternative expression is used to evaluate a sum, it is known as a **comparison test**.

EXERCISE 22D

PS 1 By using the integral test or otherwise, determine whether $\sum_{n=1}^{\infty} \frac{1}{n+2}$ converges or diverges.

P 2 Show that $\sum_{n=1}^{\infty} \frac{\ln n}{n+4}$ diverges.

PS 3 Using the integral test or otherwise, determine whether $\sum_{n=1}^{\infty} \frac{1}{n^2+1}$ converges or diverges.

P 4 Show that $\sum_{n=1}^{\infty} \frac{\ln n}{n^2}$ converges.

PS 5 Determine whether $\sum_{n=1}^{\infty} \frac{1}{e^n}$ converges or diverges.

P 6 Using the comparison test, or otherwise, show that $\sum_{n=1}^{\infty} \frac{1}{\sqrt{n^2+3}}$ diverges.

PS 7 Determine whether $\sum_{n=1}^{\infty} \frac{\ln n}{n^3}$ converges or diverges.

PS 8 Does $\sum_{n=1}^{\infty} \frac{3n^2+4}{2n^2+3n+5}$ converge or diverge?

PS 9 Evaluate whether $\sum_{n=1}^{\infty} \frac{3^n}{2^n+5^n}$ converges or diverges.

WORKED PAST PAPER QUESTION

a The curve C_1 has equation $y = -\ln(\cos x)$. Show that the length of the arc of C_1 from the point where $x = 0$ to the point where $x = \frac{1}{3}\pi$ is $\ln(2+\sqrt{3})$.

b The curve C_2 has equation $y = 2\sqrt{(x+3)}$. The arc of C_2 joining the point where $x = 0$ to the point where $x = 1$ is rotated through one complete revolution about the x-axis. Show that the area of the surface generated is $\frac{8}{3}\pi(5\sqrt{5}-8)$.

Cambridge International AS and A Level Further Mathematics 9231 Paper 1 Q8 November 2009

Answer

a Since $y = -\ln \cos x$, we can write $y = \ln \sec x$. Then $\frac{dy}{dx} = \frac{\sec x \tan x}{\sec x} = \tan x$.

Then $s = \int_0^{\frac{\pi}{3}} [1 + \tan^2 x]^{\frac{1}{2}} dx$, which simplifies to $s = \int_0^{\frac{\pi}{3}} \sec x \, dx$.

Integrating leads to $s = [\ln|(\sec x + \tan x|)]_0^{\frac{\pi}{3}} = \ln|2+\sqrt{3}| - \ln 1$,

which leads to $s = \ln(2+\sqrt{3})$.

As the answer is given in the question, we must show all steps in the working.

b From $y = 2\sqrt{x+3}$ we have $\frac{dy}{dx} = \frac{1}{\sqrt{x+3}}$.

Then $ds = \left[1 + \frac{1}{x+3}\right]^{\frac{1}{2}} dx$, which is $\left[\frac{x+4}{x+3}\right]^{\frac{1}{2}} dx$.

Next, $S = 2\pi \int_0^1 2\sqrt{x+3}\frac{\sqrt{x+4}}{\sqrt{x+3}} dx = 4\pi \int_0^1 \sqrt{x+4}\, dx$.

So $S = 4\pi\left[\frac{2}{3}(x+4)^{\frac{3}{2}}\right]_0^1$, which leads to $\frac{8}{3}\pi(5\sqrt{5}-8)$.

Checklist of learning and understanding

For some standard integrals:

- $\int \frac{1}{a^2+x^2}\,dx$ can be solved with $x = a\tan\theta$ to give $\frac{1}{a}\tan^{-1}\frac{x}{a} + c$.
- $\int \frac{1}{\sqrt{a^2-x^2}}\,dx$, can be solved with $x = a\sin\theta$ to give $\sin^{-1}\frac{x}{a} + c$.
- $\int \frac{1}{a^2-x^2}\,dx$ can be solved with $x = a\tanh\theta$ to give $\frac{1}{a}\tanh^{-1}\frac{x}{a} + c$.

For inverse functions such as $\cosh^{-1}x$, to integrate:

- Consider $\int 1 \times \cosh^{-1}x\,dx$ to use integration by parts.
- Differentiate the inverse function; integrate the '1'.
- Use integration by parts to obtain the result.

For reduction formulae with an integral such as $I_n = \int \sec^n x\,dx$:

- Split the power such that the lower power can be integrated, and the higher power can be differentiated.
- Look for the original form in your solution, such as $\int \sec^{n-2} x\,dx$ represented as I_{n-2}.

For arc length and surface area of a revolution:

- For arc length in Cartesian form, $s = \int_{x_1}^{x_2}\left[1 + \left(\frac{dy}{dx}\right)^2\right]^{\frac{1}{2}} dx$.
- For arc length in parametric form, $s = \int_{t_1}^{t_2}\left[\left(\frac{dx}{dt}\right)^2 + \left(\frac{dy}{dt}\right)^2\right]^{\frac{1}{2}} dt$.
- For arc length in polar form, $s = \int_{\theta_1}^{\theta_2}\sqrt{r^2 + \left(\frac{dr}{d\theta}\right)^2}\,d\theta$.
- For surface area of a revolution about the x-axis, $S = \int_a^b 2\pi y\,ds$, where $ds = \left[1 + \left(\frac{dy}{dx}\right)^2\right]^{\frac{1}{2}} dx$ or $ds = \left[\left(\frac{dx}{dt}\right)^2 + \left(\frac{dy}{dt}\right)^2\right]^{\frac{1}{2}} dt$.
- For surface area of a revolution about the y-axis, $S = \int_a^b 2\pi x\,ds$.

For evaluating summations:

- A summation $\sum_{n=1}^{\infty} f(n)$ can be replaced by $\int_1^{\infty} f(x)\,dx$.
- If the integral area is less than the summation area, and the integral area diverges, then the summation area also diverges.
- If the integral area is greater than the summation area, and the integral area converges, then the summation area also converges.
- For summations such as $\sum_{n=2}^{\infty}\frac{1}{n^2\ln n}$, compare this to $\sum_{n=2}^{\infty}\frac{1}{n^2}$.

END-OF-CHAPTER REVIEW EXERCISE 22

P 1 A curve has equation $y = \frac{1}{3}x^3 + 1$.

The length of the arc of the curve joining the point where $x = 0$ to the point where $x = 1$ is denoted by s.

Show that $s = \int_0^1 \sqrt{1 + x^4}\,dx$.

The surface area generated when this arc is rotated through one complete revolution about the x-axis is denoted by S. Show that $S = \frac{1}{9}\pi(18s + 2\sqrt{2} - 1)$.

[Do not attempt to evaluate s or S.]

Cambridge International AS & A Level Further Mathematics 9231 Paper 1 Q4 June 2009

P 2 Let $I_n = \int_0^1 x^n(1 - x)^{\frac{1}{2}}\,dx$, for $n \geqslant 0$.

Show that, for $n \geqslant 1$, $(3 + 2n)I_n = 2nI_{n-1}$.

Hence find the exact value of I_3.

Cambridge International AS & A Level Further Mathematics 9231 Paper 11 Q6 November 2011

3 Determine $\int \cosh^{-1} 2x\,dx$.

Hence, determine the value of $\int_{0.5}^{1} \cosh^{-1} 2x\,dx$, giving the exact solution.

Chapter 23
Complex numbers

In this chapter you will learn how to:

- prove, understand and use de Moivre's theorem for positive exponents, and also work with negative and rational exponents
- express trigonometric ratios of multiple angles in terms of powers, and express powers of $\cos\theta$ and $\sin\theta$ in terms of multiple angles
- use summation notation in conjunction with de Moivre's theorem to simplify and manipulate series of trigonometric terms
- interpret the multiplication and division of complex numbers geometrically
- determine the *n*th roots of unity and of complex expressions.

PREREQUISITE KNOWLEDGE

Where it comes from	What you should be able to do	Check your skills
AS & A Level Mathematics Pure Mathematics 3, Chapter 11	Perform basic operations on complex numbers.	1 If $z_1 = 2 + 3i$ and $z_2 = 3 - 4i$, find: a $z_1 + 2z_2$ b $z_1 z_2$ c $\frac{z_1}{z_2}$
AS & A Level Mathematics Pure Mathematics 1, Chapter 6	Use the binomial expansion.	2 Expand $\left(x^2 + \frac{1}{x^2}\right)^{10}$ in descending order, giving the first four terms.

What are complex numbers?

Complex numbers consist of two parts: a real number and an imaginary number. They enable us to work with numbers such as the square root of a negative number.

In this chapter we shall look at de Moivre's theorem for complex numbers. We shall use de Moivre's theorem to express multiple angles in terms of powers of sine and cosine. We will use summations of series to find the sum of trigonometric expressions. We shall also look at the nth roots of unity, and interpret our results geometrically.

23.1 de Moivre's theorem

From AS & A Level Pure Mathematics 3 you have seen that complex numbers can be represented in the form $z = r\cos\theta + ir\sin\theta$. This is called the **modulus argument form**.

z^2 is equal to $r^2(\cos^2\theta + 2i\sin\theta\cos\theta + i^2\sin^2\theta)$. This simplifies to $r^2(\cos^2\theta - \sin^2\theta + i\sin 2\theta)$ and so $z^2 = r^2(\cos 2\theta + i\sin 2\theta)$.

Following the same logic, $z^3 = z^2 z$ can be written as $r^3(\cos 2\theta + i\sin 2\theta)(\cos\theta + i\sin\theta)$, which is $r^3(\cos 2\theta\cos\theta + i^2\sin 2\theta\sin\theta + i(\sin 2\theta\cos\theta + \cos 2\theta\sin\theta))$, and so we have $z^3 = r^3(\cos 3\theta + i\sin 3\theta)$. So it looks as if $(\cos\theta + i\sin\theta)^n = \cos n\theta + i\sin n\theta$. Let us confirm this using proof by induction.

PROOF 23.1

Let P_k be the statement that, for some value of k, $(\cos\theta + i\sin\theta)^k = \cos k\theta + i\sin k\theta$.

Show the statement works for $n = 1$: $(\cos\theta + i\sin\theta)^1 = \cos 1\theta + i\sin 1\theta$, which clearly works.

Then considering that $(\cos\theta + i\sin\theta)^k(\cos\theta + i\sin\theta) = (\cos k\theta + i\sin k\theta)(\cos\theta + i\sin\theta)$, this leads to $\cos k\theta\cos\theta + i^2\sin k\theta\sin\theta + i(\sin k\theta\cos\theta + \cos k\theta\sin\theta)$.

Using the compound angle formulae, this simplifies to $\cos(k+1)\theta + i\sin(k+1)\theta$. Hence, $P_k \Rightarrow P_{k+1}$.

Since P_1 is true and $P_k \Rightarrow P_{k+1}$, by mathematical induction, we can then say that for all $n \geqslant 1$, $(\cos\theta + i\sin\theta)^n = \cos n\theta + i\sin n\theta$. The result is shown in Key point 23.1.

This is known as de Moivre's theorem, which can be used for all integers n, both positive and negative.

For example, $(\cos\theta + \mathrm{i}\sin\theta)^6 = \cos 6\theta + \mathrm{i}\sin 6\theta$ and $\dfrac{1}{(\cos\theta + \mathrm{i}\sin\theta)^3} = (\cos\theta + \mathrm{i}\sin\theta)^{-3}$ can be written as $\cos(-3\theta) + \mathrm{i}\sin(-3\theta) = \cos 3\theta - \mathrm{i}\sin 3\theta$.

KEY POINT 23.1

de Moivre's theorem:

If $z = \cos\theta + \mathrm{i}\sin\theta$, then $z^n = (\cos\theta + \mathrm{i}\sin\theta)^n = \cos n\theta + \mathrm{i}\sin n\theta$.
It then also follows that if $z = r(\cos\theta + \mathrm{i}\sin\theta)$,
then $z^n = r^n(\cos\theta + \mathrm{i}\sin\theta)^n = r^n(\cos n\theta + \mathrm{i}\sin n\theta)$.

WORKED EXAMPLE 23.1

Determine the value of each of the following complex numbers.

a $\left(\cos\dfrac{\pi}{4} + \mathrm{i}\sin\dfrac{\pi}{4}\right)^8$

b $\dfrac{1}{\left(\cos\left(-\dfrac{3\pi}{4}\right) + \mathrm{i}\sin\left(-\dfrac{3\pi}{4}\right)\right)^6}$

c $(4\sqrt{3} + 4\mathrm{i})^6$

d $(\sqrt{3} - \mathrm{i})^{18}$

Answer

a $\left(\cos\dfrac{\pi}{4} + \mathrm{i}\sin\dfrac{\pi}{4}\right)^8 = (\cos 2\pi + \mathrm{i}\sin 2\pi) = 1$

Using de Moivre's theorem we can multiply each $\dfrac{\pi}{4}$ by 8.

b $\dfrac{1}{\left(\cos\left(-\dfrac{3\pi}{4}\right) + \mathrm{i}\sin\left(-\dfrac{3\pi}{4}\right)\right)^6}$

$= \left(\cos\left(-\dfrac{3\pi}{4}\right) + \mathrm{i}\sin\left(-\dfrac{3\pi}{4}\right)\right)^{-6}$,

Rewrite with a negative power first.

which is $\cos\left(\dfrac{9\pi}{2}\right) + \mathrm{i}\sin\left(\dfrac{9\pi}{2}\right) = \mathrm{i}$.

Then determine the result.

c $(4\sqrt{3} + 4\mathrm{i})^6 = \left(8\cos\dfrac{\pi}{6} + 8\mathrm{i}\sin\dfrac{\pi}{6}\right)^6$,

which is $8^6(\cos\pi + \mathrm{i}\sin\pi) = -262\,144$.

Write $4\sqrt{3} + 4\mathrm{i}$ in modulus argument form. It has modulus 8 and argument $\dfrac{\pi}{6}$.

d $(\sqrt{3} - \mathrm{i})^{18} = \left(2\cos\left(-\dfrac{\pi}{6}\right) + 2\mathrm{i}\sin\left(-\dfrac{\pi}{6}\right)\right)^{18}$

Modulus is 2, argument is $-\dfrac{\pi}{6}$.

So $2^8(\cos(-3\pi) + \mathrm{i}\sin(-3\pi)) = -262\,144$.

Consider the identity $\cos(A + B) = \cos A\cos B - \sin A\sin B$. This identity can be used to determine $\cos k\theta$, but this can be time consuming. For example, $\cos 3\theta = \cos(2\theta + \theta)$ can be written as $\cos 2\theta\cos\theta - \sin 2\theta\sin\theta = (2\cos^2\theta - 1)\cos\theta - 2\sin^2\theta\cos\theta$. Finally, we get the result $\cos 3\theta = 4\cos^3\theta - 3\cos\theta$, but there is a quicker way.

From de Moivre's theorem, $\cos 3\theta + \mathrm{i}\sin 3\theta = (\cos\theta + \mathrm{i}\sin\theta)^3$. Since $\mathrm{Re}(\cos 3\theta + \mathrm{i}\sin 3\theta)$ is $\cos 3\theta$, it follows that $\cos 3\theta = \mathrm{Re}[(\cos\theta + \mathrm{i}\sin\theta)^3]$.

Now, $(\cos\theta + \mathrm{i}\sin\theta)^3 = \cos^3\theta + 3\mathrm{i}\cos^2\theta\sin\theta - 3\cos\theta\sin^2\theta - \mathrm{i}\sin^3\theta$. Equating real parts gives $\cos 3\theta = \cos^3\theta - 3\cos\theta\sin^2\theta = \cos^3\theta - 3\cos\theta(1 - \cos^2\theta) = 4\cos^3\theta - 3\cos\theta$.

This method may not seem faster for lower powers, but it is significantly faster for higher powers.

WORKED EXAMPLE 23.2

Find an expression for $\cos 5\theta$ in terms of $\cos\theta$.

Answer

Start with $(\cos\theta + i\sin\theta)^5$ expanded as	Use the binomial expansion.
$\cos^5\theta + 5i\cos^4\theta\sin\theta - 10\cos^3\theta\sin^2\theta - 10i\cos^2\theta\sin^3\theta$ $+ 5\cos\theta\sin^4\theta + i\sin^5\theta$	
Since $\text{Re}(\cos 5\theta + i\sin 5\theta) = \text{Re}(\cos\theta + i\sin\theta)^5$, we have $\cos 5\theta = \cos^5\theta - 10\cos^3\theta\sin^2\theta + 5\cos\theta\sin^4\theta$.	Equate the real part of each expression.
Using $\sin^2\theta = 1 - \cos^2\theta$ and $\sin^4\theta = (1 - \cos^2\theta)^2$	Replace the powers of sine with the powers of cosine.
we get $\cos 5\theta = 16\cos^5\theta - 20\cos^3\theta + 5\cos\theta$.	State the final answer.

TIP

Since these trigonometric expressions are so complicated, it is normally accepted that $\cos\theta + i\sin\theta$ can be written as $C + iS$. This saves both space and time.

WORKED EXAMPLE 23.3

Find $\sin 3\theta$ in terms of $\sin\theta$.

Answer

Start with $(\cos\theta + i\sin\theta)^3$. Expanding gives	Use the binomial expansion.
$\cos^3\theta + 3i\cos^2\theta\sin\theta - 3\cos\theta\sin^2\theta - i\sin^3\theta$.	
Note that $\text{Im}(\cos 3\theta + i\sin 3\theta) = \text{Im}[(\cos\theta + i\sin\theta)^3]$.	Collect the imaginary terms only.
This leads to $\sin 3\theta = 3\cos^2\theta\sin\theta - \sin^3\theta$.	Equate.
Then with $\cos^2\theta = 1 - \sin^2\theta$, we get $\sin 3\theta = 3\sin\theta - 4\sin^3\theta$.	Simplify to get an expression in sine terms only.

As well as representing $\cos k\theta$ in terms of $\cos\theta$, or $\sin k\theta$ in terms of $\sin\theta$, we can also represent $\tan k\theta$ in terms of $\tan\theta$.

Let us consider $\tan 5\theta$ to be represented in terms of $\tan\theta$. We will start with $(\cos\theta + i\sin\theta)^5$, which is $\cos^5\theta + 5i\cos^4\theta\sin\theta - 10\cos^3\theta\sin^2\theta - 10i\cos^2\theta\sin^3\theta + 5\cos\theta\sin^4\theta + i\sin^5\theta$.

Since $\tan 5\theta = \dfrac{\sin 5\theta}{\cos 5\theta}$, we can say that $\tan 5\theta = \dfrac{\text{Im}[(\cos\theta + i\sin\theta)^5]}{\text{Re}[(\cos\theta + i\sin\theta)^5]}$.

Hence, we can state that $\tan 5\theta = \dfrac{5\cos^4\theta\sin\theta - 10\cos^2\theta\sin^3\theta + \sin^5\theta}{\cos^5\theta - 10\cos^3\theta\sin^2\theta + 5\cos\theta\sin^4\theta}$.

The next step is to divide the numerator and denominator by the highest power in $\cos\theta$, so

$$\tan 5\theta = \frac{5\tan\theta - 10\tan^3\theta + \tan^5\theta}{1 - 10\tan^2\theta + 5\tan^4\theta}.$$

WORKED EXAMPLE 23.4

Find $\tan 4\theta$ in terms of $\tan\theta$.

Answer

$(\cos\theta + i\sin\theta)^4$ expands to give $\cos^4\theta + 4i\cos^3\theta\sin\theta - 6\cos^2\theta\sin^2\theta - 4i\cos\theta\sin^3\theta + \sin^4\theta$. — Use the binomial expansion.

Then $\tan 4\theta = \dfrac{\sin 4\theta}{\cos 4\theta}$ — Recall that $i^2 = -1, i^3 = -i$ and $i^4 = 1$.

$= \dfrac{4\cos^3\theta\sin\theta - 4\cos\theta\sin^3\theta}{\cos^4\theta - 6\cos^2\theta\sin^2\theta + \sin^4\theta}$ — Write $\tan 4\theta = \dfrac{\text{Im}[(\cos\theta + i\sin\theta)^4]}{\text{Re}[(\cos\theta + i\sin\theta)^4]}$.

Dividing by $\cos^4\theta$: $\tan 4\theta = \dfrac{4\tan\theta - 4\tan^3\theta}{1 - 6\tan^2\theta + \tan^4\theta}$ — Divide by the highest power of the cosine.

A very useful application of $\tan k\theta$ is to solve polynomials. Consider the quartic equation $x^4 + 4x^3 - 6x^2 - 4x + 1 = 0$. Rewrite it as $x^4 - 6x^2 + 1 = 4x - 4x^3$, and then $1 = \dfrac{4x - 4x^3}{x^4 - 6x^2 + 1}$. This is similar in structure to the trigonometric equation in Worked example 23.4.

We can substitute $x = \tan\theta$ and $\tan 4\theta = 1$. To solve this we first consider that $\tan 4\theta = 1$, then $4\theta = \dfrac{\pi}{4}, \dfrac{5\pi}{4}, \dfrac{9\pi}{4}, \dfrac{13\pi}{4}$. So $\theta = \dfrac{\pi}{16}, \dfrac{5\pi}{16}, \dfrac{9\pi}{16}, \dfrac{13\pi}{16}$, and after substituting into $x = \tan\theta$ gives the solutions $x = 0.199, 1.50, -5.03, -0.668$.

Note that there are only four solutions since our equation is a quartic. Also, if you take the next value of $\theta = \dfrac{17\pi}{16}$ it gives the same result as $\theta = \dfrac{\pi}{16}$.

WORKED EXAMPLE 23.5

By considering the form of $\tan 3\theta$, solve the cubic equation $3t^3 + 6t^2 - 9t - 2 = 0$.

Answer

Start with the expansion of $(\cos\theta + i\sin\theta)^3$, which is $\cos^3\theta + 3i\cos^2\theta\sin\theta - 3\cos\theta\sin^2\theta - i\sin^3\theta$. — 3θ tells us this is a cubic expansion.

Then $\tan 3\theta = \dfrac{\sin 3\theta}{\cos 3\theta} = \dfrac{3\cos^2\theta\sin\theta - \sin^3\theta}{\cos^3\theta - 3\cos\theta\sin^2\theta}$. — Collect real and imaginary terms.

Next, divide top and bottom by $\cos^3\theta$, giving

$\tan 3\theta = \dfrac{3\tan\theta - \tan^3\theta}{1 - 3\tan^2\theta}$. — Deduce the result.

Next, rearrange $3t^3 + 6t^2 - 9t - 2 = 0$ to $-2 + 6t^2 = 9t - 3t^3$. — Change the polynomial to match the form of $\tan 3\theta$.

which is $-2(1 - 3t^2) = 3(3t - t^3)$, so $-\dfrac{2}{3} = \dfrac{3t - t^3}{1 - 3t^2}$.

Comparing the equations, we let $t = \tan\theta$ and $\tan 3\theta = -\frac{2}{3}$.	State the $\tan 3\theta$ value.
So $3\theta = -0.5880, 2.5536, 5.6952$, which gives $\theta = -0.196, 0.8512, 1.898$.	Solve for three sequential solutions.
Hence, $t = -0.199, 1.14, -2.94$	Use the θ values to obtain the three t values.

EXERCISE 23A

1 Find the values of the following complex numbers.

a $(-\sqrt{3} - \mathrm{i})^{14}$ b $(-1 + \mathrm{i})^9$

M 2 Write $\cos 4x \cos x$ in terms of powers of $\cos x$.

3 Find the values of the following expressions giving your answer as an exact value.

a $\left(\cos\frac{\pi}{12} + \mathrm{i}\sin\frac{\pi}{12}\right)^8$ b $(\sqrt{3} + \mathrm{i})^{12}$ c $\left(\frac{1}{1+\mathrm{i}}\right)^6$

4 Using de Moivre's theorem, or otherwise, find $\cos 7\theta$ in terms of $\cos\theta$.

PS 5 Find $\tan 3\theta$ in terms of $\tan\theta$ and, hence, solve the equation $2x^3 + 9x^2 - 3 = 6x$.

P 6 Show that $\frac{(\cos\theta + \mathrm{i}\sin\theta)^6}{(\cos\theta + \mathrm{i}\sin\theta)^8}$ can be written as $\cos\theta(2\cos\theta - \sec\theta - 2\mathrm{i}\sin\theta)$.

7 Find $\frac{\sin 6\theta}{\cos\theta}$ in terms of $\sin\theta$.

P PS 8 Show that $\tan 4\theta = \frac{4\tan\theta - 4\tan^3\theta}{1 - 6\tan^2\theta + \tan^4\theta}$. Hence, determine the solutions to the equation $x^4 - 4x^3 - 6x^2 + 4x = -1$.

PS 9 By considering that $\tan 5\theta = \frac{5\tan\theta - 10\tan^3\theta + \tan^5\theta}{1 - 10\tan^2\theta + 5\tan^4\theta}$, find all solutions for the polynomial $2x^5 - 5x^4 - 20x^3 + 10x^2 + 10x = 1$.

23.2 Powers of sine and cosine

Consider the complex number $z = \cos\theta + \mathrm{i}\sin\theta$. Then by de Moivre's theorem, or otherwise, $\frac{1}{z}$ can be written as $(\cos\theta + \mathrm{i}\sin\theta)^{-1}$, and so $\frac{1}{z} = \cos\theta - \mathrm{i}\sin\theta$.

So $z + \frac{1}{z} = 2\cos\theta$ and $z - \frac{1}{z} = 2\mathrm{i}\sin\theta$.

Next we consider $z^n = (\cos\theta + \mathrm{i}\sin\theta)^n$ and $\frac{1}{z^n} = (\cos\theta + \mathrm{i}\sin\theta)^{-n}$. So it should be clear that $z^n + \frac{1}{z^n} = 2\cos n\theta$ and $z^n - \frac{1}{z^n} = 2\mathrm{i}\sin n\theta$.

From Euler's formula $\mathrm{e}^{\mathrm{i}\theta} = \cos\theta + \mathrm{i}\sin\theta$. So if $z = \mathrm{e}^{\mathrm{i}\theta}$ and $\frac{1}{z} = \mathrm{e}^{-\mathrm{i}\theta}$, then $\mathrm{e}^{\mathrm{i}\theta} + \mathrm{e}^{-\mathrm{i}\theta} = 2\cos\theta$ and $\mathrm{e}^{\mathrm{i}\theta} - \mathrm{e}^{-\mathrm{i}\theta} = 2\mathrm{i}\sin\theta$. We also have $\mathrm{e}^{n\mathrm{i}\theta} + \mathrm{e}^{-n\mathrm{i}\theta} = 2\cos n\theta$ and $\mathrm{e}^{n\mathrm{i}\theta} - \mathrm{e}^{-n\mathrm{i}\theta} = 2\mathrm{i}\sin n\theta$, as shown in Key point 23.2.

KEY POINT 23.2

Given that $z = \cos\theta + \mathrm{i}\sin\theta$ and $\frac{1}{z} = \cos\theta - \mathrm{i}\sin\theta$, then:

- $z + \frac{1}{z} = 2\cos\theta$
- $z - \frac{1}{z} = 2\mathrm{i}\sin\theta$
- $z^n + \frac{1}{z^n} = 2\cos n\theta$
- $z^n - \frac{1}{z^n} = 2\mathrm{i}\sin n\theta$

To make use of these results, we first look at $\int \cos^4\theta\,\mathrm{d}\theta$, which is quite a tricky integral to deal with.

Using $2\cos\theta = z + \frac{1}{z}$ we need to obtain $\cos^4\theta$, so let $16\cos^4\theta = \left(z + \frac{1}{z}\right)^4$.

Next, expand the right-hand side: $\left(z + \frac{1}{z}\right)^4 = z^4 + 4z^2 + 6 + \frac{4}{z^2} + \frac{1}{z^4}$. Then use $z^n + \frac{1}{z^n} = 2\cos n\theta$ and pair off the terms. So $16\cos^4\theta = 2\cos 4\theta + 8\cos 2\theta + 6$, which means we are now going to use the integral $\int \cos^4\theta\,\mathrm{d}\theta = \frac{1}{16}\int(2\cos 4\theta + 8\cos 2\theta + 6)\mathrm{d}\theta$

$= \frac{1}{32}\sin 4\theta + \frac{1}{4}\sin 2\theta + \frac{3}{8}\theta + c.$

WORKED EXAMPLE 23.6

Using complex numbers, evaluate $\int_0^{\frac{\pi}{2}} \sin^4\theta\,\mathrm{d}\theta$.

Answer

Start with $(2\mathrm{i}\sin\theta)^4 = \left(z - \frac{1}{z}\right)^4$. — Choose the appropriate identity.

Expand the right side to get:

$z^4 - 4z^2 + 6 - \frac{4}{z^2} + \frac{1}{z^4} = 2\cos 4\theta - 8\cos 2\theta + 6.$ — Expand the right side using the binomial expansion.

So $16\sin^4\theta = 2\cos 4\theta - 8\cos 2\theta + 6.$ — Note that $\mathrm{i}^4 = 1$.

So we have $\frac{1}{16}\int_0^{\frac{\pi}{2}}(2\cos 4\theta - 8\cos 2\theta + 6)\,\mathrm{d}\theta$ — Divide by the 16 from the left-hand side.

$= \left[\frac{1}{32}\sin 4\theta - \frac{1}{4}\sin 2\theta + \frac{3}{8}\theta\right]_0^{\frac{\pi}{2}}$ — Integrate.

Evaluating gives $\frac{3\pi}{16}$. — Evaluate.

EXPLORE 23.1

Explore the results of $\left(z+\frac{1}{z}\right)^n$ and $\left(z-\frac{1}{z}\right)^n$ for odd and even values of n. What do you notice? Is there a pattern? How does it affect the number of pairs of terms?

WORKED EXAMPLE 23.7

Determine the integral $\int \sin^5\theta \,d\theta$, using complex numbers.

Answer

Start with $(2i\sin\theta)^5 = \left(z-\frac{1}{z}\right)^5$.	Choose the form involving sine.
Expand the right side to get $z^5 - 5z^3 + 10z - \frac{10}{z} + \frac{5}{z^3} - \frac{1}{z^5}$.	Expand.
This is then paired up to give: $z^5 - \frac{1}{z^5} - 5\left(z^3 - \frac{1}{z^3}\right) + 10\left(z - \frac{1}{z}\right)$	Pair up terms.
Hence, $32i\sin^5\theta = 2i\sin 5\theta - 10i\sin 3\theta + 20i\sin\theta$.	Note the presence of i in every term: this will cancel.
So $\int \sin^5\theta \,d\theta = \int\left(\frac{1}{16}\sin 5\theta - \frac{5}{16}\sin 3\theta + \frac{5}{8}\sin\theta\right)d\theta$	Write the new integral.
Hence $\int \sin^5\theta \,d\theta = -\frac{1}{80}\cos 5\theta + \frac{5}{48}\cos 3\theta - \frac{5}{8}\cos\theta + c$	Integrate, taking care with negatives.

WORKED EXAMPLE 23.8

Find $\cos^6\theta - \sin^6\theta$ in the form $p\cos q\theta + r\cos s\theta$, where p, q, r, s are constants to be determined.

Answer

Let $(2\cos\theta)^6 = \left(z+\frac{1}{z}\right)^6$.

Expand the right side to get:

$64\cos^6\theta = z^6 + 6z^4 + 15z^2 + 20 + \frac{15}{z^2} + \frac{6}{z^4} + \frac{1}{z^6}$	Notice that each power of z is 2 less than the one before.
Then: $64\cos^6\theta = 2\cos 6\theta + 12\cos 4\theta + 30\cos 2\theta + 20$	Pair up terms and replace with multiple angles using $z^n + \frac{1}{z^n} = 2\cos n\theta$.
So $(2i\sin\theta)^6 = \left(z-\frac{1}{z}\right)^6$, and expanding the right side: $-64\sin^6\theta = z^6 - 6z^4 + 15z^2 - 20 + \frac{15}{z^2} - \frac{6}{z^4} + \frac{1}{z^6}$	Similarly for sine, but due to the even power there is no i in the resulting expansion.
So $-64\sin^6\theta = 2\cos 6\theta - 12\cos 4\theta + 30\cos 2\theta - 20$.	The right-hand sides are similar except alternate terms are negative.

So $\cos^6\theta - \sin^6\theta = \frac{1}{64}(4\cos 6\theta + 60\cos 2\theta)$, — Add together.

which gives $\cos^6\theta - \sin^6\theta = \frac{1}{16}\cos 6\theta + \frac{15}{16}\cos 2\theta$. — Simplify.

WORKED EXAMPLE 23.9

Find $\cos^4\theta - \sin^4\theta$ in terms of exponentials.

Answer

Since $2\cos n\theta = e^{ni\theta} + e^{-ni\theta}$ and using the previous result $16\cos^4\theta = 2\cos 4\theta + 8\cos 2\theta + 6$, we have

$\cos^4\theta = \frac{1}{16}(e^{4i\theta} + e^{-4i\theta}) + \frac{1}{4}(e^{2i\theta} + e^{-2i\theta}) + 6.$

The results for $\cos^4\theta$ and $\sin^4\theta$ have already been established.

Use the exponential form to replace the $\cos n\theta$ terms.

Similarly, $2\cos n\theta = e^{ni\theta} + e^{-ni\theta}$ in conjunction with the result $16\sin^4\theta = 2\cos 4\theta - 8\cos 2\theta + 6$.

Carry out a similar procedure for the sine portion.

So $\sin^4\theta = \frac{1}{16}(e^{4i\theta} + e^{-4i\theta}) - \frac{1}{4}(e^{2i\theta} + e^{-2i\theta}) + 6.$

Subtracting gives $\cos^4\theta - \sin^4\theta = \frac{1}{2}(e^{2i\theta} + e^{-2i\theta})$.

Subtract the results and get an unsurprising result: $C^4 - S^4 = (C^2 + S^2)(C^2 - S^2)$, which is $\cos^2\theta - \sin^2\theta = \cos 2\theta$.

EXERCISE 23B

1 Find $\sin^4\theta + 4\cos^4\theta$ in terms of cosines of multiple angles.

2 Evaluate $\int_0^{\frac{\pi}{4}} \cos^5\theta \, d\theta$.

3 Find the value of $\int_0^{\frac{\pi}{2}} (\cos^3\theta + \sin 6\theta) \, d\theta$.

M 4 Find $4\cos^5\theta$ in terms of cosines of multiple angles.

PS 5 Find $\cos^3\theta\sin^3\theta$ in terms of $\sin 6\theta$ and $\sin 2\theta$.

PS 6 Simplify $\cos^5\theta + i\sin^5\theta$, giving your answer in an exponential form, where the terms are of the form $ae^{ki\theta}$.

PS 7 Find $\cos^8\theta + \sin^8\theta$ in the form $a\cos b\theta + c\cos d\theta + e$.

M 8 Find, using complex number methods, the value of $\int_0^{\frac{\pi}{2}} \sin^7\theta \, d\theta$, giving your answer as an exact value.

23.3 The roots of unity

Consider the equation $z^3 = 1$. This equation should have three solutions. Clearly $z_1 = 1$ is a solution and, by the factor theorem, $z^3 - 1 = 0$ can be written as $(z-1)(z^2 + z + 1) = 0$. Solving the quadratic equation gives $z_2 = -\frac{1}{2} + \frac{\sqrt{3}}{2}i$ and $z_3 = -\frac{1}{2} - \frac{\sqrt{3}}{2}i$. These three solutions are known as the **cube roots of unity**.

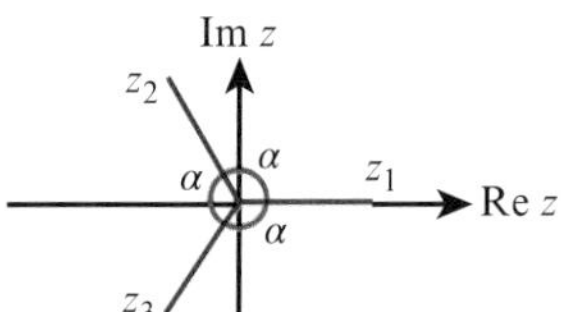

If we show these results on an Argand diagram, we see that they are spaced apart by $\frac{2\pi}{3}$ radians, and the modulus of each root is 1. We can use de Moivre's theorem instead to find the roots. Starting with $z^3 = 1$, we have $z^3 = \cos(0) + \mathrm{i}\sin(0)$. Since we know that there are three roots, we shall generalise and write the solutions as $z^3 = \cos(0 + 2k\pi) + \mathrm{i}\sin(0 + 2k\pi)$. Now let $k = 0, 1, 2$ and take the cube root of each side such that $z = \cos\left(\frac{2k\pi}{3}\right) + \mathrm{i}\sin\left(\frac{2k\pi}{3}\right)$.

So $z_1 = \cos(0) + \mathrm{i}\sin(0)$, $z_2 = \cos\left(\frac{2\pi}{3}\right) + \mathrm{i}\sin\left(\frac{2\pi}{3}\right)$, $z_3 = \cos\left(\frac{4\pi}{3}\right) + \mathrm{i}\sin\left(\frac{4\pi}{3}\right)$. These results are the same as we found previously.

In exponential form, the solutions are $z_1 = \mathrm{e}^0$, $z_2 = \mathrm{e}^{\frac{2\pi}{3}\mathrm{i}}$, $z_3 = \mathrm{e}^{\frac{4\pi}{3}\mathrm{i}}$. In this form it appears that we have a common ratio of $\mathrm{e}^{\frac{2\pi}{3}\mathrm{i}}$, which links to $1 + z + z^2$ from the algebraic result above. If we add $1 + \left(-\frac{1}{2} + \frac{\sqrt{3}}{2}\mathrm{i}\right) + \left(-\frac{1}{2} - \frac{\sqrt{3}}{2}\mathrm{i}\right)$ we get 0. We saw this from $(z - 1)(z^2 + z + 1) = 0$.

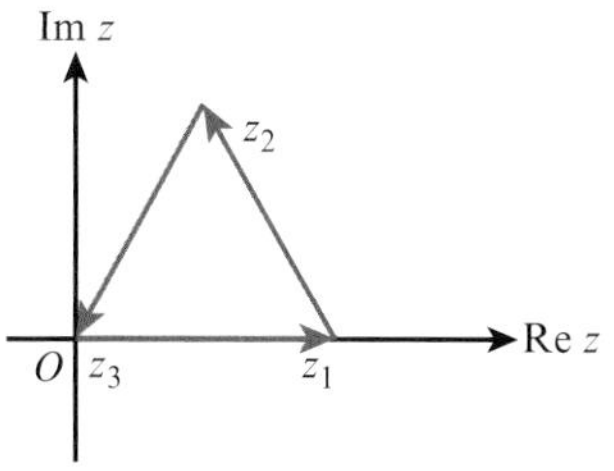

Since complex numbers behave like vectors, we can observe what happens when we add them. As you can see in the diagram, the three solutions add together to give zero, reinforcing $1 + z + z^2 = 0$.

WORKED EXAMPLE 23.10

Find, in exponential form, the four roots of $z^4 = 1$, using de Moivre's theorem. Show your results on an Argand diagram.

Answer

Let $z^4 = \cos(0) + \mathrm{i}\sin(0)$. — Recall that $\cos(0) = 1$, $\sin(0) = 0$.

Then with $k = 0, 1, 2, 3$, we have: — Adding $2k\pi$ does not change the solutions.

$z^4 = \cos(0 + 2k\pi) + \mathrm{i}\sin(0 + 2k\pi)$

Taking the 4th root of both sides: — Taking the 4th root means dividing the angle by 4.

$z = \cos\left(\frac{k\pi}{2}\right) + \mathrm{i}\sin\left(\frac{k\pi}{2}\right)$

Then the roots are $z_1 = 1$, $z_2 = \mathrm{e}^{\frac{\pi}{2}\mathrm{i}}$, $z_3 = \mathrm{e}^{\pi\mathrm{i}}$, $z_4 = \mathrm{e}^{\frac{3\pi}{2}\mathrm{i}}$. — Note the solutions are in geometric progression. Each root is $\frac{\pi}{2}$ radians from the next solution.

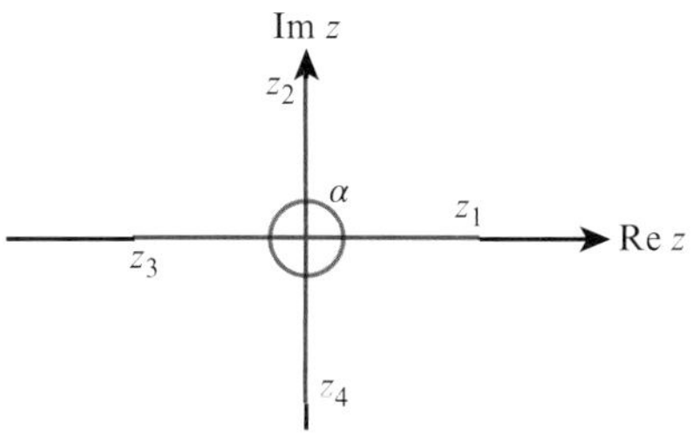

Each root has magnitude 1.

Also adding the four solutions gives the following.

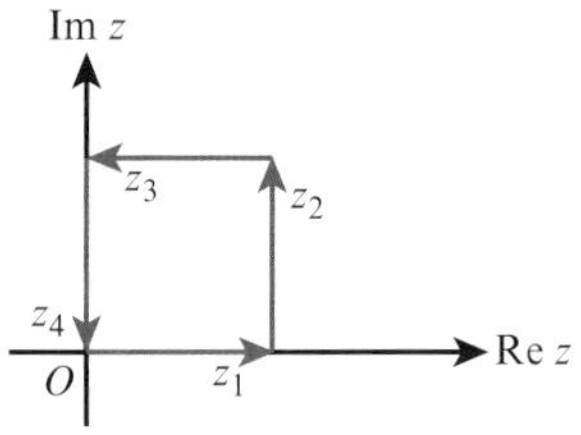

Again, adding all the solutions takes you back to zero. This implies that $1 + z + z^2 + z^3 = 0$.

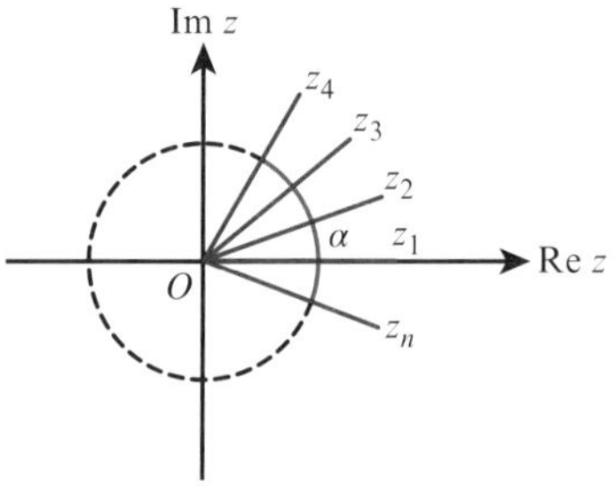

We will now try to generalise with $z^n = 1$. We know this must have n roots, so the next step is to write $z^n = \cos(0 + 2k\pi) + i\sin(0 + 2k\pi)$ for $k = 0, 1, 2, \ldots, n - 1$.

Then taking the nth roots, $z = \cos\left(\frac{2k\pi}{n}\right) + i\sin\left(\frac{2k\pi}{n}\right)$, $k = 0, 1, 2, \ldots, n - 1$.

If we let $\omega^k = \cos\left(\frac{2k\pi}{n}\right) + i\sin\left(\frac{2k\pi}{n}\right)$ for $k = 0, 1, 2, \ldots, n - 1$, then the roots can be denoted as $1, \omega, \omega^2, \ldots, \omega^{n-1}$, where ω is also $e^{\frac{2k\pi}{n}i}$.

If we show these roots on an Argand diagram, we see that the angle between successive roots is $\frac{2\pi}{n}$.

Adding all these roots together will give zero. We can also see this from $z^n - 1 = 0$ and then $(z - 1)(1 + z + z^2 + \cdots + z^{n-1}) = 0$.

These n roots are known as the **nth roots of unity**.

KEY POINT 23.3

For the equation $z^n = 1$, the nth roots of unity are $z = \cos\left(\frac{2k\pi}{n}\right) + i\sin\left(\frac{2k\pi}{n}\right)$, $k = 0, 1, 2, \ldots, n - 1$.

In exponential form these roots are $1, e^{\frac{2\pi}{n}i}, e^{\frac{4\pi}{n}i}, \ldots, e^{\frac{2(n-1)\pi}{n}i}$

TIP

Try, where possible, to use the exponential form. It is easier to write down, easier to multiply and the geometric relationship between the roots is clear.

DID YOU KNOW?

Jean-Robert Argand was an amateur mathematician who was also the manager of a bookstore. He introduced the idea of complex numbers being represented on an Argand diagram in the complex plane. He is also credited with being the first person to propose the idea of the magnitude of vectors and complex numbers, as well as direction $\vec{a}$ for vectors.

WORKED EXAMPLE 23.11

Find, in exponential form, the 7th roots of unity.

Answer

Start with $z^7 = 1$, then $z^7 = \cos(0 + 2k\pi) + i\sin(0 + 2k\pi)$,

Quote the general form for the nth roots.

where $k = 0, 1, 2, 3, 4, 5, 6$.

State the valid values of k.

Then $z = \cos\left(\frac{2k\pi}{7}\right) + \mathrm{i}\sin\left(\frac{2k\pi}{7}\right)$, where $k = 0, 1, 2, 3, 4, 5, 6$.

Write down the solutions in the correct form.

Hence, $z_1 = 1, z_2 = \mathrm{e}^{\frac{2\pi}{7}\mathrm{i}}, z_3 = \mathrm{e}^{\frac{4\pi}{7}\mathrm{i}}, z_4 = \mathrm{e}^{\frac{6\pi}{7}\mathrm{i}}, z_5 = \mathrm{e}^{\frac{8\pi}{7}\mathrm{i}}, z_6 = \mathrm{e}^{\frac{10\pi}{7}\mathrm{i}}, z_7 = \mathrm{e}^{\frac{12\pi}{7}\mathrm{i}}$.

Notice the common ratio between successive terms.

WORKED EXAMPLE 23.12

Given that $z^3 - 1 = 0$, find the solutions in $x + \mathrm{i}y$ form. Name them $1, \omega, \omega^2$.

Show that the square of one complex root is the other complex root.

Also find the value of $\omega^6 + \omega^7 + \omega^8$.

Answer

$z^3 = 1$, so $z^3 = \cos(2k\pi) + \mathrm{i}\sin(2k\pi)$, then with $k = 0, 1, 2$,

Derive the general form and write down the Cartesian complex solutions.

$z_1 = 1, z_2 = -\frac{1}{2} + \frac{\sqrt{3}}{2}\mathrm{i}, z_3 = -\frac{1}{2} - \frac{\sqrt{3}}{2}\mathrm{i}$

Denote ω and ω^2. We must have $\omega = -\frac{1}{2} + \frac{\sqrt{3}}{2}\mathrm{i}$.

Let $\omega = -\frac{1}{2} + \frac{\sqrt{3}}{2}\mathrm{i}, \omega^2 = -\frac{1}{2} - \frac{\sqrt{3}}{2}\mathrm{i}$.

Square ω to confirm it becomes ω^2.

$$\omega^2 = \left(-\frac{1}{2} + \frac{\sqrt{3}}{2}\mathrm{i}\right)^2 = \frac{1}{4} - \frac{\sqrt{3}}{2}\mathrm{i} - \frac{3}{4} = -\frac{1}{2} - \frac{\sqrt{3}}{2}\mathrm{i}$$

$\omega^6 + \omega^7 + \omega^8 = \omega^6(1 + \omega + \omega^2)$

This is zero.

Recall that $1 + \omega + \omega^2 = 0$; this is the same as $1 + z + z^2 = 0$.

There are not only roots of unity, but also nth roots of any complex number. Consider $z^4 = \mathrm{i}$. This can be written as $z^4 = \cos\frac{\pi}{2} + \mathrm{i}\sin\frac{\pi}{2}$.

Then $z^4 = \cos\left(\frac{\pi}{2} + 2k\pi\right) + \mathrm{i}\sin\left(\frac{\pi}{2} + 2k\pi\right)$.

Taking 4th roots, $z = \cos\left(\frac{\pi}{8} + \frac{k\pi}{2}\right) + \mathrm{i}\sin\left(\frac{\pi}{8} + \frac{k\pi}{2}\right)$, where $k = 0, 1, 2, 3$.

Then writing down the roots, we have $z_1 = \mathrm{e}^{\frac{\pi}{8}\mathrm{i}}, z_2 = \mathrm{e}^{\frac{5\pi}{8}\mathrm{i}}, z_3 = \mathrm{e}^{\frac{9\pi}{8}\mathrm{i}}, z_4 = \mathrm{e}^{\frac{13\pi}{8}\mathrm{i}}$.

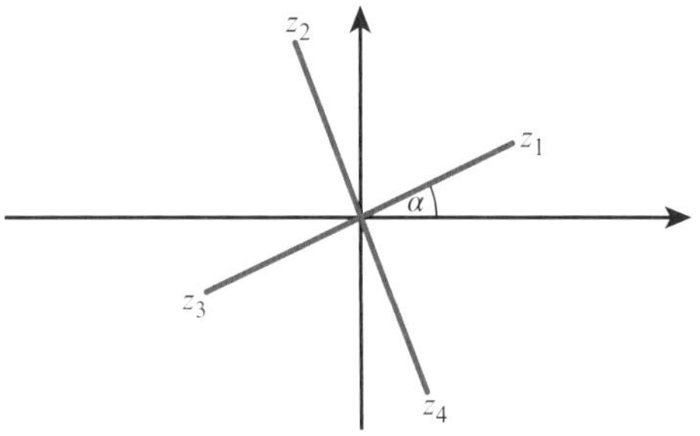

Notice that since we have four roots, they are still separated by an angle of $\frac{\pi}{2}$.

WORKED EXAMPLE 23.13

Solve $z^6 = 4 + 4\sqrt{3}\mathrm{i}$, giving all answers in the form $z = r\mathrm{e}^{\mathrm{i}\theta}$. Show all your solutions on an Argand diagram.

Answer

Since $|4 + 4\sqrt{3}\mathrm{i}| = 8$ and $\arg(4 + 4\sqrt{3}\mathrm{i}) = \frac{\pi}{3}$,

Find the modulus and argument of the complex number first.

we have $z^6 = 8\left(\cos\frac{\pi}{3} + \mathrm{i}\sin\frac{\pi}{3}\right)$

or $z^6 = 8\left[\cos\left(\frac{\pi}{3} + 2k\pi\right) + \mathrm{i}\sin\left(\frac{\pi}{3} + 2k\pi\right)\right]$, — Write the general form for the six roots.

where $k = 0, 1, 2, 3, 4, 5$.

Then $z = \sqrt{2}\left[\cos\left(\frac{\pi}{18} + \frac{k\pi}{3}\right) + \mathrm{i}\sin\left(\frac{\pi}{18} + \frac{k\pi}{3}\right)\right]$. — Take the sixth root to get z.

So the solutions are $z_1 = \sqrt{2}\mathrm{e}^{\frac{\pi}{18}\mathrm{i}}, z_2 = \sqrt{2}\mathrm{e}^{\frac{7\pi}{18}\mathrm{i}}, z_3 = \sqrt{2}\mathrm{e}^{\frac{13\pi}{18}\mathrm{i}}$,
$z_4 = \sqrt{2}\mathrm{e}^{\frac{19\pi}{18}\mathrm{i}}, z_5 = \sqrt{2}\mathrm{e}^{\frac{25\pi}{18}\mathrm{i}}, z_6 = \sqrt{2}\mathrm{e}^{\frac{31\pi}{18}\mathrm{i}}$ — Write down the six solutions. Note the difference in angle between successive roots.

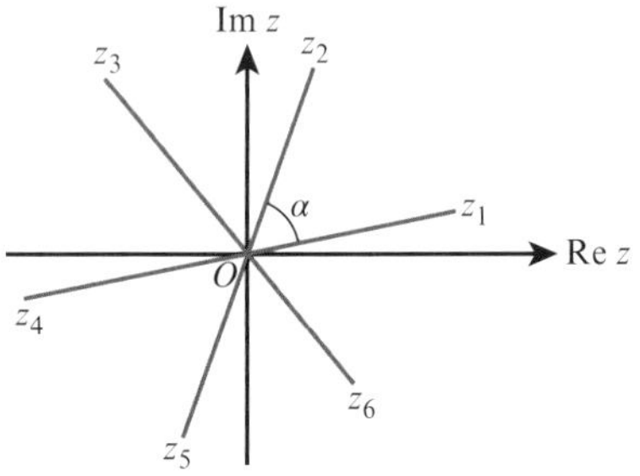

Here $\alpha = \frac{\pi}{3}$, which is of course $\frac{2\pi}{6}$.

Here are all the complex numbers added, still giving zero. — The small angle between z_1 and the real axis is $\frac{\pi}{18}$.

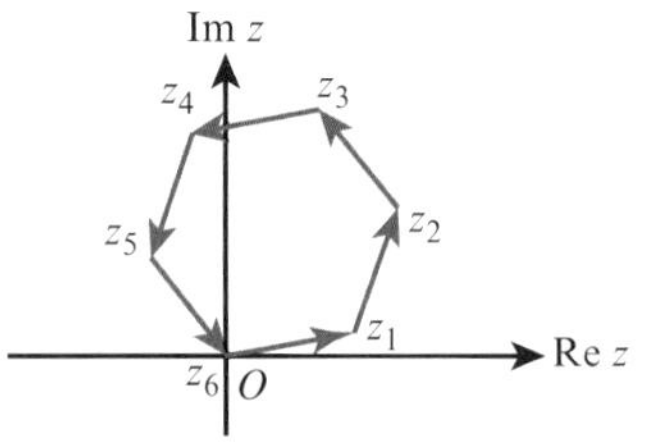

As we saw with the roots of unity, the complex solutions can still be added together to give a sum of zero.

EXERCISE 23C

1 Find the 6th roots of unity. Give your answers in integer or exponential form.

PS 2 The roots of $z^3 - 1 = 0$ are $1, \omega, \omega^2$. Determine the value of $\omega^3 + \omega^4 + \omega^5$. Otherwise, $\omega^3 = 1$, $\omega^4 = \omega$ and $\omega^5 = \omega^2$.

3 Find the roots of the equation $z^4 = 8 + 8\sqrt{3}\mathrm{i}$, giving your answers in exponential form.

4 Find the 4th roots of -16, giving each root in an exponential form.

P 5 A polynomial equation is given as $z^5 - 1 = 0$.

  a Show that 1 is one root, then factorise your polynomial into the form $(z-1)\mathrm{f}(z) = 0$, where $\mathrm{f}(z)$ is to be stated.

  b Using the four complex solutions, show that $\cos\frac{2\pi}{5} + \cos\frac{4\pi}{5} = -\frac{1}{2}$.

M 6 Solve the equation $z^8 = -8\sqrt{3} + 8\mathrm{i}$. Show all these solutions on an Argand diagram.

7 Find the roots of $z^{12} = -1$. Give your answers in exponential form.

P 8 Show that $(z - e^{i\theta})(z - e^{-i\theta}) \equiv z^2 - 2z\cos\theta + 1$.

P 9 a Write down the sixth roots of unity in exponential form.

b State the two real roots.

c The polynomial $z^6 - 1 = 0$ can be written as the product of two linear factors and two quadratic factors. Show that one of the quadratic factors is $z^2 - z + 1$ and find the other one.

PS 10 The polynomial P is given by $(z + 2 - 3i)^3 = 2 + 2i$. Given that $\omega = z + 2 - 3i$, find the roots $\omega, \omega^2, \omega^3$ and state, in terms of the z-plane, the value of $\omega + \omega^2 + \omega^3$. Sketch the three solutions on an Argand diagram.

23.4 Complex summations

Suppose we need to determine the value of $\sum_{n=0}^{N-1} \cos n\theta$. How could we begin? We could write down a few terms to get $\sum_{n=0}^{N-1} \cos n\theta = 1 + \cos\theta + \cos 2\theta + \ldots$ but this doesn't seem to help.

Recall from previous work that $\text{Re}(z) = \cos\theta$, so instead consider $\sum_{n=0}^{N-1} z^n$, which is $1 + z + z^2 + \ldots$. Now this might not seem any better, but it is a geometric sum, so $\sum_{n=0}^{N-1} z^n = \frac{z^N - 1}{z - 1}$.

Next we use $z = e^{i\theta}$ to give $\sum_{n=0}^{N-1} z^n = \frac{e^{Ni\theta} - 1}{e^{i\theta} - 1}$. Then multiplying top and bottom by $e^{-\frac{1}{2}i\theta}$ gives us $\sum_{n=0}^{N-1} z^n = \frac{e^{\left(N-\frac{1}{2}\right)i\theta} - e^{-\frac{1}{2}i\theta}}{e^{\frac{1}{2}i\theta} - e^{-\frac{1}{2}i\theta}}$. The denominator can now be written as a single term, $2i\sin\frac{1}{2}\theta$, which means we can split the result into real and imaginary parts. We, need the real part.

So with $\sum_{n=0}^{N-1} z^n = \frac{\cos\left(N - \frac{1}{2}\right)\theta + i\sin\left(N - \frac{1}{2}\right)\theta - \cos\frac{1}{2}\theta + i\sin\frac{1}{2}\theta}{2i\sin\frac{1}{2}\theta}$,

$\sum_{n=0}^{N-1} \cos n\theta$ is just the real part of the previous summation.

So $\sum_{n=0}^{N-1} \cos n\theta = \frac{\sin\left(N - \frac{1}{2}\right)\theta + \sin\frac{1}{2}\theta}{2\sin\frac{1}{2}\theta}$ or, in another form, $\frac{1}{2}\left[\sin\left(N - \frac{1}{2}\right)\theta\,\text{cosec}\,\frac{1}{2}\theta + 1\right]$.

TIP

Remember that if $z = \cos\theta + i\sin\theta$, then $\text{Re}(z) = \cos\theta$ and $\text{Im}(z) = \sin\theta$.

WORKED EXAMPLE 23.14

By considering the expansion of $\sum_{n=1}^{N} z^{2n-1}$, show that $\sum_{n=1}^{N} \cos(2n - 1)\theta = \frac{\sin 2N\theta}{2\sin\theta}$.

Answer

Start with $\sum_{n=1}^{N} z^{2n-1} = z + z^3 + z^5 + \ldots = \frac{z(z^{2N} - 1)}{z^2 - 1}$.

Then, with $z = e^{i\theta}$, $\sum_{n=1}^{N} z^{2n-1} = \frac{e^{i\theta}(e^{2Ni\theta} - 1)}{e^{2i\theta} - 1}$

to give $\frac{e^{2Ni\theta} - 1}{e^{i\theta} - e^{-i\theta}}$. — Multiply top and bottom by $e^{-i\theta}$.

So now $\sum_{n=1}^{N} z^{2n-1} = \frac{\cos 2N\theta + i\sin 2N\theta - 1}{2i\sin\theta}$.

Since $\cos(2n-1)\theta$ is the real part of z^{2n-1}, we can now write

$\sum_{n=1}^{N} \cos(2n-1)\theta = \frac{i\sin 2N\theta}{2i\sin\theta}$,

which of course is equal to $\frac{\sin 2N\theta}{2\sin\theta}$.

As well as summation forms such as $\sum_{n=0}^{N-1} z^n$, we could also deal with a summation such as $\sum_{n=0}^{N-1} (3z)^n$. To tackle this we write down a few terms first, so $\sum_{n=0}^{N-1} (3z)^n = 1 + 3z + (3z)^2 + \ldots$ shows us that the first term is 1 and the common ratio is $3z$.

So $\sum_{n=0}^{N-1} (3z)^n = \frac{(3z)^N - 1}{3z - 1}$, and if $z = e^{i\theta}$ then $\sum_{n=0}^{N-1} (3z)^n = \frac{3^N e^{Ni\theta} - 1}{3e^{i\theta} - 1}$.

The problem we have is that the previous method of multiplying, in this case by $e^{-\frac{1}{2}i\theta}$, won't work. It gives us $\frac{3^N e^{\left(N-\frac{1}{2}\right)i\theta} - e^{-\frac{1}{2}i\theta}}{3e^{\frac{1}{2}i\theta} - e^{-\frac{1}{2}i\theta}}$ but the denominator cannot be converted to only real or only imaginary numbers. So, instead, multiply top and bottom by $3e^{-i\theta} - 1$,

giving $\sum_{n=0}^{N-1} (3z)^n = \frac{(3^N e^{Ni\theta} - 1)(3e^{-i\theta} - 1)}{(3e^{i\theta} - 1)(3e^{-i\theta} - 1)}$. Then the denominator becomes $10 - 6\cos\theta$,

which is definitely real. So $\sum_{n=0}^{N-1} (3z)^n = \frac{3^{N+1}e^{(N-1)i\theta} - 3^N e^{Ni\theta} - 3e^{-i\theta} + 1}{10 - 6\cos\theta}$, and from this both real and imaginary summations can be stated.

WORKED EXAMPLE 23.15

Find, in any form, the result of $\sum_{n=1}^{N} 2^n \sin n\theta$.

Answer

Start with $\sum_{n=1}^{N} 2^n z^n = 2z + 4z^2 + 8z^3 + \ldots$.

This summation is equal to $\frac{2z[(2z)^N - 1]}{2z - 1}$. — Write down a general complex form for the summation.

Then with $z = e^{i\theta}$ we can write the summation as $\frac{2e^{i\theta}(2^N e^{Ni\theta} - 1)}{2e^{i\theta} - 1}$.	Use the exponential form to show the required expression.
Next we multiply top and bottom by $2e^{-i\theta} - 1$, so the summation is $\frac{2e^{i\theta}(2^N e^{Ni\theta} - 1)(2e^{-i\theta} - 1)}{(2e^{i\theta} - 1)(2e^{-i\theta} - 1)}$.	Multiply by an expression that reduces the denominator to a real expression.
This is then written in the form $\frac{2^{N+2}e^{Ni\theta} - 2^{N+1}e^{(N+1)i\theta} - 4 + 2e^{i\theta}}{5 - 4\cos\theta}$.	Multiply out in a form so the real or imaginary part can be found.
So, as our summation contains $\sin n\theta$, we need the imaginary part of this expression. The result is $\sum_{n=1}^{N} 2^n \sin n\theta = \frac{2^{N+2}\sin N\theta - 2^{N+1}\sin(N+1)\theta + 2\sin\theta}{5 - 4\cos\theta}$.	State the correct result, ignoring any real terms from the numerator.

Consider the summation $\sum_{n=0}^{\infty} 4^{-n}\cos\left(\frac{n\pi}{3}\right)$. Writing down a few terms will not help, so instead we consider the summation $\sum_{n=0}^{\infty}\left(\frac{z}{4}\right)^n$.

This summation looks like $1 + \frac{z}{4} + \frac{z^2}{16} + \dots$. It is a sum to infinity of the form $\frac{1}{1 - \frac{z}{4}} = \frac{4}{4 - z}$.

Let $z = e^{i\theta}$, so our sum is $\frac{4}{4 - e^{i\theta}}$.

Multiplying top and bottom by $4 - e^{-i\theta}$ changes our sum to

$$\frac{16 - 4e^{-i\theta}}{(4 - e^{i\theta})(4 - e^{-i\theta})} = \frac{16 - 4e^{-i\theta}}{16 - 4e^{i\theta} + 1 - 4e^{-i\theta}} = \frac{16 - 4e^{-i\theta}}{17 - 8\cos\theta}.$$

So we need $\mathrm{Re}\left(\frac{16 - 4e^{-i\theta}}{17 - 8\cos\theta}\right) = \frac{16 - 4\cos\theta}{17 - 8\cos\theta}$, hence

$\sum_{n=0}^{\infty} 4^{-n}\cos\left(\frac{n\pi}{3}\right) = \frac{16 - 4\cos\frac{\pi}{3}}{17 - 8\cos\frac{\pi}{3}}$. This evaluates to $\frac{14}{13}$.

WORKED EXAMPLE 23.16

Determine the value of $\sum_{n=0}^{\infty} 2^{-n}\sin\left(\frac{n\pi}{2}\right)$.

Answer

Start with $\sum_{n=0}^{\infty}\left(\frac{z}{2}\right)^n = 1 + \frac{z}{2} + \frac{z^2}{4} + \dots = \frac{1}{1 - \frac{z}{2}} = \frac{2}{2 - z}$.

Then we let $z = e^{i\theta}$, so our sum is $\frac{2}{2 - e^{i\theta}}$.

Multiply top and bottom by $2 - e^{-i\theta}$ to give a sum of

$\frac{4 - 2e^{-i\theta}}{5 - 4\cos\theta}$.

We need $\text{Im}\left(\frac{4-2e^{-i\theta}}{5-4\cos\theta}\right) = \frac{2\sin\theta}{5-4\cos\theta}$, hence

$\sum_{n=0}^{\infty} 2^{-n}\sin\left(\frac{n\pi}{2}\right) = \frac{2\sin\frac{\pi}{2}}{5-4\cos\frac{\pi}{2}}$, hence our sum works out to $\frac{2}{5}$.

EXERCISE 23D

PS 1 Given that $z = e^{i\theta}$, determine an expression for $\sum_{n=1}^{N} z^n$ in terms of exponentials.

P 2 Show that $\sum_{n=1}^{N} 3^n z^n$ can be written as:

$$\frac{(3^N e^{Ni\theta} - 1)(9 - 3e^{i\theta})}{10 - 3(e^{i\theta} - e^{-i\theta})}$$

PS 3 Expand $\sum_{n=1}^{N} z^{2n-1}$, giving your answer in trigonometric form.

PS 4 a Determine $\sum_{n=1}^{10} 4\sin(2n-1)\theta$ in terms of multiple angles of θ.

b State the value of $\sum_{n=1}^{10} 4\sin\left[\frac{(2n-1)\pi}{4}\right]$.

P 5 Show that, when N is even, the real part of $\sum_{n=1}^{N} (1 - \sec\theta e^{i\theta})^n$ is equal to $k\sin^2\theta(\tan^N\theta - 1)$, where $k = \pm 1$.

P 6 By first expanding $\sum_{n=0}^{N-1} \left(\frac{z}{3}\right)^n$, show that:

$$\sum_{n=0}^{N} 3^{-n}\cos n\theta = \frac{3^{-N+1}\cos(N-1)\theta - 3^{-N+2}\cos N\theta - 3\cos\theta + 9}{10 - 6\cos\theta}$$

PS 7 Determine the value of $\sum_{n=1}^{\infty} \left(\frac{2}{3}\right)^n \cos\left(\frac{n\pi}{3}\right)$, giving your answer in an exact form.

P 8 By considering $\sum_{n=1}^{N} z^{2n-1}$ and then using only the imaginary part of your result, show that:

$$\sum_{n=1}^{N} (2n-1)\cos\left[\frac{(2n-1)\pi}{4N}\right] = N\operatorname{cosec}\left(\frac{\pi}{4N}\right) - \operatorname{cosec}\left(\frac{\pi}{4N}\right)\cot\left(\frac{\pi}{4N}\right)$$

WORKED PAST PAPER QUESTION

By considering $\sum_{n=1}^{N} z^{2n-1}$, where $z = e^{i\theta}$, show that

$$\sum_{n=1}^{N} \cos(2n-1)\theta = \frac{\sin(2N\theta)}{2\sin\theta},$$

where $\sin\theta \neq 0$.

Deduce that

$$\sum_{n=1}^{N} (2n-1)\sin\left[\frac{(2n-1)\pi}{N}\right] = -N\operatorname{cosec}\frac{\pi}{N}.$$

Cambridge International AS & A Level Further Mathematics 9231 Paper 1 Q10 June 2008

Answer

$\sum_{n=1}^{N} z^{2n-1} = z + z^3 + z^5 + \ldots = \frac{z(z^{2N}-1)}{z^2-1}$, then let $z = e^{i\theta}$ so the sum is $\frac{e^{i\theta}(e^{2Ni\theta}-1)}{e^{2i\theta}-1}$.

Multiplying top and bottom by $e^{-i\theta}$ gives $\frac{(e^{2Ni\theta}-1)}{e^{i\theta}-e^{-i\theta}}$, so the denominator is $2i\sin\theta$.

Hence, $\sum_{n=1}^{N} z^{2n-1} = \frac{\cos 2N\theta + i\sin 2N\theta - 1}{2i\sin\theta}$, and so $\sum_{n=1}^{N} \cos(2n-1)\theta = \text{Re}\left(\frac{\cos 2N\theta + i\sin 2N\theta - 1}{2i\sin\theta}\right)$, which is $\frac{\sin(2N\theta)}{2\sin\theta}$.

Differentiating, $\left(\frac{\sin(2N\theta)}{2\sin\theta}\right)' = \frac{2N\cos(2N\theta)\times 2\sin\theta - 2\cos\theta\times\sin(2N\theta)}{4\sin^2\theta}$, which simplifies to $N\cos(2N\theta)\operatorname{cosec}\theta - \frac{1}{2}\sin(2N\theta)\operatorname{cosec}\theta\cot\theta$.

Differentiating $\cos(2n-1)\theta$ gives $-(2n-1)\sin(2n-1)\theta$.

Then if $\theta = \frac{\pi}{N}$ we have $-\sum_{n=1}^{N}(2n-1)\sin\left[\frac{(2n-1)\pi}{N}\right] = N\operatorname{cosec}\frac{\pi}{N}\cos 2\pi - \frac{1}{2}\sin 2\pi\operatorname{cosec}\frac{\pi}{N}\cot\frac{\pi}{N}$. Since the second term is equal to zero, $\sum_{n=1}^{N}(2n-1)\sin\left[\frac{(2n-1)\pi}{N}\right] = -N\operatorname{cosec}\frac{\pi}{N}$.

Checklist of learning and understanding

de Moivre's theorem:

- $(\cos\theta + \mathrm{i}\sin\theta)^n = \cos n\theta + \mathrm{i}\sin n\theta$ is de Moivre's theorem.
- $\mathrm{Re}(\cos k\theta + \mathrm{i}\sin k\theta) = \cos k\theta$
- $\mathrm{Im}(\cos k\theta + \mathrm{i}\sin k\theta) = \sin k\theta$

Powers of sine and cosine:

- $z + \frac{1}{z} = 2\cos\theta$ and $\mathrm{e}^{\mathrm{i}\theta} + \mathrm{e}^{-\mathrm{i}\theta} = 2\cos\theta$
- $z - \frac{1}{z} = 2\mathrm{i}\sin\theta$ and $\mathrm{e}^{\mathrm{i}\theta} - \mathrm{e}^{-\mathrm{i}\theta} = 2\mathrm{i}\sin\theta$
- $z^n + \frac{1}{z^n} = 2\cos n\theta$ and $\mathrm{e}^{n\mathrm{i}\theta} + \mathrm{e}^{-n\mathrm{i}\theta} = 2\cos n\theta$
- $z^n - \frac{1}{z^n} = 2\mathrm{i}\sin n\theta$ and $\mathrm{e}^{n\mathrm{i}\theta} - \mathrm{e}^{-n\mathrm{i}\theta} = 2\mathrm{i}\sin n\theta$

For roots of unity:

- If $z^n = 1$, then $z = \cos\left(\frac{2k\pi}{n}\right) + \mathrm{i}\sin\left(\frac{2k\pi}{n}\right)$, where $k = 0, 1, 2, \ldots, n-1$.
- When $z^n - 1 = 0$, $\mathrm{f}(z) = (z-1)(1 + z + z^2 + \ldots + z^{n-1})$.
- The angle between successive roots is $\frac{2\pi}{n}$.
- The value of $1 + z + z^2 + \ldots + z^{n-1}$ is 0.

For complex summations:

- For $\sum_{n=0}^{N-1} z^n = 1 + z + z^2 + \ldots$ this can be considered as a geometric sum, where z is the common ratio.
- The denominator is of two types, $\mathrm{e}^{a\mathrm{i}\theta} - \mathrm{e}^{b\mathrm{i}\theta}$ or $\alpha\mathrm{e}^{a\mathrm{i}\theta} - \beta$; multiply by a suitable exponential expression to make the denominator all real or all imaginary.

END-OF-CHAPTER REVIEW EXERCISE 23

1 Let $z = \cos\theta + \mathrm{i}\sin\theta$. Show that $1 + z = 2\cos\frac{1}{2}\theta\left(\cos\frac{1}{2}\theta + \mathrm{i}\sin\frac{1}{2}\theta\right)$.

By considering $(1 + z)^n$, where n is a positive integer, deduce the sum of the series

$\binom{n}{1}\sin\theta + \binom{n}{2}\sin 2\theta + \ldots + \binom{n}{n}\sin n\theta$.

Cambridge International AS & A Level Further Mathematics 9231 Paper 13 Q8 November 2012

2 Use de Moivre's theorem to express $\cot 7\theta$ in terms of $\cot\theta$.

Use the equation $\cot 7\theta = 0$ to show that the roots of the equation $x^6 - 21x^4 + 35x^2 - 7 = 0$ are $\cot\left(\frac{1}{14}k\pi\right)$ for $k = 1, 3, 5, 9, 11, 13$ and deduce that $\cot^2\left(\frac{1}{14}\pi\right)\cot^2\left(\frac{3}{14}\pi\right)\cot^2\left(\frac{5}{14}\pi\right) = 7$.

Cambridge International AS & A Level Further Mathematics 9231 Paper 11 Q6 June 2016

3 Let $\omega = \cos\frac{1}{5}\pi + \mathrm{i}\sin\frac{1}{5}\pi$. Show that $\omega^5 + 1 = 0$ and deduce that $\omega^4 - \omega^3 + \omega^2 - \omega = -1$.

Show further that $\omega - \omega^4 = 2\cos\frac{1}{5}\pi$ and $\omega^3 - \omega^2 = 2\cos\frac{3}{5}\pi$.

Hence find the values of $\cos\frac{1}{5}\pi + \cos\frac{3}{5}\pi$ and $\cos\frac{1}{5}\pi\cos\frac{3}{5}\pi$.

Find a quadratic equation having roots $\cos\frac{1}{5}\pi$ and $\cos\frac{3}{5}\pi$ and deduce the exact value of $\cos\frac{1}{5}\pi$.

Cambridge International AS & A Level Further Mathematics 9231 Paper 11 Q11a November 2011

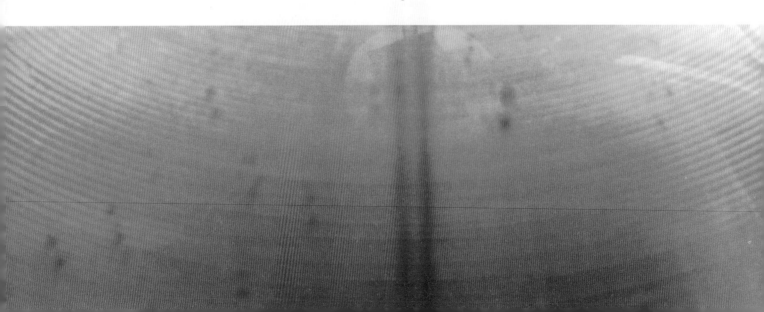

Chapter 24
Differential equations

In this chapter you will learn how to:

- determine integrating factors and solve first order differential equations
- find characteristic equations and solve second order differential equations
- use substitutions to solve first and second order differential equations.

PREREQUISITE KNOWLEDGE

Where it comes from	What you should be able to do	Check your skills
AS & A Level Mathematics Pure Mathematics 2 & 3, Chapter 10	Solve separable first order differential equations.	**1** Find the general solution of: $\frac{dy}{dx} = \frac{y^2}{x^3}$
AS & A Level Mathematics Pure Mathematics 2 & 3, Chapter 8 Chapter 19	Integrate a variety of functions.	**2** Integrate the following expressions. **a** $\int \sin^2 x \, dx$ **b** $\int x^3 \ln x \, dx$ **c** $\int \cosh 2x \, dx$
AS & A Level Mathematics Pure Mathematics 2 & 3, Chapter 4 Chapter 21	Differentiate implicitly and parametrically.	**3** **a** Given that $y = zx$, where z is a function of x, find $\frac{d^2y}{dx^2}$. **b** If $x = t^2$ and $y = t^3$, use parametric differentiation to find $\frac{d^2y}{dx^2}$.

What are differential equations?

In this chapter we shall look at first and second order linear differential equations. Differential equations relate a function to one or more of its derivatives.

Differential equations are used in a vast number of areas, including financial modelling, fluid mechanics, medicine, population growth and decay models, predator-prey models, and classical mechanics.

We shall try to understand and solve first order differential equations that are not separable, using an integrating factor. We shall then solve second order differential equations, using a trial solution that leads to an auxiliary equation. Finally, we shall use substitution methods to solve non-linear first and second order differential equations.

24.1 First order differential equations

You will have met differential equations of the form $\frac{dy}{dx} = x$ or $\frac{dy}{dx} = y^2$ in your A Level Mathematics course. These are known as first order differential equations with separable variables. It is straightforward to write them as $\int dy = \int x \, dx$ and $\int \frac{1}{y^2} \, dy = \int dx$, respectively.

But can the differential equation $x\frac{dy}{dx} + y = x$ be separated? The answer is no. No matter how we rewrite this equation, we cannot get x with dx and y with dy.

If we look closely at the left-hand side, it is actually $\frac{d}{dx}(xy)$, so now $\frac{d}{dx}(xy) = x$. Next we write $xy = \int x\,dx$ and then $xy = \frac{1}{2}x^2 + c$. So the general solution is $y = \frac{1}{2}x + \frac{c}{x}$.

Looking at another example, we have $-\frac{x}{y^2}\frac{dy}{dx} + \frac{1}{y} = x^2$. This differential equation is not separable either, but the left side can be recognised as $\frac{d}{dx}\left(\frac{x}{y}\right)$. So we now have $\frac{d}{dx}\left(\frac{x}{y}\right) = x^2$, which integrates to give $\frac{x}{y} = \frac{1}{3}x^3 + c$ and, hence, $y = \frac{3x}{x^3 + 3c}$.

WORKED EXAMPLE 24.1

Determine the general solution for the differential equation $\frac{x}{y}\frac{dy}{dx} + \ln y = x + 1$.

Answer

Note that the left-hand side is $\frac{d}{dx}(x \ln y)$. — Recognise left-hand side as $\frac{d}{dx}(x \ln y)$.

Then $\frac{d}{dx}(x \ln y) = x + 1$, and $x \ln y = \int (x + 1)\,dx$. — Write the right-hand side in integral form.

Hence, $x \ln y = \frac{1}{2}x^2 + x + c$. — Integrate.

Finally, $y = e^{\frac{1}{2}x + 1 + \frac{c}{x}}$. — Rearrange to find the general solution.

What do we do if the left-hand side is not quite in the right form? Consider the differential equation $\frac{dy}{dx} + 3y = e^{-3x}$. The left-hand side is not quite $\frac{d}{dx}(3xy)$, as this would be $3y + 3x\frac{dy}{dx}$. We need a different approach.

We shall look at a general first order differential equation in the form $\frac{dy}{dx} + Fy = G$, where F and G are functions of x.

We require the left side to be of the form $u\frac{dv}{dx} + v\frac{du}{dx}$, so we are going to multiply through by the function $I(x)$ so that $I\frac{dy}{dx} + FIy = GI$. Then we are going to match the terms with $u\frac{dv}{dx} + v\frac{du}{dx}$.

Letting $u = I$, we then find that $v = y$, $\frac{dv}{dx} = \frac{dy}{dx}$ and $\frac{du}{dx} = FI$. Now our aim is to find the function $I(x)$. Since $\frac{du}{dx} = \frac{dI}{dx}$ it follows that $\frac{dI}{dx} = FI$.

Separating variables, $\int \frac{1}{I}\,dI = \int F\,dx$, then $\ln I = \int F\,dx$, which means $I(x) = e^{\int F\,dx}$.

This is known as the **integrating factor**.

If your differential equation is written in the form $\frac{dy}{dx} + Fy = G$, then $F(x)$ is easy to spot.

We now go back to the example of $\frac{dy}{dx} + 3y = e^{-3x}$ and note that $F = 3$. Hence, $I = e^{\int 3\,dx}$, and so the integrating factor is e^{3x}.

Next we multiply through by $I(x)$, so $e^{3x}\frac{dy}{dx} + 3e^{3x}y = 1$. The left-hand side can now be written as $\frac{d}{dx}(e^{3x}y)$, so $\frac{d}{dx}(e^{3x}y) = 1$. Solving this equation leads to $e^{3x}y = x + c$, or $y = xe^{-3x} + ce^{-3x}$.

WORKED EXAMPLE 24.2

Confirm that the differential equation $x\frac{dy}{dx} + y = x$ can be solved using the integrating factor method.

Answer

For $x\frac{dy}{dx} + y = x$, let $\frac{dy}{dx} + \frac{y}{x} = 1$, then $F = \frac{1}{x}$.	Rewrite the equation in the form $\frac{dy}{dx} + Fy = G$.
So $\int \frac{1}{x}\,dx = \ln x$, then $I = e^{\ln x} = x$	Integrate $F(x)$, and state $I(x)$.
and so $x\frac{dy}{dx} + y = x$.	Multiply the rewritten equation by x.
Also we know that $\frac{d}{dx}(xy) = x$ leads to the result we saw earlier.	Show the left side can be reduced to $\frac{d}{dx}(Iy)$.

Note that in more complicated first order equations, it is generally just the functions F and G that are more complicated.

For example, if we are to solve $\frac{dy}{dx} + y\cot x = 2\cos x$, we first need to focus on $F = \cot x$.

Then $\int \cot x\,dx = \int \frac{\cos x}{\sin x}\,dx$. This integrates to give $\ln(\sin x)$, so then $I = e^{\ln \sin x} = \sin x$.

Next, we multiply through by $\sin x$ to get $\sin x\frac{dy}{dx} + y\cos x = 2\sin x\cos x$. This simplifies to give $\frac{d}{dx}(y\sin x) = \sin 2x$. Integrating both sides with respect to x leads to $y\sin x = -\frac{1}{2}\cos 2x + c$, and so the general solution is $y = -\frac{\cos 2x}{2\sin x} + c\,\mathrm{cosec}\,x$.

WORKED EXAMPLE 24.3

Find the general solution of $\cot t\frac{dy}{dt} + y = \mathrm{cosec}\,t - \sin t$.

Answer

Start with $\frac{\cos t}{\sin t}\frac{dy}{dt} + y = \frac{1}{\sin t} - \sin t$.	Rewrite the equation in the form $\frac{dy}{dt} + Fy = G$.

Multiply through by $\tan t$

$$\frac{dy}{dt} + y\tan t = \frac{1}{\cos t} - \frac{\sin^2 t}{\cos t}.$$

Simplify to get $\frac{dy}{dt} + y\frac{\sin t}{\cos t} = \cos t$.

Note $F = \frac{\sin t}{\cos t}$, — Simplify the right-hand side and state the function F.

so $I = e^{\int \frac{\sin t}{\cos t} dt} = e^{-\ln \cos t} = \sec t$. — Integrate F in order to determine I.

Multiplying through by I leads to — Multiply through by I.

$$\sec t\frac{dy}{dt} + y\sec t\tan t = 1.$$

Then $\frac{d}{dt}(y\sec t) = 1$. — Simplify the left-hand side.

Integrating gives $y\sec t = t + c$. — Integrate with respect to t.

This leads to the general solution $y = t\cos t + c\cos t$. — Obtain the general solution.

KEY POINT 24.1

For the differential equation $\frac{dy}{dx} + Fy = G$, the left-hand side will always reduce to $\frac{d}{dx}(Iy)$, where I is the integrating factor.

In order to find the constant of integration we need to know some initial conditions.

Consider the differential equation $\frac{dy}{dx} - 4y = x$ with initial conditions $y = 2$ when $x = 0$.

To solve this we shall first find the general solution, as shown in Key point 24.1.

Since $F = -4$, we can see that $I = e^{\int -4dx} = e^{-4x}$. Then $e^{-4x}\frac{dy}{dx} - 4e^{-4x}y = xe^{-4x}$, which simplifies to $\frac{d}{dx}(ye^{-4x}) = xe^{-4x}$.

For the right-hand side, we use integration by parts. Let $u = x$, $\frac{du}{dx} = 1$ and $\frac{dv}{dx} = e^{-4x}$, $v = -\frac{1}{4}e^{-4x}$.

Then $ye^{-4x} = -\frac{x}{4}e^{-4x} + \frac{1}{4}\int e^{-4x}dx$.

Completing the integration, $ye^{-4x} = -\frac{x}{4}e^{-4x} - \frac{1}{16}e^{-4x} + c$. With the initial conditions $y = 2$, $x = 0$, we have $2 = -\frac{1}{16} + c$, and so $c = \frac{33}{16}$. Hence, the solution is $y = -\frac{x}{4} - \frac{1}{16} + \frac{33}{16}e^{4x}$. When initial conditions are used the solution is known as a **particular solution**.

WORKED EXAMPLE 24.4

Find the particular solution for the differential equation $t\dfrac{dx}{dt} + 3x = t^2 + 1$, with initial conditions $x = 1, t = 1$.

Answer

Let $\dfrac{dx}{dt} + \dfrac{3}{t}x = t + \dfrac{1}{t}$, then $F = \dfrac{3}{t}$. — Divide through by t.

So $\displaystyle\int \frac{3}{t}\,dt = 3\ln t$, hence $I = e^{3\ln t} = e^{\ln t^3} = t^3$. — Use the integral of F to determine I.

Then $t^3\dfrac{dx}{dt} + 3t^2x = t^4 + t^2$. — Multiply through by I.

Left side is then $\dfrac{d}{dt}(xt^3) = t^4 + t^2$. — Simplify the left side.

Integrating both sides leads to: — Integrate both sides with respect to t.

$xt^3 = \dfrac{1}{5}t^5 + \dfrac{1}{3}t^3 + c$

Using $x = 1, t = 1$ leads to $c = \dfrac{7}{15}$. — Use the initial conditions to find c.

Hence, $x = \dfrac{1}{5}t^2 + \dfrac{1}{3} + \dfrac{7}{15t^3}$. — Divide through by t^3 to get the particular solution.

WORKED EXAMPLE 24.5

Solve the differential equation $\dfrac{dy}{dt} + y\coth t = 2e^{3t}$ that has initial conditions $y = 0, t = 0$.

Answer

Let $F = \coth t$, then: — State the function F and integrate it.

$\displaystyle\int \coth t\,dt = \int \frac{\cosh t}{\sinh t}\,dt = \ln\sinh t$

Then $I = e^{\int F\,dt} = \sinh t$, — Use $I = e^{\int F\,dt}$ to get $I = \sinh t$.

so $\sinh t\dfrac{dy}{dt} + y\cosh t = 2e^{3t}\left(\dfrac{e^t - e^{-t}}{2}\right)$. — Multiply through by $\sinh t$ and make use of $\sinh t = \dfrac{e^t - e^{-t}}{2}$.

This simplifies to give $\dfrac{d}{dt}(y\sinh t) = e^{4t} - e^{2t}$. — Simplify the expression.

Integrating, $y\sinh t = \dfrac{1}{4}e^{4t} - \dfrac{1}{2}e^{2t} + c$. — Integrate with respect to t.

Using the initial conditions, $t = 0, y = 0$, — Use the initial conditions to determine c.

leads to $c = \dfrac{1}{4}$.

Hence, $y\sinh t = \frac{1}{4}e^{4t} - \frac{1}{2}e^{2t} + \frac{1}{4}$ or

$y = \frac{1}{4\sinh t}(e^{4t} - 2e^{2t} + 1)$. Determine the particular solution.

EXERCISE 24A

1 Solve the differential equation $\frac{dy}{dx} + \frac{2}{x}y = \frac{\sin x}{x^2}$ to find the general solution.

2 Solve the differential equation $\frac{dy}{dx} + 2y = x^3e^{-2x}$ to find the general solution.

3 Solve the differential equation $\frac{dy}{dx} - 7y = e^{2x}$ to find the general solution.

M 4 The differential equation $2\frac{dx}{dt} - 4x = t$ has initial conditions $x = 1, t = 0$. Find the particular solution.

PS 5 Solve the differential equation $(x - 2)\frac{dy}{dx} - 2y = (x - 2)^4$ and find the particular solution, given that $y = 4$ when $x = 0$.

PS 6 A differential equation is such that the rate of change of y with respect to x is equal to the sum of x and y.

a Write down the differential equation.

b Find the general solution.

7 Find the general solution for the differential equation $\frac{dy}{dx} + y\tanh x = 4x$.

M 8 Given that the differential equation $\sec t\frac{dy}{dt} + y\operatorname{cosec} t = \sin^2 t\sec t$ has initial conditions $y = 0, t = \frac{\pi}{2}$, find the particular solution.

PS 9 A substance, X, is decaying such that the rate of change of the mass, x, is proportional to four times its mass. Another substance, Y, is such that the rate of change of the mass, y, is equal to $x - 2y$. Initially the values of x and y are 20 and 0, respectively.

a Find x as a function of t.

b Find y as a function of t.

c Determine the maximum value of y, giving your answer in an exact form.

24.2 Second order differential equations: The homogeneous case

Consider the first order differential equation $\frac{dy}{dx} = y$. From previous encounters with separable differential equations, our first instinct is to write $\int \frac{1}{y}\,dy = \int dx$ and then find the general solution.

We shall look at a different approach which can be extended to solve second order differential equations. If, instead, we consider that a function is equal to the derivative of itself, we can then assume that the solution must be of the form $y = Ae^{\lambda x}$, where A and λ are constants.

Next, we write the equation as $\frac{dy}{dx} - y = 0$, and if $y = Ae^{\lambda x}$ then $\frac{dy}{dx} = A\lambda e^{\lambda x}$. So our **homogeneous differential equation** becomes $A\lambda e^{\lambda x} - Ae^{\lambda x} = 0$, or $\lambda - 1 = 0$. This equation with λ is called the **auxiliary equation**.

Hence, since the only solution is $\lambda = 1$, the general solution is $y = Ae^{x}$, as shown in Key point 24.2.

KEY POINT 24.2

If the trial solution is $y = Ae^{\lambda x}$, then $A \neq 0$.

This allows us to divide the auxiliary equation by $Ae^{\lambda x}$.

WORKED EXAMPLE 24.6

Find the general solution of the differential equation $\frac{dy}{dx} + 3y = 0$.

Answer

Let $y = Ae^{\lambda x}$.	State the 'trial' solution.
Then $\frac{dy}{dx} = A\lambda e^{\lambda x}$.	Differentiate the trial solution with respect to x.
Then $A\lambda e^{\lambda x} + 3Ae^{\lambda x} = 0$, so our auxiliary equation is $\lambda + 3 = 0$ since $Ae^{\lambda x} \neq 0$.	Divide by $Ae^{\lambda x}$ and determine the auxiliary equation.
Hence, $\lambda = -3$.	State the λ value.
Then the general solution is $y = Ae^{-3x}$.	Write down the general solution.

Extending this idea to second order differential equations, consider $\frac{d^2y}{dx^2} - 3\frac{dy}{dx} + 2y = 0$.

Again, we can see that the second derivative of a function, combined with multiples of the first derivative and the function itself, leads to zero. This can happen only with an exponential function with base e.

So we try $y = Ae^{\lambda x}$, then $\frac{dy}{dx} = A\lambda e^{\lambda x}$ and $\frac{d^2y}{dx^2} = A\lambda^2 e^{\lambda x}$. So $A\lambda^2 e^{\lambda x} - 3A\lambda e^{\lambda x} + 2Ae^{\lambda x} = 0$.

Since $Ae^{\lambda x} \neq 0$, the auxiliary equation is $\lambda^2 - 3\lambda + 2 = 0$.

Then $\lambda_1 = 1, \lambda_2 = 2$, so the general solution is either $y = Ae^{x}$ or $y = Be^{2x}$.

If we start with $y = Ae^{x}$, then $\frac{dy}{dx} = Ae^{x}$, $\frac{d^2y}{dx^2} = Ae^{x}$. Substituting into the differential equation gives $Ae^{x} - 3Ae^{x} + 2Ae^{x} = 0$, and so this solution satisfies the equation.

Next try $y = Be^{2x}$, then $\frac{dy}{dx} = 2Be^{2x}$, $\frac{d^2y}{dx^2} = 4Be^{2x}$. Substituting into the differential equation gives $4Be^{2x} - 3 \times 2Be^{2x} + 2 \times Be^{2x} = 0$, and so this solution also satisfies the equation.

As both solutions are valid, we can combine them and write $y = Ae^x + Be^{2x}$ as the solution. This is known as the **complementary function**.

For example, if we consider the differential equation $\frac{d^2y}{dx^2} + 5\frac{dy}{dx} + 4y = 0$, then the first step to solving is to try $y = Ae^{\lambda x}$. Then $\frac{dy}{dx} = A\lambda e^{\lambda x}$, $\frac{d^2y}{dx^2} = A\lambda^2 e^{\lambda x}$. The auxiliary equation is then $\lambda^2 + 5\lambda + 4 = 0$. This gives two solutions, $\lambda_1 = -1, \lambda_2 = -4$.

Hence, the complementary function is $y = Ae^{-x} + Be^{-4x}$, using the formula shown in Key point 24.3. This is only possible since the differential equation is linear in y and in its derivatives.

KEY POINT 24.3

If $a\frac{d^2y}{dx^2} + b\frac{dy}{dx} + cy = 0$ has roots of auxiliary equation λ_1, λ_2, where $\lambda_1 \neq \lambda_2$, then the complementary function is $y = Ae^{\lambda_1 x} + Be^{\lambda_2 x}$.

WORKED EXAMPLE 24.7

Find the complementary function for the differential equation $\frac{d^2x}{dt^2} + 3\frac{dx}{dt} - 10x = 0$.

Answer

Try $x = Ae^{\lambda t}$, then $\frac{dx}{dt} = A\lambda e^{\lambda t}$, $\frac{d^2x}{dt^2} = A\lambda^2 e^{\lambda t}$. — Differentiate the trial solution twice with respect to t.

So $A\lambda^2 e^{\lambda t} + 3A\lambda e^{\lambda t} - 10Ae^{\lambda t} = 0$. — Substitute into the differential equation and divide by $Ae^{\lambda t}$.

Then the auxiliary equation is $\lambda^2 + 3\lambda - 10 = 0$.

The values are $\lambda_1 = -5, \lambda_2 = 2$. — State the two values of λ.

Hence, the complementary function is $x = Ae^{-5t} + Be^{2t}$. — Write down the complementary function.

Consider the differential equation $\frac{d^2y}{dx^2} + 2\frac{dy}{dx} + y = 0$. If we try $y = Ae^{\lambda x}$ as the solution, then $\frac{dy}{dx} = A\lambda e^{\lambda x}$ and $\frac{d^2y}{dx^2} = A\lambda^2 e^{\lambda x}$.

So the auxiliary equation would be $\lambda^2 + 2\lambda + 1 = 0$, or $(\lambda + 1)^2 = 0$. This means we have a repeated value of $\lambda = -1$, so can our complementary function be $y = Ae^{-x} + Be^{-x}$? No, since this is the same as $y = Ce^{-x}$. So it appears that we have 'lost' a solution somewhere.

Instead of using $y = Ce^{-x}$ we are going to try $y = F(x)e^{-x}$ as the complementary function.

So $\frac{dy}{dx} = F'(x)e^{-x} - F(x)e^{-x}$ and $\frac{d^2y}{dx^2} = F''(x)e^{-x} - F'(x)e^{-x} - F'(x)e^{-x} + F(x)e^{-x}$. We can substitute these results into the differential equation.

Thus $F''(x)e^{-x} - 2F'(x)e^{-x} + F(x)e^{-x} + 2(F'(x)e^{-x} - F(x)e^{-x}) + F(x)e^{-x} = 0$. Almost all terms cancel, so we are left with $F''(x) = 0$, and the only function that satisfies this condition is $F(x) = Ax + B$. So the complementary function is $y = (Ax + B)e^{-x}$, as shown in Key point 24.4.

To confirm that this works in our earlier problem, we get $\frac{dy}{dx} = Ae^{-x} - Axe^{-x} - Be^{-x}$, $\frac{d^2y}{dx^2} = -2Ae^{-x} + Axe^{-x} + Be^{-x}$.

Then $-2Ae^{-x} + Axe^{-x} + Be^{-x} + 2(Ae^{-x} - Axe^{-x} - Be^{-x}) + Axe^{-x} + Be^{-x} = 0$ is satisfied.

KEY POINT 24.4

If $a\frac{d^2y}{dx^2} + b\frac{dy}{dx} + cy = 0$ has roots of auxiliary equation λ_1, λ_2, where $\lambda_1 = \lambda_2 = \lambda$, then the complementary function is $y = (Ax + B)e^{\lambda x}$.

WORKED EXAMPLE 24.8

For the differential equation $\frac{d^2r}{dt^2} - 4\frac{dr}{dt} + 4r = 0$, find the complementary function.

Answer

Try $r = Ae^{\lambda t}$, then $\frac{dr}{dt} = A\lambda e^{\lambda t}$, $\frac{d^2r}{dt^2} = A\lambda^2 e^{\lambda t}$.	Differentiate the trial function twice with respect to t.
Substitute into the equation, giving: $A\lambda^2 e^{\lambda t} - 4A\lambda e^{\lambda t} + 4Ae^{\lambda t} = 0$	Substitute the results into the differential equation and cancel the $Ae^{\lambda t}$ terms.
Then $\lambda^2 - 4\lambda + 4 = 0$ leads to $\lambda = 2$.	Determine the repeated solution.
So the complementary function is $r = (At + B)e^{2t}$.	State the complementary function.

Next we shall consider a special case, the differential equation $\frac{d^2y}{dx^2} + 2\frac{dy}{dx} + 5y = 0$. This has an auxiliary equation $\lambda^2 + 2\lambda + 5 = 0$.

When solving this quadratic we get $\lambda_1 = -1 + 2i, \lambda_2 = -1 - 2i$. So the complementary function is $y = Ae^{(-1+2i)x} + Be^{(-1-2i)x}$, which can be written as $y = e^{-x}(Ae^{2ix} + Be^{-2ix})$.

This equation is not in a suitable form, so we shall use Euler's formula, $e^{ix} = \cos x + i\sin x$, to simplify our result.

Using Euler's formula, $y = e^{-x}(A\cos 2x + Ai\sin 2x + B\cos 2x - Bi\sin 2x)$, then using $C = A + B$ and $D = Ai - Bi$ leads to $y = e^{-x}(C\cos 2x + D\sin 2x)$.

For example, if the differential equation is $\frac{d^2x}{dt^2} + 4\frac{dx}{dt} + 8x = 0$, then we first try $x = Ae^{\lambda t}$, and from this we have the usual $\frac{dx}{dt} = A\lambda e^{\lambda t}$, $\frac{d^2x}{dt^2} = A\lambda^2 e^{\lambda t}$.

Then the auxiliary equation is $\lambda^2 + 4\lambda + 8 = 0$, so $\lambda = -2 \pm 2\mathrm{i}$. This means that the complementary function is $x = \mathrm{e}^{-2t}(A\cos 2t + B\sin 2t)$, as shown in Key point 24.5.

KEY POINT 24.5

If $a\frac{\mathrm{d}^2y}{\mathrm{d}x^2} + b\frac{\mathrm{d}y}{\mathrm{d}x} + cy = 0$ has roots of auxiliary equation $\lambda_1 = m + n\mathrm{i}, \lambda_2 = m - n\mathrm{i}$, then the complementary function is given by $y = \mathrm{e}^{mx}(A\cos nx + B\sin nx)$.

WORKED EXAMPLE 24.9

Find the complementary function for the differential equation $8\frac{\mathrm{d}^2y}{\mathrm{d}x^2} + 12\frac{\mathrm{d}y}{\mathrm{d}x} + 17y = 0$.

Answer

Let $y = A\mathrm{e}^{\lambda x}$, giving $\frac{\mathrm{d}y}{\mathrm{d}x} = A\lambda\mathrm{e}^{\lambda x}, \frac{\mathrm{d}^2y}{\mathrm{d}x^2} = A\lambda^2\mathrm{e}^{\lambda x}$. — Determine the first and second derivatives.

Then the auxiliary equation is $8\lambda^2 + 12\lambda + 17 = 0$ and the solutions are $\lambda_1 = -\frac{3}{4} + \frac{5}{4}\mathrm{i}, \lambda_2 = -\frac{3}{4} - \frac{5}{4}\mathrm{i}$. — Solve the auxiliary equation to obtain the λ values.

So $y = \mathrm{e}^{-\frac{3}{4}x}\left(A\cos\frac{5}{4}x + B\sin\frac{5}{4}x\right)$. — State the complementary function.

EXPLORE 24.1

Investigate what the complementary function would look like for

$\frac{\mathrm{d}^3y}{\mathrm{d}x^3} + 2\frac{\mathrm{d}^2y}{\mathrm{d}x^2} - \frac{\mathrm{d}y}{\mathrm{d}x} - 2 = 0$ and $3\frac{\mathrm{d}^3y}{\mathrm{d}x^3} - 8\frac{\mathrm{d}^2y}{\mathrm{d}x^2} + 55\frac{\mathrm{d}y}{\mathrm{d}x} - 34 = 0$.

To determine the constants *A* and *B*, we need to know a set of conditions.

For example, consider the differential equation $\frac{\mathrm{d}^2x}{\mathrm{d}t^2} + 25x = 0$ and the initial conditions $x = 0, \frac{\mathrm{d}x}{\mathrm{d}t} = 2$ when $t = 0$.

Start with $x = A\mathrm{e}^{\lambda t}$ to get $\frac{\mathrm{d}^2x}{\mathrm{d}t^2} = A\lambda^2\mathrm{e}^{\lambda t}$, then the auxiliary equation $\lambda^2 + 25 = 0$ has solutions $\lambda = \pm 5\mathrm{i}$. This leads to the complementary function $x = A\cos 5t + B\sin 5t$.

Then $x = 0, t = 0$ leads to $A = 0$, giving $x = B\sin 5t$. Differentiating gives $\frac{\mathrm{d}x}{\mathrm{d}t} = 5B\cos 5t$.

When $\frac{\mathrm{d}x}{\mathrm{d}t} = 2, t = 0$ so $B = \frac{2}{5}$. Hence, $x = \frac{2}{5}\sin 5t$. This is known as a particular solution.

The other type of conditions are known as **boundary conditions**. These differ from initial conditions in that there are two extreme values defined for the independent variable.

For example, when $x = 0, y = 1$ and when $x = 1, y = 2$.

WORKED EXAMPLE 24.10

The second order differential equation $2\frac{d^2y}{dx^2}+7\frac{dy}{dx}+3y=0$ has initial conditions $y=0$ and $\frac{dy}{dx}=\frac{5}{2}$ when $x=0$. Find the particular solution.

Answer

Start with $y=Ae^{\lambda x}$, then $\frac{dy}{dx}=A\lambda e^{\lambda x}$, $\frac{d^2y}{dx^2}=A\lambda^2e^{\lambda x}$.

The auxiliary equation is $2\lambda^2+7\lambda+3=0$. — Using the trial solution, obtain the auxiliary equation.

This leads to the solutions $\lambda_1=-3, \lambda_2=-\frac{1}{2}$. — Determine the solutions to the equation.

So $y=Ae^{-3x}+Be^{-\frac{1}{2}x}$. — State the complementary function.

When $x=0, y=0$ so $A+B=0$. — Use one initial condition.

Then differentiating gives $\frac{dy}{dx}=-3Ae^{-3x}-\frac{1}{2}Be^{-\frac{1}{2}x}$.

When $x=0, \frac{dy}{dx}=\frac{5}{2}$ gives $-3A-\frac{1}{2}B=\frac{5}{2}$. — Differentiate and use the second initial condition.

Solving the simultaneous equations gives $A=-1, B=1$. — State the solutions of the equations.

So the particular solution is $y=e^{-\frac{1}{2}x}-e^{-3x}$. — State the particular solution.

WORKED EXAMPLE 24.11

Given that the boundary conditions for the differential equation $\frac{d^2y}{dx^2}+8\frac{dy}{dx}+16y=0$ are when $x=0, y=1$ and when $x=1, y=0$, find the particular solution.

Answer

Start with $y=Ae^{\lambda x}$, then $\frac{dy}{dx}=A\lambda e^{\lambda x}$, $\frac{d^2y}{dx^2}=A\lambda^2e^{\lambda x}$. — Determine the first and second derivatives.

Then the auxiliary equation is $\lambda^2+8\lambda+16=0$, from which we obtain the repeated value $\lambda=-4$. — Solve the auxiliary equation to obtain λ.

This leads to the complementary function $y = (Ax + B)e^{-4x}$.	State the complementary function.
When $x = 0, y = 1$ gives $B = 1$, and $x = 1, y = 0$ leads to $A = -1$.	The boundary conditions enable us to find B and then A.
So $y = (1 - x)e^{-4x}$.	State the complementary function.

DID YOU KNOW?

The Black–Scholes equation in Financial Mathematics is related to the differential equation for modelling heat transfer in materials.

EXERCISE 24B

1 Find the general solution for the differential equation $\frac{d^2y}{dx^2} - 3\frac{dy}{dx} - 18y = 0$.

2 Find the general solution for the differential equation $\frac{d^2y}{dx^2} - 6\frac{dy}{dx} - 34y = 0$.

3 Find the general solution for the differential equation $\frac{d^2y}{dx^2} + 16\frac{dy}{dx} + 64y = 0$.

M 4 For the second order differential equation $a\frac{d^2y}{dx^2} + b\frac{dy}{dx} + cy = 0$, write the complementary functions for each of the following cases.

a $\lambda_1 = 2, \lambda_2 = -5$

b $\lambda_1 = -2 + 3i, \lambda_2 = -2 - 3i$

c $\lambda = 4$

PS 5 For the differential equation $\frac{d^2x}{dt^2} - 4x = 0$, determine the particular solution, given that the initial conditions are $x = 1$ and $\frac{dx}{dt} = 4$ when $t = 0$.

PS 6 Find the particular solution for the second order differential equation $9\frac{d^2r}{dt^2} - 12\frac{dr}{dt} + 4r = 0$, given that the initial conditions are $r = 2$ and $\frac{dr}{dt} = 3$ when $t = 0$.

P M 7 A differential equation is given as $\frac{d^2y}{dx^2} + 4y = 0$.

a Find the complementary function.

b Using the boundary conditions $x = 0, y = 1$ and $x = \frac{\pi}{2}, \frac{dy}{dx} = -1$, show that the particular solution is of the form $y = R\cos(2x - \alpha)$, stating the exact value of R and α, in radians, correct to 3 significant figures.

P 8 Given that $\frac{d^2s}{d\theta^2} + 7\frac{ds}{d\theta} + 6s = 0$ has initial conditions $s = 1, \frac{ds}{d\theta} = -1$ when $\theta = 0$, show that $s \to 0$ for large values of θ, and sketch the curve representing the particular solution.

24.3 Second order differential equations: The inhomogeneous case

So far we have looked at cases where the right-hand side of the equation is equal to zero.

Now we shall consider differential equations of the form $a\dfrac{d^2y}{dx^2} + b\dfrac{dy}{dx} + cy = f(x)$. These are known as **inhomogeneous differential equations**.

First we consider $\dfrac{d^2y}{dx^2} + 3\dfrac{dy}{dx} + 2y = 1$. If the right-hand side is equal to zero, then the auxiliary equation is $\lambda^2 + 3\lambda + 2 = 0$ leading to solutions $\lambda_1 = -1, \lambda_2 = -2$. The complementary function is $y = Ae^{-x} + Be^{-2x}$. But if we were to substitute the complementary function into the differential equation, we get $0 = 1$. So we need a function that deals with the 1 on the right side.

If we try $y = \dfrac{1}{2}$, then with $\dfrac{dy}{dx} = 0, \dfrac{d^2y}{dx^2} = 0$ this is actually a solution. So the next step is to try $y = Ae^{-x} + Be^{-2x} + \dfrac{1}{2}$ as the solution. Then $\dfrac{dy}{dx} = -Ae^{-x} - 2Be^{-2x}$ and $\dfrac{d^2y}{dx^2} = Ae^{-x} + 4Be^{-2x}$. Substituting into our equation, $Ae^{-x} + 4Be^{-2x} - 3Ae^{-x} - 6Be^{-2x} + 2Ae^{-x} + 2Be^{-2x} + 1 = 1$, and simplifying gives us $1 = 1$. Hence, the solution is $y = Ae^{-x} + Be^{-2x} + \dfrac{1}{2}$.

How does this solution actually work? The additional term is known as the **particular integral** (PI). The particular integral is a solution of the differential equation that deals with the right-hand side being f(x). It is of a similar form to f(x). Once we have the particular integral, the complementary function (CF) will satisfy the remaining part of the differential equation.

The result is known as a **general solution** (GS), which is normally represented by GS = CF + PI.

If the differential equation is $\dfrac{d^2y}{dx^2} + 3\dfrac{dy}{dx} + 2y = 4$ and we are not sure what is the particular integral, then we could try $y = \alpha$. With $\dfrac{dy}{dx} = 0, \dfrac{d^2y}{dx^2} = 0$ it follows that $2\alpha = 4$ and so $\alpha = 2$. As before, the complementary function is $Ae^{-x} + Be^{-2x}$.

Hence, the general solution would be $y = Ae^{-x} + Be^{-2x} + 2$.

Another example is the differential equation $\dfrac{d^2y}{dx^2} + 3\dfrac{dy}{dx} + 2y = x$. Since the right-hand side is now a linear function, it is best to try $y = \alpha x + \beta$, then $\dfrac{dy}{dx} = \alpha, \dfrac{d^2y}{dx^2} = 0$.

Substituting this into the differential equation gives $3\alpha + 2\alpha x + 2\beta = x$. So $2\alpha x = x \Rightarrow \alpha = \dfrac{1}{2}$ and $3\alpha + 2\beta = 0$. This leads to $\beta = -\dfrac{3}{4}$ and so the particular integral is $y = \dfrac{1}{2}x - \dfrac{3}{4}$.

Hence, the general solution is $y = Ae^{-x} + Be^{-2x} + \dfrac{1}{2}x - \dfrac{3}{4}$, as shown in Key point 24.6.

KEY POINT 24.6

When the right-hand side of a differential equation is a polynomial function of degree n, let the particular integral be $y = \alpha x^n + \beta x^{n-1} + \ldots$. Ensure that there are $n + 1$ terms in your polynomial.

WORKED EXAMPLE 24.12

For $\frac{d^2y}{dx^2} + 4\frac{dy}{dx} + 4y = 2 + x^2$ determine both the complementary function and the particular integral. Hence, write the general solution.

Answer

Assume the right-hand side is zero, then let $y = Ae^{\lambda x}$ so that: $\frac{dy}{dx} = A\lambda e^{\lambda x}$, $\frac{d^2y}{dx^2} = A\lambda^2 e^{\lambda x}$.

Let the right-hand side = 0 and find the complementary function in the normal way.

The auxiliary equation will be $\lambda^2 + 4\lambda + 4 = 0$. This has a repeated root of $\lambda = -2$, and so the complementary function is $y = (Ax + B)e^{-2x}$.

From the auxiliary equation state the complementary function.

For the particular integral, let $y = \alpha x^2 + \beta x + \gamma$.

For the particular integral, try a function that is in the same general form as the right-hand side.

$\frac{dy}{dx} = 2\alpha x + \beta$, $\frac{d^2y}{dx^2} = 2\alpha$

Differentiate twice with respect to x, and substitute into the differential equation.

So $2\alpha + 8\alpha x + 4\beta + 4\alpha x^2 + 4\beta x + 4\gamma = 2 + x^2$.

So $\alpha = \frac{1}{4}, \beta = -\frac{1}{2}, \gamma = \frac{7}{8}$.

Equate like terms and determine the values of the coefficients.

This means the particular integral is:

$y = \frac{1}{4}x^2 - \frac{1}{2}x + \frac{7}{8}$

State the particular integral.

Then using GS = CF + PI:

$y = (Ax + B)e^{-2x} + \frac{1}{4}x^2 - \frac{1}{2}x + \frac{7}{8}$

State the general solution.

As well as polynomials, the right-hand side can also be an exponential function. Let us look at the differential equation $\frac{d^2y}{dx^2} + 3\frac{dy}{dx} + 2y = e^{3x}$, which has the complementary function $y = Ae^{-x} + Be^{-2x}$ as before. For the particular integral we try $y = \alpha e^{3x}$, then

$\frac{dy}{dx} = 3\alpha e^{3x}$, $\frac{d^2y}{dx^2} = 9\alpha e^{3x}$.

If we substitute these results into the differential equation, $20\alpha e^{3x} = e^{3x} \Rightarrow \alpha = \frac{1}{20}$.

So $y = \frac{1}{20}e^{3x}$ is our particular integral, as shown in Key point 24.7. The general solution is $y = Ae^{-x} + Be^{-2x} + \frac{1}{20}e^{3x}$.

KEY POINT 24.7

When the right-hand side of a differential equation is an exponential function of the form $k\mathrm{e}^{\lambda x}$, try $y = \alpha\mathrm{e}^{\lambda x}$ as the particular integral.

WORKED EXAMPLE 24.13

Given that $\frac{\mathrm{d}^2y}{\mathrm{d}x^2} + 3\frac{\mathrm{d}y}{\mathrm{d}x} + 2y = \mathrm{e}^{\frac{1}{2}x} + 2x + 5$, determine the general solution.

Answer

As with previous examples, the complementary function is $y = A\mathrm{e}^{-x} + B\mathrm{e}^{-2x}$.

For the particular integral, try $y = \alpha\mathrm{e}^{\frac{1}{2}x} + \beta x + \gamma$, — For this particular integral we need to match the exponential function as well as the polynomial.

then $\frac{\mathrm{d}y}{\mathrm{d}x} = \frac{1}{2}\alpha\mathrm{e}^{\frac{1}{2}x} + \beta$ and $\frac{\mathrm{d}^2y}{\mathrm{d}x^2} = \frac{1}{4}\alpha\mathrm{e}^{\frac{1}{2}x}$. — Differentiate the particular integral twice.

Substituting gives: — Substitute into the differential equation.

$$\frac{1}{4}\alpha\mathrm{e}^{\frac{1}{2}x} + \frac{3}{2}\alpha\mathrm{e}^{\frac{1}{2}x} + 3\beta + 2\alpha\mathrm{e}^{\frac{1}{2}x} + 2\beta x + 2\gamma = \mathrm{e}^{\frac{1}{2}x} + 2x + 5$$

Solving leads to $\alpha = \frac{4}{15}, \beta = 1, \gamma = 1$. — Equate the coefficients to determine α, β and γ.

Hence, the particular solution is $\frac{4}{15}\mathrm{e}^{\frac{1}{2}x} + x + 1$, — State the particular solution.

giving $y = A\mathrm{e}^{-x} + B\mathrm{e}^{-2x} + \frac{4}{15}\mathrm{e}^{\frac{1}{2}x} + x + 1$. — Use GS = CF + PI to write down the general solution.

So far we have seen cases where the right-hand side of a differential equation is either a polynomial or an exponential function. Now we are going to look at cases where the right side is a trigonometric function.

Consider the differential equation $\frac{\mathrm{d}^2y}{\mathrm{d}x^2} + 3\frac{\mathrm{d}y}{\mathrm{d}x} + 2y = \cos 2x$, with the complementary function being $y = A\mathrm{e}^{-x} + B\mathrm{e}^{-2x}$.

For the particular integral we will try $y = \alpha\cos 2x$, with $\frac{\mathrm{d}y}{\mathrm{d}x} = -2\alpha\sin 2x$, $\frac{\mathrm{d}^2y}{\mathrm{d}x^2} = -4\alpha\cos 2x$, and then substitute this into the differential equation.

So $-4\alpha\cos 2x - 6\alpha\sin 2x + 2\alpha\cos 2x = \cos 2x$. Equating coefficients of $\cos 2x$ gives $\alpha = -\frac{1}{2}$, and equating coefficients of $\sin 2x$ we get $\alpha = 0$. As the system is inconsistent, we must now adopt a new approach.

For the particular integral we are going to try $y = \alpha\cos 2x + \beta\sin 2x$. This alternative form is required due to the cyclic nature of sine and cosine.

So $\frac{dy}{dx} = -2\alpha \sin 2x + 2\beta \cos 2x$ and $\frac{d^2y}{dx^2} = -4\alpha \cos 2x - 4\beta \sin 2x$. Substituting into the differential equation leads to $-4\alpha \cos 2x - 4\beta \sin 2x - 6\alpha \sin 2x + 6\beta \cos 2x + 2\alpha \cos 2x + 2\beta \sin 2x = \cos 2x$.

Equating coefficients of $\cos 2x$: $-2\alpha + 6\beta = 1$, and equating coefficients of $\sin 2x$: $-2\beta - 6\alpha = 0$. From these equations we obtain $\alpha = -\frac{1}{20}, \beta = \frac{3}{20}$, so the general solution is $y = A\mathrm{e}^{-x} + B\mathrm{e}^{-2x} - \frac{1}{20}\cos 2x + \frac{3}{20}\sin 2x$.

WORKED EXAMPLE 24.14

Find the general solution for $\frac{d^2h}{dt^2} - 2\frac{dh}{dt} + h = 3\sin t$.

Answer

Let the right-hand side be zero, then try $h = A\mathrm{e}^{\lambda t}$.

So $\frac{dh}{dt} = A\lambda \mathrm{e}^{\lambda t}$ and $\frac{d^2h}{dt^2} = A\lambda^2 \mathrm{e}^{\lambda t}$. — Differentiate the trial function twice.

The auxiliary equation is $\lambda^2 - 2\lambda + 1 = 0$. — Determine the auxiliary equation.

Leading to the CF: $h = (At + B)\mathrm{e}^t$. — State the complementary function.

For the PI try $h = \alpha \cos t + \beta \sin t$. — Remember the particular integral must contain both sine and cosine.

Differentiating twice:

$\frac{dh}{dt} = -\alpha \sin t + \beta \cos t, \frac{d^2h}{dt^2} = -\alpha \cos t - \beta \sin t$.

Substituting into the differential equation gives

$-\alpha \cos t - \beta \sin t + 2\alpha \sin t - 2\beta \cos t + \alpha \cos t + \beta \sin t = 3 \sin t$.

Then for $\cos t$: $-\alpha - 2\beta + \alpha = 0$ and for — Solve the simultaneous equations for α and β.

$\sin t$: $-\beta + 2\alpha + \beta = 3$, and so $\alpha = \frac{3}{2}, \beta = 0$.

So for the GS: $h = (At + B)\mathrm{e}^t + \frac{3}{2}\cos t$. — State the general solution.

When solving a second order differential equation, it is important to determine the complementary function first. There is a reason for this.

Consider the differential equation $\frac{d^2y}{dx^2} - 3\frac{dy}{dx} + 2y = \mathrm{e}^x$. By first considering that the right-hand side is zero, we have the auxiliary equation $\lambda^2 - 3\lambda + 2 = 0$. This means the complementary function is $y = A\mathrm{e}^x + B\mathrm{e}^{2x}$.

For the particular integral, we let $y = \alpha \mathrm{e}^x$, then $\frac{dy}{dx} = \alpha \mathrm{e}^x, \frac{d^2y}{dx^2} = \alpha \mathrm{e}^x$.

So $\alpha \mathrm{e}^x - 3\alpha \mathrm{e}^x + 2\alpha \mathrm{e}^x = \mathrm{e}^x$, or $0 = \mathrm{e}^x$.

This has happened because, apart from the constant, the particular integral is the same function as one of the complementary function terms. The way to deal with this is to treat it in a similar way to the repeated root case. We shall now try $y = \alpha x e^x$ as the particular integral.

So $\frac{dy}{dx} = \alpha e^x + \alpha x e^x$ and $\frac{d^2y}{dx^2} = 2\alpha e^x + \alpha x e^x$.

Now this time when we substitute into our differential equation we have $2\alpha e^x + \alpha x e^x - 3\alpha e^x - 3\alpha x e^x + 2\alpha x e^x = e^x$. This gives $\alpha = -1$.

So our general solution is $y = Ae^x + Be^{2x} - xe^x$.

WORKED EXAMPLE 24.15

Determine the general solution for the differential equation $\frac{d^2y}{dx^2} + 5\frac{dy}{dx} + 4y = 3e^{-x}$.

Answer

Let $y = Ae^{\lambda x}$.

When differentiated twice, the resulting auxiliary equation is $\lambda^2 + 5\lambda + 4 = 0$.

Use a suitable trial function to obtain the auxiliary equation.

So the complementary function is $y = Ae^{-x} + Be^{-4x}$.

Determine the complementary function.

For the particular integral try $y = \alpha x e^{-x}$.

Recognise the issue: the right-hand side is of a similar form to the CF. Adjust the particular integral.

Then $\frac{dy}{dx} = \alpha e^{-x} - \alpha x e^{-x}$ and $\frac{d^2y}{dx^2} = -2\alpha e^{-x} + \alpha x e^{-x}$.

Substituting into the differential equation gives

$-2\alpha e^{-x} + \alpha x e^{-x} + 5\alpha e^{-x} - 5\alpha x e^{-x} + 4x\alpha e^{-x} = 3e^{-x}$.

From this $\alpha = 1$.

Differentiate the particular integral and determine the value of α.

So the particular integral is given as $y = xe^{-x}$.

State the particular integral.

Hence, the general solution is $y = Ae^{-x} + Be^{-4x} + xe^{-x}$.

State the general solution.

EXPLORE 24.2

In groups or pairs, experiment with a particular integral that will work for the second order differential equation $\frac{d^2x}{dt^2} + 4x = 5\cos 2t$.

Let us look at the differential equation $\frac{d^2y}{dx^2} - 2\frac{dy}{dx} + y = e^x$. This example can pose quite a problem when trying to determine the particular integral.

First, the complementary function, obtained from $\lambda^2 - 2\lambda + 1 = 0$, is $y = (Ax + B)e^x$. We need to decide which particular integral to use: $y = \alpha e^x$ will match one term of the complementary function, as will $y = \alpha x e^x$. So we must try $y = \alpha x^2 e^x$. Differentiating, $\frac{dy}{dx} = 2\alpha x e^x + \alpha x^2 e^x$, $\frac{d^2y}{dx^2} = 2\alpha e^x + 4\alpha x e^x + \alpha x^2 e^x$, and then substituting into the differential equation gives $2\alpha e^x + 4\alpha x e^x + \alpha x^2 e^x - 4\alpha x e^x - 2\alpha x^2 e^x + \alpha x^2 e^x = e^x$. This leads to $\alpha = \frac{1}{2}$.

The particular integral is $y = \frac{1}{2}x^2 e^x$.

Hence, the general solution is $y = Be^x + Axe^x + \frac{1}{2}x^2 e^x$.

WORKED EXAMPLE 24.16

The differential equation $\frac{d^2y}{dt^2} + 8\frac{dy}{dt} + 16y = 2e^{-4t} + t$ has initial conditions $y = 1, \frac{dy}{dt} = 2$ when $t = 0$. Find the particular solution.

Answer

Let the right-hand side be zero, then try $y = Ae^{\lambda t}$. — Let the right-hand side = 0 and use a trial solution to find the auxiliary equation.

$\frac{dy}{dt} = A\lambda e^{\lambda t}$ and $\frac{d^2y}{dt^2} = A\lambda^2 e^{\lambda t}$. The auxiliary equation is $(\lambda + 4)^2 = 0$.

This leads to complementary function of $y = Ate^{-4t} + Be^{-4t}$. — Determine λ and state the complementary function.

For the particular integral, try $y = \alpha t^2 e^{-4t} + \beta t + \gamma$. — Use t^2e^{-4t} within the PI since te^{-4t} and e^{-4t} are both present in the complementary function.

Differentiating gives $\frac{dy}{dt} = 2\alpha t e^{-4t} - 4\alpha t^2 e^{-4t} + \beta$ — Differentiate the particular integral twice.

and $\frac{d^2y}{dt^2} = 2\alpha e^{-4t} - 16\alpha t e^{-4t} + 16\alpha t^2 e^{-4t}$.

Substituting into the differential equation gives

$2\alpha e^{-4t} - 16\alpha t e^{-4t} + 16\alpha t^2 e^{-4t} + 16\alpha t e^{-4t} - 32\alpha t^2 e^{-4t} + 8\beta + 16\alpha t^2 e^{-4t} + 16\beta t + 16\gamma = 2e^{-4t} + t$.

From these results we get $\alpha = 1, \beta = \frac{1}{16}, \gamma = -\frac{1}{32}$. — Use this to find the unknown constants.

So the GS is $y = Ate^{-4t} + Be^{-4t} + t^2e^{-4t} + \frac{1}{16}t - \frac{1}{32}$. — State the general solution.

With $t = 0, y = 1$ we get $B = \frac{33}{32}$. — Use initial values to find B.

Then — Differentiate, then use the other initial values to find A.

$\frac{dy}{dt} = Ae^{-4t} - 4Ate^{-4t} - \frac{33}{8}e^{-4t} + 2te^{-4t} - 4t^2e^{-4t} + \frac{1}{16}$.

Combined with $t = 0, \frac{dy}{dt} = 2$ leads to $A = \frac{97}{16}$.

So $y = \left(\frac{97}{16}t + \frac{33}{32}\right)e^{-4t} + t^2e^{-4t} + \frac{1}{16}t - \frac{1}{32}$ is the particular solution. — Write down the particular solution.

Suppose a differential equation is given as $\frac{d^2y}{dx^2} + 3\frac{dy}{dx} + 2y = x + 1$. We wish to know what happens to the solution as x becomes very large. First, we need to find the general solution.

When the right-hand side is zero, the complementary function is $y = Ae^{-x} + Be^{-2x}$. For the particular integral, we try $y = \alpha x + \beta$. After differentiating twice, and substituting into the differential equation we get $3\alpha + 2\alpha x + 2\beta = x + 1$. This leads to $\alpha = \frac{1}{2}$ and $\beta = -\frac{1}{4}$, so the particular integral is $y = \frac{1}{2}x - \frac{1}{4}$.

Now that we have established the general solution is $y = Ae^{-x} + Be^{-2x} + \frac{1}{2}x - \frac{1}{4}$, note that, when $x \to \infty$, the negative exponentials tend to zero. Hence, $y \to \frac{1}{2}x$.

WORKED EXAMPLE 24.17

Determine the general solution for $\frac{d^2y}{dx^2} + y = e^{-4x}$, and explain what happens to this solution as $x \to \infty$.

Answer

Let the right-hand side be zero and try $y = Ae^{\lambda x}$. This leads to the auxiliary equation $\lambda^2 + 1 = 0$.

Let the right-hand side = 0.

From this $y = A\cos x + B\sin x$ is the complementary function.

Determine the complementary function.

For the particular integral, try $y = \alpha e^{-4x}$.

Then $\frac{d^2y}{dx^2} = 16\alpha e^{-4x}$, which on substituting into the differential equation gives $16\alpha e^{-4x} + \alpha e^{-4x} = e^{-4x}$, which leads to $\alpha = \frac{1}{17}$.

Hence, the particular integral is $\frac{1}{17}e^{-4x}$.

Find the particular integral.

So the general solution is $y = A\cos x + B\sin x + \frac{1}{17}e^{-4x}$.

Use CF + PI to state the general solution.

Now if $x \to \infty$, $e^{-4x} \to 0$ then $y \approx A\cos x + B\sin x$.

Show the e^{-4x} term tends to zero.

This can also be written as $y = R\cos(x - \theta)$, where the constant $R = \sqrt{A^2 + B^2}$.

The addition formulae can be used to write a single trigonometric function.

So as $x \to \infty$ the function will oscillate between $-R$ and R and will have a mean value of zero.

The function clearly has a max and min value. The mean is zero because the function oscillates between its max and min values.

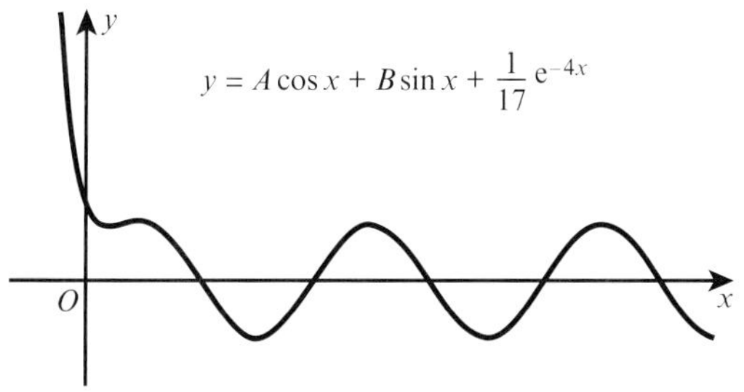

The graph shows how the function would tend towards an oscillating function.

EXERCISE 24C

1 Find the general solution for $\frac{d^2y}{dx^2} + 5\frac{dy}{dx} + 6y = -2x^2$.

PS 2 The second order differential equation $\frac{d^2r}{dt^2} - 4r = 3\cos t$ has initial conditions $r = 1, \frac{dr}{dt} = 1$ when $t = 0$.

a Find the complementary function and the particular integral.

b Hence, using the initial conditions, find the particular solution.

M 3 Given that $\frac{d^2x}{dt^2} + 2\frac{dx}{dt} + 5x = e^t + 2$ has initial conditions $x = -2, \frac{dx}{dt} = 0$ when $t = 0$, find the particular solution.

PS 4 Find the general solution of $\frac{d^2y}{dx^2} + 6\frac{dy}{dx} + 9y = x + e^{2x}$, stating $\lim_{x \to \infty} y$.

5 State, without evaluating, the correct form for the particular integral in the following cases.

a $\frac{d^2y}{dx^2} + 3\frac{dy}{dx} - 4y = 5e^x$

b $\frac{d^2y}{dx^2} + 4\frac{dy}{dx} + 4y = e^{-2x} + e^x$

c $\frac{d^2y}{dx^2} + 2\frac{dy}{dx} + 2y = 4e^{-x}\sin x$

6 Given that $\frac{d^2x}{dt^2} + 5\frac{dx}{dt} + 4x = e^{-t}$, find the general solution.

P PS 7 The initial conditions for the differential equation $4\frac{d^2h}{dt^2} - 4\frac{dh}{dt} + h = 4e^{\frac{1}{2}t}$ are $h = 0, \frac{dh}{dt} = 0$ when $t = 0$.

a Show that the particular integral must be of the form $h = \alpha t^2 e^{\frac{1}{2}t}$ and find the value of α.

b Hence, determine the particular solution.

M 8 Find the general solution for the differential equation $\frac{d^2y}{dx^2} + y = x - \cos x$. Given that the initial conditions are $y = 1, \frac{dy}{dx} = 1$ when $x = 0$, find the particular solution.

PS 9 Find the general solution for the differential equation $\frac{d^2r}{d\theta^2} + 4\frac{dr}{d\theta} + 3r = 2e^{-\theta} + e^{-3\theta}$.

PS P 10 A particle, of mass 2 kg, is dropped from rest and falls towards the ground. The resistance to motion is modelled by $5v$ N, where v is the velocity of the particle at any given time. The displacement of the particle, measured from the height where it is dropped, is denoted by x.

a Show that the equation of motion is given by $2g - 5\frac{dx}{dt} = 2\frac{d^2x}{dt^2}$, where g is the acceleration due to gravity.

b Hence, using the initial conditions, find the particular solution of this differential equation, giving your answer in terms of g.

24.4 Substitution methods for differential equations

Consider the differential equation $\frac{dy}{dx} = \frac{x+y}{x}$. This differential equation cannot be represented in the form $\frac{dy}{dx} + Fy = G$, so we need an alternative method.

First, let $\frac{dy}{dx} = 1 + \frac{y}{x}$ and then let $u = \frac{y}{x}$, or $y = ux$. The next step is to differentiate the substitution with respect to x, so $\frac{dy}{dx} = u + x\frac{du}{dx}$. The reason we differentiate is so that we can completely remove the terms $\frac{y}{x}$ and $\frac{dy}{dx}$ in the original differential equation.

Then $u + x\frac{du}{dx} = 1 + u$, which simplifies to $x\frac{du}{dx} = 1$. Then $\int du = \int \frac{1}{x} dx$, which integrates to give $u = \ln x + c$. But the solution should be $y = f(x)$, so substituting for u gives $\frac{y}{x} = \ln x + c$, or $y = x \ln x + cx$.

The original differential equation is of the form $\frac{dy}{dx} = F\left(\frac{y}{x}\right)$. To solve this type of differential equation, the substitution $u = \frac{y}{x}$ will reduce the equation to a separable form. Then we can solve it and find the general solution. We should always give the general solution using the original variables.

WORKED EXAMPLE 24.18

Using a suitable substitution, solve the differential equation $\frac{dy}{dx} = \frac{x-y}{x+y}$, giving your answer in an appropriate form.

Answer

First, write the differential equation as:

$$\frac{dy}{dx} = \frac{1 - \frac{y}{x}}{1 + \frac{y}{x}}.$$

Write in the form $\frac{dy}{dx} = F\left(\frac{y}{x}\right)$.

Note that $u = \frac{y}{x}$ and then with $y = ux$, $\frac{dy}{dx} = x\frac{du}{dx} + u$.

Differentiate the substitution with respect to x.

So $x\frac{du}{dx} + u = \frac{1-u}{1+u}$, or

$$x\frac{du}{dx} = \frac{1-u}{1+u} - u = \frac{1-2u-u^2}{1+u}.$$

Input the substitution and its derivative into the differential equation.

Then separating variables,

$$\int \frac{1+u}{1-2u-u^2} du = \int \frac{1}{x} dx.$$

Separate the variables.

Next, multiplying top and bottom by -2 gives $-\frac{1}{2}\int\frac{-2-2u}{1-2u-u^2}\,du = \int\frac{1}{x}\,dx$, which means that the left-hand side results in a logarithm.

Recognise the left-hand side as being of the form $\int\frac{kf'(u)}{f(u)}\,du$.

So $-\frac{1}{2}\ln|1-2u-u^2| = \ln x + \ln A$.

Integrate both sides. It is better to write $+c$ as $+\ln A$ to assist the combining of logs.

$\ln\left(\frac{1}{|1-2u-u^2|}\right)^{\frac{1}{2}} = \ln x + \ln A$

Use log laws $\ln A + \ln B = \ln AB$ and $n\ln A = \ln A^n$.

Then $\frac{1}{\sqrt{1-2u-u^2}} = Ax$, or $\frac{1}{1-2u-u^2} = A^2x^2$.

Equate logs then square both sides.

$1 = A^2x^2\left(1-2\frac{y}{x}-\frac{y^2}{x^2}\right)$

Change back to the original variables with $u = \frac{y}{x}$.

We can simplify this further to:

$1 = A^2(x^2 - 2xy - y^2)$

Simplify to get a general solution.

This rearranges to give the general solution $y = \pm\sqrt{c + 2x^2} - x$.

Another type of differential equation that needs substitution is the type $\frac{dy}{dx} = (x+y)^2$. We shall try the substitution $u = x + y$, then differentiate it with respect to x to get $\frac{du}{dx} = 1 + \frac{dy}{dx}$.

So $\frac{du}{dx} - 1 = u^2$, or $\frac{du}{dx} = 1 + u^2$. The next step is to write $\int\frac{1}{1+u^2}\,du = \int dx$. Recognising the standard integral on the left-hand side, we integrate to give $\tan^{-1}u = x + c$.

So $u = \tan(x+c)$, or $y = \tan(x+c) - x$.

The original differential equation is of the form $\frac{dy}{dx} = F(ax+by)$. For this case we shall generally use the substitution $u = ax + by$.

WORKED EXAMPLE 24.19

Using the substitution $u = 3y + 2x$, find a general solution for the differential equation $\frac{dy}{dx} = e^{3y+2x}$.

Answer

With $u = 3y + 2x$, we have $\frac{du}{dx} = 3\frac{dy}{dx} + 2$,

Differentiate the given substitution with respect to x.

then $\frac{1}{3}\left(\frac{du}{dx} - 2\right) = e^u$.

Substitute into the original differential equation.

Rearrange to get $\frac{du}{dx} = 3e^u + 2$.

Rearrange ready to separate variables.

Then separate variables to give $\int\frac{1}{3e^u+2}\,du = \int dx$.

To solve the integral on the left-hand side, multiply top and bottom by e^{-u}, and so $\int \frac{e^{-u}}{3+2e^{-u}}\,du = \int dx$.	Recognise that, by multiplying the top and bottom by e^{-u}, we get an integral of the form $\int \frac{kf'(u)}{f(u)}\,du$.
Then $-\frac{1}{2}\ln(3+2e^{-u}) = x + c$.	Integrate.
Rearranging gives $\ln(3+2e^{-u}) = -2(x+c)$.	Rearrange.
Then $e^{-u} = \frac{e^{-2(x+c)}-3}{2}$, so $e^{u} = \frac{2}{e^{-2(x+c)}-3}$.	Rewrite in exponential form.
Next, $u = \ln\left(\frac{2}{e^{-2(x+c)}-3}\right)$, and with $u = 3y + 2x$ we finally get the general solution $y = \frac{1}{3}\left[\ln\left(\frac{2}{e^{-2(x+c)}-3}\right) - 2x\right]$.	Take the reciprocal of both sides and take logs to get $u = f(x)$. Use substitution again, with $y = \frac{1}{3}(u-2x)$ as the general solution.

Worked example 24.20 looks at a general first order differential equation with initial conditions. We can either use the conditions $x = a, y = b$ or use $x = a, u = c$. Whichever values we use, we must still have the particular solution in the form $y = f(x)$.

WORKED EXAMPLE 24.20

Find the particular solution for the differential equation $y\frac{dy}{dx} = x - y^2$, using the substitution $u = x - y^2$ and the initial conditions $x = 0, y = \frac{1}{2}$.

Answer

Start with $\frac{du}{dx} = 1 - 2y\frac{dy}{dx}$.	Differentiate the substitution.
Then with $2y\frac{dy}{dx} = 2x - 2y^2$ the equation simplifies to $1 - \frac{du}{dx} = 2u$, or $\frac{du}{dx} = 1 - 2u$.	Substitute into the equation and rearrange.
Next $\int \frac{1}{1-2u}\,du = \int dx$ leads to $-\frac{1}{2}\ln\lvert 1-2u\rvert = x + c$.	Separate the variables and integrate.
Then using $x = 0, y = \frac{1}{2}$ we have $u = -\frac{1}{4}$, which gives $c = -\frac{1}{2}\ln\frac{3}{2}$.	Use initial conditions to find the constant of integration.

So $\frac{1}{2}\ln\lvert 1-2u\rvert - \frac{1}{2}\ln\frac{3}{2} = -x$, then $\ln\left\lvert\frac{1-2u}{\frac{3}{2}}\right\rvert = -2x$.	Rearrange and combine the logs.
Next we have $1 - 2u = \frac{3}{2}e^{-2x}$.	Remove the logarithm and use the substitution to change back into the form $y = f(x)$.
Then substituting gives $1 - 2(x - y^2) = \frac{3}{2}e^{-2x}$,	
which can be rearranged to give $y^2 = x - \frac{1}{2} + \frac{3}{4}e^{-2x}$, or $y = \pm\sqrt{x - \frac{1}{2} + \frac{3}{4}e^{-2x}}$.	State the general solution.

For second order differential equations we have only dealt with $a\frac{d^2y}{dx^2} + b\frac{dy}{dx} + cy = f(x)$.

If we have the differential equation $x\frac{d^2y}{dx^2} + 2(1-x)\frac{dy}{dx} - (2+3x)y = e^{2x}$, where $x \neq 0$, trying the standard method will not work. We need to try a substitution in order to simplify the differential equation into a more suitable form.

The suggested substitution is $u = yx$, where u is a function of x. Differentiating implicitly twice with respect to x will give $\frac{du}{dx} = y + x\frac{dy}{dx}$ and $\frac{d^2u}{dx^2} = 2\frac{dy}{dx} + x\frac{d^2y}{dx^2}$.

Rearranging these two leads to $x\frac{dy}{dx} = \frac{du}{dx} - y$ and $x\frac{d^2y}{dx^2} = \frac{d^2u}{dx^2} - 2\frac{dy}{dx}$. Substituting into the original differential equation gives $\frac{d^2u}{dx^2} - 2\frac{dy}{dx} + 2\frac{dy}{dx} - 2\left(\frac{du}{dx} - y\right) - 2y - 3u = e^{2x}$.

Cancelling terms and simplifying leads to $\frac{d^2u}{dx^2} - 2\frac{du}{dx} - 3u = e^{2x}$.

To solve this simpler differential equation, let the right-hand side be zero and try $u = Ae^{\lambda x}$. Then differentiate to get $\frac{du}{dx} = A\lambda e^{\lambda x}$ and $\frac{d^2u}{dx^2} = A\lambda^2 e^{\lambda x}$. This leads to the auxiliary equation $\lambda^2 - 2\lambda - 3 = 0$ and with $\lambda = -1, 3$ the complementary function is $u = Ae^{-x} + Be^{3x}$.

For the particular integral, try $u = \alpha e^{2x}$, and with $\frac{du}{dx} = 2\alpha e^{2x}$ and $\frac{d^2u}{dx^2} = 4\alpha e^{2x}$ the constant works out to be $\alpha = -\frac{1}{3}$. Hence, the general solution is $u = Ae^{-x} + Be^{3x} - \frac{1}{3}e^{2x}$.

Now, since $u = yx$, the general solution is $y = \frac{A}{x}e^{-x} + \frac{B}{x}e^{3x} - \frac{1}{3x}e^{2x}$.

WORKED EXAMPLE 24.21

Using the substitution $y = ux$, show that the differential equation $x^2\frac{d^2y}{dx^2} + (3x^2 - 2x)\frac{dy}{dx} + (2x^2 - 3x + 2)y = x^3e^x$ can be simplified to the differential equation $\frac{d^2u}{dx^2} + 3\frac{du}{dx} + 2u = e^x$.

Answer

Start with $y = ux$, then $\frac{dy}{dx} = u + x\frac{du}{dx}$ and $\frac{d^2y}{dx^2} = 2\frac{du}{dx} + x\frac{d^2u}{dx^2}$.

Differentiate the substitution twice with respect to x.

Then:

$$x^2\left(2\frac{du}{dx} + x\frac{d^2u}{dx^2}\right) + (3x^2 - 2x)\left(u + x\frac{du}{dx}\right) + (2x^2 - 3x + 2)ux = x^3e^x.$$

Substitute into the original differential equation.

Cancelling terms leads to $x^3\frac{d^2u}{dx^2} + 3x^3\frac{du}{dx} + 2ux^3 = x^3e^x$.

Cancel terms and simplify.

Then dividing by x^3 yields $\frac{d^2u}{dx^2} + 3\frac{du}{dx} + 2u = e^x$.

Finally, divide by x^3 to get the new differential equation.

The next type of substitution method revolves around a direct link between two variables.

For example, consider the differential equation $2y\frac{d^2y}{dx^2} + 2\left(\frac{dy}{dx}\right)^2 + 4y\frac{dy}{dx} + y^2 = x + 2$.

This is a non-linear differential equation, and we are given that $u = y^2$ is the substitution.

First, differentiate twice with respect to x to get $\frac{du}{dx} = 2y\frac{dy}{dx}$ and $\frac{d^2u}{dx^2} = 2\left(\frac{dy}{dx}\right)^2 + 2y\frac{d^2y}{dx^2}$.

Then substitute into the original differential equation to get $\frac{d^2u}{dx^2} + 2\frac{du}{dx} + u = x + 2$.

Using $u = Ae^{\lambda x}$ leads to the auxiliary equation $(\lambda + 1)^2 = 0$. So $u = (Ax + B)e^{-x}$ is the complementary function. If we try $u = \alpha x + \beta$, this leads to $u = x$ as the particular integral.

Hence, the general solution is $u = (Ax + B)e^{-x} + x$, so $y = [(Ax + B)e^{-x} + x]^{\frac{1}{2}}$.

Looking at another example, consider $3y^2\frac{d^2y}{dx^2} + 6y\left(\frac{dy}{dx}\right)^2 + 6y^2\frac{dy}{dx} + 5y^3 = e^x$ for which we shall use the substitution $w = y^3$.

First, we differentiate with respect to x to get $\frac{dw}{dx} = 3y^2\frac{dy}{dx}$ and $\frac{d^2w}{dx^2} = 6y\left(\frac{dy}{dx}\right)^2 + 3y^2\frac{d^2y}{dx^2}$.

Substitute these two results into the original differential equation to get $\frac{d^2w}{dx^2} + 2\frac{dw}{dx} + 5w = e^x$.

Let the right-hand side be zero, and with $w = Ae^{\lambda x}$ we get the auxiliary equation $\lambda^2 + 2\lambda + 5 = 0$. This has roots $\lambda_1 = -1 + 2i$ and $\lambda_2 = -1 - 2i$ so we can state that $w = e^{-x}(A\cos 2x + B\sin 2x)$ is the complementary function.

For the particular integral, we try $w = \alpha e^x$ and this leads to $\alpha = \frac{1}{8}$. Hence, the general solution is $w = e^{-x}(A\cos 2x + B\sin 2x) + \frac{1}{8}e^x$. So, finally, $y = \left[e^{-x}(A\cos 2x + B\sin 2x) + \frac{1}{8}e^x\right]^{\frac{1}{3}}$.

WORKED EXAMPLE 24.22

The initial conditions for the differential equation $2y\frac{d^2y}{dt^2} - \left(\frac{dy}{dt}\right)^2 + 8y\frac{dy}{dt} + 16y^2 = 12y^{\frac{3}{2}}t^2$ are $y = 1$ and $\frac{dy}{dt} = 4$, when $t = 0$. Given that $y > 0$, and using the substitution $z = y^{\frac{1}{2}}$, find the particular solution of the differential equation in the form $y = f(t)$.

Answer

Since $z = y^{\frac{1}{2}}$, we have $\frac{dz}{dt} = \frac{1}{2}y^{-\frac{1}{2}}\frac{dy}{dt}$ as the first derivative and $\frac{d^2z}{dt^2} = -\frac{1}{4}y^{-\frac{3}{2}}\left(\frac{dy}{dt}\right)^2 + \frac{1}{2}y^{-\frac{1}{2}}\frac{d^2y}{dt^2}$ as the second derivative.

Differentiate the substitution implicitly with respect to t, to get both first and second derivatives.

Note the link between the derivatives and the original equation.

Dividing the original differential equation by $4y^{\frac{3}{2}}$ gives:

Divide through and substitute in the first and second derivatives.

$$\frac{1}{2}y^{-\frac{1}{2}}\frac{d^2y}{dt^2} - \frac{1}{4}y^{-\frac{3}{2}}\left(\frac{dy}{dt}\right)^2 + 2y^{-\frac{1}{2}}\frac{dy}{dt} + 4y^{\frac{1}{2}} = 3t^2.$$

Hence, $\frac{d^2z}{dt^2} + 4\frac{dz}{dt} + 4z = 3t^2$.

State the new differential equation.

Let the right-hand side be zero, and try $z = Ae^{\lambda t}$.

Determine the auxiliary equation.

This gives $\lambda^2 + 4\lambda + 4 = 0$ as the auxiliary equation.

Hence, the complementary function is: $z = (At + B)e^{-2t}$.

Determine the complementary function.

For the particular integral, try $z = \alpha t^2 + \beta t + \gamma$.

Since the right-hand side is a quadratic, try $\alpha t^2 + \beta t + \gamma$.

Then with $\frac{dz}{dt} = 2\alpha t + \beta$ and $\frac{d^2z}{dt^2} = 2\alpha$, substitute into the differential equation to give $\alpha = \frac{3}{4}, \beta = -\frac{3}{2}$ and $\gamma = \frac{9}{8}$.

Differentiate twice and substitute into the original differential equation to determine the unknown constants.

So the particular solution is $z = \frac{3}{4}t^2 - \frac{3}{2}t + \frac{9}{8}$.

State the particular solution.

Hence, $z = (At + B)e^{-2t} + \frac{3}{4}t^2 - \frac{3}{2}t + \frac{9}{8}$.

State the general solution, noting this is $z = f(t)$.

When $y = 1, z = 1$ and when $\frac{dy}{dt} = 4, \frac{dz}{dt} = \frac{1}{2} \times 1 \times 4 = 2$.

Find the initial conditions based on z. This makes use of the first derivative of the substitution.

So $z = 1, t = 0$ gives $1 = B + \frac{9}{8}$. Thus $B = -\frac{1}{8}$. | Use the initial conditions to evaluate the constants A and B.

$\frac{dz}{dt} = Ae^{-2t} - 2Ate^{-2t} - 2Be^{-2t} + \frac{3}{2}t - \frac{3}{2}$,

and with $\frac{dz}{dt} = 2$,

when $t = 0$, we have $2 = A - 2B - \frac{3}{2}$.

Hence, $A = \frac{13}{4}$.

So $z = \left(\frac{13}{4}t - \frac{1}{8}\right)e^{-2t} + \frac{3}{4}t^2 - \frac{3}{2}t + \frac{9}{8}$. | State the particular solution in the form $z = f(t)$.

Since $y = z^2$, the particular solution is: | Then use $z = y^{\frac{1}{2}}$ to determine the particular solution in the form $y = f(t)$.

$y = \left[\left(\frac{13}{4}t - \frac{1}{8}\right)e^{-2t} + \frac{3}{4}t^2 - \frac{3}{2}t + \frac{9}{8}\right]^2$.

Lastly, consider the differential equation $x^2\frac{d^2y}{dx^2} + 4x\frac{dy}{dx} + 2y = \ln x$. For this differential equation we are asked to use the substitution $x = e^t$ to generate a differential equation of the form $a\frac{d^2y}{dt^2} + b\frac{dy}{dt} + cy = g(t)$. The problem here is linking x and y, so we shall use the chain rule.

Begin with $x = e^t$, then $\frac{dx}{dt} = e^t$, and then from $\frac{dy}{dx} = \frac{dy}{dt} \times \frac{dt}{dx}$ we have $\frac{dy}{dx} = e^{-t}\frac{dy}{dt}$.

Differentiating again gives $\frac{d^2y}{dx^2} = e^{-2t}\frac{d^2y}{dt^2} - e^{-2t}\frac{dy}{dt}$. Recall from Chapter 21 that $\frac{d^2y}{dx^2} = \frac{d}{dt}\left(\frac{dy}{dx}\right)\frac{dt}{dx}$. We can rearrange the derivatives $\frac{dy}{dx} = e^{-t}\frac{dy}{dt}$ into a better form: $\frac{dy}{dx} = \frac{1}{x}\frac{dy}{dt}$, or $x\frac{dy}{dx} = \frac{dy}{dt}$. The second derivative $\frac{d^2y}{dx^2} = e^{-2t}\frac{d^2y}{dt^2} - e^{-2t}\frac{dy}{dt}$ becomes $x^2\frac{d^2y}{dx^2} = \frac{d^2y}{dt^2} - \frac{dy}{dt}$.

Then from the original differential equation, $\frac{d^2y}{dt^2} - \frac{dy}{dt} + 4\frac{dy}{dt} + 2y = \ln e^t$, or $\frac{d^2y}{dt^2} + 3\frac{dy}{dt} + 2y = t$. We can now solve this differential equation.

WORKED EXAMPLE 24.23

Using the substitution $x = \frac{1}{t^2}$, show that the equation $4x^3\frac{d^2y}{dx^2} + (6x^2 + 10x^{\frac{3}{2}})\frac{dy}{dx} + 4y = \frac{1}{x}$ reduces to the equation $\frac{d^2y}{dt^2} - 5\frac{dy}{dt} + 4y = t^2$.

Answer

Start with $x = \frac{1}{t^2}$, then $\frac{dx}{dt} = -\frac{2}{t^3}$ and with $\frac{dy}{dx} = \frac{dy}{dt} \times \frac{dt}{dx}$ we get $\frac{dy}{dx} = -\frac{t^3}{2}\frac{dy}{dt}$.

Differentiate twice, making use of the chain rule.

Then $\frac{d^2y}{dx^2} = \frac{d}{dt}\left(\frac{dy}{dx}\right)\frac{dt}{dx}$ leads to $\frac{d^2y}{dx^2} = \frac{t^6}{4}\frac{d^2y}{dt^2} + \frac{3}{4}t^5\frac{dy}{dt}$.

Make use of your knowledge of both implicit and parametric differentiation.

The first derivative can be written as $\frac{dy}{dx} = -\frac{1}{2x^{\frac{3}{2}}}\frac{dy}{dt}$,

Rewrite the results to match the terms in the original equation.

and the second derivative as $4x^3\frac{d^2y}{dx^2} = \frac{d^2y}{dt^2} + 3x^{\frac{1}{2}}\frac{dy}{dt}$.

Hence

Substitute in the results, cancel terms and simplify to get the given result.

$$\left(\frac{d^2y}{dt^2} + 3x^{\frac{1}{2}}\frac{dy}{dt}\right) + (6x^2 + 10x^{\frac{3}{2}})\left(-\frac{1}{2x^{\frac{3}{2}}}\frac{dy}{dt}\right) + 4y = \frac{1}{x}$$

becomes $\frac{d^2y}{dt^2} - 5\frac{dy}{dt} + 4y = t^2$.

EXERCISE 24D

PS 1 Using the substitution $u = e^{-y}$, solve the differential equation $\frac{dy}{dx} = -(1 - e^{-y})$.

PS 2 Find the general solution for the differential equation $\frac{dy}{dx} = \frac{y^2 - x^2}{yx}$, using the substitution $u = \frac{y}{x}$.

PS 3 Solve the differential equation $\frac{dy}{dx} = \cos(x + y)$ using the substitution $u = x + y$, giving your answer as a general solution.

4 In each of the following cases, determine the first and second derivatives for y.

a $y = 2xw$, where w is a function of x

b $y = z^5$, where both y and z are functions of x

c $x = \frac{1}{t^2}$, where the variable y depends on x

P PS 5 Given that $\frac{1}{x^2}\frac{d^2z}{dx^2} + \left(\frac{3}{x^2} - \frac{4}{x^3}\right)\frac{dz}{dx} + \left(\frac{6}{x^4} - \frac{6}{x^3} - \frac{4}{x^2}\right)z = 5x - 6$, show that $y = \frac{z}{x^2}$ reduces this differential equation to $\frac{d^2y}{dx^2} + 3\frac{dy}{dx} - 4y = 5x - 6$.

Hence, find the general solution $z = f(x)$.

P PS 6 The variable y depends on x, and x and t are related by $x = e^{2t}$.

a Show that $2x\frac{dy}{dx} = \frac{dy}{dt}$ and find $\frac{d^2y}{dx^2}$.

b Find the general solution for $4x^2\frac{d^2y}{dx^2} + 8x\frac{dy}{dx} + y = 3x$.

PS 7 The variables z and x are related such that $z^2\frac{d^2z}{dx^2} + 2z\left(\frac{dz}{dx}\right)^2 + z^2\frac{dz}{dx} - 2z^3 = 4x$.

Given that $y = 2z^3$, find a differential equation relating y and x.

Hence, determine the general solution in the form $z = f(x)$.

P PS 8 The variables x and u are related by $ux = 2$. The variable y is dependent on x.

a Show that $-2\frac{dy}{du} = x^2\frac{dy}{dx}$ and $4\frac{d^2y}{du^2} = x^4\frac{d^2y}{dx^2} + 2x^3\frac{dy}{dx}$.

b Show also that $4x^4\frac{d^2y}{dx^2} + (8x^3 + 4x^2)\frac{dy}{dx} + y = \frac{2}{x}$ reduces to $16\frac{d^2y}{du^2} - 8\frac{dy}{du} + y = u$ and find the general solution in the form $y = f(u)$.

c Given that $y = 4$ and $\frac{dy}{du} = 2$ when $u = 0$, find the particular solution in the form $y = g(x)$.

WORKED PAST PAPER QUESTION

Find y in terms of t, given that $5\frac{d^2y}{dt^2} + 6\frac{dy}{dt} + 5y = 15 + 12t + 5t^2$ and that $y = \frac{dy}{dt} = 0$ when $t = 0$.

Cambridge International AS & A Level Further Mathematics 9231 Paper 1 Q8 November 2008

Answer

Let the right-hand side be equal to zero. Try $y = Ae^{\lambda t}$, then $\frac{dy}{dt} = A\lambda e^{\lambda t}$, $\frac{d^2y}{dt^2} = A\lambda^2 e^{\lambda t}$.

The auxiliary equation is $5\lambda^2 + 6\lambda + 5 = 0$. From this, $\lambda = -\frac{3}{5} \pm \frac{4}{5}i$.

So the complementary function is $y = e^{-\frac{3}{5}t}\left(A\cos\frac{4}{5}t + B\sin\frac{4}{5}t\right)$.

For the particular integral, try $y = \alpha t^2 + \beta t + \gamma$, then $\frac{dy}{dt} = 2\alpha t + \beta$, $\frac{d^2y}{dt^2} = 2\alpha$.

Then $10\alpha + 12\alpha t + 6\beta + 5\alpha t^2 + 5\beta t + 5\gamma = 15 + 12t + 5t^2$.

Hence, $\alpha = 1$, then $\beta = 0$, then $\gamma = 1$.

So the general solution is $y = e^{-\frac{3}{5}t}\left(A\cos\frac{4}{5}t + B\sin\frac{4}{5}t\right) + t^2 + 1$.
Using $y = 0$, $t = 0$ leads to $0 = A + 1$, so $A = -1$.

Then $\frac{dy}{dt} = -\frac{3}{5}e^{-\frac{3}{5}t}\left(A\cos\frac{4}{5}t + B\sin\frac{4}{5}t\right) + e^{-\frac{3}{5}t}\left(-\frac{4}{5}A\sin\frac{4}{5}t + \frac{4}{5}B\cos\frac{4}{5}t\right) + 2t$, and with $\frac{dy}{dt} = 0$ when $t = 0$, $0 = -\frac{3}{5}A + \frac{4}{5}B$, leading to $B = -\frac{3}{4}$.

Hence, the particular solution is $y = e^{-\frac{3}{5}t}\left(-\cos\frac{4}{5}t - \frac{3}{4}\sin\frac{4}{5}t\right) + t^2 + 1$.

Checklist of learning and understanding

- Make sure the equation is in the form $\frac{dy}{dx} + Fy = G$.
- To determine the integrating factor, use $I = e^{\int F\,dx}$.
- Always multiply through by the integrating factor to get $I\frac{dy}{dx} + IFy = GI$. This equation will reduce to $\frac{d}{dx}(Iy) = GI$.

For second order differential equations of the form $a\frac{d^2y}{dx^2} + b\frac{dy}{dx} + cy = f(x)$:

From the auxiliary equation $a\lambda^2 + b\lambda + c = 0$:

- If $\lambda_1 = \alpha, \lambda_2 = \beta$ then the complementary function is $y = Ae^{\alpha x} + Be^{\beta x}$.
- If $\lambda_1 = \lambda_2 = \alpha$ then the complementary function is $y = (Ax + B)e^{\alpha x}$.
- If $\lambda_1 = \alpha + \beta i, \lambda_2 = \alpha - \beta i$ then the complementary function is $y = e^{\alpha x}(A\cos\beta x + B\sin\beta x)$.

For the particular integral:

- If $f(x) = kx^2 + mx + n$ then try $y = \alpha x^2 + \beta x + \gamma$.
- If $f(x) = ke^{mx}$ then try $y = \alpha e^{mx}$.
- If $f(x) = k\cos mx$ or $f(x) = k\sin mx$, or a combination of both, then try:

$$y = \alpha\cos mx + \beta\sin mx$$

For the failure case:

- If a term in your complementary function is $Af(x)$ and the right side is $pf(x)$, then try:

$$y = \alpha x f(x)$$

- If terms in your complementary function are $Axf(x) + Bf(x)$ and the right side is $pf(x)$, then try:

$$y = \alpha x^2 f(x)$$

For differential equations requiring substitutions:

For first order differential equations:

- The differential equations will be of the form $\frac{dy}{dx} = F(x, y)$ or $\frac{dy}{dx} = F\left(\frac{y}{x}\right)$.
- Use the substitution given and differentiate once to reduce the differential equation to a separable form.

For second order differential equations:

- Use the substitution given and differentiate twice to reduce the differential equation to a form such as $a\frac{d^2u}{dx^2} + b\frac{du}{dx} + cu = f(u)$.
- For first and second order differential equations, the general solution or particular solution must be in the form of the original variables.

END-OF-CHAPTER REVIEW EXERCISE 24

1 A first order differential equation is given as $(3x+4)\frac{dy}{dx} - 3y = x$. Determine the general solution of this differential equation.

Given that $y = \frac{13}{9}$ when $x = -1$, find the value of the constant of integration.

2 Find the value of the constant k such that $y = kx^2e^{2x}$ is a particular integral of the differential equation

$$\frac{d^2y}{dx^2} - 4\frac{dy}{dx} + 4y = 4e^{2x}. \ (*)$$

Hence find the general solution of (*).

Find the particular solution of (*) such that $y = 3$ and $\frac{dy}{dx} = -2$ when $x = 0$.

Cambridge International AS & A Level Further Mathematics 9231 Paper 11 Q9 June 2016

3 Show that, with a suitable value of the constant α, the substitution $y = x^{\alpha}w$ reduces the differential equation

$$2x^2\frac{d^2y}{dx^2} + (3x^2+8x)\frac{dy}{dx} + (x^2+6x+4)y = f(x) \text{ to } 2\frac{d^2w}{dx^2} + 3\frac{dw}{dx} + w = f(x).$$

Find the general solution for y in the case where $f(x) = 6\sin 2x + 7\cos 2x$.

Cambridge International AS & A Level Further Mathematics 9231 Paper 1 Q11 June 2008

CROSS-TOPIC REVIEW EXERCISE 4

1 a You are given that $y = \operatorname{cosech}^{-1} 2x$. Show that when $x < 0$, $\frac{d^2y}{dx^2} = \frac{2}{x\sqrt{x^2+1}}$.

b Find the exact solutions of $8\cosh x - 7\sinh x = 4$.

2 The matrix **P** has eigenvector $\boldsymbol{e}$ with corresponding eigenvalue λ, and the matrix **Q** also has eigenvector $\boldsymbol{e}$ with corresponding eigenvalue μ.

a Find the corresponding eigenvalues and eigenvectors for the matrices $\mathbf{P} + \mathbf{Q}$ and $\mathbf{PQ}$.

The matrix **A** is given as $\begin{pmatrix} -1 & 4 & 6 \\ 0 & 2 & 1 \\ 0 & 0 & 5 \end{pmatrix}$.

b State the eigenvalues, and find the eigenvectors of the matrix **A**.

The matrix $\mathbf{B} = \mathbf{A} + 2\mathbf{I}$.

c Find the eigenvalues and eigenvectors of the matrices $\mathbf{A} + \mathbf{B}$ and $\mathbf{AB}$.

3 a If $y = \cosh^{-1}(2x - 3)$, show that $\frac{dy}{dx} = \frac{1}{2(x-1)(x-2)}$.

b Given that $e^{x+2y} = xy + 1$ passes through (0, 0), find the value of $\frac{d^2y}{dx^2}$ at that point.

4 Given that $I_n = \int_0^1 \sinh^n x \, dx$, show that $I_n = \frac{1}{n}[\sinh^{n-1} x \cosh x]_0^1 - \frac{n-1}{n} I_{n-2}$ for $n \geqslant 2$.

Hence, evaluate $\int_0^1 \sinh^4 x \, dx$.

5 Show that $\cos^6 \theta$ can be written in the form $a\cos 6\theta + b\cos 4\theta + c\cos 2\theta + d$. Hence, find $\int_0^{\frac{\pi}{2}} \cos^6 \theta \, d\theta$.

6 Given that $\frac{d^2y}{dx^2} - 5\frac{dy}{dx} + 4y = x^2 + e^{-2x}$ has initial conditions $y = \frac{493}{288}, \frac{dy}{dx} = \frac{181}{72}$ when $x = 0$, find the particular solution.

7 The matrix $\mathbf{A} = \begin{pmatrix} 33 & 24 \\ 48 & 57 \end{pmatrix}$ is such that $\mathbf{B}^2 = \mathbf{A}$. Using diagonalisation, or otherwise, find a matrix **B** that satisfies the condition above.

8 Given that $x = t^3 + 1, y = t^2 - t$, find $\frac{d^2y}{dx^2}$.

9 Write down an expression in terms of z and N for the sum of the series $\sum_{n=1}^{N} 2^{-n} z^n$.

Use de Moivré's theorem to deduce that $\sum_{n=1}^{10} 2^{-n} \sin\left(\frac{1}{10} n\pi\right) = \frac{1025 \sin\left(\frac{1}{10}\pi\right)}{2560 - 2048 \cos\left(\frac{1}{10}\pi\right)}$.

Cambridge International AS & A Level Mathematics 9231 Paper 1 Q7 November 2005

10 Find the eigenvalues and corresponding eigenvectors of the matrix **A**, where

$$\mathbf{A} = \begin{pmatrix} 6 & 4 & 1 \\ -6 & -1 & 3 \\ 8 & 8 & 4 \end{pmatrix}.$$

Hence find a non-singular matrix **P** and a diagonal matrix **D** such that $\mathbf{A} + \mathbf{A}^2 + \mathbf{A}^3 = \mathbf{PDP}^{-1}$.

Cambridge International AS & A Level Mathematics 9231 Paper 1 Q10 November 2003

11 The variable y depends on x and the variables x and t are related by $x = \frac{1}{t}$. Show that

$$\frac{dy}{dx} = -t^2\frac{dy}{dt} \text{ and } \frac{d^2y}{dx^2} = t^4\frac{d^2y}{dt^2} + 2t^3\frac{dy}{dt}.$$

The variables x and y are related by the differential equation

$$x^5\frac{d^2y}{dx^2} + (2x^4 - 5x^3)\frac{dy}{dx} + 4xy = 14x + 8.$$

Show that $\frac{d^2y}{dt^2} + 5\frac{dy}{dt} + 4y = 8t + 14.$

Hence find the general solution for y in terms of x.

Cambridge International AS & A Level Mathematics 9231 Paper 1 Q9 June 2004

12 The points A, B, C have position vectors $a\mathbf{i}$, $b\mathbf{j}$, $c\mathbf{k}$ respectively, where a, b, c are all positive.

The plane containing A, B, C is denoted Π.

i Find a vector perpendicular to Π.

ii Find the perpendicular distance from the origin to Π, in terms of a, b, c.

Cambridge International AS & A Level Mathematics 9231 Paper 1 Q3 June 2005

FURTHER PURE MATHEMATICS 1 PRACTICE EXAM-STYLE PAPER

1 It is given that $y = xe^{2x}$.

Prove by induction that $\frac{d^n y}{dx^n} = n \times 2^{n-1}e^{2x} + 2^n x e^{2x}$. [7]

2 Find, in terms of n, an expression for the series

$1^3 - 2^3 - 3^3 + 4^3 - 5^3 - 6^3 + \cdots + (3n-2)^3 - (3n-1)^3 - (3n)^3$. [8]

3 The cubic equation $2x^3 - 4x + 7 = 0$ has roots α, β, γ.

a Find the values of $\alpha^2 + \beta^2 + \gamma^2$ and $\frac{1}{\alpha} + \frac{1}{\beta} + \frac{1}{\gamma}$. [3]

b Find the cubic equation that has roots $\frac{1}{\alpha+2}, \frac{1}{\beta+2}, \frac{1}{\gamma+2}$. [3]

c Hence, determine the value of $\frac{\alpha\beta + \alpha\gamma + \beta\gamma + 4(\alpha + \beta + \gamma + 3)}{(\alpha+2)(\beta+2)(\gamma+2)}$. [3]

4 You are given the matrices $\mathbf{A} = \begin{pmatrix} 1 & 0 & 3 \\ 2 & 1 & -1 \\ 1 & 1 & 0 \end{pmatrix}$ and $\mathbf{B} = \begin{pmatrix} 2 & 3 & -1 \\ 0 & 5 & 1 \\ 4 & 4 & 1 \end{pmatrix}$.

a Find the inverse matrix $\mathbf{A}^{-1}$. [5]

b Hence, determine the matrix $\mathbf{C}$ in the following cases.

i $\mathbf{AC} = \mathbf{B}$ [3]

ii $\mathbf{A} + \mathbf{AC} = \mathbf{B}$ [2]

5 The curve C is given as $r = e^{-\theta}\sin\theta$ for $0 \leqslant \theta \leqslant \pi$.

a Find the maximum distance of the curve from the origin. [5]

b Sketch the curve C. [2]

c Determine the area inside the curve, giving your answer to 3 significant figures. [6]

6 A plane is given as Π_1: $3x - y + 4z = 2$.

a Find the distance of the plane from the origin. [3]

Another plane, Π_2, contains the line $\mathbf{r} = \mathbf{i} - 2\mathbf{j} + 3\mathbf{k} + (-\mathbf{i} - 2\mathbf{j} + \mathbf{k})t$ and the point $(3, 1, 1)$.

b Find the Cartesian equation of Π_2. [5]

c Find the acute angle between Π_1 and Π_2. [3]

d Find a vector that is perpendicular to the normals of Π_1 and Π_2. [3]

7 The curve C is given as $y = \frac{2x^2 + 3x - 5}{x + 2}$.

a Determine the asymptotes of C. [3]

b Show that C has no turning points. [3]

c Determine the coordinates of the points where the curve C intersects the coordinate axes. [2]

d Sketch the curve C, showing the asymptotes and intersection points. [3]

e Determine the values of x for which $y < 2$. [3]

FURTHER PROBABILITY & STATISTICS PRACTICE EXAM-STYLE PAPER

1 An experiment is carried out to investigate memory in two situations: aural and visual. A random sample of 12 students are shown 20 objects and then each student is asked to recall as many of the objects as possible. Subsequently a list of 20 different objects is read out to them and again each student is asked to recall as many as possible. The results are given below.

Student	A	B	C	D	E	F	G	H	J	K	L	M
Visual	14	15	10	9	8	13	17	12	14	7	15	6
Aural	12	13	9	10	7	14	16	10	11	8	14	5

Use a sign test to determine whether or not there is evidence that students can recall objects with greater accuracy when they are presented visually rather than aurally. Use a 5% significance level. **[8]**

2 A university librarian selects a random sample of seven students from the physics department and records the number of books each student borrows in a particular month. The results are as follows.

11, 13, 6, 8, 10, 17, 5

During the same month the librarian selects a random sample of eight students from the geography department and the number of books each of these students borrows that month is as follows.

19, 9, 20, 15, 16, 12, 14, 18

a Using the Wilcoxon rank-sum test at the 5% level of significance, test whether or not there is any difference between the median number of books borrowed by students from these two departments. **[7]**

b Explain briefly how your test would be modified if 50 students had been randomly selected from each department. **[3]**

3 Four torpedoes are fired independently from a ship at a target. Each one has a $\frac{1}{3}$ probability of hitting the target. The random variable X represents the number of hits and has probability generating function:

$$G_X(t) = \frac{1}{81}(2 + t)^4$$

a Find the mean and the variance of X. **[2]**

A second ship fires at the same target and the random variable Y, representing its number of hits, has probability generating function:

$$G_Y(t) = \frac{1}{243}(2 + t)^5.$$

Given that X and Y are independent:

b find the probability generating function of $Z = X + Y$ **[2]**

c calculate the mean and the variance of Z. **[6]**

4 The manager of a hotel collected data on the usage of the facilities at the hotel by its guests. A random sample from her records is summarised below.

Facility	Male	Female
Spa	40	68
Swimming pool	26	33
Business centre	52	31

Making your method clear, test whether or not there is any evidence of an association between gender and use of the hotel's facilities. Use a 5% significance level. **[11]**

5 A continuous random variable has probability density function f given by

$$f(x) = \begin{cases} \frac{1}{30}(x+4) & 0 \leqslant x < 2 \\ \frac{7}{96} & 2 \leqslant x < 6 \\ \frac{1}{60}(15 - x) & 6 \leqslant x \leqslant 9 \\ 0 & \text{otherwise.} \end{cases}$$

a Find $E(X)$. [3]

b Find the cumulative distribution function. [5]

c Find the median. [3]

FURTHER MECHANICS PRACTICE EXAM-STYLE PAPER

1 A particle is projected from a point O, which is on horizontal ground: the speed of projection is $20\,\text{m s}^{-1}$ and the angle of elevation is $30°$.

Find the speed and direction of the particle when it has travelled a horizontal distance of 30 m. **[5]**

2 A uniform, solid cylinder of radius $2a$ and length $7a$ has density ρ. The cylinder is attached to a hemisphere of radius $2a$ and density 2ρ. The plane face of the cylinder coincides with the plane face of the hemisphere.

This composite body is then suspended, in equilibrium, by a light string; this string is attached to a point on the rim of the plane face of the hemisphere. Find the angle which the plane face of the hemisphere makes with the vertical. **[7]**

3 A particle is travelling along a smooth, horizontal surface with speed $3u\,\text{m s}^{-1}$. It has mass $2m$ and passes through the point O when $t = 0$. An opposing force with magnitude $8t^2$ N is applied to the particle once it passes over the point O.

a Find the velocity as a function of time. **[5]**

b Find the time taken for the particle to pass through the point O again. **[4]**

4 A particle, of mass m, is resting in equilibrium on the inside surface of a smooth, circular hoop of radius $\frac{3}{2}a$. The hoop lies in a vertical plane. The particle is then projected with horizontal speed u from the lowest point on the inside of the hoop.

a Show that, for complete circles, $u \geqslant \sqrt{\frac{15}{2}ga}$. **[6]**

b Hence, find the range of values of u for which the particle does not remain in contact with the inner surface of the hoop. **[3]**

5 A particle, of mass 2 kg, is attached to one end of a light, elastic string of natural length 1.5 m and modulus of elasticity 50 N. The other end of the string is attached to a point on a ceiling. The particle is allowed to rest in equilibrium with the string taut.

a The string is pulled down a distance of 0.1 m to the point D and released. Show that, while the string is taut, the particle performs simple harmonic motion, stating the value of ω. **[6]**

Let the equilibrium position be denoted by the point E.

b Find the time taken for the particle to travel from the point D to 0.08 m above the point E. **[3]**

6 Two spheres, P and Q, of masses $2m$ and $5m$, respectively, are resting on a smooth horizontal surface. Sphere P is projected with horizontal speed $3u$ and it subsequently strikes Q directly. The coefficient of restitution between the spheres is $\frac{1}{2}$.

a Find the speed of each particle after the collision. **[6]**

b Find the loss in kinetic energy due to the collision. **[2]**

c Find the magnitude of the impulse on P due to the collision. **[3]**

FURTHER PURE MATHEMATICS 2 PRACTICE EXAM-STYLE PAPER

1 Find the general solution for $\cos x \frac{dy}{dx} - y \sin x = \cot x$, in the form $y = f(x)$. **[6]**

2 Evaluate $\int_0^{\sqrt{3}-1} \frac{1}{x^2 + 2x + 2} dx$. **[6]**

3 A system of linear equations is given as $\begin{aligned} x - 2y + z &= 0 \\ -x + 5y + z &= 2. \\ 2x - y + az &= b \end{aligned}$

a Write this set of equations as an augmented matrix and, hence, find the matrix in row echelon form. **[4]**

Find the values of a and b for each of the following cases.

b a unique solution **[1]**

c an infinite number of solutions **[1]**

d no solutions **[1]**

4 Given that $x + y^2 = \ln(xy)$, find the value of $\frac{d^2y}{dx^2}$ at the point $(-1, -1)$. **[7]**

5 By first showing that $\cosh^{-1} x$ can be written as $\ln(x + \sqrt{x^2 - 1})$, solve the quadratic equation $\cosh^2 x - 5\cosh x + 6 = 0$, giving your answers in an exact form. **[8]**

6 You are given that $I_n = \int_0^1 x^4(1 + x^3)^n dx$.

a Show that $(5 + 3n)I_n = 2^n + 3nI_{n-1}$ for $n \geqslant 1$. **[5]**

b Determine the value of I_3, giving your answer to 4 decimal places. **[4]**

7 The differential equation $\frac{d^2x}{dt^2} + \frac{dx}{dt} - 2x = 3e^t$ has initial conditions $x = 5$, $\frac{dx}{dt} = 3$ when $t = 0$.

Find the particular solution for this differential equation. **[10]**

8 Using de Moivre's theorem, show that $\tan 4\theta$ can be written in the form $\frac{4\tan\theta - 4\tan^3\theta}{1 - 6\tan^2\theta + \tan^4\theta}$. **[5]**

Hence, solve the equation $7t^4 + 20t^3 - 42t^2 - 20t = -7$, giving your answers to 3 decimal places. **[5]**

9 The matrix **A** is given as $\mathbf{A} = \begin{pmatrix} 2 & -3 & 1 \\ 0 & -1 & 1 \\ 1 & 1 & 0 \end{pmatrix}$.

a Find the eigenvalues and corresponding eigenvectors of the matrix **A**. **[8]**

b Given that $\mathbf{A} = \mathbf{PDP}^{-1}$, write down matrices for **P** and **D**. **[2]**

c Hence, determine a matrix **H**, where $\mathbf{A}^5 = \mathbf{PHP}^{-1}$. **[2]**

THE STANDARD NORMAL DISTRIBUTION FUNCTION

If Z is normally distributed with mean 0 and variance 1, the table gives the value of $\Phi(z)$ for each value of z, where

$$\Phi(z) = P(Z \leqslant z).$$

Use $\Phi(-z) = 1 - \Phi(z)$ for negative values of z.

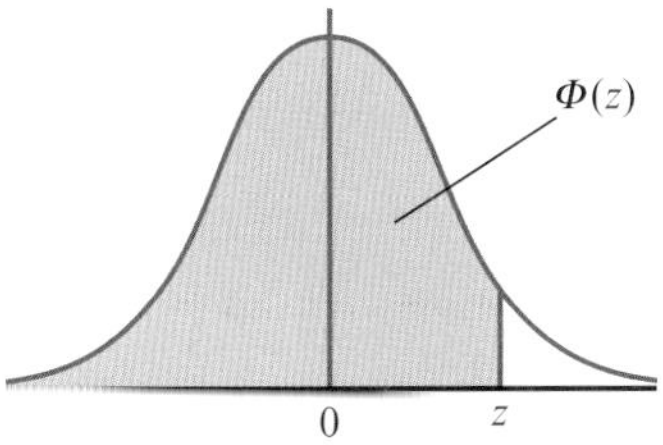

z	0	1	2	3	4	5	6	7	8	9	1	2	3	4	5	6	7	8	9
															ADD				
0.0	0.5000	0.5040	0.5080	0.5120	0.5160	0.5199	0.5239	0.5279	0.5319	0.5359	4	8	12	16	20	24	28	32	36
0.1	0.5398	0.5438	0.5478	0.5517	0.5557	0.5596	0.5636	0.5675	0.5714	0.5753	4	8	12	16	20	24	28	32	36
0.2	0.5793	0.5832	0.5871	0.5910	0.5948	0.5987	0.6026	0.6064	0.6103	0.6141	4	8	12	15	19	23	27	31	35
0.3	0.6179	0.6217	0.6255	0.6293	0.6331	0.6368	0.6406	0.6443	0.6480	0.6517	4	7	11	15	19	22	26	30	34
0.4	0.6554	0.6591	0.6628	0.6664	0.6700	0.6736	0.6772	0.6808	0.6844	0.6879	4	7	11	14	18	22	25	29	32
0.5	0.6915	0.6950	0.6985	0.7019	0.7054	0.7088	0.7123	0.7157	0.7190	0.7224	3	7	10	14	17	20	24	27	31
0.6	0.7257	0.7291	0.7324	0.7357	0.7389	0.7422	0.7454	0.7486	0.7517	0.7549	3	7	10	13	16	19	23	26	29
0.7	0.7580	0.7611	0.7642	0.7673	0.7704	0.7734	0.7764	0.7794	0.7823	0.7852	3	6	9	12	15	18	21	24	27
0.8	0.7881	0.7910	0.7939	0.7967	0.7995	0.8023	0.8051	0.8078	0.8106	0.8133	3	5	8	11	14	16	19	22	25
0.9	0.8159	0.8186	0.8212	0.8238	0.8264	0.8289	0.8315	0.8340	0.8365	0.8389	3	5	8	10	13	15	18	20	23
1.0	0.8413	0.8438	0.8461	0.8485	0.8508	0.8531	0.8554	0.8577	0.8599	0.8621	2	5	7	9	12	14	16	19	21
1.1	0.8643	0.8665	0.8686	0.8708	0.8729	0.8749	0.8770	0.8790	0.8810	0.8830	2	4	6	8	10	12	14	16	18
1.2	0.8849	0.8869	0.8888	0.8907	0.8925	0.8944	0.8962	0.8980	0.8997	0.9015	2	4	6	7	9	11	13	15	17
1.3	0.9032	0.9049	0.9066	0.9082	0.9099	0.9115	0.9131	0.9147	0.9162	0.9177	2	3	5	6	8	10	11	13	14
1.4	0.9192	0.9207	0.9222	0.9236	0.9251	0.9265	0.9279	0.9292	0.9306	0.9319	1	3	4	6	7	8	10	11	13
1.5	0.9332	0.9345	0.9357	0.9370	0.9382	0.9394	0.9406	0.9418	0.9429	0.9441	1	2	4	5	6	7	8	10	11
1.6	0.9452	0.9463	0.9474	0.9484	0.9495	0.9505	0.9515	0.9525	0.9535	0.9545	1	2	3	4	5	6	7	8	9
1.7	0.9554	0.9564	0.9573	0.9582	0.9591	0.9599	0.9608	0.9616	0.9625	0.9633	1	2	3	4	4	5	6	7	8
1.8	0.9641	0.9649	0.9656	0.9664	0.9671	0.9678	0.9686	0.9693	0.9699	0.9706	1	1	2	3	4	4	5	6	6
1.9	0.9713	0.9719	0.9726	0.9732	0.9738	0.9744	0.9750	0.9756	0.9761	0.9767	1	1	2	2	3	4	4	5	5
2.0	0.9772	0.9778	0.9783	0.9788	0.9793	0.9798	0.9803	0.9808	0.9812	0.9817	0	1	1	2	2	3	3	4	4
2.1	0.9821	0.9826	0.9830	0.9834	0.9838	0.9842	0.9846	0.9850	0.9854	0.9857	0	1	1	2	2	2	3	3	4
2.2	0.9861	0.9864	0.9868	0.9871	0.9875	0.9878	0.9881	0.9884	0.9887	0.9890	0	1	1	1	2	2	2	3	3
2.3	0.9893	0.9896	0.9898	0.9901	0.9904	0.9906	0.9909	0.9911	0.9913	0.9916	0	1	1	1	1	2	2	2	2
2.4	0.9918	0.9920	0.9922	0.9925	0.9927	0.9929	0.9931	0.9932	0.9934	0.9936	0	0	1	1	1	1	1	2	2
2.5	0.9938	0.9940	0.9941	0.9943	0.9945	0.9946	0.9948	0.9949	0.9951	0.9952	0	0	0	1	1	1	1	1	1
2.6	0.9953	0.9955	0.9956	0.9957	0.9959	0.9960	0.9961	0.9962	0.9963	0.9964	0	0	0	0	1	1	1	1	1
2.7	0.9965	0.9966	0.9967	0.9968	0.9969	0.9970	0.9971	0.9972	0.9973	0.9974	0	0	0	0	0	1	1	1	1
2.8	0.9974	0.9975	0.9976	0.9977	0.9977	0.9978	0.9979	0.9979	0.9980	0.9981	0	0	0	0	0	0	0	1	1
2.9	0.9981	0.9982	0.9982	0.9983	0.9984	0.9984	0.9985	0.9985	0.9986	0.9986	0	0	0	0	0	0	0	0	0

Critical values for the normal distribution

The table gives the value of z such that $P(Z \leqslant z) = p$, where $Z \sim N(0, 1)$.

p	0.75	0.90	0.95	0.975	0.99	0.995	0.9975	0.999	0.9995
z	0.674	1.282	1.645	1.960	2.326	2.576	2.807	3.090	3.291

Answers

1 Roots of polynomial equations

Prerequisite knowledge

1 a $y^2 + y + 3 = 0$ b $y^3 - 2y - 2 = 0$
c $9y^3 - 3y + 1 = 0$

2 a 55 b 30 c 75

3 a 1, 5, 17, 53, 161, 485 b 1, 1, 6, 16, 31, 51

Exercise 1A

1 a $\alpha + \beta = -5,\ \alpha\beta = 9$ b $\alpha + \beta = 4,\ \alpha\beta = 8$
c $\alpha + \beta = -\frac{3}{2},\ \alpha\beta = -\frac{7}{2}$

2 a $\alpha + \beta = -\frac{4}{3},\ \alpha\beta = 4$ b $-\frac{56}{9}$

3 5

4 The value of $ab = 1$. $x^2 + 3x + 1 = 0$

5 a Proof b Proof

6 $p = 2, q = 1$

7 28 and $\frac{4}{9}$

8 $x^2 + 2x - 4 = 0$ and $x^2 - 6x + 12 = 0$

9 $S_1 = -\frac{2}{3},\ S_2 = \frac{28}{9},\ S_{-1} = \frac{1}{2}$

10 a $-\frac{47}{16}$
b They are complex roots since $\alpha^2 + \beta^2 < 0$

Exercise 1B

1 a $\alpha + \beta + \gamma = -3,\ \alpha\beta\gamma = 5$
b $\alpha + \beta + \gamma = -\frac{5}{2},\ \alpha\beta\gamma = 3$
c $\alpha + \beta + \gamma = 0,\ \alpha\beta\gamma = 9$

2 a $\alpha + \beta + \gamma = 3,\ \alpha\beta + \alpha\gamma + \beta\gamma = 0$
b 9

3 a $S_2 = 4,\ S_{-1} = 0$ b $S_2 = -\frac{8}{3},\ S_{-1} = 4$
c $S_2 = -1,\ S_{-1} = \frac{5}{7}$

4 0 and 2

5 $\frac{25}{4}$ and $-\frac{137}{8}$

6 a $-a$ and $-\frac{b}{a}$
b Yes, since $\Sigma\alpha^2 = -a^2$

7 a 2 b −2

8 a Proof b $-\frac{9}{25}$

9 a $-\frac{q}{p}$ b $\frac{q^2}{p^2}$ c $-\frac{q^3}{p^3} - \frac{3r}{p}$

10 $p = 0,\ q = 1,\ r = -5$

Exercise 1C

1 a $\Sigma\alpha = 2,\ \Sigma\alpha\beta = 5$ b $\Sigma\alpha = -\frac{5}{2},\ \Sigma\alpha\beta = 0$
c $\Sigma\alpha = 0,\ \Sigma\alpha\beta = -\frac{2}{3}$

2 a $\Sigma\alpha = \frac{3}{5},\ \Sigma\alpha^2 = \frac{9}{25}$ b $\frac{1}{13}$

3 0 and $-\frac{1}{2}$, 0

4 $-\frac{239}{16}$

5 1 and 1, $-\frac{1}{2}$ and −2

6 $-6a$

7 a $-\frac{2}{3}$ and $-\frac{38}{9}$
b $\frac{118}{27}$ and $\frac{130}{81}$
c Yes, because $S_2 < 0$

8 −2, 2, 1

9 Proof

Exercise 1D

1 $x^2 + 15x + 27 = 0$

2 a $4x^2 + 12x + 49 = 0$ b $x^2 + 2x + 11 = 0$

3 $9x^2 - 20x + 14 = 0$

4 $9y^2 - 4y + 1 = 0$

5 $4y^3 - 20y^2 + 25y - 1 = 0,\ \frac{25}{2}$

6 Proof
a −3 b 3

7 Proof, $\frac{289}{64}$ and $-\frac{1}{2}$

8 $y^3 - 2y^2 + y - 16 = 0$, 50, 130, 242

End-of-chapter review exercise 1

1 Proof, $n = 1$: $\frac{7}{6}$, $n = 2$: $\frac{13}{36}, \frac{73}{216}$, Proof

2 **i** -4 **ii** 12 **iii** 4 **iv** 12

$y^4 - 4y^2 + 4 = 0$; $y = \pm\sqrt{2}$ (twice);

$x = \pm\sqrt{2} - 1$ (twice)

3 **i** Proof, $u^3 - u^2 - 13u + 93 = 0$

ii $\alpha\beta\gamma = 10$, $100v^3 - 10v^2 - 3v - 1 = 0$

2 Rational functions

Prerequisite knowledge

1 **a** $x + 3 + \frac{10}{x-3}$ **b** $\frac{1}{x-2} - \frac{1}{x-1}$

c $1 - \frac{1}{2(x+1)} + \frac{1}{2(x-1)}$

2 **a** $x = 1, y = 0$ **b** $x = -1, y = 2$

c $x = 2, x = -2, y = 0$

3 **a**

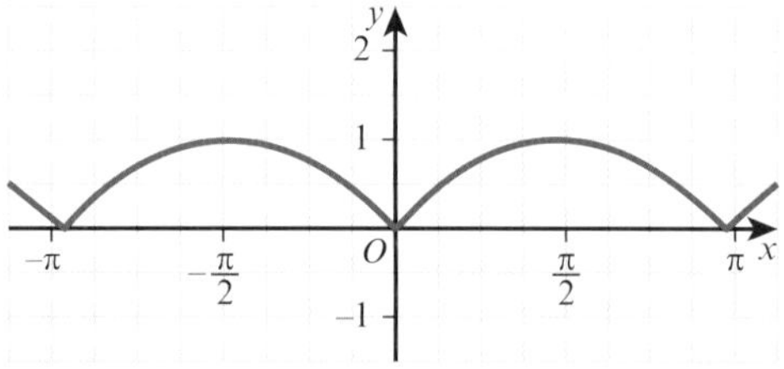

b

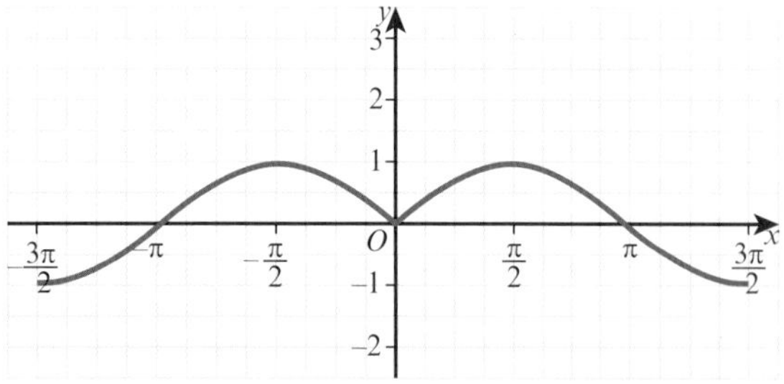

c

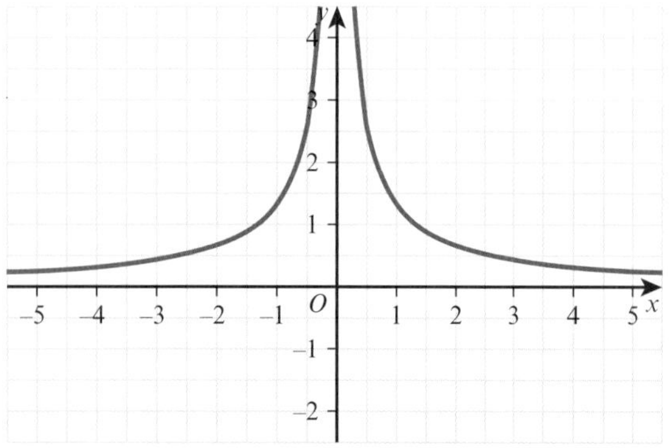

Exercise 2A

1 **a** $x = -1, x = -2, y = 0$

b $x = 2, y = 4$

c $x = -2, x = 4, y = 1$

2 $y = 2 + \frac{72}{7(x-6)} - \frac{2}{7(x+1)}$

$x = -1, x = 6, y = 2$

3 **a** 0

b 1

4 $x = 1, y = 2$

5 Intersection points are $\left(0, -\frac{1}{2}\right)$ and $\left(\frac{1}{3}, 0\right)$,

asymptotes: $x = -2$, $y = 3$

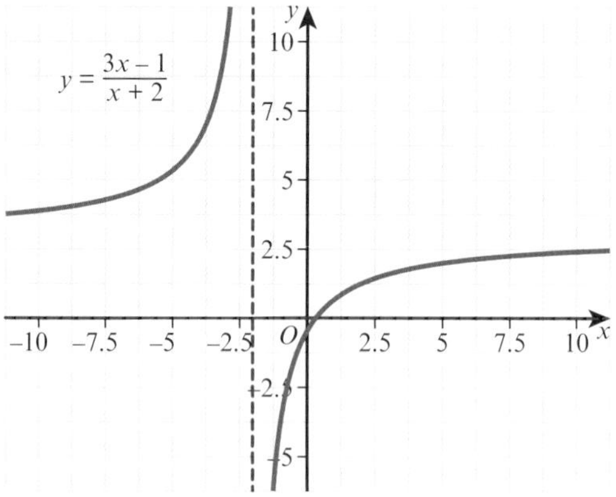

6 **a** $y = 1 + \frac{1}{x-2}$

b $x = 2, y = 1$

c Intersection points are $\left(0, \frac{1}{2}\right)$ and $(1, 0)$

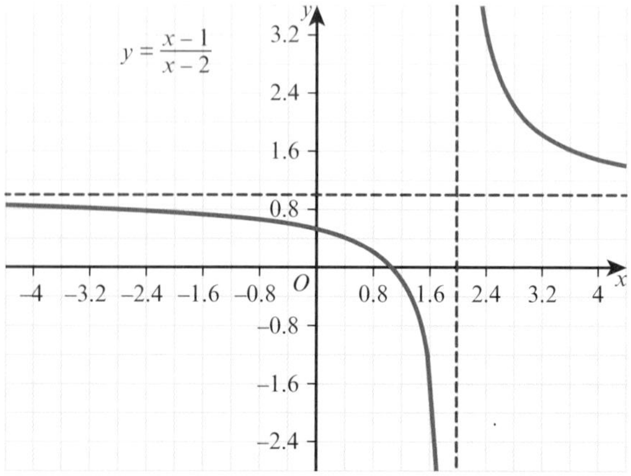

7 **a** $x = -1, x = 1, y = 0$ **b** $3 - 2\sqrt{2}, 3 + 2\sqrt{2}$

c Intersection points at $(0, -3)$ and $(3, 0)$

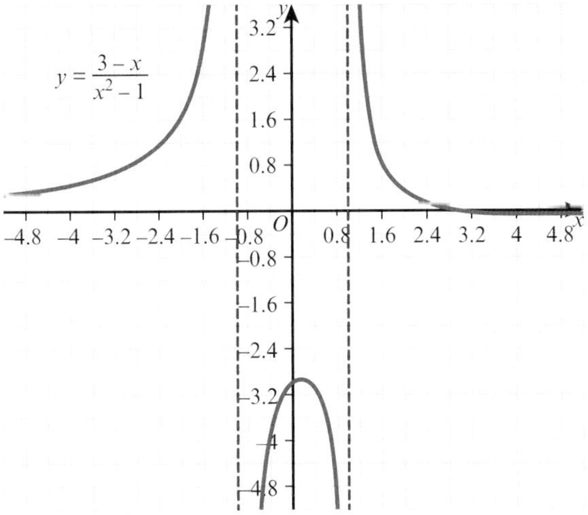

8 **a** Proof

b Intersection points at $(0, 0)$, asymptotes: $x = -3, x = 1, y = 0$

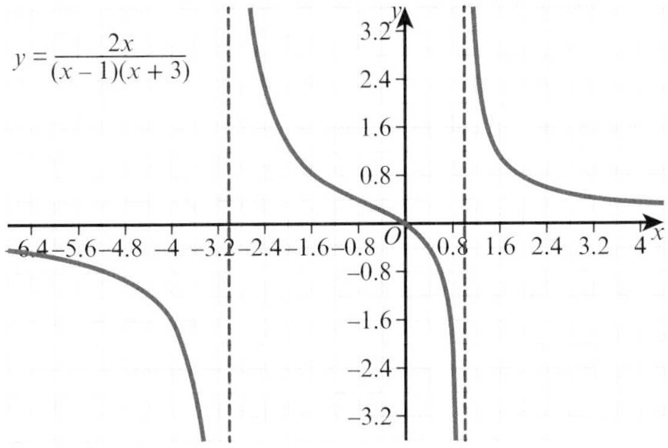

9 **a** $x = -3, x = 1, y = 1$ **b** 0

c Intersection points at $(-\sqrt{5}, 0), (\sqrt{5}, 0), \left(0, \frac{5}{3}\right)$

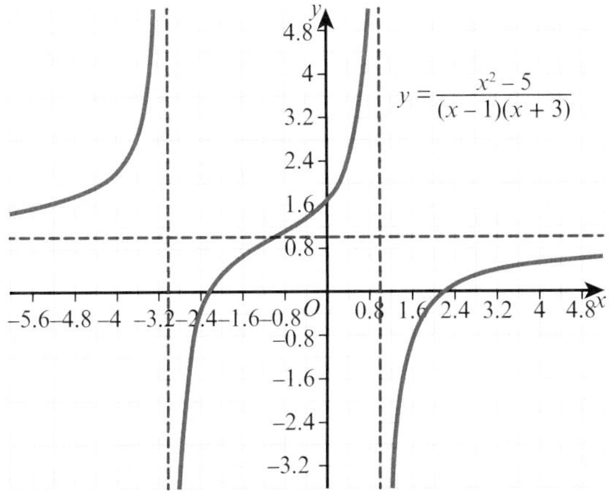

Exercise 2B

1 **a** $y = 3x - 2, x = -1$ **b** $y = x + 7, x = 4$

2 **a** 2 **b** 0

3 $y = 3x + 2 - \frac{4}{2x - 1}$

$y = 3x + 2, x = \frac{1}{2}$

4 Intersection point at $\left(0, -\frac{3}{2}\right)$, asymptotes: $x = 2, y = x + 2$

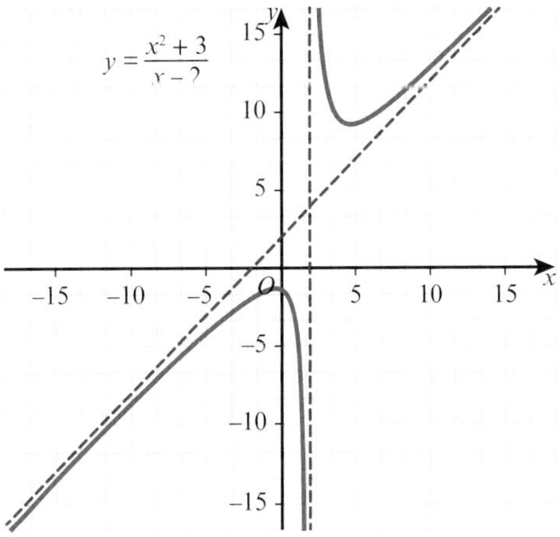

5 **a** $\lambda = 3$

b Asymptote: $x = -1$, intersection points: $(-3, 0), (0, 0)$

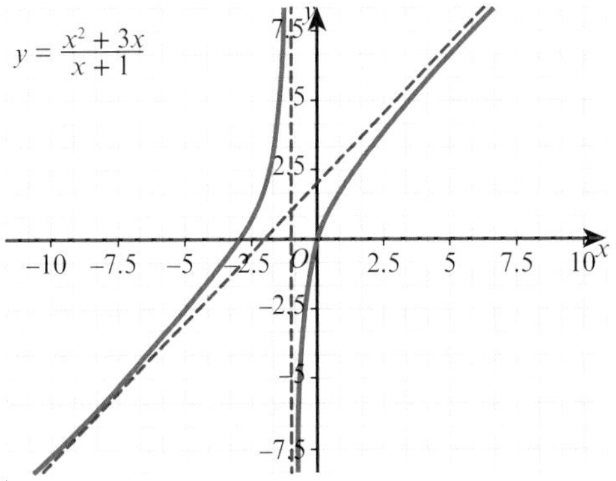

6 **a** Asymptotes: $x = 4, y = x + 2$

b Proof, $(7, 12)$

c Intersection points: $(1, 0), \left(0, -\frac{1}{4}\right)$

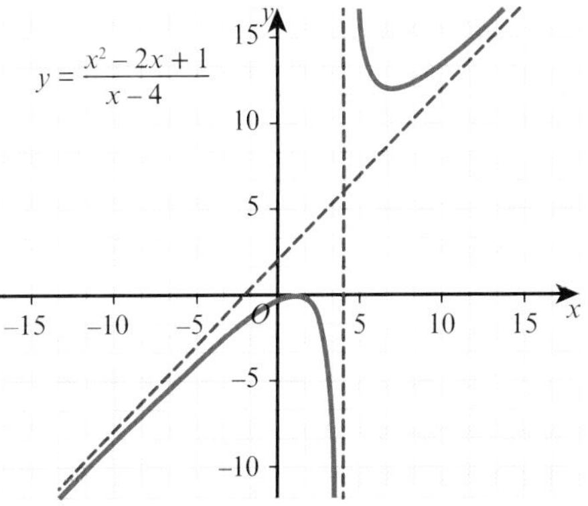

7 **a** $a = 2, b = -4$

b No turning points

c Intersection points: $(0, 4), (-1 + \sqrt{5}, 0)$ and $(-1 - \sqrt{5}, 0)$

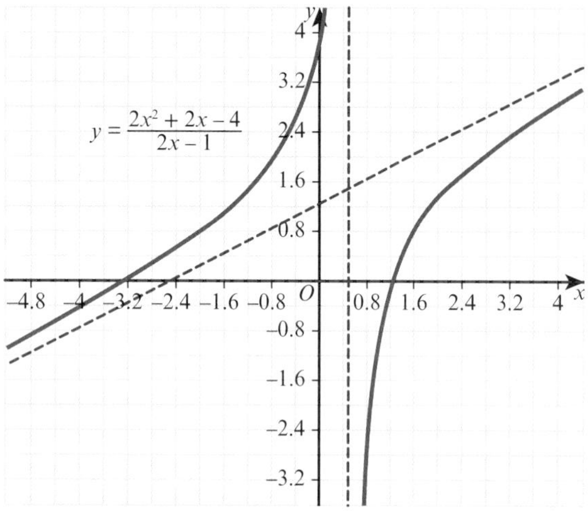

8 **a** $\alpha = -1, \beta = -2, \gamma = 7$

b Proof

c Intersection point: $\left(0, \frac{1}{3}\right)$, asymptotes: $x = 3, y = -x - 2$

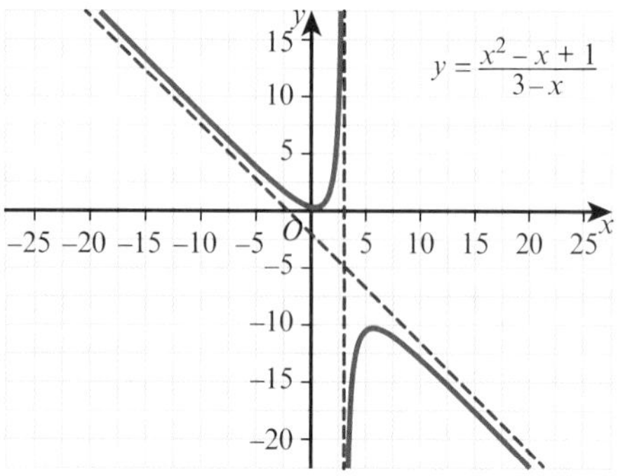

Exercise 2C

1 $-9 < x < -2$

2 $y \geqslant 0$ and $y \leqslant -12$

3 Proof

4 $x < -\frac{7}{4}, x > -1$

5 **a** $1 < y < 13$ **b** $(0, 1)$ and $(6, 13)$

6 **a** $k = \frac{4}{3}$ **b** Proof

c $\frac{25 - 4\sqrt{6}}{23} \leqslant y \leqslant \frac{25 + 4\sqrt{6}}{23}$

7 **a** $x = -2, x = 1, y = 0$ **b** Proof

c $-2 < x < -\sqrt{2}, 1 < x < \sqrt{2}$

8 $x < \frac{-\sqrt{249} - 9}{4}, -5 < x < \frac{\sqrt{249} - 9}{4}, x > 2$

Exercise 2D

1 **a** 2 **b** 0

2 **a** 2 **b** 0

3 **a** $x = -2, x = 2, y = 0$ **b** $y = 0$

4 Asymptotes: $x = -2, x = 3$ and $y = 0$, intersection points: $\left(0, -\frac{1}{6}\right)$

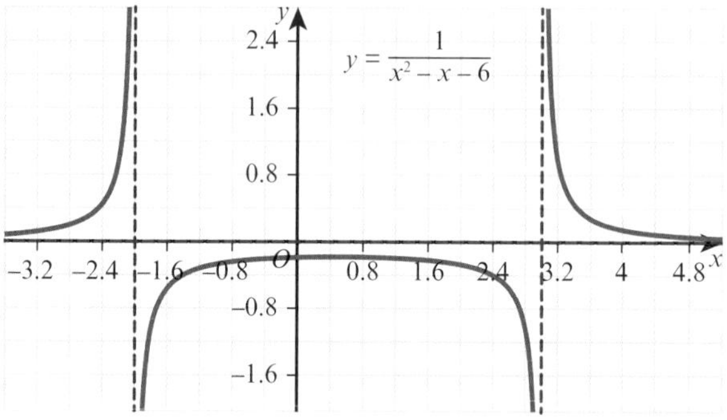

5 Intersection points: $(0, \sqrt{7}), (0, -\sqrt{7})$ and $\left(\frac{7}{3}, 0\right)$

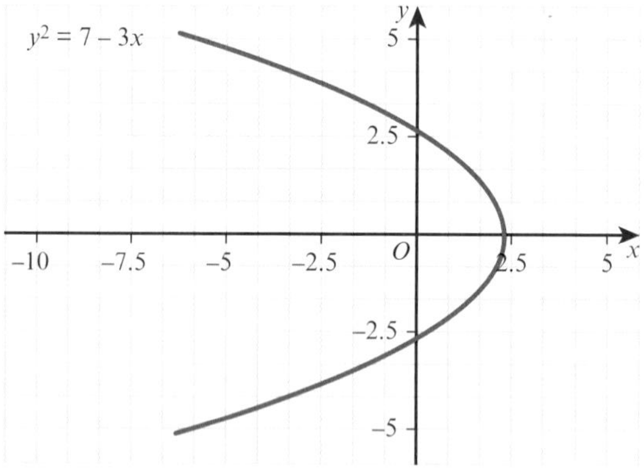

6 **a** Asymptotes: $x = -1, x = 2$ and $y = 0$, intersection points: $(0, 0)$

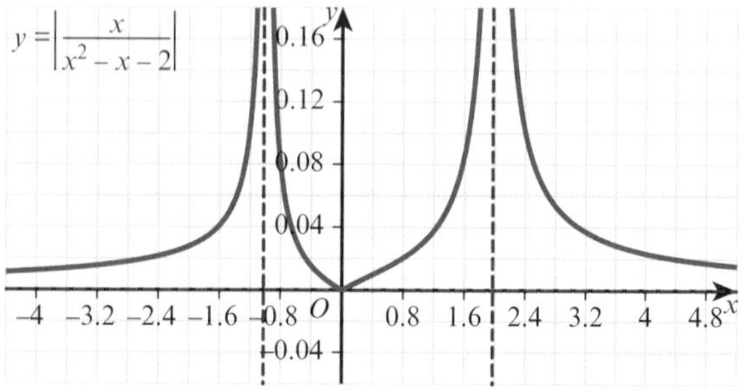

b Asymptotes: $x = -2, x = 2$ and $y = 0$, intersection points: $(0, 0)$

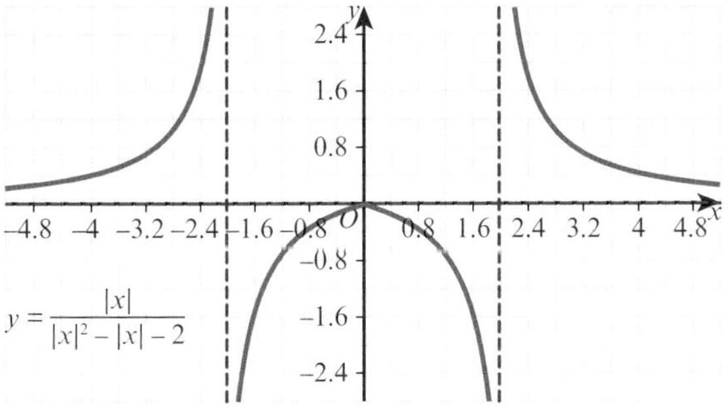

7 **a** Proof

b Proof

c Asymptotes: $x = -3, y = x - 1$ and $y = -x + 1$, intersection points: $(-1 - \sqrt{6}, 0), (-1 + \sqrt{6}, 0)$ and $\left(0, \frac{5}{3}\right)$

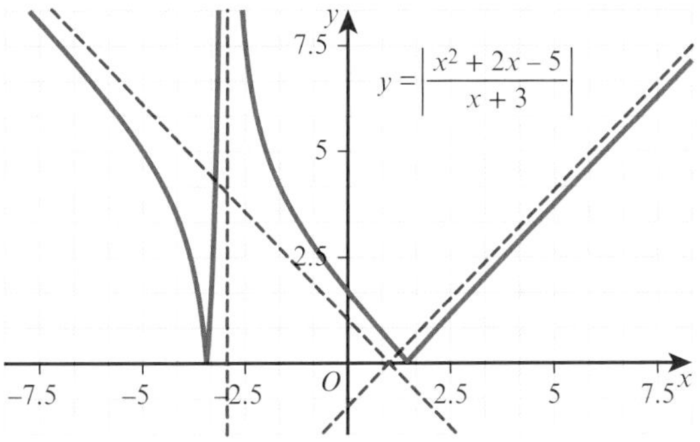

End-of-chapter review exercise 2

1 Asymptotes: $x = 3, y = x + 2$.

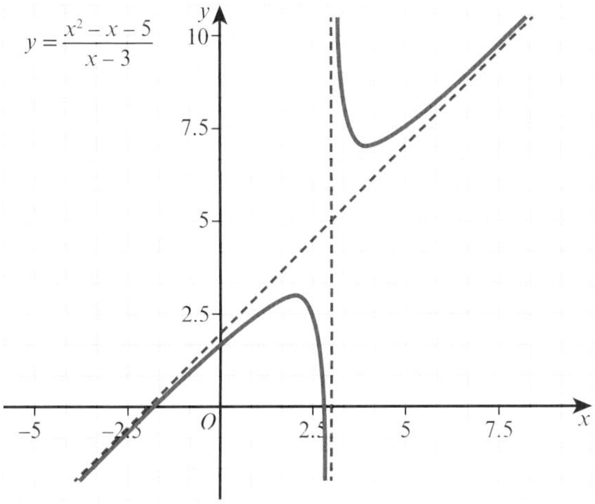

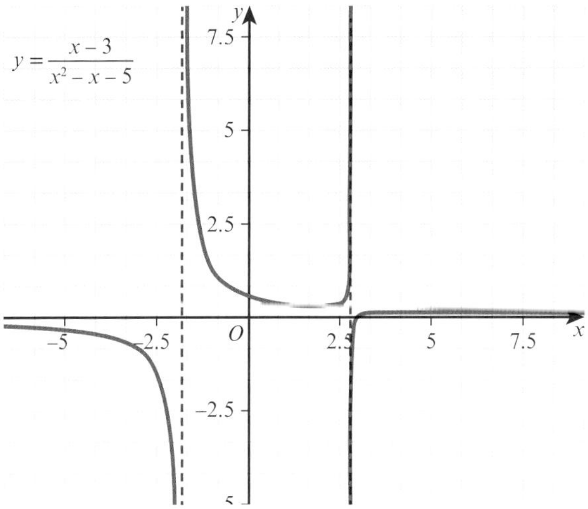

Asymptotes: $x = \frac{1 - \sqrt{21}}{2}$ and $x = \frac{1 + \sqrt{21}}{2}$.

2 Asymptotes: $x = -2, y = 2x + 1$; Proof

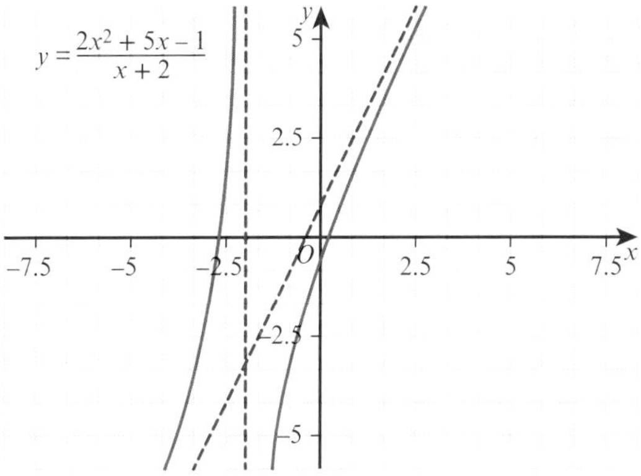

3 Asymptotes: $x = 1, y = 2$; Proof; stationary point $\left(7, \frac{25}{12}\right)$, axes intersection $(-0.5, 0), (2, 0), (0, -2)$, asymptote intersection $(4, 2)$

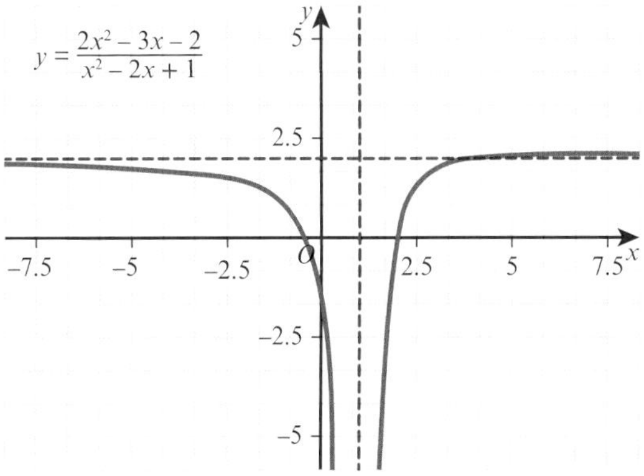

3 Summation of series

Prerequisite knowledge

1 **a** $\frac{1}{2(x-1)} - \frac{1}{2(x+1)}$

b $\frac{2}{x-2} - \frac{2}{x-1}$

2 $\frac{1}{256}$

Exercise 3A

1 Proof

2 Proof

3 $-n$

4 Proof

5 $\frac{1}{2}n(6n^2 - 9n - 5)$

6 $\frac{1}{3}n(2 + 9n + 7n^2)$

7 328 350

8 Proof, 32 760

9 204 020 000

Exercise 3B

1 $3\left(1 - \frac{1}{n}\right)$

2 Proof

3 $\frac{1}{10}$

4 $\frac{1}{4} - \frac{1}{n+4}$

5 Proof

6 Proof

$\frac{1}{2n-2} + \frac{1}{4n} - \frac{1}{4n-2}$

7 3

8 **a** $1 - \frac{1}{n-2}$ **b** 1 **c** $n > 1002$

End-of-chapter review exercise 3

1 $\frac{1}{2}\left(\frac{3}{2} - \frac{1}{n+1} - \frac{1}{n+2}\right)$

$S_\infty = \frac{3}{4}$

2 $\frac{2n(n+1)(2n+1)}{3}$, $-n(1+2n)$

3 Proof

4 Matrices I

Prerequisite knowledge

1 **a** 2 **b** -14

Exercise 4A

1 Proof

2 **a** $\begin{pmatrix} 81 & 0 \\ 16 & -5 \end{pmatrix}$

b $\begin{pmatrix} 24 & 28 \\ 4 & 18 \end{pmatrix}$

c $\begin{pmatrix} 302 & 399 \\ 57 & 79 \end{pmatrix}$

3 **a** $\begin{pmatrix} 2 & -100 & -58 \\ 6 & -44 & 6 \\ 3 & -30 & -11 \end{pmatrix}$

b $\begin{pmatrix} -25 & 9 & 6 \\ 12 & -21 & -2 \\ -3 & -9 & 8 \end{pmatrix}$

4 **a** $\begin{pmatrix} 12 \\ 20 \end{pmatrix}$

b No solution

c $(21 \quad 38)$

d No solution

5 **a** $\begin{pmatrix} 17 & 9 & -20 \\ 0 & 18 & 26 \\ 23 & -25 & -10 \end{pmatrix}$

b $\begin{pmatrix} 114 & -130 & -108 \\ 135 & -39 & -174 \\ -249 & 281 & 250 \end{pmatrix}$

c $\begin{pmatrix} 37 & 395 & -270 \\ -44 & -388 & 360 \\ 105 & 609 & -956 \end{pmatrix}$

d $\begin{pmatrix} 20 & 139 & -157 \\ -9 & 216 & 177 \\ -35 & -301 & 290 \end{pmatrix}$

6 Proof

7 $\begin{pmatrix} 0 & 9 & 18 \\ 12 & 17 & 12 \\ 172 & 231 & 48 \end{pmatrix}$

8 a $\mathbf{A}^2 = \begin{pmatrix} 4 & 0 & 0 \\ -3 & 0 & -1 \\ 3 & 0 & 1 \end{pmatrix}$, $\mathbf{A}^3 = \begin{pmatrix} 8 & 0 & 0 \\ -7 & 0 & -1 \\ 7 & 0 & 1 \end{pmatrix}$

b $\mathbf{A}^n = \begin{pmatrix} 2^n & 0 & 0 \\ 1-2^n & 0 & -1 \\ 2^n-1 & 0 & 1 \end{pmatrix}$

Exercise 4B

1 $\frac{1}{15}\begin{pmatrix} -8 & 7 \\ 9 & -6 \end{pmatrix}$

2 a $\frac{15}{2}$ b $\begin{pmatrix} 79 & -30 \\ -50 & 19 \end{pmatrix}$

3 $\frac{1}{18}\begin{pmatrix} 7 & -8 & 11 \\ 1 & 4 & -1 \\ -4 & 2 & 4 \end{pmatrix}$

4 a $\frac{1}{9}\begin{pmatrix} -5 & -7 \\ 2 & 1 \end{pmatrix}$ b $\frac{1}{52}\begin{pmatrix} 12 & -2 \\ 8 & 3 \end{pmatrix}$

c $\frac{1}{31}\begin{pmatrix} 4 & 5 \\ 3 & -4 \end{pmatrix}$ d $\frac{1}{24}\begin{pmatrix} -11 & 3 \\ 8 & 0 \end{pmatrix}$

5 $\mathbf{A}^2 = \begin{pmatrix} 7 & 10 \\ 15 & 22 \end{pmatrix}$, Proof

6 a Non-singular b Singular

7 a $\mathbf{A}^2 = \begin{pmatrix} 1 & 2 & 4 \\ 4 & 2 & 6 \\ 2 & 2 & 2 \end{pmatrix}$, $\mathbf{A}^3 = \begin{pmatrix} 5 & 6 & 8 \\ 8 & 8 & 16 \\ 6 & 4 & 8 \end{pmatrix}$

b $k = 3$

c $\mathbf{A}^{-1} = \frac{1}{4}\begin{pmatrix} 0 & 2 & -2 \\ -2 & 1 & 3 \\ 2 & -1 & 1 \end{pmatrix}$

8 $\frac{1}{20}\begin{pmatrix} -8 & -8 & -2 \\ 8 & -2 & -3 \\ 4 & 4 & 6 \end{pmatrix}$

9 $\mathbf{B} = \frac{1}{2}\begin{pmatrix} -34 & 8 & -10 & 10 \\ 18 & -2 & 4 & -6 \\ 13 & -4 & 4 & -3 \\ -8 & 2 & -2 & 2 \end{pmatrix}$

Exercise 4C

1 Proof

2 $-1, 4$

3 Proof

4 a Invertible

b Not invertible

c Invertible

5 a -12 b 0 c -96

6 Proof

7 $a = \frac{1}{2}$

8 30

Exercise 4D

1 a $\begin{pmatrix} 2 & 0 \\ 0 & -2 \end{pmatrix}$ b $\begin{pmatrix} 1 & 0 \\ 0 & -1 \end{pmatrix}$

c $\begin{pmatrix} 0 & -3 \\ -3 & 0 \end{pmatrix}$

2 a Proof; $k = -3$

b $b = 2, m = 3$

3 $\begin{pmatrix} -2 & -10 \\ 12 & -6 \end{pmatrix}$

4 a $\begin{pmatrix} 0 & 1 \\ 1 & 0 \end{pmatrix}$ b $\begin{pmatrix} -1 & 0 \\ 0 & 2 \end{pmatrix}$ c $\begin{pmatrix} 0 & -3 \\ 2 & 0 \end{pmatrix}$

5 a 24 b 111 c 48

6 a $y = \pm\frac{\sqrt{3}}{2}$ b $y = x, y = 2x$

c $y = -x, y = \frac{2}{5}x$

7 $\begin{pmatrix} 0 & -2 \\ -2 & 0 \end{pmatrix}$, points after transformation are $(-2, -2), (-4, -8)$ and $(-8, -6)$

8 a $\begin{pmatrix} 0 & 2 & 0 \\ 1 & 0 & 0 \\ 0 & 0 & 1 \end{pmatrix}$ b $\begin{pmatrix} 0 & \frac{\sqrt{2}}{4} & \frac{\sqrt{2}}{4} \\ \frac{1}{2} & 0 & 0 \\ 0 & -\frac{\sqrt{2}}{4} & \frac{\sqrt{2}}{4} \end{pmatrix}$

End-of-chapter review exercise 4

1 a $\mathbf{C} = \begin{pmatrix} -124 & -122 \\ -36 & -36 \end{pmatrix}$ b $\mathbf{D} = \frac{1}{16}\begin{pmatrix} -7 & -1 \\ 2 & -2 \end{pmatrix}$

2 a $a = -1$

b $\mathbf{A}^{-1} = \frac{1}{10}\begin{pmatrix} 16 & -16 & -6 \\ 1 & 4 & -1 \\ -2 & 2 & 2 \end{pmatrix}$

3 a $y = -\frac{1}{2}x,\ y = x$

b (1, 2), (5, 1), (4, 7)

5 Polar coordinates

Prerequisite knowledge

1 a $y = \frac{x}{2}(4 - x^2)^{\frac{1}{2}}$

b $x^2 - y^2 = 4$, or $y = \pm\sqrt{x^2 - 4}$

2 a $\frac{\pi}{8} + \frac{1}{4}$ b $\frac{e^2}{2}(e^2 - 1)$

Exercise 5A

1 $x^2 + \left(y - \frac{1}{2}\right)^2 = \frac{1}{4}$

2 $(3, 0), \left(2, \frac{\pi}{2}\right), (1, \pi), \left(2, \frac{3\pi}{2}\right)$

3

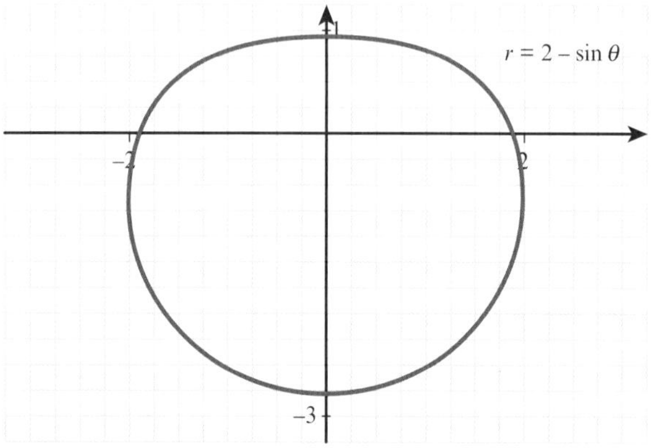

4 $r^2 = \tan\theta$

5 $\frac{\pi}{6} < \theta < \frac{5\pi}{6}$

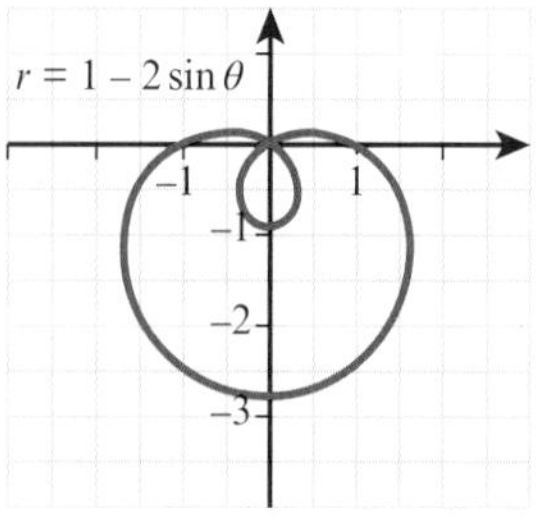

6

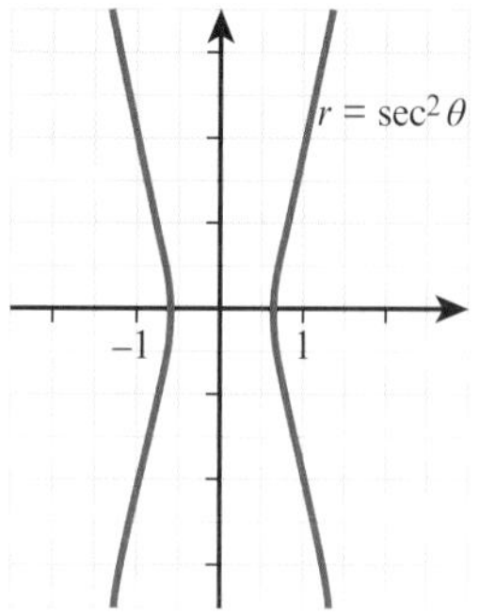

7 Proof

8

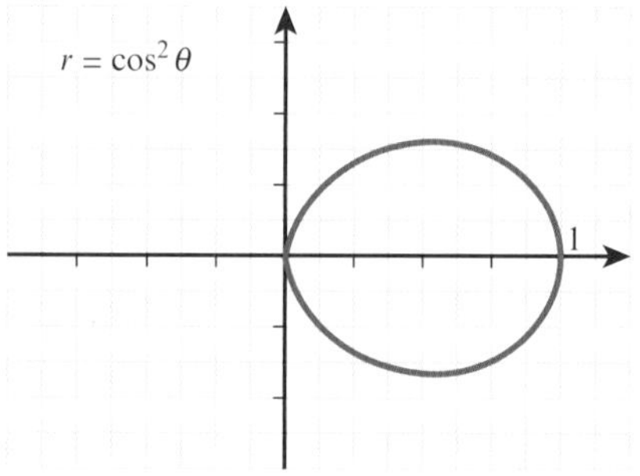

9

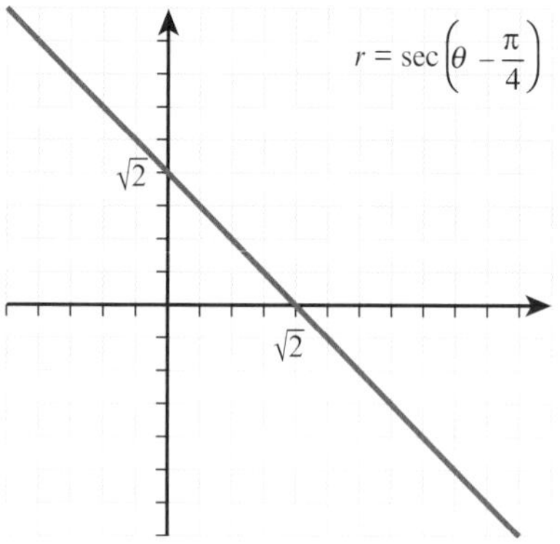

10

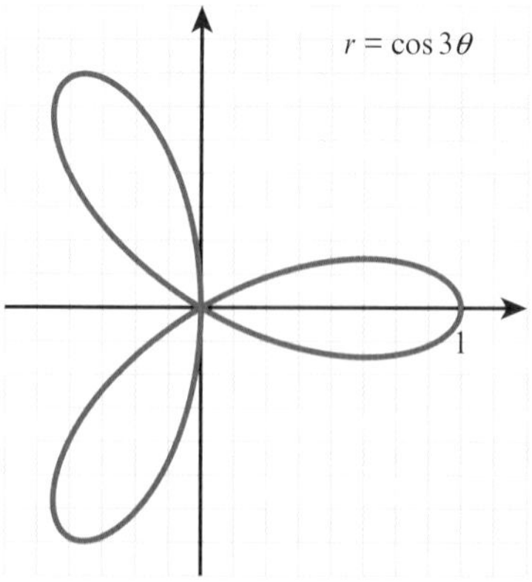

11

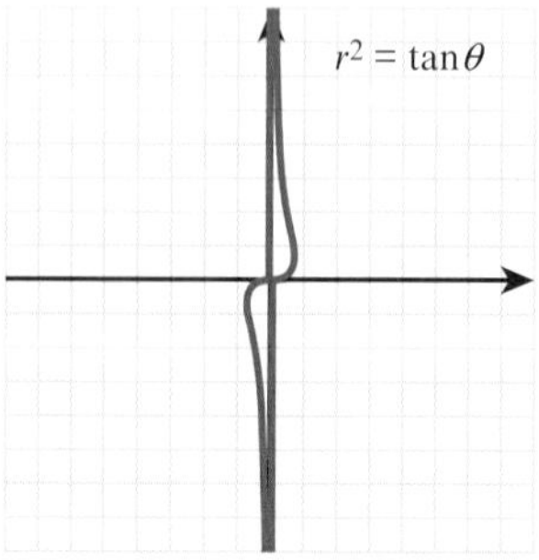

Exercise 5B

1 $\frac{7}{384}\pi^3$

2 Maximum distance $= \sqrt{2}$, at $\left(\sqrt{2}, \frac{7}{4}\pi\right)$

3 Proof

4 $\frac{e^2(e^2-1)}{4}$

5 0.658

6 2.62

7 $\frac{3\pi}{4} + \sqrt{2} + \frac{5}{4}$

8 **a** Proof **b** Proof **c** 0

9 $\frac{e^2(5e^2-1)}{8}$

End-of-chapter review exercise 5

1 **i**

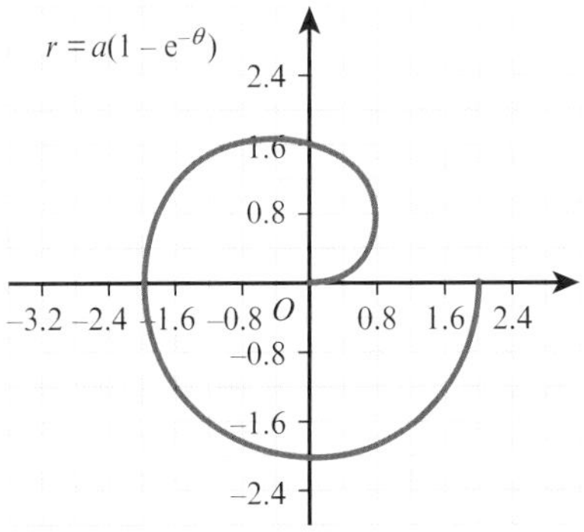

ii Proof

2 Intersections at $\left(4, \frac{\pi}{3}\right)$ and $\left(4, -\frac{\pi}{3}\right)$,

$R = \frac{22}{3}\pi - \frac{5}{2}\sqrt{3}$

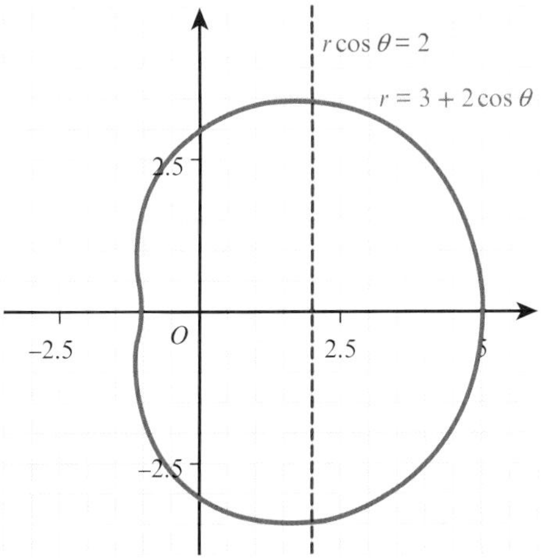

3 $\frac{dr}{d\theta} = 2\cos\theta - 2\cos 2\theta$, $\left(\frac{3}{2}\sqrt{3}, \frac{2\pi}{3}\right)$

Area: $\frac{5}{16}\pi - \frac{1}{2} - \frac{\sqrt{2}}{3}$

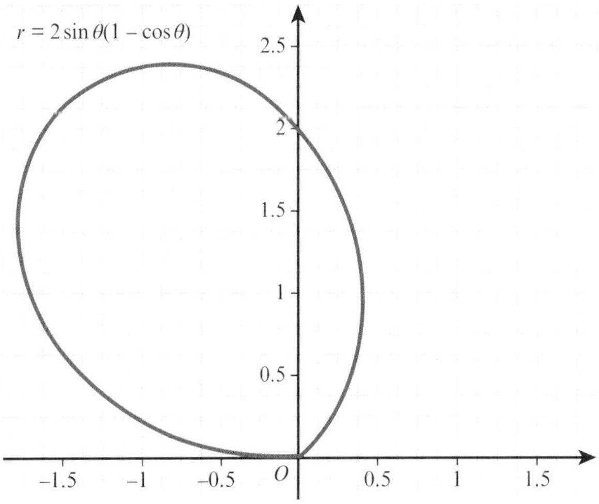

6 Vectors

Prerequisite knowledge

1 **a** $\mathbf{r} = \begin{pmatrix} 2 \\ 3 \\ 1 \end{pmatrix} + \begin{pmatrix} 1 \\ 1 \\ -2 \end{pmatrix} t$ **b** $\mathbf{r} = \begin{pmatrix} 3 \\ 0 \\ 1 \end{pmatrix} + \begin{pmatrix} 2 \\ 6 \\ 1 \end{pmatrix} t$

2 **a** 90° **b** 100.5°

Exercise 6A

1 **a** −2 **b** 1

2 2

3 $\alpha = 3, \beta = 1$

4 **a** $16\mathbf{i} + 11\mathbf{j} + 4\mathbf{k}$ **b** $-19\mathbf{i} + 7\mathbf{j} + 36\mathbf{k}$

c $101\mathbf{i} - 42\mathbf{j} + 72\mathbf{k}$ **d** $-221\mathbf{i} + 26\mathbf{j} - 52\mathbf{k}$

5 **a** $\frac{\sqrt{9787}}{2}$ **b** $\frac{\sqrt{2833}}{2}$

c $\sqrt{341}$ **d** $\frac{9\sqrt{5}}{2}$

6 $2, \frac{36}{13}$

7 **a** $\frac{281}{6}$ **b** $\frac{17}{3}$ **c** $\frac{167}{3}$

8 $m = 1$

Exercise 6B

1 a $\mathbf{r} = 2\mathbf{i} + 3\mathbf{j} + 5\mathbf{k} + (-9\mathbf{i} - 2\mathbf{j} + \mathbf{k})t$

b $\mathbf{r} = 4\mathbf{i} + \mathbf{j} + \mathbf{k} + (-9\mathbf{i} + 5\mathbf{j})t$

c $\mathbf{r} = 2\mathbf{j} + 4\mathbf{k} + (\mathbf{i} - \mathbf{j} - 5\mathbf{k})t$

2 $\mathbf{r} = \mathbf{i} + 7\mathbf{j} - 2\mathbf{k} + (-\mathbf{i} + 16\mathbf{j} + 10\mathbf{k})t$

3 $\mathbf{r} = 3\mathbf{i} - 5\mathbf{j} + \mathbf{k} + (2\mathbf{i} - 3\mathbf{j} - 2\mathbf{k})t$

4 $\frac{5\sqrt{35}}{7}$

5 $\overrightarrow{OP} = 2\mathbf{i} + 3\mathbf{j} + 2\mathbf{k}$, $\overrightarrow{OQ} = \mathbf{i} + 3\mathbf{j} + 4\mathbf{k}$

6 a Proof b $90°$ c $\frac{83\sqrt{442}}{221}$

7 a Proof b $\frac{\sqrt{66}}{33}$

8 a $a = 3$ b $b = \frac{1}{7}$

Exercise 6C

1 a $2x + 4y - 7 = 13$

b $3x + 7y + 8z = 19$

c $17x - 16y - 3z = 65$

2 $5x - z = 7$

3 $16x + 9y + 4z = 63$

4 $2x - 2y + z = 5$

5 $4\sqrt{2}$

6 $48.3°$

7 a $21.2°$ b $-x + 3y + z = 21$

8 $\mathbf{r} = \frac{5}{4}\mathbf{i} - \frac{1}{4}\mathbf{j} + (1 + 7\mathbf{j} + 4\mathbf{k})t$, $x + y - 2z = 1$

9 $\left|\frac{d - ap - bq - cr}{\sqrt{a^2 + b^2 + c^2}}\right|$

10 2.70

End-of-chapter review exercise 6

1 $\mathbf{p} = 11\mathbf{i} - 4\mathbf{j} + 3\mathbf{k}$, $\mathbf{q} = 5\mathbf{i} - 7\mathbf{j} + \mathbf{k}$

i $\frac{21\sqrt{5}}{2}$

ii $\frac{245}{2}$

2 $x + 2y + z = 3$, $70.9°$, $\mathbf{r} = -\mathbf{i} + 4\mathbf{j} + (5\mathbf{i} + \mathbf{j} - 7\mathbf{k})t$

3 $6x + 2y - 5z = 4$, E: $(2, 1, 2)$, $9.5°$

7 Proof by induction

Prerequisite knowledge

1 a $(x + 4)e^x$ b $2048\cos 4x$

2 $n^2 + 6n + 5$

3 a $\begin{pmatrix} 1 & 10 \\ 11 & 20 \end{pmatrix}$ b $\begin{pmatrix} -11 & 38 \\ -19 & 46 \end{pmatrix}$

Exercise 7A

1 Proof

2 Proof

3 Proof

4 Proof

5 a $\frac{d^2y}{dx^2} = -4\cos 2x - 8\sin 2x$

b Proof

6 a $u_2 = 18, u_3 = 34, u_4 = 66$

b Proof

7 Proof

8 Proof

9 a $\mathbf{A}^2 = \begin{pmatrix} \frac{1}{9} & 0 \\ -\frac{4}{3} & 1 \end{pmatrix}$, $\mathbf{A}^3 = \begin{pmatrix} \frac{1}{27} & 0 \\ -\frac{13}{9} & 1 \end{pmatrix}$,

$\mathbf{A}^4 = \begin{pmatrix} \frac{1}{81} & 0 \\ -\frac{40}{27} & 1 \end{pmatrix}$

b Proof c $\begin{pmatrix} 0 & 0 \\ -\frac{3}{2} & 1 \end{pmatrix}$

Exercise 7B

1 Proof

2 Proof

3 Proof

4 Proof

5 Proof

6 Proof

7 Proof

8 Proof

End-of-chapter review exercise 7

1 Proof

2 For all cases 1, $-1 + (1 + n)!$, Proof

3 Proof

Cross-topic review exercise 1

1 Proof, $\frac{1}{3}n(7n^2 - 1)$

2 **a** $S_1 = 5, S_3 = 122$

b $y^3 - 25y^2 + 10y - 1 = 0$

c 14878

3 **a** $x = -4, x = -1, y = 0$

b $\frac{dy}{dx} = \frac{-x^2 - 4x - 6}{(x^2 + 5x + 4)^2}$

c 0

d Intercepts are $(-2, 0)$, $\left(0, \frac{1}{2}\right)$

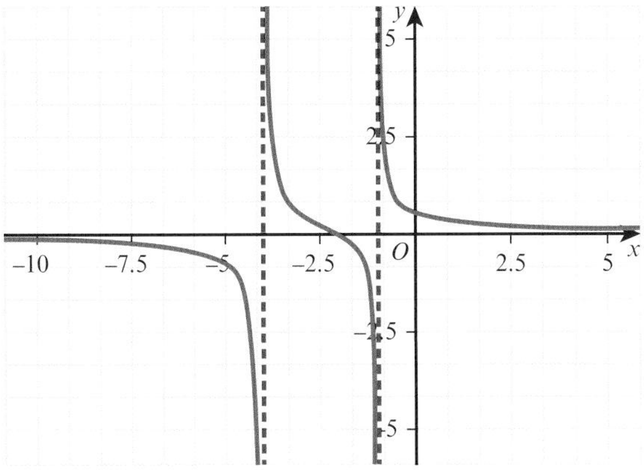

4 $\mathbf{A} = \begin{pmatrix} 1 & -2 & 3 \\ -1 & 4 & 1 \\ 2 & -2 & 9 \end{pmatrix}$ means the planes all meet at a single point

5 **a**

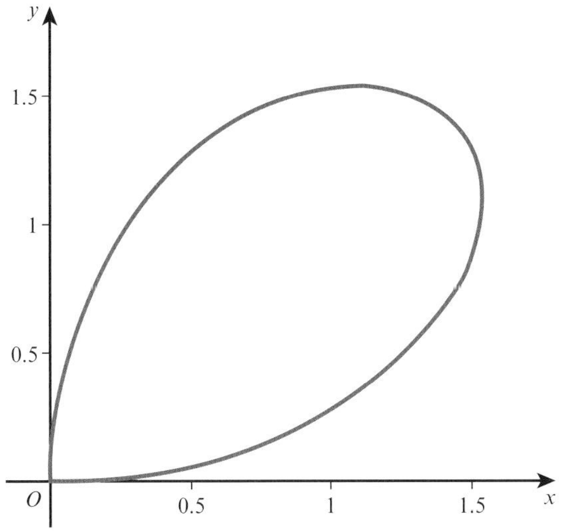

b $\frac{8\sqrt{3}}{9}$ **c** $\frac{\pi}{2}$

6 **a** $90°$ **b** $\frac{\sqrt{6}}{2}$

7 Proof

8 **a** 4 **b** Proof

9 $\frac{1}{4r-2} - \frac{1}{4r+2}; \frac{1}{2} - \frac{1}{4n+2}; \frac{1}{2}$

10 **i** $y = 5 + \frac{4}{x-2} - \frac{4}{x+3}$ **ii** $y = 1.8$

iii $x = 2, x = -3, y = 5$ **iv** $1.8 < k < 5$

11 $B = \begin{pmatrix} -\frac{1}{4} & -\frac{5}{2} & \frac{5}{2} \\ \frac{1}{2} & \frac{1}{2} & -1 \\ -\frac{1}{4} & \frac{3}{2} & -1 \end{pmatrix}$

12 Proof

8 Continuous random variables

Prerequisite knowledge

1 $E(X) = 2.3, Var(X) = 0.81$

2 $\frac{98}{3}$

Exercise 8A

1 **a** Yes, because $f(x) \geqslant 0$ and $\int f(x)dx = 1$

b No, $\int f(x)dx = 1$ but $f(x) < 0$ for some x

c Yes because $f(x) \geqslant 0$ and $\int f(x)dx = 1$

d No since $\int f(x)dx \neq 1$

2 **a**

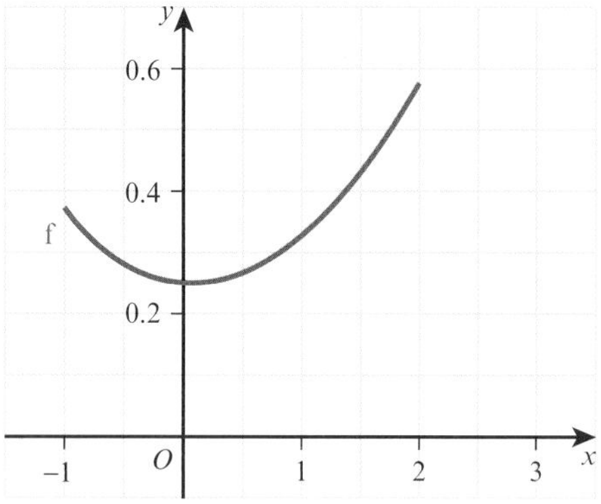

b

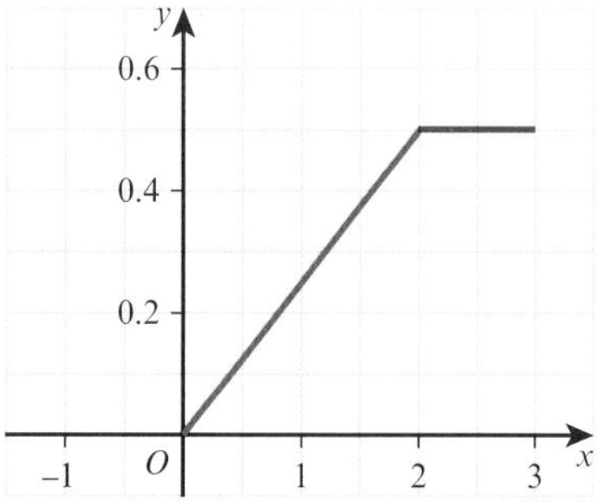

c

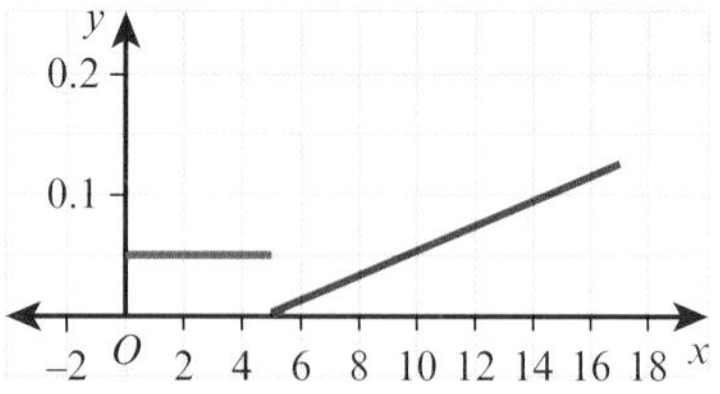

3 $k = \frac{2}{9}$

4 $k = \frac{2e^4}{e^2 - 1}$

5 **a** $k = \frac{1}{32}$ **b** 0 **c** $\frac{45}{64}$ **d** $\frac{51}{64}$

6 **a** $k = \frac{1}{15}$ **b** $\frac{7}{45}$ **c** $\frac{11}{18}$

7 $k = \frac{4}{81}$

8 $k = -\frac{1}{19}$

9 **a** $k = \frac{1}{16}$ **b** $\frac{1}{4}$ **c** $\frac{9}{32}$ **d** $\frac{23}{32}$

10 **a** $\frac{1}{36}$ **b** $\frac{1}{2}$ **c** $\frac{31}{32}$

Exercise 8B

1 $F(x) = \begin{cases} 0 & x < -4 \\ \frac{1}{95}(-3x^2 + 10x + 88) & -4 \leqslant x \leqslant 1 \\ 1 & \text{otherwise} \end{cases}$

2 $F(x) = \begin{cases} 0 & x < 2 \\ \frac{1}{27}(-68 + 54x - 12x^2 + x^3) & 2 \leqslant x \leqslant 5 \\ 1 & x > 5 \end{cases}$

3 $F(x) = \begin{cases} 0 & x < 3 \\ \frac{1}{16}(x - 3) & 3 \leqslant x \leqslant 7 \\ \frac{1}{8}(x - 5) & 7 \leqslant x \leqslant 13 \\ 1 & x > 13 \end{cases}$

4 $F(x) = \begin{cases} 0 & x < 1 \\ \frac{2}{27}(x^2 - 2x + 1) & 1 \leqslant x < 4 \\ \frac{2}{27}(-2x^2 + 22x - 47) & 4 \leqslant x \leqslant \frac{11}{2} \\ 1 & x > \frac{11}{2} \end{cases}$

5 $F(x) = \begin{cases} 0 & x < 0 \\ \frac{x}{24} & 0 \leqslant x < 5 \\ \frac{1}{48}(x^2 - 8x + 25) & 5 \leqslant x < 7 \\ \frac{1}{8}(x - 4) & 7 \leqslant x < 12 \\ 1 & x > 12 \end{cases}$

6 **a** $F(x) = \begin{cases} 0 & x < 3 \\ \frac{1}{56}(-x^2 + 24x - 63) & 3 \leqslant x \leqslant 7 \\ 1 & x > 7 \end{cases}$

b $\frac{4}{7}$ **c** $\frac{1}{2}$ **d** 4.72

7 **a** $F(x) = \begin{cases} 0 & x < 2 \\ -\frac{1}{100}(x - 11)(x - 2)^2 & 2 \leqslant x \leqslant 7 \\ 1 & x > 7 \end{cases}$

b $\frac{7}{25}$ **c** $\frac{23}{50}$

8 a $F(x) = \begin{cases} 0 & x < 4 \\ \frac{1}{180}(-x^2 + 26x - 88) & 4 \leqslant x < 7 \\ \frac{1}{540}(x^2 + 22x - 68) & 7 \leqslant x \leqslant 16 \\ 1 & x > 16 \end{cases}$

b $\frac{8}{45}$ c $\frac{59}{108}$ d 7 e $m = 10.4$

9 a $F(x) = \begin{cases} 0 & x < 6 \\ \frac{1}{99}\left(\frac{x^3}{3} - 9x^2 + 83x - 246\right) & 6 \leqslant x \leqslant 15 \\ 1 & x > 15 \end{cases}$

b 0.872 c Proof

10 a $-\frac{8}{3}$ b Proof

Exercise 8C

1 a $\frac{40}{3}$ b 200 c $\frac{200}{9}$

2 a $\frac{23}{7} = 3.286$ b 11.5 c $\frac{69}{98} = 0.704$

3 a 8.3 b 75.4 c 6.51 d 2.55

4 a $4.96 = \left(\frac{119}{24}\right)$ b $33.9 = \left(\frac{407}{12}\right)$

c 9.33 using exact values

5 $\frac{5}{64}(36 + \ln 5)$

6 $\frac{502}{7} = 71.7$

7 $\frac{e(e^2 - 2)}{2}$

8 $\frac{15}{8}\ln\left(\frac{3}{2}\right) - \frac{23}{32}$

9 $\frac{5}{3}$

10 0.482

11 a $f(x) = \begin{cases} \frac{1}{36}(3x^2 + 5) & 1 \leqslant x \leqslant 3 \\ 0 & \text{otherwise} \end{cases}$

Median, $F(2.315) < 0.5$, $F(2.325) > 0.5$, Therefore median = 2.32 correct to 3 significant figures

b Mode = 3

c $E(X) = 2.22$

d Since mean < median < mode the skew is negative.

Exercise 8D

1 $G(a) = \begin{cases} 0 & a < 0 \\ \frac{a}{400} & 0 \leqslant a \leqslant 400 \\ 1 & a > 400 \end{cases}$

2 $G(a) = \begin{cases} 0 & a < 0 \\ \frac{1}{10}(a + \sqrt[3]{a}) & 0 \leqslant a \leqslant 8 \\ 1 & a > 8 \end{cases}$

3 $G(a) = \begin{cases} 0 & a < -34 \\ \frac{-1}{285}a(34 + a) & -34 \leqslant a \leqslant -19 \\ 1 & a > -19 \end{cases}$

4 a $G(a) = \begin{cases} 0 & a < 1 \\ \frac{1}{3}(a - 1) & 1 \leqslant a \leqslant 4 \\ 1 & a > 4 \end{cases}$

b $G(b) = \begin{cases} 0 & b < 1 \\ \frac{1}{3}(b^4 - 1) & 1 \leqslant b \leqslant \sqrt{2} \\ 1 & b > \sqrt{2} \end{cases}$

5 $G(y) = \begin{cases} 0 & y < 0 \\ \frac{1}{300}(y + 20\sqrt{y}) & 0 \leqslant y \leqslant 100 \\ 1 & y > 100 \end{cases}$

6 a $F(x) = \begin{cases} 0 & x < 0 \\ -\frac{1}{16}(x^2 - 8x) & 0 \leqslant x \leqslant 4 \\ 1 & x > 4 \end{cases}$

b $G(y) = \begin{cases} 0 & y < -0 \\ -\frac{1}{144}(y^2 - 20y - 44) & -0 < y \leqslant 10 \\ 1 & y > 10 \end{cases}$

c $g(y) = \begin{cases} \frac{1}{72}(10 - y) & -0 \leqslant y \leqslant 10 \\ 0 & \text{otherwise} \end{cases}$

7 a $F(x) = \begin{cases} 0 & x < 1 \\ \frac{2(x - 1)}{x} & 1 \leqslant x \leqslant 2 \\ 1 & x > 2 \end{cases}$

b $G(y) = \begin{cases} 0 & y < \frac{1}{4} \\ \frac{2\sqrt{y} - 1}{\sqrt{y}} & \frac{1}{4} \leqslant y \leqslant 1 \\ 1 & y > 1 \end{cases}$

c $g(y) = \begin{cases} \frac{1}{2y^{\frac{3}{2}}} & \frac{1}{4} \leqslant y \leqslant 1 \\ 0 & \text{otherwise} \end{cases}$

8 **a** $G(y) = \begin{cases} 0 & y < \frac{1}{5} \\ 1 + \frac{25}{24}(y^2 - 1) & \frac{1}{5} \leqslant y \leqslant 1 \\ 1 & y > 1 \end{cases}$

b $g(y) = \begin{cases} \frac{50y}{24} & \frac{1}{5} \leqslant y \leqslant 1 \\ 0 & \text{otherwise} \end{cases}$

9 **a** $F(x) = \begin{cases} 0 & x < 0 \\ -\frac{1}{25}(x^2 - 10x) & 0 \leqslant x \leqslant 5 \\ 1 & x > 5 \end{cases}$

b $G(y) = \begin{cases} 0 & y < -5 \\ \frac{1}{100}(y + 5)^2 & -5 \leqslant y \leqslant 5 \\ 1 & y > 5 \end{cases}$

c $\frac{49}{100}$ **d** $\frac{2}{5}$

e $g(y) = \begin{cases} \frac{1}{50}(y + 5) & -5 \leqslant y \leqslant 5 \\ 0 & \text{otherwise} \end{cases}$

10 **a** $F(r) = \begin{cases} 0 & r < 1 \\ \frac{1}{25}(-r^2 + 12r - 11) & 1 \leqslant r \leqslant 6 \\ 1 & r > 6 \end{cases}$

b

$$G(A) = \begin{cases} 0 & A < \pi \\ -\left(\frac{1}{25\pi}\right)(A - 12\sqrt{A\pi} + 11\pi) & \pi \leqslant A \leqslant 36\pi \\ 1 & A > 36\pi \end{cases}$$

c $g(A) = \begin{cases} \frac{1}{25\pi}\left(\frac{6\sqrt{\pi}}{\sqrt{A}} - 1\right) & \pi \leqslant A \leqslant 36\pi \\ 0 & \text{otherwise} \end{cases}$

End-of-chapter review exercise 8

1 **i** $E(T) = 100$ **ii** 69.3 **iii** 0.819

2 **a** $k = \frac{1}{4}$

b **i** $g(y) = \begin{cases} \frac{1}{16} & 0 \leqslant y \leqslant 4 \\ \frac{1}{8\sqrt{y}} & 4 \leqslant y \leqslant 25 \\ 0 & \text{otherwise} \end{cases}$

ii Proof

iii $m_x = 3$, $m_y = 9$, hence $m_y = m_x^2$

3 **i** Proof

ii $\lambda = 0.174$, median $= \lambda^{-1}\ln 2 = 3.98$

9 Inferential statistics

Prerequisite knowledge

1 0.879

2 2.359

Exercise 9A

1 **a** $\bar{x} = 15.583$, $s^2 = 9.174$

b $\bar{x} = 145.2$, $s^2 = 177.96$

2 **a** $t_{0.95,\,10} = 1.812$ **b** $t_{0.975,\,20} = 2.086$

c $t_{0.975,\,14} = 2.145$ **d** $t_{0.995,\,24} = 2.797$

e $t_{0.9,\,7} = 1.415$ **f** $t_{0.95,\,17} = 1.740$

3 **a** H_0: $\mu = 41$, H_1: $\mu \neq 41$

b H_0: $\mu = 7.3$, H_1: $\mu > 7.3$

c H_0: $\mu = 54.2$, H_1: $\mu < 54.2$

d H_0: $\mu = 6.5$, H_1: $\mu \neq 6.5$

4 **a** $t_{0.95,\,9} = 1.833$; reject

b $t_{0.99,\,7} = 2.998$; do not reject

c $t_{0.95,\,14} = 1.761$; do not reject

d $t_{0.975,\,10} = 2.228$; reject

5 a $\bar{x} = 49.7$, $s^2 = 10.42$

b H_0: $\mu = 50.5$, H_1: $\mu < 50.5$, $t = -0.894$, $t_{0.95,\,11} = -1.796$. Do not reject H_0: The mean length is 50.5 cm, based on this sample.

6 H_0: $\mu = 60$, H_1: $\mu \neq 60$, $t = 0.494$, $t_{0.975,\,9} = 2.262$, Reject H_0: The amount of paracetamol is different from 60 mg

7 a H_0: $\mu = 175$, H_1: $\mu < 175$, $\bar{x} = 174$, $s^2 = 2.377$, $t = -1.032$, $t_{0.95,\,7} = -1.895$. Do not reject H_0: The crisp packets weigh 175 g.

b The packets that are tested cannot be sold afterwards, so as few as possible should be opened (this is called destruction testing).

8 H_0: $\mu = 5000$, H_1: $\mu > 5000$, $\bar{x} = 5004.1$, $s^2 = 36.32$, $t = 2.151$, $t_{0.95,\,9} = 1.83$

Reject H_0: The pump is giving more than 5 litres of petrol.

Exercise 9B

1 a $s_p^2 = 12.6$ b $s_p^2 = 159.86$

c $s_p^2 = 38.67$

2 a $s_p^2 = 24.68$ b $s_p^2 = 7.746$

3 a $t_{0.95,\,12} = 1.782$ b $t_{0.975,\,22} = 2.074$

c $t_{0.975,\,13} = 2.160$ d $t_{0.995,\,30} = 2.750$

e $t_{0.9,\,23} = 1.319$ f $t_{0.95,\,27} = 1.703$

4 a H_0: $\mu_x - \mu_y = 0$, H_1: $\mu_x - \mu_y \neq 0$

b H_0: $\mu_x - \mu_y = 0$, H_1: $\mu_x - \mu_y > 0$

c H_0: $\mu_x - \mu_y = 5$, H_1: $\mu_x - \mu_y > 5$

d H_0: $\mu_x - \mu_y = 6$, H_1: $\mu_x - \mu_y \neq 6$

5 NB: we are given $\sigma = 15$, H_0: $\mu_A - \mu_B = 0$, H_1: $\mu_A - \mu_B < 0$. (If more severe, A should be giving fewer marks on average.) Test statistic $= -1.7348$, $z = -1.96$. Do not reject H_0: Examiner *A* is not more severe than examiner *B*.

6 a $s_p^2 = 0.0599$ (4 decimal places)

b H_0: $\mu_M - \mu_F = 0$, H_1: $\mu_M - \mu_F > 0$, $t = 1.056$, $t_{0.95,\,16} = 1.746$

Do not reject H_0: Male Takahē birds are not significantly heavier than female Takahē birds.

7 a $s_p^2 = 15.03$

b H_0: $\mu_N - \mu_O = 10$, H_1: $\mu_N - \mu_O > 10$, $t = -0.915$, $t_{12,\,0.95} = -1.782$

Do not reject H_0: The council is correct in stating that the new route will not add more than ten minutes to the journey.

8 H_0: $\mu_B - \mu_A = 0$, H_1: $\mu_B - \mu_A \neq 0$, $t = 0.91$, $t_{0.975,\,8} = 2.306$

Do not reject H_0: There is no difference in the viscosities of the two types of honey.

Exercise 9C

1 a $\bar{d} = -0.333$, $s_d^2 = 135$

b $\bar{d} = 0.683$, $s_d^2 = 12.578$

c $\bar{d} = -5.75$, $s_d^2 = 190.93$

2 a 0.104 b −0.638 c −0.210

3 a $t_{0.975,\,10} = 2.228$ b $t_{0.95,9} = 1.833$

c $t_{0.975,\,11} = 2.201$

4 $\bar{d} = 0.0338$, $s_d^2 = 0.00183$, H_0: $\mu_d = 0$, H_1: $\mu_d > 0$, $t = 2.233$, $t_{0.975,\,7} = 2.365$

Reject H_0: The weight after the 14 days has increased significantly.

5 H_0: $\mu_d = 2$, H_1: $\mu_d > 2$, $\bar{d} = 2.225$, $s_d = 0.931589$, $t = 0.659$, $t_{0.95,\,7} = 1.895$

Do not reject H_0: The claim that participants will lose at least 2 kg in the first five weeks is not true.

6 H_0: $\mu_d = 0$, H_1: $\mu_d \neq 0$, $t = 2.934$, $t_{0.975,\,7} = 2.365$

Reject H_0: The course did not make a difference to the memory test scores.

7 H_0: $\mu_d = 0$, H_1: $\mu_d > 0$, $t = 1.057$, $t_{0.95,\,5} = 2.015$

Do not reject H_0: The visits of the psychologist have not had a positive impact on sales productivity.

Exercise 9D

1 a $t_{0.95,\,5} = 2.015$ b $t_{0.95,\,7} = 1.895$

c $t_{0.975,\,11} = 2.201$ d $t_{0.9,\,6} = 1.440$

2 a 1.061 b 1.414

c 1.563 d 0.917

3 a (10.358, 16.042) b (9.710, 16.690)
c (10.570, 15.830) d (9.276, 17.124)
e (8.455, 17.945) f (11.344, 15.056)

4 (13.32, 17.68)

5 a $\bar{x} = 7.153$, $s^2 = 0.002347$, $t_{6,\,0.975} = 2.447$, [7.108, 7.198]

b Since the confidence interval is totally above the value of 7.1, the claim by the car hire company is wrong.

6 [40.10, 46.57]

7 a [453.6, 459.3]

b The confidence interval contains 454 (just!) and so the claim is justified.

8 NB: since n is large we can use the Central Limit Theorem and we can use s^2 as an unbiased estimator for σ^2. CI: we use $z_{0.995}$, $37.2 \pm 2.576 \times \frac{3.2}{\sqrt{36}}$, [35.83, 38.57]

Exercise 9E

1 a 1.645 b 1.960
c 2.576 d 1.282

2 a $t_{0.95,\,12} = 1.782$ b $t_{0.975,\,21} = 2.080$
c $t_{0.995,\,28} = 2.763$ d $t_{0.9,\,18} = 1.330$

3 a $\sqrt{\frac{s_x^2}{n_x} + \frac{s_y^2}{n_y}} = 0.789$, confidence interval (−0.907, 1.687)

b $s_p\sqrt{\frac{1}{n_x} + \frac{1}{n_y}} = 1.546$, confidence interval (−3.350, 2.010)

c $s_p\sqrt{\frac{1}{n_x} + \frac{1}{n_y}} = 9.939$, confidence interval (−18.643, 24.303)

4 a (10.037, 14.163) b (8.87, 15.33)

5 a $s_p^2 = 1.061$
b $t_{0.9,\,20} = 1.725$, [−1.56, −0.04]

6 a [0.419, 3.081]

b Since the confidence interval is wholly above the value of 0, we can conclude that sleep deprivation does affect reaction time.

7 Since both n are large, we can use the z-statistic to do this. $z_{0.975} = 1.96$, [0.555, 1.845]

8 NB: we need to use pooled variance here. $s_p^2 = 0.0909$, [−0.590, 0.111]

End-of-chapter review exercise 9

1 a $\bar{x} = 6.1$, $s_x^2 = 1.15^2 = 1.322$, H_0: $\mu = 5.2$, H_1: $\mu > 5.2$, $t = 2.47$, $t_{0.95,\,9} = 1.83$
Reject H_0: The mean is greater than 5.2.

b H_0: $\mu_P - \mu_Q = 0$, H_1: $\mu_P - \mu_Q < 0$. Assume distributions have equal variances.
$\bar{y} = 7.0$, $s_y^2 = 1.085^2$, $s^2 = 1.118^2$, $t = 1.8$, $t_{18,\,0.95} = 1.73$
Reject H_0: Therefore mean of Q is greater.

2 H_0: $\mu = 7.5$, H_1: $\mu < 7.5$, $\bar{x} = 7.04$, $s^2 = 0.9707^2$, $t = 1.499$, $t_{0.9,\,9} = 1.383$
Reject H_0: The mean is less than 7.5.

3 $s^2 = 0.9273$; $z = 1.869$; $\alpha \leq 6.2$

10 Chi-squared tests

Prerequisite knowledge

1 0.879

2 0.181

3 0.7599

4 0.618

5 0.45

Exercise 10A

1 a 13.36 b 19.68 c 13.28 d 41.40

2 a

x_i	1	2	3	4
E_i	5	20	45	80

b

	a	b	c	d
E_i	80	80	40	40

c

x_i	2	3	4	5	6	7	8
E_i	40	40	40	40	40	40	40

3 a $\chi^2 = 8.472$
b $\chi^2 = 1.837$
c $\chi^2 = 8.494$

4 a

n	1	2	3	4
Expected frequency	32	24	16	8

b H_0: the model is a good fit
H_1: the model is not a good fit

c 4.3229

d $\nu = 4 - 1 = 3$

e $\chi_3^2(0.95) = 7.815$

f Since 4.3229 < 7.815, there is insufficient evidence to reject H_0: Therefore the model is a good fit.

5

n	O	A	B	AB
Expected frequency	100	60	40	20

H_0: The blood groups are in the proportion 5:3:2:1
H_1: The blood groups are not in the proportion 5:3:2:1

$\chi^2 = 10.5817$, $\nu = 4 - 1 = 3$, $\chi_3^2(0.95) = 7.815$

Since 10.5817 > 7.815, there is sufficient evidence to reject H_0: Therefore the blood groups in the neighbouring country are not in the proportion 5:3:2:1.

6 H_0: A uniform distribution is a good fit
H_1: A uniform distribution is not a good fit

$\chi^2 = 12.5$, $\nu = 10 - 1 = 9$, $\chi_9^2(0.95) = 16.92$

Do not reject H_0: A uniform distribution is a good fit.

Exercise 10B

1 a 25.931

b 14.817

(Or, if s is found first, $s = 14.818$ and r will then be 25.930.)

2 a 23.137

b 16.215

3 a Proof

b $r = 16.036$, $s = 11.204$

c It is necessary that each $E_i \geqslant 5$. Combining the columns in this way guarantees that.

4 $\chi^2 = 5.167$; degrees of freedom = 5. The last two columns need to be combined.

5 H_0: Binomial is a good fit
H_1: Binomial is not a good fit

$\chi^2 = 2.944$, $\chi_3^2(0.95) = 7.815$

Do not reject H_0: Binomial is a good fit.

6 H_0: Poisson $\lambda = 2.5$ is a good fit
H_1: Poisson $\lambda = 2.5$ is not a good fit

$\chi^2 = 2.944$, $\chi_5^2(0.95) = 11.070$

Reject H_0: Poisson with $\lambda = 2.5$ is not a good fit.

7 a Proof

b $p = 30.80$, $q = 15.19$

c H_0: Poisson is a good fit
H_1: Poisson is not a good fit

$\chi^2 = 11.442$, $\chi_3^2(0.99) = 11.34$

Reject H_0: A Poisson distribution is not a good model.

Exercise 10C

1 a

E_i	16	16	8	8	32

b

E_i	18	9	9	9	18	18

c

E_i
131.58
90.643
121.35
73.556
82.871

The last group has been adjusted to ensure that $\Sigma E_i = 500$.

2 a 4.156

b 2.778

c 1.299

3 a i $\nu = 9 - 1 - 1 = 7$

ii $\chi_7^2(0.95) = 14.07$

b i $\nu = 7 - 1 - 2 = 4$

ii $\chi_4^2(0.9) = 7.779$

c i $\nu = 11 - 1 = 10$

ii $\chi_{10}^2(0.975) = 20.48$

d i $\nu = 15 - 1 - 1 = 13$

ii $\chi_{13}^2(0.95) = 22.36$

4 a 0.1303

b 0.7851

c 0.0825

d 0.00202

5 H_0: Machine is equally likely to cut between 24.5 and 25.5 m

H_1: Machine is not equally likely to cut between 24.5 and 25.5 m

This could also be: H_0: L can be modelled as continuous uniform on [24.5, 25.5]

H_1: L cannot be modelled as continuous uniform on [24.5, 25.5]

$\chi^2 = 1.6$, $\nu = 4 - 1 = 3$, $\chi_3^2(0.95) = 7.815$

Do not reject H_0: Machine is equally likely to cut between 24.5 and 25.5 m.

6 H_0: $L \sim N(50, 1.5^2)$ is a good model
H_1: $L \sim N(50, 1.5^2)$ is not a good model

$\chi^2 = 223.861$, $\nu = 6 - 1 = 5$, $\chi_5^2(0.95) = 11.070$

Reject H_0: $L \sim N(50, 1.5^2)$ is not a good model for these data.

7 **a** Proof

b H_0: a normal distribution with $\mu = 47.5$ is a good model

H_1: a normal distribution with $\mu = 47.5$ is not a good model

$\chi^2 = 17.20$, $\nu = 7 - 1 - 1 = 5$, $\chi_5^2(0.995) = 16.75$

Reject H_0: A normal distribution with $\mu = 47.5$ is not a good model.

8 H_0: the model is a good fit
H_1: the model is not a good fit

$\chi^2 = 1.097$, $\nu = 5 - 1 = 4$, $\chi_4^2(0.95) = 9.488$

Do not reject H_0: The model is a good fit.

Exercise 10D

1 **a** $E_{11} = 18$, $E_{31} = 12$, $E_{33} = 8$

b $E_{12} = 18.67$, $E_{24} = 11$, $E_{13} = 24.67$

c

10.41	11.19	5.4
11.96	12.84	6.2
18.51	19.89	9.6
13.12	14.08	6.8

The shaded cells have been adjusted to ensure that rows and column add correctly.

2 **a**

12	28
18	42

$\chi^2 = 0.794$

b

31.02	34.98
62.98	71.02

$\chi^2 = 2.251$

c

30.66	35.34
25.09	28.91
62.25	71.75

$\chi^2 = 2.366$

d

28.63	7.75	31.61
19.37	5.25	21.39

The first two rows have been combined to ensure $E_{ij} \geqslant 5$.

$\chi^2 = 0.386$

3 **a** 4 **b** 6

c 6. Either the first two rows or the last two columns must be combined

4 **a**

16.18	42.82
48.82	129.18

b $\chi^2 = 5.271$

c H_0: there is no association between X and Y
H_1: there is an association between X and Y

$\nu = 1$; $\chi_1^2(0.95) = 3.481$

Reject H_0: There is an association between X and Y.

5 H_0: Age group and loan type are independent

H_1: Age group and loan type are not independent

Expected values:

Loan type	Age group			Totals
	18–25	25–35	Over 35	
Good	42.67	32.67	24.67	100
Toxic	21.3	16.3	12.3	50
Totals	64	49	37	150

$\chi^2 = 0.898$, $\nu = (2 - 1)(3 - 1) = 2$, $\chi_2^2(0.9) = 4.605$

Do not reject H_0: Age group and loan type are independent.

6 a

	N	S	E	W	Total
Selected	21	12	18	29	80
Rejected	119	108	72	121	420
Total	140	120	90	150	500

b H_0: There is no association between region and being accepted

H_1: There is an association between region and being accepted

Expected table:

22.4	19.2	14.4	24	80
117.6	100.8	75.6	126	420
140	120	90	150	500

$\chi^2 = 5.630$, $\nu = (4-1)(2-1) = 3$, $\chi_3^2(0.95) = 7.815$

Do not reject H_0: There is no association between region and being accepted.

7 H_0: There is no association between town and quality of mobile phone reception

H_1: There is an association between town and quality of mobile phone reception

$\chi^2 = 8.210$, $\nu = (3-1)(3-1) = 4$, $\chi_4^2(0.95) = 9.488$

Do not reject H_0: There is no association between town and quality of mobile phone reception.

End-of-chapter review exercise 10

1 a Mean = 1.31, variance = 1.21

Since these are roughly the same, a Poisson distribution seems appropriate.

b i $q = 20.219$

ii H_0: Poisson is a good fit, H_1: Possion is not a good fit

Need to combine last three categories.

$\chi^2 = 5.542$, $\nu = 5 - 1 - 1$, $\chi_3^2(0.9) = 6.251$

Do not reject H_0: The Poisson is a good model.

2 H_0: Car type is independent of age group
H_1: Car type is not independent of age group

Or H_0: There is no association between car type and age group

H_1: There is an association between car type and age group

χ^2 test statistic = 12.6 (1 decimal place), $\nu = 4$, $\chi_4^2(0.95) = 9.488$

Since $12.6 > 9.488$ we reject H_0: There is sufficient evidence to suggest that car type and age group are not independent (there is an association).

3 a

$2 \leqslant x < 3$	40
$3 \leqslant x < 4$	20
$4 \leqslant x < 5$	12
$5 \leqslant x < 6$	8

b H_0: f(x) is a good fit, H_1: f(x) is not a good fit

$\chi^2 = 5.7$, $\nu = 4 - 1$, $\chi_3^2(0.9) = 6.251$

Since $5.7 < 6.251$, do not reject H_0: f(x) is a good fit

11 Non-parametric tests

Prerequisite knowledge

1 0.0654 (3 sf)

Exercise 11A

1 a 11 b 14 c 9 d 6

2 a 0.0730 b 0.0898
c 0.0592 d 0.0207

3 a 0.0287 b 0.0193
c 0.0037 d 0.0539

4 a Do not reject H_0. b Reject H_0.
c Reject H_0.

5 a $E(S) = 7.5$, $Var(S) = 3.75$, $z = -1.549$
b $E(S) = 10$, $Var(S) = 5$, $z = -2.012$
c $E(S) = 7.5$, $Var(S) = 3.75$, $z = 2.066$

6 H_0: The population median is 5.2
H_1: the population median is below 5.2

Test statistic = 3, $P(X \leqslant 3) = 0.0730$

Since $0.0730 > 0.05$, do not reject H_0: There is insufficient evidence to suggest that the pH is below 5.2.

7 H_0: Population median is 11, H_1: Population median is greater than 11.

Test stat = 6, $P(X \geqslant 6 | X \sim \text{Bin}(10, 0.5)) = 0.377$

Do not reject H_0: Population median weekly pocket money has not increased from 2016 to 2017.

8 **a** H_0: The population median is 7675, H_1: The population median is not 7675.

Test statistic = 4,
$P(X \leqslant 4 | X \sim \text{Bin}(12, 0.5)) = 0.194$

Do not reject H_0: The population median is 7675.

b Median would need to be greater than 8150 (so only 2 values created a positive)

9 H_0: the population median is 60, H_1: the population median is greater than 60.

$$S^+ = 16,\ z = \frac{16.5 - \left(\frac{20}{2}\right)}{\sqrt{\frac{20}{4}}} = 2.907,\ z_{0.95} = 1.6449$$

Reject H_0: The population median time is greater than 60 minutes.

Exercise 11B

1 **a** $P = 70,\ N = 50,\ T = 50$

b $P = 8,\ N = 112,\ T = 8$

c $P = 117,\ N = 3,\ T = 3$

2 **a** 5 **b** 19

c 32 **d** 8

3 The underlying data are symmetric; the underlying data are continuous; the data are independent.

4 **a** $E(T) = 232.5$, $\text{Var}(T) = 2363.75$
$z = -1.172$

Do not reject H_0.

b $E(T) = 105$, $\text{Var}(T) = 717.5$
$z = -1.699$

Reject H_0.

c $E(T) = 410$, $\text{Var}(T) = 5535$
$z = -2.009$

Reject H_0.

5 H_0: The population median is 4, H_1: The population median is greater than 4.

$T = 4$, Critical value = 10

Reject H_0: The population median is greater than 4.

6 **a** H_0: The population median is 43, H_1: The population median is below 43.

$T = \min(1, 35) = 1$, Critical value = 8

Reject H_0: The population median is below 43.

b Wilcoxon signed-rank is preferred because the magnitudes of the differences are taken into account.

7 H_0: The population median is 11.2, H_1: The population median is greater than 11.2.
$T = \min(7, 48) = 7$, Critical value = 10

Reject H_0: The population median is 11.2.

8 H_0: The population median is 50, H_1: The population median is less than 50.

$T = 55$, $E(T) = 517.5$, $\text{Var}(T) = 7848.75$

$$z = \frac{55.5 - 517.5}{\sqrt{7848.75}}$$

$z = -5.215$

$z_{0.99} = -2.326$

Reject H_0: The population median is less than 50.

Exercise 11C

1 **a** 4 **b** 2 **c** 2

2 **a** $n = 11$

Since data points B, I, K, have a zero difference they must be ignored.

b 6

3 **a** $P(X \leqslant 3 | X \sim \text{Bin}(9, 0.5)) = 0.254$
Do not reject H_0.

b $P(X \leqslant 1 | X \sim \text{Bin}(6, 0.5)) = 0.109$
Do not reject H_0.

c $P(X \leqslant 1 | X \sim \text{Bin}(8, 0.5)) = 0.0352$
Reject H_0.

4 **a** The value of n in this case is 11, which is greater than 10 and so an approximation would be valid.

b $E(S^+) = 5.5$, $\text{Var}(S^+) = 2.75$

c $z = 0.603$

5 H_0: There is no difference in the population medians

H_1: There is a difference in the population medians

Test statistic = 2 or 8 (choose 2 to use)

$P(X \leqslant 2 | X \sim Bin(10, 0.5)) = 0.0547$

Do not reject H_0: There is no difference in the average effectiveness of the aerosols.

6 H_0: The thickness of the cornea is the same in each eye

H_1: The thickness of the cornea is different in each eye

Test statistic = 5, $P(X \geqslant 5 | X \sim Bin(7, 0.5)) = 0.227$

Since $0.227 > 0.05$, do not reject H_0: There is no difference in the thickness of the cornea.

7 H_0: The population median yields are the same

H_1: The population median yield for the new fertiliser is greater

Test statistic = 8, $P(X \geqslant 8 | X \sim Bin(10, 0.5)) = 0.0547$

Do not reject H_0: The population median yields are the same.

Exercise 11D

1 **a** $P = 15, N = 6; T = 6$

b $P = 14, N = 31; T = 14$

c $P = 15, N = 5; T = 5$

2 **a** Critical value = 3; do not reject H_0.

b Critical value = 25; reject H_0.

c Critical value = 3; do not reject H_0.

3 **a** 85.5

b 527.25

c −1.132

d Critical value = −1.96; do not reject H_0.

4 **a** H_0: the scores are the same, H_1: the scores are different.

$T = \min(16, 20) = 16$, Critical value = 5

Do not reject H_0: There is no difference between the scores of the eight students.

b The data are symmetric.

5 H_0: Phones with old and new processors are the same

H_1: Phones with the new processor are better

$T = \min(9, 46) = 9$, Critical value = 10

Reject H_0: The phones with the new processors are rated higher by customers.

6 H_0: Treatments have no difference (in the population median number of spots)

H_1: There is a difference (in the population median number of spots)

$T = \min(36, 0) = 0$, Critical value = 3

Reject H_0: There is a difference (in the population median number of spots).

7 **a** $E(T) = 232.5$ **b** $Var(T) = 2363.75$

c H_0: The pairs of identical twins have the same IQ

H_1: The pairs of identical twins have a difference in their IQ

$T = \min(272, 193) = 193$, $ts = -0.81245$, $z_{0.975} = -1.96$

Do not reject H_0: Identical twins have the same IQ.

Exercise 11E

1 **a** **i** 52 (32)

ii 32 (52)

iii 32

b **i** 75 (51)

ii 51 (75)

iii 51

c **i** $R_m = 24$ (46)

ii 46 (24)

iii 24

d **i** 25 or 30

ii 30 or 25

iii 25

2 **a** 29 **b** 45 **c** 21 **d** 16

3 **a** $E(R_m) = 99$, $Var(R_m) = 198$

b $E(R_m) = 156$, $Var(R_m) = 338$

c $E(R_m) = 72$, $Var(R_m) = 108$

d $E(R_m) = 188.5$, $Var(R_m) = 471.25$

4 **a** $E(R_m) = 186$, $Var(R_m) = 558$, $z = -1.672$

b Critical value $= -1.645$; reject H_0.

5 H_0: The calorie content of the chicken sausage is the same as the vegetarian one

H_1: The calorie content of the chicken sausage is different to the vegetarian one

$R_m = 74$, $m(n + m + 1) - R_m = 38$, $W = 38$, Critical value $= 38$

Reject H_0: The calorie content of the chicken sausage is different to the vegetarian one.

6 H_0: There is no difference in the population median length on each side of the river

H_1: There is a difference in the population median length on each side of the river

$R_m = 48$, $m(n + m + 1) - R_m = 88$, $W = 48$, Critical value $= 51$

Reject H_0: There is a difference in the lengths of the plants on the two sides of the river.

7 H_0: There is no difference in the time taken to become overripe

H_1: Chilled transport takes longer to become overripe

$R_m = 21$, $m(n + m + 1) - R_m = 39$, $W = 21$, Critical value $= 20$

Do not reject H_0: There is no difference in the time taken to become overripe.

8 H_0: There is no difference in the scores between the two sessions

H_1: There is a difference in the scores between the two sessions

$E(R_m) = 270$, $Var(R_m) = 900$, $ts = -2.483$, $P(Z \leqslant -2.483) = 0.0065$

Since we have a two-tailed test, $0.0065 < 0.01$ and so we reject H_0: There is a difference in performance between the morning session and the afternoon session.

End-of-chapter review exercise 11

1 **a** **i** Since we are comparing two sets of data, we must use a two-sample test. Since the data is not matched, we must carry out a Wilcoxon rank-sum test. To do this we must assume that the samples are independent. (The data are already continuous.)

ii H_0: there is no difference in the population medians of the two samples

H_1: The population median for returning from the dining hall is greater than the population median going to the dining hall

One-tail 5% Wilcoxon rank-sum test: Test statistic $= 94$, Critical value $= 82$

Since $94 > 82$, do not reject H_0: There is no difference in the population medians of the two samples.

b **i** The data is now matched pairs and so Wilcoxon matched-pairs signed-rank test would be appropriate.

ii H_0: The median difference of the paired values is 0

H_1: The median difference of the paired values is greater than 0

$T = 3$, Critical value for $n = 10$ is 10

Since $3 < 10$ we reject H_0: The median difference is greater than 0 and so the time taken to walk back is greater than the time to walk to the dining room.

2 H_0: There is no difference in the population medians of men's and women's cholesterol levels

H_1: There is a difference in the population medians of men's and women's cholesterol levels

$R_m = 633$, $m(n + m + 1) - R_m = 387$, $W = 387$, $E(W) = 510$, $Var(W) = 2550$

Test statistic $= -2.246$, Critical value $= -1.96$ (two-tailed 5%)

Since $-1.96 > -2.246$ reject H_0: There is a difference in the population medians of men's and women's cholesterol levels.

When drawing a stem and leaf diagram, we can see that the data are symmetric and so the assumption is justified.

3 **a** **i** The data cannot be assumed to be normal.

ii The data cannot be assumed to be from a symmetric distribution.

b H_0: The population median is 50, H_1: The population median is greater than 50

Test statistic: 11(+) or 3(−), $P(X \geqslant 11) = 0.0287$

Since $0.0287 < 0.05$, do not reject H_0: The population median is 50

12 Probability generating functions

Prerequisite knowledge

1 $\mathrm{E}(X) = 3.2$, $\mathrm{Var}(X) = 1.92$

2 $\mathrm{E}(X) = 2$, $\mathrm{Var}(X) = 2$

3 $\mathrm{E}(X) = \frac{10}{3}$, $\mathrm{Var}(X) = 7.778$

4 $\dfrac{1-\left(\frac{1}{3}\right)^n}{2}$

5 $\frac{5}{9} + \frac{20t}{27} + \frac{20t^2}{27} + \frac{160t^3}{243}$

Exercise 12A

1 a $(0.7 + 0.3t)^{20}$
b $(0.75 + 0.25t)^{10}$
c $(0.96 + 0.04t)^{50}$

2 a $\mathrm{e}^{4(t-1)}$ b $\mathrm{e}^{2.3(t-1)}$ c $\mathrm{e}^{12(t-1)}$

3 a $\frac{t}{10-9t}$ b $\frac{7t}{10-3t}$ c $\frac{2t}{5-3t}$

4 $\mathrm{G}_X(t) = \frac{t}{16}(4 + 2t + 4t^2 + t^3 + t^4 + 2t^5 + 2t^6)$

5 $\mathrm{G}_X(t) = \frac{1}{16}(t^2 + 4t^4 + 6t^6 + 4t^8 + t^{10})$

$\mathrm{G}_X(t) = \frac{t^2}{16}(1 + t^2)^4$

6

x	3	7	11
$\mathrm{P}(X = x)$	$\frac{1}{3}$	$\frac{1}{6}$	$\frac{1}{3}$

7 $X \sim \mathrm{Bin}(7, 0.2)$

8 a $\mathrm{P}(X = 0) = \frac{1}{3}$, $\mathrm{P}(X = 1) = \frac{1}{3}$, $\mathrm{P}(X = 2) = \frac{1}{6}$,
$\mathrm{P}(X = 3) = \frac{1}{12}$

b $\mathrm{P}(X = k) = \frac{1}{3 \times 2^{k-1}}$

9 $\mathrm{P}(X = x) = q^{x-1}p$, Proof

10 $k = 9$

Exercise 12B

1 a 3.9 b 15.2 c 3.9 d 3.89

2 a 3 b 7 c 3 d 1

3 $\mathrm{E}(X) = 5.3$, $\mathrm{Var}(X) = 2.21$

4 $\mathrm{E}(X) = \frac{4}{3}$, $\mathrm{Var}(X) = \frac{20}{9}$

5 a $\mathrm{G}_X(t) = \frac{t}{2-t}$
b $\mathrm{E}(X) = 2$, $\mathrm{Var}(X) = 2$

6 $\mathrm{E}(X) = \frac{q}{p}$, $\mathrm{Var}(X) = \frac{q}{p^2}$

7 $\mathrm{E}(X) = \frac{8}{3}$, $\mathrm{Var}(X) = \frac{26}{3}$

8 a $\mathrm{G}_X(t) = \frac{1}{8}(2t^2 + 3t^a + 3t^b)$
$\mathrm{G}'_X(t) = \frac{1}{8}(4t + 3at^{a-1} + 3bt^{b-1})$
$\mathrm{G}''_X(t) = \frac{1}{8}(4 + 3a(a-1)t^{a-2} + 3b(b-1)t^{b-2})$
b $a = 3, b = 7$

Exercise 12C

1 a $\frac{t}{5}(2 + 3t)$
b $\frac{1}{4}(1 + t + t^3 + t^5)$
c $\frac{t}{20}(2 + 3t)(1 + t + t^3 + t^5)$

2 a $\frac{1}{10t^2}(1 + 2t + 4t^2 + 2t^3 + t^4)$
b $\frac{t^2(1-t^5)}{5(1-t)}$
c $\frac{(1-t^5)}{50(1-t)}(1 + 2t + 4t^2 + 2t^3 + t^4)$

3 a $\mathrm{G}_X(t) = \frac{t}{10}(2 + 5t^2 + 3t^4)$
b $\mathrm{G}_Y(t) = \frac{1}{10}(3 + 4t^2 + 3t^4)$
c $\mathrm{G}_{X+Y}(t) = \frac{t}{100}(2 + 5t^2 + 3t^4)(3 + 4t^2 + 3t^4)$
d

$x + y$	1	3	5	7	9
P	0.06	0.23	0.35	0.27	0.09

4 a $\mathrm{G}_{X+Y} = \frac{6t^2}{(5-2t)(5-3t)}$

b $\frac{2}{2t-5} - \frac{3}{3t-5}$

c

k	$P(X+Y=k)$
2	$\frac{6}{25}$
3	$\frac{6}{25}$
4	$\frac{114}{625}$

5 **a** $G_{X+Y}(t) = e^{2(t-1)}(0.8 + 0.2t)^3$

b $E(X) = 2.6$

c $G''_X(t) = \frac{2e^{2t}}{125e^2}(t+4)(2t^2 + 22t + 59)$

d $Var(X+Y) = 2.48$

6 **a** Proof **b** Proof

7 **a** $\frac{3t^5}{5-2t^5}$

b $\frac{3t^8}{5-2t}$

8 **a** $\frac{e^{4(t-1)}}{t}$

b $t^3e^{4(t^{-2}-1)}$

9 **a** $G_Y(t) = \frac{3t^4}{10-7t^3}$

b Proof

c

y	$P(Y=k)$
1	0.3
4	0.21
7	0.147

Exercise 12D

1 **a** $\frac{t^4}{25}(4+t)^2$

b

y	4	5	6
$P(Y=y)$	$\frac{16}{25}$	$\frac{8}{25}$	$\frac{1}{25}$

2 **a** $\frac{1}{4}\left(\frac{1}{t} + 2 + t\right)$

b $\frac{1}{64}\left(\frac{1}{t} + 2 + t\right)^3$

c $\frac{15}{64}$

3 **a** 2

b $e^{\frac{(t-1)(5t-3)}{t}}$

4 **a** $\frac{t}{3}(1 + t + t^2)$

b $\frac{t^4}{4}(2 + t + t^2)$

c $\frac{t^5}{12}(t^4 + 2t^2 + t + 2 + t^{-1} + 2t^{-3} + t^{-4} + 2t^{-6})$

5 **a** $G_A(t) = t(0.7 + 0.3t^2)^3(0.3 + 0.7t)^4$

b $G_B(t) = \frac{3(0.7 + 0.3t)^7}{10t^3 - 7}$

c $G_C(t) = \frac{3(0.7 + 0.3t^3)^3(0.3 + 0.7t^2)^4}{10 - 7t}$

6 **a** $G_Y(t) = \frac{243t^5}{(10-7t)^5}$ **b** 0.05797

7 **a** $G_Y(t) = \frac{t^4}{10\,000}(2 + 3t + 5t^2)^4$

b $E(Y) = \frac{46}{5}$

c $Var(Y) = 2.44$

8 **a** $G_Y(t) = \frac{3t^6}{(10-9t^3)(5-4t^2)(10-7t)}$

b $\frac{21}{5000}$

End-of-chapter review exercise 12

1 $G_X(t) = \frac{5t}{36-31t}$, $E(X) = 7.2$, $Var(X) = 44.64$

2 **a** $k = 1$, $G_X(t) = \frac{et}{e-t}$

b $E(X) = \frac{e^2}{(e-t)^2}$

c $Var(X) = \frac{e^2(t^2 - 2t - 2e - 2et)}{(e-t)^4}$

3 Proof

4 Proof

Cross-topic review exercise 2

1 $s^2 = 3.00865$

$z = 1.384$

$\alpha \leqslant 8.32\%$

2 H_0: $\mu = 65$, H_1: $\mu \neq 65$

Test statistic $= -0.314$

Critical value $= t_{0.95, 7} = -1.895$

There is insufficient evidence to suggest that the sprinklers are not activated at 65°C.

3 **a** Proof

b 0.614

4 **i** [520.0, 529.2] or $524.6 \pm 4.6[1]$

ii H_0: $\mu_b - \mu_a = 0$, H_1: $\mu_b - \mu_a \neq 0$

$s^2 = 12.711$

Test statistic $= 1.52$

Critical value $= 1.64$

There is insufficient evidence to suggest a difference between the two means.

5 **a** $P(X = x) = p(1 - p)^{x-1}$

b i $G_Y(t) = p^n t^n (1 - qt)^{-n}$

ii $E(Y) = \frac{n}{p}$, $Var(Y) = \frac{nq}{p^2}$

6 H_0: No association between test results and school

H_1: An association between test results and school

Test statistic $= 3.68$

Critical value $= \chi_2^2(0.95) = 5.99$

Do not reject H_0: This is no association between test results and school.

7 H_0: There is no difference between the population medians

H_1: There is a difference between the population medians

$R_m = 48$ or 88

$W = 48$

Critical value $= 49$

Reject H_0: There is a difference in the population medians, therefore there is a difference in the average height of trees on the two sides of the river.

8 **a** Proof

b Proof

c 1.74

9 H_0: The population median is 147.50

H_1: The population median is greater than 147.50

$P = 49$, $N = 6$

$T = \min(49, 6) = 6$

Critical value $= 10$

Reject H_0: There is sufficient evidence to suggest the median is greater than 147.50.

10 **i** $100 \times {}^4C_2 \times 0.4^2 \times 0.6^2 = 34.56$

ii H_0: A binomial B(4, 0.6) is a good model.

H_1: A binomial B(4, 0.6) is not a good model.

$\chi^2 = 9.22$

$\chi_3^2(0.95) = 7.815$

Reject H_0: Probability of faulty chips is not 0.6.

11 H_0: Population median time taken = 140

H_1: Population median time taken > 140

Test statistic: $S^+ = 8\,(S^- = 2)$

$P(S^+ \geqslant 8) = 0.054688$

Do not reject H_0: the time taken to fill in the forms is 140 minutes.

13 Projectiles

Prerequisite knowledge

1 magnitude of deceleration $= 0.36\,\text{m s}^{-2}$

2 $t = 5.74\,\text{s}$ and $v = 37.4\,\text{m s}^{-1}$

Exercise 13A

1 **a** $45.62\,\text{m s}^{-1}$

b 88.68 m

c 27.17° or 62.83°

2 $42.75\,\text{m s}^{-1}$

3 $14.59\,\text{ms}^{-1} < u < 16.31\,\text{ms}^{-1}$

4 36.9°

5 $10\sqrt{2} < u < 20$

6 $7.75\,\text{m s}^{-1}$

7 **a** $\sqrt{60}\,\text{m s}^{-1}$ **b** 2.75 m

8 $6\sqrt{15}\,\text{m}$

9 2.62 s

10 **a** 2.32 s **b** $25\,\text{m s}^{-1}$

Exercise 13B

1 7.52 m

2 20 m

3 10.0 m

4 $39.9\,\text{m}\,\text{s}^{-1}$

5 30.9° below the horizontal

6 **a** 0.77 s **b** $18.1\,\text{m}\,\text{s}^{-1}$

7 27.5 m

8 Proof

9 45°, 71.6°

10 Proof

End-of-chapter review exercise 13

1 **i** Proof **ii** 38.4 m, 17.8 m

iii

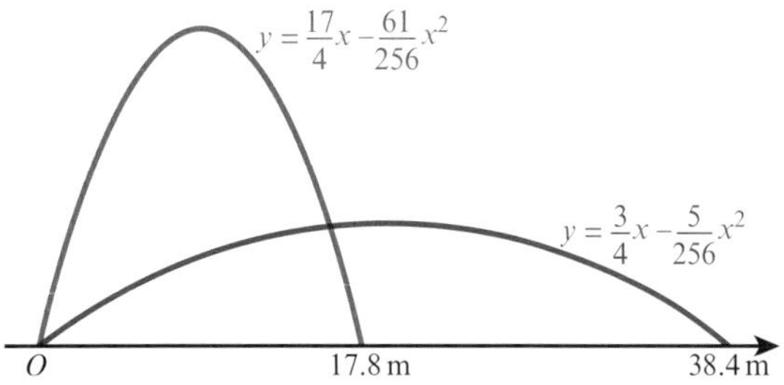

2 **i** $y = x - \frac{1}{10}x^2$

ii $x = 4.23$

iii $\theta = 8.8°$

3 **i** $k = \frac{1}{2}$, 2, Proof **ii** $t = 0.894\,\text{s}$

iii $16.3\,\text{m}\,\text{s}^{-1}$, 15.9 above the horizontal

14 Equilibrium of a rigid body

Prerequisite knowledge

1 Parallel component is $mg\sin\theta$, perpendicular is $mg\cos\theta$.

2 30°

Exercise 14A

1 1.05 kg

2 0.333 kg

3 $\frac{10}{3}$

4 **a** 6.3 N m anticlockwise

b 22.1 N m anticlockwise

c 36 N m anticlockwise

5 **a** 46.5 N m clockwise

b 12.8 N m anticlockwise

c 2.89 N m anticlockwise

6 **a** 0.119 m **b** 3.8 kg

7 $m = \frac{6}{19}M - \frac{78}{19}$

8 **a** $x = 9.78\,\text{N}$ **b** $x = 40.2\,\text{N}$

c $x = 3.20\,\text{m}$

Exercise 14B

1 $\frac{179}{58}a$ from AB, $\frac{127}{58}a$ from AC

2 5.71 from AB, 2.64 from AC

3 $1.28r$

4 $G\left(\frac{197}{81}a, \frac{127}{81}a\right)$

5 $\bar{x} = 3.04r$, $\bar{y} = 1.91r$

6 $\bar{x} = \frac{2}{2+\pi}$, $\bar{y} = 1$

7 $\bar{x} = 2.73a$, $\bar{y} = 1.82a$

8 Proof

Exercise 14C

1 $2.34r$

2 $\frac{5}{6}r$

3 $\frac{3}{4}r$

4 $\bar{x} = \frac{11}{8}a$

5 $\bar{x} = \frac{99}{28}r$

6 $k = \frac{100}{3}$

7 $\bar{x} = 6.49r$

8 $\frac{100a - 9ka}{40 + 6k}$

Exercise 14D

1 68.2°

2 29.7°

3 $\mu \geqslant \frac{1}{2\sqrt{3}}$

4 32°

5 55.8°

6 a

7 $0.474mg$, at an angle of 82.7° clockwise from the wall.

8 Topples first

9 a $\frac{11\sqrt{3}}{8}mg$ b $\frac{1}{2}r$

End-of-chapter review exercise 14

1 i 562.5 N ii 52.1° with vertical

2 i 2.12 N ii $\mu = 0.313$

3 i 0.143 m
ii a $P = 2.5$ b 0.787
iii $P = 26.0$, Proof

15 Circular motion

Prerequisite knowledge

1 Magnitude is 4.91 N, direction is 13.4° clockwise from the negative x-axis.

2 $0.832\,\mathrm{m\,s^{-2}}$

3 $21.0\,\mathrm{m\,s^{-1}}$

Exercise 15A

1 a $\frac{2}{3}\,\mathrm{rad\,s^{-1}}$ b 2 m c $4\,\mathrm{m\,s^{-1}}$

2 $\frac{10}{3}$ N

3 $3.23\,\mathrm{rad\,s^{-1}}$

4 $\omega = \sqrt{6}\,\mathrm{rad\,s^{-1}}$, 2.57 s

5 $\mu \geqslant \frac{1}{2}$

6 $20\,\mathrm{m\,s^{-1}}$

7 $2\sqrt{10}\,\mathrm{m\,s^{-1}}$

8 $m = \frac{T\tau^2}{4a\pi^2}$

9 $v = \sqrt{\frac{8ga}{3}}$

10 $\frac{3\sqrt{35}}{5} \leqslant v \leqslant \frac{\sqrt{435}}{5}$

Exercise 15B

1 $2.17\,\mathrm{m\,s^{-1}}$

2 $2.95\,\mathrm{rad\,s^{-1}}$

3 $1.96\,\mathrm{rad\,s^{-1}}$

4 $27.65\,\mathrm{m\,s^{-1}}$

5 $T_{AP} = 37.2\,\mathrm{N}$, $T_{BP} = 4.44\,\mathrm{N}$

6 $\sqrt{\frac{3ga}{2}}$

7 a $\omega = 2.99\,\mathrm{rad\,s^{-1}}$
b 28.5 per minute

8 $\mu = 0.305$

9 a $4\sqrt{2}$ N b $6.51\,\mathrm{m\,s^{-1}}$

Exercise 15C

1 48.2°

2 136.2°

3 44.0°

4 $T_{min} = 4mg$, $T_{max} = 16mg$

5 $u \leqslant \sqrt{2ga}$

6 $\frac{392}{125}$ m

7 33.6°

8 a $\sqrt{15ga}$ b $v = \sqrt{3ga}$ c $R = \frac{1}{2}mg$

9 a $v = \sqrt{\sqrt{2}ga}$ b $R_{max} = 3mg$

10 a $\sqrt{7ga}$ b $18mg$

End-of-chapter review exercise 15

1 i Proof ii $v = 5.66\,\text{m s}^{-1}$

2 i $\omega = 8.19\,\text{rad s}^{-1}$, KE $= 0.402\,\text{J}$

ii $T = 6.71\,\text{N}$, $\omega = 10.6\,\text{rad s}^{-1}$

3 i $\sqrt{\frac{1}{2}ga}$ ii $\sqrt{\frac{3}{2}ga}$

16 Hooke's law

Prerequisite knowledge

1 21.6 m

2 $12.2\,\text{m s}^{-1}$

Exercise 16A

1 a 0.45 m b 75 N c 1 N

2 0.125 m or 12.5 cm

3 $15mg$ N

4 $5mg$ N

5 1.93 m

6 $\lambda = 76.9\,\text{N}$

7 a Proof b $7\sqrt{3}g$ N

8 $\mu = \frac{3}{4}$, $x = 1.2\,\text{m}$

9 1.22 m and 1.08 m

10 a $\frac{2ka}{3}$ b $k = \frac{3}{2}$

Exercise 16B

1 a 4.17 J b 2 m c 250 N

2 Proof

3 $\lambda = 62.5\,\text{N}$, EPE $= 16\,\text{J}$

4 $\lambda = 6g$, $\frac{9}{10}g$ J

5 134.6 J

6 a Proof b $k = 2$

7 a 1.4 m b 24.5 J

8 a $\frac{175}{16}a$ b $\frac{813}{32}mga$ J

Exercise 16C

1 24.6 J

2 $1.15\,\text{m s}^{-1}$

3 a 1.07 m b 2.07 m

4 $8.32\,\text{m s}^{-1}$

5 a $15.3\,\text{m s}^{-2}$ b 38.5 J c 3.90 m

6 $4.68\,\text{m s}^{-1}$

7 a 1.13 m b $4.19\,\text{m s}^{-1}$

8 EPE $= \frac{5}{4}mga$ J, $\frac{9}{8}mga$ J

9 $\sqrt{2g}\,\text{m s}^{-1}$

End-of-chapter review exercise 16

1 i Proof ii $2.75\,\text{m s}^{-1}$

2 i $T = 6.25\,\text{N}$, Proof ii $4.90\,\text{m s}^{-1}$

3 i $\lambda = 10\,\text{N}$ ii $1.12\,\text{m s}^{-1}$

17 Linear motion under a variable force

Prerequisite knowledge

1 a $12t^3$

b $-\frac{1}{4}\cos 4t + c$

c $e^t \cos t - e^t \sin t$

2 a $v = \sqrt{\frac{2}{3}t^3 + 2c}$ b $v = e^{2e^{-x}+c}$

Exercise 17A

1 a $v = 72\,\text{ms}^{-1}$, $a = 66\,\text{ms}^{-2}$

b $v = -3\,\text{m s}^{-1}$, $a = 4\,\text{m s}^{-2}$

c $v = 7.25\,\text{m s}^{-1}$, $a = 1.6875\,\text{m s}^{-2}$

2 $8.89\,\text{m s}^{-1}$

3 $\frac{4}{9}$

4 $x = 3 - \frac{1}{t}$, cannot exceed 3 m

5 $7.8\,\text{m s}^{-1}$

6 $v = 3 - \frac{1}{3}t^3$, $x = 3t - \frac{1}{12}t^4$

7 $t = 2$

8 No, takes 136.8 m to stop.

9 9.65 m

10 Proof, $v_{max} = \frac{g}{k}$

11 **a** $\sqrt{6}$ s, or 2.45 s **b** 19.59 m

12 **a** Proof **b** 25 m s^{-1} **c** 115 m

Exercise 17B

1 **a** $v = \sqrt{\frac{2}{3}x^3 + 6x + k}$

b $v = \sqrt{e^{2x} - x^2 + k}$

c $v = \sqrt{6x + \frac{2}{x} + k}$

2 $6\sqrt{2}$ m s^{-1}

3 $v = \sqrt{3x^2 + 25}$ m s^{-1}

4 0.0671 m s^{-1}

5 $v = \sqrt{3e^{-2x} + 22}$, $\sqrt{22}$ m s^{-1}

6 4.19 m s^{-1}

7 $v^2 = 6x + 2x^2 + 4$

8 $a = \frac{40}{9\pi}$

9 **a** $v = \sqrt{32\sin\frac{x}{4} + 49}$ **b** $\sqrt{17}$ m s^{-1}

10 $v = \sqrt{\frac{3}{2}x^2 + \frac{1}{x} + \frac{27}{2}}$

End-of-chapter review exercise 17

1 **i** $x = 2.5$ m, $v = 6.12$ m s^{-1} **ii** $a = -15$ m s^{-2}

2 **i** Proof **ii** Proof **iii** 49.7 m

3 **i** $0.25v\frac{dv}{dx} = -(5 - x)$ **ii** $x = 5(1 - e^{-2t})$

18 Momentum

Prerequisite knowledge

1 $v_x = 6\sqrt{3}$ m s^{-1} and $v_y = 6$ m s^{-1}

2 105 J

Exercise 18A

1 $v_p = \frac{2}{3}u$, $v_q = \frac{8}{3}u$

2 $v = \frac{3}{5}u$

3 $\frac{51}{16}$ J

4 $e < \frac{4}{5}$

5 $e = \frac{1}{4}$, KE lost $\frac{225}{16}$ J

6 $e = \frac{1}{3}$

7 **a** Proof **b** $e = \frac{1}{2}$, $v_p = 0$

Exercise 18B

1 $0.901u$

2 $\frac{135}{32}mu^2$ J

3 $\frac{2}{11}u$

4 4.1°

5 **a** Proof **b** $\frac{63}{200}mu^2$ J

6 $v_A = 3.6$ m s^{-1}, $v_B = 0.4$ m s^{-1}, $v_C = -1.6$ m s^{-1}, No more collisions

7 Final velocity is eu

8 $\frac{3}{5}r$

9 $\frac{828}{625}mu^2$ J

10 $\frac{9}{100}mu^2$ J

End-of-chapter review exercise 18

1 $e = \frac{4 + \alpha}{3\alpha}$, Proof

2 $v_A = \frac{1}{2}u$, $v_B = \frac{3}{2}u$, $\frac{2}{5}a$

3 Proof

Cross-topic review exercise 3

1 $e = \frac{2}{3}, \frac{5}{3}m\sqrt{2gh}$

2 a 0.25 m b 1 m c Proof

3 a $\frac{20a}{24 + 3\pi}$ from AB, $\left(\frac{4 + \pi}{8 + \pi}\right)a$ from BC

b 24.6°

4 a Proof b Proof c $\frac{g}{k}$

5 a $\frac{17}{12}a$ b $2.06\sqrt{ga}$

6 a 55.2 m b 0.536 s

c 32.5° above the horizontal

7 a $v_P = \frac{u}{5}(2 - 3e), v_Q = \frac{2u}{5}(1 + e)$

b $e < \frac{2}{3}$ c $\frac{3mu^2}{5}(1 - e^2)$

19 Hyperbolic functions

Prerequisite knowledge

1 Proof

2 $x = \ln 3$

Exercise 19A

1 $\ln\left(\frac{3}{5}\right)$

2 $\ln\left(\frac{4}{3}\right), \ln\left(\frac{5}{3}\right)$

3 $\log\left(\frac{1}{33}(8 + \sqrt{97})\right)$

4 $\ln\left(\frac{2}{5}\right)$

5 $-\ln 2$ or $\ln\left(\frac{1}{2}\right)$

6

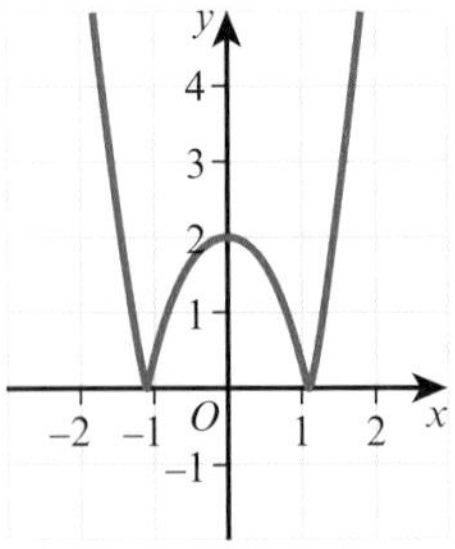

7

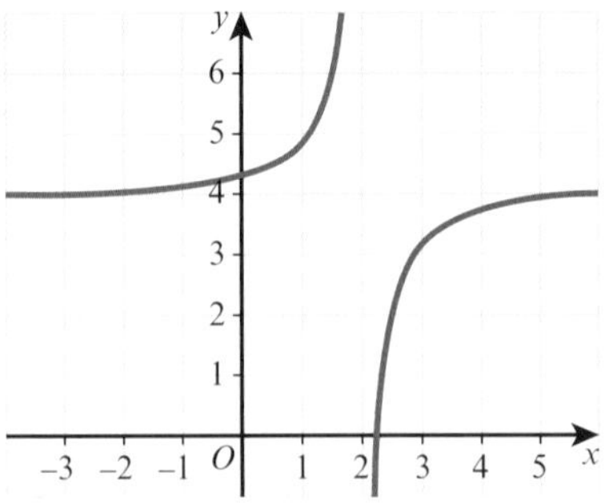

8

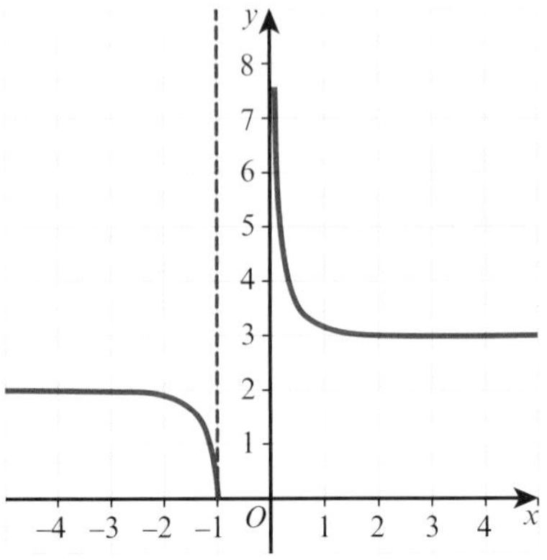

9 $\ln 3, -\ln 5$

10 $\ln\frac{1}{2}, \ln\frac{4}{3}$

11 $\ln\left(\frac{3 - \sqrt{5}}{2}\right), \ln\left(\frac{3 + \sqrt{5}}{2}\right)$

Exercise 19B

1 Proof

2 Proof

3 Proof

4 a Proof b Proof c Proof

5 Proof

Exercise 19C

1 a $\ln(3 + \sqrt{10})$ b $\frac{1}{2}\ln(5)$ c $\ln(2)$

2 a $\ln(\sqrt{10} - 3), \ln\left(\frac{\sqrt{10} - 1}{3}\right)$

b 0

c $\ln\left(\frac{1 + \sqrt{5}}{2}\right)$

3 Proof

4 Proof

5 Proof

5 Proof

6 **a** Proof **b** $\ln(\sqrt{2}+1), \ln(\sqrt{2}-1)$

End-of-chapter review exercise 19

1 $x = \ln(2+\sqrt{3}), x = \ln(2-\sqrt{3})$

2 **a** Proof **b** Proof

3 **a** Differentiate and set to 0 to give $\cosh x(4\sinh x + 1) = 0$. This only has one solution when $\sinh x = -\frac{1}{4}$ ($\cosh x = 0$ is not possible).

b $x = \ln\left(\frac{\sqrt{17}-1}{4}\right)$

20 Matrices 2

Prerequisite knowledge

1 **a** −13 **b** −7

2 **a** $\begin{pmatrix} -4 & -2 \\ -12 & 18 \end{pmatrix}$ **b** $\begin{pmatrix} 2 & -2 & 13 \\ 0 & 4 & 10 \\ -3 & 14 & 27 \end{pmatrix}$

3 **a** $\begin{pmatrix} 3 \\ 2 \\ -1 \end{pmatrix}$ **b** $\begin{pmatrix} -2 \\ 0 \\ 5 \end{pmatrix}$ **c** $\begin{pmatrix} 0 \\ 3 \\ 0 \end{pmatrix}$

Exercise 20A

1 **a** $\mathbf{e}_1$: yes with eigenvalue 5, $\mathbf{e}_2$: no

b $\mathbf{e}_1$: no, $\mathbf{e}_2$: yes with eigenvalue 1

c $\mathbf{e}_1$: yes with eigenvalue −5, $\mathbf{e}_2$: no

2 Proof; eigenvalues are −2, 5, 1 respectively.

3 **M**: eigenvalues are −1, 7 respectively.

$\mathbf{M}^2$: eigenvalues are 1, 49 respectively.

$\mathbf{M}^5$: eigenvalues are −1, 16807; eigenvectors are $\mathbf{e}_1, \mathbf{e}_2$ respectively.

4 **a** $\lambda = -1, 4, \begin{pmatrix} 1 \\ -1 \end{pmatrix}, \begin{pmatrix} 4 \\ 1 \end{pmatrix}$

b $\lambda = -4, 4, \begin{pmatrix} 3 \\ -5 \end{pmatrix}, \begin{pmatrix} 1 \\ 1 \end{pmatrix}$

5 $r = 16$

6 $\lambda = 2, 4, 5, p = 5, q = 3$

7 Proof

8 $\lambda = -3, 1, 2, \begin{pmatrix} ab-10 \\ -4b \\ 2ab \end{pmatrix}, \begin{pmatrix} 1 \\ 0 \\ 2 \end{pmatrix}, \begin{pmatrix} a \\ 1 \\ 2a \end{pmatrix}$

Exercise 20B

1 λ^2

2 Proof

3 $\lambda - 2\mu$, **e**

4 **a** $\lambda = 1, 8, \begin{pmatrix} 2 \\ 3 \end{pmatrix}, \begin{pmatrix} 1 \\ -2 \end{pmatrix}$

b $\lambda = 2, 3, \begin{pmatrix} -8 \\ 1 \end{pmatrix}, \begin{pmatrix} 1 \\ 0 \end{pmatrix}$

5 **a** $\lambda = 1, 3, 4, \begin{pmatrix} 8 \\ -6 \\ 1 \end{pmatrix}, \begin{pmatrix} 2 \\ 0 \\ -1 \end{pmatrix}, \begin{pmatrix} 1 \\ 0 \\ -1 \end{pmatrix}$, Eigenvalues of B are −2, 6, 13

b $\lambda = 1, 2, 5, \begin{pmatrix} 1 \\ -4 \\ 0 \end{pmatrix}, \begin{pmatrix} 0 \\ 1 \\ 0 \end{pmatrix}, \begin{pmatrix} 0 \\ 0 \\ 1 \end{pmatrix}$, Eigenvalues of B are −2, 1, 22

6 **a** 64, 125, −216

b $-12, -20, -42, \begin{pmatrix} 1 \\ 0 \\ -10 \end{pmatrix}, \begin{pmatrix} 1 \\ 0 \\ 0 \end{pmatrix}, \begin{pmatrix} 3 \\ 11 \\ 3 \end{pmatrix}$

7 $\lambda_1 = 3, a = -1, \lambda_2 = 2, \lambda_3 = 4, \begin{pmatrix} 2 \\ -1 \\ 1 \end{pmatrix}, \begin{pmatrix} 1 \\ 2 \\ -1 \end{pmatrix}$

8 **a** Proof **b** Proof

9 $\begin{pmatrix} \frac{3}{2} & 2 & 3 \\ \frac{1}{2} & \frac{3}{2} & \frac{3}{2} \\ -\frac{1}{2} & -1 & -1 \end{pmatrix}$

Exercise 20C

1 a Not diagonalisable

b Diagonalisable

c Not diagonalisable

2 $k \geqslant \frac{1}{7}$

3 1

4 a $\begin{pmatrix} 729 & -532 \\ 0 & 64 \end{pmatrix}$ b $\begin{pmatrix} -173 & 301 \\ -172 & 300 \end{pmatrix}$

5 a Not diagonalisable

b Not diagonalisable

c Diagonalisable

6 $\mathbf{P} = \begin{pmatrix} 3 & 1 & 1 \\ -1 & -1 & 1 \\ 0 & 2 & 0 \end{pmatrix}$, $\mathbf{H} = \begin{pmatrix} 1 & 0 & 0 \\ 0 & 1 & 0 \\ 0 & 0 & 81 \end{pmatrix}$

7 For $k = 0$: $\lambda = 0, 1, 2$ with $\begin{pmatrix} 1 \\ 0 \\ 0 \end{pmatrix}, \begin{pmatrix} 1 \\ 3 \\ -1 \end{pmatrix}, \begin{pmatrix} 1 \\ 2 \\ 0 \end{pmatrix}$.

For $k = 2$: $\lambda = 1, 2$ with $\begin{pmatrix} 1 \\ -3 \\ 1 \end{pmatrix}, \begin{pmatrix} 1 \\ 0 \\ 0 \end{pmatrix}$.

Since $k = 2$ produces only two distinct eigenvectors, it is not possible to produce a square matrix **P**, hence no inverse, hence not diagonalisable.

8 a $1, 2, -1, -2$ b $\begin{pmatrix} 1 & 0 & 0 & 273 \\ 0 & 64 & 21 & 105 \\ 0 & 0 & 1 & -315 \\ 0 & 0 & 0 & 64 \end{pmatrix}$

Exercise 20D

1 a No solutions

b Unique solution: $x = \frac{11}{5}, y = -\frac{2}{5}$

c Infinite solutions

2 a $\alpha = -\frac{4}{3}, \beta \neq 4.5$

b $\alpha = -\frac{4}{3}, \beta = 4.5$

c $\alpha \neq -\frac{4}{3}, \beta \in R$

3 a No solutions

b Unique solution: $x = \frac{7}{24}, y = \frac{1}{4}, z = \frac{1}{6}$

c Infinite solutions $\begin{pmatrix} x \\ y \\ z \end{pmatrix} = \begin{pmatrix} -\frac{7}{3} \\ \frac{2}{3} \\ 0 \end{pmatrix} + \begin{pmatrix} 13 \\ -2 \\ 3 \end{pmatrix} t$

4 $k = 7$

5 $x = \frac{5}{3}, y = -\frac{1}{3}, z = 0$

6 $\begin{pmatrix} 2 \\ 0 \\ 0 \end{pmatrix} t$

7 a 1 solution b No solutions

c Infinite solutions

End-of-chapter review exercise 20

1 $\lambda_1 = 1, \mathbf{e_1} = \begin{pmatrix} 1 \\ 2 \\ 1 \end{pmatrix}, \lambda_2 = 3, \mathbf{e_2} = \begin{pmatrix} 1 \\ 0 \\ -1 \end{pmatrix},$

$\lambda_3 = 4, \mathbf{e_3} = \begin{pmatrix} 1 \\ -1 \\ 1 \end{pmatrix}$

$\mathbf{M} = \begin{pmatrix} 1 & 1 & -1 \\ -1 & 2 & 0 \\ 1 & 1 & 1 \end{pmatrix}$

$\mathbf{D} = \begin{pmatrix} 8 & 0 & 0 \\ 0 & -1 & 0 \\ 0 & 0 & 1 \end{pmatrix}$

2 $\lambda^3 - 2\lambda^2 - \lambda + 2 = 0, \alpha = -2, \beta = -1, \gamma = 2.$

$\mathbf{A}^{-1} = \frac{1}{2}\begin{pmatrix} 2 & -2 & 4 \\ 0 & 1 & 0 \\ 0 & 1 & -2 \end{pmatrix}$

3 i $\mathbf{A} = \begin{pmatrix} \frac{3}{2} & \frac{1}{2} & \frac{1}{2} \\ \frac{3}{2} & \frac{1}{2} & \frac{3}{2} \\ -1 & 1 & 0 \end{pmatrix}$

ii $\frac{1}{2}\begin{pmatrix} 2^{2n}+1 & 2^{2n}-1 & 2^{2n}-1 \\ 2^{2n}-1 & 2^{2n}+1 & 2^{2n}-1 \\ 0 & 0 & 2 \end{pmatrix}$

21 Differentiation

Prerequisite knowledge

1 a $\frac{dy}{dx} = e^{2x} + 2xe^{2x}$ b $\frac{dy}{dx} = 4x\cos(x^2+1)$

c $\frac{dy}{dx} = \frac{2x-3}{x(x-1)}$

2 $\frac{dy}{dx} = \frac{2xy-1}{2-x^2+3y^2}$

3 $\frac{dy}{dx} = \frac{3t^2}{2t-1}$

Exercise 21A

1 a $\frac{e^x - y}{x}$

b $\frac{y^2}{e^y - 2xy}$

c $\frac{\sec^2(x+y)}{1-\sec^2(x+y)}$

2 2

3 $\frac{dy}{dx} = 1, \frac{d^2y}{dx^2} = -4$

4 $\frac{dy}{dx} = \frac{y-\cos(x+y)}{\cos(x+y)-x}$,

$\frac{d^2y}{dx^2} = \frac{2\frac{dy}{dx} + \sin(x+y)\left(1+\frac{dy}{dx}\right)^2}{\cos(x+y)-x}$

5 $\frac{dy}{dx} = -1, \frac{d^2y}{dx^2} = 2$

6 a $-\frac{y}{\alpha x}$ b Proof

7 $\frac{dy}{dx} = -\frac{5}{6}, \frac{d^2y}{dx^2} = -\frac{5}{36}$

8 a $-\frac{1}{3}$ b $-\frac{8\sqrt{3}}{9}$

Exercise 21B

1 a $-\frac{3}{4t^3}$ b $2e^{-2t}(1-t)$

2 $\frac{1}{72}$

3 $\frac{1}{3e^2}, -\frac{2}{9e^5}$

4 $-\frac{1}{24}$

5 a $e^t(t+1)$ b Proof

6 a Proof b Proof

7 $\frac{3}{4}\sec t$

8 a $2^{-\frac{1}{3}}$ b Minimum

9 a $\frac{(1+e^{4t})}{(-1+e^{4t})}$, no turning points b Proof

Exercise 21C

1 Proof

2 $\frac{2}{1-(2x+3)^2}$

3 $\frac{3x^2}{\sqrt{1-x^6}}$

4 a $\frac{dy}{dx} = 4\tanh 4x$

b $\frac{dy}{dx} = 2x\sinh(2x^2-1) + 4x^3\cosh(2x^2-1)$

c $\frac{dy}{dx} = \cosh^{-1}5x + \frac{5x}{\sqrt{25x^2-1}}$

d $\frac{dy}{dx} = \frac{1}{(x+y)^2}$

5 $\frac{d^2y}{dx^2} = 4(1+4x^2)^{-\frac{1}{2}} - 8x^2(1+4x^2)^{-\frac{3}{2}}$

6 a $\frac{dy}{dx} = 6x\sinh x^2\cosh^2 x^2$, 1 turning point

b $\frac{d^2y}{dx^2} = 6\cosh x^2[\sinh x^2\cosh x^2 + 2x^2\cosh^2 x^2 + 4x^2\sinh^2 x^2]$

7 a $\frac{dy}{dx} = \frac{b}{a\sqrt{1-b^2x^2}}$ b $\frac{dy}{dx} = \frac{b}{a(1+b^2x^2)}$

c $\frac{dy}{dx} = \frac{b}{a\sqrt{1+b^2x^2}}$ d $\frac{dy}{dx} = \frac{b}{a\sqrt{b^2x^2-1}}$

e $\frac{dy}{dx} = \frac{b}{a(1-b^2x^2)}$

8 a $t = -1, 1$ b 0

Exercise 21D

1 a $(12 + 48x^2 + 16x^4)e^{x^2}$

b $4\sin x + x\cos x$

2 $2 - 6x^2 + 15x^4$

3 1.3912819

4 a $1 + \frac{x^2}{2} + \frac{5x^4}{24} + \frac{61x^6}{720}$

b $x - \frac{x^3}{3} + \frac{x^5}{5} - \frac{x^7}{7}$

c $x + \frac{x^3}{6} + \frac{x^5}{120} + \frac{x^7}{5040}$

5 a $\frac{\pi}{2} - x + \frac{x^3}{3} - \frac{x^5}{5}$ b $1 - x^2 + x^4 - x^6$

6 a $1 - \frac{9}{2!}x^2 + \frac{81}{4!}x^4 - \frac{729}{6!}x^6$

b $x^2 + 3x^3 + 9x^4 + 27x^5$

c $1 + \frac{9x^2}{8} + \frac{27x^4}{128} + \frac{81x^6}{5120}$

7 0.198 690 10

8 a Proof b $x - \frac{x^3}{3} + \frac{2x^5}{15}$

End-of-chapter review exercise 21

1 i $\frac{3}{4}$ ii $\frac{1}{16}$

2 Proof, $-\frac{1}{16}$, maximum

3 $\frac{dy}{dx} = -\frac{1}{\sqrt{4 - x^2}}, \frac{d^2y}{dx^2} = -\frac{x}{(4 - x^2)^{\frac{3}{2}}}$.

$y \approx \frac{\pi}{2} - \frac{1}{2}x - \frac{1}{48}x^3$

22 Integration

Prerequisite knowledge

1 $\frac{e^2 + 1}{4}$

2 $-2\sqrt{2}\cos\left(\frac{x}{2}\right) + c$

Exercise 22A

1 $-\frac{2}{3}\sin^{-1}\left(\frac{3x}{5}\right) + c$

2 $\frac{\pi}{4}\tan^{-1}\frac{\pi}{4} - \frac{1}{2}\ln\left(1 + \frac{\pi^2}{16}\right)$

3 $\frac{896}{225}$

4 $2\sinh^{-1}\left(\frac{x}{\sqrt{2}}\right) + c$

5 0.962

6 17.3

7 0.266

8 $2\sin^{-1}\left(\frac{3x}{2}\right) + c$

9 $x\sinh x - \cosh x + c$

10 1.28

11 $x\sinh^{-1}x - (1 + x^2)^{\frac{1}{2}} + c$

Exercise 22B

1 $\frac{1}{4} - I_3$

2 $I_6 = 30I_4 - 5e$

3 $I_4 = \frac{16}{19} + \frac{12}{19}I_3$

4 $I_n = \frac{n-1}{n}I_{n-2}, n \geqslant 2$

5 Proof, $\frac{28}{15}$

6 a Proof b $\frac{107}{630}$

7 Proof, $\frac{2}{27}(1 + 2e^3)$

8 0.0336

9 $\frac{5\pi^2}{32}$

Exercise 22C

1 7.382

2 2π

3 $\frac{19}{3}$

4 $\frac{7}{12}$

5 199.5

6 Proof, 2.78

7 **a** Proof **b** Proof **c** 1.32

8 0.204

Exercise 22D

1 Diverges

2 Proof

3 Converges

4 Proof

5 Converges

6 Proof

7 Converges

8 Diverge

9 Converges

End-of-chapter review exercise 22

1 Proof

2 $I_3 = \frac{32}{315}$

3 $x\cosh^{-1}2x - \frac{1}{2}(4x^2 - 1)^{\frac{1}{2}} + c$, $\ln(2 + \sqrt{3}) - \frac{\sqrt{3}}{2}$

23 Complex numbers

Prerequisite knowledge

1 **a** $8 - 5\mathrm{i}$ **b** $18 + \mathrm{i}$ **c** $-\frac{6}{25} + \frac{17}{25}\mathrm{i}$

2 $x^{20} + 10x^{16} + 45x^{12} + 120x^8$

Exercise 23A

1 **a** $8192 + 8192\mathrm{i}\sqrt{3}$
b $-16 + 16\mathrm{i}$

2 $\cos x - 8\cos x^3 + 8\cos x^5$

3 **a** $-\frac{1}{2} + \frac{\sqrt{3}}{2}\mathrm{i}$ **b** 4096 **c** $\frac{\mathrm{i}}{8}$

4 $64\cos^7\theta - 112\cos^5\theta + 56\cos^3\theta - 7\cos\theta$

5 $\frac{3\tan\theta - \tan^3\theta}{1 - 3\tan^2\theta}$, $x = -5.04, -0.340, 0.876$

6 Proof

7 $32\sin^5\theta - 32\sin^3\theta + 6\sin\theta$

8 Proof, $x = -1.50, -0.199, 0.668, 5.03$

9 $-2.32, -0.593, 0.0930, 0.879, 4.44$

Exercise 23B

1 $\frac{15}{8} + \frac{3}{2}\cos 2\theta + \frac{5}{8}\cos 4\theta$

2 $\frac{43}{120}\sqrt{2}$

3 1

4 $\frac{1}{4}\cos 5\theta + \frac{5}{4}\cos 3\theta + \frac{5}{2}\cos\theta$

5 $-\frac{1}{32}\sin 6\theta + \frac{3}{32}\sin 2\theta$

6 $\frac{1}{16}\mathrm{e}^{5\mathrm{i}\theta} + \frac{5}{16}\mathrm{e}^{-3\mathrm{i}\theta} + \frac{5}{8}\mathrm{e}^{\mathrm{i}\theta}$

7 $\frac{1}{64}\cos 8\theta + \frac{7}{16}\cos 4\theta + \frac{35}{64}$

8 $\frac{16}{35}$

Exercise 23C

1 $1, \mathrm{e}^{\frac{\pi}{3}\mathrm{i}}, \mathrm{e}^{\frac{2\pi}{3}\mathrm{i}}, -1, \mathrm{e}^{\frac{4\pi}{3}\mathrm{i}}, \mathrm{e}^{\frac{5\pi}{3}\mathrm{i}}$

2 0

3 $2\mathrm{e}^{\frac{\pi}{12}}, 2\mathrm{e}^{\frac{7\pi}{12}}, 2\mathrm{e}^{\frac{13\pi}{12}}, 2\mathrm{e}^{\frac{19\pi}{12}}$

4 $z = 2\mathrm{e}^{\left(\frac{\pi}{4} + \frac{k\pi}{2}\right)\mathrm{i}}, k = 0, 1, 2, 3$

5 **a** $\mathrm{f}(z) = 1 + z + z^2 + z^3 + z^4$ **b** Proof

6 $z = \sqrt{2}\mathrm{e}^{\left(\frac{5\pi}{48} + \frac{k\pi}{4}\right)\mathrm{i}}, k = 0, 1, 2, 3, 4, 5, 6, 7$

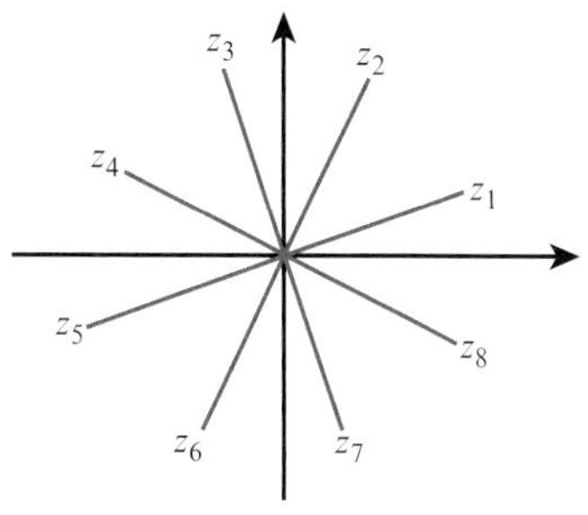

7 $z = \mathrm{e}^{\left(\frac{\pi}{12} + \frac{k\pi}{6}\right)\mathrm{i}}, k = 0, 1, \ldots, 11$

8 Proof

9 **a** $z = \mathrm{e}^{\frac{k\pi}{3}\mathrm{i}}, k = 0, 1, 2, 3, 4, 5$

b $-1, 1$ **c** Proof, $z^2 + z + 1$

10 $\omega = \sqrt{2}e^{\frac{\pi}{12}i}, \omega^2 = \sqrt{2}e^{\frac{9\pi}{12}i}, \omega^3 = \sqrt{2}e^{\frac{17\pi}{12}i}, -2 + 3i$

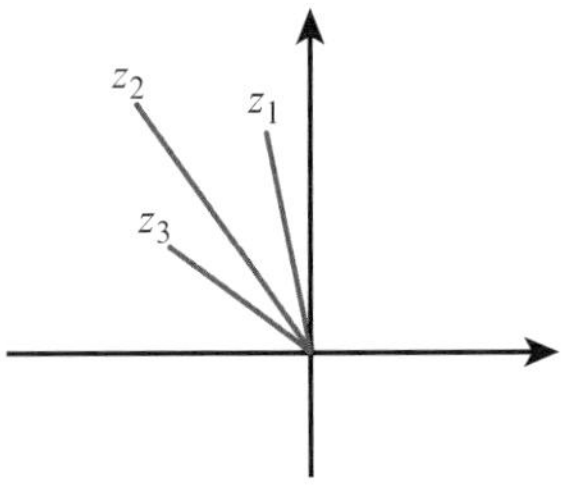

Exercise 23D

1 $\dfrac{e^{i\theta}(e^{Ni\theta} - 1)}{e^{i\theta} - 1}$

2 Proof

3 $\dfrac{\cos 2N\theta + i\sin 2N\theta - 1}{2i\sin\theta}$

4 **a** $\dfrac{2 - 2\cos 20\theta}{\sin\theta}$ **b** $4\sqrt{2}$

5 Proof

6 Proof

7 $-\dfrac{1}{7}$

8 Proof

End-of-chapter review exercise 23

1 $2^n\cos^n\dfrac{1}{2}\theta\sin\dfrac{n}{2}\theta$

2 $\cot 7\theta = \dfrac{\cot^7\theta - 21\cot^5\theta + 35\cot^3\theta - 7\cot\theta}{7\cot^6\theta - 35\cot^4\theta + 21\cot^2\theta - 1}$

3 $\cos\frac{1}{5}\pi + \cos\frac{3}{5}\pi = \frac{1}{2}, \cos\frac{1}{5}\pi\cos\frac{3}{5}\pi = -\frac{1}{4},$

$4x^2 - 2x - 1 = 0, \cos\frac{\pi}{5} = \frac{1 + \sqrt{5}}{4}$

24 Differential equations

Prerequisite knowledge

1 $y = \dfrac{2x^2}{1 - 2cx^2}$

2 **a** $\frac{1}{2}x - \frac{1}{4}\sin 2x + c$ **b** $\frac{1}{4}x^4\ln x - \frac{1}{16}x^4 + c$

c $\frac{1}{2}\sinh 2x + c$

3 **a** $\dfrac{d^2y}{dx^2} = 2\dfrac{dz}{dx} + x\dfrac{d^2z}{dx^2}$ **b** $\dfrac{3}{4t}$

Exercise 24A

1 $y = \dfrac{c - \cos x}{x^2}$

2 $y = \left(\frac{1}{4}x^4 + c\right)e^{-2x}$

3 $y = ce^{7x} - \frac{1}{5}e^{2x}$

4 $x = -\frac{1}{4}t - \frac{1}{8} + \frac{9}{8}e^{2t}$

5 $y = \dfrac{(x - 2)^4}{2} - (x - 2)^2$

6 **a** $\dfrac{dy}{dx} = x + y$ **b** $y = ce^x - x - 1$

7 $y = c\operatorname{sech} x + 4x\tanh x - 4$

8 $y = -\cot t + \frac{1}{3}\cos^2 t\cot t$

9 **a** $x = 20e^{-4t}$ **b** $y = 10e^{-2t} - 10e^{-4t}$

c $y_{max} = 2.5$

Exercise 24B

1 $y = Ae^{-3x} + Be^{6x}$

2 $y = Ae^{(3-\sqrt{43})x} + Be^{(3+\sqrt{43})x}$

3 $y = (Ax + B)e^{-8x}$

4 **a** $y = Ae^{2x} + Be^{-5x}$

b $y = e^{-2x}(A\cos 3x + B\sin 3x)$

c $y = (Ax + B)e^{4x}$

5 $x = \frac{3}{2}e^{2t} - \frac{1}{2}e^{-2t}$

6 $r = \frac{5}{3}te^{\frac{2}{3}t} + 2e^{\frac{2}{3}t}$

7 **a** $y = A\cos 2x + B\sin 2x$

b $R = \dfrac{\sqrt{5}}{2}, \alpha = 0.464$

8

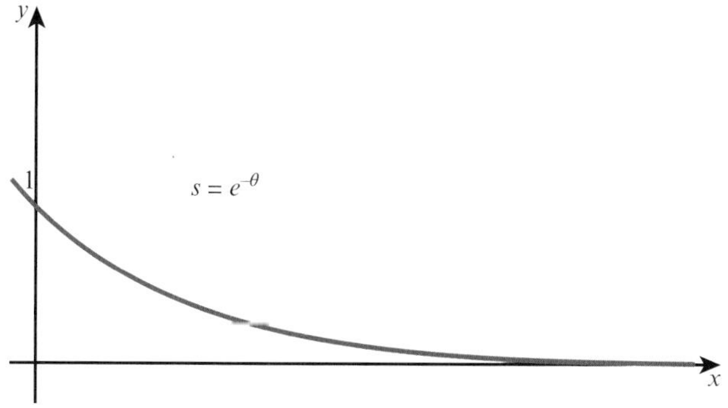

Exercise 24C

1 $y = Ae^{-2x} + Be^{-3x} - \frac{1}{3}x^2 + \frac{5}{9}x - \frac{19}{54}$

2 a $r = Ae^{-2t} + Be^{2t}$, $r = -\frac{3}{5}\cos t$

b $r = -\frac{1}{20}e^{-2t} + \frac{9}{20}e^{2t} - \frac{3}{5}\sin t$

3 $x = \frac{2}{5} + \frac{e^t}{8} - \frac{101}{40}e^{-t}\cos 2t - \frac{53}{40}e^{-t}\sin 2t$

4 $y = (Ax + B)e^{-3x} + \frac{1}{25}e^{2x} + \frac{1}{9}x - \frac{2}{27}$

$y \to \frac{x}{9}$ as $x \to \infty$

5 a $x = \frac{2}{5} + \frac{e^t}{8} - \frac{101}{40}e^{-t}\cos 2t - \frac{53}{40}e^{-t}\sin 2t$

b $y = \alpha x^2 e^{-2x} + \beta e^x$

c $y = \alpha x e^{-x}\cos x + \beta x e^{-x}\sin x$

6 $x = Ae^{-t} + Be^{-4t} + \frac{1}{3}te^{-t}$

7 a Proof, $\alpha = \frac{1}{2}$ b $h = \frac{1}{2}t^2 e^{\frac{1}{2}t}$

8 $y = A\cos x + B\sin x - \frac{1}{2}x\sin x + x$,

$y = \cos x - \frac{1}{2}x\sin x + x$

9 $r = Ae^{-\theta} + Be^{-3\theta} + \theta e^{-\theta} - \frac{1}{2}\theta e^{-3\theta}$

10 a Proof b $x = \frac{g}{5}e^{-\frac{5}{2}t} - \frac{g}{5} + \frac{2}{5}gt$

Exercise 24D

1 $y = \ln(Ae^{-x} + 1)$

2 $y = x\sqrt{c - 2\ln x}$

3 $y = 2\tan^{-1}(x + c) - x$

4 a $\frac{dy}{dx} = 2w + 2x\frac{dw}{dx}$, $\frac{d^2y}{dx^2} = 4\frac{dw}{dx} + 2x\frac{d^2w}{dx^2}$

b $\frac{dy}{dx} = 5z^4\frac{dz}{dx}$, $\frac{d^2y}{dx^2} = 20z^3\left(\frac{dz}{dx}\right)^2 + 5z^4\frac{d^2z}{dx^2}$

c $\frac{dy}{dx} = -\frac{t^4}{3}\frac{dy}{dt}$, $\frac{d^2y}{dx^2} = \frac{t^8}{9}\frac{d^2y}{dt^2} + \frac{4}{9}t^7\frac{dy}{dt}$

5 Proof, $z = Ax^2e^{-4x} + Bx^2e^x - \frac{5}{4}x^3 + \frac{9}{16}x^2$

6 a Proof, $\frac{d^2y}{dx^2} = \frac{1}{4x^2}\left(\frac{d^2y}{dt^2} - 2\frac{dy}{dt}\right)$

b $y = (At + B)e^{-t} - \frac{1}{3}e^{2t}$

7 $\frac{d^2y}{dx^2} + \frac{dy}{dx} - 6y = 24x$,

$z = \left[\frac{A}{2}e^{-3x} + \frac{B}{2}e^{2x} - 2x - \frac{1}{3}\right]^{\frac{1}{3}}$

8 a Proof

b Proof, $y = (Au + B)e^{\frac{1}{4}u} + u + 8$

c $y = \left(\frac{4}{x} - 4\right)e^{\frac{1}{2x}} + \frac{2}{x} + 8$

End-of-chapter review exercise 24

1 $y = \frac{1}{9}(3x + 4)\ln|3x + 4| + \frac{4}{9} + c(3x + 4)$, $c = 1$

2 $k = 2$, $y = Ae^{2x} + Bxe^{2x} + 2x^2e^{2x}$

$y = 3e^{2x} - 8xe^{2x} + 2x^2e^{2x}$

3 Proof, $y = x^{-2}(Ae^{-x} + Be^{-\frac{1}{2}x} - \cos 2x)$

Cross-topic review exercise 4

1 a Proof b $x = \ln 3, \ln 5$

2 a For P + Q: $\lambda + \mu$, eigenvector e. For PQ: $\lambda\mu$, eigenvector e.

b $\lambda = -1, 2, 5$, eigenvectors are

$\begin{pmatrix}1\\0\\0\end{pmatrix}, \begin{pmatrix}4\\3\\0\end{pmatrix}, \begin{pmatrix}11\\3\\9\end{pmatrix}$.

c For A + B: $\lambda + \mu = 0, 6, 12$, eigenvectors are

$\begin{pmatrix}1\\0\\0\end{pmatrix}, \begin{pmatrix}4\\3\\0\end{pmatrix}, \begin{pmatrix}11\\3\\9\end{pmatrix}$.

For AB: $\lambda\mu = -1, 8, 35$, eigenvectors are

$$\begin{pmatrix}1\\0\\0\end{pmatrix}, \begin{pmatrix}4\\3\\0\end{pmatrix}, \begin{pmatrix}11\\3\\9\end{pmatrix}.$$

3 **a** Proof **b** $\frac{dy}{dx} = -\frac{1}{2}, \frac{d^2y}{dx^2} = -\frac{1}{2}.$

4 Proof, 0.321

5 $\cos^6\theta = \frac{1}{32}\cos 6\theta + \frac{3}{16}\cos 4\theta + \frac{15}{32}\cos 2\theta + \frac{5}{16}$

$\frac{5\pi}{32}$

6 $y = \frac{2}{3}e^x + \frac{1}{3}e^{4x} + \frac{1}{4}x^2 + \frac{5}{8}x + \frac{21}{32} + \frac{1}{18}e^{-2x}$

7 $\begin{pmatrix}5 & 2\\4 & 7\end{pmatrix}, \begin{pmatrix}-5 & -2\\-4 & -7\end{pmatrix}$

8 $\frac{2-2t}{9t^5}$

9 $\frac{z\left(1-\left(\frac{z}{2}\right)^n\right)}{2-z}$

10 Eigenvalues are $-1, 2, 8$ with corresponding eigenvectors $\begin{pmatrix}4\\-9\\8\end{pmatrix}, \begin{pmatrix}5\\-6\\4\end{pmatrix}, \begin{pmatrix}1\\0\\2\end{pmatrix}.$

$\mathbf{P} = \begin{pmatrix}1 & 5 & 4\\0 & -6 & -9\\2 & 4 & 8\end{pmatrix}, \mathbf{D} = \begin{pmatrix}584 & 0 & 0\\0 & 14 & 0\\0 & 0 & -1\end{pmatrix}$

11 Proof, $y = Ae^{-\frac{1}{x}} + Be^{-\frac{4}{x}} + \frac{2}{x} + 1$

12 **i** $\begin{pmatrix}bc\\ca\\ab\end{pmatrix}$ **ii** $\frac{abc}{\sqrt{b^2c^2 + c^2a^2 + a^2b^2}}$

Further Pure Mathematics 1 practice exam-style paper

1 Proof

2 $-\frac{27}{4}n^4 - \frac{45}{2}n^3 - \frac{27}{4}n^2 + 2n$

3 **a** $4, \frac{4}{7}$

b $y^3 - 20y^2 + 12y - 2 = 0$

c 20

4 **a** $\mathbf{A}^{-1} = \frac{1}{4}\begin{pmatrix}1 & 3 & -3\\-1 & -3 & 7\\1 & -1 & 1\end{pmatrix}$

b **i** $\frac{1}{4}\begin{pmatrix}-10 & 6 & -1\\26 & 10 & 5\\6 & 2 & -1\end{pmatrix}$ **ii** $\frac{1}{4}\begin{pmatrix}-14 & 6 & -1\\26 & 6 & 5\\6 & 2 & -5\end{pmatrix}$

5 **a** $\frac{\sqrt{2}}{2e^{\frac{\pi}{4}}}$

b

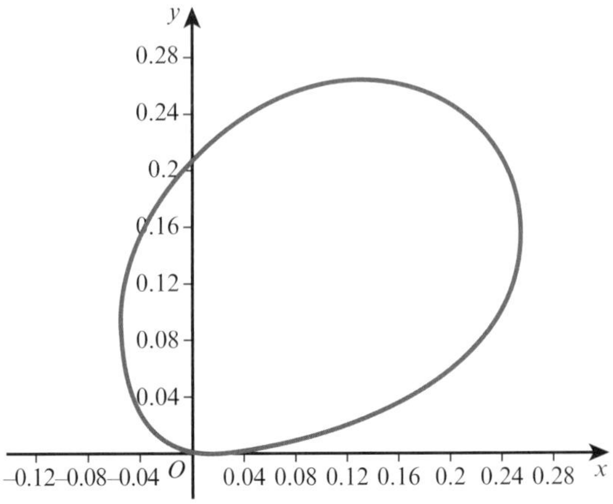

c 0.0625 (3 sf)

6 **a** $\frac{\sqrt{26}}{13}$ **b** $x + z = 4$

c 13.9° **d** $\mathbf{i} - \mathbf{j} - \mathbf{k}$

7 **a** $x = -2, y = 2x - 1$

b Proof

c $\left(0, -\frac{5}{2}\right), \left(-\frac{5}{2}, 0\right), (1, 0)$

d

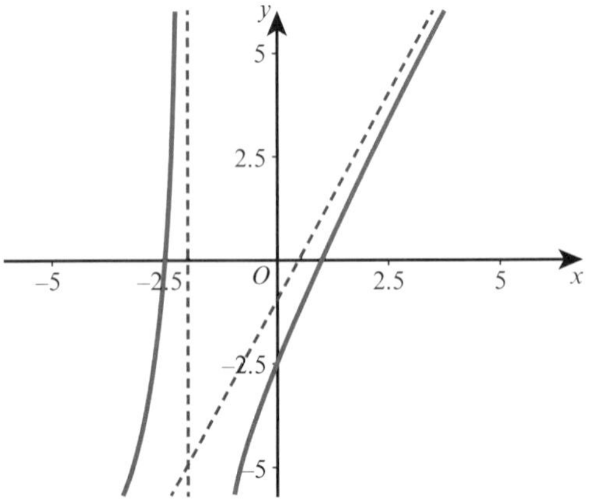

e $x < \frac{-1-\sqrt{73}}{4}, -2 < x < \frac{-1+\sqrt{73}}{4}$

Further Probability & Statistics practice exam-style paper

1 H_0: Recall for visual and aural is the same
H_1: Recall from visual is better than aural.
Test statistic: $S^+ = 9(S^- = 3)$
$P(S^+ \geqslant 9) = 0.072998$
Do not reject H_0:
Objects presented visually are not recalled more accurately than objects presented aurally.

2 a H_0: There is no difference between the population medians of the two departments
H_1: There is a difference between the population medians of the two departments
$m = 7, n = 8$
$R_m = 75$
$m(n + m + 1) - R_m = 37$
$W = 37$
Critical value = 38
Sufficient evidence to reject H_0: There is a difference in the population medians of the two departments.

b A normal approximation can be used with
$E(T) = 2525$
$\text{Var}(T) = 21042$
$T \approx N(2525, 21042)$

3 a $E(X) = \frac{4}{3}$, $\text{Var}(X) = \frac{8}{9}$

b $G_Z(t) = \frac{1}{19683}(2 + t)^9$

c $E(Z) = 3$, $\text{Var}(Z) = 2$

4 H_0: No association between gender and facilities used
H_1: An association between gender and facilities used
$\sum\left(\frac{(O - E)^2}{E}\right) = 12.7$
$\chi_2^2(0.95) = 5.991$
Reject H_0:
There is an association between gender and the facilities used at the hotel.

5 a 4.297

b $$F(x) = \begin{cases} 0 & x < 0 \\ \frac{1}{60}y(8 + y) & 0 \leqslant x < 2 \\ \frac{1}{96}(7x + 18) & 2 \leqslant x < 6 \\ \frac{1}{120}(30x - x^2 - 69) & x \geqslant 6 \\ 0 & \text{otherwise} \end{cases}$$

c Median $= \frac{30}{7}$

Further Mechanics practice exam-style paper

1 Speed $18.8\,\text{m s}^{-1}$ and direction angle 22.9° below the horizontal.

2 49.3°

3 a $v = 3u - \frac{4}{3m}t^3$ b $t = (9mu)^{\frac{1}{3}}$

4 a Proof b $\sqrt{3ga} < u < \sqrt{\frac{15}{2}ga}$

5 a $\ddot{x} = -\frac{50}{3}x$, $\omega = \sqrt{\frac{50}{3}}$

b 0.612 s

6 a $v_Q = \frac{9}{7}u$, $v_P = -\frac{3}{14}u$, opposite directions

b $\frac{135}{28}mu^2\,\text{J}$ c $\frac{45}{7}mu\,\text{N}$

Further Pure Mathematics 2 practice exam-style paper

1 $y = \sec x \ln \sin x + c \sec x$

2 $\frac{\pi}{12}$

3 a $\left(\begin{array}{ccc|c} 1 & -2 & 1 & 0 \\ 0 & 3 & 2 & 2 \\ 0 & 0 & a-4 & b-2 \end{array}\right)$

b $a \neq 4, b \in R$

c $a = 4, b = 2$

d $a = 4, b \neq 2$

4 13

5 Proof, $\ln(3 + \sqrt{8})$, $\ln(2 + \sqrt{3})$

6 **a** Proof **b** 0.9192

7 $x = e^{-2t} + 4e^{t} + te^{t}$

8 Proof, −4.129, −0.610, 0.242, 1.639

9 **a** Eigenvalues −2, 1, 2

eigenvectors $\begin{pmatrix} 1 \\ 1 \\ -1 \end{pmatrix}, \begin{pmatrix} 1 \\ 1 \\ 2 \end{pmatrix}, \begin{pmatrix} 5 \\ 1 \\ 3 \end{pmatrix}$

b $\mathbf{P} = \begin{pmatrix} 1 & 1 & 5 \\ 1 & 1 & 1 \\ -1 & 2 & 3 \end{pmatrix}, \mathbf{D} = \begin{pmatrix} -2 & 0 & 0 \\ 0 & 1 & 0 \\ 0 & 0 & 2 \end{pmatrix}$

c $\mathbf{H} = \begin{pmatrix} -32 & 0 & 0 \\ 0 & 1 & 0 \\ 0 & 0 & 32 \end{pmatrix}$

Glossary

χ^2-test: a test that can be used to look for the association between two sets of categorical data, or to perform a goodness of fit test

ρ, the Greek letter rho: density (pronounced 'row' (spelt rho))

A

Acceptance region: the values of the test statistic for which we do not reject the null hypothesis

Angle of depression: the angle formed by the line of sight and the horizontal plane for an object below the horizontal

Angle of elevation: the angle formed by the line of sight and the horizontal plane for an object above the horizontal

Angular speed: the velocity of a body rotating about a fixed point, measured as the rate of change of the angle turned per unit of time

Arithmetic sequence: a sequence in which each successive term is obtained by adding the same constant value

Asymptote: a line that a curve tends towards

Augmented matrix: a matrix that is formed by combining the columns of two matrices

Auxiliary equation: an algebraic equation of degree n that is based upon an nth degree differential equation

B

Barycentre: the point between two objects, such as planets, where the objects are perfectly balanced with each other

Boundaries: limiting or bounding lines

Boundary conditions: a set of conditions that limit the possible solutions of differential equations

Breaking equilibrium: when the net force on an object is no longer zero

C

Cardioids: a type of polar curve that is heart shaped

Catenary: a naturally occuring shape observed in cases such as telephone cables and rope bridges, modelled by the hyperbolic cosine function

Cayley–Hamilton theorem: states that every square matrix satisfies its own characteristic equation

Centre of mass: the point at which the entire mass of a body may be considered

Characteristic equation: the polynomial of degree n that relates to the eigenvalues of a square matrix

Chi-squared: a family of distributions which are used to test association and goodness of fit

Circular functions: sine, cosine and tangent are called circular functions as they are derived from the unit circle

Circular motion: motion that occurs about a fixed point where the distance is constant

Coalesce: when two objects join together upon collision; occurs when there is zero elasticity between the objects

Coefficient of restitution: the measure of how elastic the collision is between two objects

Column: a vertical collection of terms, such as in a matrix

Common perpendicular: when two or more lines or planes are such that a vector is at right angles to both of them

Comparison test: the use of a similar sum to compare against the original; this comparative sum is known to converge or diverge

Complementary function (CF): the general solution of the auxiliary equation of a linear differential equation

Composite: made up of several different parts or elements

Compressed: reduced in size due to external forces

Confidence interval: an interval for which there is a given probability that the population mean lies within that interval

Conic section: a special curve created by cutting through a right circular cone with a plane

Conical pendulum: a pendulum that performs horizontal circles about a centre that is vertically below where the string is attached

Conservation of energy: the total energy of an isolated system remains constant throughout the motion

Constraint: a rule or condition

Contingency table: a two-way table to display categorical data used in a chi-squared test

Convergent: a series is convergent if the sequence of its partial sums approaches a limit

Convolution theorem: in statistics, a theorem that allows evaluation of the probability generating function of the sum of two independent discrete random variables

Cross product: two vectors, **u** and **v**, are crossed to form a vector that is perpendicular to both **u** and **v**

Cube roots of unity: the three roots of the cubic equation $z^3 - 1 = 0$

Cubic equation: a polynomial with a leading term of power 3

Cumulative distribution function: a function that relates probability to the area under the graph for a probability density function that defines a continuous random variable

Cusp: a point on a curve at which two branches meet such that their tangents are equal

D

Deformation: the altering of the shape of an object

Degrees of freedom: the number of independent pieces of information that contribute to the estimate of a parameter

Denominator: the bottom portion of a fraction

Derivative: a function or value obtained from differentiating the original function

Determinant: a value obtained from the elements of a square matrix, usually used to represent the scaling factor from a transformation

Diagonalisable: a square matrix is known to be diagonalisable if it is similar to a diagonal matrix

Differential equation: an equation that contains the original function and at least the first derivative; the order of the differential equation is determined by the highest derivative in the equation

Differentiation: the process of finding the gradient function

Directly proportional: a relationship between two variables such that they increase in the same ratio

Discontinuity: a point on a curve in which $f(a)$ does not exist; a gap exists in the curve

Discrete uniform distribution: a distribution in which the random variable takes specific values, and each value has an equal probability

Discriminant: a function obtained from the coefficients of a polynomial, allowing the deduction of the number of roots of the polynomial in question

Displacement: the position of an object relative to its starting point, measured as a vector

E

Eigenvalue: a value obtained from solving the characteristic equation of a square matrix

Eigenvector: a vector that maps to a factor of itself when a matrix is applied to it, the direction being unchanged

Elastic: a material that has the ability to stretch beyond its natural length when a force is applied to it

Elastic potential energy (EPE): the energy stored in an elastic body that has been stretched or compressed

Element: a value in a matrix

Ellipse: a curve surrounding two focal points, where the sum of the distances of a point on the curve to these two focal points is always constant

Energy: the measure of mechanical energy stored in a system, comprising kinetic energy, potential energy and elastic potential energy

Enlargement: a transformation that increases or decreases the area or volume of an existing shape, a stretch along all coordinate axes

Equilibrium: a state in which the resultant forces on an object are zero

Extension: the extra length created when an elastic object is stretched beyond its natural length

F

Free variable: a variable that does not correspond to a pivot column in a row reduced matrix

Frustum: a right circular cone with a smaller right circular cone cut off by slicing the cone to give a larger and smaller circular face

G

General solution (GS): a solution to a differential equation with undetermined constants

H

Homogeneous differential equation: a differential equation that includes terms in only one unknown function, e.g. y, and its derivatives, e.g. $\frac{dy}{dx}, \frac{d^2y}{dx^2}$. It is possible to arrange the terms to give zero on one side of the equation

Hooke's law: a law that relates the extension of a string or spring, or the compression of a spring, to the force applied

Hyperbola: a curve surrounding two focal points, where the difference of the distances of a point on the curve to these two focal points is always constant

Hyperbolic function: hyperbolic functions are derived from the unit hyperbola

Hyperbolic identities: relationships between hyperbolic functions similar to their trigonometric equivalents

I

Implicit: a function or expression that is not expressed directly in terms of independent variables

Impulse: a force applied over a given time interval

Induction: a method of proof in which a base case is shown to be true, then successive steps are shown also to be true, completing the proof

Inertia: the resistance of any physical object to change its current state of motion

Inextensible: a spring or string that cannot be stretched beyond its natural length

Inhomogeneous differential equation: a differential equation that can include terms in two different functions. Moving all the terms in one function, e.g. $\frac{dy}{dx}, \frac{d^2y}{dx^2}$, to one side of the equation leaves a function, e.g. $f(x)$, on the other side instead of zero

Initial conditions: values that are defined or stated when the modelling of an observation is set in motion

Intersection: the point at which two or more objects, or functions, meet

Invariant: a point, or a set of points, that never change their value

Inverse matrix: a square matrix that can be multiplied by the original matrix to produce an identity matrix

Iteration: a repeat of a mathematical procedure applied to the result of a previous iteration

L

Lamina: a 2-dimensional surface with both mass and density

Limiting friction: a maximum value of static friction for which motion is impeded

Line of intersection: a line that is common to two or more planes in 3-dimensional space

Linear motion: motion that occurs in a straight line; it can be described with one spatial dimension

Logarithmic form: meaning that the answer should be written in exact form, using logarithms, usually ln

M

Matrix (plural: matrices): a rectangular array that consists of elements that are numbers or expressions, arranged in rows and columns

Model: an equation or system of equations that are used to closely resemble an observed phenomenon

Modulus of elasticity: a value that measures the resistance of an object to being stretched or compressed

Moment: a turning effect produced by a force acting at a distance on an object

Momentum: the quantity of motion of a moving body, measured as a product of its mass and velocity

N

Natural length: the original length of a spring or string before any forces act upon it

Newton's equations of motion: the set of equations that govern motion where the acceleration is constant

Newton's experimental law: a law that relates the velocities of two objects before and after collision

Non-parametric test: a test that does not require knowledge of the underlying distribution

Non-singular matrix: a matrix that has a non-zero determinant and an inverse

***n*th roots of unity:** the n solutions of the complex equation $z^n = 1$

O

Oblique: a type of asymptote that is neither horizontal nor vertical

Oblique collision: a collision in which the line of centres of the two objects is not parallel to both the objects' direction of motion

Order (of a matrix): the order of a matrix is the size of the matrix defined by the number of rows (m) and columns (n) and written $m \times n$

Osborne's rule: a rule that changes trigonometrical identities to hyperbolic identities

P

Parabola: a plane curve formed by intersecting a right circular cone with a plane that is parallel to the generator of the cone

Parabolic trajectory: a trajectory modelled by motion in a 2-dimensional plane for which the acceleration is constant

Particle: a small point mass used to represent a larger object

Particular integral (PI): a function used to convert inhomogeneous equations to homogeneous equations

Particular solution: a solution generated by given initial or boundary conditions

Percentile: a measure indicating the value below which a given percentage of observations in a group of observations fall

Perfectly elastic: a collision between two particles in which no kinetic energy is lost

Piecewise function: a function which is defined by several sub-functions, each applying to a certain interval of the domain

Polar coordinates: a 2- or 3-dimensional system for which the distance from the origin and the angle turned through are ordinates

Polynomial: a function consisting of many terms of a variable, with each term having a different non-negative integer power

Position vector: a vector that measures displacement from a given origin

Primitive: the inverse of a derivative, an indefinite integral

Probability density function: a function that describes the relative likelihood for the random variable to take on a given value

Probability generating function: a function that describes the probability of the discrete variable having a value, but in the form of a polynomial

Projectile: a particle or object that, once thrown, continues to move under its own inertia and the force of gravity

Q

Quadratic: a polynomial with a leading term of power 2

Quartic: a polynomial with a leading term of power 4

R

Rational function: an algebraic fraction in which the numerator and the denominator are polynomials

Reduced row echelon form: a matrix that has only the leading diagonal of elements that are non-zero

Reduction: a way of simplifiying an integral through integration by parts and a recurrence relation

Reflection: a transformation in which all points in the image are equidistant from a mirror line with their original positions

Rigid body: a body that remains in equilbrium in all directions

Root: a solution of an equation

Rotation: a transformation in which a plane figure rotates about a fixed point

Row: a horizontal collection of terms, such as in a matrix

Row echelon form: a matrix that has a lower triangle of zeros and a leading diagonal of non-zero elements

S

Scalar equation of a plane: the standard definition of a plane, written in the form $\mathbf{r} \cdot \mathbf{n} = \mathbf{a} \cdot \mathbf{n}$

Scalar product: the result of projecting the length of one vector parallel to the direction of another vector

Sequence: a set of mathematically ordered values or terms

Series: the sum of the terms of a sequence

Shearing: each point in a shape is displaced by an amount that is proportional to its distance from a fixed parallel invariant line

Singular matrix: a matrix that has a zero determinant, and as a consequence it cannot be inverted

Stretch: a type of transformation in which curve, or shape has either its x or y values changed by a scale factor

T

Top-heavy fraction: a fraction where the numerator's algebraic expression is the same degree or higher than that of the denominator's expression

Turning point: a point on a curve at which the gradient is equal to zero and where the gradient is of a different sign on either side of the turning point

U

Uniform: identical or consistent throughout

Unit hyperbola: a curve with the equation $x^2 - y^2 = 1$

Unit vector: a vector of magnitude 1

V

Vector determinant: *see* Determinant

Vector equation of a line: the vector representation of a line, written in the form $\mathbf{r} = \mathbf{a} + \mathbf{b}t$

Vector equation of a plane: the vector representation of a plane, written in the form $\mathbf{r} = \mathbf{a} + \mathbf{b}s + \mathbf{c}t$

Vector product: the crossing of two vectors to create a common perpendicular vector, also known as the cross product

Z

Zero matrix: a matrix that has all its elements as zeros

Index